A Guide to
Theatre in America

A Guide to Theatre in America

Compiled and Edited by
Lawrence S. Epstein

MACMILLAN PUBLISHING COMPANY
A Division of Macmillan, Inc.
NEW YORK

Collier Macmillan Publishers
LONDON

Macmillan Publishing Company
A Division of Macmillan, Inc.
866 Third Avenue, New York, N. Y. 10022

Collier Macmillan Canada, Inc.

Library of Congress Catalog Card Number: 84-19418

Printed in the United States of America

printing number
1 2 3 4 5 6 7 8 9 10

A Wecksler-Incomco Production

Library of Congress Cataloging in Publication Data
Main entry under title:

A Guide to theatre in America.

   Includes index.
   1. Theater—North America—Directories. I. Epstein,
Lawrence S.
PN2219.5.G8 1984   792'.097   84-19418
ISBN 0-02-909670-7

Contents

To everyone in theatre;
if it were easy, the whole
world would be doing it.

Introduction

An entirely new information source, *A Guide to Theatre in America* is the first arts directory to provide comprehensive information on the theatre to the general public and to the theatre community. The listings are diverse, reflecting the theatre's myriad service needs. Included are listings for schools and colleges offering degrees or certificates in theatre; libraries, archives and other collections with substantial theatre-related holdings; producers; theatres which act as producers (using their own facilities); and a variety of theatre-oriented administrative services. Important ancillary professionals such as agents, equipment suppliers, critics and publishers of theatre books are also included.

The *Guide* is divided into eighteen categories listed alphabetically, with each preceded by a brief introduction. Each category is internally divided by state and then city, with individual entries listed alphabetically under city. Listings for Canada follow those of the United States.

In compiling the *Guide,* the widest possible geographical scope was sought within parameters determined by the historical development of the American theatre. As might be expected, the greatest number of major producers, talent agents and publishers are located in New York, Los Angeles or Chicago. Users will thus find some categories weighted unevenly but unavoidably in favor of these locations. Other sections, such as suppliers, have listings more evenly distributed across the country.

In most cases individual entries are comprised of information supplied by the organization described, including any brief narrative description. Well-known groups often do not supply such narratives, since they assume that their work and purpose are already known to the public.

Because the *Guide* is arranged alphabetically and divided by subject category, only a single index is supplied. It provides quick access to individuals within organizations through an alphabetical listing of names and numbers accompanied by key contact information.

Acknowledgments

Completion of *A Guide to Theatre in America* was a difficult task, requiring the expertise (and patience) of many individuals. Glenn M. Loney of the Theatre Department of the City University of New York provided invaluable assistance, while Vincent Furfaro and Shay Kastner kept the computers running. Sally Wecksler, my agent, brought the idea to Charles E. Smith, Vice-President of Macmillan Publishing Company. Ted Mason, Associate Editor at Macmillan, gave the book its final shape. To them, and to the theatre community in general, I owe a debt of gratitude for helping me bring the diverse elements which are theatre together in this volume.

List of Acronyms

The acronym list was created from the many group affiliations acknowledged by respondents to the *Guide to Theatre* questionnaires. Because all responses to the affiliation request are included, occasional acronym duplication occurs (i.e., ACTA—Acting Coaches and Teachers Association; ACTA—American College Theatre Festival). The differences between seeming duplicates will be apparent from the accompanying text.

AA—Affiliate Artists
AAA—Arts Alliance of America
AAAE—Association of Arts Administration Educators
AAC—Association of American Colleges
AADC—American Association of Dance Companies
AAENJ—Alliance of Arts Education of New Jersey
AAM—American Association of Museums
AAO—Associated Art Organization
AASLH—American Association of State and Local History
AAT—Arts Alliance of Texas
AATCC—American Association of Textile Chemists and Colorists
AAUW—American Association of University Women
ABA—American Bus Association
ABC—Arts and Business Council
ABF—America the Beautiful Fund
ACA—American Council for the Arts
ACA—Association for Communication Administration
ACC—American Crafts Council
ACDF—American College Dance Festival Association
ACE—American Council on Education
ACHTA—American Children's Theatre Association
ACMT—Association of Civic Musical Theatres
ACOTA—American Community Theatre Association
ACT—Association of Community Theatres
ACTA—Acting Coaches and Teachers Association
ACTA—American College Theatre Association
ACTF—American College Theatre Festival
ACTH—Association for Canadian Theatre History
ACUCAA—Association of College University and Community Arts Administrators
ACUCM—Association of College and University Concert Managers

ACUCMA—Association of College and University Concert Managers and Administrators
ADG—American Dance Guild
ADTI—American Dinner Theatre Institute
AEA—Actors' Equity Association
AENJ—Arts Educators of New Jersey
AES—American Electrical Society
AETA—American Educational Theatre Association
AFA—American Federation of the Arts
AFIA—American Film Association
AFM—American Federation of Musicians
AFTRA—American Federation of Television and Radio Artists
AG—Author's Guild
AGMA—American Guild of Musical Artists
AGVA—American Guild of Variety Artists
AHA—Association of Hispanic Arts
AHD—American Hairdressers
AHFVPA—Ashford Hollow Foundation for the Visual and Performing Arts
AHSA—American Home Sewing Association
AIA—American Institute of Architects
AICT—Association of Canvas Theatres
AKT—Association of Kansas Theatres
ALA—American Library Association
AMC—American Music Center
AMCTA—American Children's Theatre Association
AMPAS—Academy of Motion Picture Arts and Sciences
ANTA—American National Theatre and Academy
ANYSAC—Alliance of New York State Arts Councils
AOADC—Association of American Dance Companies
AOCAA—Alliance of Ohio Community Arts Agencies
APA—American Playwright's Association
APO—Alpha Psi Omega

ART/NY—Alliance of Resident Theatres/New York
ASA—American Speech Association
ASCA—Alabama State Council on the Arts
ASCAH—Alabama State Council for the Arts & Humanities
ASCAP—American Society of Composers, Authors and Publishers
ASCTA—Alaska State Council on the Arts
ASOL—American Symphony Orchestra League
ASSFDC—American Society of Stage Fight Directors and Choreographers
ASTA—American Speech and Theatre Association
ASTW—American Society of Travel Writers
ATA—American Theatre Association
ATAA—Army Theatre Arts Association
ATC—American Theatre Conference
ATCA—American Theatre Critics Association
ATL—Alabama Theatre League
ATL—American Theatre League
ANTA—American National Theatre Association
ATPAM—Association of Theatrical Press Agents and Managers
ATSL—American Theatre Students League
AUCSO—American Urban and Community Symphony Orchestras
AUTA—American University Theatre Association

BBB—Better Business Bureau
BC/BS—Blue Cross/Blue Shield
BCA—Business Committee for the Arts
BCDA—British Columbia Drama Association
BDG—Broadway Drama Guild
BMI—Broadway Music, Inc.
BTA—Black Theatre Alliance

CA—Clowns of America
CAAC—California Arts Council (was CAC)
CAC—Cultural Assistance Center
CACA—Canadian Conference of the Arts
CACOA—California Confederation of the Arts
CACONFED—California Confederation of the Arts
CAEC—Combined Arts and Education Council
CAHNJ—Coalition of Arts and Humanities in New Jersey
CAI—Center for Arts Information
CAP—Citizens for the Arts in Pennsylvania
CAS—Coordinated Arts Services
CC—Costume Collection
CCA—California Council for the Arts
CCAA—Contra Costa Alliance for the Arts
CCAC—Clark County Arts Council
CCC—Chicago Chamber of Commerce
CCF—Cultural Council Foundation
CCFA—Corporate Council for the Arts
CCLM—Coordinating Council of Literary Magazines
CCM—Commission of the Arts

CCTB—Chicago Convention and Tourism Bureau, Inc.
CEA—Cincinnati Electrical Association
CELJ—Conference of Editors of Learned Journals
CETA—California Educational Theatre Association
CFDA—Cultural Facilities Development Association
CFT—Children's Film Theatre
CJOA—Consortium of Jazz Organizations and Artists
COF—Council on Foundations
CORST—Council of Resident Stock Theatres
COS—Central Opera Service
COST—Council of Stock Theatres
CSCA—Carolina Speech Communication Association
CSSA—Central States Speech Association
CTAA—Children's Theatre Association of America
CTC—California Theatre Council
CTCOA—Connecticut Commission of the Arts

DCA—City of New York Department of Cultural Affairs
DFA—Dance Films Association
DFC—Donor's Forum of Chicago

GTC—Georgia Theatre Conference

HAC—Hollywood Arts Council
HADE—Hawaii Alliance for Drama Education
HAI—Hospital Audiences, Inc.
HAU—Hebrew Actors' Union
HHAA—Historic House Association of America
HRAC—Hamilton and Regional Arts Council
HSTC—Hawaiian State Theatre Council

IAAM—International Association of Auditorium Managers
IAAPAFA—International Association of Amusement Parks, Attractions and Fair Association
IAC—Illinois Arts Council
IACFM—International Association of Concert and Festival Managers
IASLD—International Association of Set and Lighting Designers
IATSE—International Alliance of Theatrical Stage Employees and Motion Picture Machine Operators of the United States and Canada
IAU—Italian Actors' Union
IBS—Iota Beta Sigma
IDCA—Idaho Commission on the Arts
IDCCA—Illinois Department of Commerce and Community Affairs
IESA—Illumination Engineering Society of America
IHC—Illinois Humanities Council
ILCA—Illinois Cosmetology Association
INTA—Indiana Theatre Association
IOD—Institute of Outdoor Drama

IPMPI—International Photographers of the Motion Picture Industries
IS—Independent Sector
ISPAA—International Society of Performing Arts Administrators
ITA—Illinois Theatre Association
ITHS—International Thespian Society
ITI/US—International Theatre Institute of the United States

JIF—James Irving Foundation

KAT—Kentucky Arts Council
KTA—Kansas Theatre Association

LACCAD—Los Angeles City Cultural Affairs Department
LACMPAC—Los Angeles County Music and Performing Arts Commission
LATA—Los Angeles Theatre Alliance
LBPCA—Long Beach Public Corporation for the Arts
LCT—League of Chicago Theatres
LHAT—League of Historic American Theatres
LHT—League of Historical Theatres
LNYTP—League of New York Theatres and Producers
LORT—League of Resident Theatres
LTE—Legitimate Theatre Employees Union

MRC—Metropolitan Regional Council
MAC—Mississippi Arts Commission
MANA—Manufacturers's Agents National Association
MAP—Medieval Association of the Pacific
MATC—Mid-American Theatre Conference
MC—Museums Collaborative
MCA—Metropolitan Cultural Alliance
MCAH—Massachusetts Council for the Arts and Humanities
MCH—Mississippi Commission for the Humanities
MCNJ—Museum Council of New Jersey
MDA—Music Distributors Association
MEAC—Metropolitan Arts Congress
MERC—Media Equipment Resource Center
MF—Minneapolis Foundation
MHC—Minnesota Humanities Commission
MIAC—Mississippi Theatre Association
MICA—Michigan Council of the Arts
MISA—Michigan Speech Association
MITA—Michigan Theatre Association
MLA—Modern Language Association
MOG—Metropolitan Opera Guild
MOTA—Missouri State Teachers Association
MPTF—Music Performance Trust Fund
MS/B—Media Study/Buffalo

MSAB—Minnesota State Arts Board
MSCAH—Maine State Commission on the Arts and Humanities
MSPA—Maryland Society for the Performing Arts
MSRBA—Mid-States Regional Ballet Association
MST—Minneapolis Star and Tribune
MSTA—Mississippi Theatre Association
MTA—Musical Theatre Association
MUPAF—Milwaukee United Performing Arts Fund
MWA—Mystery Writers of America

NAB—National Alliance of Business
NABA—North American Ballet Association
NAC—Nebraska Arts Council
NACAA—National Assembly of Community Arts Agencies
NACC—Nashville Area Chamber of Commerce
NACM—National Association of Credit Management
NADI—National Association of Display Industries
NADSA—National Association of Dramatic and Speech Arts
NAEA—National Arts Education Association
NAEB—National Association of Educational Broadcasters
NAF—Northwest Area Foundation
NAMD—National Association of Museum Directors
NAMM—National Association of Music Merchants
NAPDF—National Association of Plastic Distributors and Fabricators
NARB—National Association for Regional Ballet
NASAA—National Assembly of State Arts Agencies
NASD—National Association of Speech and Drama
NASM—National Association of Schools of Music
NAST—National Association of Schools of Theatre
NATAS—National Association of Television Arts and Sciences
NATO—National Association of Theatre Owners
NATR—National Association of Talent Representatives
NAVA—National Audio Visual Association
NCA—National Commission on Accredition
NCA—National Costumes Association
NCACA—National Community Arts Council Association
NCACA—National Community Arts Council Association
NCAE—National Council for Arts and Education
NCAR—North Carolina Arts Council
NCBF—National City Bank Foundation
NCCR—National Committee for Cultural Resources
NCMIE—National Association of Music Importers and Exporters
NCPTA—North Carolina Professional Theatre Association
NCTA—North Carolina Theatre Association
NDC—Northwest Drama Conference

NEA—National Endowment for the Arts
NECAA—National Entertainment and Campus Activities Association
NEDTP—National Endowment Dance Touring Program
NEH—National Endowment for the Humanities
NETA—National Educational Theatre Association
NETC—New England Theatre Conference
NFFA—National Folk Festival Association
NFMC—National Federation of Music Clubs
NGD—National Graduate University
NHCA—New Hampshire Commission for the Arts
NJCAH—New Jersey Commission for the Arts and Humanities
NJSCA—New Jersey State Council on the Arts
NJTG—New Jersey Theatre Group
NJTL—New Jersey Theater League
NMC—Nashville Music Consortium
NMDE—New Mexico Drama Educators
NMDS—New Music Distribution Service
NMTA—New Mexico Theatre Association
NOA—National Opera Association
NOI—National Opera Institute
NRCA—National Research Center on the Arts
NTA—Nebraska Theatre Association
NTBA—National Tour Brokers Association
NTHA—Nevada Theater Association
NYC—New York City
NYCLCAC—New York City League of Community Arts Councils
NYFA—New York Foundation for the Arts
NYSCA—New York State Council on the Arts
NYSCH—New York State Council for the Humanities
NYSCTA—New York State Community Theatre Association

OA—Opera America
OAA—Oregon Advocates for the Arts
OAC—Ontario Arts Council (Canada)
OAC—Oregon Arts Commission
OCCA—Ohio Concerned Citizens for the Arts
OCCTA—Orange County Community Theatre Association
OCTA—Oklahoma Community Theatre Association
OIAA—Office of International Arts Affairs
ONAC—Ontario Arts Council
OOBA—Off-Off Broadway Alliance (Now ART/NY)
OR—Opportunity Resources for the Arts
ORACLE—Ohio Regional Association of Concert Lecture Enterprises
OTA—Ohio Theater Alliance

PA—Performing Artservices
PACT—Professional Association of Canadian Theatres
PAMI—Performing Arts Management Institute

PARC—Performing Arts Research Center
PCA—Pennsylvania Council on the Arts
PCCR—Publishing Center for Cultural Resources
PG—Publicists' Guild
PI—Photo International
PIPR—Public Interest Public Relations
PLOTYA—Producers' League of Theatre for Young Audiences
POA—Puppeteers of America
PPCAC—Portsmouth Community Arts Center
PUA—Publicist's Association
PW—Photo Weekly

SAC—Seattle Arts Commission
SACS—Southern Association of Colleges and Schools
SAF—Southern Arts Federation
SAG—Screen Actors' Guild
SAH—Society of Architectural Historians
SAR—Society of Authors Representatives
SBE—Society of Broadcast Engineers
SCA—Speech Communication Association
SCETA—Southern California Educational Theatre Association
SCP—SUNY College at Purchase
SCTA—South Carolina Theatre Association
SCTH—Society for Canadian Theatrical History
SDA—Southern Design Association
SDC—Society of Dyers and Colorists
SDTA—South Dakota Theatre Association
SEG—Screen Extras Guild
SERBA—South East Regional Ballet Association
SETC—Southeast Theatre Conference
SMPTE—Society of Motion Picture and Television Engineering
SPEBSQSA—Society for the Preservation and Encouragement of Barbershop Quartet Singing in America
SSDC—Society of Stage Directors and Choreographers
SSTA—Secondary School Theatre Association
STC—Southeast Theatre Conference
SWTC—South West Theatre Conference

TAG—Technical Assistance Group
TAP—Theatre Association of Pennsylvania
TC—Theater Crafts
TCA—Texas Commission of the Arts
TCB—The Conference Board
TCCBA—Theatre Communications Center of the Bay Area
TCG—Theatre Communications Group (New York)
TCS—The Costume Society
TDF—Theatre Development Fund
TEA—Theatre Equipment Association
TETA—Texas Educational Theatre Association
TFC—The Foundation Center

TGC—The Grantsmanship Center
THAP—Theta Alpha Phi
THS—Theatre Historical Society
TIA—Travel Industry of America
TNPTI—Texas Non-Profit Theatres
TO—Theatre Ontario
TPU—Theatrical Protective Union
TSE—Theatrical Stage Employees' Union
TTA—Tennessee Theatre Association
TWA—Theatrical Wardrobe Attendants Union
TWCN—The Women's Cultural Network
TWPS—The Women's Party for Survival

U/RTA—University/Resident Theatre Association
UAF—United Arts Fund
UCTA—University College Theatre Association
URTA—University Regional Theatre Association
USA—United Scenic Artists
USITT—United States Institute for Theatre Technology

VCA—Vermont Council on the Arts
VIRAC—Virginia Arts Commission

VLA—Volunteer Lawyers for the Arts
VTC—Virginia Theatre Conference
VUCG—Volunteer Urban Consulting Group

WAAA—Western Alliance of Arts Administrators
WAB—Wisconsin Arts Board
WADE—Western Association of Dramatic Educators
WATA—Washington Theatre Alliance
WEF—Westinghouse Electric Fund
WEST—Western Educational Society for Television
WESTAF—Western States Arts Foundation
WGAE—Writers' Guild of America East
WSAC—Washington State Arts Commission
WSAF—Western State Arts Association
WSCTO—Washington State Community Theatre Organization
WTA—Wisconsin Theatre Association
WVAHC—West Virginia Arts and Humanities Council
WVDCH—West Virginia Department of Culture and History
WVHF—West Virginia Humanities Foundation
WVTC—West Virginia Theatre Conference
WVUF—West Virginia University Foundation

1

Administration & Services

Under Administration & Services, a wide variety of businesses and individuals filling the ancillary needs of the industry are listed. Among these are management consultants, telephone answering services, and entertainment lawyers and accountants. The specialty of each individual or business listed can be identified through the description which follows each entry, or simply through the name given.

ARIZONA

Phoenix

George Thomas Associates
4040 East McDowell Road
Suite 218
Phoenix, AZ 85008
Tel: 602-244-8143
Address Inquiries to: George A. Thomas, Theatre Consultant, Owner
Description: Layout and equipment planning for theatres and auditoriums.

CALIFORNIA

Berkeley

Bay Area Lawyers for the Arts
c/o Hamish Sandison, Esq, 2446 Durant Avenue
Berkeley, CA 94704
Tel: 415-841-1369
Address Inquiries to: Hamish Sandison, Esq.
Description: Volunteer legal aid.

Beverly Hills

United Postal Centers
8306 Wilshire Boulevard
Beverly Hills, CA 90211
Tel: 213-650-0009
Description: Twenty-four hour mail pick up, twenty-four hour telephone message service and low cost UPS shipping.

Burbank

United Postal Centers
4219 West Olive Street
Burbank, CA 91505
Tel: 213-650-0009

Hollywood

Barries Answering Service
6546 Hollywood Boulevard
Suite 201
Hollywood, CA 90028
Tel: 213-464-8381
Description: Efficient twenty-four hours a day service. Monthly rentals of post office boxes and beepers at a reasonable price.

Hollywood Mail and Message
1523 North LaBrea
Hollywood, CA 90028
Tel: 213-876-9415
Description: Efficient telephone message service with total privacy.

United Postal Centers
8033 Sunset, West
Hollywood, CA 90046
Tel: 213-650-0009

Los Angeles

Advocates for the Arts
c/o School of Law
University of California
Los Angeles, CA 90024
Description: Volunteer legal aid.

Gelfand, Rennert and Feldman
Certified Public Accountants
1880 Century Park East
Los Angeles, CA 90067
Tel: 213-553-1707
Founded in: 1967
Member: CMA; BMA;
Description: Please see New York State entry for this listing.

Terry Ann Message Service
1551 Northwestern Avenue
Los Angeles, CA 90027
Tel: 213-467-2116; 213-466-7126
Description: Twenty-four hour message service plus all the frills for a reasonable fee.

United Postal Centers
12021 Wilshire, West
Los Angeles, CA 90025

Marina Del Rey

United Postal Centers
2554 Lincoln
Marina Del Rey, CA
Tel: 213-650-0009

Palm Springs

Gelfand, Rennert and Feldman
Certified Public Accountants
431 South Palm Canyon Drive
Palm Springs, CA 92262
Tel: 714-325-5095

Description: Please see New York State entry for this listing.

San Francisco

Gelfand, Rennert and Feldman
Certified Public Accountants
44 Montgomery Street
San Francisco, CA 94104
Tel: 415-421-8650
Founded in: 1967
Description: Please see New York State entry for this listing

Studio City

Broadway Melody Entertainment Tours
Post Office Box 1634
Studio City, CA 91604
Tel: 213-766-5875; 213-227-8370
Address Inquiries to: Vicky Francis, Director
Founded in: 1975
Description: The Broadway Melody Tours bring High School and College groups from Southern California to New York City during the winter and spring holidays for a complete package of Broadway, Off Broadway shows, Seminars and Workshops with theatre professionals. Participants also have time to explore the wilds of the Big Apple with tour guides who are New York actors, dancers and technicians taking time out from their schedules to participate with you.

CONNECTICUT

Hartford

Connecticut Volunteer Lawyers for the Arts
Connecticut Commission of the Arrts
340 Capitol Avenue
Hartford, CT 06106
Tel: 203-566-4770
Member: State of CT;
Description: Volunteer legal aid for artists.

DISTRICT OF COLUMBIA

Washington

Gerald Ness
2130 P Street, NW
Washington, DC 20037
Tel: 202-293-9042
Member: NEA;

FLORIDA

Miami

George Gill Associates
Post Office Box 610124
Miami, FL 33161
Tel: 305-891-2622
Address Inquiries to: George Gill, Partner
Muriel Gill
Founded in: 1954
Member: Florida Motion Picture and
Television Association; Illuminating
Engineering Society; USITT;
Description: George Gill Associates offers experienced consultation in lighting and staging for theatres, television, film and audiovisuals.

GEORGIA

Atlanta

Georgia Volunteer Lawyers
c/o Alston, Miller and Gaines
1220 C and S National Bank Building
Atlanta, GA 30303
Description: Volunteer legal aid.

ILLINOIS

Chicago

Bertha Masor
4200 Marine Drive
Chicago, IL 60613
Tel: 312-525-6748
Member: NEA;

Oak Park

Jerit/Boys Incorporated
The Village Mall
Oak Park, IL 60301
Tel: 312-524-2288
Description: Theatre architectural consultants.

IOWA

Sioux City

Joanne Soper
3510 Lindenwood
Sioux City, IA 51104
Tel: 712-258-0905
Member: NEA;

MARYLAND

Baltimore

Play of Light Company
2702 North Maryland Avenue
Baltimore, MD 21218
Tel: 301-366-3758
Address Inquiries to: Johanne Tessa, Director
   Description: A summer tour to France, the program is open to those with an adequate Frence language capability. The classes are in French and the study of theatre is intense. Documented, the summer session should be acceptable by colleges as 4 credit hours of French and 4 credit hours of Theatrical study.

MASSACHUSETTS

Cambridge

All the World's A Stage Travel Program
Pierre-Chriss, Department ATA 501
Box 92
Harvard Square Station
Cambridge, MA 02138
Tel: 617-876-7555
Member: ATA;
Description: Group tours for ATA members featuring theatre oriented journeys to London, Stratford-upon-Avon, Australia, Japan, Italy and America.

MINNESOTA

Minneapolis

Guthrie Management Systems
c/o The Guthrie Theater
Vineland Place
Minneapolis, MN 55403
Tel: 612-347-1100
Address Inquiries to: George Spalding
Description: A computerized system to designed for theatre box offices including electronic ledger, production administration in a completely integrated software package.

Lawyers for the Creative Arts
c/o Affiliated State Art Agencies of the
Uppeer Midwest
100 North Sixth Street
Minneapolis, MN 55403
Description: Volunteer legal aid.

NEW JERSEY

Orange

Jean Rosenthal Associates, Inc.
765 Vose Avenue
Orange, NJ 07050
Tel: 201-674-1530
Address Inquiries to: Nananne Porcher,
   President
   Clyde L. Nordheimer, P.E. Treasurer
Description: Consultant for the performing arts and fine arts.

Trenton

Cultural Law Committee
c/o New Jersey State Bar Association
172 West State Street
Trenton, NJ 08608
Description: Volunteer legal aid.

NEW MEXICO

Santa Fe

Bill Jamison
Post Office Box 1804
Santa Fe, NM 87501
Tel: 505-982-2041
Member: NEA;

NEW YORK

Brooklyn

Lawrence S. Epstein Associates
1634 59th Street
Brooklyn, NY 11204
Tel: 212-232-8468; 212-837-2881, Data
Line
Address Inquiries to: Lawrence S. Epstein,
   Consultant
   Albert A. Hartman, Systems Consultant
Founded in: 1980
Description: Lawrence S. Epstein Associates provides information to small theatrical groups planning to increase their subscription and marketing techniques through the use of personal computers.

Charles Ziff Marketing
1 Clark Street
Brooklyn, NY 10021
Tel: 212-625-6800
Address Inquiries to: Charles Ziff, Consultant
Description: A consulting firm specializing in performing arts marketing using a methodical approach developed by Mr. Ziff.

New York

Accent on Theatre Parties
246 West 44th Street
New York, NY 10036
Tel: 212-354-2062
Description: Theatre parties arranged.

Max Allentuck
165 West 46th Street
New York, NY 10036
Tel: 212-489-6530

Paul B. Berkowsky
1540 Broadway
New York, NY 10036
Tel: 212-354-4722

Buckley, Urbanski and Wells
165 West 46th Street
New York, NY 10036
Tel: 212-719-3720

Vic Cantor
1650 Broadway
New York, NY 10019

Tel: 212-581-9890
Description: Theatre parties arranged.

Center for Arts Information
1625 Broadway
New York, NY 10012
Tel: 212-677-7548
Address Inquiries to: Ellen Thurston,
Director

Color Q
370 7th Avenue, Suite 304
New York, NY 10001
Tel: 212-279-0453
Address Inquiries to: Chris Georges
Description: Composites, photo business
cards, and posters at low prices.

Crown Photo
370 West 35th Street
New York, NY 10001
Tel: 212-279-1950
Description: Specializing in theatrical, modeling, post card, interior design, fashion design, public relations and advertising industries. Complete black and white photographic reproduction services.

Di Dia/Fiore Productions
246 West 44th Street
New York, NY 10036
Tel: 212-221-4390

Frances A. Drill
165 West 46th Street
New York, NY 10036
Tel: 212-391-6660
Description: Theatre parties arranged.

Leonard Finger
1501 Broadway
New York, NY 10036
Tel: 212-944-8611

Robert Fishko
1501 Broadway
New York, NY 10036
Tel: 212-840-7840

Gatchell and Neufeld Ltd.
165 West 46th Street
New York, NY 10036
Tel: 212-575-0828

Gelfand, Rennert and Feldman
Certified Public Accountants
489 Fifth Avenue
New York, NY 10017
Tel: 212-682-0234; 213-553-1707
Founded in: 1967
Member: Country Music Association; Black
    Music Association;
Description: Business management services
for the performing arts including income
monitoring and royalty examination. Inquiries are invited from individuals with established careers and those in the process of
career advancement or their representatives. Complete confidentiality is assured.

Frank Giraldi
54 West 39 Street
New York, NY 10018
Tel: 212-840-8225

Description: Head shots and portfolios.

Joseph P. Harris Associates
15 East 48th Street
New York, NY 10017
Tel: 212-758-8730

Hopkins Associates Incorporated
56 West 22 Street
New York, NY 10010
Tel: 212-WA9-0800

Richard Horner
65 West 55th Street
New York, NY 10019
Tel: 212-245-8245

Ideal Photo Service
160 West 46th Street
New York, NY 10036
Tel: 212-819-0359
Description: Quality photo reproductions.
Resumes run on back of photos. Rush ser-
vice available at no extra cost.

Al Issac
1650 Broadway
New York, NY 10019
Tel: 212-765-5910

Robert Kamlot
c/o New York Shakespeare Festival
425 Lafayette Street
New York, NY 10003
Tel: 212-598-7140

Marvin A. Krauss
250 West 52nd Street
New York, NY 10019
Tel: 212-246-4460

James J. Kriegsmann
165 West 46th Street
New York, NY 10036
Tel: 212-382-0190; 212-382-0233
Description: Specialized in copy-work.

Bert Landsman
1650 Broadway
New York, NY 10019
Tel: 212-757-7575
Description: Theatre parties arranged.

David Lawlor
165 West 46th Street
New York, NY 10036
Tel: 212-575-7932

Bill Liberman
276 Riverside Drive
New York, NY 10025
Tel: 212-662-1290

Liz McCann and Nelle Nugent
1501 Broadway
New York, NY 10036
Tel: 212-354-9570

Leonard Mulhearn
1501 Broadway
New York, NY 10036
Tel: 212-997-1895

National Theatre Club of New York
303 West 42nd Street
New York, NY 10036

Tel: 212-586-1644
Description: Theatre parties arranged.

Dorothy Olim
1540 Broadway
New York, NY 10019
Tel: 212-869-8282

Play of the Month Guild
2 West 45th Street
New York, NY 10036
Tel: 212-575-5185
Description: Theatre parties arranged.

Albert Poland
226 West 47th Street
New York, NY 10036
Tel: 212-354-2040

Prestige Theatre Parties
165 West 46th Street
New York, NY 10036
Tel: 212-575-5050
Description: Theatre parties arranged.

Ben Rosenberg
165 West 46th Street
New York, NY 10036
Tel: 212-575-7960

Arthur Rubin
1564 Broadway
New York, NY 10036
Tel: 212-765-3906

Victor Samrock
745 Fifth Avenue
New York, NY 10022
Tel: 212-355-5727
Description: Victor Samrock is a company
manager.

Frank Scardino
1240 Lexington Avenue
New York, NY 10028
Tel: 212-737-7545
Description: Frank Scardino is a company
manager.

Richard Seader
344 West 72nd Street
New York, NY 10023
Tel: 212-877-5083
Description: Richard Seader is a company
manager.

Leonard Soloway and Allan Francis
165 West 46th Street
New York, NY 10036
Tel: 212-997-0040
Description: Soloway and Francis are theatre
consultants.

Roy Somlyo
225 West 44th Street
New York, NY 10036
Tel: 212-757-1200
Description: Roy Somlyo is a company manag-
er.

Theater Management/Ashton Springer
240 West 44th Street
New York, NY 10036
Tel: 212-221-3677

Theatre Now, Incorporated
1515 Broadway
New York, NY 10036
Tel: 212-840-4400
Description: Theatre now provides consultancy and management services.

Theatre Party Associates
234 West 44th Street
New York, NY 10036
Tel: 212-398-8370
Description: Theatre parties arranged.

Jose Vega
165 West 46th Street
New York, NY 10036
Tel: 212-489-6530
Description: Jose Vega is a company manager.

Berenice Weiler and Marilyn S. Miller
1540 Broadway
New York, NY 10036
Tel: 212-997-1139
Description: Weiler and Miller are theatre consultants.

Riverdale

Welling's, Lee Group Sales Service
3225 Johnson Avenue
Riverdale, NY 10463
Tel: 212-796-3074
Description: Theatre parties arranged.

NORTH CAROLINA
Raleigh

Charles Springman
630 North Blount Street
Raleigh, NC 27604
Tel: 919-832-0047
Member: NEA;
Description: Charles Springman is a theatre coordinator.

RHODE ISLAND
Providence

Rudy Nashan
30 Savoy Street
Providence, RI 02906
Tel: 401-274-4754
Member: NEA;
Description: Rudy Nashan is a theatre coordinator and consultant.

TENNESSEE
Nashville

Gelfand, Rennert and Feldman
Certified Public Accountants
7 Music Circle North
Nashville, TN 37203
Tel: 615-329-3333
Founded in: 1967

TEXAS
Alamo

Frances Potect
601 Austin, #1410
Alamo, TX 78516
Tel: 512-787-6756
Member: NEA;
Description: Francis Potect is a theatre administrator.

2

Agents

Talent agents act in a hundred ways as discoverers, developers, and business representatives for new and established theatre talent. They are among the most powerful people in the business.

Agents are often the first to review new talent, since busy producers, casting agents, and publishers rely on them to screen the many actors, playwrights, and other creative personnel seeking entry into the theatre world.

Equally important to aspiring and established artists is the agent's role as business representative. Dealing with a whole stable of writers, actors, and others who require financial support, agents know the intricacies of contracts better than most and can obtain the best terms. They also are constantly on the lookout for that rare commodity which is most important to their clients: work.

Playwrights should note that while unsolicited manuscripts will often be returned unopened, it is a rare agent, if he or she reads it, who will turn down a work showing true promise.

CALIFORNIA

Beverly Hills

The Artists Agency
190 North Canon Drive
Beverly Hills, CA 90210
Tel: 213-278-1200

Association Booking Corporation
292 South La Cienega
Beverly Hills, CA 90211
Tel: 213-855-8051

Beakel and Jennings Agency
427 North Canon Drive
Beverly Hills, CA 90210
Tel: 213-274-5418

David Benndett, Incorporated
2431 Briarcrest Road
Beverly Hills, CA 90210
Tel: 213-278-5657
Address Inquiries to: David Benndett, Agent
Member: AFTRA;

The Blake Agency
409 North Camden Drive
Beverly Hills, CA 90210
Tel: 213-278-6885
Member: SAG;

Harry Bloom and Associates
9460 Wilshire Boulevard
Suite 425
Beverly Hills, CA 90212

Ned Brown Incorporated
407 North Maple Drive
Beverly Hills, CA 90210
Tel: 213-276-1131

Century Artists, Ltd.
9477 Wilshire Boulevard
Beverly Hills, CA 90212
Tel: 213-273-4366

Colten, Kingsley and Associates
321 South Beverly Drive
Beverly Hills, CA 90212
Tel: 213-277-5491

Commercial Actors Agency
8500 Wilshire Boulevard
Suite 604
Beverly Hills, CA 90212
Tel: 213-553-8611
Address Inquiries to: Lew J. Deuser, Agent
Member: AGVA;

Compass Management
211 South Beverly Drive
Beverly Hills, CA 90212
Tel: 213-271-5122

Contemptorary-Korman Artists, Ltd
132 Lasky Drive
Beverly Hills, CA 90212
Tel: 213-278-8250

Werner Cosay and Associates
9744 Wilshire Boulevard
Suite 310
Beverly Hills, CA 90212
Tel: 213-550-1353

Kurt Frings Agency
9440 Santa Monica Boulevard
Beverly Hill, CA 90210
Tel: 213-274-8881

Phil Gersh Agency
222 North Canon Drive
Beverly Hills, CA 90210
Tel: 213-274-6611
Address Inquiries to: Phil Gersh, Agent

Allen Goldstein and Associates, Ltd.
9301 Wilshire Boulevard
Beverly Hills, CA 90210
Tel: 213-651-1700

Gordean Agency
9570 Wilshire Boulevard
Beverly Hills, CA 90212
Tel: 213-273-4195

Larry Grossman and Associates
211 South Beverly Drive
Beverly Hills, CA 90212
Tel: 213-550-8127

Mitchell Hamilburg Agency
292 South La Cienega Boulevard
Beverly Hills, CA 90069
Tel: 213-652-2409
Address Inquiries to: Mitchell Hamilburg,
    President
Founded in: 1937
Member: ATA; WGA;

Annette Handley
9533 Brighton Way
Beverly Hills, CA 90211
Tel: 213-273-4272

Sharon Kemp Artists Manager
9701 Wilshire
Beverly Hills, CA 90212
Tel: 213-553-9486
Address Inquiries to: Sharon Kemp, Manager
Member: SAG; AFTRA;

Irving Paul Lazar Agency
211 South Beverly Drive
Beverly Hills, CA 90212
Tel: 213-275-6153
Address Inquiries to: Irving Paul Lazar, Agent
Member: SAG; AFTRA;

The Leigh Bureau
9300 Wilshire Boulevard, Suite 555
Beverly Hills, CA 90212
Tel: 213-278-7890

Mark Levin Association
328 South Beverly Drive
Beverly Hills, CA 90212
Tel: 213-277-8881
Address Inquiries to: Mark Levine, Agent

Terry Lichtman Agency
9301 Wilshire Boulevard
Beverly Hills, CA 90210
Tel: 213-550-4550
Address Inquiries to: Terry Lichtman, Agent

M.E.W. Company
151 North San Vicente
Beverly Hills, CA 90211
Tel: 213-653-4731

Luttrel, Robinson and Associates
132 South Rodeo Drive
Beverly Hills, CA 90212
Tel: 213-275-6114

Irving Salkow Agency
9350 Wilshire Boulevard
Suite 214
Beverly Hills, CA 90212
Tel: 213-276-3141

T.K. Talent Group
119 North San Vicente Boulevard
Suite 203
Beverly Hills, CA 90211
Tel: 213-657-5031

Hillel Wasserman Agency
328 South Beverly Drive
Beverly Hills, CA 90212
Tel: 213-553-5337
Address Inquiries to: Hillel Wasserman,
    Agent
Member: SAG; AFTRA;

Burbank

Lois J. Benson Agency
2221 West Olive
Burbank, CA 91502
Tel: 213-849-5647
Address Inquiries to: Lois J. Benson, Agent
Member: SAG; AFTRA;

William Carroll Agency
2321 West Olive Avenue
Burbank, CA 91506
Tel: 213-848-9948

Carolyn Kassel Agency
2401 West Magnolia
Burbank, CA 91506
Tel: 213-761-1525
Address Inquiries to: Carolyn Kassel, Agent
Member: SAG;

Century City

William Blake Agency/West
1888 Century Park East
Century City, CA 90067
Tel: 213-274-0321
Address Inquiries to: William Blake, Agent

Member: SAG;

C.L.O.U.T. Talent Agency
1888 Century Park East
Century City, CA 90067
Tel: 213-552-3155
Member: SAG; AFTRA;

Herb Tobias and Associates
1901 Avenue of the Stars
Century City, CA 90067
Tel: 213-277-6211
Address Inquiries to: Herb Tobias, Agent
Member: AGVA;

Encino

George Michaud Agency
4950 Densmore
Encino, CA 91436
Tel: 213-981-6680
Address Inquiries to: George Michaud, Agent
Member: SAG; AFTRA;

Hollywood

Velvet Amber Agency
6515 Sunset Boulevard
Hollywood, CA 90028
Tel: 213-646-8184

Isaac Talent Agency (ITA)
6525 Sunset Boulevard, Suite 911
Hollywood, CA 90028
Tel: 213-463-3343

Julian Portman Agency
1680 North Vine Street
Suite 421
Hollywood, CA 90028
Tel: 213-463-8154

Los Angeles

Bret Adams Limited
8282 Sunset Boulevard
Los Angeles, CA 90046
Tel: 213-656-6420

Adams, Ray and Rosenberg
9200 Sunset Boulevard
Los Angeles, CA 90069
Tel: 213-278-3000

Agency for Artists
9200 Sunset Boulevard
Suite 531
Los Angeles, CA 90069
Tel: 213-278-6243

Agency for Performing Arts
9000 Sunset Boulevard
Suite 315
Los Angeles, CA 90069
Tel: 213-274-1744

Carlos Alvarado Agency
8820 Sunset Boulevard
Los Angeles, CA 90069
Tel: 213-652-0272
Address Inquiries to: Carlos Alvarado, Agent
Member: SAG; AFTRA;

Arcara, Bauman and Hiller
9220 Sunset Boulevard
Los Angeles, CA 90069

Tel: 213-271-5601
Founded in: 1976

Maxine Arnold Agency
8350 Santa Monica
Los Angeles, CA 90069
Tel: 213-650-4999
Address Inquiries to: Maxine Arnold, Agent

Irvin Arthur Associates, Ltd.
9200 Sunset Boulevard
Los Angeles, CA 90069
Tel: 213-278-5934
Founded in: 1975

Artist First, Incorporated
8230 Beverly Boulevard
Los Angeles, CA 90048
Tel: 213-653-5640

Artists Career Managment
9157 Sunset Boulevard
Los Angeles, CA 90069
Tel: 213-278-0157

The Artists Group, Ltd.
10100 Santa Monica Boulevard
Suite 310
Los Angeles, CA 90067

Miles Bohm Auer Agency
8344 Melrose Avenue
Los Angeles, CA 90069
Tel: 213-462-6416
Address Inquiries to: Miles Bohm Auer,
    Agent

Roberta Barash Agency
404 North La Cienega
Los Angeles, CA 90048
Tel: 213-820-3383
Address Inquiries to: Roberta Barash, Agent

Barr/Wilder and Associates
8721 Sunset Boulevard
Los Angeles, CA 90069
Tel: 213-652-7994

The Barskin Agency
8730 Sunset Boulevard
Los Angeles, CA 90069
Tel: 213-657-5740

Beckman/Kordus Agency
8489 West Third Street
Los Angeles, CA 90048
Tel: 213-653-5600

William Blake Agency
West Talent International
1888 Century Park East
Los Angeles, CA 90067
Tel: 213-274-0321

Nina Blanchard Agency
1717 North Highland Avenue
Los Angeles, CA 90028
Tel: 213-462-6248
Address Inquiries to: Nina Blanchard, Agent
Member: SAG; AFTRA;

J. Michael Bloom
9220 Sunset Boulevard
Los Angeles, CA 90069
Tel: 213-275-6800

Address Inquiries to: J. Michael Bloom, Agent
Member: SAG; AFTRA;

Nancee Borgnine Agency
8833 Sunset Boulevard
Suite 402
Los Angeles, CA 90069
Tel: 213-659-7272

Christine Brady Agency
11818 Wilshire Boulevard
Los Angeles, CA 90025

Brandon and Rogers Associates
9046 Sunset Boulevard
Los Angeles, CA 90069
Tel: 213-237-6173

Alex Brewis Artists Manager
8721 Sunset Boulevard
Los Angeles, CA 94107
Tel: 213-274-9874

The Calder Agency
8749 Sunset Boulevard
Los Angeles, CA 90069
Tel: 213-657-2125; 213-666-1920

The Candace Lake Office
1103 Glendon Avenue
Los Angeles, CA 90024
Tel: 213-824-9706

Roland Carriere Enterprises
5456 McConnell Avenue
Suite 140
Los Angeles, CA 90066
Tel: 213-390-7277

Gibson J. Carter Agency
9000 Sunset Boulevard
Los Angeles, CA 90069
Tel: 213-274-8813

Chandler, Raskin and Associates
8833 Sunset Boulevard
Suite 311
Los Angeles, CA 90069
Tel: 213-855-0641

Charter Management
9000 Sunset Boulevard
Los Angeles, CA 90069
Tel: 213-278-1690

Chartwell Artists
1901 Avenue of the Stars
Los Angeles, CA 90067
Tel: 212-553-3600
Member: AEA;

Chasin-Park-Citron Agency
9255 Sunset Boulevard
Los Angeles, CA 90069
Tel: 213-273-7190

Harold D. Cohen Associates
9200 Sunset Boulevard
Los Angeles, CA 90069

Carey/Phelps/Colvin Agency
1407 North La Brea
Los Angeles, CA 90028
Tel: 213-874-7780
Member: SAG; AFTRA;

Ben Conway and Associates
999 Doheny Drive
Los Angeles, CA 90069
Tel: 213-271-8133

Richard Dickens Agency
5550 Wilshire Boulevard
Los Angeles, CA 90036
Tel: 213-937-3080
Address Inquiries to: Richard Dickens, Agent
Member: SAG; AFTRA;

Elite Model Management
9255 Sunset Boulevard
Los Angeles, CA 90069
Tel: 213-274-9395
Member: SAG;

Jack Fields and Associates
9255 Sunset Boulevard
Los Angeles, CA 90069
Tel: 213-659-8414
Member: SAG; AFTRA;

Galaxy Artists
1880 Century Park East, #819
Los Angeles, CA 90067
Tel: 213-557-1218
Description: Formerly Michael McAndrews Miller, New York.

Dale Garrick International Agency
8831 Sunset Boulevard
Los Angeles, CA 90069
Tel: 213-657-2661

G. G. and Associates
439 La Cienega Boulevard
Los Angeles, CA 90048
Tel: 213-274-7661

Girard/Flaherty Agency
10889 Wilshire Boulevard
Los Angeles, CA 90024
Tel: 213-479-6591

Goldin, Dennis, Karg and Associates
470 South Vicente Boulevard
Los Angeles, CA 90048
Tel: 213-651-1700

The Granite Agency
1920 South LaCienega Boulevard
Suite 205
Los Angeles, CA 90034
Tel: 213-934-8383
Member: SAG; AFTRA;

Mauri Grashin Agency
8730 Sunset Boulevard
Los Angeles, CA 90069
Tel: 213-652-5168

Ivan Green Agency
1888 Century Park East, #908
Los Angeles, CA 90067
Tel: 213-277-1541

Grossman-Staimaster Agency
8730 Sunset Boulevard, #405
Los Angeles, CA 90069
Tel: 213-657-3040

Jeanne Halliburton Agency
5205 Hollywood Boulevard

Los Angeles, CA 90027
Tel: 213-466-6183
Address Inquiries to: Jeanne Halliburton, Agent

Jim Halsey Company
9000 Sunset Boulevard
Suite 1010
Los Angeles, CA 90069
Tel: 213-278-3397

Reece Halsey Agency
8733 Sunset Boulevard
Los Angeles, CA 90069
Tel: 213-652-2409

Hughes Agency
439 South La Cienega
Los Angeles, CA 90048
Tel: 213-550-7166
Member: SAG; AFTRA;

George B. Hunt Agency
8350 Santa Monica
Los Angeles, CA 90046
Tel: 213-654-6600
Address Inquiries to: George B. Hunt, Agent
Member: SAG; AFTRA;

Toni Kelman Association
7813 Sunset Boulevard
Los Angeles, CA 90046
Tel: 213-851-8822
Address Inquiries to: Toni Kelman, Agent
Member: AGVA;

Gene Lesser & Associates
8230 Beverly Boulevard, Suite 29
Los Angeles, CA 90048
Tel: 213-658-8321

Gilly/Levy Agency
8721 Sunset Boulevard
Los Angeles, CA 90069
Tel: 213-657-5660
Address Inquiries to: Georgia Gilly, Agent
Sidney Levy, Agent

David Libert Agency
1108 North Sherbourne
Los Angeles, CA 90069
Tel: 213-659-6776
Address Inquiries to: David Libert, Agent
Member: SAG; AFTRA;

Bessie Loo Agency
8730 Sunset Boulevard
Los Angeles, CA 90069
Tel: 213-657-5888
Address Inquiries to: Bessie Loo, Agent

Howard Love Agency
4244 Berryman Avenue
Los Angeles, CA 90066
Tel: 213-391-4090

Lynne and Reilly Artists Managers
6290 Sunset Boulevard
Los Angeles, CA 90028
Tel: 213-461-2808
Member: SAG; AFTRA;

MacArthur and Associates
6430 Sunset Boulevard
Los Angeles, CA 90028

Tel: 213-461-2727

Bob Marks Artist Management
9229 Sunset Boulevard
Suite 303
Los Angeles, CA 90069
Tel: 213-463-8191

Hazel McMillan Agency
7805 Sunset Boulevard
Los Angeles, CA 90046
Tel: 213-276-9823
Address Inquiries to: Hazel McMillan, Agent
Member: SAG;

Michele Unlimited
8060 Melrose
Los Angeles, CA 90046
Tel: 213-653-9610
Member: SAG; AFTRA;

The Morgan Agency
8462 Sunset Boulevard
Suite 3E
Los Angeles, CA 90069
Tel: 213-656-0309

Maurine Oliver and Associates
8730 Sunset Boulevard
Los Angeles, CA 90069
Tel: 213-657-1250
Address Inquiries to: Maurine Oliver, Agent

Richland Agency
1900 Avenue of the Stars
Suite 1890
Los Angeles, CA 90067
Tel: 213-553-1257

The Robinson Company
9220 Sunset Boulevard
Los Angeles, CA 90069
Tel: 213-275-4970
Member: SAG;

Jack Rose/Dorothy Day Otis Agency
6430 Sunset Boulevard
Los Angeles, CA 90028
Tel: 213-461-4911
Address Inquiries to: Dorothy Day Otis,
    Agent
    Jack Rose, Agent

Savage Agency
6212 Banner Avenue
Los Angeles, CA 90038
Tel: 213-461-8316
Member: SAG; AFTRA;

Roberts/Shiffrin Artists Agency
7466 Beverly Boulevard
Los Angeles, CA 90036
Tel: 213-937-3937

Charles H. Stern Agency
9220 Sunset Boulevard
Los Angeles, CA 90069
Tel: 213-273-6890
Address Inquiries to: Charles H. Stern, Agent
Founded in: 1960
Member: SAG; AFTRA;

Carole Stewart Agency
8230 Beverly Boulevard
Los Angeles, CA 90048

Tel: 213-655-4330
Address Inquiries to: Carole Stewart, Agent
Member: SAG; AFTRA;

Bill Sturdivant and Associates
3050 West 7th Street
Los Angeles, CA 90025
Tel: 213-382-8483
Address Inquiries to: Bill Sturdivant, Agent

H.L. Swanson, Incorporated
8523 Sunset Boulevard
Los Angeles, CA 90069
Tel: 213-652-5385

Tina/Marie Agency
1823 North Western Boulevard
Los Angeles, CA 90027
Tel: 213-469-9270
Member: SAG; AFTRA;

Topps Enterprises
1610 North Argyle
Los Angeles, CA 90028
Tel: 213-469-2591
Member: SAG;

Volman-Goldberg Company
1901 Avenue of the Stars
Suite 941
Los Angeles, CA 90067
Tel: 213-553-8919

Ruth Webb Agency
7500 Devista Drive
Los Angeles, CA 90046
Tel: 213-874-1700
Address Inquiries to: Ruth Webb, President
Founded in: 1962

Robinson/Weintraub Agency
554 South San Vincente
Los Angeles, CA 90048
Tel: 213-653-3802
Member: SAG; AFTRA;

Carolyn Williamson and Associates.
932 North La Brea Ave
Los Angeles, CA 90038
Tel: 213-851-1881
Address Inquiries to: Carolyn Williamson,
    President
Founded in: 1975

Woody's People Agency
704 North Gardne
Los Angeles, CA 90046
Tel: 213-653-7414
Member: SAG;

Wormser/Heldfond and Joseph, Agents
1717 North Highland
Los Angeles, CA 90028
Tel: 213-466-9111
Founded in: 1960
Member: SAG; AFTRA;
Description: Wormser/Heldfond and Joseph
agents obtain television commercials for actor; print jobs for actors and models; and
commercials, television shows, series and
films for young people and children (under
21 years).

Ann Wright Limited Agency
8422 Melrose Place
Los Angeles, CA 90069
Tel: 213-655-5040
Address Inquiries to: Ann Wright, Agent

Marina Del Rey

Paul Lundberg Agency, Incorporated
4676 Admiralty Way
Suite 522
Marina Del Rey, CA 90291
Tel: 213-821-8944

North Hollywood

Dietrich Agency
10850 Riverside Drive
North Hollywood, CA 91602
Tel: 213-985-4824
Member: SAG; AFTRA;

Mary Grady Artists Manager
10850 Riverside
North Hollywood, CA 91602
Tel: 213-985-9800
Address Inquiries to: Mary Grady, Agent
    Manager

Norah Sanders Agency
4737 Lankershim
North Hollywood, CA 91602
Tel: 213-769-2162
Address Inquiries to: Norah Sanders, Agent

Peggy Schaefer Agency
10850 Riverside Drive
North Hollywood, CA 91602
Tel: 213-985-5547
Address Inquiries to: Peggy Schaefer, Agent
Member: SAG; AFTRA;

Ann Waugh Talent Agency
4731 Laurel Canyon Boulevard
North Hollywood, CA 91607
Tel: 213-980-0141
Address Inquiries to: Ann Waugh, Agent
Member: SAG; AFTRA;

Billy Wood and Associates Agency
4219 Lankershim
North Hollywood, CA 91602
Tel: 213-769-1226
Address Inquiries to: Billy Wood, Agent
Member: SAG;

Pasadena

William Adrian Agency
520 South Lake Drive
Pasadena, CA 91101
Tel: 213-681-5750
Address Inquiries to: William Adrian, Agent

San Francisco

Brebner Agencies, Incorporated
161 Berry Street
San Francisco, CA 94107
Tel: 415-495-6700

Santa Maria

Gault Agency
610 West Main Street
Santa Maria, CA 93454
Tel: 805-925-0547

Sherman Oaks

Aimee Entertainment Associates
14241 Ventura Boulevard
Sherman Oaks, CA 91423
Tel: 213-872-0874
Member: SAG; AFTRA;

Connor-Corfino Associates
14241 Ventura Boulevard
Sherman Oaks, CA 91403
Tel: 213-278-8250

Studio City

The Clark Group
12835 Ventura Boulevard, Suite 13
Studio City, CA 91604
Tel: 213-761-1154

Mark Harris Management
12019 Guerin Street
Suite 4
Studio City, CA 91604
Tel: 213-760-8870

George Soares and Associates
12735 Ventura Boulevard
Studio City, CA 91604
Tel: 213-980-0400
Address Inquiries to: George Soares

Toluca Lake

Amaral Agency
10000 Riverside Drive
Toluca Lake, CA 91602
Tel: 213-980-1013

Van Nuys

Webster Artists Management
13615 Victory Boulevard
Van Nuys, CA 91404
Tel: 213-780-2558
Address Inquiries to: Erika Wain, Agent
Member: SAG; AFTRA;

DISTRICT OF COLUMBIA

Washington

Blue Star Agency
8100 Glenmore Spring Road
Washington, DC 20034
Tel: 301-585-2473

FLORIDA

Jacksonville

The Starr Agency
Post Office Box 546
Jacksonville, FL 32201
Tel: 904-743-5807
Address Inquiries to: Tara O'Neill, Relations
   Director

Morgan Starr, General Administrator
Founded in: 1977
Member: WGA;

ILLINOIS

Chicago

Austin Wahl Agency Ltd.
332 South Michigan Avenue
Chicago, Il 60604
Tel: 312-922-3329; 312-922-3331
Address Inquiries to: Thomas Wahl, President
Founded in: 1935
Description: The Austin Wahl Agency specializes in representing writers for television films, motion pictures and publication.

KENTUCKY

Louisville

Marquita Hall
5705 Maldon Drive
Louisville, KY 40216
Tel: 502-447-2099

NEVADA

Sparks

Bulbman
Post Office Box 1317
Sparks, NV 09431
Tel: 702-329-5913

NEW YORK

Forest Hills

Philip G. Spitzer Literary Agency
111-25 76th Avenue
Forest Hills, NY 11375
Tel: 212-263-7592; 212-793-4149
Address Inquiries to: Philip G. Spitzer
Founded in: 1969

New York

Act 48 Management
1501 Broadway, Suite 1713
New York, NY 10036
Tel: 212-354-4250

Buddy Altoni Esquire Incorporated
1680 North Vine Street
New York, NY 90028
Tel: 213-467-4939
Address Inquiries to: Buddy Altoni, Agent
Member: SAG; AFTRA;

Julian Bach Literary Agency
3 East 48th Street
New York, NY 10017
Tel: 212-753-2605

Bill Berger Associates, Incorporated
444 East 58th Street
New York, NY 10022

Lois Berman Agency
240 West 44th Street
New York, NY 10036
Tel: 212-581-0670
Address Inquiries to: Lois Berman, Literary
   Agent
Founded in: 1971
Member: NATAS; New York Women in
   Film; SAR;
Description: Specializes in the marketing of dramatic scripts for theatre and film. No unsolicited material accepted.

Ron Bernstein Agency
119 West 57th Street
Suite 107
New York, NY 10019
Tel: 212-759-9647; 212-265-0750
Founded in: 1976
Member: Independent Literary Association,
   Incorporated;
Description: Represents screen writers and novelists, placing their material with publishing houses, feature film companies, film producers, television producers and directors.

Lurton Blassingame
60 East 42nd Street
New York, NY 10017

Michael J. Bloom, Ltd
400 Madison Avenue
New York, NY 10017
Tel: 212-832-6900; 212-421-4200

Georges Borchardt, Incorporated
136 East 57th Street
New York, NY 10022
Tel: 212-735-5785

Brandt and Brandt Literary Agency
1501 Broadway
New York, NY 10036
Tel: 212-840-5760

Helen Brann Agency Incorporated
14 Sutton Place
New York, NY 10022
Tel: 212-751-0137

Curtis Brown, Ltd.
575 Madison Avenue
New York, NY 10022
Tel: 212-840-8272
Address Inquiries to: Curtis Brown, Agent

James Brown Associates
25 West 43rd Street
New York, NY 10036
Tel: 212-276-1131
Address Inquiries to: James Brown, Agent

Knox Burger Associates
39 ½ Washington Square South
New York, NY 10012
Tel: 212-533-2360

Career Management
119 West 57th Street
New York, NY 10019

Bertha Case
42 West 53rd Street

New York, NY 10019

Debbie Coleman
667 Madison Avenue
New York, NY 10021

Frieda Fishbein Ltd.
353 West 57th Street
New York, NY 10019
Tel: 212-247-4398; 212-265-6100
Address Inquiries to: Ms. Janice Fishbein,
    President
Founded in: 1925
Description: A literary agency representing
authors of books, plays, screenplays and
teleplays.

Blanche C. Gregory, Inc.
2 Tudor City Place
New York, NY 10017
Tel: 212-697-0828

Maxine Groffsky Literary Agency
2 Fifth Avenue
New York, NY 10011
Tel: 212-677-2720

Bertha Klausner Literary Agency
71 Park Avenue
New York, NY 10016
Tel: 212-685-2642; 212-532-8638
Address Inquiries to: Bertha Klausner,
    Literary Agent
Founded in: 1938
Member: DG; WGA;
Description: Since 1938 this agency has con-
centrated on developing young talent in ev-
ery phase of literature.

Gerald W. Purcell Associates
133 Fifth Avenue
New York, NY 10003
Address Inquiries to: Gerald W. Purcell,
    Agent

3

Awards

An important distinction to be made among the awards, prizes and scholarships listed here is that some may be solicited by the applicant, while others are awarded by a closed nominating committee with no application procedure open to the theatre community in general. Much time and effort can be saved making this distinction in advance.

Awards and other public honors can contribute greatly to the financial viability and longevity of a show, as well as to the reputation of its creator. Monetary grants lend essential support to innovative, new works by experimental or regional companies, while academic scholarships provide a foundation for students of the theatre, and for the scholars who work to preserve its history.

No recommendations are made in the *Guide* on application methodology; the scope of the awards listed is too wide. Detailed instructions should be sought from the sponsoring organization before material is submitted.

CALIFORNIA

Beverly Hills

Beverly Hills Theatre Guild
Neil Simon Playwright's Award
c/o Pamela Bohnert
Department A
329 El Camino Drive
Beverly Hills, CA 90212
Annual Budget: $5,000 prize
Description: Award for the best new American play includes $2,000 to finance a Los Angeles area showcase presentation.

Georgetown

Living Playwrights Award
Dragon Teeth Press
El Dorado National Forest
Georgetown, CA 95634
Tel: 916-333-4224
Address Inquiries to: Cornel Lengyel, Director
Description: Award is given to the most powerful poetic drama.

Hollywood

George Spelvin Award
The Masquers
1765 North Sycamore Ave.
Hollywood, CA 90028
Tel: 213-874-0840

Los Angeles

National Repertory Theatre National Play Award
Post Office Box 71011
Los Angeles, CA 90071
Annual Budget: $12,500 first prize
Description: Co-sponsored by the National Repertory Theatre and The Bilingual Foundation of the Arts, first prize includes $5,000, which will go to a professional theatre to help with the play's production.

San Francisco

Fleishacker Playwriting Contest
c/o Michael Lynch
One-Act Theatre Company
430 Mason Street
San Francisco, CA 94102
Annual Budget: $500 first prize
Description: A full production is also a part of this award, which goes to the best one-act play written by a woman.

COLORADO

Denver

National Children's Theatre Playwriting Award
Contest Editor
Pioneer Drama Service
2172 South Colorado Boulevard
Denver, CO 80222
Annual Budget: $500 first prize
Description: For 60-90 minute full-length original comedies, musicals or adaptations, which may have been previously produced.

CONNECTICUT

Hartford

Connecticut Commission on the Arts
340 Capitol Avenue
Hartford, CT 06106
Address Inquiries to: Joanne Delponte, Administrative Assistant
Annual Budget: $250-$2,500, grant range
Description: Grants for all fields of new work for developing and established Connecticut artists.

DISTRICT OF COLUMBIA

Washington

American Theatre Association
Award of Merit
1000 Vermont Avenue, NW
Washington, DC 20005
Description: Annual award given for outstanding service to educational theatre in America.

American Theatre Association
Citation for Distinguished Service to the Theaatre
1000 Vermont Avenue, NW
Washington, DC 20005
Founded in: 1963
Description: Annual award given for outstanding contribution to the theatre in America.

American Theatre Association Theatre Award
ATA, 1010 Wisconsin Avenue
Washington, DC 20007
Founded in: ATA;
Description: Two awards for outstanding research are presented at the ATA annual convention. Write ATA for nominating and procedures.

Behn and Mayorga Awards
Women's International Theatre Alliance
6205 Cromwell Drive
Washington, DC 20016
Description: Winners of this contest, which accepts unproduced and unpublished original plays, receive a staged reading at the Alliance's Skidmore College Summer Festival.

Children's Theatre Association of America
Creative Drama for Human Awarenesss Award
1000 Vermont Avenue, NW
Washington, DC 20005
Founded in: 1975

Description: Annual award which acknowledges a person or group's dedication to a non-producing creative drama program.

Children's Theatre Association of America
Zeta Phi Eta-Winifred Ward Prize
1000 Vermont Avenue, NW
Washington, DC 20005
Founded in: 1958
Description: Annual award acknowledging a children's theatre which achieves a high quality production level while stimulating community interest.

Children's Theatre Association of America
1000 Vermont Avenue, NW
Washington, DC 20005
Founded in: 1957
Description: Given to an outstanding playwright for a children's play.

Barnard Hewitt Award
American Theatre Association
1000 Vermont Avenue, NW
Washington, DC 20005
Description: Annual award given to the author of an outstanding theatre book.

Norman Lear Award
American College Theatre Festival
Kennedy Center for the Performing Arts
Washington, D.C. 20566
Address Inquiries to: Michael Kanin, Award Advisor
Description: For achievement in comedy playwriting awarded to plays entered in the Playwrighting Awards program of the American College Theatre Festival and named for the well known television producer, Norman Lear.

Audrey Wood Award in Playwriting
Department of Performing Arts
American University
Washington, DC 20016
Annual Budget: $500 prize
Description: Prize includes a full American University production.

World Theatre Award
American Theatre Association, 1000 Vermont Avenue
Washington, DC 20005
Founded in: 1967
Description: Annual award for international theatrical achievement.

FLORIDA
Boca Raton

Friends of the Caldwell Playhouse
Playwright's Competition
Post Office Box 277
Boca Raton, FL 33432
Annual Budget: $1,000 first prize
Description: Aside from the cash award, the winning author will see his play presented at the Caldwell Playhouse in Boca Raton.

Maharam Design Awards
Best Costume and Scene Design
21675 Juego Circle Villa 3A
Boca Raton, FL 33433
Founded in: 1969
Annual Budget: $200 cash award
Description: Annual award for graduate scene and costume designers.

ILLINOIS
Chicago

All-Media Dramatic Workshop Awards
c/o Karen Swanson
612 Michigan Avenue
Room 316
Chicago, IL 60611
Annual Budget: $25 per minute of playing time
Description: For original, unpublished, up-to-one-hour radio scripts of more than strictly a commercial nature.

Sergel Drama Prize
University of Chicago Theatre
5706 South University Avenue
Chicago, IL 60637
Annual Budget: $1,500 first prize
Description: Write for entry form and contest information.

KENTUCKY
Mount Sterling

ArtAct, Playwriters Competition, Incorporated
Post Office Box 754
Mount Sterling, KY 40353
Annual Budget: $500, cash prize
Description: For unpublished plays likely to appeal to a community audience.

MASSACHUSETTS
Boston

Religious Arts Guild Drama Award
25 Beacon Street
Boston, MA 02108
Description: Awarded for one unpublished one-act play that uses no more than five players in a contemporary setting. Awarded annually.

Cambridge

Hasty Pudding Theatricals
Man and Woman of the Year Awards
12 Holyoke Street
Cambridge, MA 02138
Founded in: Man, 1951; Woman, 1967
Description: Annually honors the actor and actress who have made the most outstanding contributions to entertainment.

Waltham

Community Theatre Drama Festival Award
New England Theatre Conference
50 Exchange Street
Waltham, MA 02154
Founded in: 1954
Description: Annual award to a community theatre in New England, which holds a group membership in the New England Theatre Conference, for the best production of a one act play, scene, or cutting from a three-act play.

Jack Stein Make-Up Awards
50 Exchange Street
Waltham, MA 02154
Address Inquiries to: Jack Stein
Description: Encourages excellence in theatre make-up and consists of three awards, one to a secondary school, a college, and a community theatre group in the New England area.

Moss Hart Memorial Award
New England Theatre Conference
50 Exchange Place
Waltham, MA 02154
Founded in: 1962
Description: Annual award for plays which deal with human dignity and freedom.

New England Theatre Conference
Award for Creative Achievement in the Theatrre
50 Exchange Street
Waltham, MA 02154
Founded in: 1957
Description: Honors an actor, designer, playwright or director who has made an outstanding achievement to the American theatre. Awarded annually.

MICHIGAN
Ann Arbor

Marshall Award in Musical Theatre
PTP Office
University of Michigan
League Building
227 South Ingalls
Ann Arbor, MI 48109
Annual Budget: $2,000 first prize
Description: For innovative and original full-length musicals.

MINNESOTA
Minneapolis

Christian Theatre Artist Guild
Playwriting Award
New Scripts Committee
Post Office Box 14157
Minneapolis, MN 55414
Annual Budget: $500 first prize
Description: Open to one-act plays with a Christian theme.

MISSOURI

Kansas City

Kansas City Star
Joseph Kaye Award
1729 Grand Avenue
Kansas City, MO 64108
Founded in: 1975
Description: This annual award goes to an outstanding midwestern playwright.

NEW YORK

Brooklyn

Lawrence S. Epstein Playwriting Award
1634 59th Street
Brooklyn, NY 11204
Tel: 212-232-8468
Address Inquiries to: Lawrence S. Epstein, Director
Founded in: 1984
Description: The editor of *Guide to the Theatre in America* offers a $250 award in October toward the production of a new play concerning American values.

Garden City

George Oppenheimer Playwriting Award
Newsday
550 Stewart Avenue
Garden City, NY 11530
Founded in: 1979
Annual Budget: $1,000
Description: This annual award goes to a playwright whose work is produced in New York City or on Long Island. Established in 1979 in memory of George Oppenheimer, *Newsday* drama critic.

New York

Actors' Fund Medal, Award of Merit
Actor's Fund of America
1501 Broadway
Suite 2600
New York, NY 10036
Tel: 212-221-7300

Address Inquiries to: Nedda Harrigan Logan, President
Founded in: 1882
Member: Shubert Foundation;
Annual Budget: $1,250,000
Description: The oldest theatrical charity in the world. It was founded in 1882 to aid the needy of the entertainment world, which encompassed ballet, opera, vaudeville, circus, burlesque and the legitimate stage. Since then motion pictures, radio and television have also been included.

Actor's Fund of America Medal
1501 Broadway
New York, NY 10036
Founded in: 1958
Description: Gilded bronze medal given for outstanding service to the Actor's Fund.

Actors Repertory Theatre
Annual Playwright Award
303 East 44th Street
New York, NY 10017
Description: Send a brief summary of a full length, unproduced play. A small cast production is recommended and there is a $15 entry fee.

Afro-American Total Theatre Grant
Arts Foundation, Inc.
44 West 63rd Street
Suite 6A
New York, NY 10023
Address Inquiries to: Hazel J. Bryant, Executive Director
Description: Grants to help in the productions of original musical plays. Available to U.S. citizens and nationals of Africa, Latin America and the Caribbean.

American Academy of Arts and Letters
Medal for Good Speech on Stage
633 West 155th Street
New York, NY 10032
Founded in: 1940
Description: Awarded irregularly for correct use of language in the entertainment arts.

American Academy of Arts and Letters
Award of Merit
633 West 155th Street
New York, NY 10032
Founded in: 1940
Annual Budget: $1,000, cash award
Description: For Americans who are not members of the organization, this award is given for outstanding achievement in the area of drama.

American Academy Production Award
Institute of Arts and Letters
633 West 155th Street, New York NY
Tel: 100-2 -
Founded in: 1978
Description: Established to encourage production of not-for-profit theatre in New York City.

St. Clair Bayfield Award
Actor's Equity Association
165 West 46th Street
New York, NY 10019
Tel: 212-869-8530
Address Inquiries to: Mrs. Bayfield, President
Member: AEA;

Blitzstein Award for Musical Theatre
American Academy and Institute of Arts and Letters
New York, NY 10032
Founded in: 1965
Annual Budget: $2,500, first prize
Description: Given to a composer, lyricist, or librettist to encourage the creation of new works for the musical theatre.

Brandeis University Creative Arts Awards
12 East 77th Street
New York, NY 10021
Founded in: 1957
Annual Budget: $1,000, cash award
Description: Annual award given for outstanding contributions to the theatre arts.

Business in the Arts Awards
1501 Broadway
Suite 2600
New York, NY 10036
Address Inquiries to: Edwin C. Stone, Awards Administrator
Annual Budget: $5,000 first prize, BCA Award
Description: Co-sponsored by *Forbes* magazine and the BCA, The Business-in-the-Arts Awards recognize outstanding corporate programs which support the arts. The BCA Award is a grant presented to an American arts organization for outstanding achievement in the development of business interest and support of its activities.

Clarence Derwent Awards
c/o Carl Schaeffer
410 Park Avenue
New York, NY 10022
Founded in: 1945
Description: $1,000

Creative Artists Public Service Program
Fellowships
250 West 57th Street
New York, NY 10019
Address Inquiries to: Larry Hulse, Applications Manager
Annual Budget: $3,500-$4,000, fellowship range
Description: Fellowships are available for new playwrights.

Drama Critic's Circle Musical Award
c/o Howard Kissel
275 Central Park West, New York NY
Description: For the best musical of the year.

Delia Austrian Medal
Drama League of New York
555 Park Avenue
New York, NY 1002
Tel: 212-838-5859; 212-MU8-3233
Address Inquiries to: Mrs. Edward A. Hansen, President
Founded in: 1916
Description: The Drama League is dedicated to the encouragement of public interest in drama and to encourage contemporary theatre. Their program includes lectures, theatre discussions, and Broadway and Off Broadway plays. Since 1916 the Drama League has made financial contributions to support worthwhile theatre and since 1935 has presented the Delia Austrian Medal for distinguished performance in theatre.

Clarence Derwent Awards
Actors Equity Association
165 West 46th Street
New York, NY 10019

Tel: 869-853-
Member: AEA;

Drama Desk Award
54 Charles Street
New York, NY 10014
Founded in: 1949
Description: Annually honors outstanding Broadway and Off-Broadway productions in many different categories.

Elizabeth Hull-Kate Warriner Award
234 West 44th Street
New York, NY 10036
Founded in: 1970
Annual Budget: $7,500
Description: Award goes annually to the most controversial playwright produced that year in New York City.

George Freedly Memorial Award
Theatre Library Association
111 Amsterdam Avenue
New York, NY 10023
Founded in: 1968
Description: Annual award for an outstanding written work on the field of musical theatre.

George M. Cohan Award
Catholic Actors Guild
277 West 45th Street
New York, NY 10036
Founded in: 1970
Description: Annual scholarship to a non-denominational needy school awarded for outstanding dedication to the theatre.

Rosamond Gilder Award
New Drama Forum Association
c/o Library and Museum of the
Performing Arts
Lincoln Center
New York, NY 10023
Founded in: 1978
Description: Annual award for creative achievement in writing and directing for the theatre.

Guggenheim Fellowship
John Simon Guggenheim Memorial
Foundation
90 Park Avenue
New York, NY 10016
Tel: 212-687-4470
Annual Budget: $5,000 initial grant
Description: Award given to gifted artists to further develop their creative talent. Well-known playwrights who have been recipients include Romulus Linney and Jean-Claude van Itallie.

James K. Hackett Award
City College
Department of Drama
Convent Avenue at 138th Street
New York, NY 10031
Description: Annual award to alumni and students of the City University of New York for achievement in drama.

Hampden-Edwin Booth Memorial Award
The Players
16 Gramercy Park South

New York, NY 10003
Founded in: 1978
Description: Annual award for continued dedication to the New York theatre.

INTAR Playwrights-in-Residence Lab
420 West 42nd Street
New York, NY 10036
Tel: 212-695-6134
Address Inquiries to: Maria Irene Fornes, Director

Kesselring Fund Award
15 Gramercy Park South
New York, NY 10003
Founded in: 1978
Annual Budget: $5,000 first prize; $1,000 honorable mention
Description: Established in memory of the author-actor-playwright to provide financial aid for playwrights.

George Jean Nathan Award
c/o Manufacturers Hanover Trust
600 Fifth Avenue
New York, NY 10020
Tel: 212-350-4469; 212-957-1620
Founded in: 1958

National Association of Theatre Owners
Star of the Year Awards
1500 Broadway
New York, NY 10036
Description: Grants which are awarded to stars, directors and writers of special merit.

National Gay Playwrighting Contest
c/o Terry Helbing
51 West 4th Street, #300
New York, NY 10012
Annual Budget: $250 first prize; $100 second prize
Description: Co-sponsored by the Glines, a New York based gay arts organization and the Gay Theatre Alliance, the contest is open to unpublished and unproduced one-act or full-length plays with a gay theme. Both first and second prize will be considered for production by the Glines, Robert Patrick, Doric Wilson and Eric Bentley are among the contest judges.

National Theatre Conference Citation
c/o Paul Meyers
Lincoln Center Library
111 Amsterdam Avenue
New York, NY 10023
Founded in: 1968
Description: Annual award for continued outstanding service to non-professional theatre.

New York Drama Critic's Circle Award
c/o Howard Kissel
275 Central Park West
New York, NY 10024
Founded in: 1935
Annual Budget: $1,000 cash prize
Description: Annually awarded to the author of the best new play presented on or Off-Broadway in New York City.

New York State Creative Artists Public
Service Fellowships
CAPS
c/o 250 West 57th Street, Room 1424
New York, NY 10019
Annual Budget: $3,500 for each playwright chosen.
Description: Open to play and screenwriters.

Antoinette Perry Award
250 West 57th Street
New York, NY 10022
Tel: 212-765-0609
Address Inquiries to: Isabelle Stevenson, President/Program Director
Founded in: 1947
Description: In addition to the yearly presentation of the American Theatre Wing's TONY Awards, the Wing gives grants to theatre organizations, and sponsors hospital programs and the Saturday Theatre for Children, as well as twice-yearly seminars on 'Working in the Theatre' for young professionals and students of the theatre. Dedicated to the fostering of excellence in the theatre.

Phoebe Ephron Scholarship Award
Hunter College
695 Park Avenue
New York, NY 10021
Founded in: 1981
Description: Annual award for the most promising woman playwright.

Ronato Poggioli Award
PEN American Center
47 Fifth Avenue
New York, NY 10003
Annual Budget: $3,000 first prize
Description: Given to the best English translation of an Italian play.

Pulitzer Prize
Columbia University
Graduate School of Journalism
New York, NY 10027
Tel: 212-280-3841

Saint Clair Bayfield Award
165 West 46th Street
New York, NY 10036
Founded in: 1972
Description: Awarded annually by the Actor's Equity Association to recognize an outstanding performance of Shakespeare in the New York or Connecticut area.

Saint Genesis Award
227 West 45th Street
New York, NY 10036
Founded in: 1960
Description: A service award for an individual from the performing arts who has provided special service to the Catholic Actors Guild, the theatre profession and the Church. Awarded annually.

Saint Genesis Gold Medal Award
277 West 45th Street
New York, NY 10036
Founded in: 1965

Description: Awarded irregularly for dedication to the promotion of Christian principles and the theatre profession.

Shubert Foundation Awards
234 West 44th Street
New York, NY 10036
Founded in: 1954
Description: An award for an outstanding contribution by an individual to New York theatre. Awarded annually in memory of Sam S. Shubert.

Society Of Colonial Wars Annual Award
122 East 58th Street
New York, NY 10022
Founded in: 1951
Description: This award recognizes contributions of outstanding excellence and includes an award for drama relative to Colonial Americana. Awarded annually.

Society of Stage Directors and Choreographers
Award of Merit
1501 Broadway
New York, NY 10036
Founded in: 1965
Description: This award recognizes an outstanding achievement in the performing arts. It is infrequently given.

Straw Hat Award
c/o Taplinger Associates
415 Madison Avenue
New York, NY 10017
Description: This is an award in eight categories given in the American summer theatre, awarded annually.

The Theatre World Award
c/o John Willis, Editor
190 Riverside Drive
New York, NY 10024
Founded in: 1944
Description: Established to encourage new theatrical talent, this award honors six actors and six actresses for outstanding work in a theatrical debut.

Village Voice
842 Broadway
New York, NY 10003
Founded in: 1956
Annual Budget: $1,000 best play; $1,000 standard achievement
Description: Acknowledges the outstanding achievements of the creative personnel of New York City's Off and Off-Off Broadway.

Ossining

Outer Critics Circle Performance Awards
c/o 18 Overlook Road
Ossining, NY 10562
Description: This award recognizes the best play of the New York theatre season, the performance in those plays and performances by young players. Special citations are often given to organizations for contributions to theatre. Given annually.

Staten Island

Stanley Drama Award
c/o J.J. Boies
Wagner College
Staten Island, NY 10301
Annual Budget: $800 first prize
Description: Academic or professional recommendation is required to enter this contest which accepts unproduced, full-length plays, musicals or groups of thematically related one-act plays.

NORTH CAROLINA

Greensboro

Southeastern Theatre Conference
Distinguished Career Award
1209 West Market Street
Greensboro, NC 17412
Founded in: 1960
Description: Awarded to an American from the South who has provided a special service to the American theatre annually.

Susan M. Davis Memorial Award
1209 West Market Street
Greensboro, NC 27412
Founded in: 1965
Description: Bronze plaque awarded annually to honor outstanding service to southern theatre or the Southeastern Theatre Conference.

Raleigh

Sir Walter Raleigh Cup
109 East Jones Street
Raleigh, NC 27611
Founded in: 1952
Description: Awarded annually to residents of North Carolina for works of fiction, including drama.

OHIO

Westerville

Theta Alpha Phi Medallion of Honor
58 West College Avenue
Westerville, OH 43081
Founded in: 1956
Description: Honors distinguished service to the theatre on the national level.

PENNSYLVANIA

Philadelphia

Theatre La Salle Award
20th Street and Olney Avenue
Philadelphia, PA 19141
Founded in: 1970
Description: Recognizes distinguished service to the American theatre outside of New York City. It's awarded periodically, but not more than once in a given year.

TEXAS

Houston

Country Playhouse Playwright Competition
12802 Queensbury
Town and Country Village
Houston, TX 77024
Tel: 713-467-4497
Address Inquiries to: John Newell
Founded in: 1983
Annual Budget: $750 - Full Length Play, $250 - One Act Play
Description: The Country Playhouse is a community theatre in the Houston area that offers this competition annually in the hopes of showcasing plays by neww playwrights.

Susan Smith Blackburn Prize, Incorporated
3239 Avalon Place
Houston, TX 77019
Founded in: 1979
Annual Budget: $2,000, cash award
Description: In memory of the distinguished American actress and writer, this award is given to an outstanding female playwright.

San Marcos

Southwest Theatre Conference New Play Award
Southwest Texas State University
San Marcos, TX 78666
Founded in: 1976
Annual Budget: $1,000
Description: Recognizes new plays written by residents of Texas, Oklahoma, New Mexico, Arkansas or Louisiana. It must be a full theatre production, a series of a one-act plays or a full length play previously unproduced. The award often includes a production of the play by the Permian Playhouse of Odessa, Texas.

WEST VIRGINIA

Wheeling

Towngate Theatre Playwriting Contest
Oglebay Institute, Oglebay Park
Wheeling, WV 26003
Annual Budget: $300 first prize
Description: For full length plays which have not been professionally published or produced. Judges welcome unconventional and provocative new works.

CANADA

Toronto, Ontario

Canadian Authors Association Literary Award
24 Ryerson Avenue
Toronto, Ontario, Canada M5T 2P3
Tel: 416-868-6916
Annual Budget: $5,000 cash award
Description: Annual award for a play that achieves literary excellence without sacrificing popular appeal.

Montreal, Quebec

Prix Victor Morin
82 Sherbrooke Street West
Montreal, Quebec, Canada
Founded in: 1962
Annual Budget: $500
Description: Awarded annually to an outstanding professional actor or actress whose activities have strengthened French Canadian culture.

4

Colleges & Schools

The list of colleges and schools varies widely, from those devoted solely to theatre offering certificates to mammoth state universities of which the theatre department is but a small part. It should be remembered that the absence of a degree offered in drama or theatre does not mean that a student would be cut-off from amateur theatre. A campus may have highly active theatre groups without offering a degree in the subject.

There is no appraisal given in these listings of the relative merit of specific programs, but propesctive students should consider a number of practical factors. Schools granting certificates usually offer a more intense program in an urban setting. There, students are more often taught by professionals working in the commercial theatre, which is closer at hand. On the other side, however, these schools are not accredited. They do not offer the broader education or the "college experience" which a four-year institution does. Some combination of the two may be the best solution.

ALABAMA

Andalusia

Lurleen B. Wallace State Junior College
Post Office Box 1418
Andalusia, AL 36420
Tel: 205-222-6591
Address Inquiries to: Sara McAnaulty,
Chairperson

Athens

Athens College
Department of Theatre
Athens, AL 35611
Address Inquiries to: Larry A. Saunders,
Chairman
Description: The english department supervises theatre activities.

Auburn

Auburn University
Department of Theatre
Auburn, AL 36849
Tel: 205-826-4748
Address Inquiries to: Lois Z. Garren,
Chairman
Founded in: 1919
Member: ATA; SETC; USITT;
Annual Budget: $52,000
Description: The department of theatre offers a professionally oriented undergraduate program, with a BFA degree available in performance or design/technology.

Birmingham

University of Alabama
Department of Theatre
University Station
Birmingham, AL 35294
Tel: 205-934-3236
Address Inquiries to: Dr. Ward Haarbauer,
Chairman, Performing Arts

Florence

University of North Alabama
Florence, AL 35630
Tel: 205-766-4100, Ext.247; 205-766-4100,
Ext.358
Address Inquiries to: Robert Holder, Director
Dr. Eugene Balof, Chairperson
Founded in: 1830
Member: APO;

Gadsden

Vagabond Players
Gadsden State Jr. College
Gadsden, AL 35999
Tel: 205-546-5960; 205-546-0484 ext. 255
Address Inquiries to: Marian 'Mitch' duPont,
Theatre Director
Founded in: 1973
Member: NEA; AEA; AFTRA; Alabama
Theatre League; American Film
Institute; American Speech & Theatre
Association;
Annual Budget: $1500
Description: Offers training in voice and diction, proper breathing, projection, and general effectiveness, with an emphasis on stage and television performance. Scene study is the main activity of advanced acting classes. Student theatre classes teach stagecraft and active participation in each quarter's main production. Auditioning procedures are also studied and are entered into whenever possible.

Montevallo

University of Montevallo
Department of Theatre
Montevallo, AL 35115
Tel: 205-665-2521, ext 413
Address Inquiries to: Charles C. Harbour,
Chairman
Founded in: 1896

Member: ATA; STC; ATL; ASCA;
Annual Budget: $163,000
Description: A not-for-profit theatre which sometimes tours its productions to schools and civic organizations.

Tuscaloosa

Stillman College
Tuscaloosa, AL 35402
Tel: 205-752-2548
Address Inquiries to: Janet Dill

ALASKA

Anchorage

University of Alaska, Anchorage
2533 Providence Drive
Anchorage, AK 99504
Tel: 907-279-6622
Address Inquiries to: Everett Kent, Chairman
Member: ATA;

Fairbanks

University of Alaska
College of Arts and Letters
Fairbanks, AK 99701
Tel: 907-479-7211
Address Inquiries to: Walter G. Ensign
Member: ATA;

ARIZONA

Coolidge

Central Arizona College
Signal Peak
Coolidge, AZ 85228
Tel: 602-723-4141
Address Inquiries to: Dr. Charles Hall,
Chairman
Member: ATA;

Tempe

Arizona State University
Tempe, AZ 85281
Tel: 602-965-6536
Address Inquiries to: Dr. William Arnold,
 Chairman
Member: ATA;

ARKANSAS

Batesville

Arkansas College
Post Office Box 2317
Batesville, AR 75201
Tel: 501-793-9813
Address Inquiries to: Dr. L.J. Summers,
 Chairman

Conway

University of Central Arkansas
Conway, AR 72032
Tel: 501-329-2931; 501-450-3165
Address Inquiries to: C. Robert Hawley,
 Director
Member: ATA;

Magnolia

Southern Arkansas University
Magnolia, AR 71753
Tel: 501-234-5120
Address Inquiries to: Dr. Jerry Cortez,
 Director
Member: ATA;

Pine Bluff

University of Arkansas, Pine Bluff
Cedar Street
Pine Bluff, AR 71601
Tel: 501-535-6700
Address Inquiries to: Dr. V.J. Coleman,
 Chairperson

Russeville

Arkansas Tech University
Russeville, AR 72801
Tel: 501-968-0274
Address Inquiries to: Robert Bolen, Chairman

CALIFORNIA

Alameda

College of Alameda
Department of Theatre
Alameda, CA 94501
Tel: 415-522-7221
Address Inquiries to: Fred Owens, Chairman

Alta Loma

Chaffey College
Department of Theatre
Alta Loma, CA 91701
Tel: 714-987-1737
Address Inquiries to: C.A. Sheppard,
 Chairman

Arcata

Humboldt State University
Department of Theatre
Arcata, CA 95521
Tel: 707-826-3011
Address Inquiries to: Charles Myers,
 Chairman

Azusa

Citrus College
Azusa, CA 91024
Tel: 213-355-0521
Address Inquiries to: Fredrick B. Carlson,
 Director of Theatre
Member: ATA; SCETA;
Description: A not-for-profit theatre organization.

Bakerfield

Bakersfield College
1801 Panorama Drive
Bakerfield, CA 93305
Tel: 805-395-4011
Address Inquiries to: Robert Chapman,
 Chairman
Member: ATA;

Belmont

College of Notre Dame
Department of Theatre
Belmont, CA 94002
Tel: 415-593-1601
Address Inquiries to: Robert Titlow,
 Chairman

Berkeley

University of California, Berkeley
Department of Dramatic Arts
Berkeley, CA 94720
Tel: 415-642-1677
Address Inquiries to: Donald M. Fredman,
 Chairman
Member: ATA; State of California;
Description: The Department of Dramatic Art
is in the College of Letters and Sciences.

Blue Lake

Dell'Arte School of Mime and Comedy
Department of Theatre
Blue Lake, CA 95525
Tel: 707-668-5411; 707-668-5782
Address Inquiries to: Joan Shirle, Chief
 Executive Officer and Managing
 Director, Dell'Arte Players
 Alain Schons, School Director
Founded in: 1971
Member: NEA; CAC; Mobil Corperation;
 City of Blue Lake; Theatre
 Communication Center of the Bay Area;
 CTC; CCA;
Annual Budget: $130,000
Description: The Dell'Arte School is owned
and operated by Dell'Arte Inc., which also
operates a professional theatre touring company, The Dell'Arte Players. The company
tours internationally, performing mostly
original works which emphasize contemporary ideas in a broad physical style. Members

of the company teach at the school when
not on tour. The school offers a one-year
full time training program for the committed performer. The curriculum includes
acrobatics, dance, voice, Alexander Technique, juggling, mime, commedia, clowning and mask. Intensive summer workshops in single subjects such as mask and
commedia are also offered. Students come
from all over the world.

Burbank

The Players Theatre
2811 West Magnolia Boulevard
Burbank, CA
Tel: 213-842-4755; 213-845-1193
Address Inquiries to: Donna Anderson,
 Director

Chico

California State University, Chico
Chico, CA 95929
Tel: 916-985-5351
Address Inquiries to: Dr. Lloyd S. Jones,
 Chairman
Member: ATA;

Chula Vista

Southwestern Community College
Department of Theatre
900 Otay Lakes Road
Chula Vista, CA 92010
Tel: 714-421-6700, Ext. 346
Address Inquiries to: Mr. John Newhouse,
 Chairman
Member: ATA; ACTF; SCETA;
Annual Budget: $90,000
Description: A two-year community college
located in the southwestern corner of the
U.S. Close affiliation with the Old Globe
Theatre, Starlight Civic Light Opera and local community theatre groups.

Claremont

Claremont Graduate School
10th and College
Claremont, CA 91711
Tel: 714-626-8511

Pomona College
Department of Theatre
Claremont, CA 91711
Tel: 714-621-8186
Address Inquiries to: Michael Birtwistle,
 Chairman
Founded in: 1935
Member: ATA; SCETA;

Coalinga

West Hills College
Department of Theatre
300 Cherry Lane
Coalinga, CA 93210
Tel: 209-935-0801
Address Inquiries to: Dr. Janie Jones,
 Chairperson

Compton

Compton Community College
1111 East Artesia Boulevard
Compton, CA 90221
Tel: 213-635-8081
Address Inquiries to: Pieter J. Van Niel,
Professor

Costa Mesa

Orange Coast College
Department of Theatre
2701 Fairview Road
Costa Mesa, CA 92626
Tel: 714-556-5725
Address Inquiries to: William Purkiss,
Chairman

Cupertino

De Anza College
21250 Stevens Creek Boulevard
Cupertino, CA 95014
Tel: 408-996-4567
Address Inquiries to: William Cleveland,
Administrator

Cypress

Cypress College
Department of Theatre
9200 Valley View
Cypress, CA 90630
Tel: 714-826-2220; 714-821-6320
Address Inquiries to: Kaleta Brown,
Chairperson
Member: ATA; CETA;

Davis

University of California, Davis
Department of Theatre
Davis, CA 95616
Tel: 916-752-0888; 916-752-0891
Address Inquiries to: Robert Fahrner,
Chairman
Description: UC Davis offers MA, MFA and
Ph.D programs with a distinguished faculty.
The campus features a 500 seat proscenium
theatre, 200 seat thrust stage, 100 seat arena
and 2 theatres labs in addition to close prox-
imity to the theatres of San Francisco. The
university houses a substancial theatre li-
brary and offers many performance and re-
search opportunites to its students.

El Cajon

Grossmont Community College
Department of Theatre
El Cajon, CA 92020
Tel: 714-465-1700
Address Inquiries to: Clark G. Mires,
Chairman

Fremont

Ohlone College
Department of Theatre
Post Office Box 909
Fremont, CA 94538
Tel: 415-657-2100
Address Inquiries to: G. Craig Jackson,
Chairman

Mark E. Nelson, Technical Director
Founded in: 1967
Member: ATA; USITT; State of California;
City of Fremont;
Annual Budget: $150,000

Fresno

California State University
Cedar and Shaw
Fresno, CA 93740
Tel: 209-487-9011
Address Inquiries to: Roland D. Johnson
Member: ATA;

Fresno City College
Department of Theatre
1101 East University Avenue
Fresno, CA 93741
Tel: 209-442-4600
Address Inquiries to: Tom Wright

Pacific College
Department of Theatre
Fresno, CA 93702
Address Inquiries to: James Baker, Chairman

Fullerton

Fullerton College
Department of Theatre
Fullerton, CA 92634
Tel: 714-871-8000
Address Inquiries to: Todd V. Glenn,
Chairman
Member: ATA;

Fullerton College Community Services
321 East Chapman Avenue
Fullerton, CA 92634
Tel: 714-871-8000, ext. 252
Address Inquiries to: Ted Spriggs, Jr.,
Associate Dean for Community
Relations
Jean Lester, Community Services
Coordinator
Founded in: 1961
Annual Budget: $30,000
Description: In the area of performing arts,
Fullerton College Community Services off-
ers music, dance, theatre, film-lectures and
residencies related to these areas of empha-
sis.

Gilroy

Gavilan College
Department of Theatre
5055 Santa Teresa Boulevard
Gilroy, CA 95020
Tel: 408-847-1400
Address Inquiries to: Marilyn Abad, Director

Gavilan Joint Community College
Department of Theatre
Gilroy, CA 95020
Tel: 408-842-8221
Address Inquiries to: Marylyn C. Abad,
Chairperson

Hayward

Chabot College
Department of Theatre
Hayward, CA 91245
Address Inquiries to: Glenn Leuning,
Chairman

Hollywood

Estelle Harman Actors Workshop
522 North La Brea Avenue
Hollywood, CA 90036
Tel: 213-931-8137
Member: NATTS;
Description: Cited as the most often recommended training institution. One of the
most respected drama schools and for over
two decades, a continuing source of talent
for motion pictures and television.

Golden West Studios
6429 Selma Avenue
Hollywood, CA
Tel: 213-461-4231

Los Angeles Academy of Dramatic Art
Department of Theatre
Hollywood, CA 90028
Tel: 213-467-7970
Address Inquiries to: Fredic Cook, Chairman
Member: ATA;

Huntington Beach

Golden West College
Department of Theatre
Huntington Beach, CA 92647
Tel: 714-892-7711, ext. 450
Address Inquiries to: Susan Thomas Babb,
Chairperson
Founded in: 1966
Member: ATA; USITT;
Annual Budget: $31,000

Irvine

University of California, Irvine
Department of Theatre
Irvine, CA 96717
Tel: 714-883-6614
Address Inquiries to: Robert Cohen,
Chairman

Kentfield

College of Marin
Department of Theatre
Kentfield, CA 94904
Tel: 415-457-8811
Address Inquiries to: Harvey Susser,
Chairman

La Jolla

University of California
UCSD Student Center
La Jolla, CA 92093
Tel: 714-452-4090; Art-ur -agner,
Chairman
Member: NECAA;
Annual Budget: $50,000

University of California, La Jolla
Department of Theatre
La Jolla, CA 92037

Address Inquiries to: Authur Wagner,
Chairman

La Verne

University of LaVerne
Department of Theatr
La Verne, CA 91750
Tel: 714-593-3511, Ext. 248, 364, 365;
213-629-1066
Address Inquiries to: Gay Manifold,
Department Chairman
Mick Jones, Technical Director
Founded in: 1891
Member: ATA;
Description: Curriculum includes stagecraft,
directing, lighting, costuming, theatre histo-
ry, design, playwrighting and acting. Four
major productions a year directed by faculty
and guest directors. Students also have the
opportunity to develop their own works.

Long Beach

California State University
Department of Theatre Arts
1250 Bellflower Boulevard
Long Beach, CA 90840
Tel: 213-498-5356
Address Inquiries to: Ralph W. Duckwall,
Chairman
Member: URTA;
Description: Offers the degree of MFA in costuming, lighting, scenery, make-up, and
theatre management. The Theatre Program
presents a complete season of nine or ten
productions over the spring and fall Semesters. The summer season consists of three
fully- mounted Shakespeare productions
presented in a 1,000 seat outdoor theatre.

Long Beach City College
Department of Theatre
Long Beach, CA 90808
Address Inquiries to: David Emmes,
Chairman

Los Altos

Foothill College
Department of Theatre
Los Altos, CA 94022
Tel: 415-948-8590
Address Inquiries to: Doyne Mraz,
Chairperson
Member: ATA;

Los Angeles

The Actors Workshop
6111 West Olympic Boulevard
Los Angeles, CA 90048
Tel: 213-931-4662
Address Inquiries to: Dexter Freeman,
Director
Member: OPACT
Description: Solid professional training with
continuing classes in the mornings, eve-
nings and weekends. Coaches include Danny
Goldman, Ella Smith, Scott Gourlay, Lev
Mailer, Eli Rill, Deborah Ross-Sullivan and
Logan Ramsey.

California State University
Department of Theatre
5151 State University Drive
Los Angeles, CA 90032
Tel: 213-224-3345; 213-224-3344
Address Inquiries to: Maris U. Ubans,
Chairman
Founded in: 1947
Member: ATA;
Annual Budget: $45,000
Description: This is a Department of Theatre
Arts, part of a university in the State University system; we offer BA and MA degrees; as
part of the program we produce about ten
theatrical productions a year, also some
video tape and film; we have experimental
productions as well, so students can produce
their own plays or experiment with new
works and/or new materials as part of the
educational process. The program is geared
toward preparing students for work in the
various phases of the theatrical profession.

Immaculate Heart College
Department of Theatre
Los Angeles, CA 90027
Address Inquiries to: Ruth Marie Gibbons,
Chairperson

International College
Department of Theatre
1019 Gayley Avenue
Los Angeles, CA 90024
Tel: 213-477-6761

Los Angeles City College
Department of Theatre
Los Angeles, CA 90029
Address Inquiries to: James R. McCloskey,
Chairman

Los Angeles Southwest Community
College Department of Theatre
1600 West Imperial Highway
Los Angeles, CA 90047
Tel: 213-757-9521
Address Inquiries to: Dr. Merrille Strafford,
Department Head
Member: ATA;

Loyola Marymount University
Department of Theatre
Los Angeles, CA 90045
Tel: 213-642-2837
Address Inquiries to: Robert Ackly,
Chairperson
Founded in: 1968
Member: ATA; CETA; SCETA;
Annual Budget: $28,410

Occidental College
Department of Theatre
Los Angeles, CA 90041
Tel: 213-259-2771
Address Inquiries to: Omar M. Paxon,
Chairman
Member: ATA;

University of California
Department of Theatre
405 Hilgard Avenue
Los Angeles, CA 90024

Tel: 213-825-4321
Address Inquiries to: John Young, Chairman
Member: ATA;

University of Southern California
Department of Theatre
Los Angeles, CA 90007
Tel: 415-743-2703
Address Inquiries to: W.D. Ross, Chairman
Member: ATA;

Malibu

Pepperdine University, Seaver College
Department of Theatre
24255 Pacific Coast Highway
Malibu, CA 90265
Tel: 213-456-4000

Marysville

Yuba Community College
Marysville, CA 95901
Tel: 216-742-7351
Address Inquiries to: David Wheeler,
Chairman
Member: ATA;

Modesto

Modesto Junior College
Department of Theatre
College Avenue
Modesto, CA 95350
Tel: 209-526-2000
Address Inquiries to: Joseph Stephen Collins,
Chairperson
Founded in: 1921
Member: ATA; Yosemite Community
College District;
Annual Budget: $12,000
Description: A not-for-profit theatre organiza-
tion.

Monterey

Monterey Peninsula College
Department of Theatre
Monterey, CA 93940
Tel: 408-649-1150
Address Inquiries to: Morgan Stock,
Chairman

Monterey Park

East Los Angeles College
Department of Theatre
Monterey Park, CA 91754
Tel: 213-265-8941
Address Inquiries to: Robert Eley, Chairman

Moorpark

Moorpark Community College
Department of Theatre
Moorpark, CA 93021
Tel: 805-529-2321
Address Inquiries to: Les Weider, Chairman

Mountain View

Saint Joseph's College
Department of Theatre
Mountain View, CA 94040
Address Inquiries to: Michael E. Olich,
Chairman

Napa

Napa College
Department of Theatre
2277 Napa Valley Highway
Napa, CA 94558
Tel: 707-255-2100
Address Inquiries to: Jan Molen, Director

Novato

Indian Valley College
Department of Theatre
Novato, CA 94947

Oakland

Mills College
Department of Theatre
Oakland, CA 94613
Tel: 415-632-2700
Address Inquiries to: Diana O'Hehir,
Chairperson

Oceanside

Mira Costa Community College
Department of Theatre
1 Bernard Drive
Oceanside, CA 92054
Tel: 714-757-2121
Address Inquiries to: Mary Lou Gombar,
Chairperson

Orange

Chapman College
Department of Communication
333 North Glassell
Orange, CA 92666
Tel: 714-997-6856; 714-997-6625
Address Inquiries to: Ron Thronson,
Chairperson
Member: ATA; NEA;
Annual Budget: $350,000
Description: Program designed for students
wishing to major in theatre, film, television
production or public relations. Currently
working with 125 such students. School has
a working cable television station and has
done features in film and television.

Oroville

Butte College
Department of Theatre
Route 1, Box 183A
Oroville, CA 95965
Tel: 916-895-2581
Address Inquiries to: Joseph A. Rich

Oxnard

Oxnard College
Department of Theatre
4000 South Rose Avenue
Oxnard, CA 93030
Tel: 805-488-0911, Ext. 223
Address Inquiries to: Mary Ellen Kazmark,
Chairman
Member: ATA; SCETA;
Annual Budget: $20,000
Description: Curriculum includes theatre his-
tory, acting, stage and lighting design and
childrens theatre. Four shows are given an-
nually.

Pasadena

Pasadena City College
Department of Theatre
1570 East Colorado Boulevard
Pasadena, CA 91106
Tel: 213-578-7216
Address Inquiries to: Chrystal Watson,
Chairperson

Pittsburg

Las Medanos College
Department of Theatre
Pittsburg, CA 94565
Address Inquiries to: Marian L. Shanks,
Chairperson

Pleasant Hill

Diablo Valley College
Department of Theatre
Pleasant Hill, CA 94523
Tel: 415-685-1230
Address Inquiries to: Raymond Stansbury,
Chairman
Member: ATA;

Potorsville

Potorsville College
Department of Theatre
Potorsville, CA 93257
Member:

Rancho Palos Verdes

Marymount Palos Verdes College
Department of Theatre
Rancho Palos Verdes, CA 90274
Address Inquiries to: John F. Lane, Chairman

Redding

Shasta College
Department of Theatre
Redding, CA 96001
Tel: 916-241-3523
Address Inquiries to: Judith Knowles,
Chairperson

Redlands

University of Redlands
Department of Theatre
1200 East Colton Avenue
Redlands, CA 92373
Tel: 714-793-7104
Address Inquiries to: Paul J. Little, Chairman

Redwood City

Canada College
4200 Farm Hill Boulevard
Redwood City, CA 95064
Tel: 408-429-2292
Address Inquiries to: Audrey Stanley,
Chairperson

Reedley

Reedley College
Department of Theatre
Reedley, CA 93654
Address Inquiries to: Richard H. Hoffman,
Chairman

Riverside

Riverside City College
Department of Theatre
4800 Magnolia Avenue
Riverside, CA 92506
Tel: 714-684-3240
Address Inquiries to: Gary D. Schultz,
Chairman

University of California, Riverside
Department of Theatre
Post Office Box 112
Riverside, CA 92521
Tel: 714-787-3343
Address Inquiries to: Eric Barr, Chairman
Founded in: 1959
Member: ATA; State of California;
Annual Budget: $200,000
Description: The department is designed to
provide undergraduate students with a
strong foundation in theatre arts. We offer a
wide range of courses in acting, directing,
history, criticism, literature, design and
technical theatre. In addition to the course
work, our students are regularly involved in
faculty and student directed productions and
projects. Our production facilities include
both proscenium and flexible performance
spaces equipped with some of the most
modern lighting and sound systems. Our
scene and costume shops are fully equipped
and provide students with the opportunity of
working with the full spectrum of materials
and techniques available to professional
theatres.

Rocklin

Sierra College
Department of Theatre
5000 Rocklin Road
Rocklin, CA 95677
Tel: 916-624-3333
Address Inquiries to: Loren Orr, Chairperson

Rohnert Park

Sonoma State University
Department of Theatre
Rohnert Park, CA 94928
Tel: 707-664-2474
Address Inquiries to: Judy Navas,
Chairperson
Sandy Sidwell, Department Secretary
Founded in: 1960
Member: ATA;
Description: Approaches the study of theatre
arts within a liberal arts setting. Productions
include plays, dance, concerts and experi-
mental theatre pieces. Training is in all as-
pects of theatre.

Sacramento

California State University, Sacramento
6000 J. Street
Sacramento, CA 95819
Tel: 916-454-6011
Address Inquiries to: Charles V. Hume,
Chairman
Member: ATA;

Cosumnes River College
Department of Theatre
Sacramento, CA 95823
Tel: 916-421-1000, Ext. 292
Address Inquiries to: Donna J. Sparks,
　Director
　Robert Gardiner, Technical Director
Founded in: 1971
Annual Budget: $65,000
Description: Productions include serious
dramas, one-act plays, musical theatre, caba-
ret shows and children's theatre.

Sacramento City College
Department of Theatre
Sacramento, CA 95882
Tel: 916-449-7480
Address Inquiries to: Jerry Suntherland,
　Chairman

Salinas

Hartnell Community College
Department of Theatre
Salinas, CA 93901
Address Inquiries to: Ronald C. Danko,
　Chairman

San Bruno

Skyline College
Department of Theatre
3300 College Drive
San Bruno, CA 94066
Tel: 415-355-7000
Member: ATA;

San Diego

San Diego City College
Department of Theatre
1313 Twelfth Avenue
San Diego, CA 92101
Tel: 714-238-1181
Address Inquiries to: Lyman A. Saville,
　Chairperson
Member: ATA;

United States International University
Department of Theatre
San Diego, CA 92101
Address Inquiries to: Netter Worthington,
　Chairperson
Member: ATA;

San Francisco

City College of San Francisco
Department of Theatre
50 Phelan Ave
San Francisco, CA 94112
Tel: 415-239-3100; 415-239-3132
Address Inquiries to: R. Struckman,
　Chairperson
Founded in: 1935
Member: Theatre Communication Center of
　the Bay Area;

Lone Moutain College
Department of Theatre
2800 Turk Boulevard
San Francisco, CA 94118
Tel: 415-752-7000
Address Inquiries to: James

Thomason-Bergner, Chairman

Music and Arts Institute of San Francisco
Department of Theatre
2622 Jackson Street
San Francisco, CA 94115
Tel: 415-567-1445
Address Inquiries to: Walter Teschan,
　Chairman

Performing Arts Workshop
1530 Buchanan Street
San Francisco, CA 94115

San Jacinto

Mount San Jacinto Community College
Department of Theatre
21400 Highway 79
San Jacinto, CA 92383
Address Inquiries to: Louis Canter, Dean of
　Academic Instruction

San Jose

San Jose City College
San Jose, CA 95128
Address Inquiries to: Stuart Benett, Chairman
Member: ATA;

San Jose State University
Department of Theatre Arts
San Jose, CA 95192
Tel: 408-277-2763; 408-277-2764
Address Inquiries to: Hal J. Todd, Chairman
Carol Ann Hawes, Dance Coordinator
Founded in: 1936
Member: ATA; California Educational
　Theatre Association;
Description: Combines major degree pro-
grams in drama, dance and radio-television.
Production is an important feature of the de-
partment's curriculum, which includes par-
ticipation in major plays, children's theatre,
dance concerts, musical comedies and oral
interpretation programs. The facilities include three theatres and dance, radio and
television studios.

San Luis Obispo

California Polytechnic State University
Speech Communications Department
San Luis Obispo, CA 93407
Tel: 805-546-2553
Address Inquiries to: Harry Sharp, Chairman
Founded in: 1969
Description: Speech communications depart-
ment handles theatre productions.

San Mateo

College of San Mateo
Department of Theatre
1700 West Hillsdale Boulevard
San Mateo, CA 94402
Tel: 415-574-6288

San Pablo

Compton College
Department of Theatre
San Pablo, CA 90221
Tel: 213-635-8081
Address Inquiries to: Pieter J. VanNiel,

Chairman
Member: MLA; ACTA;

Contra Costa College
Department of Theatre
San Pablo, CA 94806
Tel: 415-235-7800
Address Inquiries to: Ted Kulp, Chairman
Founded in: 1952
Member: ATA; CETA; State of California;
Description: A public community college.

San Rafael

Dominican College
Department of Theatre
San Rafael, CA 94901
Address Inquiries to: John Sowle, Chairman
Member: ATA;

Santa Ana

Santa Ana College
Department of Theatre
Santa Ana, CA 92706
Tel: 714-667-3216; 714-667-3215
Address Inquiries to: H. Robert Blaustone,
　Chairman, Speech and Communications
Founded in: 1946
Member: ATA; WEST; ASA;
Description: A varied curriculum, featuring
theatre, speech, journalism and television.

Santa Barbara

Santa Barbara City College
Department of Theatre
Santa Barbara, CA 93109
Address Inquiries to: Max Whittaker,
　Chairman

University of California, Santa Barbara
Department of Dramatic Art
Santa Barbara, CA 93106
Address Inquiries to: Rona Sande, Chair
Member: UCTA;
Description: Undergraduate and graduate
theatre programs with 9 fully mounted production, modern shops and technical equipment as well as three theatre spaces; a proscenium, studio theatre and laboratory
theatre.

Westmont College
Department of Theatre
955 La Paz Road
Santa Barbara, CA 93108
Tel: 805-969-5051
Address Inquiries to: Everett VandeBeek,
　Associate Professor

Santa Cruz

Bethany Bible College
Department of Theatre
800 Bethany Drive
Santa Cruz, CA 95060
Tel: 408-438-3800

Santa Monica

Santa Monica College
Department of Theatre
1900 West Pico Boulevard
Santa Monica, CA 90405

Tel: 213-450-5150
Address Inquiries to: Ed Gallagher, Chairman
Member: ATA; SCETA; American College
   Theatre Festival;
Annual Budget: $321,000

Santa Rosa

Santa Rosa Junior College
Department of Theatre Arts
1501 Mendocino Avenue
Santa Rosa, CA 95401
Tel: 707-527-4418; 707-527-4328
Address Inquiries to: Tom Bower,
   Chairperson
   Bob Rom, Business Manager
Founded in: 1932
Member: ATA;
Annual Budget: $45,000
Description: Prepares the beginning theatre student in the basic techniques of acting, stagecraft, lighting, costuming and makeup, culminating in full-scale productions for the community.

Saratoga

West Valley College
Department of Theatre
14000 Fruitvale
Saratoga, CA 95070
Tel: 408-867-2200
Address Inquiries to: Jack Senteney,
   Chairman

Sherman Oaks

LA Film Actors Lab
13444 Ventura Boulevard
Sherman Oaks, CA 91423
Tel: 213-789-7626
Description: Offers the professionally focused actor a unique program of on-camera workshops under the instruction of producers, directors and actors who are actively working in the film and television industry.

South Lake Tahoe

Lake Tahoe Community College
Department of Theatre
South Lake Tahoe, CA 95702
Tel: 916-541-4660
Address Inquiries to: Jeff Wentworth,
   Chairman
Founded in: 1975
Member: ATA; UCTA;
Description: Part of the California state community college system.

Stanford

Stanford University
Department of Theatre
Stanford, CA 94305
Tel: 415-497-2300
Address Inquiries to: Charles Lyons,
   Chairman
Member: ATA;

Stockton

San Joaquin Delta College
Department of Theatre
5151 Pacific Avenue
Stockton, CA 95207
Tel: 209-478-2011
Address Inquiries to: Lou Nardi, Chairman

University of the Pacific
Department of Theatre
3601 Pacific Avenue
Stockton, CA 95211
Tel: 209-946-2116; 209-946-2117
Address Inquiries to: William J. Wolak,
   Chairman
Founded in: 1970
Member: ATA;
Annual Budget: $20,000
Description: Our organization is devoted to the preparation of theatre people who are interested in gaining a good liberal arts education along with training in the arts and crafts of the theatre. We teach students in an intimate atmosphere, with adequate facilities and a fairly extensive production schedule with shows mounted on the proscenium stage and in a flexible, black-box studio. In the course of their studies, students are expected to participate in both performance and production work.

Ventura College
Department of Theatre
Stockton, CA 93003
Address Inquiries to: Sy M. Kahn, Chairman

Susanville

Lassen Community College
Department of Theatre
Susanville, CA 96130
Address Inquiries to: Joel Eis, Chairman
Member: ATA;

Turlock

California State College
Department of Theatre
801 Monte Vista
Turlock, CA 95380
Tel: 209-667-3451
Address Inquiries to: Jere D. Wade, Chairman
Founded in: 1970
Member: ATA;
Description: Theatre experience provided in an educational atmosphere.

Valencia

California Institute of the Arts
24700 McBean Parkway
Valencia, CA 91355
Tel: 805-255-1050
Address Inquiries to: Libby Appel, Dean
Founded in: 1971
Member: ATA; LATA;
Annual Budget: $500,000
Description: The aim of the theatre school is to prepare each individual for a life in the professional theatre.

College of the Canyons
26455 North Rockwell Canyon Road
Valencia, CA 91355
Tel: 805-259-7800

Van Nuys

Los Angeles Valley College
Department of Theatre
5800 Fulton Avenue
Van Nuys, CA 91401
Tel: 213-781-1200, Extension 352
Address Inquiries to: E. Peter Mauk,
   Professor
Founded in: 1949
Member: ATA;
Annual Budget: $400,000
Description: Training of students in production of theatre with accent on acting and technical problems.

Victor Ville

Victor Valley College
Department of Theatre
Victor Ville, CA 92392
Tel: 714-245-4271
Address Inquiries to: Polly Fitch, Chairperson

Visalia

College of the Sequoias
Mooney Boulevard
Visalia, CA 93277
Tel: 209-733-2050
Address Inquiries to: George C. Pappas,
   Chairman
Founded in: 1925
Member: ATA; CETA;

Walnut

Mount San Antonio College
Department of Theatre
1100 North Grand Avenue
Walnut, CA 91789
Tel: 714-598-2811
Address Inquiries to: Carter Doran,
   Instructor

West Los Angeles

Oleg Rudnik Studio
12217 Santa Monica Boulevard
West Los Angeles, CA 90025
Tel: 213-820-1670
Address Inquiries to: Oleg Rudnik, Director
Description: Powerful and effective approach. Offers beginning, intermediate and advanced courses.

Whittier

Rio Hondo College
Department of Theatre
3600 Workman Mill Road
Whittier, CA 90608
Tel: 213-692-0921
Address Inquiries to: Jean Korf, Chairperson
Member: ATA;

Woodland Hills

Pierce College
Department of Theatre
Woodland Hills, CA 91371
Tel: 213-347-0551
Address Inquiries to: Donald P. Horst,
  Chairman
Member: ATA; City of Woodland Hills;

COLORADO

Alamosa

Adams State College
Department of Theatre
Alamosa, CO 81102
Tel: 303-589-7011
Address Inquiries to: Dale E. Jeffries,
  Chairman

Colorado Springs

Colorado College
Department of Theatre
Colorado Springs, CO 80903
Tel: 303-473-2233
Address Inquiries to: William E. McMillen,
  Chairman
Member: ATA;

Denver

Colorado Women's College
Department of Theatre
Denver, CO 80220
Tel: 303-394-6012
Address Inquiries to: Marya Bednerik,
  Chairperson
Member: ATA;

Community College of Denver
Department of Theatre
1111 West Colfax Avenue
Denver, CO 80204
Tel: 303-466-8811
Description: The Community College of Denver offers several beginning courses as a part of their Communications Department. 'Oral Interpretations' and 'Reader's Theatre' are offered at the Auraria Campus.

Loretto Heights College
Department of Theatre
Denver, CO 80236
Tel: 303-936-4265
Address Inquiries to: Richard M. Clark,
  Chairman
Member: ATA;

Temple Buell College
Department of Theatre
Denver, CO 80220
Address Inquiries to: Donald E. Malmgren,
  Chairman

University of Denver
Department of Theatre
University Park
Denver, CO 80208
Tel: 303-753-2518
Address Inquiries to: Harry M. Ritchie,
  Chairman

Durango

Fort Lewis College
Department of Theatre
College Heights
Durango, CO 81301
Tel: 303-247-7410
Address Inquiries to: Kenneth E. Bordner,
  Chairman
Member: ATA;

Fort Collins

Colorado State University
Division of Theatre Arts
Johnson Hall
Fort Collins, CO 80523
Tel: 303-491-5116; 303-491-5561
Address Inquiries to: Robert E. Braddy,
  Director
Annual Budget: $70,000
Description: An academic division charged with teaching the theatrical arts and crafts. Committed to the liberal arts, students are required to enroll in a wide variety of courses in fields outside the theatrical disciplines. Students are encouraged to participate in as many of the divisions activities as possible. Productions are mounted in the University Theatre, Johnson Hall. Curriculum includes acting, directing, design, costuming, lighting, stagecraft, make-up, playwrighting and research.

Glenwood

Colorado Mountain College
Department of Theatre
Glenwood, CO 81601
Tel: 303-945-7481
Address Inquiries to: Peter Marshall,
  Chairman

Golden

Community College of Denver
Red Rocks Campus
12600 West 6th Avenue
Golden, CO 80401
Address Inquiries to: Benjamin Sweet
Description: The Community College of Denver offers several beginning courses as a part of their Communications department. Oral Interpretations and Reader's Theatre are offered at the Auraria Campus.

Greeley

Aim Community College
Department of Theatre
Greeley, CO 80631
Address Inquiries to: Don Ritter, Chairman

Gunnison

Western State College of Colorado
Department of Theatre
Gunnison, CO 81230
Tel: 303-943-2045
Address Inquiries to: Jess W. Gern, Chairman

La Junta

Otero Junior College
Department of Theatre
18th and Colorado
La Junta, CO 81050
Tel: 303-384-4446
Address Inquiries to: Ed Stafford, Chairman
Member: ATA;

Littleton

Arapahoe Community College
Department of Theatre
5900 South Santa Fe Drive
Littleton, CO 80122
Tel: 303-794-1550
Address Inquiries to: Joan E. Shields,
  Chairperson

Westminster

Community College of Denver
Department of Theatre
3645 West 112th Avenue
Westminster, CO 80030
Address Inquiries to: P.D. McLeran
Description: The Community College of Denver offers several beginning courses as a part of their Communications department. Oral Interpretations and Reader's Theatre are offered at the Auraria Campus.

CONNECTICUT

New Haven

Albertus Magnus College
Department of Theatre
700 Prospect Street
New Haven, CT 06511
Tel: 203-777-6631
Address Inquiries to: Maxine Schlingman,
  Chairperson
Member: ATA;

Southern Connecticut State College
Department of Theatre
501 Crescent Street
New Haven, CT 06515
Tel: 203-397-4432; 203-397-4431
Address Inquiries to: Daniel E. Cashman,
  Chairman
Founded in: 1954
Member: ATA; ANTA; NETC; State of CT;
Annual Budget: $30,000
Description: The department offers a BA in theatre. Students may specialize in children's theatre, design, technical theatre, performance, film/television, theatre history, dramatic literature and criticism. The department, in conjunction with the Crescent Players, stages at least four major productions a year.

New London

United States Coast Guard Academy
Department of Theatre
Mohegan Avenue
New London, CT 06320
Tel: 203-443-6045

Address Inquiries to: D.L. Janse, Director

Waterford

National Theater Institute
O'Neill Theater Center
305 Great Neck Road
Waterford, CT 06385
Tel: 203-443-5378
Description: A fully accredited intensive theatrical program especially designed for liberal arts students at the O'Neill Theater Center. The sessions are fourteen weeks and enrollment is limited.

Winsted

Northwest Connecticut Community
College Theatre
Department of Theatre
Winsted, CT 06518
Address Inquiries to: Joan Fieckenstein,
  Chairperson
Member: ATA;

DELAWARE

Dover

Wesley College
Department of Theatre
College Square
Dover, DE 19901
Tel: 302-674-4000
Address Inquiries to: James K. Young,
  Chairman

Newark

University of Delaware
Department of Theatre
Newark, Delaware 19711
Tel: 302-738-2201; 302-738-2202
Address Inquiries to: Peter T. Vagenas,
  Chairman
Founded in: 1945
Member: ATA; NAST;
Description: Offers a BA degree through the college of liberal arts and sciences where students may emphasize acting, design, technology, history/literature, or dance. University Theatre, the department producing organization, presents a five-play season and an annual dance production.

Wilmington

Brandywine College
Department of Theatre
Box 7139 Concord Dike
Wilmington, DE 19803
Tel: 203-478-3000

DISTRICT OF COLUMBIA

Washington

American University
Academy for the Performing Arts
Massachusetts Avenue at Nebraska, NW
Washington, DC 20016
Tel: 202-686-2315

Address Inquiries to: Charles Crowder,
  Chairman
Member: ATA;

Catholic University of America
Department of Theatre
Washington, DC 20064
Tel: 202-635-5353
Address Inquiries to: William H. Graham,
  Chairman
Member: ATA;

Gallaudet College
Department of Theatre
7th and Florida Avenue, NE
Washington, D.C. 20002
Tel: 202-651-5606; 202-651-5710
Address Inquiries to: David Tweedie, Acting
  Chairman
  Jo Tracie, Theatrical Coordinator
Founded in: 1963
Member: ATA;
Annual Budget: $15,000
Description: Presents three fully mounted productions and a touring show annually.

Georgetown University
Department of Theatre
State One, 3620 P Street NW
Washington, DC 20057
Tel: 202-625-4085
Address Inquiries to: Don B. Murphy,
  Chairman
Member: ATA;

George Washington University
Department of Theatre
Washington, DC 20052
Tel: 202-676-7072
Address Inquiries to: Nathan Garner,
  Chairman
Member: ATA;

Howard University
Department of Theatre
2400 Sixth Street NW
Washington, D.C. 20059
Tel: 202-636-7050; 202-636-7051
Address Inquiries to: Geoffrey W. Newman,
  Chairman
Founded in: 1949
Annual Budget: $18,000
Description: Program designed to prepare its students to persue a career in the professional or community theatre; teach drama on the secondary or college level; or pursue research in theatre arts.

Immaculata College of Washington
Department of Theatre
4300 Nebraska Avenue
Washington, DC 20016
Tel: 202-966-0040
Address Inquiries to: E. Wierdak, Chairman

Mount Vernon College
Department of Theatre
2100 Foxhill Road
Washington, DC 20007
Tel: 202-331-34444
Address Inquiries to: Julia Heflin, Chairman

University of the District of Columbia
Department of Theatre
Washington, DC 20001
Tel: 202-727-2351
Address Inquiries to: Joseph G. Gathings,
  Chairman
Member: ATA;

Washington and Jefferson College
Department of Theatre
Lincoln Street
Washington, DC 15301
Tel: 412-222-4400
Address Inquiries to: Robert L. Brindley,
  Professor of Communications, Chairman
Member: ATA;
Description: Department of Theatre.

FLORIDA

Avon Park

South Florida Junior College
Department of Theatre
Avon Park, FL 33825
Tel: 813-453-6661, Ext. 192
Address Inquiries to: Lynn MacNeil,
  Chairman

Boca Raton

Florida Atlantic University
Department of Theatre
Boca Raton, FL 33431
Tel: 305-395-5100; 305-395-2502
Address Inquiries to: Edward L. Madden,
  Chairman
Member: URTA;
Description: Offers a full range of credits towards an MFA degree. It makes complete use of its 548-seat proscenium stage and a smaller flexible studio theatre.

Bradenton

Manatee Junior College
Department of Theatre
5840 26th Street West
Bradenton, FL 33507
Tel: 813-755-1511
Address Inquiries to: John W. James,
  Chairman
Member: ATA;

Coral Gables

University of Miami
Department of Theatre
Coral Gables, FL 33124
Tel: 305-284-4474; 305-284-3178
Address Inquiries to: Herman Diers,
  Chairman
Founded in: 1939
Member: ATA; STC; FTC; Parker
  Foundation;
Annual Budget: $100,000
Description: Provides the community with exciting Shakespeare Festivals, a host of musicals, experimental productions of great plays, and a place where new young playwrights will see their work first staged. Graduates include theatrical agents, stage

managers, cinematographers and television personalities.

Deland

Stetson University
Department of Theatre
Deland, FL 32720
Tel: 904-734-4121
Address Inquiries to: James C. Wright,
    Chairman

Fort Lauderdale

Broward Community College
Department of Theatre
Fort Lauderdale, Florida 33314
Tel: 305-475-6840; 305-475-6840
Address Inquiries to: Mildred B. Mullikin,
    Chairperson
Founded in: 1960
Member: STC; ATA; Mobil Foundation;
Description: The curricular and co-curricular
programs provide the student actor or technician, with theoretical and practical experiences in theatre arts which may lead to further work in all aspects of educational and
professional theatre.

Fort Myers

Edison Community College
Department of Theatre
College Parkway
Fort Myers, FL 33901
Tel: 813-481-2121

Jacksonville

Jacksonville University
Department of Theatre
College of Fine Arts
Jacksonville, FL 32211
Tel: 904-744-3950
Address Inquiries to: Dr. Davis Sikes,
    Chairman
Member: ATA;

Lake City

Lake City Community College
Department of Theatre
Lake City, FL 32055
Tel: 904-752-1822
Address Inquiries to: Paul Ferguson,
    Chairman
Member: ATA;

Lakeland

Southeastern Bible College
Department of Theatre
Lakeland, FL 33801
Address Inquiries to: Kenneth Haddaway,
    Chairman

Marianna

Chipola Junior College
Department of Theatre
Marianna, FL 32446
Tel: 904-526-2761
Address Inquiries to: Clifford D. Herron
Member: NEA;
Annual Budget: $12,000

Miami

Barry College
Department of Theatre
11300 North East 2nd Street
Miami, Florida 33161
Tel: 305-751-0044; 305-758-3392 Ext. 223
Address Inquiries to: Patricia Minnaugh,
    Chairperson
Founded in: 1940
Member: ATA; SETA; USITT;
Annual Budget: $250,000
Description: Primarily undergraduate training
in theatre arts.

Miami-Dade Community College
Department of Theatre
300 North East 2nd Avenue
Miami, FL 33132
Tel: 305-577-6740
Address Inquiries to: Robert L. Levine,
    Chairman
Member: ATA;

Miami-Dade Community College-North
    Campus
Department of Theatre
11011 Southwest 104th Street
Miami, FL 33176
Tel: 305-596-1203
Address Inquiries to: Edward Anderson,
    Chairman

Ocala

Central Florida Community College
Department of Theatre
Post Office Box 1388
Ocala, FL 32670
Tel: 904-237-2111
Address Inquiries to: George W. Statler,
    Chairman

Orlando

Florida Technological University
Department of Theatre
Post Office Box 25000
Orlando, FL 32816
Tel: 305-275-9101
Address Inquiries to: Harry W. Smith,
    Chairman
Member: ATA;

Saint Petersburg

Eckerd College
Department of Theatre
Saint Petersburg, FL 33733
Tel: 813-867-1166
Address Inquiries to: Richard Rice,
    Coordinator
Founded in: 1958
Member: SETC;
Annual Budget: $3,000

Saint Petersburg College
Department of Theatre
Saint Petersburg, FL 33710
Tel: 813-381-6681
Address Inquiries to: Robert E. Jones,
    Chairman
Founded in: 1970
Member: ATA; STC;

Annual Budget: $12,000

Sanford

Seminole Community College
Department of Theatre
Sanford, FL 32771
Tel: 305-323-1450
Address Inquiries to: Dorothy Morrison,
    Chairperson

Sarasota

Florida State University
Asolo Conservatory Company
Post Office Drawer E
Sarasota, FL 33578
Tel: 813-711-
Address Inquiries to: Neal Kenyon, Director
Member: LORT; U/RTA;
Description: Accepts a limited number of
promising candidates for training in the
fields of acting, voice, dance, movement and
stage combat. The company performs in a
fully restored 18th century playhouse that is
part of the famed Ringling Museum.

Tallahassee

Florida School of the Arts
Department of Theatre
Tallahassee, FL 32077
Address Inquiries to: David R. Humphrey,
    Chairman
Member: ATA;

Florida State University
School of Theatre
Fine Arts Building
Tallahassee, FL 32306
Tel: 904-644-6795
Address Inquiries to: Richard G. Fallon, Dean
Member: U/RTA;
Description: Presents a complete theatrical
season utilizing its two proscenium theatres
and a flexible stage.

Tallahassee Community College
Department of Theatre
Tallahassee, FL 32304
Tel: 904-576-5181, Extension 257
Address Inquiries to: Dr. Stan DeHart,
    Artistic Director
Founded in: 1970
Member: ATA; SETC;
Description: $5,000

Tampa

Hillsborough Community College, YBOR
    Campus
Department of Theatre
Post Office Box 22127
Tampa, FL 33622
Tel: 813-879-7222
Address Inquiries to: Marvin Kirschman,
    Chairman

University of South Florida
Department of Theatre
Tampa, FL 33620
Tel: 813-974-2701; 813-974-2603
Address Inquiries to: Nancy Cole,
    Chairperson

William Lounzer, Designer and Associate
Professor
Founded in: 1958
Member: ATA;
Annual Budget: $230,000
Description: Offers a bachelors' degree in two
major areas: Performance and Design/
Technology. Students are given many op-
portunities to act, design and direct both in
class work and in the production program.
Graduates enter theatre related professions
and go onto graduate schools offering pro-
grams in their theatrical specialties.

University of Tampa
Department of Drama
401 West Kennedy
Tampa, FL 33606
Tel: 813-253-8861
Address Inquiries to: Gary Luter, Chairman
Founded in: 1977
Member: ATA; SETC;
Description: University of Tampa Theatre
produces contemporary drama, children's
theatre and musical theatre. Two to three
productions are produced annually

West Palm Beach

Palm Beach Atlantic College
Department of Theatre
West Palm Beach, FL 33401
Tel: 305-883-8592
Address Inquiries to: George J. McGee
Founded in: 1968
Member: ATA; SCA;
Annual Budget: $30,000
Description: The primary goal is to train able
and intellectually-equipped communicators.
The school strives to impart a theoretical as
well as a practical understanding of oral
communications in its artistic and societal
dimensions.

Winter Park

Rollins College
Department of Theatre
Winter Park, FL 32789
Tel: 305-646-2000; 305-646-2501
Address Inquiries to: Robert O. Juergens,
Chairman
Founded in: 1885
Member: ATA; SETC; URTA; FTC;
ACUCAA;
Annual Budget: $350,000

GEORGIA

Athens

University of Georgia
Department of Theatre
Athens, GA 30601
Tel: 404-542-2836
Address Inquiries to: Leighton M. Ballew,
Director
Member: ATA;

Atlanta

Academy Theatre School of Performing
Arts
1374 West Peachtree
Atlanta, GA 30309
Tel: 404-892-0355
Address Inquiries to: Frank Wittow, Artistic
Director

Emory University
Department of Theatre
Atlanta, GA 30322
Tel: 404-329-6187
Address Inquiries to: Fergus G. Currie,
Chairman

Georgia State University
Speech and Drama Department
University Plaza
Atlanta, GA 30303
Tel: 404-658-2921
Address Inquiries to: Lawrence J. Rifkin,
Chairperson
Member: ATA;

Mercer University, Atlanta
Department of Drama
3000 Flowers Road
Atlanta, GA 30341
Tel: 404-451-0331
Address Inquiries to: Linda Langernbruch,
Chairperson

Morehouse College
Department of Theatre
Atlanta, GA 30314
Tel: 404-681-2800

Clarkston

Dekalb Community College
Department of Theatre
555 North Indian Creek
Clarkston, GA 31907
Tel: 404-292-1520
Address Inquiries to: Mrs. Faye Clark
Member: ATA;

Columbus

Columbus College
Department of Theatre
Algonquin Drive
Columbus, GA 31907
Tel: 404-568-2030
Address Inquiries to: Dennis Ciesil,
Department Head
Member: ATA;

Decatur

Agnes Scott College
Department of Theatre
Decatur, GA 30030
Tel: 404-373-2571
Address Inquiries to: Jack T. Brooking,
Chairman
Founded in: 1965
Member: ATA; STC;
Annual Budget: $4,415
Description: A small department with a staff of
three permanent faculty members plus a
number of part time student assistants. With

a major production in the fall and spring.
The winter quarter is given over to a children's show and a series of one-acts, student directed and designed. The department offers a major in theatre and courses
which cover completely the basic areas of
Theater History, Tech/Design and Acting/
Directing. The productions are actually
produced in close cooperation with the
faculty by a student organization called
The Blackfriars.

Demorest

Piedmont College
Department of Theatre
Demorest, GA 30535
Tel: 404-723-3911

Forsyth

Tift College
Department of Theatre
Forsyth, GA 31209
Tel: 912-994-6689
Address Inquiries to: Betty Stacey, Head of
Fine Arts

Gainesville

Brenau College
Washington Street
Gainesville, GA 30501
Tel: 404-532-4341
Address Inquiries to: Elizabeth Hedrick,
Director
Member: ATA;

Gainesville Junior College
Department of Theatre
Gainesville, GA 30501
Tel: 404-536-5226
Address Inquiries to: Ed Cabell, Chairman

Macon

Macon Junior College
Department of Theatre
US 80 and I-475
Macon, GA 31206
Tel: 912-474-2700
Address Inquiries to: Dr. Charles Pecor,
Professor

Milledgville

Georgia Southern College
Department of Theatre
Milledgville, GA 30458
Tel: 912-681-5600
Address Inquiries to: Dr. Clarence McCord,
Chairman
Member: ATA;

Mount Berry

Berry College
Department of Theatre
Mount Berry, GA 30149
Tel: 404-232-5374
Address Inquiries to: Leroy Clark, Chairman
Member: ATA;

Rome

Shorter College
Department of Theatre
Shorter Hill
Rome, GA 31404
Tel: 404-232-2463
Address Inquiries to: Pauline Noble, Phd,
Drama and Speech

Savannah

Armstrong State College
Drama-Speech Section
11935 Abercorn Street
Savannah, GA 31406
Tel: 912-927-5354
Address Inquiries to: John Suchower,
Director
Founded in: 1935
Member: ATA; SETC;

HAWAII

Hilo

University of Hawaii at Hilo
Department of Theatre
Post Office Box 1357
Hilo, HI 96720
Tel: 808-961-9311
Address Inquiries to: Robert Spanabel,
Assistant Professor
Member: ATA;

Honolulu

Chaminade University
Department of Theatre
3140 Waialae Avenue
Honolulu, HI 96816
Tel: 808-732-1471
Member: ATA;

University of Hawaii
Department of Drama
1770 East West Road
Honolulu, HI 96822
Tel: 808-948-7677; 808-948-7622
Address Inquiries to: Edward A. Langhans,
Chairman
Founded in: 1950
Member: ATA;

IDAHO

Boise

Boise State University
Department of Theatre
1910 University
Boise, ID 83725
Tel: 208-385-3957; 208-385-1530
Address Inquiries to: Charles Lauterbach,
Chairman
Founded in: 1970
Member: ATA; NDC;

Coeur D'Alene

North Idaho College
Department of Theatre
1000 West Garden Avenue
Coeur D'Alene, ID 83814
Tel: 208-667-7422
Member: ATA;

Moscow

University of Idaho
Department of Theatre
Moscow, ID 83843
Tel: 208-885-6465
Address Inquiries to: Edmund M. Chavez,
Chaiman
Member: ATA;

Pocatello

Idaho State University
Department of Theatre
Pocatello, ID 83209
Tel: 208-236-2431
Address Inquiries to: Dr. Allen P. Blomquist,
Director
Member: ATA;

ILLINOIS

Aurora

Aurora College
Department of Theatre
Aurora, IL 60506
Tel: 312-892-6431
Address Inquiries to: Susan Pellowe,
Chairman

Carbondale

Southern Illinois University
Department of Theatre
Carbondale, IL 62901
Tel: 618-692-2773
Address Inquiries to: Darwin R. Payne,
Chairman
Member: ATA;

Carlinville

Blackburn College
Department of Theatre
Carlinville, IL 62626
Tel: 217-854-3231
Address Inquiries to: Thomas Anderson,
Professor
Member: ATA;

Charleston

Eastern Illinois University
Department of Theatre Arts
Charleston, IL 61290
Tel: 217-581-3110; 217-581-3121
Address Inquiries to: W. Over, Chairperson
Founded in: 1947
Member: ATA;
Annual Budget: $20,000

Chicago

Central YMCA Community College
Department of Theatre
Chicago, IL 60601
Tel: 312-222-8150
Address Inquiries to: Lorenz Boehm,
Chairman

Chicago City College, Amundsen-Mayfair
College
Department of Theatre
4626 North Knox Avenue
Chicago, IL 60630
Tel: 312-286-1323

Chicago City College, Southwest College
Department of Theatre
3939 West 79th Street
Chicago, IL 60652
Tel: 312-427-0500

Chicago State University
Department of Theatre
95th and King Drive
Chicago, IL 60628
Tel: 312-995-2190
Address Inquiries to: Sherwood Snyder,
Chairman
Member: ATA;

Columbia College Theater/Music Center
Theater-Music Center
72 East 11th Street
Chicago, IL
Tel: 312-663-9465
Description: Columbia College Theater/Music Center is dedicated to the training of tomorrow's talent.

DePaul/Goodman School of Drama
2324 North Freemont
Chicago, IL
Tel: 312-321-8374
Description: The DePaul/Goodman School of Drama offers an intensive training program in theatre skills.

De Paul University Goodman School of Drama
804 West Belden
Chicago, IL 60614
Tel: 312-321-8374
Description: Write or call the School regarding interviews and auditions.

Kennedy-King College
Department of Theatre
6800 South Wentworth Avenue
Chicago, IL 60621
Tel: 312-962-3300; 312-962-3302
Address Inquiries to: Phillip L. Williams,
Chairperson
Founded in: 1966
Member: NASD; IBS; SCA; THAP;
Annual Budget: $10,000

Malcolm X College
Theatre Program
Chicago, IL 60612
Tel: 312-942-3000
Address Inquiries to: Elizabeth Bouchard,
Chairperson

Founded in: 1970
Annual Budget: $1,000
Description: A program within the department of English and Communications with emphasis on Black drama.

Kathleen Mullady Theatre
6525 North Sheridan Road
Chicago, IL
Tel: 312-274-3000
Description: Kathleen Mullady Theatre offers training in theatre skills.

North Park College
Department of Theatre
5125 North Spaulding
Chicago, IL 60115
Tel: 312-583-2700
Address Inquiries to: Mickey Benson, Chairman

Richard Daley College
Department of Theatre
Chicago, IL 60652
Address Inquiries to: Lester Lundahl, Chairman

Roosevelt University
Department of Theatre
430 South Michigan Avenue
Chicago, IL 60605
Tel: 312-341-3720
Address Inquiries to: Yoland Lyon, Chairperson

Truman College
Department of Theatre
Chicago, IL 60640
Tel: 312-878-1700
Address Inquiries to: Charles E. Smith, Chairman

University of Chicago
Department of Theatre
5706 South University
Chicago, IL 60637
Tel: 312-753-3583
Member: ATA;

Chicago Heights

Prairie State College
Department of Theatre
Chicago Heights, IL 60411
Tel: 312-756-3110
Address Inquiries to: Richard F. Peterson, Chairman

Decatur

Millikin University
Department of Theatre
1184 West Main Street
Decatur, IL 62522
Tel: 217-424-6211; 217-424-6282
Address Inquiries to: Dr. Arthur Hopper, Chairman
Founded in: 1970
Member: ATA;
Description: Undergraduate classes in theatre and theatre production.

Richard Community College
Department of Theatre

Decatur, IL 62522
Address Inquiries to: Richard Marriott, Chairman

Richland Community College
Department of Theatre
Decatur, IL 62526
Tel: 217-875-7200 Extension 266;
     217-875-7200 Extension 262
Address Inquiries to: Winfield Scott, Chairman
     Lonn Pressnall, Associate Professor, Speech-Theatre
Founded in: 1972
Member: ITA;
Annual Budget: $5,500
Description: Produces at least three theatrical shows a year using students in the community college.

DeKalb

Northern Illinois University
Department of Theatre Arts
DeKalb, IL 60115
Tel: 815-753-1334; 815-753-1335
Address Inquiries to: Kent G. Gallagher, Chairman
Founded in: 1972
Member: ATA; SCA; ITA;
Annual Budget: $514,000

East Peoria

Illinois Central College
Department of Theatre
East Peoria, IL 61635
Tel: 309-694-5011
Address Inquiries to: Don Marine, Program Director
Member: ATA;

East Saint Louis

State Community College of East Saint Louis
Department of Theatre
East Saint Louis, IL 62201
Address Inquiries to: Michael Brodley, Chairman

Edwardsville

Southern Illinois University
Department of Theatre
Edwardsville, IL 62026
Tel: 618-692-2771
Address Inquiries to: Dr. William Vilhauer, Chairman
Member: ATA;

Elsah

Principia College
Department of Theatre
Elsah, IL 62028
Tel: 618-966-2131
Address Inquiries to: Donald Mainwarling, Chairman
Member: ATA;

Evanston

National College of Education
Department of Theatre
2840 Sheridan Road
Evanston, IL 60201
Tel: 312-256-5150
Address Inquiries to: Richard Bagg, Chairman
Member: ATA;

Galesburg

Carl Sandburg College
Department of Theatre
Galesburg, IL 61401
Tel: 309-344-2518
Address Inquiries to: John Pazereskis, Theatre Director
Founded in: 1967
Member: ATA; ITA; ISTA;
Description: Offers a two-year Associates of Arts degree with a concentration in theatre.

Ina

Rend Lake College
Department of Theatre
Rural Route 1
Ina, IL 62846
Tel: 618-437-5321
Address Inquiries to: Larry Phifer, Chairman

Lebanon

McKendree College
Department of Theatre
Lebanon, IL 62254
Tel: 618-537-4481
Address Inquiries to: Grace R. Welsh, Chairperson

Lincoln

Lincoln College
Department of Theatre
300 Keokuk Street
Lincoln, IL 62656
Tel: 217-732-3155
Address Inquiries to: Larry Cullison, Chairman
Member: ATA;

Macomb

Western Illinois University
Department of Theatre
Macomb, IL 61455
Tel: 309-298-1543; 309-298-1618
Address Inquiries to: Ms. Jerrilee Cain, Arts Coordinator
     Mr. Joseph Martinez, Artistic Director
Founded in: 1973
Member: ATA; URTA; ITA; SETC; ISTA;
Annual Budget: $45,000
Description: Four mainstage and twenty studio productions are part of the academic program. Guest artists are occasionally hired to perform, design, or direct mainstage productions. The touring theatre is part of the MFA program in acting whereby a student spends two semesters in the rehearsal and approximately 175 performances of four shows in repertory. The summer stock theatre employs 20 to 25 performers, two

directors, a choreographer, a musical director, a technical director, costume designer, scene designer and student technicians. Credit can be earned if desired, tuition waivers are available for students. Salaries and housing are provided for performers, technicians and staff. The theatre spaces include: two prosceniums, a flexible theatre and a horeshoe shaped space. In addition to regular season, a touring theatre company serves the western Illinois area.

Morton Grove

Oakton Community College
Department of Theatre
Morton Grove, IL 60053
Tel: 312-967-5120
Address Inquiries to: Dennis Berkson,
  Chairman

Normal

Illinois State University
Department of Theatre
Normal, IL 61761
Tel: 309-436-8321
Address Inquiries to: Calvin Lee Pritner,
  Chairman
Member: ATA; URTA; NAST; Illinois Arts
  Council; Illinois State U.; Illinois State
  U. Foundation;
Description: The Illinois State University produces the renowed Illinois Shakespeare Festival under the direction of Calvin Lee Pritner. Three Shakespearean productions are mounted each summer at Ewing Manor, Bloomington, in rotating repertory.

Quincy

Quincy College
Department of Theatre
1831 College Avenue
Quincy, IL 62301
Tel: 217-222-8020
Address Inquiries to: Hugh Fitzgerald,
  Chairman
Member: ATA;

River Grove

Triton College
Department of Theatre
River Grove, IL 60171
Address Inquiries to: Norman Wiegel,
  Chairman

Rockford

Rockford College
Department of Theatre
5050 East State Road
Rockford, IL 61101
Tel: 815-226-4000
Address Inquiries to: Rufus Cadigan,
  Chairman
Founded in: 1847
Member: ATA; ITA;
Annual Budget: $450,000
Description: Theatre facility including fully equipped fly system; computerized lighting board; 600 seat proscenium theatre; 200 seat black box theatre. B.A. and B.F.A. degrees offered in all areas of theatre.

Rock Island

Augustana College
Department of Theatre
639 38th Street
Rock Island, IL 61201
Tel: 309-794-7000
Address Inquiries to: Dan Spaugh, Chairman
Member: ATA;

Springfield

Lincoln Land Community College
Department of Theatre
Springfield, IL 62708
Tel: 217-786-2314
Address Inquiries to: Anthony P.J. Cerniglia,
  Chairman
Member: ATA;

Sangamon State University
Department of Theatre
Shephard Road
Springfield, IL 62708
Tel: 217-786-6600
Address Inquiries to: Guy Romans, Chairman

INDIANA

Fort Wayne

Saint Francis College
Department of Theatre
Fort Wayne, IN 46808
Tel: 219-432-3551
Address Inquiries to: Hal Gunderson,
  Chairman
Member: ATA;

Muncie

Ball State University
Department of Theatre
2000 University Avenue
Muncie, IN 47306
Tel: 317-285-4028
Address Inquiries to: E.S. Strother,
  Chairperson
Member: ATA;

Richmond

Earlham College
Department of Theatre
Richmond, IN 47374
Tel: 317-962-6561
Address Inquiries to: Henry Merrill,
  Chairman
Member: ATA;

Saint Mary of the Woods

Saint Mary of the Woods College
Department of Theatre
Saint Mary of the Woods, IN 47876
Tel: 812-535-4141
Address Inquiries to: Timothy E. Brown,
  Chairperson
  Penny Koob, Assistant
Founded in: 1840
Member: ATA; SETC; URTA; TCG; Indiana Arts Commission;
Annual Budget: $6,000
Description: A small liberal arts Catholic college for women which tries to train the student in all aspects of the theatre. Plays from all genres are produced.

Sioux Center

Dordt College
Department of Theatre
Sioux Center, IN 51250
Tel: 712-722-3771
Address Inquiries to: James Koldenhoven,
  Chairman
Member: ATA;

Upland

Taylor University
Department of Theatre
Upland, IN 46989
Tel: 317-998-2751
Address Inquiries to: James Oosting,
  Chairman
Member: ATA;

Valparaiso

Valparaiso University
Department of Theatre
University Place
Valparaiso, IN 46838
Tel: 219-464-5073
Address Inquiries to: Fred Sitton, Chairman
Member: ATA;

Vincennes

Vincennes University
Department of Theatre
1002 North First Avenue
Vincennes, IN 47591
Tel: 812-885-4256; 812-885-4580
Address Inquiries to: James Spurrier,
  Director of Theatre
Member: ATA; North Central Association of Colleges and Schools; Council of Junior Colleges; American Association of Community and Junior Colleges; National League for Nursing; INTA;
Description: Offers an A.A. or A.S. in Theatrical Production and an A.S. in Musical Theatre.

West Lafayette

Purdue University
Department of Theatre
West Lafayette, IN 47907
Tel: 317-749-2695
Address Inquiries to: Dale E. Miller,
  Chairperson
Member: ATA;

Whiting

Calumet College
Department of Theatre
Whiting, IN 46394
Tel: 219-473-4388
Member: ATA;

IOWA

Ames

Iowa State University
Department of Theatre
Ames, IA 50011
Tel: 515-294-4111
Address Inquiries to: Patrick D. Gouran,
Chairman
Member: ATA;

Cedar Rapids

Mount Mercy College
Department of Theatre
Cedar Rapids, IA 52402
Address Inquiries to: Kathleen Pudzuvelis,
Chairperson

Clarinda

Iowa Western Community College
Department of Theatre
Clarinda, IA 51632
Tel: 712-542-5117
Address Inquiries to: Delbert Smith,
Chairman

Dubuque

Loras College
Department of Theatre
1450 Alta Vista
Dubuque, IA 52001
Tel: 319-588-7127
Address Inquiries to: Donald W. Stribling,
Chairman
Member: ATA;

Iowa City

University of Iowa
Department of Drama
Iowa City, IA 52242
Tel: 319-353-5791; 319-353-6589
Address Inquiries to: Bruce Levitt, Head of
Actor Training
David Thayer, Production Manager
Member: URTA;
Description: Graduate programs available.

Iowa Falls

Ellsworth Community College
Department of Theatre
Iowa Falls, IA 50140
Member: ATA;

Le Mars

Westmar College
Department of Theatre
1002 Third Avenue Southeast
Le Mars, IA 51031
Tel: 712-546-7081
Address Inquiries to: James Fletcher,
Chairman

Marshalltown

Marshalltown Community College
Department of Theatre
Marshalltown, IA 50158
Tel: 515-752-7106
Address Inquiries to: Max G. Wiese,
Chairman

Mount Pleasant

Iowa Wesleyan College
Department of Theatre
Mount Pleasant, IA 52641
Tel: 319-385-8021
Address Inquiries to: David C. File,
Chairperson

Muscatine

Muscatine Community College
Department of Theatre
Muscatine, IA 52761
Tel: 319-263-3571; 319-263-8250
Address Inquiries to: Nancy Keel,
Chairperson
Founded in: 1929
Member: ATA; Stanley Foundation;
Annual Budget: $1,200
Description: A participant in the American
College Theatre Festival, the college mounts
three major productions a year, two recitals
and many community service productions.

KANSAS

Arkansas

Cowley County Community College
Department of Theatre
125 East Second Street
Arkansas, KS 67005
Tel: 316-442-0430
Address Inquiries to: Sydney W. Pratt,
Chairman

Baldwin City

Baker University
Department of Theatre
606 Eighth Street
Baldwin City, KS 66006
Tel: 913-594-6451
Address Inquiries to: Thelma R. Morreale,
Chairperson
Member: ATA;

Dodge City

Dodge City Community College
Department of Theatre
Dodge City, KS 67801
Address Inquiries to: F. Revitte, Chairperson

Saint Mary of the Plains College
Department of Theatre
Dodge City, KS 67801
Tel: 316-225-4171
Address Inquiries to: Harry Langdon,
Chairman
Founded in: 1952
Member: ATA; IASLD; KTA;
Annual Budget: $7,000
Description: The small department attempts
to provide a broad range of both acting and
technical training experience. All under-
graduates perform in at least two main-stage
productions annually and all work technical
crews for every production.

Emporia

Emporia State University
Department of Theatre
1200 Commercial
Emporia, KS 66801
Description: Emporia State University offer
BA, BFA and MA degrees in theatre. Students may participate in the summer repertory program which is one of the oldest programs of its kind in the mid west.

Great Bend

Barton County Community
Department of Theatre
Route 1
Great Bend, KS 67530
Tel: 316-792-2701
Address Inquiries to: Mary Misegadis,
Instructor

Hays

Fort Hays State University
Department of Theatre
Hays, KS 67601
Tel: 913-628-4226
Address Inquiries to: Suzanne Trauth,
Director
Member: ATA;

Independence

Independence Community Junior College
Department of Theatre
Box 708
Independence, KS 67301
Tel: 316-331-4100
Address Inquiries to: Margaret Doheen,
Chairperson

Kansas City

Kansas City Community College
Department of Theatre
Kansas City, KS 66112
Address Inquiries to: Laura J. Barrett,
Chairperson

Lawrence

Haskell Indian Junior College
Department of Theatre
Lawrence, KS 66044
Member: ATA;

University of Kansas
Department of Theatre
Lawrence, KS 66045

Leavenworth

Saint Mary College
Department of Theatre
Leavenworth, KS 66048
Tel: 913-682-5151
Address Inquiries to: Mary Flynn,
Chairperson

Mc Pherson

Mc Pherson College
Department of Theatre
1600 East Euclid
Mc Pherson, KS 67460
Tel: 316-241-0731

Address Inquiries to: Rick Tyler, Assistant
Professor
Founded in: 1887
Member: ATA; UCTA; AKT;
Annual Budget: $5,000

North Newton

Bethel College
Department of Drama
North Newton, KS 67117
Tel: 316-283-2500
Address Inquiries to: Arlo Kasper, Chairman
Founded in: 1912
Member: ATA; AKT; State of Kansas;
Annual Budget: $24,000
Description: Offers five major productions an-
nually plus a summer season.

Overland Park

Johnson County Community College
Department of Theatre
Overland Park, KS 66210
Tel: 913-888-8500
Address Inquiries to: James M. Williams,
Chairman

Pittsburg

Pittsburg State University
Department of Theatre
Pittsburg, KS 66762
Tel: 316-231-7000, Ext. 340
Address Inquiries to: Harold W. Loy,
Chairman
Member: ATA; AKT;
Description: The program offers BA and MA
degrees with emphasis in theatre. Academic
year major productions and repertory prod-
uctions. The Summer Resident Company
produces an annual season of thirty perfor-
mances of two musicals and one straight
play; this program is now in it's 22nd year.

Pratt

Pratt Community College
Department of Theatre
Highway 61
Pratt, KS 67124
Tel: 316-672-5641
Address Inquiries to: Edwin Gorsky,
Instructor

Salina

Kansas Wesleyan University
Department of Theatre
South Santa Fe
Salina, KS 67401
Tel: 913-827-5541, Extension 257
Address Inquiries to: Ed Guinan, Producer
Founded in: 1886
Member: ATA; UCTA;

Windfield

Southwestern College
Department of Theatre
100 College Street
Windfield, KS 67156
Tel: 316-221-4150 Extension 244
Address Inquiries to: Darnell D. Lautt,
Director of Theatre

Member: ATA; AKT;

Witchita

Wichita State University
Department of Theatre
1845 Fairmount
Witchita, KS 67208
Tel: 316-689-3368; 316-689-3360
Address Inquiries to: Richard Welsbacher,
Chairman
Founded in: 1924
Member: ATA; AKT; MATC;
Annual Budget: $33,000

KENTUCKY

Bowling Green

Western Kentucky University
Department of Theatre
Bowling Green, KY 42101
Tel: 502-745-3296
Address Inquiries to: J. Regis O'Conner,
Chairman
Member: ATA; SCA;

Danville

Centre College of Kentucky
Program in Dramatic Art
Walnut Street
Danville, KY 40422
Tel: 606-236-5211; 606-236-4692
Address Inquiries to: Cathryn Vandegriff,
Phd., Chairman
Founded in: 1946
Member: ATA;
Annual Budget: $5,000
Description: A major program in dramatic art
producing three mainstage and two studio
productions a year.

Lexington

University of Kentucky
Department of Theatre
Lexington, KY 40506
Tel: 606-257-2797
Address Inquiries to: Wallace N. Briggs,
Chairman

Louisville

Catherine Spaulding College
Department of Theatre
851 South 4th Street
Louisville, KY 40203
Tel: 502-585-9911

University of Louisville
Department of Theatre
Louisville, KY 40208
Tel: 502-588-6814
Address Inquiries to: Albert J. Harris,
Chairman
Member: ATA;

Pippa Passes

Alice Lloyd College
Department of Theatre
Pippa Passes, KY 41844
Tel: 606-368-2101

Address Inquiries to: Terry Cornett,
Professor of Drama

Richmond

Eastern Kentucky University
Department of Speech and Theater
Richmond, KY 40475
Tel: 606-622-0111; 606-622-5851
Address Inquiries to: Dr. Richard Benson,
Chairman

LOUISIANA

Grambling

Grambling State University
Department of Speech and Drama
Grambling, LA 71245
Tel: 318-247-6941; 318-247-3777
Address Inquiries to: Allen Williams,
Chairman
Member: ATA; SCA;
Annual Budget: $160,000
Description: Produces plays that tour the com-
munity.

Natchitoches

Northwestern State University
Department of Theatre
Natchitoches, LA 71457
Address Inquiries to: E. R. Black, Chairman
Member: ATA;

New Orleans

Loyola University
Department of Theatre
6363 Saint Charles Avenue
New Orleans, LA 70118
Tel: 504-865-2011
Address Inquiries to: Ernest Ferlita, Chairman
Member: ATA;

Tulane University
Department of Theatre
New Orleans, LA 70118
Tel: 504-865-6205
Address Inquiries to: M.S. Barranger,
University Chairman
Member: ATA;

Shreveport

Centenary College
Department of Theatre
2911 Centenary Boulevard
Shreveport, LA 71104
Tel: 318-869-5242; 318-869-5243
Address Inquiries to: Robert R. Buseick,
Chairman
Founded in: 1825
Member: ATA; SWTC;
Annual Budget: $15,000
Description: Award winning department dedi-
cated to producing outstanding productions
for the college and community. During the
academic year, four to six major productions
are presented as well as touring children's
productions. Advanced students are given
directorial opportunities with both the chil-
dren's productions and major productions.

Plays are selected to give actors experience with classic as well as modern plays. The community is encouraged to participate in the annual summer musicals.

MAINE

Brunswick

Bowdoin College
Division of Theatre Arts
Brunswick, ME 04011
Tel: 207-725-8731, Ext. 341
Address Inquiries to: A. Rutan, Director of Theatre
June Vail, Director of Dance
Founded in: 1903
Member: ATA; NETC;
Annual Budget: $50,000
Description: Offers an extensive program in extracurricular theatre, dance and drama, for the enjoyment and edification of their college students.

Farmington

University of Maine
Department of Theatre
Farmington, ME 04238
Tel: 207-778-6910
Address Inquiries to: John Scarcelli, Chairman

Gorham

University of Maine
Department of Theatre
College Avenue
Gorham, ME 04038
Tel: 207-839-6771
Address Inquiries to: William P. Steele, Chairman
Member: ATA;

University of Southern Maine
Department of Theatre
Gorham, ME 04038
Tel: 207-780-5481
Address Inquiries to: Walter R. Stump, Chairman
Member: ATA;

Lewiston

Bates College
Department of Theatre
Lewiston, ME 04240
Tel: 207-738-8772
Address Inquiries to: Martin Andrucki, Chairman
Member: ATA;

Orono

University of Maine, Orono
Department of Theatre
123 Lord Hall
Orono, ME 04473
Tel: 207-581-7534
Address Inquiries to: Anorld Colbath, Coordinator
Member: ATA;

Unity

Unity College
Department of Theatre
Unity, ME 04988
Tel: 207-948-3131
Address Inquiries to: Kathleen Lord, Chairperson

MARYLAND

Arnold

Anne Arundel Community College
Department of Theatre
Arnold, MD 21012
Tel: 301-647-7100
Address Inquiries to: Robert E. Kauffman, Chairman
Member: ATA;

Baltimore

College of Notre Dame of Maryland
Department of Theatre
4701 North Charles Street
Baltimore, MD 21210
Tel: 301-435-0100
Address Inquiries to: Kathleen M. Engers, Chairman
Member: ATA;

Dundalk Community College
Department of Theatre
Baltimore, MD 21222
Address Inquiries to: Walter G. Rice, Chairman
Member: ATA;

Essex Community College
Department of Theatre
7201 Rossville Road
Baltimore, MD 21237
Tel: 301-522-1420
Address Inquiries to: F. Black, Chairman
Founded in: 1957
Member: ATA; NAST;
Description: The theatre department is fully accredited by the National Assocation of Schools and Theatre. Essex is the home of Maryland's largest summer theatre, The Cockpit in Court Summer Theater, which receives funding from the Maryland Arts Council and the Baltimore County Arts Commission.

Goucher College
Department of Theatre
1021 Dulaney Valley Road
Baltimore, MD 21204
Tel: 301-825-3300
Address Inquiries to: Barry Knower, Chairman

Morgan State College
Department of Theatre
Baltimore, MD 21239
Tel: 301-323-2270
Address Inquiries to: Harmon S. Watson, Chairman
Member: ATA;

Peabody Conservatory
Theatre Department
1 East Mount Vernon Place
Baltimore, MD 21202
Tel: 301-659-8100
Address Inquiries to: Roger Brunyate, Chairman

Bethesda

Maryland Academy of Dramatic Arts and Theatre
4930 Cordell Avenue
Bethesda, MD 20814
Tel: 301-652-7999; 301-654-9820
Address Inquiries to: Ralph Tabakin, Executive Director
Founded in: 1970
Member: AEA; AFTRA; SAG; NATAS; ATA;
Description: All 'students' are performing apprentices working for professional recognition. They work with various stage, television, film, producers and agencies.

College Park

University of Maryland
Department of Theatre
College Park, MD 20742
Tel: 301-454-2740
Address Inquiries to: Dr. Rudolph E. Pugliese, Professor
Member: ATA;

Frostburg

Frostburg State College
Department of Theatre
East College Avenue
Frostburg, MD 21532
Address Inquiries to: Jack W. Vrieze, Chairman
Member: ATA;

Kensington

Capital Institute of Technology
Department of Theatre
Kensington, MD 20794

Largo

Prince Georges Community College
Department of Theatre
301 Largo Road
Largo, MD 20870
Tel: 301-336-6000
Address Inquiries to: John Handley, Associate Dean and Director
Member: ATA;

Rockville

Montgomery College
Department of Theatre
Rockville, MD 20854
Tel: 301-762-7400
Address Inquiries to: Norma Berkeley, Chairperson
Member: ATA;

Salisbury

Salisbury State College
Department of Theatre
Salisbury, MD 21801
Tel: 301-546-3261
Address Inquiries to: Leland Starnes,
Chairman
Member: ATA;

Tacoma Park

Columbia Union College
Department of Theatre
7600 Flower Avenue
Tacoma Park, MD 21901
Tel: 301-287-6060
Member: ATA;

MASSACHUSETTS

Amherst

University of Massachusetts at Amherst
Department of Theatre
112 Fine Arts Center
Amherst, MA 01003
Tel: 413-545-2214; 413-545-3490
Address Inquiries to: Virginia Scott, Graduate
Program Director
Member: URTA;
Description: A university resident theatre pro-
gram. A graduate program is available.

Boston

Leland Powers School
Department of Theatre
70 Brookline Avenue
Boston, MA 02115
Tel: 617-247-1300
Address Inquiries to: Richard C. Swan,
Chairman
Member: ATA;

Theater Workshop-Boston
551 Tremont Street
Boston, MA 02116
Tel: 617-482-4778
Address Inquiries to: Helen M. Connor,
Administrative Director
Barry Dym, President
Founded in: 1967
Annual Budget: $100,000

Chestnut Hill

Pine Manor College
Department of Theatre
400 Heath Street
Chestnut Hill, MA 02167
Tel: 617-731-7000
Address Inquiries to: Thomas B. Pegg,
Instructor

Great Barrington

Simon's Rock Early College
Department of Theatre
Alford Road
Great Barrington, MA 02130
Tel: 413-528-0771
Address Inquiries to: James Hardy

Longmeadow

Bay Path Junior College
Department of Theatre
588 Longmeadow
Longmeadow, MA 01106
Tel: 413-567-0621
Address Inquiries to: John P. Gaffney,
Chairman
Member: ATA;

Natick

Walnut Hill School of Performing Arts
912 Highland Street
Natick, MA 01760
Tel: 617-653-4312
Address Inquiries to: Mark Lindberg,
Chairman
Founded in: 1969
Description: Seating capacity 340.

North Dartmouth

Southeastern Massachusetts University
Department of Theatre
North Dartmouth, MA 02747
Tel: 617-997-9321

Springfield

Springfield College
Department of Theatre
263 Alden Street
Springfield, MA 01109
Tel: 413-788-3000
Address Inquiries to: Carroll P. Bitch,
Associate Professor
Member: ATA;

Wheaton

Regis College
Department of Theatre
235 Wellesley Street
Wheaton, MA 02193
Tel: 617-893-1820
Address Inquiries to: S. Bogan, Associate
Professor
Member: ATA;

Williamstown

Williams College
Department of Theatre
Williamstown, MA 02766
Tel: 413-597-3131
Address Inquiries to: J.B. Bucky, Director
Member: ATA;

MICHIGAN

Adrian

Siena Heights College
Department of Theatre
Adrian, MI 49221
Tel: 517-263-0371
Address Inquiries to: Glen E. Crane,
Chairman

Ann Arbor

University of Michigan
Professional Theatre Program
227 South Ingalls
Ann Arbor, MI 48109
Tel: 313-764-5350
Address Inquiries to: Walter Eysselinck,
Chairman
Jack Bender, Associate Chairman
Member: ATA;
Description: The University of Michigan offers
graduate professional training in conjunc-
tion with the resident Equity company, Mich-
igan Ensemble Theatre, and the University
of Michigan Professional Theatre Program.

Benton Harbor

Lake Michigan College
Department of Theatre
Benton Harbor, MI 49022
Tel: 616-927-3571

Big Rapids

Ferris State College, Department of
Theatre
Department of Theatre
Big Rapids, MI 49307
Tel: 616-296-9971
Address Inquiries to: Lyle Mayer, Chairman

Detroit

Mercy College of Detroit, Department of
Theatre
8200 West Outer Drive
Detroit, MI 48219
Tel: 393-531-7820
Address Inquiries to: Albert Zolton,
Chairman

University of Detroit, Marygrove College
Department of Theatre
8425 West McNichols
Detroit, MI 43221
Tel: 313-341-1838
Address Inquiries to: Dominic Missimi,
Chairman

Wayne State University
Department of Theatre
1400 Chrysler Freeway
Detroit, MI 48202
Tel: 313-961-7302
Address Inquiries to: Leonard Leone,
Chairman

Flint

University of Michigan, Flint
Department of Theatre
1321 East Court
Flint, MI 48503
Tel: 313-762-3230
Address Inquiries to: Alfred J. Loup,
Chairman
Founded in: 1967
Member: ATA; SCA;
Description: Undergraduate program of
theatre studies, producing four shows a year
on the mainstage, and several studio prod-
uctions.

Grand Rapids

Grand Rapids Baptist College
Department of Drama
1001 East Beltline, Northeast
Grand Rapids, MI 49505
Tel: 616-949-5300
Address Inquiries to: Richard Stewart, Fine
    Arts Division Chairman
Founded in: 1941

Houghton

Michigan Technological University
Department of Drama
Houghton, MI 49931
Tel: 906-487-2067
Address Inquiries to: Richard Blanning,
    Chairman
Member: ATA;

Interlochen

Interlochen Arts Academy
Department of Theatre
Interlochen, MI 49643
Tel: 616-392-5111
Address Inquiries to: Mel Mrochinski,
    Chairman
Member: ATA;

Jackson

Jackson Community College
Department of Theatre
2111 Emmons Road
Jackson, MI 49201
Tel: 517-787-0800
Address Inquiries to: G.L. Blanchard,
    Chairperson
Member: ATA;

Lansing

Lansing Community College
Department of Theatre
419 North Capitol
Lansing, MI 48914
Tel: 517-373-7400
Address Inquiries to: William A. Peterson,
    Chairman
Member: ATA;

Livonia

Schoolcraft College
Department of Theatre
18600 Haggerty Road
Livonia, MI 48151
Tel: 313-591-6400
Address Inquiries to: Lawerence W. Rudick,
    Chairman
Member: ATA;

Marquette

Northern Michigan University
Department of Theatre
Marquette, MI 49855
Tel: 906-227-2553
Address Inquiries to: James A. Panowski,
    Chairman
Member: ATA;

Monroe

Monroe County Community College
Department of Theatre
1555 South Raisinville Road
Monroe, MI 48161
Tel: 313-242-7300
Address Inquiries to: Dr. Paul Ross,
    Chairman

Rochester

Michigan Christian Junior College
Department of Theatre
800 West Avon Road
Rochester, MI 48063
Tel: 313-651-5800
Address Inquiries to: Frant Rutledge,
    Chairman
Member: ATA;

Oakland University
Department of Theatre
Rochester, MI 48063
Tel: 313-377-2030
Address Inquiries to: Dr. Raynold Allvin,
    Chairman
Member: ATA;

Olivet College
Department of Theatre
Rochester, MI 48063
Tel: 616-749-7620
Address Inquiries to: James Donohue,
    Chairman

Saginaw

Saginaw Valley State College
Department of Theatre
2250 Pierce Road
Saginaw, MI 48710
Tel: 517-793-9800
Address Inquiries to: Roland J. Keift

Spring Arbor

Spring Arbor College
Department of Theatre
Spring Arbor, MI 49283
Tel: 517-750-1200, Ext. 265
Address Inquiries to: Ester Maddox,
    Chairman
Description: Offers training in producing and
directing.

Warren

Macomb County Community College
Department of Theatre
14500 East Twelve Mile Road
Warren, MI 48093
Tel: 313-445-7000
Address Inquiries to: Donald Wing, Dean
Member: ATA;

MINNESOTA
Bemidji

Bemidji State College
Department of Theatre
Bemidji, MN 56601
Tel: 281-755-3935

Address Inquiries to: Joan Reynolds,
    Chairperson

Bloomington

Normandale Community College
Department of Theatre
Bloomington, MN 55431
Tel: 612-831-1 5001
Address Inquiries to: Linda Putnam,
    Chairman
Member: ATA;

Brainerd

Brainerd Community College
Department of Theatre
College Drive
Brainerd, MN 56401
Tel: 612-829-1791
Address Inquiries to: Bob Dryden, Chairman

Coon Rapids

Anoka-Ramsey Community College
Department of Theatre
Coon Rapids, MN 55443
Address Inquiries to: Warren W.
    Schueneman, Chairman

Duluth

College of Saint Scholastica
Department of Theatre
Duluth, MN 55811
Tel: 218-728-3631
Address Inquiries to: Robert Hasen,
    Chairman

Grand Rapids

Itasca Community College
Department of Theatre
Grand Rapids, MN 55744
Tel: 218-326-9451
Address Inquiries to: Gretchen Murphy,
    Chairperson

Hibbing

Hibbing Community College
Department of Theatre
Hibbing, MN 55746
Address Inquiries to: Vernon Benberg,
    Chairman
Member: ATA;

International Falls

Rainy River Community College
Department of Theatre
International Falls, MN 55649
Address Inquiries to: Richard Hill, Chairman

Mankato

Mankato State University
Department of Theatre
Mankato, MN 56001
Tel: 507-389-2119
Address Inquiries to: Theodore Paul,
    Chairman
Member: ATA;

Marshall

Southwest State University
Department of Speech and Theatre
Marshall, MN 56258
Tel: 507-537-7103
Address Inquiries to: Robert Ridley,
  Chairman
Member: ATA;

Minneapolis

Golden Valley Lutheran College
Department of Theatre
6125 Olson Highway
Minneapolis, MN 55422
Tel: 612-542-1245
Address Inquiries to: Paul W. Siemers,
  Chairman
Member: ATA; ACTA;
Description: Offers three productions each
year and course work in acting, history, tech-
nical theatre and directing.

Metropolitan Community College
Department of Theatre
50 Willow Street
Minneapolis, MN 55403
Tel: 612-339-9441
Address Inquiries to: Keith Jones, Chairman
Member: ATA;

University of Minnesota
Department of Theatre
Minneapolis, MN 55455
Tel: 612-373-3118; 612-373-4882
Address Inquiries to: Wendell Josal, Chair
Glenn Gadberry, Director of Graduate
  Study
Member: ATA; APA; NAST;
Description: Each summer the University
Theatre presents period musicals or melo-
dramas on the Minnesota Centennial Show-
boat and children's plays in the Peppermint
Tent. Actors and technicians for these sum-
mer theatres hold paid positions.

Monkato

Bethany Lutheran College
Department of Theatre
734 Marsh Street
Monkato, MN 56001
Tel: 507-625-2977
Address Inquiries to: Sigurd K. Lee,
  Chairperson
Member: ATA;

Morris

University of Minnesota, Morris
Department of Theatre
Morris, MN 56267
Tel: 612-589-2211
Address Inquiries to: Raymond J. Lammers,
  Speech/Theatre
Member: ATA;

Northfield

Carleton College
Department of Theatre
Northfield, MN 55057
Tel: 507-645-4431

Address Inquiries to: Edward L. Sostek,
  Chairman
Member: ATA;

Saint Olaf College
Department of Theatre
Northfield, MN 55057
Tel: 507-663-3370
Address Inquiries to: Patrick Quade,
  Chairman

Roseville

Northwestern College
Department of Theatre
Roseville, MN 55113
Tel: 612-636-4840
Address Inquiries to: Douglas M. Briggs,
  Chairman

Saint Cloud

Saint Cloud State University
Department of Theatre
Saint Cloud, MN 56301
Tel: 612-255-3229
Address Inquiries to: Ronald G. Perrier,
  Chairman
Member: ATA;

Saint Joseph

College of Saint Benedict
Department of Theatre
Saint Joseph, MN 56374
Tel: 612-363-5713
Address Inquiries to: Kerry Lafferty,
  Chairman
Member: ATA;

Saint Paul

Bethel College
Department of Theatre
Saint Paul, MN 55112
Address Inquiries to: Donald C. Rainbow,
  Chairman
Member: ATA;

College of Saint Catherine
Department of Theatre
2004 Randolph Avenue
Saint Paul, MN 55105
Tel: 612-698-5571
Address Inquiries to: Julie White,
  Chairperson
Member: ATA;

College of Saint Thomas
Department of Theatre
Saint Paul, MN 55105
Tel: 612-647-5265
Address Inquiries to: James M. Symons,
  Chairman

Concordia College
Department of Theatre
Saint Paul, MN 5504
Tel: 612-641-8266
Address Inquiries to: Jean Black, Chairperson

Hamline University
Department of Theatre
1536 Hewitt Avenue
Saint Paul, MN 55104

Tel: 612-641-2229
Address Inquiries to: James C. Ching,
  Chairman

MacAlester College
Department of Theatre
Saint Paul, MN 55101
Tel: 612-647-6221
Address Inquiries to: D. Hatfield, Chairperson
Member: ATA;

Saint Peter

Gustavus Adolphus College
Department of Theatre
Saint Peter, MN 56082
Tel: 507-931-4300
Address Inquiries to: Robert Gardner,
  Chairman
Member: ATA;

Virginia

Mesabi Community College
Department of Theatre
905 West Chestnut Street
Virginia, MN 55792
Tel: 218-741-9200
Address Inquiries to: Charles D. Rowland,
  Chairman
Member: ATA;

White Bear Lake

Lakewood Community College
Department of Theatre
White Bear Lake, MN 55110
Tel: 612-770-1331
Address Inquiries to: George F. Wade,
  Chairman

Willmar

Willmar Community College
Department of Theatre
Post Office Box 797
Willmar, MN 56201
Tel: 612-235-2131
Member: ATA;

Wiona

College of Saint Teresa
Department of Theatre
1130 West Broadway
Wiona, MN 55987
Tel: 507-454-2930
Address Inquiries to: Peter Laudry, Chairman

MISSISSIPPI

Blue Mountain

Blue Mountain College
Department of Theatre
Box 333
Blue Mountain, MS 38610
Tel: 601-685-4711
Address Inquiries to: James L. Andre,
  Chairman

Booneville

Northeast Mississippi Junior College
Department of Theatre
Booneville, MS 38829
Tel: 602-728-6208
Address Inquiries to: Mrs. William H.
  Preston, Chairperson
Member: ATA;

Brookhaven

Whitworth College
Department of Theatre
Brookhaven, MS 37601
Tel: 601-833-4311

Cleveland

Delta State University
Department of Theatre
Cleveland, MS 38733
Tel: 601-843-2434
Address Inquiries to: Willard Booth,
  Chairman
Founded in: 1938
Member: AETA; SCA; Mississippi State
  University;
Annual Budget: $100,000
Description: Performances are held in the Delta Playhouse.

Columbus

Mississippi University for Women
Department of Theatre
Columbus, MS 39701
Tel: 601-328-5067
Address Inquiries to: Guy H. Keeton,
  Chairman

Gulfport

Coast Junior College
Department of Theatre
Gulfport, MS 39501
Tel: 601-896-3355
Address Inquiries to: Donald E. Moore,
  Chairman

Hattiesburg

University of Southern Mississippi
Department of Theatre
Box 31, Southern Station
Hattiesburg, MS 39406
Tel: 601-266-7225
Address Inquiries to: Dr. I. Blaine

William Carey College
Department of Theatre
Hattiesburg, MS 39401
Tel: 601-582-5051 Extension 228
Address Inquiries to: Obra Quave,
  Chairperson
Founded in: 1906
Member: SACS; NCA; ACC; ACE; NASM;
Description: Carey Dinner Theatre is an adjunct operation of the college theatre.It operates along professional lines, but is educational and non-profit. It operates only in the summers.

Holly Springs

Rust College
Department of Theatre
Rust Avenue
Holly Springs, MS 38635
Tel: 601-252-3555
Address Inquiries to: John Johnson, Director
Member: ATA;

Jackson

Jackson State College
Department of Theatre
Jackson, MS 39217
Tel: 601-948-8533
Address Inquiries to: Edward Fisher,
  Chairman
Member: ATA;

Long Beach

Gulf Park College
Department of Theatre
Long Beach, MS 39560
Tel: 601-863-6852
Address Inquiries to: Charles F. Lembright,
  Chairman
Member: ATA;

Lorman

Alcorn State University
Department of Theatre
Lorman, MS 39096
Tel: 601-877-3711
Address Inquiries to: Jerry Bangham,
  Chairman

Mathiston

Wood Junior College
Department of Theatre
Mathiston, MS 39752
Tel: 601-263-9321
Address Inquiries to: H. Wayne Webster,
  Chairperson
Member: ATA;

Meridian

Meridian Municipal Junior College
Department of Theatre
Meridian, MS 39301
Address Inquiries to: Louise Brinson,
  Chairperson

Mississippi State

Mississippi State University
Department of Theatre
Mississippi State, MS 39762
Tel: 601-325-3320; 601-323-4746
Address Inquiries to: Dr. Dominic J. Cunetto,
  Chairman
Founded in: 1963
Member: ATA; STC; MSTA;
Description: Produces three to four major productions, plus six to eight student directed one-act plays. They host the annual North Mississippi High School Drama Festival. Usually, there is one dinner theatre production.

Moorherd

Mississippi Delta Junior College
Department of Theatre
Moorherd, MS 38761
Address Inquiries to: Suzy Patterson,
  Chairperson

Perkinston

Mississippi Gulf Coast Junior College
Department of Theatre
Perkinston, MS 39573
Tel: 601-928-5211
Address Inquiries to: Kathryn Lewis,
  Chairperson

Scooba

East Mississippi Junior College
Department of Theatre
Scooba, MS 39358
Tel: 601-476-3421
Address Inquiries to: Dayna A. Anderson,
  Chairperson
Member: ATA;

State College

Mississippi State University
Department of Theatre
State College, MS 39762
Address Inquiries to: Dominic J. Cunetto,
  Chairman

Summit

Southwest Mississippi Junior College
Department of Theatre
Summit, MS 39666
Tel: 601-428-5641
Member: ATA;

Tougaloo

Tougaloo College
Department of Theatre
Tougaloo, MS 39174
Tel: 601-982-4242
Address Inquiries to: Hollis W. Huston,
  Chairman
Member: ATA;

University

University of Mississippi
Department of Theatre
University, MS 38677
Tel: 601-232-7170
Address Inquiries to: Seldon Faulkner,
  Chairman
Member: ATA;

Wesson

Copiah-Lincoln Community Junior College
Department of Theatre
Wesson, MS 39191
Address Inquiries to: John R. Landress,
  Chairman

MISSOURI

Bolivar

Southwest Baptist College
Department of Theatre
623 South Pike
Bolivar, MO 65613
Tel: 417-326-5281

Columbia

Stephens College
Department of Theatre
East Broadway
Columbia, MO 65201
Tel: 314-442-2211
Address Inquiries to: Brett Prentiss, Head of
    Theatre
Founded in: 1937
Member: URTA;
Description: Department of theatre arts, offer-
ing BA and BFA degrees in theatre arts. Has
an 'actor-teacher' program. Performances
take place in a 300-seat proscenium theatre.

University of Missouri-Columbia
Department of Theatre
129 Fine Arts Building
Columbia, MO 65211
Tel: 314-882-2021
Address Inquiries to: Carla Waal, Director of
    Theatre
Member: ATA; SETC; MATC;
Description: The University Theatre is in the
department of Speech and Dramatic Art.

Fayette

Central Methodist College
Department of Theatre
Fayette, MO 65248
Tel: 816-248-3391
Address Inquiries to: Dr. Don Edison,
    Chairman

Fulton

Westminister College
Department of Theatre
Seventh and Westminister
Fulton, MO 65251
Tel: 314-642-3361
Member: ATA;

Joplin

Missouri Southern State College
Department of Theatre
Newman and Duquesne Roads
Joplin, MO 64801
Tel: 417-624-8100
Address Inquiries to: Milton W. Briezke,
    Director
Founded in: 1967
Member: ATA; MOTA;
Annual Budget: $5,000
Description: Provides the student with a bal-
ance of theory and practical experience.
There are two theatres on campus (one a
converted barn for small productions, the
other a new, well equipped, large theatre) in
which the students may do performance,
production and design work. There are four

major productions per year and the minor
productions of the year include two children's shows and two to ten student workshop productions.

Kansas City

Avila College
Department of Performing and Visual Arts
11901 Wornall Road
Kansas City, MO 64145
Tel: 816-942-8400; 816-942-8408 (box
office)
Address Inquiries to: William J. Louis,
    Chairman
Founded in: 1948
Member: ATA; ACTF
Annual Budget: $20,000
Description: The Performing and Visual Arts
Department at Avila College offers both tra-
ditional academic and professionally orient-
ed degrees.

University of Missouri, Kansas City
Department of Theatre
51st and Rockhill Road
Kansas City, MO 64110
Tel: 816-276-2701
Address Inquiries to: Dr. Patricia McIllrath,
    Chairperson

Liberty

William Jewell College
Department of Theatre
Liberty, MO 64068
Tel: 816-781-3806
Address Inquiries to: Dr. Georgia Bowman,
    Chairman
Member: ATA;

Marshall

Missouri Valley College
Department of Theatre
500 East College Street
Marshall, MO 65340
Tel: 816-866-6924 Extension 147
Address Inquiries to: Dr. Robert Glass,
    President
    Dr. W.H. Bearce, Academic Dean
Founded in: 1889
Member: MSTA;
Annual Budget: $4,000
Description: Provides a substantial combina-
tion of theory and practical experience.

Maryville

Northwest Missouri State University
Department of Theatre
Maryville, MO 64468
Tel: 816-582-7141
Address Inquiries to: Dr. Robert Bohlken,
    Chairman

Neosho

Crowder College
Department of Theatre
Neosho, MO 64850
Tel: 417-451-3223
Address Inquiries to: Edward N. Oathour,
    Chairman

Poplar Bluff

Three Rivers Community College
Department of Theatre
507 Vine Street
Poplar Bluff, MO 63901
Tel: 314-785-7794
Address Inquiries to: Michael Bouland,
    Chairman
Member: ATA;

Saint Joesph

Missouri Western State College
Department of Theatre
4525 Downs Drive
Saint Joesph, MO 64507
Tel: 816-271-4397
Address Inquiries to: Dr. James Mehl,
    Chairman
Founded in: 1968
Member: ATA;

Saint Louis

Saint Louis Community College at
    Meramec
    Department of Theatre
11333 Big Bend Boulevard
Saint Louis, MO 63122
Tel: 314-966-7500
Address Inquiries to: Robert Dixon, Associate
    Producer

Washington University
Department of Theatre
Saint Louis, MO 63130
Tel: 314-863-0100
Address Inquiries to: Sidney J. Friedman,
    Arts Chairman
Member: ATA;

Webster College
Department of Theatre
470 East Lockwood
Saint Louis, MO 63119
Tel: 314-968-6929
Address Inquiries to: Peter Sargent,
    Chairman
Founded in: 1925
Member: ATA; USITT; IES;
Annual Budget: $275,000

Springfield

Southwest Missouri State University
Department of Theatre
901 South National
Springfield, MO 65802
Tel: 417-836-5000
Address Inquiries to: Dr. Robert H. Bradley,
    Chairman

Tarkio

Tarkio College
Department of Theatre
Tarkio, MO 64491
Tel: 816-736-4131
Address Inquiries to: Paul J. Hustoles,
    Director of Theatre
Founded in: 1883
Member: ATA; UCTA; SETC;
Annual Budget: $150,000

Warrensburg

Central Missouri State University
Department of Theatre
Warrensburg, MO 64093
Tel: 816-429-4020; 816-429-4330
Address Inquiries to: James L. Highlander,
Professor
Member: ATA;

MONTANA

Billings

Eastern Montana College
1500 North 30th
Billings, MT 59101
Tel: 406-657-2011
Address Inquiries to: Vicki Tait, Assistant
Professor Speech/Theatre
Member: ATA;

Bozeman

Montana State University
Department of Theatre
Student Union Building
Bozeman, MT 59717
Tel: 406-994-3091
Address Inquiries to: Bruce C. Jacobsen,
Member: URTA;
Description: Department has a Shakespeare in
the Park festival and a summer program.

Dillon

Western Montana College
Department of Theatre
710 South Atlantic Street
Dillon, MT 59725
Tel: 406-683-7401
Address Inquiries to: Ellen Bush, Head of
Theatre
Founded in: 1893
Member: ATA;
Annual Budget: $4,000

Glendive

Dawson Community College
Department of Theatre
Post Office Box 421
Glendive, MT 59330
Tel: 406-365-3396
Member: ATA;

Helena

Carroll College
Little Theatre
Helena, MT 59625
Tel: 406-442-3450 Ext. 276; 406-442-3455
Address Inquiries to: Jim Bartruff, Director
Member: ATA; ACA; APO;
Annual Budget: $4,500
Description: A four year program in theatre
offering both a major and a minor in Theatre
Arts. Produces four plays annually for the
college and community of Helena.

Missoula

University of Montana
Department of Theatre
Missoula, MT 59801
Tel: 406-243-5572
Address Inquiries to: James Kriley, Chairman
Member: URTA;

NEBRASKA

Columbus

Platte Technical Community College
Department of Theatre
Box 1027
Columbus, NB 68601
Tel: 402-564-7132
Member: ATA;

Fairbury

Southeast Community College-Fairbury
Campus
Department of Theatre
924 K Street
Fairbury, NB 68352
Tel: 402-729-6148
Address Inquiries to: Terri Harris, Chairman
Member: ATA;

Lincoln

University of Nebraska, Lincoln
Department of Theatre
Lincoln, NB 68588
Tel: 402-472-2072; 402-472-1619
Address Inquiries to: Rex McGraw, Chairman
and Artistic Director
A. Richard Nichols, Chief Advisor and
Associate Artistic Director
Founded in: 1900
Member: ATA; URTA; MATC; NTA;
Annual Budget: $400,000
Description: The department trains theatre
students to the highest degree of their artis-
tic ability and offers theatrical experiences to
members of the university and community
through regular public performances.

Norfolk

Northeastern Nebraska College
Department of Theatre
Norfolk, NB 68701
Tel: 402-371-2020
Member: ATA;

North Platte

North Platte College
Department of Theatre
5th and Jeffers Street
North Platte, NB 69101
Tel: 308-532-6888
Member: ATA;

Omaha

University of Nebraska, Omaha
Department of Theatre
60th and Dodge Streets (Box 688)
Omaha, NB 68101
Tel: 402-554-2200

Address Inquiries to: Robert W. Welk,
Chairman
Member: ATA;

Scottsbluff

Hiram Scott College
Department of Theatre
Scottsbluff, NB 69361
Tel: 308-635-3761
Member: ATA;

Platte Valley Bible College
Department of Theatre
305 East 16th Street
Scottsbluff, NB 69361
Tel: 308-632-6933
Member: ATA;

Wahoo

John F. Kennedy College
Department of Theatre
Wahoo, NB 68066
Tel: 402-443-4171
Member: ATA;

NEVADA

Reno

University of Nevada, Reno
Department of Theatre
Reno, NV 89557
Tel: 702-784-6155
Address Inquiries to: Dr. Roscoe Booth,
Chairman
Member: ATA;

NEW HAMPSHIRE

Franconia

Franconia College
Department of Theatre
Franconia, NH 03580
Tel: 603-823-5545
Address Inquiries to: Ken Grantham,
Chairman
Member: ATA;

Plymouth

Plymouth State College
Department of Theatre
Plymouth, NH 93264
Tel: 603-536-1550
Address Inquiries to: Dr. Roi White, Director
of Plymouth Players
Member: ATA;

NEW JERSEY

Camden

Rutgers University
Department of Theatre
311 North Fifth Street
Camden, NJ 08102
Tel: 609-757-6246
Address Inquiries to: Zeke Berlin, Chairman

Member: ATA;

Cranford

Union College
Department of Theatre
1033 Springfield Avenue
Cranford, NJ 07016
Tel: 201-276-2600
Address Inquiries to: Donald H. Julian,
Chairman

East Orange

Upsala College
Department of Theatre
East Orange, NJ 07019
Tel: 201-266-7202; 201-266-7144
Address Inquiries to: Robert Marcazzo,
Chairman
Member: ATA;

Edison

Middlesex County College
Department of Theatre
Edison, NJ 08817
Tel: 201-548-6000, Ext. 367
Address Inquiries to: Edwin B. Drake,
Chairman
Founded in: 1966
Annual Budget: $50,000
Description: The department sponsors tour-
ing companies in theatre, dance, music and
Children's Theatre.

Glassboro

Glassboro State College
Department of Theatre
Glassboro, NJ 08028
Tel: 609-445-5288; 609-445-5787
Address Inquiries to: William Lawrence
Kushnar, Chairman
Founded in: 1968
Member: ATA; SCA
Description: Offers a B.A. degree in speech,
theatre and dance. Each includes six core
courses (Oral Interpretation, Acting, Voice
and Articulation, Stagecraft, Public Speak-
ing and Design).

Hoboken

Stevens Institute of Technology
Department of Theatre
Hoboken, NJ 07030
Address Inquiries to: Robert Reed, Chairman

Jersey City

Jersey City State College
Department of Theatre
2039 Kennedy Memorial Boulevard
Jersey City, NJ 07305
Tel: 201-547-3348
Address Inquiries to: Dr. Peter A. Teitzman,
Chairperson
Founded in: 1929
Member: ATA;

Lawrenceville

Rider College
Department of Theatre
2083 Lawrenceville Road
Lawrenceville, NJ 08648
Tel: 609-896-5168; 609-896-0800
Address Inquiries to: Patrick Chmel,
Chairman
Larry Capo, Chairman
Founded in: 1962
Member: ATA;

Madison

Drew University
Department of Theatre
36 Madison Avenue
Madison, NJ 07940
Tel: 201-377-3000
Address Inquiries to: Robert McLauglin,
Chairman
Member: ATA;

Fairleigh Dickenson University
Department of Theatre
Madison, NJ 07940
Tel: 201-377-4700
Address Inquiries to: Harvey Flaxman,
Chairman

Newark

Newark College of Arts and Sciences
Department of Theatre Arts
392 High Street
Newark, NJ 07102
Tel: 201-648-5248; 201-648-5119
Address Inquiries to: Nathan Shoehalter,
Chairman
Founded in: 1931
Member: ATA; NAEB; SCA;
Annual Budget: $10,000
Description: A liberal arts unit of Rutgers
Newark College of Arts and Sciences. Pro-
vides basic courses leading to a B.A. degree
in theatre, television/film or radio.

New Jersey Institute of Technology
Department of Theatre
Newark, NJ 07102
Tel: 201-893-42177
Address Inquiries to: William E. Gile,
Chairman
Member: ATA;

Rutgers University, Newark
Department of Theatre
392 High Street
Newark, NJ 07102
Tel: 201-648-5205
Address Inquiries to: Lester L. Moore,
Chairman

New Brunswick

Rutgers State University of New Jersey,
Department of Theatre
Mason Gross School of the Arts
New Brunswick, NJ 08903
Tel: 201-932-9891; 201-932-9816
Address Inquiries to: M. E. Comtios,
Chairman
John Bettenbender, Dean and Artistic

Director
Founded in: 1974
Description: Offers a BFA degree in acting,
design and production, and an MFA in acting, directing, design/technical, playwriting
and criticism.

Rutgers University
Mason Gross School of the Arts
New Brunswick, NJ 08903
Tel: 201-932-9816
Address Inquiries to: John Bettenbender,
Artistic Director
Dr. Mary E. Comtrois, Director-Theatre
Arts Program
Member: U/RTA;
Description: The department, has access to a
proscenium theatre with 350 seats, a flexible
theatre with 250-450 seats, a studio theatre
with 150 seats, three flexible space studio
theatres, a cabaret theatre, two scene shops,
a scene design studio, and a costume design
studio. There is a graduate program.

Rutgers University, Douglass College
Department of Theatre
New Brunswick, NJ 08903
Tel: 201-932-9721
Address Inquiries to: John Bettenbender,
Chairman

North Haledon

Salesian College
Department of Theatre
North Haledon, NJ 07508
Tel: 201-427-0452

Pamona

Stockton State College
Department of Theatre
Pamona, NJ 08239
Tel: 609-652-1776
Address Inquiries to: M.J. Rose, Chairman

Sewell

Gloucester County College
Department of Theatre
Sewell, NJ 08080
Tel: 609-468-5000
Address Inquiries to: Harry Mount, Chairman

South Orange

Seton Hall University
Department of Theatre
South Orange, NJ 07709
Tel: 201-762-9000
Address Inquiries to: Gilbert L. Rathbun,
Chairman

Toms River

Ocean County College
Department of Theatre
College Drive
Toms River, NJ 08753
Tel: 201-255-4000
Address Inquiries to: Authr Waldman,
Chairman
Member: ATA;

Trenton

Mercer County Community College
Department of Theatre
1200 Old Trenton Road
Trenton, NJ 08690
Tel: 609-586-4800
Address Inquiries to: Rosemarie Flynn,
Chairperson

Trenton State College
Department of Theatre
Pennington Road
Trenton, NJ 08625
Tel: 609-771-1855
Address Inquiries to: Harold A. Hogstrom,
Chairman
Founded in: 1931
Annual Budget: $15,000

Union

Kean College of New Jersey
Department of Theatre
Morris Avenue
Union, NJ 07083
Tel: 201-527-2107
Address Inquiries to: Doland Lumsden,
Chairman
Member: ATA;

Upper Montclair

Montclair State College
Department of Theatre
Upper Montclair, NJ 07043
Tel: 201-893-4217
Address Inquiries to: Wayne Bond, Chairman
Member: ATA;

Wayne

William Paterson College
Department of Theatre
300 Pompton Road
Wayne, NJ 07470
Tel: 201-595-2335; 201-595-2314
Address Inquiries to: Dr. Bruce Gulbranson,
Chairman
James W. Rodgers, Chairman
Founded in: 1973
Member: ATA; DG; National Drama
Therapy Association; TCG;
Annual Budget: $850,000

NEW MEXICO
Albuquerque

University of Albuquerque
Department of Theatre
Albuquerque, NM 87120
Tel: 505-842-8500
Address Inquiries to: Jim Morley, Chairman

University of New Mexico
Department of Theatre
Albuquerque, NM 87131
Tel: 505-277-4332; 505-277-2111
Address Inquiries to: Jim Morely, Chairman
Peter Prouse, Chairman
Member: ATA;

Artesia

College of Artesia
Department of Theatre
Artesia, NM 88210
Tel: 505-746-9862

Las Cruces

New Mexico State University
Department of Theatre Arts
Las Cruces, NM 88003
Tel: 505-646-4517
Address Inquiries to: Mark Medoff, Artistic
Director
J. Bruce Streett, Academic Head
Founded in: 1975
Member: ATA; SWTC; NMTA;
Annual Budget: $200,000
Description: Dedicated to education and
professional-style productions of major
plays and studio theatre.

Las Vegas

New Mexico Highlands University
Department of Theatre
Las Vegas, NM 87701
Tel: 505-425-7511
Address Inquiries to: Dr. Grady Greene,
Chairman Department of Fine Arts

Moorhead

Moorhead State University
Department of Theatre
Moorhead, NM 56560
Tel: 218-236-2762; 218-236-2126
Address Inquiries to: Mr. Richard Hanson,
Associate Director
Mrs. Kathleen Van Sickle, Box Office
Secretary
Founded in: Late 19th Century
Member: TCG; ATA; USITT;
Annual Budget: $75,000
Description: Department of theatre arts, which
mounts productions with undergraduate
students in a university setting.

Portales

Eastern New Mexico University
Department of Theatre
Portales, NM 88130
Tel: 505-562-2711; 505-562-2712
Address Inquiries to: Pat Rucker, Chairperson
Founded in: 1957
Member: ATA; NMTA; NMDE;
Annual Budget: $100,000
Description: An undergraduate theatre pro-
gram. The school produces four shows a
year with student workshops and laboratory
productions as resources permit.

Roswell

New Mexico Military Institute
Department of Theatre
501 College Aveune
Roswell, NM 88201
Tel: 505-622-6250
Address Inquiries to: Travis Reames, Public
Information Officer

Santa Fe

College of Santa Fe
Department of Theatre
Saint Michaels Drive
Santa Fe, NM 87501
Tel: 505-473-6131; 505-473-6439
Address Inquiries to: John C. Wechesser,
Chairman
Founded in: 1965
Member: ACUCCA; ATA;
Annual Budget: $150,000

Silver City

Western New Mexico University
Department of Theatre
College Avenue
Silver City, NM 88061
Tel: 605-538-6011
Address Inquiries to: James R. Donohue,
Chairman
Member: ATA;

NEW YORK
Albany

State University of New York
Department of Theatre
Albany, NY 12222
Tel: 518-457-8360
Address Inquiries to: James M. Symons,
Chairman
Member: ATA;

Alfred

Alfred University
Division of Performing Arts
Alfred, NY 14802
Tel: 607-871-2251; 607-871-2252
Address Inquiries to: James W. Chapman,
Chairman
Founded in: 1980
Member: ATA; UCTA;
Description: Dance,drama, music and speech
programs.

Amherst

Daemen College
Department of Theatre
4380 Main Street
Amherst, NY 14226
Tel: 716-839-3600
Address Inquiries to: Christopher F. Wilson,
Chairman

Annandale-on-Hudson

Bard College
Department of Drama and Dance
Annandale-on-Hudson, NY 12504
Tel: 914-758-6822, Ext. 245; 914-758-8622
Address Inquiries to: William Driver,
Professor of Drama; Director, Bard
Theatre of Drama and Dance
Founded in: 1860
Annual Budget: $21,000
Description: The college theatre, produces
plays, operas, and dance performances,
about twelve a year. It is an integral part of

the department's teaching, which is required of all majors. 15. my; e

Auburn

Cayuga County Community College
Department of Theatre
Franklin Street
Auburn, NY 13021
Tel: 315-253-7345
Address Inquiries to: Daniel C. Labeille,
  Professor of Theatre
Member: ATA;

Aurora

Wells College
Department of Theatre
Aurora, NY 13026
Address Inquiries to: Nancy Wynn,
  Chairperson

Batavia

Genesee Community College
Department of Theatre
College Road, Post Office Box 718
Batavia, NY 14020
Tel: 716-343-0055
Address Inquiries to: John R. Stork,
  Chairman

Bayside

Queensborough Community College
Department of Theatre
56th Avenue and Springfield Boulevard
Bayside, NY 11364
Tel: 212-631-6284
Address Inquiries to: Richard G. Heath,
  Chairman

Binghamton

State University of New York at
  Binghamton
Fine Arts Building, Room 233
Binghamton, NY 13905
Tel: 607-798-2630
Address Inquiries to: J.K. Urice, PhD,
  Program Director
Founded in: 1974
Member: ATA; ACA; State of New York;
Annual Budget: $150,000
Description: The major goal of the program is
to graduate students who are fully prepared
to deal with major managerial/administrative challenges in the arts, and who also have
the vision, imagination, humor and sensitivity to be effective in influencing future policy
regarding the role of the arts in a diverse,
increasingly technological, free enterprise
society.

Briarcliff Manor

Briarcliff College
Department of Theatre
Elm Road
Briarcliff Manor, NY 10510
Tel: 914-941-6400
Address Inquiries to: Harold Simmons,
  Chairman

Brockport

State University College
Department of Theatre
Brockport, NY 14420
Tel: 716-395-2478
Address Inquiries to: Clyde Basset, Chairman
Member: ATA;

Bronx

Bronx Community College
Department of Theatre
University Avenue at West 181st Street
Bronx, NY 10453
Tel: 212-367-7300
Address Inquiries to: Al Cosentino, Chairman

City University of New York
Herbert H. Lehman College
Bedford Park Boulevard West
Bronx, NY 10468
Tel: 212-960-8134; 212-960-8135
Address Inquiries to: John F. Wilson,
  Chairman
Founded in: 1968
Member: ATA; SCA; State of New York;

Bronxville

Concordia College
Department of Theatre
171 White Plains Road
Bronxville, NY 10708
Tel: 914-337-9300
Address Inquiries to: Christopher Hoyer,
  Chairman

Sarah Lawrence College
Department of Theatre
1 Meadway
Bronxville, NY 10708
Tel: 914-337-0700
Address Inquiries to: Charles Carshen,
  Chairman

Brooklyn

Brooklyn College School of Performing
  Arts
Department of Theatre
Brooklyn, NY 11210
Tel: 212-780-5800
Address Inquiries to: Benito Ortolani, Ph.D,
  Chairman
  Stephen Langley, Ph.D, Director of
  Graduate Studies
Description: Located in New York City, students have the major Broadway, Off Broadway and Off Off Broadway theatres at their
disposal. Undergraduate students work toward a BA degree in theatre arts, receive
training in all aspects of theatre, and have
numerous opp ortunities to practice their
craft throughout the year in the four Gershwin Theatre mainstage productions, directed by members of the faculty, and the many
New Theatre Workshop productions, directed by graduate students working toward an
MFA degree. Aside from directing, the college also offers graduate programs in acting,
design, criticism and arts management.

New York City Technical College
Theatreworks Program
Brooklyn, NY 11201
Tel: 212-643-5511
Address Inquiries to: Emilie A. Cozzi,
  Director
Member: ATA; SCA;

Pratt Institute
Department of Theatre
215 Ryerson Street
Brooklyn, NY 11205
Tel: 212-636-3600; 212-636-3583
Address Inquiries to: Jordan Hott, Chairman
Founded in: 1972

Brooklyn Heights

Packer Collegiate Institute
Department of Theatre
Brooklyn Heights, NY 11201
Tel: 212-875-6644
Address Inquiries to: Henry A. Wick Jr.,
  Chairman
Founded in: 1845
Annual Budget: $1.5 million
Description: Offers a full credit academic sequence of courses in all four arts which provides the student with a very strong foundation for college or professional school. A full
season of music theatre and dance performances are presented along with several art
gallery offerings each year.

Buffalo

D'Youville College
Department of Theatre
320 Porter Avenue
Buffalo, NY 14201
Tel: 716-886-8100
Address Inquiries to: Roland Brandow,
  Chairman

State University College
Department of Theatre
Buffalo, NY 14222
Tel: 716-862-5900
Address Inquiries to: Julia C. Piquette,
  Chairperson
Member: ATA;

State University of New York at Buffalo
Department of Theatre
Buffalo, NY 14214
Tel: 716-831-3742
Address Inquiries to: Saul Elkin, Chairman
Member: ATA; Pfeifer Trust;

Canton

Saint Lawrence University
Department of Theatre
Canton, NY 13617
Address Inquiries to: Dr. Phillip E. Larson,
  Chairman
Member: ATA;

Clinton

Hamilton College
Department of Theatre and Dance
Clinton, NY 13323
Tel: 315-859-4257

Address Inquiries to: Carol Bellini-Sharp
Founded in: 1981

Corning

Corning Community College
Department of Theatre
Corning, NY 14830
Tel: 607-962-9011; 607-962-9271
Address Inquiries to: Henry Moonschein,
Chairman
Founded in: 1963
Annual Budget: $4,000

Cortland

State University College
Department of Theatre
Cortland, NY 13045
Tel: 607-753-0377
Address Inquiries to: James C. Palmer,
Chairman

Elmira

Elmira College
Department of Theatre
Elmira, NY 14901
Tel: 607-734-3911
Address Inquiries to: Amnon Kabatchnik,
Chairperson
Member: ATA;

Flushing

Queens College
Department of Theatre
67-30 Kissena Boulevard
Flushing, NY 11367
Tel: 212-520-7572; 212-520-7573
Address Inquiries to: Raymond D. Gasper,
Chairman
Member: ATA;

Garden City

Adelphi University
Department of Theatre
Garden City, NY 11530
Tel: 516-294-8700
Address Inquiries to: Jaques Burdick,
Chairman
Member: ATA;

Nassau Community College
Department of Theatre
Garden City, NY 11530
Tel: 516-742-0600
Address Inquiries to: Wesley J. Jensby,
Chairman

Geneva

Hobart and William Smith Colleges
Department of Theatre
Geneva, NY 14456
Tel: 315-789-5500
Address Inquiries to: E.E. Griffth, Chairman

Glen Falls

Adirondack Community College
Department of Theatre
Glen Falls, NY 12801
Tel: 518-793-4491
Address Inquiries to: Shirley G. Weiner,

Chairman

Greenvale

C.W. Post Center of Long Island
University
Department of Theatre
Greenvale, NY 11548
Tel: 516-299-2395
Address Inquiries to: Lucille Rhodes,
Professor

Hamilton

Colgate University
Dana Arts Center
Hamilton, NY 13346
Tel: 315-824-1000, Ext. 639, 631
Address Inquiries to: Atlee Sproul, Director
Garda M. Judd, Theatre Manager
Founded in: 1819
Member: ATA; UCTA;
Description: Functions primarily to educate
students in as many aspects of dramatic liter-
ature and play production as possible. It is
also an outlet for student directors, design-
ers and playwrights, who have the oppor-
tunity to mount plays on the main stage or in
the Drama Lab.

Hempstead

Hofstra University
Department of Theatre
Fulton Avenue
Hempstead, NY 11550
Tel: 516-560-3491
Address Inquiries to: James VanWart,
Chairman

Houghton

Houghton College
Department of Theatre
Houghton, NY 14744
Tel: 716-567-2211
Address Inquiries to: Lionel Basney,
Chairman

Ithaca

Cornell University
Department of Theatre Arts
104 Lincoln Hall
Ithaca, NY 14853
Tel: 607-256-4060
Address Inquiries to: Richard Shank,
Chairman
Member: ATA; URTA;
Description: Offers a MFA degree. The University mounts a six- production main season in true repertory fashion. In addition to
productions in its 400-seat proscenium
theatre and 80/130- seat flexible theatre. It
offers workshop and summer theatre sessions.

Ithaca College
Department of Theatre Arts
Ithaca, NY 14850
Tel: 607-274-3345
Address Inquiries to: Dr. Richard M. Clark,
Chairman
Founded in: 1892

Member: ATA; NAST;

Jamaica

Saint John's University
Department of Theatre
Grand Central and Utopia Parkway
Jamaica, NY 11432
Tel: 212-969-8000
Address Inquiries to: Thomas D. Houchin,
Chairman

Keuka Park

Keuka College
Department of Theatre
Lodge Road
Keuka Park, NY 14478
Tel: 315-536-4411
Address Inquiries to: Marc A. Courchesne,
Chairman
Member: ATA;

New Delhi

State University Agricultural and
Technical College
Department of Theatre
New Delhi, NY 13753
Tel: 607-746-4216; 607-746-4222
Address Inquiries to: William Campbell,
Chairman
Founded in: 1970
Annual Budget: $9,500
Description: Campus and community theatre
organization which produces three stage
productions each academic year, usualy a
drama, a dinner theatre production and a
musical.

New Paltz

State University of New York, New Paltz
Department of Theatre
New Paltz, NY 12562
Tel: 914-257-2081; 914-257-2082
Address Inquiries to: Joesph C. Paparone,
Chairman
Frank Kraat
Member: USITT; ATA; Dramatists Guild;
Annual Budget: $20,000
Description: The theatre department is dedi-
cated to providing all students with a dynam-
ic educational experience which will result in
their becoming professionals prepared to
enter the world of theatre.

New York

American Academy of Dramatic Arts
120 Madison Avenue
New York, NY 10016
Tel: 212-686-9244
Address Inquiries to: George Cuttingham,
President and Director
Founded in: 1884
Annual Budget: $2,600,000
Description: A two year program in acting,
leading to an associates degree.

Barnard College
Department of Theatre
606 West 120th Street
New York, NY 10027

Tel: 212-280-1754
Address Inquiries to: Kenneth James, Director
Member: ATA;

City College, City University of New York
Department of Theatre
Convent Avenue and 138th Street
New York, NY 10031
Tel: 212-690-6666
Address Inquiries to: Earle R. Gister,
Chairman
Member: ATA;

Columbia University
Department of Theatre
116th Street & Broadway
New York, NY 10027
Tel: 212-280-3408
Address Inquiries to: Bernard Beckerman,
Chairman

Fordham University
Department of Theatre
Lincoln Center
New York, NY 10023
Tel: 212-841-5269
Address Inquiries to: David Davis, Chairman
Founded in: 1969
Member: ATA;

Harlem School of the Arts
Department of Theatre
645 Saint Nicholas Avenue
New York, NY 10030
Tel: 212-926-4100
Member: ATA;

Hunter College
Department of Theatre
695 Park Avenue
New York, NY 10021
Tel: 213-570-5747
Address Inquiries to: Vera Roberts,
Chairperson
Member: ATA;

Julliard School, Theatre Center
Lincoln Center
New York, NY 10023
Tel: 212-799-5000
Address Inquiries to: Michael Langham,
Director
Founded in: 1968
Description: Emphasis is on training American actors in their discipline with classical material of all periods and styles. Regular opportunities to perform in contemporary works are also provided. The school is dedicated to meeting a critical need for highly trained artists capable of handling the rigorous creative and technical demands of the modern theatre.

Lee Strasberg Theatre Institute
115 East 15th Street
New York, NY 10003
Tel: 212-533-5500
Member: NYSCA; ART/NY; TDF;
Description: An acting school based on the Stanislavski method. With many respected artists and teachers on its staff.

Marymount Manhattan College
Department of Theatre
221 East 71st Street
New York, NY 10021
Tel: 212-472-3800
Address Inquiries to: J. William Bordeau,
Artistic Director
Mary Fleisher, Managing Director
Founded in: 1947
Member: ATA;

Nat Horne Musical Theatre
440 West 42nd Street
New York, NY 10036
Tel: 212-736-7128
Address Inquiries to: Nat Horne
Lawrence Gilligan, General Manager
Founded in: 1973
Member: DTW; NEA; NYSCA; ART/NY;
TDF;
Description: Dedicated to preparing dancers for professional employment in American musical theatre. Holds classes in jazz, dance, singing and acting. There is a scholarship program for a limited number of individuals and the Dancing Plus performing company.

National Shakespeare Company
Conservatory
Post Office Box 375
Prince Station
New York, NY
Tel: 212-581-1968; 800-472-6667
Member: NAST;
Description: Professional training for the actor. Call the toll free number for information concerning auditions and qualifications.

New School for Social Research
Department of Theatre
New York, NY 11011

New York University
Tisch School of the Arts
300 South Building, 51 West 4th Street
New York, NY 10003
Tel: 212-598-4651; 212-598-2596
Address Inquiries to: Barbara
Kirshenblatt-Gimblett, Chairman
Founded in: 1968
Member: ATA;
Description: Broadly conceived, Performance Studies encompasses a full range of expressive behavior from theatre and dance to ritual and popular entertainment. It is an emerging discipline, in which theories and methods are forged to illuminate the study of these expressive forms. The curriculum combines courses in methods and theory with offerings in specialized areas. The program of study is cross cultural and interdisciplinary.

School for Creative Movement in the Arts
Department of Theatre
New York, NY 10024
Tel: 212-724-3520
Address Inquiries to: Hattie Wiener,
Chairperson

Sonia Moore Studio
485 Park Avenue
New York, NY 10022
Tel: 212-755-5120
Address Inquiries to: Sonia Moore, Director
Member: ATA;

Teachers College of Columbia University
Department of Theatre
New York, NY 10027
Tel: 212-678-3278
Address Inquiries to: Thomas J. Manning,
Chairman

Niagara Falls

Niagara University
Department of Theatre
Niagara Falls, NY 14109
Tel: 716-285-1212, Extension 526,525
Address Inquiries to: Augustine Towey,
Chairman
Dr. Sharon O. Watkinson, Publicity
Contact
Founded in: 1856
Member: ATA;
Description: Offers between six and seven major productions per year, one of which is a musical comedy. There is offered within the curriculum a full complement of theatre courses including acting, voice, speech, dance, mime, directing and courses in dramatic literature. Students may earn a BA degree.

Old Westbury

New York Institute of Technology
Department of Theatre
Old Westbury, NY 11568
Tel: 516-686-7616
Address Inquiries to: Howard Wamsley,
Chairman

Oneonta

Hartwick College
Department of Theatre
Oneonta, NY 13820
Tel: 607-432-4200
Address Inquiries to: Dr. David M. Ferrell,
Chairman
Member: ATA;

Oswego

State University of New York, Oswego
Tyler Hall
Oswego, NY 13126
Tel: 315-341-2140; 315-341-2147
Address Inquiries to: Sanford Sternlicht,
Chairman
Founded in: 1973
Member: ACTA;
Annual Budget: $10,000

Plattsburgh

State University of New York, Plattsburgh
Department of Theatre
Broad Street
Plattsburgh, NY 12901
Tel: 518-564-2000; 518-564-2181
Address Inquiries to: Charles Kline, Professor

of Theatre
Founded in: 1966
Member: ATA; NAST;
Annual Budget: $1500,000
Description: The study of theatre, like the study of the other arts, is essentially humanistic, aiming not only at acquiring a body of knowledge and certain skills but also at meaningful self-improvment through a sharpening of sense perception and the increasing ability to express inner realizations. The theatre program at Plattsburgh is the only one in State University of New York that is accredited by the National Association of the Schools of Theatre (NAST).

Potsdam

State University of New York, Potsdam
Department of Theatre
Pierrepont Avenue
Potsdam, NY 13676
Tel: 315-267-2413; 315-267-2414
Address Inquiries to: Robert W. Thayer, Dean
Founded in: 1886
Member: State of New York;
Description: Degree programs in music history, literature, and theory at the undergraduate and masters level.

Poughkeepsie

Dutchess Community College
Department of Theatre
Pindell Road
Poughkeepsie, NY 12601
Tel: 914-471-4500
Address Inquiries to: Stephen Press, Chairman

Vassar College
Department of Theatre
Poughkeepsie, NY 12603
Tel: 914-452-7000
Address Inquiries to: James B. Steerman, Chairman

Purchase

Manhattanville College
Department of Theatre
Purchase Street
Purchase, NY 10577
Tel: 914-946-9600
Address Inquiries to: James Shearwood, Director
Member: ATA;

State University of New York
Department of Theatre
Purchase, NY 10577
Tel: 914-253-5016
Address Inquiries to: Howard Stein, Chairman
Member: ATA;

Rochester

Nazareth College
Department of Theatre
4245 East Avenue
Rochester, NY 14610
Tel: 716-586-2525
Address Inquiries to: James J. Kolb, Chairman

Founded in: 1970
Member: ATA; USITT; UCTA;

Saratoga Springs

Empire State College
Department of Theatre
Saratoga Springs, NY 12866

Skidmore College
Department of Theatre
Saratoga Springs, NY 12866
Tel: 518-584-5000
Address Inquiries to: Alan Brody, Chairman
Member: ATA;

Schenectady

Schenectady County College
Department of Theatre
Schenectady, NY 12305
Address Inquiries to: G.S. Burian, Chairman
Member: ATA;

Union College
Department of Theatre
Schenectady, NY 12308
Address Inquiries to: Barry K. Smith, Chairman

Selden

Suffolk County Community College
Department of Theatre
Selden, NY 11784
Tel: 516-233-5252
Address Inquiries to: Shirley Coe, Chairperson
Member: ATA;

Staten Island

Staten Island Community College
Department of Theatre
Staten Island, NY 10301
Address Inquiries to: Benjamin Patterson, Chairman

Stone Ridge

Ulster Community College
Department of Theatre
Stone Ridge, NY 12484
Tel: 914-687-7621
Address Inquiries to: John Lawson, Chairman

Stony Brook

State University of New York, Stony Brook
Department of Theatre Arts
Stony Brook, NY 11794
Tel: 516-246-5670
Address Inquiries to: Alfred G. Brooks, Professor and Chairman
Member: URTA;
Description: It's fine arts center includes a 1,-200-seat theatre, a 2,300-seat Black Box Theatre, a 30-seat experimental theatre, and a 400-seat concert hall.

Syracuse

Lemoyne College
Department of Theatre
LeMoyne Heights
Syracuse, NY 13214

Tel: 315-446-2882
Address Inquiries to: Thomas R. Hogan, Chairman
Founded in: 1946
Member: ATA;
Annual Budget: $5,000
Description: Produces four mainstage productions. Students are asked to participate from the drama program and other academic areas not associatied with theatre. The group has a tradition of producing Shakespeare.

Onondaga Community College
Department of Theatre
Hill Campus
Syracuse, NY 13210
Tel: 315-469-7741
Member: ATA;

Syracuse University
Department of Theatre
Syracuse, NY 13210
Tel: 315-423-2708
Address Inquiries to: Arthur Storch, Chairman
Member: ATA;

Tarrytown

Marymount College
Department of Drama
Tarrytown, NY 10592
Tel: 914-631-3200; 212-898-1073
Address Inquiries to: Ronald Weyand, Chairman
Member: ACA; LTD; ATA; AEA; SAG; USA;
Annual Budget: $10,000

Troy

Hudson Valley Community College
Department of Theatre
Vandenburgh Avenue
Troy, NY 12180
Tel: 518-283-1100
Address Inquiries to: Robert Couture, Chairman
Member: ATA;

Russell Sage College
Department of Theatre
Troy, NY 12180
Tel: 518-270-2263
Address Inquiries to: Richard L. Jones, Chairman
Founded in: 1926
Member: ATA;

Utica

Mohawk Valley Community College
Department of Theatre
1101 Sherman Drive
Utica, NY 13501
Tel: 315-792-792 5000
Address Inquiries to: N.F. Sabo, Chairperson
Member: ATA;

Valhalla

Westchester Community College
Department of Theatre
Valhalla, NY 10595
Tel: 914-592-3038
Address Inquiries to: Mort Clark, Chairman

White Plains

Pace University
Department of Theatre
78 North Broadway
White Plains, NY 10603
Tel: 914-682-7000
Address Inquiries to: Beverly Brumm,
  Chairperson
Member: ATA;

NORTH CAROLINA

Ashville

University of North Carolina
Department of Theatre
University Heights
Ashville, NC 28814
Tel: 704-258-6610; 704-253-5778
Address Inquiries to: Arnold Wengrow,
  Director of Theatre
  Paul J. Sweeney, Technical Director and
  Designer
Founded in: 1970
Annual Budget: $15,000
Description: Provides an opportunity for
drama students and faculty to hone their
skills as artists and serves as an educational
resource to the Western North Carolina
community by producing plays for adult and
children's audiences representing the full
range of dramatic literature and theatrical
styles; the emphasis is on classics and 'contemporary classics,' although works of an experimental nature are also produced. The
Department of Drama offers a full range of
courses, leading to a BA degree in drama,
acting, directing, technical production, design, theatre history, and dramatic literature.

Boiling Springs

Gardner-Webb College
Department of Theatre
Boiling Springs, NC 28017
Tel: 704-434-2361
Address Inquiries to: David W. Smith,
  Chairman
Member: ATA;

Boone

Appalachian State University
Department of Communication
Boone, NC 28608
Tel: 704-262-3028; 704-262-3029
Address Inquiries to: Susan S. Cole, Director
  of Theatre
Founded in: 1899
Member: ATA; STC; DG;
Annual Budget: $19,000
Description: A liberal arts university with a

special concentration in education. The
Communication Arts Department offers
the possibility of either a BA degree or a
BS degree with a certificate. The University theatre produces four full length and up
to twelve one-act plays each year and
sponsors a children's theatre tour in the
spring. Students receive a comprehensive
background by being able to choose
courses which deal with all aspects of
theatre.

Brevard

Brevard College
Department of Theatre
Brevard, NC 28172
Tel: 704-883-8292
Address Inquiries to: Sam Cope, Chairman
Member: ATA;

Chapel Hill

University of North Carolina
Department of Theatre
Chapel Hill, NC 27514
Tel: 919-933-1132
Address Inquiries to: Arthur L. Housman,
  Chairman

Charlotte

Heritage School of Evangelism
Department of Theatre
Charlotte, NC 28279
Tel: 704-554-6061
Address Inquiries to: Thomas K. Wright,
  Chairman

Johnson C. Smith University
Department of Theatre
100-152 Beatties Ford Road
Charlotte, NC 28216
Tel: 704-372-2370
Member: ATA;

Queens College
Department of Theatre
1900 Selwyn Avenue
Charlotte, NC 28274
Tel: 704-332-7121
Address Inquiries to: Dr. Charles O. Hadley,
  Professor
Member: ATA;

University of North Carolina
Department of Theatre
Charlotte, NC 28223
Tel: 704-597-2387
Address Inquiries to: J. Spence, Chairman
Member: ATA;

Dallas

Gatson College
Department of Theatre
Dallas, NC 28034
Tel: 704-922-3136; 704-554-6080
Address Inquiries to: Thomas K. Green,
  Chairman
  Lisa Campbell, Student Assistant
Founded in: 1978
Member: ATA;
Annual Budget: $15,000

Description: A one year internship (second
year available) with emphasis on quality traditional and experimental Christian theatre.
Weekly productions take place in a 1500 seat
theatre.

Davidson

Davidson College
Department of Theatre
Davidson, NC 28036
Tel: 704-892-2000
Address Inquiries to: Rupert T. Barber,Jr.,
  Chairman
  Joseph T. Gardner,Jr., Technical
  Director
Founded in: 1963
Member: ATA; STC; NCTC;

Durham

Duke University
Drama Program
6936 College Station
Durham, NC 27708
Tel: 919-684-6285
Address Inquiries to: John M. Clum, Director
Member: ATA; STC; NCTC;
Description: Training in all aspects of theatre
through classroom and production work.

North Carolina Central University
Department of Drama
Durham, NC 27707
Tel: 919-682-2172
Address Inquiries to: Linda K. Norflett,
  Chairman
Member: ATA;

Elizabeth City

College of the Albemarle
Department of Theatre
Elizabeth City, NC 27090
Tel: 919-355-5505
Address Inquiries to: Lucy Vaughan,
  Chairman

Fayetteville

Fayetteville State University
Department of Theatre
Murchinson Road
Fayetteville, NC 28301
Tel: 919-486-1275; 919-486-1443
Address Inquiries to: Frank L. Whaley
Member: ATA; STC;

Methodist College
Department of Theatre
Raleigh Road
Fayetteville, NC 28301
Tel: 919-488-7110; 919-488-4598
Address Inquiries to: Jack Peyrose, Chairman
Member: ATA; Southern Speech
  Association; Speech Association of
  America; Methodist Church; North
  Carolina Grassroots Funding;
Annual Budget: $7,000

Greensboro

Bennett College
Department of Theatre
Greensboro, NC 27420
Tel: 914-273-4431
Address Inquiries to: Denise E. Troutman,
Chairman

Greensboro College
Department of Theatre
815 West Market Street
Greensboro, NC 27420
Tel: 919-272-7102
Address Inquiries to: Leonard Hart,
Chairman
Member: ATA;

University of North Carolina
Department of Theatre
1000 Spring Garden Street
Greensboro, NC 27412
Tel: 919-379-5562
Address Inquiries to: Tom Behm, Theatre
Division Director
Founded in: 1925
Member: ATA; NCTC; SETC; ATA; CTAA;
State of North Carolina;
Annual Budget: $200,000
Description: Combines training and practice
for students in the program. BA. BFA, MFA,
and MA degrees available.

Greenville

East Carolina University
Department of Theatre
Greenville, NC 27834
Tel: 919-757-6390
Address Inquiries to: Edgar R. Loessin,
Chairman
Founded in: 1962
Annual Budget: $30,000

Hickory

Lenior-Rhyne College
Department of Theatre
Hickory, NC 28603
Tel: 704-328-1741, Ext. 253
Address Inquiries to: Marion H. Love,
Chairman
Ray Mills, Scenic Designer
Founded in: 1976
Member: ATA; NCTA; ACUCAA;
Annual Budget: $12,500
Description: An ambitious and young organi-
zation offering a concentrated study in
theatre discipline and dramatic literature as
well as an eclectic production component.
The average year will include five-six main-
stage productions, six to ten laboratory ex-
periments, one outdoor production (usually
childrens theatre), one tour, technical assistance and/or design assistance for area arts
groups or touring companies visiting the institution, guest lectures and workshops for
area schools.

High Point

High Point College
Department of Theatre
933 Montlieu Avenue
High Point, NC 27262
Tel: 919-885-5105
Address Inquiries to: David R. Appleton,
Chairman
Paul J. Lundrigan, Assistant
Founded in: 1973
Member: ATA; NCTC; STC;

Laurinburg

Saint Andrews Presbyterian College
Department of Theatre
McCall Highway
Laurinburg, NC 28352
Tel: 919-276-3652
Address Inquiries to: Arthur McDonald,
Chairperson
Member: ATA;

Lexington

Davidson County Community College
Department of Theatre
Lexington, NC 27292
Tel: 704-249-8186; 704-249-8454
Address Inquiries to: Dorthea D. Burkhark,
Chairman
Founded in: 1970
Member: ATA; Davidson Council for
Creative Arts;

Mars Hill

Mars Hill College
Department of Theatre
Mars Hill, NC 28754
Tel: 704-689-1203
Address Inquiries to: James W. Thomas,
Chairman
Member: ATA;

Misenheimer

Pfeiffer College
Department of Theatre
Misenheimer, NC 28109
Tel: 704-463-7343
Address Inquiries to: James B. Wood,
Chairman
Member: ATA;

Pembroke

Pembroke State University
Department of Theatre
Pembroke, NC 28372
Tel: 919-521-4214, Extension 287;
919-521-0778, Box Office
Address Inquiries to: E. Morris, Chairman
Founded in: 1887
Member: ATA; SETC; NCTC;
Annual Budget: $17,000

Raleigh

Meredith College
Department of Theatre
Hillborough Street
Raleigh, NC 27611
Tel: 919-883-6461
Address Inquiries to: Nancy Truesdale,
Chairman
Member: ATA;

North Carolina State University
Department of Theatre
Raleigh, NC 27607
Address Inquiries to: Charles Martin,
Chairman
Member: ATA;

Peace College
Department of Theatre
15 East Peace Street
Raleigh, NC 27604
Tel: 919-832-2881
Address Inquiries to: Terrence McGovern,
Chairman

Rocky Mount

North Carolina Wesleyan College
Department of Theatre
Highway 301 North
Rocky Mount, NC 27801
Tel: 919-422-7121
Address Inquiries to: Ralph Traxier III,
Chairman
Member: ATA;

Salisbury

Catawa College
Department of Theatre
West Innes Street
Salisbury, NC 28144
Tel: 704-637-4417
Address Inquiries to: Hoyt M. McCachren,
Chairman
Founded in: 1925
Member: ATA; NCTC; STC; ATA;
Annual Budget: $8,000

Livingstone College
Department of Theatre
701 West Monroe
Salisbury, NC 28144
Tel: 704-633-7960
Address Inquiries to: Clyde Williams,
Chairman
Member: ATA;

Whiteville

Southeastern Community College
Department of Theatre
Whiteville, NC 28472
Address Inquiries to: C.L. Wellborne,
Chairman

Winston-Salem

North Carolina School of the Arts
Department of Theatre
Post Office Box 12189
Winston-Salem, NC 27107
Tel: 919-784-7170
Address Inquiries to: Malcolm Morrison,
Chairman
Member: ATA;

Salem College
Department of Theatre
Winston-Salem, NC 27108
Tel: 919-723-7961

Address Inquiries to: Mary Homrighous, Chairman

Wake Forest University
Department of Theatre
Box 7264 Reynolda Station
Winston-Salem, NC 27109
Tel: 919-761-5294; 919-761-5295
Address Inquiries to: Harold C. Tedford, Director
Donald H. Wolfe, Chairman
Founded in: 1940
Member: ATA; STC; NCTC;
Description: Serves as a training ground for future performers and technicians but, it also provides a series of plays for the general benefit of the entire university community. It is fundamentally an educational theatre.

NORTH DAKOTA
Fargo

North Dakota State University
Department of Theatre
Fargo, ND 58203
Tel: 701-237-8011
Address Inquiries to: Frederick G. Walsh, Chairman
Member: ATA;

OHIO
Berea

Baldwin-Wallace College
Department of Theatre
275 Eastland Road
Berea, OH 44017
Tel: 216-826-2900
Address Inquiries to: Dr. James A. Ross, Head
Member: ATA;

Canton

Kent State University
Professional Arts Center
6000 Frank Avenue
Canton, OH 44720-7599
Tel: 216-499-9600
Address Inquiries to: Dr. William Bittle, Dean
Mr. Phillip Robb, Theatre Department Head
Founded in: 1973
Annual Budget: $5,000
Description: Offers a wide variety of classes and performance opportunities to students in music, theatre, fine art, and dance. Under the guidance of highly talented and qualified faculty, the student gains not only a working knowledge of his area, but also experiences a multitude of professional advancement opportunities.

Cleveland

Ursuline College
Department of Theatre
2550 Lander Road
Cleveland, OH 44124

Tel: 216-449-4200
Address Inquiries to: Dr. Mary P. Daley, Chairman
Member: ATA;

Cleveland Heights

Fairmount Center for Performing Arts
Department of Theatre
1925 Coventry Road
Cleveland Heights, OH 44118
Tel: 216-932-2000
Address Inquiries to: Kenneth Long
Member: ATA;

Columbus

Ohio State University
Department of Theatre
1849 Cannon Drive
Columbus, OH 43210
Tel: 614-422-5821
Address Inquiries to: Dr. Firman H. Brown, Chairman
Member: U/RTA;
Description: Department has a graduate program and many varied performance spaces for productions offering BA, BFA, MA, MFA and Ph.D programs.

Granville

Denison University
Department of Theatre
Granville, OH 43023
Tel: 614-587-0810
Address Inquiries to: Dr. Bruce Halverson, Chairman, Department of Theatre and Cinema
Member: ATA;

Huron

Bowling Green State University, Firelands
Department of Theatre
901 Rye Beach Road
Huron, OH 44839
Tel: 419-433-5560
Address Inquiries to: Dr. Ronald Ruble, Chair, Humanities Department
Member: ATA;

Kent

Kent State University
Department of Theatre
Kent, OH 44242
Tel: 216-672-2760
Address Inquiries to: Dr. William H. Zucchero, Cooridinator
Member: ATA;

Mount Saint Joesph

Mount Saint Joseph on the Ohio College
Department of Theatre
5700 Delhi Road
Mount Saint Joesph, OH 45051
Tel: 513-244-4863
Member: ATA;

Toledo

Mary Manse College
Department of Theatre
2436 Parkwood
Toledo, OH 43620
Tel: 419-243-9421
Member: ATA;

Willoughby

School of Fine Arts
Department of Theatre
38660 Mentor Avenue
Willoughby, OH 44094
Tel: 216-951-7500
Address Inquiries to: Timothy Ryan, Chairman
Member: ATA;

Wooster

College of Wooster
Department of Theatre
Wooster, OH 44691
Tel: 216-264-1234
Address Inquiries to: Gerald Sanders, Chairman
Member: ATA;

OKLAHOMA
Alva

Northwestern Oklahoma State University
Department of Theatre
Alva, OK 73717
Tel: 405-327-1700
Address Inquiries to: John Barton, Chairman, Speech Department
Member: ATA;

Goodwell

Panhandle State University
Department of Theatre
Goodwell, OK 73939
Tel: 405-349-2611 Extension 255
Address Inquiries to: Jim Roach, Chairman
Member: ATA;

Miami

Northeastern Oklahoma Agricultural and Mechnical College
Department of Theaatre
2nd and 1, North East
Miami, OK 74354
Tel: 918-542-8441
Address Inquiries to: Shirl White, Chairman
Member: ATA;

Tishomingo

Murray State College
Department of Theatre
Tishomingo, OK 73460
Tel: 405-371-2371
Address Inquiries to: Fred Poe, Chairman
Member: ATA;

Tonkawa

Northern Oklahoma College
Department of Theatre
1220 East Grand
Tonkawa, OK 74563
Tel: 405-628-2581
Address Inquiries to: James Morgan,
  Chairman
Member: ATA;

Tulsa

University of Tulsa
Department of Theatre
600 South College
Tulsa, OK 74104
Tel: 918-939-6351
Address Inquiries to: Dr. Nancy Vunovich,
  Chairman
Member: ATA;

OREGON
Ashland

Southern Oregon College
Department of Theatre
1250 Siskiyou Boulevard
Ashland, OR 97520
Tel: 503-482-3311
Member: ATA;

Gresham

Mount Hood Community College
Department of Theatre
26000 Southeast Stark Street
Gresham, OR 97030
Tel: 503-667-1561
Address Inquiries to: Gael Tower, Division
  Chaiperson
Member: ATA;

Mount Angel

Colegio Cesar Chevez
Department of Theatre
Mount Angel, OR 97362
Tel: 503-843-2234
Address Inquiries to: Carl Ritchie, Chairman
Member: ATA;

Pendleton

Blue Mountain Community College
Department of Theatre
Post Office Box 100
Pendleton, OR 97801
Tel: 503-276-1260
Member: ATA;

Portland

Concordia College
Department of Theatre
2811 Northeast Holman
Portland, OR 97211
Tel: 503-284-1148
Address Inquiries to: Hans Spalteholz,
  Chairman
Member: ATA;

University of Portland
Department of Theatre
5000 North Willamette Boulevard
Portland, OR 97203
Tel: 503-283-7228
Address Inquiries to: Paul S. Melhuish,
  Chairman
Member: ATA;

Warner Pacific College
Department of Theatre
2219 Southeast 68th Street
Portland, OR 97215
Tel: 503-775-4368
Address Inquiries to: Mary Boyce, Chairman
Member: ATA;

Weatherford

Southwestern State College
Department of Theatre
Weatherford, OR 73096
Tel: 405-772-5511
Address Inquiries to: Dr. G. Bellamy,
  Chairman, English Department
Member: ATA;

PENNSYLVANIA
Allentown

Cedar Crest College
Department of Theatre
Allentown, PA 18104
Tel: 215-437-4471
Address Inquiries to: Marianna Loosemore,
  Professor of Drama and Speech,
  Chairperson
Member: ATA;

Muhlenberg College
Center for the Arts and Theatre
Allentown, PA 18104
Tel: 215-433-3191
Address Inquiries to: Charles Richter,
  Chairman
Member: ATA;

Annville

Lebanon Valley College
Department of Theatre
Annville, PA 14003
Tel: 717-867-3561
Address Inquiries to: Anna D. Faber,
  Chairperson

Aston

Our Lady of Angels College
Humanities Department
Aston, PA 19014
Tel: 215-GL9-0905
Address Inquiries to: Jeanette Clare,
  Chairperson

Beaver Falls

Geneva College
Department of Theatre
Beaver Falls, PA 15010
Tel: 412-846-1103
Address Inquiries to: Harry Farra, Chairman

Bethlehem

Lehigh University
Department of Theatre
Bethlehem, PA 18015
Tel: 215-861-3640
Address Inquiries to: Jeffrey Milet, Chairman
Member: ATA;

Moravian College
Department of Theatre
Bethlehem, PA 18018
Tel: 215-865-0741; 214-861-1489
Address Inquiries to: Jack R. Ramsey,
  Chairman
Member: ATA;

Northampton Community College
Department of Theatre
Bethlehem, PA 18017
Address Inquiries to: Norman Roberts,
  Chairman

Bloomsburg

Bloomsburg State College
Bloomsburg, PA 17815
Tel: 717-389-3817
Address Inquiries to: Michael Mchale,
  Director of Theatre
Member: ATA;

Bradford

University of Pittsburgh
Department of Theatre
Bradford, PA 16791
Tel: 814-362-3801
Address Inquiries to: Patty Bianco,
  Chairperson

Bryn Mawr

Cushing Junior College
Department of Theatre
Bryn Mawr, PA 19010
Address Inquiries to: Carol C. Sherman,
  Chairperson

Byrn Mawr

Bryn Mawr College
Department of Theatre
Merion Avenue
Byrn Mawr, PA 19010
Tel: 215-525-1000
Address Inquiries to: Robert A. Buttman,
  Chairman
Member: ATA;

California

California State College
Department of Theatre
California, PA 15419
Tel: 412-938-4220
Address Inquiries to: Robert Cowan,
  Chairman
Member: ATA;

Cambridge Springs

Alliance College
Department of Theatre
Cambridge Springs, PA 16403
Tel: 814-398-4611

Address Inquiries to: Marylou Brenner

Carlisle

Dickinson College
Department of Theatre
Carlisle, PA 17013
Tel: 717-243-5121
Address Inquiries to: David Brubaker,
Chairman
Member: ATA;

Center Valley

Allentown College of Saint Francis De
Sales
Department of Theatre
Station Avenue
Center Valley, PA 18034
Tel: 215-282-1100
Address Inquiries to: Gerard Schubert,
Department Head
Member: ATA;

Chester

PMC College
Department of Theatre
Chester, PA 19013
Address Inquiries to: Charles B. Smith,
Chairman
Description: Now part of Widener University.

Widener University
Department of Theatre
Chester, PA 19013

Cheyney

Cheyney State College
Department of Theatre
Cheyney, PA 19319
Tel: 215-399-2000
Address Inquiries to: Edythe S. Bagley,
Director
Member: ATA;

Clarion

Clarion State College
Department of Theatre
165 Warwick Boyd Fine Arts Center
Clarion, PA 16214
Tel: 814-226-2282
Address Inquiries to: Alice M. Clover
Member: ATA;

Clarks Summit

Baptist Bible College
Department of Theatre
578 Venard Road
Clarks Summit, PA 18411
Tel: 717-587-1172
Member: ATA;

Collegeville

Ursinus College
Department of Theatre
Collegeville, PA 19426
Tel: 215-489-4111
Address Inquiries to: Joyce Henry,
Chairperson

Dallas

Collegium Misericordia
Theatre Arts College
Dallas, PA 18612
Tel: 717-675-2181
Address Inquiries to: Walter C.J. Anderson,
Chairman

East Stroudsburg

East Stroudsburg State College
Department of Theatre
East Stroudsburg, PA 18301
Tel: 717-424-3233
Address Inquiries to: J.J. Brennan, Chairman
Member: ATA;

Edinboro

Edinboro State College
Department of Drama
Edinboro, PA 16444
Tel: 814-732-2736; 814-732-2537
Address Inquiries to: Thomas Stanko,
Chairman
Founded in: 1981
Member: ATA;
Annual Budget: $15,000

Elizabethtown

Elizabethtown College
Department of Drama
Elizabethtown, PA 17022
Tel: 717-367-1151
Address Inquiries to: Jack P. Sederholm,
Chairman

Erie

Behrend College
Department of Theatre
Erie, PA 16563
Tel: 814-898-1511
Address Inquiries to: Paul Iddings

Gannon University
Department of Drama
Perry Square
Erie, PA 16541
Tel: 814-871-7327
Address Inquiries to: William Steckler,
Chairman
Member: ATA;

Mercyhurst College
Department of Theatre
Erie, PA 16546
Tel: 814-864-0681
Address Inquiries to: Igor Stalsky, Chairman
Member: ATA;

Gettysburg

Gettysburg College
Department of Theatre
Post Office Box 428
Gettysburg, PA 17325
Tel: 717-334-3131
Address Inquiries to: Emile O. Schmidt,
Chairperson
Member: ATA;

Glenside

Beaver College
Department of Theatre
Glenside, PA 19038
Tel: 215-884-3500
Address Inquiries to: Rosary O'Neil,
Chairperson
Judith Elder
Member: ATA;

Grantham

Messiah College
Department of Theatre
Grantham, PA 17027
Tel: 717-766-2511
Address Inquiries to: Dr. Norman Bert,
Chairman
Member: ATA;
Description: Department of Theatre.

Greensburg

Seton Hill College
Department of Theatre
Greensburg, PA 15601
Tel: 412-834-2200
Address Inquiries to: Eugene A. Saraconi,
Chairman
Member: ATA;
Description: Department of Theatre.

Greenville

Thiel College
Department of Theatre
Greenville, PA 16125
Address Inquiries to: William A. Robinson,
Chairman

Gwynedd Valley

Gwynedd Mercy College
Department of Theatre
Gwynedd Valley, PA 19437
Tel: 215-646-7300
Address Inquiries to: Jules Tasca,
Chairperson
Founded in: 1963
Member: NTC;

Haverford

Haverford College
Department of Theatre
Haverford, PA 19041
Tel: 215-649-9600
Address Inquiries to: Robert A. Buttman,
Chairman
Member: ATA;

Huntington

Juniata College
Department of Theatre
Huntington, PA 16652
Tel: 814-643-4310
Address Inquiries to: Doris P Goehring,
Chairperson

Indiana

Indiana University
Department of Theatre
Theatre by the Grove
Indiana, PA 15705
Tel: 412-357-2965
Address Inquiries to: A. Lockrow, Chairman
Beverly Young, Business Manager -
    Theatre By the Grove
Founded in: 1976
Member: ATA; SETC; SCA; USITT;
Annual Budget: $20,000
Description: A Department of Theatre in the
School of Fine Arts. Orientation is toward
degree programs and pre-professional pro-
grams.

Johnstown

University of Pittsburgh
Department of Theatre
Johnstown, PA 15904
Tel: 814-266-9661
Address Inquiries to: Rodney H. Eatman,
    Chairman

Kutztown

Kutztown State College
Department of Theatre
College Hill
Kutztown, PA 19530
Tel: 215-683-4400
Address Inquiries to: Dr. Annette Mazzaferri,
    Chairperson
Founded in: 1966
Member: SCA; ECA; AAUW;
Annual Budget: $3,000
Description: Students can major in theatre
with a fine arts emphasis or a liberal arts
emphasis. The department sponsors three
active theatre organizations: Drama Club,
Readers' Theatre and Sunshine Players
(plays for children).

Lancaster

Franklin and Marshall College
Department of Drama
Post Office Box 3003
College Avenue
Lancaster, PA 17604
Tel: 717-291-4016
Address Inquiries to: Gordon M. Wickstrom,
    Chairman
Founded in: 1899
Member: ATA;
Annual Budget: $22,000

LaPlume

Keystone Junior College
Department of Theatre
LaPlume, PA 18440
Tel: 717-945-5141
Address Inquiries to: Michael Allen,
    Chairman

Latrobe

Saint Vincent College
Department of Theatre
Latrobe, PA 15650
Tel: 412-539-9761
Address Inquiries to: Joseph Reilly, Director
Member: ATA;
Description: Department of Theatre.

Lewisburg

Bucknell University
Department of Theatre
Lewisburg, PA 17837
Tel: 717-523-1271
Address Inquiries to: Harvey M. Powers,
    Chairman
Member: ATA;

Lincoln

Lincoln University
Department of Theatre
Lincoln, PA 18015
Tel: 215-691-7000
Address Inquiries to: H. Barrett Davis,
    Chairman
Member: ATA;
Description: Department of Theatre.

Lock Haven

Lock Haven State College
Department of Theatre
Lock Haven, PA 17745
Tel: 717-893-2136
Address Inquiries to: Betty Wisnewski,
    Chairperson
Member: ATA;

Loretto

Saint Francis College
Department of Theatre
Loretto, PA 15940
Tel: 814-472-7000
Address Inquiries to: Kenny Resinski,
    Chairman

Mansfield

Mansfield State College
Department of Theatre
Mansfield, PA 16933
Tel: 717-662-4415
Address Inquiries to: A. Vernon Lapps,
    Chairman
Member: ATA;

Meadville

Allegheny College
Department of Drama
Meadville, PA 16335
Address Inquiries to: William F. Walton,
    Chairman
Member: ATA;

Media

Delaware County Community College
Department of Theatre
Media, PA 19063
Tel: 215-353-5400
Address Inquiries to: Carol Thon,
    Chairperson

Millersville

Millersville State College
Department of Theatre
Millersville, PA 17751
Tel: 717-872-5411
Address Inquiries to: Robert H. Fogg,
    Chairman
Member: ATA;
Description: Department of Theatre.

Moylan

Hedgerow Theatre School
Rose Valley Road
Moylan, PA 19065
Tel: 215-566-9892
Address Inquiries to: Rose Schulman,
    Director of Theatre Education
Member: ATA;
Description: Department of Theatre.

Nanticoke

Luzern College
Department of Drama
Nanticoke, PA 18634
Address Inquiries to: John Pisanesch,
    Chairman

Newtown

Bucks County Community College
Department of Performing Arts
Newtown, PA 18940
Tel: 215-968-8084
Member: ATA;

New Wilmington

Westminster College
Department of Theatre
New Wilmington, PA 16142
Tel: 412-946-8761
Address Inquiries to: Walter E. Sheid,
    Chairman

Philadelphia

Chestnut Hill College
Department of Theatre
Philadelphia, PA 19118
Tel: 215-214- 4210
Member: ATA;

Drexel University
Department of Theatre
32nd and Chestnut Street
Philadelphia, PA 19104
Tel: 215-895-2528
Address Inquiries to: Michael L. Rabbitt,
    Chairman

Saint Joseph's College
Department of Fine Arts and English
Philadelphia, PA 19131
Address Inquiries to: Francis R. Olley,
    Chairman
Member: ATA;

Temple University
Department of Theatre
Philadelphia, PA 19122
Tel: 212-787-8413

Address Inquiries to: Wal Cherry, Chairman
Member: ATA;

University of Pennsylvania
Department of Theatre
Philadelphia, PA 19104
Tel: 215-243-5000
Address Inquiries to: Janice Silberman,
   Chairman
Member: ATA;
Description: Department of Theatre.

Pittsburgh

Carlow College
Department of Theatre
Pittsburgh, PA 15213
Tel: 412-683-4800; 412-578-6036
Address Inquiries to: Richard M. Berlin,
   Chairman

Carnegie-Mellon University
Department of Theatre
Pittsburgh, PA 15213
Tel: 412-587-2392
Member: ATA;

Chatham College
Department of Theatre
Woodland Road
Pittsburgh, PA 15232
Tel: 412-441-8200
Address Inquiries to: Jack H. Neeson,
   Chairman

Duquesne University
Department of Theatre
Pittsburgh, PA 15219
Tel: 412-434-6460
Address Inquiries to: Eva C. Robotti,
   Chairman Speech Communication and
   Theatre
Member: SCA;

Point Park College
201 Wood Street
Pittsburgh, PA 15222
Tel: 412-391-4100
Address Inquiries to: Mark Lewis, Chairman

Robert Morris College
Department of Theatre
Pittsburgh, PA 15219
Tel: 412-264-9300
Address Inquiries to: Thomas V. Gaydos,
   Chairman

University of Pittsburgh
Department of Theatre
Cathedral of Learning
Pittsburgh, PA 15260
Tel: 412-633-
Address Inquiries to: Attilio Favorini,
   Chairman

Radnor

Cabrini College
Department of Performing Arts
Radnor, PA 19087
Tel: 215-687-2100
Address Inquiries to: Frank Saul, Chairman

Reading

Albright College
Department of English
Reading, PA 19604
Address Inquiries to: Lynn Morrow,
   Chairperson
Member: ATA;

Saint Davids

Eastern College
Department of Communication Arts
Fairview Drive
Saint Davids, PA 19087
Tel: 215-688-3300
Address Inquiries to: Gordon C. Bennett,
   Chairman
   Becky Bourne, Director
Founded in: 1970
Annual Budget: $1,500
Description: Does not offer a major in theatre,
but does offer a high-quality co-curricular
program including two major productions
per year.

Scranton

Marywood College
Department of Theatre
Scranton, PA 18509
Tel: 717-343-6521
Address Inquiries to: George F. Perry,
   Chairman
Member: ATA;

University of Scranton
Department of Theatre
Box 18
Scranton, PA 18510

Selinsgrove

Susquehanna University
Department of Communications
Selinsgrove, PA 17870
Tel: 717-374-9700
Address Inquiries to: Larry D. Augustine,
   Chairman

Shippensburg

Shippensburg State College
Department of Theatre
Shippensburg, PA 17257
Tel: 717-532-1732
Address Inquiries to: James M. St. Claire,
   Chairman

Slippery Rock

Slippery Rock State University
Department of Theatre
Slippery Rock, PA 16057
Address Inquiries to: Milton E. Resinski,
   Chairman

Swarthmore

Swarthmore College
Department of Theatre
Swarthmore, PA 19081
Tel: 215-447-7149
Address Inquiries to: Lee Devin, Chairperson

University Park

Pennsylvania State University
Department of Theatre Arts
103 Arts Building
University Park, PA 16802
Tel: 814-865-7586
Address Inquiries to: Douglas N. Cook,
   Chairman
Member: ATA;

Villanova

Villanova University
Department of Theatre
Villanova, PA 19085
Tel: 215-645-4760
Address Inquiries to: Wesley M. Truitt,
   Chairman
Member: ATA;

Waynesburg

Waynesburg College
Department of Theatre
Waynesburg, PA 15370
Tel: 412-627-8191
Address Inquiries to: Alonso Alegria,
   Chairman
Member: ATA;

West Chester

West Chester State College
Department of Theatre
West Chester, PA 19380
Tel: 215-436-2500
Address Inquiries to: William Morehouse,
   Chairman

West Mifflin

Community College of Allegheny County
Department of Theatre
West Mifflin, PA 15122
Tel: 412-469-1100
Address Inquiries to: Anna B. Wyma,
   Chairperson
Member: ATA;

Wilkes-Barre

King's College
Department of Theatre
Wilkes-Barre, PA 18711
Tel: 717-826-5900, extension 762, 763
Address Inquiries to: Carl E. Wagner,
   Chairman
Founded in: 1969
Annual Budget: $16,000

Wilkes College
Department of Theatre
Wilke-Barre, PA 18072
Tel: 717-824-4651
Address Inquiries to: Jay D. Siegfried,
   Chairman
Member: ATA;

Williamsport

Lycoming College
Department of Theatre
Williamsport, PA 17701
Tel: 717-326-1951
Address Inquiries to: Robert F. Falk,
　Chairman
Member: ATA;
Description: Department of Theatre.

York

York College of Pennsylvania
Department of Theatre
Country Club Road
York, PA 17405
Tel: 717-846-7788
Address Inquiries to: Richard D. Farrell,
　Chairman

RHODE ISLAND
Barrington

Barrington College
Department of Theatre
Middle Highway
Barrington, RI 02806
Tel: 401-246-1200 Extension 146
Address Inquiries to: William I. Han, Director
Member: ATA;
Description: Department of Theatre.

Bristol

Roger Williams College
Department of Theatre
Bristol, RI 02809
Tel: 401-253-1000
Address Inquiries to: William Grandgeorge,
　Area Coordinator
Member: ATA;
Description: Department of Theatre.

Kingston

University of Rhode Island
Department of Theatre
Kingston, RI 02881
Tel: 401-792-1000
Address Inquiries to: James W. Flannery,
　Chairman
Member: ATA;
Description: Department of Theatre.

SOUTH CAROLINA
Anderson

Anderson College
Department of Theatre
316 Boulevard
Anderson, SC 29204
Tel: 803-256-4287
Member: ATA;
Description: Department of Theatre.

Charleston

Baptist College at Charleston
Department of Theatre
Box 10087
Charleston, SC 29411
Tel: 803-797-4011
Member: ATA;
Description: Department of Theatre.

Clinton

Presbyterian College
Department of Fine Arts
South Broad Street
Clinton, SC 29325
Tel: 803-833-2820
Address Inquiries to: Dale O. Rains,
　Chairperson

Columbia

Benedict College
Department of Theatre
Columbia, SC 29204
Tel: 803-779-4930
Address Inquiries to: William C. West,
　Chairman
Member: ATA;
Description: Department of Theatre.

University of South Carolina
Department of Theatre and Speech
The Horseshoe
Columbia, SC 29208
Tel: 803-777-4288; 803-777-5208
Address Inquiries to: Patti P. Gillespie,
　Chairman
　Susan Roof, Business Manager
Member: ATA; ACA; SCA;

Conway

Coastal Carolina College
Department of Theatre
Conway, SC 29526
Tel: 803-347-3161
Address Inquiries to: Michael Fortner,
　Director
Member: ATA;

Due West

Erskine College
Department of English
Due West, SC 29639
Tel: 803-379-2131
Address Inquiries to: J. Bruce Carlock,
　Chairman
Member: ATA;

Florence

Francis Marion College
Department of Theatre
Post Office Box 7500
Florence, SC 29501
Tel: 803-669-4121
Address Inquiries to: Dennis C. Sanderson,
　Chairman
Founded in: 1973
Member: SETC; ATA;

Gaffney

Limestone College
Department of Theatre
College Drive
Gaffney, SC 29340
Tel: 803-489-7151
Address Inquiries to: Charles R. Hannum,
　Chairman

Greenville

Bob Jones University
Department of Theatre
Wade Hampton Boulevard
Greenville, SC 29614
Tel: 803-242-5100 Extension 238
Address Inquiries to: Dewitt Jones, Chairman,
　Department of Theatre
Member: ATA;

Furman University
Department of Drama
Greenville, SC 29613
Tel: 803-294-2051; 803-294-2125
Address Inquiries to: Philip G. Hill, Chairman
Founded in: 1935
Member: ATA; STC; SCTA;
Annual Budget: $120,000
Description: Undergraduate liberal arts college producing four or five major productions annually and a varying number of laboratory theatre productions.

Greenwood

Lander College
Department of Speech and Theatre
Stanley Avenue
Greenwood, SC 29646
Tel: 803-229-8211; 803-229-8213
Address Inquiries to: Harvey M. Jeffreys
Frank E. Jackson
Founded in: 1970
Member: ATA; SETC; SCTA; CSCA;
Annual Budget: $15,000
Description: A four-year liberal arts college offering a BA in speech and theatre. Presents four major productions each year and several minor productions.

Hartsville

Coker College
Department of Theatre
Hartsville, SC 29550
Tel: 803-332-1381
Address Inquiries to: Robert Bloodworth,
　Chairman
Member: ATA;

Newberry

Newberry College
Department of Theatre
Newberry, SC 29108
Tel: 803-276-8104
Address Inquiries to: Kenneth R. Robbins
Member: ATA; ASSFDC; STC;
Annual Budget: $10,000
Description: The Speech and Theatre department prepares individuals for graduate studies, the seminary and occupations which demand a high level of communication

skills. Five major theatre productions are mounted yearly giving the student's ample opportunities to learn practical aspects of speech and theatre. They also offer an arts management program in which students have opportunities to work with professional theatres, museums and civic arts organizations.

Orangeburg

South Carolina State College
Department of Theatre
College Avenue
Orangeburg, SC 29117
Tel: 803-536-7123
Address Inquiries to: Frank M. Mundy, Chairman

Rock Hill

Winthrop College
Department of Theatre
319 Kinard Boulevard
Rock Hill, SC 29733
Tel: 803-323-2171
Address Inquiries to: Chris Reynolds, Chairman
Member: ATA;

SOUTH DAKOTA

Aberdeen

Northern State College
Department of Drama
Jay and 12th Street
Aberdeen, SD 57401
Tel: 605-622-2503
Address Inquiries to: Richard Norquist, Chairman

Brookings

South Dakota State University
Department of Theatre
Brookings, SD 57006
Tel: 605-688-6131
Address Inquiries to: Pugsley Hall

Huron

Huron College
Department of Theatre
Huron, SD 57350
Tel: 605-352-8721
Address Inquiries to: Avi Seaver, Ph.D.
Founded in: 1883
Member: ATA;
Annual Budget: $2,000
Description: Produces a full-length play each regular term. A play for young audiences is produced in January and tours the area public schools. A summer theatre production is also mounted. Huron College has a modern, 260 seat proscenium theatre with an excellent shop adjoining the stage.

Madison

Dakota State College
Humanities Department
Madison, SD 57042
Tel: 605-256-3551
Address Inquiries to: David P. Johnson, Chairman

Mitchell

Dakota Wesleyan University
Department of Theatre
Mitchell, SD 57301
Tel: 605-996-6511
Address Inquiries to: Michael Turchen, Chairman

Sioux Falls

Augustana College
Department of Speech and Drama
29th and Summit
Sioux Falls, SD 57102
Tel: 605-336-5526
Address Inquiries to: Gary Reed, Chairman

Sioux Falls College
Department of Humanities
1501 South Prairie
Sioux Falls, SD 57101
Tel: 605-331-6709
Address Inquiries to: Perry W. Patterson, Chairman

Spearfish

Black Hills State College
Department of Theatre
1200 University Street
Spearfish, SD 57783
Tel: 605-642-6268
Address Inquiries to: Albin W. Sandau, Chairman
Member: ATA;

Springfield

University of South Dakota, Springfield
Department of Theatre
Springfield, SD 57062
Tel: 605-369-5414
Address Inquiries to: Virgil Petrik, Chairman

Vermillion

University of South Dakota, Vermillion
Department of Theatre
Vermillion, SD 57069
Tel: 605-677-5418
Address Inquiries to: Ronald L. Moyer, Chairman
Founded in: 1935
Member: ATA; MATC; USITT; SDTA;
Annual Budget: $45,000, plus staff salaries
Description: Offers B.F.A. and M.A. degrees. Programs within the B.F.A. are preprofessional performance (acting, directing, dance), preprofessional production (scenic, costume, lighting), general theatre and drama and theatre education (secondary). Production facilities include a 450-seat proscenium theatre, a 100-seat 'black-box' theatre, dance studio, design studio, and well-equipped scenic and costume shops.

The Department presents a varied season of plays, musicals and dance concerts, which periodical tour the state. Associated with the Black Hills Playhouse where they produce their summer stock season.

Yankton

Mount Mary College
Department of Oral Communication
1100 West 8th
Yankton, SD 57078
Tel: 605-668-1533
Address Inquiries to: Catherine McGovern, Chairperson
Founded in: 1935
Member: ATA; SDTA;
Annual Budget: $1,000
Description: A small Benedictine college that presents about three productions a year.

Yankton College
Department of Theatre
12th and Douglas Avenue
Yankton, SD 57078
Tel: 605-665-3661
Address Inquiries to: Ambrose P. Schenk, Chairman
Member: ATA;

TENNESSEE

Athens

Tennessee Wesleyan College
Department of Theatre
Post Office Box 112
Athens, TN 37303
Tel: 615-745-5093
Address Inquiries to: L. E. Whiting, Chairman

Chattanooga

University of Tennessee, Chattanooga
Department of Theatre
323 Fine Arts Building
Chattanooga, TN 37402
Tel: 615-755-4374; 615-755-4297
Address Inquiries to: Fred Behringer, Chairman
Founded in: 1886
Member: ATA;

Clarksville

Austin Peay State University
Department of Theatre
Clarksville, TN 37040
Tel: 615-648-7378
Address Inquiries to: I. Filippo, Chairman
Founded in: 1963
Member: ATA; TTA; SCA;

Columbia

Columbia State Community College
Department of Theatre
Columbia, TN 38401
Tel: 615-388-0120
Member: ATA;

Cookeville

Tennessee Technological University
Department of Theatre
Cookeville, TN 38501
Tel: 615-528-3478
Address Inquiries to: M.L. McKay, Chairman

Dayton

Bryan College
Department of Theatre
Dayton, TN 37321
Tel: 775-204-, ext. 286
Address Inquiries to: Rachel R. Morgan,
  Chairperson
Member: SETC;
Description: A small Christian liberal arts college. The theatre bill is limited to one major production a year, plus several one-act plays. It has a company that appears in area churches.

Greenville

Tusculum College
Department of Theatre
Tusculum Station
Greenville, TN 37743
Tel: 615-639-2701
Address Inquiries to: David F. Behan,
  Chairman
Member: ATA;

Henderson

Freed-Hardeman College
Department of Communication/Theatre
158 East Main Street
Henderson, TN 38340
Tel: 901-989-4611
Address Inquiries to: Henry A. McDaniel Jr.,
  Director of Theatre
  Gerald Fulkerson, Chairman
Founded in: 1950
Member: ATA; SETC; TTA;
Description: The department has a childrens theatre touring group called the Pied Pipers Company II. The group tours hospitals, retardation centers, burn wards, elementary schools and other facilities for children.

Jackson

Jackson State Community College
Department of Theatre
Post Office Box 2467
Jackson, TN 38301
Tel: 901-424-3520
Address Inquiries to: Dr. C.D. Culver,
  Chairman
Member: ATA;

Lambuth College
Department of Theatre
Jackson, TN 38301
Tel: 901-427-6743
Address Inquiries to: Jesse B. Byrum,
  Chairperson

Lane College
Department of Theatre
545 Lane Avenue
Jackson, TN 38301

Tel: 901-424-4600
Address Inquiries to: R.H. Antrum, Chairman

Union University
Department of Theatre Arts
North 45 Bypass
Jackson, TN 38301
Tel: 901-668-1818
Address Inquiries to: N. Stevenson,
  Chairperson
Member: ATA;

Jefferson Street

Carson-Newman College
Communication Arts Department
Russel Street
Jefferson Street, TN 37760
Tel: 615-745-9061
Address Inquiries to: John Welton, Director
  of Drama
Founded in: 1851
Annual Budget: $2,700
Description: One act plays, children's theatre productions, and reader's theatre productions are done in drama classes. Three additional major productions are staged each year and are open to all interested student actors and technicians.

Johnson City

East Tennessee State University
Department of Theatre
ETSU Station
Johnson City, TN 37601
Address Inquiries to: Jack Peyrouse,
  Chairman
Member: ATA;

Knoxville

Knoxville College
Department of Theatre
901 College Street
Knoxville, TN 37921
Tel: 615-546-0751
Member: ATA;

University of Tennessee, Knoxville
Department of Theatre
Cumberland Avenue
Knoxville, TN 37916
Tel: 615-974-2591
Address Inquiries to: Ralph G. Allen, Ph.D,
  Chairman, Department of Theatre
Member: ATA;

Martin

University of Tennessee, Martin
Department of Theatre
Martin, TN 38237
Tel: 901-587-7133
Address Inquiries to: William Snyder,
  Chairman
Member: ATA;

McKenzie

Bethel College
Department of Theatre
Cherry Street
McKenzie, TN 38201
Tel: 901-352-5896

Address Inquiries to: Rodney Higginbotham,
  Chairman
Founded in: 1980
Member: ATA; STC;
Annual Budget: $1,800
Description: A small, private, church-related liberal arts college. A number of speech theatre courses are offered and there are three major productions per school year.

Memphis

Christian Brothers College
Department of Theatre
650 East Parkway South
Memphis, TN 38104
Tel: 901-278-0100
Address Inquiries to: Thomas Schumacher,
  Director
Member: ATA;

Lemoyne-Owen College
Department of Theatre
807 Walker Avenue
Memphis, TN 38126
Tel: 901-948-6626
Address Inquiries to: I.D. Thompson,
  Chairman
Member: ATA;

Southwestern at Memphis
Department of Theatre
2000 North Parkway
Memphis, TN 38112
Address Inquiries to: R.S. Hill, Chairman
Member: ATA;

Milligan College

Milligan College
Department of Theatre
Milligan College, TN 37682
Address Inquiries to: William Moorhouse,
  Chairman

Nashville

Belmont College
Department of Theatre
1900 Belmont Boulevard
Nashville, TN 37203
Tel: 615-383-7001
Address Inquiries to: Dr. Jerry L. Warren,
  Chairman
Member: ATA;

Fisk University
Department of Theatre
17th Avenue N
Nashville, TN 37203
Tel: 615-329-8765
Address Inquiries to: Gladys I. Forde,
  Chairman

George Peabody College
Department of Drama
21st Avenue South
Nashville, TN 37203
Tel: 615-327-8121
Address Inquiries to: Willard C. Booth,
  Chairman

Scarritt College for Christian Workers
Department of Theatre

19th and Grand Avenue
Nashville, TN 37203
Tel: 615-327-2700
Address Inquiries to: James H. Warren,
    Associate Professor
Member: ATA;

Trevecca Nazarene College
Department of Theatre
333 Murfreesboro Road
Nashville, TN 37210
Tel: 615-244-6000 Extension 374
Address Inquiries to: Dr. Barbara McClain,
    Chairperson
Member: ATA;

Vanderbuilt University
Department of Drama and Speech
Nashville, TN 37235
Tel: 615-033- 2404
Address Inquiries to: Cecil D. Jones Jr.,
    Chairman

Sewanee

University of the South
Department of Theatre
Sewanee, TN 37375
Tel: 615-598-5931
Address Inquiries to: Frank M. Miller,
    Chairman
Founded in: 1972
Member: ATA; STC; ACA;
Annual Budget: $66,000

TEXAS

Abilene

Henderson County Junior College
Abilene, TX 79601
Tel: 915-677-7281
Address Inquiries to: George Oliver, Director
    of Theatre

Alpine

Sul Ross State University
Alpine, TX 79830
Tel: 915-837-8221
Address Inquiries to: George Bradley,
    Chairman
Member: ATA;

Amarillo

Amarillo College
Department of Theatre
Amarillo, TX 79178
Tel: 806-376-5111
Address Inquiries to: Terral S. Lewis,
    Chairman
Member: ATA;

Amarillo Theatre Centre and Academy
Box 2424
Amarillo, TX 79109
Tel: 806-355-9991
Address Inquiries to: Roger Thomas,
    Executive Director
Founded in: 1926
Member: TNPTI; ATA;
Annual Budget: $150,000

Description: Five conventional shows and
three children's shows are mounted annually.

Austin

Huston-Tillotson College
Department of Theatre
1820 East 8th Street
Austin, TX 78702
Tel: 512-476-7421

University of Texas, Austin
Department of Theatre
Austin, TX 78712
Tel: 512-471-5793
Address Inquiries to: Coleman A. Jennings,
    Chairman
Member: URTA;
Description: The department offers approxi-
mately 20 productions along with the Shoe-
string Theatre, a production lab for play-
wrights. Features include the Summer
Theatre Program, Dance Repertory Theatre
and The London Stage Project. Scholar-
ships, assistantships and grants to students
are availble.

Baytown

Lee College
Department of Fine Arts
Post Office Box 818
Baytown, TX 77520
Tel: 713-427-5611
Address Inquiries to: T.E. Bowlett, Chairman

Borger

Frank Phillips College
Department of Theatre
Borger, TX 79007
Tel: 806-274-5311
Address Inquiries to: John P. Banard,
    Chairman

Brazosport

Brazosport College
Department of Theatre
Post Office Drawer 955
Brazosport, TX 7754
Tel: 713-265-6131
Address Inquiries to: Tom Kinney, Chairman
Member: ATA;

Brownsville

Texas Southmost College
Department of Theatre
Brownsville, TX 78520
Tel: 512-541-1241
Address Inquiries to: Anna Miller,
    Chairperson
Member: DCA;

Cisco

Cisco Junior College
Department of Fine Arts
Cisco, TX 76437
Address Inquiries to: Mary A. Reed,
    Chairman

Corpus Christi

Corpus Christi State University
Department of Theatre
Post Office Box 6010
Corpus Christi, TX 78411
Tel: 512-991-6810
Address Inquiries to: Dr. Miriam
    Wagenschein, Dean, College of Arts and
    Humanities
Member: ATA;

Dallas

Bishop College
Department of Theatre
3837 Simpson and Stuart Street
Dallas, TX 75241
Tel: 214-376-4311
Address Inquiries to: Dr. Jack Gilber,
    Chairman
Member: ATA;

El Centro College
Department of Theatre
Main and Lamar Street
Dallas, TX 75202
Address Inquiries to: Phillip H. Jackman

Richland College
Department of Theatre
12800 Abrams Road
Dallas, TX 75081
Tel: 214-746-4550
Address Inquiries to: Bob Dyer, Instructor

Denison

Grayson County College
Department of Theatre
6101 Highway 691
Denison, TX 75020
Tel: 214-893-6834
Address Inquiries to: Dr. Charles McAdams,
    Director Division of Fine Arts

Denton

Denton Community College
Department of Theatre
Denton, TX 76402
Member: ATA;

Texas Womens University
Denton, TX 76204
Tel: 817-382-2315
Address Inquiries to: M. Don Ryan, Chairman
Member: ATA;

Edinburg

Pan American University
Department of Communication
Edinburg, TX 78935
Tel: 512-381-3581
Address Inquiries to: Marian Monta,
    Chairperson
Member: ATA;

El Paso

University of Texas, El Paso
Department of Theatre
El Paso, TX 79968
Tel: 915-747-5666
Address Inquiries to: Dr. H.N. Williams,

Chairman
Member: DCA;

Fort Worth

Tarrant County Junior College, South
  Campus
Department of Theatre
5301 Campus Drive
Fort Worth, TX 76119
Tel: 817-534-4861
Address Inquiries to: Dr. Gwendel Mulkey,
  Chairman

Texas Wesleyan College
Department of Theatre
Post Office 3277
Fort Worth, TX 76105
Tel: 817-534-0251
Address Inquiries to: Mason Johnson,
  Chairman
Member: DCA;

Houston

San Jacinto College
Department of Theatre
5800 Uvalde
Houston, TX 77049
Tel: 713-458-4050
Address Inquiries to: Perry Riley, Chairman
Member: ATA;

Texas Southern University
Department of Theatre
3201 Wheeler Avenue
Houston, TX 77004
Tel: 713-527-7360
Address Inquiries to: Carlton W. Molete,
  Chairman
Member: ATA;

University of Houston, Central Campus
Department of Theatre
4800 Calhoun
Houston, TX 77004
Tel: 713-749-1011
Address Inquiries to: Sidney Berger,
  Chairman

University of Houston, Downtown College
Department of Theatre
1 Main Street
Houston, TX 77002
Tel: 713-749-1011
Address Inquiries to: John Biggers, Artistic
  Director

Huntsville

Sam Houston State University
Department of Speech and Drama
136 Sunset Lake Drive
Huntsville, TX 74430
Tel: 713-295-7687
Address Inquiries to: Charles A. Schmidt,
  Chairman

Hurst

Tarrant County Junior College Northeast
Department of Theatre
828 Harwood Road
Hurst, TX 76053
Address Inquiries to: Doyle D. Smith,

Chairman
Member: ATA;

Jacksonville

Lon Morris College
Department of Theatre
Lon Morris College Station
Jacksonville, TX 75766
Tel: 214-586-2471
Address Inquiries to: Ruth Alexander,
  Chairperson
Member: ATA;

Jefferson City

Carson-Newman College
Department of Theatre
Russel Street
Jefferson City, TX
Address Inquiries to: D. Petrik, Chairman

Kerrville

Schreiner College
Department of Fine Arts
Post Office Box 4498
Kerrville, TX 78028
Tel: 512-896-5411
Address Inquiries to: Andrew J. Ritch,
  Chairman

Killeen

Central Texas College
Department of Theatre
Killeen, TX 76541
Address Inquiries to: Terry Eyman,
  Chairperson

Lubbock

Lubbock Christian College
Department of Theatre
Lubbock, TX 79407
Tel: 806-792-3221
Address Inquiries to: June Bearden, Chairman

Texas Tech University
Department of Theatre Arts
Post Office Box 4298
Lubbock, TX 79409
Tel: 806-742-3601
Address Inquiries to: Richard A. Weaver,
  Director of Theatre
Member: ATA;

Marshall

East Texas Baptist College
Department of Theatre
1209 North Grove
Marshall, TX 75670
Tel: 214-938-3911
Address Inquiries to: Steven J. Peters,
  Chairman

Memphis

Memphis State University
Department of Drama
Memphis, TX 38152
Tel: 901-454-2565
Address Inquiries to: Richard A. Rice,
  Director of Theatre
Member: URTA;

Description: The department has a main
theatre with 400 seats, a flexible proscenium,
a graduate program available.

Mesquite

Eastfield College
Department of Theatre
3737 Motley Drive
Mesquite, TX 75150
Tel: 214-746-3100
Address Inquiries to: Robert Erwin, Theatre
  Director
Member: ATA;

Nacogdoches

Stephen F. Austin State University
Department of Theatre
6204 SFA
Nacogdoches, TX 75961
Tel: 713-569-4004
Address Inquiries to: Thomas K. Heino,
  Chairman
Member: ATA;

Odessa

Odessa College
Department of Theatre
Post Office Box 3752
Odessa, TX 79760
Tel: 915-337-5381
Address Inquiries to: Jane Ann Crum,
  Chairperson
Founded in: 1946
Member: ATA; ACTF; TETA;
Annual Budget: $33,000

Paris

Paris Junior College
Department of Theatre
2400 Clarksville Street
Paris, TX 75460
Tel: 214-785-7661
Address Inquiries to: Ray E. Karrer,
  Chairman

Plainview

Wayland Baptist University
Department of Theatre
1900 W 7th Street
Plainview, TX 79072
Tel: 806-296-5521
Address Inquiries to: Roland W. Myers,
  Chairman
Member: ATA;

Prairie View

Prairie View A and M College
Department of Theatre
Prairie View, TX 77445
Tel: 713-857-2356
Address Inquiries to: Ted Shine, Chairman

San Angelo

Angelo State University
Department of Drama
San Angelo, TX 76902
Tel: 915-942-2031; 915-942-2032
Address Inquiries to: Raymond E. Carver,
  Chairman

Founded in: 1966
Member: ATA; TETA; SWTC;
Annual Budget: $50,000

San Antonio

Our Lady of the Lake College
Department of Theatre
411 South West 24th Street
San Antonio, TX 78285
Tel: 512-434-6711
Address Inquiries to: Richard Slocum,
    Chairman

San Antonio College
Department of Theatre
1300 San Pedro Avenue
San Antonio, TX 78284
Tel: 512-734-5381
Address Inquiries to: Ron Lucke, Chairman
Member: ATA;

San Antonio Little Theatre and Academy
Post Office Box 12356
San Antonio, TX 78212
Tel: 512-732-8101
Address Inquiries to: Joe Salek, Manager

Trinity University
Department of Drama
715 Stadium Drive
San Antonio, TX 78284
Tel: 512-736-8511
Address Inquiries to: James M. Symons,
    Speech and Drama Department
Member: ATA;

Sherman

Austin College
Department of Theatre
Sherman, TX 75090
Tel: 214-892-9101
Address Inquiries to: W.D. Narramore,
    Chairman
Member: ATA;

Snyder

Western Texas College
Department of Theatre
Snyder, TX 79549
Tel: 915-573-8511
Address Inquiries to: Charles A. Holland,
    Chairman

Temple

Temple Junior College
Department of Theatre
2600 South First Street
Temple, TX 76501
Tel: 817-773-9961
Address Inquiries to: J. Bryant Reeves,
    Chairperson
Member: ATA;

Texarkana

Texarkana College
Department of Theatre
1024 Tucker
Texarkana, TX 75501
Tel: 214-838-4541
Address Inquiries to: Mildred Parsons,

Chairperson

Texas City

College of the Mainland
Department of Theatre
8001 Palmer Highway
Texas City, TX 77590
Tel: 713-938-1211
Address Inquiries to: Jack Westin, Theatre
    Coordinator
Member: ATA;

Tyler

Texas College
Department of Theatre
Tyler, TX 75701
Tel: 214-594-3200
Address Inquiries to: P. Irwin, Chairman
Member: DCA;

Vernon

Vernon Regional Junior College
Department of Drama
4400 College Drive
Vernon, TX 76384
Tel: 817-552-6291
Address Inquiries to: Kay Cook, Chairperson
Member: ATA;

Waco

Baylor University
Department of Theatre
Waco, TX 76703
Tel: 817-755-1861
Address Inquiries to: Bill G. Cook, Chairman
Founded in: 1946
Member: ATA; SWTC; TETA;
Annual Budget: $25,000

McLennan Community College
Department of Theatre
1400 College Drive
Waco, TX 76708
Tel: 817-756-6551
Address Inquiries to: James Henderson,
    Instructor

Paul Quinn College
Department of Theatre
Waco, TX 75704
Tel: 817-753-8081

Weatherford

Weatherford College
Department of Theatre
308 East Park
Weatherford, TX 76086
Tel: 817-594-5471, Ext. 36
Address Inquiries to: Jim Ramp, Chairman,
    Department of Speech and Drama
Member: DCA;

UTAH

Cedar City

Southern Utah State College
Department of Theatre Arts
351 West Center
Cedar City, UT 84750
Tel: 801-856-3636
Address Inquiries to: Fred C. Adams,
    Chairman

Ephraim

Snow College
Department of Theatre
140 East College Avenue
Ephraim, UT 84627
Address Inquiries to: Richard P. Haslam,
    Chairman

Logan

Utah State University
Department of Theatre
Logan, UT 84321
Tel: 801-752-4100
Address Inquiries to: W. Vosco Call,
    Chairperson
Member: ATA;

Ogden

Weber State College
Department of Theatre
3750 Harrison Boulevard
Ogden, UT 84415
Tel: 801-626-6431
Address Inquiries to: T. Leonard Rowley

Salt Lake City

University of Utah
Department of Theatre
College of Fine Arts
Salt Lake City, UT 84112
Tel: 801-581-6356
Address Inquiries to: Keith Engar, Chairman

Westminister College
Department of Theatre
1840 South 13th Street East
Salt Lake City, UT 84105
Tel: 801-484-1651
Address Inquiries to: Jay W. Lees, Chairman
Member: DCA;

VERMONT

Bennington

Bennington College
Department of Theatre
Bennington, VT 05201
Tel: 802-442-5401
Address Inquiries to: Leroy Logan, Chairman
Member: DCA;

Burlington

University of Vermont
Department of Theatre
Burlington, VT 05405
Tel: 802-656-2095
Address Inquiries to: Edward J. Feidner,

Chairman
Member: ATA;

Johnson

Johnson State College
Department of Performing Arts
Johnson, VT 05656
Tel: 802-635-2356
Address Inquiries to: Ralph Carter, Chairman
Member: DCA;

Northfield

Norwich University
Department of English/Theatre
Northfield, VT 05663
Tel: 802-485-5011
Address Inquiries to: Carlton F. Berry, Jr.,
   Chairman

Plainfield

Goddard College
Department of Theatre
Plainfield, VT 05667
Tel: 802-454-8311
Address Inquiries to: Catherine Michelson,
   Chairman
Member: DCA;

Poultney

Green Mountain College
Department of Theatre
Poultney, VT 05764
Tel: 802-287-9313
Address Inquiries to: Saul Elkin, Chairman
Member: DCA;

Winooski

Saint Michaels College
Department of Theatre
56 College Parkway
Winooski, VT 05404
Tel: 802-655-2000
Address Inquiries to: Joane Ratageb,
   Chairperson

VIRGINIA

Blacksburg

Virginia Polytechnic Institute
Department of Theatre
Blacksburg, VA 24061
Tel: 703-951-5200
Address Inquiries to: Donald A. Drapeau,
   Chairman
Member: DCA;

Buena Vista

Southern Seminary Junior College
Department of Theatre
Buena Vista, VA 24416
Tel: 703-261-6181
Address Inquiries to: William H. Rough,
   Chairman
Member: DCA;

Charlottesville

University of Virginia
Department of Theatre
Charlottesville, VA 22903
Tel: 804-924-3326
Address Inquiries to: George Black, Chairman
Member: DCA;

Emory

Emory and Henry College
Department of English
Emory, VA 24327
Address Inquiries to: H. Alan Pickrell,
   Chairman

Fairfax

George Mason University
Department of Theatre
4400 University Drive
Fairfax, VA 22030
Tel: 703-323-2450
Address Inquiries to: Jack L. Jenkins,
   Chairman
Member: ATA;

Farmville

Longwood College
Department of Theatre
Farmville, VA 23901
Tel: 804-392-9371
Address Inquiries to: Dr. Patton Lockwood,
   Chairman
Member: DCA;

Ferrum

Ferrum College
Department of Theatre
Post Office Box 85
Ferrum, VA 24088
Tel: 703-365-2121
Address Inquiries to: R. Rex Stephenson,
   Chairman
Member: ATA;

Fredericksburg

Mary Washington College
Department of Dramatic Arts
Fredericksburg, VA 22401
Tel: 703-820-6320
Address Inquiries to: Roger Kenvin,
   Chairman
Member: DCA; ATA;

Hampton

Hampton Institute
Department of Drama
Hampton, VA 23668
Tel: 804-727-5401
Address Inquiries to: Timothy E.
   Roseborough, Chairman

Hollins College

Hollins College
Department of Theatre
Post Office Box 9602
Hollins College, VA 24020
Tel: 703-362-6518
Address Inquiries to: Thomas Atkins,

Chairman

Lynchburg

Lynchburg College
Department of Dramatic Arts
Lynchburg, VA 24501
Tel: 804-845-9071
Address Inquiries to: Robert C. Hailey,
   Chairman
Member: DCA;

Richmond

Virginia Commonwealth University
901 West Franklin Street
Richmond, VA 23284
Address Inquiries to: Kenneth Campbell,
   Chairman
Member: DCA;

WASHINGTON

Pullman

University of Washington
Department of Theatre
Pullman, WA 99164
Tel: 509-335-4581
Address Inquiries to: Director Wadleigh,
   Chairman
Member: DCA;

Seattle

Cornish Institute of Allied Arts
Department of Theatre
710 East Roy
Seattle, WA 98102
Tel: 206-323-1400
Address Inquiries to: Julian Schembri,
   Chairman
Member: DCA;

Seattle Pacific University
Department of Theatre
3307 3rd Avenue West
Seattle, WA 98119
Tel: 206-281-2036
Address Inquiries to: James Chapman,
   Director
Member: DCA;

Seattle University
Department of Theatre
11th and Spring
Seattle, WA 98122
Tel: 206-626-6336
Address Inquiries to: David M. Butler,
   Chairman
Member: DCA;

Spokane

Fort Worth College of the Holy Names
Department of Theatre
West 4000 Randolph Road
Spokane, WA 99204
Tel: 509-328-2970
Address Inquiries to: Robert Welch,
   Chairman
Member: DCA;

WEST VIRGINIA

Athens

Concord College
Department of Theatre
Athens, WV 24712
Tel: 304-384-3115
Address Inquiries to: Ronald L. Burgher,
Chairman
Member: DCA;

Bluefield

Bluefield College
Department of Theatre
Bluefield, WV 24605
Tel: 703-327-7137
Address Inquiries to: Charles R. Hannum,
Chairman
Member: DCA;

Buckhannon

West Virginia Wesleyan College
Department of Drama
Buckhannon, WV 26201
Tel: 304-473-8044
Address Inquiries to: Charles J. Presar,
Chairman
Member: ATA;

Charleston

Morris Harvey College
Department of Theatre
Charleston, WV 25304
Address Inquiries to: Kenneth Slattery,
Chairman

Fairmont

Fairmont State College
Department of Theatre
Fairmont, WV 26554
Tel: 304-367-4219
Address Inquiries to: JoAnn Lough,
Chairperson

Huntington

Marshall University
Department of Theatre
Huntington, WV 25701
Tel: 304-696-6786
Address Inquiries to: Elaine A. Novak,
Chairperson

Institute

West Virginia State College
Department of Communications
Box 28, Theatre Institute
Institute, WV 25112
Tel: 304-766-3197
Address Inquiries to: David Wohl, Chairman
Founded in: 1975
Member: ATA; SETC; WVHD;
Annual Budget: $100,000
Description: A generalist program in communications, providing education in the areas of theatre, film, television, and speech.

Morgantown

West Virginia University
Department of Theatre
Morgantown, WV 26506
Tel: 304-293-4022
Address Inquiries to: Jon Whitmore,
Chairman
Member: ATA; ACA; SETC; WVTC;
WVDCH; WVUF; Benedum Foundation,
Pittsburgh;

Parkersburg

Ohio Valley College
Department of Theatre
Parkersburg, WV 25304
Tel: 304-485-7384
Address Inquiries to: Steven Frye, Chairman

Parkersburg Community College
Department of Theatre
Parkersburg, WV 26101
Tel: 304-424-8266
Address Inquiries to: Phil Haynie, Chairman

Salem

Salem College
Department of Theatre
Salem, WV 26426
Tel: 304-782-5217
Address Inquiries to: Susana Morton,
Chairperson

Shepherdstown

Shepherd College
Department of Theatre
Shepherdstown, WV 25443
Tel: 304-876-2735
Address Inquiries to: Bruce L. Partin,
Chairman

Wheeling

Wheeling College
Department of Theatre
Post Office Box 18
Wheeling, WV 26003
Address Inquiries to: Charles F. Braun,
Chairman

Willimson

Southern West Virginia Community
College
Department of Theatre
Willimson, WV 25601
Tel: 304-235-2800
Address Inquiries to: James D. Bartlett,
Chairman

WISCONSIN

Appleton

Lawrence University
Department of Theatre
Post Office Box 599
Appleton, WI 54911
Tel: 414-739-3681
Address Inquiries to: Richard France,
Chairman

Member: ATA;

Beloit

Beloit College
Department of Theatre
Beloit, WI 53511
Tel: 608-365-3391
Address Inquiries to: Carl G. Balson, Director
Member: ATA;

Fond Du Lac

Marian College
Department of Theatre
45 South National Avenue
Fond Du Lac, WI 54935
Tel: 414-921-3900
Address Inquiries to: H.J. Linborg,
Chairperson

Janesville

University of Wisconsin Center
Department of Theatre
Rock County
Janesville, WI 53545
Tel: 608-755-2811
Address Inquiries to: Bob Holt, Chairman

Kenosha

Carthage College
Department of Theatre
Kenosha, WI 53140
Tel: 414-551-8500
Address Inquiries to: T. Shandy Holland,
Chairman

University of Wisconsin, Parkside
Department of Dramatic Arts
Post Office Box 2000
Kenosha, WI 53140
Tel: 414-553-2522
Address Inquiries to: Leon J. VanDyke,
Chairman
Founded in: 1976
Member: ATA; WTA; MAP; DCA;
Annual Budget: $12,000

La Crosse

University of Wisconsin
Department of Theatre
1725 State Street
La Crosse, WI 54601
Tel: 608-785-8523
Address Inquiries to: Richard Tinapp,
Chairman

Viterbo College
Department of Theatre
815 South 9th Street
La Crosse, WI 54601
Tel: 608-784-0040
Address Inquiries to: Phillip Recher,
Chairman
Member: DCA; ATA;

Madison

Edgewood College
Department of Performing Arts
855 Woodrow Street
Madison, WI 53711
Tel: 608-257-4861

Address Inquiries to: Jewell P. Fitzgerald, Chairperson

Madison Area Technical College
Department of Theatre
211 North Carroll Street
Madison, WI 53703
Tel: 608-266-5054
Address Inquiries to: Michael Barber, Chairman

University of Wisconsin
Department of Theatre
Madison, WI 53706
Tel: 608-263-6320
Address Inquiries to: Edward Kamarck, Chairman

Manitowoc

Silver Lake College
Department of Theatre
2406 South Alverno Road
Manitowoc, WI 54220
Tel: 414-684-6691
Address Inquiries to: Martin F. Lavin, Chairman

University of Wisconsin, Manitowoc
Department of Theatre
705 Viebahn Street
Manitowoc, WI 54220
Tel: 414-682-8251
Address Inquiries to: David H. Semmes, Assistant Professor
Member: DCA;

Marshfield

University of Wisconsin, Marshfield
Department of Theatre
Marshfield, WI 54449
Tel: 715-387-1147
Address Inquiries to: Greg Rindfleisch, Chairman

Milwaukee

Alverno College, Department of Theatre
3401 South 39th Street
Milwaukee, WI 53215
Tel: 414-671-5400
Address Inquiries to: H.C. Timm, Chairman
Member: ATA;

Cardinal Stritch College
Department of Theatre
6801 North Yates Road
Milwaukee, WI 53217
Tel: 414-352-5400, Ext. 291
Address Inquiries to: Rose Klassen, Chairperson
David Oswald, Director
Founded in: 1977
Member: ATA; ACA; WTA;
Annual Budget: $50,000
Description: Offers majors in theatre and interpersonal communications.

Concordia College
Department of Humanities
Milwaukee, WI 53140
Tel: 414-344-3400
Address Inquiries to: David Eggebrecht, Chairman

Marquette University
Department of Theatre Arts
615 North 11th Street
Milwaukee, WI 53233
Tel: 414-224-7504
Address Inquiries to: Robert Klassen, Chairman
Member: ATA;

University of Wisconsin, Milwaukee
School of Fine Arts
Milwaukee, WI 53201
Tel: 414-963-4762
Address Inquiries to: Sanford Robbins, Chairman
Member: DCA;

University of Wisconsin, Milwaukee
Training Program
Post Office Box 413
Milwaukee, WI 53201
Tel: 414-936-4947
Address Inquiries to: Robert W. Corrigan, Dean
Description: The UWM's Professional Theatre Training Program offers undergraduate programs in Costume Construction, Stage Management and Technical Production. Write for information regarding these intensive and disiplined theatre programs.

Oshkosh

University of Wisconsin, Oshkosh
Department of Theatre
Oshkosh, WI 54901
Tel: 414-424-4422
Address Inquiries to: Gloria Lind, Coordinator
Member: DCA;

Richland Center

University of Wisconsin, Richland Center
Department of Theater
Richland Center, WI 53581
Tel: 608-647-6186
Address Inquiries to: Margaret Jean Birkett, Chairman

Ripon

Ripon College
Department of Drama
Ripon, WI 54971
Tel: 414-748-8136; 414-748-7525
Address Inquiries to: Edmund Roney, Ph.D.
Founded in: 1851
Member: ATA; WTA;

River Falls

University of Wisconsin, River Falls
Department of Theatre
River Falls, WI 54022
Tel: 715-425-3911
Address Inquiries to: Dr. Jerald Carstens, Chairman
Member: DCA;

Sheboygan

Lakeland College
Department of Theatre
Sheboygan, WI 53081
Tel: 414-565-2111
Address Inquiries to: James Crawford, Chairman

Stevens Point

University of Wisconsin, Stevens Point
Department of Theatre
2100 Main Street
Stevens Point, WI 54481
Tel: 715-346-0123
Address Inquiries to: Seldon Faulkner, Chairman
Member: DCA;

Watertown

Northwestern College
Department of Theatre
Watertown, WI 53094
Tel: 414-261-4352
Address Inquiries to: Sylvester Quam, Chairperson

Waukesha

Carroll College
Department of Theatre Arts
Waukesha, WI 53186
Tel: 414-547-1211
Address Inquiries to: David Molthen, Chairman
Founded in: 1896
Member: ATA; WTA;
Annual Budget: $23,500
Description: Offers majors in theatre arts and theatre education. The curriculum represents a survey approach to theatre and requires courses in various areas of theatre. The Carroll Players, Wisconsin's oldest active theatre producing organization, presents three mainstage productions annually in the Otteson Theatre. Productions of experimental and one-act plays are presented in a separate studio season.

West De Pere

Saint Norbert College
Department of Humanities and Fine Arts
West De Pere, WI 54115
Tel: 414-337-3110
Address Inquiries to: Kelly Callam, Chairperson
Founded in: 1967
Member: ATA; USITT;
Annual Budget: $5,000

WYOMING

Casper

Casper College
Department of Theatre
125 College Drive
Casper, WY 82601
Tel: 307-268-2216
Address Inquiries to: Tom Empey, Chairman

Member: ATA;

Cheyenne

Laramie County Community College
Department of Theatre
Cheyenne, WY 82001
Tel: 307-634-5853
Address Inquiries to: Nick Panopoulos,
    Chairman

Laramie

University of Wyoming
Box 3951, University Station
Laramie, WY 82071
Tel: 307-766-2197
Address Inquiries to: C. W. Bahs, Chairman
Member: ATA;

Powell

Northwest Community College
Department of Theatre
Powell, WY 82435
Address Inquiries to: Kermit Herd, Chairman
Member: ATA;

Riverton

Central Wyoming College
Department of Theatre
Riverton, WY 82501
Tel: 307-856-9291
Address Inquiries to: Robin Cole,
    Chairperson
Member: ATA;

CANADA

Calgary, Alberta

University of Calgary
Department of Drama
2500 University Drive, NW
Calgary, Alberta, Canada T2N 1N4
Tel: 403-284-5421
Address Inquiries to: Douglas McCullough
Founded in: 1967
Member: ATA;

Edmonton, Alberta

University of Alberta
Department of Theatre
Edmonton, Alberta, Canada T6G 2C9
Tel: 403-432-2771
Address Inquiries to: James McTeague,
    Chairman
Founded in: 1947

Lethbridge, Alberta

University of Lethbridge
Department of Dramatic Arts
4401 University Drive
Lethbridge, Alberta, Canada T1K 3M4
Tel: 403-329-2675
Address Inquiries to: Richard Epp, Chairman
Founded in: 1971
Annual Budget: $200,000
Description: A four year B.A. or B.Ed. pro-
gram focusing on drama as an integral part
of the liberal arts. Curriculum includes per-

formance, design, directing, theoretical
criticism, history, developmental drama
and children's theatre. Students have the
opportunity of doing half of their course
work in theatre.

Vancouver, British Columbia

University of British Columbia
Department of Theatre
2075 Wesbrook
Vancouver, British Columbia, Canada V6T
1W5
Tel: 604-228-3880; 604-228-2678
Address Inquiries to: John Brockington,
    Chairman
Founded in: 1958
Member: ATA; CTC; ATTI; BCDA; WADE;
    Society for Canadian Theatre History;
    AEA;
Description: The department of theatre exists
within the faculty of art and the liberal arts
tradition. The BA degree can be taken in
theater or film and offers a program ba-
lanced between practical and academic work.
The BFA degree can be taken in acting and/
or technical/design. This degree provides a
greater emphasis on professional training
within the liberal arts context. The MA and
PhD degrees are structured academically in
theatre history, dramatic literature and criticism. The MFA in theatre is a professional
training degree in either directing or design. All graduate degrees have strictly limited enrollment. They admit one or two students each year in order to give them fullest
attention.

Victoria, British Columbia

University of Victoria
Department of Theatre
Post Office Box 1700
Victoria, British Columbia, Canada V8W
2Y2
Tel: 604-477-6911; 604-721-7992
Address Inquiries to: Barbara M. McIntrye,
    Chairperson
Founded in: 1966
Member: ATA;

Brandon, Manitoba

Brandon University
Department of Theatre
Brandon, Manitoba, Canada
Tel: 204-728-9520
Address Inquiries to: Cedric Vendiback,
    Chairman
Founded in: 1972

Antigonish, Nova Scotia

Saint Francis Xavier University
Department of Theatre
Antigonish, Nova Scotia, Canada
Address Inquiries to: John C. Rapsey,
    Chairman

Halifax, Nova Scotia

Dalhousie University
Department of Theatre
Halifax, Nova Scotia, Canada B3H 3J5
Tel: 902-424-2233; 902-424-2234
Address Inquiries to: Peter Perina,
    Chairperson
    L.H. Lawrence, Chairperson
Founded in: 1969

Downsview, Ontario

York University
Department of Theatre
4700 Keele Street, Room 206A
Downsview, Ontario, Canada M3J 1P3
Tel: 416-667-2247; 416-667-3237
Address Inquiries to: Don Rubin, Chairman
Founded in: 1968
Member: ATA;
Description: York University offers a four year
degree program in all aspects of perfor-
mance and a Master of Fine Arts. Special
courses are offered in the summer for ac-
tors.

Guelph, Ontario

University of Guelph
Department of Drama
Guelph, Ontario, Canada N1G 2W1
Tel: 519-824-4120
Address Inquiries to: Leonard Conolly,
    Chairman
Founded in: 1966
Description: Offers a comprehensive under-
graduate education in all aspects of drama
and theatre, leading to a BA degree. Gradu-
ates enter various fields including theatre,
teaching and higher education.

Hamilton, Ontario

McMaster University
Department of Theatre
Hamilton, Ontario, Canada
Tel: 416-525-9140, extension 4660, 4661
Address Inquiries to: Nathalie D. Emmett,
    Director
    Douglas Duncan Ph.D, Academic
    Chairman
Founded in: 1971
Member: ATA; ACUCAA; OAC; Hamilton
    and Regional Arts Council;
Annual Budget: $84,811

Kingston, Ontario

Queens University
Department of Theatre
Kingston, Ontario, Canada K7L 3N6
Tel: 613-547-6261
Address Inquiries to: J.R. Euringer, Chairman
Founded in: 1948

Saint Catherines, Ontario

Brock University
Department of Theatre
Saint Catherines, Ontario, Canada L25
Tel: 416-684-7201
Address Inquiries to: M.J. Miller, Chairperson

Toronto, Ontario

University of Toronto
University College Program in Drama
79 Saint George Street
Toronto, Ontario, Canada M5S 1A1
Tel: 416-978-4418; 416-978-8601
Address Inquiries to: Stephen Martineau,
  Chairman
Founded in: 1975
Annual Budget: $70,000
Description: A program sponsored by the college of the university, not a department of faculty of arts and sciences. Enrollment is limited to 80 students. Specializes in coordinating academic and practical work.

Waterloo, Ontario

University of Waterloo
Department of Theatre
Humanities, Room 148
Waterloo, Ontario, Canada N2L 3G1
Tel: 519-885-1211
Address Inquiries to: W.R. Chadwick,
  Chairman
Founded in: 1972

Windsor, Ontario

University of Windsor
Department of Dramatic Arts
Windsor, Ontario, Canada N9B 3P4
Tel: 519-253-4232
Address Inquiries to: George L. Neilson,
  Director
Founded in: 1958
Member: ATA; Association for Canadian
  Theatre History; Theatre Ontario;

Montreal, Quebec

Concordia University
Department of Theatre
Loyola Campus, 7141 Sherbrooke Street
  West
Montreal, Quebec, Canada H4B 1R6
Tel: 514-482-0320; 514-879-5855
Address Inquiries to: Norma Springford,
  Chairperson
  Don Childs, Chairman
Founded in: 1981
Description: Concordia University, formed after the merger of Sir George Williams and Loyola Universities, offers a full range of undergraduate theatre activities in a production oriented department offering intensive training programs in performance and scenography at the undergraduate level.

Regina, Saskatchewan

University of Regina
Department of Theatre
Regina, Saskatchewan, Canada S4S 0A2
Tel: 306-584-4866
Address Inquiries to: Gabriel Prendergast,
  Chairman
Founded in: 1966

Saskatoon, Saskatchewan

University of Saskatchewan
Department of Theatre
Saskatoon, Saskatchewan, Canada
Tel: 306-343-2656
Address Inquiries to: D.F. Nalbach, Chairman
Founded in: 1945

5

Councils & Service Organizations

Arts Councils and service organizations ordinarily operate in a specific geographic area. Their function is to provide a variety of services to local non-profit theatre groups with worthwhile projects but little experience. Among these services are the coordination of box office activities, the creation of a mailing list for potential subscribers, technical advice for backstage operations, the organization of theatre festivals, and general administrative advice. The services rendered by these often under-financed groups contribute immeasurably to the health of the non-commercial theatre.

One service which these community service groups provide is of particular importance: giving advice on grant proposals and applications. Since service group budgets are as a rule not large enough to grant significant cash awards, their experience in dealing with large foundations which render such assistance can be pivotal.

ALABAMA

Abbeville

Abbeville Arts Council
Post Office Box 172
Abbeville, AL 36310
Tel: 205-585-2598
Address Inquiries to: Jeanie R. Rane,
  Executive Director
Founded in: 1974
Member: ACA;
Annual Budget: $10,000
Description: Sponsors concert series, peformances and tours of performing arts groups.

Albertville

Mountain Valley Council on the Arts
Post Office Box 592
Albertville, AL 35950
Tel: 205-593-7505
Address Inquiries to: Martha Robertson,
  President
Founded in: 1970.
Member: ACA;
Annual Budget: 10,000
Description: Aids other organizations in such areas as grants, administrative services, technical assistance, and information services as well as providing equipment for loan.

Andalusia

LBW Community Arts Council
Post Office Box 1418
Andalusia, AL 36420
Tel: 205-222-6591
Address Inquiries to: Rubye DelPlunkett,
  Executive Director
Founded in: 1973
Member: ACA;
Annual Budget: $10,000
Description: Provides a variety of services to performing arts groups which includes artists registry, box office services and promotion.

Anniston

Anniston Council on the Arts
Post Office Box 1252
Anniston, AL 36201
Tel: 205-237-6767
Address Inquiries to: Marguerite Turner,
  President
Founded in: 1973
Member: ACA;
Annual Budget: $10,000
Description: Sponsors performances, tours and arts festival.

Ashland

Clay County Arts and Crafts League
Post Office Box 566
Ashland, AL 36251
Tel: 205-354-2183
Address Inquiries to: Dora Smith, President

Atmore

Atmore Council of Fine Arts
102 South Pensacola
Atmore, AL 36502
Tel: 205-368-3640
Address Inquiries to: Dayton Long, President
Founded in: 1976
Member: ACA;
Annual Budget: $10,000
Description: A private arts council sponsoring performances, tours and arts festival.

Birmingham

Greater Birmingham Arts Alliance
Post Office Box 2152
Birmingham, AL 35201
Tel: 205-251-1228
Address Inquiries to: Jack Horlacher,
  Executive Director
Founded in: 1968
Member: ACA;

Annual Budget: $50,000
Description: Offers a variety of services to not for profit performing arts organizations. They can offer professional advice on administration, cooperative mailing lists, artists registration and other important services.

Brewton

Brewton Arts Council
Post Office Box 432
Brewton, AL 36426
Tel: 205-867-4832
Address Inquiries to: Hermione Holzborn,
  Secretary

Butler

Choctaw County Arts Council
1106 Cliff Road
Butler, AL 36904
Tel: 205-459-3666
Address Inquiries to: Patsy Griffith, Chairman
Founded in: 1974
Annual Budget: $50,000

Centre

Cherokee County Arts Council
Post Office Box 366
Centre, AL 35906
Tel: 205-927-3337
Address Inquiries to: Estelle Smith, Executive
  Director

Centreville

Centreville/Brent Arts Council
Post Office Box 398
Centreville, AL 35094
Tel: 205-926-4631
Address Inquiries to: Mary L. Moseley,
  President

Chatom

Washington County Arts and Crafts
  Association
Post Office Box 278
Chatom, AL 36518
Tel: 205-847-2714
Address Inquiries to: Jessie Blouke, President

Clanton

Chilton County Arts and Humanities
  Council
100 First Avenue
Clanton, AL 35045
Tel: 205-366-2921
Address Inquiries to: Harvey Clapp, President

Chilton County Fine Arts Guild
100 First Avenue
Clanton, AL 35045
Tel: 205-366-2921
Address Inquiries to: Harvey Clapp, President
Founded in: 1972
Member: ACA;
Annual Budget: $10,000
Description: Aids performing artists by offer-
ing grants, workshops and providing arts
services to area schools.

Cullman

Cullman Community Arts Council
217 Convent Road, Northeast
Cullman, AL 35055
Tel: 205-734-1089
Address Inquiries to: Kay Yager, Chairman

Decatur

Decatur Arts Council
Post Office Box 173
Decatur, AL 35601
Tel: 205-355-3422
Address Inquiries to: Carolyn Locklear,
  President

Demopolis

City of Demopolis Arts Committee
400 South Main
Demopolis, AL 36732
Tel: 205-289-0396
Address Inquiries to: Mrs. G.B. Strong,
  Chairman

Dothan

Arts and Humanities Council
Post Office Box 1369
Dothan, AL 36301
Tel: 205-792-2914
Address Inquiries to: Roy W. Watford,
  President
Founded in: 1972
Member: ACA;
Annual Budget: $10,000
Description: Provides a coordinated mailing
list and information services to not for profit
performing arts groups.

Enterprise

Coffee County Arts Alliance
Post Office Box 848
Enterprise, AL 36330
Tel: 205-347-2623
Address Inquiries to: Nancy Cowart Brunson,
  President
Founded in: 1974
Member: ACA;
Annual Budget: $10,000
Description: Sponsors performances and arts
services to area public schools.

South Alabama Junior College Consortium
Council on the Arts
Post Office Box 1300
Enterprise, AL 36330
Tel: 205-347-5431
Address Inquiries to: Shirley Woodie,
  Coordinator
Founded in: 1973
Member: ACA;
Annual Budget: $10,000
Description: Sponsors performances and
tours.

Eufala

Eufaula Arts Council
403 North Randolph
Eufala, AL 36027
Tel: 205-687-3121
Address Inquiries to: Mrs. Sam Snead,
  President

Florala

Florala Area Arts Council
602 East Fifth Avenue
Florala, AL 36442
Tel: 205-858-3227
Address Inquiries to: Robert Rodwell,
  Chairman

Florence

Florence City Arts Commission
Kennedy-Douglas Arts Center
217 East Tuscaloosa Street
Florence, Al 35630
Tel: 205-764-7271
Address Inquiries to: Barbara Kimberlin,
  Coordinator
Member: AAM; City of Florence;
Annual Budget: $30,000

Foley

Performing Arts Association
Post Office Box 295
Foley, Al 36535
Tel: 205-943-0364
Address Inquiries to: Carter Lee, President

Fort Deposit

Community Arts and Activities
  Commission
Post Office Box 280
Fort Deposit, AL 36032
Tel: 205-227-4940
Address Inquiries to: Mrs. Henry F.
  Crenshaw, Chairman
Founded in: 1973

Member: ACA;
Annual Budget: $10,000
Description: Provides several services of use
to not for profit performing arts organizations including information, box office services, and technical assistance.

Fort Payne

Dekalb County Arts Council
Post Office Box 520
Fort Payne, AL 35967
Tel: 205-845-0714
Address Inquiries to: Charles Shipp,
  President

Gadsden

Gasden Council on the Arts
Public Relations Director
Republic Steel
Gadsden, AL 35904
Tel: 205-543-6400
Address Inquiries to: Phil Williams, Chairman

Gardendale

Gardendale Cultural Arts Council
Post Office Box 38
Gardendale, AL 35071
Tel: 205-631-5679
Address Inquiries to: LeAnn Belcher
Founded in: 1974
Member: ACA;
Description: Gardendale Cultural Arts Council
sponsors arts festivals, workshops and pro-
vides information services to performing
artists.

North Arts Council
425 Albert Drive
Gardendale, AL 35071
Tel: 205-631-7438
Address Inquiries to: Nelda Atchley, President

Grant

Grant Arts and Humanities Council
Post Office Box 70
Grant, AL
Tel: 205-728-4205
Address Inquiries to: Jo McBride, Vice
  President

Greensboro

Hale County Council for the Arts
Post Office Box 490
Greensboro, AL 36774
Tel: 205-624-8793
Address Inquiries to: William J. Heron,
  President
Founded in: 1975
Member: ACA;
Annual Budget: $10,000
Description: Providing aid to Performing Art-
ists in the Greensboro area.

Greenville

Greenville City Arts Commission
Post Office Box 507
Greenville, AL 36037
Tel: 205-382-3111
Address Inquiries to: W.E. Hardin, President

Heflin

Cleburne Arts and Crafts League
Route 4, 101 Evans Bridge Road
Heflin, AL 36264
Tel: 205-463-7917; 205-463-2223
Address Inquiries to: Clara Roach, President
Founded in: 1969
Member: ACA;
Annual Budget: $10,000
Description: Sponsors an artists in schools program and offers coordinated mailing lists and information services to not for profit performing arts organizations.

Huntsville

The Arts Council
Von Braun Civic Center
Huntsville, AL 35801
Tel: 205-533-6565
Address Inquiries to: Ramona Baker,
Executive Director
Founded in: 1963
Member: ACA; BCA; FEDAPT; NASAA;
NACAA;
Annual Budget: $80,000
Description: Offers information services, technical assistance, administration, box office, arts management and grantsmanship. There are 83 organizational members on the council whose purpose is the development and coordination of cultural and artistic activities.

Jackson

Jackson Arts and Crafts Association
331 High Acres Drive
Jackson, AL 36545
Tel: 205-246-3545
Address Inquiries to: Mrs. H.W. Porter,
President

Jasper

Jasper Arts Council
Post Office Box 622
Jasper, AL 35501
Tel: 205-384-3461
Address Inquiries to: Sis Grant, President

Livingston

Sumter County Fine Arts Council
Post Office Drawer 1038
Livingston, AL 35470
Tel: 205-652-2298
Address Inquiries to: Irene Bruce, President

Luverne

Crenshaw County Arts Council
Post Office Box 388
Luverne, AL 36049
Tel: 205-335-5174
Address Inquiries to: Dr. Warren Williams,
President

Marion

Commission on the Arts and Humanities
213 Polk Street
Marion, AL 36756
Tel: 205-683-2871

Address Inquiries to: Woody S. Moore,
Chairman

Mobile

Allied Arts Council of Metropolitan
Mobile
401 Auditorium Drive
Mobile, AL 36602
Tel: 205-432-9796
Address Inquiries to: Charles Manchester,
Executive Director
Founded in: 1955
Member: ACA;
Annual Budget: $10,000
Description: Sponsors a weekly radio program as well as offering an artists registry, coordinated mailing list, and centralized box office services.

Monroeville

Monroe County Arts Council
Post Office Box 924
Monroeville, AL 36460
Tel: 205-575-3282
Address Inquiries to: Patricia W. Stewart,
President
Founded in: 1975
Member: ACA;
Annual Budget: $10,000
Description: Sponsors festivals and tours.

Montevallo

Shelby County Arts Council
410 Meadow Road
Montevallo, AL 35115
Tel: 205-665-4132
Address Inquiries to: Janet Seaman, President

Montgomery

Alabama Assembly of Community Arts
Councils
500 East Boulevard, Suite 119
Montgomery, AL 36109
Tel: 205-272-5175
Address Inquiries to: Marlo Bussman,
Executive Director
Description: A state arts organization.

Alabama State Council on the Arts
322 Alabama Avenue
Montgomery, AL 36104
Tel: 205-832-6758

Arts Council of Montgomery
1010 Forest Avenue
Montgomery, Al 36106
Tel: 205-265-8593
Address Inquiries to: JoAnna Boske,
Administrative Officer
Founded in: 1979
Member: ACA;
Annual Budget: $10,000
Description: Provides information services and the loan of equipment to performing arts organizations through the city of Montgomery, department of parks and recreation.

Jasmine Hill Arts Council
Post Office Box 6001

Montgomery, AL 36106
Tel: 205-265-2837; 205-263-1440
Address Inquiries to: Taylor Dawson,
President
Founded in: 1976
Member: SAF; ASCAH; Blount Foundation;
Description: A community council sponsoring performances of Shakespeare, folk festivals and various performing groups.

Oneonta

Oneonta Civic Arts Committee
1910 Lincoln Avenue
Oneonta, AL 35121
Tel: 205-625-3916
Address Inquiries to: Diane Palmer, Chairman

Ozark

Dale County Council on the Arts
Post Office Box 971
Ozark, AL 36360
Tel: 205-774-6232
Address Inquiries to: Dorothy Crowley,
President
Founded in: 1976
Member: Friends of the Library; Women's
Guild; Alabama State Council on the
Arts and Humanities;

Pell City

Greater Pell City Arts Council
Post Office Box 169
Pell City, Al 35125
Tel: 205-522-5873
Address Inquiries to: Cliff Morrison,
President

Phenix City

Phenix City Arts Council
Post Office Box 1132
Phenix City, AL 36867
Tel: 404-561-0364
Address Inquiries to: Jared T. Davis,
President
Founded in: 1975
Member: ACA;
Annual Budget: $10,000
Description: Sponsors an artists in residence program and an arts festival.

Prattville

Prattville Council on the Arts
Post Office Box 178
Prattville, AL 36067
Tel: 205-365-6727
Address Inquiries to: Judd Sparling, President
Founded in: 1973
Member: ACA;
Annual Budget: $10,000
Description: Aids performing arts organizations by providing information services, a coordinated mailing list and help with grants and proposals.

Prichard

Prichard Arts and Humanities Congress
4559 Old Citronelle Highway
Prichard, AL 36613
Address Inquiries to: John Andrews,

President

Rockford

Coosa County Arts Council
Route 2
Rockford, AL 35136
Tel: 205-377-4540
Address Inquiries to: Sally Holland, President

Russellville

Franklin County
Arts and Humanities Council
Post Office Box 879
Russellville, AL 35653
Tel: 205-332-1830
Address Inquiries to: Joe Gilliland, President
Founded in: 1976
Member: ACA;
Description: Sponsors an artists in schools program, and a children's theatre program.

Samson

Geneva County Arts and Crafts
Association
Post Office Box 62
Samson, AL 36477
Address Inquiries to: David Malstream, President

Scottsboro

Jackson County Arts Council
Benham Avenue
Scottsboro, AL 35768
Tel: 205-259-1874
Address Inquiries to: Ann Bittel, President
Founded in: 1971
Member: ACA;
Annual Budget: $10,000
Description: Offers artist in residence programs and sponsors performances and tours. Additionally, the council provides aid with management and administration, a coordinated mailing list and information services.

Selma

Council on the Arts and Humanities
820 King Street
Selma, AL 36701
Tel: 205-874-4061
Address Inquiries to: Carl Morgan, President

Sylacauga

Area Council on the Arts and Humanities
Post Office Box 21
Sylacauga, AL 35150
Tel: 205-249-2700; 205-245-5383
Address Inquiries to: Gladys T. Brown, President
Founded in: 1973
Member: Alabama State Council on the Arts and Humanities; SAF;
Annual Budget: $22,000

Talladega

Talladega Arts Council
Post Office Box 263
Talladega, AL 35160
Founded in: 1974

Member: ACA;
Description: Sponsors performances, tours and an arts festival. The council also provides not for profit groups with a coordinated mailing list, information services and aid with management and administration.

Tallassee

McCraney Arts Council
622 Hudson Place
Tallassee, AL 36078
Tel: 205-283-4606
Address Inquiries to: Edwin Watkins, Chairman

Thomasville

Thomasville Arts and Humanities Council
Post Office Box 107
Thomasville, AL 36784
Tel: 205-636-5731
Address Inquiries to: Jerry McCrory, President

Troy

City of Troy Council on the Arts and Humanities
Post Office Box 606
Troy, AL 36081
Tel: 205-566-3685
Address Inquiries to: Evelyn Watsol, President

Tuscaloosa

Arts and Humanities Council
Tuscaloosa County
Post Office Box 1117
Tuscaloosa, AL 35401
Tel: 205-758-8083
Address Inquiries to: Tom Boozer, Executive Director
Founded in: 1970
Member: ACA;
Annual Budget: $10,000
Description: Provides a great variety of services to performing arts organizations. In addition to loans of equipment, an artist registry, coordinated mailing list and information services are provided.

Tuskegee Institute

Southern Vocational Arts Council
1323 Adams Street
Tuskegee Institute, AL 36088
Tel: 205-727-0792
Address Inquiries to: Merci leeTapley, President

Union Springs

Bullock County Arts Council
Route 1
Post Office Box 255
Union Springs, AL 36089
Tel: 205-474-3385
Address Inquiries to: Mrs. George L. McMillan, Chairman
Founded in: 1973
Member: ACA;
Description: Organized under the auspices of the Bullock County Public Schools the Arts

Council sponsors performances, tours and arts festivals.

Wadley

Southern Appalachia Consortium Arts Council
Southern Union State Junior College
Wadley, AL 36276
Tel: 205-395-2211 Extension 39
Address Inquiries to: Dr. Herschel D. Love, Coordinator
Founded in: 1974
Member: ACA;
Annual Budget: $10,000
Description: Organized under the auspices of the Southern Appalachia Consortium the council provides a coordinated mailing list, information services and aids in the creation of grant applications and proposals.

ALASKA

Anchorage

Alaska State Council on the Arts
360 K Street
Anchorage, AK 99501
Tel: 907-279-3824

Anchorage Arts Council
419 West 7th Avenue
Anchorage, AK 99501
Tel: 907-274-7324
Address Inquiries to: Carol A. Derfner, Executive Director

Fillipino Community of Anchorage
Post Office Box 2132
Anchorage, AK 99510
Tel: 907-344-4430
Address Inquiries to: Rita Jenkins, President

Sitka

Southeast Alaska Regional Arts Council
c/o Sitka Community College, Box 2133
Sitka, AK 99835
Tel: 907-747-6653
Address Inquiries to: Marlene Lund, Executive Director
Description: A state arts council.

ARIZONA

Anaheim

Anaheim Arts Cowncil
Post Office Box 3757
Anaheim, AZ 92803

Bisbee

Bisbee Council on the Arts
Post Office Box 451
Bisbee, AZ 85603
Tel: 602-432-7071
Address Inquiries to: Cora Thorp, Chairman
Founded in: 1969
Annual Budget: $50,000

Cochise Fine Arts Council
Post Office Box 1783
Bisbee, AZ 85603
Tel: 602-432-9951
Address Inquiries to: Bonnie Pettit, President
Founded in: 1969
Annual Budget: $10,000

Flagstaff

Flagstaff Art Association
Post Office Box 1901
Flagstaff, AZ 86001
Tel: 602-774-0822
Address Inquiries to: Robert F. Topp,
  President
Annual Budget: $10,000

Globe

Gila County Fine Arts Association
Post Office Box 1738
Globe, AZ 85501
Tel: 602-425-7611
Address Inquiries to: Noel Gillespie,
  President
Founded in: 1953
Annual Budget: $10,000

Kingman

Kingman Commission on the Arts
113 Spring Road
Kingman, AZ 86403

Phoenix

Arizona Commission on the Arts
6330 North Seventh Street
Phoenix, AZ 85014
Tel: 602-271-5884

Phoenix Art Council
1202 North Third Street
Phoenix, AZ 85004
Tel: 602-271-9052
Address Inquiries to: Wink Blair, Executive
  Director
Founded in: 1960
Annual Budget: $10,000

Prescott

Prescott Council on the Arts
Post Office Box 61
Prescott, AZ

Scottsdale

Scottsdale Center for the Arts
7383 Scottsdale Mall
Scottsdale, AZ 85251
Tel: 602-994-2301; 602-994-2304
Member: ACUCAA; AAM; City of
  Scottsdale;
Annual Budget: $1,200,000
Description: Supports a variety of performing
arts activities.

Sedona

Sedona Arts Center
Post Office Box 569
Sedona, AZ 86336
Tel: 602-282-3809
Address Inquiries to: George Moritz,

President
Founded in: 1951
Annual Budget: $50,000

Tubac

Tubac Center for the Arts
Post Office Box 282
Tubac, AZ 85640
Tel: 602-398-2371
Address Inquiries to: Doris A. Fouch,
  Director
Founded in: 1972
Annual Budget: $50,000

Tucson

Pima County Arts Council
c/o Pima County Parks Department
1204 West Silverlake
Tucson, AZ 85713
Tel: 602-792-8306
Address Inquiries to: John Zeeb, Arts
  Supervisor
Founded in: 1947
Annual Budget: $100,000

Tucson Commission on the Arts
Post Office Box 27210
Tucson, AZ 85726

ARKANSAS

Hot Springs

Fine Arts Council of Hot Springs
815 Whittington Avenue
Hot Springs, AR 71901
Tel: 501-623-0836
Address Inquiries to: Richard Smith,
  President
Founded in: 1946
Annual Budget: $50,000

Jonesboro

Jonesboro Fine Arts Council
Post Office Box 224
Jonesboro, AR 72401
Tel: 501-932-1151
Address Inquiries to: Roberta P. Priest,
  Executive Secretary

Little Rock

Arkansas Art Center
Post Office Box 2137
MacArthur Park
Little Rock, AR 72203
Tel: 501-372-4000
Address Inquiries to: Townsend Wolfe,
  Director
Founded in: 1960
Annual Budget: $1,000,000

State Office of Arts and Humanities
404 Train Station Square
Little Rock, AR 72201
Tel: 501-371-2539

Magnolia

Magnolia Arts Council
128 South Jackson, Drawer A
Magnolia, AR 71753
Tel: 501-234-3550
Address Inquiries to: Oliver Clegg, President

Pine Bluff

Pine Arts Council
2001 Country Club Lane
Pine Bluff, AR 71601
Tel: 501-535-1655
Address Inquiries to: Mrs. Louis L. Ramsay,
  President

Stuttgart

Grand Prairie Art Council
Post Office Box 65
Stuttgart, AR 72160
Tel: 501-673-8586; 501-673-7278
Address Inquiries to: Mrs. Mike Crum,
  President
  Mrs. Neil Maynard, Chairman
Founded in: 1964
Annual Budget: $10,000
Description: A multi disciplinary organization
involved with visual art, crafts and creative
writing.

West Memphis

West Memphis Fine Arts Center
Post Office Box 1434
West Memphis, AR 72301
Tel: 501-735-6923
Address Inquiries to: Jerry L. Davis, President
Founded in: 1972
Annual Budget: $10,000

CALIFORNIA

Anaheim

Anaheim Parks Department
Arts Section
630 North Anaheim Boulevard
Anaheim, CA 92805
Tel: 714-533-1460
Address Inquiries to: Patsy L. Ray, Recreation
  Supervisor

Arroyo Grande

Pismo Beach Arts Council
1545 Hillcrest Street
Arroyo Grande, CA 93420
Address Inquiries to: Mrs. Q.H. Alexalder,
  President

Artesia

Fine Arts Associates
17822 Summer Avenue
Artesia, CA 90701
Address Inquiries to: Mrs. Marvin Eckles,
  President

Bakersfield

Arts Council of Bakersfield
2 Hidden Lane
Bakersfield, CA 93309

Barstow

Barstow Convention and Cultural Center
Post Office Box 319
Barstow, CA 92311

Bellflower

Bellflower Cultural Arts Council
9729 East Flower
Bellflower, CA 90706
Tel: 213-867-1744
Address Inquiries to: Claire S. Thompson,
  President
Founded in: 1964
Annual Budget: $50,000

Belmont

San Mateo County Arts Council
Twin Pines Cultural Center
1219 Ralston Avenue
Belmont, CA 94002
Tel: 415-593-1816
Address Inquiries to: William Nemoyten,
  Executive Director
Founded in: 1972
Annual Budget: $100,000

Berkeley

Berkeley Civic Art Commission
Berkeley Art Center
1275 Walnut Street
Berkeley, CA 94709
Tel: 415-849-4120
Address Inquiries to: Mrs. Foster Foreman,
  President
Founded in: 1959
Annual Budget: $50,000

Burbank

Burbank Fine Arts Federation
110 West Clark
Post Office Box 4459
Burbank, CA 91510
Address Inquiries to: Betsy Lueke

Carmel

Carmel Cultural Commission
Post Office Box 5066
Carmel, CA 93921
Tel: 408-624-3996
Address Inquiries to: Richard Tyler, Cultural
  Director
Founded in: 1965
Annual Budget: Cultural center for the
  peninsula and the home of several
Description: Cultural center for the peninsula
and the home of several performing and
presenting organizations.

Claremont

Claremont Intercultural Council
Claremont Courier
112 Harvard Street
Claremont, CA 91711

Tel: 714-621-4761; 714-621-4762
Address Inquiries to: Martin Weinberger
Member: Claremont Colleges;
Annual Budget: $75,000
Description: Provides intercultural relations
and promotion of the arts.

Compton

Compton Cultural Commission
City Hall
600 North Alameda Avenue
Compton, CA 90221

Corte Mafera

Marin Art Commission
Post Office Box 248
Corte Mafera, CA 94925

Davis

Civic Arts Division/City of Davis
212 D Street
Davis, CA 95616
Tel: 916-756-3740
Address Inquiries to: Donald E. Knaub, Civic
  Arts Coodinator
Founded in: 1973
Annual Budget: $100,000

Eureka

Humboldt Arts Council
Post Office Box 221
Eureka, CA 95501
Tel: 707-443-3413
Address Inquiries to: Mrs. Arthur Johnson,
  President
Founded in: 1966
Annual Budget: $50,000

Fresno

Parks and Recreation Department
Cultural Arts Division
Room 102, 2425 Fresno Street
Fresno, CA 93721
Tel: 209-488-1012
Address Inquiries to: Christopher Curcio,
  Supervisor
Founded in: 1975
Annual Budget: $100,000

Glendora

Allied Arts Council
1500 Compromise Line Road
Glendora, CA 91740
Tel: 213-335-1782
Address Inquiries to: Dr. Alberta Babcock,
  Chairman
Founded in: 1959
Annual Budget: $10,000

Hemet

Ramona Pageant Association
Post Office Box 755
Hemet, CA 92343
Tel: 714-658-3111
Address Inquiries to: Frank Regur, Chairman
Founded in: 1923
Annual Budget: $100,000

Hollywood

Melrose Theatre Association
7420 Melrose Avenue
Hollywood, CA 90028

Huntington Beach

Golden West Cultural Programs Series
15744 Golden West Street
Huntington Beach, CA 92647

LaCrescenta

Glendale Regional Arts Council
Post Office Box 8292
LaCrescenta, CA 91214
Tel: 213-249-6510
Address Inquiries to: Kathryn B. Hull,
  President
Founded in: 1974
Annual Budget: $10,000

Lakewood

Lakewood Cultural Arts Council
Post Office Box 158
Lakewood, CA 90714
Tel: 213-866-9771
Address Inquiries to: Barbara Moore,
  Recreation Supervisor
Founded in: 1975
Annual Budget: $10,000

Long Beach

Long Beach Regional Arts Council
130 Pine Avenue
Long Beach, CA 90802
Tel: 213-436-6822
Address Inquiries to: Sheriden Beebe,
  President
Founded in: 1968
Annual Budget: $50,000

Los Angeles

Municipal Arts Department
City Hall, Room 1500
Los Angeles, CA 90012
Tel: 213-485-2433
Address Inquiries to: R. Kenneth Ross,
  General Manager
Founded in: 1911
Annual Budget: $100,000

Performing Arts Council
Music Center of Los Angeles County
135 North Grand Avenue
Los Angeles, CA 90012
Tel: 213-972-7265
Address Inquiries to: Joseph Clapsaddle,
  Chairman
Founded in: 1965
Annual Budget: $100,000

University of California at Los Angeles
Arts Council
405 Hilgard Avenue
Los Angeles, CA 90024
Tel: 213-825-3264
Address Inquiries to: Mrs. Walter Richman,
  President
Founded in: 1953
Annual Budget: $100,000

Mill Valley

Mill Valley Arts Commission
Post Office Box 132
Mill Valley, CA 94941
Tel: 415-383-6664
Address Inquiries to: Evelyn Topper,
   Chairperson
Founded in: 1965
Annual Budget: $10,000

Newport

Newport Beach City Arts Commission
3300 Newport Boulevard
Newport, CA 92663
Tel: 714-640-2110
Address Inquiries to: Ladislaw Reday,
   Chairman
Founded in: 1960
Annual Budget: $10,000

Oakland

Alameda County Art Commission
c/o Office of Administration
1730 Franklin, Suite 200
Oakland, CA 94612
Tel: 415-874-6751
Address Inquiries to: Jean R. Wente,
   Chairperson
Founded in: 1965
Annual Budget: $100,000

Palo Alto

City Arts Department
250 Hamilton Avenue
Palo Alto, CA 94306
Tel: 405-329-2122
Address Inquiries to: Allan Longacre,
   Director
Founded in: 1966
Annual Budget: $100,000

Pittsburg

Pittsburg Arts and Cultural Commission
Post Office Box 1518
Pittsburg, CA 94565
Tel: 415-439-4978
Address Inquiries to: Dennis Flannery,
   Director
Founded in: 1975

Pleasant Hill

Pleasant Hill Arts Council
3300 North Main Street
Pleasant Hill, CA 94523
Tel: 415-934-6050
Address Inquiries to: Toni Crawford, Director
Founded in: 1974
Annual Budget: $10,000

Rohnert Park

Rohnert Park Cultural Arts Corporation
435 Southwest Boulevard
Rohnert Park, CA 94928
Tel: 707-795-5416
Address Inquiries to: Marion McMullan,
   President
Founded in: 1972
Annual Budget: $10,000

San Bernadino

Arrowhead Allied Arts Council
Post Office Box 103
San Bernadino, CA 92402
Tel: 714-888-1495
Founded in: 1966
Member: ACA; Inland Empire Cultural
   Foundation;
Annual Budget: $50,000

San Carlos

San Carlos Fine Arts Committee
Civic Center
666 Elm Street
San Carlos, CA 94070
Tel: 415-593-8011
Address Inquiries to: Gary W. Bush,
   Chairman
Founded in: 1970
Annual Budget: $10,000

San Francisco

California Arts Council
Post Office Box 795
San Francisco, CA 94101
Tel: 415-346-1062

San Francisco Arts Commission
c/o City Hall
San Francisco, CA 94102
Tel: 415-558-3465; 415-558-3463
Address Inquiries to: Joan Ellison, Director
Founded in: 1932
Annual Budget: $800,000
Description: Supports the varied and exciting
performing arts activities of the city.
Through its Dance and Theatre Committee
and Music Committee the commission
sponsors events and organizations, such as
the Civic Chorale, San Francisco Blues Festi-
val, theatres and performing arts series.

Theatre Communications of the Bay Area
2940 16th Street
San Francisco, CA 97103
Tel: 415-621-0427
Founded in: 1976
Member: TCCBA;
Description: A multi-resourse information
center offering publications, conferences,
workshops, talent file, job bank, and the Bay
Area Theatre Alliance, a coalition of local
theatre companies. *Call Board Magazine,* is a
regular trade magazine centered in the S an
Francisco Bay Area including articles by local artists, playwrights, critics, as well as
production schedules, job listings, training
and rental space information. Every two
years BATA publishes *Theatre Directory of the
Bay Area,* a professional resource guide.
Sources of Publicity, is a media guide listing
radio, television and publication contacts
and deadlines for Bay Area media outlets
providing publicity for performing arts
groups.

San Franciso

Foundation Center
312 Sutter Street
San Franciso, CA 94108
Tel: 415-397-0902; 800-424-9836
Description: Field Office of The Foundation
Center, call for a schedule of services and
hours.

San Jose

Council of Arts, Greater San Jose
123 South Third Street
San Jose, CA 95113
Tel: 408-279-1131
Address Inquiries to: Val Ramsey, President
Founded in: 1971
Annual Budget: $10,000

Fine Arts Commission
291 South Market Street
San Jose, CA 95113
Tel: 408-277-5144
Founded in: 1962
Annual Budget: $100,000

San Luis Obispo

Civic and Fine Arts Association
Post Office Box 264
San Luis Obispo, CA 93406
Tel: 805-595-2341
Address Inquiries to: Lucille Fabbri, President
Founded in: 1961
Annual Budget: $10,000

Santa Cruz

Santa Cruz County Arts Committee
701 Ocean Street
Santa Cruz, CA 95060
Tel: 408-425-2394
Address Inquiries to: Keith Kelly, Director
Founded in: 1974
Annual Budget: $50,000

Santa Rosa

Sonoma County Arts Council
1049 Fourth Street
Santa Rosa, CA 95404
Tel: 707-528-8220
Address Inquiries to: Alan Milner, President
Founded in: 1965
Annual Budget: $100,000

Topanga

Community Arts Development Group
125 South Topanga Canyon Boulevard
Topanga, CA 90290
Tel: 213-455-1351
Address Inquiries to: James A. Boivin,
   President
Founded in: 1975
Annual Budget: $50,000

COLORADO

Aurora

The National Writer's Club
1450 South Havana, Suite 620
Aurora, Colorado 80012
Description: A not for profit organization offering services and support to writers.

Denver

Colorado Council on the Arts
1550 Lincoln Street
Denver, CO 80201
Tel: 303-866-5433

CONNECTICUT

East Haddam

League of Historic Theatres
Post Office Box A
East Haddam, CT 06423
Description: The League was established to encourage preservation of the performing arts and it's unique facilities. They have helped to save and bring attention to theatre, music halls, opera houses, film theatres, and movie palaces, all of which are part of America's heritage.

Hartford

Connecticut Commission on the Arts
340 Capitol Avenue
Hartford, CT 06106
Tel: 203-566-4770
Description: Works in close cooperation with the New England Foundation for the Arts.

DELAWARE

Wilmington

Alumni Theatre Association
721 Halstead Road
Wilmington, DE 19803
Tel: 302-478-2588
Address Inquiries to: Thomas M. Marshall, President
Founded in: 1968
Annual Budget: $25,000

Delaware State Arts Council
9th and French Streets
Wilmington, DE 19801
Tel: 302-571-3548

DISTRICT OF COLUMBIA

Washington

Advocates for the Arts
2000 P Street
Washington, DC 20036
Tel: 202-659-5161
Member: ACA; NACAA; NEA;
Description: Helps community arts agencies with advice concerning the planning and presentation of seminars and membership campaigns. Advocates for the Arts maintains offices in New York and Washington D.C.

American Theatre Association
1010 Wisconsin Avenue, NW
Washington, DC 20005
Tel: 202-342-7530
Address Inquiries to: Bernard S. Rosenblatt, President
Margaret Lynn, Executive Director
Member: ACA; NACAA; NEA;
Description: The 48th Annual Convention of ATA will be held in San Franciso from August 12 to 15th. ATA, one of the largest and oldest theatre organizations in the U.S. is the parent organization for the ACTA (American Community Theatre Association), ATAA (Army Theatre Arts Asscociation), CTAA (Children's Theatre Association of America), SSTA (Secondary School Theatre Assocation) and the UCTA (University and College Theatre Association).

Commission on the Arts and Humanities
1012 14th Street, NW
Washington, DC 20005
Tel: 202-724-5613

Foundation Center, Washington DC Collection
1001 Connecticut Avenue
Washington, DC 20036
Tel: 202-331-1400; 800-424-9836, Publication
Description: One of two national libraries maintained by the Foundation Center, headquartered in New York.

National Assembly of State Arts Agencies
1010 Vermont Avenue NW, Suite 316
Washington, DC 20005
Tel: 202-347-6352; Eli-abe-h Michel
Member: ACA; NACCA; NEA;
Description: NASAA is a not for profit membership organization of state arts councils. It is dedicated to the growth of the arts and represents the collective concerns of its member agencies while providing forums for the review of national arts policies.

National Endowment for the Arts
2401 E Street
Washington, DC 20506
Tel: 202-682-5400
Address Inquiries to: Frank Hotsoll, Chairman
Hugh Southern, Deputy Chairman of Programs
Founded in: 1965
Annual Budget: $12,000,000
Description: It is suggested that information regarding the NEA be made in writing. In a time of decreasing government funding, the National Endowment continues to provide an increasing number of programs and is the largest single source of arts support. The goals of the NEA are preservation of cultural heritage, strengthening of America's cultural institutions and assistance to developing artists.

National Endowment for the Humanities
806 15th Street
Washington, DC 20506
Tel: 202-786-0438
Address Inquiries to: William J. Bennett, Chairman
Geoffrey Marshall, Deputy Chairman
Description: The NEH supports historical, critical and theoretical studies or closely related projects. Write for program requirements and deadlines.

University and College Theatre Association
1010 Wisconsin Avenue, NW
Suite 360
Washington, DC 20007
Address Inquiries to: Donald L. Loeffler, President
Roger Gross, Vice President
Member: ATA; CELJ;
Description: U/CTA is one of the sub groups the of American Theatre Association. *Theatre Journal*, published in March, May October and December is available to members and to non-members by subscription.

FLORIDA

Orlando

Florida League of the Arts
76 West Church Street
Orlando, FL 32801
Tel: 305-843-2787
Address Inquiries to: Dr. J. Warren, President
Description: A state arts council.

Pensacola Beach

Florida Theatre Conference
100 Narvaez Drive
Pensacola Beach, FL 32561
Address Inquiries to: Rebecca Rankin

Tallahassee

Fine Arts Council of Florida
Department of State, The Capitol
Tallahassee, FL 32304
Tel: 904-487-2980; 904-488-4343

GEORGIA

Atlanta

Georgia Council for the Arts
225 Peachtree Street NE
Atlanta, GA 30303
Tel: 404-656-3990

Southern Arts Federation
255 Peachtree Street, NE
Atlanta, GA 30303
Tel: 404-577-7244
Description: Representing Alabama, Georgia, Kentucky, Mississippi, Carolina, South Carolina and Tennessee.

Crawfordville

Georgia Theatre Conference
Pembroke Hall
Crawfordville, GA 30631
Address Inquiries to: Mrs. Bolton Lunceford

Saint Simons Island

Island Arts Center
Post Office Box 673
Saint Simons Island, GAM 31522
Tel: 912-638-8770; 912-638-8771
Founded in: 1954
Member: ACA; NACAA; GAMG;
Annual Budget: $60,000
Description: A multi-faceted organization sponsoring classes, exhibits, programs for senior citizens.

HAWAII
Honolulu

Hawaii State Arts Council
University of Hawaii
2530 Dole Street, 4th Floor
Honolulu, HI 96822
Tel: 808-948-8242

IDAHO
Boise

Idaho State Commission on the Arts
State House
Boise, Idaho 83720
Tel: 208-384-2119

ILLINOIS
Chicago

Illinois Arts Council
111 North Wabash Avenue
Chicago, IL 60602
Tel: 312-435-6765

INDIANA
Bloomington

National Center for Research in the Arts
Indiana University
Bloomington, IN 47401
Tel: 812-337-0798
Member: ACA; NACCA; NEA;

Farmland

Delaware County Council for the Arts
Post Office Box 4883
Farmland, IN 47340
Address Inquiries to: Jean Slaughter

Flora

Fine Arts Committee
304 North Center Street
Flora, IN 46929
Tel: 219-967-3671

Address Inquiries to: Karen Rieffel

Gary

Greater Gary Arts Council
504 Broadway, Suite 1037
Gary, IN 46402
Tel: 219-885-8444
Address Inquiries to: John Cleveland,
  Executive Director

Huntingburg

Huntingburg Arts Committee
Route 2
Post Office Box 232-A
Huntingburg, IN 88351
Tel: 812-683-2324
Address Inquiries to: Robert Schroeder,
  Chairman

Indianapolis

Hillside Cultural Center
Post Office Box 88351
Indianapolis, IN 46208
Tel: 317-925-9861
Address Inquiries to: Ron Taylor, Director

Indiana Arts Commission
155 East Market
Indianapolis, IN 46204
Tel: 317-633-5649

Lafayette

Lafayette Art Center
101 South Ninth Street
Lafayette, IN 47901
Tel: 317-742-4470
Address Inquiries to: Suzanne Stafford,
  Director

IOWA
Des Moines

Iowa State Arts Council
State Capitol Building
Des Moines, IA 50319
Tel: 515-281-5297

KANSAS
Topeka

Association of Community Arts Councils
509A Kansas Avenue
Topeka, KS 6603
Tel: 913-296-4092
Address Inquiries to: Romalyn Tilghman,
  Executive Director
Description: A state arts council.

Kansas Arts Commission
117 West 10th Street
Topeka, KS 66612
Tel: 913-296-3335

KENTUCKY
Corbin

Fine Arts Association of SE Kentucky
1210 Pine Street
Corbin, KY 40701
Tel: 606-528-4824
Address Inquiries to: Mrs. Harold Wortman,
  Chairperson
  Betty Hamilton, Program Chairperson
Founded in: 1960
Member: KAT; SAF;
Annual Budget: $18,000

Elizabeth

Hardin County Arts Council
Post Office Box 903
Elizabeth, KY 42701
Address Inquiries to: Linda Dorsey,
  Chairperson
Founded in: 1976

Frankfort

Kentucky Arts Commission
100 West Main Street
Frankfort, KY 40601
Tel: 502-564-3757

Lexington

Lexington Council of the Arts
755 Brookhill Drive
Lexington, KY 40502
Address Inquiries to: Marilyn Moosenick,
  Chairperson
Founded in: 1971
Annual Budget: $10,000

Louisville

Greater Louisville Fund for the Arts
511 West Broadway
Louisville, KY 40202
Tel: 502-582-1821
Address Inquiries to: Allan Cowen, Executive
  Director
Founded in: 1948
Annual Budget: $100,000

Owensboro

Owensboro Arts Commission
122 East 18th Street
Owensboro, KY 42301
Tel: 502-685-3141
Address Inquiries to: Mary Hood, Executive
  Director
Founded in: 1975
Annual Budget: $50,000

Paducah

City-County Arts Council
Post Office Box 301
Paducah, KY 42001
Tel: 502-444-7713
Address Inquiries to: Don Hayes, Executive
  Director
Founded in: 1974
Annual Budget: $50,000

LOUISIANA
Alexandria

Rapides Art Council
Post Office Box 1064
Alexandria, LA 71301
Tel: 318-443-3219
Address Inquiries to: Mrs. Ledoux Provosty,
President
Founded in: 1973
Annual Budget: $10,000

Baton Rouge

Louisiana State Arts Council
Post Office Box 44247
Baton Rouge, LA 70804
Tel: 504-342-6467

Lafayette

Acadiana Arts Council
Post Office Box 53762
Lafayette, LA 70505
Tel: 318-233-7060
Address Inquiries to: Tom Boozer, Executive
Director
Founded in: 1975
Member: ACA; NACAA; NASAA;
Association of Louisiana Arts and
Artists; Atlantic Richfield; Gulf; We Shall
Overcome Fund; Heymann Foundation;
Annual Budget: $300,000
Description: Coordinates, promotes, sup-
ports, encourages, and advances creative
and charitable not-for-profit activities.

New Orleans

Louisiana Council for the Performing Arts
7524 Saint Charles Avenue
New Orleans, LA 70118
Tel: 504-527-5070

MAINE
Augusta

Forum-A
University of Maine, Augusta
Augusta, ME 04330
Tel: 207-662-7131, Ext. 212
Address Inquiries to: Bronwen Tudor,
Executive Director
Founded in: 1970
Member: University of Maine at Augusta;
Maine State Commission on the Arts
and Humanities;
Annual Budget: $60,000
Description: A community arts organization
based at the University of Maine at Augusta.
Sponsors performances in dance, music,
and theatre.

Maine State Commission on the Arts and
Humanities
State House
Augusta, ME 04330
Tel: 207-289-2724

Carabassett Valley

Mountain Arts Council
RFD
Carabassett Valley, ME 04982
Tel: 207-235-2505; 207-235-2212
Address Inquiries to: Constance Page,
Chairperson
Founded in: 1975
Annual Budget: $15,000

Farmington

Arts Institute of Western Maine
Corner of Main and Anson Streets
Farmington, ME 04938
Tel: 207-778-3475
Address Inquiries to: Mrs. Donna Green,
President
Mrs. Katherine Merrill, Treasurer
Founded in: 1973
Member: Title 4;
Description: Sponsors the Stagecoach
Theatre, which tours productions to the
towns of Western Maine during the summer
months.

Hebron

Phoenix Council
Hebron Academy
Hebron, ME 04238
Tel: 207-966-2100
Address Inquiries to: Marilyn Ackley,
Coordinator
Founded in: 1973
Annual Budget: $10,000

Oquossoc

Rangeley Friends of the Performing Arts
Review Committee
Oquossoc, ME 04964
Tel: 207-864-3617
Address Inquiries to: Sara Guffey, President
Founded in: 1969
Annual Budget: $10,000

Portland

Greater Portland Arts Council
334 Fore Street
Portland, ME 04111
Tel: 207-774-5743
Address Inquiries to: Joseph Lovegren,
President
Founded in: 1962
Annual Budget: $10,000

MARYLAND
Baltimore County

Hatford County Cultural Advisory
Commission
Essex Community College
Baltimore County, MD 21237
Tel: 301-682-6000
Address Inquiries to: Dr. Joseph Mego,
President
Founded in: 1974
Annual Budget: $10,000

Baltimore

County Commission on the Arts and
Sciences
124 Olde Courthouse
Baltimore, MD 21204
Tel: 301-494-2757
Address Inquiries to: Lois K. Baldwin,
Executive Director
Founded in: 1975
Annual Budget: $10,000
Description: Formerly The Baltimore County
Arts Council.

Maryland Arts Council
15 West Mulberry
Baltimore, MD 21210
Tel: 301-685-6740

Bethesda

Montgomery County Arts Council
6400 Democracy Boulevard
Bethesda, MD 20034
Tel: 301-468-4172
Address Inquiries to: Eliot Pfanstiehl,
Coordinator
Founded in: 1976

Cambridge

Dorchester Arts Center
120 High Street
Cambridge, MD 21613
Tel: 301-228-8870
Address Inquiries to: Jesse Hester
Founded in: 1970

Cumberland

Allegheny Arts Council
8 Green Street
Cumberland, MD 21502
Tel: 301-777-9137
Address Inquiries to: L. South, Arts
Coordinator
Founded in: 1976
Annual Budget: $30,000

La Plata

Charles County Arts Council
Post Office Box 368
La Plata, MD 20646
Tel: 301-934-9305
Address Inquiries to: Nancy Lipscomb,
Program Specialist
Founded in: 1975
Annual Budget: $50,000

Riverdale

Maryland National Capital Park/Planning
Commission
Arts Division
6600 Kenilworth Avenue
Riverdale, MD 20737
Tel: 301-699-2450; 301-699-2452
Address Inquiries to: Shirley McReynolds,
Administration Specialist
JoAnn Uzel, Performing Arts Program
Director
Founded in: 1967
Member: ACUCAA; Cultural Alliance of
Greater Washington; NACAA;

Annual Budget: $583,000
Description: Strives to meet the needs of the artistic community and provide citizens with opportunities for arts experiences during their leisure time. They offer a variety of services to individual artists and performers and to county-based dance, music, theatre and visual arts groups. Specialists in each discipline are available to provide consultation and technical assistance.

Westminster

Carroll County Arts Council
129 East Main Street
Westminster, MD 21157
Tel: 301-848-7272
Address Inquiries to: Naomi Benzil, Executive Director
Founded in: 1964
Member: American Council for the Arts;
Annual Budget: $28,000
Description: An organization dedicated to creating and nurturing a climate for the arts in Carroll County. It operates an arts center which is used as a performance space.

Williamsport

Washington County Arts Council
202 Oak Circle
Williamsport, MD 21740
Tel: 301-733-5600
Address Inquiries to: Juanita Aukeman, President
Founded in: 1968
Annual Budget: $50,000

MASSACHUSETTS

Amherst

Arts Extension Service
University of Massachusetts
Amherst, MA 01003
Tel: 413-545-2360
Address Inquiries to: Robert Lynch, Director
Founded in: 1973
Member: ACA; NCACA;
Annual Budget: $100,000
Description: A community development program which has been working to meet the needs of continuing education in the arts since 1973. By providing non financial support in the forms of services, programs and educational offerings, AES reaches individuals and organizations involved in developing arts interests on local and national levels.

Boston

Associated Foundation of Greater Boston
294 Washington Street
Suite 501
Boston, MA 02108
Member: ACA; NACAA; NEA;

Boston Center for the Arts
539 Tremont Street
Boston, MA 02116
Tel: 617-426-5000
Address Inquiries to: Royal Cloyd, President

Founded in: 1970
Member: Greater Boston Chamber of Commerce; Massachusetts Cultural Alliance; National Trust for Historic Preservation;
Annual Budget: $300,000
Description: Designed to meet the needs of professional artists in a unique urban community setting. The eight-building complex contains rehearsal halls, two theatres, a dozen performing arts groups and the Boston Ballet. Upon completion of all facilities, the Center will be self-supporting.

Commonwealth Council on the Arts and Humanities
14 Beacon Street
Boston, MA 02108
Tel: 617-723-3851

Massachusetts Assembly of Community Arts Councils
Council on the Arts and HHumanities
1 Ashburton Place
Boston, MA 02108
Tel: 617-727-3668
Address Inquiries to: Mia Goldman, Executive Director
Description: A state arts organization.

Mayor's Office of Cultural Affairs
The Boston Foundation, Room 208
City Hall Plaza
Boston, MA 02201
Tel: 617-725-3000
Address Inquiries to: Helen Rees, Director
Founded in: 1970
Annual Budget: $100,000

Metropolitan Cultural Alliance
250 Boylston Street
Boston, MA 02116
Tel: 617-247-1460
Address Inquiries to: Lawrence Chvany, Executive Director
Founded in: 1972
Annual Budget: $100,000

North End-Waterfront Arts Council
20 Paramenter Street
Boston, MA 02113
Tel: 617-227-2927
Address Inquiries to: Priscilla B. Dewey, Executive Director
Founded in: 1975
Annual Budget: $50,000

Cambridge

New England Foundation for the Arts
25 Mount Auburn Street
Cambridge, MA 02138
Tel: 617-492-2914

Dover

Charles River Creative Arts Program
56 Center Street
Dover, MA 02030
Tel: 617-785-0068
Address Inquiries to: Priscilla B. Dewey, Executive Director
Founded in: 1970

Annual Budget: $100,000

Greenfield

Arts Council of Franklin County
Post Office Box 364
Greenfield, MA 01301
Tel: 413-774-3131
Address Inquiries to: Mary K. Hoffman, Executive Director
Founded in: 1972
Annual Budget: $50,000

Haverhill

Merrimack Valley Council on the Arts
4 Summer Street
Haverhill, MA 08130
Tel: 617-373-0421
Address Inquiries to: George Capron, Executive Director
Founded in: 1972
Annual Budget: $50,000

Monterey

Southern Berkshire Community Arts Council
Post Office Box 232
Monterey, MA 02145
Tel: 413-528-3747
Address Inquiries to: Bette Seigerman, Executive Director
Founded in: 1974
Annual Budget: $50,000

Quincy

South Shore Cultural Alliance
36 Miller Stile Road
Quincy, MA 02169
Tel: 479-111-
Address Inquiries to: James Simpson, President
Founded in: 1975

Waltham

Waltham Arts Council
205 Bacon Street
Waltham, MA 02154
Tel: 617-893-8050
Address Inquiries to: Dr. Frederick Stokely, President
Founded in: 1976
Annual Budget: $50,000

Wapole

Wapole Arts Council
Post Office Box 182
Wapole, MA 02081
Tel: 617-668-6882
Address Inquiries to: Suzanne P. Bassett, President
Founded in: 1972
Annual Budget: $10,000

Worcester

Worcester Cultural Commission
253 Belmont Street
Worcester, MA 01605
Tel: 617-799-1325; 617-799-1326
Address Inquiries to: Stephen A. Kokolis, Executive Director

Robert C. Maher, Chairman
Founded in: 1979
Member: ACA; NACAA; MCA;
Annual Budget: $50,000
Description: The primary function of this not-for-profit city agency is audience development and cultural programming. It is funded by government and corporate sources. It publishes listings of local cultural events and develops city cultural programs, such as festivals and public art projects, with other community agencies.

MICHIGAN

Adrian

Croswell Opera House and Fine Arts Association
Post Office Box 724
Adrian, MI 49221
Tel: 517-263-5674; 517-263-6415
Address Inquiries to: Robert A. Soller,
Managing Director
Founded in: 1967
Member: League of Historic American
Theatres (Charter Member);
Annual Budget: $185,000
Description: Operates the Croswell House, the third oldest continually operating theatre in the United States, as a community arts center. Programs include a summer musical theatre program, a town hall lecture series, youth theatre series, a winter community theatre program and a community chorus. It sponsors performances of ballet, chorus, orchestra, drama and variety programming. The facility can be rented for various purposes and is equipped to show 35 MM motion pictures. It is a not-for-profit group which receives grants from both public and private sources.

Albion

Albion Community Arts Program
Post Office Box 588
Albion, MI 49224
Tel: 517-629-8072
Address Inquiries to: Mary Moore, Director
Founded in: 1970
Annual Budget: $10,000

Ann Arbor

Ann Arbor Arts Association
117 West Liberty
Ann Arbor, MI 48104
Tel: 313-994-8004
Address Inquiries to: William P. Milne,
President
Founded in: 1909
Annual Budget: $10,0000

Bad Axe

Thumb Council for the Arts
Post Office Box 63
Bad Axe, MI 48913
Tel: 517-269-7604
Address Inquiries to: Jeanette Herrington,

President
Founded in: 1975
Annual Budget: $10,000

Battle Creek

Battle Creek United Arts Council
450 North Avenue
Battle Creek, MI 49016
Tel: 616-965-3931
Address Inquiries to: Marguerite Yarger,
Executive Director
Founded in: 1964
Annual Budget: $10,000

Bellevue

Bellevue Community Arts Council
201 West Street
Bellevue, MI 49021
Tel: 616-763-9413
Address Inquiries to: Darwin Kuhl, Director
Founded in: 1975
Annual Budget: $10,000

Birmingham

Birmingham-Bloomfield Art Association
1516 South Cranbrook Road
Birmingham, MI 48009
Tel: 313-644-0866
Address Inquiries to: Ken Gross, Executive
Director
Founded in: 1956
Annual Budget: $10,0000

Cass City

Cass City Arts Council
4618 Kennebec Drive
Cass City, MI 48726
Tel: 517-872-3465
Address Inquiries to: Holly Althaver,
President
Founded in: 1974
Annual Budget: $10,000

Cheboygan

Cheboygan Area Arts Council
Post Office Box 95
Cheboygan, MI 49721
Tel: 616-627-2739
Address Inquiries to: Christine Driscoll,
President
Founded in: 1971
Annual Budget: $50,000

Dearborn

Dearborn Community Arts Council
Post Office Box 572
Dearborn, MI 48126
Address Inquiries to: Robert Dotten,
Chairman
Founded in: 1969
Annual Budget: $10,000

Detroit

Michigan Council for the Arts
1200 6th Avenue
Detroit, MI 48226
Tel: 313-256-3717

Southeast Michigan Arts Forum
2735 West Warren
Detroit, MI 48208
Tel: 313-898-6340
Address Inquiries to: Shirley Harbin, Director
Founded in: 1959
Member: Michigan Arts Forum;
Annual Budget: 50,000
Description: A not-for-profit organization whose primary function is to disseminate information about cultural events. It issues an Arts Directory in which all the activities of seven counties are listed.

East Lansing

Michigan Association of Community Arts
Agencies
608 Whitehills Drive
East Lansing, MI 48823
Tel: 517-355-2300
Address Inquiries to: Thomas Turk, President
Description: A state arts council.

Greenville

Greenville Creative Arts Council
409 South Lauray
Greenville, MI 48838
Tel: 616-754-4264
Address Inquiries to: Ruth Hansen,
Chairperson
Founded in: 1973
Annual Budget: $10,000

Holly

Holly Fine Arts Council
111 College Street
Holly, MI 48442
Tel: 313-634-7341
Address Inquiries to: Dan Rolls, Executive
Director
Founded in: 1973
Annual Budget: $10,000

Ironwood

Upper Peninsula Arts Coordinating Board
1000 Norway
Ironwood, MI 49855
Tel: 906-228-8521
Address Inquiries to: Vivian Lasich, President
Founded in: 1974
Annual Budget: $10,000

Ishpeming

Peninsula Arts Appreciation Council
Post Office Box 273
Ishpeming, MI 49849
Tel: 906-486-4401
Address Inquiries to: Clyde Colberg,
President
Founded in: 1972
Annual Budget: $50,000

Lansing

Metropolitan Lansing Fine Arts Council
507 South Grand Avenue
Lansing, MI 48933
Tel: 517-487-2424
Address Inquiries to: Robert W. Jones,
Executive Director

Founded in: 1964
Annual Budget: $10,000

Menominee

Menominee Arts Council
1502 First Street
Menominee, MI 49858
Tel: 906-863-2524
Address Inquiries to: John B. Henes,
President
Founded in: 1972

Midland

Midland Center for the Arts
1801 West Saint Andrews Road
Midland, MI 48640
Tel: 517-631-5930
Address Inquiries to: Don Jaeger, Executive
Director
Founded in: 1966
Annual Budget: $100,000

Monroe

Monroe City-County Fine Arts Council
1555 South Raisinville Road
Monroe, MI 48161
Tel: 313-242-7300
Address Inquiries to: Robert P. Merkel,
President
Founded in: 1967
Member: Michigan Council of the Arts;
Annual Budget: $10,000
Description: Funded by corporations, city and
county governments, the council makes
grants in music and architecture to deserv-
ing local talent. It also holds visual arts con-
tests for community artists.

Mount Pleasant

Community Arts Council
812 Oakland Drive
Mount Pleasant, MI 48858
Tel: 517-722-2543
Address Inquiries to: Martha L. Joynt,
President
Founded in: 1975
Annual Budget: $10,000

Muskegon

Greater Muskegon Council for the Arts
1336 Sanford Street
Muskegon, MI 49443
Tel: 616-773-1115
Address Inquiries to: Carlo V. Spataro,
Executive Director
Founded in: 1972
Annual Budget: $10,000

Oak Park

Oak Park Arts and Cultural Commission
14200 Oak Park Boulevard
Oak Park, MI 48237
Tel: 313-548-7230
Address Inquiries to: Irving Stollman,
President
Founded in: 1975
Annual Budget: $1,000

Petoskey

Crooked Tree Arts Council
461 East Mitchell
Petoskey, MI 49770
Tel: 616-347-4337; 616-347-7870
Address Inquiries to: Jack Perry, Chairman
Susan Storm, President
Founded in: 1972
Annual Budget: $20,000
Description: This not-for-profit organization
is funded by government, foundation and
private sources. It operates a community
arts center which provides performances of
music, drama and dance; a sales and show
gallery for visual arts; and classes in drama,
dance, music, painting, pottery and cooking
for adults and children.

Plymouth

Plymouth Community Arts Council
332 South Main Street
Plymouth, MI 48170
Tel: 313-455-5260
Address Inquiries to: Mrs. David Wood,
Administrator
Founded in: 1969
Annual Budget: $50,000

Pontiac

Pontiac Arts Council
47 Williams Street
Pontiac, MI 48053
Tel: 313-333-7849
Address Inquiries to: Ian R. Lyons, President
Founded in: 1966
Annual Budget: $10,000

Port Huron

Seaway Arts Council
Saint Clair County Community College
323 Erie St.
Port Huron, MI 48060
Tel: 313-982-3881
Address Inquiries to: Patti Stockhausen,
Director
Founded in: 1971
Annual Budget: $50,000

Rochester

Rochester Arts Commission
Post Office Box 328
Rochester, MI 48063
Address Inquiries to: Thomas Patterson,
Co-Chairperson
Mrs. Thomas Patterson, Co-Chairperson
Founded in: 1965
Annual Budget: $50,000

Rockford

Rockford Area Arts Commission
c/o Municipal Building
Rockford, MI 49341
Tel: 616-866-2213
Address Inquiries to: Bette Young,
Chairperson
Founded in: 1975

Roscommon

Roscommon Chamber Music Society
Post Office Box 88
Roscommon, MI 48653
Tel: 517-275-5826
Address Inquiries to: Julia Borak, President
Founded in: 1969
Annual Budget: $10,000

Sterling Heights

Sterling Heights Cultural Commission
40555 Utica Road
Sterling Heights, MI 48078
Tel: 313-268-8500
Address Inquiries to: John Clinton,
Administator
Founded in: 1973

Sturgis

Sturgis Art Council
201 North Nottawa Road
Sturgis, MI 49091
Tel: 616-651-8541
Address Inquiries to: Carl Aiken, Director
Founded in: 1974
Member: Michigan Association of
Community Arts Agencies;
Annual Budget: $30,000
Description: A not-for-profit community arts
organization.

Traverse City

Traverse City Arts Council
Post Office Box 681
Traverse City, MI 49684
Tel: 616-946-2881
Address Inquiries to: Mrs. Paul Russell,
President
Founded in: 1966
Annual Budget: $10,000

Warren

Warren Cultural Commission
29500 Van Dyke City Hall
Warren, MI 48093
Tel: 313-573-9500
Address Inquiries to: Jan Pierce, Executive
Director
Founded in: 1970
Annual Budget: $50,000

MINNESOTA

Bemedji

North Country Arts Council
c/o Bemedji State University
Box 128
Bemedji, MN 56601
Tel: 218-755-2065
Founded in: 1974
Annual Budget: $50,000

Canby

Canby Southwest Association
Arts and Humanities Council
606 Oscar North
Canby, MN 56220

Tel: 507-223-5962
Address Inquiries to: R. A. Jones

Edgerton

Ederton Fine Arts Federation
Post Office Box 401
Edgerton, MN 56128
Tel: 507-442-8281
Address Inquiries to: John Vandermaten
Founded in: 1974
Annual Budget: $10,000

Grand Rapids

Grand Rapids Performing Arts Council
Post Office Box 512
Grand Rapids, MN 55744
Tel: 218-326-8512
Founded in: 1964
Annual Budget: $15,000
Description: Schedules and sponsors workshops for community schools and holds a youth talent festival.

Little Falls

Area Arts Council
120 First Street, NE
Little Falls, MN 56345
Tel: 612-232-5155
Address Inquiries to: Glen Kraywinkle,
  Manager
Founded in: 1971

Luverne

Council for Arts in Rock County
110 Virginia Street
Luverne, MN 56165
Tel: 507-283-2598
Address Inquiries to: Ruth H. Okarski,
  Coordinator
Founded in: 1973
Member: Southwest Arts and Humanities
  Council; Citizens for the Arts;
Annual Budget: $3,500

Marshall

Marshall Arts Association
606 South First Street
Marshall, MN 56258
Address Inquiries to: Pat Peterson, President
Founded in: 1970
Annual Budget: $10,000

Southwest Minnesota Arts Council
Post Office Box 583
Marshall, MN 56258
Tel: 507-537-6201
Address Inquiries to: Mary Martin, Executive
  Director
Founded in: 1974
Annual Budget: $100,000

Minneapolis

Minneapolis Arts Commission
302 City Hall
Minneapolis, MN 55415
Tel: 612-348-5486
Address Inquiries to: Melisande Charles,
  Executive Director
Founded in: 1975

Annual Budget: $50,000

Minnesota State Arts Council
314 Clifton Avenue
Minneapolis, MN 55403
Tel: 612-874-1335

Montevideo

Montevideo Arts Council
513 North Ninth Street
Montevideo, MN 56265
Address Inquiries to: Mary Birkey, President
Founded in: 1975
Annual Budget: $10,000

Northfield

Northfield Arts Guild
Post Office Box 21
Northfield, MN 55057
Tel: 507-645-8877; 507-645-8878
Address Inquiries to: Sue Shepard,
  Administrator
  Marie B. Sathrum, Program Manager
Founded in: 1956
Annual Budget: $120,000
Description: Facilities include a dance studio, theatre and recital room all in a restored historical register building. Program includes twelve 12 theatre productions a year.

Owatonna

Owatonna Arts Council
Post Office Box 134
Owatonna, MN 55060
Tel: 507-451-9990
Address Inquiries to: Mary E. Leach,
  President
Founded in: 1974
Annual Budget: $50,000

Saint Cloud

Saint Cloud Community Arts Council
Post Office Box 323
Saint Cloud, MN 56302
Tel: 612-252-2105
Address Inquiries to: David J. Borgert,
  President
Founded in: 1969
Member: Minnesota Citizens for the Arts;
  St. Cloud Area Chamber of Commerce;
  St. Cloud Downtown Association;
Annual Budget: $20,000
Description: Provides administrative services to the local arts community.

Saint Paul

Compas
700 Saint Paul Building
6 West 5th Street
Saint Paul, MN 55102
Tel: 612-227-8241
Address Inquiries to: Molly LaBerge,
  Executive Director
Founded in: 1974
Annual Budget: $100,000

Saint Paul Ramsey Arts Council
30 East Tenth Street
Saint Paul, MN 55101
Tel: 612- 22- 8241

Address Inquiries to: Marlow G. Burt,
  Executive Director
Founded in: 1952
Annual Budget: $100,000

South Saint Paul

South Saint Paul Civic Arts Commission
125 Third Avenue
South Saint Paul, MN 55075
Tel: 451-278-
Founded in: 1974
Annual Budget: $1,000

Thief River Falls

Thief River Falls Arts Council
1524 Cartway Drive
Thief River Falls, MN 56701
Tel: 218-681-5916
Address Inquiries to: Dolores Forney,
  President
Founded in: 1975
Annual Budget: $10,000

Tracey

Tracey Arts Council
Tracey Community Foundation
Tracey, MN 56175
Tel: 507-629-3437
Address Inquiries to: Steve Snyder,
  Community Education Director
Founded in: 1975

West Saint Paul

Dakota County Fine Arts Society
436 Ruby Drive
West Saint Paul, MN 55118
Founded in: 1960
Annual Budget: $50,000

MISSISSIPPI

Biloxi

Greater Gulf Coast Arts Council
Post Office Box 4091
Biloxi, MS 39531
Tel: 601-388-1976
Address Inquiries to: Jeanette Westfall,
  President
Founded in: 1970
Annual Budget: $60,000
Description: A programming and service organization for other arts groups.

Charleston

Charleston Council on Arts
423 East Main
Charleston, MS 38921
Tel: 601-647-3382
Address Inquiries to: Mrs. E.J. Miller,
  President
Founded in: 1976

Fulton

Itawamba County Arts Council
310 Cedar Street
Fulton, MS 38843
Tel: 601-862-4926

Address Inquiries to: Dr. W.T. Edmonson,
President
Founded in: 1976
Annual Budget: $10,000

Jackson

Mississippi Arts Commisssion
Post Office Box 1314
Jackson, MS 39205
Tel: 601-354-7336

Yazoo City

Yazoo Arts Council
Post Office Box 985
Yazoo City, MS 39194
Tel: 601-746-6062
Address Inquiries to: Betty DeCell, President
Founded in: 1976
Annual Budget: $10,000

MISSOURI
Cuba

Cuba Arts Council
Route 1, Box 242
Cuba, MO 65453
Address Inquiries to: Michael Bottom,
President
Founded in: 1966
Annual Budget: $10,000

Kansas City

Mid-America Arts Alliance
20 West 9th Street, Suite 550
Kansas City, MO 64105
Tel: 816-421-1388
Description: Arts Council for the states of Arkansas, Kansas, Missouri Nebraska and Oklahoma.

Maryville

Nodaway Arts Council
Post Office Box 55
Maryville, MO 64468
Tel: 816-582-5687
Address Inquiries to: David Shestak,
President
Founded in: 1966
Annual Budget: $10,000

Nevada

Community Council on the Arts
1212 North Olive Street
Nevada, MO 64772
Tel: 417-667-3994
Address Inquiries to: Warran Hargus,
President
Founded in: 1973
Annual Budget: $10,000

St. Louis

Missouri State Council on the Arts
111 South Bemiston
St. Louis, MO 63105
Tel: 314-721-1672

Unionville

Putnam County Arts Council
1817 Putnam
Unionville, MO 63565
Tel: 816-947-2284
Address Inquiries to: Glen H. Lochead,
Chairman
Founded in: 1973

MONTANA
Anaconda

Copper Village Museum and Arts Center
Post Office Box 29
Anaconda, MT 59711
Tel: 406-563-3604
Address Inquiries to: Mary Brimhall, Director
Founded in: 1971
Annual Budget: $10,000

Chester

Liberty County Arts Council
Post Office Box 555
Chester, MT 59522
Tel: 406-759-5476
Address Inquiries to: Helen Aaberg, Project
Director
Founded in: 1967
Member: Montana Performing Arts
Consortium; Montana Institute of the
Arts;
Annual Budget: $10,000

Missoula

Montana Assembly of Community Arts
Council
Montana Arts Council
235 Pine Street
Missoula, MT 59801
Tel: 406-543-8286
Address Inquiries to: David E. Nelson,
President
Description: A state arts council.

Montana State Arts Council
235 East Pine Street
Missoula, MT 59801
Tel: 406-543-8286

NEBRASKA
Crawford

Crawford Cultural Center
337 Second Street
Crawford, NB 69339
Tel: 308-665-2389
Address Inquiries to: Gary Aten

Grand Island

Grand Island Area Arts Council
111 West Second Street
Grand Island, NB 68801
Tel: 308-384-2130
Address Inquiries to: Beth Baird, Chairperson
Founded in: 1975
Annual Budget: $10,000

Hastings

Association for the Visual Arts
1001 North Saint Joseph
Hastings, NB 68901
Address Inquiries to: Lois Brink, President

Kearney

Kearney Area Arts Council
Post Office Box 2001
Kearney, NB 68847
Tel: 308-234-4949
Address Inquiries to: Germaine Oldfather,
President
Barbara Wild, Administrator
Founded in: 1975
Member: Kearney Area Chamber of
Commerce;
Annual Budget: $30,000
Description: Sponsors approximately twenty events annually, ranging from a full length theatre production to an afternoon workshop. KAAC sponsors local and area artists as well as touring groups.

Lincoln

Lincoln Community Arts Council
Room 508, Center Building
Lincoln, NB 68508
Tel: 402-477-5930
Address Inquiries to: Jaqueline A. Hall,
Executive Director
Founded in: 1968
Member: NAC; Lincoln Area Agency on
Aging; Lincoln Community Arts Fund
Corporation;
Annual Budget: $45,000

McCook

McCook Area Arts Council
1205 East Third Street
McCook, NB 69001
Tel: 308-345-6303, Ext. 65
Address Inquiries to: Richard L. Driml,
Chairman
Founded in: 1966
Member: NAC;
Annual Budget: $10,000

Neligh

Neligh Arts Council
Post Office Box 194
Neligh, NB 69756
Tel: 402-887-5090
Address Inquiries to: Lynn Morrison,
President
Founded in: 1975
Annual Budget: $10,000

Norfolk

Norfolk Arts Council
501 Norfolk Avenue
Norfolk, NB 68701
Address Inquiries to: Richard Klass

North Platte

North Platte Area Art Council
c/o Chamber of Commerce
Post Office Box 968
North Platte, NB 69101
Tel: 308-532-6888
Address Inquiries to: Colin Taylor, President

Omaha

Metropolitan Arts Council
Post Office Box 1077
Omaha, NB 68101
Tel: 402-341-7910
Address Inquiries to: Gloria Bartek, Executive
Director
Founded in: 1966
Annual Budget: $350,000
Description: Provides arts programs and services to the people in the Omaha metropolitan area and works in partnership with government and business to create a public/private support system for all the arts. The present programs include: neighborhood arts, in which performing artists give classes, workshops and performances throughout Douglas County; and Arts for Special Audiences, which offers classes, workshops, and performances for those not ordinarily involved in the arts including the deaf and hearing impaired, senior citizens, the handicapped and the retarded.

Nebraska Arts Council
7367 Pacific Street
Omaha, NE 68114
Tel: 402-554-2122

Nebraska Assembly of Community Arts
Council
8448 West Center Road
Omaha, NB 68124
Tel: 402-554-2122
Address Inquiries to: Kenneth Maupin,
President
Description: A state arts council.

Ord

Loup Valley Arts Council
607 North 22nd
Ord, NB 68862
Tel: 308-728-3874
Address Inquiries to: Martie Brady, President

Scottsbluff

West Nebraska Art Center
Post Office Box 62
Scottsbluff, NB 69361
Tel: 308-632-2226
Address Inquiries to: Richard Crom,
Executive Director
Founded in: 1966
Member: Nebraska Assembly of Community
Arts Councils; Nebraska Museums
Coalition; ACA; NACAA;
Annual Budget: $100,000

Seward

Seward Arts Council
1160 Eastridge
Seward, NB 68434
Address Inquiries to: Charlene Berns,
President

Stromburg

Stromsburg Area Arts Council
416 Main Street
Stromburg, NB 68666
Address Inquiries to: Pat Carlson

Valentine

North Central Nebraska Area Arts Council
527 North Hall
Valentine, NB 62901
Tel: 402-376-3234
Address Inquiries to: Jack Erickson, President
Founded in: 1971
Annual Budget: $10,000

Verdigre

Verdigre Arts Council
Post Office Box C
Verdigre, NB 68783
Address Inquiries to: Mrs. James Carlson,
President

York

York Area Arts Council
11 Fairview Drive
York, NB 68467
Address Inquiries to: Bill Rathe, President

NEVADA

Las Vegas

Allied Arts Council
821 Las Vegas Boulevard, North
Las Vegas, NV 89101
Tel: 702-384-1208
Address Inquiries to: Naomi Fine, President
Founded in: 1961
Annual Budget: $10,000

Las Vegas Arts Council
Post Office Box 1506
Las Vegas, NV 87701
Tel: 505-425-7400
Address Inquiries to: John Gavahan, President

Nevada Alliance for the Arts
821 Las Vegas Boulevard
Las Vegas, NV 89101
Tel: 702-384-1208
Address Inquiries to: Zel Lowman, President
Description: A state arts council.

Reed Whipple Cultural Arts Center
821 Las Vegas Boulevard
Las Vegas, NV 89101
Tel: 702-386-6211
Address Inquiries to: Iris Newman,
Supervisor
Founded in: 1973
Annual Budget: $100,000

Reno

Nevada State Council on the Arts
560 Mill Street
Reno, NV 89502
Tel: 702-784-6231

Sierra Arts Foundation
Post Office Box 2814
Reno, NV 89505
Tel: 702-329-1234
Address Inquiries to: Barbara Wright,
President
Founded in: 1971
Annual Budget: $10,000

NEW HAMPSHIRE

Andover

Creative Arts Association of Andover
Post Office Box 71
Andover, NH 03216
Tel: 603-735-5371
Address Inquiries to: Winslow Eaves,
President
Founded in: 1962
Member: New Hampshire Commision on
the Arts;
Annual Budget: $5,000

Chocorua

Arts Council of Tamworth
Post Office Box 71
Chocorua, NH 03817
Address Inquiries to: Robert Lloyd, President
Founded in: 1966
Annual Budget: $10,000

Concord

New Hampshire Commission on the Arts
40 North Main Street
Concord, NH 03301
Tel: 603-271-2789
Description: Works in close cooperation with
the New England Foundation for the Arts.

Franconia

Lafayette Arts Council
Post Office Box E
Franconia, NH 03580
Tel: 603-823-8056
Address Inquiries to: Donald Anderson

Hanover

Friends of the Hopkins Center
Dartmouth College
Hanover, NH 03755
Tel: 603-646-2006
Address Inquiries to: Drewry Logan,
President
Sybil B. Williamson, Executive Secretary
Founded in: 1968
Annual Budget: $50,000
Description: An organization of people interested in the arts and willing to help encourage their growth at Dartmouth College. Supports Outreach Programs, student projects, and the sponsorship of visiting artists in

drama, music and dance through fund raising benefits.

Jefferson

North County Arts Council
White Mountain Center for the Arts
Post Office Box 145
Jefferson, NH 03583
Tel: 603-586-7754
Address Inquiries to: Allan Knotts, Director

White Mountains Center for the Arts
Post Office Box 145
Jefferson, NH 03585
Tel: 603-586-7754
Address Inquiries to: John Goyette, Executive
    Director
Founded in: 1972
Annual Budget: $100,000

Keene

Cheshire Arts Council
East Surry Road
Keene, NH 03431
Tel: 603-352-5159
Address Inquiries to: Ruth Ewing, President

Grand Monadnock Regional Arts Council
31 Central Square
Keene, NH 03431
Tel: 603-924-3271
Address Inquiries to: Sara Germain, Director

Lancaster

Lancaster Arts Council
White Moutain Regional High School
Lancaster, NH 03584
Tel: 603-788-2076
Address Inquiries to: Leonard Hall

Lebanon

The Arts Exchange
16 Whipple Building
Lebanon, NH 03766
Tel: 603-448-4353
Address Inquiries to: Clinton Baer, Executive
    Director
Description: A community arts council.

Friends of Lebanon Opera House
74 Prospect Street
Lebanon, NH 03766
Tel: 603-448-2966
Address Inquiries to: Mrs. Clark Griffiths,
    President

Lincoln

Lincoln Arts Council
Pollard Road
Lincoln, NH 03251
Tel: 603-745-2289
Address Inquiries to: Rachel Adams,
    President

Littleton

Littleton Arts Council
Fowler Hill Road
Littleton, NH 03561
Tel: 603-444-5014
Address Inquiries to: Virginia Stewart

Manchester

Federated Arts of Manchester
148 Concord Street
Manchester, NH 03104
Tel: 603-668-6186
Address Inquiries to: Dolly Harrison,
    Executive Director

Manchester Institute of Arts and Sciences
148 Concord Street
Manchester, NH 03101
Tel: 603-623-0313
Address Inquiries to: James K. Boatner,
    Executive Director

Merrimack Valley Arts Council
148 Concord Street
Manchester, NH 03104
Tel: 603-668-6186
Address Inquiries to: Dolly Harrison,
    President
Founded in: 1976
Annual Budget: $50,000

Saint Anselm's Commission on the Arts
Saint Anselm's Drive
Manchester, NH 03102
Tel: 603-669-1030; 603-237-1030
Address Inquiries to: Eugene Rice, Executive
    Director

Meriden

New Hampshire West Council for the Arts
Review Committee
Meriden, NH 03770
Tel: 603-469-3232
Address Inquiries to: Aidron Duckworth,
    Director

Nashua

Arts and Sciences Center
14 Court Street
Nashua, NH 03060
Tel: 603-883-1506
Address Inquiries to: Ann L. Carner,
    Executive Director
Founded in: 1958
Annual Budget: $100,000

Newport

Library Arts Center
58 North Main Street
Newport, NH 03773
Tel: 03 -63 -040
Address Inquiries to: Audrey Sylvester,
    Director
Founded in: 1967
Annual Budget: $50,000

Peterborough

Sharon Arts Center
Route 2, Post Office Box 361
Peterborough, NH 03458
Tel: 603-924-7256
Address Inquiries to: Alan Erdoffy, Executive
    Director
Founded in: 1946
Annual Budget: $100,000

Pittsfield

Pittsfield Area Arts Council
32 Manchester Street
Pittsfield, NH 03263
Address Inquiries to: Dr. Jay D. Clark,
    President
Founded in: 1974
Annual Budget: $10,000

Wolfeboro

Governor Wentworth Arts Council
Post Office Box 743
Wolfeboro, NH 03894
Tel: 603-569-2744
Address Inquiries to: Jean Puff, President
Founded in: 1926
Annual Budget: $5,000
Description: Governor Wentworth Arts Council serves the artists and the community in the area.

NEW JERSEY

Annandale

Hunterdon County Cultural Commission
Route 1
Annandale, NJ 08801
Address Inquiries to: Walter J. Young

Belvedere

Warren County Cultural Commission
County Court House
Belvedere, NJ 07823
Address Inquiries to: Irene N. Street

Cape May

Mid-Atlantic Center for the Arts
Post Office Box 164
Cape May, NJ 08204
Address Inquiries to: Ray Schultz, President

Cape May Court House

Cape May Cultural Commission
35 Romney Place
Cape May Court House, NJ 08210
Tel: 609-465-5937
Founded in: 1968

Clinton

Hunterdon Art Center
Old Stone Mill
7 Center Street
Clinton, NJ 08809
Address Inquiries to: Lawrence Carlbon,
    President

Edison

Edison Recreational Center
Municipal Boulevard, Plainfield Avenue
Edison, NJ 08817
Tel: 201-287-0900
Address Inquiries to: Tricia Campbell,
    Director
Founded in: 1973
Annual Budget: $50,000

Middlesex County Arts Council
37 Oakwood Avenue
Edison, NJ 08817
Tel: 201-549-4684
Address Inquiries to: Estelle Hasenberg,
     Executive Director
Founded in: 1969
Annual Budget: $100,000

Haddon Township

Camden County Cultural Commission
250 South Park Drive
Haddon Township, NJ 08108
Tel: 609-858-0063
Address Inquiries to: Gail Greenberg,
     Executive Director
     Grace Dodge, Assistant
Founded in: 1972
Member: County of Camden;
Annual Budget: $100,000
Description: The commission is charged with
developing public interest in state and local
history and aid in the visual and performing
arts.

Jersey City

Hudson County Office of Cultural Affairs
595 Newark Avenue
Jersey City, NJ 07306
Tel: 201-659-5062
Address Inquiries to: Charles K. Robinson,
     Executive Director
Founded in: 1975
Annual Budget: $100,000

Lawrence

Lawrence Arts Council
Municipal Square
Lawrence, NJ 08648
Tel: 609-883-0873
Address Inquiries to: Beverly Nester,
     President
Founded in: 1971
Annual Budget: $10,000

Madison

Arts Council of Morris
Drew University
Madison, NJ 07940
Tel: 201-377-6622
Address Inquiries to: Barbara Keefauver,
     Executive Director
Founded in: 1973
Annual Budget: $50,000

Mount Holly

Burlington County Cultural and Heritage
     Commission
49 Rancocas Road
Mount Holly, NJ 08060
Tel: 609-261-5068
Address Inquiries to: David A. Miller,
     Administrator
     Margaret Shirk, Exhibit Artist
Founded in: 1970
Member: ACA; NEA; NJCAH; Federal Arts
     Alliance of N.J.; National Trust; N.J.
     Historical Society; American Association
     for State and Local History; Victorian

Society; N.J. Museums Council; County
     of Burlington; State of New Jersey;
Annual Budget: $50,000
Description: The commission is both an arts
producing and arts facilitating public agency
servicing Burlington and its forty five identified arts organizations. Programs include a
summer performing arts series.

Newark

Essex County Division of Cultural Affairs
115 Clifton Avenue
Newark, NJ 07039
Tel: 201-482-6400; 201-482-0967
Address Inquiries to: Liz DelTufo, Director
Founded in: 1980
Member: EPACA; NJSCA;
Annual Budget: $50,000
Description: A part of the Essex County Divi-
sion of cultural affairs, the division is the
only recognized official body of the state of
New Jersey to fully represent the county as
its arts organization. Promotes, coordinates,
evaluates and supports most of the maj or
county cultural events and provides mini-
grants and resourses wherever possible.

North Brunswick

Middlesex County Cultural Commission
841 George Road
North Brunswick, NJ 08902
Tel: 201-745-4489
Address Inquiries to: Jeffrey A. Kesper,
     Administrator
     Anna M. Aschkenes, Assistant
     Administrator
Founded in: 1971
Member: ACUCAA; AASLH; AAM; AENJ;
     AAENJ; NAEA; MCNJ; FNJPB; SAH;
     HHAA;
Annual Budget: $50,000
Description: A public service organization re-
sponsible for developing county wide pro-
grams in the arts and in the cultural values,
goals and traditions of the community, the
state and the nation.

Paramus

Bergen County Cultural Commission
Bergen Community College, 400 Paramus
Road
Paramus, NJ 07652
Tel: 201-477-1500
Address Inquiries to: Dean loisMarshall,
     President
Founded in: 1968
Annual Budget: $50,000

Princeton

Princeton Arts Council
44 Nassau Street
Princeton, NJ 08540
Tel: 609-921-7185
Address Inquiries to: Anne D. Reeves,
     Executive Director
Founded in: 1969
Annual Budget: $10,000

Red Bank

Monmouth Arts Center
99 Monmouth Street
Red Bank, NJ 07701
Tel: 201-842-9000
Address Inquiries to: Rick Eckart, Manager
Description: A state arts council.

Monmouth County Arts Council
99 Monmouth Street
Red Bank, NJ 07701
Tel: 201-842-9000
Address Inquiries to: Sharon Burnham,
     Director
Founded in: 1971
Annual Budget: $100,000

Trenton

New Jersey State Council on the Arts
27 West State Street
Trenton, NJ 08625
Tel: 609-292-6130

NEW MEXICO

Artesia

Artesia Arts Council
Post Office Box 782
Artesia, NM 88210
Tel: 505-746-3226
Address Inquiries to: Russell Floore,
     President
Founded in: 1975
Annual Budget: $10,000

Roswell

Roswell Area Arts Council
1708 West Third Street
Roswell, NM 88201
Tel: 505-662-7648
Address Inquiries to: Charles Southard,
     President

Sante Fe

Western States Arts Foundation
141 East Palace Avenue
Sante Fe, NM 57501
Tel: 505-998-1166

NEW YORK

Albany

Albany City Arts Office
Department of Human Resources
75 New Scotland Avenue
Albany, NY 12208
Tel: 518-472-6147
Address Inquiries to: Sandra Seifter, Arts
     Coordinator
Founded in: 1973

The Arts Center
1069 Scotland Road
Albany, NY 12201
Tel: 518-438-7895
Address Inquiries to: Maria Faina,
     Coordinator

Founded in: 1969
Annual Budget: $100,000

Arkville

Erpf Catskill Cultural Center
Route 28
Arkville, NY 12406
Tel: 904-586-3326
Address Inquiries to: John B. Hopkins,
  Executive Director
Founded in: 1975
Member: Regional Conference of Historical
  Agencies; NYSCA;
Annual Budget: $130,000
Description: A multi arts organization. Performing activities include Childrens Theatre (Community Experimental Repertory Theatre, Poughkeepsie).

Athens

Greene County Council on the Arts
Post Office Box 126
Athens, NY 12015
Tel: 518-734-3792
Address Inquiries to: Dean Crane, President
Founded in: 1975
Annual Budget: $50,000

Binghamton

Roberson Center for the Arts and
  Sciences
30 Front Street
Binghamton, NY 13905
Tel: 607-772-0660
Address Inquiries to: Duane Truex, Executive
  Director
  Laura B. Martin, Assistant
  Director/Programming
Founded in: 1954
Member: American Association of
  Museums; NYSCA;
Annual Budget: $1,200,000
Description: A performing arts center and historical museum.

Brooklyn

Brooklyn Arts and Culture Association
200 Eastern Parkway
Brooklyn, NY 11238
Tel: 212-783-4469; 212-783-3077
Address Inquiries to: Charlene Victor,
  President
  Chuck Reichenthal, Program/Publicity
  Director
Founded in: 1965
Member: NYCLCAC; NYSCA; NCACA;
Annual Budget: $450,000
Description: Works in over 2,400 locations in Brooklyn schools, parks, streets, religious, civic, cultural and educational institutions. Its services include providing monthly newsletters, cultural calendars, performances, festival exhibitions, seminars, artistic workshops, scholarships, film festivals, technical assistance and workshops, equipment loans, bookkeeping, publicity, exposure, small financial grants to the Brooklyn visual and performing artist and art organizations.

Buffalo

Arts Development Services
237 Main Street
Buffalo, NY 14203
Tel: 716-856-7520
Address Inquiries to: Maxine N.
  Brandenburg, Executive Director
Founded in: 1973
Annual Budget: $100,000

Corning

Chemung Valley Arts Council
171 Cedar Street
Corning, NY 14830
Tel: 607-967-5871
Address Inquiries to: Charlene Holland,
  Executive Director
Founded in: 1972
Member: ACA; NACAA; NYSCA; NYSCA;
  Taylor Wine Company and Foundation;
  New York State Parks Department;
  Corning Glass Foundation; Gannett
  Foundation; Lindau Foundation; New
  York State Division for Youth; Steuben
  County; Ingersoll Rand Corperation;
  Tripp Foundation;
Annual Budget: $50,000
Description: An arts information service providing technical assistance to over forty not-for-profit organizations and clearing house for booking performances.

Cortland

Council on the Arts for Cortland
19 Main Street
Cortland, NY 13045
Tel: 607-753-0722
Address Inquiries to: Janet B. Steck,
  Executive Director
Founded in: 1974
Annual Budget: $50,000

Delhi

Delaware County Council on the Arts
c/o Delhi College, 149 Bush Hall
Delhi, NY 13753
Tel: 607-746-4161
Address Inquiries to: William Tastle,
  Chairman
Founded in: 1975
Annual Budget: $50,000

Elmsford

Town of Greenburgh Arts and Cultural
  Committee
Post Office Box 205
Elmsford, NY 10523
Tel: 914-478-3559; 914-682-5200
Address Inquiries to: Madeleine Gutman,
  Executive Director
Founded in: 1965
Member: NYSCA; Dance Films Association;
  American Association for the
  Advancement of the Humanities;
  Committee for the Visual Arts; Young
  Filmakers; Meet the Composer Poets
  and Writers;
Annual Budget: $25,000

Description: Presents a world arts and humanities schedule of poetry, music and dance in ten monthly admission free concerts and two lecture series. Purpose is to preserve, continue and enrich the multi-cultural artistic and intellectual traditions representative of the finest achievements of human endeavor which have formed the basis of social organization of all peoples throughout history by organizing and presenting performances, exhibitions, seminars and conferences, led by qualified specialists within and without the township.

Freeport

The Arts Council at Freeport
Post Office Box 97
Freeport, NY 11520
Tel: 516-223-2522; 516-223-4769
Address Inquiries to: Lila Diringer, Executive
  Director
Founded in: 1975
Member: NYSCA; NYSCA; NEA; Nassau
  County Forum for the Arts; Freeport
  Chamber of Commerce; LI Tourism
  Commission; Nassau County Office of
  Cultural Development; Village of
  Freeport; Freeport Public Schools;
Annual Budget: $100,000
Description: Offers art services to local arts organizations and individual artists offer workshops in the arts, trips, festivals, and showcases for young performers.

Genesee

Genesee Valley Council on the Arts
4241 Lakeville Road
Genesee, NY 14454
Tel: 716-245-5401
Address Inquiries to: Nancy O'Dea, Executive
  Director
  Barbara Dechario, Assistant
Founded in: 1966
Member: ACA;
Annual Budget: $500,000

Glen's Falls

Lower Adirondack Regional Arts Council
Post Office Box 659
Glen's Falls, NY 12801
Tel: 518-789-1144
Address Inquiries to: Joyce Smith, Executive
  Director
Founded in: 1972
Member: Albany League of the Arts;
  Alliance; Empire State Crafts Alliance;
  Glenn Falls Foundation;
Annual Budget: $50,000
Description: A clearing house for the arts in the Glenn Falls region.

Gloversville

Fulton County Arts Council
40 North Main Street
Gloversville, NY 12078
Tel: 518-725-6248
Address Inquiries to: Joanne Vedder,
  Executive Director
Founded in: 1974

Annual Budget: $50,000

Guilderland Center

Guilderland League of Arts
Post Office Box 305
Guilderland Center, NY 12085
Tel: 716-456-2913
Address Inquiries to: Elaine Luzine, President
Founded in: 1975
Annual Budget: $10,000

Hastings-on-Hudson

Hastings Creative Arts Council
Post Office Box 193
Hastings-on-Hudson, NY 10706
Tel: 914-478-2814
Address Inquiries to: Carolyn Zinn, Executive
   Director
Founded in: 1963
Annual Budget: $50,000

Hauppauge

County of Suffolk Office of Cultural Affairs
County Center, Veterans Memorial
   Highway
Hauppauge, NY 11787
Tel: 516-979-2987
Address Inquiries to: Nicholas Ullrich,
   Program Coordinator
Founded in: 1974
Annual Budget: $100,000

Hempstead

Department of Parks and Recreation
Hempstead Executive Plaza
50 Clinton Street
Hempstead, NY 11550
Tel: 516-489-5000
Address Inquiries to: George Leonard,
   Supervisor
Founded in: 1975
Annual Budget: $100,000

Herkimer

Herkimer County Arts Council
Post Office Box 25
Herkimer, NY 133350
Tel: 315-866-0300
Address Inquiries to: Robert Grinnell,
   President
Founded in: 1975
Annual Budget: $10,000

Hopewell Junction

Taconic Art Center
Post Office Box 383
Hopewell Junction, NY 12533
Tel: 914-226-9266
Address Inquiries to: Robert Ramage,
   President
Founded in: 1972
Annual Budget: $50,000

Huntington

Alliance of New York State Arts Councils
198 New York Avenue
Huntington, NY 11743
Tel: 516-423-1818
Address Inquiries to: Elizabeth H. Howard,
   Secretary

Huntington Arts Council
12 New Street
Huntington, NY 11743
Tel: 516-271-8423
Address Inquiries to: Ashley Kiebitz,
   Executive Director
Founded in: 1963
Annual Budget: $100,000

Islip

Islip Town Council on the Arts
Post Office Box 85
Islip, NY 11751
Tel: 516-581-2448
Address Inquiries to: Lillian Barbush,
   Chairman
Founded in: 1974
Annual Budget: $10,000

Ithaca

Center for the Arts at Ithaca
313 North Tioga Street
Ithaca, NY 14580
Tel: 607-273-8588
Address Inquiries to: Thomas Niederkorn,
   Chairman
Founded in: 1964
Annual Budget: $100,000

Jamaica

Queens Council on the Arts
161-04 Jamaica Avenue
Jamaica, NY 11432
Tel: 212-291-1100
Address Inquiries to: Jean Weiss, Executive
   Director
   Carol McCully, Program Services
Founded in: 1966
Member: ACA; NYSCA; NEA; NYSCA;
   Department of Cultural Affairs of the
   City of New York;
Annual Budget: $250,000
Description: An arts service organization
providing management support services
and program services. Goal is to stimulate
artistic and cultural activities in the borough
of Queens.

Jamestown

Jamestown Area Arts Council
Municipal Building
Jamestown, NY 14701
Address Inquiries to: John Alpaugh,
   Chairman
Founded in: 1975

Kingston

Ulster County Council for the Arts
95 Maiden Lane
Kingston, NY 12401
Tel: 914-339-4330
Address Inquiries to: Helen Vukasin,
   Executive Director
Founded in: 1974
Annual Budget: $50,000

Loch Sheldrake

Sullivan County Council for the Arts
Review Committee
Loch Sheldrake, NY 12759
Tel: 914-434-5750
Address Inquiries to: Allan Dampman,
   President
Founded in: 1974
Member: NYSCA; ACA; ACUCAA; Sullivan
   County Community College; NYSCA;
Annual Budget: $50,000
Description: Closely associated with Sullivan
County Community College. In the summer
presents a six week 'mini-Chautauqua' of
lectures, dances, theatre, and concerts, both
professional and amateur. During the fall-
spring period it presents a series of five or
six professional performances and an equal
number of local or amateur performances.

Mahopach

Putnam Arts Council
Post Office Box 156
Mahopach, NY 10541
Tel: 914-628-3664
Address Inquiries to: Julia Rotta, Executive
   Director
Founded in: 1963
Annual Budget: $50,000

Mamaroneck

Mamaroneck Council on the Arts
169 Mount Pleasant Avenue
Mamaroneck, NY 10543
Tel: 914-698-7400
Address Inquiries to: Gloria Landes,
   Executive Director
Founded in: 1972
Annual Budget: $50,000

New Berlin

New Berlin Art Forum
Post Office Box 329
New Berlin, NY 13411
Tel: 607-847-9810; 607-847-8890
Address Inquiries to: Mary Ellis, Executive
   Director
Founded in: 1974
Member: The Alliance; Chenango County
   Council of the Arts;
Annual Budget: $10,000
Description: A presenting organization.

Newburgh

Greater Newburgh Arts Council
427 Grand Street
Newburgh, NY 12550
Tel: 914-562-9028
Address Inquiries to: N. Terry Holbert,
   Chairman
Founded in: 1969
Annual Budget: $10,000

New Rochelle

New Rochelle Council on the Arts
45 Wellington Avenue
New Rochelle, NY 10804
Tel: 914-632-9227

Address Inquiries to: Eleanor Wakin,
Executive Director
Founded in: 1976
Annual Budget: $10,000

New York

Advocates for the Arts
570 Seventh Avenue
New York, NY 10018
Tel: 212-354-6655
Member: ACA; NACAA; NEA;
Description: The New York office of the Washington D.C. service organization. See Washington D.C. entry.

Affiliate Artists
155 West 68th Street
New York, NY 10023
Tel: 212-874-6021
Member: ACA; NACAA; NEA;
Description: A professional service organization serving the not-for- profit sector of the performing arts.

Alliance of Resident Theatres, New York
325 Spring Street
New York, NY 10013
Tel: 212-989-5257
Address Inquiries to: Janes S. Moss,
Executive Director
Elizabeth Gardella, Director of Planning
and Development
Description: Originally the Off Off Broadway Theatre Association (OOBA), The Alliance of Resident Theatres New York, ART/NY, offers administrative advice, special services, student placements and internships. ART/NY should be considered the hub of Off Off Broadway Theatre, dedicated to encouraging the not-for-profit professional theatre as a significant component of New York's cultural and economic life.

American Council on the Arts
570 5th Avenue
New York, NY 10018
Tel: 212-354-6655
Address Inquiries to: Milton Rhodes,
President
William Keens, Executive Director
Founded in: 1960
Description: The ACA is involved in matters of arts advocacy, national policy issues, arts management and administration. Many publications and services are available.

Associated Actors and Artists of America
165 W. 46th Street
New York, NY 10036
Tel: 212-869-0358
Address Inquiries to: Frederick O'Neal,
President
Founded in: 1910
Description: An umbrella organization for jurisdicational disputes between the different theatrical unions.

Association of Theatre Artists
54 Nagle Avenue
New York, NY 10040
Tel: 212-569-6200

Member: NYSCA; ART/NY; TDF;

Business Committee for the Arts
1775 Broadway
New York, NY 10019
Tel: 212-664-0600
Address Inquiries to: Judith A. Jedlicka,
President
Founded in: 1966
Description: A national not for profit organization of business leaders committed to supporting the arts and encouraging new and increased support from the business community.

Chinese-American Arts Council
45 Canal Street
New York, NY 10002
Tel: 212-431-9740; 212-284-6083
Address Inquiries to: Alan Chow, Director
Olga Tong, Newsletter Editor
Founded in: 1975
Member: NYSCA; ACA; NEA; DCA;
Annual Budget: $75,000
Description: Serves as a booking agent of Asian-American performing artists and maintains an information center concerning artists listed. The council also produces 'total' Chinese theatre and offers demonstrations of Chinese theatre and Chinese Musical Instrument theatre. A newsletter and calander of events with profiles of artists and performances is available.

Dance Theater Workshop
219 West 19th Street
New York, NY 10011
Tel: 212-691-6500
Address Inquiries to: Robert Applegarth,
Associate Director
Founded in: 1965
Annual Budget: $650,000
Description: Founded in 1965 as a choreographers' cooperative, the Dance Theater has grown to be a membership organization providing production facilities and artist sponsorship programs as well as a broad spectrum of pre-production, promotional and technical serv ices to the community of independent dance artists in New York.

Department of Cultural Affairs
830 Fifth Avenue
New York, NY 10021
Tel: 212-360-8211
Address Inquiries to: Bess Myerson,
Commissioner
Founded in: 1962

Dramatists Guild
234 West 44th Street
New York, NY 10036
Tel: 212-398-9366
Address Inquiries to: David E. LeVine,
Executive Director
Peter Stone, President
Founded in: 1920
Description: The Dramatists Guild is a professional association of playwrights, composers and lyricists. For more that 50 years the Guild has protected their rights and im-

proved the conditions by which its members work. All theatre writers, produced or not, are encouraged to become members of the Guild which also publishes *The Dramatists Guild Quarterly.*

Educational Facilities Laboratories
850 Third Avenue
New York, NY 10022
Tel: 212-751-6214
Member: ACA; NACCA; NEA;

Federation for the Extension and
Development of the American Theatre
(FEDAPTT)
1500 Broadway
New York, NY 10036
Tel: 212-575-7660

The Foundation Center
777 Seventh Avenue
New York, NY 10106
Tel: 212-975-1120; 800-424-9836,
Publication
Description: The Foundation Center's free libraries contain the materials neccessary to investigate funding sources. Many services and publications are available to save time and aid s organizations and individuals who cannot visit one of the libraries or regional collections. An associate program is a fee service for those who require immediate and frequent access to Foundation information by toll free line.

Foundation for the Extension and
Development of the American Professional
Theatre (FEDAPT)
165 West 46th Street, Suite 310
New York, NY 10036
Tel: 212-869-9690
Address Inquiries to: Fred Vogel, Executive
Director
Jessica L. Andrews, Director Theatre
Division

Harlem Cultural Council
2349 Seventh Avenue
New York, NY 10030
Tel: 212-862-3000
Address Inquiries to: Geanie Faulkner,
Executive Director
Founded in: 1964
Annual Budget: $100,000

League of New York Theatres and
Producers
266 West 47th Street
New York, NY 10036
Tel: 212-764-1122
Address Inquiries to: Harvey Sabinson,
Executive Director
Richard Barr, President
Founded in: 1932
Description: The League serves over 250 Broadway Producers and Theatre Owners.

League of OffBroadway Theatres and
Producers
1540 Broadway, Suite 711
New York, NY 10036
Tel: 212-869-8282

Address Inquiries to: Paul Libin, President
Paul Berkowsky, Vice President 10.
Description: Off Broadway Theatre Owners
and Producers are members of this organization which aims to encourage Off Broadway productions in New York.

Lower Manhattan Cultural Council
32 Broadway
New York, NY 10004
Tel: 212-269-0320
Address Inquiries to: Frederick S. Taylor,
    Executive Director
Founded in: 1973
Annual Budget: $130,000

National Assembly of Community Arts
    Agencies
American Council for the Artss
570 Seventh Avenue
New York, NY 10018
Tel: 212-354-6655
Member: ACA; NACCA; NEA;

New York State Council on the Arts
80 Centre Street
New York, NY 10013
Tel: 212-488-2892
Founded in: 1960
Annual Budget: $39,000,000
Description: The New York State Council on
the Arts was the original State Council
founded in 1960. Because of New Yorks example there was an increase to 22 Councils
by 1966. Since the programs of NYSCA are
so vast, it is best to contact the Theatre Program of the Council directly.

Opportunity Resources for the Arts, (OR)
1501 Broadway
New York, NY 10036
Tel: 212-575-1688
Address Inquiries to: Freda Mindlin,
    Executive Director
    Linda Sweet, Director of Visual Arts
Description: Opportunity Resources for the
Arts helps arts organizations search for qualified administrative staffs. Administrators
may keep their resumes on file with OR for
a small fee for access by theatres across the
country.

Public Arts Council
25 Central Park West
New York, NY 10009
Tel: 212-586-7527
Address Inquiries to: Doris Fredman,
    Chairperson
Founded in: 1972
Annual Budget: $100,000

Theatre Communications Group (TCG)
355 Lexington Avenue
New York, NY 10017
Tel: 212-697-5230
Address Inquiries to: Peter Zeisler, Director
Terence Nemeth, Publications Director
Founded in: 1961
Description: Theatre Communications Group
is a national service organization for not for
profit professional theatre groups. Known
for many services and its publication *Theatre*

Communications, TCG offers job listings service, fellowships in performing arts management and advisory consultation services.

Theatre Development Fund
1501 Broadway
New York, NY 10036
Tel: 212-221-0013, General Office;
212-221-0885, Administrative Office
Address Inquiries to: Hugh Southern,
    Executive Director
Founded in: 1967
Description: Founded to invigorate the production of plays in commercial theatre, TDF
subsidizes low cost admissions to Broadway,
Off and Off Off Broadway productions
through its ticket voucher program to special groups such as students, seniors and union members. TDF now operates a TKTS
(tickets) h in Times Square, Bryant Park and
downtown Brooklyn where discount tickets
can be obtained by anyone with the time to
wait in the long and increasingly popular
lines.

Theatre Library Association
111 Amsterdam Avenue
New York, NY 10023
Tel: 212-870-1600

Niagara Falls

Niagara Council of the Arts
Box 937, Falls Station
Niagara Falls, NY 14303
Tel: 716-278-8881; 716-278-8147
Address Inquiries to: Jacquie Allen, Executive
    Director
Founded in: 1969
Member: NYSCA; ACA; Niagara
    Educational Foundation; NY Foundation;
Annual Budget: $225,000
Description: Fosters and promotes the arts in
Niagara County. For the past twelve years
the council has attempted to identify the cul-
tural needs of the community and develop
the artistic and financial resources to pro-
duce programs.

North Tonawanda

Tonawanda's Council on the Arts
Carnegie Cultural Center
240 Goundry Street
North Tonawanda, NY 14120
Tel: 716-694-4400
Address Inquiries to: Shirley Zerby, President
Founded in: 1966
Annual Budget: $10,000

Norwich

Chenango County Council on the Arts
47 South Broad Street
Norwich, NY 13815
Tel: 607-334-3286
Address Inquiries to: Earl Sincerbox,
    Chairman
Founded in: 1975

Olean

Olean Community Arts Council
Post Office Box 141
Olean, NY 14760
Tel: 716-373-2522
Address Inquiries to: Earl Hodges, Executive
    Director
Founded in: 1975
Annual Budget: $50,000

Oneonta

Oneonta Community Arts Center
Post Office Box 20
Oneonta, NY 13820
Tel: 607-433-2555
Address Inquiries to: Lee Tawny, Executive
    Director
Founded in: 1955
Annual Budget: $10,000

Upper Catskill Community Council of the
    Arts
Old Milne Library, Room 101A
State University
Oneonta, NY 13820
Tel: 607-432-2070
Address Inquiries to: Leonard Ryndes,
    Executive Director
Founded in: 1969
Annual Budget: $50,000

Oyster Bay

Cultural and Performing Arts Division
Department of Community Services
Town Hall-Audrey Avenue
Oyster Bay, NY 11771
Address Inquiries to: Lois Manning,
    Executive Director
Founded in: 1975
Annual Budget: $50,000

Penn Yan

Yates County Arts Council
200 Main Street
Penn Yan, NY 14527
Tel: 315-536-8439; 315-536-7318
Address Inquiries to: Barbara L. Burke,
    President
Founded in: 1975
Annual Budget: $3,000
Description: The organization was reorganized in 1981 since it became clear there is a
need for an active unit to serve as a resource;
cooperate with other organizations, business and industry for art promotion; promote workshops at all age levels and activate
marketing in arts, crafts and bookings. Also
involved with the three area school systems
and Kevka College. They are especially interested in tourism and art promotion.

Troy

Central New York Community Arts
Council
800 Park Avenue
Troy, NY 13501
Tel: 315-789-5039
Address Inquiries to: Phillipa Kennedy,
    Executive Director

Founded in: 1966
Annual Budget: $100,000

NORTH CAROLINA

Albermarie

Stanley County Arts Council
Post Office Box 909
Albermarie, NC 28001
Tel: 704-982-8116
Address Inquiries to: Patricia B. Hartley,
    Executive Director
Founded in: 1974
Annual Budget: $50,000

Ashville

Arts Councils of Western North Carolina
Post Office Box 507
Ashville, NC 28802
Tel: 704-258-0710
Address Inquiries to: Deborah Austin,
    Administrator
Founded in: 1976
Member: Association of North Carolina
    Arts Councils; American Council For the
    Arts;
Annual Budget: $80,000
Description: An umbrella service organization
for arts groups and artists in Buncombe
County.

Civic Arts Council
8 Beaver Point Drive
Ashville, NC 28804
Tel: 704-667-6967
Address Inquiries to: Dr. James P. Parker
Founded in: 1953
Annual Budget: $50,000

Belmont

Gatson Fine Arts Council
Post Office Box 565
Belmont, NC 28012
Tel: 704-825-5146
Address Inquiries to: Mrs. W. W. Styers,
    President
Annual Budget: $15,000

Candor

Montgomery County Arts Council
Post Office Box 206
Candor, NC 27229
Tel: 919-974-4774
Address Inquiries to: Mrs. Bennie Hollers,
    President
Founded in: 1971
Annual Budget: $10,000

Charlotte

Arts and Science Council
110 East Seventh Street
Charlotte, NC 28202
Tel: 704-372-9664
Address Inquiries to: Halsey M. North,
    Executive Director
Founded in: 1959
Annual Budget: $100,000

Clinton

Sampson Arts Council
Post Office Box 841
Clinton, NC 28328
Tel: 919-592-7184
Address Inquiries to: Mossette Butler,
    President
Founded in: 1973
Annual Budget: $50,000

Currituck

Currituck County Arts Council
Post Office Box 111
Currituck, NC 27929
Tel: 919-232-2311
Address Inquiries to: Barbara Snowden,
    President
Founded in: 1975
Annual Budget: $10,000

Danbury

Stokes County Arts Council
Post Office Box 56
Danbury, NC 27106
Tel: 919-593-8159
Address Inquiries to: Mike Killam, Executive
    Director
Founded in: 1974
Annual Budget: $50,000

Dunn

Harnett County Arts Council
1011 North Orange Avenue
Dunn, NC 28334
Tel: 919-892-8344
Address Inquiries to: Claudine Whitaker,
    President
Founded in: 1975

Durham

Durham Arts Council
810 West Proctor Street
Durham, NC 27707
Tel: 919-682-5519
Address Inquiries to: James McIntyre,
    Executive Director
Founded in: 1954
Annual Budget: $100,000

Edenton

Chowan Arts Council
108 South Granville Street
Edenton, NC 27932
Tel: 919-482-4112
Address Inquiries to: Louise Darby, Chairman
Founded in: 1970
Annual Budget: $10,000

Elizabethtown

SE North Carolina Arts Council
Route 2
Post Office Box 211
Elizabethtown, NC 28337
Tel: 919-588-4898
Address Inquiries to: Ann Hood, Executive
    Director
Founded in: 1966
Annual Budget: $10,000

Fayetteville

Arts Council of Fayetteville
Post Office Box 318
Fayetteville, NC 28302
Tel: 919-323-1776
Address Inquiries to: Carolyn Carlson,
    Executive Director
Founded in: 1974
Annual Budget: $100,000

Forest City

Performing Arts Guild
Post Office Box 44
Forest City, NC 28043
Tel: 704-245-8676
Address Inquiries to: Matthew McEnnerney,
    Executive Director
Founded in: 1971
Annual Budget: $100,000

Franklin

Macon County Cultural Arts Council
Post Office Box 726
Franklin, NC 28734
Tel: 704-524-7683
Address Inquiries to: Jinny Jones, Executive
    Director
Founded in: 1975
Description: The Council's primary purpose is
to encourage active, county-wide participa-
tion in, and appreciation of, the arts. This is
achieved by promoting and coordinating
programs representing all facets of the arts:
music, theatre, dance, literary and visual.

Graham

Alamance County Arts Council
135 West Elm Street
Graham, NC 27253
Tel: 919-226-4495; 919-226-4496
Address Inquiries to: Alex Hutchins,
    Executive Director
Founded in: 1956
Member: North Carolina Association of
    Arts Councils; National Assembly of
    Community Arts Agencies; American
    Council for the Arts;
Annual Budget: $50,000
Description: Promotes the arts within the
county through eight major organizations
which include The Alamance Childrens Theater and The Sword of Peace, which produces outdoor dramas. Each spring they
have a ten day festival of the arts which incor-
porates all facets of the arts. They also work
with other agencies within the county ot co-
sponsor as many activities as possible each
year. They arrange for artists to donate their
time and work and teach their art form in the
school system.

Greensboro

North Carolina Association of Arts
Councils
712 Summit Avenue
Greensboro, NC 27405
Tel: 919-274-2436
Description: A state arts council.

Hayesville

Clay County Historical and Arts Council
Post Office Box 5
Hayesville, NC 28904
Tel: 404-896-2244
Address Inquiries to: Jane Moore, President
Founded in: 1974
Annual Budget: $10,000

Hickory

Hickory Arts Council
Post Office Box 1004
Hickory, NC 28601
Tel: 704-328-1741
Address Inquiries to: Dr. Robin Gatwood,
President
Founded in: 1959
Annual Budget: $10,000

High Point

High Point Arts Council
220 East Commerce Street
High Point, NC 27260
Tel: 919-882-0710; 919-882-9721
Address Inquiries to: Jon K. Gossett,
Executive Director
Founded in: 1963
Annual Budget: $90,000

Kenansville

Duplin County Arts Council
Post Office Box 36
Kenansville, NC 28349
Tel: 919-296-1341
Address Inquiries to: Regina Whaley,
Executive Director
Founded in: 1975
Annual Budget: $50,000

Kinston

Community Council for the Arts
Post Office Box 3554
Kinston, NC 28501
Tel: 919-527-2517
Address Inquiries to: S. Cone, Executive
Director
Founded in: 1965
Member: North Carolina Association of
Arts Councils; National Association of
Community Arts Agencies;
Annual Budget: $120,000

Manteo

Sea and Sound Arts Council
Post Office Box 1029
Manteo, NC 27954
Address Inquiries to: John Riddick, President
Founded in: 1975
Member: North Carolina Association of
Arts Councils;
Annual Budget: $10,000

Mar Hills

Madison County Arts Council
Route 3, California Creek Road
Mar Hills, NC 28754
Tel: 704-689-4168
Address Inquiries to: Dr. Grover L. Angel,

President
Founded in: 1976

Mocksville

Davie County Arts Council
Post Office Box 744
Mocksville, NC 27028
Tel: 704-634-2188
Address Inquiries to: Ervin Riley, President
Founded in: 1975
Annual Budget: $10,000

Morganton

Burke Arts Council
115 East Meeting Street
Morganton, NC 28655
Tel: 704-433-7282
Address Inquiries to: June J. Hollingsworth,
Executive Director
Karen Barnes, Associate Director
Founded in: 1974
Member: North Carolina Association of
Arts Councils;
Annual Budget: $20,000

Mount Airy

Surry Arts Council
Post Office Box 141
Mount Airy, NC 27030
Tel: 919-786-7998
Address Inquiries to: Don Nance, Director
Founded in: 1968
Annual Budget: $10,000

New Bern

Craven Community Arts Council
Post Office Box 596
New Bern, NC 28560
Tel: 919-638-2577; 919-637-4064
Address Inquiries to: Mrs. Stevie Zaytoun,
President
Mrs. Georgia Carmichael, Executive
Director
Founded in: 1974
Member: North Carolina Association of
Arts Councils;
Annual Budget: $47,000

Pittsboro

Pittsboro Arts Advisory Committee
Post Office Box 753
Pittsboro, NC 27312
Tel: 919-542-4642
Address Inquiries to: Billie Shambley,
Executive Director
Founded in: 1975
Annual Budget: $5,000

Raleigh

North Carolina Department of Cultural
Resourses
Review Committee
Raleigh, NC 27611
Tel: 919-733-7897

Rocky Mount

Chamber of Commerce Arts Council
Post Office Box 392
Rocky Mount, NC 27801
Tel: 910-442-5111
Address Inquiries to: Jack Matkin, President
Founded in: 1971
Annual Budget: $10,000

Shelby

Cleveland County Arts Council
First National Bank, Box 168
Shelby, NC 28150
Tel: 704-482-3831
Address Inquiries to: J.G. Creech, Chairman
Founded in: 1975

Smithfield

Johnston County Arts Council
Post Office Box 1298
Smithfield, NC 27577
Tel: 919-934-7494
Address Inquiries to: Richard Williams,
President
Founded in: 1970
Annual Budget: $10,000

Soul City

Soul City Cultural Arts and Historical
Society
Post Office Box 38
Soul City, NC 27553
Tel: 919-456-3111
Address Inquiries to: Janice Crump, Cultural
Arts Planner
Founded in: 1974
Annual Budget: $10,000

Spruce Pine

Toe River Arts Council
408 Altpass Road
Spruce Pine, NC 28777
Tel: 704-765-2652
Address Inquiries to: Susan Larson, Director
Founded in: 1976
Member: Alliance for Arts Education; North
Carolina Association of Arts Councils;
National Assembly of Community Arts
Agencies;
Annual Budget: $43,000

Statesville

Iredell Arts Council
Post Office Box 134
Statesville, NC 28677
Tel: 704-873-6100; 704-873-6400
Address Inquiries to: Norma Morrison,
President
Founded in: 1975
Member: North Carolina Arts Council;
North Carolina Association of Arts
Councils;
Annual Budget: $25,000

Sylva

Jackson County Arts Council
43 Falls Circle
Sylva, NC 28779
Tel: 704-586-6166
Address Inquiries to: Linda Kotila, President
Founded in: 1975

Trenton

Jones County Arts Council
Post Office Box 69
Trenton, NC 28585
Tel: 919-448-3131
Address Inquiries to: Rena Henderson,
   President
Founded in: 1975
Annual Budget: $10,000

Washington

Beaufort County Arts Council
Post Office Box 634
Washington, NC 27889
Tel: 919-946-2504
Address Inquiries to: Rose Lewis, Director
Founded in: 1971
Member: North Carolina Association of
   Arts Councils; National Assembly of
   Community Arts Agencies;
Annual Budget: $45,000
Description: Approximately one-half of their
budget is generated through classes, mem-
berships, and special events.

Williamston

Martin County Arts Council
Post Office Box 1134
Williamston, NC 27892
Tel: 919-792-1575; 919-792-4361
Address Inquiries to: Alton Hopewell,
   Chairman
Founded in: 1975
Member: North Carolina Association of
   Arts Councils;
Annual Budget: $10,000
Description: Sponsors a performance series
and plans and manages a spring arts festival
consisting of a day which includes perfor-
mances in an amphitheatre. They also spon-
sor classes and support the local community
theatre group.

Wilson

Arts Council of Wilson
205 Gray Street
Wilson, NC 27893
Tel: 919-291-4329
Address Inquiries to: Vicky E. Bell, Director
Founded in: 1967
Annual Budget: $50,000

Yadkinville

Yadkin Arts Council
Route 3, Box 142
Yadkinville, NC 27055
Tel: 919-679-2941
Address Inquiries to: William Casstevens,
   Executive Director
Founded in: 1975

Annual Budget: $10,000

NORTH DAKOTA

Fargo

Lake Agassiz Arts Council
Post Office Box 742
Fargo, ND 58107
Tel: 701-237-6133
Address Inquiries to: Linda Short, Office
   Manager
Founded in: 1970
Member: NACA;
Annual Budget: $80,000
Description: Provides advocacy services, Unit-
ed Arts fund drive, hotline for art events,
and technical assistance. Publishes monthly
arts activity calendar.

State Council on the Arts and Humanities
North Dakota State University
Fargo, ND 58102
Tel: 701-237-7143

OHIO

Akron

International Society of Performing Arts
Administrators
c/o Clinton E. Nortton, President
Thomas Performing Arts Hall
University of Akron
Akron, OH 44325
Tel: 216-375-7595
Address Inquiries to: Clinton E. Norton,
   President
Member: ACA; NACCA; NEA;

Bryan

Bryan Fine Arts Council
Post Office Box 525
Bryan, OH 43506
Tel: 419-636-1144
Address Inquiries to: Beverly Lindsay,
   President
Founded in: 1973
Annual Budget: $10,000

Chillicothe

Scioto Society
Post Office Box 73
Chillicothe, OH 45601
Tel: 614-775-4100
Address Inquiries to: W.L. Mundell, President
   Marion Waggoner, Vice President
Founded in: 1970
Member: NETC; STC; OTA; NTBA; ABA;
   TIA;
Annual Budget: $650,000
Description: Concerned with the cultural, his-
torical, educational and economic develop-
ment of a tri-county area along the Scioto
River Valley of Southern Ohio. Affiliate Cor-
porations are: Tecumseh Productions, In-
corporated, The Scioto Valley Arts Council,
The Scioto Society Convention and Visitors'
Bureau.

Cleveland

Buckeye Woodland Community Service
10613 Lamontier
Cleveland, OH 44104
Tel: 216-368-1070
Address Inquiries to: Thomas Gannon,
   Executive Director
Founded in: 1975
Annual Budget: $100,000

Foundation Center Field Office
739 National City Bank Building
Cleveland, OH 44114
Tel: 216-861-1933; 800-424-9836,
   Publications
Address Inquiries to: Jeanne Bohlen, Director
   Description: A national service organization
providing factual information on philan-
thropic giving with a nationwide network of
reference libraries to aid in identifying foundation programs that correspond with your
needs.

Great Lakes Arts Alliance
11424 Bellflower
Cleveland, OH 44106
Tel: 216-229-1098
Description: Arts Councils for the states of Il-
linois, Michigan and Ohio.

Columbus

Greater Columbus Arts Council
33 North Third Street
Columbus, OH 43215
Tel: 614-234-2606
Address Inquiries to: Tim Sublette, Executive
   Director
Founded in: 1970
Annual Budget: $100,000

Ohio State Arts Council
50 West Broad Street
Columbus, OH 43215
Tel: 614-466-2613

Elyria

Lorain County Arts Council
140 Middle Avenue
Elyria, OH 44035
Tel: 216-323-7120
Address Inquiries to: Constance Mateer,
   Executive Director
Founded in: 1967
Annual Budget: $50,000

Fayette

Fayette Community Fine Arts Council
Post Office Box 355
Fayette, OH 43521
Tel: 419-237-2683
Address Inquiries to: Tom Spiess,
   Co-Chairman
Founded in: 1973
Annual Budget: $10,000

Jackson

Jackson County Arts Council
200 Grandview
Jackson, OH 45640
Address Inquiries to: Lily Goldstayn, Director

Founded in: 1975
Annual Budget: $10,000

Lima

Council For the Arts of Greater Lima
Post Office Box 1124, Memorial Hall
Lima, OH 45802-1124
Tel: 419-225-9165
Address Inquiries to: Brian E. Tingle,
    Executive Director
Founded in: 1966
Member: ACA; ACUCAA; NACAA;
    ORACLE; OCCA;
Annual Budget: $90,000
Description: A community Arts Council with
twenty three member organizations serving
Lima, Allen County and the contiguos four
counties. Provides services for members
and programming such as Children's
Theatre Season-touring representative
companies, artists in schools and communi-
ty, a major outdoor summer performing and
visual arts and crafts festival, concerts in the
parks and dance.

Lithopolis

Lithopolis Area Fine Arts Association
Post Office Box 187
Lithopolis, OH 43136
Tel: 614-837-4765
Address Inquiries to: Thomas E. Rehl,
    Program Director
Founded in: 1973
Member: AOCAA; ORACLE;
Annual Budget: $12,000
Description: Provides Cultural Enrichment for
the community through the sponsorship of
numerous vocal, instrumental and dramatic
programs.

Marietta

Marietta Arts Council
c/o WMOA Radio, Box 708
Marietta, OH 45750
Tel: 614-373-1490
Address Inquiries to: Ray H. Rosenblum,
    President
Founded in: 1971

Marion

Greater Marion Arts Council
Post Office Box 448
Marion, OH 43302
Tel: 614-387-2732
Address Inquiries to: Larry Dussault,
    President
Founded in: 1966
Annual Budget: $10,000

Middleton

Arts in Middleton
Post Office Box 441
Middleton, OH 45042
Address Inquiries to: Jerome D. Judd,
    President
Founded in: 1965

Parma

Parma Area Fine Arts Council
7441 West Ridgewood Drive
Parma, OH 44129
Tel: 216-888-4514
Address Inquiries to: Thomas P. Clark,
    President
Founded in: 1962
Annual Budget: $50,000

Piqua

Piqua Fine Arts Foundation
400 North Wayne Street
Piqua, OH 45356
Tel: 513-773-4198
Address Inquiries to: Britton B. Wood,
    Chairman
Founded in: 1970
Annual Budget: $10,000

Sandusky

North Central Ohio Arts Council
Post Office Box 332
Sandusky, OH 44870-0002
Tel: 419-627-8791
Address Inquiries to: Ann M. Johnson,
    Executive Director
Founded in: 1975
Member: National Association of
    Community Arts Agencies; Alliance of
    Ohio Community Arts Agencies; Ohio
    Regional Association of Concert and
    Lecturee Enterprises;
Annual Budget: $100,000
Description: Purpose is to broaden cultural life
in Erie, Huron and Ottawa counties in all
disciplines. It coordinates programs, does
research in the arts and tries to increase
public awareness of art programs.

Springfield

Springfield Arts Council
Post Office Box 745
Springfield, OH 45501
Tel: 513-324-2712
Address Inquiries to: J. Chris Moore,
    Executive Director
    Lisa Dichersm, Assistant Director
Founded in: 1967
Member: OTA; ACUCAA;
Annual Budget: $140,000
Description: An outdoor summer festival, free
to the general public, incorporating a variety
of performing arts. Their artist series is for
visiting artists/groups on tour and usually
includes a lecturer, a ballet, a holiday pro-
gram, something musical and a drama. They
also have artist residencies through the
school year.

OKLAHOMA

Oklahoma City

Oklahoma Arts and Humanities Council
Jim Thorpe Building
Oklahoma City, OK 73105
Tel: 405-521-2931

OREGON

Coos Bay

Coos Art Museum
515 Market Street
Coos Bay, OR 97420
Tel: 503-267-3901
Address Inquiries to: Maggie Karl, Director

Coquille

Coquille Valley Art Association
587 North Elliot
Coquille, OR 97423
Tel: 503-396-3968
Address Inquiries to: Viki Smith

Depoe Bay

Oregon Coast Council for the Arts
Post Office Box 67
Depoe Bay, OR 97341
Tel: 503-265-8823
Address Inquiries to: Jeff Ouderkirk

Enterprise

Eastern Oregon Arts Council
Route 1, Post Office Box 219
Enterprise, OR 97828
Tel: 503-426-3393
Address Inquiries to: Eva Slinker, President

Eugene

Lane Regional Arts Council
795 Williamette Street
Room 416
Eugene, OR 97401
Tel: 503-485-2278
Address Inquiries to: Karen Johnson,
    Executive Director
Founded in: 1976
Member: NACAA; OAA; OAC; City of
    Eugene;
Annual Budget: $75,000
Description: A not-for-profit community ser-
vice organization providing referral infor-
mation and technical assistance to profes-
sional artists. Coordinates county wide arts
in education program, joint services for
member arts organizations and promotes
arts organizations throughout the state.

Maude Kerns Art Center
1910 15th Avenue, East
Eugene, OR 97403
Tel: 503-345-1571
Address Inquiries to: Leslie Copland, Director
Founded in: 1951
Member: Lane Regional Arts Council; OAA;
Annual Budget: $60,000
Description: A private not-for-profit art orga-
nization sponsoring art classes, exhibition
galleries, gifts shops, rental sales galleries,
special festivals and performing arts events.

Forest Grove

Valley Art Association
2120 Main Street
Forest Grove, OR 97110
Tel: 503-357-3703
Address Inquiries to: Lois Chambers

Klamath

Klamath Arts Association
Post Office Box 995
Klamath, OR 97601
Tel: 503-884-6157
Address Inquiries to: Beth Grigg, Secretary

Klamath Arts Council
Post Office Box 1703
Klamath, OR 97601
Tel: 503-882-1503
Address Inquiries to: Lynn Schrader,
President

La Pine

Central Oregon Arts Association
Post Office Box 175
La Pine, OR 97739
Tel: 503-536-2770
Address Inquiries to: Mary Gordon

Madras

Central Oregon Arts Association
456 Fifth
Madras, OR 97741
Address Inquiries to: Barbara Shadduck

Monmouth

Monmouth-Independence Community Art
Association
Post Office Box 114
Monmouth, OR 97361
Tel: 503-838-2834
Address Inquiries to: Ruth Culbertson

Prineville

Central Oregon Arts Society
Route 1, Box 1207
Prineville, OR 97754
Address Inquiries to: Cora Houston

Roseburg

Roseburg Art Association
17 Royal Oaks
Roseburg, OR 97470
Tel: 503-673-5871
Address Inquiries to: Marilyn Woodrich

Salem

Oregon Arts Commission
316 Oregon Building, 494 State Street
Salem, OR 97301
Tel: 503-378-3625

Roberts Arts Center
3626 River Road
Salem, OR 97303
Tel: 503-378-9060
Address Inquiries to: Bill Rowe

Salem Arts Commission
555 Liberty Street SE
Salem, OR 97301
Tel: 503-588-6261; 503-588-6294
Address Inquiries to: Paul Koch, Chair
Founded in: 1976
Annual Budget: $750
Description: Advisory Commission to the
Salem City Council on matters related to the
arts. A not-for-profit organization.

The Dalles

Dalles Art Association
Post Office Box 882
The Dalles, OR 97058
Tel: 503-296-4759
Address Inquiries to: Mary Hopkins, Director

PENNSYLVANIA

Allentown

Valley Arts Council
Post Office Box 4504
Allentown, PA 18105
Tel: 215-776-0204
Address Inquiries to: Janet Goloub, Executive
Director
Founded in: 1973
Annual Budget: $20,000
Description: An umbrella and advocacy orga-
nization for performing, literary and visual
arts promoting art and artists of the Lehigh
Valley.

Altonna

Blair County Arts Foundation
1208 12th Avenue
Altonna, PA 16601
Tel: 814-944-9434
Address Inquiries to: Eleanor Steckman,
Executive Secretary
Founded in: 1960
Annual Budget: $100,000

Ambler

Rising Sun Cultural Arts Program
Post Office Box 182
Tennis and Hendricks
Ambler, PA 19002
Tel: 215-646-2015
Address Inquiries to: Barbara Freebody,
Executive Director
Founded in: 1972
Annual Budget: $100,000

Avoca

NE Pennsylvania Arts Alliance
Post Office Box 777
Avoca, PA 18641
Tel: 717-655-5581
Address Inquiries to: Howard Grossman,
Executive Director
Founded in: 1975
Annual Budget: $10,000

Bethlehem

Bethlehem Fine Arts Commission
c/o City Hall
10 E Church Street
Bethlehem, PA 18018
Tel: 215-865-7000
Founded in: 1963
Annual Budget: $50,000

Butler

Butler County Music and Arts Association
Post Office Box 504
Butler, PA 16001
Address Inquiries to: Jay Upperman,
President
Founded in: 1963
Description: Sponsors music and arts festivals
during the third weekend in July.

Carlisle

Mid-Susquehanna Arts in Education
Council
54 Parker Street
Carlisle, PA 17013
Tel: 717-783-2554
Address Inquiries to: Janet Figler, Executive
Director

Corry

Corry Area Fine Arts Council
209 North Center Street
Corry, PA 16406
Address Inquiries to: Ann Gould, President
Founded in: 1972
Annual Budget: $10,000

Doylestown

Bucks County Council on the Arts
Room 315, Building G
Neshaminy Manor Center
Doylestown, PA 18901
Tel: 215-343-2800
Address Inquiries to: Anita Subers, Executive
Director
Founded in: 1974

Erie

Arts Council of Erie
801 French Street
Erie, PA 16501
Tel: 814-452-3427
Address Inquiries to: Gregory G. Gibson,
Executive Director
Founded in: 1960
Annual Budget: $50,000

Harrisburg

Greater Harrisburg Arts Council
114 Walnut Street
Harrisburg, PA 17101
Tel: 717-234-5454
Address Inquiries to: Phyllis Moffett,
Chairman
Founded in: 1968
Annual Budget: $100,000

Pennsylvania Council on the Arts
2001 North Front Street
Harrisburg, PA 17102
Tel: 717-783-8466

Hazelton

Greater Hazelton Fine Arts Council
Mezzanine-Northeastern Building
Hazelton, PA 18201
Tel: 717-455-7555; 717-459-2975
Address Inquiries to: President
Founded in: 1964

Member: CAP;
Annual Budget: $10,000

Honesdale

Wayne County Creative Arts Council
843 Main Street
Honesdale, PA 18431
Tel: 717-253-3080
Address Inquiries to: Arthur Fasshauer,
  President
Founded in: 1973
Annual Budget: $10,000

Huntingdon

Greater Huntingdon Fine Arts Council
Post Office Box 216
Huntingdon, PA 16652
Tel: 717-253-3080
Address Inquiries to: Lynn Streightoff
Founded in: 1972
Annual Budget: $10,000

Indiana

Indiana Arts Council
915 School Street
Indiana, PA 15701
Tel: 412-687-2397
Address Inquiries to: J. Bent

Johnstown

Johnstown Arts Council
Post Office Box 402
Johnstown, PA 15907
Tel: 814-536-1333
Address Inquiries to: Maryanne Larison

King of Prussia

Upper Merion Cultural Center
700 Moore Road
King of Prussia, PA 19406
Tel: 215-337-1393
Address Inquiries to: Constance Focht,
  President
Founded in: 1961
Member: EPACA;

Lebanon

Lebanon Valley Council on the Arts
Post Office Box 786
Lebanon, PA 17042
Address Inquiries to: Mrs. Russell C. Hatz

Levittown

Middletown Township Arts Commission
Middletown Township Building
Route 413
Levittown, PA 19058

Lewisburg

Lewisburg Council on the Arts
Post Office Box 418
Lewisburg, PA 17837
Address Inquiries to: Barbara Dugan

Lewiston

Mifflin-Juniata Arts Festival Council
542 Electric Avenue
Lewiston, PA 17044
Address Inquiries to: Carol Genc

Meadville

Meadville Council on Arts
Post Office Box 337
Meadville, PA 16335
Tel: 814-336-5051
Address Inquiries to: Kay E. Kleeman,
  Executive Director
Founded in: 1975
Annual Budget: $20,000
Description: Operates a community arts cen-
ter with programs in art, crafts, dance and
theatre and is a clearinghouse for arts infor-
mation.

Mercer

Mercer Chamber of Commerce
R.D. 6, Box 6765
Mercer, PA 16137
Tel: 412-748-3532; 412-662-3980
Address Inquiries to: Adelaine Courtney,
  Chairperson;
Founded in: 1950
Member: Pennsylvania Chamber of
  Commerce;
Annual Budget: $9,085

Montrose

Susquehanna County Arts Council
75 Church Street
Montrose, PA 18801
Tel: 717-278-3950
Founded in: 1976

Philadelphia

Chinese Cultural and Community Center
125 North Tenth Street
Philadelphia, PA 19107
Tel: 215-NA3-6767
Address Inquiries to: T.T. Chang, President,
  Board of Trustees
  Barbara Hussong, Acting Executive
  Director
Founded in: 1955
Description: Offers cultural and social service
programs to the Chinese community, tour-
ists and non-Chinese residents of the Dela-
ware Valley.

Pittsburgh

Arts and Crafts Center of Pittsburgh
Fifth and Shady Avenue
Pittsburgh, PA 15232
Tel: 412-361-0873
Address Inquiries to: Audrey Bethel,
  Executive Director
Founded in: 1944
Annual Budget: $100,000

Reading

Berks County Arts Council
Post Office Box 854
Reading, PA 19603
Tel: 215-755-2104
Address Inquiries to: Carolyn Ramsey,
  President
Founded in: 1971
Annual Budget: $10,000
Description: Sponsors five outdoor arts and

crafts shows a year in conjunction with
other programs and different locations in
Berks County.

Sharon

Mayor's Committee on the Arts
Redevelopment Authority
10 Vine Street
Sharon, PA 16146
Address Inquiries to: John J. Higgins,
  Chairman
Founded in: 1972
Annual Budget: $10,000

State College

Art Alliance of Central Pennsylvania
Post Office Box 493
State College, PA 16801
Address Inquiries to: Delores Cooper

Stroudsburg

Monroe County Arts Council
County Courthouse
Monroe Street
Stroudsburg, PA 18360
Tel: 717-992-5157
Address Inquiries to: Mr. Tom Breslauer,
  President
Founded in: 1975
Annual Budget: $3,500
Description: An organization of individual
members and groups in the county who are
interested in and related to the arts.

Susquehanna

Mayor's Council on the Arts
Borough Building, Exchange Street
Susquehanna, PA 18847
Tel: 717-853-4625
Address Inquiries to: Jeanne Rodriguez,
  Executive Director
Founded in: 1974
Annual Budget: $10,000

Wayne

Wayne Art Center
413 Maplewood Avenue
Wayne, PA 19087
Tel: 215-688-3553
Address Inquiries to: Ginna Clark, President
Founded in: 1930
Annual Budget: $50,000

Wellsboro

Tioga County Arts Council
37 Pearl Street
Wellsboro, PA 16901
Tel: 717-724-1708
Address Inquiries to: Mary Keene

York

Mayor's Office Arts Program of York
50 West King Street
York, PA 17405
Tel: 717-843-8841
Address Inquiries to: Ann Marden, Executive
  Director
Founded in: 1974
Annual Budget: $10,000

PUERTO RICO

San Juan

Instituto de Cultura Puertorriquena
Apartado Postal 4184
San Juan, PR 00905

RHODE ISLAND

Lincoln

Lincoln Council on the Arts
Post Office Box 213
Lincoln, RI 02865
Tel: 401-725-4990
Address Inquiries to: Carol Beagan, President
Founded in: 1969
Annual Budget: $10,000

Providence

Assembly of Community Arts Councils
Rhode Island Council on the Arts
334 Westminster Mall
Providence, RI 02903
Tel: 401-277-3880
Description: A state arts council.

Rhode Island State Council on the Arts
344 Westminster Mall
Providence, RI 401 277 3880

United Arts Rhode Island
45 Arcade Building
Providence, RI 02903
Tel: 401-351-2451
Address Inquiries to: Jane Phelps, Executive
  Director
Founded in: 1962
Annual Budget: $100,000

Westerly

The Center for the Arts
119 High Street
Westerly, RI 02891
Tel: 401-596-2854
Address Inquiries to: Jeffrey James, Director
Founded in: 1974
Member: ACA; ASOL; TCG;
Annual Budget: $240,000

SOUTH CAROLINA

Abbeville

Abbeville Arts Commission
Post Office Box 852
Abbeville, SC 29620
Tel: 803-459-2157
Founded in: 1971

Anderson

Anderson County Arts Council
405 North Main Street
Anderson, SC 29621
Tel: 803-224-8811
Address Inquiries to: Sue Parks, Executive
  Director
Founded in: 1973
Annual Budget: $50,000

Bennettsville

Marlboro Area Arts Council
927 East Main Street
Bennettsville, SC 29512
Tel: 803-479-2192
Address Inquiries to: Lucy McIntire,
  Executive Director
Founded in: 1970
Annual Budget: $50,000

Columbia

Assembly of Community Arts Agencies
South Carolina Arts Commission
829 Richland Street
Columbia, SC 29201
Tel: 803-758-3442
Address Inquiries to: James H. Williams,
  President
Description: A state arts council.

South Carolina Arts Commission
829 Richland Street
Columbia, SC 29201
Tel: 803-339-6646

Easley

Easley Arts Council
Post Office Box 841
Easley, SC 29640
Tel: 802-859-5351
Address Inquiries to: Mason Garrett
Founded in: 1973

Greenville

Metropolitan Arts Council
301 College Street
Greenville, SC 29601
Tel: 803-232-2402
Address Inquiries to: Bobbi Wheless,
  Executive Director
Founded in: 1973
Annual Budget: $50,000

Greenwood

Greenwood Council of the Arts
210 West Cambridge Avenue
Greenwood, SC 29646
Tel: 803-223-2546
Address Inquiries to: Dr. Jane Bolen,
  Executive Director
Founded in: 1975
Annual Budget: $10,000

Newberry

Newberry Arts Council
1508 College Street
Newberry, SC 29108
Tel: 803-276-5012
Address Inquiries to: William Canine,
  Chairman
Founded in: 1975
Annual Budget: $10,000

Spartanburg

Arts Council of Spartanburg County
385 South Spring Street
Spartanburg, SC 29301
Tel: 803-583-2776
Address Inquiries to: Georgia K. Allen,

Executive Director
Founded in: 1968
Annual Budget: $100,000

Walhalla

Oconee County Arts Commission
Post Office Box 217
Walhalla, SC 29691
Tel: 803-638-5049
Address Inquiries to: Elva Brown, Executive
  Director
Founded in: 1966
Annual Budget: $12,000,000

SOUTH DAKOTA

Aberdeen

Aberdeen Arts Council
1112 South Washington
Aberdeen, SD 57401
Tel: 605-662-2350
Address Inquiries to: Beth Wray, President
Founded in: 1963
Annual Budget: $50,000

Chamberlain

Missouri Valley Arts Council
Post Office Box 549
Chamberlain, SD 57325
Tel: 605-734-5871; 605-734-6530
Address Inquiries to: David Larson, President
Founded in: 1974
Annual Budget: $10,000

Eagle Butte

Sioux Nation Arts Council
Post Office Box 73
Eagle Butte, SD 57625
Tel: 605-964-2811
Address Inquiries to: Sidney J. Keith, Head
  Chief
Founded in: 1972
Annual Budget: $10,000

Faulkton

Faulkton Area Arts Council
Post Office Box 70
Faulkton, SD 57538
Tel: 605-598-4187
Address Inquiries to: Linda Bartholomew,
  Executive Director
Founded in: 1975
Annual Budget: $10,000

Hot Springs

Hot Springs Arts Council
505 North River
Hot Springs, SD 57747
Tel: 605-745-6696; 605-745-4225
Address Inquiries to: Beulah Donnell, Chief
  Administrator and Treasurer
Founded in: 1975
Annual Budget: $10,000
Description: Sponsors the Main Street Arts
and Crafts Festival. Operates the art center
which includes an art gallery and an auditori-
um for rent. The Arts Council Players have

presented a weekly melodrama the past two summers as well as other plays.

Huron

Huron Area Arts Council
1742 McClellan Drive, SW
Huron, SD 57350
Tel: 605-352-8651
Address Inquiries to: G. Hoffman, President
Founded in: 1974
Annual Budget: $10,000

Marion

Freeman Area Arts Council
Route 2
Marion, SD 57043
Tel: 605-648-3474
Address Inquiries to: Phyllis Schrag, President
Founded in: 1975
Annual Budget: $10,000

Pierre

Short Grass Arts Council
Post Office Box 757
Pierre, SD 57501
Tel: 605-224-7402
Address Inquiries to: Polly Nelson, President
Founded in: 1974
Annual Budget: $10,000

Rapid City

Rapid City Fine Arts Council
713 Seventh Street
Rapid City, SD 57701
Tel: 605-394-4101; 605-394-4102
Address Inquiries to: Ruth Brennan, Executive Director
Founded in: 1968
Member: American Council for the Arts; National Assembly of Community Arts Agencies; Foundation for the Arts in South Dakota; S.D. Museum Association; Association of Art Museums;
Annual Budget: $50,000

Sioux Falls

Sioux Empire Arts Council
1817 South Sherman
Sioux Falls, SD 57105
Tel: 605-336-2850
Address Inquiries to: Roy Loftesness, President
Founded in: 1969
Annual Budget: $2,000

South Dakota Arts Council
108 West 11th Street
Souix Falls, SD 57102
Tel: 605-339-6646

Watertown

Watertown Area Arts Council
912 North Broadway
Watertown, SD 57201
Tel: 605-886-5542
Address Inquiries to: Marion Tangren, Chairman

Florence Bruhn
Founded in: 1968
Annual Budget: $10,000
Description: Aims to enhance the cultural life of the community. It co-sponsors art, music and drama workshops in the school and coordinate a weekend production for the community which includes a variety show and melodrama.

TENNESSEE

Chattanooga

Allied Arts Fund of Greater Chattanooga
16 Pattern Parkway
Chattanooga, TN 37402
Tel: 615-266-7318
Address Inquiries to: Lynn Grimsley, Chairperson
Founded in: 1969
Member: United Art Fund;
Annual Budget: $450,000

Cookeville

Cookeville Arts Council
Breen Lane
Cookeville, TN 38501
Address Inquiries to: Dr. Kermit Breen, Chairman
Founded in: 1972
Annual Budget: $10,000
Description: A not-for-profit service organization.

Covington

Tipton County Art Association
Post Office Box 575
Covington, TN 38019
Address Inquiries to: Bill Nolen, President
Founded in: 1970
Annual Budget: $10,000

Hendersonville

Hendersonville Arts Council
Post Office Box 1006
Hendersonville, TN 37075
Tel: 615-824-4881
Founded in: 1975
Annual Budget: $50,000
Description: A service organization.

Martin

Martin Arts Commission
Post Office Box 197
Martin, TN 38237
Tel: 901-587-9502
Address Inquiries to: Max Pentecost, Chairman
Description: A service organization

Maryville

Smoky Mountain Passion Play Association
108 ½ Magnolia Street
Maryville, TN 37801
Tel: 615-984-4111
Address Inquiries to: Carl M. Koontz, President

Founded in: 1972
Annual Budget: $100,000

Memphis

Memphis Arts Council
Post Office Box 40682-9990
Memphis, TN 38104
Tel: 901-278-2950
Address Inquiries to: Sally Thomason, Executive Director
Founded in: 1963
Annual Budget: $800,000
Description: The United Fund for the Arts of Memphis.

Nashville

Assembly of Community Arts Councils
Tennessee Arts Commission
Capitol Hill Building
Nashville, TN 37219
Tel: 615-741-1701
Address Inquiries to: Maureen Franklin, President
Description: A state arts council.

Tennessee Arts Commission
222 Capitol Hill Building
Nashville, TN 37219
Tel: 615-741-1701

Oak Ridge

Arts Council of Oak Ridge
Post Office Box 324
Oak Ridge, TN 37830
Address Inquiries to: Lamar C. Toomer, President
Founded in: 1955
Annual Budget: $50,000
Description: A not-for-profit service organization.

Sparta

Arts Guild of Sparta
Post Office Box 305
Sparta, TN 38583
Tel: 615-761-2367
Address Inquiries to: Mrs. Edsel England, Executive Director
Founded in: 1973
Annual Budget: $10,000
Description: A service organization.

Sweetwater

Sweetwater Valley Citizens for the Arts
Post Office Box 188
Sweetwater, TN 37874
Tel: 615-337-6014
Address Inquiries to: Mary Greenhoe, Executive Director
Founded in: 1974
Annual Budget: $10,000

Tullahoma

Tullahoma Fine Arts Center
401 South Jackson Street
Tullahoma, TN 37388
Tel: 615-455-1234; 615-455-0097
Address Inquiries to: Lucie F. Hollis, Executive Director

Frank Hightower, Jr.
Founded in: 1968
Member: Tennessee Arts Commission; Tennessee Alliance of Community Arts Agencies; National Association of Community Arts Agencies;
Annual Budget: $60,000
Description: Promotes the fine arts and enhances the quality of life through the arts. The Center also has a membership gallery where artist members may display their works.

TEXAS
Austin

Texas Commission on the Arts and Humanities
Post Office 13406, Capitol
Austin, TX 78711
Tel: 512-475-6593

College Station

Arts Council of Brazos Valley
Post Office Drawer CL
College Station, TX 77840
Tel: 713-244-8883
Address Inquiries to: Phyllis Dozier, Executive Director
Founded in: 1970
Annual Budget: $50,000

Corpus Christi

Corpus Christi Arts Council
Post Office Box 6683
Corpus Christi, TX 78411
Founded in: 1949
Annual Budget: $50,000
Description: A service organization

Fort Worth

Arts Council of Fort Worth and Tarrant County
2505 West Lancaster
Fort Worth, TX 76107
Tel: 817-738-7191
Address Inquiries to: John W. Sims, Executive Director
Founded in: 1964
Member: Texas Arts Alliance; American Council for the Arts; National Assembly of Community Arts Councils; Texas Assembly of Arts Councils;
Annual Budget: $879,000
Description: A fund which raises money for seven different performing arts groups, including the Fort Worth Theatre.

Houston

Combined Arts Corporate Campaign
c/o R.F. Dini Associates
600 Jefferson
Suite 502
Houston, TX 77002
Tel: 713-654-9217
Address Inquiries to: Richard Dini, Executive Director

Founded in: 1973
Annual Budget: $100,000
Description: A service organization.

Houston Cultural Affairs Council
Post Office Box 1562
Houston, TX 77001
Address Inquiries to: Molly Parkerson, Executive Director
Founded in: 1964
Description: A service organization.

Texas Assembly of Arts Councils
c/o Charles Lansden, President
1100 Milam Building, 25th Floor
Houston, TX 77002
Tel: 713-651-1313
Address Inquiries to: Herb Haslam, Executive Director
Description: A state arts council.

Lake Jackson

Brazosport Fine Arts Council
Post Office Box 684
Lake Jackson, TX 77566
Tel: 713-265-6427
Address Inquiries to: R.L. Bryant, President
Founded in: 1964

San Antonio

Arts Council of San Antonio
235 East Commerce
San Antonio, TX 78205
Tel: 512-224-5532
Address Inquiries to: Robert Canon, Executive Director
Founded in: 1964
Annual Budget: $100,000
Description: A service organization.

Temple

Cultural Activities Center
Post Office Box 3292
Temple, TX 76501
Tel: 817-773-9926
Address Inquiries to: Thomas L. Turk, Executive Director
George Prater, Visual Arts Director
Founded in: 1958
Member: National Assembly of Community Arts Agencies; Association of College University and Community Arts Administrators; American Council for the Arts;
Annual Budget: $250,000
Description: A community arts agency, as well as a performing and creative arts center.

UTAH
Salt Lake City

Utah State Division of Fine Arts
609 East South Temple Street
Salt Lake City, UT 84102
Tel: 801-533-5895

VERMONT
Montpelier

Vermont Council on the Arts
136 State Street
Montpelier, VT 05602
Tel: 802-828-3291

VIRGINIA
Annandale

Association for Communication Administration
5105 Backlick Road, Suite E
Annandale, VA 22003
Tel: 703-053-
Address Inquiries to: Theodore Clevenger, President
Robert N. Hall, Staff Coordinator
Member: ATA; UCTA;
Description: Affiliated with the Association of American Colleges, the Cheif Administrators Program of the UCTA of ATA and the Speech Communication Association.

Richmond

Commission for the Arts and Humanities
400 East Grace Street
Richmond, VA 23219
Tel: 804-783-4492

WASHINGTON
Kent

Kent Civic Arts Commission
Post Office Box 223
Kent, WA 98031
Address Inquiries to: Marie Crew, Secretary
Founded in: 1975
Annual Budget: $10,000

Kettle Falls

Old Mission Gallery Arts Council
Kettle Falls Realty, East 250 Third
Kettle Falls, WA 99141
Tel: 509-738-6225
Address Inquiries to: Jean Link, Executive Director
Founded in: 1974
Annual Budget: $10,000

Kirkland

Creative Arts League
620 Market Street
Kirkland, WA 98033
Tel: 206-822-7161
Address Inquiries to: Donna Schill, Executive Director
Founded in: 1962
Annual Budget: $50,000

Lynwood

Arts Alliance of Washington State
c/o Edmonds Community College
2000 68th Avenue W
Lynwood, WA 98036

Tel: 206-775-8551
Address Inquiries to: Nancy N. Meier,
    President
Description: A state arts council.

Mountlake Terrace

Mountlake Terrace Arts Commission
23204-58th Street
Mountlake Terrace, WA 98043
Tel: 206-774-7007
Address Inquiries to: Christine Gibson,
    Secretary
Founded in: 1971
Annual Budget: $10,000

Ocean Shores

Associated Arts of Ocean Shores
Post Office Box 241
Ocean Shores, WA 98043
Address Inquiries to: Barbara Shores,
    Executive Director
Founded in: 1974
Annual Budget: $50,000

Olympia

Washington State Arts Commission
1151 Black Lake Boulevard
Olympia, WA 98504
Tel: 206-753-3860

Raymond

Willapa Harbor Arts Commission
544 BAllentine
Raymond, WA 98577
Tel: 206-942-2944
Address Inquiries to: Robert Hannan, Vice
    President
Founded in: 1975
Annual Budget: $10,000

Redmond

Sammamish Arts Association
Post Office Box 604
Redmond, WA 98052
Founded in: 1974
Annual Budget: $10,000

Renton

Renton Municipal Arts Commission
Municipal Building, 200 Mill Avenue
Renton, WA 98055
Tel: 206-235-2591
Founded in: 1965
Annual Budget: $10,000

Richland

Allied Arts Council of the Mid-Columbia
    Region
Post Office Box 735
Richland, WA 99352
Tel: 509-943-0525
Founded in: 1968
Annual Budget: $50,000

Seattle

Allied Arts of Seattle
107 South Main Street
Seatlle, WA 98104
Tel: 206-624-0432

Address Inquiries to: Alice Rooney, Executive
    Secretary
Founded in: 1954
Annual Budget: $50,000

Burien Arts Association
421 Southwest 146th
Seattle, WA 98166
Tel: 206-244-7808
Address Inquiries to: Dorothy Harper,
    President
Founded in: 1966
Annual Budget: $10,000

Corporate Council for the Arts
421 Skinner Building
Seattle, WA 98101
Tel: 206-682-3663
Address Inquiries to: Robert E. Gustavson,
    Executive Director
Founded in: 1969
Annual Budget: $100,000

King County Arts Commission
Room W-140, County Courthouse
Seattle, WA 98104
Tel: 206-344-4040
Address Inquiries to: Yankee Johnson,
    Executive Secretary
Founded in: 1966
Annual Budget: $100,000

Performing and Visual Arts
100 Dexter Avenue North
Seattle, WA 98109
Tel: 206-625-4021
Address Inquiries to: Theresa Cooper,
    Executive Director
Founded in: 1920
Annual Budget: $100,000

Seattle Arts Commission
305 Harrison Street
Seattle, WA 98109
Tel: 206-625-4223
Address Inquiries to: John Blaine, Executive
    Secretary
Founded in: 1971
Annual Budget: $100,000

Snohomish

Snohomish Arts Commission
1009 First Street
Snohomish, WA 98290
Tel: 206-568-3115
Address Inquiries to: Mary Waltz, Executive
    Director
Founded in: 1975
Annual Budget: $10,000

Tacoma

Allied Arts of Tacoma
600 Commerce Street
Tacoma, WA 98402
Address Inquiries to: Kathryn Haley,
    President
Founded in: 1961
Annual Budget: $50,000

Tacoma-Pierce County Civic Arts
    Commission
705 South Ninth, Suite 105
Tacoma, WA 98492
Tel: 206-593-4754
Address Inquiries to: Richard Trapp,
    President
Founded in: 1965
Annual Budget: $100,000

Vancouer

Cooperative Arts Council of Clark County
Post Office Box 1995
Vancouer, WA 98663
Tel: 206-696-8171
Address Inquiries to: Donald G. Senecal,
    Chairman
Founded in: 1975
Annual Budget: $10,000

Walla Walla

Allied Arts Council of Walla Walla Valley
109 South Palouse Street
Walla Walla, WA 99362
Tel: 509-529-5978
Address Inquiries to: Peggy Hoyt, Executive
    Director
Founded in: 1967
Annual Budget: $10,000

Wenatchee

Allied Arts Council of North Central
    Washington
Post Office Box 573
Wenatchee, WA 98801
Founded in: 1964
Annual Budget: $10,000

Yakima

Allied Arts Council of the Yakima Valley
5000 West Lincoln Avenue
Yakima, WA 98902
Tel: 509-966-0930
Address Inquiries to: Tom Tomlinson,
    Executive Director
Founded in: 1960
Annual Budget: $50,000

WEST VIRGINIA

Buckhannon

Upshur County Center for the Creative
Arts
Post Office Box 639
Buckhannon, WV 26201
Tel: 304-472-6109
Founded in: 1974
Annual Budget: $50,000

Charleston

Charleston Performing Arts Council
Post Office Box 2749
Charleston, WV 25330
Tel: 304-348-8173
Address Inquiries to: Jane Thieling, President
Founded in: 1974
Annual Budget: $50,000

West Virginia Arts and Humanities
  Council
Science and Cultural Center
Capitol Complex
Charleston, WV 25305
Tel: 304-348-7311

Clarksburg

Clarksburg-Harrison County Cultural
  Foundation
127 West Main Street
Clarksburg, WV 26301
Tel: 304-662-1366
Address Inquiries to: Ulysses Buffington,
  President
Founded in: 1973
Annual Budget: $50,000

Franklin

Pendleton County Committee for the Arts
Post Office Box 572
Franklin, WV 268017
Tel: 304-358-2506
Address Inquiries to: Thomas Firor, President
Founded in: 1975
Annual Budget: $10,000

Hinton

Three Rivers Arts Council
Ewart Miller Building
Hinton, WV 25951
Tel: 304-466-1224
Address Inquiries to: David Ziegler, President
Founded in: 1975

Logan

Logan County Council for the Arts
Post Office Box 218
Logan, WV 25601
Tel: 304-752-1324
Address Inquiries to: David Compton,
  President
Founded in: 1973
Description: A service organization.

Moorefield

Fine Arts Committee
Hardy County Library Association
Post Office Box 653
Moorefield, WV 26836
Tel: 304-538-6560
Address Inquiries to: Bruce Macbeth,
  Chairman
Founded in: 1975
Annual Budget: $10,000

Philippi

Barbour County Arts and Humanities
  Council
100 Keyes Avenue
Philippi, WV 26416
Tel: 304-457-1700
Address Inquiries to: Carl Hatfield, President
Founded in: 1976
Description: A service organization.

Summit Point

Jefferson County Arts Council
Post Office Box 120
Summit Point, WV 25446
Tel: 304-725-4335
Address Inquiries to: Mrs. John VanTol
Founded in: 1975
Annual Budget: $50,000
Description: A service organization

Weirton

Weirton Area Arts Council
Post Office Box 482
Weirton, WV 26062
Tel: 304-748-7110
Address Inquiries to: Marvin Levendorf,
  President
Founded in: 1974
Annual Budget: $10,000
Description: A service organization.

WISCONSIN

Janesville

Rock Prairie Arts Council
Post Office Box 1494
Janesville, WI 53545
Tel: 608-752-5713
Address Inquiries to: Nancy Raufman,
  Executive Director
Founded in: 1974
Annual Budget: $50,000
Description: A service organization.

Madison

City Cultural Affairs Committee
202 Monona Avenue
Madison, WI 53703
Tel: 608-266-4611; 608-255-8177
Address Inquiries to: Lynn A. Hellmuth,
  Chairman
  Linda Lewis, Staff Liaison, Mayor's
  Office
Founded in: 1974
Annual Budget: $20,000
Description: Serves as a liaison between the
City and area residents involved in the arts.
Working to encourage the growth and ac-
cessibility of all of the art forms in Madison,
the Committee annually awards the City's
Artgrants and Mallgrants.

Wisconsin Arts Board
123 West Washington Avenue
Madison, WI 53702
Tel: 608-266-6959

Mellen

Ashland-Bayfield Arts Council
Post Office Box 577
Mellen, WI 54546
Address Inquiries to: Suzanne Stringe,
  Executive Director
Founded in: 1974
Annual Budget: $10,000
Description: A service organization

Milwaukee

Milwaukee Art Commission
City Hall-Room 205
200 E Well Street
Milwaukee, WI 53202
Tel: 414-278-2371
Address Inquiries to: Lillian Leenhouts,
  Chairman
Founded in: 1938
Annual Budget: $10,000

United Performing Arts Fund
929 North Water Street
Milwaukee, WI 53202
Tel: 414-237-7121
Address Inquiries to: William J. Murphy,
  Executive Director
Founded in: 1967
Annual Budget: $100,000

Racine

Racine Arts Council,Inc.
Post Office Box 263
Racine, WI 53401
Tel: 414-553-2367
Address Inquiries to: Mr. Dave Pedersen,
  President
Founded in: 1967
Description: An educational service organiza-
tion.

Watertown

Watertown Arts Council
Post Office Box 204
Watertown, WI 53180
Tel: 414-261-6913
Address Inquiries to: Mrs. Al Maas, President
Founded in: 1964
Annual Budget: $10,000
Description: A service organization

WYOMING

Caspar

Wyoming Council on the Arts
Post Office Box 3033
Caspar, WY 82601
Tel: 307-265-5434

Kemmerer

Kemmerer Council on the Arts
613 Emerald
Kemmerer, WY 83101
Tel: 307-877-6652
Address Inquiries to: Audrey Pfisterer,
  President
Founded in: 1974
Annual Budget: $10,000

Riverton

Arts in Action Council
501 Southridge Drive
Riverton, WY 82501
Tel: 347-856-9565
Address Inquiries to: Robert C. Kirtley,
  Executive Director
Founded in: 1971

Annual Budget: $10,000

Rock Springs

Sweetwater County Community Fine Arts
  Center
400 C Street
Rock Springs, WY 82901
Tel: 347-382-4599
Address Inquiries to: Al Keeny, Director
Founded in: 1939
Annual Budget: $50,000

CANADA

Edmonton, Alberta

Alberta Culture Council
CN Tower, 10004-104 Avenue
Edmonton, Alberta, Canada T5J 0K5
Tel: 403-427-2553
Address Inquiries to: Gordon Gordey

Vancouver, British Columbia

Vancouver Professional Theatre Alliance
c/o New Play Centre
1512 Anderson Street
Vancouver, British Columbia, Canada V6H
  3R6
Address Inquiries to: Pamela Hawthorn

Victoria, British Columbia

British Columbia Cultural Fund
Ministry of Provincial Secretary and
  Government Services
Cultural Services Branch
Victoria, British Columbia, Canada
  V8W2Y2
Tel: 604-387-5848
Address Inquiries to: Thomas G. Fielding

Winnipeg, Manitoba

Manitoba Arts Council
555 Main Street
Winnipeg, Manitoba, Canada R3B 1C3
Tel: 204-944-2237
Address Inquiries to: Ernest Stigant

Fredericton, New Brunswick

New Brunswick Cultural Development
  Branch
Room 414, Centennial Building
Fredericton, New Brunswick, Canada E3B
  5H1
Tel: 506-453-3610
Address Inquiries to: John Saunders

Saint John's, Newfoundland

New Foundland and Labrador Arts
  Council
Prince Philip Drive, Box 1854
Saint John's, Newfoundland, Canada A1C
  5P9
Tel: 709-722-7711
Address Inquiries to: Edythe Goodridge

Newfoundland Cultural Affairs
Prince Philip Drive, Box 1854
Saint John's, Newfoundland, Canada A1C
  5P9

Tel: 709-737-3650
Address Inquiries to: John Perlin

Halifax, Nova Scotia

Dramatists' Co-Op of Nova Scotia
Box 3608, South Post Office
Halifax, Nova Scotia, Canada B3J 3K6
Tel: 902-423-8116
Address Inquiries to: Christopher Heide

Nova Scotia Cultural Affairs Division
Post Office Box 864
Halifax, Nova Scotia, Canada B3J 2V2
Tel: 902-424-4378
Address Inquiries to: Michael Ardenne

Sydney, Nova Scotia

Canadian Child and Youth Drama
  Association
318 Towerview Place
Sydney, Nova Scotia, Canada B1S 3B8
Tel: 902-539-1995
Address Inquiries to: Theresa MacKinnon

Downsview, Ontario

Association for Canadian Theatre History
Department of Theatre
York University
4700 Keele Street
Downsview, Ontario, Canada M3J 1P3
Tel: 416-667-3975
Address Inquiries to: Ross Stuart

Ottawa, Ontario

Canada Council
Post Office Box 1047
255 Albert Street
Ottawa, Ontario, Canada K1P 5V8
Tel: 613-237-3400

Canada Council on the Arts
151 Sparks Street
Ottawa, Ontario, Canada K1P 5V8
Tel: 613-237-3400

Canada Council Touring Office
Post Office Box 1047
Ottawa, Ontario, Canada K1P 5V8
Tel: 613-238-7413
Address Inquiries to: John Cripton

Canadian Conference of the Arts
141 Laurier Avenue West, Suite 707
Ottawa, Ontario, Canada K1P 5J3
Tel: 613-356-
Address Inquiries to: John Hobday

Department of External Affairs
125 Sussex Drive
Ottawa, Ontario, Canada K1A 0G2
Tel: 613-992-9948
Address Inquiries to: Jacques Montpetit

Secretary of State, Arts and Culture
66 Slater Street
Ottawa, Ontario, Canada K1A 0M5
Tel: 613-996-3711
Address Inquiries to: Ann Dadson

Toronto, Ontario

Canadian Independent Theatrical
  Producers
c/o 94 Belmont Street
Toronto, Ontario, Canada M5R 1P3
Tel: 416-922-0084
Address Inquiries to: Peter Peroff
Heinar Pillar

Co-ordinated
137 Yonge Street
Toronto, Ontario, Canada M5C 1W6
Tel: 416-368-1024
Address Inquiries to: Peter Main

Council for Business and the Arts in
  Canada
Box 7, Suite 1507, 401 Bay Street
Toronto, Ontario, Canada M5H 2Y4
Tel: 416-869-3016
Address Inquiries to: Arnold Edinborough

Council of Drama in Education
336 Markham Street
Toronto, Ontario, Canada M6G 2K9
Address Inquiries to: Dennis Mills
Margie Marmor

International Theatre Institute
c/o Professional Association of Canadian
  Theatres
3 Church Street
Suite 301
Toronto, Ontario, Canada
Tel: 416-366-0159
Address Inquiries to: Curtis Barlow

Ontario Arts Council
151 Bloor Street West
Toronto, Ontario, Canada M5S 1T6
Tel: 416-961-1660
Address Inquiries to: William Lord

Ontario Ministry of Culture and
  Recreation
77 Bloor Street West
Toronto, Ontario, Canada M7A 2R9
Tel: 416-965-7690
Address Inquiries to: David Spence

Performing Arts Publicists Association
9 Humewood Court, Suite 22
Toronto, Ontario, Canada M6C 1C9
Tel: 416-656-4820
Address Inquiries to: D.R. Jellis

Professional Association of Canadian
  Theatres
3 Church Street, Suite 301
Toronto, Ontario, Canada M5E 1M2
Tel: 416-366-0159
Address Inquiries to: Curtis Barlow

Theatre Ontario
8 York Street, 7th Floor
Toronto, Ontario, Canada N5J 1R2
Tel: 416-366-2938
Address Inquiries to: Don Herbertson

Toronto Drama Bench
c/o Theatre Ontario, 8 York Street, 7th
  Floor
Toronto, Ontario, Canada M5J 1R2

Tel: 416-366-2938
Address Inquiries to: Jeniva Berger

Toronto Theatre Alliance
25 Lennox Avenue
Toronto, Ontario, Canada M6G 3W6
Tel: 416-536-1101
Address Inquiries to: Keith Turnbull
Cathy Smalley

Wintario
Ministry of Culture and Recreation
77 Bloor Street West
Toronto, Ontario, Canada M7A 2R9
Tel: 416-965-0617
Address Inquiries to: R.E. Second

Charlottetown, P.E.I.

Prince Edward Island, Cultural Affairs
Post Office Box 2000
Charlottetown, P.E.I., Canada C1A 7N8
Tel: 902-894-4738
Address Inquiries to: T. Earl Hickey

Montreal, Quebec

ASSITEJ-Canadian Centre
4808 Saint Denis Street
Montreal, Quebec, Canada H2J 2L6
Tel: 514-288-9343
Address Inquiries to: Susan Rubes
Yvon Lorendeau

Quebec, Quebec

Quebec Ministry of Cultural Affairs
955 chemin St-Louis
Quebec, Quebec, Canada G1A 1A3
Tel: 418-643-2110
Address Inquiries to: Pierre Cantin

Regina, Saskatchewan

Saskatchewan Arts Board
200 Lakeshore Drive
Regina, Saskatchewan, Canada S4S 0B3
Tel: 306-565-4056
Address Inquiries to: Joy Cohnstaedy

6
Critics

Below is a nationwide listing of those men and women who contribute so much to the success or demise of new theatre productions. They vary in power and influence, from the New York firstnight critic who can sink a million dollar show with one paragraph, to the local reporter extolling the latest dinner theatre production.

Bigcity critics have always been a powerful influence; but recently, the importance of regional theatre reviewers has increased along with the quality of regional productions. Many of the urban and regional critics listed here belong to the American Theatre Critics Association (ACTA).

ALABAMA
Anniston

Randy Hall
216 West 10th Street
Anniston, AL 36201
Member: ATCA;
Description: Randy Hall is a critic for the *Anniston Star.*

Montgomery

Judith R. Helms
327 Rose Lane
Montgomery, AL 36104

ARIZONA
Phoenix

Michael Dixon
c/o *The Phoenix Gazette*
Post Office Box 1950
Phoenix, AZ 85001
Member: ATCA;

Gerald M. Kane
c/o KMCR-FM
5624 North 12th Street
Phoenix, AZ 85014
Member: ATCA;

Richard Pontizuis
c/o *The Phoenix Gazette*
120 East Van Buren Street
Phoenix, AZ 85004
Member: ATCA;

Tempe

Roberta Bender
607 East Loyola Drive
Tempe, AZ 85282
Member: DCA;

Tucson

John Peck
Post Office Box 1449
Tucson, AZ 85702
Member: DCA;

CALIFORNIA
Anaheim

Karl Wray
c/o *Anaheim Bulletin*
Post Office Box 351
Anaheim, CA 92805

Berkeley

Erik Beuersfeld
c/o KPFA, 2207 Shattuck Avenue
Berkeley, CA 97704
Member: ATCA;

Carol Egan
1610 Milvia Street
Berkeley, CA 94709

Joanna G. Harris
2714 Woolsey Street
Berkeley, CA 94705
Member: DCA;

Burlingame

Janice Ross
1917 Devereux Drive
Burlingame, CA 94010
Member: DCA;

Corona Del Mar

Janice Plastino
1307 Santanella Terrace
Corona Del Mar, CA 92625
Member: DCA;

Fresno

Janet Singer
4803 North Hulbert
Fresno, CA 93705
Member: DCA;

Hollywood

David Galligan
c/o *Hollywood Drama-Logue*
1456 North Gordon Street
Hollywood, CA 90028
Tel: 213-464-5079
Description: David Galligan writes the 'Inside Hollywood' column for *Hollywood Drama-Logue.*

Wendy Loring
1967 North Wilcox
Hollywood, CA 90068

Kensington

Marti Keller
c/o *Independent & Gazette*
637 Wellesley Street
Kensington, CA 94708
Member: ATCA;

Rella Lossy
c/o *East Bay Review*
96 Highland Boulevard
Kensington, CA 94708
Member: ATCA;

Los Angeles

Martin Bernheimer
Los Angeles Times
Times Mirror Square
Los Angeles, CA 90053

Sylvie Drake
c/o *Los Angeles Times*
Times Mirror Square
Los Angeles, CA 90053
Member: ATCA;

Nancy Mason Hauser
6906 Pacific View
Los Angeles, CA 90068
Member: DCA;

Ray Holland
3738 West Monon
Los Angeles, CA 90027
Member: ATCA;

Edward K. Kaufman
c/o *Santa Monica Outlook*
10354 Louisiana Avenue
Los Angeles, CA 90025
Member: ATCA;

Ray Loynd
c/o *Herald Examiner*
1111 South Broadway
Los Angeles, CA 90027
Member: ATCA;

Martin A. David
3365 Hamilton Way
Los Angeles, CA 90026

Ron Pennington
c/o *Hollywood Reporter*
4148 Tracy Street
Los Angeles, CA 90027
Member: ATCA;

Jay Stanley
c/o *Quote Magazine*
3720 Clayton Avenue
Los Angeles, CA 90027
Member: ATCA;

Dan Sullivan
Los Angeles Times
Times Mirror Square
Los Angeles, CA 90053
Member: ATCA;

Viola Hegyi Swisher
345 South Curson Avenue
Los Angeles, CA 90036
Member: DCA;

David Vaughn
3223 Kingsley
Los Angeles, CA 90020
Tel: 213-380-5546
Member: DCA;

Lawrence Christon
c/o *Los Angeles Times*
Times Mirror Square
Los Angles, CA 90053
Member: ATCA;

Menlo Park

James Dillon
202 Santa Margarita
Menlo Park, CA 94025
Tel: 415-327-7532

Modesto

Leo Stutzin
c/o *Modesto Bee*
1215 Fordham
Modesto, CA 95350
Member: ATCA;

North Hollywood

Charles Faber
c/o *The Advocate*
10805-4 Blix Street
North Hollywood, CA 91602
Member: ATCA;

Gillian Rees
10642 Whipple Street, #1
North Hollywood, CA 91602
Member: DCA;

Oakland

Jonathan Kamin
c/o Bay Arts Press Service
3132 Sheffield Avenue
Oakland, CA 94602

Robert Taylor
c/o *Oakland Tribune*
Post Office Box 24424
Oakland, CA 94623
Member: ATCA;

Marilyn Tucker
570 El Dorado Avenue
Oakland, CA 94611
Member: DCA;

Ontario

Marge Gross
c/o *The Ontario Daily Report*
Post Office Box 4000
Ontario, CA 91761
Member: ATCA;

Riverside

T.E. Foreman
c/o *The Press & Enterprise*
Post Office Box 792
Riverside, CA 92502

Sacramento

William Glackin
c/o *Sacramento Bee*
Post Office Box 15779
Sacramento, CA 95813
Member: ATCA;

Richard Simon
c/o *Sacramento Union*
301 Capitol Mall
Sacramento, CA 95812
Member: ATCA;

Billy Von Veal
1414 Q Street, #2
Sacramento, CA 916 441 6534
Member: DCA;

San Diego

Frances L. Bardacke
c/o *San Diego Magazine*
815 Manhattan Court
San Diego, CA 92109
Member: ATCA;

Welton Jones
c/o *San Diego Union*
Post Office Box 191
San Diego, CA 92112

Eileen Sondak
6344 Lake Lomond Drive
San Diego, CA 92119
Member: DCA;

San Francisco

Alan Brown
620 28th Street
San Francisco, CA 94131

Stanley Eichelbaum
c/o KQED
515 Kansas Street
San Francisco, CA 94107

Carolyn Evans
1933 Greenwich Street
San Francisco, CA 94123

Stanley Friedman
c/o Channel 6
674 Greenwich Street
San Francisco, CA 94133

Pamela Gaye
199 Carl
San Francisco, CA 94117
Member: DCA;

Ruth Clark Lert
19 Valleta Court
San Francisco, CA 94131
Member: DCA;

Leland Sanford Meyergrove
Post Office Box 6149
San Francisco, CA 94101

Jeanne Miller
c/o *San Francisco Examiner*
110 5th Street
San Francisco, CA 94103

Steve Warren
c/o *Creative Loafing*
635 Ellis Street, #34
San Francisco, CA 94109

Bernard Weiner
c/o *San Francisco Chronicle*
5th and Mission Streets
San Francisco, CA 94119

San Mateo

Barbara Bladen
c/o *San Mateo Times*
1080 South Amphlet
San Mateo, CA 94402

G.S. Tagashira
800 North Delaware, Apt. 102
San Mateo, CA 94401
Member: DCA;

Santa Monica

Claudia Chapline
522 Santa Monica Boulevard
Santa Monica, CA 90401
Description: Institute for Dance and Experimental Art.

Leo Mishkin
220 San Vicente Boulevard
Santa Monica, CA 80402
Member: ATCA;

South Pasadena

Tony Scott
c/o *Daily Variety*
609 Prospect Avenue
South Pasadena, CA 91030
Member: ATCA;

Stanford

Martin Esslin
c/o Drama Department, Stanford
   University
Stanford, CA 94305
Member: ATCA;

Stockton

Steven Scott-Orr
205 West Robinhood Drive
Stockton, CA 95207
Member: DCA;

West Los Angeles

Linda Tomko
1515 Beloit, #6
West Los Angeles, CA 90025
Member: DCA;

COLORADO

Boulder

Marda Kirn
Post Office Box 356
Boulder, CO 80306

Denver

Barbara Mackay
c/o *Denver Post*
Post Office Box 1709
Denver, CO 80201

CONNECTICUT

Bethel

Fran Sikorski
c/o Acorn Press Publications
12 Midway Drive
Bethel, CT 06801
Member: OCC;

Cheshire

Ernestine Stodelle
855 North Brooksvale
Cheshire, CT 06410
Member: DCA;
Description: Ernestine Stodelle is dance critic
for *The New-Haven Register.*

Fairfield

Lisa Faye Kaplan
c/o *Fairpress*
611 Fairfield Beach Road
Fairfield, CT 06430

Member: OCC;
Description: Arts and Entertainment Editor of
Fairpress.

Ruth Lampland Ross
c/o *Bridgeport Post-Telegram*
Post Office Box 554 South Benson Road
Fairfield, CT 06430
Member: OCC;
Description: Free Lance critic

Greenwich

Leslie Martin
197 Stanwich Road
Greenwich, CT 06830
Member: DCA;

Hartford

Malcolm Johnson
285 Broad Street
Hartford, CT 06115
Member: ATCA;
Description: Mr. Johnson is a theatre critic for
the *Hartford Courant.*

Steve Kemper
c/o *Hartford Advocate*
203 Newbury Street
Hartford, CT 06114
Member: OCC;

Nancy Pappas
285 Broad Street
Hartford, CT 06115
Member: DCA;

Meriden

Phyllis Donovan
169 Tulip Drive
Meriden, CT 06450
Member: ATCA;
Description: Phyllis Donovan is a theatre critic
for the *Meriden Record.*

New Fairfield

Linda Triegel
c/o *Citizen News* Route 4, Box 605
New Fairfield, CT 06810
Member: OCC;

New Haven

Michael A. Bertin
c/o *New Haven Journal Courier*
470 Prospect Street, #54
New Haven, CT 06511
Member: OCC;

Newtown

Jack Gaston Kipp
c/o *The Newtown Bee*
4 Nettleton Avenue
Newtown, CT 06470
Member: OCC;
Description: A freelance critic.

Markland Taylor
Hanover Road
Newtown, CT 06470
Member: ATCA;
Description: Markland Taylor is theatre critic
in the New Haven area.

Ridgefield

Tom A. Killen
c/o *Darien News*
39 Boulder Hill Road
Ridgefield, CT 06877
Member: OCC;

Southport

Tim Holly
c/o *Bridgeport Post-Telegram*
Box 154
Southport, CT 06490
Member: OCC;

Stamford

Sarey Bernstein
355 Cascade Road
Stamford, CT 06903
Member: OCC;
Description: Freelance critic

Trumbull

Joseph Pronechon
c/o *Trumbull News, Monroe and Eastern
Couriers*
82 Woolsey Avenue
Trumbull, CT 06611
Member: OCC;

West Hartford

Edgar Kloten
19 Red Top Drive
West Hartford, CT c/o *Trumbull News
Monroe and Eastern Couriers*
Member: ATCA; OCC;
Description: Mr. Kloten is a theatre critic for
the *West Hartford News.*

Westport

Gloria Cole
c/o *Stamford Advocate Compass*
20 Appletree Trail
Westport, CT 06880
Member: OCC;
Description: Editor of *Stamford Advocate Compass.*

Allen Lewis
4 Elwil Drive
Westport, CT 06880
Member: ATCA;
Description: Allen Lewis is theatre critic for
the *New Haven Register.*

West Simsbury

John Balmer
115 West Mountain Road
West Simsbury, CT 06092
Member: ATCA;
Description: Mr. Balmer is a theatre critic for
the *Farmington Valley Herald.*

DELAWARE

Wilmington

Philip F. Crosland
831 Orange Street
Wilmington, DE 19899
Member: ATCA;
Description: Philip F. Crosland is a theatre
critic for the *Wilmington News Journal.*

Patrick Stoner
c/o WHYY-TV
5th and Scott Streets
Wilmington, DE 19899
Member: ATCA;

DISTRICT OF COLUMBIA

Washington

Cynthia Barkley
Kennedy Center
Washington, DC 20566
Member: DCA;

Bonnie Brooks
NEA-Dance Program
Washington, DC 20506

Richard L. Coe
2101 Connecticut Avenue NW
Washington, DC 20008
Member: ATCA;
Description: Richard Coe is a theatre critic for
the *Washington Post.*

Rhoda Grauer
2401 E Street NW
Washington, DC 20506
Member: DCA;
Description: The NEA Dance Program.

George Jackson
1435 4th Street SW
Washington, DC 20024
Member: DCA;

James Lardner
1150 15th Street NW
Washington, DC 20071
Member: ATCA;
Description: James Lardner is a theatre critic
for *The Washington Post.*

Davey Marlin-Jones
40001 Brandywine Street NW
Washington, DC 20016
Member: ATCA;
Description: Davey Marlin-Jones is the theatre
critic for WTOP-TV, Washington, DC.

Jean Nordhaus
623 East Capitol Street SE
Washington, DC 20003

Geraldine Otremba
3161 Adams Mill Road
Washington, DC 20010
Description: Kennedy Center.

Julie Van Camp
901 6th Street SW, #106A
Washington, DC 20024

Member: DCA;

FLORIDA

Fort Lauderdale

Robert Keaton
506 South West Riverside Drive
Fort Lauderdale, FL 33312
Member: ATCA;
Description: Robert Keaton is a critic for the
Fort Lauderdale News.

Fort Meyers

Maureen Bashaw
c/o *News Press*
1456 Linwood
Fort Meyers, FL 33901
Member: ATCA;

Miami

Christine Arnold
c/o *Miami Herald*
Herald Plaza
Miami, FL 33101
Member: ATCA;
Description: Christine Arnold is a critic for the
Miami Herald.

Sam Hirsch
c/o WTVJ TV
316 North Miami Avenue
Miami, FL 33128
Member: ATCA;

James Roos
Miami Herald
Miami, FL 33101
Member: DCA;
Description: A critic for the *Miami Herald.*

Saint Petersburg

Mary Nic Shenk
Saint Petersburg Times
Saint Petersburg, FL
Member: DCA;

Sarasota

Nina Brigham
c/o *Sarasota Journal*
Postal Drawer 1719
Sarasota, FL 33578
Member: ATCA;

Marcia Corbino
c/o *Sarasota Herald Tribune*
Sarasota, Fl 33578
Member: ATCA;

St. Petersburg

Dorothy Smiljanich
Post Office Box 1121
St. Petersburg, FL 33578
Member: ATCA;
Description: Dorothy Smiljanich is a critic for
the *St. Petersburg Times.*

GEORGIA

Atlanta

Stuart Culpepper
1864 Windemere Drive, North East
Atlanta, GA 30324
Member: ATCA;
Description: Stuart Culpepper is a reviewer for
the *Atlanta Gazette.*

Mercy Sandberg-Wright
1842 Walthall Drive NW
Atlanta, GA 30324
Member: ATCA;
Description: Mercy Sandberg-Wright is a crit-
ic for the *Atlanta Gazette.*

Helen C. Smith
c/o *Atlanta Constitution*
Atlanta, GA 30303
Member: ATCA;

Barbara Thomas
c/o *Atlanta Journal*
72 Marietta Street NW
Atlanta, Ga 30303
Member: ATCA;

Decatur

George Beiswanger
2109 Spring Creek Road
Decatur, GA 30033
Member: DCA;

Savannah

Krys Keller
Post Office Box 1088
Savannah, GA
Member: ATCA;
Description: Krys Keller is a critic for the
Savannah Morning News.

ILLINOIS

Chicago

Ann Barzel
3950 North Lake Shore Drive
Chicago, IL 60613
Member: DCA;

Lawrence Bommmer
c/o *Chicago Illinoian*
2616 North Clark Street
Chicago, IL 60614
Member: ATCA;

Earl Calloway
c/o *Daily Defender*
2400 South Michigan Avenue
Chicago, IL 60616
Member: ATCA;

Claudia Cassidy
c/o WFMT
33 East Bellvue Place
Chicago, IL 60611
Member: ATCA;

Dick Christensen
Chicago Tribune
435 North Michigan Avenue

Chicago, IL 60657
Member: DCA;

Beth Genne
2147 West Farwell
Chicago, IL 60645
Member: DCA;

Alanna Barr Gordon, Gordon Editorial
  Services
6603 North Damen
Chicago, IL 60645
Member: DCA;

Christine Koyama
c/o *Chicago Magazine*
500 North Michigan Avenue
Chicago, IL 60611
Member: ATCA;

Valerie Scher
842 West Lill
Chicago, IL 60614
Member: DCA;

Bury St. Edmund
c/o *The Reader*
12 East Grand Street
Chicago, IL 60611
Member: ATCA;

Glenna Syse
c/o *Chicago Sun-Times*
401 North Wabash
Chicago, IL 60611
Member: ATCA;

Peoria

Lynn Matluck
1227 West Swan Curve
Peoria, IL 61615

Urbana

Diana Snyder
4-305 Krannert Center
Urbana, IL 61801
Member: DCA;

Waukegan

Dan Zeff
c/o *News-Sun,* 100 West Madison
Waukegan, IL 60085
Member: ATCA;

INDIANA

Indianapolis

Patrick Corbin
c/o *The Indianapolis Star*
307 North Pennsylvania Street
Indianapolis, IN 46206
Member: ATCA;

Charles J. Ferruzza
28 West 54th Street
Indianapolis, IN 46208
Member: DCA;

Marshall

Dr. Gustav Varga
Dance Department
Southwest State University
Marshall, IN 56258
Member: DCA;

Muncie

William T. Liston
c/o *Muncie Star*
RR 3, Box 186Y
Muncie, IN 47302
Member: ATCA;

IOWA

Iowa City

Judith Green
41 ½ South Summit Street
Iowa City, IA 52240
Member: DCA;

Jennifer Martin
University of Iowa Dance Program
North Hall 107
Iowa City, IA 52242
Member: DCA;

KENTUCKY

Louisville

William Mootz
c/o *Louisville Courier Journal*
525 West Broadway
Louisville, KY 40202
Member: ATCA;

Dudley Saunders
c/o *Louisville Times*
525 West Broadway
Louisville, KY 40202
Member: ATCA;

LOUISIANA

Shreveport

David Connelly
222 Lake Street
Shreveport, LA 71180

MAINE

Brunswick

Deanne Smeltzer
82 Federal Street
Brunswick, ME 04011
Member: DCA;

June Adler Vail
1 Oakland Street
Brunswick, ME 04011
Member: DCA;

MARYLAND

Baltimore

Lou Cedrone,Jr.
c/o *Baltimore Sun*
Calvert and Center Streets
Baltimore, MD 21203
Member: ATCA;

Kathy Ellin
8000 Longmeadow Road
Baltimore, MD 21208
Member: DCA;

R.H. Gardner
c/o *Baltimore Sun*
Calvert and Center Streets
Baltimore, MD 21203
Member: ATCA;

R.P. Harriss
c/o *Baltimore News American*
Lombard and South Streets
Baltimore, MD 21203
Member: ATCA;

Sarah Penno Lord
6219 Falls Road
Baltimore, MD 21209
Member: ATCA;
Description: Sarah Penno Lord is a theatre
critic for the *Baltimore News American.*

Bethesda

Elizabeth A. Smigel
5807 Ridgefield Road
Bethesda, MD 20016
Member: DCA;

Chevy Chase

Alice Wilding-White
6710 Hillandale Road
Chevy Chase, MD 20815
Member: DCA;

Columbia

Carolyn Keleman
10291 Wilde Lake Terrace
Columbia, MD 21044
Member: DCA;

Frederick

Edward I. Campbell
234 East Third Street
Frederick, MD 21209
Member: ATCA;
Description: Edward I. Campbell is a theatre
critic for the *Frederick News Post.*

Rockville

Richard D. Freed
6201 Tuckerman Lane
Rockville, MD 20852
Member: ATCA;

Silver Springs

Charles Christopher Mark
9214 Three Oaks Drive
Silver Springs, MD 20901
Member: ATCA;
Description: Charles Mark is a theatre critic

and publisher of Arts Reporting Service.

MASSACHUSETTS

Amherst

Anita Page
84 McClellan Street
Amherst, MA 01002
Member: DCA;

Arlington

Leila Sussman
34 Hamilton Road
Arlington, MA 02174
Member: DCA;

Auburndale

Caldwell Titcomb
67 Windermere Road
Auburndale, MA 02116
Member: ATCA;

Boston

Carolyn Clay
100 Massachusetts Avenue
Boston, MA 02115
Member: ATCA;
Description: Carolyn Clay is the theatre critic
for the *Boston Phoenix.*

Thor Eckert Jr.
One Norway Street
Boston, MA 02115
Member: ATCA;
Description: Mr. Eckert is a theatre critic for
the *Christian Science Monitor.*

Kevin Kelly
135 Morrisey Boulevard
Boston, MA 02107
Member: ATCA;
Description: Mr. Kelly is a theatre critic for the
Boston Globe.

T.M. Sarno
Post Office Box 1817
Boston, MA 02105
Member: DCA;

Brookline

Iris M. Fanger
190 Dudley Street
Brookline, MA 02146

Cambridge

Sharon Basco
395 Broadway
Cambridge, MA 02139
Member: DCA;

Debra Cash
5 Upland Road
Cambridge, MA 02140

Arthur Friedman
929 Massachusetts Avenue
Cambridge, MA 02139
Member: ATCA;
Description: Mr. Friedman is a theatre critic
for the *Real Paper.*

Malden

Joan Lautman
104 Summer Street
Malden, MA 02148
Member: ATCA;
Description: Joan Lautman is a theatre critic
for the *Boston Ledger.*

Melrose

Brian S. McNiff
151 Upham Street
Melrose, MA 02176
Member: ATCA;
Description: Mr. McNiff is a theatre critic for
the *Worcester Telegram.*

Needham

Christine Temin
90 Forest Street
Needham, MA 02192
Member: DCA;

Newburyport

Carolyn G. Toleczki
56 Kent Street
Newburyport, MA 01950
Member: DCA;

Northampton

Karen Nelson
10 West Street
Northampton, MA 01060

Pittsfield

Milton Bass
33 Eagle Street
Pittsfield, MA 01201
Member: ATCA;
Description: Mr. Bass is a theatre critic for the
Berkshire Eagle.

Springfield

Thomas G. Hart
1860 Main Street
Springfield, MA 01101
Member: ATCA;
Description: Mr. Hart is a theatre critic for the
Springfield Daily.

Stockbridge

Allison Tracy
Post Office Box 751
Stockbridge, MA 01262
Member: DCA;

Waltham

John Bush Jones
Brandeis University
Waltham, MA 02254
Member: ATCA;
Description: Mr. Jones is a theatre critic for
Theatre Arts.

Worcester

Norma Adler
20 Wabash Avenue
Worcester, MA 01604
Member: DCA;

MICHIGAN

Allendale

Christine Loizeaux
7270 Pierce Street
Allendale, MI 49401

Ann Arbor

Susan I. Nisbett
837 West Huron Street
Ann Arbor, MI 48103

Marianne Danks Rudnicki
1737 Orchard Street
Ann Arbor, MI 48103
Member: DCA;

Detroit

Jay Carr
c/o *Detroit News*
615 Lafayette Boulevard
Detroit, MI 48231
Member: ATCA;

Lawrence DeVine
c/o *Detroit Free Press*
321 West Lafayette Boulevard
Detroit, MI 48321
Member: ATCA;

Flint

David Graham
c/o *The Flint Journal*
200 East First Street
Flint, MI 48502
Member: ATCA;

Kalamazoo

Don W. Carlson
c/o *Kalamazoo Gazette*
2516 Kensington Drive
Kalamazoo, MI 49008
Member: ATCA;

Heintz, Diane
1841 Oakland Drive
Kalamazoo, MI 49008

MINNESOTA

Burnsville

Lucille Johnsen Stelling
c/o *Freeway News*
12600 Parkwood Drive
Burnsville, MN 55337
Member: ATCA;

Minneapolis

Don Morrison
c/o *Minneapolis Star*
Fifth and Portland Avenues
Minneapolis, MN 55415
Member: ATCA;

Thomas Russell
1530 South 6th Street, Apt. 2000
Minneapolis, MN 55454
Member: DCA;

Linda Shapiro
95 Bedford Street Southeast
Minneapolis, MN 55414
Member: DCA;

R. Michael Steele
c/o *Minneapolis Tribune*
Fifth and Portland Avenues
Minneapolis, MN 55415
Member: ATCA;

Melinda Ward
Walker Art Center, Vineland Place
Minneapolis, MN 55403
Member: DCA;

North Mankato

Tim DeMarce
1121 Lake Street
North Mankato, MN 56001

Saint Louis Park

Judith Brin Ingber
2526 Kipling Avenue South
Saint Louis Park, MN 55416

Saint Paul

Cynthia Gehrig
Jerome Foundation
First National Bank Building
Saint Paul, MN 55101
Member: DCA;

Carol Nuckols
Ft. Worth Star Telegram
200 Wet Avenue
Saint Paul, MN 55105

St. Paul

John Harvey
c/o *St. Paul Pioneer Press*
55 East 4th Street
St. Paul, MN 55101
Member: ATCA;

David Hawley
c/o *St. Paul Pioneer Press*
55 East 4th Street
St. Paul, MN 55101
Member: ATCA;

MISSOURI

Kansas City

Robert W. Butler
c/o *Kansas City Star*
1729 Grand Avenue
Kansas City, MO 64108
Member: ATCA;

Harry Haskell
4618 Warwick Blvd.
Kansas City, MO 64112
Member: DCA;

Patty Moore
610 West 62nd Street
Kansas City, MO 64113

Madelyn Voights
6641 Linden Road
Kansas City, MO 64113
Member: DCA;

St. Louis

James Evans
880 Tuxedo Boulevard
St. Louis, MO 63119

Frank Hunter
c/o *St. Louis Globe-Democrat*
710 North 12th Street
St. Louis, MO 63101
Member: ATCA;

Herb Metz
c/o KSD-TV
40 North Kings Highway
St. Louis, MO 63108
Member: ATCA;

Judith Newmar
c/o *St. Louis Post Dispatch*
900 North 12th Boulevard
St. Louis, MO 63101
Member: ATCA;

Joe Pollack
c/o *St. Louis Post Dispatch*
710 North 12th Street
St. Louis, MO 63101
Member: ATCA;

NEBRASKA

Larchmont

Walter Kerr
1 Beach Avenue
Larchmont, New York 10538
Member: ATCA;
Description: Walter Kerr is a freelance theatre critic, formerly with *The New York Times.*

Omaha

Leroy Perkins
4875 F. Street
Omaha, NB 68117
Member: DCA;
Description: Sun Newspapers.

Mary T. Smith
6536 Wirt Street
Omaha, NB 68104
Member: DCA;

NEW JERSEY

Atlantic City

William Green
c/o *Atlantic City Press*
Atlantic City, NJ 10024
Member: OCC;

Atlantic Highlands

Joan Pikula
71 Bay Avenue
Atlantic Highlands, NJ 07716
Member: DCA;

Clifton

Joan Finn
17 Janice Terrace
Clifton, NJ 07013
Member: ATCA;
Description: Joan Finn is theatre critic for the *Montclair Times.*

Englewood

Dorothy Thom
369 Tryon Avenue
Englewood, NJ 07631
Member: DCA;

Hoboken

Lynn Asinof
909 Hudson Street
Hoboken, NJ 07030
Member: DCA;

Millburn

Joseph Gale
Post Office Box 636
Millburn, NJ 07041
Member: DCA;

Morristown

Fran Wood
800 Jefferson Road
Morristown, NJ 07054
Member: ATCA;
Description: Fran Wood is theatre critic for the *Daily Record.*

Newark

Bette Spero
c/o *The NewarkStar Ledger*
StarLedger Plaza
Newark, NJ 07101
Member: ATCA;

New Brunswick

Ernest Albrect
123 How Lane
New Brunswick, NJ 08903
Member: ATCA;
Description: Ernest Albrect is theatre critic for the *Home News.*

New Milford

Gordon Tretick
c/o *The Ridgewood News*
313 Concors Place
New Milford, NJ 07646
Member: OCC;

Oakland

Robert L. Daniels
5 Cedar Street
Oakland, NJ 07436
Member: ATCA;
Description: Robert L. Daniels is theatre critic for *The Week Ahead.*

Perth Amboy

Vincent Zito
173 High Street
Perth Amboy, NJ 08861
Member: ATCA;

Princeton

Barbara Fox
86 Cedar Lane
Princeton, NJ 08540
Tel: 609-921-2774
Member: DCA
Description: Trenton Times critic

Michael Robertson
15 Henderson Avenue
Princeton, NJ 08540
Member: DCA;

Somerville

Jean Ogden
Post Office Box 1170
Somerville, NJ 08876
Member: ATCA;
Description: Jean Ogden is theatre critic for
WBRW radio.

Tinton Falls

Valerie Sudol
5206 Asbury Avenue
Tinton Falls, NJ 07724
Member: DCA;

Titusville

Gilda Morigi
c/o *American Jewish Life*
Post Office Box 178
Titusville, NJ 08560
Member: OCC;

Trenton

Ted Otten
Post Office Box B
Trenton, NJ 08690
Member: DCA;
Description: Mercer County Community College critic.

West Orange

Elaine Shein Jaskol
27 Rutgers Street
West Orange, NJ 07052
Member: DCA;

Woodbridge

Mirko Tuma
1 Hoover Way
Woodbridge, NJ 07095
Member: ATCA;

NEW MEXICO

Albuquerque

Pamela Beerer
3939 Rio Grande Boulevard Northwest
Albuquerque, NM 87107
Member: DCA;

Santa Cruz

Nicole Plett
Santa Fe New Mexican
Post Office Box 273
Santa Cruz, NM 87567
Member: DCA;

Santa Fe

Allan N. Pearson
Post Office Box 4684
Santa Fe, NM 87502
Member: DCA;

NEW YORK

Albany

Mary Anne Leonard
457 Ontario Street
Albany, NY 12208
Tel: 518-454-5460
Member: DCA;
Description: Knickerbocker News, Albany

Brightwaters

Dawn Lillie Horwitz
57 Woodland Drive
Brightwaters, NY 11718

Bronx

Roxanne Artesana
1332 Metropolitan Avenue, #4G
Bronx, NY 10462
Member: DCA;

Brooklyn

Dee Bailey
812 Carroll Street
Brooklyn, NY 11215
Member: DCA;

Marvadene Brock
196 8th Avenue
Brooklyn, NY 11215

Robert Greskovic
304 Washington Avenue
Brooklyn, NY 11205

Marilyn Hunt
79 State Street
Brooklyn, NY 11201

Barry Laine
134 Henry Street
Brooklyn, NY 11201
Member: DCA;

Ellen Lampert
39 Plaza Street
Brooklyn, NY 11217
Member: DCA;
Description: Brooklyn Academy of Music,
Public Relations

Julinda Lewis
64 Hart Street
Brooklyn, NY 11206
Member: DCA;
Description: A critic and teacher on theatre and
dance.

Al Pischl
1801 East 26th Street
Brooklyn, NY 10024
Member: DCA;

Roberta Plutzik
195 Hicks Street
Brooklyn, NY 11201
Member: ATCA;
Description: Roberta Plutzik is a freelance
theatre critic.

Annette Rivera
449 State Street
Brooklyn, NY 11217
Member: DCA;

Francine Roland
8711 24th Avenue
Brooklyn, NY 11214
Member: DCA;

Diane J. Rosenthal
595 7th Street
Brooklyn, NY 11215
Member: DCA;

Hazel B. Solomon
441 Maple Street
Brooklyn, NY 11215
Member: DCA;

Sharon True
388 Clinton Street
Brooklyn, NY 11231
Member: DCA;

Lesley Valdez
572 7th Street
Brooklyn, NY 11215
Member: DCA;

Hal Wiener
2128 East 29th Street
Brooklyn, NY 11229
Member: DCA;

Buffalo

Terry Doran
218 Main Street
Buffalo, NY 14240
Member: ATCA;
Description: Terry Doran is a theatre critic for
the *Buffalo Evening News.*

Jayne S. Freeman
184 Barton Street
Buffalo, NY 14240
Member: ATCA;
Description: Jayne Freeman is a theatre critic
for WNED-TV in Buffalo.

Clinton

Sondra Lomax
Department of Theatre and Dance
Hamilton College
Clinton, NY 13303

Geneseo

Herbert Simpson
12 Oak Street
Geneseo, NY 14454
Member: DCA;

Hempstead

Howard B. Lord
Post Office Box 700
Hempstead, NY 11551
Member: ATCA;
Description: Howard B. Lord is a theatre critic
for the *Long Island Catholic.*

Hewlett

Arlene Epstein
c/o *South Shore Journal*
109 Pierrepont Avenue
Hewlett, NY 11557
Member: OCC;
Description: Arts Editor of *South Shore Journal.*

Huntington Station

Allan Wallach
64 Long Street
Huntington Station, NY 11746
Member: ATCA;
Description: Allan Wallach is a theatre critic
for *Newsday.*

Ithaca

Karen Fink
414 Cayuga Heights Road
Ithaca, NY 14850

Long Beach

Joseph S. King
c/o *Independent Voice*
9 Kerrigan Street
Long Beach, NY 11516
Member: OCC;

Long Island City

Janice Berman Alexander
Newsday
Long Island City, NY 11747
Member: DCA;

Loudonville

Lisa F. Hillyer
181 Merards Road
Loudonville, NY 12211
Member: DCA;

Mamaroneck

Kathie Beals
400 Carroll Avenue
Mamaroneck, NY 10543
Member: ATCA;
Description: Kathie Beals is a theatre critic for
the Westchester- Rockland Newspapers.

Moses Schonfeld
c/o WRTN Radio
1175 Greacent Point Road
Mamaroneck, NY 10543
Member: OCC;

Middletown

Marie Ann Dulzer
102 Sycamore Drive
Middletown, NY 10940
Member: ATCA;
Description: Marie Ann Dulzer is a theatre
critic for the *Times Herald Record.*

Mount Kisco

Amy Bardsley
Indian Hill Road
Mount Kisco, NY 10549
Member: DCA;

Kay Bardsley
Indian Hill Road
Mount Kisco, NY 10549
Member: DCA;

New Rochelle

Eileen Ulman Spitz
2 Woodcut Lane
New Rochelle, NY 10804
Member: DCA;

New York

Reba Adler
108 West 69th Street
New York, NY 10023
Member: DCA;

Frances Alenikoff
537 Broadway
New York, NY 10012
Member: DCA;

Zita Allen
c/o A. Mberi
2155 Adam Clayton Powell Boulevard
New York, NY 10027
Member: DCA;

Jack Anderson
110 Thompson Street
New York, NY 10011
Member: DCA;

Helen Atlas
119 West 57th Street
New York, NY 10019
Member: DCA;

Peter A. Bailey
2289 5th Avenue
New York, NY 10037
Member: ACTA;
Description: Peter A. Bailey is a freelance
theatre critic who also works with the Black
Theatre Alliance (BTA).

Sally Banes
359 Canal Street
New York, NY 10013
Member: DCA;

Clive Barnes
450 West End Avenue
New York, NY 10024
Member: ACTA; DCA;
Description: Clive Barnes is theatre critic for
the *New York Post.*

Patricia Barnes
450 West End Avenue
New York, NY 10024
Member: DCA;

John Beaufort
424 East 52nd Street
New York, NY 10022
Member: ATCA;

Description: John Beaufort is a theatre critic
for the *Christian Science Monitor.*

Nancy Becker
2 Wooster Street
New York, NY 10013
Member: DCA;

Madeleine Beckman
131 Thompson Street
New York, NY 10012
Member: DCA;

Gina Bella
32 Thompson Street, #6
New York, NY 10013
Member: DCA;

Byron Belt
50 West 67th Street
New York, NY 10023
Member: DCA;

Shelly Berg
69 Fifth Avenue
New York, NY 10003
Member: DCA;

Miriam Berkeley
Dover Publications
180 Varick Street
New York, NY 10004
Tel: 212-255-3755; 212-877-2924
Member: DCA

Frederic Berliner
c/o TGIF Entertainment/Casting
24 Fifth Avenue
New York, NY 10011
Member: OCC;
Description: New York City Editor of *T.G.I.F.*

Ira Bilowit
55 West 42nd Street
New York, NY 10036
Member: ATCA;
Description: Ira Bilowit is a theatre critic for
the *New York Theatre Review.*

Betty Blake
Theatre Information Bulletin
4 Park Avenue, Suite 21D
New York, NY 10016
Member: OCC;

Eileen Blumenthal
842 Broadway
New York, NY 10003
Member: ATCA;
Description: Eileen Blumenthal is a theatre
critic for the *Village Voice.*

Theresa Bowers
333 West 88th Street
New York, NY 10024

Townsend Brewster
c/o *Harlem Cultural Review*
171-29 103rd Road
New York, NY 11433
Member: OCC;

Craig Bromberg
117 Varick Street
New York, NY 10013

Tel: 212-989-7189
Description: Instep/Dance Scope Magazine

Virginia Brooks
460 Riverside Drive
New York, NY 10027

Holly Brubach
112 West 76th Street
New York, NY 10023

Noel Carroll
359 Canal Street
New York, NY 10013

Aaron Cohen
345 East 19th Street
New York, NY 10003
Tel: 212-673-7286
Member: DCA;

William Como
Dance Magazine
1180 6th Avenue
New York, NY 10036

C.C. Conner
444 East 84th Street
New York, NY 10028

Robert Cornfield
145 West 79th Street
New York, NY 10024

Margaret Croyden
250 West 94th Street
New York, NY 10025
Member: ACTA;
Description: Margaret Croyden is a freelance theatre critic.

Dennis Cunningham
51 West 52nd Street
New York, NY 10019
Member: ATCA;
Description: Dennis Cunningham is a theatre critic for WCBS-TV.

Glenne Currie
220 East 42nd Street
New York, NY 10017
Member: ATCA;
Description: Glenne Currie is a theatre Critic for United Press International.

Gautam Dasgupta
92 Saint Marks Place
New York, NY 10003
Member: ATCA;
Description: Gautam Dasgupta is editor of the *Performing Arts Journal.*

Karen Davidov
272 First Avenue, #11D
New York, NY 10009

Curt Davis
c/o *New York Post*
349 West 45th Street
New York, NY 10036
Member: OCC;

Mary Day
34 West 38th Street
New York, NY 10018

Tim Debaets
Pavia and Harcourt, 63 Wall Street
New York, NY 10005

Didier DeLaunoy
155 East 34th Street
New York, NY 10016
Member: ATCA;
Description: Didier DeLaunoy is a theatre critic for *The Black American.*

Edwin Denby
145 West 21st Street
New York, NY 10011

Jennifer Dunning
233 West 77th Street
New York, NY 10024

Patricia Egan
30 West 46th Street
New York, NY 10036

Barbara Engelbrecht
77 Hudson Street
New York, NY 10013
Tel: 212-732-2962
Member: DCA;

Michael Feingold
842 Broadway
New York, NY 10003
Member: ATCA;
Description: Michael Feingold is a theatre critic for the *Village Voice.*

Ellen Foreman
110 West 94th Street
New York, NY 10025
Member: ACTA;
Description: Ellen Foreman is theatre critic for *Black American.*

Mario Fratti
145 West 55th Street
New York, NY 10019
Member: ATCA;
Description: Mario Fratti is theatre critic for the *Paese Sera.*

Phyllis Funke
484 West 43rd Street, #35Q
New York, NY 10036
Member: ACTA;
Description: Phyllis Funke is a freelance theatre critic.

Josefina Garcia
162 East 80th Street, #3A
New York, NY 10021
Member: DCA;

Rosamond Gilder
24 Grammercy Park
New York, NY 10003
Member: ATCA;

Brendan Gill
25 West 43rd Street
New York, NY 10036
Member: ATCA;
Description: Brendan Gill is a theatre critic for *The New Yorker* magazine.

Victor Gluck
c/o *Wisdom's Child*
97-50 Queens Boulevard, #C-4
New York, NY 11374
Member: OCC;

Nancy Goldner
5 West 86th Street
New York, NY 10024
Member: DCA;

Eric Gordon
c/o *New Haven and Fairfield Advocates*
174 West 89th Street, #5B
New York, NY 10024
Member: OCC;

Alexis Greene
200 East 15th Street
New York, NY 10003
Member: DCA;

Marjorie Gunner
101 West 57th Street
New York, NY 10019
Member: ATCA;
Description: Marjorie Gunner is theatre critic for the *Bronx Home News.*

Mel Gussow
28 West 10th Street
New York, NY 10011
Member: ATCA;
Description: Mel Gussow is a theatre critic for the *New York Times.*

Cathryn G. Harding
3 Stuyvesant Oval
New York, NY 10009
Tel: 212-473-0380; 215-645-5607

William Harris
514 Broadway
New York, NY 10012
Member: ATCA;

Jan Hartman
c/o Virginia Brooks
460 Riverside Drive
New York, NY 10027
Member: DCA;

Henry Hewes
1326 Madison Avenue
New York, NY 10028
Member: ACTA;
Description: Henry Hewes writes theatre criticism for many well known publicatons.

Holly Hill
15 West 11th Street
New York, NY 10011
Member: ATCA;
Description: Holly Hill is a theatre critic for the *New York Theatre Review.*

Catherine Hughes
79 West 12th Street
New York, NY 10011
Member: ATCA;
Description: Catherine Hughes is a theatre critic for the *America.*

Richard Hummler
154 West 46th Street
New York, NY 10036
Member: ATCA;
Description: Richard Hummler is theatre critic for *Variety.*

Dan Isaac
30 West 88th Street
New York, NY 10024
Member: ACTA;
Description: Dan Isaac is the drama editor for the *East Side Express.*

Judith Jacobs
39A Gramercy Park North
New York, NY 10010
Member: DCA;

Robert Jacobson
1865 Broadway
New York, NY 10023
Member: DCA;
Description: Robert Jacobson is the Editor-in-Chief of *Ballet News.*

Cynthia Lee Jenner
3 East 9th Street
New York, NY 10003
Member: ATCA;
Description: C. Lee Jenner is a theatre critic for Courier-Life Publications.

Jeremy Gerard
62 East 87th Street
New York, NY 10028
Member: ACTA;
Description: Jeremy Gerard is theatre critic for *Our Town.*

Wendy Jophet
c/o Landa, 117 East 77th Street
New York, NY 10021
Tel: 212-535-7301

Ted Kalem
1271 Avenue of the Americas
New York, NY 10020
Member: ATCA;
Description: Ted Kalem is theatre critic for the *Time Magazine.*

Austin Kane
c/o *Hollywood Drama-Logue*
330 West 45th Street
New York, NY 10036
Tel: 212-582-4240
Description: Austin Kane writes the column 'Circling Manhattan' for *Hollywood Drama-Logue.*

Julia L. Keefer
408 East 78th Street
New York, NY 10021
Member: DCA;

Anna Kisselgoff
61 West 113th Street
New York, NY 10025
Member: DCA;
Description: Dance critic for *The New York Times.*

Howard Kissel
7 East 12th Street
New York, NY 10003
Member: ATCA;
Description: Howard Kissel is theatre critic for *Womens Wear Daily.*

Stewart Klein
205 East 67th Street
New York, NY 10021
Member: ATCA;
Description: Stuart Klein is a theatre critic for WNEW-TV.

Jack Kroll
444 Madison Avenue
New York, NY 10022
Member: ATCA;
Description: Jack Kroll is a theatre critic for *Newsweek* magazine.

Pat Lamb
17 West 67th Street
New York, NY 10023
Member: ATCA;
Description: Pat Lamb is theatre critic for *Womensweek.*

Judy Landon
357 East 57th Street
New York, NY 10022
Member: DCA;

Karla Layden
c/o *Community News*
437 East 76th Street
New York, NY 10021
Member: OCC;

Leo Lerman
350 Madison Avenue
New York, NY 10017
Member: ATCA;
Description: Leo Lerman ia a theatre critic for *Vogue.*

Elenore Lester
245 East 21st Street
New York, NY 10010
Member: ATCA;

James Leverette
83 Macdougal Street
New York, NY 10012
Member: ATCA;

Emory Lewis
360 West 22nd Street
New York, NY 10011
Member: ATCA;
Description: Emory Lewis is theatre critic for *The Bergen Record.*

Mary Ann Liebert
500 East 85th Street
New York, NY 10021
Tel: 212-988-0743
Description: Manhattan East newspaper

Pia Lindstrom
c/o WNBC, 30 Rockefeller Plaza
New York, NY 10020
Member: ATCA;
Description: Pia Lindstom is a theatre critic for

WNBC-TV.

Frank Lipsius
27 West 55th Street
New York, NY 10019
Member: ATCA;
Description: Frank Lipsius is theatre critic for *The Financial Times.*

Valentina Litvinoff
9 East 17th Street
New York, NY 10003

Glenn Loney
3 East 71st Street
New York, NY 10021
Member: ATCA;
Description: Glenn Loney is a theatre critic for *Opera News, Theatre Crafts, Players, Ballet News, Los Angeles Time, Ddance Magazine, Smithsonian,* and *Theatre Journal.*

Cindy Lyle
49 West 16th Street
New York, NY 10011

Patricia MacKay
250 West 57th Street
New York, NY 10019
Member: ATCA;
Description: Patricia MacKay is the editor of *Theatre Crafts Magazine.*

Billy Mahoney
Julliard School, Dance Division
Lincoln Center Plaza
New York, NY 10023

Elva Mangold
c/o *East Side Weekly*
40 Park Avenue
New York, NY 10016
Member: OCC;
Description: Critic for the *East Side Weekly, Queens Tribune,* and *News World.*

Joan Marlone
c/o Proscenium Productions
4 Park Avenue
New York, NY 10016
Member: OCC;

Bonnie Marranca
92 Saint Marks Place
New York, NY 10003
Member: ATCA;
Description: Bonnie Marranca is one of the editors of the *Performing Arts Journal.*

John Martin
200 West 58th Street, #110
New York, NY 10019
Member: DCA;

Jacqueline Maskey
105 West 73rd Street
New York, NY 10023
Member: DCA;

Francis Mason
46 Morton Street
New York, NY 10014
Member: DCA;

Katy Matheson
205 West 15th Street, #3V
New York, NY 10011
Member: DCA;

Annette Michelson
141 Wooster Street
New York, NY 10012

Martita Middence
127 West 79th Street
New York, NY 10024

Richard Miller
c/o Garrett Enterprises
1560 Broadway
New York, NY 10036
Tel: 1 8-0 2-3 6600; 212-575-1000
Member: OCC;
Description: A nationally syndicated columnist.

Sarah Montague
119 Bank Street
New York, NY 10014

Erika Munk
249 West 13th Street
New York, NY 10011
Member: ATCA;
Description: Erika Munk is a theatre critic for
the *Village Voice.*

Don Nelson
220 East 42nd Street
New York, NY 10017
Member: ATCA;
Description: Don Nelson is a theatre critic for
the *New York Daily News.*

Barbara Newman
150 West 96th Street, #15F
New York, NY 10025

Joan T. Nourse
780 Riverside Drive
New York, NY 10032
Member: ATCA;
Description: Joan Nourse is a theatre critic for
Dramascope.

Julius Novick
3 Washington Square
New York, NY 10012
Member: ATCA;
Description: Julius Novick is a theatre critic for
the *Village Voice.*

Jean Nuchtern
411 West End Avenue
New York, NY 10024

Edith Oliver
25 West 43rd Street
New York, NY 10036
Member: ATCA;
Description: Edith Oliver is a theatre critic for
The New Yorker magazine.

Hilary Ostlere
401 First Avenue
New York, NY 10010

Kay Perper
152 West 58th Street

New York, NY 10019
Member: DCA;

Janis Pforsich
521 East 87th Street
New York, NY 10028
Member: DCA;

Richard Philp
Dance Magazine
1180 6th Avenue
New York, NY 10036
Member: DCA;

Robert Pierce
117 Perry Street
New York, NY 10014
Member: DCA;

Gary Pollard
159 Maiden Lane
New York, NY 10038
Member: DCA;

Henry Popkin
54 King Street
New York, NY 10014
Member: ATCA;

Leonard Probst
30 Rockefeller Plaza
New York, NY 10020
Annual Budget: ATCA;
Description: Leonard Probst is a theatre critic
for WNBC-TV.

Gerald Rabkin
304 East 6th Street
New York, NY 10003
Member: ATCA;
Description: Gerald Rabkin is theatre critic for
the *New Statesman.*

Alan Rich
755 Second Avenue
New York, NY 10017
Member: ATCA;
Description: Alan Rich is a theatre critic for
New York Magazine.

Frank Rich
229 West 43rd Street
New York, NY 10036
Member: ACTA;
Description: Theatre critic for *The New Times.*

Allen Robertson
c/o Howlett
48 West 89th Street
New York, NY 10024
Member: DCA;

Lillie Rosen
622 East 20th Street
New York, NY 10009
Member: DCA;

Peter Rosenwald
1125 Fifth Avenue
New York, NY 10028
Member: DCA;

Charles Ryweck
c/o *Hollywood Reporter*

1501 Broadway
New York, NY 10036
Member: ATCA;

Hubert Saal
Newsweek
444 Madison Avenue
New York, NY 10022
Member: DCA;
Description: A critic for *Newsweek.*

Verna Sabelle
21 East 66th Street
New York, NY 10021
Member: ATCA;
Description: Verna Sabelle is a theatre critic
for *M.D. Magazine.*

Michael Sander
c/o 866 Third Avenue
New York, NY 10022
Member: ACTA;
Description: Critic for *Hollywood Drama–Logue*
in New York.

Leo Sauvage
270 West End Avenue
New York, NY 10023
Member: ATCA;
Description: Leo Sauvage is theatre critic for
Les Nouvelles Literaires

Marion Sawyer
258 West 22nd Street
New York, NY 10022
Member: DCA;
Description: A critic for *Chelsea-Clinton News.*

Bonnie Scheibman
29 North Moore Street
New York, NY 10003
Member: DCA;

Richard J. Scholem
Post Office Box 740
New York, NY 11746
Member: ATCA;
Description: Richard Scholem is a theatre critic for WNYC Radio.

Luise Scripps
1 West 72nd Street
New York, NY 10023
Member: DCA;

Barnett Serchuk
785 West End Avenue, #2B
New York, NY 10025
Member: DCA;

Christopher Sharp
7 East 12th Street
New York, NY 10003
Member: ATCA;
Description: Christopher Sharp is theatre critic for Fairchild Publications.

Maury Sherman
442 10th Avenue, #4FN
New York, NY 10001
Member: DCA;

Don Shewey
514 Broadway
New York, NY 10012

Member: ATCA;

Marcia B. Siegel
244 West 72nd Street
New York, NY 10023
Member: DCA;

Jill Silverman
16 Charles Street
New York, NY 10014
Member: DCA;

Linda Small
23-15 98th Street
New York, NY 11369
Member: DCA;

Amanda Smith
241 East 76th Street
New York, NY 10021
Member: DCA;

Claudia Soifer
71 First Avenue
New York, NY 10003
Member: DCA;

Sally R. Sommer
9 West 10th Street
New York, NY 10011
Tel: 212-673-9303
Member: DCA;

Nancy Spector
463 West Street
New York, NY 10014
Member: DCA;

Lee Edward Stern
Manning, Selvage and Lee
99 Park Avenue
New York, NY 10016
Member: DCA;

Norma McLain Stoop
1 Lincoln Plaza, #23D
New York, NY 10023
Member: DCA;

Burt Supree
60 East 7th Street
New York, NY 10003
Member: DCA;

Dorothy Swerdlove
c/o Billy Rose Collection
New York Public Library
111 Amsterdam Avenue
New York, NY 10023
Member: OCC;
Description: Head of Billy Rose Collection, NY
Public Library

Sy Syna
187 Chrystie Street
New York, NY 10002
Member: ATCA;
Description: Sy Syna is a theatre critic for the
Other Paper.

Linda Szmyd
Judson Hall-New York University
53 Washington Square
New York, NY 10012
Member: DCA;

William Talbot
c/o Samuel French, Inc.
25 West 45th Street
New York, NY 10036
Member: OCC;

Eric Taub
353 West 51st Street, Apartment 1-2
New York, NY 10019
Member: DCA;

Walter Terry
170 West End Avenue
New York, NY 10023
Member: DCA;

Rose Ann Thom
522 West End Avenue
New York, NY 10024
Member: DCA;

Pauline Tish
48 Grove Street
New York, NY 10014
Member: DCA;

Tobi Tobias
38 West 96th Street
New York, NY 10025
Member: DCA;

Suzanne Walther
127 West 78th Street
New York, NY 10024
Member: DCA;

Debbie Wasserman
41 West 72nd Street
New York, NY 10023
Member: ACTA;
Description: Debbie Wasserman is a theatre
critic for the *New York Theatre Review.*

Amy E. Waterman
11 Waverly Place, #8C
New York, NY 10003
Member: DCA;

Douglas Watt
220 East 42nd Street
New York, NY 10017
Member: ATCA;
Description: Ernest Leogrande is a theatre
critic for the *New York Daily News.*

Carmen Kelly Webster
c/o Yonkers, Tuchahoe Papers
34-29 80th Street
New York, NY 11172
Member: OCC;

Bert Wechsler
c/o *Our Town*
215 East 80th Street
New York, NY 10021
Member: OCC;

Andrew Mark Wentkin
70 West 71st Street
New York, NY 10023
Member: DCA;

Ross Wetzsteon
842 Broadway
New York, NY 10003

Member: ATCA;

Gerald Wilk
74-02 Kessel Street
New York, NY 11375
Member: ATCA;
Description: Gerald H. Wilk is theatre critic for
Die Deutche Buhne.

John A. Willis
c/o *Theatre World*
190 Riverside Drive
New York, NY
Member: OCC;
Description: Editor of *Theatre World, Dance
World, Screen World*

Edwin Wilson
55 Central Park West
New York, NY 10023
Member: ACTA;
Description: Edwin Wilson is theatre critic for
The Wall Street Journal.

Barton Wimble
Box 616, Ansonia Station
New York, NY 10023
Member: DCA;

Enid Wooward
320 East 54th Street
New York, NY 10022
Member: DCA;

Peter Wynne
115 East 9th Street
New York, NY
Member: ATCA;
Description: Peter Wynne is theatre critic for
The Record.

Robert Yohn
135 West 14th Street
New York, NY 10011
Member: DCA;

Suzanne Youngerman
250 West 99th Street
New York, NY 10025
Member: DCA;

Elizabeth Zimmer
31 East 30th Street
New York, NY 10016
Member: DCA;

D'lela Zuck
22 West 77th Street
New York, NY 10024
Member: DCA;

Northport

Elsa Posey Novak
21 Marion's Lane
Northport, NY 11768

Poughkeepsie

Mindy Aloff
1 Wing Road
Poughkeepsie, NY 12603
Member: DCA;

Jeffery Borak
Post Office Box 1231

Poughkeepsie, NY 11746
Member: ATCA;
Description: Jeffrey Borak is a theatre critic for the *Poughkeepsie Journal.*

Rochester

Judith Cox
1055 Meios Street
Rochester, NY

Jilana Van Meter
129 Lake Lea Road
Rochester, NY 14617
Member: DCA;

Sea Cliff

Robert Lyons
c/o *Mineola American*
45 Laurel Avenue
Sea Cliff, NY 11579
Member: OCC;

South Nyack

Pamela Sommers
123 Piermont Avenue
South Nyack, NY 10960
Tel: 914-358-5921
Member: DCA;

Staten Island

Jane Gardner
19 Occident Avenue
Staten Island, NY 10304
Member: DCA;

Norman Nadel
234 College Avenue
Staten Island, NY 10314
Member: ATCA;
Description: Norman Nadel is theatre critic for Newspaper Enterprises.

Syosset

Stephanie Miles
45 Belevedere Drive
Syosset, NY 11791

Syracuse

Nevart Apikian
125 Parkway Drive
Syracuse, NY 13207
Member: ATCA;
Description: Nevart Apikian is a theatre critic for the *Syracuse Post Standard.*

David Feldman
102 Euclid Terrace
Syracuse, NY 13210
Member: ATCA;
Description: David Feldman is a theatre critic for the *Syracuse Post Standard.*

Valley Cottage

Marian F. Wolbers
Post Office Box 23
Valley Cottage, NY 10989
Member: DCA;

West Hempstead

Frank J. Ucciardo
c/o WBAB Radio
538 Chesman Street
West Hempstead, NY 11552
Member: OCC;

White Plains

Kathie Beals
1 Gannett Drive
White Plains, NY 10604
Member: DCA;
Description: A critic for the Westchester Rockland Newspapers.

Jacques Le Sourd
c/o Westchester-Rockland Papers
One Gannett Drive
White Plains, NY 10604
Member: ATCA;

Elaine Schettino
c/o TGIF Entertainment/Casting
320 East Columbus Avenue
White Plains, NY 10604
Member: OCC;
Description: Associate Editor of *T.G.I.F.*

NORTH CAROLINA
Charlotte

Jo Ann Rhetts
Post Office Box 2138
Charlotte, NC 28233
Member: ATCA;
Description: Jo Ann Rhetts is a reviewer for the *Charlotte Observer.*

Hendersonville

Mary Jo Padgett
334 Third Avenue West
Hendersonville, NC 28739
Member: DCA;

NORTH DAKOTA
Fargo

Sylvia Paine
Post Office Box 2020
Fargo, ND 58107
Member: DCA;
Description: A critic for *Forum.*

OHIO
Akron

Donald Rosenberg
Akron Beacon Journal
Akron, OH
Member: DCA;
Description: A critic for the *Akron Beacon Journal.*

Cincinnati

Tom McElfresh
c/o *The Cincinnati Enquirer*
617 Vine Street
Cincinnati, OH 45201
Member: ATCA;

Jerry Stein
c/o *Cincinnati Post*
800 Broadway
Cincinnati, OH 45202
Member: ATCA;

Cleveland

Peter Bellamy
c/o *The Plain Dealer*
2476 Kenilworth Road
Cleveland, OH 44106
Member: ATCA;

Tony Mastroianni
c/o *Cleveland Press*
901 Lakeside Avenue
Cleveland, OH 44114

Wilma Salisbury
1801 Superior Avenue
Cleveland, OH 44114
Member: DCA;

Columbus

Edward Fisher
c/o *Columbus Dispatch*
34 South Third Street
Columbus, OH 43216
Member: ATCA;

Lorain

Howard Gollop
c/o *Lorain Journal*
1657 Broadway
Lorain, OH 44052
Member: ATCA;

Toledo

Norman Dresser
c/o *Toledo Blade*
3028 Pemberton Drive
Toledo, OH 43606
Member: ATCA;

Anne L. Skalski
2828 Pemberton Drive
Toledo, OH 43606
Member: DCA;

Valley View

Jackie Demaline
c/o *Sun Newspapers*
5510 Cloverleaf Parkway
Valley View, OH 44125
Member: ATCA;

OREGON
Medford

Alvin Reiss
c/o *The Mail Tribune*
Post Office Box 1108
Medford, OR 97501
Member: ATCA;

Monmouth

Ray Miller
c/o Creative Arts Department
Oregon College of Education
Monmouth, OR 97361

Phoenix

Greg McKeen
c/o KTVL-TV, Box 97
Phoenix, OR 97535
Member: ATCA;

Portland

Holly Johnson
c/o *The Oregonian*
2425 NW Lovejoy Street
Portland, OR 97210
Member: ATCA;

Arnold Marks
c/o *Oregon Journal*
1320 SW Broadway
Portland, OR 97201
Member: ATCA;

Louise Steinman
3850 SW 41st Street
Portland, OR 97202
Member: DCA;

PENNSYLVANIA
Abington

Michael Elkin
1062 Highland Avenue
Abington, PA 19001
Member: ATCA;
Description: Michael Elkin is a theatre critic
for the *Jewish Exponent.*

New Kensington

Kathleen-Gail Atkinson
146 Warren Drive
New Kensington, PA 15068
Member: DCA;

Phiadelphia

Gerald Weales
208 South 43rd Street
Phiadelphia, PA 19103
Member: ATCA;
Description: Gerald Weales is a freelance
theatre critic.

Philadelphia

Richard Rutherford
936 Irving Street
Philadelphia, PA 19107
Member: DCA;

Ann Vachon
Temple University
Dance Department
Philadelphia, PA 19122
Member: DCA;

Daniel Webster
Philadelphia Inquirer
Philadelphia, PA
Member: DCA;
Description: A critic for the *Philadelphia Inquirer.*

Pittsburgh

George Anderson
50 Boulevard of the Allies
Pittsburgh, PA 15222
Member: ATCA;
Description: George Anderson is a theatre
critic for the *Pittsburgh Post Gazette.*

Edward Blank
c/o *Pittsburgh Press*
24 Boulevard of the Allies
Pittsburgh, PA 15230
Member: ATCA;

RHODE ISLAND
Newport

Martha Smith
3 Division Street
Newport, RI 02840
Tel: Mar-ha -mith
Member: ATCA;
Description: Martha Smith is theatre critic for
the *Providence Journal.*

Providence

William K. Gale
75 Fountain Street
Providence, RI 02902
Member: ACTA;
Description: Mr. Gale is a theatre critic for the
Providence Journal.

James L. Seavor
10 Dorrance Street
Providence, RI 02903
Member: ATCA;

SOUTH DAKOTA
Sioux Falls

Marshall Fine
c/o *Sioux Falls Argus Leader*
200 South Minnesota Avenue
Sioux Falls, SD 57102
Member: ATCA;

TENNESSEE
Memphis

Edwin Howard
c/o *Memphis Star Scimitar*
495 Union Avenue
Memphis, TN 37202
Member: ATCA;

Robert Jennings
c/o *Memphis Commercial Appeal*
Memphis, TN 38101
Member: ATCA;

Howell Pearre
c/o *Memphis Magazine*
750 Adams Avenue
Memphis, TN 38105
Member: ATCA;

Nashville

Clara Hieronymous
c/o *The Tennessean*
1100 Broad Street
Nashville, TN 37202
Member: ATCA;

Sara Sprott Morrow
c/o *The Nashville Banner*
1100 Broad Street
Nashville, TN 37202
Member: ATCA;

Alan Nelson
c/o *The Nashville Banner*
1100 Broad Street
Nashville, TN 37202
Member: ATCA;

TEXAS
Austin

Judi Hazlett
8603 Donna Trail
Austin, TX 78758
Member: DCA;

Nancy Kaufman
3102 West Avenue
Austin, TX 78705
Member: DCA;

Suzanne Shelton
1 Nob Hill Circle
Austin, TX 78746
Member: DCA;

Dallas

John Branch
5200 Belmont, Apartment 219
Dallas, TX 75206

Sean Mitchell
c/o *Dallas Times Herald*
3428 McFarlin
Dallas, TX 75205
Member: ATCA;

Patsy Swank
c/o KERA-Channel 13
Harry Hines Boulevard

Dallas, TX 75201
Member: ATCA;

Diane Werts
c/o *Dallas News*
927C Shadyside Lane
Dallas, TX 75223
Member: ATCA;

Winifred Widener
6816 Del Norte
Dallas, TX
Member: DCA;

El Paso

Joan Quarm
1520 Upson
El Paso, TX 79902
Member: DCA;

Fort Worth

Susan Petty
1309 Montgomery
Fort Worth, TX 76107
Member: DCA;

Friendswood

Susan H. Dauphin
c/o KUHF-FM
111 Royal Court
Friendswood, TX 77546
Member: ATCA;

Houston

William Albright
c/o *Houston Post*
4747 Southwest Freeway
Houston, TX 77001
Member: ATCA;

Rowland Bachman
Jones Hall
615 Louisiana
Houston, TX 77002
Address Inquiries to: Houston Ballet
Member: DCA;

Ira J. Black
c/o KLEF-FM
5353 West Alabama, Suite 410
Houston, TX 77056
Member: ATCA;

Elizabeth Elam
3030 Lafayette
Houston, TX 77005

Joanna Friesen
1509 Hawthorne
Houston, TX 77006
Member: DCA;

Steve Hogner
2010 Park, #5
Houston, TX 77019
Member: DCA;

Ann Holmes
c/o *Houston Chronicle*
801 Texas Street
Houston, TX 77002
Member: ATCA;

San Antonio

Lonnie Martin
Post Office Box 23219
San Antonio, TX 78223
Member: DCA;

Victoria

Daniel Ray Goddard
c/o *Victoria Advocate*
811 ½ West Stayton
Victoria, TX 77901
Member: ATCA;

Wharton

R.L. Cowser Jr.
920 Center
Wharton, TX 77488

Wichita Falls

Martha Steimel
1611 Singleton
Wichita Falls, TX 76302
Tel: 817-767-4673
Member: DCA;

UTAH

Salt Lake City

Rodger M. Barrow
Building 509, University of Utah
Salt Lake City, UT 84112
Member: DCA;

Octavia Haines
607 East 2nd Avenue
Salt Lake City, UT 801 355 5281
Description: Chronicle, U. of Utah

VERMONT

Burlington

Sharry Underwood
Redrock 12, 161 Austin Drive
Burlington, VT 05401
Member: DCA;

VIRGINIA

Ashland

Jon D. Longaker
133 Beverly Road
Ashland, VA 23005
Member: ATCA;
Description: Edward Campbell is critic for the *Frederick News Post.*

Newport News

David Nicholson
10344 Warwick Boulevard
Newport News, VA 23601

Richmond

Roy Proctor
333 East Grace Street
Richmond, VA 23219
Member: ATCA;
Description: Roy Proctor is a theatre critic for the *Richmond News Leader.*

Frances Wessells
2020 Stuart Avenue
Richmond, VA 23220
Member: DCA;

WASHINGTON

Seattle

Carole Beers
Seattle Times
Fairview Avenue North and Johns
Seattle, WA 98111
Member: DCA;
Description: A critic for the *Seattle Times.*

Maxine Cushing Gray
Northwest Arts
Post Office Box 97
Seattle, WA 98125
Member: DCA;
Description: A critic for the *Northwest Arts.*

Maggie Hawthorne
Seattle Post Intelligencer
6th and Wall
Seattle, WA 98121
Member: DCA;

Stephen Heck
4412 50th Avenue
Seattle, WA 98116
Member: DCA;

Wayne Johnson
c/o *Seattle Times*
Fairview Avenue North and Johns
Seattle, WA 98111
Member: ATCA;

Sandra Kurtz
1005 North 42nd Street
Seattle, WA 98103
Member: DCA;

Coby Larsen
1517 Magnolia Way West
Seattle, WA 98199

Lori Powell
924 20th Avenue
Seattle, WA 98112
Member: DCA;

Laura Shapiro
2006 24th Avenue East
Seattle, WA 98112
Member: DCA;

WEST VIRGINIA
Morgantown

Byron Nelson
1496 Woodland Drive
Morgantown, WV 26505
Member: ATCA;
Description: Byron Nelson is the theatre critic for the *Morgantown Dominion Post.*

WISCONSIN
Madison

Angela LaMaster
32 Sherman Terrace, #3
Madison, WI
Member: DCA;

Milwaukee

Laura M. Beaumont
2523 West Vogel Avenue
Milwaukee, WI 53212
Member: DCA;

Wynne Delacoma
Post Office Box 661
Milwaukee, WI 53201

Jay Joslyn
c/o *Milwaukee Sentinel*
198 North Fourth Street
Milwaukee, WI 53201
Member: ATCA;

Louise M. Kenngott
Post Office 661
Milwaukee, WI 53213
Member: DCA;

Dominique Noth
c/o *Milwaukee Journal*
3464 North Murray Avenue
Milwaukee, WI 53201
Member: ATCA;

Shorewood

Curtis Carter
2609 East Menlo
Shorewood, WI 53211

CANADA
Vancouver, British Columbia

Leland Windreich
3787 West 4th Avenue, #203
Vancouver, British Columbia, Canada V6R 1P4
Member: DCA;

Edmonton, Alberta

Carolyn Heiman
9910 112th Street
Edmonton Alta, Canada T5K 1L6
Member: DCA;

Winnipeg, Manitoba

Casimer Carter
71 Kennedy Street, #4
Winnipeg, Manitoba, Canada R3C 1S5

Downsview, Ontario

Laurel Quinlan
17 Four Winds Drive
Downsview, Ontario, Canada M3J 1K7
Member: DCA;

Oakville, Ontario

Michael Crabb
392 Pine Avenue
Oakville, Ontario, Canada L6J 2K3

Ottawa, Ontario

Burf Kay
89 Fifth Avenue
Ottawa, Ontario, Canada K1S 2M3
Member: DCA;

Toronto, Ontario

William Littler
1 Yonge Street
Toronto, Ontario, Canada
Description: Toronto Star.

Dianne Woodruff
351 Berkeley Street
Toronto, Ontario, Canada M5A 2X6
Member: DCA;

Waterloo, Ontario

Diana Taplin
University of Waterloo
Waterloo, Ontario, Canada N2L 3G1
Member: DCA;

Willowdale, Ontario

Gail E. Vanstone
185 Shaughnessy Boulevard, #602
Willowdale, Ontario, Canada M2J 1K2
Member: DCA;

7
Directors & Choreographers

The director and choreographer are often the key to a production's success, providing the core of originality around which the rest of the show's elements must revolve. This section provides a nationwide listing of members of the Society of Stage Directors and Choreographers (SSDC), although, again, a majority of these reside in the New York metropolitan area. The term "Director", "Choreographer", or "Director-Choreographer" follows the individual's name in the entry, denoting his or her specialization. A choreographer is one who composes and arranges dance for a production. A director has more far-reaching responsibilities; for action, lighting, music, and rehearsals.

ALABAMA

Anniston

Martin L. Platt, Director
POB 141
Anniston, AL 36202
Tel: 205-236-7503; 205-237-3822

ARKANSAS

Tuscon

Ellen Ray, Director-Choreographer
7046 East 5th Street
Tuscon, AR 85710

CALIFORNIA

Beverly Hills

Eric Berry, Director
Henderson/Hogan Agency
217 South Beverly Drive
Beverly Hills, CA 90212
Tel: 213-274-7815

Jeffrey Chambers, Director
c/o Irv Schecter Company
404 North Roxbury
Beverly Hills, CA 90212
Tel: 213-278-8070

John Clark, Director
612 North Alpine Drive
Beverly Hills, CA 90210

Peter R.J. Deyell, Director
9300 Wilshire Boulevard, #470
Beverly Hills, CA 90212
Tel: 213-274-5316

Michel M. Grilikhes, Director
420 Walker Drive
Beverly Hills, CA 90210
Tel: 213-271-0102

Lawrence Kasha, Director
2229 Gloaming Way
Beverly Hills, CA 90210
Tel: 213-276-1761

Elanie May, Director
8909 West Olympic Boulevard, Suite 200
Beverly Hills, CA 90211
Tel: 213-855-0505

Harvey Medlinsky, Director
9555 West Olympic Boulevard
Beverly Hills, CA 90212
Tel: 213-552-9090

David Schroeder, Director
215 South La Cienega Boulevard, Suite 200
Beverly Hills, CA 90211
Tel: 213-855-1201

Tad Tadlock, Director-Choreographer
c/o Sam Haskell
William Morris Agency
151 El Camino Drive
Beverly Hills, CA 90212
Tel: 213-859-4441

Joel Zwick, Director
c/o Irv Schechter Company
404 North Roxbury
Beverly Hills, CA 90213

Century City

Robert Greenwald, Director
1901 Avenue of the Stars
Century City, CA 90066
Tel: 213-552-9455

Encino

Devra Korwin, Director-Choreographer
16425 Bosque Drive
Encino, CA 91436
Tel: 213-990-1941

Hollywood

Ralph Beaumont, Director-Choreographer
6702 Hillpark Drive
Hollywood, CA 90068
Tel: 213-876-7597

Kevin Carlisle, Director-Choreographer
2022 North Sycamore Avenue
Hollywood, CA 90069
Tel: 213-874-6171

Ron Davis, Choreographer
c/o Creative Dance Foundation
6565 Sunset Boulevard Suite 218
Hollywood, CA 90028
Tel: 213-462-6565

Joel Mondeaux, Director
2033 Cheremova Avenue
Hollywood, CA 90068
Tel: 213-465-7471

Jack Ragotzy, Director
2057 Castilian Drive
Hollywood, CA 90068
Tel: 213-851-0019

Huntington Beach

David Emmes, Director
16871 Sea Witch Lane
Huntington Beach, CA 92699
Tel: 714-957-2602

Los Angeles

Leland Ball, Director
2300 Laurel Canyon Boulevard
Los Angeles, CA 90046
Tel: 213-656-2210

John Bowab, Director
1342 North Hayworth Avenue
Los Angeles, CA 90046
Tel: 213-278-7616

Ann Bowen, Director
1950 North Normandie Avenue
Los Angeles, CA 90027
Tel: 213-664-9381; 213-550-6366, Peri Winkler

Jack Bunch, Director-Choreographer
9000 Sunset Boulevard
Los Angeles, CA 90069
Tel: 213-273-0744

Gilbert Cates, Director
9200 Sunset Boulevard
Los Angeles, CA 90069

Tony Charmoli, Director-Choreographer
1271 Sunset Place Drive
Los Angeles, CA 90069

Tel: 213-855-0181

Gordon Davidson, Director
135 North Grand Avenue
Los Angeles, CA 90012
Tel: 213-972-7388

Joseph Hardy, Director
1888 Century Park East
Los Angeles, CA 90067
Tel: 213-277-4545

Peter H. Hunt, Director
1799 Westridge Road
Los Angeles, CA 90049
Tel: 213-472-1863

Rob Iscove, Director-Choreographer
9200 Sunset Boulevard, Suite 428
Los Angeles, CA 90069
Tel: 213-275-6135

Glenn Jordan, Director
1888 Century Park East
Los Angeles, CA 90067

Daniel Mann, Director
8730 Sunset Boulevard
Los Angeles, CA 90069
Tel: 213-657-3040

Steve Meyer, Director
830 North Wilcox
Los Angeles, CA 90038
Tel: 213-465-9579

Lynne Morris, Choreographer
9046 Sunset Boulevard
Los Angeles, CA 90069
Tel: 213-271-5693

Anthony Newley, Director
9255 Sunset Boulevard, Suite 1101
Los Angeles, CA 90069
Tel: 213-278-6880

Ron Palillo, Director
c/o Creative Artists-Ron Meyers
1888 Century Park East
Los Angeles, CA 90067
Tel: 213-277-4545

Tony Richardson, Director
1478 North King's Road
Los Angeles, CA 90069
Tel: 213-656-5314

Lee D. Sankowich, Director
7456 Melrose Avenue
Los Angeles, CA 90046
Tel: 213-653-4667

George Schaefer, Director
1801 Avenue of the Stars
Los Angeles, CA 90067
Tel: 213-553-6205

Buddy Schwab, Director-Choreographer
8730 Ashcroft Avenue
Los Angeles, CA 90048
Tel: 213-652-8082

Claude Thompson, Choreographer
1111 Hacienda Place
Los Angeles, CA 90069
Tel: 213-274-9475

Los Angelos

Frances Coppola
573 West Windsor Boulevard
Los Angelos, CA 9004
Tel: 213-467-1520

Malibu

William Glover, Director
30119 Harvester Road
Malibu, CA 90265
Tel: 213-457-9923

George Roy Hill, Director
27580 Winding Way
Malibu, CA 90265

North Hollywood

William Bartman, Director
5517 Corteen Place
North Hollywood, CA 91607
Tel: 213-462-8955

Carle Bensen, Director
5746 Fulcher
North Hollywood, CA 91601
Tel: 213-506-1595

David Gold, Director-Choreographer
6623 ½ Whitsett Avenue
North Hollywood, CA 91606
Tel: 213-985-8941; 213-874-2200

David Jason, Director
5030 Riverton, #7
North Hollywood, CA 91601

Ken Letner, Director
4418 Simpson, #1
North Hollywood, CA 91607
Tel: 213-769-1929

Walter Painter, Director-Choreographer
4823 Ben Avenue
North Hollywood, CA 91607
Tel: 213-477-2075

San Francisco

William Ball, Director
c/o American Conservatory Theatre, 450
Geary Street
San Francisco, CA 94102
Tel: 415-771-3880

Milt Commons, Director
655 Stockton Street
San Francisco, CA 94108

R.G. Davis, Director
611 Rhode Island Street
San Francisco, CA 94107
Tel: 415-647-2982; 212-724-7400

Michael Smuin, Director-Choreographer
378 18th Avenue
San Francisco, CA 94121
Tel: 415-751-2141

Donald Weissmuller, Choreographer
111 Joost Avenue
San Francisco, CA 94138
Tel: 415-JU6-9073

San Fransisco

William J. Browder, Director
1480 Page Street
San Fransisco, CA 94117
Tel: 451-621-8628

Allen Fletcher, Director
450 Geary Street
San Fransisco, CA 94108
Tel: 415-771-3880

San Jose

Milton Lyon, Director
2225 McLaughlin, Apartment #1
San Jose, CA 95122
Tel: 408-297-1463

Santa Monica

Danny Daniels, Director-Choreographer
310 Wilshire Boulevard
Santa Monica, CA 90401

Ben Martin, Director
1505 Harvard
Santa Monica, CA 90404
Tel: 213-829-1656

Sherman Oaks

Harry Cauley, Director
3660 Glenridge Drive
Sherman Oaks, CA 91423
Tel: 213-784-3241

Studio City

Norman Cohen, Director
4327 Laurel Grove Avenue
Studio City, CA 91604
Tel: 213-769-0234; 213-461-3726, Francine
Witkin

Nick DeCarlo, Director-Choreographer
4111 Tuhunga Avenue, Apartment 15
Studio City, CA 91604
Tel: 213-762-6614

Joanne Divito, Director-Choreographer
12654 Moorpark, Apartment 10
Studio City, CA 91604
Tel: 213-760-7570

Bernard Erhard, Director
12100 Valley Spring Lane
Studio City, CA 91604
Tel: 213-506-0014

Dorothy Holland, Director-Choreographer
12431 Landale
Studio City, CA 91604
Tel: 213-760-0734

Nancy Walker, Director
3702 Eureka Drive
Studio City, CA 91604
Tel: 213-760-8474

Van Nuys

Will Mackenzie, Director
13109 Chandler Boulevard
Van Nuys, CA 91401
Tel: 213-997-6031

Al Rossi, Director
15744 Gault Street
Van Nuys, CA 91406
Tel: 213-902-1538

West Covina

Gary Davis, Director
2500 East Thackery
West Covina, CA 91791
Tel: 213-967-7839

West Hollywood

David Nillo, Director-Choreographer
728 North Doheny Drive
West Hollywood, CA 90069
Tel: 213-276-7441

Woodland Hills

Jeff Blekner, Director
4815 Dunman Avenue
Woodland Hills, CA 91364
Tel: 213-887-5938

Chad Block, Director-Choreographer
5117 Llano Drive
Woodland Hills, CA 91364

COLORADO

Denver

Edward Payson Call, Director
1050 13th Street
Denver, CO 80204
Tel: 303-893-4200

CONNECTICUT

Darien

Don Enoch, Director
29 Lakeside Avenue
Darien, CT 06820
Tel: 203-655-4799

Fairfield

Stuart Vaughan, Director
111 Wheeler Park Avenue
Fairfield, CT 06432
Tel: 203-374-8940

New Haven

David Hammond, Director
228 Park Street, #11
New Haven, CT 06520
Tel: 212-873-4806; 212-873-4802

Rowayton

Dennis Cole, Director-Choreographer
46 Roton Avenue
Rowayton, CT 06835
Tel: 203-853-7337

Stafford Springs

Charles Werner Moore, Director
Post Office Box 206
Stafford Springs, CT 06076
Tel: 203-875-7255

Stamford

Del Tenny, Director
351 Erkshine Road
Stamford, CT 06903
Tel: 212-581-0177; 203-322-7352
Address Inquiries to: 203 324 6781

Stratford

Mary Hunter Wolf, Director
American Shakespeare Theatre
Stratford, CT 06497
Tel: 203-378-7321; 212-WO - 3900

West Cornwall

Larry Gates, Director
River Road
West Cornwall, CT 06976
Tel: 212-697-6339

West Redding

Morton Da Costa, Director
20 Dorethy Road
West Redding, CT 06896
Tel: 203-938-2438

DELAWARE

Wilmington

James M. Jamieson,
Director-Choreographer
209 West 14th Street
Wilmington, DE 19801
Tel: 302-656-8969

DISTRICT OF COLUMBIA

Washington

Louis W. Scheeder, Director
201 East Capital Street, SE
Washington, DC 20003
Tel: 202-547-3230

Robert Graham Small, Director
1742 Church Street NW
Washington, DC 20036
Tel: 203-232-1122

FLORIDA

Fort Pierce

Richard Vath, Director
c/o Indian River, 3209 Virginia
Fort Pierce, FL 33450

Lakeland

Mary Friday, Choreographer
719 East Palmetto
Lakeland, FL 33801
Tel: 813-686-2631

Lake Worth

James Malcolm, Director-Choreographer
4564 Holly Lake Drive
Lake Worth, FL 33463
Tel: 305-968-4564; 212-246-8484

Naples

Ruth Clark Everitt, Director
132 Lake Point Lane
Naples, Fl 33942
Tel: 813-775-5615

Palm Beach

Ruth Clark-Everitt, Director
418 B Australian
Palm Beach, FL 33480
Tel: 305-655-1240; 305-833-1484

Sarasota

Jim Hoskins, Director-Choreographer
Post Office Box Drawer E
Sarasota, FL 33578
Tel: 813-355-7115

Neal Kenyon, Director-Choreographer
Post Office Box Drawer E
Sarasota, FL 33578
Tel: 813-355-7115

Carolyn Michel, Director
800 South Boulevard of Presidents
Sarasota, FL 33577
Tel: 212-JU6-6300; 813-388-1576

ILLINOIS

Chicago

Sheldon Patinkin, Director
1060 West Albion Avenue
Chicago, IL 60626
Tel: 312-973-0221

Steven Schachter, Director
2851 North Halsted
Chicago, IL 60607
Tel: 312-975-2314

Des Plaines

Brian Lynch, Choreographer
9359 Bay Colonial, #3N
Des Plaines, IL 60016
Tel: 312-827-6751

Evanston

Tony Mockus, Director
2717 Woodbine Avenue
Evanston, IL 60201
Tel: 312-864-6565; 312-583-5000

La Grange Park

Chuck Likar, Director
1209 Meadowcrest
La Grange Park, IL 60525
Tel: 312-352-8003

Oak Park

Rudy Hogenmiller, Choreographer
1000 South Taylor
Oak Park, IL 60304
Tel: 312-383-2360

Skokie

Ronna Kaye, Director
5145 West Fairview Lane
Skokie, IL 60077

Wilmette

Richard S. Kordos, Director
800 Chilton
Wilmette, IL 60091
Tel: 312-251-1901

INDIANA

Indianopolis

Edward J. Stern, Director
3726 Totem Lane
Indianapolis, IN 46208
Tel: 317-635-5277

West Lafayette

Jim O'Connor, Director
435 Robinson
West Lafayette, IN 47906
Tel: 317-494-5811

LOUISIANA

New Orleans

Tony Bevinetto, Director-Choreographer
135 Country Club Drive
New Orleans, LA 70124
Tel: 504-482-0092

Jack M. Payne, Director-Choreographer
1118 Ursulines Street
New Orleans, LA 70116
Tel: 504-586-9604

MARYLAND

Baltimore

Robert Minford, Director
3925 Beech Avenue
Baltimore, MD 21211
Tel: 301-243-0150; 301-235-8000

Carl Schurr, Director
1216 John Street
Baltimore, MD 21217
Tel: 301-462-5249

Chevy Chase

Leo Brady, Director
3605 Dunlop Street
Chevy Chase, MD 20015
Tel: 301-652-6512

Virginia Freeman, Director-Choreographer
6822 Delaware Street
Chevy Chase, MD 20015
Tel: 301-645-0416; 202-547-3230

James D. Waring, Director
153 Quincy Street
Chevy Chase, MD 20015
Tel: 301-654-8161

MASSACHUSETTS

Boston

Robert C. Gilman,
Director-Choreographer
46 The Fenway, Apartment 8
Boston, MA 02215
Tel: 212-787-3362; 617-261-5163

Cambridge

Lester W. Thompson, Jr., Director
31 Linnaear Street
Cambridge, MA 02140
Tel: 617-354-3460

Weston

David F. Wheeler, Director
271 Glen Road
Weston, MA 02193
Tel: 617-235-4382

Williamsburg

Gemze De Lappee, Choreographer Gemze
De
83 Village Hill Avenue R
Williamsburg, MA 01096
Tel: 413-268-3172

MICHIGAN

Kalamazoo

Robert L. Smith, Director
3734 Barrington Drive
Kalamazoo, MI 49007
Tel: 616-375-2278

Oak Park

Christine Zevan, Choreographer
25547 Lincoln Terrace Drive
Oak Park, MI 48237
Tel: 313-967-1724; 313-352-1796

Redford Twp.

David Davis, Director
14830 Seneca
Redford Twp., MI 48239

MINNESOTA

Champlin

Larry Whiteley, Director-Choreographer
11260 West River Road
Champlin, MN 55316
Tel: 612-421-1291

Mankato

Ronald C. Olauson, Director
719 South Broad
Mankato, MN 56001
Tel: 507-388-7447; 507-389-2118

Minneapolis

John Command, Director-Choreographer
1511 West 33rd Street
Minneapolis, MN 55408
Tel: 612-825-7667

Charles Nolte, Director
1927 East River Terrace
Minneapolis, MN 55414
Tel: 612-335-2520

MISSOURI

Kansas City

James W. Assad, Director
5406 Harrison Street
Kansas City, MO 64110
Tel: 816-333-5522

St. Louis

Wallace K. Chappell, Director
130 Edgar Road, Box 28030
St. Louis, MO 63119
Tel: 314-968-7340

Jane Conzelman, Director-Choreographer
12426 Ridgefield Drive
St. Louis, MO 63131
Tel: 314-965-3430

Gavin Webb, Director
820 South LaClede Station Road
St. Louis, MO 63119
Tel: 314-962-3722

NEVADA

Sparks

Gary Giocomo, Choreographer
3102 Bristle Branch Drive
Sparks, NV 89431
Tel: 702-331-1228

NEW JERSEY

Englewood

Harry Eggart, Director
21 Hillside Avenue
Englewood, NJ 07631
Tel: 201-568-4421

Jersey City

Michael Heaton, Director
195 South Street
Jersey City, NJ 07307
Tel: 201-653-4578; 212-246-0430

Madison

Paul Barry, Director-Fencing
Choreographer
c/o N.J. Shakespeare Festival
Madison, NJ 07940
Tel: 201-377-5330

Montclair

James A. Baffico, Director
216 Midland Avenue
Montclair, NJ 07042
Tel: 201-783-3490

Paula Kay Pierce, Director
75 Gates Avenue

Montclair, NJ 07042
Tel: 201-746-5941; 212-895-7080

Frederick Rolf, Director
177 Midland Avenue
Montclair, NJ 07042
Tel: 201-744-5526

Orange

Harold Scott, Director
300 Oakwood Avenue
Orange, NJ 07050
Tel: 201-673-7924

Paramus

Pat Julian, Director
116 Arnot Place
Paramus, NJ 07652
Tel: 201-262-5179; 201-244-4270

Pennington

Robert Lanchester, Director
137 South Main Street
Pennington, NJ 08534
Tel: 609-737-9629

Ridgefield Park

Thom Molyneaux, Director
244 Teaneck Road
Ridgefield Park, NJ 07660
Tel: 212-228-0900; 201-641-1040

Secaucus

Warren Kliewer, Director
281 Lincoln Avenue
Secaucus, NJ 07094
Tel: 201-863-6436

Teaneck

Sheldon Epps, Director
165 Van Buskirk Road
Teaneck, NJ 07666
Tel: 201-833-2841

Union

Anna Faix, Choreographer
1944 Axton Avenue
Union, NJ 07083
Tel: 201-686-7087

Wall

Frank Rollins Harrison, Director
167 Tilton's Corner Road
Wall, NJ 07719
Tel: 212-541-7600

NEW YORK

Amityville

Del Hughes, Director
30 Norman Avenue
Amityville, NY 11701
Tel: 516-264-2234

Babylon

Greg McCaslin, Director
121 Wyandanch Avenue
Babylon, NY 11702
Tel: 516-661-3631; 212-730-1188

Bayside Hills

Donald Christy, Director
58-34 215th Street
Bayside Hills, NY 11364
Tel: 212-224-7574

Brooklyn

Michael Bergmann, Director
99 Commercial Street
Brooklyn, NY 11222
Tel: 212-289-2508

Nadine Charlsen
1634 59th Street
Brooklyn, NY 11204
Tel: 212-236-0258

Ted Cornell, Director
One Fulton Street
Brooklyn, NY 11201
Tel: 212-643-9749

Jay Fox, Director-Choreographer
830 President Street
Brooklyn, NY 10215
Tel: 212-789-1727

J.F. Guadagni, Director
16 Stanton Road
Brooklyn, NY 11235
Tel: 212-332-7440

Carol Kastendieck,
Director-Choreographer
114 Clinton Street, 6A
Brooklyn, NY 11201
Tel: 212-MA4-1325

Wiliam Koch, Director-Choreographer
52 Clark Street, #5A
Brooklyn, NY 11201
Tel: 212-875-5784

Mario Martone, Director
1586 East 94th Street
Brooklyn, NY 11236
Tel: 212-531-1376; 212-531-9495

Victor Raider-Wexler, Director
164 Hall Street
Brooklyn, NY 11205
Tel: 212-622-0983; 212-840-1234

Ronald Roston, Director
129 Amity Street
Brooklyn, NY 11201
Tel: 212-858-9831

M. David Samples, Director
441 14th Street
Brooklyn, NY 11215

Rudy Tronto, Director-Choreographer
356 Dean Street
Brooklyn, NY 11217
Tel: 212-834-1095

Bonnie Walker, Choreographer
830 President Street
Brooklyn, NY 11215
Tel: 212-789-1727

Sims Wyeth
474 Third Street
Brooklyn, NY 11215
Description: Member; AFTRA, SAG, AEA,
Dramatists Guild.

Buffalo

Neal Du Brock, Director
168 North Street
Buffalo, NY 14201
Tel: 716-882-8858

Corona

Frank Scaringi, Director
40-20 Junction Boulevard
Corona, NY 11368
Tel: 212-TW9-0700

East Hampton

Alan Schneider, Director
41 Gingerbread Lane
East Hampton, NY 11937
Tel: 516-324-4267; 714-745-9449

Elmont

Ronald G. Russo, Director-Choreographer
2070 Renfrew Avenue
Elmont, NY 11003
Tel: 516-345-5256

Franklin Square

Cyprienne Gabel, Director-Choreographer
1096 Woodcliff Drive
Franklin Square, NY 11010
Tel: 516-561-1919, Home; 212-757-6300,
Service

Garden City

John Cappeletti, Director
25 Spruce Street
Garden City, NY 11530
Tel: 516-741-3874

Glen Head

Michael R. Martorella, Director
56 Smith Street
Glen Head, NY 11545
Tel: 516-671-0350

Hauppauge

Vic D'Amore, Director-Choreographer
41 Roosevelt Boulevard
Hauppauge, NY 11787
Tel: 516-586-4460

Hempstead

James Van Wart, Director
Hofstra University
Hempstead, NY 11550
Tel: 516-560-3281

Irving on the Hudson

Robert Lewis, Director
Matthiessen Park
Irving on the Hudson, NY 10533
Tel: 914-591-9217

Monsey

Henry Le Tang, Choreographer
7 Eleanor Place
Monsey, NY 10952
Tel: 914-357-7194; 212-974-9332

Mount Vernon

Dan Held, Director
2 Wales Place
Mount Vernon, NY 10552
Tel: 914-664-8394

Nanuet

Ted Forlow, Director-Choreographer
90 East Townline Road
Nanuet, NY 10954
Tel: 914-623-2549

New Rochelle

Ossie Davis, Director
Post Office Box 1318
New Rochelle, NY 10802
Tel: 914-235-6867

New York

Peter Anastos, Director-Choreographer
David Singer, 3 East 54th Street
New York, NY 10022
Tel: 212-308-2320

Julie Arenal, Director-Choreographer
205 East 10th Street
New York, NY 10003
Tel: 212-840-1234

Norman Ayrton, Director
c/o Juilliard School, Drama Division
Lincoln Center
New York, NY 10023
Tel: 212-799-5000 extension 251

Karin Baker, Director-Choreographer
41 Central Park West
New York, NY 10023
Tel: 212-799-7122

Word Baker, Director
333 West 56th Street, #9A
New York, NY 10019
Tel: 212-247-6484

Ted S. Bank, Director-Choreographer
535 Hudson, #4A
New York, NY 10014
Tel: 212-929-7119; 212-840-1234

Richard Barri, Director
344 West 89th Street
New York, NY 10024
Tel: 212-877-7507

Robert Barton, Director
320 West 90th Street, #2A
New York, NY 10024
Tel: 212-799-8549, Home; 212-582-4240, Service

Cash Baxter, Choreographer-Director
316 West 79th Street
New York, NY 10024
Tel: 212-787-9158

Margery Beddow, Director-Choreographer
514 West End Avenue, #11B
New York, NY 10024
Tel: 212-877-3756

Andre Belgrader, Director-Choreographer
84 Charles Street
New York, NY 10014
Tel: 212-675-7656

David H. Bell, Director-Choreographer
240 West 98th Street, Apartment 4D
New York, NY
Tel: 212-864-7911; 212-730-1188

Peter Bennett, Director
223 West 20th Street, Apartment 5A
New York, NY 10011
Tel: 212-243-8599

Tony Berk, Director
60 West 66th Street, Apartment 19G
New York, NY 10023
Tel: 212-362-3545; 212-764-1711

Zeke Berlin, Director
59 West 10th Street
New York, NY 10011
Tel: 212-254-0803

Melvin Bernhardt, Director
c/o Milton Goldman ICM
40 West 57th Street
New York, NY 10019
Tel: 212-556-5703

Valerie Bettis, Director-Choreographer
22 West 15th Street
New York, NY 10011
Tel: 212-982-7414

Patricia Birch, Director-Choreographer
c/o Franklin Weissberg
505 Park Avenue
New York, NY 10022
Tel: 212-532-5100

John Bishop, Director
11 Riverside Drive
New York, NY 10023
Tel: 212-362-6133

Stuart Bishop, Director
c/o Honey Sanders
229 West 42nd Street
New York, NY 10036
Tel: 212-947-5555

David Black, Director
251 East 51st Street
New York, NY 10022
Tel: 212-733-1188

Steven A. Bohm, Director-Choreographer
c/o Creative Theatre International
60 East 42nd Street
New York, NY 10017
Tel: 212-687-0586

Todd Bolender, Director-Choreographer
c/o Paul Szilard Productions
161 West 73rd Street
New York, NY 10023
Tel: 212-799-4756

Jack V. Booch, Director
300 West 49th Street, Apartment 610
New York, NY 10019
Tel: 212-246-0990

DeVeren Bookwalter, Director
134 West 4th Street, Apartment 3
New York, NY 10012
Tel: 212-673-3153

George Boyd, Director
Luis Sanjurjo I.C.M., 40 West 57th Street
New York, NY 10019

Julianne Boyd, Director
25 Fifth Avenue
New York, NY 10003
Tel: 212-533-3759

Ed Brazo, Choreographer
259 West 12th Street
New York, NY 10014
Tel: 212-989-9643; 212-840-1234

John R. Briggs, Director
400 West 43rd Street, Apartment 44L
New York, NY 10036
Tel: 212-564-2347

Robert Brink, Director
149 West 95th Street, Apartment 3B
New York, NY 10025
Tel: 212-840-1234

Dennis Brite, Director
57 First Avenue
New York, NY 10003
Tel: 212-477-4681

Dennis De Brito, Director
c/o Scott Hudson, Eric Ross Associates
60 East 42nd Street
New York, NY 10017
Tel: 212-687-9797

Amie Brockway, Director
460 West 49th Street
New York, NY 10019
Tel: 212-977-2639

Charles David Brooks
Director-Choreographer
400 West 43rd Street, Apartment 14A
New York, NY 10036
Tel: 212-244-6187

Arvin Brown, Director
Clifford Stevens STE Representation
888 Seventh Avenue
New York, NY 10019
Tel: 212-246-1030

Jamie Brown, Director
400 West 43rd Street, Apartment 26R
New York, NY 10011
Tel: 212-989-9691

Perry Bruskin, Director
490 West End Avenue
New York, NY 10024

Tel: 212-724-4531

Colin Bucksey, Director
232 West 2nd Street
New York, NY 10011
Tel: 212-989-9691

George Bunt, Director
c/o Hesseltine/Baker Ltd
165 West 46th Street #409
New York, NY 10036
Tel: 212-921-4460

Helen Butleroff, Choreographer
Box 553, Gracie Station
New York, NY 10028
Tel: 212-988-6695

Jason Buzas, Director
156 Franklin Street
New York, NY 10013
Tel: 212-925-3733

Joseph Calarco, Director
888 Eighth Avenue, #7J
New York, NY 10019
Tel: 212-247-4328

John Calvert, Director-Choreographer
18 Bank Street
New York, NY 10014
Tel: 212-691-3385

Leonard Cariou, Director
c/o Clifford Stevens, STE Representation
888 Seventh Avenue
New York, NY 10019
Tel: 212-246-1030

Patricia Carmichael, Director
307 West 4th Street
New York, NY 10014
Tel: 212-989-9762

Kay Carney, Director-Choreographer
396 Bleeker Street
New York, NY 10014

Larry Carpenter, Director
52 Bank Street, Apartment #6
New York, NY 10014
Tel: 212-929-7595

Vinnette Carroll, Director
227 West 17th Street
New York, NY 10011
Tel: 212-924-7820

Donald Carter, Director
321 East 54th Street
New York, NY 10022
Tel: 212-755-7275; 212-840-1234

Forrest Carter, Director
33 East 70th Street
New York, NY 10021
Tel: 212-288-4378

Elowyn Castle, Director
325 West 71st Street, Apartment #6B
New York, NY 10023
Tel: 212-362-0138; 212-840-1234

Tony Catanese
400 West 43rd Street, Apartment 37-O
New York, NY 10036

Tel: 212-564-8756

Christopher Catt, Director
10 West 87th Street, Apartment #1A
New York, NY 10024
Tel: 212-874-7778

Fred Chalfy
327 West 55th Street, Apartment 2A
New York, NY 10019
Tel: 212-244-4270

David Chambers, Director
905 West End Avenue
New York, NY 10025
Tel: 212-663-1582

Martin Charnin, Director
350 Fifth Avenue
New York, NY 10001
Tel: 212-947-7600

Dorothy Chernuck, Director
220 East 52nd Street
New York, NY 10022
Tel: 212-752-8437

Alfred Christie, Director
405 East 45th Street
New York, NY 10022
Tel: 212-759-7977

Leonardo Cimino, Director
119 West 57th Street
New York, NY 10019
Tel: 212-245-1919

Peter Coe
Lantz Office
888 Seventh Avenue
New York, NY 10106
Tel: 212-586-0200

Alexander H. Cohen, Director
225 West 44th Street
New York, NY 10036
Tel: 212-757-1200

Edward M. Cohen, Director
949 West End Avenue
New York, NY 10025
Tel: 212-864-5861

Joseph Conforti, Director
49 Park Avenue
New York, NY 10017
Tel: 212-575-9611

Tom Conti, Director
c/o Lionel Larner
850 Seventh Avenue
New York, NY 10019
Tel: 212-246-3105

Kevin Conway, Director
25 Central Park West
New York, NY 10023
Tel: 212-582-9235

Roderick Cook, Director
Monty Silver, 200 West 57th Street
New York, NY 10019
Tel: 212-765-4040

Robert M. Cooper, Director
1414 Avenue of the Americas

New York, NY 10019
Tel: 212-688-5825

Frank Corsaro, Director
33 Riverside Drive
New York, NY 10021
Tel: 212-874-1058; 212-697-9680, Jay Jullien

Morton Da Costa, Director
c/o Colton-Weissberger
505 Park Avenue
New York, NY 10022
Tel: 212-532-5100

Ken Costigan, Director
Ambrose Company
1466 Broadway, #1610
New York, NY 10036
Tel: 212-921-0230

Edie Cowan, Choreographer
c/o The Shukat Company Ltd.
340 West 55th Street
New York, NY 10019
Tel: 212-582-7614

Warren Crane, Director
77 Park Avenue
New York, NY 10017
Tel: 212-686-1714

Kimothy Cruse, Director
c/o Triad Entertainment Enterprises
315 East 72nd Street, #19G
New York, NY 10021
Tel: 212-628-5915; 213-464-8381

Leslie B. Cutler, Director
344 West 72nd Street
New York, NY 10023
Tel: 212-362-1813

Grover Dale, Director-Choreographer
c/o Eric Schepard, ICM
40 West 57th Street
New York, NY 10019
Tel: 212-556-5706

John Henry Davis, Director
196 West 10th Street, Apartment 1D
New York, NY 10014
Tel: 212-929-5735

Lennard De Carl, Director
484 West 43rd Street, Apartment 21T
New York, NY 10036
Tel: 212-840-1234

Michael A. Del Medico, Director
17 West 67th Street
New York, NY 10023
Tel: 212-787-5572; 212-874-7226

Jon-Michael Delon, Director-Choreographer
300 Mercer Street, Apartment 32C
New York, NY 10003
Tel: 212-475-1588

Reginald Denham, Director
100 West 57th Street
New York, NY 10019
Tel: 212-421-4100

Margaret Denithorne, Director
142 West 87th Street, Apartment #C2
New York, NY 10024
Tel: 212-874-()99 Home; 212-724-7400
Service

John Dexter, Director
Metropolitan Opera House, Lincoln
Center
New York, NY 10023
Tel: 212-799-3313

Glenda Dickerson, Director
3647 Broadway, Apartment 8A
New York, NY 10031
Tel: 212-368-8486

Crandall Diehl, Director-Choreographer
101-B East 97th Street
New York, NY 10029
Tel: 212-289-7683

Joe Donavan, Director-Choreographer
400 West 58th Street
New York, NY 10019
Tel: 212-581-6092; 212-586-6300

David A. Dorwart, Director
255 West 23rd Street, Apartment #FE
New York, NY 10011
Tel: 212-807-9845; 212-799-9099

Robert Drivas, Director
376 Bleeker Street
New York, NY 10014
Tel: 212-243-3076

John Driver, Director
c/o William Carver
Helen Merrill Agency
337 West 22nd Street
New York, NY 10011
Tel: 212-924-6314

Dan Duckworth, Director
701 Seventh Avenue, Apartment #9W
New York, NY 10036
Tel: 212-757-6300

Val Dufour, Director-Choreographer
40 West 22nd Steet
New York, NY 10010
Tel: 212-243-4573

Doreen Dunn, Choreographer
340 West 72nd Street
New York, NY 10023
Tel: 212-582-4240

Jeffrey Dunn, Director
857 Ninth Avenue
New York, NY 10019
Tel: 212-245-3166

Lyle Dye Jr., Director
245 West 107th Street, Apartment 10F
New York, NY 10025
Tel: 212-662-1085

Leslie Eberhard, Director
2109 Broadway, Apartment 12-126
New York, NY 10023
Tel: 212-595-1102; 212-586-6300

Jack Eddleman, Director-Choreographer
162 Ninth Avenue
New York, NY 10019
Tel: 212-989-3154

Susan Einhorn, Director
319 West 82nd Street
New York, NY 10024
Tel: 212-787-6832; 212-421-4100

Rina Elisha, Director
120 West 86th Street
New York, NY 10024
Tel: 212-724-6934

Robert Elston, Director
112 Charlton Street
New York, NY 10014
Tel: 212-691-4029

Jean Erdman, Choreographer-Director
316 East 88th Street
New York, NY 10029
Tel: 212-534-6363

Andre Ernotte, Director
455 West 23rd Street, #6F
New York, NY 10011
Tel: 212-741-3719

Ken Eulo, Director
140 West 79th Street, Suite 7E
New York, NY 10024
Tel: 212-724-8292

George W. Faison, Director-
Choreographer
615 West End Avenue
New York, NY 10024
Tel: 212-595-0693

Jim Fargo, Director
148 West 16th Street
New York, NY 10011
Tel: 212-691-3044

Arthur Faria, Director-Choreographer
101 West 12th Street
New York, NY 10011
Tel: 212-929-0129

John Fearnley, Director
484 West 43rd Street, Apartment 36-C
New York, NY 10036
Tel: 212-695-4162

Marianne Fearn, Director
149 West 12th Street
New York, NY 10011
Tel: 212-924-7928

Gene Feist, Director
333 West 23rd Street
New York, NY 10011
Tel: 212-924-7160

George Ferencz, Director
400 Madison Avenue
New York, NY 10017
Tel: 212-832-6900

Dolores M. Ferraro, Director
130 East 18th Street, Apartment 5G
New York, NY 10003
Tel: 212-260-5592; 212-840-1234

Felix Fibich, Choreographer
50 West 97th Street
New York, NY 10025
Tel: 212-865-3935

Miriam Fond, Director-Choreographer
888 8th Avenue
New York, NY 10019
Tel: 212-586-7938

Ron Forella, Director-Choreographer
108 West 73rd Street
New York, NY 10023
Tel: 212-580-7501

Charles Forsythe, Director
1841 Broadway, Apartment 1206
New York, NY 10023
Tel: 212-486-6544

Allan Fox, Director
50 West 97th Street, #14D
New York, NY 10025
Tel: 212-662-6531

Aaron Frankel, Director
425 Riverside Drive
New York, NY 10025
Tel: 212-633-5381

Ruella Frank, Choreographer
113 West 95th Street
New York, NY 10025
Tel: 212-622-3322

Burry Fredrik, Director
45 West 54th Street
New York, NY 10019
Tel: 212-246-0175; 203-227-9349

Daniel Freudenberger, Director
330 East 79th Street, Apartment 5B
New York, NY 10028
Tel: 212-288-8469

Joel J. Friedman, Director
80 First Avenue
New York, NY 10009

Martin Fried, Director
420 West End Avenue
New York, NY 10024
Tel: 212-799-1549

Lynne Gannaway, Director-Choreographer
201 West 89th Street
New York, NY 10024
Tel: 212-873-4062; 212-840-1234

Troy Garza, Director
201 West 70th Street, Apartment 29H
New York, NY 10023
Tel: 212-580-7770

Ella Gerber, Director
329 East 58th Street
New York, NY 10022
Tel: 212-688-2356

Gino Giglio, Director
56 Seventh Avenue
New York, NY 10011
Tel: 212-929-2797; 212-582-3750

Bill Gile, Director
29 Bank Street

New York, NY 10014
Tel: 212-741-7363

Paul Glover, Director-Choreographer
308 East 79th Street
New York, NY 10021
Tel: 212-744-3301

Charles Goddertz, Choreographer
230 West 99th Street
New York, NY 10025
Tel: 212-846-6525

John Going, Director
170 West 73rd Street, Apartment 11a
New York, NY 10023
Tel: 212-362-8481

Cliff Goodwin, Director
230 Thompson Street
New York, NY 10012
Tel: 212-982-5291

Mark Gordon, Director
323 West 83rd Street
New York, NY 10024
Tel: 212-799-1631; 212-586-6300

Marvin Gordon, Director-Choreographer
387 Bleeker Street
New York, NY 10014
Tel: 212-243-6434

Bick Goss, Choreographer
201 West 85th Street
New York, NY 10024
Tel: 212-799-2726

Charles Gray, Director
132 East 19th Street
New York, NY 10003
Tel: 212-982-1147

Daryl Gray, Choreographer
200 West 70th Street
New York, NY 10023

Jerry Grayson, Director
415 West 24th Street, Apartment 6D
New York, NY 10011
Tel: 212-929-5797; 212-582-0260

Edward M. Greenberg, Director
161 East 79th Street
New York, NY 10021
Tel: 212-737-7515

Thomas Gruenewald, Director
1650 Broadway, #1005
New York, NY 10019
Tel: 212-581-5766

Serge Gubelman, Director-Choreographer
75 Chambers Street
New York, NY 10007

William, Guild, Director
31 West 82nd Street, Apartment 2F
New York, NY 10024
Tel: 212-799-5917

Gerald Gutierrez, Director
62 East 55th Street
New York, NY 10022
Tel: 212-355-4165

John Hagan, Director
430 West 44th Street
New York, NY 10036
Tel: 212-246-8021; 212-354-4250

Nola J. Hague, Director
870 West 181 Street, #57
New York, NY 10033
Tel: 212-781-9601

Peter J. Hajduk, Director
21 Gramercy Park South, Apartment 3C
New York, NY 10003
Tel: 212-533-7984

Jack Hallett, Director
72 East 93rd Street
New York, NY 10028
Tel: 212-586-6300

William Hammerstein, Director
598 Madison Avenue
New York, NY 10022
Tel: 212-486-7373

Richard Harden, Director
574 West End Avenue
New York, NY 10024
Tel: 212-873-7661

Jay Harnick, Director
465 West End Avenue
New York, NY 10024
Tel: 212-787-8497; 212-575-8459

Judith Haskell, Director-Choreographer
340 West 57th Street
New York, NY 10019
Tel: 212-245-2915

Sandra C. Hastie, Director
136 West 4th Street, Apartment 2A
New York, NY 10012

June Havoc, Director
1650 Broadway, #406
New York, NY 10019
Tel: 212-541-5250

Bob Heath, Choreographer
325 West 45th Street
New York, NY 10036
Tel: 212-246-0430; 212-245-6197

Bob Herget, Director-Choreographer
119 West 57th Street
New York, NY 10019
Tel: 212-765-5260

Bill Herndon, Director
119 West 57th Street
New York, NY 10019
Tel: 212-CI5-1919

Bolen High, Director
353 West 45th Street
New York, NY 10036

Gregory Allen Hirsch, Director
301 East 10th Street
New York, NY 10009
Tel: 212-260-6155

Randal Hoey, Director
162 West 56th Street, #405
New York, NY 10019

Tel: 212-246-9529

David Holdgreiwe,
Director-Choreographer
2130 Broadway, #2404
New York, NY 10023
Tel: 212-246-8484

Robert Bruce Holley, Director
174 West 76th Street, #12G
New York, NY 10023
Tel: 212-799-7251

Hanya Holm, Director
45 West 54th Street
New York, NY 10019
Tel: 212-CI6-9776

Fritz Holt, Director
230 West 55th Street
New York, NY 10019
Tel: 212-246-2550

Jack Horner, Director
400 West 43rd Street, Apartment 17A
New York, NY 10036
Tel: 212-594-8589; 212-JU6-3700

Donald Howarth, Director
c/o Shannon, J.E.
309 East 81st Street
New York, NY 10028
Tel: 212-794-2758

Richard J. Hughes Jr., Director
40 West 22nd Street
New York, NY 10010
Tel: 212-691-4367

Pamela Hunt, Director-Choreogrpher
152 East 94th Street, #6A
New York, NY 10028
Tel: 212-860-3145

William E. Hunt, Director
1650 Broadway
New York, NY 10019
Tel: 212-582-6762

Gregory S. Hurst, Director
140 Riverside Drive, 4C
New York, NY 10024
Tel: 212-874-3656; 215-434-6110

Alfred Hyslop, Director
30 Waterside Plaza, Apartment 27D
New York, NY 10010
Tel: 212-684-5626

Tod Jackson, Director-Choreographer
60 West 68th Street
New York, NY 10023
Tel: 212-873-7606; 212-765-6373

Marty Jacobs, Director
230 Riverside Drive, #10D
New York, NY 10025
Tel: 212-865-1812

Robert Johanson, Director-Choreographer
310 West 94th Street, #2B
New York, NY 10025
Tel: 212-666-4469

Bernard Johnson, Director-Choreographer
176 West 87th Street

New York, NY 10024
Tel: 212-580-1874; 212-580-1888

Louis Johnson, Director-Choreographer
14 Morton Street, #4
New York, NY 10014
Tel: 212-243-5714

Ernestine M. Johnston, Director
40 West 135th Street, #11R
New York, NY 10037
Tel: 212-840-1234

James Earl Jones, Director
390 West End Avenue
New York, NY 10017
Tel: 212-877-0627

Walton Jones, Director
400 Madison Avenue
New York, NY 10017
Tel: 212-832-6900

Makram Joubran, Director-Choreographer
62 West 56th Street, #3A
New York, NY 10019
Tel: 212-757-2549; 212-PL2-7676

Jonas R. Jurasas, Director
133 West 17th Street, #1A
New York, NY 10011
Tel: 212-255-1902

Robert Kalfin, Director
407 West 43rd Street
New York, NY 10036
Tel: 212-877-0627; 212-877-0556

Garson Kanin, Director
200 West 57th Street
New York, NY 10019

Steven Kaplan, Director
400 West 43rd Street, #45A
New York, NY 1036
Tel: 212-736-5269

Richard Karp, Director
115 East 9th Street
New York, NY 10003
Tel: 212-477-2368; 212-575-1115

Janice Kasni, Choreographer
101 West 57th Street
New York, NY 10019
Tel: 212-279-9321

Barnet Kellman, Director
48 West 27th Street
New York, NY 10001
Tel: 212-685-4632

Raphael Kelly, Director
168 East 89th Street
New York, NY 10028
Tel: 212-840-0512

Voigt Kempson, Director-Choreographer
527 Madison Avenue, #1106
New York, NY 10022
Tel: 212-888-6711

Harold J. Kennedy, Director
20 West 72nd Street
New York, NY 10023
Tel: 212-TR7-3800

David Kitchen, Director-Choreographer
333 East 17th Street
New York, NY 10003
Tel: 212-247-5834

Joseph Klein, Director
28 West 87th Street
New York, NY 10024
Tel: 212-874-5789

Edward Kovens, Director
200 West 15th Street, 18A
New York, NY 10011
Tel: 212-929-3125

Danya Krupska, Director-Choreographer
564 West 52nd Street
New York, NY 10019
Tel: 212-247-2945

Basil Langton, Director
41 West 69th Street
New York, NY 10023
Tel: 212-799-5254; 213-472-1630

Dick Latessa, Director
250 West 57th Street
New York, NY 10019
Tel: 212-246-2166

Sue Lawless, Director
340 West 57th Street
New York, NY 10019
Tel: 212-245-2915

Paul Lazarus, Director
382 Central Park West
New York, NY 10025
Tel: 212-662-3147

Loi Leabo, Director-Choreographer
30 Greenwich Avenue, #1A
New York, NY 10011
Tel: 212-691-2920; 212-929-5814

Wilford Leach, Director
425 Lafayette Street
New York, NY 10003
Tel: 212-598-7100

Irving Lee, Director-Choreographer
251 West 57th Street
New York, NY 10019
Tel: 212-581-7240

Susan Lehman, Director
220 West 71st Street
New York, NY 10023
Tel: 212-840-1234; 212-595-9208

Zoya Leporska, Director-Choreographer
40 West 86th Street
New York, NY 10024
Tel: 212-362-4474; 212-582-4240

Gene Lesser, Director
19 West 87th Street
New York, NY 10024
Tel: 212-595-6497

Rhoda Levine, Director-Choreographer
18 East 8th Street
New York, NY 10003
Tel: 212-254-5543

Stephen Levi, Director
519 Second Avenue
New York, NY 10016
Tel: 212-889-2504

Daniel Lewis, Choreographer
32 Jones Street
New York, NY 10014
Tel: 212-789-1644

Will Lieberson, Director
205 West 89th Street
New York, NY 10024
Tel: 212-787-0862; 212-221-9088

Ron Link, Director
277 West 10th Street
New York, NY 10014
Tel: 212-741-1355; 212-661-2820

John Lithgow, Director
562 West End Avenue, #3A
New York, NY
Tel: 212-580-2954

Robert H. Livingston, Director
347 West 39th Street
New York, NY 10018
Tel: 212-947-0430

Peter Lobdell, Director-Choreographer
43 West 27th Street
New York, NY 10001
Tel: 212-679-7683

Bill Ludel, Director
170 West 74th Street
New York, NY 10023
Tel: 212-877-0227

Salem Ludwig, Director
70 La Salle Street, Apartment MH
New York, NY 10027
Tel: 212-866-4718

Dorothy Lyman, Director
17 Pomander Walk
New York, NY 10025
Tel: 212-222-4181

Will MacAdam, Director
549 East 12th Street
New York, NY 10009
Tel: 212-477-2171

Davey Marlin-Jones, Director
853 7th Avenue
New York, NY 10019
Tel: 212-JU2-1280

Luis Martinez, Director
37-49 75th Street
New York, NY 11372
Tel: 212-355-9817

Jeffrey Martin, Director
574 West End Avenue, #45
New York, NY 10024
Tel: 212-362-9213

William Martin, Director
222 West 83rd Street
New York, NY 10024
Tel: 212-724-1548

Peter Masterson, Director
162 West 56th Street
New York, NY 10019
Tel: 212-246-9029

Ada Brown Mather, Director
265 West 11th Street
New York, NY 10014
Tel: 212-924-6398

Billy Matthews, Director
11 East 80th Street
New York, NY 10021
Tel: 212-288-5604

Otto Maximillian, Director-
Choreographer
442 West 42nd Street
New York, NY 10036
Tel: 212-564-8406

Janet McCall, Director
349 West 44th Street
New York, NY 10036
Tel: 212-757-1633; 212-840-1234

Diane McIntyre, Choreographer
580 St. Nicholas Avenue, #4H
New York, NY 10030
Tel: 212-690-3647

Hale Mckeen, Director
315 West End Avenue
New York, NY 10023
Tel: 212-TR7-0449

Lynne Meadow, Director
321 East 73rd Street
New York, NY 10021
Tel: 212-288-2500

Andrew Mendelson, Director
321 East 13th Street, Apt. 12A
New York, NY 10003
Tel: 212-593-1640; 212-673-7732

Jeff Meredith, Director
145 West 71st Street
New York, NY 10023
Tel: 212-874-4522

Bert Michaels, Director-Choreographer
316 West 79th Street
New York, NY
Tel: 212-873-5356

Richard Michaels, Director
211 West 106th Street
New York, NY 10025
Tel: 212-666-1793

Marcia Milgrom, Director-Choreographer
23 West 73rd Street
New York, NY 10021
Tel: 212-595-6683

Agnes George De Mille,
Director-Choreographer
c/o William Morris Agency, Samuel! Liff
1350 Avenue of the Americas
New York, NY 10019
Tel: 212-586-5100

Philip Minor, Director
229 East 21st Street
New York, NY 10010

Tel: 212-674-7172

Rand Mitchell, Director-Choreographer
1505 Broadway, Suite 2907
New York, NY 10036
Tel: 212-840-1234

Richard Mogavero, Director
328 West 88th Street
New York, NY 10024
Tel: 212-877-8679

John Montgomery,
Director-Choreographer
303 West 74th Street
New York, NY 10023
Tel: 212-724-2446; 212-582-0176

Robert Moore, Director
575 Madison Avenue
New York, NY 10022
Tel: 212-PL9-4580

Sonia Moore, Director
485 Park Avenue
New York, NY 10022
Tel: 212-PL5-5120

Ted Mornel, Director
158 West 15th Street
New York, NY 10011
Tel: 212-989-3807; 212-354-4250

Jeffrey B. Moss, Director
850 7th Avenue
New York, NY 10019
Tel: 212-586-7344

Syeus Mottel, Director
140 West 79th Street
New York, NY 10024
Tel: 212-LY5-0505; 212-541-7090

Tony Napoli, Director
68 West 83rd Street
New York, NY 10024
Tel: 212-724-5935

David Nash, Director-Choreographer
515 Broadway, 6th Floor
New York, NY 10012
Tel: 212-925-0162

Ronald Nash, Director
400 West 43rd Street, #40R
New York, NY 10036
Tel: 212-736-4759

Richard Natkowski,
Director-Choreographer
133 West 71st Street
New York, NY 10023
Tel: 212-580-9482

Jeffrey K. Neill, Director-Choreographer
57 West 75th Street, #2F
New York, NY 10023
Tel: 212-877-7906

Ed Nolfi, Director-Choreographer
54 West 70th Street
New York, NY 10023
Tel: 212-595-0239

Jay Norman, Choreographer
119 West 71st Street

New York, NY 10023
Tel: 212-787-0775; 212-247-6168 Tom
Currie

Douglas Norwick, Choreographer
396 Bleecker Street
New York, NY 10014
Tel: 212-924-1494

Jack O'Brien, Director
c/o Wender and Associates
30 East 60th Street
New York, NY 10022
Tel: 212-832-8330

Charles Olsen, Director
100 West 94th Street
New York, NY 10025
Tel: 212-865-9475

Stuart Ostrow, Director
c/o Linden and Deutsch
110 Park Avenue
New York, NY 10022

Joseph Patton, Director-Choreographer
726 8th Avenue
New York, NY 10036
Tel: 212-221-3797

Kent Paul, Director
155 East 93rd Street
New York, NY 10028

James Pentecost, Director
711 West End Avenue, #5MS
New York, NY 10025
Tel: 212-864-2085

Michael Perrier, Choreographer
303 West 74th Street, #5F
New York, NY 10023

Robert Pesola, Director
39 East 12th Street
New York, NY 10003
Tel: 212-777-9210

William Peters, Director
825 West End Avenue
New York, NY 10025
Tel: 212-662-2773; 212-LT1-6470

Art Pingree, Director
155 East 75th Street, #5E
New York, NY 10021
Tel: 212-988-2681

Stephen Porter, Director
44 Gramercy Park West
New York, NY 10010
Tel: 212-674-2189

Otto Preminger, Director
711 Fifth Avenue
New York, NY 10022
Tel: 212-838-6100

David Pressman, Director
333 Central Park West
New York, NY 10025

Don Price, Director-Choreographer
260 Riverside Drive
New York, NY 10025
Tel: 212-866-5680

Hal Prince, Director
1270 Avenue of the Americas, #2410
New York, NY 10020
Tel: 212-399-0960

Ellis Rabb, Director
20 West 64th Street, #27R
New York, NY 10023

Lee Rachman, Director
201 West 89th Street
New York, NY 10024
Tel: 212-362-7656

Karl Reichman, Director-Choreographer
165 West 91st Street
New York, NY 10024
Tel: 212-730-1188

Robin Reseen, Choreographer
c/o Judy Leverone
24 West 95th Street
New York, NY 10025
Tel: 212-864-0786

Nancy Rhodes, Director
484 West 43rd Street, #20H
New York, NY 10036
Tel: 212-594-7880; 212-575-1558

Byron Ringland, Director
77 Washington Place
New York, NY 10011
Tel: 212-228-2961

Jerome Robbins, Director-Choreographer
1212 Avenue of the Americas
New York, NY 10036
Tel: 212-586-4700

Dana Roberts, Director
484 West 43rd Street, #35E
New York, NY 10036
Tel: 212-695-2599; 212-874-2424

Cliff Robertson, Director
870 U.N. Plaza
New York, NY 10017
Tel: 212-980-6868

Scott Robinson, Director-Choreographer
323 West 75th Street, #C
New York, NY 10023
Tel: 212-362-8775

Steve Robman, Director
1540 Broadway
New York, NY 10036
Tel: 212-730-0787

Dennis Rosa, Director-Choreographer
65 East 55th Street
New York, NY 10022
Tel: 212-355-4165

Philip Rose, Director
157 West 57th Street
New York, NY 10019

Stuart Ross, Director-Choreographer
484 West 43rd Street, #35T
New York, NY 10036
Tel: 212-868-2943; 212-228-0900

William Ross, Director
1697 Broadway

New York, NY 10019
Tel: 212-582-6585

Michael E. Rudman, Director
30 East 60th Street
New York, NY 10022
Tel: 212-832-8330

Frank Ruella, Choreographer
113 West 95th Street, #4F
New York, NY 10025
Tel: 212-662-3322

Amy Saltz, Director
484 West 43rd Street, #17B
New York, NY 10036
Tel: 212-736-5345

Al Santoli
666 West End Avenue, Suite 9H
New York, NY 10025
Tel: 212-362-6616

Isaac Schambelan, Director
306 West 18th Street
New York, NY 10011
Tel: 212-840-1234; 212-243-4337

Terry Schreiber, Director
120 Riverside Drive
New York, NY 10024
Tel: 212-874-7509

Michael A. Schultz, Director
1180 Avenue of the Americas
New York, NY 10036
Tel: 212-575-1313

Douglas R. Seale, Director
1 University Place, #14C
New York, NY 10003
Tel: 212-GR3-8516

Connie Shafer, Choreograher
528 East 85th Street
New York, NY 10028
Tel: 212-734-8207; 914-338-4210

Zara Shakow, Director
160 West 73rd Street
New York, NY 10023
Tel: 212-TR4-0729; 212-TR7-6700

Dennis Shearer, Choreographer
201 West 89th Street
New York, NY 10024
Tel: 212-873-0894; 212-582-4240

Nelson Sheeley, Director
433 West 21st Street
New York, NY 10011
Tel: 212-675-3884

Isaiah Sheffer, Director
194 Riverside Drive
New York, NY 10025
Tel: 212-799-3631

Lewis Shena
484 West 43rd Street, #23P
New York, NY 10036
Tel: 212-564-0832

Geoffrey Sherman, Director
850 7th Avenue
New York, NY 10019

Tel: 212-581-4490

Lee Sherman, Director-Choreographer
245 West 25th Street
New York, NY 10001
Tel: 212-243-3274

Paul Shyre, Director
905 West End Avenue
New York, NY 10025
Tel: 212-663-1586

John Sillings, Director
146 West 76th Street
New York, NY 10023
Tel: 212-799-7970

Robert D. Simons, Director
465 Madison Avenue
New York, NY 10022
Tel: 212-832-2800

Loukas Skipitaris, Director
32-19 38th Street
New York, NY 11103
Tel: 212-721-7610

Jo Jo Smith, Director-Choreographer
1733 Broadway
New York, NY 10019
Tel: 212-586-2940

James F. Smock, Choreographer
c/o Honey Sanders Agency
229 West 42nd Street
New York, NY 10036
Tel: 212-947-5555

Robert Speller, Director-Choreographer
343 West 14th Street, Apartment 5FW
New York, NY 10014
Tel: 212-989-1632; 212-840-1234

Tony Stevens, Director-Choreographer
190 Riverside Drive
New York, NY 10024
Tel: 212-840-1234

Anthony Stimac, Director
7 Stuyvesant Oval
New York, NY 10009
Tel: 212-674-0490

Harold Stone, Director
106 East 85th Street
New York, NY 10028
Tel: 212-628-4459

Ted Story, Director
142 West 11th Street
New York, NY 10011
Tel: 212-255-3084

Hailla Strauss, Choreographer
201 West 70th Street
New York, NY 10023
Tel: 212-595-7922

Roger Sullivan, Director
345 Riverside Drive, #6G
New York, NY 10025
Tel: 212-864-5972

Eugene Taylor, Director
431 West 44th Street
New York, NY 10036

Tel: 212-582-2756

Hiram Taylor, Director-Choreographer
40 First Avenue, #14C
New York, NY 10009
Tel: 212-228-1272

Gerald M. Teijelo, Jr., Director-
Choreographer
564 West 52nd Street, #3W
New York, NY 10019
Tel: 212-765-5681

Lee Theodore, Director-Choreographer
4 East 75th Street
New York, NY 10021
Tel: 212-879-5750

Shepard Traude, Director
711 Fifth Avenue
New York, NY 10022
Tel: 212-688-2500; 212-873-1579

Russell Treyz, Director-Choreographer
107 Bedford Street
New York, NY 10014
Tel: 212-924-7151; 212-840-1234

Rudy Troutman, Director
3 Sheridan Square, #16B
New York, NY 10014
Tel: 212-243-6797

John Ulmer, Director
25 East 10th Street
New York, NY 10003
Tel: 212-673-1798

Shari Upbin, Director-Choreographer
45 East 89th Street
New York, NY 10024
Tel: 212-289-4173; 212-724-2800

Porter Van Zandt, Director
118 West 79th Street
New York, NY 10024
Tel: 212-877-8202

Henry Velez, Director
12 Bank Street
New York, NY 10014
Tel: 212-989-3684

Frank Wagner, Director-Choreographer
140 West 55th Street, #6B
New York, NY 10019
Tel: 212-757-3696

Stanley Waren, Director
465 West End Avenue
New York, NY 10024
Tel: 212-877-3770

Janet Watson, Choreographer
55 West 95th Street, #54
New York, NY 10025
Tel: 212-222-6137

Marc B. Weiss, Director
255 West 90th Street
New York, NY 10024
Tel: 212-877-6750

Thomas Edward West, Director
425 West 45th Street, Apartment #2RW
New York, NY 10036

Tel: 212-586-8588

Arthur Whitelaw, Director
132 East 38th Street
New York, NY 10016
Tel: 212-532-9321

Onna White, Director-Choreographer
c/o Abe Newborn
1365 York Avenue
New York, NY 10028
Tel: 212-861-4635

B.J. Whiting, Director
417 East 65th Street
New York, NY 10021
Tel: 212-288-0215; 212-245-2915

Arthur R. Williams, Director
c/o Roger Brian Cowan, Esq.
110 East 42nd Street
New York, NY 10017
Tel: 212-682-3570

Liz Williamson, Choreographer
1270 5th Avenue, #5T
New York, NY 10029
Tel: 212-348-7318

Noel Willman, Director
18 East 68th Street, #4C
New York, NY 10021
Tel: 212-737-7667

John W. Wilson, Director-Choreographer
114 East 28th Street
New York, NY 10016
Tel: 212-532-3764

Walt Witcover, Director
105 West 13th Street
New York, NY 10011
Tel: 212-691-4367

George Wojtasik, Director
711 East 11th Street, #8F
New York, NY 10009
Tel: 212-869-9266

William Woodman, Director
320 West End Avenue, 4-B
New York, NY 10023
Tel: 212-580-2838; 541-943-

Moni Yakim, Director
220 West 71st Street
New York, NY 10023
Tel: 212-873-6065

Ira Zuckerman, Director
231 West 18th Street
New York, NY 10011
Tel: 212-741-0844; 212-JU6-6300

Stephen Zuckerman, Director
162 West 56th Street, Suite 405
New York, NY 10019
Tel: 212-246-9029

Nyack

John Stix, Director
727 Route 9 West
Nyack, NY 10960
Tel: 914-359-6376; 212-752-7676

Pawling

Joseph Stockdale, Director
5 Coulter Avenue
Pawling, NY 12564
Tel: 914-855-9186

Putnum Valley

Buck Heller, Director-Choreographer
R.R. No. 1, Box 22C
Putnum Valley, NY 10579

Riverdale

Dennis Dennehy, Director-Choreographer
4525 Henry Hudson Parkway
Riverdale, NY 10471
Tel: 212-548-4699

Rockville Centre

Lynne Corbett, Director-Choreographer
1215 Waterveiw Drive
Rockville Centre, NY 11570
Tel: 516-536-7874

Scarsdale

Marnel Sumner, Director
5 Chedworth Road
Scarsdale, NY 10583
Tel: 914-472-2512

Spring Valley

Stone Widney, Director
243 McNamara Road
Spring Valley, NY 10977
Tel: 914-354-3728

Suffern

Robert Pagent, Director-Choreographer
38 Route 306
Suffern, NY 10901
Tel: 914-354-4038

Syracuse

Arthur Storch, Director
820 East Genesee Street
Syracuse, NY 13210
Tel: 315-423-4008

White Plains

Peter Birch, Director-Choreographer
797 North Street
White Plains, NY 10605

NORTH CAROLINA
Raleigh

Jay Huguely
318 Polk Street
Raleigh, NC
Tel: 919-821-0410; 919-821-0498

Salisburg

Hubert W. Rolling, Director
126 Ackert Avenue
Salisburg, NC 28144
Tel: 704-633-5471; 704-633-3877

OHIO

Bay Village

Vincent Dowling, Director
30869 Lake Road
Bay Village, OH 444140
Tel: 216-835-3951

Cincinnati

James Farnsworth,
Director-Choreographer
3203 Golden Avenue, #307
Cincinnati, OH 45226
Tel: 513-321-3766; 513-241-8989

Michael Murray, Director
c/o Cincinnati Playhouse
962 Mt. Adams Circle
Cincinnati, OH 45202

Cleveland Heights

Mitchell Bradley Fields, Director
3654 Grosvenor
Cleveland Heights, OH 44118
Tel: 216-321-2006

Paul Lee, Director
2541 Overlook Road, #7
Cleveland Heights, OH 44106
Tel: 216-371-0560

PENNSYLVANIA

Gouldsboro

Erma Duricko, Director
Post Office Box 406
Gouldsboro, PA 18424
Tel: 717-842-4104

Philadelphia

Robert Hedley, Director
2009 Pine Street
Philadelphia, PA 19103
Tel: 215-LA5-7652

Irene Lewis, Director
220 South 16th Street
Philadelphia, PA 19102

Holgar Linden, Choreographer
1615 Sansom Street
Philadelphia, PA 19103
Tel: 215-561-4159

Pittsburgh

Don Brockett, Director-Choreographer
5600 Darlington Road
Pittsburgh, PA 15217
Tel: 421-521-8738

Gregory Lehane, Director
5435 Claybourne, #805
Pittsburgh, PA 15352
Tel: 412-687-1589

Myron Howard Nadel, Choreographer-
Director
4920 Centre Avenue, #503
Pittsburgh, PA 15219
Tel: 412-621-9987; 412-578-2392

TENNESSEE

Gatlinburg

Don MacPherson, Director-Choreographer
461 Parkway
Gatlinburg, TN 37738
Tel: 615-436-4054; 615-436-4039

TEXAS

Amarillo

Larry Randolph, Director
Post Office Box 30520
Amarillo, TX 79120

Austin

Lathan Sanford, Director-Choreographer
Post Office Box 764A
Austin, TX 78737
Tel: 512-288-2252; 512-471-7544

Dallas

Mesrop Kesdekian, Director
3625 Fairfax Street
Dallas, TX 75209
Tel: 214-522-7288

Evie McGhee, Choreographer
Post Office Box 26188
Dallas, TX 75226
Tel: 214-565-1116

Buff Shurr, Director-Choreographer
13771 North Central, #802
Dallas, TX 75243
Tel: 214-690-4537

Sally Soldo, Choreographer
c/o Kim Dawson Agency
1143 Apparel Mart
Dallas, TX 75207
Tel: 214-638-2414

Annabelle Weenick, Director
c/o Peggy Taylor Talent
3616 Howell
Dallas, TX 75204
Tel: 214-526-4800

Fort Worth

Bruce Lea, Choreographer
3719 Shelby Drive
Fort Worth, TX 76109
Tel: 817-921-2842

Florine Pulley, Director-Choreographer
5532 Hightower Street
Fort Worth, TX 76112
Tel: 817-451-4003

Carl Tressler, Director-Choreographer
3824 Shellbrook Drive
Fort Worth, TX 76109
Tel: 817-924-9306

Irving

Steve Riley, Director-Choreographer
3900 Acapulco
Irving, TX 75062
Tel: 212-799-7233

UTAH

Provo

Tad Danielewski, Director
1280 Cedar Avenue
Provo, UT 84604
Tel: 801-374-2856

VIRGINIA

Alexandria

Terry Kester, Director
5600 Seminary
Alexandria, VA 22311
Tel: 703-931-6727

McLean

David Dannenbaum, Director
1939 Kennedy Drive, #108
McLean, VA 22102
Tel: 703-356-7268

WASHINGTON

Seattle

Margaret Booker, Director
c/o Intiman Theatre Company, Box 4246
Seattle, WA 98104
Tel: 206-624-4541

Clayton Corzatte, Director
2520 11th Avenue West
Seattle, WA 98119
Tel: 206-282-0386

Gregory Falls, Director
The Highlands
Seattle, WA 98177
Tel: 206-364-7421

Robert Loper, Director
2641 East Helen
Seattle, WA 98112
Tel: 206-323-3382; 206-542-4239

Jack Sydow, Director
6527 51st Avenue, NE
Seattle, WA 98115
Tel: 206-522-6095; 206-543-5140

WISCONSIN

Madison

Richard E. Hughes, Director
501 Prospect Avenue
Madison, WI 53711
Tel: 608-251-0644

Milwaukee

John Dillon, Director
929 North Water Street
Milwaukee, WI 53202
Tel: 414-273-7121

CANADA

Stratford, Ontario

John S. Hirsch, Director
Stratford Shakespeare Festival
Stratford, Ontario, Canada
Tel: 519-271-4040

Toronto, Ontario

Michael Bawtree, Director
286 Sherbourne Street
Toronto, Ontario, Canada M5A 2S1
Tel: 416-922-7441

8
Facilities

The performance spaces listed here are those which are generally available for rental by touring companies or individual performers. The schedules of some facilities and their willingness to rent space sometimes depends on whether they are currently producing their own shows. Inquiries should be made well before a planned event.

The size of the facility is noted in the entry, while costs, subject to rapid changes, are omitted. Specific information concerning stage design, number of dressing rooms etc., should be obtained at the address given.

ALABAMA

Anniston

Anniston Little Theatre
1620 Leighton Avenue
Anniston, AL 36201
Tel: 205-236-8342
Address Inquiries to: ALT Board of Directors
Founded in: 1921

Birmingham

Bell Auditorium University of Alabama
13th Street and Seventh Avenue
Birmingham, AL 35294
Tel: 205-934-3236
Address Inquiries to: Dr D. Ward Haarbauer, Manager
Founded in: 1950

Jefferson Civic Center
1 Civic Center Plaza
Birmingham, AL 35202
Tel: 205-328-8160
Address Inquiries to: Randy Godwin, Manager
Founded in: 1972-74

Southern College Theatre
800 Eighth Avenue West
Birmingham, AL 35204
Tel: 205-328-5250, Ext. 324
Address Inquiries to: John Michael Warburton, Manager
Founded in: 1970

Town and Gown Theater
University of Alabama
Birmingham, AL 35294
Founded in: 1950

Birmington

Jewish Community Center
3960 Montclair Road
Birmington, AL 35223
Tel: 205-879-0411
Address Inquiries to: Harold E. Katz, Manager
Founded in: 1958

Florence

Zodiac Theatre
Post Office Box 622
Florence, AL 35630

Huntsville

Von Braun Civic Center
700 Monroe Street, SW
Huntsville, AL 35801
Tel: 205-533-1953
Address Inquiries to: Cliff Wallace, Manager

Mobile

Mobile Municipal Theatre
401 Auditorium Drive
Mobile, AL 36601
Tel: 205-438-7261
Address Inquiries to: Buddy Clewis, Manager
Founded in: 1965

Mobile Theatre Guild
14 North Lafayette Street
Mobile, AL 36604
Tel: 205-433-7513
Address Inquiries to: Tom Pocase, Manager

Pixie Playhouse
Post Office Box 845
Langham Park
Mobile, AL 36608
Tel: 205-344-1537
Address Inquiries to: Mrs. Marty Bruner

Montevallo

Depot-In-The-Park
Orr Municipal Park
Montevallo, AL 35115
Tel: 205-665-1591
Address Inquiries to: Dr. Charles E. Majur

Palmer Auditorium
University of Montevallo
Montevallo, AL 35115
Tel: 205-665-2521
Address Inquiries to: Professor W. T. Chichester, Department of Speech and Theatre

Talladega

Harwell Auditorium
414 Oak Street
Talladega, AL 35160
Tel: 205-362-2203
Address Inquiries to: Pearino Gaither, Manager

University

Morgan Hall Auditorium
c/o Clark Box 2906
University, AL 35486
Tel: 205-348-7007
Address Inquiries to: James Clark, Manager

CALIFORNIA

Baldwin Park

Baldwin Civic Auditorium
14403 East Pacific Avenue
Baldwin Park, CA 91706

Burbank

Golden Mall Playhouse
226 East Tujunga Avenue
Burbank, CA 91502
Tel: 213-843-7529
Address Inquiries to: Pamela Gilmore, Manager
Founded in: 1922

Castro Valley

Chanticleers Playhouse
Post Office Box 2021
Castro Valley, CA 94546

Dominguez Hills

California State College Playbox
1000 East Victoria Street
Dominguez Hills, CA 90247
Tel: 213-532-4300
Address Inquiries to: Marshall Bialosky, Manager
Founded in: 1977

University Theatre
1000 East Victoria Street
Dominguez Hills, CA 90474
Tel: 213-532-4300, Ext. 383
Address Inquiries to: Jack A. Vaughn,
  Chairman
Founded in: 1977

Fresno

Fresno Convention Center Theatre
700 M Street
Fresno, CA 93721
Tel: 209-488-1515
Address Inquiries to: Robert A. Schoettler,
  Executive Director
Founded in: 1966

University Theatre
California State University, Fresno
Fresno, CA 93740
Tel: 209-294-3987; 209-294-2216
Founded in: 1911
Member: ATA;
Annual Budget: $50,000
Description: Four theatres on campus: 450-
seat Joan W. Wright Theatre; 200-seat Arena
Theatre; 200-seat Child Drama Center; 6000
capacity Amphitheatre.

Fullerton

California State University Theatre
800 North College Boulevard
Fullerton, CA 92634
Tel: 714-870-3628
Address Inquiries to: Charles Redmon, Jr.,
  Chairman
Founded in: 1965

Jupiter Theatre
516 North Harbor Boulevard
Fullerton, CA 92632
Tel: 714-525-4725
Address Inquiries to: Darr Branch, Manager
Founded in: 1972

Hollywood

Hollywood Center Theatre
1451 North Las Palmas Avenue
Hollywood, CA 90028

Zephyr Theatre
7458 Melrose Avenue
Hollywood, CA 90046
Tel: 213-852-9399
Address Inquiries to: Barbara Epstein,
  Executive Director

Long Beach

California State University Little Theatre
150 Bellflower Boulevard
Long Beach, CA 90840
Tel: 213-498-4540
Address Inquiries to: Fred Kobus
Founded in: 1953

Long Beach Convention Center Arena
300 East Ocean Boulevard
Long Beach, CA 213 436 3636
Tel: 213-436-3636
Address Inquiries to: Dick Shaff, Manager
Founded in: 1962

School of Fine Arts Auditorium
California State University
Long Beach, CA 90840
Tel: 213-498-4364
Address Inquiries to: A. James Bravar,
  Manager
Founded in: 1955

Los Angeles

The Groundlings
7307 Melrose Avenue
Los Angeles, CA 90046
Tel: 213-934-4747
Member: AEA; CAC; CFA; CTC; LATA;
Description: A professional showcase theatre.
Seating capacity of 99.

Shubert Theatre
2020 Avenue of The Stars
Los Angeles, CA 90067
Tel: 213-553-6711
Address Inquiries to: Edward Parkinson,
  General Manager
Founded in: 1972

Theatre West
3333 Cahuenga Boulevard
Los Angeles, CA 90068
Tel: 213-851-4839
Member: AEA; CAC; CFA; CTC;
  Consortium for Human Services; LATA;
Annual Budget: $30,000
Description: Seating capacity of 204

North Hollywood

Theatre Exchange
11855 Hart Street
North Hollywood, CA 91605
Tel: 213-765-9005
Member: AEA; CAC; CFA; CTC; LATA;
Description: Seating capacity of 58.

Sherman Oaks

Actors Alley
4334 Van Nuys Boulevard
Sherman Oaks, CA 91403
Tel: 213-986-7440
Member: AEA; CAC; CFA; CTC; LATA;
Description: Seating capacity of 75.

CONNECTICUT

Bridgeport

Andre and Clara Theatre
84 Iranistan Avenue
Bridgeport, CT 06602
Tel: 203-576-4397
Founded in: 1972
Description: University of Bridgeport facility.

Sharon

Sharon Playhouse
Route 396
Sharon, CT 0609

Westport

Westport Country Playhouse
25 Powers Court
Westport, CT 06880

FLORIDA

Delray Beach

Delray Beach Playhouse
Post Office Box 1056
Delray Beach, FL 33444
Tel: 305-272-1281
Address Inquiries to: Alfred V. Garguilo,
  Manager
Founded in: 1948

Miami

Parker Playhouse
Post Office Box 4603
Miami, FL 33338
Tel: 305-764-1441
Address Inquiries to: Zev Bufman, Producer
Founded in: 1968
Annual Budget: $100,000

Titusville

Titusville Playhouse
Post Office Box 1234
Titusville, FL 32780
Tel: 305-267-9684
Address Inquiries to: David Jache, President
Founded in: 1965
Member: FTC;
Annual Budget: $10,000

Vero Beach

Riverside Theatre
Post Office Box 3788
Vero Beach, FL 32960
Tel: 305-567-8860
Address Inquiries to: Steve Stahl, Manager
Helen Fricker, Assistant Manager
Founded in: 1972

GEORGIA

Jekyll Island

Jekyll Island Amphitheatre
201 Old Plantation Road
Jekyll Island, GA 31520
Tel: 912-635-2236
Address Inquiries to: William R. Workman
Founded in: 1972

HAWAII

Honolulu

Fort Ruger Theatre
Makapu and Aloha Avenues
Honolulu, HI 96816
Tel: 808-734-0274
Address Inquiries to: Mrs. Robin J. Beasley,
  Chairman
Founded in: 1940

Manoa Valley Theatre
2833 East Manoa Road
Honolulu, HI 96822
Tel: 808-988-6131
Address Inquiries to: Joy S. Dalzell, Manager
Founded in: 1926

Wahiawa

Schofield Drama Center
Recreation Services, Schofield Barracks
Wahiawa, HI 96786
Tel: 808-655-0891
Address Inquiries to: Joe L. Craver, Manager
Founded in: 1961

IDAHO
McCall

Alpine Playhouse
Post Office Box 753
McCall, ID 83638
Tel: 208-634-9945
Address Inquiries to: Cory Hormaechea,
    President
Founded in: 1966
Member: ICA;
Annual Budget: $5,000

Pocatello

Frazier Auditorium
Idaho State University
Pocatello, ID 83201
Tel: 208-236-3695
Address Inquiries to: David W. Alkofer,
    Manager
Founded in: 1924

ILLINOIS
Chicago

Court Theatre
University of Chicago
Chicago, IL 60637
Tel: 312-753-3581
Address Inquiries to: D. Nicholas Rudall,
    Chairman
Member: ATA;

Galesburg

Eleanor Abbott Ford Center
Knox College
Galesburg, IL 61401
Tel: 309-343-0112
Address Inquiries to: R. C. Whitlatch,
    Manager
Founded in: 1964
Description: Seating capacity 950.

Marengo

Shady Lane Playhouse
Route 20 West
Marengo, IL 60152

Normal

Illinois State University
Department of Theatre
Normal, IL 61761
Tel: 309-436-6683
Address Inquiries to: Calvin Lee Printer,
    Chairman
Member: URTA;
Description: The department has access to a
450 seat proscenium theatre, a 135 seat
thrust theatre, and a dinner theatre. Gradu-
ate programs are available.

Illinois State University Auditorium
Illinois State University
Normal, IL 61761
Tel: 309-438-2222
Address Inquiries to: Randy Greene, Manager
Founded in: 1973
Description: Seating capacity 3,500.

Peoria

Peoria Players Theatre House
4300 North University Avenue
Peoria, IL 61614
Tel: 309-688-4473
Address Inquiries to: Jerry Johnson, Vice
    President
    Bonnie White, Secretary
Founded in: 1956
Description: Seating capacity 390.

Rockford

The New American Theatre
118 South Main Street
Rockford, IL 61108
Tel: 815-963-9454
Address Inquiries to: J.R. Sullivan, Artistic
    Director
Description: Seating capacity 450.

Rock Island

Centennial Hall
Augustana College
Rock Island, IL 61201
Tel: 309-794-7306
Address Inquiries to: Michael C. Shawgo,
    Director of Public Events
Founded in: 1959
Description: Seating capacity 250.

Saint Charles

Pheasant Run Playhouse
Post Office Box 64
Saint Charles, IL 60174
Tel: 312-584-1454
Address Inquiries to: Carl Stohn Jr., President
Founded in: 1964
Annual Budget: $100,000

Wheaton

Wheaton College Performing Arts Center
Wheaton College
Wheaton, IL 60187
Tel: 312-682-5098

Winnetka

Recital Hall
300 Green Bay Road
Winnetka, IL 60093
Tel: 312-446-3822
Founded in: 1955

Zion

Zion Passion Play Amphitheatre
Dowie Memorial Drive
Zion, IL 60099
Tel: 312-746-2221
Address Inquiries to: Roger Ottersen,
    Manager
Founded in: 1968
Description: Seating capacity 1,200.

INDIANA
Bloomington

Indiana University Auditorium
Indiana University
Bloomington, IN 47401
Tel: 812-337-1103
Address Inquiries to: Lawrence Davis,
    Manager
Founded in: 1941
Description: Seating capacity 2,803.

Indiana University Theatre
Indiana University
Bloomington, IN 47401
Tel: 812-337-9053
Founded in: 1941
Description: Seating capacity 385.

Evansville

Evansville Civic Theatre
717 North Fulton Avenue
Evansville, IN 47708
Tel: 812-423-2060
Address Inquiries to: Dick Engbers, Manager
Founded in: 1908
Description: Seating capacity 185.

Fort Wayne

Community Center for the Performing
Arts
303 East Main Street
Fort Wayne, IN 46802
Tel: 219-422-4226
Address Inquiries to: Mary B. Brant, Manager
Founded in: 1973
Description: Seating capacity 680.

Embassy Theatre
121 West Jefferson
Fort Wayne, IN 46802
Tel: 219-424-5665
Address Inquiries to: Rick Hammet, Manager
Description: Seating capacity 3000.

Foellinger Outdoor Theater in Franke
Park
1 East Main Street
Fort Wayne, IN 46802
Tel: 219-482-2785
Address Inquiries to: Robert E. Behr,

Manager
Founded in: 1949
Description: Seating capacity 3000.

Fort Wayne Performing Arts Center
324 Penn Avenue
Fort Wayne, IN 46805

Scottish Rite Auditorium
431 West Berry Street
Fort Wayne, IN 46802
Tel: 219-423-2593
Address Inquiries to: John Lombard, Manager
Founded in: 1958
Description: Seating capacity 1,197.

Goshen

John S. Umble Center
1700 South Main Street
Goshen, IN 46526
Tel: 219-593-3161
Address Inquiries to: J. Robert Kreider,
   Manager
Founded in: 1977
Description: Seating capacity 250.

Greencastle

DePauw Speech Hall
DePauw University
Greencastle, IN 46135
Tel: 317-653-9721
Address Inquiries to: Robert O. Weiss,
   Manager
Founded in: Constructed 1885, converted
   1927.
Description: Seating capacity 450.

De Pauw University Performing Arts
Center
De Pauw University
Greencastle, IN 46135
Tel: 317-653-9721
Address Inquiries to: Robert O. Weiss,
   Manager
Founded in: Constructed 1975.
Description: Depauw University Performing
Arts Center has a total seating capacity 1,-
950.

Indianapolis

Anthenaeum Turners Building
401 East Michigan Street
Indianapolis, IN 46204
Tel: 317-635-6336
Address Inquiries to: John Waymire, Manager
Founded in: Constructed 1898, converted
   1972.
Description: Seating capacity 396.

Brown Theatre
Hilton University
49th Street at Boulevard Place
Indianapolis, IN 46204
Tel: 317-926-1581
Address Inquiries to: Robert L. Young, Jr.,
   Manager
Founded in: 1954
Description: Seating capacity 4,004

Clowes Memorial Hall
4600 Sunset Avenue

Indianapolis, IN 46208
Tel: 317-924-6321
Address Inquiries to: Sidney H. Weedman,
   Manager
Founded in: Constructed 1963.
Description: Seating capacity 2,200.

West Lafayette

Purdue University
Loeb Playhouse/Stewart Theatre
West Lafayette, IN 47907
Tel: 317-749-2649
Address Inquiries to: Dale E. Miller, Director
   of Theatre
Member: URTA;
Description: Graduate programs available.

IOWA
Akron

Ye Olde Opera House
Post Office Box 341
Akron, IA 51001

Ames

C.Y. Stephens Auditorium
Iowa State University
Ames, IA 50011
Tel: 515-294-3347
Address Inquiries to: Richard D. Snyder,
   Manager
Founded in: Constructed 1969.
Description: Seating capacity 2,749.

T.H. Benton Auditorium
Iowa State Center
Ames, IA 50011
Tel: 515-294-3347
Address Inquiries to: Dr. Richard D. Snyder,
   Manager
Founded in: 1969
Description: Seating capacity 440.

Decorah

Luther College Field House
Speech and Theater Department
Decorah, IA 52101
Tel: 319-387-1245
Address Inquiries to: Paul Henzler, Manager
Founded in: 1964
Description: Seating capacity 4,000.

Iowa City

Hancher Auditorium
The University of Iowa
Iowa City, IA 52242
Tel: 319-353-6251
Address Inquiries to: James Wockenfuss,
   Manager
Founded in: 1972
Description: Seating capacity 2,684

Marshalltown

Martha Ellen Tye Playhouse
Fisher Community Center
Marshalltown, IA 50158
Tel: 515-752-4164
Address Inquiries to: Sandy Schlesinger,

Manager
Founded in: 1959
Description: Seating capacity 450.

Mount Pleasant

Iowa Wesleyan Chapel Auditorium
Iowa Wesleyan College
Mount Pleasant, IA 52641
Tel: 319-385-8021
Address Inquiries to: Miriam Messer,
   Manager
Founded in: Constructed 1880.
Description: Seating capacity 800.

Ottuma

Ottuma Heights College
Grandview and Elm Street
Ottuma, IA 52501
Address Inquiries to: J. Solloway, Manager

Sioux City

Sioux City Municipal Auditorium
401 Gordon Drive
Sioux City, IA 51101
Tel: 712-279-6157
Address Inquiries to: Harold C. Hansen,
   Manager
Founded in: 1950
Description: Seating capacity 4,781.

Spirit Lake

Okoboji Summer Theatre
Post Ofice Box 341
Spirit Lake, IA 53160
Tel: 712-332-2773
Address Inquiries to: Fred R. Homertz,
   Manager
Founded in: 1930
Description: Seating capacity 450.

KANSAS
Great Bend

Great Bend City Auditorium
1214 Stone
Great Bend, KS 67530
Tel: 316-793-3755
Address Inquiries to: Carol Soden, Manager
Description: Seating capacity 2,500.

Hays

Felton-Stuart Theatre
Fort Hays State College
Hays, KS 67601
Tel: 913-628-5361

Hays Art Center
112 East 11th
Hays, KS 67601
Tel: 913-625-7522
Address Inquiries to: Carol J. Hall, Manager
Founded in: Converted 1977.

Lawrence

Hoch Auditorium
University of Kansas
Lawrence, KS 66045
Tel: 913-864-3421

Address Inquiries to: James Moeser, Manager
Founded in: 1925

Leavenworth

Xavier Theatre
4100 South 4th Trafficway
Leavenworth, KS 66048
Tel: 913-682-5151
Address Inquiries to: Carolgene Burd,
  Manager
Description: Seating capacity 440.

Lindsberg

Burnett Center for Performing Arts
Bethany College
Lindsberg, KS 67456
Tel: 913-227-3312
Address Inquiries to: Piet Knentsch, Manager
Founded in: 1973.
Description: Seating capacity 301.

Presser Hall Auditorium
Bethany College
Lindsberg, KS 67456
Tel: 913-227-3312 extension 42
Address Inquiries to: A.J. Pearson, Manager
Founded in: 1929
Description: Seating capacity 1,902.

Manhattan

Manhattan Civic Theatre
423 Houston
Manhattan, KS 66502
Tel: 913-776-8591
Founded in: Converted 1976.
Description: Seating capacity 120.

Manhattan Community House
4th and Humbolt
Manhattan, KS 66502
Tel: 913-776-4714
Founded in: 1920
Description: Seating capacity 150.

Vassar

Vassar Playhouse
Post Office Box 5
Vassar, KS 66543
Tel: 913-828-3249
Address Inquiries to: Bruce Rogers, Manager
Veda Rogers, Manager
Founded in: 1930
Description: Seating capacity 195.

Whippoorwill Showboat
Post Office Box 5
Vassar, KS 66543
Tel: 913-828-3249
Description: Seating capacity 50.

Wichita

Century 11 Convention Hall
225 West Douglas
Wichita, KS 67202
Tel: 316-264-9121
Address Inquiries to: James F. Clancy,
  Manager
Founded in: 1969
Description: Seating capacity 661.

Century 11 Theatre
225 West Douglas
Wichita, KS 67202
Tel: 316-264-9121
Address Inquiries to: James F. Clancy,
  Manager
Founded in: 1969
Description: Seating capacity 661.

Witchita

Alexander Auditorium
Friends University
1500 University
Witchita, KS 67213
Tel: 316-263-9131
Address Inquiries to: William Wade Perry,
  Manager
Founded in: 1965
Description: Seating capacity 485.

KENTUCKY

Ashland

Paramount Arts Center
Winchester and 12th
Ashland, KY 41101
Tel: 606-324-3175
Address Inquiries to: Linda L. Ball, Manager
Founded in: 1931
Description: Seating capacity 1,309.

Danville

Pioneer Playhouse of Kentucky
Danville, KY 40422
Tel: 606-236-2747
Address Inquiries to: Eben Henson, Manager
Founded in: 1950
Description: Seating capacity 1,200.

Lexington

Diner's Playhouse
434 Interstate Avenue
Lexington, KY 40505
Tel: 606-299-8407
Address Inquiries to: Christopher Parsons,
  President
Founded in: 1973
Member: Southeastern Theatre Association;
Annual Budget: $100,000

Mitchell Fine Arts Center
Transylvania University
Lexington, KY 40508
Tel: 606-233-8179
Address Inquiries to: Gary Anderson,
  Manager
Founded in: 1969
Description: Seating capacity 1,050.

Louisville

Actors Theatre of Louisville
316-320 West Main Street
Louisville, KY 40202
Tel: 502-584-1265
Address Inquiries to: Alexander Speer,
  Manager
Founded in: 1972
Description: Seating capacity 641.

Maysville

Maysville Players Opera House
116 2nd Street
Maysville, KY 41056
Tel: 606-564-3666
Address Inquiries to: Mary Anderson, Rental
  Manager
Founded in: 1898
Description: Seating capacity 450.

Milligan College

Seeger Memorial Chapel
Milligan College
Milligan College, KY 37682
Tel: 615-929-0116
Address Inquiries to: Dr. John A. Dowd,
  Manager
Founded in: 1966
Description: Seating capacity 1,275.

Pineville

Pine Mountain Park Amphitheatre
Pineville, KY 40977
Tel: 606-337-3800
Address Inquiries to: Preston Slusher,
  Manager
Founded in: 1935

LOUISIANA

Baton Rouge

Baton Rouge Little Theater
Post Office Box 1943
Baton Rouge, LA 70821
Tel: 504-924-6496
Address Inquiries to: Mrs. E.J. Maginnis,
  Manager
Founded in: 1961
Description: Seating capacity 425.

Natchitoches

Grand Encore Amphitheatre
LA Highway 6 East
Post Office Box 1714
Natchitohes, LA 71457
Tel: 318-357-1714
Address Inquiries to: W. Charxes Park,
  Manager
Founded in: 1976
Description: Seating capacity 1,375.

Northwestern State University
Little Theatre
Fine Arts Building
Natchitoches, LA 71457
Tel: 318-357-6196
Address Inquiries to: E. Robert Black,
  Manager
Founded in: 1937
Description: Seating capacity 300.

New Orleans

Dixon Hall
Tulane University
New Orleans, LA 70118
Tel: 504-897-3491

Description: Seating capacity 1,000.

MASSACHUSETTS

Cambridge

Agassiz Theater
Radcliffe College
Cambridge, MA 02138
Founded in: Converted 1977.
Description: Seating capacity 400.

Dennis

Cape Playhouse
Route 6A
Dennis, MA 02638
Tel: 617-385-3838
Address Inquiries to: Angelo Del Rossi,
   Director
   Lamont E. Smith, Managing Director
Founded in: 1927
Annual Budget: $100,000

Dover

Festival Theatre
56 Centre Street
Dover, MA 02030
Tel: 617-785-1260
Address Inquiries to: Priscilla B. Dewey,
   Manager
   Peter Dewey, Manager
Founded in: 1977
Description: Seating capacity 700.

Easthampton

The Williston Theatre
Williston-Northampton School
Easthampton, MA 01027
Tel: 413-527-1520
Address Inquiries to: George B. Dunnington,
   Business Manager
Founded in: 1958
Description: Seating capacity 340.

East Wareham

Agawam Hall
Depot Street
East Wareham, MA 02538

Falmouth

Highfield Theatre
Drawer F
Falmouth, MA 02541
Tel: 617-548-0668
Address Inquiries to: Robert A. Haslun,
   Manager
Founded in: 1890
Description: Seating capacity 601.

Groton

Lawrence Academy Theatre
Powderhouse Road
Groton, MA 01450
Tel: 617-448-3344
Address Inquiries to: William Harman,
   Manager
Founded in: 1965
Description: Seating capacity 400.

Medford

Tufts Arena Theater
Tufts University
Medford, MA 02155
Tel: 617-623-3880
Address Inquiries to: Eric Forsythe, Manager
Founded in: 1890
Description: Seating capacity 380.

Melrose

Melrose Memorial Hall
Main Street
Melrose, MA 02176
Address Inquiries to: George Hume, Manager
Founded in: 1912
Description: Seating capacity 1,060.

Nahant

Knights of Columbus Hall
Relay Road
Nahant, MA 01908
Address Inquiries to: Anthony DellaGrotte,
   Manager
Description: Seating capacity 200.

Newton Centre

Pomroy Playhouse, The
84 Eldredge Street
Newton Centre, MA 02158
Tel: 617-244-9538
Address Inquiries to: Marilyn Krassin,
   Manager
Description: Seating capacity 250.

Orleans

Orleans Arena Theatre
Old Town Hall, Main Street
Orleans, MA 02653
Tel: 617-255-9929
Address Inquiries to: John Kelly, Executive
   Director
Founded in: 1873
Description: Seating capacity 160.

Plymouth

Old Colony Theater
Main Street
Plymouth, MA 02360
Tel: 617-746-7474
Address Inquiries to: Robert W. York
Founded in: 1914
Description: Seating Capacity 750.

Salem

Salem Cultural Arts Center
32 Derby Square
Salem, MA 01970
Tel: 617-744-4580
Address Inquiries to: Robert Murray,
   Manager
Founded in: 1840

South Yarmouth

Yarmouth Playhouse
250 Old Main Street
South Yarmouth, MA 02664

Springfield

Springfield Civic Center
1277 Main Street
Springfield, MA 01103
Tel: 413-781-7080
Address Inquiries to: Jerry Healy, Manager
Founded in: 1972

Vineyard Haven

Katherine Cornell Memorial Theatre
Vineyard Haven, MA 02568
Address Inquiries to: Josephine Crowell,
   Town Clerk
Founded in: 1700
Description: Seating capacity 150.

West Springfield

Horace A. Moses Building-Stage/West
Eastern State Grounds
1511 Memorial Avenue
West Springfield, MA 01089
Tel: 413-736-7092
Address Inquiries to: Stephen E. Hays,
   Manager
Founded in: 1925

Worcester

Worcester Foothills Theatre
6 Chatham Street
Worcester, MA 01608
Tel: 617-754-3314
Address Inquiries to: Lindon Rankin,
   Company Manager
   Marc P. Smith, Executive Producer
Founded in: 1920
Description: Seating capacity 149.

Worcester Jewish Community Center
633 Salisbury Street
Worcester, MA 01608
Tel: 617-756-7109
Address Inquiries to: Lester Kaplan,
   Executive Director
   Fran Ross, Program Director
Founded in: 1967
Annual Budget: $1,000,000
Description: Seating capacity 280.

Worcester Memorial Auditorium
Worcester, MA 01608
Tel: 617-752-6703
Address Inquiries to: Clifton Robertson,
   Manager
Founded in: 1933
Description: Seating capacity 3,008.

MICHIGAN

Ann Arbor

Arena Theatre
Freize Building
State Street at Washington
Ann Arbor, MI 48104
Tel: 313-764-5387
Founded in: 1959
Description: Seating capacity 175.

Mendelssohn Theatre
227 South Ingalls
Ann Arbor, MI 48104
Tel: 313-763-1085
Address Inquiries to: Alfred Stuart, Manager
Founded in: 1928
Description: Seating capacity 702.

Power Center for the Performing Arts
121 Fletcher Street
Ann Arbor, MI 48109
Tel: 313-763-3333
Address Inquiries to: Ralph P. Beebe,
    Manager
Founded in: 1971
Description: Seating capacity 1,414.

Trueblood Theatre
State Street at Washington
Ann Arbor, MI 48104
Tel: 313-764-5687
Address Inquiries to: Opal Bailey, Rental
    Manager
Founded in: 1961
Description: Seating capacity 699.

Battle Creek

W.K. Kellogg Auditorium
West Van Buren at McCamley Street
Battle Creek, MI 49014
Founded in: 1935
Description: Seating capacity 2,400.

Charlotte

Charlotte Civic Theatre
Post Office Box 231
Charlotte, MI 48813

East Lansing

Michigan State University
Performing Arts Center
East Lansing, MI 48824
Tel: 517-355-6690
Address Inquiries to: Frank C. Rutledge,
    Chairman
Member: URTA;
Description: Department has a graduate pro-
gram. Performances take place in the Fair-
child Theatre, which has a 676-seat capacity
and a proscenium thrust stage, in Arena
Theatre, which has a 215-seat capacity and
The Studio Theatre, which has a 100-seat
capacity.

MISSISSIPPI
Meridian

Meridian Junior College Theatre
5500 Highway 19, North
Meridian, MS 39301
Tel: 601-483-8241
Address Inquiries to: Ronnie Miller, Director
Founded in: 1976
Member: MTA; STC;
Annual Budget: $14,000
Description: Seating capacity 600.

Meridian Little Theatre
Post Office Box 3055, North Station
Meridian, MS 38301
Tel: 601-482-6371
Address Inquiries to: Jimmy Pigford, Resident
    Director
Founded in: 1976
Member: NEA; Mississippi Little Theatre
    Association; STC;
Description: Seating capacity 400.

Natchez

Natchez Little Theatre
Post Office Box 1232
Natchez, MS 39120
Tel: 601-442-2233
Address Inquiries to: Mrs. Forrest R.
    Colebank, President
Founded in: 1948
Description: Seating capapcity 245. A not-for-
profit facility available for rental.

State College

Lee Hall Auditorium
Mississippi State University
State College, MS 39762
Tel: 601-325-5646
Address Inquiries to: Gaddis Hunt, Manager
Founded in: 1900
Description: Seating capacity 1,200.

Tupelo

Tupelo Community Theatre
1014 Main Street
Tupelo, MS 38801
Tel: 601-842-4518
Address Inquiries to: John Pittmon, Manager
Founded in: Converted 1976.
Description: Seating capacity 225.

MISSOURI
Kansas City

Danciger Auditorium
8201 Holmes Road
Kansas City, MO 64131
Tel: 816-361-5200
Address Inquiries to: Paula Simkins, Manager
Founded in: 1962
Description: Seating capacity 499.

Goppert Theatre
11901 Wornall Road
Kansas City, MO 64145
Tel: 816-942-8400
Address Inquiries to: Dr. William J. Louis,
    Manager
Founded in: 1974
Description: Seating capacity 500.

Kansas City Convention Center
301 West 13th Street
Kansas City, MO 64145
Tel: 816-421-8000
Address Inquiries to: Harold R. Peterson,
    Manager
Founded in: 1936
Description: Seating capacity 2,572.

Kansas City Municipal Auditorium
1310 Wyandotte Street
Kansas City, MO 64105
Tel: 816-421-8000
Address Inquiries to: Harold Peterson
Description: Seating capacity 2,572.

(Kansas City) Starlight Theatre Summer
Series
c/o Starlight Theatre Association
4600 Starlight Road
Kansas City, MO 64132
Tel: 816-333-9481
Founded in: 1950
Description: Located in the heart of the 1,700
acre Swope Park, this 8,000 seat outdoor
theatre offers professional Broadway-type
musicals and concerts by major name entertainers from June-September. The facility
which seats almost 8,000 people, may be
made available to outside producers/pro-
moters. Interested parties should contact
the theatre.

Lyric Theatre
11th and Central
Kansas City, MO 64105
Tel: 816-471-4933
Address Inquiries to: James Sutherland,
    Manager
Founded in: 1930
Description: Seating capacity 1700.

Parkville

Bell Road Barn Playhouse
6008 Bell Road
Parkville, MO 64152
Tel: 816-587-0218
Address Inquiries to: Jenkin R. David,
    Manager
Founded in: 1954
Description: Seating capacity 100.

Park College Little Theatre
Park College
Parkville, MO 64152
Tel: 314-741-2000
Address Inquiries to: Jim Cox, Manager
Founded in: 1950
Description: Seating capacity 228.

Point Lookout

Jones Auditorium
School of the Ozarks
Point Lookout, MO 65726
Tel: 417-334-6411
Address Inquiries to: Dr. Graham Clark,
    President
Founded in: 1968
Description: Seating capacity 980.

Saint Louis

Plantation Playhouse
Saint Louis, MO 63138
Address Inquiries to: Michael Moss, Producer

Sikeston

Sikeston Activity Center
201 South Kings Highway
Sikeston, MO 63801
Tel: 314-471-4113
Address Inquiries to: Charles F. Church,
   Manager
Founded in: 1890
Description: Seating capacity 380.

Springfield

Landers Theatre
311 East Walnut Street
Springfield, MO 65806
Tel: 417-869-1334
Address Inquiries to: Paula Thompson,
   General Manager
Founded in: 1909
Description: Seating capacity 500.

MONTANA

Missoula

Masquer Theater
Department of Drama
University of Montana
Missoula, MT 59801
Tel: 406-243-4481
Address Inquiries to: James D. Kriley,
   Manager
Founded in: 1903
Member: ATA; NAST;
Description: Seating capacity 1,300.

NEBRASKA

Lincoln

University of Nebraska
Department of Theatre
103 Temple Building
12th and R Streets
Lincoln, NB 68508
Tel: 402-472-1606; 402-472-2072
Address Inquiries to: Rex McGraw, Chairman
Member: U/RTA;
Description: The department of theatre has access to 3 production facilities.

Norfolk

Norfolk City Auditorium
Norfolk, NB 68701
Tel: 371-808-; 371-456-
Founded in: 1930
Annual Budget: $54,855

Omaha

Omaha Civic Auditorium
1804 Capitol Avenue
Omaha, NB 68102
Tel: 402-346-1323
Address Inquiries to: Charles Mancuso,
   Manager
Founded in: 1955

Orpheum Theater
409 South 16th Street
Omaha, NB 68102
Tel: 402-346-1323
Address Inquiries to: Charles J. Mancuso,
   Manager
Founded in: 1927
Description: Seating capacity 2,761.

York

Yorkshire Playhouse
Post Office Box 413
York, NE 68467

NEVADA

Las Vegas

Las Vagas Convention Center
3150 South Paradise Road
Las Vegas, NV 89109
Tel: 702-735-2323
Address Inquiries to: Gene Stephens,
   Manager
Founded in: 1959
Description: Seating capacity 7,392 in the
Main Hall.

Reed Whipple Cultural Arts Center
821 Las Vegas Boulevard North
Las Vegas, NV 89101
Tel: 702-386-6386
Address Inquiries to: Pat Marchese, Manager
Founded in: 1961
Description: Seating capacity 300.

NEW HAMPSHIRE

Greenville

Lakes Region Playhouse
Route 11 and 11B
Greenville, NH 03246
Tel: 603-293-7561
Description: Seating capacity 600.

Mason

Mason Town Hall
Mason, NH 03048
Tel: 603-878-2613
Founded in: 1850

Milford

Souhegan Valley Theatre
Mount Vernon Street
Milford, NH 03055
Address Inquiries to: T.C. Lorden, Manager
Founded in: 1975
Description: Seating capacity 500.

Nashua

Arts and Science Center
14 Court Street
Nashua, NH 03060
Tel: 603-883-1506
Address Inquiries to: George Lubeley, Rental
   Manager
Founded in: 1973
Description: Seating capacity 250.

North Conway

Eastern Slope Playhouse
North Conway, NH 03860
Tel: 603-356-5776
Founded in: 1917
Description: Seating capacity 162.

Plymouth

Ernest L. Silver Hall
Plymouth State College
Plymouth, NH 03264
Tel: 603-536-1550
Address Inquiries to: Arthur Hanson,
   Manager
Founded in: 1955
Description: Seating capacity 600.

Wolfeboro

Wolfeboro Playhouse
Post Office Box 288
Wolfeboro, NH 03894

NEW JERSEY

Caldwell

Caldwell College Student Union Building
Caldwell College
Caldwell, NJ 07006
Tel: 201-228-4424
Address Inquiries to: Sister M. Mildred,
   Manager
Founded in: 1968
Description: Seating capacity 1,500.

Clinton

The Hunterton Art Center
Old Stone Mill
7 Center Street
Clinton, NJ 08809
Tel: 201-735-8415
Address Inquiries to: Jane Reading, President
   Linda C. Buki, Executive Director
Founded in: 1953
Member: AAM; NEA; NEH; NJSCA;
Annual Budget: $150,000
Description: Art space consists of three art
galleries and contemporary craft shop. Occasional theatre and dance performances.

Dover

Dover Little Theatre
Post Office Box 82
Elliott Street
Dover, NJ 07801
Tel: 201-366-9890
Address Inquiries to: Mrs. Joan M. Munson,
   President
Founded in: Converted 1965.
Description: Seating capacity 165.

East Orange

Halfpenny Playhouse/Upsala Theatre
Edgerton Terrace
East Orange, NJ 07019
Address Inquiries to: Teri Gaalipeau,
   Manager
Founded in: 1960

Description: Seating capacity 575.

Hackensack

Orrie De Nooyer Auditorium
200 Hackensack Avenue
Hackensack, NJ 07061
Tel: 201-343-6000
Address Inquiries to: John Beddoe, Manager
Founded in: 1966
Description: Seating capacity 1,021.

Holmdel

Garden State Arts Center
Post Office Box 116
Holmdel, NJ 07733
Address Inquiries to: John Carson, Manager
Founded in: 1968
Description: Seating capacity 5,040.

Jersey City

Roosevelt Stadium
Charles K. Robinson
Department of Human Resources
30 Baldwin Avenue
Jersey City, NJ 07304
Tel: 201-332-1800
Address Inquiries to: Al Keenan, Manager
Founded in: 1937
Description: Seating capacity 35,000.

5 Corners Library Auditorium
Network and Summit Avenues
Jersey City, NJ 07306
Address Inquiries to: Ben Grimm, Librarian

Lawrenceville

Rider College Cultural Programs
Post Office Box 6400
Lawrenceville, NJ 08648
Tel: 608-896-0800
Address Inquiries to: Sarah-Ann Harnick,
  Director
Description: Seating capacity 458

Middlesex

Foothill Playhouse
Beechwood Avenue
Middlesex, NJ 08846
Tel: 201-356-0462
Address Inquiries to: Stanley F. Klein,
  Manager
Founded in: 1947

Montclair

The Whole Theater Company
544 Bloomfield Avenue
Montclair, NJ 07042
Tel: 201-744-2996; 201-744-2989
Address Inquiries to: Robert Alpaugh,
  Manager
Founded in: Converted 1977
Annual Budget: $710,000
Description: Seating capacity 190.

Moorestown

The Theater
Post Office Box 330
Moorestown, NJ 08057
Tel: 609-234-9737

Address Inquiries to: Charles Buckwald,
  Business Manager
Founded in: 1925
Description: Seating capacity 275.

Mount Holly

Mount Holly Recreation Center
Brainerd Street
Mount Holly, NJ 08060
Tel: 609-267-0178
Address Inquiries to: Donald Pulzynski,
  Manager
Founded in: 1900
Description: Seating capacity 250.

Paterson

Paterson Library Auditorium
250 Broadway
Paterson, NJ 07501
Tel: 201-279-4200
Address Inquiries to: Sylvia Jaroslow,
  Manager
Founded in: 1968
Description: Seating capacity 150.

Smithville

Smithville Theatre
Route 9
Smithville, NJ 08201

Titusville

Open Air Theatre
Post Office Box 1776
Titusville, NJ 08560
Tel: 609-737-9721; 609-446-0301
Address Inquiries to: Jack M. Rees, Manager
Founded in: 1964
Annual Budget: $84,000
Description: The theatre, which operates from
June thru August, presents Shakespearean
plays, operettas and musical comedies. Seat-
ing capacity 800.

Trenton

Artists Showcase Theatre
1150 Indiana Avenue
Trenton, NJ 08611
Tel: 609-392-2433
Address Inquiries to: Byron Steele, Artistic
  Director
Founded in: 1911
Description: Seating capacity 125.

New Jersey State Museum Auditorium
205 West State Street
Trenton, NJ 08626
Tel: 609-292-6300
Address Inquiries to: Leah P. Sloshberg,
  Manager
Founded in: 1954
Description: Seating capacity 416.

Trenton War Memorial Auditorium
West Lafayette Street
Trenton, NJ 08608
Tel: 609-393-4866
Address Inquiries to: Frank Gogdan, Manager
Founded in: 1930
Description: Seating capacity 1,926.

Woodbury

Sketch Club Playhouse
Glover and Logan Streets
Woodbury, NJ 08096
Tel: 609-848-8089
Founded in: Converted 1952
Description: Seating capacity 99.

NEW MEXICO
Hobbs

The Playhouse
1700 North Grimes
Hobbs, NM 88240
Tel: 505-393-9524
Address Inquiries to: Frank Rose, Vice
  President
Founded in: 1962

Las Cruces

New Mexico State University Little
  Theatre
New Mexico State University
Las Cruces, NM 88003
Tel: 505-646-2421
Address Inquiries to: Clark Rogers, Manager
Founded in: 1962
Description: Seating capacity 420.

Roswell

Pearson Auditorium
1900 North Main Street
Roswell, NM 88201
Tel: 505-622-6250; 505-623-9338
Address Inquiries to: Junso Ogawa, Major
Founded in: 1940
Member: NECAA; ASCAP; BMI;
Annual Budget: $10,000
Description: The auditorium is set aside for
the Roswell Symphony Orchestra Concerts,
the Roswell Community Concert Association Series, regular movies for the cadets,
and various other forms of entertainment
and educational programs. It is available for
rental.

Santa Fe

Saint Francis Auditorium
Museum of New Mexico
Santa Fe, NM 87501
Tel: 505-827-2351
Address Inquiries to: Donald Strel, Rental
  Manager
Description: Seating capacity 500.

NEW YORK
Albany

Albany Civic Auditorium
19 Clinton Avenue
Albany, NY 12207
Tel: 518-465-3333
Address Inquiries to: Evelyn E. Knoll,
  Director
Founded in: 1929
Description: Seating capacity 2,901.

Albany Civic Theatre
235 Second Avenue
Albany, NY 12209

Page Hall
Washington Avenue
Albany, NY 12207
Tel: 513-457-7600
Address Inquiries to: Donald Bielecki,
  Manager
Description: Seating capacity 2,800.

State University of New York
Performing Arts Center
1400 Washington Avenue
Albany, NY 12222
Tel: 518-457-8608
Address Inquiries to: Michael T. Sheehan,
  Manager
Founded in: 1967
Description: Seating capacity total of 1,260.

Alexandria Bay

Alexandria Bay Convention Hall
James Street
Alexandria Bay, NY 13601
Tel: 315-482-3320
Address Inquiries to: David A. Golden,
  Manager
Founded in: 1930
Description: Seating capacity 200.

Alfred

Major Holmes Auditorium
Harder Hall, Alfred University
Alfred, NY 14802
Tel: 607-871-2411
Address Inquiries to: William E. Emrick,
  Manager
Founded in: 1973
Description: Seating capacity 422.

McLane Center
Alfred University
Alfred, NY 14802
Tel: 607-871-2193
Address Inquiries to: Richard Powers,
  Director
Founded in: 1972
Description: Seating capacity 2,500.

State University of New York
Department of Campus Activities
Performing Arts Center
Alfred, NY 14802
Tel: 607-871-6326; 607-871-6115
Address Inquiries to: John Larsen, Chairman
Member: ATA; NECAA; ;

Susan Howell Hall
Alfred University
Alfred, NY 14802
Tel: 607-871-2193
Address Inquiries to: Mary Kay Lewis,
  Manager
Founded in: 1954
Description: Seating capacity 125.

Bayside

Queensborough Community College
Theatre
Springfield Boulevard
Bayside, NY 11364
Tel: 212-631-6321
Address Inquiries to: Darrel Calvin, Manager
Founded in: 1970
Description: Seating capacity 875.

Brooklyn

Brooklyn Center for the Performing Arts
Brooklyn College
Campus Road at Hillel Place
Brooklyn, NY 11210
Tel: 212-780-5296, Operations and Rentals;
212-780-5291, Programming
Address Inquiries to: Dan Swartz, General
  Manager
  Richard Grossberg, Assistant General
  Manager (contact for rentals)
Founded in: 1953
Member: ACUCAA; Avon Foundation;
  ISPAA; NEA; NYSCA; Robert Sterling
  Clark Foundation;
Description: BCBC annually presents a variety
of arts programs during the season from
September through June. In Whitman Hall,
seating 2,500, BCBC presents the Great Art-
ists series of performances by international-
ly known concert artists, orchestras and
dance companies. The 500 seat Gershwin
Theatre is used for theatre and recital pro-
grams. Both theatres are available to producers.

Chautauqua

Chautauqua Amphitheatre
Chautauqua Lake
Chautauqua, NY 14722
Tel: 715-357-5635
Description: Seating capacity 6,500.

Clinton

Minor Theatre
Hamilton College
Clinton, NY 13323
Tel: 315-853-5511
Founded in: 1890
Description: Seating capacity 236.

Crompond

Martha Guinsberg Pavilion
Baron De Hirsh Road
Crompond, NY 10517
Tel: 914-528-5402
Founded in: 1956
Description: Seating capacity 800.

Delhi

The Little Theatre
State University Agricultural and
Technical College
Delhi, NY 13753
Tel: 607-746-4216
Address Inquiries to: William Campbell,
  Manager
Founded in: 1972

Description: Seating capacity 336.

Elmont

West Nassau Youth Center
One Plainfield Avenue
Elmont, NY 11033
Tel: 516-328-8358
Address Inquiries to: Ronald G. Russo,
  Manager
Founded in: Converted 1970.
Description: Seating capacity 400.

Flushing

Queens Theatre in the Park
Flushing Meadow Park
Flushing, NY 11368
Tel: 212-596-5700
Member: City of New York; NEA; NYSCA;
  ART/NY; TDF;
Annual Budget: $200,000
Description: Operated as a program of the
Queens Cultural Assocation. As a center for
performing arts, it is utilized for theatre and
dance presentations.

Fredonia

Michael C. Rockefeller Arts Center
State University College
Fredonia, NY 14063
Tel: 716-673-3217
Address Inquiries to: Edward A. DeDee,
  Manager
Founded in: 1969
Description: Has a total seating capacity of 1,-
800.

Ithaca

Dillingham Center
Ithaca College
Ithaca, NY 14850
Tel: 607-274-3345
Address Inquiries to: Firman H. Brown, Jr.,
  Chairman
Founded in: 1968
Description: Seating capacity 535.

Dillingham Center for the Performing Arts
Ithaca College
Ithaca, NY 14850
Tel: 607-274-3345
Address Inquiries to: Firman Brown, Manager
Founded in: 1968
Description: Seating capacity 350.

Jamestown

Little Theatre Building
18-24 East Second Street
Jamestown, NY 14701
Tel: 716-483-1095
Address Inquiries to: Marshall B. Dahlin,
  Manager
Founded in: 1900
Description: Seating capacity 440.

Lackawanna

Boland Memorial Theatre
500 Martin Road
Lackawanna, NY 14218
Tel: 716-826-1500

Address Inquiries to: Matthew V. Oreskovic,
Manager
Founded in: 1957
Description: Seating capacity 1,040.

Lindenhurst

Studio Theatre
141 South Welwood Avenue
Lindenhurst, NY 11757
Tel: 516-884-1877
Address Inquiries to: Mike Engel, Manager
Description: Seating capacity 175.

Little York

Pavilion Theatre
Dwyer Memorial Park, Route 281
Little York, NY 13087
Tel: 607-749-4044
Founded in: 1800
Description: Seating capacity 250.

Mamaroneck

Emelin Theatre
Library Lane
Mamaroneck, NY 10543
Tel: 914-698-3045
Address Inquiries to: Norman Kline, Manager
Founded in: 1972
Description: Seating capacity 280.

New York

American Place Theatre
111 West 46th Street
New York, NY 10036
Tel: 212-246-0393
Address Inquiries to: Lawrence Wein, Owner
Founded in: 1971
Description: The American Place Theatre
building houses Wynn Handman's theatre
company providing a 299 seat mainstage
and a 100 seat cafe theatre in addition to
administrative offices.

Astor Place Theatre
434 Layfayette Street
New York, NY 10003
Tel: 212-254-4370
Address Inquiries to: Albert Poland, Owner
Founded in: 1969
Description: The original Astor family lived in
the building, which is opposite the Astor Library (which houses the New York Shakespeare Festival). Total seating capacity in the
theatre is 299.

Bouwerie Lane Theatre
330 Bowery
New York, NY 10012
Tel: 212-677-0060
Address Inquiries to: Eve Admanson,
Director
Founded in: 1971
Member: ART/NY; TDF; NYSCA;
Description: Housing the Jean Cocteau Rep-
ertory, the theatre seats 140 which is in the
off off broadway contract catagory.

Cherry Lane Theatre
38 Commerce Street
New York, NY 10014

Tel: 212-989-2020
Address Inquiries to: Andrea Carroad, Owner
Founded in: 1924
Description: Seating 124, the Cherry Lane
Theatre is a well known fixture of Green-
which Village theatre life.

Harold Clurman Theatre
412 West 42nd Street
New York, NY 10036
Tel: 212-575-9654
Address Inquiries to: Jack Garfein, Director
Founded in: 1978
Member: AEA; TDF; CRT/NY;
Description: Named in honor of Harold Clur-
man, the building is part of the 42nd Street
Theatre Row development and houses 100
in the main theatre and 75 in its workshop
area. The thatre company presents plays and
runs a workshop series.

Cunningham Dance Theatre
463 West Street
New York, NY 10014
Tel: 212-691-9751
Member: NYSCA; ART/NY; TDF;
Description: Space available for perfor-
mances.

Dance Gallery
242 East 14th Street
New York, NY 10003
Tel: 212-685-5972
Member: NYSCA; ART/NY; TDF;
Description: Space available for perfor-
mances.

Dia Art Foundation
155 Mercer Street
New York, NY 10012
Tel: 212-260-2110
Member: NYSCA; ART/NY; TDF;
Description: Space available for perfor-
mances.

Hunter College Studio Theatre
930 Lexington Avenue at 69th Street
New York, NY 10021
Tel: 212-570-5434
Member: NYSCA; ART/NY; TDF;
Description: Space available for perfor-
mances.

Loeb Student Center
566 LaGuardia Place
New York, NY 10012
Tel: 212-598-2022
Member: NYSCA; ART/NY; TDF;
Description: Space available for perfor-
mances.

The Music Box Theatre
239 West 45th Street
New York, NY 10036
Tel: 212-246-4636
Address Inquiries to: Norman Stone, Owner
Shubert Organization
Founded in: 1921
Description: The Music Box was built by com-
poser Irving Berlin and his producer Sam H.
Harris. It opened with the Music Box Revue
of 1921 and currently seats 1010.

Westside Arts Theatre/Chelsea Theatre
Center
407 West 43rd Street
New York, NY 10036
Tel: 212-541-8394
Member: AEA; TDF;
Description: The Chelsea Theatre Company is
housed in the Cheryl Crawford Theatre (210
seats) and the plant contains a smaller 190
seat theatre. The Company has won 23
Obies and taken many of its productions to
Broadway.

YM-YWHA
1395 Lexington Avenue
New York, NY 10028
Tel: 212-427-6000
Member: NYSCA; ART/NY; TDF;
Description: Space available for perfor-
mances.

Scarsdale

YM-YWHA-Westchester
999 Wilmot Road
Scarsdale, NY 10583

Staten Island

Snug Harbor Cultural Center
Richmond Avenue
Staten Island, NY 10301
Tel: 212-448-2500; Mic-eal-Sheehan,
Executive Director
Founded in: 1976
Annual Budget: $800,000
Description: Snug Harbor is a performing and
visual arts center set in the Historical Land-
mark district. Facilities include a 900 seat
procenium, 250 seat recital hall, and an out-
door performance area for 12,000.

Woodstock

Woodstock Playhouse
Post Office Box 396
Woodstock, NY 12498

NORTH CAROLINA

Charlotte

Rowe Theatre
UNCC Department of Creative Arts
Charlotte, NC 28223
Tel: 707-597-2477
Address Inquiries to: Marvin Crosland,
Manager
Founded in: 1971
Description: Seating capacity 337.

UNCC, Department of Creative Arts
Hwy 49 UNCC Station
Charlotte, NC 28233
Tel: 704-597-2322
Founded in: 1971
Description: A total seating capaciy of 750.

Manteo

Waterside Theatre
Post Office Box 40
Manteo, NC 27954
Tel: 919-473-2127
Address Inquiries to: G. Page Meekins,
 Manager
Founded in: 1937
Description: Seating capacity 1,776.

Mount Airy

Mount Airy Fine Arts Center
Post Office Box 141
Mount Airy, NC 27030
Founded in: Converted 1967.
Description: Seating capacity 300.

Raleigh

Raleigh Amphitheatre
301 Pogue Street
Raleigh, NC 27607
Tel: 919-832-3519
Address Inquiries to: Anthony Dingman,
 Manager
Founded in: 1940
Description: Seating capacity 260.

Wilmington

Sarah Graham Kenan Auditorium
UNC-W, Post Office Box 3725
Wilmington, NC 28401
Tel: 919-791-9695
Address Inquiries to: Doug W. Swink,
 Manager
Founded in: 1970
Description: Seating capacity 982.

Winston-Salem

James G. Hanes Community Center
Theatre
610 Coliseum Drive
Winston-Salem, NC 27106
Tel: 919-722-2585
Address Inquiries to: McCoy Hill, Manager
Founded in: 1957
Description: Seating capacity 420.

Reynolds Auditorium
Hawthorne Road
Winston-Salem, NC 27104
Tel: 919-727-2180
Address Inquiries to: Michael Pelech,
 Manager
Founded in: 1960
Description: Seating capacity 1,920.

NORTH DAKOTA

Grand Forks

Chester Fritz Auditorium
Box 8282, University Station
Grand Forks, ND 58202
Tel: 701-777-3076; 701-777-4211
Address Inquiries to: Linda Rohde, Director
Founded in: 1972
Member: ACUCAA;
Annual Budget: $310,000

Description: Seating capacity 2,416

La Moure

La Moure County Auditorium
La Moure County Memorial Park
La Moure, ND 58451
Founded in: 1930
Description: Seating capacity 800.

OHIO

Canton

Canton Memorial Civic Center
1101 North Market Avenue
Canton, OH 44702
Tel: 216-489-3090; 216-489-3000
Address Inquiries to: Louis Sebald, Manager
Founded in: 1952
Annual Budget: $300,000
Description: The building is used for all types
of events; private parties, graduations,
proms, wedding receptions, festivals, bas-
ketball games, circus, dog shows and trade
shows.

Columbus

Veterans Memorial Auditorium
Columbus, OH 43125

Dayton

Montgomery County Memorial Hall
125 East First Street
Dayton, OH 45422
Tel: 513-223-7581
Address Inquiries to: Barbara A. Hayde,
 Director
Founded in: 1910
Annual Budget: $200,000
Description: A public facility available for lease
by any profit or not for profit group or individual. The activities at the Hall range
from dance recitals to Broadway plays. They
have recently installed the finest sound system and a computerized lighting system with
meeting and catering facilities for groups of
all sizes. The building houses the administrative offices of the Dayton Opera, Dayton
Philharmonic and Dayton Ballet and is the
performance space for the Trotwood Circle
Chidrens Theatre.

Dover

Schoenbrunn Amphitheatre
Box 275
Dover, OH 44622
Tel: 216-339-1132
Address Inquiries to: Rachel Redinger,
 Manager
Founded in: 1969
Member: NTBA;
Annual Budget: $400,000
Description: Seating capacity 1,600

Zanesville

Zanesville Art Center
1145 Maple Avenue
Zanesville, OH 43701
Tel: 614-452-0741
Address Inquiries to: Dr. Charles Dietz,
 Director
Founded in: 1936

OKLAHOMA

Oklahoma City

Oklahoma Theatre Center
400 West Sheridan
Oklahoma City, OK 73102
Tel: 405-239-6884
Address Inquiries to: Penny Alfred, Business
 Manager
Founded in: 1968
Member: ATA; OCTA; ACA;
Annual Budget: $400,000

Tulsa

Leta Chapman Theatre
University of Tulsa
600 South College
Tulsa, OK 74104
Tel: 918-592-6000
Address Inquiries to: Dr. Nancy Vunovich,
 Director of Theatre
Founded in: 1975
Member: ATA;
Description: Seating capacity 411

Theatre Two
University of Tulsa
600 South College
Tulsa, OK 74104
Tel: 918-592-6000
Address Inquiries to: Dr. Nancy Vunovich,
 Director of Theatre
Founded in: 1975
Member: ATA;
Description: Seating capacity 175

Tulsa Performing Arts Center
Third and Cincinnati
Tulsa, OK 74103
Tel: 918-581-5641
Address Inquiries to: Bob C. Mayer, Acting
 Manager
 Warren Houtz, Technical Director
Founded in: 1977
Member: IAAM; ACUCAA; ISPA;
Annual Budget: $1,000,000
Description: Major activity is in renting and
servicing four theatres and an art gallery.
Their largest theatre seats 2,400 (Chapman
Music Hall); John Williams Theatre seats
429; Studio I seats 288 and Studio II seats
200.

OREGON

Ashland

Oregon Shakespearean Festival
Association
15 South Pioneer Street
Drawer 158
Ashland, OR 97520
Tel: 503-482-2111
Address Inquiries to: Jerry Turner, Producing
   Director
   William W. Patton, General Manager
Member: U/RTA;
Description: Performance spaces include The
Angus Bowmer Theatre, an indoor, 600 seat,
open stage and The Black Swan Theatre, a
flexible, 138-156 seat arena patterned after
the 1559 Fortune Theatre of Shakespeare's
London.

Corvallis

Oregon Memorial Union Lounge
Oregon State University
Corvallis, OR 97330
Tel: 754-241-; 754-210-
Address Inquiries to: George Stevens
Founded in: 1928

University Foundation Center
Austin Auditorium
Oregon State University
Corvallis, OR 97331 3102
Tel: 503-754-2402
Address Inquiries to: Jim Schupp, Manager
Founded in: 1981
Annual Budget: $350,000
Description: A conference center as well as
performing arts hall. The auditorium is
acoustically excellent with a capacity of 1200,
making it very intimate and desirable as per-
forming facility.

PENNSYLVANIA

Scranton

University of Scranton Student Center
Linden Street and Monroe Avenue
Scranton, PA 18505
Tel: 717-761-7841
Address Inquiries to: Jim Santos, Manager
Founded in: 1953
Description: Has a seating capacity of 6,700.

University Park

Pennsylvania State University
Department of Theatre
103 Arts Building
University Park, PA 16802
Tel: 814-865-7586
Address Inquiries to: Douglas N. Cook,
   Chairman
   Roger N. Cook, Graduate Coordinator
Member: URTA;
Description: The department's Playhouse
Theatre has a 450 seat capacity and a pros-
cenium thrust stage; The Pavilion Theatre
has a 250 seat capacity and an arena stage;
The Kern Dinner Theatre has a 200 seat

capacity.

Pennsylvania State University Auditorium
Pennsylvania State University
University Park, PA 16802
Tel: 814-863-0388
Address Inquiries to: William E. Crocken,
   Manager
Founded in: 1974
Description: Seating capacity 2,599

Playhouse Theatre
Arts Building, Penn. State University
University Park, PA 16803
Tel: 814-863-0381
Address Inquiries to: John R. Bayless,
   President
Founded in: 1963
Description: Seating capacity 500.

Schwab Auditorium
103 University Auditorium, Penn. State
University
University Park, PA 16802
Tel: 814-863-0388
Address Inquiries to: Robert W. Baisley,
   Manager
Founded in: 1902
Description: Seating capacity 1,135.

SOUTH CAROLINA

Columbia

Drayton Hall
University of South Carolina
Columbia, SC 29208
Tel: 803-777-4288; 803-777-5208
Address Inquiries to: Patti P. Gillespie
Description: Seating capacity 400.

Conway

Upstage Company
Coastal Carolina College
Conway, SC 29526
Tel: 803-347-3161
Address Inquiries to: Michael Fortner,
   Manager
Founded in: 1968
Description: Seating capacity 150.

SOUTH DAKOTA

Rapid City

Rushmore Plaza Civic Center
444 Mount Rushmore Road North
Rapid City, SD 57701
Tel: 605-394-4115
Address Inquiries to: Jack Beckman, Manager
Founded in: 1977
Description: Seating capacity 1,774.

Vermillion

Warren M. Lee Center for the Fine Arts
University of South Dakota
Vermillion, SD 57069
Tel: 605-677-5481
Address Inquiries to: Wayne S. Knutson,
   Manager

Founded in: 1974
Description: Seating capacity of 820.

Slagle Auditorium
University of South Dakota
Vermillion, SD 57069
Tel: 605-677-5481
Address Inquiries to: Cheryl L. Beeck,
   Director, Arts Outreach
Member: ACA;
Description: Seating capacity 2,200.

TENNESSEE

Chattanooga

Chattanooga Memorial Auditorium
399 McCallie Avenue
Chattanooga, TN 37402
Tel: 615-266-2642
Address Inquiries to: Clyde M. Hawkins,
   Manager
Founded in: 1924
Description: Seating capacity 4,843.

Tivoli Theatre
Broad Street
Chattanooga, TN 37402
Tel: 615-267-1676
Address Inquiries to: Clyde Hawkins,
   Manager
Founded in: 1921
Description: Seating capacity 1,806.

Clarksville

Margaret Fort Theatre
Austin Peay State University
Clarksville, TN 37040
Tel: 615-648-7378
Address Inquiries to: Dr. Joe Flippo, Manager
Founded in: 1974
Member: ATA; SCA;
Annual Budget: $20,000
Description: Seating capacity 196.

Lebanon

Cumberland College Auditorium
South Greenwood Street
Lebanon, TN 37087
Tel: 615-444-2562
Address Inquiries to: Kenneth J. Hawkins,
   Manager
Founded in: 1920, converted 1966.

Memphis

C B C Theatre/Auditorium
650 East Parkway South
Memphis, TN 38104
Tel: 901-278-0100, ext. 270
Address Inquiries to: Susan-Lynn Johns,
   Manager
Founded in: 1958
Member: Memphis Arts Council;
Description: Seating capacity is 639.

Cook Convention Center-Dixon-Myers
Hall
235 North Main
Memphis, TN 38103
Tel: 901-523-2982

Address Inquiries to: Carl D. Patterson,
Executive Director
Founded in: 1974
Description: Seating capacity 4,361.

Memphis Children's Theatre
2599 Avery Avenue
Memphis, TN 28112
Tel: 901-275-0835
Founded in: 1960
Description: Seating capacity 200.

Memphis State University
Department of Drama
Memphis, TN 38152
Tel: 901-454-2565
Address Inquiries to: Richard A. Rice,
Director of Theatre
Member: URTA;
Description: Department has access to The
Main Theatre, which seats 400.

Theatre Memphis
630 Perkins Extended
Memphis, TN 38117
Tel: 901-682-8323
Address Inquiries to: Sherwood Lohrey,
Manager
Founded in: 1975
Description: Seating capacity 425.

Nashville

Nashville War Memorial Auditorium
7th and Union Streets
Nashville, TN 37219
Tel: 615-741-3132
Address Inquiries to: James Drake, Manager
Founded in: 1920
Description: Seating capacity 2,100.

Tennessee Performing Arts Center
505 Deaderick Street
Nashville, TN 37219
Tel: 615-741-7975; 615-741-5633
Address Inquiries to: Mr. Warren K.
Sumners, Managing Director
Mr. Bruce Andrus-Hughes, Director of
Operations
Founded in: 1978
Member: ACUCAA; IAAM; NACC; NMC;
Annual Budget: $2,000,000
Description: Presents touring performing
arts. Rentals to touring acts, private video
tapings and national meetings. Educational
outreach: Nashville Institute for the Arts.
Constituent Groups: Nashville Symphony
Orchestra, Acting Studio, Circle Players,
and Friend s of Music. Total seating capacity
of 3,796.

TEXAS

Beaumont

Lamar University Theatre
Post Office Box 10044
Lamar University
Beaumont, TX 77710
Tel: 713-898-8927
Founded in: 1961

Description: Seating capacity 538.

Brownsville

Friendship Garden Pavilion
Post Office Box 911
Brownsville, TX 78520
Tel: 512-542-3367
Address Inquiries to: Arthur S. Greiner,
Manager
Founded in: 1954
Description: Seating capacity 3,500.

Jacob Brown Auditorium
Post Office Box 911
Brownsville, TX 78520
Tel: 512-542-3367
Address Inquiries to: Arthur S. Greiner,
Manager
Founded in: 1954
Description: Seating capacity 2,193.

Carthage

Q M Martin Auditorium
Panola Junior College
Carthage, TX 75633
Tel: 214-693-3836
Address Inquiries to: Charles Langlotz,
Manager
Founded in: 1973
Description: Seating capacity 650.

Cisco

Kendrick Amphitheater
Route 2, Box 46
Cisco, TX 76537
Tel: 817-629-2732
Address Inquiries to: J.H. Kendrick, Manager
Founded in: 1965
Description: Houses a not-for-profit religious
pageant, a diorama and a museum. It has a
seating capacity of 1,800.

Corsicana

Warehouse Living Arts Center
202 East Collin
Corsicana, TX 75110
Tel: 214-872-5421
Address Inquiries to: Cranston Dodds,
Artistic Director
Founded in: 1860
Member: Texas Non Profit Theatre
Association;
Annual Budget: $46,000
Description: Seating capacity 130

Dallas

Bob Hope Theatre
Southern Methodist University
Dallas, TX 75275
Tel: 214-692-2558
Address Inquiries to: Richard G. Ayers,
Manager
Founded in: 1968
Description: Seating capacity 392.

Caruth Auditorium
Owen Arts Center
Southern Methodist University
Dallas, TX 75275
Tel: 214-692-2713

Address Inquiries to: Dorothea Kelley,
Manager
Founded in: 1968
Description: Seating capacity 100.

Dallas Convention Center
Dallas, TX 75202
Tel: 214-658-7000
Address Inquiries to: W.W. Vanderslice,
Manager
Founded in: 1957
Description: Has a total seating capacity of 11,-
139.

Dallas Theatre Center
Down Center Stage
3636 Turtle Creek Boulevard
Dallas, TX 75219
Tel: 214-526-0107
Address Inquiries to: Paul Baker, Manager
Founded in: 1964

Dallas Theatre Center
Kalita Humphreys Theatre
3636 Turtle Creek Boulevard
Dallas, TX 75219
Tel: 214-526-8210; 214-526-8857
Address Inquiries to: Paul Baker, Artistic
Director
Founded in: 1959
Annual Budget: $2 million
Description: Seating capacity 516.

Fair Park Bandshell
Dallas, TX 75226
Address Inquiries to: Wayne Gallagher,
Manager
Founded in: 1936
Description: Seating capacity 3,792.

Margo Jones Experimental Theatre
Southern Methodist University
Dallas, TX 75275
Tel: 214-692-2558
Address Inquiries to: Richard G. Ayers,
Manager
Founded in: 1968
Description: Seating capacity 150.

McFarlin Memorial Auditorium
6400 Hillcrest Avenue
Dallas, TX 75205
Tel: 214-699- 3129
Address Inquiries to: Bob Moxley, Manager
Founded in: 1926
Description: Seating capacity 2,409.

Mountain View College Arena Theatre
4849 West Illinois Avenue
Dallas, TX 75211
Tel: 214-746-4132
Address Inquiries to: J. Sharon Griffith,
Manager
Founded in: 1971
Description: Seating capacity 550.

Denton

Denton Main Auditorium
Post Office Box 23865
TWU Station
Denton, TX 76204
Tel: 817-387-8422

Founded in: 1930
Description: Seating capacity 2,400.

Firehouse Theatre
221 North Elm
Denton, TX 76201
Tel: 817-382-7014
Address Inquiries to: Cranston H. Dodds,
    Manager
Founded in: 1921
Description: Seating capacity 276.

North Texas State University Theatre
North Texas State University
Denton, TX 75203
Tel: 817-788-2560
Address Inquiries to: Hattie Fansler, Manager
Founded in: 1968
Description: Seating capacity 612.

Redland Auditorium
Texas Women's University
Denton, TX 76204
Tel: 817-387-1412
Address Inquiries to: Dr. J.W. Eberly,
    Manager
Founded in: 1960
Description: Seating capacity 350.

Fort Worth

Casa Manana
3101 West Lancaster
Fort Worth, TX 76112
Tel: 817-332-9319
Address Inquiries to: Bud Franks, Manager
Founded in: 1958
Description: Seating capacity 1,832

Ed Landreth Auditorium
School of Fine Arts
Texas Christian University
Fort Worth, TX 76129
Tel: 817-926-2461
Address Inquiries to: Al Loyd, Manager
Founded in: 1949
Description: Seating capacity 1,235.

Reynolds Auditorium, Cowden Hall
Southwestern Baptist Theological
Seminary
Fort Worth, TX 76122
Tel: 817-923-1921
Founded in: 1926
Description: Seating capacity 500.

Tarrant County Convention Center
Theater
1111 Houston Street
Fort Worth, TX 76102
Tel: 817-332-9222
Address Inquiries to: Louis C. Owen, CFE
    (Executive Director)
Founded in: 1968
Member: IAAM;
Annual Budget: $2,000,000
Description: Seating capacity 3,054.

Texas Christian University Theatre
Landreth Hall
School of Fine Arts
Fort Worth, TX 76129
Tel: 817-926-2461

Address Inquiries to: Dr. Henry Hammack,
    Manager
Founded in: 1949
Description: Seating capacity 218.

Texas Wesleyan Fine Arts Auditorium
Texas Wesleyan College
Box 3277
Fort Worth, TX 76105
Tel: 817-534-0251
Address Inquiries to: Donald W. Bellah,
    Manager
Founded in: 1923
Description: Seating capacity 750.

Truett Auditorium
Southwestern Baptist Theological
Seminary
Fort Worth, TX 76122
Tel: 817-923-1921
Address Inquiries to: Wayne Evans, Vice
    President
Founded in: 1948
Description: Seating capacity 1,300.

William Edrington Scott Theatre
3505 West Lancaster
Fort Worth, TX 76107
Tel: 817-738-1938
Address Inquiries to: Bill Garber, Manager
Founded in: 1966
Description: Seating capacity 493.

Livingston

Sundown Theatre
Route 3, Box 640
Livingston, TX 77351
Tel: 713-563-4391
Address Inquiries to: Alan Levey, Manager
Founded in: 1975

Odessa

Odessa College Fine Arts Center
Odessa College
Post Office Box 3752
Odessa, TX 79760
Tel: 915-337-5381
Address Inquiries to: Wally Jackson, Manager
Founded in: 1946
Description: A seating capacity total of 935.

San Antonio

Laurie Auditorium
Trinity University
San Antonio, TX 78284
Tel: 512-736-8119
Address Inquiries to: John L. McFadden,
    Manager
Founded in: 1971
Description: Seating capacity 2,965. Used
mainly for musical performances and avail-
able for rental.

San Antonio Convention Center
Post Office Box 1898
San Antonio, TX 78297
Tel: 512-225-6351
Address Inquiries to: Francis W. Vickers,
    Manager
Founded in: 1968
Description: A total seating capacity of 12,800.

Trinity University Fine Arts Center
Trinity University
715 Stadium Drive
San Antonio, TX 78284
Tel: 512-225-6351
Address Inquiries to: Paul Baker, Manager
Founded in: 1966
Description: A total seating capacity of 610.

UTAH

Manti

Manti Temple Grounds
Manti, UT 84642
Tel: 801-835-2333
Address Inquiries to: R. Morgan Dyreng,
    Manager
Founded in: 1885

Ogden

Weber State College Fine Arts Center
Main Auditorium
3750 Harrison Boulevard
Ogden, UT 84408
Tel: 801-399-5941
Address Inquiries to: Dr. Herbert Cecil,
    Manager
Founded in: 1964
Description: Seating capacity 1,800.

Salt Lake City

Kingsbury Hall
University of Utah
Salt Lake City, UT 84112
Tel: 801-581-7808
Address Inquiries to: Paul Cracroft, Manager
Founded in: 1928
Description: Seating capacity 1,919.

Salt Palace
100 Southwest Temple
Salt Lake City, UT 84111
Tel: 801-521-6060
Description: Seating capacity 14,000.

Springdale

Zion Bicentennial Amphitheatre
Springdale, UT 84111
Founded in: 1976
Description: Seating capacity 2,500.

VERMONT

Brattleboro

Brattleboro Museum and Art Center
Post Office Box 800
Brattleboro, VT 05301
Tel: 802-257-0124
Address Inquiries to: W. Rod Faulds, Director
    Gail Lynde, Administrative Assistant
Founded in: 1915
Description: Various theatre groups have used
this facility to present plays, play readings,
poetry readings and puppet shows. The gal-
lery space is usually opened for single per-
formances.

Burlington

Ira Allen Chapel
University of Vermont
Burlington, VT 05401
Tel: 802-656-3040
Address Inquiries to: Dr. William Metcalfe,
Chairman
Founded in: 1925
Description: Seating capacity 1,025.

Royall Tyler Theatre
University of Vermont
Burlington, VT 05401
Tel: 802-656-2095
Address Inquiries to: Edward J. Feidner,
Dircetor
Founded in: 1901
Description: Seating capacity 300.

Putney

Windham College Theatre
Windham College Parkway
Putney, VT 05346
Tel: 802-387-5511
Address Inquiries to: Paul Nelsen, Manager
Founded in: 1972
Description: Seating capacity 410.

Winooski

Saint Michael's Playhouse
56 College Parkway
Winooski, VT 05404
Tel: 802-655-2000, Extension 2449
Address Inquiries to: Donald Rathgeb,
Director
Founded in: 1947

VIRGINIA

Bristol

Virginia Fine Arts Center Little Theatre
Virginia Intermont College
Bristol, VA 24201
Tel: 703-669-6101
Address Inquiries to: Stephen Hamilton,
Manager
Founded in: 1981
Description: Seating capacity 160.

Colonial Heights

Swift Creek Mill Playhouse
Post Office Box 41
Colonial Heights, VA 23834
Tel: 703-748-5203
Address Inquiries to: Warner Callahan,
Director
Founded in: 1966

Hampton

Hampton Coliseum
Post Office Box 7309
Hampton, VA 23666
Tel: 804-838-5650
Address Inquiries to: Andrew D. Greenwell,
Manager
Founded in: 1969
Description: Seating capacity 10,953.

Hanover

Barksdale Theatre
Hanover Tavern
Hanover, VA 23069
Tel: 804-838-5650
Address Inquiries to: David and Nancy
Kilgore
Muriel McAuley
Founded in: 1953
Member: VIRAC; Chesapeake Foundation;
Continental Financial Services; Best
Products Foundation;
Annual Budget: $75,000

Harrisonburg

Mintzer Auditorium
Municipal Building
Main Street
Harrisonburg, VA 22801
Address Inquiries to: Marvin Milam, Manager
Founded in: 1968
Description: Seating capacity 100.

Hollins College

Bradley Hall
Hollins College
Hollins College, VA 24020
Tel: 703-362-6512
Address Inquiries to: Dr. John Diercks,
Chairman
Founded in: 1958

Little Theater
Hollins College
Hollins College, VA 24020
Address Inquiries to: Tom Atkins, Manager
Founded in: 1925
Description: Seating capacity 700.

McLean

McLean Center Theatre
7211 Van Ness Court
McLean, VA 22101
Tel: 703-356-1061
Address Inquiries to: Clarissa Jaffe, Artistic
Director
Founded in: 1970

Middletown

Wayside Theatre
Middletown, VA 22645
Tel: 703-869-1782
Address Inquiries to: Lou Furman, Manager
Founded in: 1930
Description: Seating capacity 260.

Newport News

Christopher Newport College Campus
Center Theatre
Shoe Lane
Newport News, VA 23606
Tel: 804-599-7005; 804-599-7088
Address Inquiries to: Skelly Warren, Theatre
Manager
Founded in: 1973
Description: Seating capacity 377.

Norfolk

Norfolk Scope Cultural/Convention
Center
Scope Plaza
Norfolk, VA 23510
Tel: 804-441-2764
Address Inquiries to: C.E. Bell, Manager
Founded in: 1971
Member: IAAM;
Annual Budget: $2,120,000.
Description: Seating capacity: 11,584 (Convention Hall); Chrysler Hall (2,363); Exhibition Hall (60,000 Square Feet)

Norfolk Theatre Center
345 West Freemason Street
Norfolk, VA 23510
Tel: 804-627-1234
Address Inquiries to: Stan Febyszn, Artistic
Director
Founded in: 1968
Annual Budget: $100,000

Old Dominion Center Theatre
Old Dominion University
Norfolk, VA 23508
Tel: 804-489-6210
Address Inquiries to: Lew Derrickson,
Manager
Description: Seating capacity 1,800.

Old Dominion Technology Theatre
Old Dominion University
46th and Hampton Boulevard
Norfolk, VA 23508
Tel: 804-440-4373; 804-440-4423
Address Inquiries to: John Meng, Technical
Director
Founded in: 1968
Annual Budget: $75,000
Description: A theatre and auditorium available for all the performing arts utilitized by the university and community. The theatre has a procenium house with 396 seats, a stage array 27 by 35 feet wide, with a small orchestra pit and 30 lines of counterweight wit h up-to-date lighting and sound.

Orkney Springs

Orkney Springs Pavilion
Orkney Springs Hotel
Orkney Springs, VA 22845
Tel: 703-856-2610
Address Inquiries to: Miles Portlock, Owner
Founded in: 1976
Description: Seating capacity 1,700.

Radford

Radford College Studio Theatre
Norwood Street
Radford, VA 24141
Tel: 703-731-5152
Address Inquiries to: Mary B. Gallagher,
Manager
Founded in: 1972
Description: Seating capacity 500.

Richmond

Playhouse 3200
3200 West Broad Street
Richmond, VA 23230
Tel: 703-353-8975
Address Inquiries to: Bill Reed, Manager
Founded in: 1971

WASHINGTON

Centralia

Centralia College Theatre
Post Office Box 634
Centralia, WA 98531
Tel: 206-736-9391
Address Inquiries to: Phillip R. Wickstrom,
    Manager
Founded in: 1972
Description: Seating capacity 170.

Fort Lewis

Centurion Playhouse
Building 5300
Music and Theatre Branch, RSD
Fort Lewis, WA 98433
Tel: 206-968-3402
Address Inquiries to: Nicholas Credgington
Description: Seating capacity 200.

Omega Center for the Performing Arts
Building 5226
Music and Theatre Branch, RSD
Fort Lewis, WA 98433
Tel: 206-968-4097
Address Inquiries to: Gary Bankes, Manager
Description: Seating capacity 200.

Kirkland

Northwest College Learning Center
Northwest College
Kirkland, WA 98033
Tel: 206-822-8266
Address Inquiries to: Owen Hodges, Manager
Founded in: 1965

Lake Chelan

Apple Core Playhouse
Post Office Box P
Lake Chelan, WA 98816
Tel: 509-682-2814
Address Inquiries to: Matt Love, Manager
Founded in: 1975
Description: Seating capacity 150.

Spectrum Theatre of Allied Arts
118 East Johnson
Lake Chelan, WA 98816
Tel: 509-682-5041
Address Inquiries to: Donovan Gray, Manager
Founded in: 1974
Description: Seating capacity 200.

Olympia

Theatre Art Nouveau
Post Office Box 613
Olympia, WA 98501
Tel: 206-491-6504
Address Inquiries to: Ken Olendory, Manager

Founded in: 1930
Description: Seating capacity 200.

Port Townsend

Key City Playhouse
Post Office Box 194
Port Townsend, WA 98368
Tel: 206-385-3721
Address Inquiries to: Vern Jones, Presdent
Founded in: 1880
Description: Seating capacity 99.

Seattle

A Contemporary Theatre
100 West Roy Street
Seattle, WA 98119
Tel: 206-285-3220; 206-285-3220
Address Inquiries to: Louise Cummings,
    Administrator
Founded in: 1913
Member: NEA; SAC; King County Arts
    Commission; WSAC;
Annual Budget: $1,200,000
Description: Seating capacity 423.

Bathouse Theatre
7312 West Green Lake Drive
Seattle, WA 98103
Tel: 206-524-9110
Address Inquiries to: John Chambless,
    Manager
Founded in: Converted 1970.
Description: Seating capacity 130.

McKinley Auditorium
3307 3rd Avenue
Seattle Pacific College
Seattle, WA 981193
Tel: 206-281-2051
Description: Seating capacity 500.

Onstage Theatre
17171 Bothell Way
Seattle, WA 98155
Tel: 206-364-7128
Founded in: 1969
Description: Seating capacity 111.

Seattle Center
305 Harrison Street
Seattle, WA 98109
Tel: 206-625-4227; 206-625-4254
Address Inquiries to: Jack Fearey, Director
Rod Payne, Marketing and Sales Director
Founded in: 1962
Annual Budget: $8,500,000
Description: Facilities and respective seating
capacities are as follows: Coliseum: 15,000;
Arena: 6,200; Opera House: 3,100; Play-
house: 900; Bagley Wright Theatre: 850. A
home for The Seattle Symphony Orchestra,
The Seattle Opera, Pacific Northwest Ballet,
and The Seattle Repertory Theatre.

Seattle Center Arena
305 Harrison
Seattle, WA 98109
Tel: 206-625-4254
Address Inquiries to: Jack Feary, Manager
Founded in: 1927
Description: Seating capacity 15,000.

Seattle Center Opera House
305 Harrison
Seattle, WA 98109
Tel: 206-625-4254
Address Inquiries to: Rod Payne, Manager
Founded in: 1927
Description: Seating capacity 3,100.

Seattle Pacific University
Demaray Hall
3rd West and West Bertona
Seattle, WA 98119
Founded in: 1967
Description: Seating capacity 225.

Seattle Public Library-Main Branch
1000 Fourth Avenue
Seattle, WA 98104
Tel: 206-625-2665
Address Inquiries to: Ronald A. Dubblerly,
    City Librarian
    Mary E. Kleir, Secretary, Management
    Services Division
Description: Seating capacity 200.

Seattle University Auditorium
12th and East Columbia
Seattle, WA 98122
Address Inquiries to: George Behan,
    President
Founded in: 1967
Description: Seating capacity 100.

The Skid Road Theatre
Pioneer Square Performing Arts
Association
102 Cherry Street
Seattle, WA 98104
Tel: 206-622-0251
Address Inquiries to: Susan C. Richardson,
    General Manager
Founded in: 1890
Description: Seating capacity 125.

Spokane

Gene Russell Theatre
Gonzaga University
Spokane, WA 99202
Tel: 509-328-4200
Address Inquiries to: David A. Haraway,
    Manager
Founded in: 1968
Description: Seating capacity 226.

Walla Walla

Cordiner Hall
Whitman College
Walla Walla, WA 99362
Tel: 509-529-5100
Address Inquiries to: Francis Mills, Manager
Founded in: 1943
Description: Seating capacity 202.

Yakima

Warehouse Theatre
5000 West Lincoln
Yakima, WA 98908
Tel: 509-966-0930
Address Inquiries to: Mrs. Stuart Semon,
    Manager
Description: Seating capacity 254.

WEST VIRGINIA

Charleston

W.B. Geary Auditorium
University of Charleston
2300 MacCorkle Avenue SE
Charleston, WV 25304
Tel: 304-346-9471
Address Inquiries to: David L. Lottrall,
Director of Auditorium Services
Terry Moran, Director of Student
Activities
Founded in: 1951
Description: With a seating capacity of 1,000,
the auditorium is utilized for all kinds of performing arts activities.

Huntington

Huntington Galleries
Park Hills
Huntington, WV 25701
Tel: 304-529-2701
Address Inquiries to: James Lawhorn,
Manager
Founded in: 1972
Description: The Huntington Galleries has a
total seating capacity of 1,050.

Keith-Albee Theatre
925 4th Avenue
Huntington, WV 25720
Tel: 304-523-0185
Address Inquiries to: Dan Johnson, General
Manager
Founded in: 1928
Member: NATA;
Description: Seating capacity 1,800.

Morgantown

West Virginia University Arts Center
West Virginia University
Morgantown, WV 26506
Tel: 304-293-4642
Address Inquiries to: John W. Ellis, Manager
Founded in: 1968
Description: Seating capacity 1,500.

West Liberty

Hall of Fine Arts Theater
West Liberty State College
West Liberty, WV 26074
Tel: 304-336-8006; 304-336-8003
Address Inquiries to: Alfred R deJaager,
Manager
Founded in: 1950
Description: Seating capacity 480. The theater
is used mainly for music.

West Liberty College Hall
West Liberty State College
West Liberty, WV 26074
Tel: 304-336-8006
Address Inquiries to: Alfred R. DeJaager,
Manager
Founded in: 1970
Description: Seating capacity 480.

WISCONSIN

Appleton

Lawrence University Music-Drama Center
115 North Park Avenue
Appleton, WI 54911
Tel: 414-739-3681
Founded in: 1950

Green Bay

University Theatre
University of Wisconsin Green Bay
Green Bay, WI 54302
Tel: 414-465-2256; 414-465-2217
Address Inquiries to: Tom Birmingham,
Manager
Linda Erwin, House and Box Office
Manager
Founded in: 1974
Member: NEA; ACUCAA;
Annual Budget: $74,500
Description: The home of performing arts series. The program budget is used mainly for
artists fees and the theatre, which is flexible,
holds 482.

La Crosse

Mary E. Sawyer Auditorium
5th and Vine Streets
La Crosse, WI 54601
Tel: 608-784-5652
Founded in: 1955
Description: Seating capacity 4,100.

Madison

Madison Area Technical College
Department of Musical Theatre
211 North Carroll
Madison, WI 53703
Tel: 608-266-5054
Founded in: 1971
Annual Budget: $25,000
Description: In the process of putting together
a two year Associate degree program. This
program will focus on performance as well
as the technical aspects of theatre.

Regina Theatre
Edlewood College
855 Woodrow
Madison, WI 53711
Tel: 608-257-4861
Address Inquiries to: Jewell Fitzgerald,
Manager
Description: Seating capacity 100.

Manitowoc

Silver Lake College Fine Arts Theatre
Silver Lake College, 2406 South Alverno
Road
Manitowoc, WI 54220
Tel: 414-684-6691
Address Inquiries to: Sheila O'Connor,
Manager
Founded in: Remodeled 1973.
Description: Seating capacity 175.

Marchfield

Fine Arts Auditorium
2000 West Fifth Street
Marchfield, WI 54449
Tel: 715-387-1147
Address Inquiries to: Peter Hendler, Manager
Founded in: 1970
Description: Seating capacity 450.

Menomonie

Mabel Tainter Memorial Theater
205 Main Street
Menomonie, WI 54751
Tel: 715-235-9725
Address Inquiries to: Kathleen Dickson,
Building Administrator
Founded in: 1890
Member: LHAT;
Description: Seating capacity 330.

Milwaukee

Robert Cooley Auditorium
Milwaukee Technical College
1015 North Sixth Street
Milwaukee, WI 53203
Tel: 414-278-6300; 414-278-6310
Address Inquiries to: Wilford P. Quirmbach,
Auditorium Coordinator, President,
Wisconsin Secondary School Theatre
Association
Founded in: 1918
Member: WTA;
Annual Budget: Subject to MATC approval
Description: With a seating capacity of 1,800,
the Cooley Auditorium is primarily a facility
used for state and cultural events. MATC
policy states that programs held in the
school must be educational or cultural, free
of charge, and open to the public.

Milwaukee County War Memorial
Performing Arts Center
929 North Water Street
Milwaukee, WI 53202
Tel: 414-273-7121
Address Inquiries to: Archie A. Sarazin,
Manager
Founded in: 1969
Annual Budget: $2,000,000
Description: A major multi purpose facility
comparable to the Lincoln and Kennedy centers. It serves as the home for the Milwaukee
Symphony Orchestra, Milwaukee Repretory
Theatre and Music for Youth. The Florentine Opera Company, Skylight Comic Opera, Milwaukee Ballet Company, Chicago
Symphony Orchestra and the Bel Canto
Chorus also perform at the center. The complex includes Uihlien Hall (seating 2,331),
Charles P. Vogel Recital Hall (seating 482)
and the Todd Wehr Theater (seating 504).
Peck Pavlion, a permanen t outdoor theatre
with seating for 375 and full sound and lighting is located on the Center's riverfront
grounds.

Mount Mary College Theater Arts Center
Mount Mary College
Milwaukee, WI 53220

Tel: 414-258-4810
Address Inquiries to: Maynard Samsen,
 Manager
Founded in: 1954
Description: Seating capacity 878.

Skylight Theatre
813 North Jefferson Street
Milwaukee, WI 53202
Tel: 414-271-8815
Address Inquiries to: Clair Richardson,
 Manager
Founded in: 1962
Description: Seating capacity 235.

Water Street Theatre
1247 North Water Street
Milwaukee, WI 53202
Tel: 414-278-0555
Founded in: 1971
Description: Seating capacity 99.

Racine

Racine Memorial Hall
72 Seventh Street
Racine, WI 53404
Tel: 414-636-9169
Address Inquiries to: Norman C. McPhee,
 Manager
Founded in: 1976
Description: Seating capacity 405.

Racine Theatre Guild
2519 Northwestern Avenue
Racine, WI 53404
Tel: 414-633-1250
Address Inquiries to: Norman C. McPhee,
 Manager
Founded in: 1976
Description: Seating capacity 405.

Ripon

Benstead Theatre
Rodman Center for the Arts
Ripon College
Ripon, WI 54971
Tel: 414-748-8136
Address Inquiries to: Edmund Roney,
 Manager
Founded in: 1972
Description: Seating capacity 99.

Demmer Concert Hall
Rodman Center for the Arts
Ripon College
Ripon, WI 54971
Tel: 414-748-8120
Address Inquiries to: Raymond Stahura,
 Manager
Founded in: 1972
Annual Budget: $3,000
Description: Seating capacity 250.

Sheboygan

John Michael Kohler Arts Center
608 New York Avenue
Sheboygan, WI 53081
Tel: 414-458-6144
Address Inquiries to: Ruth DeYoung Kohler,
 Manager
 Craig McDaniel, Curator of Performing

Arts
Founded in: 1970
Description: Seating capacity 162.

University of Wisconsin Fine Arts Theater
University of Wisconsin Sheboygan
Box 719, Lower Falls Road
Sheboygan, WI 53081
Tel: 414-459-3750
Address Inquiries to: Dean F. Graunke,
 Manager
Founded in: 1970
Description: Seating capacity 400.

Whitewater

Barnett Theatre Center for the Arts
University of Wisconsin at Whitewater,
8000 Main Street
Whitewater, WI 53190
Tel: 414-472-1561
Address Inquiries to: Gene Wilson, Chairman
Founded in: 1971
Description: Seating capacity 412.

WYOMING

Laramie

University of Wyoming
Fine Arts Center Concert Hall
University of Wyoming
Laramie, WY 82070
Founded in: 1972

CANADA

Saint John's, Newfoundland

The Arts and Culture Centre
Post Office Box 1854, Prince Philip Drive
Saint John's, Newfoundland, Canada A1C
5P9
Tel: 709-737-3650
Address Inquiries to: John C. Perlin
 Richard Stoker
Founded in: 1967

Halifax, Nova Scotia

Theatre 707
1707 Brunswick Street
Halifax, Nova Scotia, Canada
Tel: 902-429-7777
Address Inquiries to: Weldon Boma
 John Wright
Founded in: 1978

Toronto, Ontario

Bayview Playhouse
1605 Bayview Avenue
Toronto, Ontario, Canada M4G 3B5
Tel: 416-481-6191
Address Inquiries to: Peter Peroff, General
 Manager
Description: Rented out to touring companies.

Harbourfront Studio Theatre
235 Queen's Quay West
Toronto, Ontario, Canada M5J 2G8
Tel: 416-364-7127; 416-869-8412

Address Inquiries to: Roy Higgins,
 Performing Arts Manager
 Fiona McCall, Director of
 Communications
Founded in: 1979
Description: A theatre space.

Pauline McGibbon Cultural Centre
86 Lombard Street
Toronto, Ontario, Canada M5C 1M3
Tel: 416-363-7929
Address Inquiries to: Joanne Ruderfer,
 Director
Founded in: 1979
Description: Performance space available.

Music Hall Theatre
147 Danforth Avenue
Toronto, Ontario, Canada M4K 1N2
Tel: 416-463-1186
Description: Rents space on a show-by-show
basis.

Poor Alex Theatre
296 Brunswick Avenue
Toronto, Ontario, Canada M5S 2M7
Tel: 416-920-8370
Address Inquiries to: Gwen Brooks, Manager
Founded in: 1963
Description: The Poor Alex Theatre is rented
to theatre companies.

Quebec City, Quebec

Grand Theatre du Quebec
269 boulevard Saint Cyrille East
Quebec City, Quebec, Canada G1R 2B3
Tel: 418-643-8111, Administrative;
418-643-8131, Box Office
Address Inquiries to: Ulric Breton,
 Programming
 Jean-Charles Latour, Director
Founded in: 1971
Description: A building containing two
theatres which are available for rental to
touring companies.

9

Theatre Festivals

The festival is an increasingly popular event in North American theatre. There is no set tradition as to the contents of a festival; it can be a celebration of Shakespeare's plays, an introduction to new playwrights, twentieth century comedy—the variety is endless.

Festivals also provide an important opportunity for inexperienced creative and technical personnel to gain professional experience in a less forbidding setting than the New York theatre community. As the reorganization of theatre grows and marketing techniques become increasingly sophisticated, more festivals and hence greater opportunity for aspiring theatre professionals will arise.

ALABAMA

Anniston

Alabama Shakespeare Festival
Post Office Box 141
Anniston, AL 36201
Tel: 205-236-7503; 205-237-2332 (Summer Box Office)
Address Inquiries to: Josephine E. Ayers,
  Executive Producer
  Martin L. Platt, Artistic Director
Founded in: 1972
Member: TCG; LORT;
Annual Budget: $600,000
Description: Held for five weeks in July-August in the Anniston High School Auditorium, this festival presents plays by Shakespeare and classical plays. They are performed by a professional repertory company in two air-conditioned theatres: The Festival Theatre at 12th Street and Woodstock Avenue and The Act Playhouse at 1020 Noble Street in downtown Anniston.

Birmingham

Birmingham Festival of Arts
1927 First Avenue North
Suite 1004
Birmingham, AL 35203
Tel: 205-323-5461, Ext. 52
Address Inquiries to: Sara C. Crowder,
  Executive Secretary
Founded in: 1951
Annual Budget: Over $100,000
Description: A voluntary, non-commercial endeavor to increase international and human understanding by bringing local ethnic groups and foreign citizens together to exhibit the cultural achievements of other nations and peoples.

Fort Deposit

Calico Fort Arts and Crafts Fair
Post Office Box 310
Fort Deposit, AL 36032
Address Inquiries to: Mrs. W. H. Lee
Description: Includes children's theatre presentations and Indian dancers.

Mobile

Arts and Crafts Week, Fairhope
Mobile Chamber of Commerce
Post Office Box 2187
Mobile, AL 36601
Description: The Fairhope Arts and Crafts Week is held in mid to late March and features, in addition to arts and crafts exhibitions, theater and dance programs.

Talladega

Talladega Arts Festival
Talladega College
Talladega, AL 35160
Address Inquiries to: Dr. Roland Braithwaite,
  Dean of the College
Description: The Festival is held in early to April on the campus of Talladega College. In addition to concerts, recitals, lectures and art exhibitions, plays and dance presentations are featured.

Tuscaloosa

Tuscaloosa Heritage Celebration
Tuscaloosa County Preservation Society
Post Office Box 1665
Tuscaloosa, AL 35403
Tel: 205-758-2238
Founded in: 1970
Annual Budget: $45,000
Description: Runs for one week in early to April and features a number of events celebrating the history of Tuscaloosa including theatre presentations.

ALASKA

Haines

Lynn Canal Community Players
Post Office Box 75
Haines, AK 99827
Tel: 907-766-2540; 907-766-2763
Address Inquiries to: Gail Gregg, President
David Nanney, Managing Director
Founded in: 1957
Member: ASCTA; Alaska Arts Southwest;
  CFDA;
Annual Budget: $10,000
Description: Hosts the Alaska State Community Theatre Drama Festival every two years in April. The program for the 1983 festival (April 4-10) includes one-act productions by over 18 community theatres.

ARIZONA

Flagstaff

Flagstaff Summer Festival
Post Office Box 1607
Flagstaff, AZ 86001
Description: Held for seven weeks from June to August. Covering presentations in all the performing arts, the festival includes plays, dance companies and children's theatre.

Phoenix

Greater Phoenix Summer Festival
Phoenix Chamber of Commerce
805 North Second Street
Phoenix, AZ 85004
Description: Held yearly from June through August and features concerts, ballet and theatre performances.

Yuma

Garces Celebration of the Arts
248 Madison Avenue
Yuma, AZ 85364
Description: Held in early May, and in addition to concerts and fine arts exhibitions, includes performances of dance and drama.

ARKANSAS

Heber Springs

Ozark Frontier Trail Festival
Chamber of Commerce
Heber Springs, AR 72543
Description: Held for three days in mid-Octo-

ber or early November and begins with the performance of a play.

CALIFORNIA

Fullerton

Medieval Festival, Fullerton
University Activities Center
California State University
Fullerton, CA 92634
Address Inquiries to: Charmaine Coker,
   Medieval Festival Coordinator
Description: Celebrates medieval traditions by bringing them to life in the form of music, art, sports tournaments and productions of plays.

La Mirada

Fiesta de Artes, La Mirada
Post Office Box 232
La Mirada, CA 90638
Description: Held for 10 days in late June the festival includes theatre and dance presentations.

Long Beach

Long Beach Heritage Week
Chamber of Commerce
121 Linden Avenue
Long Beach, CA 90802
Description: Held for eight days in early May and includes a number of attractions including theatrical productions.

Los Angeles

Inter Arts Festival, Torrance
Southern California Visitors Council
705 West Seventh Street
Los Angeles, CA 90017
Description: Held for nine days in mid-October and features the production of one play.

Summer Drama Festival
Director, Summer Drama Festival
Occidental College
1600 Campus Road
Los Angeles, CA 90041
Tel: 213-259-2772
Founded in: 1960
Member: ATA; SCETA;
Annual Budget: $60,000
Description: During July and August the students of Occidental College perform six plays in repertory. The emphasis is on Shakespeare, Shaw and Gilbert and Sullivan. Plays are directed by graduates of the drama department.

San Diego

National Shakespeare Festival
Old Globe Theatre, Balboa Park
Box 2171
San Diego, CA 92112
Description: From June to September productions of Shakespeare are presented, preceded by a one-half hour program of Elizabethan music.

San Diego Festival of the Arts
340 San Gorgonio
San Diego, CA 92106
Address Inquiries to: Mrs. Bea Evenson
Description: Held yearly for eleven days in August or September in Balboa Park. The entertainment, all held outdoors and without charge, includes every type of performing group, including plays, dance groups and mimes.

San Jose

Summer Repertory Theatre Festival
San Jose State University
Department of Theatre Arts
San Jose, CA 95192
Tel: 408-277-2763
Founded in: 1935
Member: ATA; State of California;
Description: On Thursdays through Sundays throughout July, three plays are presented in three theatres.

San Rafael

Marin Shakespeare Festival
Dominican College
San Rafael, CA 94901
Description: From July to September, two of Shakespeare's plays are presented Thursday through Sunday.

Santa Maria

PCPA Theatrefest
Post Office Box 1700
Santa Maria, CA 93456
Tel: 213-925-4009; 213-925-3288
Address Inquiries to: Donovan Marley,
   Producing Director
   Barbara Sellers, Associate Producer
Founded in: 1965
Annual Budget: 2.3 million
Description: The result of a unique partnership between Alan Hancock and the Solvang Theatrefest, PCPA is a repertory theatre company performing in three theatres located in adjoining communities. Provides an opportunity for student actors to work in a professiona l environment.

COLORADO

Boulder

Colorado Shakespeare Festival (Boulder)
Department of Theatre and Dance
University of Colorado
Boulder, CO 80309
Tel: 303-492-7355; 303-492-8181
Address Inquiries to: Daniel S.P. Yang,
   Producing Director
Founded in: 1958
Member: U/RTA;
Description: It is the seventh theatre group in the world to complete the entire Shakespearean Canon of 37 plays. For five weeks in July and August, it presents three Shakespearean plays in repertory.

Denver

Central City Opera and Drama Festival
910 16th Street
Suite 636
Denver, CO 80202
Description: Held for sixteen days during June and July. Produces operas and concerts as well as theatrical productions, including Gilbert and Sullivan operettas.

Red Rocks Music and Drama Festival
Colorado Visitors Bureau
225 West Colfax Avenue
Denver, CO 80202
Description: Held from June through August and presents plays and concerts in an outdoor amphitheater.

Steamboat Springs

Steamboat Summer Arts
Steamboat Springs Council of the Arts
Post Office Box 1913
Steamboat Springs, CO 80477
Description: Held for one month during July and August, features dance and drama productions and workshops.

Winter Theatre Festival
Steamboat Springs Council of the Arts
Post Office Box 1913
Steamboat Springs, CO 80477
Description: From December to April, during the skiing season, a number of plays are presented on weekends.

CONNECTICUT

New Haven

Yale Festival of Undergraduate Drama
Box 902A, Yale Station
New Haven, CT 06520
Description: This festival is held for three days in March. Various drama groups are invited to compete.

New London

Puppeteers of America Festival
New London Chamber of Commerce
1 Whale Oil Row
New London, CT 06320
Description: Seminars held in August, consisting of seminars on puppetry and including performances of puppet shows.

Norwich

Norwich Rose-Arts Festival
One Constitution Plaza
Norwich, CT 06360
Description: Held for one week in late June and early July in a tent on the Norwich Chelsea Parade. It features many different types of exhibits and entertainments, including plays and a variety show.

Westport

White Barn Theatre Festival (Westport)
Newtown Avenue
Westport, CT 06880
Tel: 203-227-3768
Description: During July and August plays are presented by companies from all over the world. International works are presented occasionally.

DISTRICT OF COLUMBIA

Washington

American College Theatre Festival
Kennedy Center for the Performing Arts
Washington, DC 20566
Tel: 202-254-3437; 202-872-0466
Member: ATA; John F. Kennedy Center
  Corporate Fund;
Description: Held in April for two weeks, the festival presents the best college productions chosen from over 350 entries around the country. Each of the 10 plays is presented for two performances.

Shakespeare Summer Festival
1000 Sixth Street SW
Washington, DC 20034
Description: During July and August, plays of Shakespeare are presented on Sundays in various parks in the city.

FLORIDA

Gainesville

Gainesville Spring Arts Festival
Santa Fe Community College
Gainesville, FL 32601
Address Inquiries to: Barbara Kirkpatrick
Description: Held for four days in May and features, among its many attractions, performances of plays.

Hollywood

Seven Lively Arts Festival, Hollywood
Lively Arts Festival
2030 Polk Street
Hollywood, FL 33200
Address Inquiries to: Mrs. Jane Rose
Description: Held for nine days in April. It features exhibitions and performances in all the arts including theatre and dance productions.

Miami Beach

ShakespearebytheSea
North Shore Community Center
Miami Beach, FL 33139
Description: During July and August plays of Shakespeare are presented outdoors.

Ormand Beach

Florida Theatre Festival
681 North Halifax
Ormand Beach, FL 32074
Address Inquiries to: Bud Siefred

Description: Held in June for four days, the Florida Theatre Festival presents plays by community groups in the state. Seminars are also conducted.

Pensacola

Pensacola Festival Fever Days
Pensacola-Escambia Development
Commission
803 North Palafox
Pensacola, FL 32501
Address Inquiries to: Bill Mathers
Description: Held in Pensacola for two days in September it features many exhibitions and performances, including plays, dance presentations, country skits and Shakespeare.

Tampa

Festival of the Hill, Tampa
University Center Program Office
University of South Florida
Tampa, FL 33620
Tel: Fra- La-a, Program Director
Description: Held for two days in November and features many different exhibitions and entertainments including theatre, dance performances and a circus.

HAWAII

Honolulu

InterArts Hawaii
University of Hawaii Foundation
Bachman Hall
Honolulu, HI 96822
Tel: 808-948-8259; 808-737-3387
Founded in: 1957
Member: NEA; NEH;
Description: A program of the University of Hawaii Foundation which includes the visual arts, dance, drama and theatre, literature and music. Beginning in late May, InterArts presents many performances and exhibitions (both asian and western) in conjunction with credit and/or non-credit courses conducted by distinguished visiting artists.

IDAHO

Coeur d'Alene

Citizens Council for the Arts
Art on the Green
Post Office Box 901
Coeur d'Alene, ID 83814
Tel: 208-664-9052; 208-664-2259
Address Inquiries to: Opal Brooten,
  Chairperson
  Sue Flammia
Founded in: 1968
Annual Budget: $13,000
Description: For 14 years, the annual Art on the Green Festival has promoted arts in the schools through concerts, visual and performing arts presentations.

ILLINOIS

Downers Grove

Festival of American Community Theaters
in Spokane
c/o David M. Gooder
1341 Turvey Road
Downers Grove, IL 60515
Address Inquiries to: David M. Gooder,
  ACTA President
Description: Held for several days at different times each year in different locations, the festival presents nine winning productions by community theatres from around the country. It includes discussions with critics and theatre leaders.

East Peoria

ICC Fine Arts Festival
Illinois Central College
2129 High View Road
East Peoria, IL 61611
Description: Held in late April or early May for up to twelve days. Among its many features are theatrical performances and dance productions.

Normal

Theatre Festival
Illinois State University
Normal, IL 61761
Description: Presented for two days in February at the University, this festival presents productions of theatre and drama.

Peoria

Peoria Spring Arts Festival
Bradley University
1501 West Bradley Avenue
Peoria, IL 61606
Description: Held for two days in April and consists of performances by Bradley University students, faculty and alumni. Among the presentations are plays, mime, dramatic and interpretive readings and dancing.

Rockford

Rockford Arts Festival
Rockford Council for the Arts and
Sciences
401 South Main
Rockford, IL 61103
Description: Consists of four one-day festivals held in June and July in various parks in Rockford. Among its events are street theatre productions, square dancing and barbershop quartet singing.

INDIANA

Fort Wayne

Fort Wayne Fine Arts Festival
c/o Fort Wayne Arts Foundation
232 ½ West Wayne Street
Fort Wayne, IN 46802
Description: Held in July and August and features, among its many events, theatre-in-

the-round productions, dance presentations and puppet shows.

Kokomo

Kokomo Creative Arts Festival
2510 Elaine Court
Kokomo, IN 46901
Address Inquiries to: Mrs. Dwight Callaway
Description: Held at the end of April and features, among its attractions, theatre and dance presentations.

IOWA

South Clinton

Riverboat Days
Clinton Chamber of Commerce
333 Fourth Avenue
South Clinton, IA 52732
Description: A three day festival in July presented on the Showboat Rhododendron. Among its events are plays presented by the Rhododendron Players.

KENTUCKY

South Union

Shaker Festival, South Union
Shakertown
South Union, KY 42283
Address Inquiries to: Miss Julia Neal, Publicity Chairman
Description: This ten day festival, held in July, features a pageant that retells the history of the Shaker Society.

MARYLAND

Baltimore

3400 On Stage
Shriver Hall
Johns Hopkins University
Baltimore, MD 21218
Description: Held for three days in April, this festival, sponsored by the Student Council, features many outdoor events including some theatrical presentations.

Bowie

Bowie Festival of Fine Arts
Bowie State College Humanities Division
Bowie, MD 20715
Description: Held for one week in May and includes, among its many events, some dramatic productions.

MASSACHUSETTS

Boston

Boston Festival of Arts
Greater Boston Chamber of Commerce
125 High Street
Boston, MA 02110
Description: Held outdoors in June and July, the festival features many events in the visual and performing arts, including theatre and dance presentations.

Summerthing, Boston
603 City Hall Annex
23 Court Street
Boston, MA 02108
Description: This festival brings cultural events and entertainment to Boston neighborhoods and is presented outdoors in various parks throughout the city. Among its offerings are theatre and dance presentations.

Manomet

Plymouth Drama Festival
National Association of Dramatics
Post Office Box 997
Manomet, MA 02345
Tel: 617-224-3697
Address Inquiries to: Franklin Trask, Ph.D., Founder and Administrator
Founded in: 1936
Annual Budget: $20,000
Description: Held June through September, the festival presents plays and concerts. The oldest summer theatre in America where hundreds of alumni have gone on to theatrical stardom.

Stockbridge

Berkshire Theatre Festival
East Main Street
Stockbridge, MA 01262
Tel: 413-298-3618
Address Inquiries to: Allan Albert, Artistic Director
  Thomas Urquhart, Managing Director
Founded in: 1965
Member: AEA;
Annual Budget: $100,000

Williamstown

Williamstown Theatre Festival
Post Office Box 517
Williamstown, MA 01267
Description: Held for two months during the summer, the festival has a professional resident company and a cabaret. Many plays are presented not often done in the commercial theatre.

MICHIGAN

Grand Rapids

Grand Rapids Festival of Arts
Arts Council of Greater Grand Rapids
126 College, SE
Grand Rapids, MI 49502
Tel: 616-454-9221
Founded in: 1968
Annual Budget: $1,100,000
Description: Held for three days in June, the emphasis of this Grand Rapids Fesitival is on all of the arts available in the metropolitan area. Events include five outdoor stages for music, dance, theatre and other perfor-

mances, arts and crafts sales, film and writers contests, chamber music and childrens theatre.

Kalamazoo

Kalamazoo Festival Playhouse
Theatre Arts Department
Kalamazoo College
Kalamazoo, MI 49007
Description: Presented at Kalamazoo College during July and August, the festival presents plays acted by students supplemented by local amateurs.

MISSISSIPPI

Jackson

Delta Arts and Crafts Festival
Yazoo City
Travel Department
Agricultural/Industrial Board
Box 849
Jackson, MS 39205
Description: A one day event held in early May. Among its attractions are theatrical presentations.

MISSOURI

Kansas

Women's Jazz Festival
Post Office Box 22321
Kansas, MO 64113
Tel: 816-361-1901
Address Inquiries to: Carol Comer, Executive Director
  Dianne Gregg, President
Founded in: 1977
Member: NAJE; KCAC;
Annual Budget: 104,000
Description: A non-profit corporation whose purpose is to create a market for the growing number of female jazz artists and to stimulate an interest in jazz in general. Accomplishments will be achieved by continuing sponsorship of concerts, clinics, workshops, a lecture/film series, invitationals, scholarships, directories and competitions.

NEW HAMPSHIRE

Andover

Creative Arts Association of Andover
Arts and Crafts Festival
Post Office Box 71
Andover, NH 03216
Tel: 603-735-5371
Address Inquiries to: Winslow Eaves, President
Member: NHCA;
Annual Budget: $2,000
Description: Held in July for two days, the Andover Arts and Crafts Festival includes fine arts exhibits and crafts.

Hanover

Congregation of the Arts
Hopkins Center
Dartmouth College
Hanover, NH 03755
Description: Presented in June and August. Although the emphasis is on music, performances of plays are included.

Milford

Souhegan Theatre Council
American Stage Festival
Post Office Box 225
Milford, NH 03055
Tel: 603-673-6896
Founded in: 1971
Member: AEA; NETC;
Annual Budget: $100,000

NEW JERSEY

Woodbridge

Shakespeare Festival of Woodbridge
428 South Park Drive
Woodbridge, NJ 07095
Tel: 201-634-2496
Address Inquiries to: Leon A. Seyglinski,
Director
Founded in: 1961
Annual Budget: $10,000

NEW MEXICO

Farmington

Farmington Arts Festival
Chamber of Commerce, Box 267
Farmington, NM 87401
Description: Held in October and includes some theatrical presentations.

Las Cruces

New Mexico Shakespeare Festival
New Mexico State University
Las Cruces, NM 88003
Description: Presented during June and July, the festival emphasizes the plays of Shakespeare, but also presents productions by other authors as well as an evening of ballet.

NEW YORK

Bronx

Hostos Arts Festival
Hostos Community College
475 Grand Concourse
Bronx, NY 10451
Description: The talents of students and members of the community are displayed during this three day May festival. Among the many events are dramatic and dance presentations.

Hempstead

Shakespeare Festival
Department of Drama
Hofstra University
Hempstead, NY 11550
Description: Presented in March for five weeks in a replica of the Globe Theater, the festival presents plays by, or about Shakespeare, as well as exhibits, concerts and films relating to the bard.

Ithaca

Ithaca Spring Festival
Cornell University
Public Information Office
Ithaca, NY 14850
Description: Held for four days in April and May at Cornell University, the festival has a different theme each year. Among its presentations are plays, various types of dance performances and puppet shows.

New York

New York Shakespeare Festival
425 Lafayette Street
New York, NY 10003
Tel: 212-598-7100
Address Inquiries to: Joseph Papp, Producer
Robert Kamlot, General Manager
Founded in: 1954
Description: Presented during June-August in Central Park, the festival presents plays by Shakespeare and other authors.

Potsdam

Crane School of Music
State University College
Potsdam, NY 13676
Tel: 315-267-2413; 315-267-2415
Address Inquiries to: Robert Thayer, Dean of
Music
Arthur Unsworth, Associate Dean of
Music
Founded in: 1886
Description: The Spring Festival, held March through May
the festival includes some dramatic and dance presentations. The school is a component of the State University College of Arts and Science, Potsdam, a unit of the State University of New York. It is a complex of five buildings and houses a music theater and concert hall, serving the needs of students, faculty and northern New York State inhabitants.

Syracuse

Syracuse Festival of the Arts
Syracuse University
Syracuse, NY 13210
Description: Held in late April and early May at Syracuse University. Among its events are drama and dance presentations.

Utica

Utica Arts Festival
Munson-Williams-Proctor Institute
310 Genesee Street
Utica, NY 13502
Description: This festival, held for ten days in July and includes some dance and drama presentations.

NORTH CAROLINA

Charlotte

Charlotte Festival in the Park
Charlotte Chamber of Commerce, Public Relations Department, 222 South Church Street
Charlotte, NC 28202
Description: Held for six days in September in Freedom Park. Features continuous entertainment on a number of stages. Included are plays, children's theatre, magicians and clowns.

NORTH DAKOTA

Bismarck

Chataqua
Post Office Box 948
Bismarck, ND
Tel: 701-663-1948
Address Inquiries to: Everett Albers
Frank Vyzralek
Description: Performances are reenactments of historical events, and are intended to stimulate interest in our heritage and the humanities.

International Festival of the Arts, Dunseith
North Dakota State Highway Department
Bismarck, ND 58505
Tel: 800-437-2077; 701-224-2525
Address Inquiries to: Assistant Travel
Director
Description: This festival, held in June and July, includes some outdoor performances of drama and dance.

Fargo

Trollwood Park
914 Main Avenue
Fargo, ND 58102
Tel: 701-232-6424; 701-241-1350
Description: Throughout the summer there are plays, art festivals, workshops and demonstrations, band concerts, an International Jugglers Convention, jazz festivals and much more.

Lamoure

Lamoure Summer Theatre
Lamoure, ND
Tel: 701-883-4401
Description: Performers are high school or college students, and adults from the area.

Medora

Medora Musical
Medora, ND 8645
Tel: 800-437-2070; 701-632-4444
Description: A musical extravaganza performed nightly from mid June through Labor Day weekend. Famed stage personalities and novelty acts and the Burning Hills singers and dancers.

OHIO
Cleveland

Cleveland Summer Arts Festival
11125 Magnolia Drive
Cleveland, OH 44106
Description: Held from June through August, this Cleveland festival provides free entertainment and training in the arts, including dramatic and dance presentations. Performers include the Cleveland Ballet Guild and the Ballet Russe of Cleveland. Workshops in thea tre and dance are also conducted.

Great Lakes Shakespeare Festival
Ohio Theatre Playhouse Square
Cleveland, OH 44115
Tel: 216-228-1225
Address Inquiries to: Vincent Dowling,
   Artistic Director
   Mary Bill, Managing Director
Founded in: 1962
Member: OTA; AAA; TCG; LORT; OCCA;
   GLAA;
Annual Budget: $900,000

Toledo

Crosby Festival of the Arts
c/o Beverlee Anderson
5403 Elmer Drive
Toledo, OH 43615
Description: The festival which is held for two days in June, features competitive events in the arts including theatre and dance presentations.

Willoughby

Annual Outdoor Arts Festival
School of Fine Arts
38660 Mentor Avenue
Willoughby, OH 44094
Tel: 216-951-7500
Address Inquiries to: Mrs. Nancy Saxon,
   Public Relations
   Mrs. Doris Foster, Festival Coordinator
Founded in: 1957
Description: Held for three days in late July, this festival offers a variety of continuous entertainment.

OKLAHOMA
Stillwater

Southwest Cultural Heritage Festival
Oklahoma State University
Stillwater, OK 74078
Tel: 405-624-6217; 405-624-6142
Address Inquiries to: Edward P. Walkiewicz,
   Festival Coordinator 1982
   Gwendolyn C. Powell, Arts Coordinator
   1982
Founded in: 1981
Member: Oklahoma State University; NEA;
   NEH;
Annual Budget: $67,000
Description: Held in October on the campus of the university, the varied presentations in this festival include theatrical presentations, concerts, and other musical events, art exhibits, dance, fiction and poetry readings, films and script readings.

Tahlequah

Trail of Tears
Director
Tsa-La-Gi
Box 515
Tahlequah, OK 74464
Description: Shown for two months from late June-August, the drama reenacts part of Cherokee history.

OREGON
Ashland

Oregon Shakespearean Festival
Post Office Drawer 158
Ashland, OR 97520
Tel: 503-482-2111
Address Inquiries to: Jerry Turner, Artistic
   Director
   William Patton, Executive Director
Founded in: 1935
Member: TCG; AAA; ATA; NEA; Ford
   Foundation; W.R.Grace; others;
Annual Budget: $3,400,000
Description: Presents productions ranging from Shakespeare to modern, tragedy, comedy, drama, and farce, in three theatres: the 1173 seat Elizabethan (outdoor), the 601 seat Angus Bowner, and the Black Swan, a 140 seat 'black box' theatre. The company also underta kes an actors-in-schools program which reaches 180,000 students.

PENNSYLVANIA
Pittsburgh

Black Week Festival (Pittsburgh)
Black Action Society
University of Pittsburgh
Pittsburgh, PA 15213
Description: The Black Week Festival is held on the campus of the University of Pittsburgh, for one week in November. It features, among its many events, theatrical and

dance presentations.

University Park

Festival of American Theatre
Penn State University
137 Arts Building
University Park, PA 16801
Description: Operating for six weeks from June to August, the festival presents a variety of American plays.

Nittany Mountain Summer Festival
University Arts Services
Penn State University
111 Arts Building,
University Park, PA 16802
Description: Held for three weeks during July and August at Pennsylvania State University. This visual and performing arts festival features classical and modern dance works by the Pennsylvania Ballet. Held in conjunction with this festival is the Festival of American Theatre.

TEXAS
Austin

Fine Arts Festival
University of Texas
College of Fine Arts
Austin, TX 78712
Tel: 512-471-1655; 512-471-1656
Description: The Fall Festival of the Arts is held in October, and the Spring Festival in April. Each event lasts one week and is held on campus and in various areas within the city of Austin. Events include Dance and Drama (one-act plays) productions. The events are held throughout each day outside and in shopping malls.

Fort Worth

Fine Arts Festival
School of Fine Arts
Texas Christian University
Fort Worth, TX 76129
Founded in: 1942
Description: The festival is held in the spring semester, generally around February and/or March. In addition to the musical events and a play, there is generally a faculty art exhibition.

Galveston

Festival USA on the Strand
Galveston County Cultural Arts Council
Post Office Box 1105
Galveston, TX 75550
Description: Occurs in August and features, among its cultural events, theatre and dance presentations.

Houston

The Houston Festival
1950 West Gray #6
Houston, TX 77019
Tel: 713-521-9329; 713-521-9559
Address Inquiries to: Jackson C. Hinds

Britt D. Davis, President
Founded in: 1979
Member: Cooper Industries Foundation;
Shell Companies Foundation; Houson
Chronicle Foundation; Brown
Foundation; Houston Endowment;
Crooker Charitable Foundation; Texas
Commerce Bank Foundation; State of
Texas; City of Houston; federal;
corporate; private;
Annual Budget: $470,000
Description: A 10 day celebration of the per-
forming and visual arts held in late March. A
celebration of the city, focusing on the arts,
situated in and around downtown Houston
and sponsored by the city, the Chamber of
Commerce, the Greater Houston Conven-
tion and Visitors Council, and the Cultural
Arts Council of Houston.

Houston Shakespeare Festival
University of Houston
Department of Drama
Houston, TX 77004
Tel: 713-749-1427
Address Inquiries to: Sidney L. Berger,
Chairman
Member: URTA;
Description: From June through August, the
Houston Shakespeare Festival prepares and
presents two full scale productions. The
plays are presented in the city's Miller Out-
door Theatre, a fully equipped facility which
seats 2,000.

Odessa

Globe of the Great Southwest Shakespeare
Festival
2808 Shakespeare Road
Odessa, TX 79761
Tel: 915-332-1586; 915-332-1587
Address Inquiries to: David Weaver Jr.,
Business Manager
Founded in: 1958
Member: TCA;
Annual Budget: $92,000
Description: Hosts the annual Odessa Shake-
speare Festival each Spring in February and
March utilizing professional and student act-
ing companies such as the National Shake-
speare Company, North Texas State Univer-
sity, and Texas Christian University. In the
remainder of the year, the Globe hosts a va-
riety of classical and educational plays.

Round Top

Shakespeare at Winedale
Box 11
Round Top, TX 78954
Tel: 713-278-3530
Address Inquiries to: James B. Ayres
Founded in: 1970
Annual Budget: $20,000
Description: Students from the University of
Texas and from colleges and universities in
the U.S. study Shakespeare through perfor-
mance. Only students who have no experi-
ence in performance may apply. Six weeks of
intensive reading, analysis of texts, and writ-

ing taught by correspondance; six weeks
of study at Winedale, in a theatre, daily
from 7 a.m. to 1 a.m., seven days a week.
Performances free to the public. Three
plays per summer. Capacity of theatre is
350.

UTAH

Cedar City

Utah Shakespearean Festival
Southern Utah State College
351 West Center
Cedar City, UT 84720
Tel: 801-586-7880, Administration Office;
801-586-7878, Box Office
Address Inquiries to: Fred C. Adams,
Producing Director
Founded in: 1959
Member: ATA; U/RTA;
Annual Budget: $300,000
Description: Produces three plays in repertory
on the Adams Memorial Shakespeare
Theatre stage during July and August.

Salt Lake City

The Morman Miracle Pageant
420 A Street
Salt Lake City, UT 84103
Tel: 801-835-2333; 801-835-1094
Address Inquiries to: R. Morgan Dyreng,
General Chairman
Macksene S. Rux, Director
Founded in: 1967
Annual Budget: $20,000
Description: It is historically and religiously
authentic and portrayed in true pageant
form.

VERMONT

Burlington

Champlain Shakespeare Festival
University of Vermont
Burlington, VT 05405
Tel: 802-656-2094
Founded in: 1959
Member: University of Vermont;
Annual Budget: $16,000

VIRGINIA

Bristol

Bristol Spring Arts Festival
Bristol Chamber of Commerce
Box 1039
Bristol, VA 24201
Description: Held in April, the festival includes
performances of ballet and plays.

Richmond

Festival of Arts (Richmond)
Department of Recreation and Parks
900 East Broad Street
Richmond, VA 23219

Description: Held from June-August, the Festival of Arts includes performances of
Shakespeare, children's productions, and
appearances by the Richmond Ballet.

Roanoke

Festival-in-the-Park Incorporated
(Roanoke)
Post Office Box 12745
Roanoke, VA 24028
Tel: 703-342-2640
Address Inquiries to: James E. Webster,
President
Robert Hooper, Vice President
Founded in: 1968
Member: Roanoke Valley Arts Council;
Annual Budget: $15,000
Description: Sponsors and organizes the fol-
lowing festival events: 'The Festival on the
River', which includes a gala stage show and
is held on the last Sunday in May. At the
Amphitheatre Stage continuous perfor-
mances of dance, theatre and music.

Vienna

Wolf Trap Farm Park
Post Office Box 12
Vienna, VA 22180
Description: Held from June to September,
the Wolf Trap Festival features many performing arts attractions, including productions of plays, musicals and ballet.

Williamsburg

An Occasion for the Arts
Post Office Box 363
Williamsburg, VA 23185
Description: This one-day October festival in-
cludes the presentation of a play.

WASHINGTON

Seattle

Burien Arts Festival
1626 Southwest 156th
Seattle, WA 98166
Description: This three-day June festival of the
fine and performing arts includes theatre
and dance presentations.

Edmonds Art Festival
Post Office Box 9344
Seattle, WA 98109
Address Inquiries to: J. Ward Phillips,
President
Description: Held for three days in June, this
festival includes performances of plays.

CANADA

Banff, Alberta

The Banff Centre
Banff, Alberta, Canada T0L 0C0
Description: Runs a training program in
theatre design and technology, and presents
a summer festival.

Banff Festival of the Arts
Post Office Box 1020
Banff, Alberta, Canada
Tel: 403-762-6255; 403-762-6300
Address Inquiries to: Thomas M. Kouk,
   Manager of Theater Events
Founded in: 1930
Member: ACUCAA; IAAM;
Description: Held in August, the festival features evening performances of drama, musicals, dance, opera, music and more.

Saint John's, Newfoundland

Saint John's Provincial Drama Festival
Newfoundland Department of Tourism
Confederation Building
Saint John's, Newfoundland, Canada
Description: Presented in April for six days, the festival presents competitive productions by several amateur theatre companies.

Shakespearean Production Festival
Newfoundland Department of Tourism
Confederation Building
Saint John's, Newfoundland, Canada
Description: For six days in April, Shakespearean plays are presented.

Halifax, Nova Scotia

Nova Scotia Festival of the Arts
Dalhousie Art Centre
6101 University Avenue
Halifax, Nova Scotia, Canada
Description: Held for one week in August, includes performances of drama, dance, puppet shows and magicians.

Niagara on the Lake, Ontario

Shaw Festival
Post Office Box 774
Niagara on the Lake, Ontario, Canada L0S 1J0
Tel: 416-468-2153; 416-468-3201
Address Inquiries to: June Faulkner, General
   Manager
   Janette Hickin, Publicity Director
Founded in: 1962
Description: The Shaw Festival presents the works of George Bernard Shaw and his contemporaries.

Stratford, Ontario

Stratford Festival
Post Office Box 520
Stratford, Ontario, Canada N5A 6V2
Tel: 519-271-4040; 416-273-1600
Address Inquiries to: Anne Selby, Publicity
   Director
   Leonard McHardy, Publicity Director
Founded in: 1953
Description: Held from June to October, the festival presents productions of plays by Shakespeare and other authors on three seperate stages. Also presents many musical events.

Charlottetown, Prince Edward Island

Charlottetown Festival
Box 848
Charlottetown, Prince Edward Island,
Canada C1A 7L9
Tel: 902-892-2464; 902-892-1267
Founded in: 1964
Annual Budget: $3,000,000
Description: Original Canadian musical theatre is presented during the summer months with support provided by government, private and corporate sources.

Quebec City, Quebec

Festival d'ete de Quebec
26 Rue St Pierre, C.P. 24, Succ B.
Quebec, Quebec, Canada G1K 7A1
Tel: 418-692-4540
Founded in: 1967
Annual Budget: $925,000
Description: The Quebec Summer Festival aims to support creativity in all the performing arts ranging from theatre, to mime and clowns. It is a international event, now in its 18th year.

Summer Festival
Tourist and Convention Bureau
60 d'Auteuil Street
Quebec, Quebec, Canada
Description: Held for 11 days in July, this festival includes some theatrical presentations.

10
Foundations

Foundations vary in size, as do arts councils and service organizations. On the whole, however, they can provide access to far greater amounts of money, and the scope of their activities is at least the nation, if not the world.

Individuals usually have little luck applying to foundations for financial assistance. The decision makers at foundations are oriented toward projects conceived by non-profit groups, so an individual's association with one of these is the best way to insure a hearing for a worthwhile concept related to theatre.

ALABAMA
Birmington

Parisian Stores, Alabama
1101 North 26th Street
Birmington, AL 35234
Tel: 205-251-1300
Address Inquiries to: Emil Hess, Chairman of the Board
Founded in: 1886
Annual Budget: $100,000
Description: Has supported theatre, dance, arts councils and performing arts centers.

Southern Natural Gas Company
Post Office Box 2563
Birmington, AL 35202
Tel: 205-325-7578
Annual Budget: $98,000
Description: Has supported music, dance, arts councils and community art programs.

ARIZONA
Phoenix

Southwest Forest Industries
Post Office Box 7548
Phoenix, AZ 85012
Tel: 602-279-5381
Annual Budget: $22,000
Description: Has supported theatre, dance, arts councils and cultural and performing arts centers.

Valley National Bank of Arizona
Post Office Box 71
Phoenix, AZ 85001
Tel: 602-261-2321
Annual Budget: $307,000
Description: Has supported theatre, music, arts service organizations and cultural and performing arts centers.

ARKANSAS
El Dorado

Murphy Oil Corporation
Corporate Headquarters
El Dorado, AR 71730
Tel: 501-862-6411
Annual Budget: $54,000
Description: Has supported music, cultural and performing arts centers.

CALIFORNIA
Los Angeles

Cyprus Mines Corporation
555 South Flower Street
Los Angeles, CA 90071
Tel: 213-489-3700
Annual Budget: $250,000
Description: Has supported theatre, dance, arts councils and performing arts centers.

Security Pacific Foundation
333 South Hope Street
Los Angeles, CA 90051
Tel: 213-613-6688
Address Inquiries to: Carol Taufer, President
Founded in: 1977
Annual Budget: $2,750,000
Description: Supports theatre, dance, arts councils and cultural and performing arts centers. Currently supportive of community efforts to employee matching gift programs. Support substantively for California based organizations.

Union Bank Foundation
Box 3100 Terminal Annex
Los Angeles, CA 90051
Tel: 213-687-6120
Annual Budget: $350,000
Description: Have supported music, public TV/radio and cultural and performing arts centers.

Whittaker Corporation
10880 Wilshire Boulevard
Los Angeles, CA 90024
Tel: 213-475-9411

Annual Budget: $43,000
Description: Has supported museums and cultural and performing arts centers.

Newport Beach

Pacific Mutual Life Insurance Company
700 Newport Center Drive
Newport Beach, CA 92663
Tel: 714-640-3014
Founded in: 1868
Annual Budget: $345,000
Description: Has supported theatre, dance, and cultural and performing arts centers, primarily in southern California.

Oakland

The Clorox Company
1221 Broadway
Oakland, CA 94612
Tel: 415-271-7747
Address Inquiries to: Contributions Program Coordinator
Annual Budget: $350,000
Description: Has supported theatre, dance, arts councils and performing arts centers.

Kaiser Aluminum and Chemical Corporation
300 Lakeside Drive
Oakland, CA 94643
Tel: 415-271-5569
Annual Budget: $372,000
Description: Has supported theatre, dance, arts councils and performing arts centers.

Palo Alto

Hewlett Packard Company
1501 Page Mill Road
Palo Alto, CA 94304
Tel: 415-856-3053
Annual Budget: Not available
Description: Has supported theatre, dance, arts councils and performing arts centers.

Riverside

Bourns Foundation
1200 Columbia Avenue
Riverside, CA 92507
Tel: 714-781-5599

Description: Has supported arts councils and cultural organizations.

San Diego

San Diego Gas and Electric Company
Post Office Box 1831
San Diego, CA 92112
Tel: 714-232-4252 ext. 1606
Annual Budget: $152,000
Description: Has supported community arts programs and arts councils and consolidated arts funds drive.

The Wickes Corporation
110 West A Street
San Diego, CA 92101
Tel: 714-238-0304
Annual Budget: $141,000
Description: Has supported theatre, music, arts councils and consolidated arts fund drives.

San Francisco

BankAmerica Foundation
Post Office Box 37000
San Francisco, CA 94137
Tel: 415-622-8674
Address Inquiries to: Jean Higuera, Program Assistant
Annual Budget: $2,802,000
Description: Has supported art councils and cultural organizations.

Foremost-McKesson Foundation
1 Post Street
San Francisco, CA 94104
Tel: 415-983-8673
Annual Budget: $690,000
Description: Has supported theatre, dance, and cultural organizations.

Levi Strauss Foundation
Two Embarcadero Center
San Francisco, CA 94106
Tel: 415-544-6000
Annual Budget: $700,000
Description: Has supported theatre, music and community arts programs.

Pacific Telephone Company
140 New Montgomery Street
San Francisco, CA 94105
Tel: 415-542-4063
Founded in: 1906
Annual Budget: $2,300,000
Description: Has supported theatre, dance, arts councils and cultural and performing arts centers. Focus of support on performing arts organizations located in California and Nevada only.

Potlatch Corporation
One Maritime Plaza
San Francisco, CA 94119
Tel: 415-981-5980
Annual Budget: $600,000
Description: Has supported music, dance, art councils and performing arts centers.

Standard Oil Company of California
225 Bush Street
San Francisco, CA 94104

Tel: 415-894-7700
Annual Budget: $5,060,000
Description: Has supported theatre, dance, arts councils and cultural and performing arts centers.

Wells Fargo Bank
464 California Street
San Francisco, CA 94144
Tel: 213-683-7056
Annual Budget: $600,000
Description: Has supported theatre, arts councils and cultural and performing arts centers.

COLORADO

Colorado Springs

Colorado Interstate Gas Company
Post Office Box 1087
Colorado Springs, CO 80944
Tel: 303-473-2300, ext. 421
Annual Budget: $70,000
Description: Has supported theatre, dance, arts councils and performing arts centers.

Denver

Ideal Basic Industries
950 17th Street, Box 8789
Denver, CO 80201
Tel: 303-623-5661
Annual Budget: $118,000
Description: Has supported arts, music and museum programs.

Mountain Bell
931 14th Street
Denver, CO 80226
Tel: 303-624-3908
Annual Budget: $788,000
Description: Has supported theatre, dance, arts councils and performing arts centers.

United Bank of Denver, N.A.
1740 Broadway
Denver, CO 80202
Tel: 303-861-8811
Annual Budget: Not available
Description: Has supported theatre, dance, arts councils and cultural and performing arts centers.

CONNECTICUT

Farmington

Heublein Foundation
Munson Road
Farmington, CT 06032
Tel: 203-677-4061
Annual Budget: Not available
Description: Has supported arts councils and cultural and performing arts centers.

Greenwich

General Reinsurance Corporation
600 Steamboat Road
Greenwich, CT 06830
Tel: 203-622-4383

Annual Budget: $94,000
Description: Has supported theatre, arts councils and performing arts centers.

Hartford

Aetna Life and Casualty
151 Farmington Avenue
Hartford, CT 06156
Tel: 203-273-2465; 203-273-7589
Address Inquiries to: Robert H. Roggeveen, Administrator of Public Service Programs
Founded in: 1972
Annual Budget: $8,200,000
Description: Has supported the arts on a limited basis. New grants are restricted to the Greater Hartford area and to the twelve cities participating in the Foundation's Focus program.

Connecticut General Insurance Corporation
Hartford, CT 06152
Tel: 203-243-8811
Founded in: 1977
Description: Has supported various arts organizations including Hartford Stage, Hartford Symphony and Greater Hartford Arts Council.

Connecticut Mutual Life Insurance Company
140 Garden Street
Hartford, CT 06115
Tel: 203-549-4111
Address Inquiries to: George S. Wachtel, Director of Communications
Founded in: 1977
Annual Budget: $500,000
Description: Has supported various organizations and activities.

Phoenix Mutual Life Insurance Company
One American Row
Hartford, CT 06115
Tel: 203-278-1212 ext 5359
Founded in: 1851
Annual Budget: $400,000
Description: Has supported arts councils, consolidated arts funds drives and public TV/radio.

The Traveler's Insurance Company
One Tower Square
Hartford, CT 06115
Tel: 203-277-2508
Annual Budget: $1,100,000
Description: Supported theatre, dance, arts councils and cultural and performing arts centers.

United Technologies Corporation
One Financial Plaza
Hartford, CT 06101
Tel: 203-728-7000
Address Inquiries to: Gordon Bowman, Director of Corporate Creative Programs
Annual Budget: $2,721,000
Description: Has supported theatre, dance, arts councils and cultural and performing

arts centers.

Meriden

Insilco Foundation
1000 Research Parkway
Meriden, CT 06450
Tel: 203-634-2066
Annual Budget: $118,000
Description: Has supported theatre, music and cultural organizations.

Old Greenwich

Condec Corporation
1700 East Putnam Avenue
Old Greenwich, CT 06870
Tel: 203-637-4511
Address Inquiries to: Herbert Gladstone, Vice President and Treasurer
Founded in: 1976
Annual Budget: $117,000
Description: Has supported various arts organizations, including Hartman Theater, West Hill High School Junior Symphony, Greenwich High School Junior Symphony, Lincoln Center for the Performing Arts and WNET Channel 13.

Stamford

General Telephone and Electronics Foundation
One Stamford Forum
Stamford, CT 06904
Tel: 203-357-2157
Annual Budget: $3,300,000
Description: Has supported cultural and performing arts centers.

Olin Corporation Charitable Trust
120 Long Ridge Road
Stamford, CT 06904
Tel: 203-356-3301; 203-356-3021
Address Inquiries to: Carmella V. Piacentive
Founded in: 1945
Description: Has supported theatre, music, arts councils and community arts programs.

Xerox Foundation
Post Office Box 1600
Stamford, CT 06904
Tel: 203-329-8711
Annual Budget: $8,000,000
Description: Has supported allied organizations, national and local arts councils and cultural and performing arts centers, as well as public television and national art exhibitions.

Windsor Locks

The Dexter
Corporation Foundation
One Elm Street
Windsor Locks, CT 06096
Tel: 203-623-9801
Annual Budget: $100,000
Description: Has supported arts councils and cultural organizations.

DELAWARE
Wilmington

Columbia Gas System;
20 Montchanin Road
Wilmington, DE 19807
Tel: 302-429-5000
Annual Budget: $504,709
Description: Has supported theatre, dance, arts councils andd performing arts centers.

Delmarva Power and Light Company
800 King Street
Wilmington, DE 19899
Tel: 302-429-3410
Annual Budget: $129,000
Description: Has supported the preservation of historic sites.

DISTRICT OF COLUMBIA
Washington

Government Employees Insurance Company
GEICO PLAZA
Washington, DC 20076
Tel: 301-986-2006
Annual Budget: $75,000
Description: Has supported theatre and cultural and performing arts centers.

Potomac Electric Power Company
1900 Pennsylvania Avenue NW
Washington, DC 20068
Tel: 202-872-3187
Annual Budget: $186,000
Description: Has supported theatre, music and cultural and performing arts centers.

FLORIDA
Miami

Bacardi Imports
2100 Biscayne Boulevard
Miami, FL 33137
Tel: 305-573-8511
Address Inquiries to: Jose F. Castellanos, Director of the Art Gallery
Description: Has supported theatre, dance, arts councils and performing arts centers.

Southeast Banking Corporation
100 South Biscayne Boulevard
Miami, FL 33131
Tel: 305-577-3033; 305-577-3134
Address Inquiries to: Jean H. Johnson, Director of the Fine Arts Department
Founded in: 1974
Annual Budget: Not available
Description: Has supported museums, public TV/radio and cultural and performing arts centers. Southeast is acquiring a large contemporary art collection.

Orlando

Sentinel Star Community Association
Box 2833, 633 N Orange Avenue
Orlando, FL 32802
Tel: 305-420-5275
Annual Budget: $90,000
Description: Has supported theatre, dance, arts councils and cultural and prforming arts centers.

GEORGIA
Atlanta

Southern Bell Telephone and Telegraph Company
Post Office Box 2211
Atlanta, GA 30301
Tel: 404-529-6276
Annual Budget: Not available
Description: Has supported theatre, arts councils and cultural and performing arts centers.

Columbus

Gas Light Company of Columbus
Post Office Box 1657
Columbus, GA 31902
Tel: 404-322-8891
Annual Budget: $15,000
Description: Has supported theatre, dance, arts councils and performing arts centers.

HAWAII
Honolulu

Alexander and Baldwin, Incorporated
Post Office Box 3440
Honolulu, HI 96801
Tel: 808-525-6640
Address Inquiries to: Gregg Perry, Vice President
Annual Budget: $236,000
Description: Supports cultural and performing arts centers.

ILLINOIS
Chicago

Amoco Foundation
200 East Randolph Drive
Chicago, IL 60601
Tel: 312-856-6305
Annual Budget: $5,750,000
Description: Amoco Foundation is the corporate foundation for arts support of Standard Oil Company (Indiana). They have supported music, dance, arts councils and cultural and performing arts centers.

Borg-Warner Foundation, Inc.
200 South Michigan Avenue
Chicago, IL 60604
Tel: 312-322-8656
Annual Budget: $715,000
Description: Has supportd arts councils and

cultural organizations.

Central Telephone and Utilites
Corporation
5725 East River Road
Chicago, IL 60631
Tel: 312-399-2767
Address Inquiries to: Robert W. Smith,
    Contributions Administrator
Founded in: 1976
Annual Budget: $138,000
Description: Supports various arts organizations.

Commonwealth Edison Company
Post Office Box 767
Chicago, IL 60690
Tel: 312-294-3062
Annual Budget: $1,247,000
Description: Has supported theatre, dance,
arts councils and performing arts centers.

Consolidated Foods Corporation
135 South LaSalle
Chicago, IL 60603
Tel: 312-726-6414
Address Inquiries to: Curtis G. Linke,
    Director of Public Affairs
Founded in: 1977
Annual Budget: $290,000
Description: Has supported arts organizations, including, the Chicago Symphony, the
Lyric Opera, Chicago Art Institute, the
Chicago Historical Society, Public Television, the Ravinia Playhouse, the Field Museum and the Contemporary Art Museum.

Container Corporation of America
One First National Plaza
Chicago, IL 60603
Tel: 312-786-5340
Address Inquiries to: John G. Egan, Vice
    President and Foundation Manager
Founded in: 1977
Annual Budget: $652,000
Description: Has supported various art forms,
cultural organizations and activites. Arts organizations supported include Chicago Art
Institute, Arts Council of Fort Worth and
Tarrant County, Chicago Theater Coalition,
Lyric Opera and National Corporate Fund
for Dance.

Harris Bank Foundation
111 West Monroe Street
Chicago, IL 60690
Tel: 312-461-6660
Address Inquiries to: H. Kris Ronnow,
    Secretary and Treasurer
Founded in: 1953
Member: TCB; DFC;
Annual Budget: $250,000
Description: Has supported educational, cultural, social service and community development projects. The Foundation and Contributions activities are premised on the assumption that the bank invests a portion of
its profits into programs and projects that
help to maintain and upgrade the quality of
life in the Chicago area.

Hart, Schaffner and Marx Foundation
101 North Wacker Drive
Chicago, IL 60606
Tel: 312-372-6300
Address Inquiries to: Kay C. Nalbach, Vice
    President
Description: Has supported art institutes, museums and educational television.

IC Industries Incoporated
111 East Wacker Drive
Chicago, IL 60601
Tel: 312-565-3074
Annual Budget: Not available
Description: Has supported arts councils and
cultural and performing arts centers.

Illinois Bell Telephone Company
225 West Randolph Street
Chicago, IL 60606
Tel: 312-427-4691
Address Inquiries to: Steve Hines, Manager
    of Contributions
Annual Budget: $145,000
Description: Has supported arts councils and
cultural and performing arts centers. Grants
are determined by comparison with other
companies of similar size and importance
are doing in the community.

Inland Steel-Ryerson Foundation
30 West Monroe Street
Chicago, IL 60603
Tel: 312-346-0300
Annual Budget: $1,648,000
Description: Has supported theatre, arts councils and cultural and performing arts centers.

International Harvester Foundation
401 North Michigan Avenue
Chicago, IL 60611
Tel: 312-836-2100
Annual Budget: $1,250,000
Description: Has supported cultural and performing arts centers.

Jewel Foundation
5725 East River Road
Chicago, IL 60631
Tel: 312-693-6000
Annual Budget: $453,000
Description: Has supported arts councils, museums and music.

Pullman Foundation Incorporated
200 South Michigan Avenue
Chicago, IL 60604
Tel: 312-322-7057
Annual Budget: $400,000
Description: Has supported theatre, music,
arts councils and performing arts centers.

Quaker Oats Foundation
345 Merchandise Mart Plaza
Chicago, IL 60654
Tel: 312-222-6981
Annual Budget: $754,000
Description: Has supported theatre, dance,
arts education and performing arts centers.

Santa Fe Railway Foundation
80 East Jackson Boulevard
Chicago, IL 60604
Tel: 312-427-4900
Annual Budget: $823,000
Description: Has supported music, public TV/
radio and cultural and performing arts centers.

The Sears-Roebuck Foundation
Sears Tower, D/703, 40-6
Chicago, IL 60684
Tel: 312-875-8331; 312-875-8336
Annual Budget: $3,000,000
Description: Has supported theatre, dance,
arts councils and cultural and performing
arts centers.

United Airlines Foundation
Post Office Box 66100
Chicago, IL 60666
Tel: 312-952-5714
Annual Budget: $628,000
Description: Has supported music, dance, arts
councils and cultural and performing arts
centers.

Glenview

Kraft Incoporated
Kraft Court
Glenview, IL 60025
Tel: 312-998-2418
Annual Budget: $1,005,000
Description: Has supported theatre, arts councils and performing arts centers.

Signode Foundation
3600 Westlake Avenue
Glenview, IL 60025
Tel: 312-276-8500
Annual Budget: $200,000
Description: Has supported arts service organizations, music and cultural and performing arts centers.

Zenith Radio Corporation
1000 Milwaukee Avenue
Glenview, IL 60025
Tel: 312-391-8181
Address Inquiries to: William A. Nail,
    Executive Secretary of Corporate
    Contributions Committee
Founded in: 1918
Annual Budget: $450,000
Description: Has supported public TV/radio,
music, and libraries.

Libertyville

International Minerals and Chemical
Corporation
IMC Plaza
Libertyville, IL 60048
Tel: 312-362-8100
Annual Budget: $500,000
Description: Has supported theatre, arts councils and cultural and performing arts centers.

Lincolnshire

Trans Union Corporation
90 Half Day Road
Lincolnshire, IL 60015
Tel: 312-295-4233
Annual Budget: $221,000
Description: Supported music, public TV/radio and cultural and performing arts centers.

Long Grove

Kemper Insurance Companies
Long Grove, IL 60049
Tel: 312-540-2536
Annual Budget: $208,000
Description: Has supported arts programs, music and public TV/radio.

Moline

John Deere Foundation
John Deere Road
Moline, IL 61256
Tel: 309-752-4667
Annual Budget: $2,237,000
Description: Has supported arts councils and cultural organizations.

Oak Brook

McDonald's Corporation
McDonald's Plaza
Oak Brook, IL 60521
Tel: 312-887-6594
Annual Budget: $985,000
Description: Has supported community education projects and cultural and performing arts centers.

Peoria

Central Illinois Light Company
300 Liberty Street
Peoria, IL 61602
Tel: 309-672-5260
Address Inquiries to: Harriet M. Ringel,
    Community Relations Manager
Founded in: 1976
Annual Budget: $58,000
Description: Has contributed funds for television and the Landmarks Association.

Rolling Meadows

Gould Foundation
10 Gould Center
Rolling Meadows, IL 60008
Annual Budget: $825,000
Description: Has supported art councils and performing arts centers.

Schaumburg

Motorola Foundation
1303 East Algonquin Road
Schaumburg, IL 60196
Tel: 312-576-6200
Annual Budget: $618,000
Description: Has supported community arts programs, music and public TV/radio.

Springfield

Franklin Life Insurance Company
Franklin Square
Springfield, IL 62713
Tel: 217-528-2011, ext. 513
Annual Budget: Not available
Description: Has supported arts councils and performing arts centers.

INDIANA

Fort Wayne

Central Soya Foundation
1300 Fort Wayne National Bank Building
Fort Wayne, IN 46802
Tel: 219-422-8541
Address Inquiries to: Richard J. Sawyer, Vice
    President
Annual Budget: $463,000
Description: Has supported arts councils and cultural organizations.

The Lincoln National Life Foundation
1300 South Clinton, Box 1110
Fort Wayne, IN 46801
Tel: 219-427-3928; 219-427-3271
Address Inquiries to: Marilyn A. Vachon, Vice
    President and Secretary
Founded in: 1962
Annual Budget: $100,000
Description: It no longer funds arts councils, music and performing arts centers, but directs its support to education through minority scholarships and the Lincoln Museum. Exceptions are the completion of a $750,000 endowment for operations of the Fort Wayne Bota nical Garden/Plant Conservatory and short term, interest free loans to three local performing arts theatre organizations.

Indianapolis

Eli Lily and Company Foundation
307 East McCarty Street
Indianapolis, IN 46206
Tel: 317-261-2489
Annual Budget: $1,200,000
Description: Has supported theater, arts councils and performing arts centers.

Indiana Bell Telephone Company
220 North Meridian Street
Indianapolis, IN 46204
Tel: 317-265-2595
Founded in: 1924
Annual Budget: $800,000
Description: Has supported art museums, opera, theatre, dance, arts councils and performing arts centers.

The Indiana National Bank
One Indiana Square
Indianapolis, IN 46266
Tel: 317-266-6398
Annual Budget: Not available
Description: Has supported theatre, dance, arts councils and performing arts centers.

Indianopolis

Indianapolis Power and Light Company
25 Monument Circle, Box 1595B
Indianapolis, IN 46206
Tel: 317-635-6868
Annual Budget: Not available
Description: Has supported cultural and performing arts centers, music and museums.

Jasper

The Habig Foundation
1549 Royal Street
Jasper, IN 47546
Tel: 812-482-1600
Annual Budget: Not available
Description: The Habig foundation is the corporate foundation for arts support of Kimball International Incorporated. They have supported arts councils, and cultural and performing arts centers.

IOWA

Davenport

Iowa-Illinois Gas and Electric Company
206 East Second Street
Davenport, IA 52801
Tel: 319-326-7038
Annual Budget: Not availabale
Description: Has supported theatre, dance, arts councils and performing arts centers.

Des Moines

The Bankers Life
711 High Street
Des Moines, IA 50307
Tel: 515-247-5098
Annual Budget: $380,000
Description: Has supported theatre, dance, arts councils and performing arts centers.

Iowa Power and Light Company
823 Walnut
Des Moines, IA 50309
Tel: 515-281-2345
Annual Budget: $183,000
Description: Has supported theatre, music, museums and performing arts centers.

KANSAS

Shawnee Mission

Yellow Freight System Foundation
10990 Roe Avenue
Shawnee Mission, KS 66207
Tel: 913-383-3000
Annual Budget: $275,000
Description: Has supported theatre, dance, public TV/radio and cultural and performing arts centers.

KENTUCKY

Louisville

Glenmore Distilleries Company
1700 Citizens Plaza
Louisville, KY 40202
Tel: 502-636-5211
Annual Budget: Not available
Description: Has supported theatre, concerts, arts fund drives and arts councils.

MAINE

Augusta

Central Maine Power Company
Edison Drive
Augusta, ME 04336
Tel: 207-623-3521
Annual Budget: $43,000
Description: Has supported theatre, dance, arts councils and performing arts centers.

MARYLAND

Baltimore

Baltimore Gas and Electric Company
Post Office Box 1475
Baltimore, MD 21203
Tel: 301-234-7437
Address Inquiries to: George W. Gephart,
  Manager of Corporate Communications
Annual Budget: $587,000
Description: Has supported theatre, dance, arts councils and performing arts centers.

Noxell Foundation
Post Office Box 1799
Baltimore, MD 21203
Tel: 301-666-2662
Annual Budget: $110,000
Description: Has supported music, dance, arts education and cultural and performing arts centers.

Hunt Valley

McCormick and Company Fund
11350 McCormick Road
Hunt Valley, MD 21031
Tel: 301-667-7383
Annual Budget: $185,000
Description: Has supported arts and education scholarships and cultural and performing arts centers.

MASSACHUSETTS

Boston

Boston Edison Company
800 Boylston Street
Boston, MA 02199
Tel: 617-424-2266
Annual Budget: $222,000
Description: Has supported theatre, dance, arts councils and performing arts centers.

The Boston Globe
135 Morrisey Boulevard
Boston, MA 02107
Tel: 617-929-2881
Annual Budget: $250,000
Description: Has supported theatre, dance, arts councils and performing arts centers.

The Eastern Associated Foundation
One Beacon Street
Boston, MA 02108
Tel: 617-742-9200
Annual Budget: $400,000
Description: Has supported arts service and cultural organizations.

Gillette Charitable and Educational Foundation
Prudential Tower Building
Boston, MA 02106
Tel: 617-421-7725
Annual Budget: $960,000
Description: Has supported cultural institutions and arts organizations.

New England Mutual Life
501 Boylston Street
Boston, MA 02117
Tel: 617-266-3700, ext. 2730
Annual Budget: $375,000
Description: Has supported theatre, music and cultural and performing arts centers.

New England Telephone Company
185 Franklin Street
Boston, MA 02107
Tel: 617-743-2384
Annual Budget: $625,000
Description: Has supported dance, music, arts councils and arts service organizations.

Cambridge

Polaroid Foundation
750 Main Street
Cambridge, MA 02139
Tel: 617-864-6000, ext. 3597
Founded in: 1971
Annual Budget: $1,600,000
Description: Has supported theatre, dance, arts councils and performing arts centers.

Lexington

Itek Corporation
10 Maguire Road
Lexington, MA 02173
Tel: 617-276-2645
Annual Budget: $70,000
Description: Has supported community arts programs, museums and public television.

Westwood

William Underwood Company
One Red Devil Lane
Westwood, MA 02090
Tel: 617-329-5300
Description: Supported theatre, dance, arts councils and cultural and performing arts centers.

Worcester

Norton Company Charitable Corporation
1 New Bond Street
Worcester, MA 01606
Tel: 617-853-1000
Annual Budget: $560,000
Description: Has supported music, public TV/radio, arts councils and arts funds drives.

MICHIGAN

Battle Creek

Battle Creek Gas Company
23 East Michigan Mall
Battle Creek, MI 49016
Tel: 616-968-8111
Annual Budget: $8,000
Description: Has supported theatre, dance, arts councils and performing arts centers.

Detroit

Chrysler Corporation Fund
Post Office Box 1919
Detroit, MI 48288
Tel: 313-956-5317
Annual Budget: $2,600,000
Description: Has supported arts councils and cultural organizations.

General Motors Foundation
3044 West Grand Boulevard
Detroit, MI 48202
Tel: 313-556-4260
Annual Budget: Not avalable
Description: Has supported arts councils and cultural organizations.

Michigan Bell Telephone Comapny
444 Michigan Avenue
Detroit, MI 48226
Tel: 313-223-7878
Annual Budget: $600,000
Description: Has supported theatre, arts councils and performing arts centers.

Michigan Consolidated Gas Company
One Woodward Avenue
Detroit, MI 48226
Tel: 313-965-2430, ext. 369l
Annual Budget: $433,000
Description: Has supported theatre, arts programs and performing arts centers.

NBD Charitable Trust
Post Office Box 116
Detroit, MI 48232
Annual Budget: $695,000
Description: Has supported music, arts councils and cultural and performing arts.

Jackson

Consumers Power Company
212 West Michigan Avenue
Jackson, MI 49201
Tel: 517-788-0430
Address Inquiries to: H.E. Spieler, Manager
  of Region Public Affairs
Founded in: 1977
Annual Budget: $350,000

Description: Has supported various art forms, cultural organizations, and activities. Organizations supported on an on-going basis include Detroit Institute for the Arts, Michigan Opera Theatre, Meadowbrook Music Theatre, Michigan Foundation for the Arts, Grand Rapids Center for the Performing Arts, Ella Sharpe Museum, Jackson Symphony, Battle Creek Arts Center in Jackson, The Battlecreek Center and Grand Rapids Center.

MINNESOTA

Arden Hills

Land O'Lakes Foundation
4001 Lexington Avenue North
Arden Hills, MN 55112
Tel: 612-481-2222
Founded in: 1921
Annual Budget: $45,000
Description: Has supported regional arts activities.

Chaska

Green Giant Foundation
Hazeltine Gates Office Building
Chaska, MN 55318
Tel: 612-448-2828
Annual Budget: $205,000
Description: Has supported arts councils and cultural/performing arts centers.

Duluth

Minnesota Power and Light Company
30 West Superior Street
Duluth, MN 55802
Tel: 218-722-2641
Annual Budget: $94,000
Description: Has supported theatre, dance, arts councils and performing arts centers.

Hopkins

The Tonka Foundation
10505 Waysata Boulevard
Hopkins, MN 55343
Tel: 612-544-9171
Annual Budget: $91,000
Description: Supported theatre, music, arts councils and cultural and performing arts centers.

Minneapolis

Dayton Hudson Foundation
777 Nicollet Mall
Minneapolis, MN 55402
Tel: 612-370-6554
Annual Budget: $5,254,000
Description: Has supported arts councils and cultural organizations.

The Donaldson Foundation
Post Office Box 1299
Minneapolis, MN 55440
Tel: 612-698-0391
Annual Budget: $120,000
Description: Has supported arts councils and cultural organization.

General Mills Foundation
Post Office Box 1113
Minneapolis, MN 55440
Tel: 612-540-3337
Address Inquiries to: Dr. James P. Shannon, Vice President and Executive Director
Founded in: 1954
Member: FC; IS;
Annual Budget: $5,110,000
Description: Has supported cultural organizations and public broadcasting in Minneapolis and St. Paul, Minnesota and in other communities where General Mills has major employee concentration.

Honeywell Fund
Post Office Box 524
Minneapolis, MN 55440
Tel: 612-870-6822
Founded in: 1958
Annual Budget: $4,500,000
Description: Supports non-profit organizations in health, welfare, education and the arts. It's focus is on education and funds go to four-year degree granting colleges in computer science, engineering, and business administration, which operate in their major manufacturing communities. Since education is the funds main thrust, support to the arts is being decreased to less than 10% of it's total budget. It funds on a geographic basis.

Jostens Foundation
5501 Norman Center Drive
Minneapolis, MN 55437
Tel: 612-830-3324
Annual Budget: $75,000
Description: Has supported theatre, arts councils and performing arts centers.

Multifoods Charitable Foundation
1200 Multifoods Building
Minneapolis, MN 55402
Tel: 612-340-3302
Annual Budget: $575,000
Description: Has supported theatre, arts councils and cultural and performing arts centers.

Munsingwear Incorporated
718 Glenwood Avenue
Minneapolis, MN 55405
Tel: 612-340-4710
Annual Budget: $121,000
Description: Has supported theater, dance, arts councils and performing arts centers.

Northwest Bancorporation
1200 Northwestern Bank Building
Minneapolis, MN 55480
Tel: 612-372-8393
Annual Budget: $80,000
Description: Has supported theatre, music, arts councils and performing arts centers.

Northwestern National Bank of Minneapolis
7th and Marquette Avenue
Minneapolis, MN 55400
Tel: 612-372-8954
Annual Budget: $660,000

Description: Has supported theatre, dance arts councils and performing arts centers.

Peavey Company
730 Second Avenue, South
Minneapolis, MN 55402
Tel: 612-370-7612
Annual Budget: $435,000
Description: Has supported theater, dance, arts councils and performing arts centers.

The Pillsbury Company Foundation
3290 Pillsbury Center
Minneapolis, MN 55402
Tel: 612-330-8379; 612-330-8573
Annual Budget: $3,050,000
Description: Has supported theatre, music, arts councils and performing arts centers.

Saint Paul

H.B.Fuller Company, Corporate Headquaters
2400 Kasota Avenue
Saint Paul, MN 55108
Tel: 612-645-3401
Annual Budget: $357,000, $37,000 to performing arts
Description: Has supported arts education, scholarships and art programs in the public school system. The company has a policy of matching employee contributions to any accredited college, university or high school in the United States. The corporate fund has made contributions to the Duck Soup Players, Guthrie Theatre, Minneapolis Society of Fine Arts, Minneapolis Orchestral Association, Minnesota Public Radio, the St. Paul Arts Fund and many other arts activties in the communities where H.B. Fuller employees reside.

The Saint Paul Companies
385 Washington Street
Saint Paul, MN 55102
Tel: 612-221-7769
Annual Budget: $766,000
Description: Has supported theatre, arts councils and cultural and performing arts centers.

MISSOURI

Kansas City

Kansas City Southern Industries
114 West 11th Street
Kansas City, MO 64105
Tel: 816-556-0303
Annual Budget: $155,000
Description: Has supported theatre, music and cultural and performing arts centers.

Missouri Public Service Company
10700 East 50 Highway
Kansas City, MO 64138
Tel: 816-353-5018
Annual Budget: $64,000
Description: Has supported theatre, visual arts and cultural and performing arts centers.

United Telecommunications
Post Office Box 11315
Kansas City, MO 64112
Tel: 913-384-7314
Annual Budget: $285,000
Description: Has supported music, dance, arts councils and cultural and performing arts centers.

Saint Joseph

Saint Joseph Light and Power Company
520 Francis Street
Saint Joseph, MO 64505
Tel: 816-233-8888
Annual Budget: Not available
Description: Has supported music, community arts programs and arts service organizations.

Saint Louis

Monsanto Fund
800 North Lindbergh
Saint Louis, MO 63119
Tel: 314-694-4391
Annual Budget: $5,000,000
Description: Has supported theatre, dance, arts councils and performing arts centers.

Pet Milk Foundation
400 South Fourth Street
Saint Louis, MO 63166
Tel: 314-621-5400
Annual Budget: $400,000
Description: Has supported music, arts councils and cultural and performing arts centers.

The Seven-Up Company Charitable Trust
121 South Meramec
Saint Louis, MO 63105
Tel: 314-889-7777
Annual Budget: not available
Description: Has supported music, libraries, arts councils and arts fund drives.

Southwestern Bell Telephone Company
1010 Pine Street
Saint Louis, MO 63101
Tel: 314-247-8585
Annual Budget: $2,390,000
Description: Has supported theatre, dance, arts councils and cultural and performing arts centers.

Union Electric Charitable Trust
Post Office Box 87
Saint Louis, MO 63166
Tel: 314- 62- 3222
Annual Budget: $630,000
Description: Has supported public TV/radio, dance, arts councils and consolidated arts fund drives.

St. Louis

Chromalloy American Foundation
120 South Central
St. Louis, MO 63105
Tel: 314-726-9200
Annual Budget: $350,000
Description: Has supported arts councils and cultural organizations.

NEBRASKA
Dakota City

Iowa Beef Processors, Incorporated
Dakota City, NE 68731
Tel: 402-494-2061 ext. 351
Annual Budget: $35,000
Description: Has supported community arts programs, music and visual arts.

Lincoln

Bankers Life Nebraska
Cotner at O Street
Lincoln, NE 68501
Tel: 402-467-1120
Address Inquiries to: Harry P. Seward, Chairman and Chief Executive Officer
Annual Budget: $12,000
Description: Has supported theatre, dance, arts councils and performing arts centers.

Omaha

ConAgra Charitable Foundation
Kiewit Plaza
Omaha, NE 68131
Tel: 402-346-8004
Annual Budget: $123,000
Description: Has supported arts councils and cultural organizations.

Northwestern Bell Telephone Company
100 South Nineteenth Street
Omaha, NE 68102
Tel: 402-422-3507
Annual Budget: $1,680,000
Description: Has supported theatre, music, public TV/radio and cultural and performing arts centers.

NEVADA
Las Vegas

Nevada Power Company
Post Office Box 230
Las Vegas, NV 89151
Tel: 702-385-5733
Annual Budget: $17,500
Description: Has supported theatre, dance, arts councils and consolidated arts fund drives.

Southwest Gas Corporation
Post Office Box 15015
Las Vegas, NV 89114
Tel: 702-876-7241; 702-876-7222
Address Inquiries to: Judith Ford, Vice President and Corporate Secretary
Founded in: 1931
Annual Budget: Not available
Description: Has supported arts service organizations, community arts programs and visual arts.

NEW HAMPSHIRE
Concord

The New Hampshire Charitable Fund
One South Street
Concord, NH 03310
Tel: 603-225-6641
Member: ACA; NACCA; NEA;

Manchester

Merchants Savings Bank
Hampshire Plaza
Manchester, NH 03105
Tel: 603-668-5111
Annual Budget: $60,000
Description: Has supported theatre, arts councils and performing arts centers.

NEW JERSEY
Morris Plains

Warner-Lambert Foundation
201 Tabor Road
Morris Plains, NJ 07950
Tel: 201-540-2000
Annual Budget: $1,800,000
Description: Has supported theatre, dance, arts councils and cultural and performing arts centers.

Murray Hill

Bell Telephone Laboratories
600 Mountain Avenue
Murray Hill, NJ 07974
Tel: 201-582-6254
Annual Budget: $17,000
Description: Has supported theatre, dance, arts councils and performing arts centers.

Newark

Mutual Benefit Life Insurance Company
520 Broad Street
Newark, NJ 07101
Tel: 201-481-8106
Annual Budget: Not available
Description: Has supported music, public TV/radio and cultural and performing arts centers.

New Jersey Bell Telephone Company
540 Broad Street
Newark, NJ 07101
Tel: 201-649-3132
Annual Budget: $600,000
Description: Has supported theatre, dance, arts councils and performing arts centers.

Prudential Insurance Company of America
Prudential Plaza
Newark, NJ 07101
Tel: 201-877-7311
Annual Budget: $3,360,000
Description: Has supported theatre, dance, arts councils and performing arts centers.

Parsippany

BASF Wyandotte Corporation
100 Cherry Hill Road
Parsippany, NJ 07054
Tel: 201-282-3300
Address Inquiries to: Robert B. Semple,
  Chairman of the Board
Annual Budget: $250,000
Description: Has supported theatre, dance,
arts councils and performing arts centers.

Interpace Foundation
260 Cherry Hill Road
Parsippany, NJ 07054
Tel: 201-335-1111
Annual Budget: $100,000
Description: Has supported community arts
programs, museums and music.

NEW MEXICO

Albuquerque

Albuquerque National Bank
303 Roma North West
Albuquerque, NM 87103
Tel: 505-765-2104
Address Inquiries to: Lillian Dolde, Vice
  President
Annual Budget: $95,000
Description: Supports art councils and cultural
organizations.

Santa Fe

Theatre Arts Corporation
905 Saint Frances Drive
Santa Fe, NM 87501
Tel: 505-983-9815
Address Inquiries to: Robert Garrison,
  Artistic Director
Founded in: 1963

NEW YORK

Brooklyn

The Lincoln Savings Bank
531 Broadway
Brooklyn, NY 11206
Tel: 212-764-1416
Annual Budget: $55,000
Description: Has supported community arts
programs, dance and state and local arts
agencies.

Mineola

LILCO Charitable Trust
250 Old Country Road
Mineola, NY 11501
Tel: 516-228-2070
Annual Budget: $371,000
Description: Has supported cultural and per-
forming arts centers, music and public TV/
radio.

New York

Abex Foundation
530 Fifth Avenue
New York, NY 10036
Tel: 212-560-3200
Address Inquiries to: O.B. Cottle, Treasurer
Annual Budget: $181,000
Description: Has supported various perform-
ing arts activities. They are the foundation of
the Abex Corporation.

ACF Foundation, Incorporated
750 Third Avenue
New York, NY 10017
Tel: 212-986-8600
Address Inquiries to: Robert W. Montgomery,
  Assistant Secretary
Founded in: 1954
Annual Budget: $386,841
Description: A small foundation with limited
funds which are directed mainly to organiza-
tions where the corporation has facilities.

Arts and Communications Counselors
110 East 59th Street
New York, NY 10022
Tel: 212-593-6475
Address Inquiries to: Nina Kaiden Wright,
  President
Founded in: 1959

Avon Product Foundation
9 West 57th Street
New York, NY 10019
Tel: 212-593-5605
Address Inquiries to: Glenn Clarke, Director
Annual Budget: $1,050,500
Description: Has supported arts councils and
cultural organizations.

Babcock and Wilcox
161 East 42nd Street
New York, NY 10017
Tel: 212-687-6700
Address Inquiries to: S.W.Boone, Vice
  President of Public Affairs
Annual Budget: $500,000
Description: Has supported theatre, dance,
arts councils and performing arts centers.

Bankers Trust Company
280 Park Avenue
New York, NY 10017
Tel: 212-977-6270
Address Inquiries to: Ronald G. Wickham,
  Assistant Vice President
Annual Budget: $2,200,000
Description: Supported theatre, dance, arts
councils and performing arts centers.

The Bristol-Myers Fund
345 Park Avenue
New York, NY 10022
Tel: 212-644-2403
Annual Budget: $2,006,000
Description: Has supported arts councils and
cultural organizations.

Chase Manhattan Bank, N. A.
One Chase Manhattan Plaza
New York, NY 10015
Tel: 212-552-4411

Founded in: 1958
Annual Budget: $2,300,000
Description: Has supported theatre, dance,
arts councils and performing arts centers
based in New York City.

Chemical Bank
20 Pine Street
New York, NY 10005
Tel: 212-770-2147
Annual Budget: $1,169,000
Description: Has supported theatre, dance,
arts councils and performing arts centers.

Citicorp and Citibank, N.A.
399 Park Avenue
New York, NY 10043
Tel: 212-559-8182
Annual Budget: $2,365,497
Description: Has supported theatre, dance,
arts councils and performing arts centers.

Cluett, Peabody and Company
510 Fifth Avenue
New York, NY 10036
Tel: 212-697-6100
Description: Has supported theatre, dance,
arts councils and performing arts centers.

The Duplan Foundation
1430 Broadway
New York, NY 10018
Tel: 212-354-8500
Description: Their support priority is to mu-
seums.

Equitable Life Assurance
1285 Avenue of the Americas
New York, NY 10019
Tel: 212-554-1057
Annual Budget: $2,470,000
Description: Has supported arts education/
scholarships as well as museums and librar-
ies

Foundation for Dance Promotion
87 Fifth Avenue
New York, NY 10003
Tel: 212-675-2452
Address Inquiries to: Ann Kearns

Frederick W. Richmond Foundation
743 Fifth Avenue
New York, NY 10022
Tel: 212-752-1668
Annual Budget: $90,000
Description: Has supported theatre, dance,
arts councils and cultural and performing
arts centers.

Freeport Minerals Company
200 Park Avenue
New York, NY 10017
Tel: 212-578-9297
Annual Budget: $87,000
Description: Has supported arts centers and
facilities such as Lincoln Center for the Per-
forming Arts.

Grace Foundation
1114 Avenue of the Americas
New York, NY 10036
Tel: 212-764-6003

Annual Budget: $1,578,000
Description: Has supported arts councils and consolidated arts funds drives.

Indian Head Foundation
1211 Avenue of the Americas
New York, NY 10036
Tel: 212-764-3280
Annual Budget: $91,000
Description: Has supported arts programs and facilities such as Lincoln Center for the Performing arts.

International Paper Company Foundation
220 East 42nd Street
New York, NY 10017
Tel: 212-490-6580
Annual Budget: $1,380,498
Description: Has supported art councils and facilities such as Lincoln Center for the Performing Arts.

International Telephone and Telegraph
320 Park Avenue
New York, NY 10002
Tel: 212-752-6000
Annual Budget: Not available
Description: Has supported dance, public television and radio.

Joseph E. Seagram and Sons, Incorporated
375 Park Avenue
New York, NY 10022
Tel: 212-572-7000
Annual Budget: $719,000
Description: Has supported theatre, music and community arts programs.

Lever Brothers Company Foundation
390 Park Avenue
New York, NY 10022
Tel: 212-688-6000 ext. 8038
Annual Budget: $235,000
Description: Has supported theatre, arts councils and performing arts centers.

Manufacturers Hanover Foundation
350 Park Avenue
New York, NY 10022
Tel: 212-350-4067
Annual Budget: $1,547,000
Description: Has supported cultural and performing arts centers as well as museums and libraries.

Metropolitan Life Foundation
One Madison Avenue
New York, NY 10010
Tel: 212-578-3515
Annual Budget: $1,665,000
Description: Has supported theatre, dance, arts councils and performing arts centers.

Mobil Foundation, Incorporated
150 East 42nd Street
New York, NY 10017
Tel: 212-883-4725
Annual Budget: $4,000,000
Description: Has supported theater, dance, performing arts centers and public TV/radio.

Morgan Guaranty Trust Company
23 Wall Street
New York, NY 10015
Tel: 212-483-2090
Annual Budget: $2,500,000
Description: Has supported theatre, dance arts councils and performing arts centers.

National Bank of North America
44 Wall Street
New York, NY 10005
Tel: 212-623-8640
Annual Budget: $200,000
Description: Has supported theatre, dance, arts councils and performing arts centers.

National Corporate Fund for the Dance, Inc.
130 West 56th Street
New York, NY 10019
Tel: 212-582-0130
Address Inquiries to: Judith A. Jedlickc, President
  Carolyn L. Stolper, Associate Director
Founded in: 1972
Annual Budget: $600,000
Description: A national not-for-profit organization which conducts an annual united appeal in the business community for major American dance companies including: American Ballet Theatre, San Francisco Ballet, The Joffrey Ballet, Alvin Ailey American Dance Theatre, The Feld Ballet, Merce Cunningham Dance Company, The Paul Taylor Dance Company and the Twyla Tharp Dance Foundation. Over two hundred corporations subscribe to the fund which helps to support seven of America's great dance companies.

New York Telephone Company
1095 Avenue of the Americas
New York, NY 10036
Tel: 212-395-7715
Annual Budget: $1,500,000
Description: Has supported theatre, dance, arts councils and facilities such as Lincoln Center for the Performing Arts.

New York Times Company Foundation
229 West 43rd Street
New York, NY 10036
Tel: 212-556-1091
Address Inquiries to: President
Annual Budget: $656,000
Description: Has supported theatre, dance, arts councils and cultural and performing arts centers.

Norlin Foundation
200 Park Avenue
New York, NY 10017
Tel: 212-986-8900
Annual Budget: $135,000
Description: Has supported music, public TV/radio and cultural and performing arts centers.

Philip Morris Incorporated
100 Park Avenue
New York, NY 10017
Tel: 212-679-1800
Annual Budget: $1,100,000

Description: Has supported theatre, dance, arts councils and performing arts centers.

Saks Fifth Avenue-Gimbel Brothers Foundation
1275 Broadway
New York, NY 10001
Tel: 212-564-3300, ext. 207
Annual Budget: $435,000
Description: Has supported performing arts centers.

SCM Corporation
299 Park Avenue
New York, NY 10017
Tel: 212-752-2700
Annual Budget: Not available
Description: Has supported in-facility exhibitions or performances.

Singer Company Foundation
30 Rockefeller Plaza
New York, NY 10020
Tel: 212-581-4800
Annual Budget: $450,000
Description: Has supported arts education/scholarships and cultural and performing arts centers.

Squibb Corporation
40 West 57th Street
New York, NY 10019
Tel: 212-489-4753
Annual Budget: $550,000
Description: Has supported visual arts, arts councils and cultural and performing arts centers.

J. Walter Thompson Company Fund
420 Lexington Avenue
New York, NY 10017
Tel: 212-867-1000
Annual Budget: $100,000
Description: Supported theatre, dance, arts councils and performing arts centers.

Union Carbide Corporation
270 Park Avenue
New York, NY 10017
Tel: 212-551-4229
Annual Budget: $2,645,000
Description: Has supported theatre, dance, arts councils and cultural and performing arts centers.

United States Trust Company of New York
45 Wall Street
New York, NY 10005
Tel: 212-425-4500
Annual Budget: $165,000
Description: Has supported music, dance and cultural and performing arts centers.

Western Electric Fund
222 Broadway
New York, NY 10038
Tel: 212-669-2649
Founded in: 1953
Annual Budget: $7,000,000
Description: Has supported theatre, dance, arts councils and cultural and performing arts dance centers located in those cities

where its corporate sponsor has major facilities.

Purchase

Pepsi Company Foundation
Purchase, NY 10577
Tel: 914-253-2900
Annual Budget: $680,000
Description: Has supported visual arts, arts councils and performing arts centers.

Rochester

Eastman Kodak Company
343 State Street
Rochester, NY 14650
Tel: 716-724-3127
Founded in: 1880
Description: Has supported arts councils and cultural organizations.

Gannet Foundation
55 Exchange Street
Rochester, NY 14614
Tel: 716-262-3315
Annual Budget: $5,600,000
Description: Has supported arts councils and cultural organizations.

Lincoln First Bank of Rochester
One Lincoln First Square
Rochester, NY 14643
Tel: 716-262-4428
Annual Budget: $180,000
Description: Has supported community arts programs, galleries and music.

Sybron Community Fund
1100 Midtown Tower
Rochester, NY 14604
Tel: 716-546-4040
Annual Budget: $635,000
Description: Supported theatre, music, arts councils and community arts programs

Tarrytown

Technicon Corporation
511 Benedict Avenue
Tarrytown, NY 10583
Tel: 914-631-8000
Description: Supported arts councils and consolidated arts fund drives.

White Plains

General Foods Corporation
250 North Street
White Plains, NY 10625
Tel: 914-683-2400
Annual Budget: $1,800,000
Description: Has supported theatre, dance, arts councils and performing arts centers.

NORTH CAROLINA

Charlotte

NCNB Corporation
Post Office Box 120
Charlotte, NC 28255
Tel: 704-374-8885
Annual Budget: Not available

Description: Has supported museums, arts councils and cultural and performing arts centers.

Durham

Liggett Group
Post Office Box 1886
Durham, NC 27702
Tel: 919-471-7645
Annual Budget: $672,000
Description: Has supported theater, arts councils and performing arts centers.

Fayetteville

North Carolina Natural Gas Corporation
150 Rowan Street
Fayetteville, NC 28301
Tel: 919-483-0315
Annual Budget: $18,000
Description: Has supported music, museums and historic preservation.

Greensboro

Blue Bell Foundation
335 Church Court
Greensboro, NC 27401
Tel: 919-373-3962
Annual Budget: $200,000
Description: Has supported arts councils and facilities for the performing arts.

Marion

Currier Piano Company, Incorporated
100 South Clay Street
Marion, NC 28752
Tel: 704-652-3424
Description: Has supported arts/education scholarships, community arts programs and music.

Winston-Salem

Hanes Corporation
Post Office Box 5416
Winston-Salem, NC 27103
Tel: 919-744-3700
Annual Budget: $468,000
Description: Has supported artists' workshops/studios, art councils and arts fund drives.

Hanes Dye and Finishing Company
Post Office Box 202
Winston-Salem, NC 27102
Tel: 919-725-1391
Annual Budget: 5% of profit (before taxes)
Description: Has supported theatre, dance, arts councils and performing arts centers.

R. J. Reynolds Industries, Incorporated
Reynolds Boulevard
Winston-Salem, NC 27102
Tel: 919-748-2643
Annual Budget: Not available
Description: Has supported theatre, dance, arts councils and performing arts centers.

The Wachovia Corporation
Post Office Box 3099
Winston-Salem, NC 27102
Tel: 919-748-5923

Annual Budget: Not available
Description: Has supported music, dance, arts councils and cultural and performing arts centers.

OHIO

Akron

General Tire Foundation
One General Street
Akron, OH 44329
Tel: 216-798-3440
Annual Budget: $730,000
Description: Has supported arts councils and performing arts centers.

Cincinnati

The Baldwin Foundation
1801 Gilbert Avenue
Cincinnati, OH 45202
Tel: 513-852-7965
Address Inquiries to: James E. Schwab, Treasurer
Description: Has supported arts councils and cultural organizations.

Cincinnati Bell
225 East Fourth Street
Cincinnati, OH 45202
Tel: 513-397-2495
Annual Budget: $160,000
Description: Has supported theatre, dance, arts councils and performing arts centers.

Frisch's Restaurants
2800 Gilbert Avenue
Cincinnati, OH 45206
Tel: 513-559-5200; 513-961-2660
Address Inquiries to: Louis J. Ullman, Vice President of Finance
Founded in: 1947
Annual Budget: $100,000
Description: Has supported theatre, dance, arts councils and performing arts centers.

The John Shillito Company
Seventh and Race Streets
Cincinnati, OH 45202
Tel: 513-852-6878
Annual Budget: $205,000
Description: Has supported theatre, dance, arts councils and cultural and performing arts centers.

Taft Broadcasting Company
1906 Highland Avenue
Cincinnati, OH 45219
Tel: 513-721-1414
Annual Budget: $100,000
Description: Supported theatre, music, arts councils and public TV/radio.

Cleveland

Cleveland Trust Company
900 Euclid Avenue
Cleveland, OH 44101
Tel: 216-687-5969
Annual Budget: $600,000
Description: Has supported theare, dance, arts

councils and performing arts centers.

Eaton Charitable Fund
100 Erieview Plaza
Cleveland, OH 44114
Tel: 216-523-5000
Description: Has supported arts councils and cultural organizations.

The Hanna Mining Company
100 Erieview Plaza
Cleveland, OH 44114
Tel: 216-523-3200
Annual Budget: Not Available
Description: Has supported theatre and cultural and performing arts centers.

The Lamson and Sessions Foundation
2000 Bond Court
1300 E. Ninth Street
Cleveland, OH 44114
Tel: 216-781-5000
Annual Budget: $80,000
Description: Has supported music, public TV/radio, and cultural and peforming arts centers.

National City Bank
623 Euclid Avenue
Cleveland, OH 44114
Tel: 216-861-4900
Annual Budget: $320,000
Description: Has supported theater, dance arts councils and performing arts centers.

Sohio Corporate Contributions Program
The Midland Building
Cleveland, OH 44115
Tel: 216-575-5702
Annual Budget: $15,000,000
Description: The Standard Oil Company (Ohio) supports the arts through its Corporate Contribution Program.

TRW Foundation
23555 Euclid Avenue
Cleveland, OH 44117
Tel: 216-383-2412
Annual Budget: $2,100,000
Description: Supported theatre, dance, arts councils and cultural and performing arts centers.

Dayton

NCR Foundation
Dayton, OH 45479
Tel: 513-449-2171
Annual Budget: $940,000
Description: Has supported theatre, dance, arts councils and music.

Third National Bank and Trust Company
34 North Main Street
Dayton, OH 45402
Tel: 513-226-6354
Annual Budget: $60,000
Description: Supported music, dance, arts councils and arts service organizations.

Newton

Maytag Company Foundation
Newton, OH 50208
Tel: 615-792-7000, ext. 8216
Annual Budget: $204,000
Description: Has supported theater, dance and cultural and performing arts centers.

Wickliffe

The Lubrizol Foundation
29400 Lakeland Boulevard
Wickliffe, OH 44092
Tel: 216-943-4200
Annual Budget: $404,000
Description: Has supported theatre, arts councils and performing arts center.

OKLAHOMA

Bartlesville

Phillips Petroleum Foundation
Bartlesville, OK 74004
Tel: 918-661-5660
Annual Budget: $2,180,000
Description: Has supported theatre, dance, arts councils and performing arts centers.

Oklahoma City

Kirkpatrick Foundation
1300 North Broadway
Oklahoma City, OK 73103
Tel: 405-235-5621
Address Inquiries to: Eleanor J. Maurer,
    Personal Executive
    Mr. John E. Kirkpatrick, Chairman of
    Board
Founded in: 1955
Annual Budget: $75,000
Description: Supports religious, charitable, scientific, literary, or educational undertakings within the United States and possessions.

Tulsa

WILLCO Foundation
One Williams Center
Tulsa, OK 74103
Tel: 918-588-2111
Address Inquiries to: B.F. Boddie, Vice
    President
Founded in: 1974
Annual Budget: Not available
Description: Has supported visual arts, arts councils and cultural and performing arts centers. WILLCO foundation will also match employee gifts to arts organizations from $25 to $500 each annually.

OREGON

Portland

Omark Industries, Incorporated
2100 Southeast Milport Road
Portland, OR 97222
Tel: 503-654-6531
Annual Budget: $122,000

Description: Has supported theatre, music, visual arts and cultural and performing arts centers.

Portland General Electric Company
121 Southwest Salmon Street
Portland, OR 97204
Tel: 503-226-8511
Annual Budget: $325,000
Description: Has supported theatre, music, arts councils and performing arts centers.

PENNSYLVANIA

Allentown

Air Products and Chemicals, Incorporated
Post Office Box 538
Allentown, PA 18105
Tel: 215-398-6587
Address Inquiries to: Stewart H. Stabley,
    Executive Secretary of Corporate
    Contributions
Annual Budget: $798,000
Description: Has supported various art forms and cultural organizations.

Pennsylvania Power and Light Company
2 North 9th Street
Allentown, PA 18013
Tel: 215-821-5375
Annual Budget: $360,000
Description: Has supported libraries, museums and public TV/radio.

Hershey

The Hershey Fund
19 East Chocolate Avenue
Hershey, PA 17033
Tel: 717-534-4235
Annual Budget: Not available
Description: Has supported music, public TV/radio and theatre.

Philadelphia

ARA Services Incorporated
Independence Square West
Philadelphia, PA 19106
Tel: 215-574-5379
Address Inquiries to: Bruce C. Boyce,
    Secretary of Corporate Contributions
    Committee
Description: Supports local arts endeavors primarily and is sensitive to community needs.

Bell of Pennsylvania
One Parkway
Philadelphia, PA 19102
Tel: 215-466-3376
Annual Budget: $552,000
Description: Has supported theatre, dance, arts councils and performing arts centers.

Girard Bank
1 Girard Plaza
Philadelphia, PA 19101
Tel: 215-585-3918
Annual Budget: $455,000
Description: Has supported theatre, dance,

arts councils and performing arts centers.

INA Foundation
1600 Arch Street
Philadelphia, PA 19101
Tel: 215-241-4369
Annual Budget: $700,000
Description: Has supported theatre, music and cultural/performing arts centers.

Philadelphia National Bank
Broad and Chestnut Streets
Philadelphia, PA 19101
Tel: 215-629-4181
Annual Budget: $610,000
Description: Has supported theatre, dance, arts councils and performing arts centers.

Provident Mutual Life Insurance Company of Philadelphia
4601 Market Street
Post Office Box 7378
Philadelphia, PA 19101
Tel: 215-474-7000
Annual Budget: $177,000
Description: Has supported theatre, music, visual arts and public TV/radio.

Rohm and Haas Company
Independence Mall West
Philadelphia, PA 19105
Tel: 215-592-2863
Annual Budget: $730,000
Description: Has supported arts councils and consolidated arts fund drives.

Pittsburgh

Duquesne Light Company
435 Sixth Avenue
Pittsburgh, PA 15219
Tel: 412-471-4300, ext. 6279
Annual Budget: $285,000
Description: Has supported theatre, dance, arts councils and performing arts centers.

Gulf Oil Foundation
7th and Grant Street
Pittsburgh, PA 15219
Tel: 412-263-5188
Annual Budget: $5,523,000
Description: Has supported cultural/performing arts centers and public television/radio.

Mellon Bank Foundation
Mellon Square
Pittsburgh, PA 15230
Tel: 412-232-6266
Founded in: 1974
Annual Budget: $1,423,000
Description: Has supported music, theatre, dance, museums and libraries.

Mine Safety Appliances Company
Charitable Trust
600 Penn Center Boulevard
Pittsburgh, PA 15235
Tel: 412-273-5046
Annual Budget: Not available
Description: Has supported theatre, dance, arts programs and public TV/radio.

Pittsburgh National Foundation
Fifth Avenue and Wood Street
Pittsburgh, PA 15222
Tel: 412-355-2830
Annual Budget: $282,000
Description: Has supported theatre, dance, community arts programs and performing arts centers.

Rockwell International
600 Grant Street
Pittsburgh, PA 15219
Tel: 412-565-2407
Annual Budget: Not available
Description: Has supported theatre, visual arts and cultural and performing arts centers.

United States Steel Foundation
600 Grant Street
Pittsburgh, PA 15230
Tel: 412-433-5238
Address Inquiries to: James T. Hosey, Vice President
William A. Gregory, Jr., Assistant Executive Director
Founded in: 1953
Annual Budget: $6,600,000
Description: Has supported theatre, dance, arts councils and cultural and performing arts centers.

Westinghouse Electric Fund
Westinghouse Building, Gateway Center
Pittsburgh, PA 15222
Tel: 412-255-3017
Address Inquiries to: C.M. Springer, Executive Director
Founded in: 1952
Annual Budget: $3,200,000
Description: Has supported theatre, dance, arts councils and consolidated arts fund drives.

Warren

United Refining Company
Post Office Box 780
Warren, PA 16365
Tel: 814-723-1500
Annual Budget: $36,000
Description: Has suppoted music, community arts programs and cultural and performing arts centers.

RHODE ISLAND

Providence

Textron Inc.
40 Westminster Street
Providence, RI 02903
Tel: 401-421-2800
Description: Supported music, public TV/radio and cultural and performing arts centers.

Warwick

Warwick Arts Foundation
Post Office Box 726
Warwick, RI 02888
Tel: 401-942-2399

Address Inquiries to: Ruby Shalansky, Administator
Founded in: 1963
Annual Budget: $10,000

SOUTH CAROLINA

Columbia

South Carolina National Bank
101 Greystone Boulevard
Columbia, SC 29226
Tel: 803-765-3756
Address Inquiries to: Virginia M. Grose, Vice President
Founded in: 1834
Description: Has supported theatre, arts councils and arts fund drives within the state of South Carolina. The bank also has a corporate art collection and purchases from artists who have or have had some connection with South Carolina.

Fort Mill

Springs Mills, Incorporated
Fort Mill, SC 29715
Tel: 803-547-2901
Address Inquiries to: Robert L. Thompson, Jr., Director of Public Affairs
Founded in: 1887
Annual Budget: Not available
Description: Supports visual arts, and community arts programs. Its major interests are the sponsorship of photographic exhibitions developed by the Museum of Modern Art, and a large regional (Carolina's) art exhibition and traveling art show.

Greenville

Riegel Textile Corporation Foundation
Green Gate Park, Suite 800
Greenville, SC 29607
Tel: 803-242-6050
Annual Budget: $280,000
Description: Has supported theatre, arts councils and community arts programs.

SOUTH DAKOTA

Rapid City

Black Hills Power and Light Company
Post Office Box 1400
Rapid City, SD 57709
Tel: 605-348-1700
Description: Has supported theatre, dance, arts councils and performing arts centers.

Sioux Falls

National Bank of South Dakota
Post Office Box 1308
Sioux Falls, SD 57101
Tel: 605-339-8646
Annual Budget: $100,000
Description: Has supported theater, arts councils and cultural and performing arts centers.

TENNESSEE

Nashville

Nashville Gas Company
814 Church Street
Nashville, TN 37203
Tel: 615-254-0611
Annual Budget: $36,000
Description: Has supported theatre, public TV/radio and cultural and performing arts centers.

National Life and Accident Insurance Company
National Life Center
Nashville, TN 37250
Tel: 615-749-1462
Annual Budget: $408,000
Description: Has supported theatre, arts councils and performing arts centers.

TEXAS

Austin

The Hogg Foundation
The University of Texas
Austin, TX 78712
Tel: 512-471-5041
Member: ACA; NACCA; NEA;

Canyon

Texas Panhandle Heritage Foundation, Incorporated
Post Office Box 268
Canyon, TX 79015
Tel: 806-655-2181
Address Inquiries to: Raymond Raillard, Executive Vice President
Founded in: 1961
Annual Budget: $100,000
Description: The foundation was created to construct an ampitheatre with sound and lights to be used to house the dramatic production of 'TEXAS', written by playwright Paul Green, in order to preserve and promote the history of the Texas Panhandle.

Dallas

The LTV Corporation
Post Office Box 5003
Dallas, TX 75222
Tel: 214-746-7728
Annual Budget: $1.8 million
Description: Has supported theatre, cultural and performing arts centers and dance.

Republic National Bank of Dallas
Post Office Box 5961
Dallas, TX 75222
Tel: 214-653-5742
Annual Budget: $730,000
Description: Has supported theatre, dance, arts councils and performing arts centers.

Triangle Pacific Corporation
4255 LBJ Freeway
Dallas, TX 75234
Tel: 214-661-2800
Annual Budget: $25,000

Description: Supported theatre, music, public TV/radio and cultural and performing arts centers.

Houston

Shell Oil Companies Foundation, Inc. Two Shell Plaza
Post Office Box 2099
Houston, TX 77001
Tel: 713-241-3616
Annual Budget: $4,000,000
Description: Has supported theatre, dance, arts councils and cultural and performing arts centers.

Transco Companies
2700 South Post Oak Road
Houston, TX 77056
Tel: 713-626-8100 ext. 719; 713-871-2455
Annual Budget: $104,000
Description: Supported theatre, visual arts, arts councils and cultural and performing arts centers.

Sugarland

Imperial Sugar Company
Post Office Box 9
Sugarland, TX 77478
Tel: 713-491-9181
Annual Budget: Not available
Description: Has supported arts councils, museums and historic preservation.

Southwestern Group Financial, Incorporated
333 Southwestern Boulevard
Sugar Land, TX 77478
Tel: 713-494-6071
Annual Budget: Not available
Description: Has supported theatre, opera, public arts agencies and community arts programs.

VERMONT

Montpelier

National Life Insurance Company
National Life Drive
Montpelier, VT 05602
Tel: 802-223-3431 ext. 205
Annual Budget: $68,000
Description: Has supported cultural and performing arts centers, libraries and public TV/radio.

VIRGINIA

Middletown

Wayside Foundation for the Arts
Wayside Theatre
Middletown, VA 22645
Tel: 703-869-1782
Address Inquiries to: Dr. William McCoy, Manager
Founded in: 1963
Member: AEA;
Annual Budget: $100,000

Richmond

Universal Leaf Tobacco Company
Post Office Box 25099
Richmond, VA 23260
Tel: 804-359-9311
Annual Budget: $100,000
Description: Has supported music, dance, arts councils and cultural and performing arts centers.

WASHINGTON

Seattle

Boeing Charitable Trust
7755 East Marginal Way
Seattle, WA 98124
Tel: 206-655-2835
Annual Budget: $1,004,000
Description: Has supported arts councils and cultural organizations.

Pacific Northwest Bell Telephone Company
1600 Bell Plaza
Seattle, WA 98191
Tel: 206-345-4766
Annual Budget: $563,000
Description: Has supported theatre, music, arts councils and community arts programs.

Safeco Insurance Companies
Safeco Plaza
Seattle, WA 98185
Tel: 206-545-5708
Annual Budget: $496,000
Description: Has supported arts councils, community arts programs and Public TV/radio.

Seattle First National Bank
1001 Fourth Avenue
Seattle, WA 98104
Tel: 206-583-4194
Annual Budget: $510,000
Description: Has supported theatre, arts councils and cultural and performing arts centers.

Washington Natural Gas Company
815 Mercer Street
Seattle, WA 98111
Tel: 206-622-6767
Annual Budget: Not available
Description: Has supported music, arts councils and arts education/scholarships.

Tacoma

Weyerhaeuser Company Foundation
Tacoma, WA 98401
Tel: 206-593-7153
Annual Budget: $2,822,000
Description: Has supported theatre, arts councils and cultural and performing arts centers.

WISCONSIN

Manitowoc

Manitowoc Company Incorporated
Post Office Box 66
Manitowoc, WI 54220
Tel: 414-684-6621
Annual Budget: Not Available
Description: Has supported theatre, visual arts and museums.

Milwakee

Joseph Schlitz Brewing Company
235 West Galena Street
Milwakee, WI 53212
Tel: 414-271-7434
Annual Budget: Not available
Description: Has supported public TV and radio.

Milwaukee

Universal Foods Foundation, Incorporated
433 East Michigan Street
Milwaukee, WI 53201
Tel: 414-271-6755
Annual Budget: $47,000
Description: Has supported theatre, music, arts councils and cultural and performing arts centers.

Wisconsin Telephone Company
722 North Broadway
Milwaukee, WI 53202
Tel: 414-678-2384
Annual Budget: $340,000
Description: Has supported public TV/radio, arts councils and cultural and performing arts centers.

Neenah

Kimberly-Clark Foundation
North Lake Street
Neenah, WI 54956
Tel: 414-729-1212
Annual Budget: $850,000
Description: Has supported theatre, arts councils and cultural and performing arts centers.

Wausau

Wausau Area Performing Arts Foundation
Post Office Box 783
Wausau, WI 54401
Tel: 715-842-0988
Address Inquiries to: Robert J. Hankins, Executive Director
Founded in: 1972
Annual Budget: $100,000

Wausau Insurance Companies
2000 Westwood Drive
Wausau, WI 54401
Tel: 715-842-6092
Address Inquiries to: Roger Drayna, Public Relations Director
Founded in: 1911
Annual Budget: $250,000
Description: Has supported theatre, arts councils and cultural organizations.

Wisconsin Rapids

Consolidated Papers, Inc.
c/o Consolidated Civic Foundation, Inc.
Wisconsin Rapids, WI 54494
Tel: 715-442- 3368
Address Inquiries to: Daniel P. Meyer, President
Founded in: 1951
Annual Budget: $400,000
Description: Has supported various art forms, cultural organizations and activities. Arts organizations supported include Community Arts Council of South Wood County, Community Concerts, Community Players, Hopa Arts Festivals and McMillan Memorial Library.

11

Libraries & Collections

Libraries and collections, as the keepers of theatre history, also serve as conduits to future generations for developments in 20th century theatre. Herein are listed the major collections, both public and privately administered, which have significant theatre holdings.

Larger collections, such as the New York Public Library or the Yale University libraries, are in general the most useful to researchers. Smaller collections should not be ignored, however, as they may possess equivalent or better collections in a specialized area. The Folger Shakespeare Library in Washington, D.C. is a good example.

Students and scholars of the theatre should remember that there are usually restrictions on the use of university libraries and private collections by unaffiliated persons. The administrator of the institution in question should be contacted regarding any research privileges sought.

ALABAMA

Mobile

Mobile Public Library Special Collections
Division
7001 Government Street
Mobile, AL 36130

Montgomery

Alabama Department of Archives and
History Manuscripts Division
Montgomery, AL 36130

ARIZONA

Tucson

Tucson Public Library Fine Arts Room
200 South Sixth Avenue
Tucson, AZ 85721

CALIFORNIA

Berkeley

University of California Special Collections
Berkeley, CA 94720

Davis

University of California, Davis Shields
Library
Davis, CA 95616

Denver

Denver Public Library
1357 Broadway
Denver, CA 80203
Member: ACA; NACCA; NEA;
Description: A research library containing information of interest to performing arts researchers.

Hollywood

Academy of Motion Picture Arts and
Sciences
9038 Meelrose Avenue
Hollywood, CA 90069

Irvine

University of California
Special Collections
Irvine, CA 92713

Long Beach

California State University
Special Collections
1250 Bellflower Boulevard
Long Beach, CA 90840

Los Angeles

Institute of the American Musical
840 North Larrabee Street
Los Angeles, CA 90069

Los Angeles Public Library
630 West Fifth Street
Los Angeles, CA 90071

Music Center Operating Company
Archives
135 North Grand Avenue
Los Angeles, CA 90012

University of California, Los Angeles
Theatre Arts Library
Los Angeles, CA 90024

University of Southern California
Special Collections Department
University Park
Los Angeles, CA 90007
Member:

University Research Library
University of California
Los Angeles, CA 90024
Member: ACA; NACCA; NEA;
Description: A research library of great value

to performing arts researchers.

Pasadena

Pasadena Public Library
Fine Arts Division
285 East Walnut Street
Pasadena, CA 91101

Riverside

University of California, Riverside
University Library
4045 Canyon Crest Drive
Post Office Box 5900
Riverside, CA 92507

San Diego

San Diego Public Library
820 E Street
San Diego, CA 92101
Member: ACA; NACCA; NEA;
Description: A starting place for performing
arts researchers in San Diego.

San Francisco

California Historical Society
2090 Jackson Street
San Francisco, CA 94109

San Francisco Public Library
530 Kearny Street
San Francisco, CA 94108
Member: ACA; NACCA; NEA;
Description: Contains information of special
value to performing arts researchers.

Santa Barbara

University of Santa Barbara
Special Collections
Santa Barbara, CA 93106

Stanford

Stanford University
Drama Library
Stanford, CA 94305

Valencia

California Institute of the Arts
24700 McBean Parkway
Valencia, CA 91355

COLORADO

Denver

Colorado Historical Society
1300 Broadway
Denver, CO 80203

CONNECTICUT

Hartford

Connecticut Historical Society
One Elizabeth Street
Hartford, CT 06105

Hartford Public Library
500 Main Street
Hartford, CT 06103
Member: ACA; NACCA; NEA;
Description: Contains information of importance to performing arts researchers.

New Haven

Yale University
Crawford Theatre Collection
New Haven, CT 06520

Yale University, Drama Library
Box 1903A, Yale Station
New Haven, CT 06520

Waterford

Eugene O'Neill Theater Center
305 Great Neck Road
Waterford, CT 06385

DELAWARE

Wilmington

Historical Society of Delaware
505 Market Street
Wilmington, DE 19801

DISTRICT OF COLUMBIA

Washington

Folger Shakespeare Library
201 East Capitol Street
Washington, DC 20003

Georgetown University, Lauinger Library
37th and O Street, NW
Washington, DC 20057

Kennedy Center for the Performing Arts
Library of Congress Performing Arts

Library
Washington, DC 20506

Library of Congress
Rare Books and Special Collections
Washington, DC 20540

National Theatre Library/Archives
1321 E Street, Northwest
Washington, DC 20004

FLORIDA

Gainesville

University of Florida, Belknap Collection
210 Library West
Gainesville, FL 32611

Jacksonville

Jacksonville Public Library
122 North Ocean Street
Jacksonville, FL 32203
Member: ACA; NACCA; NEA;
Description: Contains a section of interest to performing arts researchers

Miami

Miami-Dade Public Library
Florida Collection
One Biscayne Boulevard
Miami, FL 33132
Member: ACA; NACCA; NEA;
Description: A Research Library containing useful information for Performing Arts researchers.

Sarasota

Ringling Museum of Art
Art Research Library
Post Office Box 1838
Sarasota, FL 33578

Tallahassee

Charles MacArthur Center for American Theatre
Florida State University
Tallahassee, FL 32304

GEORGIA

Atlanta

Atlanta Public Library
126 Carnegie Way, NW
Atlanta, GA 30303
Member: ACA; NACCA; NEA;
Description: The starting point for Performing Arts researchers in Georgia.

HAWAII

Honolulu

Thomas Hale Hamilton Library
Humanities Division
2550 The Mall
Honolulu, HI 96822
Member: ACA; NACCA; NEA;

ILLINOIS

Chicago

Chicago Historical Society
Clark Street and West North Avenue
Chicago, IL 60614

Chicago Public Library
Special Collections
425 North Michigan Avenue
Chicago, IL 60611

Lake Forest

Northwestern University Library
Special Collections Department
1935 Sheridan and College Roads
Lake Forest, IL 60045

IOWA

Mount Pleasant

Museum of Repertoire America
Midwest Old Threshers
Mount Pleasant, IA 52641

KANSAS

Lawrence

University of Kansas
Watson Memorial Library
Lawrence, KS 66045

Topeka

Topeka Public Library Gallery of Fine Arts
1515 West Tenth Street
Topeka, KS 66604
Tel: 913-233-3040
Address Inquiries to: James C. Marvin, Librarian
Tom Muth, Assistant Librarian
Founded in: 1870
Member: AAM; ACA; ALA; KMA; MPLA; MPMA; NACCA; NEA;
Annual Budget: $1,500,000
Description: Topeka Public Library provides some information on the arts, holds a year round gallery Exhibition program and runs collection program for the fine arts.

KENTUCKY

Louisville

Louisville Free Public Library
Forth and York Streets
Louisville, KY 40203
Member: ACA; NACCA; NEA;

University of Louisville
University Library
2301 South 3rd Street
Louisville, KY 40208

LOUISIANA

New Orleans

New Orleans Public Library
Art and Music Division
219 Loyola Avenue
New Orleans, LA 70140

Tulane University, Tilton Library
7001 Freret
New Orleans, LA 70118

MAINE

Boothbay

Boothbay Theatre Museum
Corey Lane
Boothbay, ME 04537

Orono

University of Maine
Raymond H. Fogler Library
Special Collections
Orono, ME 04469

Portland

University of Maine
Center for Research and Advanced Study
246 Deering Avenue
Portland, ME 04102
Member: ACA; NACCA; NEA;

MARYLAND

Baltimore

Enoch Pratt Free Library
400 Cathedral Street
Baltimore, MD 21201
Member: ACA; NACCA; NEA;

Maryland Historical Society
201 West Monument Street
Baltimore, MD 21204

Towson

Goucher College
Julia Rogers Library
Dulaney Valley Road
Towson, MD 21204

MASSACHUSETTS

Boston

Bostonian Society, Old State House
206 Washington Street
Boston, MA 02109

Boston Public Library
Copley Square
Boston, MA 02117

Boston University, Mugar Library
771 Commonwealth Avenue
Boston, MA 02215

Emerson College, Abbot Memorial Library
303 Berkeley Street

Boston, MA 02116

Cambridge

Harvard University
Houghton Library
Cambridge, MA 02138

Radcliffe College, Schleslinger Library
3 James Street
Cambridge, MA 02138

Medford

Tufts University
Cohen Arts Center
Medford, MA 02155

Northampton

Smith College
Werner Josten Library for the Performing
Arts
Northampton, MA 01063

South Hadley

Mount Holyoke College
Williston Memorial Library
South Hadley, MA 01075

Waltham

American Jewish Historical Society
2 Thornton Road
Waltham, MA 02154

Brandeis University
University Library, Drama Division
Waltham, MA 02154

Worcester

American Antiquarian Society
185 Salisbury Street
Worcester, MA 01609

MICHIGAN

Ann Arbor

University of Michigan
University Library
Department of Rare Books and Special
Collections
Ann Arbor, MI 48109

Dearborn

Henry Ford Centennial Library
1501 Michigan Avenue
Dearborn, MI 48126
Member: ACA; NACCA; NEA;

Detroit

Detroit Institute of Arts, Research Library
5200 Woodward Avenue
Detroit, MI 48202

Detroit Public Library, Performing Arts
Department
5201 Woodward Avenue
Detroit, MI 40202

Purdy Library
Wayne State University
Detroit, MI 48202

Member: ACA; NACCA; NEA;

University of Michigan
Department of Special Collections
520 Woodward Avenue
Detroit, MI 48202

Wayne State University
General Library
Detroit, MI 48202

East Lansing

Michigan State University
Special Collections Division
East Lansing, MI 48824

Flint

Flint Public Library, Drama Department
1026 East Kearsley Street
Flint, MI 48502

Grand Rapids

Grand Rapids Public Library
Library Plaza
Grand Rapids, MI 49502
Member: ACA; NACCA; NEA;

Marshall

American Museum of Magic
107 East Michigan Avenue
Marshall, MI 49068

MINNESOTA

Minneapolis

Guthrie Theatre Foundation
725 Vinaland Place
Minneapolis, MN 55403

Minneapolis College of Art and Design
200 East 25th Street
Minneapolis, MN 55404

Minneapolis Public Library and
Information Center
Literature and Language DDepartment
300 Nicollet Mall
Minneapolis, MN 55401

Minneapolis Public Library Sociology
Department
300 Nicollet Mall
Minneapolis, MN 55401
Member: ACA; NACCA; NEA;

Saint Paul

Minnesota Historical Society
Cedar Street and Central Avenue
Saint Paul, MN 55101

Saint Paul Public Library
90 West 4th Street
Saint Paul, MN 55102

MISSISSIPPI

Jackson

Mississippi Department of Archives and
History
Drama Department
Jackson, MS 39217

MISSOURI

Columbia

Missouri Historical Society
University of Missouri
Columbia, MO 65201

Kansas City

University of Missouri
Kansas City Playhouse, Room 300
Kansas City, MO 64110

St. Louis

Washington University
Drama Department
St. Louis, MO 63130

NEBRASKA

Lincoln

Nebraska State Historical Society
1500 R Street
Lincoln, NE 68508

University of Nebraska at Lincoln
Drama Library
Lincoln, NE 68508

NEW HAMPSHIRE

Hanover

Dartmouth College
Baker Library
Hanover, NH 03755

NEW JERSEY

Princeton

Princeton University
William Seymour Theatre Collection
Princeton, NJ 08540

West Long Beach

Monmouth College
Murry and Leonie Guggenheim Memorial
Library
West Long Beach, NJ 07764

NEW YORK

Binghamton

State University of New York
Glenn G. Bartle Library
Binghamton, NY 13901

Brockport

State University of New York
Drake Memorial Library
Brockport, NY 14420

Brooklyn

Brooklyn College Library
Avenue H at Bedford Avenue
Brooklyn, NY 11210

Brooklyn Public Library
Grand Army Plaza
Brooklyn, NY 11238

Clinton

Hamilton College
Drama Department Library
Clinton, NY 13323

Corning

Corning Community College
Arthur A. Houghton Library
Corning, NY 14830

Hempstead

Hofstra University
Drama Department Library
Hempstead, NY 11550

Ithaca

Cornell University
Drama Department Library
Ithaca, NY 14853

Jamaica

Queensborough Public Library, Art and
Music Division
89-11 Merrick Boulevard
Jamaica, NY 11432

New Rochelle

New Rochelle Public Library, Fine Arts
Department
662 Main Street
New Rochelle, NY 10805

New York

American Academy of Arts and Letters
633 West 155th Street
New York, NY 10032

American Academy of Dramatic Arts
120 Madison Avenue
New York, NY 10016

Armstead-Johnson Foundation for Theatre
Research
c/o Hotel Chelsea
222 West 23rd Street
New York, NY 10011

Columbia University, Special Collections
525 Broadway
New York, NY 10027

International Theatre Institute of the
United States
1860 Broadway
New York, NY 10023

Juilliard School
Lila Acheson Wallace Library
Lincoln Center
New York, NY 10023

Metropolitan Museum of Art
Lewisohn Reference Library
Fifth Avenue at 82d Street
New York, NY 10028

Museum of Broadcasting
1 East 53d Street
New York, NY 10022

Museum of the City of New York
Fifth Avenue at 103d Street
New York, NY 10029

Neighborhood Playhouse School of the
Theatre
Lewisohn Library
340 East 54th Street
New York, NY 10022

New York Historical Society
170 Central Park West
New York, NY 10024

New York Public Library, Arts Research
Center
111 Amsterdam Avenue
New York, NY 10023

New York University Library, Special
Collections
70 Washington Square South
New York, NY 10012

Paul Robeson Archives
157 West 57th Street, Suite 403
New York, NY 10018

The Players, New York
16 Gramercy Park South
New York, NY 10003
Tel: 212-475-6116
Address Inquiries to: Louis A. Rachow,
   Curator
Founded in: 1888
Description: Edwin Booth founded The Play-
ers which not only houses the club but the
Walter Hampden-Edwin Booth Theatre Col-
lections. You must contact the curator, Louis
A Rachow, editor of *Theatre and Performing Arts
Collections*, before visiting.

Radio City Music Hall Archives
1260 Avenue of the Americas
New York, NY 10020

Shubert Archive
234 West 44th Street
New York, NY 10036
Description: The complete collection of corre-
spondence and memorabilia of the Shubert
Brothers. The collection is still being collat-
ed and is not open to the public at this time.

Walter Hampden-Edwin Booth Theatre
Library
16 Gramercy Park
New York, NY 10003

Queens

Queens College Library
65-30 Kissena Boulevard
Queens, NY 11367

Queens Historical Society
143-35 37th Avenue
Queens, NY 11354

Rochester

University of Rochester
Department of Rare Books, Manuscripts
and Archives
Rochester, NY 14627

Schenectady

State Museum, S.U.N.Y.
Division of Historical Services
Schenectady, NY 12306

Stonybrook

State University of New York, Stony
Brook
Special Collections
Stonybrook, NY 11794

Yonkers

American Museum of Comedy
William Treadwell Library
Yonkers, NY

NORTH CAROLINA

Chapel Hill

Institute of Outdoor Drama
University of North Carolina
202 Graham Memorial 052-A
Chapel Hill, NC 27514

University of North Carolina
Wilson Library
Chapel Hill, NC 27514

Winston-Salem

North Carolina School of the Arts
Semens Library
200 Waughtown Street
Winston-Salem, NC 27107

OHIO

Cincinnati

Public Library of Cincinnati and Hamilton
County
Art and Music Department
800 Vine Street
Cincinnati, OH 45202

Columbus

Ohio University Theatre Research
Institute
1712 Neil Avenue
Columbus, OH 43210

Kent

Kent State University Library
Department of Special Collections
Kent, OH 44242

OKLAHOMA

Norman

University of Oklahoma Drama Library
550 Parrington Oval
Norman, OK 73019

PENNSYLVANIA

Philadelphia

The Free Library of Philadelphia
Logan Square
Philadelphia, PA 19103
Tel: 215-686-5322
Address Inquiries to: Keith Doms, Director
Marie A. Davis, Deputy Director
Founded in: 1891
Member: ACA; NA; NACCA; NEA;
Annual Budget: $18,588,151

Historical Society of Pennsylvania
1300 Locust Street
Philadelphia, PA 19107

Temple University
Special Collections Department
Philadelphia, PA 19122

Pittsburgh

Carnegie Library of Pittsburgh, Art
Division
4400 Forbes Avenue
Pittsburgh, PA 15213

University of Pittsburgh, Special
Collections
363 Hilman Library
Pittsburgh, PA 15260

University Park

Pennsylvania State University
Fred Lewis Pattee Library
University Park, PA 16801

York

Historical Society of York County
Special Collections Department
York, PA 17405

RHODE ISLAND

Providence

Brown University, John Hay Library
20 Prospect Street
Providence, RI 02912

Rhode Island Historical Society
52 Power Street
Providence, RI 02906

Rhode Island School of Design
2 College Street
Providence, RI 02903

SOUTH CAROLINA

Charleston

South Carolina Historical Society
Fireproof Building
Charleston, SC 29401

TENNESSEE

Knoxville

University of Tennessee, Knoxville
Special Collections
Knoxville, TN 37916

Nashville

Public Library of Nashville and Davidson
County
Eighth Avenue, North and Union
Nashville, TN 37203

TEXAS

Austin

University of Texas
Hoblitzelle Theatre Arts Library
Austin, TX 78712

Dallas

Dallas Public Library
1954 Commerce Street
Dallas, TX 75201

Dallas Public Library, Fine Arts Division
1954 Commerce Street
Dallas, TX 75201

Southern Methodist University
McCord Theatre Collection
Dallas, TX 75275

Fort Worth

Fort Worth Public Library
Arts Division
Fort Worth, TX 76102

Texas Christian University, Mary Couts
Burnett Library
Drawer E.
Texas Christian University Station
Fort Worth, TX 76129

Houston

University of Houston, Anderson Library
4800 Calhoun Boulevard
Houston, TX 77004

San Antonio

San Antonio Public Library
Drama Division
San Antonio, TX 78205

Trinity University
715 Stadium Drive
San Antonio, TX 78212

UTAH

Provo

Brigham Young University
Clark Library
Provo, UT 84601

Salt Lake City

Salt Lake City Public Library, Information
Services
209 East Fifth Street
Salt Lake City, UT 84111
Tel: 801-363-5733

University of Utah
Drama Library
Salt Lake City, UT 84112

VERMONT

Montpelier

State of Vermont
Libraries Reference Service
111 State Street
Montpelier, VT 05602
Tel: 802-828-3261

VIRGINIA

Fairfax

Research Center for the Federal Theatre
Project
George Mason University
4400 University Drive
Fairfax, VA 22030

Richmond

Richmond Public Library
Performing Arts Division
101 East Franklin Street
Richmond, VA 23219
Tel: 808-649-4256

Virginia Historical Society
Special Collections Department
Richmond, VA 23219

Williamsburg

College of William and Mary
Drama Library
Williamsburg, VA 23185

WASHINGTON

Seattle

Seattle Public Library
100 Fourth Avenue
Seattle, WA 98104
Tel: 206-624-3800
Founded in: 1890
Annual Budget: $10,500,000

University of Washington Libraries
Drama Library BH-20
Seattle, WA 98195

Spokane

Gonzaga University, Crosby Library
East 502 Boone Avenue
Spokane, WA 99258

WEST VIRGINIA

Charleston

Kanawha County Public Library
123 Capitol Street
Charleston, WV 25301
Tel: 304-343-4646

WISCONSIN

Madison

University of Wisconsin, Memorial Library
728 State Street
Madison, WI 53706

Wisconsin Center for Film and Theatre
Research
1220 Linden Drive
Madison, WI 53706

Milwaukee

Marquette University Memorial Library
1415 West Wisconsin Avenue
Milwaukee, WI 53233
Tel: 307-634-5853

Milwaukee Public Library
814 West Wisconsin Avenue
Milwaukee, WI 53233

University of Wisconsin, Milwaukee
2311 East Hartford Avenue
Milwaukee, WI 53201

Oshkosh

University of Wisconsin, Polk Library
800 Algoma Boulevard
Oshkosh, WI 54901

WYOMING

Cheyenne

Laramie County Community College
Library
1400 East College Drive
Cheyenne, WY 82001
Tel: 307-634-5853

Laramie

University of Wyoming
William Robertson Coe Library
Laramie, WY 82070

CANADA

Calgary, Alberta

University of Calgary
2920 24th Avenue, NW
Calgary, Alberta, Canada T2N 1N4

Edmonton, Alberta

University of Alberta
Cameron Library
Edmonton, Alberta, Canada T6G 2J8

Vancouver, British Columbia

Vancouver Public Library
Language and Literature Division
750 Burrard Street
Vancouver, British Columbia, Canada V6Z
IX5

Sackville, New Brunswick

Mount Allison University
Ralph Pickard Bell Library
Sackville, New Brunswick, Canada E0A
3C0

Hamilton, Ontario

McMaster University, Mills Memorial
Library
Division of Archives and Research
Collections
Hamilton, Ontario, Canada L8S 4L6

Kingston, Ontario

Queens University at Kingston
Douglas Library
Kingston, Ontario, Canada K7L 5C4

Niagra Falls, Ontario

Houdini Magical Hall of Fame
1019 Centre Street
Niagra Falls, Ontario, Canada

North London, Ontario

University of Western Ontario
1151 Richmond Street
North London, Ontario, Canada N6A 3K7

Ottawa, Ontario

National Library of Canada
395 Wellington Street
Ottawa, Ontario, Canada K1A 0N3

Public Archives of Canada Library
395 Wellington Street
Ottawa, Ontario, Canada K1A 0N3

Stratford, Ontario

Stratford Shakespeare Festival Foundation
Archives and Collections
Post Office Box 520
Stratford, Ontario, Canada N5A 6V2

Toronto, Ontario

Metropolitan Toronto Library
Theatre Department
789 Yonge Street
Toronto, Ontario, Canada M4W 2G8

University of Toronto, Fisher Library
120 Saint George Street
Toronto, Ontario, Canada M5S 1A5

Montreal, Quebec

McGill University Libraries
3459 McTavish Street
Montreal, Quebec, Canada H3A 1Y1

12

Press Agents

Press agents perform two functions: they represent shows and they represent individual performers. The roles are not mutually exclusive; most agents have a roster of clients that includes celebrities and shows of all types.

In general, the press agent creates and oversees the advertising campaign of a show, arranges for maximum media attention to be given its stars, and supervises all relations with the press, including critics. Personal press agents are utilized by famous or almost famous theatre personalities to maximize their media exposure and to enhance, protect, or repair their public image.

Users of the *Guide* searching for a press agent in their locale will find that this section is a nationwide listing, and that all agents are members of ATPAM (Association of Theatrical Press Agents and Managers), a professional organization. Most agents are located in the major metropolitan areas, especially New York and Los Angeles. An experienced, well connected press agent in the theatrical hub, however, can be invaluable for the attention he or she can draw to a worthwhile regional production.

CALIFORNIA

Beverly Hills

Allen-Rolontz and Associates
201 North Robinson Boulevard, Suite C
Beverly Hills, CA 90211
Tel: 213-274-6793

Bar-Lor Associates
428 North Palm Drive
Beverly Hills, CA 90210
Tel: 213-278-1998

Belson and Klass Associates
211 South Beverly Drive
Beverly Hills, CA 90212
Tel: 213-274-9169
Member: Association of Talent Agents;

Blowitz and Canton Company
9350 Wilshire Boulevard, Suite 200
Beverly Hills, CA 902010
Tel: 213-275-9443

Dick Brooks, Unlimited
9465 Wilshire Boulevard
Beverly Hills, CA 90212
Tel: 213-273-8477

Wally Cedar Associates
Post Office Box 265
Beverly Hills, CA 90213
Tel: 213-550-7627

Jack Chutuk and Associates
9908 Santa Monica Boulevard
Beverly Hills, CA 90212
Tel: 213-552-1773

Cottman/Mazza
8484 Wilshire Boulevard, Suite 900
Beverly Hills, CA 90211
Tel: 213-655-4740

Dennis Davidson Associates
211 South Beverly Drive, Suite 200
Beverly Hills, CA 90212
Tel: 213-275-8505

The Flaire Agency
8693 Wilshire Boulevard, Suite 204
Beverly Hills, CA 90211
Tel: 213-659-6721

Gardiner and Associates
124 North Clark Drive, Suite 306
Beverly Hills, CA 90211
Tel: 213-659-3069

Gardiner/Fitzgerald/Smith
119 North San Vicente Boulevard
Beverly Hills, CA 90211
Tel: 213-936-2138

Goldberg/Ehrlich Enterprises,
   Incorporated
9701 Wilshire Boulevard, Suite 800
Beverly Hills, CA 90212
Tel: 213-550-5935

Mortie Guterman Agency
190 North Canon Drive, Suite 202
Beverly Hills, CA 90210
Tel: 213-652-3961

Guttman and Pam, Ltd.
120 El Camino Drive, Suite 104
Beverly Hills, CA 90212
Tel: 213-278-6775

Steve Jaffe Public Relations
9454 Wilshire Boulevard, Suite 405
Beverly Hills, CA 90212
Tel: 213-273-2501

Milton Kahn Associates, Incorporated
433 North Camden Drive, Suite 400
Beverly Hills, CA 90210
Tel: 213-550-6338

Chicki Kleiner Public Relations
1665 North Beverly Drive
Beverly Hills, CA 90210
Tel: 213-278-7797

Susan Meyer Public Relations
350 North Palm Drive
Beverly Hills, CA 90210
Tel: 213-278-4357

David Mirsch Enterprises
280 South Beverly Drive, Suite 311
Beverly Hills, CA 90212
Tel: 213-275-9485

Burbank

Lee Merrin and Associates
1200 Riverside Drive, Suite 233
Burbank, CA 91506
Tel: 213-845-6655

Cypress

Good Company Talent Agency
5400 Orange Avenue, Suite 126
Cypress, CA 90630
Tel: 213-598-2741

Encino

Phil Paladino Public Relations
16055 Ventura Boulevard, Suite 800
Encino, CA 91436
Tel: 213-501-3744

Hollywood

Tim Barker Public Relations
6525 Sunset Boulevard, 4th Floor
Hollywood, CA 90028
Tel: 213-461-2888

Bart-Milander Associates, Incorporated
6671 Sunset Boulevard, Suite 1574
Hollywood, CA 90028
Tel: 213-658-5454

Frank H. Berend and Associates
1635 Vista Del Mar
Hollywood, CA 90028
Tel: 213-464-5241

Elayne Blythe and Associates
1727 North Sycamore Avenue
Hollywood, CA 90028
Tel: 213-874-3644

Children's Talent Guild
1741 North Ivar Street, Suite 119
Hollywood, CA 90028
Tel: 213-466-7161

Columbia Artists Management
Incorporated (C.A.M.I.)
7060 Hollywood Boulevard, Suite 304
Hollywood, CA 90028
Tel: 213-462-6623

G.M.A.
1741 North Ivar Street, Suite 119
Hollywood, CA 90028
Tel: 213-466-7161

Jolly Public Relations
1585 Crossroads of the World, Suite 119
Hollywood, CA 90028
Tel: 213-469-4631

Kline Communications Corporation
1741 North Ivar Street, Suite 204
Hollywood, CA 90028
Tel: 213-462-6371

The Laufer Company
7060 Hollywood Boulevard
Hollywood, CA 90028
Tel: 213-467-3111

Susan Patricola Public Relations
6525 Sunset Boulevard, Suite 407
Hollywood, CA 90028
Tel: 213-461-2888

Irvine

Sonny Hayes Celebrity Center
2102 Business Center Drive
Irvine, CA 92715
Tel: 213-852-1888

Los Angeles

Bob Abrams and Associates
2030 Prosser Avenue
Los Angeles, CA 90025
Tel: 213-475-7739

Agee, Stevens and Acree, Incorporated
1474 North Kings Road
Los Angeles, CA 90069
Tel: 213-654-0941

APL Publicity
8732 Sunset Boulevard, Suite 220
Los Angeles, CA 90069
Tel: 213-657-6932

Hella Asch Communications
2385 Roscomore Road, Suite E16
Los Angeles, CA 90024
Tel: 213-476-7765

The Associated Literary Agency
8961 Sunset Boulevard, Suite 2A
Los Angeles, CA 90069
Tel: 213-273-6416

Elaine Auerbach Incorporated
8939 Cadillac Avenue
Los Angeles, CA 90034
Tel: 213-839-2179; 213-202-8788

Ricky Barr Agency
8833 Sunset Boulevard, Suite 308
Los Angeles, CA 90069
Tel: 213-652-7994

Berkhemer and Kline
261 South Figueroa Street, Suite 250
Los Angeles, CA 90012
Tel: 213-620-5711

Barbara Best, Incorporated
511 North San Vicente Boulevard
Los Angeles, CA 90048
Tel: 213-652-8025

Billings, M/S Publicity, Ltd.
8833 Sunset Boulevard, Suite 310
Los Angeles, CA 90069
Tel: 213-657-2027

The Blaine Group
180 South Sycamore Avenue, Suite 202
Los Angeles, CA 90036
Tel: 213-938-2577

Henri Bollinger Public Relations
9200 Sunset Boulevard, Suite 601
Los Angeles, CA 90069
Tel: 213-274-8483

Walter South Boxer Public Relations
9031 Phyllis Avenue
Los Angeles, CA 90069
Tel: 213-271-7720

Bracy and Schulz
3127 Ettrick Street
Los Angeles, CA 90027
Tel: 213-466-4666

Paul Brandon and Associates
9046 Sunset Boulevard
Los Angeles, CA 90069
Tel: 213-273-6173

Howard Brandy
521 Westbourne Drive
Los Angeles, CA 90048
Tel: 213-657-7940

Braverman-Mirisch, Incorporated
9255 Sunset Boulevard, Suite 308
Los Angeles, CA 90069
Tel: 213-274-5204

Jim Bridges Agency
933 North La Brea Avenue
Los Angeles, CA 90038
Tel: 213-874-3274

Tom Brocato and Associates,
Incorporated
6380 Wilshire Boulevard, Suite 1411
Los Angeles, CA 90048
Tel: 213-653-9570

Broder/Kurland Agency
9046 Sunset Boulevard, Suite 202
Los Angeles, CA 90069
Tel: 213-274-8921

The Brokaw Company
9255 Sunset Boulevard, Suite 411
Los Angeles, CA 90069
Tel: 213-273-2060

Jan Brown Public Relations
932 North Larrabee Street
Los Angeles, CA 90069
Tel: 213-855-0621

The Buddy Goldberg Company
Melros Avenue, Suite 305
Los Angeles, CA 90046
Tel: 213-852-1777

Carl Byoir and Associates, Incorporated
900 Wilshire Boulevard, Suite·1114
Los Angeles, CA 90017
Tel: 213-627-6421

Michael Catalano Public Relations
884 North Beverly Glen
Los Angeles, CA 90024
Tel: 213-474-5930

Chadwick Company
1841 Outpost Drive
Los Angeles, CA 90068
Tel: 213-851-1500

Esme Chandlee Public Relations
9021 Melrose Avenue, Suite 207
Los Angeles, CA 90069
Tel: 213-276-2369

Rita Chandler Associates Inc.
8833 Sunset Boulevard, Suite 405
Los Angeles, CA 90069
Tel: 213-855-0641

Brando Crespi and Associates
971 North La Cienega Boulevard, Suite
206
Los Angeles, CA 90069
Tel: 213-657-2010

Bernyce Cronin and Associates
539 South La Cienega Boulevard
Los Angeles, CA 90048
Tel: 213-273-8144

Judi Davidson Publicity
2020 Avenue of the Stars
Los Angeles, CA 90067
Tel: 213-557-3066

Donna Lee Davies Agency
3518 Cahuenga Boulevard West, Suite 318
Los Angeles, CA 90068
Tel: 213-850-0143

Dean, Joel and Associates and Joel Dean
and Associates
8961 Sunset Boulevard
Los Angeles, CA 90069
Tel: 213-550-8903

Girard Mitchell Digney
1023 Hancock Avenue, Suite 315
Los Angeles, CA 90069
Tel: 213-659-6328

Michael B. Druxman and Associates
8831 Sunset Boulevard, Suite 406
Los Angeles, CA 90069
Tel: 213-652-5592

Famous Toby Mamis Ent., Incorporated
(FTM)
9165 Sunset Boulevard, Suite 203
Los Angeles, CA 90069
Tel: 213-550-0130

Elizabeth A. Ferrell Associates
2451 Green Valley Road
Los Angeles, CA 90046
Tel: 213-654-4175

First Impressions
1462 North Stanley Avenue, Suite 212
Los Angeles, CA 90046
Tel: 213-876-3436

Patricia Fitzgerald Company
9026 Harratt Street
Los Angeles, CA 90069
Tel: 213-273-0020

Maury Foladare and Associates
8350 Santa Monica Boulevard, Suite 206A
Los Angeles, CA 90069
Tel: 213-654-5031

Frank Liberman and Associates,
Incorporated
9021 Melrose Avenue, Suite 308
Los Angeles, CA 90069
Tel: 213-278-1993; 213-276-5716
Address Inquiries to: Frank Liberman,
President, ATPAM
Member: PUA; AMPAS; ATPAM;

Freeman and Doff, Incorporated
8732 Sunset Boulevard, Suite 250
Los Angeles, CA 90069
Tel: 213-659-4700

The Garrett Company
8732 Sunset Boulevard, Suite 220
Los Angeles, CA 90069
Tel: 213-657-1711

Gloria Geale and Associates
9000 Sunset Boulevard, Suite 814
Los Angeles, CA 90036
Tel: 213-657-2125

Michael Gershman Communications
9229 Sunset Boulevard, Suite 601
Los Angeles, CA 90069
Tel: 213-278-4930

The Goddard Company
8833 Sunset Boulevard, Suite 400
Los Angeles, CA 90069
Tel: 213-657-4433

Sheldon Goldman Talent Agency
6363 Wilshire Boulevard, Suite 115
Los Angeles, CA 90048
Tel: 213-651-4576

Gotler Agency
9100 Sunset Boulevard, Suite 360
Los Angeles, CA 90069
Tel: 213-273-2811

Greene's Creative Expressions
439 South La Cienega Boulevard,
#110-112
Los Angeles, CA 90048
Tel: 213-278-9902

Jacquelin Green
7803 Sunset Boulevard
Los Angeles, CA 90046
Tel: 213-657-4629

Richard Gully
838 North Doheny Drive
Los Angeles, CA 90069
Tel: 213-273-3838

Hanson and Schwam Public Relations
9229 Sunset Boulevard, Suite 603
Los Angeles, CA 90069
Tel: 213-278-1255

Harshe-Rotman and Druck, Incorporated
3345 Wilshire Boulevard, Suite 909
Los Angeles, CA 90010
Tel: 213-385-5271

Hecht Harman Vukas Creative
Communications
1032 Hilldale Avenue
Los Angeles, CA 90069
Tel: 213-278-9339

Skip Heinecke Reflections, Incorporated
8961 Sunset Boulevard, Suite B
Los Angeles, CA 90069
Tel: 213-859-0833

Hill and Knowlton, Incorporated
5900 Wilshire Boulevard, Suite 1200
Los Angeles, CA 90036
Tel: 213-937-7460

Joe Hoenig and Associates
9056 Santa Monica Boulevard, Suite 201
Los Angeles, CA 90069
Tel: 213-276-3121

ICPR
9255 Sunset Boulevard, 8th Floor
Los Angeles, CA 90069
Tel: 213-550-8211

Sam Jacoby and Associates
8033 Sunset Boulevard, Suite 370
Los Angeles, CA 90046
Tel: 213-876-9784

The James Agency
971 North La Cienega Boulevard, Suite
204
Los Angeles, CA 90069
Tel: 213-659-2386

Noreen Jenny Communicates
Post Office Box 35149
Los Angeles, CA 90035
Tel: 213-657-7072

Bernard F. Kamins
11236 Cashmere Street
Los Angeles, CA 90049
Tel: 213-476-2888

Kramer and Reiss Public Relations
9100 Sunset Boulevard, Suite 240
Los Angeles, CA 90069

Tel: 213-273-3242

Laurence Laurie and Associates
8899 Beverly Boulevard, Suite 906
Los Angeles, CA 90048
Tel: 213-274-0851

Michael Levine
3630 Wilshire Boulevard, Suite 202
Los Angeles, CA 90010
Tel: 213-387-8113

Levinson Associates
927 North La Cienega Boulevard
Los Angeles, CA 90069
Tel: 213-657-8800

Lewis Company, Ltd.
650 North Bronson Avenue
Los Angeles, CA 90004
Tel: 213-469-1600

Frank Liberman and Associates
9021 Melrose Avenue, Suite 308
Los Angeles, CA 90069
Tel: 213-278-1993

Lippin and Grant, Incorporated
8124 West Third Street, Suite 204
Los Angeles, CA 90048
Tel: 213-653-5910

Lipsman and Associates
8961 Sunset Boulevard, Suite 2E
Los Angeles, CA 90069
Tel: 213-273-3200

Samuel Lurie
1405 North Laurel Avenue
Los Angeles, CA 90046
Tel: 213-656-1425
Member: ATPAM;

Mahoney/Wasserman and Associates
117 North Robertson Boulevard
Los Angeles, CA 90048
Tel: 213-550-3922

Bruce Merrin Organization
9000 Sunset Boulevard, Suite 610
Los Angeles, CA 90069
Tel: 213-550-8094

Norman J. Millen Public Relations
8430 Santa Monica Boulevard, Suite 210
Los Angeles, CA 90069
Tel: 213-654-8853

Morgan Company
2472 North Beachwood Drive
Los Angeles, CA 90068
Tel: 213-466-9757

Palmer and Simes Public Relations
9034 Sunset Boulevard, Suite 250
Los Angeles, CA 90069
Tel: 213-278-2361

David F. Parry and Associates
5900 Wilshire Boulevard, Suite 1240
Los Angeles, CA 90036
Tel: 213-938-7138

Pickwick/Maslansky/Koenigsberg Public
Relations, Incorporated (PMK)
8642 Melrose Avenue, Suite 200

Los Angeles, CA 90069
Tel: 213-854-3500

Sandy Pollock
9007 Rangely Avenue
Los Angeles, CA 90048
Tel: 213-271-8459

PRA (Public Relations Associates)
552 Norwich Drive
Los Angeles, CA 90048
Tel: 213-659-0380

Tom Brocato and Associates,
   Incorporated
6380 Wilshire Boulevard, Suite 1411
Los Angeles, CA 90048
Tel: 213-653-9570
Address Inquiries to: Thomas Brocato,
   President, ATPAM
Member: ATPAM;

Bill Watters and Associates
1271 Saint Ives Place
Los Angeles, CA 90069
Tel: 213-272-0148
Founded in: 1952
Member: ATPAM;
Description: ATPAM press agents representing many organizations and individuals in performing arts, theatre and film.

Mission Hills

Stanley Musgrove Public Relations
11010 Arleta Avenue
Mission Hills, CA 91340
Tel: 213-465-2027; 213-782-3092

North Hollywood

Laurence Frank and Company
4605 Lankershim Boulevard, Suite 220
North Hollywood, CA 91602
Tel: 213-508-6111

Garon, Bob Public Relations
11104 La Maida Street
North Hollywood, CA 91601
Tel: 213-760-0042

Mike Marx Enterprises
11130 Huston Street
North Hollywood, CA 91601
Tel: 213-506-8488

Palos Verdes

Wayne Coombs Agency
75 Malaga Cove Plaza
Palos Verdes, CA 90274
Tel: 213-377-0420

Pasedena

All Talent Agency
2437 East Washington Boulevard
Pasadena, CA 91104
Tel: 213-797-2422

San Diego

Rose Perius
c/o Continental Promotions, 2749 Erie
San Diego, CA 92117
Tel: 714-298-8858; 714-276-6521
Address Inquiries to: Rose Perius, ATPAM

Member: ATPAM;

San Francisco

Kolmar Raush Associates
3216 Geary Boulevard
San Francisco, CA 94118
Tel: 415-387-1727
Address Inquiries to: Hanns Kolmar, ATPAM
Virginia Kolmar, ATPAM
Founded in: 1952
Member: ATPAM;

Sherman Oaks

Aleon Bennet and Associates
13455 Ventura Boulevard, Suite 212
Sherman Oaks, CA 91423
Tel: 213-990-8070

Estelle Endler Associates
3920 Sunny Oak Road
Sherman Oaks, CA 91403
Tel: 213-783-7110

Mamakos and Associates
4348 Van Nuys Boulevard, Suite 207
Sherman Oaks, CA 91403
Tel: 213-788-0164

Charles Pomerantz, Ltd.
15300 Ventura Boulevard, Suite 412
Sherman Oaks, CA 91403
Tel: 213-872-0080

Studio City

Luis Alvarez
11264 Sunshine Terrace
Studio City, CA 91604
Tel: 213-877-8779; 213-339-5907
Address Inquiries to: Luis Alvarez
Member: ATPAM;

Career Artists International
11030 Ventura Boulevard, Suite 3
Studio City, CA 91604
Tel: 213-980-1315

David Gest and Associates
13251 Ventura Boulevard, Suite 2C
Studio City, CA 91604
Tel: 213-986-7474

Lilly Lipton International
3217 Dona Emilia Drive
Studio City, CA 91604
Tel: 213-656-6842

Rae Lynn Public Relations
3670 Buena Park Drive
Studio City, CA 91604
Tel: 213-761-6994

Toluca Lake

Michael Logan Public Relations
4321 Cahuenga Boulevard
Toluca Lake, CA 91602
Tel: 213-985-0647

Paul Marsh and Associates
Post Office Box 2119
Toluca Lake, CA 91602
Tel: 213-761-3750

West Covina

Carrolls Agency, Incorporated
2100 Kings Crest Drive
West Covina, CA 91791
Tel: 213-966-6327

Westlake Village

Coast Enterprises
Post Office Box 4621
Westlake Village, CA 91359
Tel: 213-889-9714

The Charles A. Moses Company
32108 Beachlake Lane
Westlake Village, CA 91361
Tel: 213-707-1360

COLORADO
Denver

V.R. Gagnon
350 Jersey Street
Denver, CO 80220
Tel: 303-322-1989; 303-388-2836
Member: ATPAM;

MASSACHUSETTS
Boston

Terese M. Sarno
Post Office Box 1817
Boston, MA 02105
Address Inquiries to: Terese M. Sarno,
   ATPAM
Member: ATPAM;

West Medford

Dance Plant, Incorporated
Post Office Box 66
West Medford, MA 02156
Tel: 617-395-2199
Address Inquiries to: Diane Pariser, Director
Francine Smith, Director

NEW YORK
Brooklyn

Tom Kerrigan
1 Montague Terrace
Brooklyn, NY 11201
Tel: 212-624-1193
Founded in: 1972
Member: ATPAM;

Floral Park

Rima Corben
270 14 L Grand Central Parkway
Floral Park, NY 11005
Tel: 212-225-5141
Address Inquiries to: Rima Corben, ATPAM
Member: ATPAM;

Little Neck

Capricorn Management
34-12 255th Street
Little Neck, NY 11363
Tel: 212-631-9229

New York

Ted Goldsmith
125 West 12th Street
New York, NY 10011
Tel: 212-929-7226
Address Inquiries to: Ted Goldsmith, Press
  Agent
Member: ATPAM;

New York

Harold Abbey
165 West 57th Street
New York, NY 10019
Tel: 212-841-9678
Address Inquiries to: Harold Abbey, Press
  Agent

Clarence Allsopp
55 West 42 Street, Room 1547
New York, NY 10036
Address Inquiries to: Clarence Allsopp,
  ATPAM
Member: ATPAM;

Alpert/Levine Public Relations
1501 Broadway, Suite 1502
New York, NY 10036
Tel: 212-354-5940
Address Inquiries to: Michael Alpert, ATPAM
  Marilyn LeVine, ATPAM
Founded in: 1967
Member: ATPAM;
Description: Publicity and press representatives.

Howard Atlee
1560 Broadway, Suite 507
New York, NY 10036
Tel: 212-575-9415
Address Inquiries to: Howard Atlee, ATPAM
Member: ATPAM;

Leslie Brooke Bailey
c/o New York City Ballet, New York State
  Theatre
  Lincoln Center
New York, NY 10023
Tel: 212-877-4700

Susan Bloch
165 West 66th Street
New York, NY 10023
Tel: 212-873-0706

Phillip Bloom
1995 Broadway
New York, NY 10023
Tel: 212-243-5363
Address Inquiries to: Phillip Bloom, Press
  Agent

Herbert Breslin
119 West 57th Street
New York, NY 10019
Tel: 212-246-5480
Address Inquiries to: Herbert Breslin, Press

Agent
Stanley Brody
649 East 14th Street
New York, NY 10009
Tel: 212-228-7863
Address Inquiries to: Stanley Brody, Press
  Agent

Mary Bryant
165 West 46th Street
New York, NY 10036
Tel: 212-575-1166
Address Inquiries to: Mary Bryant, Press
  Agent

Canaan Associates
51 East 42 Street, Suite 1503
New York, NY 10017
Tel: 212-682-4155
Member: ATPAM;

Barbara Carroll
1501 Broadway
New York, NY 10036
Tel: 212-391-6994
Address Inquiries to: Barbara Carroll, Press
  Agent

Bruce Cohen
2054 Broadway
New York, NY 10023
Tel: 212-580-9548
Address Inquiries to: Bruce Cohen, Press
  Agent

Peter Conway
155 West 68th Street
New York, NY 10023
Tel: 212-799-5998

Patt Dale
159 West 53rd Street
New York, NY 10019
Tel: 212-245-5855
Address Inquiries to: Patt Dale, Press Agent

Danceservices
New York, NY 10023
Tel: 212-580-4500
Address Inquiries to: Judith Finell, President

Harry Davies
350 West 57th Street
New York, NY 10019
Tel: 212-247-8522
Address Inquiries to: Harry Davies, Press
  Agent

Virginia Donaldson
c/o New York City Ballet, New York State
  Theatre
  Lincoln Center
New York, NY 10023
Tel: 212-TR - 4700

Alan L. Eichler
333 West 14th Street
New York, NY 10014
Tel: 212-929-1130
Address Inquiries to: Alan L. Eichler, Press
  Agent

Max Eisen
234 West 44th Street
New York, NY 10036
Tel: 212-391-1072
Address Inquiries to: Max Eisen, Press Agent

Joshua Ellis
45 West 34th Street
New York, NY 10001
Tel: 212-947-0515
Address Inquiries to: Joshua Ellis, Press
  Agent

Bill Evans
165 West 46th Street
New York, NY 10036
Tel: 212-489-6530
Address Inquiries to: Bill Evans, Press Agent

Richard Falk
1472 Broadway
New York, NY 10036
Tel: 212-221-0043
Address Inquiries to: Richard Falk, Press
  Agent
Founded in: 1940
Annual Budget: $100,000

Nini Finklestein
850 Third Avenue, 14th Floor
New York, NY 10022
Tel: 212-752-1408
Address Inquiries to: Nini Finklestein, Press
  Agent

Becky Flora
247 West 21st Street
New York, NY 10011
Tel: 212-242-7379
Address Inquiries to: Becky Flora, Press
  Agent

Chester Fox
3 West 57th Street
New York, NY 10019
Tel: 212-371-1799
Address Inquiries to: Chester Fox, Press
  Agent

Charles France
57 West 75th Street
New York, NY 10023
Tel: 212-362-9243
Address Inquiries to: Charles France, Press
  Agent

Jane Friedman
250 West 57th Street
New York, NY 10107
Tel: 212-245-5587
Address Inquiries to: Jane Friedman, Press
  Agent

Irene Gandy
234 West 44th Street
New York, NY 10036
Tel: 212-391-1072
Address Inquiries to: Irene Gandy, Press
  Agent

Robert Ganshaw
157 West 57th Street
New York, NY 10019
Tel: 212-489-6745

Address Inquiries to: Robert Ganshaw, Press
Agent

Faith Geer
485 West 22nd Street
New York, NY 10011
Tel: 212-243-3353
Address Inquiries to: Faith Geer, Press Agent

Edwin & Michael Gifford
1211 Park Avenue
New York, NY 10028
Tel: 212-427-7600
Address Inquiries to: Edwin Gifford, Press
Agent
Michael Gifford, Press Agent

John Gingrich
130 West 56th Street
New York, NY 10019
Tel: 212-757-8060
Address Inquiries to: John Gingrich, Press
Agent

Barbara Glenn
234 West 44th Street
New York, NY 10036
Tel: 212-391-1072
Address Inquiries to: Barbara Glenn, Press
Agent

Mark Goldstaub
312 West 48th Street
New York, NY 10036
Tel: 212-582-2879
Address Inquiries to: Mark Goldstaub, Press
Agent
Member: ATPAM;

Frank Goodman Publicity
1776 Broadway
New York, NY 10019
Tel: 212-246-4180
Address Inquiries to: Frank Goodman,
Publicist
Arlene Goodman, Vice President
Founded in: 1956
Member: ATPAM;
Annual Budget: $500,000
Description: Specialists in entertainment public relations for theatre, television and film.

Meg Gordean
c/o Gurfman and Murtha Associates
162 West 56th Street
New York, NY 10019
Tel: 212-245-4771
Address Inquiries to: Meg Gordean, ATPAM
Member: ATPAM;

Marian Graham
135 East 50th Street
New York, NY 10022
Tel: 212-753-7110
Address Inquiries to: Marian Graham, Press
Agent
Member: ATPAM;

Peter Gravina
115 East 92nd Street
New York, NY 10028
Tel: 212-369-7086
Member: ATPAM;

Jan Greenberg
420 Riverside Drive
New York, NY 10025
Tel: 212-864-3306
Address Inquiries to: Jan Greenberg, Press
Agent
Member: ATPAM;

Gurtman and Murtha Associates,
Incorporated
162 West 56th Street
New York, NY 10019
Tel: 212-245-4771; 212-245-4772
Address Inquiries to: James Murtha, ATPAM
Bernard Gurtman, ATPAM
Founded in: 1970
Member: Friars Club; ATPAM;
Description: The firm also acts as a management and booking firm for artists.

Wendy Hanson
1001 Park Avenue
New York, NY 10028
Tel: 212-734-3406
Address Inquiries to: Wendy Hanson, Press
Agent
Member: ATPAM;

Lewis Harmon
205 West 57th Street
New York, NY 10019
Tel: 212-247-0354
Address Inquiries to: Lewis Harmon
Member: ATPAM;

Shirley Herz
165 West 48th Street
New York, NY 10036
Tel: 212-221-8466
Address Inquiries to: Shirley Herz, Press
Agent
Member: ATPAM;

Ruth Hider
310 West 56th Street
New York, NY 10019
Tel: 212-757-6734
Address Inquiries to: Ruth Hider, Press Agent
Member: ATPAM;

Virginia Holden
4 East 88th Street
New York, NY 10028
Tel: 212-534-5382
Address Inquiries to: Virginia Holden, Press
Agent
Member: ATPAM;

Mae Hong
525 East 14th Street
New York, NY 10009
Tel: 212-475-7393
Address Inquiries to: Mae Hong, Press Agent
Member: ATPAM;

Fred Hoot
230 West 55th Street
New York, NY 10019
Tel: 212-246-3346
Address Inquiries to: Fred Hoot, Press Agent
Member: ATPAM;

John Howlett
48 West 89th Street
New York, NY 10024
Tel: 212-799-3003
Address Inquiries to: John Howlett, Press
Agent
Member: ATPAM;

Betty Lee Hunt
1501 Broadway
New York, NY 10036
Tel: 212-354-0880
Address Inquiries to: Betty Lee Hunt, Press
Agent
Member: ATPAM;

Virginia Hymes
465 West End Avenue
New York, NY 10024
Tel: 212-873-8616
Address Inquiries to: Virginia Hymes, Press
Agent
Member: ATPAM;

Jacksina and Freedman
1501 Broadway
New York, NY 10036
Tel: 212-921-7979
Address Inquiries to: Judy Jacksina, Press
Agent
Member: ATPAM;

Ellen Jacobs
252 West 73rd Street
New York, NY 10023
Tel: 212-496-8353
Address Inquiries to: Ellen Jacobs, ATPAM
Kathy Ellin, assistant
Founded in: 1980
Member: ATPAM;
Description: Press agents primarily devoted to developing and establishing press contacts and relations for clients as a means of keeping them in the public eye. Work entails publicizing upcoming concerts, performances and exhibits and also creating special events to engage the interest of the media, and conceiving wide variety of press and promotional materials for clients.

Jean Dalrymple Associates
150 West 55th Street
New York, NY 10019
Tel: 212-246-7820
Address Inquiries to: Jean Dalrymple, Owner,
ATPAM
Homer Poupart, Associate, ATPAM
Member: ATPAM;

Diane Judge
38 East 38th Street
New York, NY 10016
Tel: 212-685-2690
Address Inquiries to: Diane Judge, Press
Agent
Member: ATPAM;

Mark Kappel
252 West 76th Street
New York, NY 10023
Tel: 212-724-3889
Member: ATPAM;

KLS Management, Ltd.
76 Pearl Street
New York, NY 10004
Tel: 212-741-0368
Address Inquiries to: Kaylynn Sullivan,
　Director, ATPAM
Member: ATPAM;

Warren Knowlton
45 West 34th Street
New York, NY 10001
Tel: 212-947-0515
Address Inquiries to: Warren Knowlton, Press
　Agent
Member: ATPAM;

Marvin Kohn
234 West 44th Street
New York, NY 10036
Tel: 212-398-0022
Address Inquiries to: Marvin Kohn, Press
　Agent
Member: ATPAM;

Richard Kornberg
New York Shakespeare Festival
425 Lafayette Street
New York, NY 10003
Tel: 212-598-7100
Address Inquiries to: Richard Kornberg,
　Press Agent
Member: ATPAM;

Seymour Krawitz
850 Seventh Avenue
New York, NY 10019
Tel: 212-CI - 1120
Address Inquiries to: Seymour Krawitz,
　ATPAM
Founded in: 1953
Member: ATPAM;

Robert W. Larkin
250 West 82nd Street, #31
New York, NY 10024
Tel: 212-595-4630
Member: ATPAM;

Ellen Levene
42 Perry Street
New York, NY 10014
Tel: 212-255-7997
Founded in: 1977

The Massimo Agency
1841 Broadway, Suite 1105
New York, NY 10023
Tel: 212-265-1003
Founded in: 1978
Member: ATPAM;

Pentacle
200 W 72nd St., Suite 20
New York, NY 10023
Tel: 212-580-8107
Address Inquiries to: Mara Greenberg,
　Director
　Ivan Sygoda, Company Director
Founded in: 1975
Member: ATPAM;
Annual Budget: $125,000

Performing Artservices, Incorporated
463 West Street
New York, NY 10014
Tel: 212-989-4953
Member: ATPAM;

Susan Schulman and Associates
1501 Broadway
New York, NY 10036
Member: ATPAM;

Staten Island

Michael T. Sheehan
914 Richmond Terrace
Staten Island, NY 10301
Tel: 212-448-2500
Address Inquiries to: Michael T. Sheehan,
　ATPAM Executive Director
Founded in: 1976
Member: ATPAM;

PENNSYLVANIA

Philadelphia

F. Randolph Associates
1300 Arch Street
Philadelphia, PA 19107
Tel: 215-567-6662
Address Inquiries to: F. Randolph Swartz,
　ATPAM
Member: ATPAM;
Description: Press agents that also develop
products for the performing arts, manage-
ment consultant and ad agency. See also,
listing under suppliers.

CANADA

Toronto,Ontario

Marcia McClung
c/o National Ballet of Canada
157 King Street East
Toronto,Ontario, Canada M5C 1G9
Tel: 416-362-1041
Address Inquiries to: Marcia McClung,
　Publicity Director, ATPAM
Member: ATPAM;

13

Producers

The role of "producer" in the theatre of the 1980's, is a difficult one to define. There are basically two types. The first is an active participant in fundraising and organizing a show, while the other is a "producer" in name only, acting primarily as a source of cash and prestige. Increasingly, this role is filled not just by wealthy individuals, but by major corporations especially motion picture companies.

In addition to the entries listed here, the "Theatre" category should be consulted, especially by those living outside of the major metropolitan areas. Regional, community, and summer theatres frequently act as their own producers, often with considerable success. They are more easily approached than the major producing organizations, which very often return unsolicited material unopend. If the aspiring playwright, composer, or lyricist is determined to enter the urban market however, it is best to contact a well-established agent, listed under a separate heading, "Talent Agents".

CALIFORNIA

Beverly Hills

Lawrence Kasha
2229 Gloaming Way
Beverly Hills, CA 90210
Tel: 213-276-1760

Kaslan Productions
1119 Gloaming Way
Beverly Hills, CA 90210
Tel: 213-276-1760

Hollywood

Rapport Entertainment Corporation
1023 North Labrea Avenue
Hollywood, CA 90028
Tel: 213-876-9033
Address Inquiries to: Richard Stobie, General
  Manager
Founded in: 1968
Annual Budget: $5,000

Los Angeles

Mike Merrick
9200 Sunset Boulevard
Los Angeles, CA 90069
Tel: 213-278-1211

NEW YORK

New York

George Abbott
1270 Avenue of the Americas
New York, NY 10020
Tel: 212-399-0960

Doris Cole Abrahams
c/o Transart Productions
1501 Broadway
New York, NY 10036
Tel: 212-869-9669

Roger Ailes
230 Central Park South
New York, NY 10019
Tel: 212-765-3022

Alexander H. Cohen, Producer
225 West 44th Street
New York, NY 10036
Tel: 212-764-1900
Description: Broadway Producer.

Allen, Friedman, Nichols, and Meyer
Regency Communication, Limited
405 Park Avenue
New York, NY 10022
Tel: 212-935-1717
Description: Broadway Producers.

AMAS Repertory Theatre
1 East 104th Street
New York, NY 10029
Tel: 212-369-8000

American Place Theatre
111 West 46th Street
New York, NY 10036
Tel: 212-246-3730
Address Inquiries to: Wynn Handman,
  Artistic Director

American Theatre Productions
c/o Thomas W. Mallow
1500 Broadway
New York, NY 10036
Tel: 212-391-8160

Craig Anderson and Associates
1501 Broadway
New York, NY 10036
Tel: 212-944-5970

A.N.T.A.
245 West 52nd Street
New York, NY 10019
Tel: 212-757-4133

Lyn Austin
18 East 68th Street
New York, NY 10021
Tel: 212-371-9610

Azenverg, Bradley, Krauss and Siders
165 West 46th Street
New York, NY 10036
Tel: 212-489-6530
Description: Broadway Producers.

Bill Baird
41 Union Square
New York, NY 10003
Tel: 212-989-9840

Barry M. Brown and Fritz Holt, Producers
250 West 52nd Street
New York, NY 10019
Tel: 212-807-0982
Description: Broadway producers.

Ira Bernstein
15 East 48th Street
New York, NY 10017
Tel: 212-758-8730

Joseph Beruh
1650 Broadway
New York, NY 10019
Tel: 212-765-5910

David Black Productions, Incorporated
251 East 51st Street
New York, NY 10022
Tel: 212-753-1188

Bloomgarden, Bloomgarden and Marsolais
275 Central Park West
New York, NY 10024
Tel: 212-787-5481
Description: Broadway producers.

Rufus Botzow
35 West 76th Street
New York, NY 10023
Tel: 212-362-1196

Charles Bowden Productions
919 Third Avenue
New York, NY 10022
Tel: 212-371-5450

Frederick Brisson
745 5th Avenue
New York, NY 10022
Tel: 212-724-2526
Description: Broadway producer.

Jeff G. Britton
c/o One Star Ltd.
1501 Broadway
New York, NY 10036
Tel: 212-944-0448

Robert A. Buckley
165 West 46th Street
New York, NY 10036
Tel: 212-719-3720

Zev Bufman Entertainment
1466 Broadway
New York, NY 10036
Tel: 212-719-5000; 305-673-8011

Courtney Burr
5 Tudor City Place
New York, NY 10017
Tel: 212-687-0987

Callahan, Springer and
Stephens-Weitenhoffer
Little Theatre, 240 West 44th Street
New York, NY 10036
Tel: 212-221-3677
Description: Broadway producers.

Arthur Cantor, Producer
234 West 44th Street
New York, NY 10036
Tel: 212-664-1290
Description: In addition to theatre, Mr. Cantor has a film booking company and does advance public relations.

Carousel Communications Corporation
c/o Richard Bell and J. Lloyd Grant
1414 Avenue of the Americas
New York, NY 10019
Tel: 212-688-4112

The Cates Brothers
119 West 57th Street
New York, NY 10019
Tel: 212-765-1300

Cheryl Crawford, Moe Septee, Chelsea
Theatre
400 East 52nd Street
New York, NY 10022
Tel: 212-759-5484
Description: Broadway producers.

Circle in the Square
1633 Broadway
New York, NY 10019
Tel: 212-581-3270
Address Inquiries to: Ted Mann, Producer
Description: Broadway Producer

Circle Repertory Company
161 Avenue of the Americas
New York, NY 10013

Tel: 212-691-3210

City Center of Music and Drama
1860 Broadway
New York, NY 10023
Tel: 212-399-0550

David Cogan
350 Fifth Avenue
New York, NY 10118
Tel: 212-947-7600

Robert Colby
37 West 57th Street
New York, NY 10019
Tel: 212-759-8730

CSC Repertory
136 East 13th Street
New York, NY 10003
Tel: 212-477-5808

D/H Productions
250 West 57th Street, #1913
New York, NY 10019
Tel: 212-582-5656
Address Inquiries to: Richard Humphrey
Description: Producers of Broadway and Off Broadway theatre; film packagers.

Hoburn Management Corporation
c/o Howard J. Burnett/Maggi Burnett
235 East 48th Street
New York, NY 10017
Tel: 212-980-6760

Charles Hollerith Jr.
18 West 55th Street
New York, NY 10019
Tel: 212-586-6295

Fritz Holt
250 West 52nd Street
New York, NY 10019
Tel: 212-807-0982

Richard Horner Associates
65 West 55th Street
New York, NY 10019
Tel: 212-245-8245

Robert Jani Productions
c/o Radio City Music Hall
1260 Avenue of the Americas
New York, NY 10020
Tel: 212-246-1532

Kaslan Productions
353 West 56th Street
New York, NY 10019
Tel: 212-246-2342

Kaufman/Lerner Productions
105 West 55th Street
New York, NY 10019
Tel: 212-757-5825

Norman Kean
240 West 47th Street
New York, NY 10036
Tel: 212-586-7870

King-Hitzig Productions
665 Fifth Avenue
New York, NY 10022
Tel: 212-644-0602

Jay Kingwill
226 West 47th Street
New York, NY 10036
Tel: 212-354-1239

Joseph Kipness
c/o Kippys Productions, Charlotte Dicker
261 West 44th Street
New York, NY 10036
Tel: 212-719-3540

Terry Allen Kramer
711 Fifth Avenue
New York, NY 10022
Tel: 212-832-8000

Marvin A. Krauss
250 West 52nd Street
New York, NY 10019
Tel: 212-246-4460

David S. Landay
353 West 56th Street
New York, NY 10019
Tel: 212-246-2342

Edgar Lansbury
1650 Broadway
New York, NY 10019
Tel: 212-765-5910

Steve Leber and David Krebs
65 West 55th Street
New York, NY 10019
Tel: 212-765-2600

Orin Lehman
67 East 82nd Street
New York, NY 10028
Tel: 212-734-6450

Jack Lenny
140 West 58th Street
New York, NY 10019
Tel: 212-582-0270

Alan Jay Lerner
420 Madison Avenue
New York, NY 10017
Tel: 212-679-2211

Herman Levin
424 Madison Avenue
New York, NY 10017
Tel: 212-758-3344

Bill Liberman
276 Riverside Drive
New York, NY 10025
Tel: 212-662-1290

James Lipton
159 East 80th Street
New York, NY 10021
Tel: 212-535-9500

Burton L. Litwin
1776 Broadway
New York, NY 10019
Tel: 212-245-1100

Lester Lockwood
325 West End Avenue
New York, NY 10023
Tel: 212-787-4111

Joshua Logan
435 East 52nd Street
New York, NY 10022
Tel: 212-752-1910

Lucille Lortel
60 West 57th Street
New York, NY 10019
Tel: 212-757-8359

John Lotas
355 Lexington Avenue
New York, NY 10017
Tel: 212-661-5355

Edwin S. Lowe Productions
375 Park Avenue
New York, NY 10152
Tel: 212-421-5800

Manhattan Theatre Club
321 East 73rd Street
New York, NY 10021
Tel: 212-288-2500

Elliot Martin
152 West 58th Street
New York, NY 10019
Tel: 212-245-4176

Elizabeth Mc Cann and Nelle Nugent
1501 Broadway
New York, NY 10036
Tel: 212-354-9570

David Merrick
1515 Broadway
New York, NY 10036
Tel: 212-398-9875

Arthur R. Mills Associates
47 West 68th Street
New York, NY 10023
Tel: 212-787-1066

Jerome Minskoff
1350 Avenue of the Americas
New York, NY 10019
Tel: 212-765-9700

Lee A. Minskoff
1350 Avenue of the Americas
New York, NY 10019
Tel: 212-765-9700

Ruth Mitchell
1270 Avenue of the Americas
New York, NY 10020
Tel: 212-399-0960

Music Fair Productions
32 East 57th Street
New York, NY 10022
Tel: 212-759-2810

Nederlander Productions
1564 Broadway
New York, NY 10036
Tel: 212-765-3096

Negro Ensemble Company
424 West 55th Street
New York, NY 10019
Tel: 212-575-5860

Lore Noto
181 Sullivan Street
New York, NY 10022
Tel: 212-832-7010

Gerard Oestreicher
680 Madison Avenue
New York, NY 10021
Tel: 212-838-3000

Dorothy Olim Associates, Inc.
1540 Broadway
New York, NY 10036
Tel: 212-869-8282

Lester Osterman
1650 Broadway
New York, NY 10019
Tel: 586-557-

Joseph Papp
c/o N.Y. Shakespeare Festival
425 Lafayette Street
New York, NY 10003
Tel: 212-598-7100

Hildy Parks
225 West 44th Street
New York, NY 10036
Tel: 212-757-1200

Phoenix Theatre
1540 Broadway
New York, NY 10036
Tel: 212-730-0787
Address Inquiries to: T. Edward Hambleton,
   Managing Director

Producer's Collaborative
240 West 44th Street
New York, NY 10036
Tel: 212-390-1030
Address Inquiries to: Lindsay Gambini
Mark B. Simon
Founded in: 1983
Description: Young producers looking for
properties and options.

Producers Foundation/Association
2095 Broadway, Suite 405
New York, NY 10023
Tel: 212-496-9121; 212-496-9122/¾
Address Inquiries to: Joel Peel, Artistic
   Director
   John Smith, Managing Director
Founded in: 1964
Member: AEA; ACUCAA; NAPAMA;
Annual Budget: $300,000
Description: Producers Foundation/Associa-
tion is recognized as one of the finest theatre
companies performing for young audiences.
They are proud of the reputation they have
earned over the last twelve years, and strive
to bring the best in educational, professional, and englightening theatre to young peo-
ple-from kindergarten through college.
Aside from their book shows, they present
the finest artists in dance, puppetry, mime
and country western. They tour extensively
throughout the United States with their
musical theatre, and the award winning Joffrey Ballet concert Group.

Richard Adler, Producer
870 United Nations Plaza
New York, NY 10017
Tel: 212-838-5907
Address Inquiries to: Richard Adler, Producer
   Description: Broadway Producer.

Richard Barr, Charles Woodward and
Terry Speigel, Producers
226 West 47th Street
New York, NY 10036
Tel: 212-354-7470
Description: Broadway producers.

Steven Beckler and Thomas C. Smith,
Producers
225 West 84th Street, Apartment 2A
New York, NY 10024
Tel: 212-799-0634
Description: Broadway producers.

Pound Ridge

Stuart Ostrow
Post Office Box 188
Pound Ridge, NY 10576
Tel: 914-764-4432

14

Publications & Publishers

The listings in this section encompass two areas of print media: magazines and newspapers which specialize in or devote considerable space to theatre; and book publishers with a significant number of theatre titles in print.

The magazines listed vary widely, from a technical publication such as *Theatre Crafts* to a more general entertainment daily, *Variety*. The publishers are equally varied, from Samuel French, Inc., which publishes only plays, to companies publishing on a wide variety of subjects, including theatre, such as Macmillan, Inc.

Writers submitting material to be considered for publication should follow some simple steps. They should address a query letter to the appropriate editor, with an outline of the proposed article or book. With the latter, a sample chapter is best. Return postage should always be included. Consider carefully the description offered with each entry before mailing, since knowing the orientation of a publisher can save unnecessary postage, wasted time, and needless rejection notices.

ALABAMA

University

University of Alabama Press
Post Office Box 2877
University, AL 35486

ARIZONA

Tuscon

University of Arizona Press
Post Office Box 3398
Tuscon, AZ 85722

CALIFORNIA

Berkeley

East Bay Review
East Bay Performance
1800 Dwight Way
Berkeley, CA 94703
Description: Published bi-weekly.

University of California Press
2223 Fulton Street
Berkeley, CA 94720

Beverly Hills

Performing Arts
K and K Publishing, Incorporated
9348 Santa Monica Boulevard
Beverly Hills, CA 90210
Description: Published monthly.

Claremont

Mime Journal
Pomona College Theatre Department
Claremont, CA 91711
Description: Mime Journal is back in print with features and articles especially related to the art of mime.

Hollywood

Channel One
c/o Robert L. Smith
1229 Highland Avenue
Hollywood, CA 90038
Description: Published quarterly.

Daily Variety
1400 North Cahuenga Boulevard
Hollywood, CA 90028
Description: Published five times per week.

Hollywood Reporter
6715 Sunset Boulevard
Hollywood, CA 90028
Description: Published daily.

T.G.I.F.
T.G.I.F. Enterprises
Box 1683
Hollywood, CA 90028
Description: Published bi-weekly.

Los Angeles

Creative Actors Association
1626 North Wilcox, #300
Los Angeles, CA 90028
Description: Publishers of the *Entertainment Handbook*, an alphabetical and geographical directory.

Hollywood Drama-Logue
Post Office Box 38771
Los Angeles, CA 90028
Tel: 213-464-5079
Address Inquiries to: Bill Bordy, Publisher
Lee Melville, Editor-in-Chief
Description: A major Hollywood casting and production news publication with theatre reviews from across the country.

John Offord Publications
9200 Sunset Boulevard
Los Angeles, CA 90069
Description: Offerings such as *British Alternative Theatre Directory* and *British Theatre Directory* are available from the U.S. office of John Offord Publications.

Visual Resources Incorporated
Post Office Box 45734
Los Angeles, CA 90045
Description: Publishers of *The VRI Slide Library of World Theatre.* Other presentations available include: Classical Theatre, Medieval Theatre, Renaissance Theater, Baroque Theater, 18th and 19th Century Theater, 20th Century Theater and the Survey of the History of Euopean Theater Arts from the Greeks to the Present.

Mountain View

Habibi
c/o Robert C. Zalot, Post Office Box 4081
Mountain View, CA 94040
Description: Published monthly.

Palo Alto

Mayfield Publishing Company
285 Hamilton Avenue
Palo Alto, CA 94301
Tel: 415-326-1640
Description: Publishers of *Theatre Brief Edition.*

San Diego

Applause
San Diego Applause Magazine, Incorporated
454 Olive Street
San Diego, CA 92103
Description: Published monthly.

San Francisco

A.C.T.
Arts and Leisure Publications
950 Battery
San Francisco, CA 94111
Description: Published monthly.

Performing Arts Magazine
Theatre Publications
651 Brannan Street
San Francisco, CA 94107
Description: Published monthly.

Public Management Institute
358 Brannan Street
San Francisco, CA 94107
Tel: 415-896-1900
Description: The publishers of *The Directory of Corporate Philanthropy,* a directory and guide to corporate funding for the arts.

San Francisco Theatre Magazine
631 Union Street
San Francisco, CA 94133
Description: Published quarterly.

COLORADO

Denver

Pioneer Drama Service
2172 South Colorado Boulevard
Denver, CO 80222
Address Inquiries to: Shubert Fendrich, Editor
Founded in: 1961
Description: A major play publisher for the high school educational market. This house has adapted many plays from the public domain to this market and their catalog is strong on musicals as well.

New Haven

Theatre
Box 2046 Yale Station
New Haven, Connecticut 06520
Description: Published three times per year.

CONNECTICUT

Rowayton

New Plays for Children
Post Office Box 273
Rowayton, CT 06853

DELAWARE

Newark

University of Delaware Press
326 Hullihen Hall
Newark, DE 19711
Tel: 302-738-1149
Address Inquiries to: James Merrill, Director
Julien Yoseloff, ISBN Contact
Description: Publishes books on the arts and on a wide variety of scholarly subjects. Included in their titles are some plays and

books on drama and the theatre.

DISTRICT OF COLUMBIA

Washington

ATA Publications
1029 Vermont Avenue, NW
Washington, DC 20005
Description: Publishes *Theatre Journal* four times per year and *Theatre News* ten times per year.

Communication Arts International
Kayward Publications
Box 1933
Washington, DC 20013
Description: Published quarterly.

Cultural Post
NEA
2401 E Street, NW
Washington, DC 20506
Description: Published bi-monthly.

Howard University Press
2900 Van Ness Street, NW
Washington, DC 20008

Three Continents Press
1346 Connecticut Avenue NW, Suite 1131
Washington, DC 20036
Tel: 202-457-0288
Address Inquiries to: Donald E. Herdeck, President, Editor and Domestic and Foreign Rights and Permissions
Harold Ames Jr., Executive Vice President
Description: Publishes books on a large variety of subjects including some on the drama.

Unicorn Times
930 F Street NW, Suite 511
Washington, DC 20004
Description: Published monthly.

Washington International Arts Letter
Post Office Box 9005
Washington, DC 20003
Description: Published ten times per year.

W.P.A.S. Museletter
Washington Performing Arts Scoeity
425 13th Street NW
Washington, DC 20004

FLORIDA

Gainesville

University Presses of Florida
15 Northwest 15th Street
Gainesville, FL 32603

Tallahasee

Apalachee Quarterly
Post Office Box 20106
Tallahasee, FL 32304
Description: Printed by DDB Press, the quarterly will print original one-act plays. The author will receive copies.

GEORGIA

Athens

University Of Georgia Press
Athens, GA 30602

Clarkston

Dekalb Literary Arts Journal
DeKalb College
555 Indian Creek Drive
Clarkston, GA 30021
Description: One-act plays are accepted and the author will be provided with copies.

HAWAII

Honolulu

University Press of Hawaii
2840 Kolowalu Street
Honolulu, HI 96822

ILLINOIS

Champaign

University of Illinois Press
54 East Gregory Drive
Box #5081, Station A
Champaign, IL 61820

Chicago

Black Stars
c/o John H. Johnson
820 South Michigan Avenue
Chicago, IL 60605
Description: Published monthly.

Chicago Magazine
500 North Michigan
Chicago, IL 60611
Tel: 312-751-7150
Address Inquiries to: Christine Newman, Book Review and Fiction Editor
Description: *Chicago Magazine* publishes excerpts from books on the performing arts.

Dramatic Publishing Company
4150 North Milwaukee Avenue
Chicago, IL 60641
Tel: 312-545-2062
Address Inquiries to: Christopher Sergel, President

Ebony
820 South Michigan Avenue
Chicago, IL 60605
Tel: 312-322-9320
Address Inquiries to: Herbert Nipson, Executive Editor
Description: *Ebony* occasionally offers articles on the performing arts and reviews.

Stagebill Group
B and B Enterprises, Incorporated
500 North Michigan Street
Chicago, IL 60611
Description: Published monthly.

University of Chicago Press
5801 South Ellis Avenue
Chicago, IL 60637

Dekalb

Players Magazine
National Collegiate Players
University Theatre
Dekalb, Illinois 60115
Description: Published bi-monthly.

Elgin

Performance Publishing Company
978 North McLean Boulevard
Elgin, IL 60120
Description: An educational publishing house offering a catalog especially strong in musicals.

INDIANA

Bloomington

Indiana University Press
10th and Morton Streets
Bloomington, IN 47405

Indianapolis

Child Life Magazine
Post Office Box 567B
Indianapolis, IN 46206
Description: Plays of 500 to 700 words for classroom productions by children are accepted. Writing should be for a 7 to 11 year old audience and there is a payment of about 4 cents a word upon publication.

Muncie

Ball State University Forum
Ball State University
Muncie, IN 47306
Address Inquiries to: Frances Mayhew Rippy, Editor
Dick A. Renner, Editor
Description: Will accept one-act play and provide copies for the author.

IOWA

Ames

Iowa State University Press
South State Avenue
Ames, IA 50010

Cedar Rapids

Heuer Publishing Company
Postal Drawer 248
Cedar Rapids, IA 52406
Address Inquiries to: J. Vincent Heuer, Editor
Description: Plays for high school production are accepted and a fee is paid on publication.

KANSAS

Lawrence

Regents Press of Kansas
303 Carruth-O'Leary
Lawrence, KS 66045

Liberal

Leisure Times
c/o James S. Head
16 South Kansas
Liberal, KS 67901
Description: Published weekly.

KENTUCKY

Lexington

Around The Town
c/o Wallace C. Jones
Post Office Box 27
Lexington, KY 40502
Description: Published monthly.

University Press of Kentucky
Lexington, KY 40506

LOUISIANA

Baton Rouge

Louisiana State University Press
Baton Rouge, LA 70803

New Orleans

Anchorage Press
Post Office Box 8067
New Orleans, LA 70182
Tel: 504-283-8868
Address Inquiries to: Orlin Carey, Editor
Anne R. Gowdy, Editorial Advisor
Founded in: 1935
Description: Through 48 years the Anchorage Press has been publishing and distributing plays. Call or write for the latest listings.

MARYLAND

Baltimore

Johns Hopkins University Press
34th and North Charles Streets
Baltimore, MD 21218

Lanham

University Press of America
4720 Boston Way
Lanham, MD 20706
Tel: 301-459-3366
Address Inquiries to: James E. Lyons, Managing Editor
Founded in: ATA;
Annual Budget: University Press of America is a large publisher of books
Description: University Press of America is a large publisher of books on the humanities and social sciences and along with American Theatre Association arranges for books to

be published with the ATA imprint. Hundreds of theatrical books and mongraphs are available.

Silver Spring

Forecast
c/o Richard W. Mostow
8615 Ramsey Avenue
Silver Spring, MD 20910
Description: Published monthly.

MASSACHUSETTS

Amherst

University of Massachusetts Press
Post Office Box 429
Amherst, MA 01004

Boston

Plays
8 Arlington Street
Boston, MA 02116
Description: Published eight times per year.

Routledge and Kegan Paul
9 Park Street
Boston, MA

Cambridge

Harvard University Press
79 Garden Street
Cambridge, MA 02138

MIT Press
28 Carleton Street
Cambridge, MA 02142

New Boston Review
Boston Critic
10 B Mount Auburn Street
Cambridge, MA 02138
Tel: 617-492-5478; 617-492-5486
Description: The *Review* occasionally publishes reviews in the performing arts and articles on the subject.

Medford

Prologue
Tufts University
Arena Theatre
Medford, MA 02155
Tel: 617-623-3880 (box office);
617-628-5000 ext237 (office)
Address Inquiries to: Peter D. Arnott, Chairman
Founded in: 1910
Member: ACTF; ACA; ATA; NETC;
Description: Published three times per year.

MICHIGAN

Ann Arbor

Cinegram Film and Video News
c/o Peter F. Kuchnicki
512 South Main
Ann Arbor, MI 48104
Description: Published monthly.

UMI Research Press
300 North Zeeb Road
Ann Arbor, MI 48106
Tel: 313-761-4700; 800-521-0600, Order
Line
Description: Write or call the toll free number
for the latest listings from UMI Research
Press.

University Of Michigan Press
839 Greene Street
Ann Arbor, MI 48106

MINNESOTA
Minneapolis

Madhatter Press
3101 Twelfth Avenue South, #5
Minneapolis, MN 55407
Description: The Madhatter Press has pub-
lished such books as, *From the Neck Up*, by
Denise Dreher.

University of Minnesota Press
2037 University Avenue Southeast
Minneapolis, MN 55414

Vanilla Press
2400 Colfax Avenue South
Minneapolis, MN 55405
Tel: 612-374-4726
Address Inquiries to: Jean-Marie Fisher,
   President, Sales Manager and Rights
   and Permissions
   Thomas Redshaw, Editorial Board
   Chairman
Description: Publishes paperback books on
several subjects including some drama titles.

MISSISSIPPI
Jackson

University Press Of Mississippi
3825 Ridgewood Road
Jackson, MS 39211

MISSOURI
Columbia

Saturday Review
Post Office Box 6024
Columbia, MO 65205
Tel: 314-875-3003
Address Inquiries to: Jeff Gluck, Publisher
Bruce Van Wyngarden, Editor
Description: The *Saturday Review* publishes ar-
ticles on a number of subjects including arti-
cles on the performing arts and reviews of
theatre and dance productions.

University of Missouri Press
Post Office Box 1644
Columbia, MO 65205

Fenton

The Puppetry Journal
The Puppeteers of America, Incorporated
2015 Novem Drive
Fenton, MO 63026
Description: Published bi-monthly.

NEBRASKA
Hartsdale

Public Service Materials Center
111 North Central Avenue
Hartsdale, New York 10530
Description: Publications include *Where Ameri-
ca's Large Foundations Make Their Grants* and *The
Corporate Fund Raising Directory.*

Lincoln

University of Nebraska Press
318 Nebraska Hall
Lincoln, NE 68588

New York

Penguin Books
625 Madison Avenue
New York, New York 10022

NEW HAMPSHIRE
Salem

Marion Boyars Publishers
99 Main Street
Salem, NH 03079
Tel: 617-686-6407
Address Inquiries to: Marion Boyars,
   President
Description: Publishers of dramatic literature.

NEW JERSEY
Atlantic City

Atlantic City Magazine
1616 Pacific Avenue, Suite 214
Atlantic City, NJ 08401
Description: Published quarterly.

Chatham

New Jersey Music and Arts
572 Main Street
Chatham, NJ 07928
Description: Published 10 times per year.

Clifton

James T. White and Company
1700 State Highway 3
Clifton, NJ 07013
Tel: 201-773-9300
Address Inquiries to: William H. White,
   President
   Raymond D. McGill, Editor-in-Chief
Description: Publishes books on the perform-
ing arts including some titles on the theatre.

Engelwood Cliffs

Salem Press
550 Sylvan Avenue
Engelwood Cliffs, NJ 07632
Tel: 201-871-3700
Address Inquiries to: Frank N. Magill,
   President and Editor-in-Chief
   Arthur Friese, Executive Vice President
   and Domestic and Foreign Rights and
   Permissions
Description: Salem Press publishes reference
books for school and public libraries on a
variety of subjects including drama. In 1980
five titles were published.

Englewood Cliffs

Prentice-Hall/Spectrum Books
c/o D. Karrel
Englewood Cliffs, NJ 07632

Metuchen

Scarecrow Press, Incorporated
52 Liberty Street
Metuchen, NJ 08840

Princeton

Princeton Book Company, Publishers
Post Office Box 109
Princeton, NJ 080540
Tel: 201-297-8370

Rockleigh

Longwood Division
Allyn and Bacon, Incorporated
Link Drive
Rockleigh, NJ 07647
Description: Publishers of such books as *Stage
Management* and *Acting for the Camera.*

Teaneck

Somerset House
417 Maitland Avenue
Teaneck, NJ 07666
Tel: 201-833-1795
Description: Publishers of *Theatre in Focus*, a
pictorial history of world theatre on slides
and color microfiche. Accompanying texts
included.

Totowa

Rowman and Littlefield
81 Adams Drive
Totowa, NJ 07512

NEW MEXICO
Santa Fe

National Arts Jobbank
141 East Palace Avenue
Santa Fe, NM 87501
Tel: 505-988-1166
Address Inquiries to: Karen Kinnett Hyatt,
   Development Director
   Helen E. Lyons, Editor
Founded in: 1981
Member: WSAF;
Description: A monthly listing of jobs available

in the performing and visual arts, primarily for arts administrators, technicians, artists in residence and interns.

NEW YORK

Ancram

Ancram Standard
Ancram Restoration, Incorporated
Ancram, NY 12502
Description: Published monthly.

Bronx

Fordham University Press
University Box L
Bronx, NY 10458

Brooklyn

Brooklyn College Arts Management Circle
Brooklyn College
Department of Theatre
Brooklyn, NY 11210
Address Inquiries to: Robert L. Hess,
    President
    Leslie S. Jacobson, Dean, Graduate
    Division
Founded in: 1983
Description: A Directory of graduates of the MFA Performing Arts Management Program of Brooklyn College. The Directory is a networking source for those working in the Management field in all the arts.

Educational Theatre Guide
Nostrand and Flatbush at Hillel Road
Brooklyn College
Brooklyn, NY 11210
Tel: 212-434-1900

Performance-Management
Brooklyn College, Department of Theatre
Brooklyn, NY 11210
Address Inquiries to: Stephen Langley, Ph.D,
    Program Director
Founded in: 1978
Description: A performing arts management newsletter produced by the students of the Brooklyn College M.F.A. program in Performing Arts Administration.

Cape Vincent

Academic Book Club, (ABC)
Post Office Box 399
Cape Vincent, NY 13618
Description: A book club that offers books not readily available in local bookstores.

Elmsford

Pergamon Press
Maxwell House, Fairview Park
Elmsford, NY 10523

Garden City

Fireside Theatre Book Club
501 Franklin Avenue
Garden City, NY 11530
Description: A theatre book club which offers a wide selection of plays and theatre books

mailed to your home or office on a subscription basis.

Ithaca

Cornell University Press
124 Roberts Place
Ithaca, NY 14850

Melville

American Record Guide
One Windsor Place
Melville, NY 11747
Tel: 516-673-9312
Description: Publishes reviews of classical records and of books on music.

New York

A and W Publishers Incorporated
95 Madison Avenue
New York, NY 10016
Tel: 212-725-4970
Address Inquiries to: Lawrence D. Alexander,
    President
Description: Publishers of theatre books.

Abel
Abel News Agencies
300 West 17th Street
New York, NY 10011
Description: Published monthly.

Applause Theatre Books
100 West 67th Street
New York, NY 10023
Tel: 212-595-4735
Address Inquiries to: Glenn Young
Founded in: 1980
Description: Applause Theatre Books has one of the largest theatre book selections available. As mail order specialists handling books from all publishers, they would be pleased to have you phone or write for there extensive catalog.

Art and the Law
36 West 44th Street
New York, NY 10036
Tel: 212-575-1150
Address Inquiries to: Judith Stein, Book
    Review Editor
Description: Art and the Law publishes articles on legal issues in the arts and reviews of books on related subjects.

ART/New York
325 Spring Street
New York, NY 10013
Tel: 212-989-5257
Description: Recent publications include *Will it Make a Theatre?* and *New York's Other Theatre*, a guide to Off-Off Broadway.

Arts Management
Radius Group, Incorporated
408 West 57th Street
New York, NY 10019
Description: Published five times per year.

Backstage
165 West 46th Street
New York, NY 10036
Tel: 212-947-0020

Address Inquiries to: Allen Zwerdling, Editor
George L. George, Book Review Editor
Description: Backstage publishes listings of theatrical and dance auditions, articles on, and reviews of theatrical and dance productions and reviews of books on the performing arts.

Billboard
Billboard Publications, Incorporated
1515 Broadway
New York, NY 10036
Description: Published weekly.

Broadway Play Publishing, Inc.
249 West 29th Street
New York, NY 10001
Tel: 212-563-3820
Description: Write or call BPPI for the lastest catalog, including new titles such as *Summit Conference* and *Looking Glass*.

Cambridge University Press
32 East 57th Street
New York, NY 10022
Description: Recent books listed include *Ingmar Bergman, Four Decades in the Theatre.*

Center for Arts Information
625 Broadway
New York, NY 10012
Description: Publishes directories, mailing lists and management aides and for the arts.

Changes
Changes Publications, Incorporated
Box 631
Cooper Station
New York, NY 10003
Description: Published monthly.

Columbia University Press
562 West 113th Street
New York, NY 10025

Da Capo Press
233 Spring Street
New York, NY 10013
Tel: 212-620-8000
Description: Publishers of books relating to film and theatre covering topics such as criticism, history, biographies and reference.

Dance Magazine
1180 Avenue of the Americas
New York, NY 10036
Tel: 212-921-9300
Address Inquiries to: William Como, Editor
Description: Dance Magazine publishes articles on every aspect of dance and reviews and photographs of dance productions.

Dance Scope
1133 Broadway
New York, NY 10010
Tel: 212-691-4564
Address Inquiries to: H.B. Kronen
Description: Dance Scope publishes serious articles on the dance.

Drama Book Specialists Publishers
821 Broadway
New York, NY 10003
Tel: 212-582-1475

Address Inquiries to: Ralph Pine, President
Description: A wide selection of theatre books availble by mail or by dropping in to the shop when in New York. DBS publishes as well as carryies large stock for immediate shipment. Recent titles include *Stagecraft* and *Market the Arts!*.*

Drama Review
New York University School of the Arts
51 West Fourth Street
New York, NY 10012
Description: Published quarterly.

Drama Review, The
New York University
51 West Fourth Street
New York, NY 10012
Tel: 212-598-2597
Address Inquiries to: Michael Kirby, Editor
Description: The Drama Review accepts articles on all aspects of the theatre.

Dramatists Play Service
440 Park Avenue South
New York, NY 10016
Tel: 212-683-8960
Address Inquiries to: Samuel Taylor, President

Edinburgh University Press
562 West 113th Street
New York, NY 10025

Entertainment
Cobra Communications Limited
Post Office Box 62, Planetarium Station Station
New York, NY 10024
Description: Published bi-weekly.

Equity News
AEA, 1500 Broadway
New York, NY 10036
Description: Published nine times per year.

The Foundation Center
888 7th Avenue
New York, NY 10106
Tel: 800-424-9836; 212-975-1120
Description: Past publications have included the *Directory of Evaluation Consultants.* If you visit New York and are investigating grant support a visit to the Center would be a worthwhile investment.

Samuel French, Inc.
25 West 45th Street
New York, NY 10036
Founded in: 1830
Description: The largest and oldest theatrical publishers in the United States, French has offices in New York, Hollywood, Toronto and London. The best way to work with the company is to request their latest catalog of over 400 pages listing plays and musicals. If you do not find a particular play in the catalog, call the French office, since they also hold the rights to thousands of additional works.

Harper's
2 Park Avenue

New York, NY 10016
Tel: 212-481-5220
Address Inquiries to: Lewis H. Lapham, Editor
Description: Harper's Magazine offers reviews and occasionally does articles on the performing arts.

Holt, Rinehart and Winston
383 Madison Avenue
New York, NY 10017
Description: One of America's largest publishing houses with many theatre titles. Orders should be sent to Post Office Box 36, Lavalette, NJ 08735.

International Alliance of Theatrical Stage Employees Official Bulletin
1515 Broadway
New York, NY 10036
Description: Published quarterly.

International Contact Book
c/o Celebrity Service, Incorporated
171 West 57th Street
New York, NY 10019
Description: This publication list names and addresses for celebrities in the United States and abroad.

Interview
860 Broadway
New York, NY 10003
Description: Published monthly.

Alfred A. Knopf
Random House, Inc.
201 East 50th Street
New York, NY 10022

Lodestar Books
2 Park Avenue
New York, NY 10016

Longman Incorporated
1560 Broadway
New York, NY 10036
Description: Past publications include, *Children and Drama* by Nellie McCaslin, *Creative Drama in the Classroom,* and *Longman Anthology of American Drama,* by Lee A. Jacobus.

Macmillan Publishing Company
A division of Macmillan, Incorporated
866 Third Avenue
New York, NY 10022
Description: Publishers of theatre reference books including *Guide to the Theatre in America,* and *The Enjoyment of Theatre,* by Kenneth M. Cameron and Pattie P. Gillespie.

Mandate
Modernismo Publications, Incorporated
155 Avenue of the Americas
New York, NY 10013
Description: Published monthly.

McGraw-Hill Book Company
1221 Avenue of the Americas
New York, NY 10020
Description: Past publications were *The Theatre Experience,* by Edwin Wilson, and *History of Film,* by Beaver.

Metropolitan Opera Guild
1865 Broadway
New York, NY 10023
Description: Recent Information on *Ballet News* and *OPera News.*

Mime, Mask and Marionette
Marcel Dekker Incorporated
270 Madison Avenue
New York, NY 10016
Description: Published quarterly.

Musical Show
Tams Witmark Music Library, Incorporated
270 Madison Avenue
New York, NY 10016
Description: Published six times per year.

New American Library
1633 Broadway
New York, NY 10019

New York Literary Forum
Post Office Box 262, Lenox Hill
New York, NY 10020

New York Theatre Critics Review
Proscenium Publications
4 Park Avenue
New York, NY 10016
Description: Published thirty times per year.

New York Theatre Review
55 West 42nd Street
New York, NY 10036
Tel: 212-221-6078
Description: The *New York Theatre Review* publishes articles on the theatre and reviews of the New York season.

Performing Arts Journal
Box 858, Stuyvesant Station
New York, NY 10009
Description: Published three times per year.

Playbill
71 Vanderbilt Avenue
New York, NY 10169
Description: The theatre audiences guide to Broadway shows with details of the cast and credits for each production along with its well known stories and features. *Playbill* is now available through subscribtion with delivery monthly

Plays in Progress
c/o TCG 355 Lexingon Avenue
New York, NY 10017
Tel: 212-697-5230
Description: A service of the Theatre Communications Group, Plays in Progress offers a subsription that provides an opportunity to read new plays before they are produced.

Pocket Books
1230 Avenue of the Americas
New York, NY 10020

Random House, Incorporated
201 East 50th Street
New York, NY 10022

Red Dust Incorporated
Box 630, Gracie Station
New York, NY 10028
Tel: 212-348-4388
Address Inquiries to: Joanna Gunderson,
   Rights and Permissions
   Warren Gunderson, Co-Publisher
Description: Red Dust publishes new works by
new writers including some plays. In 1980
four titles were published.

Richards Rosen Press Incorporated
29 East 21st Street
New York, NY 10010
Tel: 212-777-3017
Address Inquiries to: Richard Rosen,
   President
   Ruth C. Rosen, Secretary-Treasurer
Description: Richards Rosen publishes books
for the trade and the library, including a se-
ries for theatre students. In 1980 it pub-
lished 36 titles.

Show Business
Leo Shull Publications
134 West 44th Street
New York, NY 10036
Description: Published weekly, this trade
newspaper provides casting and production
news.

Showcase
c/o Jack Winter
180 East End Avenue
New York, NY 10028
Description: Published monthly.

Slide Presentations, Publishers
175 Fifth Avenue
New York, NY 10010
Tel: 212-677-2200; 212-744-2730
Address Inquiries to: Stephen Arnold Sbarge
Founded in: 1974

Thames and Hudson, Inc.
500 Fifth Avenue
New York, NY 10110
Description: Recent titles include *The Irish
Theatre.*

Theatre Arts Books
153 Waverly Place
New York, NY 10014
Tel: 212-675-1815
Address Inquiries to: George Zournas,
   Director, Editor and Foreign Rights and
   Permissions
   Rosamond Gilder, Contracts
Description: Theatre Arts publishes books on
the theatre and related subjects inclucing
American Dialects, Foreign Dialects, and *Dialects
for the Stage.*

Theatre Communications
355 Lexington Avenue
New York, NY 10017
Tel: 100-7; 212-697-5230
Address Inquiries to: Jim O'Quinn, Editor
Laura Ross, Associate Editor
Member: TCG;
Description: *Theatre Communications is the
monthly newletter published by the Theatre

Communcations Group featruing aritcles,
news and job listings.

Theatre Crafts
250 West 57th Street, Suite 312
New York, NY 10019
Tel: 212-582-4110
Address Inquiries to: Patricia MacKay,
   Publisher/Editor
   Susan Wallach, Associate Editor
Description: Published bi-monthly, a major
production-oriented trade magazine and the
most useful for those involved in the techni-
cal aspects of theatre. Well known for the
Theatre Crafts Directory.

The Drama Review
721 Broadway, Room 600
New York, NY 10003
Description: Published quarterly.

Urizen Books
66 West Broadway
New York, NY 10007
Tel: 212-962-3413
Address Inquiries to: Michael Roloff,
   President, Editor and Rights and
   Permissions
   Wieland Shulz-Keil, Editor
Description: Publishes both literary and schol-
arly books including some titles on the
theatre.

Variety
154 West 46th Street
New York, NY 10036
Description: One of the major weekly newspapers of the entertainment industry.

Viking Press
625 Madison Avenue
New York, NY 10022
Tel: 212-755-4330
Address Inquiries to: Irving Goodman,
   President
   Theodore Flam, Treasurer and
   Contracts
Description: Publishes general fiction and
nonfiction books on a variety of subjects in-
cluding some on drama.

Village Voice
842 Broadway
New York, NY 10012
Description: A major weekly publication of the
New York area, providing comprehensive
Broadway, Off-Broadway and Off-Off-
Broadway listings and in-depth reviews by
major New York theatre critics.

Weekly Theatrical Calendar
Celebrity Service, Incorporated
171 West 57th Street
New York, NY 10019

Queens

AUM Publications
Post Office Box 32433
Queens, NY 11431
Tel: 212-523-3471
Address Inquiries to: Carl Brown, President
Description: Publishers of plays and dramatic

literature.

Schenectady

Kite
416 Smith Street
Schenectady, NY 12305
Description: Published weekly.

NORTH CAROLINA
Asheville

Arts Journal
324 Charlotte Street
Asheville, NC 28801
Description: Published monthly.

Durham

Duke University Press
Box 6697, College Station
Durham, NC 27708

NORTH DAKOTA
Grand Forks

Theatre History Studies
University of North Dakota
Grand Forks, ND

OHIO
Cincinnati

Dramatics
International Thespian Society
3368 Central Parkway
Cincinnati, Ohio 45225
Description: Published five times per year.

Cleveland

Free Lance
6005 Grand Avenue
Cleveland, OH 44104
Tel: 216-431-7118
Address Inquiries to: Casper L. Jordan,
   Editor
   Ruissell Atkins, Editor

Third Sector Press
2000 Euclid Avenue
Cleveland, OH 44118
Tel: 216-932-6066
Address Inquiries to: Wendy Franklin,
   Publisher
Description: Publishers of *Philanthropy and Mar-
keting* and other books useful for fund rai-
sing.

Franklin

Eldridge Publishing Company
Post Office Drawer 216
Franklin, Ohio 45006
Description: One of the oldest educational
publishing houses, Eldridge has many holdings suiltable for elementary school and
church groups.

Kent

Kent State University Press
Drama Library
Kent, OH 44242

PENNSYLVANIA

Allentown

Today Magazine
c/o F. Alan Shirk
2230 Fairview
Allentown, PA 18104
Description: Published monthly.

Pittsburgh

Carnegie Magazine
Carnegie Institute, 4400 Forbes Avenue
Pittsburgh, PA 15213
Description: Published monthly.

TEXAS

Forth Worth

U.S. Small Business Administration
Post Office Box 15434
Forth Worth, TX 76119
Tel: 800-433-7212; 800-792-8901, Texas
only
Description: Publishers of management aides,
small marketing aides and small business
bibliographies for small business organizations.

Houston

Houston Scene
4000 San Jacinto
Houston, TX 77004
Description: Published monthly.

Performing Arts Magazine
11 Greenway Plaza Suite 620
Houston, TX 77046
Description: Published monthly.

Schulenburg

I.E. Clark
Saint John's Road, Box 246
Schulenburg, TX 78956
Tel: 713-743-3232
Description: Publishers of plays and books for
the theatre. Write for a catalog of offerings.

UTAH

Provo

Brigham Young University Press
209 UPB
Provo, UT 84602

VIRGINIA

Reston

American Alliance for Recreation and
Dance
1900 Association Drive
Reston, VA 22091
Tel: 703-476-3481
Description: Many publications concerning
Dance movement that would be helpful in
theatre are available from the 40,000 mem-
ber Alliance.

CANADA

Burnaby, British Columbia

Playboard
Archway Publishers, 7560 Lawrence Drive
Burnaby, British Columbia, Canada V5A
1T6
Description: Published monthly.

Surrey, British Columbia

Event
Kwantlen College, Box 9030
Surrey, British Columbia, Canada V3T
5H8
Address Inquiries to: Leona Gom, Editor
Description: Short dramatic pieces are accept-
ed and a small payment is made upon publi-
cation.

Vancouver, British Columbia

Talonbooks
201-1019 East Cordova
Vancouver, British Columbia, Canada M5J
1R2
Tel: 604-255-5915
Address Inquiries to: Peter Hay

University of British Columbia Press
303-6344 Memorial Road
Vancouver, British Columbia, Canada V6T
1W5

Victoria, British Columbia

Press Porcepic
560 Johnson Street, #235
Victoria, British Columbia, Canada

Winnipeg, Manitoba

House Programme
Manitoba Theatre Centre, 174 Market
Winnipeg, Manitoba, Canada R3B OP8
Description: Published six times per year.

Montreal

McGill- Queen's University Press
McGill University
Montreal, Canada M5S 1A6

Saint John's, Newfoundland

Newfoundland Herald
c/o Geoffery W. Stirling, Box 2015
Saint John's, Newfoundland, Canada A1C
5R7
Description: Published weekly.

Downsview, Ontario

Canadian Theatre Review
CTR Publications, 200 B Administrative
Studies
York University
Downsview, Ontario, Canada M3J 1P3
Description: Published quarterly.

Canadian Theatre Review Publications
York University, 4700 Keele Street
Downsview, Ontario, Canada M3J 1P3
Tel: 416-667-3768
Address Inquiries to: Don Rubin
Description: Publishers of books as well as
Canadian Theatre Review, a monthly theatre
magazine featuring articles and plays.

Guelph, Ontario

Canadian Drama/L'Art Dramatique
Canadien
Department of English
University of Guelph
Guelph, Ontario, Canada
Tel: 519-821-4120
Address Inquiries to: Eugene Benson

Ottawa, Ontario

Arts Bulletin
141 Laurier Avenue West, Suite 707
Ottawa, Ontario, Canada K1P 5J3
Tel: 613-238-3561
Address Inquiries to: Ann Heard

Stratford, Ontario

Fanfares
Stratford Shakespearean Festival of
Canada, Festivals Theatre, Post Office
Box 520
Stratford, Ontario, Canada N5A 6V2
Description: Published quarterly.

Toronto, Ontario

University of Toronto, Massey College
Toronto, Ontario, Canada M5S 2E1
Tel: 416-978-2092
Address Inquiries to: Jill Levenson

Performing Arts in Canada
52 Avenue Road
Toronto, Ontario, Canada M5R 2G3
Description: Published quarterly.

Playwrights Canada
8 York Street, 6th Floor
Toronto, Ontario, Canada M5J 1R2
Tel: 416-363-1581
Address Inquiries to: Shirley Gibson

Samuel French, Inc.
80 Richmond Street East
Toronto, Ontario, Canada M5C 1P1
Tel: 416-363-3536
Address Inquiries to: Ms. N. Parsons
Description: A Canadian branch of Samuel
French.

Scene Changes
Theatre Ontario, 8 York Street, 7th Floor
Toronto, Ontario, Canada M5J 1R2
Tel: 416-366-2938

Address Inquiries to: Jeniva Berger

That's Showbusiness
191 Church Street
Toronto, Ontario, Canada M5B 1Y7
Description: Published semi-monthly.

Theatrebooks Limited
659 Yonge Street, 2nd Floor
Toronto, Ontario, Canada M4Y 1Z9
Tel: 416-922-7175
Address Inquiries to: John Harvey

Theatre History in Canada
Massey College, University of Toronto
Toronto, Ontario, Canada M5S 2E1
Address Inquiries to: Ann Saddlemyer
Richard Plant

Toronto Calendar Magazine
CUC Publishing Limited
65 Front Street, East
Toronto, Ontario, Canada M5E 1B6
Description: Published monthly.

Vancouver Calendar Magazine
CUC Publishing, 65 Front Street, East
Toronto, Ontario, Canada M5E 1B6
Description: Published monthly.

Montreal, Quebec

Echos-Vedettes
c/o Pierre Peladeau
225 East Roy Street
Montreal, Quebec, Canada H2W 1H5
Description: Published weekly.

Jeu, Cahiers de Theatre
Post Office Box 1600, Station E
Montreal, Quebec, Canada H2T 3B1
Tel: 514-523-1757
Address Inquiries to: Lorraine Hebert

Les Presses de l'Universite de Montreal
C.P. 6128 Succursale A
Montreal, Quebec, Canada H3C 3J7

Montreal Calendar
2100 Guy Street, Suite 400
Montreal, Quebec, Canada H3H 2M8
Description: Published monthly.

Montreal Ce Mois
2100 Guy Street, Suite 400
Montreal, Quebec, Canada H3H 2M8
Description: Published monthly.

Montreal-Nord, Quebec

VLB Editeur
5840 Boulevard Gouin Est
Montreal-Nord, Quebec, Canada
Tel: 514-326-5029
Address Inquiries to: Victor-Levy Beaulieu

Quebec, Quebec

Les Presses de l'Universite Laval
Cite universitaire, C.P. 2447
Quebec, Quebec, Canada G1K 7R4

15

Suppliers

The "Suppliers" section is the longest in the *Guide*, with almost 2000 entries. The information contained here will assist managers of regional, academic, and traveling theatre companies in assessing any areas' available equipment and services, and where these can be purchased.

The description ending each entry provides details on what supplies are available from the dealer in question; anything from onstage fog and rain to a complete sound system, and how these technical foundations to a staged illusion may be purchased or rented.

ALABAMA

Birmingham

American Lighting
Number 28, 2nd Avenue N
Birmingham, AL 35204
Tel: 203-322-0570
Description: Suppliers of lighting and technical equipment.

Huntsville

Luna Tech
822 Demasters Street
Huntsville, AL 35801
Tel: 205-533-1487; 205-533-1489
Address Inquiries to: Tom DeWille, President
Bill McBride, General Manager
Member: APA; USITT;
Description: Manufactures the PYROPAK system of pyrotechnic special effects, and produces indoor and outdoor pyrotechnic displays. Supplier of custom lighting systems.

Madison

Hammond Industries
8000 Madison Pike
Madison, AL 35758
Tel: 205-772-9626; 205-772-3870
Address Inquiries to: Paul L.P. Twist,
National Sales Manager
Founded in: 1977
Description: Supplier of lighting and sound equipment.

ALASKA

Anchorage

Alaska Stagecraft
Post Office Box 4-2556
1025 Orca S7
Anchorage, AK 99509
Tel: 907-276-5671
Description: Suppliers of lighting and technical equipment.

JTC Sound and Light Company
2911 Spenard Road
Anchorage, AK 99503

Tel: 907-274-1549
Description: Suppliers of lighting and technical equipment

Eagle River

Mark IV Enterprises
Post Office Box 89
Eagle River, AK 99577
Tel: 907-688-2133
Description: Suppliers of lighting and technical equipment.

ARIZONA

Mesa

Leslie Sales
25 Three Fountains
Mesa, AZ 85203
Tel: 602-969-5729
Address Inquiries to: Chuck Leslie
Description: Manufacturer of tapes for film processing.

Phoenix

F.G. Lighting Sales
Post Office Box 20186
Phoenix, AZ 85036
Tel: 602-277-7901
Address Inquiries to: Frank Galia
Bob Dunnerman Sr.
Description: Supplier of lighting equipment.

Globe Ticket Company
3118 West Thomas Road, Suite 705
Phoenix, AZ 85017
Tel: 602-278-3559
Description: Suppliers of lighting and technical equipment.

Intermountain Specialty Equipment Company
2643 East University Drive, #111
Phoenix, AZ 85034
Tel: 602-267-9404
Description: Manufacturer of stage equipment

J.R. Russell Electric
120 E. Missouri Avenue
Phoenix, AZ 85102

Tel: 602-279-6454
Address Inquiries to: John Russell, Owner
Description: Supplier of complete lines of sound and lighting equipment.

J.R. Russell
1045 East Canelback Road
Phoenix, AZ 85014
Tel: 602-266-6918
Address Inquiries to: J.R. Russell, Owner
John Ravert, General Manager
Founded in: 1966
Member: AES; USITT; NAVA;
Description: Design, engineering, sales, rental of stage lighting/sound, sets, display and decorating services to theatre, schools, churches, conventions and organizations.

Stage Sound
4708 East Van Buren
Phoenix, AZ 85008
Tel: 602-275-6060
Description: Supplier of sound equipment. Rentals available.

S.W. Audio Systems
2213 East Indian School Road
Phoenix, AZ 85016
Description: Supplier of lighting equipment.

Tempe

Tempe Sales Company
412 West Broadway
Tempe, AZ 85281
Tel: 602-967-4811

Tucson

Arizona Cine Equipment Company
1660 E. Winsett Street #220
Tucson, AZ 85719
Tel: 602-623-8268
Address Inquiries to: Lee Oliver
Founded in: 1972
Description: Rental, retail and service business catering to the needs of the motion picture, theatrical and convention industries. It provides expendables from gels to lamps, muslin, paints, sound systems, lighting, audio-visual, video.

ARKANSAS

Fort Smith

Joe Udouj
Post Office Box 1851
Fort Smith, AR 72901
Tel: 501-783-1468
Address Inquiries to: Joe Udouj
Description: Supplier of tickets and ticket racks.

Weldon, Williams, and Lick
Post Office Box 168
Fort Smith, AR 72902
Tel: 501-783-4113
Address Inquiries to: Bill Kelso, Assistant Sales Manager
Description: Manufacturer of tickets and ticket racks.

Little Rock

Bylites
Post Office Box 3131
1118 West Markham Street
Little Rock, AR 72203
Tel: 501-372-4535
Description: Suppliers of lighting and technical equipment.

CALIFORNIA

Berkeley

Dharma Trading Company
1918 University Avenue
Berkeley, CA 94704
Tel: 415-841-7722
Description: Supplier of dyes, fabric paints and ready-to-dye fabrics by mail order.

Beverly Hills

Dazian's Incorporated
165 South Robertson Boulevard
Beverly Hills, CA 90211
Tel: 213-657-8900; 213-655-9691
Description: Supplier of theatrical fabrics and supplies.

Brisbane

Cinema Services
3866 Bayshore
Brisbane, CA 94005
Tel: 415-469-5220
Description: Supplier of lighting equipment.

Burbank

Colortran, Incorporated
1015 Chestnut Street
Burbank, CA 91502
Tel: 213-843-1200
Address Inquiries to: Thomas L. Pincu, Vice President
Member: NAB; USITT; SMPTE; IES;

Koessler Sales Company, Incorporated
2010 West Burbank Boulevard
Burbank, CA 91506
Tel: 213-849-5716
Description: Supplier of sound equipment and intercom systems.

Lowel-Light Mfg., Incorporated
3407 West Olive Avenue
Burbank, CA 91505
Tel: 213-846-7740
Address Inquiries to: Roy Low, Western Regional Sales Manager
Description: Supplier of lighting equipment.

Burlingame

Carelli-EMA
1588 Gilbreth Road
Burlingame, CA 94010
Tel: 415-697-6286
Description: Supplier of electrical outlet strips and utility carts.

Chatsworth

Marantz Company, Incorporated
20525 Nordoff Street
Chatsworth, CA 91311
Tel: 213-998-9333
Address Inquiries to: Joseph S. Tushinsky
Description: Supplier of sound equipment.

Sundance Lighting Corporation
9801 Variel Avenue
Chatsworth, CA 91311
Tel: 213-882-4321
Address Inquiries to: James L. Moody, President
Christine Hagerman, Executive Managing Director
Founded in: 1976
Member: IES; PERS; USITT;
Annual Budget: $1,000,000
Description: Supplier of lighting equipment, design for lighting and scenes, leasing, rental and construction.

Superscope, Incorporated
20525 Nordhoff Street
Chatsworth, CA 91311
Tel: 213-998-9333
Address Inquiries to: Charlie Farrington, Director of Corporate Communications
Description: Manufacturer of sound equipment.

Culver City

Wavelength Incorporated
11505 West Jefferson Boulevard
Culver City, CA 90230
Tel: 213-390-9801
Description: Wavelength supplies lighting and technical equipment.

Cupertino

Nova Stage Lighting
10121 Emperial Avenue
Cupertino, CA 95014
Tel: 408-996-7954
Description: Suppliers of lighting and technical equipment.

Daly City

Duro-Test Light Center
347a Serramonte Plaza
Daly City, CA 94015
Tel: 415-994-3393
Address Inquiries to: Don Adams, General Sales Manager
Description: Supplier of light bulbs and spot lights.

El Cajon

Musician Supply Company
1001 Vernon Way
El Cajon, CA 92020
Tel: 714-448-7137
Address Inquiries to: Robert Eastman
Description: Supplier of sound equipment.

Encino

Ideal Wig Company
18075 Ventura Boulevard
Encino, CA 91316
Tel: 213-345-1226
Address Inquiries to: Herb Orlins
Description: See New York entry.

Fullerton

Fullerton Civic Light Opera Company, Incorporated
218 West Commonwealth Avenue
Fullerton, CA 92632
Tel: 714-526-3832
Address Inquiries to: Jan Duncan, Assistant General Manager
Harriet Dasher, Production Manager
Founded in: 1971
Annual Budget: $250,000
Description: Supplier of scenery and costumes.

Gardenia

Unger Sales Associates
1604 W. 139th Street
Gardenia, CA 90249
Tel: 213-538-2811
Description: Supplier of electrical outlet strips and utility carts.

Glendale

Richard Arnold and Associates
331 West Arden Avenue
Glendale, CA 91203
Tel: 213-240-3677
Address Inquiries to: Richard Arnold
Description: Manufacturer of tapes for film processing.

Marvin Jacobs Optical Engineering
4527 San Fernando Road
Glendale, CA 91204
Tel: 213-244-0838
Address Inquiries to: Howard Stucker
Description: Manufacturer of theatre sound effects and control consoles.

Mel Audio and Video
1122 E. Chevy Chase Drive
Glendale, CA 91205
Tel: 213-245-7708

Description: Supplier of intercom mixers.

Hawthorne

Thermodyne International, Ltd.
12600 Yukon Avenue
Hawthorne, CA 90250
Tel: 213-679-0411
Address Inquiries to: W.C. Wolf, Sales
Manager
Description: Manufacturer of shipping cases.

Hollywood

Cine 60 Incorporated
6430 Sunset Boulevard
Hollywood, CA 90028
Tel: 213-461-3046
Address Inquiries to: Evan Green, Branch
Manager
Description: Manufacturer of lighting and
camera equipment.

Ciro Equipment, Corporated
6820 Romaine Street
Hollywood, CA 90038
Tel: 213-467-1296
Address Inquiries to: Barry Green, President
Description: Manufacturer of tapes for film
processing.

Coast Recording Equipment Supply
Incorporated
6114 Santa Monica Boulevard
Hollywood, CA 90038
Tel: 213-462-6058
Address Inquiries to: Jerry Cubbage
Founded in: 1973
Description: Supplier of sound equipment.

Alan Gordon Enterprises, Inc.
1430 North Cahuenga Boulevard
Hollywood, CA 90028
Tel: 213-466-3561
Address Inquiries to: Grant Loucks, President
Ted Lane, Sales Manager
Founded in: 1946
Member: SMPTE;
Description: Manufacturer, retailer and dis-
tributor of movie equipment.

Mole-Richardson Company
937 North Sycamore Avenue
Hollywood, CA 90038
Tel: 213-851-0111
Address Inquiries to: Howard R. Bell, Vice
President, Sales
Description: Manufacturer of generators,
transformers, microphones and special
effects.

Olesen
1535 Ivar Ave
Hollywood, CA 90028
Tel: 213-461-4631
Description: Supplier of lighting equipment.

Plastic Reel Corp. of America
7165 Willoughby Avenue
Hollywood, CA 90046
Tel: 213-851-7532
Address Inquiries to: Carole Pinker, Office
Manager
Description: Manufacturer of reels and reel ac-

cessories.

See Factor Pacific, Incorporated
1420 Beachwood Drive
Hollywood, CA 90028
Tel: 213-469-7214
Address Inquiries to: Tony Mazzucchi, Vice
President
Description: Supplier of portable lighting and
intercom systems.

Stage Lighting Distributors
1653 North Argyle
Hollywood, CA 90028
Tel: 213-466-8324
Description: Supplier of lighting and technical
stage equipment.

Visual Resources Incorporated
6233 Hollywood Boulevard
Hollywood, CA 90028
Description: Supplier of slides, catalogues and
handbooks for theatre and dance.

Huntington Beach

Daryl Braun Associates
15691 Container Lane
Huntington Beach, CA 92647
Tel: 213-594-8764
Address Inquiries to: Daryl Braun
Description: Supplier of lighting equipment.

Imperial Beach

VRI Slide Library, Incorporated
Post Office Box 1208
Imperial Beach, CA 92032
Description: The VRI Library offers collec-
tions of slides from Greek Theatre to Mod-
ern Theatre.

Inglewwood

Jack Berman Company, Incorporated
8925 South LaCienga Boulevard
Inglewwood, CA 90301
Tel: 213-649-6101; 910-328-6184
Address Inquiries to: Jack Berman
Description: Supplier of sound equipment.

Irvine

Jiffy Mixer Company, Incorporated
17981-G Sky Park Circle
Irvine, CA 92714
Tel: 714-557-1272
Address Inquiries to: Ursula Gries, General
Manager
Description: Manufacturer of a specialized
tool for mixing paints.

Long Beach

KT Electronics
3306 Lime Avenue
Long Beach, CA 90807
Tel: 213-424-0979; 213-427-8963
Founded in: 1951
Member: IEEE; all sound publications;
Description: Supplier of intercom systems,
microphone preamplifiers and mixers.

Los Alamitos

Broom's Electronics, Incorporated
3403 Cerritos Avenue
Los Alamitos, CA 90720
Tel: 213-598-3314
Description: Manufacturer of commercial
sound equipment.

Los Angeles

Belden Communications
Preferred Distributing
1114 North Sycamore Avenue
Los Angeles, CA 90028
Tel: 213-461-4201
Address Inquiries to: Bud McKinney,
President
Description: A regional branch office.

H.S. Eales Company
Post Office Box 45465
Los Angeles, CA 90045
Tel: 213-776-4410
Address Inquiries to: H.S. Eales
Founded in: 1964
Member: USITT; CETA;
Description: Supplier of lighting equipment.

Four Star Stage Lighting, Incorporated
3935 North Mission Road
Los Angeles, CA 90031
Tel: 213-221-5114
Address Inquiries to: Bob Kruggel
Don Savarese
Description: Supplier of lighting equipment.

Galaxy Stage Lighting
5421 Santa Monica Boulevard
Los Angeles, CA 90029
Tel: 213-464-9283
Description: Suppliers of lighting and techni-
cal equipment.

Globe Ticket Company
Post Office Box 90656
Los Angeles, CA 90009
Tel: 213-774-4210
Description: Supplier of tickets and ticket
equipment.

Iddings Paint Company
3486 Union Pacific Avenue
Los Angeles, CA 90023
Tel: 213-268-4744
Address Inquiries to: Joseph E. Bates,
General Manager
Description: Manufacturer of paints and col-
ors.

LA Stage Lighting
1450 Venice Boulevard
Los Angeles, CA 90019
Description: Supplier of lighting.

Litelab
5200 Venice Boulevard
Los Angeles, CA 90019
Tel: 213-936-6206
Address Inquiries to: Vincent G. Finnegan Jr.,
National Sales Manager
Founded in: 1975
Member: NAMM; Asid Industry Foundation;
Description: The largest manufacturer and

supplier of lighting systems to the entertainment market also manufacturing architectural fixtures for the architecture and design market.

S.A.E. (Scientific Audio Electronics)
701 E. Macy Street
Los Angeles, CA 90012
Tel: 213-489-7600
Address Inquiries to: Michael Joseph,
   Director of Marketing
Description: Manufacturer of sound equipment.

Skirpan Lighting Control Corporation
1155 North LaCienega Boulevard
Los Angeles, CA 90069
Tel: 213-657-6383
Address Inquiries to: Robert A. Slutske,
   Manager, West Coast Operations
Description: Supplier of lighting equipment.

Strand Century Incorporated
5432 West 102nd Street
Los Angeles, CA 90045
Tel: 213-776-4600
Address Inquiries to: Gene Murphy, Vice
   President, Sales and Marketing
Founded in: 1929
Member: USITT; NAB;
Description: Manufacturer of a full range of lighting, dimming and control equipment for permanent and touring theatrical operations.

Technical Audio/Visual Services,
Incorporated
5569 West Washington Boulevard
Los Angeles, CA 90016
Tel: 213-938-2858
Address Inquiries to: Michael M. Murray,
   President
Description: Supplier of media and audio equipment, motion picture projectors, screens and lenses.

Textile Resources
3763 Durango Avenue
Los Angeles, CA 90034
Tel: 213-838-9179
Address Inquiries to: Joan Ericson, General
   Manager
Description: Supplier of dyes and fabrics.

Video Systems Network, Incorporated
12530 Beatrice Street
Los Angeles, CA 90066
Tel: 213-871-0677
Description: Supplier of intercom systems, and microphone preamplifiers and mixers.

Westlake Audio
6311 Wilshire Boulevard
Los Angeles, CA 90048
Tel: 213-655-0303
Description: Supplier of sound equipment.

Hyman Hendler and Sons
763 South Los Angeles Street
Los Angeles, CA 90014
Tel: 213-627-9348

Description: Wide selections of fabrics and trims offering fireproofing and bonding.

Montebello

Teac Corporation of America
7733 Telegraph Road
Montebello, CA 90640
Tel: 213-726-0303
Address Inquiries to: Tay Hotta, Advertising
   Manager
Founded in: 1966
Member: NAMM; AES; NAB; NAVA;
Description: Supplier of tape recorders and mixers.

North Hollywood

Audiotronics
7428 Bellaire
North Hollywood, CA 91605
Tel: 213-765-2645
Address Inquiries to: G. Grindinger, Director
   of Corporation
Description: Audiotronics supplies audio visual equipment.

Cetec Gauss
13035 Saticoy Street
North Hollywood, CA 91605
Tel: 213-875-1900
Address Inquiries to: Mort Fujii, President
Ken McKenzie, National Sales Mgr., Gauss
   Loudspeakers
Description: Manufacturer of sound systems and equipment.

Filmways Audio Services
5540 Cleon Avenue
North Hollywood, CA 91601
Tel: 213-877-9711
Description: Supplier of intercom systems, microphone preamplifiers and mixers.

RTS Systems, Incorporated
4167 Fair Avenue
North Hollywood, CA 91602
Tel: 213-980-0511
Address Inquiries to: Douglas Leighton,
   President
Description: Maufacturer of intercom systems, microphone preamplifiers and mixers.

Sig Frends Beauty Supply Company
5202 Laurel Canyon Boulevard
North Hollywood, CA 91607
Description: Supplier of professional make-up.

Sound Chamber
12041 Burbank Boulevard
North Hollywood, CA 91607
Tel: 213-985-1376; 213-761-1454
Address Inquiries to: Diane H. Roth, Sales
   and Marketing
Founded in: 1976
Description: Supplies amplifiers, lighting and other technical equipment. It specializes in the design and implementation of custom audio and lighting systems throughout the world.

Theatre Vision
5426 Fair Avenue
North Hollywood, CA 91601
Tel: 213-769-0928
Address Inquiries to: Richard Meduitz
John Chuck
Founded in: 1977
Member: ATA; CETA; NAB; USITT;
Description: Rental and sales of lighting equipment. Suppliers of fabrics, paints and custom dyes.

Tri-Tronics Incorporated
4019 Tujunga Avenue
North Hollywood, CA 91604
Tel: 213-871-0677
Description: Supplier of intercom systems, and microphone preamplifiers and mixers.

Oakland

L.P. Marketing
2036 Livingston Street, #5
Oakland, CA 94606
Tel: 415-532-5600
Address Inquiries to: Larry Peterson
Description: Manufacturer of sound systems and equipment.

Pasadena

Rupert, Gibbon and Spider
470 Maylin Street
Pasadena, CA 91105
Tel: 213-792-0600
Address Inquiries to: Bea Katz, Office
   Manager
Description: Supplier of dyes and paints.

Pleasanton

Moulthrop Sales, Incorporated
7080 Commerce Drive
Pleasanton, CA 94566
Tel: 415-846-0550
Description: Supplier of sound equipment and intercom systems.

Redondo Beach

Smith-Victor Corporation
2810 Spreckels Lane
Redondo Beach, CA 90278
Tel: 213-371-6541
Description: Manufacturer of lighting equipment.

Redwood City

Weishaar Ashe and Associates
550 Price Avenue, Suite #4
Redwood City, CA 94063
Tel: 415-364-9802
Description: Supplier of sound equipment.

Sacramento

Sacramento Theatrical
212 13th Street
Sacramento, CA 95814
Tel: 916-447-7444
Address Inquiries to: John Cox
Description: Supplier of lighting equipment.

Skip's Music, Incorporated
2740 Auburn Boulevard
Sacramento, CA 95821
Description: Supplies music and amplification equipment, and stage lighting.

San Carlos

Stagecraft Industries, Incorporated
913 Tanklage Road
San Carlos, CA 94070
Tel: 415-592-8885
Address Inquiries to: Dan McIrvin, Manager
Description: Manufacturer of stage equipment.

San Diego

Audio Specialists of San Diego
1357 7th Avenue Suite A
San Diego, CA 92110
Tel: 714-231-3984
Description: Supplier of intercom systems and sound equipment.

Al Radick
Post Office Box 26667
San Diego, CA 92126
Tel: 815-886-3135
Address Inquiries to: Al Radick
Description: Supplier of folding stages and portable dance floors.

San Diego Stage and Lighting Supply
2002 State Street
San Diego, CA 92101
Tel: 714-235-8379
Address Inquiries to: Robert DeMent,
   President
   Lori Rubinstein, General Manager
Founded in: 1976
Description: A service and supply organization combining rentals and sales to the theatre industry.

San Fernando

Superscope Tape Duplicating Products
455 Fox Street
San Fernando, CA 91340
Tel: 213-365-1191
Address Inquiries to: M. Ned Padwa
Description: Supplier of sound equipment.

San Francisco

Charles A. Blakely Company
646 First Street
San Francisco, CA 94107
Tel: 415-431-5563
Address Inquiries to: Chuck Blakely
Description: Supplier of lighting equipment.

California Theatrical Supply
745 Polk Street
San Francisco, CA 94109
Tel: 415-928-5824; 415-957-1686
Address Inquiries to: Richard M. Barulich,
   General Manager
Founded in: 1976
Member: NOA; ATA; USITT;
Description: U.S. distributors for Kryolan and Brandel makeup as well as the best quality wig materials.

Clear-Com Intercom Systems (CCI)
1111 17th Street
San Francisco, CA 94107
Tel: 415-861-6666
Address Inquiries to: Ed Fitzgerald, Sales
   Director
   Peter Giddings, Marketing Director
Founded in: 1968
Description: A manufacturer of hard wired, hands-free intercom systems specially designed for the theatrical and auditorium business.

Dance Art Company, Serbin Company
222 Powell Street
San Francisco, CA 94102
Tel: 415-392-4912; 415-392-4913
Founded in: 1926
Description: Supplier of theatrical equipment including feathers, beads, sequins, fabrics, wigs, beards, masks, small props, makeup, jewels, tiaras, dancewear, dance shoes, glitter, fog machines and cobweb machines.

Flynns Fabric Design Supplies
1154 Howard Street
San Francisco, CA 94103
Tel: 415-621-5968, Flynns; 415-431-8214, Fibrec
Address Inquiries to: Michael W. Flynn, Sales
   Manager
   Darryl E. Brooks, Assistant Sales
   Manager
Founded in: 1969
Description: Supplier of a wide variety of dyes, textile paints, fabrics for dying and printing, books, etc.

Frap Company
Post Office Box 40097
San Francisco, CA 94114
Tel: 415-431-9350
Address Inquiries to: Cindy Portlock, Sales
   Manager
Description: Manufacturer of sound equipment.

Guitar Center
928 Van Ness Avenue
San Francisco, CA 94109
Tel: 415-441-4020
Address Inquiries to: John Root
Description: Supplier of sound equipment.

Holzmueller Corporation
2545 16th Street
San Francisco, CA 94103
Tel: 415-864-7800
Description: Supplier of lighting equipment.

Kryolan Corporation
747 Polk Street
San Francisco, CA 94109
Tel: 415-928-5824; 415-957-1686
Address Inquiries to: Richard M. Barulich
Founded in: 1975
Description: U.S. distributor of Kryolan and Brandel makeup.

Phoebus Company, Incorporated
145 Bluxome Street
San Francisco, CA 94107

Tel: 415-543-7626
Address Inquiries to: John Tedesco, President
Description: Supplier of lighting and technical equipment.

Sound Genesis
2001 Bryant Street
San Francisco, CA 94110
Tel: 415-285-8900
Description: Supplier of intercom systems and sound equipment.

Stahl and Stahl
101 Kansas Street, #114
San Francisco, CA 94103
Tel: 415-626-3037
Description: Supplier of theatrical fabrics and supplies.

San Jose

Dick Knell
2533 Cottle Avenue
San Jose, CA 95125
Tel: 408-267-0720
Address Inquiries to: Dick Knell
Description: Manufacturer of tapes for film processing.

Musson Theatrical, Incorporated
582 Stockton Avenue
San Jose, CA 95126
Tel: 408-296-0210
Description: Suppliers of lighting and technical equipment.

San Luis Obispo

Teatronics, Incorporated
101 Suburban Road
San Luis Obispo, CA 93401
Tel: 805-544-3555
Description: Manufacturers lighting equipment and the latest in solid state computerized lighting boards.

San Rafael

Dharma Trading Company
Post Office Box 916
San Rafael, CA 94902
Tel: 415-456-1211; 415-841-7722
Address Inquiries to: R. Robel, Manager
Description: Supplier of dyes, fabric paints and ready-to-dye fabric by mail order.

Santa Clara

Memorex Corporation
Post Office Box 1000
Santa Clara, CA 95052
Tel: 408-987-1072
Address Inquiries to: J.C. Higgins, Product
   Manager
Description: Manufacturer of audio and video tape.

The Superior Electric Company
1333 Lawrence Expressway
Santa Clara, CA 95051
Tel: 408-985-1435
Description: Supplier of electrical equipment.

Toluca Lake Station

Hammond Industries
Post Office Box 2229
Toluca Lake Station, CA 91602
Tel: 213-846-0500
Address Inquiries to: Derek Allen, West Coast
  Sales Manager
Description: Supplier of lighting and sound
equipment.

Torrance

Sharp Electronics Corporation
1047 Carson Boulevard
Torrance, CA 90502
Description: Manufacturer of television cameras and equipment.

Tustin

Jim Coffey
14352 Ehlen Way
Tustin, CA 92680
Tel: 714-832-6152
Address Inquiries to: Jim Coffey
Description: Supplier of stage shells and staging.

Van Nuys

Kryolan Corporation
14316 Victory Boulevard
Van Nuys, CA 91401
Tel: 213-789-1465; 213-787-5054
Address Inquiries to: Siegfried H. Geike,
  Secretary
Description: Manufacturer of professional
make-up.

West Covina

Norcostco California Costume
2101 West Garvey Avenue North
West Covina, CA 91790
Tel: 213-960-4711
Member: ATA;
Description: Supplies lighting equipment, theatrical makeup, stage supplies and costumes

Woodland Hills

Elmo Manufacturing Corporation
Post Office Box 828
Woodland Hills, CA 91367
Tel: 213-346-4500
Address Inquiries to: Chuck Logan
Description: Supplier of projectors.

The Great American Market
Box 178, 21133 Costanso Street
Woodland Hills, CA 91364
Tel: 213-883-8182
Address Inquiries to: Mofid Bissada, Sales
  Manager
Founded in: 1975
Member: NAB;
Description: Manufactures a line of unique
items for the motion picture, television,
theatre and concert stage. Starstrobe,
Colormax, Great American Patterns and the
Scene Machine are a few spectral products
that we supply. They also provide a custom
design servic e for special effects and projections.

The Superior Electric Company
6150 Canoga Avenue
Woodland Hills, CA 91367
Tel: 213-999-2150
Description: Supplier of electrical equipment.

COLORADO

Boulder

Studio Six Projects
3844 Orion Court
Boulder, CO 80302
Tel: 303-447-8286
Description: Supplier of lighting equipment.

Colorado Springs

Electronic Sound Products
3320 Chelton Loop South
Colorado Springs, CO 80909
Tel: 303-597-9350; 303-599-5264
Founded in: 1976
Description: Sales, rental and installation of
sound and lighting systems.

Stage Engineering and Supply
325 Karen Lane
Colorado Springs, CO 80901
Tel: 303-635-2935
Address Inquiries to: Dave Hand
Description: Supplier of lighting equipment.

Denver

B and B Electronic Products
500 South Quebec
Denver, CO 80237
Tel: 303-773-6700
Address Inquiries to: Bob Nelson
Description: Manufacturer of sound systems
and equipment.

Bozak, Incorporated
c/o Gedney Company
476 East 58th Avenue
Denver, CO 80216
Tel: 303-572-1900
Address Inquiries to: J.A. Gedney, Sales
  Manager
Description: A regional branch office.

Hiwest Lighting Specialties
2785 North Speer Boulevard, Suite 250
Denver, CO 80211
Tel: 303-433-8824
Description: Supplier of lighting equipment.

Johns-Manville Sales Corporation
Ken-Caryl Ranch
Denver, CO 80217
Tel: 303-979-1000
Address Inquiries to: D.G. Meredith, Market
  Manager
Description: Manufacturer of power supplies.

McCloud and Raymond Company
2020 South Pontiac Way
Denver, CO 80222
Tel: 303-756-1589
Description: Supplier of sound and intercom
systems.

Scowcroft and Associates
4895 Joliet Street Unit #D
Denver, CO 80239
Tel: 303-371-5280
Description: Supplier of sound equipment.

Theatrix, Incorporated
5138 East 39th Avenue
Denver, CO 80207
Tel: 303-388-9345
Address Inquiries to: Bob Bauer, President
Pete Happe, Marketing/Sales
Description: Supplier of lights and dimming
systems.

Walter Engineering Associates
880 Bonnie Brae Boulevard
Denver, CO 80209
Tel: 303-777-5585
Description: Supplier of electrical outlet strips
and utility carts.

Englewood

Intermountain Specialty Equipment
Company
Post Office Box 1158
Englewood, CO 80150
Tel: 303-773-1444
Description: Manufacturer of stage equipment.

Littleton

Electro-Tek Sales, Incorporated
991 West Quarles Drive
Littleton, CO 80123
Tel: 303-623-3370
Description: Manufacturer of commercial
sound equipment.

CONNECTICUT

Bedford Heights

Cercone-Vincent Associates, Inc.
5020 Richmond Road
Bedford Heights, CT 44146
Tel: 216-292-2550
Address Inquiries to: Paul Vincent
Description: Supplies theatrical, television and
lighting equipment.

Bethel

The Cutawl Company
Bethel, CT 06801
Tel: 203-792-8622
Address Inquiries to: Kent Kristensen, Sales
  Maager
Founded in: 1922
Description: Manufactures the Cutawl Machine and has world wide sales to the theatre
design industry.

Bristol

The Superior Electric Company
383 Middle Street
Bristol, CT 06020
Tel: 203-582-9561
Address Inquiries to: J. McMahon, Sales
Description: Manufacturer of electrical equip-

ment.

East Windsor Hill

Frank E. Brown Company, Inc.
Post Office Box 417
East Windsor Hill, CT 06028
Description: Manufacturer of lighting and supplier of stage and studio equipment.

Meriden

Show Lighting Corporation
26 South George Street
Meriden, CT 06450
Tel: 203-238-2000
Address Inquiries to: Will Hevey
Description: Supplier of lighting control systems.

Milford

Connecticut Theatre Supply/Theatre
Concepts
282 Woodmont Road
Milford, CT 06460
Tel: 203-877-4507
Address Inquiries to: John Petrafesa
Founded in: 1974
Description: Supplier of lighting control systems and general theatrical supplies.

Putnam

Superwinch, Incorporated
Connecticut Route 52 at Exit 95
Putnam, CT 06260
Tel: 203-928-7787
Address Inquiries to: Phyllis Racine,
    Customer Service Manager
Description: Manufacturer of winches and hoists for use in theatre.

South Norwalk

Bozak, Incorporated
587 Connecticut Avenue
South Norwalk, CT 06854
Tel: 203-838-6521
Address Inquiries to: Ron Coll, Vice
    President
Description: Supplies loudspeakers and electronics.

Trumbull

Colortran, Incorporated
24 Lake Avenue
Trumbull, CT 06611
Tel: 203-261-7835
Address Inquiries to: Charles Davidson,
    Manager
Member: NAB; USITT; SMPTE; IES;
Description: A regional branch office.

Wallingford

Herm Robbins Associates
34B Pilgrims Harbor
Wallingford, CT 06492
Tel: 203-265-5045
Address Inquiries to: Herm Robbins
Description: Supplier of lighting equipment.

Waterbury

Concert Lighting Company
437 Watertown Avenue
Waterbury, CT 06708
Tel: 203-573-1517
Address Inquiries to: Frank J. Esposito,
    Owner
Description: Manufacturer and supplier of neon, flash boxes and fog machines.

West Haven

Robert Reiss Associates
70 Jessie Drive
West Haven, CT 06516
Tel: 203-933-8542
Address Inquiries to: Robert Reiss
Description: Supplier of sound equipment.

DISTRICT OF COLUMBIA

Washington

National Stage Lighting
1232 9th Street, NW
Washington, DC 20001
Tel: 202-483-7090
Address Inquiries to: Neil Fleitell
Description: Supplier of lighting equipment.

FLORIDA

Ft. Lauderdale

Teco, Incorporated
1033 North East 44th Street
Post Office Box 23280
Ft. Lauderdale, FL 33334
Tel: 305-772-0242; 305-947-8751
Address Inquiries to: Chub Puia
Description: Supplier of lighting equipment.

Hialeah

Apollo Lights and Sound
1514 East 4th Avenue
Hialeah, FL 33010
Tel: 305-887-8899
Description: Sound and lighting equipment for the stage.

Miguel A. Lopez
825 West 31st Street
Hialeah, FL 33012
Tel: 305-822-6853
Address Inquiries to: Miguel A. Lopez
Description: Supplier of commercial sound equipment.

Maitland

Hutto-Hawkins-Peregoy
139 Candace Drive
Maitland, FL 32751
Tel: 305-831-2474
Description: Supplier of sound equipment.

Miami

George Gill Associates
Post Office Box 610124
Miami, FL 33161
Tel: 305-891-2622
Address Inquiries to: George Gill, Partner
Member: USITT;
Annual Budget: $2,000,000
Description: George Gill, Eastern Manager of ColorTran Industries, became associated with the visual communications industry in 1931 when he took an interest in theatrical effects while attending New York University.

Image Devices Incorporated
1825 North East 149th Street
Miami, FL 33181
Tel: 305-945-1111
Address Inquiries to: Bill Reiter, Associate
Description: Supplier of film and video equipment.

Lite-Trol Service Company, Incorporated
12229 North East 13th Court
Miami, FL 33161
Tel: 305-891-1581
Address Inquiries to: Rick Rudolph, Vice
    President.
Description: Repairs lighting systems.

Stage Equipment and Lighting,
Incorporated
Post Office Box 61000F
Miami, FL 33161
Tel: 305-891-2010
Address Inquiries to: Mike Grosz, Vice
    President, Technical Consultant
    Rick Rudolph, Technical Consultant
Description: Supplier of stage and lighting equipment, fluorescent paints, phosphorescent tapes and paints.

World Wide Products, Incorporated
10818 North West 6th Court
Miami, FL 33168
Tel: 305-754-5475
Description: Supplier of sound and intercom systems.

North Miami

Dazian's Incorporated
1785 Broad Causeway, Suite No. 9
North Miami, FL 33181
Tel: 305-893-3430; 305-893-3431
Description: Supplier of theatrical fabrics and supplies.

North Miami Beach

John Barry
815 North East 172nd Terrace
North Miami Beach, FL 33162
Address Inquiries to: John Barry
Description: Supplier of wireless microphones.

Orlando

John W. Carroll
1133 Marlowe Avenue
Orlando, FL 32809
Tel: 305-855-1993

Address Inquiries to: John W. Carroll
Description: Manufacturer of commercial sound equipment.

Discount Music Center
456 North Orange Avenue
Orlando, FL 32801
Tel: 305-843-2025
Description: Suppliers and renters of lighting, music systems and other technical equipment. Discount also repairs equipment.

Photomart
6327 South Orange Avenue
Orlando, FL 32809
Description: Supplier of wireless microphones.

Gene A. Rowell
1222 Country Club Drive
Orlando, FL 32804
Tel: 305-425-6228
Address Inquiries to: Gene A. Rowell
Description: Supplier of microphone and audio equipment.

Pensacola

Grice Electronics
Post Office Box 1911
320 East Gregory Street
Pensacola, FL 32501
Tel: 904-477-8100
Description: Electronic supplies for the stage, including lighting and sound systems.

Pinellas Park

Discovery Sound and Light
4988 73rd Avenue North
Pinellas Park, FL 33565
Tel: 813-546-5518
Description: Suppliers of sound systems and stage lighting.

Frank C. McPherson Associates
Post Office Box 800
Pinellas Park, FL 33565
Tel: 813-577-3300
Address Inquiries to: Frank C. McPherson
Description: Supplier of lighting equipment.

Plantation

Capron Lighting and Sound
991 South State Road 7
Plantation, FL 33317
Tel: 305-792-8812
Address Inquiries to: Howard Packer, Vice President
Description: Manufacturer of lighting and supplier of stage and studio equipment.

Erich Gompertz and Associates
941 South West 70th Avenue
Plantation, FL 33314
Tel: 305-583-5819
Address Inquiries to: Erich Gompertz
Description: Manufacturer of tapes for film processing.

Sarasota

Michael Chafee Enterprises
2215 Alpine Avenue
Sarasota, FL 33579
Tel: 813-621-7725
Address Inquiries to: Mike Chafee
Description: Manufacturer of sound systems and equipment.

St. Petersburg

John F. Thompson Company
5003 Brittany Drive South
St. Petersburg, FL 33715
Tel: 813-866-0045
Address Inquiries to: John F. Thompson
Founded in: 1962
Member: ERA;
Description: Supplier of sound equipment.

Tampa

Bay Stage Lighting
310 South MacDill Avenue
Tampa, FL 33609
Tel: 813-877-1089
Address Inquiries to: Sam Marino
Description: Supplier of lighting control systems.

Design Line
5485 Jet Port Industrial Boulevard
Tampa, FL 33614
Tel: 813-886-5073
Description: Supplier of lighting equipment, flourescent paints, phosphorescent tapes and paints.

Welaka

Hartman and Associates, Incorporated
Box 459, Beecher's Point
Welaka, FL 32093
Tel: 904-467-9296
Description: Manufacturer of lighting equipment.

GEORGIA

Atlanta

Afera
1848 Briarwood Road
Atlanta, GA 30329
Description: Supplier of wireless microphones.

Bozak Incorporated
3819 Oakcliff Industrial Court
Atlanta, GA 30340
Tel: 404-448-3790
Address Inquiries to: David Roddey, Manager
Description: A regional branch office.

Cassandra Henning
Division of L and M Stagecraft
1446 Mayson Street
Atlanta, GA 30324
Tel: 404-875-2683; 404-872-6686
Address Inquiries to: Cassandra Henning
Description: Supplier of lighting equipment and audio/visual equipment.

Design Lighting Systems
4200 Perimeter Park South
Atlanta, GA 30341
Tel: 404-457-2594
Description: Supplier of lighting equipment.

Duro-Test Light Center
1950 Century Boulevard NE, Suite 4
Atlanta, GA 30345
Tel: 404-633-0132
Address Inquiries to: Marion Croom, Vice President-Sales
Description: Supplier of light bulbs and spot lights.

Globe Ticket Company
Post Office Box 82759, Hapeville Branch
Atlanta, GA 30354
Tel: 404-766-0286
Description: Supplier of tickets and ticket equipment.

Herschel-Harrington Scenic and Lighting Studio
132-A Tenth North East
Atlanta, GA 30309
Tel: 404-892-0065
Address Inquiries to: Charles Walker
Description: Supplier of lighting equipment.

Hollingsworth and Still
1611 Perimeter Center East
Atlanta, GA 30346
Tel: 404-394-3270
Description: Supplier of electrical outlet strips and utility carts.

Image Devices Incorporated
1615 Phoenix Boulevard
Atlanta, GA 30349
Tel: 404-996-0000
Address Inquiries to: Steve Brinson
Description: Supplier of film and video equipment.

Millar Electronics, Incorporated
3110 Maple Drive NE, Room 110
Atlanta, GA 30305
Tel: 404-261-6160; 404-261-6161
Description: Supplier of sound equipment.

Norcostco-Atlanta Costume
2089 Monroe Drive, NE
Atlanta, GA 30324
Tel: 404-874-7511
Member: ATA;
Description: Supplier of lighting equipment, theatrical make-up, stage supplies and costumes.

Chamblee

Technical Systems Reps
2065 Peachtree Industrial Court, Suite 215
Chamblee, GA 30341
Tel: 404-457-0426
Description: Supplier of sound and intercom systems.

Hampton

M.W. Productions
Route 2, Box 130
Hampton, GA 30228
Tel: 404-955-2742
Description: Manufacturer of PYROPAK materials, and supplier of custom lighting systems.

Marietta

Bob Branand
2926 Missy Drive
Marietta, GA 30060
Tel: 404-993-1282; 404-993-1283
Description: Supplier of folding stages and portable dance floors.

Roswell

Henry W. Phillips Company
110 Mansel Circle
Roswell, GA 30075
Tel: 404-992-3070
Address Inquiries to: Henry W. Phillips
Founded in: 1970
Member: ERA;
Description: Supplier of sound equipment.

Stone Mountain

Roger Anderson
635 Navarre Drive
Stone Mountain, GA 30087
Tel: 404-469-2864
Address Inquiries to: Roger Anderson
Description: Supplier of stage shells and staging.

Tucker

El Rep Sales
4508 Bibb Boulevard, Suite B4
Tucker, GA 30004
Tel: 404-938-7108
Address Inquiries to: Ben Van De Kreke
Founded in: 1969
Description: Manufacturer of sound systems and equipment and manufacturer's electronics representative.

HAWAII
Honolulu

American Seating Company
352 Ward Avenue
Honolulu, HI 96814
Tel: 808-537-6608

Electronic Services, Incorporated
690-G Kakoi Street
Honolulu, HI 96816
Tel: 808-847-4891
Address Inquiries to: Craig Maddox
Description: Supplier of lighting equipment.

Lee Gaber Company
Post Office Box 8237
Honolulu, HI 96815
Tel: 808-839-9059
Address Inquiries to: Lee Gaber
Description: Supplier of sound equipment.

Gene Piety Factors
861 Mapunapuna Street
Honolulu, HI 96802
Tel: 808-839-9059
Address Inquiries to: Gene Piety
Description: Supplier of electrical outlet strips and utility carts.

Kailua

Eggshell Lighting Company
1120 Hele Street
Kailua, HI 96734
Tel: 808-262-9605
Description: Supplier of lighting and technical equipment.

IDAHO
Caldwell

Caxton Printers, Ltd.
Post Office Box 700
Caldwell, ID 83605
Tel: 208-459-7421
Description: Manufacturer of stage equipment.

ILLINOIS
Addison

Classic Communications
47 East Fullerton
Addison, IL 60101
Tel: 312-279-8082
Address Inquiries to: David Skrudland
Founded in: 1965
Member: NAVA; AMI;
Description: Supplies audio-visual hardware, programming equipment and screens.

Barrington

Modular Sound Systems
22 North Pepper Road
Barrington, IL 60010
Tel: 312-382-4550
Address Inquiries to: Jim Wischmeyer
Description: Supplies speaker systems and audio equipment.

Pro Audio Sales
111 South Drive Tower Lakes
Barrington, IL 60010
Tel: 312-381-4559
Address Inquiries to: Brian Tucker
Description: Manufacturer of sound systems and equipment.

Berwyn

Figatner-Scott Company
6217 West Cermak Road
Berwyn, IL 60402
Tel: 312-484-2800
Description: Supplies paints, wall coverings, art supplies and picture framing.

Irvin H. Raditz and Company
7115 West Roosevelt
Berwyn, IL 60402
Tel: 312-788-1079
Description: Irvin H. Raditz and Company supplies make-up and costume accessories.

Champaign

American Scenic Company
Post Office Box 862
#2 Henson Place
Champaign, IL 61820
Tel: 217-351-6253
Description: Supplier of lighting equipment.

Ancha Electronics
713 Edgebrook
Champaign, IL 61820
Tel: 217-398-6600; 217-398-6601
Address Inquiries to: Robert F. Ancha, President
Founded in: 1964
Description: Ancha Electronics, a company founded by its president, Robert F. Ancha in 1964, is a group of professional communications engineers and consultants. Virtually every conceivable communications application is available to their clientele. They specialize in system design and installation. As designers they prefer the challenges of satisfying functional needs to the routine marketing of electronic equipment.

J.R. Russell Electric
714 South Niel
Champaign, IL 61820
Tel: 217-356-8700
Address Inquiries to: Ronald E. Johnson, Vice President
Description: Supplier of complete lines of sound and lighting equipment.

Chicago

The Arcus Ticket Company
348 North Ashland Avenue
Chicago, IL 60607
Tel: 312-733-7440
Address Inquiries to: Harold Gannon
Description: Prints and sells all kinds of tickets.

Art Drapery Studios
6252 North Pulaski
Chicago, IL 60646
Tel: 312-736-9700
Address Inquiries to: George F. Petterson Mike Neben
Description: Supplies stage equipment and furnishings, and installs stage rigging.

Bailey's Incorporated
25 West Van Buren Street
Chicago, IL 60605
Tel: 312-939-2172
Address Inquiries to: Ray Gnat
Description: Supplies military clothing, shoes and camping clothes.

Ballantyne Flamproofing Company
2722 North Lincoln Avenue
Chicago, IL 60614
Tel: 312-348-7770
Address Inquiries to: William J. Ballantyne, President

Ray Roach, Product Sales
Founded in: 1939
Description: Supplies and services products to fire retard-cloth, paper and display items.

Becker Studios
2824 West Taylor Street
Chicago, IL 60612
Tel: 312-722-4040
Address Inquiries to: Brian Becker, Treasurer
Founded in: 1903
Member: IATSE;
Description: Becker Studios are custom designers and builders of scenery, drops, displays; serving legitmate theatre, industial, multimedia and trade shows, commercials, films, television and conventions.

Behrend's Incorporated
541 North Franklin
Chicago, IL 60610
Tel: 312-527-3060
Address Inquiries to: Jack Behrend
Founded in: 1953
Member: SMPTE;
Description: Supplies 16mm and 35mm picture projectors, slide projectors, speakers, microphones and programmers.

Belden Communications
25 West 45th Street, Room 1206
Chicago, IL 60612
Tel: 212-730-0172
Address Inquiries to: Paula Boxer,
  Advertising and Marketing Director
Description: Belden Communications supplies discharge lights.

B.J. Seaman and Company
1801 South Lumber
Chicago, IL 60634
Tel: 312-666-6580; 312-733-7911
Address Inquiries to: B.J. Seaman
Founded in: 1961
Description: Supplies fabrics: e.g. Muslins, cheesecloths, silouette cloth, burlaps, meshes, nettings, floor coverings, back drops, flat coverings, webbings, and tapes. Services: cutting, sewing, grometting, printing, painting, and repairing.

Broadway Costumes
932 West Washington
Chicago, IL 60607
Tel: 312-829-6400
Address Inquiries to: R.W. Kondor, President
R.C. Schramm, Vice President, General
  Manager
Founded in: 1886
Annual Budget: $500,000
Description: Supplier of costumes and actor's accessories.

Channon Corporation
1343 West Argyle
Chicago, IL 60640
Tel: 312-475-4700
Address Inquiries to: Max F. Roller, President
  Description: Manufacturer of stage equipment, stage curtains and gym dividers.

Chicago Hair Goods
428 South Wabash Avenue
Chicago, IL 60605
Tel: 312-427-8600
Address Inquiries to: Nathan L. Goldstein,
  President
Member: ATA;
Description: Distributor and manufacturer of wigs, moustaches, beards, and hairpieces for men, women and children.

Chicago Scenic Studios
2217 West Belmont Avenue
Chicago, IL 60618
Tel: 312-942-1483, Shop; 312-477-8366, Office
Address Inquiries to: Robert F. Doepel
Founded in: 1978
Member: USITT;
Description: Supplies complete production services, rental, design, management, supervision and fabrication of sets, costumes, props and lights. The shop is located at 213 N. Morgan Street, Chicago, IL, 60607.

Chicago Spotlight
4036 West Waveland
Chicago, IL 60641
Tel: 312-777-8824
Address Inquiries to: Dawn Hollingsworth,
  Sales Manager
Description: Supplies spotlights and associated support equipment.

Chicago's Recycle Shop
5308 North Clark
Chicago, IL 60660
Tel: 312-878-8525
Description: Supplies authentic vintage clothing, jewelry, props and furniture.

Chicago Tanning Company
1500 West Cortland Street
Chicago, IL 60622
Tel: 312-486-8180
Address Inquiries to: Tina Caldwell
Description: Supplies leather, grain, suede, deerskin, sheepskin and chamois.

Comco Plastics of Illinois
4920 South Monitor Avenue
Chicago, IL 60638
Tel: 312-496-1800; 312-581-3000
Address Inquiries to: Kay Carroll, Branch
  Manager
Founded in: 1945
Member: NAPDF;
Description: Supplies plastic fabrications.

Contemporary Quilt and Fabrics
2863 North Clark Street
Chicago, IL 60657
Tel: 312-528-0360
Description: Supplies quilting kits, stencils, patterns and cotton fabrics.

Costumes Unlimited
814 North Franklin
Chicago, IL 60610
Tel: 312-642-0200
Address Inquiries to: Jack W. Kirkby,
  President

Description: Supplier of costumes for productions, conventions, photographers and film studios.

Dazian's Incorporated
400 North Wells Street
Chicago, IL 60610
Tel: 312-467-1991
Description: Supplier of theatrical fabrics and supplies.

Decorators Supply Corporation
3610-12 South Morgan Street
Chicago, IL 60609
Tel: 312-847-6300
Address Inquiries to: Jack Maingast
Description: Supplies interior architectural details, wall applicate and wall panels.

Diversitronics, Incorporated
415 North State Street
Chicago, IL 60610
Tel: 312-644-3816
Address Inquiries to: Larry Cada
Description: Supplies high intensity strobe lights and special effects systems.

Eager Plastics
3701 South Halsted Street
Chicago, IL 60609
Tel: 312-927-3484; 312-927-3515
Address Inquiries to: Peter Cumerford, Sales
  and Technical Service
Founded in: 1977
Description: Supplies fiberglass cloth, polyester and epoxy resins, latex mold making rubber, silicon RTV, related materials suitable for sculpture resin art, resin stained glass, stage props, fiberglass scenery, fiberglass mountains, water falls and lakes.

Foamcraft Incorporated
947 West Van Buren Street
Chicago, IL 60607
Tel: 312-243-6262
Address Inquiries to: Bernard L. Joseph
Description: Supplies flexible foams.

Fraerman Yard Goods and Draperies
Company
314 West Adams Street
Chicago, IL 60606
Tel: 312-236-6886; 312-236-6887
Address Inquiries to: Irving M. Shepard,
  President
  Gary Melonian, Vice President and
  General Manager
Founded in: 1933
Member: American Home Sewing
  Association; Chicago Chamber of
  Commerce;
Description: Supplies woolens, silks, cottons, velvet drapery, metallics, polyesters and every other kind of fabric a performing arts group could require.

Furniture Leasing Service
819 North Clark Street
Chicago, IL 60610
Tel: 312-642-0600
Description: Supplies and rents residential and office furniture.

George B. Carpenter and Company
401 North Ogden
Chicago, IL 60647
Tel: 312-666-8700
Address Inquiries to: Mazella Jackson
Darlene Runyon
Description: Supplies cordage, scenery fabrics, artists canvas, grommets and finishing tools.

G. Fishman's Sons, Incorporated
1101 South Desplaines Street
Chicago, IL 60607
Tel: 312-922-7250; 312-922-725½ /3
Address Inquiries to: Frank Henkin
Founded in: 1904
Description: Supplies fabrics of all kinds and related trimmings.

Grand Stage Lighting Company
630 West Lake Street
Chicago, IL 60606
Tel: 312-332-5611; 800-621-2181
Address Inquiries to: Dawn Hollingsworth
Description: Suppliers of lighting equipment, make-up, hi-fi goods and disco products.

Hall's Rental Service, Incorporated
3950 West Devon Avenue
Chicago, IL 60659
Tel: 312-982-9200
Description: Supplies china, silver, glassware, antique silver and copper tables.

House of Drane
410-20 North Ashland Avenue
Chicago, IL 60622
Tel: 312-829-8686
Description: Supplies costumes, masks and adult novelties.

Ray R. Hutmacher Associates, Inc.
7205 West Pratt
Chicago, IL 60631
Tel: 312-631-3248
Address Inquiries to: Ray R. Hutmacher
Description: Supplier of sound equipment.

Izzy Rizzy's House of Tricks
6034 South Pulaski
Chicago, IL 60629
Tel: 312-735-7370
Description: Supplies costumes, magic tricks, ventriloquist dummies and puppets.

Joseph Lumber Company
2001 North Narragansett
Chicago, IL 60639
Tel: 312-622-3000
Description: Supplies lumber, building materials, paint and hardware.

Kennedy-Webster Electric Company
133 North Jefferson Street
Chicago, IL 60606
Tel: 312-876-1612
Address Inquiries to: Catherine Heber
  Gradert
Founded in: 1912
Description: Distributors of all types of light bulbs.

Lighting Associates
2626 Lakeview, Suite 2008
Chicago, IL 60614
Tel: 312-348-6767
Address Inquiries to: Sylvia Price,
  Secretary/Treasurer
Description: Supplier of lighting symbol templates.

National Electric Supply
5311 North Kedzie Avenue
Chicago, IL 60625
Tel: 312-463-1470
Address Inquiries to: Rob Ramsden
Description: Supplies lamps, fixtures and videotapes.

Odd's 'N Ends Unlimited
932 West Washington Boulevard
Chicago, IL 60607
Tel: 312-666-2660
Address Inquiries to: R.W. Kondor, President
R.C. Schramm, Manager
Founded in: 1977
Description: Supplies costume needs: fabrics, jewelry, imported ethnic costumes, weapons and accessories.

Perle Roland Perfume Shop
946 West Rush Street
Chicago, IL 60611
Tel: 312-944-1432
Address Inquiries to: Mary Wall
Founded in: 1964
Description: Supplies theatrical makeup, perfumes, colognes and toiletries for men and women.

Petersen Brothers Plastics
2041 West Belmont
Chicago, IL 60618
Tel: 312-528-6161
Description: Supplies plastic rods, tubes and cement.

Progress Feather Company
657 West Lake Street
Chicago, IL 60606
Tel: 312-726-7443
Address Inquiries to: Melville Beswick
Founded in: 1913
Description: Supplies feathers of all kinds.

Rauland-Borg
3535 West Addison Street
Chicago, IL 60618
Tel: 312-267-1300
Address Inquiries to: Carl Dorwaldt
Description: Supplies professional sound systems.

R. Nyren Company
2222 West Diversey
Chicago, IL 60647
Tel: 312-276-5515
Address Inquiries to: R. Nyren
Description: Supplies textile trimmings, fringes and cords.

Sanders Lighting Templates
5830 West Patterson Avenue
Chicago, IL 60618
Tel: 312-736-9551; 312-725-4345

Address Inquiries to: Richard J. Sanders Sr.,
  President
Founded in: 1980
Member: AIA; USITT; ATA;
Description: Supplies stage and television lighting templates, as well as scene designers and sound system templates. They also carry a full line of other templates under the name of Sanders Templates, for architects, draftsmen and computer programmers.

Saul S. Siegal Company
847 West Jackson Boulevard
Chicago, IL 60607
Tel: 312-738-3400
Address Inquiries to: Leon Siegel
Sidney Moltz
Description: Supplies fabrics and drapes.

S. Hirsh and Sons
621-23 West Randolph Street
Chicago, IL 60606
Tel: 312-263-5213
Description: Supplies authentic period clothing, and military costumes.

Standard Photo Supply
43 East Chicago Avenue
Chicago, IL 60611
Tel: 312-440-4920
Address Inquiries to: Bob Aberg
Description: Supplies photographic and graphic arts supplys.

Taubman Textiles
2845 West 48th Street
Chicago, IL 60632
Tel: 312-523-6351
Address Inquiries to: John Zita
Description: Supplies backdrop cloths.

Thunderbird Products Company
1042 West Van Buren
Chicago, IL 60607
Tel: 312-733-2340
Address Inquiries to: Lydia Ellis
Description: Supplies giftwares and indian type beadwork for costumes.

Walbrunn Paint Company
1846 West 95th Street
Chicago, IL 60643
Tel: 312-445-2267

Widl Video
5425 West Diversey
Chicago, IL 60639
Tel: 312-622-9606
Address Inquiries to: Jerry O'Connell
Description: Supplies cables, connectors and adaptors.

Crystal Lake

Dimatronics Incorporated
171 South Main Street
Crystal Lake, IL 60014
Tel: 815-455-4400
Address Inquiries to: Richard Latronica, Vice
  President
  Mary Czajka, Sales Service Production
Founded in: 1972
Description: Supplies dimming systems,and

provides service, repair and consultation on new equipment.

Elk Grove Village

Audio Visual Techniques
1380 Louis Avenue
Elk Grove Village, IL 60007
Tel: 312-956-8300
Description: Supplies rental, sales and service of audio-visual equipment.

A World of Plastic
1517 South Elmhurst Road
Elk Grove Village, IL 60007
Tel: 312-956-6161
Address Inquiries to: Phil Mansole
Description: Supplies and fabricates acrylic and Lucite products.

Duro-Test Sales and Service
1200 Kirk Street
Elk Grove Village, IL 60007
Tel: 312-766-0042
Address Inquiries to: Harley Jones
Description: Specializes in decorative bulbs for all commercial and industrial applications.

Upstaging, Incorporated
1001 Nicholas Boulevard
Elk Grove Village, IL 60007
Tel: 312-640-1185
Description: Supplier of lighting equipment.

Visuals Ltd.
1485-C Landmeier Road
Elk Grove Village, IL 60007
Tel: 312-640-1185
Address Inquiries to: Gary Carone
Description: Supplies theatrical lighting and touring systems.

Evanston

Midwest Stage Lighting
2104 Central
Evanston, IL 60201
Tel: 312-328-3966
Description: Supplies stage and concert lighting systems and effects.

Shure Brothers, Incorporated
222 Hartrey Avenue
Evanston, IL 60204
Tel: 312-866-2547
Address Inquiries to: Pat Dalton, National Sales Manager
Description: Supplier of sound equipment and high-fidelity components.

Galesburg

Putnam Color and Dye
Post Office Box 1267
Galesburg, IL 61401
Tel: 309-343-6181
Address Inquiries to: John Flaherty
Description: Supplies dyes, paints, arts and crafts materials.

Glen Ellyn

The Superior Electric Company
799 Roosevelt Road
Glen Ellyn, IL 60137
Tel: 312-858-2960
Description: Supplier of electrical equipment.

Glenview

American Mobile Video
946 Golfview Road
Glenview, IL 60025
Tel: 312-729-6280
Description: Supplier of intercom systems, microphone preamplifiers and mixers.

Groveland

Loren Benbow and Associates
Post Office Box 244
Groveland, IL 61535
Tel: 309-387-6556
Address Inquiries to: Loren Benbow
Description: Supplier of lighting equipment.

Highland Park

R-Columbia Product Company, Incorporated
2008 St. Johns Avenue
Highland Park, IL 60035
Tel: 312-432-7915
Address Inquiries to: Irving Rozak, President
Description: Manufacturer of headphones and microphones.

Itasca

Superscope Chicago, Incorporated
1300 Norwood Avenue
Itasca, IL 60143
Tel: 312-569-2147
Address Inquiries to: Henry Werch
Description: Supplier of sound equipment.

Lincolnwood

Research Technology International
4700 Chase Avenue
Lincolnwood, IL 60646
Tel: 312-677-3000; 800-323-7520
Address Inquiries to: Ray L. Short Jr., President
  Tom Boyle, National Sales Manager
Founded in: 1969
Member: NAB; SMPTE; NAVA; NMA; NARMC; NRB;
Description: Manufacturer of film cleaning equipment, film editing and care supplies, and videotape evaluator/cleaners. Supplier of film and video accessories, supplies, storage and furniture. Write for their catalog featuring over 1200 items.

Lombard

Northwestern Theatre Association
146 Eisenhower Lane, North
Lombard, IL 60148
Tel: 312-629-4165
Address Inquiries to: Kevin Brady
Description: Supplier of lighting equipment.

Strand Century, Incorporated
303 West Greenfield
Lombard, IL 60148
Tel: 312-629-1664
Address Inquiries to: Larry Brown, Regional Manager
Description: Supplier of lighting equipment.

McHenry

Mar Ray Costume Shops
3923 West Main Street
McHenry, IL 60050
Tel: 815-385-6077
Address Inquiries to: Marge Olszewski
Founded in: 1968
Member: NCA; Clowns of America;
Description: A collection of costumes for rental. Theatrical makeup, novelties, hats, and dance supplies are available for sale-- retail only.

Naperville

Tech Theatre Incorporated
Post Office Box 401
Naperville, IL 60540
Tel: 312-971-0855
Address Inquiries to: Dana Howard
Description: Supplier of lighting equipment.

Normal

Richard Seniff
R.R. #8, Post Office Box 87
Normal, IL 61761
Tel: 309-452-2089
Address Inquiries to: Richard Seniff
Description: Supplier of stage shells and staging.

Northbrook

Ansell-Simplex Ticket Company
2970 Maria Avenue
Northbrook, IL 60062
Tel: 312-291-0696
Address Inquiries to: Joel Meagher, Salesman
  David Prober, Executive Sales Director
Founded in: 1906
Description: Supplies tickets of all kinds. Terms and discounts available to eligible companies, schools and individuals.

William M. Linz Associates, Inc.
821 Skokie Boulevard
Northbrook, IL 60062
Tel: 312-498-9600
Address Inquiries to: William M. Linz
Description: Supplier of sound and intercom systems.

Major Corporation
455 Academy Drive
Northbrook, IL 60062
Tel: 312-564-4550
Address Inquiries to: Dan Aberson, Sales Engineer
Description: Manufacturer of lighting and control equipment.

Oak Brook

Johns-Manville Sales Corporation
2222 Kensington Court
Oak Brook, IL 60521
Tel: 312-887-7400
Address Inquiries to: F.K. O'Connell, District
   Sales Manager
Description: Manufacturer of power supplies.

Oak Park

Herman Leis and Son
6739 West North Avenue
Oak Park, IL 60302
Tel: 312-524-0424
Address Inquiries to: Walter Kurt Leis,
   Owner
Founded in: 1932
Description: Supplies hairpieces.

Palatine

F.P.C. Corporation
615 West Colfax
Palatine, IL 60067
Tel: 312-359-3838
Address Inquiries to: Patrick Kamins
Description: Supplies hot melt glue, glue guns,
pop rivets and pop rivet tools.

Mar Ray Costume Shop
557 N. Hicks Rd.
Palatine Mall
Palatine, IL 60067
Tel: 312-991-0777
Address Inquiries to: Marge Olszewski
Founded in: 1968
Member: NCA; Clowns of America;
Description: A collection of costumes for rent-
al. Theatrical makeup, novelties, hats, and
dance supplies are available for sale-- retail
only.

Park Forest South

International Honeycomb Corporation
1149 Central Avenue
Park Forest South, IL 60466
Tel: 800-323-9161; 312-534-6595
Founded in: 1972
Member: USITT;
Description: Supplies kraft panels for scenery.
Known for its lightweight flats.

River Grove

Hala Kahiki
2832 River Road
River Grove, IL 60171
Tel: 312-456-3222
Address Inquiries to: Rose Marie Stieg
Description: Supplies Hawaiian costumes,
musical instruments and decorations.

Rosemont

Rent Com Incorporated
9550 Berwyn
Rosemont, IL 60018
Tel: 312-678-0071
Address Inquiries to: Ron Steinberg
Dan Evans
Founded in: 1971
Member: AES; AMI;

Annual Budget: $1 million
Description: Supplies sound, video and projection service.

Savanna

FaceMakers, Incorporated
140 Fifth Street
Savanna, IL 61074
Tel: 815-273-3944
Address Inquiries to: Mrs. St. George
Hobart C. Carstairs, Executive Secretary
Founded in: 1972
Member: NCA;
Description: The largest supplier of animal
and character costumes in the United States,
featuring original designs (over 200 differ-
ent animals) and custom making facilities.
Animal costumes are available for purchase
and rental. A catalogue is available.

Schaumburg

William Wawak Company
2235 Hammond Drive
Schaumburg, IL 60195
Tel: 312-397-4850
Address Inquiries to: William F. Wawak
Description: Supplies sewing and tailoring
items.

Schiller Park

Polyform Products Company
9420 West Byron Street
Schiller Park, IL 60176
Tel: 312-678-4836
Description: Supplies oven baking modeling
compounds.

Skokie

Dance Barre Inc.
4935 Oakton
Skokie, IL 60077
Tel: 312-674-5064
Founded in: 1975
Description: Supplies leotards, tights, skate-
dresses, jazz pants, exercise and gymnastic
shoes.

Springfield

Brent Theatrical Lighting
12 Whippoorwill Road
Rural Route 6
Springfield, IL 62707
Tel: 217-546-9608
Description: Supplier of lighting and technical
equipment for the stage.

H.M. Kloppenburg and Sons
1529 South MacArthur Blvd.
Springfield, IL 62704
Description: Manufacturer of lighting and
supplier of stage and studio equipment.

Summit

The Feed Store
5408 South Harlem
Summit, IL 60501
Tel: 312-458-1327
Address Inquiries to: Joesph G. Bestwina
Description: Supplies hay, burlap bags, corn

and wheat stalks.

Wheeling

Foster Sound Incorporated
505 Harvester Court
Wheeling, IL 60090
Tel: 312-541-7510
Address Inquiries to: June Bart
Description: Supplies professional audio
equipment, designs and installs sound rein-
forcement systems.

INDIANA
Anderson

Lumatrol Corporation
409 Citizens Bank Building
Anderson, IN 46016
Tel: 317-649-0606
Address Inquiries to: Lowell Davidson
Jim Bittner

Carmel

Midwest Representatives and Associates
30 East Main Street
Carmel, IN 46032
Tel: 317-844-4555
Description: Supplier of sound equipment.

Griffith

Smith-Victor Corporation
301 North Colfax
Griffith, IN 46319
Tel: 219-924-6136; 800-348-9862
Address Inquiries to: R.B. McCullough, Sales
   Department
Founded in: 1874
Member: National Association of
   Photographic Manufacturers; National
   Audio-Visual Association; Photographic
   Marketing Association;
Description: Manufacturer of lighting equip-
ment; supplies video and photographic ac-
cessories.

Huntington

Bozak
c/o Bob Hoke Sales, Inc.
56 Belair Drive
Post Office Box 771
Huntington, IN 46750
Tel: 219-356-1555
Description: A regional branch office.

Indianapolis

Indiana Electrical Sales
5160 East 65th Streeet
Indianapolis, IN 46220
Tel: 317-849-3880
Address Inquiries to: Gary Herder
George Ransford
Description: Supplier of lighting equipment.

Merrill Stage Equipment
6520 Westfield Boulevard
Indianapolis, IN 46220
Tel: 317-255-4666
Address Inquiries to: Frank E. Merrill, Owner

Founded in: 1946
Member: USITT; American National Standards Institute; American Theatre Association; Indiana Theatre Association;
Description: Supplies equipment for educational and community theatres around Indiana, including lighting, scenic, intercom equipment and make-up.

Stage Tech
5602 Elmwood Drive, Suite 216
Indianapolis, IN 46239
Tel: 317-788-9715
Description: Suppliers of lighting and technical equipment.

Sukup and Cox, Incorporated
2060 East 54th Street
Indianapolis, IN 46220
Tel: 317-253-5501
Description: Supplier of sound and intercom systems.

Tipton Sound and Lighting
36 South Pennsylvania
Indianapolis, IN 46204
Tel: 317-631-2703
Address Inquiries to: David L. Tipton, President
Founded in: 1975
Annual Budget: $250,000
Description: Supplies and rents and repairs sound systems, lighting and other technical equipment for the stage.

Middlebury

Gohn Brothers
Post Office Box 111
Middlebury, IN 46540
Tel: 219-825-2400
Address Inquiries to: Lamar E. Gohn
Description: Supplies Amish 'work' clothes, suits, overcoats, quilting and yard goods.

Newberg

Eckert Lighting
605 Adams Street
Newberg, IN 47630
Tel: 812-853-5825
Description: Supplier of lighting and technical equipment.

Notre Dame

Sing-Sing Lighting
Post Office Box 664
Notre Dame, IN 46556
Tel: 219-232-5707
Address Inquiries to: Mike Whalen
Description: Supplier of lighting equipment.

Vincennes

Iris Stage Lighting Company
22 North 4th Street
Vincennes, IN 47591
Tel: 812-882-1346
Description: Suppliers of lighting and technical equipment.

Wabash

Wabash Instrument Company
1801 Grand Street
Wabash, IN 46992
Tel: 219-563-8406
Address Inquiries to: Shethar Davis, President
Description: Manufacturer of psychedelic lighting.

Warsaw

Da-Lite Screen Company, Incorporated
3100 State Road 15 North
Post Office Box 629
Warsaw, IN 46580
Tel: 219-267-8101; 219-Tel-x 23 2649
Address Inquiries to: Elmer J. Danch, Director, Advertising and Sales Promotion
Founded in: 1909
Member: PMA; NAVA;
Description: Manufacturer of slide and movie projection screens and accessories.

Peabody ABC Corporation
Post Office Box 77
Warsaw, IN 46580
Tel: 219-267-5166
Address Inquiries to: Donald R. Clemens
Description: Supplies jute, burlap and laminated PVC.

IOWA

Atlantic

Kimian Sales Company, Incorporated
1804 Sycamore Street
Atlantic, IA 50022
Tel: 712-243-1626
Description: Supplier of sound equipment and intercom systems.

Davenport

River Cities Sound
1025 West Fourth Street
Davenport, IA 52802
Tel: 319-323-7398
Address Inquiries to: Frank A. Holst, Partner
Mark A. Zimmerman, Partner
Founded in: 1976
Annual Budget: $176,000
Description: Supplier of sound systems, lighting, and equipment for all kinds of presentations.

Des Moines

Beams Company
2318 Harding Road Station 14B
Des Moines, IA 50314
Tel: 515-255-1148
Address Inquiries to: Tim Eakins
Description: Manufacturer of sound systems and equipment.

Midwest Equipment Company of Iowa
Post Office Box 1093
Des Moines, IA 50311
Tel: 515-255-3116
Description: Supplier of lighting equipment.

KANSAS

Kansas City

Direct Safety Company
511 Osage
Kansas City, KS 66110
Tel: 913-281-0504
Address Inquiries to: Gary Ashwill, General Manager
Description: Supplier of safety equipment.

Overland Park

Gary Pendleton
10329 Ash
Overland Park, KS 66207
Tel: 913-381-5035
Address Inquiries to: Gary Pendleton
Description: Supplier of tickets and ticket racks.

Shawnee Mission

Beams Company
11503 West 75th Street
Shawnee Mission, KS 66214
Tel: 913-631-0301
Address Inquiries to: Mike Eakins
Description: Manufacturer of sound systems and equipment.

Fred Kohnken
Post Office Box 15227
Shawnee Mission, KS 66222
Tel: 913-341-5071
Address Inquiries to: Fred Kohnken
Description: Supplier of folding stages and portable dance floors.

Wichita

SECT Theatrical Supply, Incorporated
1909 East Central
Wichita, KS 67214
Tel: 316-267-4377
Address Inquiries to: Steve Butler
Description: Supplier of lighting equipment, intercoms and make-up.

Theatrical Services
128 South Washington
Wichita, KS 67202
Tel: 316-263-4415
Founded in: 1976
Description: Suppliers and renters of lighting, technical equipment and costumes. Theatrical make-up is also available.

KENTUCKY

Covington

Theatre House Incorporated
400 West Third Street
Covington, KY 41012
Tel: 606-431-2414
Address Inquiries to: Roger Hartman
June Hartman
Founded in: 1955
Description: Supplies drapes, drops and scenery flats.

Louisville

Falls City Theatre Equipment Company
427-429 South Third Street
Louisville, KY 40202
Tel: 502-584-7375
Address Inquiries to: Bill Carrol
Description: Supplier of lighting eqipment.

LOUISIANA

Baton Rouge

Ford Theatrical Lighting
2633 Lydia Avenue
Baton Rouge, LA 70808
Tel: 504-343-9412
Description: Manufacturer of PYROPAK materials, and supplier of custom lighting systems.

Jefferson

Somar, Incorporated
Post Office Box 10543
Jefferson, LA 70181
Tel: 504-733-9535
Description: Supplier of lighting equipment.

Kenner

Dave Kotatek
10 Sadine Court
Kenner, LA 70062
Tel: 504-721-9865
Address Inquiries to: Dave Kotatek
Description: Supplier of tickets and ticket racks.

Metairie

Rapco Associates, Incorporated
Post Office Box 7885
4515 Shores Drive, Suite 202
Metairie, LA 70010
Tel: 504-887-9500
Address Inquiries to: Robert A. Philibert, President
  Jack Brignac, Vice President
Founded in: 1976
Description: Supplier of lighting equipment.

MARYLAND

Baltimore

David H. Brothers, Company
19 Old Court Road
Baltimore, MD 21208
Tel: 301-764-7189
Address Inquiries to: David H. Brothers
Description: Supplier of sound equipment and intercom systems.

Life-Like Products
1600 Union Avenue
Baltimore, MD 21211
Tel: 301-889-1023
Address Inquiries to: Ed Freeman, Vice President of Sales
Description: Manufacturer of scenic and landscaping materials.

The Theatre Service Group
1792 Union Avenue
Chipper Mill Park
Baltimore, MD 21211
Tel: 301-467-1225
Address Inquiries to: Richard Antisdel
Description: Supplier of lighting equipment.

Bladensburg

Professional Sound Systems of Maryland
5303 Taussig Road
Bladensburg, MD 20710
Description: Supplier of wireless microphones.

Bowie

Al Lever and Associates
12607 Waverly Place
Bowie, MD 20715
Tel: 301-262-7678
Address Inquiries to: Elayne Lever
Founded in: 1969
Member: PTN; PW; PI;
Annual Budget: $85,000
Description: Manufacturer of tapes for film processing.

College Park

The Superior Electric Company
7100 Baltimore Avenue
College Park, MD 20740
Tel: 301-277-3235
Description: Supplier of electrical equipment.

Forest Hill

Hurley Screen Corporation
1515 Melrose Lane
Forest Hill, MD 21050
Tel: 301-838-0036; 301-838-0037
Address Inquiries to: Timothy Joel, Production Manager
Description: Manufacturer of screens for theatrical use.

Hyattsville

Design Theatrical
5027 36th Avenue
Hyattsville, MD 20782
Tel: 301-699-9356; Ira-Kol-aister
Description: Supplier of lighting equipment.

Laurel

Chesapeake Lighting Associates, Incorporated
29 C Street
Laurel, MD 20707
Tel: 301-792-2266; 301-953-1266
Founded in: 1978
Description: Supplier of lighting equipment representing Electro Controls, Incorporated and Litelab, Incorporated in the Maryland, D.C., and Northern Virginia.

Rockville

Colortran, Incorporated
958 Paulsboro Drive
Rockville, MD 20850
Tel: 301-340-7405
Address Inquiries to: James Munn, Manager

Member: NAB; USITT; SMPTE; IES;
Description: A regional branch office.

Silver Spring

Earl Dinsmore Company
111 Eldrid Drive
Silver Spring, MD 20904
Description: Manufacturer of lighting and supplier of stage and studio equipment.

R and R Stagelighting
622 Mississippi Avenue
Silver Spring, MD 20910
Tel: 301-589-9025
Description: Supplier of lighting equipment.

Rollerwall Incorporated
Post Office Box 757
Silver Spring, MD 20901
Tel: 301-649-4422
Address Inquiries to: S. Elbaum, President
Member: BBB;
Description: Manufacturer of paint rollers. Designs paint rollers and applicators for use in wallprinting wallpaper patterns directly on walls.

Tacoma Park

Kinetic Artistry
7216 Carroll Avenue
Tacoma Park, MD 20012
Tel: 301-270-6666
Address Inquiries to: Eric Sepler
Description: Supplier of lighting equipment.

MASSACHUSETTS

Boston

Boston Light Source
63-1 Commercial Wharf
Boston, MA 02110
Description: Manufacturer of lighting and supplier of stage and studio equipment.

Dazian's Incorporated
420 Boylston Street
Boston, MA 02116
Tel: 617-266-5040
Description: Supplier of theatrical fabrics and supplies. Inclusive of stage drapery fabrics and all types of scenery fabrics.

Major Theatre Equipment
28 Piedmont Street
Boston, MA 01116
Description: Supplier of fluorescent paints, and phosphorescent tapes and paints.

Montgomery-Ames Associates
263 Summer Street
Boston, MA 02110
Tel: 617-423-2978
Description: Supplier of lighting equipment.

Jack Stein Make-Up Center
80 Boylston Street
Boston, MA 02116
Tel: 617-542-7865; 617-542-8334
Address Inquiries to: Sophie Stein, Manager
Founded in: 1954

Member: NCA;

Description: Supplier of cosmetics. The staff will assist in suggesting what make-up to use for a particular production and how to do character make-up.

Tracy Costumes
63 Melcher Street
Boston, MA 02210
Tel: 617-542-9100
Address Inquiries to: Michael Carnaby, Owner
Description: Rents costumes to amateur and professional companies, including high schools and colleges. Specializes in costumes for Gilbert and Sullivan operettas. Sheet music and scenery also available.

Cambridge

Roctronics Entertainment Lighting
22-TC Wendell Street
Cambridge, MA 02138
Tel: 617-826-8888
Address Inquiries to: Dr. Richard Iacobucci, President
Founded in: 1965
Annual Budget: $200,000
Description: Pioneers in the design and manufacture of innovative equipment. Roctronics aims to solve performing arts problems with durable low-cost solutions. The company invented color synthesis used in composing harmonious colors for musical productions.

Fall River

Hanoud Associates
711 County Street
Fall River, MA 02723
Tel: 617-675-2489
Address Inquiries to: Paul Hanoud
Description: Manufacturer of sound systems and equipment.

Framingham

George Mitchell
6 Adams Road
Framingham, MA 01701
Tel: 617-872-7610; 612-941-1700
Address Inquiries to: George Mitchell
Tom McCarthy, Sales Coordinator
Founded in: 1952
Member: IAAM; ACWI; NASB; NSF;
Annual Budget: 12,000,000
Description: Supplier of mobile folding stages, portable dance floors and folding tables designed to perform in a professsional manner, but not require the luxury of permanent space. May be folded and moved by one person.

Lowell

Research Council of Makeup Artists
52 New Spaulding Street
Lowell, MA 01851
Tel: 617-459-9864
Address Inquiries to: Vincent J.R. Kehoe, President
Founded in: 1963

Member: NATAS; SMPTE;
Description: All RCMA foundations, countershadings, shadings, cheeckcolors, lipcolors and any special shades are manufactured in their own laboratory using specially designed machines and under Mr. Kehoe's direct supervision. This machinery is adjustable to specific grinds and exact timing, thereby maintaining better color fidelity than foundations made with a roller mill or blender type machinery.

Natick

Jonel Sales Associates, Incorporated
215 Oak Street
Natick, MA 01760
Tel: 617-653-3736
Description: Manufacturer of commercial sound equipment.

Needham

Mullin Technical Sales Company, Incorporated
945 Great Plain Avenue
Needham, MA 02192
Tel: 617-444-4780; 617-444-4740
Description: Supplier of sound equipment.

Needham Heights

Capron Lighting and Sound
278 West Street
Needham Heights, MA 02194
Tel: 617-444-8850
Address Inquiries to: John C. Gates, Customer Services
Description: Manufacturer of lighting and supplier of stage and studio equipment.

Newton

Lake Systems
55 Chapel Street
Newton, MA 02160
Tel: 617-244-6881
Address Inquiries to: Frank Demayo, Vice President
Founded in: 1951
Description: Supplier of intercom systems, microphone preamplifiers, mixers, theatre lighting and sound reinforcement systems.

Salem

D.I.M. Lighting Company
Cedar Hill Road
Salem, MA 01970
Tel: 617-744-8859
Address Inquiries to: John Iwanicki, Sales
Normand Dionne, Sales
Description: Manufacturer of headset systems, amplifiers and lighting equipment.

Somerville

Charles H. Stewart and Company
8 Clarendon Avenue
Somerville, MA 02144
Tel: 617-625-2407
Address Inquiries to: Earl Stewart, Owner
Founded in: 1866
Member: THS; NETC; LHT; USITT;
Description: Supplier of stage equipment.

South Boston

Virgolight Incorporated
72 K Street
South Boston, MA 02127
Tel: 617-269-1445
Description: Manufacturer of lighting control equipment.

Stockbridge

Limelight Productions, Incorporated
Post Office Box 816, Yale Hill
Stockbridge, MA 01262
Tel: 413-298-3771
Address Inquiries to: William Beautyman, Jr., President
Founded in: 1971
Member: USITT; NETC;
Description: A sales and rental company carrying a full range of products for theatrical and related applications. Represents most of the major lighting manufacturers, and sells all types of lighting accessories.

Wellesley Hills

Michael Scott Company, Incorporated
20 Walnut Street
Wellesley Hills, MA 02181
Tel: 617-235-0102
Address Inquiries to: Michael Scott
Description: Supplier of sound and intercom systems.

The Superior Electric Company
6 Abbott Road
Wellesley Hills, MA 02181
Tel: 617-237-0750
Description: Supplier of electrical equipment.

Woburn

Globe Ticket Company
222 New Boston Street
Woburn, MA 01801
Tel: 617-935-7150
Description: Supplier of tickets and ticket equipment.

Worcester

David Clark Company Incorporated
360 Franklin Street
Worcester, MA 01604
Tel: 617-756-6216
Address Inquiries to: George R. Conlon, Product Manager, Communications
Description: Manufacturer of headset systems and communications systems.

MICHIGAN

Ann Arbor

Alternative Light
2972 Gale Road
Ann Arbor, MI 48105
Tel: 313-994-5700
Address Inquiries to: William Davis
Description: Supplier of lighting equipment.

Bloomfield Hills

R.J. Hetzel
2893 Aldgate Drive
Bloomfield Hills, MI 48013
Tel: 313-333-7672
Address Inquiries to: R.J. Hetzel
Description: Manufacturer of power supplies.

Dearborn

Lynch's Incorporated
939 Howard Street
Dearborn, MI 48124
Description: Supplier of professional make-up.

Detroit

Globe Ticket Company
9675 Bryden Street
Detroit, MI 48204
Tel: 313-931-6720
Description: Supplier of tickets and ticket equipment.

Runnel Studios
4767 14th Street
Detroit, MI 48204
Tel: 313-898-4266
Address Inquiries to: Dean Wickline
Description: Supplier of lighting equipment.

The Superior Electric Company
Prudential Building
20820 Greenfield Road
Detroit, MI 48237
Tel: 313-967-1011
Description: Supplier of electrical equipment.

Ferndale

Hiltronics, Incorporated
380 Hilton Road
Ferndale, MI 48220
Tel: 313-398-5556
Description: Supplier of sound equipment.

Hamburg

James Fackert Cae Incorporated
Post Office Box 430
Hamburg, MI 48139
Tel: 313-231-9373
Address Inquiries to: James H. Fackert, Chief Engineer/ President
John Malek, Marketing Manager
Founded in: 1973
Member: USITT; AES;
Description: Manufacturer of lighting control consoles, special effects and dimmers.

Highland

Garrick Associates
3925 Loch Drive
Highland, MI 48031
Tel: 313-887-2140
Address Inquiries to: Harris Garrick
Description: Manufacturer of tapes for film processing.

Okemos

Crites and Associates, Incorporated
Post Office Box B
Okemos, MI 49426
Tel: 517-349-1040
Description: Supplier of lighting equipment.

Pleasant Ridge

Shalco, Incorporated
23716 Woodward Avenue
Pleasant Ridge, MI 48069
Tel: 313-547-4771
Description: Supplier of sound equipment and intercom systems.

Plymouth

J. Malcolm Flora, Incorporated
165 W. Liberty
Plymouth, MI 48170
Tel: 313-453-4295; 313-453-0065
Description: Supplier of sound equipment.

Rochester

Bozak, Incorporated
Post Office Box 410
Rochester, MI 48063
Tel: 313-652-2520
Description: A regional branch office.

Southfield

R. Milsk Company
22420 Telegraph Road
Southfield, MI 48034
Tel: 313-354-3310
Address Inquiries to: R. Milsk
Description: Supplier of electrical outlet strips and utility carts.

Troy

Superscope Detroit, Incorporated
591 Executive Drive
Troy, MI 48084
Tel: 313-588-7200
Address Inquiries to: Dick Isola
Description: Supplier of sound equipment.

MINNESOTA

Edina

Mel Foster Technical Sales, Inc.
7611 Washington Avenue, South
Edina, MN 55435
Tel: 612-941-9800
Address Inquiries to: Gene Foster
Founded in: 1924
Description: Supplier of sound equipment and manufacturers' representatives'.

M.E.R. and Associates
7317 Cahill Road
Edina, MN 55435
Address Inquiries to: Bob McGinnis
Karen Russo
Description: Manufacturer of sound systems and equipment.

Maple Grove

RC Sales
7127 Willow Road
Maple Grove, MN 55369
Tel: 612-425-5543
Description: Supplier of commercial sound equipment.

Minneapolis

Consolidated Photographic Sales
4548 Ewing Avenue North
Minneapolis, MN 55422
Tel: 612-535-2254
Address Inquiries to: David Tearle
Description: Manufacturer of tapes for film processing.

Felland-Coombe and Association
6524 Walker Street
Minneapolis, MN 55246
Tel: 612-929-1679
Description: Supplier of lighting equipment.

Norcostco, Incorporated
3203 North Highway 100
Minneapolis, MN 55422
Tel: 612-533-2791
Member: ATA;
Description: Supplier of lighting equipment, theatrical make-up, stage supplies and costumes.

D. Peterson and Associates
5603 Lyndale Avenue
Minneapolis, MN 55419
Tel: 612-861-6051
Description: Supplier of electrical outlet strips and utility carts.

Clark R. Gibb Company
1311 West 25th Street
Minneapolis, MN 55405
Tel: 612-377-1200
Address Inquiries to: Clark R. Gibb
Description: Supplier of sound and intercom systems.

Sico, Incorporated
7525 Cahill Road
Minneapolis, MN 55435
Tel: 613-941-1700
Address Inquiries to: Harold J. Wilson, President
Andrew J. Shea, Vice President, Sales and Marketing
Founded in: 1951
Description: Manufacturer of folding stages and portable dance floors. Sisco Equipment is designed to make multiple use of space and to be handled and set up by one person.

Stage-Brite
695 Lowry Avenue North East
Minneapolis, MN 55418
Tel: 612-788-9476
Address Inquiries to: Glenn F. Nellist, National Sales Manager
Description: Supplier of lighting equipment.

Telex Communications, Incorporated
9600 Aldrich Avenue South
Minneapolis, MN 55420

Tel: 612-884-4051
Address Inquiries to: Tom Johnson, Director of Sales, A/V Products
Greg Dzubay, Product Manager, Broadcast and Professional Audio Products
Description: Manufacturer of sound equipment and intercom systems.

Theatrical Rigging Systems, Incorporated
4060 West Broadway
Minneapolis, MN 55422
Tel: 612-533-3311
Address Inquiries to: James T. Kunz, President
Description: Supplier of lighting and dimming equipment.

Minnetonka

Clark Gibb Company
11100 Ren Road West
Minnetonka, MN 55343
Tel: 612-932-3950
Description: Manufacturer of lighting equipment.

Owatonna

Jerry Sebring
505 14th Street, SE
Owatonna, MN 55060
Tel: 507-451-5220
Address Inquiries to: Jerry Sebring
Description: Supplier of stage shells and staging.

Wenger Corporation
555 Park Drive
Owatonna, MN 55060
Tel: 800-533-0393
Address Inquiries to: Thomas R. Springmeyer, Market Manager
Dick Hegle, Market Manager
Description: Manufacturer of stage shells and staging.

MISSOURI

Ballwin

Bozak, Incorporated
c/o Centurian Marketing, Box 1011
Ballwin, MO 63011
Tel: 314-227-7229
Address Inquiries to: John Shaw, Manager
Description: A regional branch office.

Kansas City

Allied Theatre Crafts
224 West 5th Street
Kansas City, MO 64015
Tel: 816-421-3980
Description: Supplier of lighting, technical equipment and costumes.

Associated Theatrical Contractors
307 West 80th Street
Kansas City, MO 64114
Tel: 816-523-1655
Address Inquiries to: Tom Stewart, Manager
Description: Supplies lighting control systems, patch panels and lighting fixtures.

A.T.C.
307 West 80th Street
Kansas City, MO 64114
Tel: 816-523-1655
Address Inquiries to: Frank Stewart
Description: Supplier of lighting equipment.

Belsaw, Incorporated
315 West Port Road
Kansas City, MO 64111
Description: Supplier of wood and insulation products.

SECT Theatrical Supplies, Incorporated
406 E. 18th Street
Kansas City, MO 64108
Tel: 816-471-1239
Address Inquiries to: Steve Butler, President
Bill Kosman, Rental Manager
Founded in: 1975
Member: LTG Dimensions;
Description: A full service theatrical supply house providing stage lighting, hardware, make-up, dimmer boards, special effects, trusses, lifts, intercom systems and scenic materials.

Theatre Lighting Center
809 East 31st Street
Kansas City, MO 64109
Tel: 816-561-1611
Address Inquiries to: Norm Pattee
Description: Supplier of lighting, technical equipment, and costumes.

Raytown

Merten Co., Incorporated
9805 East 53rd Street
Raytown, MO 64133
Tel: 816-358-7777
Description: Supplier of lighting equipment.

Springfield

Associated Theatrical Contractors
1904 C East Meadowmere
Springfield, MO 65804
Tel: 417-862-4725
Description: Supplier of lighting, technical, and sound equipment and stage costumes.

St. Louis

Forristal-Young Sales Company
8986 Manchester
St. Louis, MO 63144
Tel: 314-968-9975
Founded in: 1953
Member: ERA; IEEE;
Description: Supplier of O.E.M. components (electronic), commercial sound systems, and CATV security systems and components.

Kathrinus-Kelly and Company
7852 Big Bend Boulevard
St. Louis, MO 63119
Tel: 314-968-3800
Description: Supplier of electrical outlet strips and utility carts.

Archie Smith
4482 Lindell Boulevard
St. Louis, MO 63108
Tel: 314-533-8458
Address Inquiries to: Archie Smith
Description: Supplier of tickets and ticket racks.

Street Louis

Brotherton Lighting Service
7150 Garesche
Street Louis, MO 63136
Description: Supplier of lighting equipment.

Volland Studios, Incorporated
1425 Hanley Industrial Court
Street Louis, MO 63105
Tel: 314-962-5555
Address Inquiries to: R. Michael Volland, President
Description: Supplier of stage equipment.

Union

P and B Lighting, Incorporated
Post Office Box 303
Union, MO 63084
Tel: 314-394-2663; 314-583-5863
Address Inquiries to: Wayne Whittier, Director of Sales and Marketing
Description: Supplier of dimming equipment lighting systems and fixtures.

Video TechniLites, Incorporated
Post Office Box 226
Union, MO 63084
Tel: 314-583-9914; 314-583-3754
Address Inquiries to: Rich Bay, President
Buck Krieger, Vice President
Founded in: 1981
Description: Supplier of lighting equipment for performing arts, industrial accounts, fairs and shows.

Wing Industries, Incorporated
Highway UU and Neier Road
Union, MO 63084
Tel: 314-583-5863
Description: Supplier of lighting, technical equipment and stage costumes.

MONTANA

Great Falls

Northern School Supply Company
Post Office Box 431
Great Falls, MT 59403
Tel: 406-453-4374
Description: Manufacturer of stage equipment.

Missoula

R.W. Wages Agency
Box 5356
Missoula, MT 59806
Tel: 406-549-3283
Address Inquiries to: Wayne Wages
Description: Supplier of lighting equipment.

NEBRASKA

Lincoln

R.W. Changstrom and Associates
Route #8
Lincoln, NE 68506
Tel: 402-723-3367
Address Inquiries to: Bob Changstrom
Tom Changstrom
Description: Supplier of lighting equipment.

Mexico

Lambda Platform Systems
5739 West Main Street
Mexico, New York 13114
Tel: 315-963-3330
Description: Flexible platforms, seating and staging light enough to be handled by two people but strong enough to hold hundreds.

Omaha

Electric Specialties Company
Post Office Box 14042, West Omaha
Omaha, NE 68114
Tel: 402-391-6000
Description: Supplier of lighting equipment.

Omaha Stage Equipment, Incorporated
3873 Leavenworth Street
Omaha, NE 68105
Tel: 402-345-4427
Address Inquiries to: Mary Bledsoe, President
Mel Walling, Vice President
Founded in: 1981
Annual Budget: $1,000,000
Description: Manufactures and installs a variety of equipment for the stage, including curtains, tracks, dimmer switchboards, spotlights, and rigging.

NEVADA

Las Vegas

Cinema Services
3050 Sheridan Street
Las Vegas, NV 89102
Tel: 702-876-4667
Address Inquiries to: Jimmy Brennan
Description: Supplier of lighting equipment.

Design Concepts
5365 Polaris Avenue
Las Vegas, NV 89118
Tel: 702-736-8333
Address Inquiries to: Fred Joseph
Description: Supplier of lighting equipment.

Reno

DeGraffenreid Associates
Box 3518
Reno, NV 89505
Tel: 702-826-2313
Address Inquiries to: Dean DeGraffenreid
Description: Supplier of lighting equipment.

NEW HAMPSHIRE

Concord

Mikan Theatricals
55 Walker Street
Concord, NH 03301
Address Inquiries to: Daniel Kiley
Description: Supplier of dimmers, lighting equipment and makeup.

Hampton

Mikan Theatricals
54 Tide Mill Road
Hampton, NH 03842
Tel: 603-926-2744; 617-542-9101
Address Inquiries to: Michael Carnaby, Owner
Description: Supplies Bob Vielly, Ben Nye and Mehron Makeup. They import beards and mustaches from England. They also deal in Altman, Rozio, Teatronics, LMI, TTI, Iddings scenery paint, Spectrum dimmers and lighting equipment, technical books and hardware. Mikan Theatricals also owns and operates Tracy Costumes in Boston.

Londonderry

Associated Systems
Post Office Box 333
Londonderry, NH 03053
Tel: 603-434-0731
Description: Supplier of sound equipment.

Peterborough

Brookstone Company
Vose Farm Road
Peterborough, NH 03458
Description: Supplier of wood and insulation products.

NEW JERSEY

Atlantic City

Bash Theatrial Lighting
1515 A Pacific Avenue
Atlantic City, NJ 08404
Address Inquiries to: James Cannon, Manager
Description: A regional branch office.

Atlantic Highlands

Audio Visual Laboratories, Incorporated
500 Hillside Avenue
Atlantic Highlands, NJ 07716
Tel: 201-291-4400
Address Inquiries to: Sylvia Costa, Director of Marketing
Description: Visual Laboratories supplies multi-image programming systems and accessories.

Barrington

Edmund Scientific Company
7782 Edscorp Building
Barrington, NJ 08007
Tel: 609-547-3488
Description: Supplier of lighting equipment and scientific products by mail order.

Bloomingdale

Central/Shippee, Incorporated
46 Star Lake Road
Bloomingdale, NJ 07403
Tel: 201-838-1100; 800-631-8968
Address Inquiries to: Donald A. Hubner, Vice President-Sales
Founded in: 1928
Description: Manufacturer of flameproof felt in eighty colors for costumes and set design.

Carlstadt

Plastic Reel Corporation of America
640 S. Commercial Avenue
Carlstadt, NJ 07072
Tel: 201-933-9125; 212-541-6464
Address Inquiries to: Keith Leenig, Customer Service Manager
Description: Manufacturer of reels and reel accessories.

Cherry Hill

Landy Associates Incorporated
1890 East Marlton Pike
Cherry Hill, NJ 08003
Tel: 609-424-4660
Address Inquiries to: James E. Landy, President
Founded in: 1970
Description: Supplier of intercom systems, microphone preamplifiers and mixers as well as broadcast equipment to schools, radio and television stations.

Wes Ostlund
136 Partree Road
Cherry Hill, NJ 08003
Tel: 609-424-2067
Address Inquiries to: Wes Ostlund
Description: Supplier of stage shells and staging.

Edison

Astrup Company
Post Office Box 995
Edison, NJ 08818
Tel: 201-225-1776
Founded in: 1876
Description: Supplies flame and non-flame resistant scenery fabrics, cordage and rope.

Elmwood Park

Strand Century, Incorporated
20 Bushes Lane
Elmwood Park, NJ 37347
Tel: 201-791-7000
Address Inquiries to: Bob Dente, Regional Manager
Description: Supplier of lighting control systems.

Englewood Cliffs

Johns-Manville Sales Corporation
600 Sylvan Avenue
Englewood Cliffs, NJ 07632
Tel: 215-543-0701
Address Inquiries to: G.N. Carozza, District Sales Manager
Description: Manufacturer of power supplies.

Florham Park

Charles Beseller Company
8 Fernwood Road
Florham Park, NJ 07932
Tel: 201-822-1000
Address Inquiries to: John R. Lucas,
Sales/Manager
Description: Supplies projectors and sound
filmstrip viewers.

Hillside

Wireworks Corporation
380 Hillside Avenue
Hillside, NJ 07205
Tel: 201-686-7400
Address Inquiries to: Larry J. Williams
Description: Manufacturer of microphone and
audio equipment.

Maplewood

Robart-Green Commpany
17-21 Newark Way
Maplewood, NJ 07040
Tel: 201-761-7400
Address Inquiries to: Dan Greenfield
Arnie Robinson
Description: Supplier of lighting equipment.

Montclair

Electro-Chemical Products Corporation
89 Walnut Street
Montclair, NJ 07042
Tel: 201-746-2633; 201-243-6825
Address Inquiries to: Michael Fain,
Secretary/Treasurer
Founded in: 1951
Member: SMPTE;
Description: Manufacturer of film cleaners.

Newark

Canrad-Hanovia, Incorporated
100 Chestnut Street
Newark, NJ 07105
Tel: 201-589-4300
Address Inquiries to: B. Gorlin, Vice
President
Description: Supplier of Spot-Lite glow-in-
the-dark tape.

North Bergen

Bash Theatrical Lighting
2012 86th Street
North Bergen, NJ 07047
Tel: 201-869-1400; 212-279-9265
Address Inquiries to: Robert Cannon,
President
Don Stern, Vice President
Founded in: 1976
Description: Bash Theatrical Lighting supplies
Altman units, x-rays and spotlights.

Duro-Test Corporation
2321 Kennedy Boulevard
North Bergen, NJ 07047
Tel: 201-867-7000
Address Inquiries to: Lawrence H. Johnson,
Vice President
Description: Supplier of light bulbs and spot
lights.

Northvale

Comprehensive Video Supply Corporation
148 Veterans Drive
Northvale, NJ 07647
Tel: 201-767-7990; 800-526-0242
Address Inquiries to: Ted Jacoby, Customer
Service Manager
Description: Manufacturer and supplier of
video equipment.

Paramus

Sharp Electronics Corporation
10 Keystone Place
Paramus, NJ 07652
Tel: 201-265-5600
Address Inquiries to: Robert Garbutt,
Manager, Professional Products Dept.
Description: Manufacturer of television cam-
eras and equipment.

Park Ridge

Creative Technology, Incorporated
Post Office Box 334
50 Colony Avenue
Park Ridge, NJ 07656
Tel: 201-573-1225
Description: Supplier of lighting and technical
equipment and stage costumes.

Pleasantville

Atlantic City Stage Lighting Company
28 Old Turnpike
Pleasantville, NJ 08232
Tel: 609-641-8447
Address Inquiries to: Tricia Anastasia,
President
Description: Atlantic City Stage Lighting sup-
plies lighting equipment for stage, TV, casi-
nos and color media.

Princeton

Films for the Humanities
Post Office Box 2053
Princeton, NJ 08540
Tel: 201-329-6912
Address Inquiries to: Harold Mantell,
President
Description: Supplier of sound effects.

Somerville

BML Stage Lighting Company,
Incorporated
27 Steele Avenue
Somerville, NJ 08876
Tel: 201-725-0810
Address Inquiries to: Eric Moskowitz
Description: Supplier of lighting equipment.

South Orange

Sonny Simberkoff Associates, Inc.
71 Valley Street
South Orange, NJ 07079
Tel: 201-763-7900
Description: Supplier of sound equipment.

Stirling

Thermoplastic Processes
Valley Road
Stirling, NJ 07980
Tel: 201-647-1000
Address Inquiries to: Henry Tancke, Sales
Manager
Description: Manufacturer of shields for
fluorescent lamps and plastic extrusions.

Westville

SGL Waber Electric
300 Harvard Avenue
Westville, NJ
Tel: 609-456-5400
Address Inquiries to: Carl Guenther,
Marketing Manager
Description: Supplier of electrical outlet strips
and utility carts.

Whippany

Norcostco, Incorporated
375 Route 10
Whippany, NJ 07981
Tel: 201-539-5169
Member: ATA;
Description: Supplier of lighting equipment,
theatrical make-up, stage supplies and cos-
tumes.

NEW MEXICO

Albuquerque

Albuquerque Civic Light Opera
Association
4201 Ellison Northeast
Albuquerque, NM 87109
Tel: 505-345-6577
Address Inquiries to: Chris Stromme, Scenery
Nancy Ruth Weart, Costumes
Description: Suppliers of lighting equipment,
technical equipment and costumes.

C.T. Carlburg and Associates
Incorporated
2530 Washington North East
Albuquerque, NM 87110
Tel: 505-888-3883
Address Inquiries to: Carl T. Carlberg,
Owner/Manager
Founded in: 1955
Member: Electronic Representatives
Association/Chicago; Rio Grande
Electronic Representatives
Association/Albuquerque; Association of
Commerce and Industry/Albuquerque;
Description: Supplier of electrical outlet strips
and utility carts representing manufacturers
of electronic components and instruments.
Technical sales to manufacturers, govern-
ment agencies, educational institutions and
product distributors.

Spectra Dynamics
415 Marble North West
Albuquerque, NM 87102
Tel: 505-843-7202
Description: Manufacturer and supplier of

lighting, technical equipment and props. Rentals available.

Alburquerque

Mixed Media Productions
12204 Palm Springs Court, NE
Alburquerque, NM 87111
Tel: 505-298-9600; 505-296-0096
Description: A recording studio and supplier of theatrical lighting and sound equipment. Licensed for electrical contracting in New Mexico.

NEW YORK

Baldwinsville

Ferrini-Konarski Associates, Incorporated
7335 State Fair Boulevard
Baldwinsville, NY 13027
Description: A manufacturer's representative specializing in industrial lighting. Complete line of theatrical lighting available.

Bardonia

N.R. Associates
74 Westlyn Drive
Bardonia, NY 10954
Tel: 914-623-6299; 914-623-2063
Address Inquiries to: Norman Rothman
Founded in: 1955
Description: Manufacturer of tapes for film processing.

Bellmore

Ticket Craft Incorporated
1925 Bellmore Avenue
Bellmore, NY 11710
Tel: 516-826-1500; 800-645-4944
Address Inquiries to: Barbara Caporaso, Vice President
Description: Manufacturer of theatre tickets.

Bohemia

Lycian Stage Lighting
385 Central Avenue
Bohemia, NY 11716
Tel: 516-589-3939
Address Inquiries to: Richard F. Logothetis, President
Description: Manufacturer of lighting equipment.

Bronx

Feller Precision, Incorporated
378 Canal Place
Bronx, NY 10451
Tel: 212-292-1004
Address Inquiries to: Arthur Soyk, Office Manager
Description: Manufacturer of sound equipment.

Four Star Stage Lighting
585 Gerard Avenue
Bronx, NY 10451
Tel: 212-993-0471
Address Inquiries to: Vickie Wallace
John Mahoney

Description: Supplier of lighting equipment and fluorescent paints, and phosphorescent tapes and paints.

Buffalo

Costumes Unlimited, Incorporated
1685 Elmwood Avenue
Buffalo, NY 14207
Tel: 716-873-0709; 412-281-3277
Address Inquiries to: James W. Disbrow, Treasurer
Founded in: 1974
Description: Manufacturer of custom uniforms and outfits.

Dion Products
78 Amber Street
Buffalo, NY 14220
Tel: 716-823-4381
Address Inquiries to: Gerald J. Dion, Owner
Description: Manufacturer of lighting equipment.

Litelab
251 Elm Street
Buffalo, NY
Tel: 716-856-4300
Address Inquiries to: Vincent G. Finnegan Jr., National Sales Manager
Founded in: 1975
Member: NAMM; Asid Industry Foundation;
Description: The largest manufacturer and supplier of lighting systems to the entertainment market. Also manufactures architectural fixtures for the architecture and design market.

Commack

Landau and Mack, Incorporated
66 Commack Road
Commack, NY 11725
Tel: 516-499-2775
Description: Supplier of sound equipment.

Cornwall-on-Hudson

Costume Armour, Incorporated and Christo-Vac
Post Office Box 325
Shore Road
Cornwall-on-Hudson, NY 12520
Tel: 914-534-9120
Address Inquiries to: Mary Novellino, Vice President
Founded in: 1966
Description: Supplier of theatrical armor for both sale and rental.

Deerpark

Stage Lighting Discount Corporation
70 Haight Street
Deerpark, NY 11729
Tel: 516-242-7865
Address Inquiries to: Jack Foster, Sales
Description: Supplier of lighting and control equipment.

Theatrical Services and Supplies, Incorporated
205C Brook Avenue
Deer Park, NY 11729

Tel: 516-242-5454
Address Inquiries to: Robert F. Bayer, President
Description: Supplier of sound and lighting systems, scenery and makeup.

East Bloomfield

R.E. Nicholson
75 West Main Street
East Bloomfield, NY 14443
Tel: 716-657-6145
Address Inquiries to: R.E. Nicholson
Description: Manufacturer of stage equipment.

East Meadow

Bestek
386 Newbridge Avenue
East Meadow, NY 11554
Tel: 516-794-3953
Description: Supplier of lighting, sound, technical equipment and stage costumes.

East Rochester

D.O. Industries, Incorporated
317 East Chestnut
East Rochester, NY 14445
Tel: 716-385-4920
Address Inquiries to: Richard Kassle, Operations Manager
David Goldstein, President
Founded in: 1972
Description: Supplier of optical products.

The Superior Electric Company
533 West Commercial Street
East Rochester, NY 14445
Tel: 716-381-9210
Description: Supplier of electrical equipment.

Elmont, Long Island

F. Edwin Schmitt Company, Incorporated
Post Office Box 165
Elmont, Long Island, NY 11003
Tel: 516-437-8150
Address Inquiries to: F. Edwin Schmitt
Description: Supplier of sound equipment.

Farmingdale

Farralane
66 Commerce Drive
Farmingdale, NY 11735
Description: Suppliers of lighting, sound, technical equipment and stage costumes.

Flushing

Bettan Sales Incorporated
77-15 164th Street
Flushing, NY 11366
Tel: 212-591-7600
Description: Supplier of sound equipment and intercom systems.

Glen Head

Lite-Trol Service Company, Incorporated
72 Glenwood Road
Glen Head, NY 11545
Tel: 516-671-5288
Address Inquiries to: Eugene Rudolph,

President
Description: Repairs lighting control systems.

Irvington-on-Hudson

Kamar Products, Incorporated
2 South Buckhout Street
Irvington-on-Hudson, NY 10533
Tel: 914-591-8700
Address Inquiries to: Robert Reibel, President
Founded in: 1962
Description: Manufacturer of 'glassless' mirrors.

Ithaca

Ithaca Theatre Lighting, Incorporated
1001 West Seneca Street
Ithaca, NY 14850
Tel: 607-272-2131
Address Inquiries to: Ron Colvin, Vice
President
Description: Manufacturer of lighting equipment.

Jackson Heights

Pro Audio Marketing
Post Office Box 153
Jackson Heights, NY 11372
Tel: 212-898-0200
Address Inquiries to: Stan Sommers
Description: Manufacturer of sound systems
and equipment.

Jericho

ATS Ticket Service
Post Office Box 159
375 North Broadway
Jericho, NY 11753
Tel: 516-433-7227
Description: Suppliers of quality tickets, they
also design and print your tickets for your
specific needs.

Johnsburg

Creative Stage Lighting Company
Post Office Box 51
Johnsburg, NY 12843
Tel: 518-251-3302
Address Inquiries to: George Studnicky,
General Manager
Lily M. Studnicky, Administrative
Assistant
Founded in: 1977
Description: Offers lighting equipment and
suppplies for sale or rental. Available are
touring and one night lighting systems for
musical, theatrical and industrial events.
Creative Stage Lighting Company works directly with any agencies, facilities, theatres
or schools

Liverpool

Ferrini-Konarski Associates, Incorporated
300 Tulip Street
Liverpool, NY 13088
Address Inquiries to: 315 635 3232
716 235 3065
Founded in: 1974
Description: A manufacture representative
specializing in industrial lighting. Has a

complete line of theatrical lighting.

Jack Mesnick Sales
13 Juneberry Lane
Liverpool, NY 13088
Tel: 315-622-3211
Address Inquiries to: Jack Mesnick
Founded in: 1972
Member: ERA;
Description: Supplier of commercial sound
equipment, including Paso, Superex, and
Dyna Systems.

Long Island City

Broadway Productions, Incorporated
51-02 27th Street
Long Island City, NY 11101
Tel: 212-392-0020
Address Inquiries to: Joseph Maceda, Vice
President

Kliegl Brothers
32-32 48th Avenue
Long Island City, NY 11101
Tel: 212-786-7474
Address Inquiries to: Michael Connell, Sales
Manager
Founded in: 1896
Member: USITT; SMPTE; NAB;
Description: Manufactures lighting equipment, hardware and dimming systems.

Mutual Hardware Corporation
5-45 49th Avenue
Long Island City, NY 11101
Tel: 212-361-2480
Address Inquiries to: Vincent Mallardi,
President
Founded in: 1935
Member: USITT;
Description: Supplier of scenic paints, fog machines and theatrical hardware, such as
tracks, curtains and casters.

Murry Rosenblum Sound Associates, Inc.
21-36 33rd Road
Long Island City, NY 11106
Tel: 212-728-2654
Address Inquiries to: Murry Rosenblum,
President
Description: Supplier of wireless microphones.

Manlius

Brown Lighting Sales
3214 Sunridge Drive
Manlius, NY 13104
Tel: 315-682-8916
Address Inquiries to: Bob Brown
Description: Supplier of lighting equipment.

Monroe

Rauland-Borg Corporation
40 High Ridge Road
Monroe, NY 10950
Tel: 914-783-4151
Address Inquiries to: Walter J. Spencer
Description: Supplier of sound and communications equipment.

Nanuet

Swivelier, Incorporated
33 Route 304
Nanuet, NY 10954
Tel: 914-623-3471
Address Inquiries to: Irv Schucker, Sales
Manager
Description: Manufacturer of lighting equipment.

Newburgh

Macbeth Sales Corporation
R.D. #3
Jeanne Drive
Newburgh, NY 12550
Tel: 914-564-6300; 800-431-9980
Address Inquiries to: Wendell T. Gill,
National Sales Manager
Description: Supplier of xenon bulbs.

New City

Stage Lighting Discount Corporation
5 Ferndale Road
New City, NY 10956
Tel: 914-634-9494
Address Inquiries to: R. Ritz, Sales
Description: Supplier of lighting and control
equipment.

New Hyde Park

Elmo Manufacturing Corporation
70 New Hyde Park Road
New Hyde Park, NY 11040
Tel: 516-775-3200
Address Inquiries to: Frank A. Brill, National
Sales Manager
Founded in: 1921
Member: NAVA; SMPTE;
Description: Manufacturer of motion picture
projectors.

New Rochelle

American Stage Lighting
1331-C North Avenue
New Rochelle, NY 10804
Tel: 914-636-5538
Description: Supplier of lighting, technical
equipment and stage costumes. Also supplies fluorescent paints, and phosphorescent
tapes and paints.

New York

Alcone Company, Incorporated
575 8th Avenue
New York, NY 10018
Tel: 212-594-3980
Member: ATA; USITT; SETC;
Description: Supplier of lighting and all types
of theatrical equipment except costumes.

Barbizon Electric Company, Incorporated
426 West 55th Street
New York, NY 10019
Tel: 212-586-1620
Address Inquiries to: Sam Resnick, Manager
Joe Houseman, Manager
Description: Barbizon Electric supplies a full
line of SSTV lamps.

Brooks-Van Horn Costume Company
117 West 17th Street
New York, NY 10011
Tel: 212-989-8000
Address Inquiries to: Arthur Gerald,
   President
Description: Manufacturer and rental of theatrical costumes.

Camera Mart, Incorporated
456 West 55th Street
New York, NY 10019
Tel: 212-757-6977
Address Inquiries to: Jeff Wohl, Sales
   Manager
Description: Supplier of Wireless Microphones, film, photographic and video equipment.

Carroll Sound, Incorporated
895 Broadway
New York, NY 10036
Tel: 212-868-4120
Address Inquiries to: Garry S. Bratman, Vice
   President
   Joseph D. Gulas, General Manager
Founded in: 1945
Member: NAMM; MDA; NCMI;
Description: Export and import wholesale musical instruments, particularly percussive and sound effects.

Cine 60 Incorporated
630 Ninth Avenue
New York, NY 10036
Tel: 212-586-8782
Address Inquiries to: Don F. Civitillo,
   Marketing Manager
Description: Manufacturer of lights and camera equipment.

Colortran, Incorporated
600 West End Avenue, #1A3
New York, NY 10024
Tel: 212-874-2122
Address Inquiries to: Les Zellan, Manager
Member: NAB; USITT; SMPTE; IES;
Description: A regional branch office.

Costume Pattern Service
428 West 44th Street
New York, NY 10036
Tel: 212-246-5769
Address Inquiries to: Barbara L. Callahan,
   Partner
Description: Supplies male and female patterns by mail order.

Dazian's Incorporated
40 East 29th Street
New York, NY 10016
Tel: 212-686-5300
Address Inquiries to: Norman Friedlander,
   President
Founded in: 1842
Member: LNYTP;
Description: Supplier of theatrical fabrics and supplies.

Devlin Productions, Incorporated
150 West 55th Street
New York, NY 10019

Tel: 212-582-5572
Address Inquiries to: Sandra Devlin,
   President
Description: Supplier of video production equipment.

Duro-Test Light Center
One Times Square
New York, NY 10036
Tel: 212-391-8190
Address Inquiries to: Stan Spiegel, General
   Sales Manager
Description: Supplier of light bulbs and spot lights.

Manny Feris
76 Ninth Avenue, Room 1531
New York, NY 10011
Tel: 212-924-7783; 212-625-4357
Address Inquiries to: Manny Feris
Description: Full range of theatrical equipment: Dimmers, control consoles, patch panels, lighting instruments and special effects.

Gothic Color Company, Incorporated
727-729 Washington Street
New York, NY 10014
Tel: 212-929-7493; 212-929-7494
Address Inquiries to: Moe Schwartz, Manager
   Description: Supplier of dyes and paints.

Ideal Wig Company
38 Pearl Street
New York, NY 10004
Tel: 212-269-6610
Address Inquiries to: Bill Zauder, Manager,
   Theatrical H.G. Div.
Description: Supplier of hair goods, beards, moustaches and wigs.

Imagineering Incorporated
234 West 44th Street
New York, NY 10036
Description: Supplier of lighting equipment.

Bob Kelly Cosmetics Inc.
151 West 46th Street
New York, NY 10036
Tel: 212-245-2237
Address Inquiries to: Bob Kelly, President
Description: Manufacturer and distributor of theatrical cosmetics.

Lighting Services, Incorporated
150 East 58th Street
New York, NY 10022
Tel: 212-838-8633
Address Inquiries to: John G. Churko,
   National Sales Manager
Description: Manufacturer of lighting equipment.

Litelab Corporation
76 Ninth Avenue
New York, NY 10011
Tel: 212-675-4357
Address Inquiries to: Vincent G. Finnegan Jr.,
   National Sales Manager
Founded in: 1975
Member: NAMM; Asid Industry Foundation;
   Description: The largest manufacturer and supplier of lighting systems to the entertain-

ment market. Also manufactures architectural fixtures for the architecture and design market.

Lowel-Light Mfg., Incorporated
475 Tenth Avenue
New York, NY 10019
Tel: 212-947-0950
Address Inquiries to: Art Kramer, Sales
   Manager
   Marvin Seligman, Vice President
Founded in: 1959
Member: PMPEA; SMPTE; NAB; NAVA;
Description: Manufactures portable, location lighting equipment for motion picture, television, video and still application.

M and J Trimming Company
1008 Sixth Avenue
New York, NY 10018
Tel: 212-391-9072
Address Inquiries to: Ralph Sutton, Manager
Description: Supplier of beads, trim, feathers, laces and rhinestones.

Manny's Music
156 West 48th Street
New York, NY 10036
Tel: 212-747-0576
Address Inquiries to: Henry Goldrich
Description: Supplier of sound equipment.

Masque Sound and Recording
Corporation
331 West 51st Street
New York, NY 10019
Tel: 212-245-4623
Founded in: 1936
Description: Supplier of intercom systems, sound equipment and amplification for use on stage. Also rents equipment.

Maxine Fabrics Company
417 Fifth Avenue
New York, NY 10016
Tel: 212-685-1790
Address Inquiries to: Steve Koslin, President
Description: Supplier of fabrics and patterns.

Mayer and Fisher, Incorporated
15 West 38th Street
New York, NY 10018
Tel: 212-840-8438
Address Inquiries to: Harry Mayer
Description: Supplier of fabrics.

Plastic Reel Corporation of America
43 West 61st Street
New York, NY 10023
Tel: 212-541-1950
Address Inquiries to: Ray Fincke
Description: Manufacturer of reels and reel equipment.

Rose Brand Textile Fabrics
517 West 34th Street
New York, NY 10001
Tel: 212-594-7424; 800-223-1624
Address Inquiries to: George Jacobstein,
   General Manager
   Steven Safer, Sales Manager
Description: Supplier of theatrical curtains, draperies and tapes.

See Factor, Incorporated
84 Thomas Street
New York, NY 10013
Tel: 212-732-1464; 710-581-4327
Address Inquiries to: Elliot B. Krowe, Vice
President
Description: Supplier of portable lighting and
intercom systems.

Stagelight Cosmetics
630 Ninth Avenue
New York, NY 10036
Tel: 212-757-4851
Address Inquiries to: Mark Genauer,
President
Description: Manufacturer of theatrical cos-
metics.

Stage Lighting Distributors Corporation
346 West 44th Street
New York, NY 10036
Tel: 212-489-1370; 516-669-1616
Description: Carries major brands of lighting
and other technical equipment.

M. Stein Cosmetics Company
430 Broome Street
New York, NY 10013
Tel: 212-226-2430
Address Inquiries to: Mr. Roffer, Vice
President
Description: Supplier of theatrical cosmetics.

Alfred Stern
408 West 57th Street
New York, NY 10019
Tel: 212-246-9866
Address Inquiries to: Alfred Stern
Description: Supplier of costumes

Strobelite Company, Incorporated
10 East 23rd Street
New York, NY 10010
Tel: 212-677-9220
Address Inquiries to: R. Andersen, Sales
Manager
O. Shatts, Purchasing
Founded in: 1924
Member: IES;
Description: Manufacturer of fluorescent
paints, and phosphorescent tapes and
paints. Supplies glow in the dark effects on
costumes, props and scenery, activated by
blacklights.

Theatre Marketplace
Post Office Box 181
New York, NY 10024
Tel: 212-724-0248
Address Inquiries to: Harris Goldman,
President
Description: Supplier of illuminated pens and
clipboards.

Times Square Lighting
318 West 47th Street
New York, NY 10036
Tel: 212-245-4155
Description: Supplier of lighting equipment.

Times Square Theatrical Supply
Corporation
318 West 47th Street

New York, NY 10036
Tel: 212-245-4155; 212-541-5045
Founded in: 1930
Member: USITT; ATA; NADI; NAMM;
Description: Supplier of fluorescent paints,
and phosphorescent tapes, and paints. Ma-
jor supplier of theatrical and studio lighting,
lighting systems, make-up, special effects,
glow tapes, curtains and dance floors. Times
Square rents and leases equipment.

Visual Resources, Incorporated
152 West 42nd Street, Suite 1219
New York, NY 10036
Address Inquiries to: Larry Qualls
Description: Supplier of slides, catalogues and
handbooks for theatre and dance.

Zauder Bros., Incorporated
902 Broadway
New York, NY 10010
Tel: 212-228-2600
Address Inquiries to: Fred Zauder, Vice
President
Description: Manufacturer of makeup, wigs
and beards for the theatre.

Ossining

Theatre Production Service
26 South Highland Avenue
Ossining, NY 10562
Tel: 914-941-0357
Description: Supplier of theatrical equipment
including lighting, makeup, sound effects
and wigs.

Pelham

Paso Sound Products, Incorporated
14 First Street
Pelham, NY 10803
Tel: 914-738-4800
Address Inquiries to: Paul Mastrangelo,
Executive Vice President
Description: Manufacturer of commercial
sound equipment.

Plainview

Listec Television Equipment Corporation
39 Cain Drive
Plainview, NY 11803
Tel: 516-694-8963
Address Inquiries to: Bruce Ballantyne
Description: Supplier of theatre sound effects
and control consoles.

Port Chester

Rosco Labs, Incorporated
36 Bush Avenue
Port Chester, NY 10573
Tel: 914-937-1300
Address Inquiries to: Stan Miller, President
Member: ATA; SMPTE;
Description: One of the world's largest manu-
facturers of color filters for film, theatre and
television.

Richmond Hill

Rubie's Costume Company Incorporated
1 Rubie Plaza
Richmond Hill, NY 11418
Tel: 202-846-1008
Address Inquiries to: Joel Beige, Vice
President, Sales
Founded in: 1947
Member: AETA; NCA; USITT;
Description: Supplier of costumes, make-up,
and props for the theatre. Send for a free,
large and comprehensive catalogue.

Rochester

Ferrini-Konarski Associates, Incorporated
1008 South Plymouth Avenue
Rochester, NY 14608
Description: A manufacture representative
specializing in industrial lighting. Complete
line of theatrical lighting available.

South Salem

Television Equipment Associates
Post Office Box 260
South Salem, NY 10599
Tel: 914-763-8893
Address Inquiries to: B. Pegler, President
Description: Manufacturer of intercom head-
sets.

Spring Valley

Video Components
601 South Main Street
Spring Valley, NY 10977
Description: Supplier of shipping cases.

Syracuse

J.R. Clancy Incorporated
7041 Interstate Island Road
Syracuse, NY 13209
Tel: 315-451-3440
Address Inquiries to: J.R. Clancy
Description: Manufacturer of rigging and the-
atrical hardware.

Lewis and Dunnigan Company,
Incorporated
104 Jamesville Road
Syracuse, NY 13214
Tel: 315-446-5522
Member: ERA; VIP;
Description: Manufacturers representative for
sound and intercom systems.

Walden

Packaged Lighting Systems, Incorporated
Post Office Box 285
Walden, NY 12586
Tel: 914-778-3515
Address Inquiries to: Hy Hilzen, Director of
Technology
Description: Manufacturer of lighting equip-
ment.

Wantagh

Chic Lighting
1550 Wantagh Avenue
Wantagh, NY 11793
Tel: 516-752-9824

Description: Supplier of lighting, sound, technical equipment and stage costumes.

West Babylon

Stage Lighting Discount Corporation
548 Sunrise Highway
West Babylon, NY 11704
Tel: 516-669-1616; 212-489-1370
Description: Carries major brands of lighting and other technical equipment.

Whitestone

Baschnagel Brothers, Incorporated
150-25 14th Avenue
Whitestone, NY 11357
Tel: 212-767-1919
Address Inquiries to: Robert Baschnagel Jr.,
   President
   Carol Baschnagel, Vice President
Founded in: 1900
Description: Baschnagel Brothers manufacturers and supplies custom and stock sheet metal custom ticket racks.

Woodside

Skirpan Lighting Control Corporation
61-03 32nd Avenue
Woodside, NY 11377
Tel: 212-274-7222
Address Inquiries to: Robert L. Benson,
   Director of Marketing
Description: Manufacturer of lighting equipment.

Superscope New York, Incorporated
37-04 57th Street
Woodside, NY 11377
Tel: 212-446-7227
Address Inquiries to: Joe Deo
Description: Supplier of sound equipment.

Yonkers

Altman Stage Lighting
57 Alexander Street
Yonkers, NY 10701
Tel: 914-476-7987
Description: Supplier of lighting and technical equipment and stage costumes.

Jack Brown Electronic Sales
207 Rosedale Road
Yonkers, NY 10910
Tel: 914-779-7330
Address Inquiries to: Jack Brown
Description: Supplier of electrical outlet strips and utility carts.

Fedigan Lighting Associates
12 Fanshaw Avenue
Yonkers, NY 10705
Tel: 914-968-6636
Address Inquiries to: Jim Fedigan
Description: Manufacturer of lighting control systems.

NORTH CAROLINA

Chapel Hill

A and E Sales
3 Cedronella Drive, Route 2
Chapel Hill, NC 27514
Description: Supplier of lighting equipment.

Charlotte

E.C. Gatewood
3120 Arundel Drive
Charlotte, NC 28209
Tel: 704-523-3499
Address Inquiries to: E.C. Gatewood
Description: Manufacturer of power supplies.

The Superior Electric Company
5600 Executive Center Drive
Charlotte, NC 28212
Tel: 704-535-5846
Description: Supplier of electrical equipment.

Durham

Carrington Electrical Sales
2203 Alabama Avenue
Durham, NC 27705
Tel: 919-286-7951
Description: Supplier of lighting equipment.

Greensboro

D. Rick Hershberger
3403 Overton Drive
Greensboro, NC 27408
Tel: 919-288-2742
Address Inquiries to: Rick Hershberger
Description: Manufacturer of tapes for film processing.

Stage Decoration and Supplies,
Incorporated
1204 Oakland Avenue
Post Office Box 5463
Greensboro, NC 27403
Tel: 919-275-6488
Address Inquiries to: W.R. Taylor, President
Leslie Martin, Production Manager
Description: Manufacturer of stage equipment.

Standard Theatre Supply Company
125 Higgins Street
Greensboro, NC 27406
Description: Supplier of wireless microphones.

Tom Teeter
901 Forest Hill Drive
Greensboro, NC 27401
Tel: 919-855-6238
Address Inquiries to: Tom Teeter
Description: Supplier of tickets and ticket racks.

Matthews

Carrington Elecrical Sales
Post Office Box 6
Matthews, NC 28105
Tel: 704-882-1195
Description: Supplier of lighting equipment.

Morganton

Grand Piano Company
Post Office Box 1238
Morganton, NC 28665
Address Inquiries to: Dennis Kincaid
Description: Supplier of sound equipment.

NORTH DAKOTA

Fargo

Northern School Supply Company
Post Office Box 2627
Fargo, ND 58102
Tel: 701-293-3210
Description: Manufacturer of stage equipment.

OHIO

Amherst

Amherst Fabric and Trim
205 North Leavitt Road
Amherst, OH 44001
Tel: 216-988-2116
Address Inquiries to: Howard Mowcomber
Description: Specializes in trims, metallic fabric and bridal fabrics.

Amherst Lumber Company
700 Mill Avenue
Amherst, OH 44001
Tel: 216-988-4431
Address Inquiries to: Floyd Blevins
Rocky Rossini
Description: Manufactures mini-barns and mill work.

Aurora

Calico Corners
196 South Chillicothe Road
Aurora, OH 44202
Tel: 216-562-8558
Founded in: 1951
Description: Supplies decorative fabrics, slipcovers, drapery and upholstery.

Beachwood

Fabri-Centers of America
23550 Commerce Park Road
Beachwood, OH 44122
Tel: 216-464-2500
Address Inquiries to: Michael Feuer
Description: Supplies retail fabrics.

Bedford Heights

Cercone Vincent Associates, Incorporated
5020 Richmond Road
Bedford Heights, OH 44146
Tel: 216-292-2550
Address Inquiries to: Samuel P. Cercone,
   President
   Paul E. Vincent, Vice President
Founded in: 1976
Member: Society of Broadcast Engineers;
   United States Institute of Theatre
   Technology;

Description: A complete performance lighting company, offering lighting system design, supply of equipment and installation when required. Short or long term rentals are available. Offices are located in Pittsburgh, PA and Cleveland, OH.

Beechwood

Electronic Salesmasters
24100 Chagrin Boulevard
Beechwood, OH 44122
Tel: 216-831-9555
Description: Supplier of electrical outlet strips and utility carts.

Canton

Janson Industries
1200 Garfield Avenue SW
Canton, OH 44706
Tel: 216-455-7029; 216-455-2241
Address Inquiries to: Richard W. Janson
Founded in: 1935
Description: Manufacturer of stage equipment including stage curtains, track systems, counterweight equipment and stage lighting systems. The firm has pioneered innovative installation procedures and has many patents in theatre applications. An electronics divisio n provides turnkey installations of television, projection and simulation systems.

Cincinnati

Aufdemkampe Hardware Company
2000 Central Parkway
Cincinnati, OH 45214
Tel: 513-381-3200
Founded in: 1904
Description: Distributors of hardware, power tools and machinery.

Beck Studios, Incorporated
5614 Wooster Pike
Cincinnati, OH 45227
Tel: 513-271-0080
Address Inquiries to: Merrel B. Ludlow

Cappel Display Company, Incorporated
920 Elm Street
Cincinnati, OH 45202
Tel: 513-621-0952
Address Inquiries to: John Cappel
Ray Cappel
Description: Supplies decorations and novelties for all types of productions including opera, television and schools.

General Display Corporation
112 West Court Street
Cincinnati, OH 45202
Tel: 513-241-5251
Description: Supplies many theatre tools and honeycomb panels.

H.C. King and Associates, Incorporated
800 Compton Road
Cincinnati, OH 45231
Tel: 513-521-5511
Address Inquiries to: H.C. King
Founded in: 1927
Member: IES;

Description: Supplier of lighting equipment.

Uchtman Associated
7923 Mitchell Farm Lane
Cincinnati, OH 45242
Tel: 513-984-8886
Member: MANA; IESA; CEA;
Description: Agents for lighting, major dimming equipment and energy saving equipment.

The Wilson Paint Company
1616 Harrison Avenue
Cincinnati, OH 45214
Tel: 513-251-5300
Address Inquiries to: William R. Powell
Dennis Hock

Cleveland

Astrup Company
2937 West 25th Street
Cleveland, OH 44113
Tel: 216-696-2800
Founded in: 1876
Description: Supplies flame and non-flame resistant scenery fabrics, cordage and rope.

Bilt-Rite Fabrics, Incorporated
16121 Euclid Avenue
Cleveland, OH 44112
Tel: 216-451-2900
Address Inquiries to: Ralph Klaiman,
President
Description: Supplies upholstery, drapery fabrics and discontinued patterns.

Dodd Company, The
13123 Shaker Square
Cleveland, OH 44120
Tel: 216-561-1500
Address Inquiries to: Alex B. Glendinning
Description: Photographic and art supplies, camera and projector repair.

General Electric Lamp Products Division
Nela Park
Cleveland, OH 44112
Tel: 216-266-2121
Address Inquiries to: C.N. Clark
Description: Manufacturer of lamps.

Imtech, Incorporated
6862 Engle Road
Cleveland, OH 44130
Tel: 216-826-3400
Description: Supplier of sound and intercom systems.

Industrial Safety Products, Incorporated
5775 Canal Road
Cleveland, OH 44125
Tel: 216-524-0360
Address Inquiries to: Mark Castro
Description: Supplies safety caps, glasses, muffs and face shields.

Krause Costume Company
2439 Superior Avenue
Cleveland, OH 44114
Tel: 216-241-6466
Address Inquiries to: Thomas Gerseny,
Manager
Melvin Gerseny, President

Founded in: 1867
Member: NOA; NCA; MOG; TCS;
Description: Supplier of theatrical, masquerade and operatic wardrobes on a rental basis. They also handle makeup, hats, wigs and various other accessories on a retail basis. The company ships all over the country and deals with both civic and educational institutions.

L and M Stagecraft, Incorporated
2110 Superior Avenue
Cleveland, OH 44114
Tel: 216-621-4752
Address Inquiries to: Charles A. McDougall,
President
Tom Corrigan
Description: Supplier of lighting equipment, audio/visual equipment and draperies.

Mutual Display
1748 East 27th Street
Cleveland, OH 44114
Tel: 216-621-3685
Address Inquiries to: Hal Moses
Description: Supplies stage props, screens, and backgrounds.

Sheffield Bronze Paint Corporation
17814 South Waterloo Road
Cleveland, OH 44119
Tel: 216-481-8330
Address Inquiries to: Herbert Mintz
Founded in: 1927
Description: Supplies aluminium paints and indoor/outdoor paints.

Taffy's
701 Beta Drive
Cleveland, OH 44143
Tel: 216-461-3360
Description: Supplies outfitting costumes.

Transilwrap Company of Cleveland
5905 Cloverleaf Parkway
Cleveland, OH 44125
Tel: 216-524-4160
Description: Supplies plastics for lighting, skylights and mirrors.

Columbus

Mandabach-Lehner Company
155 South Hamilton Road
Columbus, OH 43213
Tel: 614-235-0265
Founded in: 1975
Member: ERA;
Description: Supplier of sound equipment.

McFadden Sales, Incorporated
4645 Executive Drive
Columbus, OH 43220
Tel: 614-459-1280
Description: Supplier of sound equipment.

Theatre Magic
1282 Nantucket
Columbus, OH 43220
Tel: 614-459-3222
Address Inquiries to: Richard Huggins
Beverly Huggins
Founded in: 1975

Annual Budget: $80,000
Description: Supplies special effects equipment to theatres, television and Broadway productions. Retail equipment includes a remote and a manual fog machine (by Fog Masters), a cobweb spinner, and both custom and stock projection patterns. Consultation available for any special effects needs.

Dayton

The Joyce-Cridland Company
Post Office Box 1630
Dayton, OH 45401
Tel: 513-294-6261
Address Inquiries to: Gregory W. Furlong,
   Manager, Field Sales
   John M. Miller, Vice President,
   Marketing
Founded in: 1873
Member: United States Institute of Theater
   Technology; Material Handling Institute;
   Petroleum Equipment Institute;
   Equipment Tool Institute; Automotive
   Lift Institute; National Association of
   Manufacturers;
Description: Manufactures stage and orchestra pit lift equipment powered hydraulically or by screw jacks.

Klopf Audio/Video Company
3381 Successful Way
Dayton, OH 45414
Tel: 513-236-5500
Address Inquiries to: Brooke McCarter
Description: Supplies audio and video communications.

Elyria

Loomis Camera Company
413 Broad Street
Elyria, OH 44035
Tel: 216-322-3325
Address Inquiries to: Marvin Smith
Description: Supplies photo equipment.

Findlay

Joe Flavell
1539 Brookside Drive
Findlay, OH 45848
Tel: 419-422-4235
Address Inquiries to: Joe Flavell
Description: Manfacturer of staging.

Loveland

Newco Products, Incorporated
11605 Lebanon Road
Loveland, OH 45040
Tel: 513-683-1825
Address Inquiries to: Nancy Rozzi
   Art Rozzi
Founded in: 1954
Description: Supplies flash powder and original Newco Photographic flash powder also NPII, two component flash powder for theatrical special effects.

Medina

J.B. Parent Company
Great Northern Building
4986 Gateway Drive
Medina, OH 44256
Tel: 216-725-8871
Address Inquiries to: Pat Parent
Description: Manufacturer of sound systems and equipment.

James H. Podolny Co.
124 W. Washington Street
Medina, OH 44256
Tel: 216-725-8814
Address Inquiries to: James H. Podolny
Description: Supplier of commercial sound equipment.

The Superior Electric Company
124 West Washington Street
Medina, OH 44256
Tel: 216-725-8887
Description: Supplier of electrical equipment.

Toledo

Concession Supply Company
1016 North Summit Street, Box 1007
Toledo, OH 43697
Tel: 419-241-7711
Address Inquiries to: Brad Brockway,
   President
   Bob Brockway, Vice President
Founded in: 1905
Member: NACM; IAAAFA;
Description: A manufacturing and sales organization. They have a manufacturing facility as well as sales room and display items. About 10% of our sales are international and we cover all of the states in the United States. They are also a complete one-stop-service for concession and theatrical items.

Kneisley Electric Company, The
Box 4692
Toledo, OH 43620
Tel: 419-241-1219
Address Inquiries to: Clint Ewell
Founded in: 1935
Member: NAVA; TEA;
Description: Manufactures xenon lamp conversions for strong trouper spotlights.

Strong Electrical Corporation
87 City Park Avenue
Toledo, OH 43697
Tel: 419-248-3741
Address Inquiries to: Gene Schaefer
Founded in: 1926
Description: Supplies spotlights.

Warren

Sound Creations
1309 Bingham Northwest
Warren, OH 44485
Tel: 216-399-8752
Address Inquiries to: Al Galo
Description: Supplies professional sound equipment.

Washingtonville

White Product Company
200 East Main Street
Washingtonville, OH 44490
Tel: 216-747-8116; 216-427-6542
Address Inquiries to: John J. Gavura,
   President
Description: Supplier of wood and insulation products.

Youngstown

Sam Bohm Associates
2821 Belmar Drive
Youngstown, OH 44505
Tel: 216-759-7866
Description: Manufacturer of tapes for film processing.

Masters Costumes
303 Federal Plaza West
Youngstown, OH 44503
Tel: 216-744-2571
Address Inquiries to: Beverly Darling,
   Manager
Description: Masters Costumes sells and rents costumes, makeup and hair goods.

OKLAHOMA

Oklahoma City

Audio Associates
2419 Classen
Oklahoma City, OK 73106
Tel: 405-524-3232
Description: Suppliers of lighting, technical and sound equipment. Rentals are available.

Capitol Stage Equipment Company
3121 North Pennsylvania
Oklahoma City, OK 73112
Tel: 405-524-9552
Address Inquiries to: Larry Thompson
Description: Supplier of lighting equipment.

Oklahoma City Scenic Company
Post Office Box 1147
Oklahoma City, OK 73101
Tel: 405-232-6176
Description: Supplier of lighting equipment.

S.E.B. Paint Company
115 Northeast 10th Street
Oklahoma City, OK 73104
Tel: 405-232-0153
Description: Supplier of scenic paints and accessories.

Tulsa

Audio-Visual Enterprises
2109 East 51st Street
Tulsa, OK 74105
Tel: 918-743-6427
Description: Suppliers of lighting, technical and audio-video equipment.

Walter S. Brewer Company
2216 East 56th Place
Tulsa, OK 74105
Tel: 918-749-9894

Description: Supplies, rents and manufactures lighting and technical equipment.

The Crosby Group
Post Office Box 3128
Tulsa, OK 74101
Tel: 918-834-4611
Address Inquiries to: Dick Cast, Advertising
  Manager
Description: Suppliers of lighting and technical equipment. Rentals available.

Ford Audio and Acoustics, Incorporated
4715 East 41st Street
Tulsa, OK 74135
Tel: 918-663-4730
Description: Suppliers of lighting, technical and audio-visual equipment.

Panoak Lighting Systems
6809 East 40th Street
Tulsa, OK 74145
Tel: 918-664-1111
Address Inquiries to: L.S. Bostic, General
  Manager
Description: Supplier of lighting and technical equipment.

Studio West, Incorporated
421 South Rockford
Tulsa, OK 74120
Tel: 918-582-3512
Address Inquiries to: C.E. West, President
Carolyn West, Secretary/Treasurer
Description: Supply and rent theatre, studio and television lighting. Also carries color media, fixtures, adapter, wiring devices and communications systems.

OREGON

Eugene

Back Stage Lighting
878 Pearl Street
Eugene, OR 97400
Address Inquiries to: Greg Long
Description: Supplier of lighting equipment.

Hillsboro

Electronics Diversified, Incorporated
1675 Northwest 216th Street
Hillsboro, OR 97123
Tel: 503-645-5533
Address Inquiries to: Luis Walsh, Marketing
  Manager
Description: Manufacturer of lighting equipment.

Portland

Earl and Brown Company
7719 Southwest Capitol Highway
Portland, OR 97219
Tel: 503-245-2283
Address Inquiries to: Ken Baldwin
Description: Manufacturer of sound systems and equipment.

Hollywood Lights, Incorporated
0625 SW Florida
Portland, OR 97219

Tel: 503-244-5808; 503-245-2236
Address Inquiries to: Tom Neal, President
James Robinson, Rental and Sales
  Manager
Founded in: 1940
Description: Supply and rent lighting and electrical services for theatre, t.v., tradeshows and conventions.

Don McClain
1345 Northeast 109th
Portland, OR 97220
Tel: 503-253-5527
Address Inquiries to: Don McClain
Description: Supplier of lighting equipment.

Stagecraft Industries, Incorporated
13022 North West Kearney Street
Portland, OR 97209
Tel: 503-226-7351
Address Inquiries to: Ronald W. Hill, Sales
  Representative
Description: Manufacturer of stage equipment.

Dale G. Weber Co.
1226 S.E. 7th Avenue
Portland, OR 97214
Tel: 503-234-7671
Address Inquiries to: Dale G. Weber
Description: Supplier of commercial sound equipment.

PENNSYLVANIA

Allentown

Automatic Devices Company
212 South 12th Street
Allentown, PA 18103
Tel: 215-797-6000
Address Inquiries to: Donald R. Heller, Vice
  President
Description: Supplies stage curtains, lighting and gym dividers.

Bala Cynwyd

McMannus Enterprises
111 Union Avenue
Post Office Box 150
Bala Cynwyd, PA 19004
Tel: 215-664-8600; 800-523-0348
Address Inquiries to: Stephen Lister
Founded in: 1966
Member: ATA; USITT;
Description: Supplier of intercom systems, audio control consoles, lighting control consoles and special effects. Supplier of a full range of theatre, film and television equipment and supplies. Sales and rentals.

Blue Bell

The Superior Electric Company
650 Blue Bell West
Blue Bell, PA 19422
Tel: 215-248-5770
Description: Supplier of electrical equipment.

Emmaus

Sport Seating Company, Incorporated
1540 Chestnut Street
Emmaus, PA 18049
Tel: 215-967-5450
Address Inquiries to: William R. Nixon,
  Executive Vice President
Description: Manufacturer of theatre seats.

Flourtown

Bond Lumetech, Ltd.
Post Office Box 95
Flourtown, PA 19031
Tel: 215-247-6104
Description: Supplier of lighting equipment.

Glenside

Richard Lewis Sales
222 South Easton Road
Glenside, PA 19038
Tel: 215-886-1555; 215-886-1556
Address Inquiries to: Richard Lewis
Founded in: 1950
Member: ERA;
Description: Manufacturer of commercial sound equipment.

Healdsburg

Ruppert, Gibbon and Spider
718 College Street
Healdsburg, PA 945448
Tel: 707-433-9577
Description: Supplier of paints and dyes for theatre.

Holland

Par-Nell Sales Co.
7 Patricia Road
Holland, PA 18966
Tel: 215-355-9330
Description: Supplier of commercial sound equipment.

Horsham

Globe Ticket Company
680 Blair Mill Road
Post Office Box 365
Horsham, PA 19044
Tel: 215-657-4230
Address Inquiries to: J.E. Betterly, Marketing
  Manager
Description: Manufacturer of tickets and ticket equipment.

King of Prussia

Memorex Corporation
741 Fifth Avenue
King of Prussia, PA 19406
Address Inquiries to: D. Miller, Regional
  Representative
Description: Manufacturer of audio and video tape.

Newtown Square

George M. Conneen Company, Inc.
24 South Newtown Street Road
Newtown Square, PA 19073
Tel: 215-353-2241; 215-353-2242

Address Inquiries to: George M. Conneen
Description: Supplier of sound equipment and intercom systems.

Oreland

Diversified Lighting
120 Pennsylvania Avenue
Oreland, PA 19075
Tel: 215-887-7480
Address Inquiries to: Warren Goff, President
Joseph J. Petro, Theatrical Lighting Specialist
Founded in: 1967
Description: Manufacturer and representative of lighting, supplier of stage and studio equipment, and can also layout and plan lighting and controls.

Variable Electric Products, Incorporated
1504 Walnut Avenue
Post Office Box 115
Oreland, PA 19075
Tel: 215-884-5375
Address Inquiries to: Joe Vetter
Description: Supplier of lighting equipment.

Philadelphia

Samuel K. Macdonald, Inc.
1531 Spruce Street
Philadelphia, PA 19102
Tel: 215-545-1205
Address Inquiries to: Samuel K. Macdonald
Description: Supplier of sound equipment.

Magnetic Recorders
1533-35 Cherry Street
Philadelphia, PA 19102
Tel: 215-563-2010
Description: Supplier of intercom systems, microphone preamplifiers and mixers.

Richard S. Pass Associates
9003 Eastview Road
Philadelphia, PA 19152
Tel: 215-464-9444
Address Inquiries to: Richard S. Pass
Description: Supplier of microphone and audio equipment.

Charles Shestack Associates
8400 Bustleton Avenue, Suite 200
Philadelphia, PA 19152
Tel: 215-745-4044
Address Inquiries to: Charles Shestack
Description: Manufacturer of tapes for film processing.

South African Feather Company, Incorporated
401 N. Broad Street, Suite 242
Philadelphia, PA 19108
Tel: 215-925-5219; 215-925-5220
Address Inquiries to: Ronald Isserman, Vice President
Description: Manufacturer of feathers.

Pittsburgh

Fred T. Beaudry and Associates, Incorporated
1520 Northway Mall
Post Office Box 15155
Pittsburgh, PA 15237
Tel: 412-364-0788
Address Inquiries to: Fred Beaudry
Founded in: 1971
Description: Supplier of lighting equipment representing Colortran Incorporated, Burbank, California (manufacturers of lighting instruments, dimming, and control equipment) and The Peter Albrecht Corporation, Milwaukee, Wisconsin (manufacturers of automatic stage systems).

Buhl Optical
1009 Beech Avenue
Pittsburgh, PA 15233
Tel: 412-321-0076
Address Inquiries to: Ira Stapsy, President
Description: Supplier of projectors and projection lenses.

Cercone Vincent Associates, Incorporated
2741 Noblestown Road
Pittsburgh, PA 15205
Tel: 412-922-0901
Address Inquiries to: Samuel P. Cercone, President
Paul E. Vincent, Vice President
Founded in: 1976
Member: Society of Broadcast Engineers; United States Institute of Theatre Technology;
Description: A complete performance lighting company, offering lighting system design, supply of equipment and installation when required. Short or long term rentals are available. Offices are located in Pittsburgh, PA and Cleveland, OH.

Costumes Unlimited Pittsburgh, Incorporated
1031 Forbes Avenue
Pittsburgh, PA 15219
Tel: 412-281-3277
Address Inquiries to: Jadene Deems, Manager
Founded in: 1896
Description: A major activity is rental of costumes. They sell the complete line of Stein's and Ben Nye makeup in addition hundreds of masks and novelty items. Costumes Unlimited also specializes in custom contract sewing.

Daquelente Brothers
8150 Perry Highway
Pittsburgh, PA 15237
Tel: 412-364-3700
Description: Supplier of lighting equipment.

Ekedahl Tool and Supply Company
Post Office Box 13198
Pittsburgh, PA 15243
Tel: 412-531-2850
Address Inquiries to: Stephen M. Goldman
Description: Supplier of tools and furniture.

Flexitrol Lighting
237 Morrison Drive
Pittsburgh, PA 15216
Tel: 412-531-4733
Address Inquiries to: Bob Miller
Description: Supplier of lighting equipment.

Globe Ticket Company
Post Office Box 11272
Pittsburgh, PA 15238
Tel: 412-361-8013
Description: Supplier of tickets and ticket equipment.

Rochester

Frank E. Davis Associates
524 Virginia Avenue
Rochester, PA 15704
Tel: 412-774-2133
Address Inquiries to: Frank E. Davis
Pat Leahy
Founded in: 1940
Description: Supplier of stage lighting equipment and accessories. Theatrical lighting equipment, stage curtains, stage settings and all related items. Follow spotlights and special effects.

Scranton

Harrils Theatrical Service
101 South Main Street
Scranton, PA 18510
Description: Supplier of fluorescent paints, and phosphorescent tapes and paints.

State College

EMS Products
242 South Gill Street
State College, PA 16801
Tel: 814-237-6702
Address Inquiries to: Delbert Boarts, Owner
Vonny Boarts, Business Manager
Founded in: 1973
Description: Supplier of the 'telephone ringer', a sound effect device.

Wescosville

Lehigh Electric Products Company
R.D. 1, Box J1, Route 222
Wescosville, PA 18106
Tel: 215-395-3386
Address Inquiries to: Lloyd H. Jones, Vice President
Founded in: 1962
Member: USITT;
Description: Manufactures a broad line of lighting control and distribution equipment for theatre, television and architectural applications. Equipment includes dimmers, control consoles, patch panels, connector strips, plug-in boxes and floor pockets.

PUERTO RICO

Carolina

Duro-Test International Corporation
Post Office Box 1893
Carolina, PR 00628
Tel: 809-768-2711; 809-762-1485
Address Inquiries to: Robert Joseph, General Manager
Jose Morales, Sales Administrator
Founded in: 1929
Description: Supplier of light bulbs and spot

lights.

Westinghouse Electric Supply Company
Box 144, La Ceramica Annex
Carolina, PR 00630
Address Inquiries to: Federico Garcia, Sales
  Department
Description: Supplier of lighting equipment.

RHODE ISLAND
Bristol

Brett Theatrical, Ltd.
91 Beach Road
Bristol, RI 02809
Tel: 401-253-5624
Address Inquiries to: Roger Brett, President
Description: Supplier of stage and flooring.

Cranston

Albert Sydney and Associates
143 Hoffman Avenue
Cranston, RI 02920
Tel: 401-943-3530
Address Inquiries to: Albert Sydney
Description: Manufacturer of tapes for film
processing.

Providence

**Connecticut Theatre Supply/ Theatre
Concepts**
40 Richmond Street
Providence, RI 02903
Tel: 401-331-7288
Address Inquiries to: John Petrafesa
Founded in: 1974
Description: Supplier of lighining systems
and general theatrical supplies.

Westerly

Payne Motion Picture Service
20 High Street
Westerly, RI 02891
Tel: 401-596-4739
Address Inquiries to: Gerald Payne
Description: Supplier of lighting equipment.

TENNESSEE
Antioch

Mike Jones
314 Cane Ridge Drive
Antioch, TN 37013
Tel: 615-331-2164
Address Inquiries to: Mike Jones
Description: Supplier of tickets and ticket
racks.

Knoxville

TERI Productions
600 Atlantic Avenue
Knoxville, TN 37917
Tel: 615-546-2082
Address Inquiries to: Jim Coatney
Description: Supplier of lighting equipment.

Theatrical Equipment Rental, Incorporated
600 Atlantic Avenue
Knoxville, TN 37917
Tel: 615-546-2082
Address Inquiries to: James E. Coatney,
  President
Description: Supplier of concert stages, light-
ing systems, costumes, paint and makeup.

Memphis

Audiotronics, Incorporated
3750 Old Getwell Road
Memphis, TN 38118
Tel: 901-362-1350
Address Inquiries to: H.S. Kendrick, Vice
  President
Description: Audiotronics supplies audio con-
trol consoles.

Dover Corporation/Elevator Division
Post Office Box 2177
Memphis, TN 38101
Tel: 601-393-2110
Address Inquiries to: Robert L. Snowden,
  Marketing Services Manager
Description: Supplier of stage lifts.

L.D.A. Sales
2221 Freemont
Memphis, TN 38114
Tel: 901-743-3111
Address Inquiries to: Sam Spraeberry
Bill Griffin
Description: Supplier of lighting equipment.

Media Equipment Company
795 South Main Street
Memphis, TN 38101
Tel: 901-774-6300; 901-388-3436
Address Inquiries to: William O'Rork,
  President
Founded in: 1977
Annual Budget: $300,000
Description: Supplier of wireless micro-
phones. Consults, rents and services most
types of production equipment.

Nashville

Collin Finney
807 Bradford Avenue
Post Office Box 40927
Nashville, TN 37024
Tel: 615-383-1358
Address Inquiries to: Collin Finney
Description: Supplier of lighting equipment.

Interstate Lighting
1421 4th Avenue N
Nashville, TN 37210
Tel: 615-259-4696
Description: Manufacturer of PYROPAK
materials, and supplier of custom lighting
systems.

TEXAS
Arlington

Bob Curtis
708 Lincoln Green Drive
Arlington, TX 76011
Tel: 817-261-6859
Address Inquiries to: Bob Curtis
Description: Manufacturer of tickets and ticket
racks.

J.L. Leary
3600 W. Pioneer Pkwy., Suite 12
Arlington, TX 76103
Tel: 817-274-6411
Address Inquiries to: J.L. Leary
Description: Manufacturer of power supplies.

Austin

Decor Electronics Corporation
4711 East Fifth Street
Austin, TX 78702
Tel: 512-385-0277
Address Inquiries to: Paul J. Anderson,
  Manager-Marketing
Description: Manufacturer of lighting equip-
ment and switchboards.

Carrollton

Atmos Corporation
Box 173
Carrollton, TX 75006
Tel: 214-242-6581
Address Inquiries to: Ed Eley, Sales Manager
Description: Supplies dimming controls and
systems.

Carrolton

Prescolite Lite Control
Post Office Box 173
Carrolton, TX 75006
Tel: 214-242-6581
Description: Supplier of lighting and technical
equipment. Rentals available.

Dallas

Bozak, Incorporated
c/o Charles Lucas Sales Company
Post Office Box 24632
Dallas, TX 75224
Tel: 214-330-8181
Description: A regional branch office.

**Commercial Plastics and Supply
Corporation**
2200 Vantage Street
Dallas, TX 75207
Tel: 214-631-8170
Description: Supplies and rents lighting and
technical equipment.

The Crockett Sales Company
2204 Griffin
Dallas, TX 75202
Tel: 214-748-8209
Description: Supplier of sound equipment.

Dallas Stage
2813 Florence
Dallas, TX 75204
Tel: 214-630-0297

Address Inquiries to: Jim Bradford
Founded in: 1975
Description: Supplier of lighting equipment.

Dazian's Incorporated
2014 Commerce Street
Dallas, TX 75201
Tel: 214-748-3450
Founded in: 1842
Member: ATA; USITT; TETA;
Description: Supplier of theatrical fabrics and supplies. The oldest and largest supplier in this field selling retail and wholesale to all.

Victor Duncan, Inc.
2659 Fondren
Dallas, TX 75206
Tel: 214-369-1165
Address Inquiries to: Lee A. Duncan,
   President
   Frank Marasco, Vice President
Founded in: 1960
Description: The firm is a completely equipped rental, sales and service company, specializing in films and video production equipment and accessories. Operates repair and maintenance facilities in Chicago, Dallas, and Detroit.

Globe Ticket Company
Post Office Box 47284
Dallas, TX 74247
Tel: 214-631-3450
Description: Supplier of tickets and ticket equipment.

Edwin Jones Company
6445 Prestonshire
Dallas, TX 75225
Tel: 214-789-9447
Address Inquiries to: Edwin Jones
Description: Supplier of lighting equipment.

Little Stage Lighting Company
10507 Harry Hines Boulevard
Dallas, TX 75220
Tel: 214-358-3511
Address Inquiries to: Margaret Little, Office
   Manager
   Don Webster, Sales Manager
Founded in: 1926
Member: IES; USITT;
Annual Budget: $1,000,000
Description: Founded by Harry Little in 1926 as a retail and sales organization for drapes, scenery and lighting. The company changed direction when William Little, proprietor, assumed management of the business. It now manufacturers, distributes and rents stage lighting equipment and supplies, including spots, floods, scoops and color media.

Charles Lucas Sales Company
Post Office Box 24632
Dallas, TX 75224
Tel: 214-330-8181
Address Inquiries to: Charles Lucas
Description: Supplier of sound equipment.

Jack F. McKinney Sales Co.
1303 Chemical Street

Dallas, TX 76207
Tel: 214-631-9450
Address Inquiries to: Jack F. McKinney
Description: Supplier of commercial sound equipment.

Mike Sanders and Associates
6060 North Central Expressway
Dallas, TX 75225
Tel: 214-696-2885
Address Inquiries to: Mike Sanders
Description: Supplier of lighting, technical equipment and theatrical souveniers.

Norcostco-Texas Costume
2125 North Horwood Street
Dallas, TX 75201
Tel: 214-748-4581
Member: American Theatre Association;
Description: Supplier of lighting equipment, theatrical make-up, stage supplies and costuming.

Peter Wolf Concepts
5200 East Grand Avenue
Dallas, TX 75223
Tel: 214-823-2862

Plastic Reel Corporation of America
1234 Roundtable Drive
Dallas, TX 75247
Tel: 214-634-7774
Address Inquiries to: Linda Aylem, Customer
   Service Manager
Description: Manufacturer of reels and reel equipment.

Don Robinson
1921 Moser #220
Dallas, TX 75206
Tel: 214-233-0731
Address Inquiries to: Don Robinson
Description: Supplier of stage shells and staging.

J.Y. Schoonmaker Company
10710 Sand Hill Road
Dallas, TX 75238
Tel: 214-349-1650
Address Inquiries to: J.Y. Schoonmaker
Description: Supplier of sound equipment and intercom systems.

Showtrol
2220 Shorecrest Drive
Dallas, TX 75235
Tel: 214-358-4527
Description: Supplier and manufacturer of lighting and technical equipment.

The Superior Electric Company
2530 Walnut Hill Lane, #164
Dallas, TX 75229
Tel: 214-350-1368
Description: Supplier of electrical equipment.

Superscope Texas, Incorporated
3214 Beltling Road
Dallas, TX 75234
Tel: 214-241-9712
Address Inquiries to: Bill Boksa
Description: Supplier of sound equipment.

Peter Wolf Associates, Inc.
8181 Hoyle
Dallas, TX 75227
Tel: 214-388-3461
Address Inquiries to: Mary McCullough,
   Promotion Manager
   Ary Arlon, Sales, Public Relations
Description: Manufacturer of stage equipment.

Wyborny Sales Company, Incorporated
9450 Skillman Suite 113
Dallas, TX 75243
Tel: 214-348-9657
Address Inquiries to: Jim Hancock
Description: Manufacturer of sound systems and equipment.

El Paso

Production Services
6016 G-3 Doniphan
El Paso, TX 79932
Tel: 915-584-6903
Description: Supplies and services lighting, technical, sound equipment and special effects.

Garland

Kempsell Associates
Post Office Box 2333
Garland, TX 75040
Tel: 214-278-3188
Description: Manufacturer of tapes for film processing.

Houston

Don Buergler
10031 Greencreek Drive
Houston, TX 77070
Tel: 713-524-2271
Address Inquiries to: Don Buergler
Description: Manufacturer of tickets and ticket racks.

Concert Lighting
2301 Dumble
Houston, TX 77023
Tel: 713-926-1249
Address Inquiries to: Howard Kells
Description: Supplier of lighting, sound, and staging for concerts, shows and conventions.

First Electric, Incorporated
6400 West Oark, Suite 289
Houston, TX 77057
Tel: 713-789-9447
Founded in: 1975
Member: IES; USITT;
Description: Supplier of lighting equipment.

Houston Cinema and Sound Equipment
3732 North Shepard
Houston, TX 77018
Tel: 713-691-4379
Address Inquiries to: John Gasche
Description: Supplier of sound equipment.

Industrial Audio/Video, Inccorporated
2617 Bissonnet
Houston, TX 77005

Tel: 713-524-1956
Description: Suppliers of intercom and sound equipment.

Klopf Audio/Video Company
2617 Bissonnet
Houston, TX 77005
Tel: 513-236-5500
Description: Supplier of intercom systems, and microphone preamplifiers and mixers.

Lighting and Electrical Sales
2116 Canada Dry
Houston, TX 77023
Tel: 713-923-7781
Description: Supplier of lighting equipment.

Nunn Electric Supply Company
Post Office Box 1454
Houston, TX 77001
Description: Supplier of lighting equipment.

Performing Arts Supply Company
10161 Harwin Drive, Suite 115
Houston, TX 77036
Tel: 713-776-8900
Address Inquiries to: Bonnie Ambrose, President
Description: Supplier of lighting, technical equipment, make-up and costumes. Rentals available.

Southern Importers
4825 San Jacinto Street
Houston, TX 77004-5620
Tel: 713-524-8236
Address Inquiries to: M.A. Frost III, President Sam Cohen, Vice President
Founded in: 1915
Description: Supplier of lighting, technical equipment, special effects costumes and fabrics. Also supplier of seasonal decorations and ballasts.

Wyrborny Sales Company, Incorporated
9630 Clairewood Suite B2A
Houston, TX 77036
Tel: 713-772-0961
Address Inquiries to: Nill Speegle
Description: Manufacturer of sound systems and equipment.

Irving

Memorex Corporation
1621 Walnut Hill
Irving, TX 75062
Address Inquiries to: D. Meyers
Description: Manufacturer of audio and video tape.

New Braunfels

Pran Incorporated
1001 Broadway
New Braunfels, TX 78130
Tel: 512-625-2376
Description: Supplier of lighting and technical equipment.

Rowlett

Colortran, Incorporated
3805 Cheyenne Drive
Rowlett, TX 75088
Tel: 214-375-4211
Address Inquiries to: Mel Rimmer, Manager
Member: NAB; USITT; IES; SMPTE;
Description: A regional branch office.

San Antonio

Costumes
4501 McCullough
San Antonio, TX 78212
Tel: 512-822-3373
Description: Supplier of costumes, hair goods and accessories.

Texas Scenic
5423 Jackson Drive
San Antonio, TX 78228
Tel: 512-684-0091
Description: Supplier of fluorescent paints, and phosphorescent tapes and paints.

Texas Scenic Company, Incorporated
Post Office Box 28297
San Antonio, TX 78228
Tel: 512-684-0091
Description: Manufacturer of PYROPAK materials, and supplier of custom lighting systems.

Thomas-Redwine, Incorporated
427 Breesport
San Antonio, TX 78216
Tel: 512-349-2131
Address Inquiries to: Jack Thomas Bill Redwine
Description: Supplier of lighting equipment.

San Marcos

Decor Electronics
Post Office Box 606
San Marcos, TX 78666
Tel: 512-392-6041
Description: Suppliers of lighting and technical equipment. Rentals available.

Schulenberg

I.E. Clark, Incorporated
Post Office Box 246
Schulenberg, TX 78956
Tel: 713-743-3232
Description: Suppliers of lighting and technical equipment.

UTAH

Salt Lake City

B and B Electrical Products Incorporated
2605 East and 3300 South
Salt Lake City, UT 84109
Tel: 801-486-3943
Address Inquiries to: Richard Hansen
Description: Manufacturer of sound systems and equipment.

Electro Controls, Incorporated
2975 South 300 West
Salt Lake City, UT 84115
Tel: 801-487-9861
Address Inquiries to: Hyrum Mead, Vice President, Lighting Systems Group
Founded in: 1946
Member: NAB; USITT;
Description: Manufacturer of control dimmers, distribution and lighting instruments for theater and television. Also a manufacturer of dimmers and control for architectural and residential lighting systems.

Ria Corporation
50 East Malvern Avenue
Salt Lake City, UT 84115
Tel: 801-486-8822
Description: Supplier of intercom systems and sound equipment.

Rual Industries, Incorporated
1700 South 740 West
Salt Lake City, UT 84104
Tel: 801-972-1317; 801-972-1318
Address Inquiries to: Robert Green, Operations Manager
Founded in: 1973
Member: USITT;
Description: Manufacturer of electrical control distribution equipment.

Stage Light-Tronics
2536 South 700 East
Salt Lake City, UT 84106
Tel: 801-485-9886
Address Inquiries to: Paul C. Whitehead, Owner
Description: Supplier of lighting and control equipment.

VERMONT

Bennington

Bob Davidson
Post Office Box 962
Bennington, VT 05201
Tel: 802-447-0311
Address Inquiries to: Bob Davidson
Description: Supplier of staging and stage shells.

VIRGINIA

Alexandria

Richard S. Pass Associates
200 North Pickett Street #514
Alexandria, VA 22304
Tel: 703-370-9888
Address Inquiries to: Richard S. Pass
Description: Supplier of microphone and audio equipment.

Annandale

Maylett Associates
4747 Kandel Court
Annandale, VA 22003
Tel: 703-354-6055; 703-354-5368

Address Inquiries to: William Maylett, President
Founded in: 1971
Member: IEEE; SMPTE;
Annual Budget: $150,000
Description: Specializes in television consultation, broadcast engineering, design and maintenence of intercom equipment.

Strand Century, Incorporated
4618 Conwell Drive
Annandale, VA 22003
Tel: 703-941-9025
Address Inquiries to: Gene Hanna, Regional Manager
Description: Supplier of lighting equipment.

Falls Church

Potomac Lighting
105 North Virginia Avenue
Falls Church, VA 22046
Tel: 703-534-4550
Address Inquiries to: Chuck N. Osher
Mike McGiffin
Founded in: 1978
Description: Sales representatives for dimming equipment and stage lighting of all makes working with architects and designers to furnish equipment for new and remodeled theatres.

Reston

Sphere Associates
11250-14 Roger Bacon Drive
Reston, VA 22090
Tel: 703-471-1230
Address Inquiries to: Ted Bennet
Description: Manufacturer of sound systems and equipment.

Richmond

VESCO
Post Office Box 9566
Richmond, VA 23228
Tel: 804-266-5811
Description: Supplier of lighting equipment.

Roanoke

VESCO
924 Ridgecrest Road
Roanoke, VA 24019
Tel: 704-366-9749
Description: Supplier of lighting equipment.

Virginia Beach

VESCO
Post Office Box 7130
Virginia Beach, VA 23457
Tel: 804-426-6426
Description: Supplier of lighting equipment.

WASHINGTON

Bellevue

Seaport Marketing
2054 127th South East
Bellevue, WA 90085
Tel: 206-641-5721

Address Inquiries to: John Mayer
Description: Supplier of sound equipement.

Stagecraft Industries, Incorporated
Post Office Box 660
Bellevue, WA 98009
Tel: 206-454-3089; 503-226-7351
Address Inquiries to: Calvin C. McIrvin, President
William S. Walter, Vice President
Founded in: 1929
Description: The Northwest's largest and oldest theatrical supply house, Stagecraft manufactures and installs rigging, drapes and portable stages.

Olympia

Capitol Communication Incorporated
Post Office Box 481
Olympia, WA 98507
Tel: 206-943-5378
Address Inquiries to: Denny Bradley
Description: Supplier of lighting equipment.

Seattle

Cerulean Blue, Ltd.
Post Office Box 5126
Seattle, WA 98105
Tel: 206-625-9647
Address Inquiries to: Ron Granich, President
Ann Marie Patterson, Vice President/Sales Manager
Founded in: 1972
Member: SDA; AATCC; SDC; ACC;
Description: Wholesale and retail of textile art supplies, industrial dyestuffs, auxiliary chemicals, prepared fabrics, tools, books and paints. Can provide excellent technical advise.

Clear Light Systems Company
608 19th Avenue East
Seattle, WA 98112
Tel: 206-322-8811
Address Inquiries to: Gary Christenson, Owner
Description: Manufacturer of lighting systems and supplier of intercom systems.

Earl and Brown Company, Incorporated
320 Second West
Seattle, WA 98119
Tel: 206-284-1121
Address Inquiries to: Mike Earl
Description: Manufacturer of sound systems and equipment.

Fleehart and Sullivan, Incorporated
Post Office Box 77008
Seattle, WA 98133
Tel: 206-522-1533; 910-444-2275
Description: Supplier of sound equipment.

Lighting Specialties Division of D.A. Olson Company
5001 25th Avenue, NE
Seattle, WA 98105
Tel: 206-522-6594
Address Inquiries to: Leon Zornes, Vice President
Lucinda Denninger, Designer

Description: Manufacturer of lighting equipment.

Northern Light
7420 181st Place South West
Seattle, WA 98020
Tel: 206-774-9217
Description: Supplier of sound and lighting equipment.

Pacnor Marketing
815 West Ewing Street
Seattle, WA 98119
Tel: 206-284-8020
Description: Supplier of electrical outlet strips and utility carts.

Petek Sales
1541 Westlake Avenue North
Seattle, WA 98109
Tel: 206-285-9006
Address Inquiries to: Gary Petek
Member: IES;
Description: Supplier of lighting equipment.

P.N.T.A.
316 Westlake Avenue, North
Seattle, WA 98109
Tel: 206-622-7850
Address Inquiries to: Mac Perkins
Description: Supplier of lighting equipment.

RTP Enterprises
11812-8th Avenue, NW
Seattle, WA 98177
Tel: 206-362-1146
Description: Manufacturer of tapes for film processing.

Spokane

Blount Products, Incorporated
Post Office Box 14001
Spokane, WA 99214
Tel: 509-926-3918
Description: Manufacturer of stage equipment.

Tacoma

Globe Ticket Company
Post Office Box 11067
Tacoma, WA 98411
Tel: 206-474-0721
Description: Supplier of tickets and ticket equipment.

Jim Trotter
Post Office Box 44316
Tacoma, WA 98444
Tel: 206-531-1201
Address Inquiries to: Jim Trotter
Description: Supplier of stage shells and staging.

WEST VIRGINIA

Fairmont

Masquers/Town and Gown Players
Fine Arts Department
Fairmont State College
Fairmont, WV 26554

Tel: 304-367-4248; 304-367-4240
Address Inquiries to: Jo Ann Lough,
  Production Manager
Description: Limited costume and stage
equipment rental to other theatrical organizations.

Nitro

Midwest Telecommunications
300 First Avenue
Nitro, WV 25143
Tel: 502-491-2888
Description: Supplier of intercom systems and
sound equipment.

WISCONSIN

Brookfield

Voss-Dent and Associates
4420 Coral Drive
Brookfield, WI 53005
Description: Manufacturer of lighting and
supplier of stage and studio equipment.

Eau Claire

Disco Explosion
Highway 93 South
Eau Claire, WI 54701
Tel: 715-834-6360
Description: Supplier of lighting equipment.

Hartland

Ericksen Lighting Sales
103 North Avenue
Hartland, WI 53029
Tel: 414-367-5920
Description: Supplier of lighting equipment.

Madison

Road Grator
328 West Gorham
Madison, WI 53703
Tel: 608-257-0678
Description: Supplier of lighting equipment.

State Historical Society of Wisconsin
816 State Street
Madison, WI 53706
Tel: 608-262-0459
Address Inquiries to: Joan Severa, Curator of
  Costumes and Textiles
Description: Supplier of patterns for women's
costumes.

Milwaukee

Arjay Lighting Sales
3832 North Hubbard
Milwaukee, WI 53212
Tel: 414-961-1690
Address Inquiries to: Russ Card
Description: Supplier of lighting equipment.

Cameo House, Ltd.
3828 W. North Avenue
Milwaukee, WI 53208
Tel: 414-449-1281
Address Inquiries to: R.O. Memmel,
  President

Description: Supplier of moldmaking material
for making stage props.

Kerwin, Incorporated
5024 North Ardmore Avenue
Milwaukee, WI 53217
Tel: 414-964-7777
Description: Supplier of lighting equipment.

Mid-West Scenic and Stage Equipment
Company, Ltd.
224 East Bruce Street
Milwaukee, WI 53204
Tel: 414-276-2707
Address Inquiries to: John R. Dolphin,
  President
  Mike McDonald
Founded in: 1967
Member: USITT;
Description: A complete one stop shop for
items related to stagecraft, theatre design,
lighting and scenic elements for the theatre.
Furnishes and installs theatrical equipment,
stage lighting and stage scenery. Manufactures supplies and rents stage equipment.
Services include the fabrication of odd theatrical events.

New Berlin

State Wide Lighting Incorporated
21516 West Greenfield Avenue
New Berlin, WI 53151
Address Inquiries to: Gordon Pearson
Description: Manufacturer of lighting equipment.

CANADA

Calgary, Alberta

Electro Controls
7035 Farrell Road, Southeast
Calgary, Alberta, Canada T2H OT3
Tel: 403-255-7716
Address Inquiries to: Mark Russell, National
  Sales Manager
Founded in: 1957
Description: Manufacturer of stage lighting
and control equipment.

Strand Sound
1437 45th Avenue NE
Calgary, Alberta, Canada T2A 2M9
Description: Supplier of sound equipment.

Edmonton, Alberta

Lighting by Monty
11528 89th Street
Edmonton, Alberta, Canada
Tel: 403-477-5077
Address Inquiries to: A.E. Montgomery
Description: Supplier of lighting equipment.

Vancouver, British Columbia

Kelly-Deyong Sound
2145 West Broadway
Vancouver, British Columbia, Canada V6K
2C7
Address Inquiries to: Gary Musgrave,
  Manager

Description: Supplier of intercom systems.

Nana Distributors Ltd.
1612 West 3rd Avenue
Vancouver, British Columbia, Canada V6J
1K2
Tel: 604-734-4511
Description: Supplier of theatre sound effects
and control consoles.

Richmond Sound Design Ltd.
1234 West 6th Avenue
Vancouver, British Columbia, Canada V6H
1A5
Tel: 604-734-1217; 604-734-0705
Address Inquiries to: Charles Richmond,
  President
Founded in: 1972
Member: AES; USITT;
Description: Manufacturer of theatre sound
effects and control consoles. my; e

Calgary, Alberta

Electro Controls
7035 Farrell Road, South East
Calgary, Alberta, Calgary Canada
Tel: 403-255-7716

Brampton, Ontario

Elmo Canada Manufacturing Corporation
44 West Drive
Brampton, Ontario, Canada L6T 3T6
Tel: 416-453-7880
Address Inquiries to: Paul MacMahon
Description: Supplier of projectors.

Holophane-Manville Canada Incorporated
1620 Steeles Avenue
Brampton, Ontario, Canada L6T 1A5
Tel: 416-793-3111
Address Inquiries to: C.S. Buckland, Presidnet
Founded in: 1898
Member: IES;
Description: Manufacturer of power, commercial and industrial lighting equipment.

Don Mills, Ontario

The Pringle Group
30 Scarsdale Road
Don Mills, Ontario, Canada M3B 2R7
Address Inquiries to: Lee White
Steve Parsons
Description: Supplier of sound equipment.

Malton, Ontario

Hammond Industrial Imports
7270 -1 Torbram Road
Malton, Ontario, Canada L4T 3Y7
Address Inquiries to: Carmel Doherty,
  General Manager
Description: Supplier of lighting and sound
equipment.

Markham, Ontario

Moyer Vico Corporation
Equipment Division
250 Steelcase Road East
Markham, Ontario, Canada L3R 2S3
Tel: 416-495-1685
Address Inquiries to: Cy Bulkis, Sales

Manager
Description: Supplier of folding and portable dance floors.

Mississauga, Ontario

Superscope Canada, Ltd.
3710 Nashua Drive
Mississauga, Ontario, Canada L4V 1M5
Tel: 416-676-1720
Address Inquiries to: Steven Hertzberg
Description: Supplier of sound equipment.

Ottawa, Ontario

Stage Lighting Ottawa
2097 Street Lawrence Boulevard
Ottawa, Ontario, Canada
Address Inquiries to: Len Stone
Description: Supplier of lighting equipment.

Pickering, Ontario

Simmonds and Sons, Ltd.
975 Dillingham Road
Pickering, Ontario, Canada L1W 3B2
Tel: 416-839-8041
Address Inquiries to: A.C. Simmonds
Description: Supplier of sound equipment.

Rexdale, Ontario

Duro-Test Electric Ltd.
419 Attwell Drive
Rexdale, Ontario, Canada M9W 5W5
Tel: 416-675-1623; 416-675-1624
Address Inquiries to: Douglas Peace, Vice
   President
   Georges Merson, National Accounts
Founded in: 1954
Description: Supplier of light bulbs and spot lights, designed for commercial/industrial use.

Life-Like Products, Ltd.
24 Ronson Drive
Rexdale, Ontario, Canada M9W 1B4
Address Inquiries to: Barry Altbaum,
   President
Description: Manufacturer of scenic and landscaping materials.

Scarborough, Ontario

Telak Electronics Ltd.
690 Progress Avenue, Unit 3
Scarborough, Ontario, Canada M1H 3A6
Tel: 416-438-3804
Description: Supplier of sound and intercom systems.

Toronto, Ontario

The American Superior Electric Co., Ltd.
38 Torlake Crescent
Toronto, Ontario, Canada M8Z 1B3
Tel: 416-255-2318
Description: Supplier of electrical equipment.

Dover Corporation/Elevator Division
126 John Street
Toronto, Ontario, Canada M5V2E3
Description: Supplier of stage lifts.

Efston Line
3500 Bathurst Street
Toronto, Ontario, Canada M6A 2C6
Tel: 416-787-5140
Address Inquiries to: Evan Efston
Description: Supplier of scientific products by mail order.

Levitt Safety Ltd.
33 Laird Drive
Toronto, Ontario, Canada M4G 389
Description: Supplier of headset systems and communications systems.

Lumitrol Limited
5 Walker Avenue
Toronto, Ontario, Canada M4V IG3
Tel: 416-921-6060; 416-921-6688
Address Inquiries to: Bruce Whitehead,
   President
Founded in: 1974
Description: Supplier of lighting, dimmers, drapes, stage rigging, electrical supplies and spots. Lumitrol will provide theatre engineering, design and consultation for theatres and schools.

Struthers Paint Company
491 Church Street
Toronto, Ontario, Canada M4Y 2C6
Tel: 416-924-6271

Toronto 2B, Ontario

Malabar Ltd.
14 McCaul Street
Toronto 2B, Ontario, Canada M5T 1V6
Tel: 416-598-2581
Address Inquiries to: Geoffrey Curtis, General
   Manager
Founded in: 1922
Description: Supplies both retail and wholesale make-up, retail dance supplies, and costumes for opera, theatre, musicals and film.

Waterloo, Ontario

Rauland-Borg Corporation
244 Murdock
Waterloo, Ontario, Canada N2J 2M7
Tel: 519-885-1043
Address Inquiries to: Roy Henning
Description: Supplier of sound and communications equipment.

Dorval, Quebec

Omnimedia Corporation
9653 Cote de Liesse
Dorval, Quebec, Canada H9P 1A3
Tel: 514-636-9971
Description: Manufacturer of sound systems and equipment.

Granby, Quebec

Westinghouse Electric Corporation
Post Office Box 519
Granby, Quebec, Canada

Tel: 514-378-0470
Address Inquiries to: Mike McAuliffe, General
   Manager
Description: Supplier of lighting equipment.

Montreal, Quebec

Johnny Brown
2019 Mansfield Street
Montreal, Quebec, Canada
Address Inquiries to: Johnny Brown
Description: Supplier of fluorescent paints, and phosphorescent tapes and paints.

Duro-Test Electric Ltd.
Post Office Box 255
Place Bonaventure
Montreal, Quebec, Canada H5A 1B2
Tel: 514-861-1529
Address Inquiries to: John Wright, Sales
   Manager
Description: Supplier of light bulbs and spot lights.

La Salle Audio
2500 Bates Road
Montreal, Quebec, Canada H3S 1A6
Tel: 514-342-4503
Address Inquiries to: Jacques Bogos, Vice
   President
Description: Supplier of intercom systems.

Paco Electronics, Ltd.
45 Stinson Street
Montreal, Quebec, Canada H4N 2E1
Tel: 514-748-6787
Address Inquiries to: William Cohen, General
   Manager
Description: Manufacturer of commercial sound equipment.

Radio Service Incorporated
2500 Bates Road
Montreal, Quebec, Canada H3S 1A6
Tel: 514-342-4503
Address Inquiries to: Jacques Bogos
Description: Supplier of sound mixing consoles.

16
Theatre

For this section, a theatre is defined as a group which has its own facility and acts as its own producer. From time to time, it may rent or otherwise make available its facilities to other performing artists.

The theatres described here vary considerably. Aside from wide geographic distribution, there are great differences in orientation, from traditional community theatres in the Midwest to the avant garde, off off Broadway theatres of New York. Wherever possible, a description of the work of the theatre involved is provided.

ALABAMA

Anniston

Anniston Little Theatre
Post Office Box 1454
Anniston, AL 36202
Tel: 205-236-8342
Address Inquiries to: Bruce Howard, Director
  George H. Deyo, President
Founded in: 1927
Annual Budget: $10,000 - $24,999
Description: Promotes dramatic art and culture in the community.

Shakespeare Festival
Post Office Box 141
Anniston, AL 36201

Bay Minette

Bay Minette Little Theatre
Post Office Box 93
Bay Minette, AL 36507

Birmingham

Asphalt Players
Post Office Box 7377
Birmingham, AL 35223
Tel: 205-879-0411
Address Inquiries to: Robert C. Lott, Director
Founded in: 1976
Description: Provides quality theatre experiences for youth performers and audiences of the total community during the summer and fosters workshops during the school year.

Birmingham Children's Theatre
Post Office Box 1362
Birmingham, AL 35201
Tel: 205-324-0470
Address Inquiries to: James L. Rye
Founded in: 1947

Celebrity Dinner Theatre
1446 Montgomery Highway
Birmingham, AL 35216
Tel: 205-823-3000
Address Inquiries to: James L. Wilcoxen,
  President/General Manager
  Naomi Wilcoxen, Vice
  President/Manager

Founded in: 1971
Center Players
3960 Montclair Road
Birmingham, AL 35213

Jaceo Community Theatre - Black Fire
  Company
1823 Avenue E Ensley
Birmingham, AL 35218
Tel: 205-780-7510, Ext. 24
Address Inquiries to: Donna Edwards Todd,
  Artistic Director
  Benny Anthony Rivers, Administrative
  Assistant
Founded in: 1971
Annual Budget: $10,000 - $24,999
Description: Provides theatrical training for financially disadvantaged youths and exposes them and the community to quality arts experiences.

Jewish Community Center Players
3960 Montclair Road
Birmingham, AL 35223
Tel: 205-879-0411
Address Inquiries to: Irving Stern, Director
Founded in: 1958
Annual Budget: $10,000 - $24,999
Description: Brings the best of Broadway plays to Bermingham.

Samford Masquers
800 Lake Shore Drive
Birmingham, AL 35209

Town and Gown
1116 South 26th Street
Birmingham, AL 35205

Centre

Cherokee Playhouse
Pine Hill Drive
Centre, AL 35960

Chicksaw

Civic Theatre
Post Office Box 11102
Chicksaw, AL 36611

Dothan

Southeast Alabama Community Theatre
Post Office Box 2127
Dothan, AL 36301
Tel: 205-792-8428
Founded in: 1974
Annual Budget: $25,000 - $49,999
Description: Provides the area communities with the opportunity to participate in theatrical productions for public performances.

Eufaula

Eufaula Little Theatre
Post Office Box 199
Eufaula, AL 36027

Fairhope

Am Players Company
1112 Oak Avenue
Fairhope, AL 63532

Florence

Gingerbread Playhouse
Post Office Box 1324
Florence, AL 35630

Summer Workshop Theatre
Box 738, University Station
Florence, AL 35630

Zodiac Players Theatre
Post Office Box 249
Florence, AL 35630

Foley

Baldwin Chamber Theatre
Post Office Box 1162
Foley, AL 36535

Fort Rucker

Fort Rucker Recreation Center
Theatre Division
Post Office Box 516
Fort Rucker, AL 36362
Member: CTAA;

Gadsden

Gadsden Civic Theater
310 North 27th Street
Post Office Box 901
Gadsden, AL 35904
Tel: 205-547-7960
Address Inquiries to: Mary Hardin, President
Basil Gilchrist, Vice President
Founded in: 1960
Annual Budget: $10,000 - $24,999
Description: To enrich the lives of our citizens by providing live theatre for their participation, involvement and entertainment.

Greenville

Greenville Little Theatre
401 College Street
Greenville, AL 36037

Hartselle

Hartselle Little Theatre
Post Office Box 204
Hartselle, AL 35640

Huntsville

Broadway Theatre League
208 White Street Northeast
Huntsville, AL 35801

Huntsville Little Theatre
700 Monroe Street
Huntsville, AL 35801
Tel: 205-533-6565
Address Inquiries to: Robert James, President
Charles Jackson, Vice President
Founded in: 1949
Annual Budget: $10,000 - $24,999
Description: To foster, encourage and promote education and interest in dramatic arts and broaden and improve the members' proficiency in theatre arts.

Little Theatre
3703 College Park
Huntsville, AL 35805

Mobile

Alabama League
Community Theatre Division
1067 Cloverdale Drive
Mobile, AL 36606
Address Inquiries to: Ms. Sandi Mayer

Children's Musical Theatre
Post Office Box 66407
Mobile, AL 36660
Member: CTAA;

Dixie Players
Post Office Box 8145
Mobile, AL 36608

Mobile Theatre Guild
Post Office Box 1265
Mobile, AL 36601
Tel: 205-433-7513
Address Inquiries to: Tom Pochase, Managing Resident Director;
Jerry L. Carre, President
Founded in: 1951
Member: ATL; STC;

Annual Budget: Over $100,000
Description: To bring to the community at large the best in musicals, dramas, and comedies and provide local talent with a place to perform.

New Ensemble Players
603 Delaware Street
Mobile, AL 36603

Pixie Players
Post Office Box 81
Mobile, AL 36608
Tel: 205-344-1537
Address Inquiries to: Marty Brunner,
Executive Director
Margaret Dennis, President
Founded in: 1959
Member: AAC; ATL; STC;
Annual Budget: $10,000 - $24,999
Description: Provides live theatre for children while training them in theatre arts.

Stage Door Theatre
Holiday Inn I-65
Mobile, AL 36609

1st Theatre Company of the South
4151 Vega Drive
Mobile, AL 36609

Montevallo

Shelby Community Theatre
188 Shashonee Drive
Montevallo, AL 35115

Shelly County Community Theatre
Post Office Box 33
Montevallo, AL 35115
Tel: 205-344-1537
Address Inquiries to: Charles E. Majure,
Artistic Director
Founded in: 1972
Annual Budget: $500.00 - $999.00
Description: To encourage the cultural and educational development of Shelby County by promoting the legitimate theatre as a permanent and vital art form.

Montgomery

Montgomery Little Theatre
432 South Goldwaite
Montgomery, AL 36104

Shakespeare Players
Post Office Box 511
Montgomery, AL 36101

Prichard

Prichard Players
140 West Petum
Prichard, AL 36610

Scottsboro

Scottsboro Community Theatre
408 College Street
Scottsboro, AL 35768

Tuscaloosa

Tuscaloosa Players
Post Office Box 2028
Tuscaloosa, AL 35401

Wesleyan Players
Post Office Box 2056
Tuscaloosa, AL 35401

Tuscumbia

Ivy Green Theatre
300 W Worth Common
Tuscumbia, AL 35674
Tel: 205-383-4066
Address Inquiries to: Lurline Cook, Chairman
Mildred Kimbrough, Secretary
Founded in: 1961
Annual Budget: $1,000 - $4,999
Description: Sponsers William Gibson's 'The Miracle Worker' at the birthplace of Helen Keller in Tuscumbia each summer.

Miracle Worker Theatre
303 East 6th Street
Tuscumbia, AL 35674

Vestavia

Holiday Dinner Theatre
1447 Montgomery Highway
Vestavia, AL 35216

ALASKA

Anchorage

Anchorage Community Theatre
2600 Minnesota Drive
Anchorage, AK 99501

Ketchikan

First City Players
Post Office Box 3160
Ketchikan, AK 99901

Kodiak

Cry of the Wild Ram
Post Office Box 1792
Kodiak, AK 99615

Skagway

Poverty Players
Skagway, AK 99840

ARIZONA

Phoenix

Arizona Community on the Arts
6330 North 7th Street
Phoenix, AZ 85014

Little Theatre
25 East Coronade Road
Phoenix, AZ 85003

Phoenix Children's Theatre
Post Office Box 7504
Phoenix, AZ 85011

Sombrero Playhouse
4747 North 7th Street
Phoenix, AZ 85014

Scottsdale

Scottsdale Community Players
Post Office Box 127
Scottsdale, AZ 85252

Tucson

Playbox Community Theatre
Post Office Box 12098
Tucson, AZ 85711

Tom Thumb Players Company
4737 East Towner
Tucson, AZ 85712
Address Inquiries to: Lester Netzky

ARKANSAS

Batesville

The Arkansaw Traveller
Post Office Box 2053
Batesville, AR 75201

Crossett

Little Theatre
1207 Cypress
Crossett, AR 71630

Eldorado

Little Theatre
524 North Madison
Eldorado, AR 71730

Eureka Springs

The Great Passion Play
Post Office Box 471
Eureka Springs, AR 72632

Fort Smith

Fort Smith Little Theatre
2101 S H Street
Fort Smith, AR 72901

Hot Spring

Community Players
815 Whittington
Hot Spring, AR 71901

Hot Springs

Hernando Desoto
Post Office Box 1259
Hot Springs, AR 71901

Hot Springs National Park

Park Players, Ltd.
Post Office Box 1259
Hot Springs National Park, AR 71901
Tel: 501-767-2351
Address Inquiries to: Keath North, Producer
Robert Simpson, Manager
Founded in: 1978
Annual Budget: 100,000
Description: Summerstock presentations in
1500 seat outdoor amphitheatre. Emphasis
on previously unproduced musical comedies

for general audiences.

Little Rock

Community Theatre of Little Rock
Post Office Box 1
Little Rock, AR 72203

Pine Bluff

Little Theatre
1300 West 12th Avenue
Pine Bluff, AR 71601

CALIFORNIA

Alameda

Little Theatre
1409 High Street
Alameda, CA 95701

Alhambra

Masque Players
1316 West Pine
Alhambra, CA 91801
Address Inquiries to: A. Eggleston

Alhamra

Readers Theatre
900 South Almansor
Alhamra, CA 91801

Altadena

Theatre Americana
Post Office Box 245
Altadena, CA 91001

Anaheim

Ana Cultural Center
931 North Harbor Boulevard
Anaheim, CA 92805

Ana Modjeska Players
Post Office Box 3354
Anaheim, CA 92802
Address Inquiries to: C. Gonzales

Disneyland Players
2314 East Alden
Anaheim, CA 92806

Fremont Adult Theatre
608 West Lincoln Avenue
Anaheim, CA 92805

Parks and Recreation Theatre
630 North Anaheim Boulevard
Anaheim, CA 92805

Antioch

Community Theatre
Post Office Box 638
Antioch, CA 94509
Address Inquiries to: T. Beagle

Arcadia

Arcadia Repertory Theatre
180 Campus Drive
Arcadia, CA 91006

Bakersfield

Bakersfield Community Theatre
Post Office Box 1283
Bakersfield, CA 93302

First Nighters
3621 Pickwood Drive
Bakersfield, CA 93306

Barstow

Barstow Community Players
Barstow, CA 92311
Address Inquiries to: O.E. Goldsmith

Berkeley

Committee for Arts and Lectures
University of California
101 Zellerbach Hall
Berkeley, CA 94720
Tel: 415-642-0212
Address Inquiries to: Susan S. Farr, Manager
Louis Spisto, Business Manager
Founded in: 1906
Member: WAAA; IAAM; ACUCAA;
Annual Budget: $2,000,000
Description: C.A.L. presents professional per-
forming arts for the campus and the com-
munity. The emphasis of the program is on
classical music and dance. Programs are
presented in Zellerbach Hall, Wheeler
Auditorium, Hertz Hall, and the Greek
Theatre.

Community Theatre Arts
2212 Woolsey Street
Berkeley, CA 94705

Florence Schwimley Little Theatre
2246 Milvia
Berkeley, CA 94720
Address Inquiries to: Robert Onstad,
    Chairman
Founded in: 1930

Magic Theatre
2980 College Avenue
Berkeley, CA 94705

The Theatre
2980 College Avenue
Berkeley, CA 94705

Beverly Hills

Actors and Directors Laboratory
254 South Robertson Boulevard
Beverly Hills, CA 90211
Tel: 213-652-6483
Address Inquiries to: Jack Gafrein, Artistic
    Director
Founded in: 1968

All Saints Theatre
504 North Camden Drive
Beverly Hills, CA 90210

Atelier Workshop
153 South Crescent Drive
Beverly Hills, CA 90212
Address Inquiries to: M. Renner

Beverly Hills Playhouse
254 South Robertson

Beverly Hills, CA 90211

The Friars
9990 Santa Monica
Beverly Hills, CA 90212

Roxbury Recreational Center
471 South Roxbury Drive
Beverly Hills, CA 90212

Theatre 40
241 Moreno Drive
Beverly Hills, CA 90210
Tel: 213-277-4221
Address Inquiries to: Flora Plumb, President
Emile Hamaty, Controller
Founded in: 1964
Member: CTC; LATA;
Annual Budget: $30,000
Description: A group of classically-trained professional actors and directors, with diversified backgrounds in regional and New York theatres. For the past 20 years they have presented over 60 fully-mounted production of the Classics -- both American and International -- as well as west-coast premieres. Seating capacity of 99.

Bonita

Chula Vista Playhouse
4180 Acacia
Bonita, CA 92002
Address Inquiries to: P. Smith

Borrego Springs

Deanza Players
Borrego Elementary School
Borrego Springs, CA 19801

Buena Park

Bird Cage Theatre
Knotts Berry Farm
Buena Park, CA 95247

Burbank

Aghape Players
139 Golden Mall
Burbank, CA 91502
Member: AEA; CAC; CFA; CTC; LATA;

Burbank Little Theatre
1111 West Olive
Burbank, CA 91503

Burbank Theatre Guild
c/o Burbank Little Theatre
1100 West Clark
Burbank, CA 91506
Tel: 213-843-9400
Founded in: 1952
Annual Budget: $25,000
Description: Live Theatre seating 175 people. Open Friday and Saturday evenings. Curtain at 8:30PM.

Center Stage Theatre
2043 North Evergreen Street
Burbank, CA 91505
Tel: 213-843-7529
Address Inquiries to: Walter Gilmore, Technical Director
Founded in: 1972

Annual Budget: $50,000

Civic Light Opera
Post Office Box 201
Burbank, CA 91503

Players Theatre
2811 West Magnolia Boulevard
Burbank, CA 91505

Players Theatre Company
2811 West Magnolia Boulevard
Burbank, CA 91505
Tel: 213-842-4755; 213-845-1193
Address Inquiries to: Donna Anderson, Artistic Director
Founded in: 1971
Member: ACTA;
Annual Budget: $30,000
Description: Players Theatre Company is a non-professional theatre company.

Tracy Theatre
701 North San Fernando Boulevard
Burbank, CA

Camarillo

Camarillo Community Theatre
1605 East Burnley
Camarillo, CA 93010

Campbell

Gaslighter Theatre
400 East Campbell Avenue
Campbell, CA 95008

Campton

Roberson Players
123 North Rose Avenue
Campton, CA 90221

Canoga Park

Free Comedy Workshop
20561 Haynes
Canoga Park, CA 91306

Lanark Drama Workshop
21816 Lanark
Canoga Park, CA 91304
Address Inquiries to: W. Spendlooe

Orbit Players
8500 Fallbrook Avenue
Canoga Park, Ca 91304

Carmel

Children's Experimental Theatre
Post Office Box 3381
Carmel, CA 9321
Address Inquiries to: Marcia G. Hovick

Carpinteria

Carpinteria Theatre
Carpinteria Junior High School
Carpinteria, CA 93013

Carson

Playbox Theatre
1000 East Victoria Street
Carson, CA 90746

Chatsworth

Valley Theatre of Performing Arts
21340 Devonshire Street
Chatsworth, CA 91311

Chula Vista

South Bay Players
1147 Dixon Drive
Chula Vista, CA 92011

Claremont

Garrison Theatre
10th and Columbia
Claremont, CA 91711

Mexican Players
Post Office Box 149
Claremont, CA 91711

Clayton

Stagecoach Players
Post Office Box 206
Clayton, CA 94517

Colton

Colton Little Theatre
Mount Vernon
Colton, CA 92324

Compton

Church Theatre Group
4603 Rosecrans Avenue
Compton, CA 90222

Concord

Concord Little Theatre
5289 Pine Hollow Road
Concord, CA 94521

Willows Theatre
1975 Diamond Boulevard
Concord, CA 94519
Tel: 415-671-3065; 415-671-3066
Address Inquiries to: James L. Jester, Producer/Manager
Founded in: 1977
Member: TCCBA; ATA; ACUCAA; CCAA;
Annual Budget: $200,000
Description: Operates primarily as a community theatre. Also produces a childrens' performing arts series, a film series, opera and ballet -- approximately 200 events per year.

Corona

Little Theatre
953 East Francis
Corona, CA 91720

Coronado

Coronado Community Playhouse
1121 G Avenue
Coronado, CA 92118

Costa Mesa

Civic Playhouse
Post Office Box 1200
Costa Mesa, CA 92626
Address Inquiries to: P. Tambellini

Newport Players
526 Center Street
Costa Mesa, CA 92626

South Coast Repertory Theatre
1827 Newport Blvd
Costa Mesa, CA 92627

Covina

Masque Players
629 Darfield Avenue
Covina, CA 91724
Tel: 213-966-9360
Address Inquiries to: John Steward, President
Founded in: 1960

Culver City

Mathison Singers
4133 Tilden Avenue
Culver City, CA 90230

United Methodist Church Theatre
4464 Sepulveda Boulevard
Culver City, CA 90230

Cupertino

Community of Faith Drama
18601 Runo Court
Cupertino, CA 95014

Del Mar

San Dieguito Little Theeatre
Post Officee Box 643
Del Mar, CA 92014

Denair

Central Valley Players
3548 Santa Fe
Denair, CA 95316

Diamond Point

Diamond Bar Players
23818 Twin Pin Lane
Diamond Point, CA 91766

Downey

Downey Civic Light Opera Association
Post Office Box 429
Downey, CA 90241
Tel: 213-923-1714; 213-861-3994
Address Inquiries to: Margaret Glenn,
  President
Founded in: 1955
Member: ATA;
Annual Budget: $200,000

Dramedians
8024 Cole
Downey, CA 90242
Address Inquiries to: J. Davies

Gay Nineties Theatre
8024 Cole Street
Downey, CA 90242

Gold Crown Dinner Theatre
7676 Fireston Boulevard
Downey, CA 90241
Tel: 213-861-7117
Address Inquiries to: Myrl Svela, President
Founded in: 1971

Public Inter Forum
Post Office Box 405
Downey, CA 90201

Theatre Workshop
8450 2nd Street
Downey, CA 90241

El Cerrito

Contra Catsa Civic Theatre
951 Pomona Avenue
El Cerrito, CA 94530

Encino

Little Theatre Group
4935 Balboa
Encino, CA 91316

Temple Drama Group
15739 Ventura Boulevard
Encino, CA 91316

Fair Oaks

Footlighter Theatre
7170 Linda Sue Way
Fair Oaks, CA 95628

Folsom

Sutter Gaslighters
720 Sutter Street
Folsom, CA 95630

Fontana

Fathers Childs Theatre
9116 Sierra Avenue
Fontana, CA 92335

Fontana Mummers
Post Office Box 1630
Fontana, CA 92335

Fort Bragg

Footlighter Little Theatre
Post Office Box 575
Fort Bragg, CA 95437

Foster City

Hillbarn Thetre
1285 Hillsdale Blvd.
Foster City, CA 94404

French Gulch

French Gulch Theatre
Main Street
French Gulch, CA 96033

Fresno

Fresno Community Theatre
Post Office Box 1308
Fresno, CA 93715
Tel: 209-233-6213; 209-233-6214
Address Inquiries to: Chuck Carson,
  Development Director
  Bruce Parker, Technical Director
Founded in: 1955
Member: CTC;
Annual Budget: $80,000
Description: A community theatre giving the general public an opportunity to benefit themselves by having the opportunity to perform in productions and to assist in all other functions for the production.

Fullerton

Footlighters
119 Buena Vista
Fullerton, CA 92633

Muckenthaler Center
1201 Malvern Avenue
Fullerton, CA 92633

Garden Grove

Schherazade Players
12174 Euclid
Garden Grove, CA 92640

Theatre As You Like It
12002 Robert Lane
Garden Grove, CA 92640

Glendale

Glendale Center Theatre
324 North Orange
Glendale, CA 91203

Little Theatre Verdugo
1611 Arboles Drive
Glendale, CA 91207

Versailles Room Theatre
1010 North Glendale
Glendale, CA 91206

Granada Hills

North Valley Community Theatre
16601 Rinaldi
Granada Hills, CA 91344

Hanford

Kings Players, Incorporated
514 East Visalia Street
Hanford, CA 93230
Tel: 209-584-7241
Address Inquiries to: Joyce Wegley, President
Founded in: 1962
Annual Budget: $5,000
Description: The Kings Players is a not-for-profit amateur theatre group.

Hawthorne

Genesis Darte Theatre
5435 West 142nd Place
Hawthorne, CA 90250

Hemet

Ramon Outdoor Playhouse
Post Office Box 755
Hemet, CA 92343
Tel: 714-658-3111
Founded in: 1923
Description: A historical outdoor drama based on Helen Hunt Jackson's novel *Ramona*.

Hidden Hills

Hidden Hills Players
5791 Jed Smith Road
Hidden Hills, CA 91302
Address Inquiries to: C. Brown

Hollywood

Aquarius Theatre
6230 Sunset Boulevard
Hollywood, CA 90028

The Cast Theatre Incorporated
804 North El Centro Avenue
Hollywood, CA 90038
Tel: 213-462-9872, Production Office;
  213-462-0265, Box Office
Address Inquiries to: Ted Schmitt, President
Randy J. Clifton, Artistic Director
Founded in: 1976
Member: LATA; HAC; CTC; AEA; CAC;
Annual Budget: $10,000
Description: The CAST Theatre is a generating station for new theatre. Dedicated to the development of new playwrights through the production of their origingal plays, the CAST Theatre is a not-for-profit, tax-exempt California educational corporation, based in Hollywood.

Company of Angels
5846 Waring Avenue
Hollywood, CA 90038

The Group Theatre
1276 Van Ness
Hollywood, CA 90028
Tel: 213-466-2273
Address Inquiries to: Lonny Chapman,
  Artistic Director
  Don Furnaux, Chairman
Annual Budget: $25,000

Hollywood Actors Theatre
1715 North Cahuenga Boulevard
Hollywood, CA 90028
Member: AEA; CAC; CFA; CTC; LATA;
Description: A professional showcase theatre.

Mark Taper Forum Laboratory
2580 Cahuenga Boulevard
Hollywood, CA 90068
Tel: 213-972-7357
Address Inquiries to: Erik Brenmark,
  Manager
Founded in: 1931

Masquers Club
1765 North Sycamore Street
Hollywood, CA 90028
Tel: 213-374-0840
Founded in: 1925

Metropolitan Theatre
649 North Pointsettia Place
Hollywood, CA 90048

Nosotros
1314 North Wilton Place
Hollywood, CA 90026
Tel: 213-465-4167
Address Inquiries to: Jerry G. Velasco,
  President
Founded in: 1970
Annual Budget: $80,000
Description: Nosotros was formed to further the goals of persons of Spanish-speaking origin in the motion picture and television industry by providing a theatrical showcase.

Pilot Theatre for the Performing Arts
6600 Santa Monica Boulevard
Hollywood, CA 90038
Member: AEA; CAC; CFA; CTC; LATA;
Description: A professional showcase theatre center.

Princess Theatre
870 North Vine
Hollywood, CA 90038

Seis Actores
1715 Cahuenga
Hollywood, CA 90028

Shepard Theatre Workshop
6468 Santa Monica Boulevard
Hollywood, CA 90038
Tel: 213-462-9033
Address Inquiries to: Richmond Shepard,
  Director
Founded in: 1978
Description: Three small theatres producing many shows throughout the year.

Sunset Theatre Workshop
7350 Sunset Boulevard
Hollywood, CA 90046

Trans-American Video Theatre
1514 North Vine Street
Hollywood, CA 90028

Huntington Beach

Golden West College Community Theatre
15744 Golden West Street
Huntington Beach, CA 92647
Tel: 714-892-7711
Address Inquiries to: Wallace Huntoon,
  Chairman
Founded in: 1970

Huntington Beach Playhouse, Incorporated
Post Office Box 451
Huntington Beach, CA 92648
Tel: 714-847-4465; 714-536-9072
Address Inquiries to: Paul Sullivan, President
Founded in: 1963
Member: OCCTA; HBCC;
Annual Budget: $20,000

Playhouse
Post Office Box 251
Huntington Beach, CA 92646
Address Inquiries to: N.R. Murphy

Huntington Park

Huntington Park Civic Theatre
3401 East Florence Avenue
Huntington Park, CA 90255
Tel: 213-582-6162
Address Inquiries to: Eileen Henehan,
  President
Founded in: 1947
Annual Budget: $5,000

Hyde Park

Lamoille County Plays
Hyde Park Opera High School
Hyde Park, CA 91304

Inglewood

Centinela Playhouse
400 West Beach
Inglewood, CA 90302
Address Inquiries to: J. Schwartz

Irvine

Street Theatre
University of California
Irvine, CA 92664

Irving

Penrod-Plastino Movement Theatre
4645 Greentree
Irving, CA 97215
Tel: 714-552-7472
Address Inquiries to: Alex Delgado,
  Recreation Department
Founded in: 1970
Member: AADC;
Annual Budget: $1,000

Kensington

Squirrel Hill Theatre
1 Lawson Road
Kensington, CA 94707

La Canada

YMCA Theatre Group
1930 Foothill
La Canada, CA 91011

Laguna Beach

Festival of the Arts
1455 Terrace Way
Laguna Beach, CA 92651
Tel: 714-494-8021
Address Inquiries to: Douglas Rowe, Director

Laguna Moulton Community Playhouse
606 Laguna Canyon Road
Laguna Beach, CA 92651
Tel: 714-494-8021
Address Inquiries to: Douglas Rowe, Manager
Founded in: 1924
Annual Budget: $100,000

Stop-Gap
630 Anita Street
Laguna Beach, CA 92651
Address Inquiries to: Don R. Laffoon

La Jolla

Theatre Research and Development
904 Silverado
La Jolla, CA 92037

Lakewood

Lakewood Little Theatre
5050 Clark Avenue
Lakewood, CA 90712

Lakewood Players Incorporated
1150 South Independence
Lakewood, CA 80226

Sunshine Company
4253 Ladoga
Lakewood, CA 90713

Lodi

Tokay Players
11 South Sacramento Street
Lodi, CA 94240

Lomita

Chapel Theatre
2222 Lomita Boulevard
Lomita, CA 90717
Address Inquiries to: J. Vogel

Long Beach

C B Demille Theatre
7025 Parkcrest
Long Beach, CA 90808

Center Players
2601 Grand Avenue
Long Beach, CA 90815
Address Inquiries to: H. Nalibow

Center Players
Long Beach Jewish Community Center
3801 East Willow Street
Long Beach, CA 90815
Tel: 213-426-7601; 213-636-5970
Founded in: 1960
Member: LBPCA;
Annual Budget: $10,000
Description: Center Players presents two
productions per year plus theater work-
shops.

Community Players
5021 Anaheim Street
Long Beach, CA 90804
Address Inquiries to: S. Reed

Denalee Productions
3070 Montair Avenue
Long Beach, CA 90808
Tel: 213-425-1759
Address Inquiries to: Dennis W. King,
   Chairman
Founded in: 1972
Annual Budget: $5,000

Hay Penny Players
2760 Studebaker Road
Long Beach, CA 90815

International Theatre Company
California State University
Long Beach, CA 90805

Lakewood Theatre
7025 Parkcrest
Long Beach, CA 90808

Long Beach Community Players
5021 East Anaheim Street
Long Beach, CA 90804
Tel: 213-438-0356
Address Inquiries to: James N. Naylor,
   Administrator
Founded in: 1929
Annual Budget: $100,000

Luminarias of Torr
5021 East Anaheim
Long Beach, CA 90804

Temple Studio Theatre
5021 Anaheim Street
Long Beach, CA 90804

Los Angeles

Actors Forum
3365 ½ Cahuenga Boulvard West
Los Angeles, CA 90068
Tel: 213-850-9016
Member: AEA; CAC; CFA; CTC; LATA;
Description: Seating capacity of 50.

Actors of America
1750 Canfield Street
Los Angeles, CA 90035
Address Inquiries to: G. Jaffray

Actors Repertory Company
5625 North Figuera
Los Angeles, CA 90027

Actors Studios West
8341 Delongpre
Los Angeles, CA 90069

Afro American Culture
4309 Broadway
Los Angeles, CA 90037

Amen Players
10508 West Pico
Los Angeles, CA 90064

American National Theatre and Academy
Post Office Box 3221
Los Angeles, CA 90028
Address Inquiries to: Lisabeth Fielding,
   Executive Secretary
Founded in: 1957
Annual Budget: $25,000

Anna Bing Arnold Theatre
5905 Wilshire Boulevard
Los Angeles, CA 90036

ANTA
Post Office Box 3221
Los Angeles, CA 90028

Argo Center of Cultural Art
4276 Crenshaw Boulevard
Los Angeles, CA 90008
Address Inquiries to: D. Becker

Assistance League
1370 St. Andrews Place
Los Angeles, CA 90028

Awarehouse Theatre
3327 South Sepulveda
Los Angeles, CA 90034
Address Inquiries to: T. Ewings

Black Collect Theatre
4309 South Broadway
Los Angeles, CA 90037

Brentwood Pres. Players
12000 San Vincente
Los Angeles, CA 90049

Burbage Theatre Ensemble
Century City Playhouse
10508 West Pico Boulevard
Los Angeles, CA 90064
Member: AEA; CAC; CFA; CTC; LATA;

Call Board
8451 Melrose Place
Los Angeles, CA 90069
Address Inquiries to: D. Cooper

Casa Italiana
1501 North Broadway
Los Angeles, CA 90012

Cellar Theatre
102 South Vermont
Los Angeles, CA 90004

Center Playhouse
5870 West Olympic
Los Angeles, CA 90036
Address Inquiries to: B. Mullen

Century City Playhouse
10508 West Pico
Los Angeles, CA 90064

Character Circle Players
2114 West Manchester
Los Angeles, CA 90047

Chemin De Fer Theatre
102 South Vermont
Los Angeles, CA 90004

Children's Theatre Festival
6253 Hollywood Boulevard, #222
Los Angeles, CA 90028
Address Inquiries to: Celeste Anlauf
Member: CTAA;

City Theatre Project
2653 Hollyridge Drive
Los Angeles, CA 90028
Tel: 213-464-5031
Address Inquiries to: John David Garfield,
   Artistic Director
Founded in: 1974
Annual Budget: $5,000

Comedia II Productions
130 South La Brea
Los Angeles, CA 90036

Community Theatre
155 Washington Boulevard
Los Angeles, CA 90015

Company Theatre
1653 South La Cienega Boulevard
Los Angeles, CA 90035
Tel: 213-274-5153
Address Inquiries to: Peter A. Chernack,
   Executive Director
Founded in: 1967
Member: AEA; CAC; CFA; CTC; LATA;
Annual Budget: 100,000
Description: A professional showcase theatre
company.

Contempo Theatre
10886 Leconte
Los Angeles, CA 90024

Credibility Gap
8162 Melrose Avenue
Los Angeles, CA 90046

Cultural Arts Center
3224 Riverside Drive
Los Angeles, CA 90027

Address Inquiries to: P. Martin

CW and Company
6468 Santa Monica
Los Angeles, CA 90038

East West Players
4424 Santa Monica Boulevard
Los Angeles, California 90029
Tel: 213-660-0366
Description: Seating capacity of 99.

Ebony Showcase Theatre
4720 West Washington Boulevard
Los Angeles, CA 90016

Evergreen Stage Company
11747 Mayfield Avenue
Los Angeles, CA 90049
Tel: 213-659-2802

Facets
2727 West 6th Street
Los Angeles, CA 90057

Falcon Studio Theatre
5526 Hollywood Boulevard
Los Angeles, CA 90028

Felicia Mahood Players
11338 Santa Monica Boulevard
Los Angeles, CA 90025
Tel: 826-478-6238
Address Inquiries to: Sherman E. Sanders,
Producer
Founded in: 1973
Annual Budget: $1,000

Fifth Studio Theatre
4157 West 5th Street
Los Angeles, CA 90020
Member: AEA; CAC; CFA; CTC; LATA;
Description: A professional theatre company.

Foundation for the Junior Blind Group
5300 Angelus Vista Boulevard
Los Angeles, CA 90043
Description: A theatre for the blind.

Geneva Players
3300 Wilshire
Los Angeles, CA 90005
Address Inquiries to: D. Rolf

Golden Gate Theatre
5156 Whittier Boulevard
Los Angeles, CA 90022

Greek Theatre
2700 North Vermont Avenue
Los Angeles, CA 90027

The Groundlings
1089 North Oxford Avenue
Los Angeles, CA 90029
Tel: 213-462-4415
Address Inquiries to: Gary Austin, Artistic
Director
Founded in: 1974
Member: LATA;
Annual Budget: $25,000

Holiday Stage
855 North Vermont Avenue
Los Angeles, CA 90029

Holmes Theatre Group
5910 Locksley Place
Los Angeles, CA 90028

Horeshoe Stage
7458 Melrose
Los Angeles, CA 90046

Horseshoe Stage
7458 Melrose
Los Angeles, CA 90046
Address Inquiries to: I. Rogers

Huntington Hartford Theater
1615 Vine Street
Los Angeles, CA 90028
Tel: 462-666-

Hyperion Theatre
1835 Hyperion Avenue
Los Angeles, CA 90027
Member: AEA; CAC; CFA; CTC; LATA;
Description: A professional showcase theatre.

Inner City Cultural Center
1308 South New Hampshire Avenue
Los Angeles, CA 90006
Member: AEA; CAC; CFA; CTC; LATA;
Description: A professional theatre and cultur-
al center.

Italian American Drama Group
1051 North Broadway
Los Angeles, CA 90012
Tel: 213-664-7435
Address Inquiries to: Angelo Bertolino,
Organizer
Founded in: 1966
Annual Budget: $1,000

Junior Programs
Box 24572
Los Angeles, CA 90024

Kentwood Players
8301 North Hindrey Avenue
Los Angeles, CA 90045
Tel: 213-645-5156
Founded in: 1950
Annual Budget: $10,000

L.A. Press Club Theatre
Los Angeles Press Club
600 North Vermont Avenue
Los Angeles, CA 90004

League of La Theatre
1024 South Tobertson Boulevard
Los Angeles, CA 90035

Lee Strasberg Institute
6757 Hollywood Boulevard
Los Angeles, CA 90028

Lewis Comedy Rumors
6142 Carlos
Los Angeles, CA 90028

Los Angeles Actors' Theatre
1089 North Oxford
Los Angeles, CA 90029
Tel: 213-464-5500
Member: AEA; CAC; CFA; CTC; LATA;
Description: A professional showcase theatre.

Los Angeles Feminist Theatre
8700 Skyline Drive
Los Angeles, CA 90046
Tel: 213-656-9044
Address Inquiries to: Sarah Sappington Kuhn,
Founder and Artistic Director
Founded in: 1970
Annual Budget: $5,000

The Los Angeles Free Shakespeare
Festival
Post Office Box 1951
Los Angeles, CA 90038
Tel: 213-469-3974
Address Inquiries to: Peg Yorkin, Managing
Director
Founded in: 1973
Annual Budget: $100,000

Los Angeles Gazebo Theatre One,
Incorporated
515 Westmount Drive
Los Angeles, CA 90048
Tel: 213-657-3270
Description: See Santa Barbara Gazebo
Theatre One, Inc. listing.

Mafundi Institute
1827 East 103rd Street
Los Angeles, CA 90002

Mandala Productions
649 North Poinsettia
Los Angeles, CA 90036

Matrix Theatre
7657 Melrose Avenue
Los Angeles, CA 90046
Tel: 213-653-3279
Member: AEA; CAC; CFA; CTC; LATA;
Description: A professional showcase theatre.
Seating capacity of 99.

Melrose Theatre Association
733 North Seward Street
Los Angeles, CA 90038
Tel: 213-465-1885
Member: AEA; CAC; CFA; CTC; LATA;
Description: A professional showcase theatre.
Seating capacity of 80.

Meredith Experimental Theatre
649 Pointsetta
Los Angeles, CA 90046

Merrick Theatre Academy of Drama
870 North Vine Street
Los Angeles, CA 90038

Met Theatre
649 North Poinsettia Place
Los Angeles, CA 90036
Tel: 213-932-8614
Member: AEA; CAC; CFA; CTC; LATA;
Description: A professional showcase theatre.
Seating capacity is open.

Municipal Art Gallery Theatre
4804 Hollywood Boulevard
Los Angeles, CA 90027

New Artef Players
8816 ½ Sunset Boulevard
Los Angeles, CA 90069

Member: AEA; CAC; CFA; CTC; LATA;
Description: A professional showcase theatre.

New Mercury Theatre
1451 North Las Palmas
Los Angeles, CA 90046

New Playwrights Foundation
1707 North Kenmore
Los Angeles, CA 90027
Member: AEA; CAC; CFA; CTC; LATA;
Description: A professional showcase theatre
for new actors and playwrights.

New Playwrights Theatre
6468 Santa Monica
Los Angeles, CA 90038

New Theatre Ensemble
666 ½ North Robertson
Los Angeles, CA 90067

New Theatre, Incorporated
c/o Martin Magner
1282 Burnside Avenue
Los Angeles, CA 90019
Member: AEA; CAC; CFA; CTC; LATA;
Description: A professional showcase theatre.

Nine O'Clock Players
1367 North Andrews Place
Los Angeles, CA 90028
Tel: 213-469-1973, Assistance League
Switchboard; 213-499-1970
Address Inquiries to: Mrs. Lynn P. Raitnover,
  Chairman
  Mrs. John Grey, Production Chairman
Founded in: 1929
Description: An auxiliary of the Assistance
League of Southern California. Produces
two plays a year (a fall production and a
spring production) for children. Nearly 10,-
000 children experience theatre through
these productions. Handicapped and under-
priviledged children are admitted free of
charge.

Nomads Theatre
6525 West Sunset Blvd
Los Angeles, CA 90028

Nosotros
1314 North Wilton Place
Los Angeles, CA 90028
Tel: 213-465-4167
Member: AEA; CAC; CFA; CTC; LATA;
Description: A professional showcase theatre.
Seating capacity of 67.

Occidental Center Plays
1150 South Olive
Los Angeles, CA 90035

Odyssey Theatre Ensemble
c/o Odyssey Theatre Foundation
12111 Ohio Avenue
Los Angeles, CA 90025
Tel: 213-826-1626; 213-879-5221
Address Inquiries to: Ron Sossi, Managing
  and Artistic Director
Founded in: 1969
Member: TCG; CAC; CCA; LATA; CTC;
  NEA; LACCAD; LACMPAC; JIF;
Annual Budget: $250,000

Description: Offers an exciting alternative to
the large commercial theatre in Los Angeles.
Since its inception, the Odyssey has consist-
ently presented innovative, quality productions which have earned it a national and
international reputation. It is now breaking
new ground by establishing the nation's first
International Experimental Theatre Center.

Off The Wall
1204 North Fairfax
Los Angeles, CA 90046
Member: AEA; CAC; CFA; CTC; LATA;
Description: An off-beat professional theatre.

Ohh Poo Pah Doo
7561 Sunset Boulevard
Los Angeles, CA 90046

Operation Bootstrap
4171 South Central Avenue
Los Angeles, CA 90011

Orpheun Theatre Corporation
1025 Palm Drive
Los Angeles, CA 90069
Member: AEA; CAC; CFA; CTC; LATA;
Description: A professional theatre corpora-
tion.

Overland Express Company
3700 Barham
Los Angeles, CA 90068

Oxford Theatre
1089 North Oxford Avenue
Los Angeles, CA 90029

Palm Court
Alexandria Hotel
Spring at 5th Street
Los Angeles, CA 90013

Parlando Compnay
6468 Santa Monica
Los Angeles, CA 90038

Patriotic Hall
1816 South Figueroa
Los Angeles, CA 90015

Pelic Theatre
8451 Melrose Place
Los Angeles, CA 90069

Penny Gaffers Dramatic Society
6111 West Olympic
Los Angeles, CA 90029

Pitschel Players
8162 Melrose Blvd
Los Angeles, Ca 94133

Pixie Players-Plummer Park
1300 North Vista
Los Angeles, CA 90046
Tel: 213-876-1725
Address Inquiries to: John Angelo, Drama
  Director

Players Ring Gallery
8325 Santa Monica Boulevard
Los Angeles, CA 90069

The Playhouse
940 South Figueroa

Los Angeles, CA 90015

Plays For Living
1345 South Burlington Avenue
Los Angeles, CA 90006

Playwrights Group
7420 Melrose
Los Angeles, CA 90046

Plummer Mummers
1200 North Vista
Los Angeles, CA 90046
Address Inquiries to: J. Angelo

Provisional Theatre
1816 North Vermont
Los Angeles, CA 90027
Tel: 213-644-1450
Address Inquiries to: Barry Opper, Manager
Founded in: 1972

Ralph Frued Playhouse
MacGowen Hall
University of California, Los Angeles
Los Angeles, CA 90014

Remsen Bird Hillside Theatre
1600 Campus Road
Los Angeles, CA 90041
Tel: 213-259-2772
Address Inquiries to: Dean Brigida Kanuer,
  Manager
Founded in: 1925

The Revelation
1915 Rodeo Road
Los Angeles, CA 90018

Roxy Theatre
9009 Sunset Boulevard
Los Angeles, CA 90069

Saint Albans Theatre Group
580 Hilgard Avenue
Los Angeles, CA 90024

Saint Genesis Players
4510 Finley
Los Angeles, CA 90027

Sal Ponti Theatre
1835 Hyperion
Los Angeles, CA 90027

Sayers Players
1451 North Las Palmas
Los Angeles, CA 90028

Scorpio Rising Theatre
426 North Hoover Street
Los Angeles, CA 90026
Member: AEA; CAC; CFA; CTC; LATA;
Description: A professional showcase theatre
center.

Shakespeare Society of America
Globe Playhouse
1107 North King's Road
Los Angeles, CA 90069
Member: AEA; CAC; CFA; CTC; LATA;
Description: A professional, Shakespearean
theatre.

Sinai Temple Theatre
10400 Wilshire Boulevard

Los Angeles, CA 90024

Society to Save the Stage
Post Office Box 69A07
Los Angeles, CA 90069
Tel: 282-948-
Address Inquiries to: Rosemary Lazarou,
  Managing Director
  Tim Doyle, Resident Director and
  House Manager
Description: Provides experience and exposure that would not otherwise be available for both professional and beginning performers and technicians.

Staircase Company
6111 West Olympic Boulevard
Los Angeles, CA 90048

Steven North Workshop
498 Saint Pierre Road
Los Angeles, CA 90024

Steve Peck Theatre Arts
2855 South Robertson
Los Angeles, CA 90034

Studio Theatre Playhouse
1944 Riverside Drive
Los Angeles, CA 90039

Sydney Mason Workshop
133 North Mansfield
Los Angeles, CA 90036

Synergy Trust
1835 Hyperion
Los Angeles, CA 90027

Tara Players
10508 West Pico Boulevard
Los Angeles, CA 90064

Temple Maskers
4000 West Slausen Avenue
Los Angeles, CA 90043

Theatre of Light
6817 Franklin Avenue
Los Angeles, CA 90028
Member: AEA; CAC; CFA; CTC; LATA;

Theatre of Watts
1743 East 122nd Street
Los Angeles, CA 90059

Three Arts Studio
7233 Santa Monica
Los Angeles, CA 90046
Address Inquiries to: F. Wyka

Touring Artists Group
5907 Fourth Avenue
Los Angeles, CA 90043

Troupers Playhouse
1627 North La Brea
Los Angeles, Ca 90028

Watts Tower Theatre
1727 East 107th Street
Los Angeles, CA 90002

Westchester Playhouse
8301 South Hindry Avenue
Los Angeles, CA 90045
Address Inquiries to: A. Marcom

West Coast Theatre Company
Post Office Box 38217
Los Angeles, CA 90038

Westwood Players
10886 Le Conte Avenue
Los Angeles, CA 90024
Tel: 213-477-4907
Address Inquiries to: Leonard Buzz Blair,
  Producer
Founded in: 1974
Annual Budget: $100,000

Womanspace
11007 Venice Boulevard
Los Angeles, CA 90034

Womens Center Theatre
2021 North Western
Los Angeles, CA 90027

Womens Ensemble
10508 West Pico
Los Angeles, CA 90064

Yamashiro Dinner Theatre
1999 North Sycamore
Los Angeles, CA 90068

Manteca

Community Theatre
14410 Modoc Court
Manteca, CA 95336

Marysville

Sutter Buttes Regional Theatre Group
629 G Street
Marysville, CA 95901

Millbrae

Millbrae Players
255 Broadway
Millbrae, CA 94030

Modesto

Modesto Community Theatre
1111 Cambridge Court
Modesto, CA 95350

Monterey Park

Amphi Theatre
Barnes Park
Monterey Park, CA 91754

Montery Park Little Theatre
350 South McPherrin
Monterey Park, CA 91754

Murphys

Black Bart Players
Murphys, CA 95247

Napa

Pretenders Playhouse
Post Office Box 525
Napa, CA 94558

North Hollywood

Apolladoros Musicals
5643 Rhodes Avenue
North Hollywood, CA 91607

Barones Dinner Theatre
10123 Riverside Drive
North Hollywood, CA 90064

Film Actors Workshop
5004 Vineland
North Hollywood, CA 91601
Tel: 213-766-5108
Address Inquiries to: Tony Barr, Supervisor
  Barbara Barr, Administrator
Description: All scenes performed on-camera in our complete video department.

Group Repertory Theatre
11043 Magnolia Boulevard
North Hollywood, CA 91601
Tel: 213-760-9766
Member: AEA; CAC; CFA; CTC; LATA;
Description: A professional showcase theatre company. Seating capacity of 80.

Pact
11855 Hart Street
North Hollywood, CA 91605

Rep
3759 Cahuenga West
North Hollywood, CA 91604

Shakespeare Ensemble
5000 Colfax Avenue
North Hollywood, CA 91601

Synthaxis Theatre Company
4219 Lankershim Boulevard
North Hollywood, CA 91602
Member: AEA; CAC; CFA; CTC; LATA;

The Theatre
5118 Lankershim Blvd.
North Hollywood, CA 91601

Northridge

Megaw Theatre
17601 Saticoy Street
Northridge, CA 91324
Member: AEA; CAC; CFA; CTC; LATA;
Description: A professional showcase theatre.

Norwalk

Southern California Conservatory Theatre
11110 East Alondra Boulevard
Norwalk, CA 90650
Tel: 213-860-2451, ext 343; 213-924-2100
Address Inquiries to: Fred Fate, Producing
  Director
  Kevin Sales, Assistant Producer
Founded in: 1977
Annual Budget: $250,000
Description: An intense summer training program. In addition to performing in three shows each summer, the actors attend classes in all aspects of the performing arts.

Novato

Community Players
906 Machin Avenue
Novato, CA 94947

Oakland

Oakland Civic Theatre
1502 Lakeside Avenue
Oakland, CA 94612

Ojai

Ojai Art Center
Post Office Box 33
Ojai, CA 93023

Ontario

Gallery Theatre
C Street and Lemon
Ontario, CA 91786

Harlequin Theatre
126 East C Street
Ontario, CA 91761

Oxnard

Cabrillo Music Theatre
1801 Tehama
Oxnard, CA 93030

Plaza Players
1265 South H Street
Oxnard, CA 93030

Pacific Palisades

Saint Matthews Players
030 Bienvenida
Pacific Palisades, CA 90272

Palm Springs

Civic Theatre
538 North Palm Canyon Drive
Palm Springs, CA 92262
Address Inquiries to: M. Mc Laughlin

Palo Alto

Manhattan Playhouse
Manhattan and Bayshore
Palo Alto, CA 94303

Palo Alto Children's Theatre
1305 Middlefield Road
Palo Alto, CA 94301
Address Inquiries to: Patricia Briggs

Palos Verdes

Palos Verdes Players
2514 Via Tejon
Palos Verdes, CA 90274

Panorama City

Panorama Music Workshop
8600 Hazeltine Avenue
Panorama City, Ca 91402

Pasadena

Hoffman Players
1588 North Holliston
Pasadena, CA 91104

Pasadena Arts Center Theatre
360 North Arroyo Boulevard
Pasadena, CA 91103
Member: AEA; CAC; CFA; CTC; LATA;
Description: A professional showcase theatre
arts center.

Puppeteers of America
5 Cricklewood Path
Pasadena, CA 91107
Founded in: 1937
Description: A national not-for-profit corporation dedicated to the promotion and development of the art of puppetry.

Sierra Madre Studio
17 West Dayton Street
Pasadena, CA 91105

Spectrum Productions
Cal Tech
Pasadena, CA 91109

Throop Players
300 South Los Robles
Pasadena, CA 91106
Address Inquiries to: P. Barr

Pismo Beach

Footlighters
767 Price Canyon
Pismo Beach, CA 93449
Address Inquiries to: B. Skeen

Pomona

Temple Theater Group
3033 North Towne Avenue
Pomona, CA 91767

Porterville

Porterville Barn
Post Office Box 108
Porterville, CA 93257

Poway

Tumbleweed Western Theatre
12204 Boulder View
Poway, CA 92064

Redlands

Footlighters
Post Office Box 444
Redlands, CA 92373

Grove Theatre
Vine Street
Redlands, CA 92373

Redondo Beach

Golden Hull
555 Fishermans Wharf
Redondo Beach, CA 90277

Rialto

Rialto Playhouse
1539 North Clifford Street
Rialto, CA 92376

Riverside

Riverside Children's Theatre
Post Office Box 2744
Riverside, CA 92516
Address Inquiries to: Gary T. Gerdes

Riverside Community Players
4026 14th Street
Riverside, CA 92501

Ross

Riverside Community Players
Post Office Box 626
Ross, CA 94957

Ross Valley Players
Post Office Box 626
Ross, CA 94957

Rowland Heights

Row Heights Community Theatre
1845 Nowell Avenue
Rowland Heights, CA 91748

Sacramento

Civic Theatre
1419 H Street
Sacramento, CA 95814

Sacramento Music Circus
1419 H Street
Sacramento, CA 95184

San Bernardino

California Theatre
Post Office Box 606
San Bernardino, CA 92402

San Clemente

Community Theatre
202 Cabrillo
San Clemente, CA 92627
Address Inquiries to: J. Applegett

Sebastions West Theatre
140 Pico Avenue
San Clemente, CA 92672

San Diego

Actors Quarter
480 Elm Street
San Diego, CA 92101

Carter Center Stage
Balboa Park
San Diego, CA 92101

Mission Playhouse
3960 Mason Street
San Diego, CA 92110

Northshores Advertising School
3366 Park Ave
San Diego, CA 92103

Off-Broadway Theatre
314 F Street
San Diego, CA 92101

Old Globe Theatre
Simon Edison Center
Post Office Box 2171
San Diego, CA 92112
Tel: 714-231-1941; 714-231-1942
Address Inquiries to: Craig Noel, Executive
Producer
Jack O'Brien, Artistic Director
Founded in: 1935
Member: FEDAPT; CAC; CTC;
CACONFED; CAEC; LORT; TCG;
Annual Budget: $3,776,000
Description: From June to September, profes-

sional productions of Shakespeare, and other classics, are presented in the three theatres, The Old Globe Theatre, Cassius Carter Center, Stage and Festival Stage, of the Simon Edison Center for Performing Arts. A fully professional winter season of eight major plays is held from December to May.

Puppet Playhouse
3903 Voltaire Street
San Diego, CA 92107

San Diego Community Theatre
Post Office Box 2171
San Diego, CA 92112

San Diego Repertory Theatre
1620 Sixth Avenue
San Diego, CA 92101

Southeast Community Theatre
150 South 49th Street
San Diego, CA 92113

San Francisco

Pitschel Players
756 Union Street
San Francisco, CA 94133

San Francisco Actors Ensemble
2940 16th Street, Studio B-1
San Francisco, CA 94103
Tel: 415-861-9015
Address Inquiries to: Stefani Priest, Executive Director
Founded in: 1971
Annual Budget: $50,000

Shadowplayers
745 Buchanan
San Francisco, CA 94102

San Gabriel

Lindy Theatre
320 ½ South Mission Drive
San Gabriel, CA 91776

Players USA
Post Office Box 771
San Gabriel, CA 91776
Tel: 213-281-1286
Founded in: 1971

Sangab Mission Players
Post Office Box 1155
San Gabriel, CA 91776

San Gabriel Little Theatre
320 South Mission
San Gabriel, CA 91776

Womens Drama Group
261 Junipero Serra
San Gabriel, CA 91776

San Jose

California Young People's Theatre
6840 Chiala Lane
San Jose, CA 95129

San Jose State University
Company Comique
Theatre Arts Department
San Jose, CA 95192
Tel: 408-277-2763; 408-277-2764
Address Inquiries to: Hal J. Todd, Artistic Director
Founded in: 1976
Member: ATA; TCG; TCCBA; CETA;
Annual Budget: $38,000
Description: A not-for-profit, non-professional theatre organization.

San Luis Obispo

Central Coast Children's Theatre
Post Office Box 925
San Luis Obispo, CA 93406

Little Theatre
Post Office Box 122
San Luis Obispo, CA 93406

San Marino

Hunting Community Players
1700 Huntington Drive
San Marino, CA 91108
Address Inquiries to: C. Stephens

Saint Edmunds Players
Post Office Box 8138
San Marino, CA 91108

San Pedro

Aprenda Players
2007 Avenue Aprenda
San Pedro, CA 90700
Address Inquiries to: D. Draper

Galilean Players
580 West 6th Street
San Pedro, CA 90731
Address Inquiries to: E. Bridges

Santa Ana

Anaheim Theatre
520 Linwood
Santa Ana, CA 92701

Harlequin Dinner Playhouse
3503 South Harbor Boulevard
Santa Ana, CA 92704

Marquee Theatre
1227 Raymer
Santa Ana, CA 92704

Phillips Hall/Santa Ana College
17th at Bristol
Santa Ana, CA 92706
Tel: 714-667-3395; 714-667-3216
Address Inquiries to: Nicholas J. D'Antoni, Manager
  Sheryl Donchey, Theatre Arts Department Chairman
Founded in: 1954
Member: UCTA; SCETA; USITT; ATA;
Annual Budget: 23,000

Santa Barbara

Alcehama Productions
914 Santa Barbara Street
Santa Barbara, CA 93101

Lobero Theatre Foundation
33 East Canon Berdito
Santa Barbara, CA 93101

Performing Arts Center
Santa Barbara High School
Santa Barbara, CA 93101

Santa Barbara Gazebo Theatre One
631 Alameda Padre Serra
Santa Barbara, CA 93103
Tel: 805-962-6587; 213-657-3270
Address Inquiries to: Jack Nakano, Artistic Director
Founded in: 1974
Member: LATA; NEA;
Annual Budget: $50,000
Description: Two projects now in operation: California Youth Theatre and The Shakespeare Video Society.

Santa Barbara Repertory Theatre
James R. Garvin Memorial Theatre
Santa Barbara City College
Santa Barbara, CA 93109
Tel: 805-965-0581, Ext. 375
Address Inquiries to: B. Pope Freeman, PhD, Managing Director
Member: URTA;
Description: A summer repertory theatre with flexible seating and staging.

Youth Theatre Productions
Post Office Box 1027
Santa Barbara, CA 93102

Santa Maria

Civic Theatre
1660 McClelland Drive
Santa Maria, CA 93454

Pac Cons Performing Arts
Allan Hancock College
Santa Maria, CA 93354

Santa Maria Theatre
Post Office Box 1868
Santa Maria, CA 93456
Address Inquiries to: K. George

Santa Monica

Group Studio Theatre
1211 Montana
Santa Monica, CA 90403

Group Theatre
1211 4th Street
Santa Monica, CA 90401
Address Inquiries to: T. Roter

Morgan Theatre
2627 Pico Boulevard
Santa Monica, CA 90405
Tel: 213-828-7519

Pelican Players
1220 1220 2nd Street
Santa Monica, CA 90401

Public Words Theatre
235 Hill Street
Santa Monica, CA 90405
Member: AEA; CAC; CFA; CTC; LATA;
Description: A professional, public, showcase theatre.

Santa Monica Group Theatre
1211 4th Street
Santa Monica, CA 90401
Member: AEA; CAC; CFA; CTC; LATA;
Description: A professional showcase theatre.

Theatre Arts Commission
1008 11th Street
Santa Monica, CA 90403

Unitarian Church Players
18th and Arizona
Santa Monica, CA 90404

Unity Players
1245 4th Street
Santa Monica, CA 90401

Santa Rosa

Actor's Theater for Children
3625 Yale Drive
Santa Rosa, CA 95405
Tel: 707-545-4307
Address Inquiries to: Walter McGauley,
   Executive Director
Founded in: 1971
Member: CTA;
Annual Budget: $5,000

Santa Rosa Players
3625 Yale Drive
Santa Rosa, CA 95405

Saratoga

Lyric Players
22100 Mount Eden
Saratoga, CA 95070

Seal Beach

Peppermint Playhouse
124 Main Street
Seal Beach, CA 90740

Sierra Madre

Baker Street Productions
139 Esperanza
Sierra Madre, CA 91204
Address Inquiries to: Michael Dunngan,
   Manager
Founded in: 1969

Heinks Memorial Theatre Players
526 West Highland
Sierra Madre, CA 91024
Address Inquiries to: M. Dunnigan

Simi

Horizon Players
585 East Street
Simi, CA 93065

South Lake Tahoe

Tahoe Valley Players
Post Office Box 1165
South Lake Tahoe, CA 95702

Spring Valley

Spring Valley Theatre
9602 Memory Lane
Spring Valley, CA 92077

Stanton

Stanton Community Theatre
Stanton Parks and Recreation
Stanton, CA 90680

Stockton

Stockton Civic Theatre
Post Office Box 1701
Stockton, CA 95201

Studio City

Hollywood Theater Company
12838 Kling Street
Studio City, CA 91604
Tel: 213-984-1867
Address Inquiries to: Rai Tasco, Director
Founded in: 1972

Studio City Little Theatre
12621 Rye Street
Studio City, CA 91604

Theater East Company
12655 Ventura Boulevard
Studio City, CA 91604
Tel: 213-766-6111
Address Inquiries to: Indus Arthur, President
Founded in: 1961
Member: AEA; LATA;
Annual Budget: $25,000

Tarzana

Covenant Players
Lindlay and Burbank
Tarzana, CA 91356

Tehachapi

Community Theatre
Zella Young Star PT
Tehachapi, CA 93561

Thousand Oaks

The Conejo Players
Post Office Box 1695
Thousand Oaks, CA 91320
Address Inquiries to: T. Waters

Topanga

Mermaid Tavern Players
20421 West Callon Drive
Topanga, CA 90290

Topanga Playhouse
1440 North Topanga
Topanga, CA 90290

Torrance

Hampton Players
1522 Cravens Avenue
Torrance, CA 90501
Address Inquiries to: L. Gillespie

Thomas More Theatre Company
5430 Torrance Boulevard
Torrance, CA 90503
Tel: 213-540-2021
Address Inquiries to: John R. Carrol,
   Chairman
Founded in: 1960
Annual Budget: $1,000

Tujunga

Ascension Players
10154 Mountain
Tujunga, CA 91042
Address Inquiries to: J. Ferstead

Turlock

Gaslight Players
Turlock, CA 95380
Address Inquiries to: Lou Cinelli

Tustin

Pacific Group Theatre
Post Office Box 301
Tustin, CA 92680

Tustin Thespian Troupe
1750 Laguana Road
Tustin, CA 92680

Upland

Garrick Players
1615 2nd Avenue
Upland, CA 91786

Valencia

Cal Arts Theatre Ensemble
24700 McBean Parkway
Valencia, CA 91355
Tel: 805-255-1050
Member: AEA; CAC; CFA; CTC; LATA;

Van Nuys

Congregational Church Theatre
14115 Magnolia Blvd.
Van Nuys, CA 91403

People in Motion
14800 Sherman Way
Van Nuys, CA 91405

Repertory West
5310 Fulton
Van Nuys, CA 91401

Vayermo

Saint Andrews Priory
14120 East Pallet Creek
Vayermo, CA 93563

Venice

Hippovideo: the Foundation for
   Multi-Media and the Arts
117 Sunset Avenue
Venice, CA 90291
Tel: 213-396-7114
Address Inquiries to: Jack Paritz, Artistic
   Director
Founded in: 1974
Annual Budget: $5,000
Description: Multi-media theatrical presentation.

Venice Free Theatre II
1513 Ocean Front Walk
Venice, CA 90291

Ventura

Ojai Little Theatre Group
Post Office Box 699
Ventura, CA 93001

PZ Players Theatre
Post Office Box 43
Ventura, CA 93001

Victorville

Community Center Theatre
15619 8th Street
Victorville, CA 92392

West Hollywood

Callboard Theatre
8451 Melrose Place
West Hollywood, CA 90069
Member: AEA; CAC; CFA; CTC; LATA;
Description: A professional showcase theatre.

Westlake

Westlake Theatre Company
31761 Village School
Westlake, CA 91360

Westminister

Long Beach Childrens Theatre
15451 Vermont
Westminister, CA 92683

Westminster

Westminter Community Theatre
14131 Dumont Lane
Westminster, CA 92683

Whittier

Whittier Community Theatre
Post Office Box 601
Whittier, CA 90605
Address Inquiries to: M. J. Calvin

Yuba City

Sutter Buttes Theatre
Post Office Box 386
Yuba City, CA 95991

Yucaipa

Yucaipa Little Theatre
11837 Peach Tree Circle
Yucaipa, CA 92399

Yucca Valley

Yucca Valley Players
7625 Jemez Trail
Yucca Valley, CA 92284

COLORADO

Arvada

Arvada Festival Playhouse
5665 Wadsworth Boulevard
Arvada, CO 80002

Boulder

The Actors Theatre
2439 Kalmia Avenue
Boulder, CO 80302
Tel: 313-449-7528
Address Inquiries to: Frank Georgianna,
    Artistic Director
Founded in: 1975
Annual Budget: $5,000

Nomad Players Inc
Post Office Box 1604
Boulder, CO 80302

Breckenridge

Backstage Theatre
Post Office Box 97
Breckenridge, CO 80424
Tel: 303-453-0199; 303-453-2297
Address Inquiries to: Allyn Mosher, Manager
Founded in: 1974
Annual Budget: $30,000
Description: A not-for-profit community
theatre, supported by private donations and
run on a volunteer basis. Open five nights a
week, eight months a year in the ski town of
Breckenridge.

Colorado Springs

Civic Theatre
321 North Tejon Street
Colorado Springs, CO 80902

Commerce City

Adams County Community Theatre
Post Office Box 1022
Commerce City, CO 80022

Cripple Creek

Imperial Players
Imperial Hotel
Cripple Creek, CO 80813
Tel: 303-689-2292
Address Inquiries to: Robert C. Burroughs
Danny Griffith, Musical and Olio Director
Founded in: 1947
Description: Famous for performances of
American Melodrama, the Imperial Players
were chosen to be filmed in performance by
the Public Broadcasting System. The players
use only the authentic scripts of 19th century
America.

Denver

Actors' 'Studio 7' of Gaslight Theatre
4201 Hooker Street
Denver, CO 80211
Tel: 303-455-6077; 303-427-5125
Address Inquiries to: R. Paul Willett,
    Producer
Founded in: 1964
Annual Budget: $25,000

Bonfils Theatre
Colfax At Elizabeth
Denver, CO 80206

Colorado Children's Theatre
1750 Willow Street
Denver, CO 80220

Address Inquiries to: D.E. Malmgren
Member: CTAA;

Denver Center for the Performing
    Arts-Bonfils Theatre
East Colfax at Elizabeth
Denver, CO 80206
Tel: 303-322-7725, Box Office;
    303-399-5418, Other Departments
Address Inquiries to: Henry E. Lowenstein,
    Producer
    Ted Ross, Production Manager
Founded in: 1929
Member: USITT; ANTA; TCG; URTA;
    ATA; SCA; NTC; USITT; Rocky
    Mountain Institute for Theatre
    Technology, Inc.; NEA;
Annual Budget: $100,000
Description: Offers non-professional actors a
fully staffed professional theatre in which to
work. There are two theatre spaces within
the Bonfils: a proscenium stage which seats
550 in the auditorium and Bo-Bans Cabaret
which seats up to 98 people. In recent years
the Bonfils has offered a wide range of plays
including new works and Denver premieres.
The programming has reflected the increasing strength and importance of minority
theatre in America and has offered opportunities to actors of all cultures. The Bo-
Bans Cabaret, the Bonfils Theatre for Children, the Bonfils Theatre School, and the
community outreach programs like Creative
Drama Program and Festival Caravan have
all contributed to the organization's success.

Eden Theatrical Workshop
410 Franklin Street
Denver, CO 80205

Elitch Gardens Theatre
4620 West 38th Avenue
Denver, CO 80212

Nubian House Theatre
3401 High Street
Denver, CO 80205

Saints And Sinners
1324 Monoco Parkway
Denver, CO 80222
Address Inquiries to: M. Sefton

Durango

Durango Civic Players
85 Folsom Place
Durango, CO 81301

Estes Park

Estes Park Community Theatre
Estes Park, CO 80517

The Summertree Players
Post Office Box 480
Estes Park, CO 80517
Tel: 913-584-6512; 303-586-6100
Address Inquiries to: Margaret Sullivan,
    General Manager
    Douglas Koth, Promotional Director
Founded in: 1977
Annual Budget: 30,000
Description: A professional non equity tour-

ing company employing actors from the Western states, touring contemporary plays, melodrama's and variety shows. Many shows are performance ready at any time of the year and bookings for any size audience, large and small, are accepted. The company is also available for residencies and work shops throughout the year. The Summertree Players can be found at Estes Park, Colorado where they are traditionally in residence during the summer.

Florence

Red Brick Players
Post Office Box 87
Florence, CO 81226

Fort Collins

Probe Theatre
1101 West Oak
Fort Collins, CO 80521

Fort Morgan

Morgan City Players
Post Office Box 157
Fort Morgan, CO 80701
Address Inquiries to: J. Long

Grand Junction

Colorado West Players
3746 G Road
Grand Junction, CO 81501

Gunnison

Western Players
Post Office Box 989
Gunnison, CO 81230

La Junta

Picketwire Players
8th and San Juan
La Junta, CO 81050
Tel: 303-384-9912; 303-384-7591
Address Inquiries to: Sharon Kolomitz,
  President
Founded in: 1968
Annual Budget: $25,000
Description: A totally self-supporting community theatre with a seating capacity of 390. Three to four productions are mounted annually plus a summer musical.

LaPorte

Foothills Civic Theatre
Post Office Box 319
LaPorte, CO 80535
Tel: 303-484-8182
Address Inquiries to: Nancy Johnson,
  President
  Charles J. Mullen, Company Manager
Founded in: 1974
Annual Budget: $50,000
Description: A not-for-profit community based theatre composed of a board of Directors, an auxiliary guild, a manager, secretary, and innumerable hard-working and dedicated volunteers working in all aspects of theatre production. Produces five major productions during its season as well as

many community service projects.

Littleton

Columbine Players
Post Office Box 1003
Littleton, CO 80102

Heritage High School Theatre
7109 South Gallup
Littleton, CO 80120
Address Inquiries to: G.R. Rains

Longmont

Potpourri Players, Ltd.
17 University Circle
Longmont, CO 80501
Tel: 303-772-1430
Address Inquiries to: Maria Bennett,
  President
Founded in: 1957
Annual Budget: $5,000

Montrose

Magic Circle Players
Post Office Box 1214
Montrose, CO 81401

North Glenn

Catharsis 2
9813 Alamo Drive
North Glenn, CO 80221

Pueblo

Broadway Theatre League of Pueblo,
  Incorporated
Post Office Box 3145
Pueblo, CO 81005
Tel: 303-545-4721; 303-542-1211
Address Inquiries to: Mr. Robert Hawkins,
  President
Founded in: 1960
Member: ACUCAA; Pueblo County; CFI
  Steel Corporation; The Farley
  Foundation; The Thatcher Foundation;
Annual Budget: $50,000

The Impossible Players
126 South Oneida
Pueblo, CO 81002
Tel: 303-542-6969
Address Inquiries to: Robert VanSickle
Founded in: 1966

USC Summer Theatre
2200 North Bonforts Boulevard
Pueblo, CO 81001
Tel: 303-549-2169; 303-584-3227
Address Inquiries to: Dr. Ken Plonkey,
  Director of Theatre
Founded in: 1970
Member: ATA; USITT;
Annual Budget: $12,500
Description: A university summer stock theatre combining professional, non-equity actors and technicians with graduate and undergraduate students in a company whose members are both actors and technicians. Scholarships and a few paid positions available.

Westminster

North Glenn Community Theatre
9215 Stuart Street
Westminster, CO 80030

CONNECTICUT

Avon

Avon Playmakers
128 Climax Road
Avon, CT 06001

Bloomfield

C G Theatre
900 Cottage Grove Road
Bloomfield, CT 06002

Branford

Post Road Players
159 Linden Avenue
Branford, CT 06405

Bridgeport

Polka Dot Playhouse
Post Office Box 50
Bridgeport, CT 06601
Tel: 203-374-1777
Address Inquiries to: Irene Ballok, President
Founded in: 1954
Member: NETA;
Annual Budget: $25,00

Brookfield

Country Players
Post Office Box 1000
Brookfield, CT 06804

Chaplin

Miniature Opera Theatre
Post Office Box 275
Chaplin, CT 06235

Chesire

Community Theatre
Post Office Box 149
Chesire, CT 06410

Collinsville

Canton Benefit Productions
West Road Route
Collinsville, CT 06022

Hartford Community Players
Warner Road
Collinsville, CT 06022

Cos Cob

Connecticut Circle Players
40 Catrock Road
Cos Cob, CT 06087
Tel: 203-869-6416
Address Inquiries to: Helga Kopperl,
  Producer
Founded in: 1971
Annual Budget: $5,000

East Haven

Footlight Players
54 Cliff Street
East Haven, CT 06512

Enfield

Enfield Stage Company
211 Hazard Avenue
Enfield, CT 06082

Glastonbury

Fire and Thorn Repertory Theatre
2183 Main Street
Glastonbury, CT 06033

Groton

Pfizer Players
Eastern Point Road
Groton, CT 06340

Hamden

Hamden On Stage
52 Wilbert Street
Hamden, CT 06514

Hartford

Aetna Players
151 Farmington Avenue
Hartford, CT 06156

Hartford Stagers
196 Palm Street
Hartford, CT 06112

The Thalians
140 Garden Street
Hartford, CT 06105

Hebron

Greater Hartford Churches
Route 1
Hebron, CT 06248

Podium Players
Route 1, East Street
Hebron, CT 06248

Lakeville

Oblong Valley Players
Post Office Box 1582
Lakeville, CT 06039
Address Inquiries to: K. Lee Collins

Madison

Nutmeg Players
21 Stonewall Lane
Madison, CT 06443

Manchester

Community Players
205 Oak Street
Manchester, CT 06040

G and S Workshop
61 Bruce Road
Manchester, CT 06040

Little Theatre
Post Office Box 1405
Manchester, CT 06040

Manchester Gilbert and Sullivan Workshop
Post Office Box 626
Manchester, CT 06040
Tel: 203-646-8299

Milford

Stratford G and S Company
21 Sunset Avenue
Milford, CT 06460

New Britian

Rep Theatre
Post Office Box 437
New Britian, CT 06050

New Canaan

Town Players
Post Office Box 201
New Canaan, CT 06840

New Fairfield

Candlewood Area Theatre
New Fairfield, CT 06810

New Haven

Albertus Summer Theatre
700 Prospect Street
New Haven, CT 06511
Tel: 203-865-9697
Address Inquiries to: Albert De Fabio Jr.,
  Manager
Founded in: 1974

Curtain Raisers
66 Fulton Street
New Haven, CT 06512

Hill Parents Association
Post Office Box 7005
New Haven, CT 06511
Tel: 203-777-6371
Address Inquiries to: Kenny Kiensler,
  President
Founded in: 1966
Annual Budget: $5,000

Long Wharf Theatre
222 Sargent Drive
New Haven, CT 06511
Tel: 203-787-4284; 203-787-4282 (Box
  Office)
Address Inquiries to: Arvin Brown, Artistic
  Director
  M. Edgar Rosenblum, Executive
  Director
Founded in: 1965
Member: LORT; TCG; AAA; NHAC; AEA; ;
  Description: Long Wharf Theatre works un-
der a LORT B/D contract with Actors Equity
Association, and has contracts with the So-
ciety of Stage Directors and Choreogra-
phers.

Renaissance Theatre Company
217 Greenwich Avenue
New Haven, CT 06519

Summer Theatre of Greater New Haven
700 Prospect Street
New Haven, CT 06511
Tel: 203-624-7481

Address Inquiries to: J. Robert Jennings,
  Director
Founded in: 1974

Yale Repertory Theatre
222 York Street
New Haven, CT 06511
Tel: 203-436-1587
Address Inquiries to: Robert Brustein, Artistic
  Director
Founded in: 1966
Member: LORT;
Annual Budget: $100,000

New Milford

Community Theatre
29 Church Street
New Milford, CT 06776

Creative Arts Center Theatre
Post Office Box 165
New Milford, CT 06776

Newton

Town Players, Incorporated
Post Office Box 211
Newton, CT 06470
Address Inquiries to: David Brown, Buisness
  Manager
Founded in: 1951

Nichols

Country Theatre
71 Hilltop Drive
Nichols, CT 06611

Oakville

Clockwork Repertory Theatre
133 Main Street
Oakville, CT 06779
Tel: 203-274-7247
Address Inquiries to: Harold J. Pantley,
  Executive Director
  Mark J. Kravetz, Artistic Director
Founded in: 1977
Member: LHAT; ATA; NETC;
Annual Budget: $120,000
Description: A 170 seat repertory theatre with
a six month season beginning in November.

Old Greenwich

Connecticut Playmakers
Post Office Box 705
Old Greenwich, CT 06870

Pleasant Valley

Pleasant Valley Players
Post Office Box 44
Pleasant Valley, CT 06063

Portland

Portland Players
3 Penny Corner Road
Portland, CT 06480

Ridgefield

Ridgefield Workshop
Post Office Box 59
Ridgefield, CT 06877

Rowayton

Art Center Showcase
145 Rawayton Avenue
Rowayton, CT 06853

Sherman

Sherman Players
Jericho Road
Sherman, CT 06784
Tel: 203-354-3622
Address Inquiries to: Frank B. Rogers,
    President
Founded in: 1925

Southbury

Southbury Playhouse
Post Office Box 361
Southbury, CT 06488
Tel: 203-264-8215; 203-264-8216
Address Inquiries to: W. Thomas Littleton,
    Producer
    Fred P. Steinharter, Managing Director
Founded in: 1969

Southington

Southington Community Theatre
Post Offfice Box 411
Southington, CT 06489

Stonington

Stonington Players
45 Main Street
Stonington, CT 06378

Stratford

American Shakespeare
    Theatre/Connecticut Center for the
    Performing Arts (Strratford)
1850 Elm Street
Stratford, CT 06497
Tel: 203-378-7321; 212-966-3900
Address Inquiries to: Peter Coe, Artistic
    Director
    William W. Goodman, Chairman of the
    Board
Founded in: 1955
Member: AEA; ATPAM;
Description: From June to September plays by
Shakespeare and other authors are presented. There is an internship program for management oriented students. From September through May the theatre presents pre
and post broadway productions. April and
May represent the Student Audience Season, which features a full length and traditional Shakespeare production presented
for students throughout an eight state area.
In the 22 years of the Student Audience Season, over 2,750,000 students have been introduced to Shakespeare.

Little Theatre at Booth Park
1344 East Main
Stratford, CT 06497

Suffield

Suffield Players
1136 Mapleton Avenue
Suffield, CT 06078

Torrington

Amateur Community Theatre
Meadowbrook Lane
Torrington, CT 06790

Torrington Civic Theatre
Prospect Street
Post Office Box 925
Torrington, CT 06790

Washington

Dramalites, Incorporated
Washington, CT 06793
Tel: 203-868-7482
Address Inquiries to: James Kelly, President
Founded in: 1930
Annual Budget: $5,000

Waterbury

Civic Theatre of Waterbury
Post Office Box 85
Waterbury, CT 06702
Tel: 203-756-6666
Address Inquiries to: Ralph E. Aronheim,
    President
Founded in: 1927
Annual Budget: $50,000

Waterford

National Theatre of the Deaf
Little Theatre
305 Great Neck Road
Waterford, CT 06385
Tel: 203-442-0066; 203-443-7406
Address Inquiries to: David Hays, Director
    Delos Mark Scism, Tour Director
Founded in: 1967
Member: U.S. Department of Education;
Annual Budget: $1,000,000
Description: All performances are for general
audiences and are simultaneously spoken
and signed. Performs in schools and provides introductory and advanced workshops
in visual theatre including movement, kinetic imagery, sign and mime and also creative
drama, storytelling and sign language for
the stage. Company has performed in fifty
states, had twelve tours abroad, three films
and numerous national and international
television appearances and appeared at the
1984 Summer Olympic Games.

Watertown

Oakville Players
116 Claxton Avenue
Watertown, CT 06795

West Hartford

Center Players
335 Bloomfield Avenue
West Hartford, CT 06107

Mark Twain Masquers
170 Kingswood
West Hartford, CT 06119
Tel: 203-232-7808
Address Inquiries to: David Young, Artistic
    Director
Founded in: 1932
Member: ATA; ACTA;
Annual Budget: $60,000

West Redding

Redding Players
Route 3 Moutain Road
West Redding, CT 06896

Wethersfield

Community Players
32 Fotte Path Lane
Wethersfield, CT 06109

Wilton

Wilton Playshop
Post Office Box 363
Wilton, CT 06897

Windsor

Windsor Jesters
Post Office Box 7
Windsor, CT 06095

DELAWARE

Centerville

Brandywiners
8725 Kennett Pike
Centerville, DE 19807
Address Inquiries to: W. Peuchen

Claymont

Wilmington Drama League
2309 Wilson Avenue
Claymont, DE 19703
Address Inquiries to: D. Farrar

Dover

Singing Players-Dover
333 Pennsylvania Avenue
Dover, DE 19901
Address Inquiries to: M. Storey

Greenville

Theatre Arts Group
4403 Kennett Pike
Greenville, DE 19807

Millsboro

Possum Point Players
205 Washington Street
Millsboro, DE 19966

Wilmington

Arena Stages
19 Lindsey Place
Wilmington, DE 19809
Address Inquiries to: R. Grass

Christina Cultural Arts
88 East 7th Street
Wilmington, DE 19801
Address Inquiries to: D. Gray

Delaware Dinner Theatre
1014 Delaware Avenue
Wilmington, DE 19806

Lyceum Players
Post Office Box 3659
Wilmington, DE 19807
Address Inquiries to: V. Clarke

Wilmington Black Theatre
313 North Broom Street
Wilmington, DE 19805
Address Inquiries to: J. P. Powell

DISTRICT OF COLUMBIA

Washington

Arena Stage
6th and Maine Avenue SW
Washington, DC 20024
Tel: 202-554-9066
Address Inquiries to: Lee G. Rubenstein,
President
Founded in: 1950
Member: LORT; TCG; NEA; Morris and
Gwendoln Cafritz Foundation,
Incorporated; Ford Foundation; The
Phillip L. Graham Fund; The George
Preston Marshall Foundation; Public
Welfare Foundation; The Shubert
Foundation; Atlantic Richfield;
Annual Budget: $3,000,000
Description: One of the oldest acting ensembles in the United States. Performs new American plays, premieres of important European plays, classics in modern interpretations, new musical works, recent plays that proved unsuccessful in the commercial theatre. Presented in Arena's triplex of modern, intimate playhouses. The resident acting company is supplemented by actors engaged for one or more plays each season.

Back Alley Theatre
1365 Kennedy Street, NW
Washington, DC 20011

Bleeker Street Players
3622 Ordway Street, NW
Washington, DC 20016
Address Inquiries to: R. Kainer

Borrowed Time Productions
Post Office 23330 L'Enfant
Washington, DC 20024

Bridge Street Players
3115 P Street, NW
Washington, DC 20007
Address Inquiries to: J. Fry

British Embassy Players
3100 Massachusetts NW
Washington, DC 20008
Address Inquiries to: S. Johnson

Chevy Chase Players
5601 Connecticut, NW
Washington, DC 20015

Coffee House Players
1658 Columbia Road, NW
Washington, DC 20009

DC Community Theatre
2826 Newton Street, SE
Washington, DC 20018
Address Inquiries to: Evelyn Seralio

Earth Onion Theatre
1531 Q Street NW
Washington, DC 20009

Fillmore Arts Center
35th Street, SO Streets, NW
Washington, DC 20007
Member: CTAA;

Folger Theatre Group
201 East Capitol Street
Washington, DC 20003
Tel: 202-547-3230
Address Inquiries to: Louis W. Scheeder,
President
Founded in: 1970
Member: AEA;

Ford's Theatre Society
511 10th Street
Washington, DC 20004
Tel: 202-638-2941
Address Inquiries to: Frakie Hewitt, Executive
Producer
Founded in: 1968

Foundry Players
1500 16th Street NW
Washington, DC 20036
Address Inquiries to: J. Griffin

Kennedy Center for the Performing Arts
Alliance for Arts Education
Washington, DC 20566
Address Inquiries to: Jack Kukuk

Library Theatre, Incorporated
418 Seventh Street, NW
Washington, DC 20004
Address Inquiries to: Jo Hodgin

National Theatre Of Deaf
Post Office Box 974
Washington, DC 20002

Unitarian Players
2900 Connecticut NW
Washington, DC 20008
Address Inquiries to: P. Talbot

Washington Theatre Club
1101 23rd Street
Washington, DC 20037
Tel: 202-296-2386
Address Inquiries to: Stephen Aaron,
Producer
Founded in: 1963

FLORIDA

Anna Maria

Island Players
Anna Maria, FL 33501
Tel: 813-778-5755
Address Inquiries to: Mrs. Jay J. Uber,
President
Founded in: 1948

Atlantic Beach

Players By the Sea
1135 East Coast Drive
Atlantic Beach, FL 32003

Boca Raton

Boca Raton Theatre
5500 Northwest 2nd Avenue
Boca Raton, FL 33432

Caldwell Playhouse
Post Office Box 277
Boca Raton, FL 33432

Bradenton

Manatee Players
Post Office Box 748
Bradenton, FL 33505

Bradon

The Village Players
Post Office Box 349
Bradon, FL 33511
Tel: 813-677-0666
Address Inquiries to: Eileen Wyland,
President
Founded in: 1970
Annual Budget: $5,000

Brandon

Village Players
Post Office Box 349
Brandon, FL 33511

Cape Coral

Cape Coral Community Theatre
Post Office Box 974
Cape Coral, FL 33904

Clearwater

Little Theatre
302 Seminole Street
Clearwater, FL 33515

Royalty Players
820 Jasmine Way
Clearwater, FL 33516

Clermont

Citrus Actors Theatre
199 Orange Avenue
Clermont, FL 32711

Cocoa

Cocoa Village Players
Post Office Box 1750
Cocoa, FL 32922

Ropps Follies
6500 June Drive

Cocoa, FL 32922

Cocoa Beach

Surfside Playhouse
Post Office Box 53
Cocoa Beach, FL 32931

Coral Gables

Merry Go Round Players
235 Alcazar
Coral Gables, FL 33134

Daytona Beach

Daytona Playhouse
100 Jessamine Boulevard
Daytona Beach, FL 32018
Tel: 904-255-2431; 904-255-2432
Address Inquiries to: Jack Reed, Managing
   Director
   Ann Heflin, President, Board of
   Directors
Founded in: 1947
Member: ATA; STC; FTC;
Annual Budget: $100,000
Description: Primary function is the prod-
uction of six shows per season (Sept 1-June
15). The schedule offers two musicals and
four straight plays.

Deland

Deland Players
Post Office Box 5417
Deland, FL 32720

Shoestring Theatre
Post Offfice Box 554
Deland, FL 32720

Eustis

Bay Street Players
Post Office Box 1406
Eustis, FL 32726

Fort Lauderdale

Fort Lauderdale Children's Theatre,
Incorporated
Post Office Box 4779
Fort Lauderdale, FL 33338
Tel: 305-763-6882
Address Inquiries to: Nancy Yole, Artistic
   Director
   Carol Auger, President
Founded in: 1952
Member: ATA; CTC; SETC; FTC;
Annual Budget: $50,000
Description: A not-for-profit corporation set
up to teach all phases of theatre to youngsters between the ages of 7 and 18. In classes
the students learn some theatre history,
stage movement, acting, motivation, building a character and the personal discipline
necessary in the arts. Under professional
supervision, the youngsters act in several
productions each year, work the front of
house, help build and paint sets and light
shows. Essentially, a children's producing
theatre for children.

Fort Lauderdale Theatre
Post Office Box 4779
Fort Lauderdale, FL 33304

Fort Pierce

Saint Lucie Community Theatre
Post Office Box 1233
Fort Pierce, FL 33450

Ft. Myers Beach

Beach Players
Post Office Box 2336
Ft. Myers Beach, FL 33931

Edison Players
Post Office Box 282
Ft. Myers, FL 33902

Gainesville

Gainesville Little Theatre
Post Office Box 14233
Gainesville, FL 32601

Hippodrome Theatre
1540 Northwest 53rd Avenue
Gainesville, FL 32601

Hippodrome Theatre, In-Education
25 SE 2nd Place
Gainesville, FL 32601

Hollywood

Hollywood Playhouse
Little Theatre of Hollywood
2640 Washington Street
Hollywood, FL 33020
Tel: 305-922-0404; 305-927-4239
Address Inquiries to: Richard Atkinson,
   President
   Marianne Mavrides, Executive Director
Founded in: 1948
Annual Budget: $125,000
Description: A cultural organization dedicated
to bringing live theatre into the community.

Jacksonville

A Company of Players
2532 Park Street
Jacksonville, FL 32204

Alhambra Dinner Theatre
12000 Beach Boulevard
Jacksonville, Fl 32216
Tel: 904-641-1212
Address Inquiries to: W.C. Hartigan,
   Executive Director
Founded in: 1967

Jupiter

Coastal Players
Post Office Box 1641
Jupiter, FL 33458

Kissimmee

Osceola Players
Post Office Box 861
Kissimmee, FL 32741

Lake City

Lake City Community Theatre
Post Office Box 566
Lake City, FL 32055

Lakeland

Lakeland Little Theatre
Post Office Box 1869
Lakeland, FL 22802
Tel: 813-682-8442; 813-686-2565
Founded in: 1952
Member: FTC; ATC;
Annual Budget: $40,000
Description: Mounts five shows a year with a
volunteer staff.

Lake Wales

Black Hills Passion Play of America
Post Office Box 71
Lake Wales, FL 33853

Largo

Largo Recreation Department
Post Office Box 296
Largo, FL 33540

Spanish TR Playhouse
21 Pinda Palm West
Largo, FL 33540

Lehigh Acres

Lehigh Players
Post Office Box 74
Lehigh Acres, FL 33936

Mandarin

Mandarin Players
Post Office Box 164
Mandarin, FL 32064

Miami

Coconut Grove Childrens Theatre
Department of Theatre
3043 Grand Avenue
Post Office Box 331002
Miami, FL 33133
Tel: 305-442-0489
Address Inquiries to: Cornelia Dozier,
   Creative Director
   Kathy Suergiu, Arts Co-ordinator
Founded in: 1973
Member: ATA; CTA; STC; ITHS; BTA;
   CTAA;
Annual Budget: $75,000

Spotlight Players South
8365 186th Street
Miami, FL 33157
Tel: 305-258-9511
Address Inquiries to: Morton Mattaway,
   Chairman
Founded in: 1971
Annual Budget: $10,000

Naples

Naples Players
580 Palm Circle
Naples, FL 33940

New Smyrna Beach

Little Theatre
Post Office Box 14
New Smyrna Beach, FL 32069

North Miami Beach

North Miami Beach Community Theatre
Victory Park Civic Center
North Miami Beach, FL 33161

North Miami Beach Recreation
  Department
17011 NE 19th Avenue
North Miami Beach, FL 33162

North Winter Park

Ballet Royal
1295 Park Avenue
North Winter Park, FL 32789

Ocala

Marion Players
Post Office Box 455
Ocala, FL 32670

Orange Park

Orange Park Community Theatre
Post Office Box 391
Orange Park, FL 32073

Orlando

Central Florida Civic Theatre
1010 Princeton Street
Orlando, FL 32802

Once Upon a Stage
3376 Edgewater
Orlando, FL 32804
Tel: 305-425-8400
Address Inquiries to: Milton Rovine,
  Executive Producer
Founded in: 1972

Pied Piper Players
1009 Plato Avenue
Orlando, FL 32809

Palm Beach

Platform Players
Post Office Box 2543
Palm Beach, FL 33480

Royal Poinciana Plaza
Post Office Box 231
Palm Beach, FL 33480
Tel: 305-833-0705, Executive Office;
  305-659-3310, Box Office
Address Inquiries to: Zev Bufman, Producer
Ron Wicknick, Director of Theater
  Operations
Founded in: Present location since 1957.
Member: AEA;
Description: Under the producership of Mr.
Bufman, the Playhouse is a union theater
presenting the best in pre-Broadway, national, international and bus and truck productions to the community, Florida and the
United States.

Panama City

Kaleidoscope Theatre
Post Office Box 4272
Panama City, FL 32401
Tel: 904-763-6878
Address Inquiries to: Sandy Grissom,
  President
  Lois Carter, Vice President
Founded in: 1972
Annual Budget: $5,000

Pensacola

Pensacola Little Theatre
Post Office Box 415
Pensacola, FL 32502

Pinellas Park

Showboat Dinner Theatre
Post Office Box 516
Pinellas Park, FL 33565

Plantation

Circle of Friends Children's Theatre
428 North West 70th Avenue, #136
Plantation, FL 33317
Address Inquiries to: Dini Sterngold
Member: CTAA;

Pompano Beach

Pompano Players, Incorporated
Post Office Box 2045
Pompano Beach, FL 33061
Tel: 305-946-4646
Address Inquiries to: Don Ridenour,
  President
  Aili Simpson, First Vice President
Founded in: 1959
Member: Florida Theatre Conference;
Annual Budget: $25,000

Port Charlotte

Charlotte Players
Post Office Box 2187
Port Charlotte, FL 32952

Sanibel

Pirate Playhouse
Route 1, Post Office Box 581
Sanibel, FL 33957

Sarasota

Asolo State Theatre
Post Office Drawer East
Sarasota, FL 33578
Tel: 813-355-7115
Address Inquiries to: Richard G. Fallen,
  Executive Director
Founded in: 1960

Florida Studio Theatre
4619 Bay Shore Drive
Sarasota, FL 33580
Tel: 813-355-4096
Address Inquiries to: Jon W. Spelman,
  Artistic Director
  Marty Arden, Managing Director
Founded in: 1973
Annual Budget: $100,000

Golden Apple Dinner Theatre
25 North Pineapple Avenue
Sarasota, FL 33577
Tel: 813-266-2646
Address Inquiries to: Robert Turoff,
  Producer, Director and General
  Manager
Founded in: 33577

The Players
Post Office Box 2277
Sarasota, FL 33578
Tel: 813-958-1577
Address Inquiries to: Frank J. Holroyd,
  President
Founded in: 1930
Annual Budget: $100,000

Satellite Beach

Satellite Youth Player
Post Office Drawer 2479
Satellite Beach, FL 32937

Siesta Key

Actors Theatre
4857 Primrose Path
Siesta Key, FL 33578

St. Petersburg

Palisades Theatre Company
Post Office Box 10717
St. Petersburg, FL 33733

Saint Petersburg Little Theatre
Post Office Box 13175
St. Petersburg, FL 33733

Stuart

Martin City Players
Post Office Box 1894
Stuart, FL 33494

Tallahassee

Tallahassee Little Theatre
Post Office Box 3262
Tallahassee, FL 32303
Tel: 904-224-8474
Address Inquiries to: Charles Wellborn,
  President
  Inge Schwartz, Vice President
Founded in: 1948
Annual Budget: $25,000

Tampa

Bartke's Dinner Theatre
2500 Rocky Point Drive
Tampa, FL 33607
Tel: 813-884-0478
Address Inquiries to: Bill Bartke, Producer
  and General Manager
Founded in: 1968

Spanish Little Theatre
1704 Seventh Avenue
Tampa, FL 33605
Tel: 813-248-3594
Address Inquiries to: Rene J. Gonzalez,
  Founder and Artistic Director
Founded in: 1959

Tampa Community Theatre
Post Office Box 124
Tampa, FL 33601

Tampa Players
Post Office Box 124
Tampa, FL 33601
Tel: 813-877-2684
Address Inquiries to: Bill Lelbach, President
Zenobia Alvarer, Vice President
Founded in: 1925
Member: FTC; SETC;
Annual Budget: $20,000
Description: Critically acclaimed theatre presenting 'Off-Broadway' style comedy.

Titusville

Titusville Playhouse
Post Office Box 1234
Titusville, FL 32780

Venice

Venice Little Theatre
140 West Lampre Avenue
Venice, FL 33595

The Venice Little Theatre
Tampa Avenue
Venice, FL 33595
Tel: 813-488-2419; 813-488-1115
Address Inquiries to: Jack Taylor,Theatre
Administrator
Courtney Sweeting, Technical Director
Founded in: 1950
Annual Budget: $195,000
Description: A 2,200 member community theatre serving the West Coast of Florida from Bradenton to Fort Myers.

Vero Beach

Vero Beach Theatre Guild
Post Office Box 4019
Vero Beach, FL 32960
Tel: 305-562-1621
Address Inquiries to: Helen M. Fricker,
Production Coordinator
Linda Middleton, Secretary
Founded in: 1958

West Palm Beach

Actors Workshop
1451 South Olive
West Palm Beach, FL 33401

Winterhaven

Community Theatre
Post Office Box 1615
Winterhaven, FL 33880

Winter Park

Annie Russell Theatre
Box 37
Rollins College
Winter Park, FL 32789
Tel: 305-646-2501
Address Inquiries to: Steven S. Neilson,
Assistant Professor/Business Manager
Founded in: 1931
Member: ACUCAA; SETC; ATA; Florida
Theatre Conference;

Annual Budget: $100,000

GEORGIA

Albany

Albany Little Theatre
Post Office Box 552
Albany, GA 31702
Tel: 912-439-7141
Address Inquiries to: Woody Pyeatt,
Managing Director
Tom Pattison, President
Founded in: 1933
Member: GTC; SETC; ATA; GCAH;
Annual Budget: $75,000

Georgia Theatre Conference
Post Office Box 1865
Albany, GA 31702

Athens

Georgia Resident Theatre Company
University of Georgia
Athens, GA 30602
Tel: 404-542-2836
Address Inquiries to: August W. Staub,
Chairman
W. Joseph Stell, Production Manager
Founded in: 1937
Member: ATA; SETC; UCTA; NAST; NTC;
Annual Budget: $100,000

Town and Gown Players
Post Office Box 1255
Athens, GA 30601

Atlanta

Academy Theatre
3317 Piedmont Road Northeast
Atlanta, GA 30305
Tel: 404-261-8550
Address Inquiries to: Frank Wittow,
Artistic/Executive Director
Nancy Hager, General Manager
Founded in: 1956

Alliance Theatre Company
15 16th Street North East
Atlanta, GA 30309

Alliance Theatre Company/Atlanta
Children's Theatre
12801 Peachtree Street NE
Atlanta, GA 30309
Tel: 404-898-1132
Address Inquiries to: Bernard Harvard,
Managing Director
Fred Chappell, Artistic Director
Founded in: 1969
Member: AEA;
Annual Budget: $2,334,342
Description: One of the ten top resident theatre companies in the country. Each season, it presents six productions on its mainstage, drawn from current musicals, dramas and comedies as well as the classical theatre. Other programs include a Studio Season of new and experimental works, an active Children's Theatre program, an Acting School,

an annual touring production, and many special events.

Atlanta Children's Theatre
Post Office Box 77324
Atlanta, GA 30357
Tel: 404-892-7607
Address Inquiries to: Charles L. Doughty,
Executive Director
Betty Blondeau, Educational Director
Founded in: 1968
Member: AEA;
Annual Budget: $100,000

Atlanta Civic Center
Post Office Box 11748
Atlanta, GA 30305

Georgia Community for the Arts
225 Peachtree NE
Atlanta, GA 30303

Southern Arts Federation
225 Peachtree Street, #712
Atlanta, GA 30303

Columbus

Columbus Little Theatre
Post Office Box 1622
Columbus, GA 31920

The Readers
6202 Parkway Avenue
Columbus, GA 31904

Springer Theatre Company
Post Office Box 1622
Columbus, GA 31902
Tel: 404-324-1100; 404-324-5717
Founded in: 1961
Annual Budget: $110,000
Description: The state theatre of Georgia.

Dalton

Dalton Creative Arts
Old Firehouse Theatre
Dalton, GA 30702

Dalton Little Theatre, Inc.
700 South Thornton Avenue
Dalton, GA 30702

Gainesville

Gainesville Civic Theatre
Post Office Box 264
Gainesville, GA 30501

Macon

Macon Little Theatre
Post Office Box 7121
Macon, GA 31204
Address Inquiries to: M.P. Hatfield

Marietta

Barn Dinner Theatre
1690 Terrell Mill Road
Marietta, GA 30060

Newnan

Newnan Playmakers
Post Office Box 225
Newnan, GA 30263

Savannah

Little Theatre
1717 Gwinnett Street
Savannah, GA 31404

Thomson

Thomson Players Inc.
Post Office Box 844
Thomson, GA 30824

Waycross

Waycross Little Theatre
Waycross Recreation Center
Waycross, GA 31501

HAWAII

Honolulu

Hawaii Performing Arts Company
2833 East Manda Road
Honolulu, HI 96822-1893
Tel: 808-988-6131; 808-988-7388
Address Inquiries to: Dwight T. Martin,
   Managing Director
   Deborah Hopkinson, Marketing Director
Founded in: 1969
Member: ACTA; HSTC; HADE;
Annual Budget: $140,000
Description: Six mainstage productions per
season (two musicals, two comedies, two
dramas). Previews manually interpreted and
sign language for hearing impaired audi-
ence members. Studio series (experimental)
productions on Monday and Tuesday. First
non-professional company in United States
licensed to produce Bernard Pomerance's
'The Elephant Man'. Volunteer actors, designers, technicians and house management

Hawaii Street Foundation-Culture
250 South King
Honolulu, HI 96813

Honolulu Community Theatre
Makapuu and Aloha Avenue
Honolulu, HI 96816
Tel: 808-734-0274; 808-737-8108
Address Inquiries to: Ms. Robin R. Beasley,
   Manager
Founded in: 1915
Member: ATA;
Annual Budget: $285,000
Description: The second oldest community
theatre in the U.S. performing continuously
all year with seven to eight productions in
their 500 seat theatre. Professional staff of
eight full-time with large volunteer support.

Kailua

Honolulu Community Theatre
616 Uluhala Street
Kailua, HI 96744

Winward Theatre Guild
Post Office Box 624
Kailua, HI 96734
Tel: 808-254-2356
Address Inquiries to: Robert D. Riska,
   Director
Founded in: 1967

IDAHO

Boise

Boise Little Theatre, Incorporated
Post Office Box 2603
Boise, ID 83701
Tel: 208-342-5104
Founded in: 1947

Coeur D'Alene

Coeur D'Alene Community Theatre
Post Office Box 622
Coeur D'Alene, ID 83814
Tel: 208-667-1323
Address Inquiries to: Robert E. Moe, General
   Manager
Founded in: 1964
Annual Budget: $70,000
Description: Members of the company can
gain valuable experience in all aspects of
repertory musical theatre while providing
quality entertainment for eastern Washington and western Montana. Each company
member must be willing to do technical and
other related theatre chores as well as perform. Full-time company members receive
room and board stipends. Those who take
on positions of responsibility, such as directors, stage managers, costume, receive additional monies.

Gooding

Gingnol Puppet Theater
Gooding High School
Route 1
Gooding, ID 83330
Tel: 208-934-4831
Address Inquiries to: Claire Major, Director
Founded in: 1971

Idaho Falls

Community Players Inc.
290 North Bellin Road
Idaho Falls, ID 83401

Nampa

Canyon Players
203 Lake Lowell Avenue
Nampa, ID 83651

Pocatello

Pocatello Community Theatre
Post Office Box 4308
Pocatello, ID 83201

Preston

Preston Community Players
Blocks Men's Store
Preston, ID 83263

Twin Falls

Magic Valley Little Theatre
Post Office Box 3
Twin Falls, ID 83301

Wallace

Valley Community Theatre
Box 866
195 King Street
Wallace, ID 83873
Tel: 208-753-5792
Address Inquiries to: Ray H. Giles, President
Founded in: 1966
Annual Budget: $1,000

ILLINOIS

Alton

Alton Little Theatre
1225 Fairway Drive
Alton, IL 62002

Antioch

Palette Masque Lyre
877 Main Street
Antioch, IL 60002

Arlington Heigh

North West Hospital Players
800 West Central Road
Arlington Heigh, IL 60005

Off-Broadway Players
Post Office Box 3
Arlington Heigh, IL 60006

Arlington Heights

Village Theatre Incorporated
Post Office Box 32
Arlington Heights, IL 60006
Tel: 312-259-3200
Address Inquiries to: Jack R. Behl, President
   Grace Seaman, Vice President
Founded in: 1949
Annual Budget: $1,000

Bloomingdale

Rustic Barn Dinner Theatre
Route 20, Lake Street
Bloomingdale, IL 62220
Address Inquiries to: Kermit Allen, Producer

Bloomington

Community Players
Post Office Box 20
Bloomington, IL 61701

Canton

Fulton Company Playhouse
Post Office Box 344
Canton, IL 61520

Chicago

All Mini Theatre
4315 West 63rd Street
Chicago, IL 60629

Apollo Theatre Center
2540 North Lincoln Avenue
Chicago, IL
Tel: 312-935-6100
Founded in: 1978
Description: The Apollo Theatre Center presents contemporary plays.

Arie Crown
McCormick Place on the Lake
Chicago, IL
Tel: 312-791-6000
Description: Arie Crown Theatre presents musicals, ballets, concerts and operettas featuring celebrities.

The Beverly Players
2153 West 11th Street
Chicago, Il 60643

Black Arts Celebration
1020 South Wabash Avenue 200
Chicago, IL
Tel: 312-663-9580
Description: Black Arts Celebration is an organization with a philosophy of 'education through entertainment'. They offer workshops and classes in drama, dance, music and writing.

Black Ensemble Theatre Corporation
1655 North Burling
Chicago, IL
Tel: 312-751-0263
Description: The Black Ensemble Theatre Corporation strives to enhance the knowledge of black lifestyles and bridge the cultural gap between races. They present educational theatre and theatre for the deaf as well as traditionally staged theater.

The Blackstone Theatre
60 East Balbo Drive
Chicago, IL
Tel: 312-977-1700
Founded in: 1910
Description: The Blackstone Theatre presents many fine theatrical productions.

Body Politic Theatre
2261 North Lincoln Avenue
Chicago, IL
Tel: 312-871-3000
Description: Body Politic Theatre is Chicago's oldest off-Loop theatre. Hits presented in the past include *Lunching, Banjo Dancin'* and *Macbeth.*

Center Youth Theatre
3003 West Touhy
Chicago, IL 60645
Tel: 312-761-9100
Address Inquiries to: Douglas L. Lieberman, Director/Producer
Tillie Hanson, Associate Producer
Founded in: 1962
Annual Budget: $25,000

Chicago City Theatre Company
410 South Michigan
Chicago, IL
Tel: 312-663-3618
Description: Chicago City Theatre Company is a professional resident theatre company.

Chicago Community Theatre
410 South Michigan
Chicago, IL 60605

Child's Theatre Company
2245 North Clifton Avenue
Chicago, IL
Tel: 312-281-3020
Description: Child's Theatre Company presents original plays and adaptations of children's stories. They also offer workshops in creative drama.

Civic Theatre/Civic Opera House
20 North Wacker Drive
Chicago, IL
Tel: 312-346-0270
Description: Civic Theatre/Opera House presents a variety of musical productions throughout the year.

The Commons Theatre Company
6443 North Sheridan Road
Chicago, IL
Tel: 312-465-3030

Drury Lane East McCormick Place
175 East Chestnue
Chicago, IL 60611

Earth Theatre
109 West Hubbard
Chicago, IL 60610

Eugene Field Park Theatre
5100 North Ridgeway
Chicago, IL 60625
Tel: 312-478-1210
Address Inquiries to: Gene Falcetta, Director/Producer
Founded in: 1965

First Chicago Center
Dearborn and Madison
Chicago, IL
Tel: 312-732-4470
Description: First Chicago Center is a theater that presents plays and concerts.

Free Street Theater
59 West Hubbard
Chicago, IL 60610
Tel: 312-822-0460
Address Inquiries to: Patrick Henry, Producer/Artistic Director
Glynn Lowrey, General Manager
Founded in: 1969
Member: AEA;
Annual Budget: $100,000

Goodman Theatre
200 South Columbus Drive
Chicago, IL
Tel: 312-443-3800
Description: Goodman Theatre is Chicago's oldest established producing theatre. They present new works as well as revivals. They

also offer workshops, seminars, lectures and discussions.

Imagination Theater, Incorporated
7535 North Washtenaw Avenue
Chicago, IL 60645
Tel: 312-262-4195
Address Inquiries to: George Crenshaw
Description: A touring educational theatre.

Kenneth Sawyer Goodman Memorial Theatre
200 South Columbus Drive
Chicago, IL 60603
Tel: 312-236-3238
Address Inquiries to: Ken Myers, Executive Director
Founded in: 1925

Kuumba Theatre
218 S. Wabash
Chicago, IL
Tel: 312-269-8061

Lincoln Park Theatre
2021 North Stockton Drive
Chicago, IL 60614

Loop Players
64 East Lake Street, Third Floor
Chicago, IL
Tel: 312-269-8061
Description: Loop Players presents five major productions, a variety show and summer tours annually.

Magic Circle Theatre
615 West Wellington Avenue
Chicago, IL 60657
Tel: 312-929-0542
Address Inquiries to: Guy Giarrizzo, Artistic and Producing Director
Robert Perry, Chairman
Founded in: 1971
Member: Chicago Theatre Alliance;
Annual Budget: $100,000
Description: A children's community theatre.

National Radio Theatre
612 North Michigan Avenue, Suite 316
Chicago, IL 60611
Address Inquiries to: Yuri Rasovsky, Producer
Description: Original radio scripts are accepted at varying fees.

Old Town Players
1718 North Northpark
Chicago, IL 60614
Tel: 312-645-0145
Address Inquiries to: Gertrude Soltker, President
Renata Alleluka, Vice President
Founded in: 1933
Member: ATA;
Annual Budget: $25,000

Ridge Park Players
106th Longwood Avenue
Chicago, IL 60643

The Shubert Theatre
22 West Monroe Street
Chicago, IL
Tel: 312-977-1700

Founded in: 1906
Description: The Shubert Theatre presents Broadway musicals and dramas.

South Side Community Arts Center
3831 South Michigan
Chicago, IL 60653

Theatre First
Merchandise Market
Post Office Box 3545
Chicago, IL 60654

Theatre-Lincoln Park Church
600 West Fullertoon
Chicago, IL 60614

Union Park Drama Department
1501 West Randolph
Chicago, IL 60607

Washington Park Field House
5531 King Drive
Chicago, IL 60637

World Playhouse
410 Michigan Avenue
Chicago, IL
Tel: 312-922-3555
Founded in: 1898
Description: The World Playhouse Theatre presents recitals, concerts, lectures and plays.

Clinton

Community Players
Clinton, IL 61727

Cory

Fox Trails Theatre Company
9008 Cory Road
Cory, IL 60013

Danville

Red Mask Players
James Gill
Danville, IL 61832

DeKalb

Players Magazine
Northern Illinois University
DeKalb, IL 60115
Address Inquiries to: M. Pallen

Stage Coach Players
Post Office Box 511
DeKalb, IL 60115

Des Plaines

Des Plaines Theatre
620 Lee Street
Des Plaines, IL 60016

Divine Word Seminary

Techny Theater
Divine Word Seminary, IL 60062

Downers Grove

Grove Players
Post Office Box 92
Downers Grove, IL 60515

Elgin

Elgin Community Theatre
Post Office Box 208
Elgin, IL 60120

Elk Grove

Masque and Staff
523 Ridgewood
Elk Grove, IL 60007

Elmhurst

Elmhurst Community Theatre
102 Fellows Court
Elmhurst, IL 60126

Elmwood

Elmwood Park Little Theatre
8201 Fullerton
Elmwood, IL 60635

Evanston

Hillel Drama Workshop
1740 Judson
Evanston, IL 60201

Zeta Phi Eta
518 Greenwood Boulevard
Evanston, IL 60201
Address Inquiries to: Gertrude Breen

Flossmor

Parents Without Partners Players
3712 Beach Street
Flossmor, IL 60422
Address Inquiries to: D. Schlay

Franklin Park

Franklin Park Players
9560 Franklin Avenue
Franklin Park, IL 60131

Freeport

Winneshiek Theatre Group
1410 West Stephenson
Freeport, IL 61032

Galena

Galena Art Theatre
c/o Sue Corbett
212 Bouthillier
Galena, IL 61036
Tel: 815-777-1367
Address Inquiries to: Mark Rosenthal, Presidnent
   Lisa Willey, Vice President
Founded in: 1961
Annual Budget: $1000

Galesburg

Prairie Players Civic Theatre
652 West Losey Street
Galesburg, IL 61401

Geneva

Playmakers Incorporated
Post Office Box 372
Geneva, IL 60134

Harvard

Harvard Players
Post Office Box 156
Harvard, IL 60033

Highland Park

Performing Arts Workshop
881 Apple Tree Lane
Highland Park, IL 60035
Address Inquiries to: Eileen Boevers

Hinsdale

Hinsdale Players
Post Office Box 312
Hinsdale, IL 60521
Address Inquiries to: Denny E. Wise, President

Joliet

Curbside Playhouse
427 North Chicago Street
Joliet, IL 60432

Lake Forest

Academy Festival Theatre
Barat College
Lake Forest, IL 60045
Tel: 312-234-6750
Address Inquiries to: William Gardner, Producer
Founded in: 1973

Lake Forest Country Day School Theatre
270 South Western
Lake Forest, IL 60045
Address Inquiries to: Phyllis Mount

Lake Zurich

Country Players
777 White Birch Lane
Lake Zurich, IL 60047

Libertyville

Cabriolet Dinner Theatre
Routes 21 and 63
Libertyville, IL 60048
Tel: 312-367-1313
Address Inquiries to: William Earley, President
Founded in: 1974

Village Players
Post Office Box 426
Libertyville, IL 60048

Lincolnwood

Lincolnwood Theatre
6742 North Kilpatrick
Lincolnwood, IL 60645

Lombard

Discovery Theater
13th and Luther
Lombard, IL 60148
Address Inquiries to: Le Roy Kennel, Director
   Description: A children's theatre.

Lombard Park District
120 West Maple
Lombard, IL 60148

Macomb

Community Theatre
736 Auburn Drive
Macomb, IL 61455

Western Illinois Summer Music Theatre
Department of Theatre
Western Illinois University
Macomb, IL 61235
Tel: 309-762-3631
Address Inquiries to: Gene Kozlowski,
    Coordinator
Founded in: 1972
Annual Budget: $25,000

Mahomet

Mahomet Community Theatre
303 Main Street
Mahomet, IL 61853

Maywood

Coleman Puppet Theatre
1516 Second Avenue South
Maywood, IL 61455
Tel: 312-344-2920
Address Inquiries to: F.R. Coleman, Director
Founded in: 1947

Mendota

Mendota Community Theatre
Post Office Box 304
Mendota, IL 61342
Address Inquiries to: J.W. Richards, Manager
Founded in: 1953
Annual Budget: $10,000

Moline

Playcrafters
Coaltown Road and 49th
Moline, IL 61265
Address Inquiries to: W. McWilliam

Mount Carmel

Civic Theatre
403 Cherry Street
Mount Carmel, IL 62863

Mount Carroll

Timber Lake Playhouse Company
Post Office Box 29
Mount Carroll, IL 61053
Tel: 815-244-8844
Founded in: 1962
Annual Budget: $100,000

Mt. Morris

Blackhawk Players
Community Gym
Mt. Morris, IL 61054

Mt. Morris Community Players
Community Gym
Mt. Morris, IL 61054

Northbrook

Northbrook Civic Theatre
Post Office Box 534
Northbrook, IL 60062
Tel: 312-498-2178

Address Inquiries to: Peggy Kent, President
Frank Miley, Vice President
Founded in: 1968

Northlake

Northlake Community Theatre
55 East North Street
Northlake, IL 60164

Palatine

Village Theatre
Village Inn
1719 Rand
Palatine, IL 60067

Park Ridge

Peeko Puppet Productions
Post Office Box 363
Park Ridge, IL 60068
Tel: 312-823-8778
Address Inquiries to: Billie Logan, Owner
Ellie Reed, Owner
Founded in: 1957

Pekin

Pekin Players
Post Office Box 686
Pekin, IL 61554

Peoria

Corn Stock Theatre
Post Office Box 412
Peoria, IL 61610

Peoria Players
4300 North University
Peoria, IL 61614

Petersburg

Great American People Show
Summer: Box 401; Off Season: Box 2178
Summer: Petersburg; Off Season:
    Champaign, IL Summer: 61675; Off
    Season: 618820
Tel: 217-632-7754
Address Inquiries to: John Ahart, Ph.D.,
    Artistic Director
    Jean Hahn, Treasurer
Founded in: 1976
Member: ITA; NEH; IHC; IAC; IDCCA;
Annual Budget: $125,000
Description: Acclaimed by critics and audiences alike, the award winning, Great American People Show produces historical dramas and documentaries in repertory.

Hollow Theatre
New Salem State Park
Petersburg, IL 62675

Your Obedient Servant Theatre
Post Office Box 401
Petersburg, IL 62675

Pontiac

Vermillion Players
Pontiac, IL 61764

Princeton

Burlesque Company Little Theatre
Princeton, IL 61356

Quincy

Progressive Playhouse
1515 Jersey Street
Quincy, IL 62301

Quincy Community Little Theatre
Post Office Box 554
Quincy, IL 62301

River Forest

Tempo Players
7900 West Division Street
River Forest, IL 60305

Rockford

New American Theatre
117 South Wyman Street
Rockford, IL 61108
Tel: 815-963-9454
Address Inquiries to: J.R. Sullivan, Artistic
    Director
    Patricia Heaselden, Business Manager
Founded in: 1972
Annual Budget: $100,000

Skokie

Skokie Players
3808 Fargo Avenue
Skokie, IL 60076

Summit

Candelight Dinner Playhouse
5620 South Harlem Avenue
Summit, IL 60501
Tel: 312-735-7400
Address Inquiries to: William Pullins,
    President

Wauconda

Wauconda Players
350 Larkdale
Wauconda, IL 60084

Waukegan

Waukegan Community Theatre
Post Office Box 97
Waukegan, IL 60085

West Dundee

Chateau Louise Resort Theatre
West Dundee, IL 60118

Western Springs

Theatre of Western Springs
Hampton at Hillgrove, Box 29
Western Springs, IL 60558
Tel: 312-246-4043
Address Inquiries to: Val Bettin, Artistic
    Director
    Julie Mills, Chairperson
Founded in: 1929
Member: ATA; ACTA;
Annual Budget: $100,000

Woodstock

Woodstock Opera House
Post Office Box 175
Woodstock, IL 60098

Zion

Zion Passion Play
Dowie Memorial Drive
Zion, IL 60099
Tel: 312-746-2221
Address Inquiries to: Roger Otterson,
  President
Founded in: 1935
Annual Budget: $25,000

INDIANA

Alexandria

Alexandria Community Theatre
Route 1
Post Office Box 341
Alexandria, IN 46001
Tel: 317-724-2927
Address Inquiries to: James R. Moore,
  Chairman
  Judy Donahue, Vice Chairperson
Founded in: 1969
Annual Budget: $5,000

Anderson

Anderson Civic Theatre
2414 South Jackson Street
Anderson, IN 46014

Auburn

Auburn Community Theatre
Auburn, IN 46706
Address Inquiries to: J. Outland

Bedford

Little Theatre
1510 2nd Street
Bedford, IN 47421

Bristol

Elkhart Civic Theatre
Bristol House
Post Office Box 252
Bristol, IN 46507

Clarksville

Little Theatre
301 East Montgomery Avenue
Clarksville, IN 47131

Evansville

Civic Theatre
Post Office Box 804
Evansville, IN 47701

Evansville Civic Theatre
717 North Fulton
Evansville, IN 47710
Tel: 812-423-2616
Address Inquiries to: Dick Engbers, President
Founded in: 1924
Annual Budget: $25,000

Old Courthouse Community Theatre
Old Couthouse
Evansville, IN 47708
Founded in: 1971
Annual Budget: $1,000

Repertory People of Evansville
Old Courthouse
Evansville, IN 47708
Tel: 812-423-2060
Address Inquiries to: Thomas E. Angermeier,
  President
  Randal K. Boarman, Vice President
Founded in: 1975
Annual Budget: $10,000

Fort Wayne

Arena Theatre
816 Ewing Street
Fort Wayne, IN 46802
Tel: 219-742-0135
Address Inquiries to: Robert E. Behr,
  President
  Wayne Schaltenbrand, Vice President
Founded in: 1974

Arena Theatre Incorporated
826 Ewing Street
Fort Wayne, IN 46802

First Presbyterian Theatre
300 West Wayne Webster
Fort Wayne, IN 46802

Fort Wayne Civic Theatre
303 East Main Street
Fort Wayne, IN 46802
Address Inquiries to: Richard Casey

Theatre Workshop
Park Board
1 East Main Street
Fort Wayne, IN 46802
Tel: 219-423-7015
Address Inquiries to: Robert E. Behr,
  Recreation Supervisor
Founded in: 1964

Youtheatre
303 East Main Street
Fort Wayne, IN 46802
Address Inquiries to: Harvey Cocks

Gary

The Company Players
3729 Broadway
Gary, IN 46409
Address Inquiries to: Bryan Fonseca

Greenfield

Haasier Heartland Repertory Theatre
Post Office Box 25
Greenfield, IN 46140

Greensburg

Tree County Players
321 North Franklin
Greensburg, IN 47240
Address Inquiries to: B. Barne

Indianapolis

Atheneum Players
5044 East 10th Street
Indianapolis, IN 46201

Bluff Players
8321 Palmetto Lane
Indianapolis, IN 46217
Address Inquiries to: G. Kruggel

Booth Tarkington Civic Theatre
1200 West 38th Street
Indianapolis, IN 46322
Address Inquiries to: Ron Rucker

Footlight Musicals
Box 68
1847 North Alabama
Indianapolis, IN 46202

Mud Creek Players
9550 East 86th Street
Indianapolis, IN 46256

Starlight Musical Incorporated
Post Office Box 40517
Indianapolis, IN 46240
Tel: 317-926-1581
Founded in: 1945
Annual Budget: $1,000,000
Description: A summer outdoor theatre, cov-
ered with proscenium stage, operates six
weeks in July and August. It is a full Equity
company using 'name' entertainers in both
Broadway and variety shows.

Lafayette

Civic Theatre
20 Mayberry Court
Lafayette, IN 47904

New Castle

First Nighters
Post Office Box 23
New Castle, IN 47362

Noblesville

Hamilton Company Players
R S Street Road 238 East
Noblesville, IN 46060

Peru

Olde Olsen Memorial Theatre
Post Office Box 580
Peru, IN 46970

Richmond

Richmond Civic Theatre
1003 East Main
Richmond, IN 47374

Tell City

Tell City Community Players
City Hall
Tell City, IN 47586

Terre Haute

Community Theatre
25th and Washington
Terre Haute, IN 47803

Happiness Bag Players
1519 South 7th Street
Terre Haute, IN 47802
Address Inquiries to: Sydney Stowe

Valparaiso

Community Theatre
1907 Berkely Drive
Valparaiso, IN 46383

IOWA

Ames

Actors Incorporated
318 ½ Main Street
Ames, IA 50010
Address Inquiries to: W.E. Wagner

Bettendorf

Bettendorf Community Theatre
2204 Grant Street
Bettendorf, IA 52722

Britt

Hancock Company Little Theatre
581 Center Street
Britt, IA 50423

Burlington

Players Workshop
1431 Grove Street
Burlington, IA 52601

Carroll

Carroll Community Theatre
1748 Quinit Avenue
Carroll, IA 51401
Address Inquiries to: A. Minnich

Cedar Rapids

Children's Theatre
Post Office Box 1583
Cedar Rapids, IA 52403
Member: CTAA;

Community Theatre
1124 3rd Street
Cedar Rapids, IA 52401

Charles City

The Story Point
Post Office Box 142
Charles City, IA 50616

Cherokee

Cherokee Community Theatre
Post Office Box 702
Cherokee, IA 51012

Clinton

Clinton Community Theatre
Post Office Box 286
Clinton, IA 52732

Conrad

Whistle Stop Players
Post Office Box 59
Conrad, IA 50621

Council Bluffs

Chanticleer Incorporated
Post Office Box 304
Council Bluffs, IA 51501

Des Moines

Drama Workshop
Bell Avenue and Casady Drive
Des Moines, IA 56315
Address Inquiries to: J. Thompson

Dubuque

The Barn Community Theatre
Flora Park
Dubuque, IA 52001

Durant

Tri-County Playcast
Post Office Box 881
Durant, IA 52747

Eldora

Eldora Community Theatre
Post Office Box 284
Eldora, IA 50627

Elkader

Opera House Players
Post Office Box 421
Elkader, IA 52043

Forest City

The Brick Street Theatre Company
506 South Clark
Forest City, IA 50436

Fort Dodge

Hawkeye Community Theatre
Post Office Box 32
Fort Dodge, IA 50501

Grinnell

Grinnell Community Theatre
Post Office Box 110
Grinnell, IA 50112

Humboldt

Castle Theatre Incorporated
108-3rd Street
Humboldt, IA 50548

Iowa City

Iowa City Community Theatre
Post Office Box 827
Iowa City, IA 52240

Lemars

Lemars Community Theatre
Post Office Box 45
Lemars, IA 51031

Maquoketa

Peace Pipe Players
Route 1
Maquoketa, IA 52060

Marshalltown

Community Theatre/Hoelscher
1503 South 2nd Street
Marshalltown, IA 50158

Mason City

Community Theatre
Post Office Box 549
Mason City, IA 50401

Mechanicsville

Black Masque Players
Post Office Box 49
Mechanicsville, IA 52306

Muscatine

Muscatine Masquers
Post Office Box 502
Muscatine, IA 52761

Newton

Community Theatre
Post Office Box 195
Newton, IA 50208

Red Oak

Red Oak Junior High
308 Corning Street
Red Oak, IA 51566

Shenandoah

South West Iowa Theatre Group
Post Office Box 212
Shenandoah, IA 51601

Sibley

Off-Off Broadway
823 3rd Avenue
Sibley, IA 51249

Sioux City

Sioux City Community Theatre
Post Offfice Box 512
Sioux City, IA 51102

Spirit Lake

Okoboji Summer Theatre
Post Office Box 391
Spirit Lake, IA 51360

Storm Lake

Buena Vista Community Theatre
110 West 2nd Street
Storm Lake, IA 50588
Address Inquiries to: M. Kestel

Waterloo

Black Hawk Children's Theatre
Box 4261
Waterloo, IA 50704

Waterloo Community Playhouse
Post Office Box 433
Waterloo, IA 50704

Tel: 319-235-0367

Address Inquiries to: Charles Stilwill

Description: The Waterloo Community Players is an active community theatre with its own *Callboard* newsletter and an active subscription program.

Waukon

Allamakee Community Players
Waukon, IA 52172

Williamsburg

Lotor Players
Post Office Box 153
Williamsburg, IA 52361

Winterset

Apple Tree Players
Winterset, IA 50273

KANSAS

Abilene

Abilene Community Theatre
1000 West 1st Street, City Building
Abilene, KS 67140

Atchison

Atchison Community Theatre
Post Office Box 175
Atchison, KS 66002
Address Inquiries to: J. Dubois

Augusta

Augusta Community Theatre
Post Office Box 175
Augusta, KS 67010
Address Inquiries to: J. Sandfort

Coffeyville

Coffeyville Community Theatre
1505 Highland
Coffeyville, KS 67337
Address Inquiries to: J. Veron

Concordia

Brown Grand Community Theatre
333 East 16th Street
Concordia, KS 66901
Address Inquiries to: K. Church

Council Grove

Otitiani Study Club
Post Office Box 145
Council Grove, KS 66846
Address Inquiries to: M. Keyser

Dodge City

Way Off-Broadway Players
Post Office Box 1284
Dodge City, KS 67801
Address Inquiries to: M. Barnes

Fort Scott

Fort Scott Community Theatre
2108 South Horton
Fort Scott, KS 66701
Address Inquiries to: R. Peterson

Fredonia

Fredonia Players
Post Office Box 355
Fredonia, KS 66736

Garden City

Garden City Community Theatre
c/o Garden City High School
Garden City, KS 67846

Great Bend

Great Bend Civic Theatre
1019 Morphy
Great Bend, KS 67530
Address Inquiries to: A. Rebein

Hays

Short Grass Players
204 West 7th Street
Hays, KS 67601
Address Inquiries to: J. Phillip

Hutchinson

Hutchinson Community Theatre
108 East Sherman
Hutchinson, KS 67501

Junction City

Little Theatre
Post Office Box 305
Junction City, KS 66441
Address Inquiries to: D. Werts

Kingman

Prairie Players
241 Avenue H West
Kingman, KS 67068
Address Inquiries to: B. Giertz

Lawrence

Lawrence Community Theatre
Post Office Box 3205
Lawrence, KS 66044
Address Inquiries to: M. Doveton

Seem-To-Be-Players
630 Elm
Lawrence, KS 66044
Address Inquiries to: Richard Averill

Leawood

Tomahawk Drama Service League
10311 High Drive
Leawood, KS 66206

Liberal

Liberal Community Theatre
510 North Jordan
Liberal, KS 67901
Address Inquiries to: D. Spady

Lyons

Rice City Community Theatre
205 South Pioneer
Lyons, KS 67554

Madison

Verdigris Valley Players
Madison, KS 66860
Address Inquiries to: W. B. Crone

Manhattan

Manhattan Community Theatre
Post Office Box 1142
Manhattan, KS 66502
Address Inquiries to: R. Sanline

Newton

Newton Community Theatre
616 Park Road
Newton, KS 67114
Address Inquiries to: M. Smith

Olathe

Olathe Community Theatre
Post Office Box 144
Olathe, KS 66061

Paola

Paola Civic Theatre
609 East Wea
Paola, KS 66071
Address Inquiries to: L. Morterson

Pittsburg

Pittsburg Community Theatre
Post Office Box 236
Pittsburg, KS 66762

Quinter

Prairie Theatre
Rural Route 1
Quinter, KS 67752
Address Inquiries to: Mrs. D.A. Crist

Salina

Salina Community Theatre
228 ½ East Republic
Salina, KS 66604
Address Inquiries to: L. Borden

Shawnee Mission

The Barn Players
5164 Merriam Drive
Shawnee Mission, KS 66203

Community Children's Theatre of Kansas
6431 Wenonga
Shawnee Mission, KS 66203
Address Inquiries to: John B. Keller
Member: CTAA;

Topeka

Adult Community Theatre
215 East 7th Street
Topeka, KS 66603

Topeka Civic Theatre
Post Oofice Box 893
Topeka, KS 66601

Address Inquiries to: D. Bachmann

Valley Center

Valley Center Players
809 North Colby
Valley Center, KS 67147
Address Inquiries to: D. Dellinger

Vassar

Vassar Playhouse
Route 1
Vassar, KS 66543

Wellington

Wellington Community Theatre
Post Office Box 573
Wellington, KS 67152
Address Inquiries to: D. Pressgrove

Wichita

The Crown Players
1407 North Armour
Wichita, KS 67026
Address Inquiries to: T. Morris

Wichita Community Theatre
110 South Battin
Wichita, KS 67218
Address Inquiries to: M. J. Teall

KENTUCKY

Bardstown

The Stephen Foster Story
Post Office Box D
Bardstown, KY 40004

Berea

Wilderness Road
College Post Box 2355
Berea College
Berea, KY 40404

Bowling Green

Bowling Green Community Theatre
Covington Woods Park
Bowling Green, KY 42101

Carcassonne

The Little Shepherd of Kingdom Come
Post Office Box 7
Carcassonne, KY 41806

Fort Campbell

Fort Campbell Community Theatre
42nd and Indiana Avenue
Fort Campbell, KY 42223

Fulton

Fulton Community Theatre
304 5th Street
Fulton, KY 42041

Harrodsburg

The Legend of Daniel Boone
Post Office Box 365
Harrodsburg, KY 40330
Address Inquiries to: John C. Allison, General

Manager

Lexington

Dixie Theatre
422 Hart Road
Lexington, KY 40502

Lexington Children's Theatre
Division of the Living Arts and Science
Center
Post Office Box 11833
Lexington, KY 40512
Tel: 606-252-1381
Address Inquiries to: Mrs. William Rogers,
President
Doreen Heard, Artistic Director
Founded in: 1939
Member: ATA; CTAA;
Annual Budget: $50,000

Lexington Church Theatre
311 East Main Street
Lexington, KY 40507

Musical Theatre Society
2235 Bahama Drive
Lexington, KY 40505

Studio Players Incorporated
1008 Gainesway Drive
Lexington, KY 40501
Address Inquiries to: E. Krislov

Louisville

Actors Theatre of Louisville, Incorporated
316-320 West Main Street
Louisville, KY 40202
Tel: 502-584-1265
Address Inquiries to: Mrs. Cyrus L.
Mackinnon, President
Founded in: 1964
Member: LORT;
Description: One of the most renowned of the
Regional theatres, it has introduced many
new playwrights to Broadway. The annual
Actor's Theatre of Louisville Playwright's
festival draws theatre goers and critics from
around the country.

Blue Apple Production
Box 4261
Louisville, KY 40204

Louisville Children's Theatre
St. Francis Center
2117 Payne Street
Louisville, KY 40206

Louisville Youth Theatre
Post Office Box 8115
Louisville, KY 40208

Maysville

Maysville Players
116 North 2nd Street
Maysville, KY 41056
Tel: 606-564-3666
Address Inquiries to: Louise O. Bellows,
President
Bill Marshall, Vice President
Founded in: 1961
Annual Budget: $50,000

Paducah

Market House Theatre
Paducah, KY 42001
Address Inquiries to: Paul Meier

Pineville

The Book of Job
Pineville, KY 40977
Tel: 606-337-3800
Address Inquiries to: Preston Slusher,
General Manager
Orlin Corey, Director
Founded in: 1959

Radcliff

Hardin Company Playhouse
952 Sunset Drive
Radcliff, KY 40160

Russellville

Logan Company Community Theatre
345 South Main Street
Russellville, KY 42276

Somerset

Cumberland Players
207 Cherokee
Somerset, KY 42501

Whitesburg

Roadside Theatre
Post Office Box 743
Whitesburg, KY 41858

LOUISIANA

Alexandria

Cenla Community Theatre
Post Office Box 225
Alexandria, LA 71301

Baton Rouge

Baton Rouge Little Theatre
Post Office Box 1943
Baton Rouge, LA 70821
Tel: 504-924-6496
Address Inquiries to: Lee Edward, Manager
Founded in: 1946
Member: ACTA;
Annual Budget: $100,000

Bossier City

Gaslite Players
1807 Bayou Circle
Bossier City, LA 71010
Address Inquiries to: N. Abraham

Covington

Playmakers Incorporated
1018 West 18th Avenue
Post Office Box 372
Covington, LA Post Office Box 372

Eunice

Players Theatre Incorporated
Post Office Box 909
Eunice, LA 70535
Address Inquiries to: Doris Stagg, President
John L. Uzzo, Vice President
Annual Budget: $5,000

Fort Polk

Fort Polk Theatre Guild
Building 1801
Fort Polk, LA 71459
Member: CTAA;

Lake Charles

Artistic Civic Theatre
518 Ford Street
Lake Charles, LA 70601

Natchitoches

Louisiana Cavalier
Post Office Box 1714
Natchitoches, LA 71457

New Orleans

Dashiki Theatre
3564 Virgil Boulevard
New Orleans, LA 70113
Address Inquiries to: T. Gilliam

Free Southern Theatre
1240 Dryodes Street
New Orleans, LA 70133
Address Inquiries to: J. Oneil

Gallery Center Theatre
1500 Canal
New Orleans, LA 70140

Le Petit Theatre
616 Saint Peter Street
New Orleans, LA 70116

Shreveport

Little Theatre
812 Margaret Place
Shreveport, LA 71101

MAINE

Augusta

Augusta Players
Augusta Mental Health Institute
Augusta, ME 04330
Address Inquiries to: Mrs. Betty Sambrook

Maine State Community On Arts
146 State Street
Augusta, ME 04330

Bangor

Bangor Civic Theatre
188 Broadway
Bangor, ME 04401

Hebrew Community Drama
38 Somerset Street
Bangor, ME 04401

Bath

Bath Civic Theatre
Bath, ME 14530
Address Inquiries to: J. Patrick Montgomery

Berwick

Beaver Dam Little Theatre
Berwick, ME 03901

Boothbay Harbor

Reg Little Theatre
Boothbay Harbor, ME 04538

Bridgton

Homestead Players, Bridgton Community
  Theatre
39 North High Street
Bridgton, ME 04009

Bristol

Bristol Footlighters
Bristol, ME 04539

Brunswick

Brunswick Music Theatre/Coastal Theatre
  Workshop
Post Office Box 656
Brunswick, ME 04011
Tel: 207-725-8769; 207-882-7607
Address Inquiries to: Victoria Crandall,
  Executive and Artistic Director
  Bennett Katz; President, Board of
  Directors, CTW
Founded in: Coastal Theatre Workshop,
  1978; Brunswick Music Theatre,
Member: AEA; MSCAH; Time, Inc.;
Annual Budget: $400,000
Description: A professional summer stock
theatre which runs an eleven week season of
five musicals from June to September.

Brunswick Workshop Theatre
5 Bank Street
Brunswick, ME 04011

Pine Tree Players
Naval Air Station
Brunswick, ME 04011

Camden

Camden Civic Theatre
Post Office Box 362
Camden, ME 04843

Cape Elizabeth

Ram Island Art Center
Ram Island Farm
Cape Elizabeth, ME 04107

Damariscotta

Area Recreation Hall
Post Office Box 501
Damariscotta, ME 04543

Lewiston

Community Center
125 Webster Street
Lewiston, ME 04240

Millinocket

Millinocket Community Theatre
188 Highland Avenue
Millinocket, ME 04462

Newcastle

Damcastle Players
Newcastle, ME 04553

Portland

Portland Players
420 Cottage Road
Portland, ME 04106

Searsport

Ebbtide Players
East Maine Street
Searsport, ME 04974

Waterville

Waterville Players
Augusta Road
Waterville, ME 04901
Address Inquiries to: Mrs. C. B. Loubier

Waterville Playshop
Post Office Box 75
Waterville, ME 43566

Wilton

Sandy River Players
Wilton, ME 04294

MARYLAND

Accokeek

Accokeek Theatre Workshop
Route 1
Apple Valley
Accokeek, MD 20607
Address Inquiries to: A. Lawless

Adelphi

The Adelphians
9539 Riggs Road
Post Office Box 748
Adelphi, MD 20783
Address Inquiries to: J. Robertson

Annapolis

Colonial Players
108 East Street
Annapolis, MD 21401
Address Inquiries to: J. Williams

Baltimore

Arena Players
406 Orchard Street
Baltimore, MD 21201

Liberty Community Theatre
7909 Brookford Circle
Baltimore, MD 21208
Address Inquiries to: A. East Clayman

Mid-Towne Players
20th and St. Paul Streets
Baltimore, MD 21218

Saint Mathews Players
Loch Raven Boulevard
Baltimore, MD 21239

Spotlighters Theatre
817 Saint Paul Street
Baltimore, MD 21202

Urban Services Cultural Arts Project
1400 Orleans Street
Baltimore, MD 21231
Address Inquiries to: Norman Ross

Bel Air

Edwin Booth Theatre
401 Thomas Run Road
Bel Air, MD 21014

Susque Festival Theatre
401 Thomas Run Road
Bel Air, MD 21014
Address Inquiries to: J. Lemlich

Bethesda

Cedar Lane Stage
9601 Cedar Lane
Bethesda, MD 20014

Free Association
8707 Cranbrook Court
Bethesda, MD 20817
Tel: 301-365-0037
Address Inquiries to: Margaret Ramsey,
     Artistic Director
Founded in: 1974
Member: DTW;
Annual Budget: $5,000
Description: A group of dancers, actors and
musicians representing a broad spectrum of
training in dance and theatre. Their im-
provisations flow between theatre and
dance, making an amalgamated form some-
where between dance, theatre and imaginis-
tic performance. Free Association is available for residencies and workshops for
theatre, voice and movement.

G Spelvin Experience Theatre
4930 Cordell Avenue
Bethesda, MD 20014

Maryland Childrens' Theatre
4930 Cordell Avenue
Bethesda, MD 20814
Tel: 301-652-7999; 301-654-9820
Address Inquiries to: Ralph Tabakin, Director
     M.H. Dnrerr, Prnducer
Founded in: 1970
Member: AFTRA; SAG; ATA; AEA;
     NATAS; UCTA; AFL/CIO; MSPA;
     ACHTA; WHATA;
Description: Write, produce, and perform theatrical productions involving youth and tee-
nagers in order to advance the education
and comprehension of the young. They also
assist theatrical producers and educational
organizations on a fee basis in scripting, editing, and producing educational curricula
guide-lines and tour productions includes
live staging, film, and television.

Montgomery Players
7723 Groton Road
Bethesda, MD 20014
Address Inquiries to: A. Kullen

Potomac Playhouse
4949 Battery Lane
Bethesda, MD 20014
Address Inquiries to: A. Lynn

Bowie

Belair Community Theatre
Post Office Box 604
Bowie, MD 20715

Musicomedy Productions
2211 Hindle
Bowie, MD 20715
Address Inquiries to: P. Fischer

Camp Springs

Suratts Stage Door
6609 Napoli Road
Camp Springs, MD 20031

Cheverly

Cheverly Community Theatre
6401 Forest Road
Cheverly, MD 20785

Chevy Chase

Library Theatre
6805 Florida Street
Chevy Chase, MD 20015
Address Inquiries to: C. Adler

Clinton

PR George Little Theatre
5906 Bedford Lane
Clinton, MD 20735
Address Inquiries to: S. Delaurier

Columbia

Columbia Community Theatre
Other Barn/Oakland ML
Columbia, MD 21045

Shoestring Players
10622 Fable Row
Columbia, MD 21044

Theatre Upstairs
10622 Fable Row
Columbia, MD 21044
Address Inquiries to: P. Carlson

Cumberland

South Lee Street Players
14 South Lee Street
Cumberland, MD 21502

Trojan Playhouse
Willowbrook Road
Cumberland, MD 21502
Address Inquiries to: F. Pfeiffer

Dundalk

Dundalk Community Theatre
7200 Sollers Point Road
Dundalk, MD 21222

Essex

Cockpit In Court
7201 Rossville Boulevard
Essex, MD 21221

Frederick

Frederick Town Players
501 Prospect Boulevard
Frederick, MD 21701
Address Inquiries to: William E. Main

Gaithersburg

Montgomery Players
Post Office Box 812
Gaithersburg, MD 20760

Rockville Music Theatre
56 Nina Court
Gaithersburg, MD 20760
Address Inquiries to: T. Reed

Glen Echo

Adventure Theatre
Glen Echo Park
Glen Echo, MD 20768

Greenbelt

MAD Productions
Code 63 Goddard SFC
Greenbelt, MD 20771
Address Inquiries to: S. Martin

Hyattsville

Chris-Mar Players
6914 Freeport Street
Hyattsville, MD 20784
Address Inquiries to: D. Grimes

Publick Playhouse
5445 Landover Road
Hyattsville, MD 20784
Address Inquiries to: D. Herbert

Kansas City

Goppert Theatre
11901 Wornall Road
Kansas City, MD 64145
Tel: 816-942-8400
Address Inquiries to: Dr. William J. Louis,
     Manager/Chairman
Founded in: 1974
Member: ACTA;
Annual Budget: $22,000
Description: Dedicated to the training of per-
forming and visual arts students in a liberal
arts setting while being responsive to the
needs of the professional areas.

Laurel

Gingerbread Players
422 Montgomery Street
Laurel, MD 20810
Address Inquiries to: J. Nigh

Oakland

Garrett City Playhouse
Box 304
Oakland, MD 21250

Randallstown

Mattew Players
East McChurch Street
Randallstown, MD 21133
Address Inquiries to: Albert Levy

Reistertown

Reister Community Theatre
Post Office Box 215
Reistertown, MD 21136

Riverdale

Prince George Playhouse
6600 Kenilworth Avenue
Riverdale, MD 20840
Address Inquiries to: D. Herbert

Rockville

Chelm Players
6125 Montrose Road
Rockville, MD 20852
Address Inquiries to: K. Hopkins

Holy Cross Players
801 Rockville Pike, #405
Rockville, MD 20852
Address Inquiries to: Mrs. Betty Keate

Parkland Community Theatre
4610 West Frankfort Drive
Rockville, MD 20853
Address Inquiries to: R. Moock

Rockville Little Theatre
208 Upton Street
Rockville, MD 20850
Address Inquiries to: J. Moser

Triangle Theatre Company
13915 Flint Rock Road
Rockville, MD 20853
Address Inquiries to: R. Sage

Silver Spring

Bel Pre Players
2605 Baywood Court
Silver Spring, MD 20906
Address Inquiries to: L. Hickman

Burtonsville Players
3413 Kilkenny Street
Silver Spring, MD 20904
Address Inquiries to: A. Sperling

Calverton Players
3413 Kilkenny Street
Silver Spring, MD 20904
Address Inquiries to: A. Sperling

Glenmont Players
3608 Isabil Street
Silver Spring, MD 20906
Address Inquiries to: S. Stewart

Montgomery Savoyards
403 Lexington Drive
Silver Spring, MD 20901
Address Inquiries to: Hanlon

Sandy Spring Theatre Group
16029 Chester Mill
Silver Spring, MD 20906
Address Inquiries to: S.W. Parrish

Silver Spring Stage
10145 Colesville Road
Silver Spring, MD 20901

Sykesville

Mechanicsville Repertory Theatre
7349 Springfield Avenue
Sykesville, MD 21784
Address Inquiries to: F. Edwards

Takoma Park

Seasoned Players
7017 16th Avenue
Takoma Park, MD 20012
Address Inquiries to: H. Blutstein

Upper Marlboro

Marlboro Masquers
9122 Old Burton Circle
Upper Marlboro, MD 20870
Address Inquiries to: E. Cummings

Westminster

The Carroll Players
Church of the Ascension
Westminster, MD 21157

MASSACHUSETTS

Abington

Abington Little Theatre
Post Office Box 71
Abington, MA 02351

Action

Little Theatre Workshop
5 Orchard
Action, MA 01720

Arlington

Friends of Drama
22 Academy Street
Arlington, MA 02174

Auburndale

Club Players
283 Melrose Street
Auburndale, MA 02166

Barnstable

Comedy Club
Barnstable, MA 02630

Bedford

Bedford Players
4 Rodney Road
Bedford, MA 01730
Tel: 617-275-8147
Address Inquiries to: William Moonan,
  President
Founded in: 1970

Boston

Boston Foundation
1 City Hall
Boston, MA 02201

The Charles Playhouse
76 Warrenton Street
Boston, MA 02116

Crosswalk Theatre for Children
300 Congress Street
Boston, MA 02210
Member: CTAA;

Kenyon Martin Mime Troupe-National
  Mime Theatre
419 Boylston, Suite 510
Boston, MA 02116
Tel: 617-353-1440
Address Inquiries to: Fran McCarthy,
  Manager
Founded in: 1965
Annual Budget: $25,000

OM Theatre Workshop Boston
Boston Center for the Arts
557 Tremont Street
Boston, MA 02116
Tel: 617-482- 4778
Founded in: 1967

Pilgrims Theatre Company
645 Boylston Street
Boston, MA 02116

Pocket Mime Theatre
Post Office Box 269
Boston, MA 02117
Tel: 617-266-2770
Address Inquiries to: Jeffrey Bernstein,
  President
  Douglas R. Haley, General Manager
Founded in: 1970
Annual Budget: $100,000

Stage 1 Theatre Laboratory
551 Tremont Street
Boston, MA 02116
Tel: 617-426-8492
Address Inquiries to: Kaleel Sakakeeny,
  Artistic Director
Founded in: 1967

Theatre Company of Boston
551 Tremont Street
Boston, MA 02116
Tel: 617-423-7193
Founded in: 1963

Theatre Two and Theatre Two Workshops
376 Boyleston
Boston, MA 02116
Tel: 617-864-1700
Address Inquiries to: Joe Polinsky, President
Charles Koro, Vice President
Founded in: 1970
Annual Budget: $10,000

Brighton

Circle Players
50 Sutherland Road
Brighton, MA 02135

Cambridge

Brattle Street Players
42 Brattle Street
Cambridge, MA 02138

Cambridge Ensemble
1151 Massachusetts Avenue
Cambridge, MA 02138
Tel: 617-876-2544
Address Inquiries to: Barbara Bregstein,
     President
Founded in: 1973
Annual Budget: $50,000

Caravan Theatre
1555 Masachusetts Avenue
Cambridge, MA 02138
Tel: 617-868-8520
Address Inquiries to: Bobbi Ausubel,
     President
     Stan Edelson, Vice President
Founded in: 1965
Annual Budget: $50,000

Harvard Summer Repertory Theatre
Loeb Drama Center
64 Brattle Street
Cambridge, MA 02138
Tel: 617-495-2668
Address Inquiries to: George Hamlin,
     Producing Director
Founded in: 1961
Member: AEA; URTA;
Description: Produces three or four profes-
sional staged dramas each summer season.
An AEA company, the cast includes known
and established performers as well as some
apprentices and students. The Loeb Drama
Center is a fully staffed and equipped theatre
on the campus of Harvard University.

New England Foundation For The Arts
15 Mount Auburn Street
Cambridge, MA 02138

The People's Theatre
1253 Cambridge Street
Cambridge, MA 02138
Tel: 617-547-4930
Address Inquiries to: James Wiliams,
     Program Coordinator
     Chris Connaire, President
Founded in: 1964
Annual Budget: $25,000

Proposition Workshop
245 Hampshire Street
Cambridge, MA 02139
Tel: 617-661-1776
Address Inquiries to: Allan Albert, President
Founded in: 1968
Annual Budget: $100,000

Silk Purse Players
Acorn Park
Cambridge, MA 02140

Canton

Canton Community Club
627 Pleasant Street
Canton, MA 02021

Canton Informal Players
54 Lewis Street
Canton, MA 02021

Cohasset

Cohasset Drama Club
Post Office Box 225
Cohasset, MA 02025

Davers

Davers Community Theatre
20 Colby Road
Davers, MA 01923

Dorchester

Carney Hospital Little Theatre
2100 Dorchester Avenue
Dorchester, MA 02122

Community Players
150 American Legion Highway
Dorchester, MA 02122

Eastham

The Fishermans Players
Methodist Church
Eastham, MA 02642

Easthampton

Williston Summer Theatre
Williston-Northampton School
Easthampton, MA 01027
Tel: 413-527-1520
Address Inquiries to: Ellis B. Baker, Director
Founded in: 1970
Annual Budget: $25,000

East Longmeadow

Community Theatre
Post Office Box 47
East Longmeadow, MA 01028

East Somerville

Peabody Players
93 Broadway
East Somerville, MA 02143

Fall River

Little Theatre Of Fall River
Post Office Box 1282
Fall River, MA 02722

Falmouth

Falmouth Players
63 Elm Street
Falmouth, MA 02540

Falmouth Playhouse
Falmouth, MA 02540
Tel: 617-563-6622
Address Inquiries to: Sidney Gordon,
     Manager
     Dr. Stephen Langley, Managing Director
Founded in: 1949

Fitchburg

Stratton Players
60 Wallace Avenue
Fitchburg, MA 01420

Framingham

Chateau De Ville Dinner Theatre
2 Dinsmore Avenue
Framingham, MA 01701
Address Inquiries to: Gerald Roberts,
     Producer

Grafton

Grafton Players Club
63 Keith Hill Road
Grafton, MA 01519

Granby

Homesteaders
78 Amherst Street
Granby, MA 01033

Greenfield

Arena Civic Theatre Inc.
Post Office Box 744
Greenfield, MA 01301
Tel: 413-773-8111
Address Inquiries to: Ann Christern,
     Managing/Artistic Director
     Roger Seward, President
Founded in: 1971
Annual Budget: $25,000

Harvard

Harvard Players
West Bear Hill Road
Harvard, MA 01451

Haverhill

Universalist-Unitarian Drama
Universalist Church
Haverhill, MA 01830

Hingham

Hingham Civic Chorus
20 Porter Coves Road
Hingham, MA 02043

Holden

Players Club
808 Main Street
Holden, MA 01520

Hollistion

Curtain Timers
40 Roy Avenue
Hollistion, MA 01746

Hopedale

Hopedale Little Theatre
18 Bancroft Park
Hopedale, MA 01747

Hyannis

Cape Cod Melody Tent
Hyannis, MA 02601
Tel: 617-775-5630; 617-775-9100
Address Inquiries to: William Carmen,
     Producer, Managing Director
     Beverly Carmen, Director
Founded in: 1946
Member: AEA;
Description: Produces three to five musicals

each year, with a star in the lead and five to seven weeks of variety shows featuring a weekly concert with a major star.

Hyde Park

Neponset Valley Players
1137 River Street
Hyde Park, MA 02136

Jamaica Plain

Footlight Club
7A Eliot Street
Jamaica Plain, MA 02130

Jefferson

Worcester Children's Theatre
1782 Wachasett Street
Jefferson, MA 01522
Tel: 617-829-3411
Address Inquiries to: Linda B. Robbins,
President
Edward Herson, Vice President
Founded in: 1969
Annual Budget: $25,000

Lawrence

Garrett Players
11 Halsey Street
Lawrence, MA 01843

Lexington

Premiere Performing Company
Post Office Box 252
Lexington, MA 02173

Lowell

Delphic Drama Studio
826 Chelmsford Street
Lowell, MA 01851

Footlighters
28 Fleming Street
Lowell, MA 01851

Lynn

Magic Lantern Player
64 Mansfield Street
Lynn, MA 01904

Lynnfield

Spotlighters
Post Office Box 4
Lynnfield, MA 01940

Malden

Curtain Time Players
45 Willow Street
Malden, MA 02151

Marblehead

Marblehead Little Theatre
Post Office Box 284
Marblehead, MA 01945

Marion

Marion Art Center Players
Post Office Box 602
Marion, MA 02738

Medfield

Center for Creative Arts
31 Park Street
Medfield, MA 02052

Melrose

Discovery Workshop
486 Main Street
Melrose, MA 02176
Tel: 617-665-8870
Address Inquiries to: Claire E. DiMeo,
President
Claire DiMeo Jr., Treasurer
Founded in: 1971
Member: NETC; NEA;
Annual Budget: $25,000

Melrose Community Players
Post Office Box 114
Melrose, MA 02176

North Shore Discovery Workshop
486 Main Street
Melrose, MA 02176
Tel: 617-665-8870
Address Inquiries to: Claire E. DiMeo,
President
Founded in: 1971
Member: NETC;

Middleboro

Cranberry Players
105 Plymouth
Middleboro, MA 02346

Milton

Milton Players
Post Office Box 1
Milton, MA 02186

Nahant

Peninsula Players of Nahant
65A Basspoint Road
Nahant, MA 01908
Tel: 617-581-1078
Address Inquiries to: Zane Knoy, President
Martin J. Blatz, Vice President
Founded in: 1972
Member: NETC;
Annual Budget: $10,000

Natick

Natick Drama Workshop
5 Summer Street
Natick, MA 01760
Address Inquiries to: Richard L. Gaudette,
General Manager
Founded in: 1966
Annual Budget: $25,000

Needham

Needham Community Theatre
Post Office Box 242
Needham, MA 02192

Needham Drama Workshop
5 Manning Street
Needham, MA 02194
Tel: 617-444-1178
Address Inquiries to: Dick Power, Manager

Joseph P. Lombard, President
Founded in: 1970
Annual Budget: $5,000

Needham Youth Summer Theatre
651 Central Avenue
Needham, MA 02194
Tel: 617-444-7351
Address Inquiries to: Harriet Mermes,
President
Founded in: 1968
Annual Budget: $10,000

Wig and Whiskers
236 Greendale Road
Needham, MA 02192

New Bedford

Your Theatre
100 R Parker Street
New Bedford, MA 02740

Newbury

New Essex Players
4 Maple Terrace
Newbury, MA 01950

Newton Centre

Country Players
Post Office Box 9
Newton Centre, MA 02159

Newton Country Players
Post Office Box 9
Newton Centre, MA 02161
Tel: 617-244-2160
Address Inquiries to: James M. Sloane,
President
Larry Morris, Vice President
Founded in: 1955
Annual Budget: $10,000

Piccadilly Square Theatre Company
93 Union Street
Newton Centre, MA 02159
Tel: 617-237-2679
Address Inquiries to: Anita Sangiolo,
President
Muriel Dolan, Vice President
Founded in: 1974
Annual Budget: $10,000

Northampton

Circle Players
Post Office Box 6
Northampton, MA 01060

North Andover

Raytheon Drama Ad
17 Arnis Street
North Andover, MA 01845

North Attleboro

Attleboro Little Theatre
Post Office Box 946
North Attleboro, MA 02760

North Quincy

Parker School Children's Theatre
148 Billings Road
North Quincy, MA 02171
Address Inquiries to: Eugene W. Creedon

North Wilbraham

Wilbraham Community Theatre
23 Brainard Road
North Wilbraham, MA 01095

Norwood

Curtain Timers
50 Longfellow Road
Norwood, MA 02062

Oak Bluffs

Marthas Vineyard
Little Theatre
Oak Bluffs, MA 02557

Orleans

Orleans Arena Theatre
Old Town Hall, Main Street
Orleans, MA 02653
Tel: 617-255-0695
Address Inquiries to: Elizabethe B. Argo,
    Producer/Director
    Emma C. Pettengill, Business Manager
Founded in: 1950
Member: NETC;
Annual Budget: $50,000

Peabody

Puppet Studio and Little Theatre
    Marionettes
67 Lake Shore Road
Peabody, MA 01960
Tel: 617-595-4455
Address Inquiries to: Dorothy Rankin,
    Director
Founded in: 1944

Pittsfield

Towne Players
2 Partridge Road
Pittsfield, MA 01201

Plymouth

National Association of Dramatics
White Horse Beach
Plymouth, MA 02381
Tel: 617-224-3967
Address Inquiries to: Dr. A. Franklin Trask,
    President
    L. Alison Hawley, Treasurer
Founded in: 1936

Quincy

Center Players
10 Merrymount Road
Quincy, MA 02169

Community Players
51 Edwards Street
Quincy, MA 02169

Reading

Quannapowitt Players
Post Office Box 12-T
Reading, MA 01867

Richmond

Robbins-Zust Marionettes and Theatre
East Road
Richmond, MA 01254
Tel: 413-698-2591
Address Inquiries to: Richard L. Robbins,
    President
    Ann Carter-Cox, Vice President
Founded in: 1971
Annual Budget: $25,000

Rockport

Cape Ann Players
Post Office Box 95
Rockport, MA 01966

Roxbury

Negro Repertory Theatre
14 Crawford Street
Roxbury, MA 02119

Sidewalk Theatre Players
14 Crawford Street
Roxbury, MA 02119

Sangus

Towncriers
115 Forest Street
Sangus, MA 01906

Scituate

Scituate Dramateurs
8 Lawson Road
Scituate, MA 02066

Sharon

Sharon Masquers
Sharon Community Center
Sharon, MA 02067

Sharon Players
Gorwin Drive
Sharon, MA 02067

Sherborn

Sherborn Players
Everett Street
Sherborn, MA 01770

Shirley

Shirley Little Theatre
Benjamin Road
Shirley, MA 01464

Shrewsbury

Theatre Six
85 Crescent Street
Shrewsbury, MA 01545

Springfield

Actors Repertory Theatre
201 Woodlawn Street
Springfield, MA 01108

Center Players
1160 Dickinson Street
Springfield, MA 01108

Dominique's Puppeteers and Mimi-Magic
    Players
187 Bowdoin Street
Springfield, MA 01109

Dunbar Players
33 Oak Street
Springfield, MA 01109

Faith Church Players
52 Summer Avenue
Springfield, MA 01108

Stoughton

The Little Theatre
247 Prospect Street
Stoughton, MA 02072

Wedded Ring Players
Congregational Church
Stoughton, MA 02072

Sudbury

Sudbury Players
Post Office Box 18
Sudbury, MA 01776

Sutton

Sutton Community Players
Boston Road
Sutton, MA 01527

Swansea

Community Children's Theatre
Post Office Box 207
Swansea, MA 02777
Tel: 617-678-6351
Founded in: 1968
Member: NETC;
Annual Budget: $1,000

Truro

Wellfleet Players
North Pamet Road
Truro, MA 02666

Wakefield

Theatre Ensemble
4 Central Street
Wakefield, MA 01880

Waltham

New England Theatre Conference
c/o M. Phillips
50 EXC Street
Waltham, MA 02154

Watertown

Phillips Players
111 Mount Auburn Street
Watertown, MA 02172

Wellesley Hills

Amateurs Incorporated
10 Sawyer Road
Wellesley Hills, MA 02181

Wellesley

Wellesley Children's Theatre
4 Mansfield Road
Wellesley, MA 02181
Tel: 617-235-5–29
Address Inquiries to: Ilene Magnus,
    Producer/Director
Founded in: 1949

Westfield

Westfield Little Theatre
4 Lothrop Avenue
Westfield, MA 01085

Weston

Drama Workshop
483 Boston Post Drive
Weston, MA 02193

Friendly Society
313 Boston Post Road
Weston, MA 02193

West Roxbury

Stagecrafters
29 Meredith Street
West Roxbury, MA 02132

West Springfield

Stage/West
1511 Memorial Avenue
West Springfield, MA 01089
Tel: 413-781-4470
Address Inquiries to: Stephen E. Hayes,
    Producing Director
Founded in: 1967
Annual Budget: $750,000
Description: A professional resident theatre
presenting seven plays annually.

Storrowton Theatre
Exposition Park
West Springfield, MA 01089
Tel: 413-732-1105
Address Inquiries to: Michael P. Iannucci,
    Manager
Founded in: 1959
Annual Budget: $100,000
Description: Seating capacity of 2300.

Weymouth

Curtain Call Theatre
Post Office Box 191
Weymouth, MA 02188

Wilbraham

Springfield Profile Ensemble Theatre
586 Main Street
Wilbraham, MA 01095
Tel: 413-596-8449
Address Inquiries to: Florea M. Britch,
    President
    Carroll P. Britch, Vice President
Founded in: 1971
Annual Budget: $5,000

Winchester

Unitarian Players
Winchester Unitarian
Winchester, MA 01890

Winchester Summer Theatre
31 Mystic Avenue
Winchester, MA 01890

Worcester

Cathedral Players
12 Shirley Street
Worchester, MA 01610

Huntington Players
10 Irving Street
Worcester, MA 01609

Wesley Pretenders
114 Main Street
Worcester, MA 01608

Worcester Foothills Theatre Company
Post Office Box 236
Worcester, MA 01602
Tel: 617-754-3314
Address Inquiries to: Cushing C. Bozenhard,
    Chairman
    Marc P. Smith, President
Founded in: 1974
Member: TCG; Arts and Sciences
    Development Service; MCAH;
Annual Budget: $250,000

MICHIGAN

Adrian

Croswell Players
Post Office Box 724
Adrian, MI 49221

Allegan

Allegan Community Players
Post Office Box 202
Allegan, MI 49010

Allen Park

Allen Park Civic Theatre
16850 Southfield
Allen Park, MI 48101

Alpena

Alpena Civic Theatre
401 River Street
Alpena, MI 49707

Ann Arbor

Ann Arbor Black Theatre
1655 Newport Road
Ann Arbor, MI 48104

Ann Arbor Civic Theatre
201 Mulholland
Ann Arbor, MI 48103

University of Michigan
Mendelssohn Theatre
Ann Arbor, MI 48104
Tel: 313-764-6300
Address Inquiries to: Dr. Walter Eysselinck,
    Chairman
Member: AEA; ATA; URTA; ACUCAA;
    UCTA;
Annual Budget: $100,000

Augusta

Barn Theatre
Augusta, MI 49012

Battle Creek

Battle Creek Civic Theatre
12 East Michigan Mall
Battle Creek, MI 49014

Bay City

Bay City Players
Post Office Box 1
Bay City, MI 48706

Birmingham

Village Players
Post Office Box 172
Birmingham, MI 48012

Bloomfield Hills

Will-O-Way Repertory Theatre
775 West Long Lake Road
Bloomfield Hills, MI 48013

Brighton

Livingston Players
Post Office Box 52
Brighton, MI 48116

Capac

Detroit Sign Company
13794 Bryce
Capac, MI 48014

Cedar Springs

Cedar Springs Players
Post Office Box 209
Cedar Springs, MI 49319

Cheboygan

Northland Players
Post Office Box 515
Cheboygan, MI 49721

Clawson

Stagecrafters
Post Office Box 11
Clawson, MI 48017

Dearborn

Dearborn Civic Theater
City Hall Annex East
Dearborn, MI 48126

Dearborn Heights

Beta Sigma Fellowship
23369 Longview
Dearborn Heights, MI 48127
Address Inquiries to: B. Roys

Dear Heights Community Theatre
1801 North Beech Daly

Dearborn Heights, MI 48126

Detroit

Afro-Centric Theatre
14223 Faust
Detroit, MI 48223

Black Artist Manifesto
18971 Prairie
Detroit, MI 48221

B. Pugh Productions
16606 Fairfield
Detroit, MI 48221

Cathedral Theatre
510 Temple
Detroit, MI 48202

Cochran Players
2773 East Larned-101
Detroit, MI 48207
Address Inquiries to: D. Hayes

Concept East
5826 Hazlett Street
Detroit, MI 48210
Tel: 313-875-3150
Address Inquiries to: L. Smith, Executive
    Director
Founded in: 1961

Concerned Artists
14684 Stoepel
Detroit, MI 48238

Detroit Crusade
3015 East Outer Drive
Detroit, MI 48234
Address Inquiries to: S. Holmes

Eswad Tabia
12027 Wilshire
Detroit, MI 48213

Lavice and Company
17191 Murray Hill
Detroit, MI 48235

Mausi
Post Office Box 4096
Detroit, MI 48204

North Rosendale Park Player
18241 Scarsdale
Detroit, MI 48223

Park Players
18445 Scarsdale
Detroit, MI 48223

Players Club
3321 East Jefferson
Detroit, MI 43207

Quality Players
15034 Ardmore
Detroit, MI 48227

Rappa House Theatre
96 East Fisher Freeway
Detroit, MI 48201
Address Inquiries to: J. Nimmons

Rosedale Community Players
21428 Grand River
Detroit, MI 48219

Theatre Arts
3321 East Jefferson
Detroit, MI 48207

East Detroit

East Detroit Civic Theatre
Post Office Box 94
East Detroit, MI 48021

Escanaba

Players De Noc
Post Office Box 45
Escanaba, MI 48920

Farmington Hills

Farmington Players
25521 Crystal Spring
Farmington Hills, MI 48018

Fenton

Fenton Villiage Players
801 North Road
Fenton, MI 48430

Flint

Flint Youth Theatre
924 East Sixth Street
Flint, MI 48503
Address Inquiries to: Ann Elgood
Member: CTAA;

Star Musical of Flint
1241 East Kearsley Street
Flint, MI 48502

Franklin

Franklin Village Players
Post Office Box 594
Franklin, MI 48025

Fremont

Fremont Civic Theatre
Route 2, Box 102
Fremont, MI 49412

Grand Haven

Central Park Players
Post Office Box 564
Grand Haven, MI 48417

Grand Rapids

Community Circle Theatre
Post Office Box 1613
Grand Rapids, MI 49501

Grand Rapids Civic Theatre
737 Leonard Northwest
Grand Rapids, MI 49504

Hartland

Hartland Players
Post Office Box 204
Hartland, MI 48029

Holland

Holland Community Theatre
Post Office Box 234
Holland, MI 49423

Jackson

Clark Lake Players
Post Office Box 343
Jackson, MI 49204

Lansing

Lansing Civic Players
Post Office Box 16117
Lansing, MI 48901

Lincoln Park

Lincoln Civic Theatre
1600 McLain
Lincoln Park, MI 48146

Livonia

Wayne-Westland Theatre
35042 Hees
Livonia, MI 48150

Manistee

Manistee Civic Players
Post Office Box 32
Manistee, MI 49660

Marquette

Marquette Community Theatre
Post Office Box 735
Marquette, MI 49855

Marshall

Marshall Civic Theatre
Post Office Box 102
Marshall, MI 49068

Monroe

Monroe Community/Repertory Theatre
Post Office Box 581
Monroe, MI 48161

Muskegan

Port City Playhouse
1336 Sanford Street
Muskegan, MI 49441
Address Inquiries to: Robert Fritsch

New Baltimore

Anchor Community Theatre
50976 Washington
New Baltimore, MI 48047

Oak Park

Oak Park Community Theatre
14300 Oak Park Blvd
Oak Park, MI 48237

Ridgefield Players
8501 West Ten Mile Road
Oak Park, MI 48237

Okemos

Community Circle Players
4208 South Okemos Road
Okemos, MI 48864

Ortonville

Brandon Stage
280 Linda K Lane
Ortonville, MI 48462
Address Inquiries to: E. Thornton

Oscoda

Shoreline Players
Post Offfice Box 395
Oscoda, MI 48750

Owasso

Owasso Community Players
Post Office Box 32
Owasso, MI 48867

Petoskey

Little Traverse Civic Theatre
Post Office Box 51
Petoskey, MI 49770

Pewamo

Pewamo-Westph Community Players
Post Office Box 254
Pewamo, MI 48873

Pontiac

Pontiac Theatre IV
Post Office Box 1154
Pontiac, MI 48056

Port Austin

Port Austin Community Players
Rail Road Street
Port Austin, MI 48467

Port Huron

Port Huron Little Theatre
Post Office Box 821
Port Huron, MI 48060

Portland

Portland Civic Players
231 Maple
Portland, MI 48875

Richmond

Richmond Community Theatre
Division Road
Richmond, MI 48062

Rochester

Avon Players
1185 Washington Road
Rochester, MI 48063

Romeo

Romeo Players
Romeo Youth Community Center
Romeo, MI 48065

Roseville

Roseville Community Theatre
15250 Martin
Roseville, MI 48066
Address Inquiries to: R. Morrison

Saginaw

Pit and Six Balcony Theatre
805 North Hamilton
Saginaw, MI 48602 ·
Address Inquiries to: Ralph Maffongelli

Saint Clair Shores

Saint Clair Shores Players
Post Office Box 234
Saint Clair Shores, MI 48083

Saint Joseph

Twin City Players
Post Office Box 243
Saint Joseph, MI 49085

Saint Louis

Gratiot Company Players
Post Office Box 143
Saint Louis, MI 48880

Saline

Saline Area Players
Post Office Box 334
Saline, MI 48176

Saugatuck

Red Barn Theatre
Saugatuck, MI 49453

Southfield

Saint Bede Players
19239 Somerset
Southfield, MI 48076

Southfield Civic Theatre
26000 Evergreen
Southfield, MI 48076

Southgate

The Lion Company
Post Office Box 1026
Southgate, MI 48195

Southgate Community Theatre
Post Offfice Box 1090
Southgate, MI 48195

Sterling Heights

Sterling Heights Players
8777 Lozon Street
Sterling Heights, MI 48078

Tawas City

Tawas Community Theatre
301 West Elm
Tawas City, MI 48763

Tecumseh

Tecumseh Players
Post Office Box 94
Tecumseh, MI 49286

Three Rivers

Three Rivers Community Theatre
Post Office Box 157
Three Rivers, MI 49039

Traverse City

Production Company
143 East 8th Street
Traverse City, MI 49684

Traverse City Civic Players
148 East 8th Street
Traverse City, MI 49684

Trenton

Trenton Community Theatre
2447 West Jefferson
Trenton, MI 48183

Troy

Troy Players
Post Office Box 284
Troy, MI 48099

Waterford

Lakeland Players
Post Office Box 379
Waterford, MI 48095

West Bloomfield

Farm Family Players
7072 Edinborough
West Bloomfield, MI 48033

Wyandotte

Wyandotte Community Theatre
Post Office Box 135
Wyandotte, MI 48192

Ypsilanti

Ypsilanti Players
Post Office Box 595
Ypsilanti, MI 48197

MINNESOTA

Akeley

Leech Lake Community Theatre
Route 2, Post Office Box 50
Akeley, MN 56433
Address Inquiries to: Hellen Vollman

Albert Lea

Albert Lea Community Theatre
Post Office Box 115
Albert Lea, MN 56007

Anoka

Anoka Theatre Ensemble
1500 South Ferry Street
Anoka, MN 55303
Address Inquiries to: Paul Pierce

Appleton

Appleton Theatre Board
Route 3, Post Office Box 63
Appleton, MN 56208
Address Inquiries to: P. Hegland

Baudette

Stage of the Woods
Baudette, MN 56623

Bertha

Bertha Community Theatre
Bertha, MN 56437
Address Inquiries to: Tim Hjelmeland

Blaine

Blaine Community Theatre
Blaine Senior High School
University Avenue and Highway 242
Blaine, MN 55434

Blue Earth

Blur Earth Town and Country Players
312 North Holland Street
Blue Earth, MN 56013
Address Inquiries to: Mike Ellingsen

Community Players
215 North Galbraith
Blue Earth, MN 56013

Burnsville

Community Theatre of Burnsville
Post Office Box 1051
Burnsville, MN 55337

Canby

Canby Community Players
Canby, MN 56220

Chanhassen

Chanhassen Civic Theatre
7607 Huron Avenue
Chanhassen, MN 55317

Chaska

Chaska Civic Theatre
110914 Van Hersen Circle
Chaska, MN 55318
Address Inquiries to: Ruth Stevenson

Chokio

Chokio Community Theatre
Chokio, MN 55101
Address Inquiries to: Neal Hofland

Cloquet

Blackthorn Theatre
323 4th Street
Cloquet, MN 55720

Cloquet Community Players
23 Third Street
Cloquet, MN 55720

Coon Rapids

Coon Rapids Theatre
10951 Crooked Lake Boulevard
Coon Rapids, MN 55432

Cottage Grove

Stage Door Theatre
8370 Gookview Avenue South
Cottage Grove, MN 55016

Crookston

Crookston Community Theatre
Post Office Box 264
Crookston, MN 56716

Detriot Lakes

Playhouse 412
Post Office Box 1112
Detriot Lakes, MN 56501

Duluth

Daisy Hill Theatre
1023 West 6th Street
Duluth, MN 55802
Address Inquiries to: R.J. Jensen

Duluth Playhouse
506 West Michigan Street
Duluth, MN 55802

East Grand Forks

East Grand Forks Community Theatre
Community Education
East Grand Forks, MN 56721
Address Inquiries to: Terry White

Edina

Edina Theatre Company
555 West 70th Street
Edina, MN 55435
Address Inquiries to: Nancy Anderson

Elk River

Elk River Community Theatre
310 King Street
Elk River, MN 55330
Address Inquiries to: Clifford Lundberg

Fairmont

Civic Summer Theatre
Post Office Box 169
Fairmont, MN 56031
Address Inquiries to: Terry Anderson

Faribault

Faribault Community Theatre
1130 Nortwest First Avenue
Faribault, MN 55021

Forest Lake

Masquers Theatre Company
Post Office Box 367
Forest Lake, MN 55025

Fridley

Fridley Summer Theatre
6000 West Moore Lake Drive
Fridley, MN 55432

Glencoe

Buffalo Creek Players
Rural Route 2
Glencoe, MN 55336
Address Inquiries to: Alvin Hoff

Grand Marais

Grand Marais Playhouse
Grand Marais, MN 55604
Address Inquiries to: Jean Thomas

Grand Rapids

Grand Rapids Players
Post Office Box 26
Grand Rapids, MN 55744
Address Inquiries to: Dr. Vernon Erickson

Granite Falls

Granite Falls Community Theatre
Community Education Office
Granite Falls, MN 56241

Hastings

Hastings Community Players
Post Office Box 284
Hastings, MN 55033

Herman

Agassiz Theatre
Herman, MN 56248

Hibbing

Hibbing Area Theatre
607 East Howard
Hibbing, MN 55778
Address Inquiries to: Bob Valeri

Houston

Houston Community Theatre
Houston, MN 55943
Address Inquiries to: Mrs. Gary Schmidt

Hutchinson

Mill Pond Players
Route 4
Hutchinson, MN 55350
Address Inquiries to: Dan Martens

Isle

Mille Lacs Community Theatre
Isle, MN 56342
Address Inquiries to: Jay Anderson

Lake Benton

Lake Benton Opera House
Post Office Box 1
Lake Benton, MN 56149

Lakeville

Lakeville Civic Theatre
Community School Office
Lakeville, MN 55044

Le Sueur

Le Sueur Community Theatre
115 Sunset Circle
Le Sueur, MN 56058
Address Inquiries to: John Eje

Litchfield

Litchfield Community Theatre
126 North Marshall Avenue
Litchfield, MN 55355

Luverne

Green Earth Players
Post Office Box 207
Luverne, MN 56156

Madison

Prairie Arts Group
721 Parkview Lane
Madison, MN 56256
Address Inquiries to: Mercene Holzemer

Mahnomen

Mahnomen Community Theatre
Mahnomen, MN 56557

Mankato

Fine Arts Community Theatre
104 Hannah Street
Mankato, MN 56001
Address Inquiries to: Mary Austermann

Maple Plain

Orono Ensemble Theatre
Main Street
Maple Plain, MN 55359

Marshall

Four Winds Community Theatre
800 Hackberry Street #12
Marshall, MN 56285

Milaca

Milaca Players
Milaca, MN 56353
Address Inquiries to: Jack Palmer

Minneapolis

Acting Company Musical Theatre
2317 Grand Avenue South
Minneapolis, MN 55405

Alive and Trucking Theatre
116 East 32nd Street
Minneapolis, MN 55408
Tel: 612-823-1022

At the Foot of the Mountain
3144 Tenth Avenue, South
Minneapolis, MN 55407
Tel: 612-375-9487; 612-825-2820
Address Inquiries to: Martha Boesing, Artistic
    Director
    Phyllis Jane Rose, Managing Director
Founded in: 1974
Member: TWCN; TCG; TWPS; All the
    Good Old Girls; M-R/AAS/C;
    Minneapolis A.R.T. Exchange; MSAB;
    NEA; MHC; BC/BS; FBSF; GMF; HB
    Fuller Co.; John G. Kinnard & Co.;
    Land-O-Lakes; MST; Bremer
    Foundation; Butler Foundation; Jostens
    Foundation; MF; NAF; UAF; Whitney
    Foundation; NCBF; Piper, Jaffrey &
    Hopwood;
Description: The oldest continuously produc-
ing professional women's theatre in the U.S.

Center Stage of the JCC
4330 Cedar Lake Road
Minneapolis, MN 55416

The Children's Theatre Company
2400 Third Avenue
Minneapolis, MN 55404
Tel: 612-874-0500
Address Inquiries to: John Clark Donahue,
    Artistic Director
Description: Internships at The Children's
Theatre Company and School provide high
school graduate, college students and adult
professionals the opportunity to work and
study in the areas of performing, production, and administration.

Experimental Theatre
1430 Washong Avenue South
Minneapolis, MN 55404

Gilbert and Sullivan Very Light Opera
Company
1715 West Franklin
Minneapolis, MN 55405
Address Inquiries to: Richard Fishel

Mill City Theatre
345 13th Avenue NE
Minneapolis, MN 55413

Minnesota Singers Theatre
2501 Pleasant Avenue South
Minneapolis, MN 55404

New Coffeehouse Theatre
1521 University Avenue SE
Minneapolis, MN 55414

Out And About Theatre Company
307 West 15th Street #44
Minneapolis, MN 55403
Address Inquiries to: Richard Rehse

Park Square Theatre
3400 15th Avenue South
Minneapolis, MN 55101

Pillsbury Waite Cultural Arts
720 East 26th Street
Minneapolis, MN 55404
Address Inquiries to: Keith Masuda

Powderhorn Players
3400 15th Avenue South
Minneapolis, MN 55407

Real Community Theatre
3307 Columbus Avenue
Minneapolis, MN 55407
Address Inquiries to: Judy Cooper

Taproot Theatre
1523 Portland Avenue South
Minneapolis, MN 55404
Address Inquiries to: Frank Siegle

Minnetonka

Minnetonka Theatre
14300 Excelsior Boulevard
Minnetonka, MN 55343
Address Inquiries to: David Allan

Montevideo

Village Players
Post Office Box 106
Montevideo, MN 56265
Address Inquiries to: Jon Skaalen

Mora

Mora Area Community Theatre
1235 South Union
Mora, MN 55051
Address Inquiries to: Ms. Pat Johnson

Nevis

Northern Lights Players
Route 2
Nevis, MN 56467
Address Inquiries to: Kathy Hueur

New Hope

New Hope Musical Theatre
3801 Xylon Avenue North
New Hope, MN 55428

Off-Broadway Musical Theatre
8955 47-½ Avenue North
New Hope, MN 55428
Address Inquiries to: Wendy L. Anderson

New London

New London-Spicer Summer Theatre
Post Office Box 158
New London, MN 56273

New Prague

New Prague Community Theatre
Post Office Box 61
New Prague, MN 56071

New Ulm

Hermannstraum
Post Office Box 461
New Ulm, MN 56073

Pioneer Players
622 Cantor Street
New Ulm, MN 56073
Address Inquiries to: June Benson

North Branch

Crossroads Theatre Company
Post Office Box 499
North Branch, MN 55056

Olivia

Renville County Arts Centre
Post Office Box 25
Olivia, MN 56277
Address Inquiries to: Patricia Kadlerek

Ortonville

Big Stone Community Theatre
229 South East 2nd Street
Ortonville, MN 56278
Address Inquiries to: Rosemary Biel

Owatonna

Little Theatre of Owatonna
Post Office Box 64
Owatonna, MN 55060

Park Rapids

Park Rapids Summer Theatre
Fishbrook Lane
Park Rapids, MN 56470

Perham

Good Time Players
Route 1, Box 370
Perham, MN 56573

Prior Lake

Prior Lake Players
Post Office Box 321
Prior Lake, MN 55372

Redwood Falls

Cabaret Players
Post Office Box 351
Redwood Falls, MN 56283

Redwood Falls Community Players
Post Office Box 22
Redwood Falls, MN 56283

Rochester

Rochester Civic Theatre
Mayo Park
Rochester, MN 55901
Tel: 507-282-8401; 507-282-7633
Address Inquiries to: Robert A. Birch,
    Managing Director
Founded in: 1952
Member: ATA; ACTA;
Annual Budget: $140,000

Southeastern Minnesota Regional
    Development Commission
301 Marquette Bank Building
Rochester, MN 55901
Description: Sponsors of regional theatre.

Roseau

Uffda Players
Post Office Box 225
Roseau, MN 56751

Rosemount

Playhouse 196
3160 145 Street West
Rosemount, MN 55024
Address Inquiries to: Bob Rhodes

Saint Cloud

County Sterns Theatre Company
917 ½ Germain Street
Saint Cloud, MN 56301

Troupe Theatre Incorporated
Post Office Box 553
Saint Cloud, MN 56301

Saint James

Saint James Summer Theatre
10th Avenue North
Saint James, MN 56081

Saint Paul

Bush Theatre
690 Cleveland Avenue South
Saint Paul, MN 55101
Address Inquiries to: Karen West Welch

Chimera Theatre Company
30 East 10th Street
Saint Paul, MN 56221

Address Inquiries to: Dale Huffington

Duck Soup Players
948 Carmel Court
Saint Paul, MN 55112
Address Inquiries to: Pat Bettendorf

Echo Theatre Company
1241 Juliet Avenue
Saint Paul, MN 55105
Address Inquiries to: John Coughlin

Saint Peter

Saint Peter Community Players
306 Elm
Saint Peter, MN 56082

Spring Valley

Brave Community Theatre Company
Post Office Box 95
Spring Valley, MN 55975

St. Paul

At Random
1817 Achland Avenue
St. Paul, MN 55104

Capitol City Theatre
617 South Smith Avenue
St. Paul, MN 55107
Address Inquiries to: Maureen Nieman

Climb, Incorporated
529 Jackson Street, Suite 227
St. Paul, MN 55101
Member: CTAA;

Park Square Theatre
400 Sibley Street
St. Paul, MN 55101

Stanchfield

Braham Community Theatre
RR 2, Box 46
Stanchfield, MN 55080
Address Inquiries to: Vern Heise

Starbuck

Minnewaska Showstoppers
Route 2
Starbuck, MN 56381
Address Inquiries to: Victor Vatthauer

Stillwater

Stillwater Community Theatre
3rd and Pine Street
Stillwater, MN 55416

Tower

Northern Lights Player
Post Office Box 200A
Tower, MN 55790

Trimont

Trimont Summer Community Theatre
Post Office Box 133
Trimont, MN 56176

Wadena

Madhatters Community Theatre
609 2nd Street
Wadena, MN 56482
Address Inquiries to: Mrs. Lillian Bradford

Waseca

Waseca Players
304 North East 6th
Waseca, MN 56093
Address Inquiries to: R. P. Madel

Waverly

Unicorn Community Theatre
Waverly High School
Waverly, MN 55390

West Saint Paul

Glass Theatre Company
1037 Bidwell
West Saint Paul, MN 55118

White Bear Lake

Lakeshore Players
Post Office Box 8562
White Bear Lake, MN 55110

Willmar

Willmar Community Theatre
Rural Route 4
Willmar, MN 56201
Address Inquiries to: Dave Dorsey

Winona

Winona Community Theatre
Post Office Box 735
Winona, MN 55987
Address Inquiries to: Jeannie Morrison

Worthington

Grassroots Theatre
Nobles Public Library
Post Office Box 166
Worthington, MN 56187

MISSISSIPPI

Bay Street Louis

Bay Street Louis Little Theatre
Post Office Box 342
Bay Street Louis, MS 39520

Biloxi

Biloxi Little Theatre
Post Office Box 955
Biloxi, MS 39533
Address Inquiries to: Henry Horne

Sheffield Ensemble Theatre
Post Office Box 1394
Biloxi, MS 39533

Canton

Canton Community Players
229 East North Street
Canton, MS 39046
Address Inquiries to: Joann Gordon

Cleveland

Cleveland Community Theatre
Post Office Box 44
Cleveland, MS 38732
Address Inquiries to: Linda Ross

Little Theatre
Post Office Box 587
Cleveland, MS 38732

Columbus

Columbus Community Theatre
Post Office Box 83
Columbus, MS 39701
Address Inquiries to: Beverly Kissinger

Corinth

Corinth Theatre Arts, Inc.
Post Office Box 127
Corinth, MS 38834
Address Inquiries to: Doug Hammond

Ellisville

Ellisville State School
Fine Arts Department
Ellisville, MS 39437
Member: CTAA;

Greenville

Delta Center Stage
Post Office Box 14
Greenville, MS 38701
Address Inquiries to: Albert Watson

Grenada

Grenada Fine Arts Playhouse
Post Office Box 867
Grenada, MS 38901
Address Inquiries to: Charles Calhoun

Gulfport

Center Stage
Post Office Box 153
Gulfport, MS 39501

Gulfport Little Theatre
Post Office Box 567
Gulfport, MS 39501

Hattiesburg

Hattiesburg Little Theatre
Post Office Box 1291
Hattiesburg, MS 39401
Address Inquiries to: Mary Gandy

Jackson

New Stage Theatre
Post Office Box 4792
Jackson, MS 39216
Address Inquiries to: Suzanne Chiles

Puppet Arts Theatre
5144 Old Canton Road
Jackson, MS 39211
Address Inquiries to: Peter Zapletal

Sun Rise Theatre
760 Wingfield Street
Jackson, MS 39209
Address Inquiries to: Furahaa Saba

Laurel

Laurel Little Theatre
Post Office Box 2131
Laurel, MS 39440
Address Inquiries to: Mary Ann Sumrall

Long Beach

Center Stage
229 Klondyke Road
Long Beach, MS 39560
Address Inquiries to: Natalie N. Howard

Louisville

Communications Center
Post Office Box 760
Louisville, MS 39339

Meridian

Meridian Little Theatre
Post Office Box 3055
Meridian, MS 39301
Address Inquiries to: Jimmy Pigfird

Natchez

Natchez Little Theatre
Post Office Box 1232
Natchez, MS 39120
Address Inquiries to: Edgar Wilkins

Stage 67
Post Office Box 1051
Natchez, MS 39120

Ocean Springs

Mississippi Repertory Theatre
810 Iberville Drive
Ocean Springs, MS 39564
Address Inquiries to: Marco St John

Oxford

Oxford Little Theatre
520 North Lamar
Oxford, MS 38655
Address Inquiries to: Mrs. James Elkins

Pascagoula

Paspoint Little Theatre
Post Office Box 231
Pascagoula, MS 39567
Address Inquiries to: Tommy Jackson

Sardis

Panola Playhouse
Post Office Box 13
Sardis, MS 38666
Address Inquiries to: James R. Major

Starkville

Starkville Community Theatre
Post Office Box 1254
Starkville, MS 39759

Tupelo

Tupelo Community Theatre
611 North Thomas Street
Box 1094
Tupelo, MS 38801
Tel: 601-842-4518
Address Inquiries to: Art Eckersley, President

Mrs. Walter Fleishhacker, Vice President
Founded in: 1969
Annual Budget: $10,000

Waynesboro

Waynesboro Little Theatre
Post Office Box 281
Waynesboro, MS 39367
Address Inquiries to: Mrs. Dan Lomax

Yazoo City

Yazoo Playhouse
Post Office Box 664
Yazoo City, MS 39194

MISSOURI

Branson

The Shepherd of the Hills
Route 1
Branson, MO 65616

Clinton

Clinton Repertory Theatre
Democrat
Clinton, MO 64735
Address Inquiries to: J. Whiter

Columbia

Maplewood Barn Theatre
701 Manor Drive
Columbia, MO 65201
Address Inquiries to: Phyllis Pearson

De Soto

On Stage Players
419 Amvets Drive
De Soto, MO 63020
Address Inquiries to: Jo Ann Hawkins

Jefferson City

Little Theatre
1105 Moreau
Jefferson City, MO 65101

Kansas City

Foolkiller Incorporated
3820 Campbell
Kansas City, MO 64109
Address Inquiries to: C. Leighton

Missouri Repertory Theatre
5100 Rockhill Road
Kansas City, MO 64110
Tel: 816-276-2701
Address Inquiries to: Patricia McIlrath,
   Chairman
Member: URTA;
Description: A professional repertory theatre
company.

Resident Theatre
8201 Holmes Road
Kansas City, MO 64131

Resident Theatre/Jewish Community
Center
8201 Holmes Road
Kansas City, MO 64131

Tel: 816-361-5200
Address Inquiries to: Paula Simkins,
   Managing Director
   James Coleman, Technical Director
Founded in: 1931
Annual Budget: $25,000

Unicorn Theatre Workshop
3514 Jefferson
Kansas City, MO 64111
Address Inquiries to: Diana Mange

Waldorf Astoria Playhouse
Tiffany's Attic Dinner Playhouse
5028 Main Street
Kansas City, MO 64112
Tel: 816-523-1706; 816-361-2661
Address Inquiries to: Dennis Hennessy,
   Producer
   Richard Carrother, Co-Producer
Founded in: 1972
Member: USITT;

Kenton

Canton Festival Theatre
Route 2
Kenton, MO 63435
Address Inquiries to: K. Miller

Kirksville

Traveller's Community Theatre
411 South Halliburton
Kirksville, MO 63501
Address Inquiries to: Pat Severns

Lookout

Beacon Hill Theatre School
Ozark Point
Lookout, MO 65726

Louis

Rattling the Chains Theatre
c/o Barbara Cloyd
1039 Pinegate Street
Louis, MO 63122
Tel: 314-965-1854

Maryville

Community Theatre
North West Missouri State
Maryville, MO 64468
Address Inquiries to: R. West

Nevada

Nevada Community Theatre
223 West Cherry Street
Nevada, MO 64772
Address Inquiries to: Adele Ausink

Parkville

Actors Prologue Repertory Theatre
Park College
Parkville, MO 64152
Tel: 314-741-2000
Address Inquiries to: James Cox II, Managing
   Director
Founded in: 1977
Description: $10,000

Bell Road Barn Playhouse
6008 Bell Road
Parkville, MO 64152
Tel: 816-587-0218
Address Inquiries to: Jenkin K. David,
   President
   Barbara David, Vice President
Founded in: 1954

Point Lookout

Act One Players
School of the Ozarks
Point Lookout, MO 65726
Tel: 417-334-6411
Founded in: 1960
Annual Budget: $10,000

Beacon Hill Theatre
School of the Ozarks
Point Lookout, MO 65726
Tel: 417-334-6411, ext. 339, summer;
   417-334-6411, ext. 437, all year
Address Inquiries to: James L. Meikle,
   Manager
Founded in: 1960
Member: ATA; USITT; SCA;
Description: A summer theatre under the
guidance of the School of the Ozarks pre-
senting a six week season of six shows. The
theatre has a seating capacity of 980.

Beacon Hill Theatre Company
School of the Ozarks
Point Lookout, MO 65726
Tel: 417-334-6411
Founded in: 1960

Saint Joseph

Saint Joseph Community Theatre
627 North 25th Street 110
Saint Joseph, MO 64506

Saint Louis

City Players
3207 Washington Avenue
Saint Louis, MO 63108
Address Inquiries to: Irma Tucker

Municipal Theatre Association
Forest Park
Saint Louis, MO 63112
Tel: 314-361-1900, General Office;
   314-367-8686, Box Office
Address Inquiries to: Edwin R. Culver
Founded in: 1919
Description: The Muny is the oldest (63 years)
and the largest (almost 12,000 seats) of all
outdoor musical theatres in the United
States. It makes 1,500 free seats available to
the public for every performance.

The Repertory Theatre of Saint Louis
130 Edgar Road
Post Office Box 28030
Saint Louis, MO 63119
Tel: 314-968-7340; 314-968-4925, Box
Office
Address Inquiries to: Wallace Chappell,
   Artistic Director
   Mathew B. Librach, Director of
   Marketing

Founded in: 1967
Member: Ford Foundation; LORT; TCG;
   Shubert Foundation; NEA; Missouri
   Arts Council; St. Louis City Arts and
   Humanities Commission; Arts and
   Education Council of St. Louis;
Annual Budget: $2,000,000
Description: In 1981, the Lorretto-Hilton
Theatre was reorganized as The Repertory
Theatre of Saint Louis. The company uses
the facilities of the Lorretto-Hilton Center
on the campus of Webster College, featuring
a mainstage and studio theatre program.
One of America's vibrant regional theatres.

Sedalia

Sedalia Community Theatre
717 West 6th Street
Sedalia, MO 65301
Address Inquiries to: Ginger Swearingen

Sikeston

Sikeston Little Theatre
835 William Street
Sikeston, MO 63801
Address Inquiries to: H. Terrell

Springfield

Springfield Little Theatre
311 East Walnut Street
Springfield, MO 65806
Tel: 417-869-1334
Address Inquiries to: Dr. Robert Bradley,
   President
   Michael Lampe, Manager
Founded in: 1935
Member: ATA;

St. Louis

R B Harrison Players
4730 Penrose Street
St. Louis, MO 63115
Address Inquiries to: V. Wamble

MONTANA

Bozman

Loft Theatre
1522 West Main
Bozman, MT 59715

Butte

Butte Community Theatre
1924 Carolina
Butte, MT 59701

Deerlodge

Deerlodge Community Theatre
710 Kentucky
Deerlodge, MT 59722

Dillon

Wapiti Players
Gleed Building
Dillon, MT 59725

Fort Benton

Fort Benton Community Theatre
1st State Bank
Fort Benton, MT 59442

Hamilton

Hamilton Little Theatre
Post Office Box 302
Hamilton, MT 59840

Hardin

Hardin Community Theatre
626 West 4th
Hardin, MT 59034

Hayre

Badlands Players
Hayre, MT 59501

Jordan

Driftwood Players
Jordan, MT 59337

Livingston

Blue Slipper Theatre
516 North F Street
Livingston, MT 59047

Park Drama Group
647 North San Vicente
Livingston, MT 59047

Miles City

Barn Players
121 North 12th Street
Miles City, MT 59301
Address Inquiries to: H. Boe

Missoula

Montana Repertory Theatre
Department of Drama-Dance
University of Montana
Missoula, MT 59812
Tel: 406-243-6809; 406-243-5572
Address Inquiries to: Steven Wing, Director
Founded in: 1968
Member: TCG; NEA; Montana Arts
   Council; University of Montana
   Foundation; Champion International
   Corporation;
Annual Budget: $175,000
Description: A professional touring company
which visits the western states from February through April.

Novi

Stage 1
Post Office Box 181
Novi, MT 48050

Romeo

Black Swan Players
11316 South Crestline
Romeo, MT 48065
Address Inquiries to: D. Weaver

Sidney

Gaslight Theatre Players
Post Office Box 50
Sidney, MT 59270

NEBRASKA

Auburn

Auburn Community Theatre
1712 J
Auburn, NE 68305

Aurora

Aurora Community Theatre
Post Office Box 462
Aurora, NE 68818

Beatrice

Beatrice Community Players
420 North 13th Street
Beatrice, NE 68310

Bellevue

Bellevue Little Theatre
2301 Lloyd Street
Bellevue, NE 68008

Blair

Blair Community Theatre
Post Office Box 426
Blair, NE 68008

Boystown

Boys Town Community Theatre
Boystown, NE 68010
Address Inquiries to: Al Pallon

Broken Bow

Broken Bow Community Playhouse
Post Office Box 726
Broken Bow, NE 68822

Columbus

Platte Valley Playhouse
Post Office Box 1161
Columbus, NE 68601

Creighton

Main Street Theatre
Creighton, NE 68729

Curtis

Curtis Little Theatre
Post Office Box 85
Curtis, NE 69025

David City

Alpine Community Players
Post Office Box 150
David City, NE 68632

Falls City

Falls City Community Theatre
Falls City, NE 68355

Fremont

Fremont Community Players
Post Office Box 1004
Fremont, NE 68025

Gordon

Gordon Community Theatre
Gordon, NE 69343

Gothenburg

Gothen Community Playhouse
Post Office Box 15
Gothenburg, NE 06756

Grand Island

GILT
Post Office Box 182
Grand Island, NE 68801

Hastings

Hastings Community Theatre
Post Office Box 922
Hastings, NE 68949

Hebron

Thayer County Theatre
Post Office Box 14
Hebron, NE 68370

Holdrege

Prairie Players
Holdrege, NE 68949

Lexington

Third Century Community Theatre
Lexington, NE 68850
Address Inquiries to: Mike Bacon

Lincoln

Lincoln Community Playhouse
2500 South 56th Street
Lincoln, NE 68506
Tel: 402-489-9608
Address Inquiries to: John R. Wilson,
   Manager
   Carol McVey, Administrator
Founded in: 1938
Member: ACT;

Nebraska Repertory Theatre
103 Temple Building
12th and R Streets
Lincoln, NB 68508
Tel: 402-472-1606,2072
Address Inquiries to: Rex McGraw, Chairman
Member: U/RTA;
Description: A repertory theatre with a summer season.

Nebraska City

Little Theatre Nebraska City
Post Office Box 392
Nebraska City, NE 68410

Norfolk

Norfolk Community Theatre
Post Office Box 164
Norfolk, NE 68701

North Platte

North Platte Community Theatre
306 West Circle Drive
North Platte, NE 69101

Omaha

Center Stage
333 South 132nd Street
Omaha, NE 68154

Emmy Gifford Children's Theatre
3504 Center Street
Omaha, NE 68105
Member: CTAA;

Firehouse Dinner Theatre
11th and Jackson
Omaha, NE 68102
Tel: 402-346-8833
Address Inquiries to: Richard L. Mueller,
Manager
Founded in: 1903
Description: Seating capacity 304.

Norton Theatre
520 South 10th Street
Omaha, NE 68102

Omaha Community Playhouse
6915 Cass Street
Omaha, NB 68132
Tel: 402-553-4890
Address Inquiries to: Marion Mooberry,
Manager
Founded in: 1959
Description: Seating capacity 500.

Puppet Theater Museum
511 South 11th
Omaha, NB 68102
Tel: 402-342-1313
Address Inquiries to: Sam Ridge, President
Paul Mesner, Vice President
Founded in: 1977
Member: NEA; PA;
Description: Seating capacity 80.

Westroads Dinner Theatre
46 Town Hall Road
Omaha, NB 68114
Tel: 402-397-0300
Address Inquiries to: Gary Bandringa,
Executive Producer
Stephen B. Woolverton, Executive
Producer
Founded in: 1971
Description: Seating capacity of 500.

Osceola

Osceola Community Theatre
Osceola, NE 68651

Plymouth

Encore Community Playhouse
Post Office Box 206
Plymouth, NE 68424

South Sioux City

South Sioux City Players
214 West 31st
South Sioux City, NE 68776

Wauneta

Wauneta Art Players
Crystal Theatre
Wauneta, NE 69045

York

Yorkville Players
York, NE 68467

NEVADA

Boulder City

Boulder Repertory Theatre
700 6th Street
Boulder City, NV 89005

Carson City

Proscenium Players, Inc.
Post Office Box 1165
Carson City, NV 89701
Tel: 702-882-4503
Address Inquiries to: Dee Ann Lien, President
Judy Reeder, Vice President
Founded in: 1966
Member: ACTA;

Las Vegas

Casino Theatre
Union Plaza Hotel
1 Main Street
Las Vegas, NV 89101

Charleston Heights Library Arts Center
800 Brush Street
Las Vegas, NV 89107

Meadows Playhouse
Post Office Box 19666
Las Vegas, NV 89119

Rainbow Company Children's Theatre
821 Las Vegas Blvd. North
Las Vegas, NV 89101

Whipples Arts Center
821 Las Vegas Blvd.
Las Vegas, NV 89101

Reno

Reno Little Theater
Post Office Box 2088
Reno, NV 89505
Tel: 702-329-0661; 702-322-3244
Address Inquiries to: Jerry L. Frank,
Producing Director
Eleanor E. Cowan, Business Manager
Founded in: 1935
Member: ACTA; NTHA;
Annual Budget: $40,000
Description: Welcomes all who wish to exercise their dramatic arts, whether it be on stage, backstage, or in one of the many jobs which make up the production of a play.

South Lake Tahoe

South Lake Tahoe Players
Post Office Box 13271
South Lake Tahoe, NV 95702

NEW HAMPSHIRE

Amherst

Amherst Players
Post Office Box 312
Amherst, NH 03031

Concord

Community Players
Post Office Box 681
Concord, NH 03301

New Hampshire Arts Commission
North Main Phenix Hall
Concord, NH 03301

Dover

Garrison Players
88 Spruce Lane
Dover, NH 03820

East Swanzey

The Old Homestead
Post Office Box 6
East Swanzey, NH 03446

Exeter

Exeter Players
Post Office Box 504
Exeter, NH 03833

Franklin

Twin River Players
82 Pleasant Street
Franklin, NH 03235

Hennker

MYS Productions
Hennker, NH 03442

Keene

Keene Summer Theatre
Keene State College
Keene, NH 03431
Tel: 603-357-4041

Lancaster

Colonel Town Players
Lancaster, NH 03584

Milford

American Stage Festival
Post Office Box 225
Milford, NH 03055

Mulford

Souchegan Players
North River Road
Mulford, NH 03055

Nashua

Actor Singers
4 Brookline Street
Nashua, NH 03060

New Boston

Manchester Players
New Boston, NH 03070

New Boston Players
New Boston, NH 03070

New London

New London Barn Players
Post Office Box 285
New London, NH 03257
Tel: 603-526-4631
Address Inquiries to: Steven Mendelson,
  Business Manager
Founded in: 1933
Member: NETC;

North Conway

Mount Washington Valley Theatre
  Company
Eastern Slope Playhouse
North Conway, NH 03860
Tel: 603-356-5776
Address Inquiries to: Paula Young, President
Jeffrey Nelson, Producer
Founded in: 1972

Resort Players
North Conway, NH 03860

Peterborough

Peterborough Players
Box 1
Peterborough, NH 03458
Tel: 603-924-3601
Address Inquiries to: Sally Stearns Brown,
  Managing Director
Founded in: 1933

Pittsfield

Pittsburg Players
Sunset Hill Road
Pittsfield, NH 03263

Whitfield

Weathervane Theatre
Whitfield, NH 03598
Tel: 603-837-9010
Address Inquiries to: Thomas B. Haas,
  Artistic Director
Founded in: 1965

Wilton

Andy's Summer Playhouse
Box 601
Wilton, NH 03086
Tel: 603-654-2613
Address Inquiries to: Jane K. Ernst, Managing
  Director
Founded in: 1961
Description: The only children's theatre of its
type in New Hampshire.

NEW JERSEY

Aberdeen

Beth Ahm Community Players
550 Lloyd Road
Aberdeen, NJ 07747

Audobon

Drama Spot Repertory Company
167 Carlisle Road
Audobon, NJ 08106

Beach Haven

Joseph P. Hays Surflight Summer Theatre
Box 155
Beach Haven, NJ 08008
Tel: 609-492-9477; 609-492-4112
Address Inquiries to: Eleanor C. Miller,
  Producer
Founded in: 1950
Description: Presenting Broadway musicals
June to September with a 21 member resi-
dent company and a new show each week.

Beach Haven Terrace

Surflight Summer Theatre
29 West Indiana Avenue
Beach Haven Terrace, NJ 08008
Tel: 609-492-4112; 609-492-9477
Address Inquiries to: Eleanor C. Miller,
  Producer
Founded in: 1950
Description: Professional non-Equity Summer
Theatre employing a 21 member resident
company.

Belvedere

Country Gate Players
114 Greenwich Street
Belvedere, NJ 07823

Bergenfield

Stagecrafters
153 Elder Avenue
Bergenfield, NJ 07621
Tel: 201-385-1298
Address Inquiries to: Mrs. John Lydecker,
  Resident Director
Founded in: 1952

Bloomfield

Bloomfield Civic Theatre
84 Broad Street
Bloomfield, NJ 07003

Bordentown

New Bordentown Community Player
272 Ward Avenue 7L
Bordentown, NJ 08505
Address Inquiries to: D. Starr

Chatham

Chatham Community Players
North Passaic Avenue, Box 234
Chatham, NJ 07928

Cherry Hill

Burlington City Footlight
9 Paper Mill Road
Cherry Hill, NJ 08003

Stage Left
Kings Highway North
Cherry Hill, NJ 08034

Chester

Chester Theatre Group
Post Office Box 38
Chester, NJ 07930

Cranford

Celebration Playhouse
118 South Avenue
Cranford, NJ 07016

Cranford Drama Club
78 Winans Avenue, Box 511
Cranford, NJ 07016

Cranford Dramatic Club
78 Winans Avenue
Cranford, NJ 07016
Tel: 201-276-7611
Address Inquiries to: Carl R. Peterson,
  President
  William Powers, Vice President
Founded in: 1919
Annual Budget: $30,000
Description: A non-professional structured lit-
tle theatre group producing four shows each
year including one musical. A childrens
theatre is also offered before Christmas.
Dedicated to offer the community a well-
rounded program and help members deve-
lop their acting skills. Directors come from
the membership.

Demarest

Demarest Little Theatre
Post Office Box 113
Demarest, NJ 07627

Dover

Dover Little Theatre
Box 82
Elliot Street
Dover, NJ 07801
Tel: 201-366-9890
Address Inquiries to: Miss John M. Munson,
  President
  Edward Holl, Vice President
Founded in: 1933

East Orange

Yates Musical Theatre for Children
19 Morse Avenue
East Orange, NJ 07017
Member: AEA;
Description: An AEA theatre for young audi-
ences.

Englewood

Creative Theatre for Children
30 North Van Brunt Street
Englewood, NJ 07631
Member: CTAA;

Essex Fells

Playcrafter Caldwell
Post Office Box 191
Essex Fells, NJ 07021

Fanwood

The Philathalians
33 Elm Avenue
Fanwood, NJ 07023

Fort Dix

Lakeside Music and Theatre
Nashville and Tennessee Avenue
Fort Dix, NJ 08640

Fort Lee

Palisades Players
177 Main Street
Fort Lee, NJ 07024

GreenBrook

Philathalians of Fanwood
4055 Rock Avenue EXT
GreenBrook, NJ 08812

Hackensack

New Dimension Theatre Studio
c/o YMHA of Bergen County
Hackensack, NJ 07601
Tel: 201-489-5900
Address Inquiries to: L. Rosenberg, President
   P. Fuller, Vice President
Founded in: 1961
Annual Budget: $50,000

Haddonfield

Musicrafters-Camden
Post Office Box 247
Haddonfield, NJ 08033

Payton Players
Washington Avenue
Haddonfield, NJ 08033

Plays and Players
Post Office Box 145
Haddonfield, NJ 08033

Haddon Heights

Road Company of Audubon
302 8th Avenue
Haddon Heights, NJ 08035
Address Inquiries to: Ted Eisner

Hillside

Hillside Community Players
1422 Maple Avenue
Hillside, NJ 07205
Tel: 201-926-1050
Address Inquiries to: Barbara A. Sasovetz,
   President
Founded in: 1967

Holmdel

Holmdel High School, Theatre Activity
   Fund
Crawford Corner Road
Holmdel, NJ 07733

Jersey City

Hudson County Public Theatre
244 New York Avenue
Jersey City, NJ 07307
Tel: 201-653-7143
Address Inquiries to: Robert D. Flach,
   President
   Joseeph Di Conzo, Vice President
Founded in: 1973
Annual Budget: $25,000

Kearny

Jerz Company
100 Laurel Avenue
Kearny, NJ 07032
Tel: 201-991-2938; 201-991-0950
Founded in: 1963
Member: AEA; PLOTYA; NJTG; CAHNJ;
Annual Budget: $67,500
Description: An AEA theatre for young audi-
ences as well as for mature audiences. The
Jerz Company presents original musical re-
views on history and science.

Leonia

Players Guild of Leonia
Post Office Box 131
Leonia, NJ 07605
Founded in: 1919

Livingston

Livingston Community Players
Post Office Box 158
Livingston, NJ 07039

Madison

The New Jersey Shakespeare Festival
Drew University
Madison, NJ 07940
Tel: 201-377-4487; 201-377-5330,
   Administrative
Address Inquiries to: Paul Barry, Artistic
   Director
   Ellen Barry, Producing Director
Founded in: 1910
Member: TCG; AEA; NJTG; FEDAPT; AAA;
   Description: An Actor's Equity repertory
theatre committed to the presentation of
classic theatre. The Festival is one of the few
true repertory companies remaining in the
country where plays are offered in nightly
rotation by resident professional actors.
They prsent not only the works of Shake-
speare, but also a variety of classic dramatic
literature both new and old.

Magnolia

Stage Door Theatre
607 Beverly Drive
Magnolia, NJ 08049

Matawan

Creative Productions
2 Beaver Place
Matawan, NJ 07747
Tel: 201-566-6985
Address Inquiries to: Walter L. Born, Director
Founded in: 1970

Mavesink

Monmouth Players
Monmouth Avenue
Mavesink, NJ 07752

Medford Lakes

Log Cabin Players
Vaughn Community House
Medford Lakes, NJ 08055

Merchantville

Merchantville Player
120 South Center Street
Merchantville, NJ 01809

Millburn

Paper Mill Playhouse
Brookside Drive
Millburn, NJ 07041
Tel: 201-379-3636
Address Inquiries to: John W. White Jr.,
   Chairman
Founded in: 1934

Montclair

The Whole Theatre Company
544 Bloomfield Avenue
Montclair, NJ 07042
Tel: 201-744-2989; 201-744-2996
Address Inquiries to: Robert Alpaugh,
   General Manager
   Arnold Mittelman, President
Founded in: 1971
Member: AEA; FEDAPT; TCG;

Montville

Barn Theatre
Skyline Drive
Montville, NJ 07045

Moorestown

New Jersey Theatre League
306 Collins Avenue
Moorestown, NJ 08057

New Brunswick

George Street Playhouse
414 George Street
New Brunswick, NJ 08901
Tel: 201-846-2895; 201-246-7717
Founded in: 1974
Member: AAA; ACA; LORT; TCG;
   FEDAPT;

Northfield

Atlantic Community Theatre
Jackson and Fuae Avenues
Northfield, NJ 08225

Nutley

Nutley Little Theatre
47 Erie Place, Box 131
Nutley, NJ 17110

Nyack

Elmwood Players
16 Park Street
Nyack, NJ 10960

Oradell

Bergen Community Players
298 Kindermack Road
Oradell, NJ 07649

Bergen County Players
298 Kinderkamack Road
Oradell, NJ 07649
Tel: 201-261-4200 Ext. 4203
Founded in: 1932
Member: NJTL; AA;
Annual Budget: $50,000
Description: Seating capacity 210.

Palmyra

Bridge Players
211 East Broad Street
Palmyra, NJ 08065

Paterson

Genesis Repertory Company
39 Broadway
Paterson, NJ 07509

The Learning Theatre
Post Office Box 2144
Paterson, NJ 07509
Tel: 201-345-3220
Address Inquiries to: Deborah Sheehan,
    Executive Director
    Irene Sterling, Artistic Director
Founded in: 1972
Member: ATA; CTAA;
Annual Budget: $125,000
Description: Creates and tours original participation plays for children. Dedicated to enriching the quality of childrens theatre by making it a part of the learning process and by offering an opportunity to participate in the creative process.

Pennington

Pennington Players
Post Office Box 144
Pennington, NJ 08534

Princeton

McCarter Theatre
91 University Place
Princeton, NJ 08546

Rahway

Revelers Dramatic Club
168 Main Street West
Rahway, NJ 07065

Ramsey

Ramsey Players
46 North Central Avenue
Ramsey, NJ 07446
Tel: 201-327-4058
Founded in: 1960

Ridgewood

Village Players
Post Office Box 332
Ridgewood, NJ 07451

Rockaway

Bell and Barter Theatre
Church and Wall Streets
Rockaway, NJ 07866

Roosevelt

Peacock Puppet Theater
Britton House
Roosevelt, NJ 08555
Tel: 609-448-2605
Address Inquiries to: Robert E. Mueller,
    Artistic Director
Founded in: 1967
Description: A small professional puppet group dedicated to serious puppetry and childrens theatre.

Runnemede

Laughingstock Company
219 East Clements Bridge Road
Runnemede, NJ 08078

Springfield

Springfield Community Players
Sarah Bailey Civic Center, Church Hall
Springfield, NJ 07081
Tel: 201-399-2293
Address Inquiries to: Shelley Wolfe, President
    Rita Giller, Vice President
Founded in: 1969
Annual Budget: $5,000

Spring Lake

Pine Tree Players
Post Office Box 567
Spring Lake, NJ 07762

Suffern

Antrim Players
Spookrock Road
Suffern, NJ 10901
Address Inquiries to: B. Freeman

Summit

Craig Theatre
6 Kent Place
Summit, NJ 07901

Tenafly

Community Theatre
Post Office Box 135
Tenafly, NJ 07670

Titusville

Washington's Crossing Association
Post Office Box 1776
Titusville, NJ 08560
Address Inquiries to: Jack Borden, President

Trenton

Shakespeare '70 Incorporated
121 Grand Street
Trenton, NJ 08611
Tel: 609-392-1704
Address Inquiries to: Gerald Edward
    Guarnieri, Executive Director
    John F. Erath, Ph.D., Director
Founded in: 1970
Member: NJTL;
Annual Budget: $25,000
Description: Produced at the Artists Showcase Theatre in Trenton, the Open Air Theatre in Titusville, New Jersey and on college and high school stages. Specializes in musicals with classical themes or settings. The company is drawn from educators, students and professionals in related fields such as broadcasting. Two of their board members appear in films, commercials, and television soaps.

Turnersville

Spotliters
803 Westminister Blvd
Turnersville, NJ 08012

Upper Montclair

Studio Players-Essex
14 Alvin Place
Upper Montclair, NJ 07043

Vineland

Cumerland Players
Post Office Box 494
Vineland, NJ 08360

Wayne

Packanack Players
Post Office Box 657
Wayne, NJ 07470

Westfield

Community Players
1000 North Avenue
Westfield, NJ 07090

West Orange

New Jersey Theatre League
54 Nestro Road
West Orange, NJ 07052
Tel: 201-731-7011
Founded in: 1948

West Paterson

Theatre Arts Repertory Company
21 Mt. Pleasant Avenue
West Paterson, NJ 07242

Willingboro

Willingboro Theatre of the Performing
    Arts
Post Office Box 398
Willingboro, NJ 08046
Tel: 609-387-3226
Address Inquiries to: Kathleen Bishop,
    President
    Jacki Seaman, Vice President
Founded in: 1973

Annual Budget: $10,000

Woodbury

Sketch Club Players
Glover and Logan
Box 674
Woodbury, NJ 08096
Tel: 609-848-8089
Address Inquiries to: Charles Dougherty,
  Production Vice President
  Sally Bouchaud, President
Founded in: 1933
Annual Budget: $10,000

NEW MEXICO

Alameda

Corrales Community Theatre
Star Rite
Alameda, NM 87114

Albequerque

Classics Theatre Company
9728 Academy NW
Albequerque, NM 87114

Albuquerque

Albuquerque Dance Theatre
805 Tijeras Northwest
Albuquerque, NM 87102

Cedar Crest

Barn Dinner Theatre
Post Office Box 257
Cedar Crest, NM 87008
Address Inquiries to: R.M. Hager, Producer

Clayton

Clayton Players
Clayton, NM 88415
Address Inquiries to: J. Chilocote

Clovis

Young Peoples Theatre
2106 Wallace
Clovis, NM 88101

Corrales

Corrales Adobe Theatre
Post Office Box 546
Corrales, NM 87048
Tel: 505-898-3323
Address Inquiries to: Rita Elliott, President
Founded in: 1958

Farmington

Masquers
618 South Mesa Verde
Farmington, NM 87401

Gallup

Gallup Community Theatre
Post Office Box 1032
Gallup, NM 87301
Address Inquiries to: E. Mc Daniel

Hobbs

Hobbs Community Players
1700 North Grimes
Hobbs, NM 88240
Tel: 505-393-9524
Address Inquiries to: Donna Erwin, President
Founded in: 1963

Hobbs Community Playhouse
Post Office Box 2153
Hobbs, NM 88240

Las Cruces

Las Cruces Community Theatre
Post Office Box 1281
Las Cruces, NM 88001
Tel: 505-523-1200
Address Inquiries to: N.B. Sanford
Founded in: 1963

Los Alamos

Don Juan Playhouse
80 Cascabel
Los Alamos, NM 87544
Address Inquiries to: M. Downer

Light Opera Company
3112 Villa
Los Alamos, NM 87544

Raton

New Mexico School of Performing Arts
Post Office Box 1146
Raton, NM 87740

Roswell

Roswell Community Little Theatre
1100 North Virginia
Roswell, NM 88201
Tel: 505-622-6322
Founded in: 1961

San Cristobal

Magic Tortoise Theatre
Post Office Box 111
San Cristobal, NM 87564

Sandoval

Corrales Adobe Theatre
Post Office Box 128
Sandoval, NM 87048

Santa Fe

Theatre Arts Corporation
724 Canyon Road
Santa Fe, NM 87501
Tel: 505-983-9815
Address Inquiries to: Robert Garrison,
  Artistic Director

NEW YORK

Albany

Black Experience Ensemble
5 Homestead Avenue
Albany, NY 12203
Tel: 518-452-3306
Address Inquiries to: Mars Hill, Director

Founded in: 1968

Drama Workshop
Whitehall Road
Albany, NY 12208

Empire State Youth Theatre Institution
Empire State Plaza
Alevel Meeting Center
Albany, NY 12223
Member: CTAA;

Episcopal Actors Guild
498 Clinton Avenue
Albany, NY 12206

Merri Moppets
1014 Central Avenue
Albany, NY 12801

Willett Players
362 State Street
Albany, NY 12210

Alexandria Bay

1000 Islands Summer Theatre
Alexandria Bay, NY 13601
Tel: 315-482-3320
Address Inquiries to: Dr. G.F. Reidenbaugh,
  Producer
Founded in: 1972

Auburn

Auburn Children's Theatre
West Genesee Street
Auburn, NY 13021

Auburn Civic Theatre
Post Office Box 506
Auburn, NY 13021
Tel: 315-252-5876
Address Inquiries to: Susan C. Riford,
  Executive Director
Founded in: 1958

Auburn Players Community Theatre
Post Office Box 543
Auburn, NY 13021
Address Inquiries to: Barbara S. Melanson,
  President
  Michael J. Lobisco, Vice President
Founded in: 1961

Baldwin

South Shore Repertory
c/o Mrs Grace Turkesher
988 Lydia Place
Baldwin, NY 11510

Barneveld

Playhouse on the Hill
c/o Ijams
Route 28
Barneveld, NY 13304
Tel: 315-896-4441
Address Inquiries to: Maitland T. Ijams,
  President
  Edwain B. Barrett, Secretary
Founded in: 1971

Bell Harbor

Cooky's
Post Office Box 215
Bell Harbor, NY 11694

Bellmore

Players Workshop
c/o Sy Kaplan
2706 Karen Street
Bellmore, NY 11710

Bellport

Bellport Playcrafters
36 Bellport Lane
Bellport, NY 11713

Binghampton

Civic Theatre
30 Front Street
Binghampton, NY 13905

Bohemia

Connetquot Drama Society
High School 7th Street
Bohemia, NY 11716

Bowmanville

Lancaster Community Players
Post Office Box 101
Bowmanville, NY 14026

Brentwood

Brentwood Players
55 Van Buren Street
Brentwood, NY 11717

Bronxville

Loft and Film Theatre Circle
84 Kraft Avenue
Bronxville, NY 10708

Seven Arts Society
Reformed Church of Bronxville
Bronxville, NY 10708
Tel: 914-337-6776
Address Inquiries to: Bob McIntyre, President
    Ruth Relyea, Vice President
Founded in: 1957

Brooklyn

Adelphian Players
8515 Ridge Boulevard
Brooklyn, NY 11209
Tel: 718-273-3781
Address Inquiries to: Russell Bonanno,
    Artistic Director
    Lawrence Berrick, Technical Director
Founded in: 1964

The Alonzo Players
395 Clinton Avenue
Brooklyn, NY 11238
Tel: 718-622-9058
Address Inquiries to: Cecil Alonzo, Executive
    Director
    Oliver Leigh, Vice Chairman
Founded in: 1968

Billie Holiday Theatre
1368 Fulton Street
Brooklyn, NY 11216
Tel: 718-636-0919
Founded in: 1972
Member: ATA; BTA; NYSCA; ART/NY;
    TCG; TDF;
Annual Budget: $500,000
Description: Brings professional Black theatre
to the black community. It educates new
black artists and technicians. The theatre
produces a forty week season with two resident companies and includes a children's
company, The Bubble Gum Players.

Chelsea Theatre Center of Brooklyn
30 Lafayette Avenue
Brooklyn, NY 11216
Tel: 718-783-5110
Address Inquiries to: Oliver Rea, Chairman of
    Board

Dume Spanish Theatre
41-17 Greenpoint Avenue
Brooklyn, NY
Tel: 212-729-3880; 718-729-3880
Member: NYSCA; ART/NY; TDF;
Description: An emphasis on Cuban theatre
and Hispanic culture performed in Spanish.

Festival Repertory Company
1401 Flatbush Avenue
Brooklyn, NY 11210
Tel: 718-859-9459
Address Inquiries to: Adele Waterman,
    Producer
    Paul Furman, Executive Director
Founded in: 1970

Gallery Players
Old First Church
Carroll Street and Seventh
Brooklyn, NY 11215
Tel: 718-499-8239
Member: BACA; private funding;
Description: A theatre in Park Slope present-
ing classics, children's theatre and musicals,
as well as originals. Now in it's 16th season,
it is the community's oldest theatre compa-
ny.

George Gershwin Theatre
Flatbush and Nostrand Avenues
Brooklyn College
Brooklyn, NY 11210
Tel: 718-859-1180
Member: NYSCA; ART/NY; TDF;
Description: Space available for perfor-
mances.

The Glines
28 Willow Street
Brooklyn, NY 11201
Tel: 718-522-5567
Address Inquiries to: John Glines, Executive
    Producer
    Lawrence Lane; Managing Director
Founded in: 1976
Member: DCA; NEA; NYC; NYSCA;
Annual Budget: $100,000
Description: Dedicated to the creation and
production of works that deal openly with

the gay experience. They produce every-
thing from staged readings to full scale off
off broadway productions.

Heights Players
26 Willow Place
Brooklyn, NY 11201
Tel: 718-237-2752
Founded in: 1956
Member: NYSCA; ART/NY; TDF;
Description: A community Off Off Broadway
group located in Brooklyn Heights.

Kings Theater Guild
304 East 3rd Street
Brooklyn, NY 12223
Tel: 718-844-4241
Address Inquiries to: Liz Peart, President
Mike Newson, Secretary

On Stage Repertory Company
c/o Advent Lutheran Church
Avenue P at East 12th Street
Brooklyn, NY 11229
Tel: 718-743-6819
Address Inquiries to: Robert P. Elleman,
    Artistic Director
    Leslie D. Fisherman, Executive Director
Founded in: 1973
Member: ART/NY; NYSCA; TDF;
Description: Aims to bring theatre to Brooklyn
at prices Brooklynites can afford.

Puppet Theatre of War
2753 West 15th Street
Brooklyn, NY 11224
Tel: 718-373-2810
Address Inquiries to: Barton Lane, Director
Founded in: 1972

Redwood Players
655 East 81st Street
Brooklyn, NY 11209

Ryan Repertory Company
2445 Bath Avenue
Brooklyn, NY 11214
Tel: 718-373-5208
Address Inquiries to: Barbara Parisi
Jonathan Rosenblum
Founded in: 1972
Member: BACA Decentralization Program;
    Irene Ryan Foundation; ART/NY; TDF;
Description: Presents original musical come-
dies and straight plays.

Buffalo

Amana Actors
584 Broden Road
Buffalo, NY 14225

Amherst Players
1752 Parker Boulevard
Buffalo, NY 14225

Rooftop Players Little Theatre
200 Norwood Avenue
Buffalo, NY 14222

Saint Ann's Little Theatre
376 Herman Street
Buffalo, NY 14223

Studio Arena Theatre
681 Main Street
Buffalo, NY 14203
Tel: 716-856-5650
Address Inquiries to: Frank T. Stone,
  Chairman
  Weles V. Moot, Jr., Chairman
Founded in: 1927
Member: TCG; AEA;

Towne Players
232 Hartford Avenue
Buffalo, NY 14223

Chappaqua

Drama Group
Post Office Box 106
Chappaqua, NY 10514

Clinton

Adirondack Playhouse
Playhouse on the Hill
Clinton, NY 13323

Copenhagen

Camden Community Players
Cobb Road
Copenhagen, NY 13626

Corning

Corning Summer Theatre
Post Office Box 51
Corning, NY 14830
Tel: 607-936-4634
Address Inquiries to: Dorothy Chernuck,
  Producer
Founded in: 1951
Annual Budget: $400,000
Description: A professional summer theatre
relying on corporate support, private dona-
tions and box office receipts.

Cortland

Cortland Repertory Theatre
Post Office Box 783
Cortland, NY 13045
Tel: 607-753-6161
Address Inquiries to: David J. Yaman,
  Producer
  Rochelle L. Ray, General Manager
Founded in: 1971
Annual Budget: $100,000

Deer Park

Arena Players Repertory
269 West 18th Street
Deer Park, NY 11729

East Aurora

Aurora Players
Post Office Box 206
East Aurora, NY 14052

Eastchester

Town Hall Community Theatre
South Andrew Road
Eastchester, NY 10709

East Hampton

Guild Hall Players
c/o E.E. McDonough
39 Buell Lane
East Hampton, NY 11937

East Rochester

Barry Tuttle Summer Theatre
East Rochester, NY 14603
Address Inquiries to: Barry Tuttle

Elmira

Elmira Little Theatre
Post Office Box 761
Elmira, NY 14902

Elmont

YMCA Nassau Youth Theatre Company
1 Plainfield Avenue
Elmont, NY 11033
Tel: 516-328-8358
Address Inquiries to: Ronald Russo, Theatre
  Arts Director
  Judy A. Babajko, Chairperson
Founded in: 1972

Elmsford

An Evening Dinner Theatre
11 Clearbrook Road
Elmsford, NY 10523
Tel: 914-592-2268
Address Inquiries to: William B. Stutler,
  Manager
  Robert J. Funking, Manager
Founded in: 1974
Member: AEA;

Fishkill

Cecilwood Theatre
Route 52, Box 56
Fishkill, NY 12524

Fredonia

Dunkirk-Fredonia Players
54 A Berry Road
Fredonia, NY 14063

Freeport

Mohawk Players, Inc.
c/o J. Schrader
178 Craig Avenue
Freeport, NY 11520

Garden City

Adelphi University
Olmstead Theatre
Garden City, NY 11530

Garden City Little Theatre
c/o Sal Catania, 85 Stewart Avenue
Garden City, NY 11530

Little Theatre
85 Stewart Avenue
Garden City, NY 11530

Glen Falls

Adirondack Children's Troupe
Star Route, Pilot Knob Road
Glen Falls, NY 12801
Address Inquiries to: Katie Blossom

Glen Head

Glen Players, Inc.
Post Office Box 174
Glen Head, NY 11545
Tel: 516-676-3515
Founded in: 1949

Gouverneur

Community Players
Barney Street Road
Gouverneur, NY 13642

Greenwood Lake

Greenwood Lake Little Theatre
Post Office Box 744
Greenwood Lake, NY 10925

Guilderland

Guilderland Community Theatre
Post Office Box 181
Guilderland, NY 12084

Hamburg

Hamburg Little Theatre
Post Office Box 5
Hamburg, NY 14075

Hartsdale

Fort Hill Players
1115 The Colony
Hartsdale, NY 10530

Westchester Repertory
94 Pinewood Garden
Hartsdale, NY 10530

Huntington

Huntington Township Theatre Group
Post Office Box 824
Huntington, NY 11743

Village Green Summer Playhouse
25A and Park Avenue
Huntington, NY 11743
Tel: 516-549-4065
Address Inquiries to: Richard Allen, Board
  Chairman
  David Johnson, Producer
Founded in: 1974
Annual Budget: $100,000

Ithaca

Ithaca Repertory Theater
313 North Tioga Street
Ithaca, NY 14850
Tel: 607-273-8588
Address Inquiries to: Thomas Niedeerkorn,
  Chairman
  Ruth Houghton, Vice President
Founded in: 1970
Annual Budget: $100,000

Jamestown

Little Theatre of Jamestown
18-24 East 2nd Street
Jamestown, NY 14701

Jeericho

Plays and Players
5 Hazlewood Drive
Jeericho, NY 11753

Jericho

Jericho Community Theatre
c/o Mrs. Mimi Gruber
54 Bounty Lane
Jericho, NY 11753

Johnstown

Colonial Little Theatre
Post Office Box 283
Johnstown, NY 12095

Kenmore

Jim Menke Marionette Theatre
99 Northwood Drive
Kenmore, NY 14233
Tel: 716-876-7869
Address Inquiries to: James E. Menke, Jr.,
  Producer, Director
Founded in: 1950
Member: PA;

Kingston

Coach House Players
12 Ausgusta Street
Kingston, NY 12401
Address Inquiries to: Kay Finn, Business
  Manager
  Wendell Scherer, President
Founded in: 1950
Member: NYSCA;
Annual Budget: $25,000.

Lackawanna

Phoenix Players
500 Martin Road
Lackawanna, NY 14218
Tel: 716-826-1500
Address Inquiries to: Matthew V. Oreskovic,
  Drama Director and Fine Arts Director
Founded in: 1971
Annual Budget: $25,000

Lake George

Lake George Dinner Theatre
Route 9
Lake George, NY 12845
Tel: 518-668-5787
Address Inquiries to: David Eastwood,
  Producer
Founded in: 1968
Annual Budget: $50,000

Lake Placid

Lake Placid Center for Music, Drama and
  Art;
Saranac Avenue at Fawn Ridge
Lake Placid, NY 12946
Member: AEA;

Description: An AEA theatre for young audiences.

Lakeview

South Shore Drama Group
c/o Mrs. Blanch Rothstein
322 Glen Road
Lakeview, NY 11570

Latham

Calvary Methodist Church
14 Belle Avenue
Latham, NY 12110

Footlighters
13 Belle Avenue
Latham, NY 11210

Latham Community Players
Post Office Box 345
Latham, NY 11210
Tel: 518-869-7339
Address Inquiries to: Donald Countermine,
  President
Founded in: 1958

Lewiston

Niagara Falls Little Theatre, Inc.
419 Tryon Drive
Lewiston, NY 14092
Tel: 716-282-9119
Address Inquiries to: Warren Hartburg,
  Chairman
  Mrs. Eileen Paron, Vice Chairman
Founded in: 1926
Member: NYSCA; NYSCA;
Annual Budget: $25,000

Lindenhurst

List Theatricals 'Studio Theatre'
141 South Welwood Avenue
Lindenhurst, NY 11757
Tel: 516-884-1877
Address Inquiries to: Mike Engel, Artistic
  Director
Founded in: 1962
Annual Budget: $25,000

Liverpool

Clay Towne Players
4016 Bay Park Drive
Liverpool, NY 13088

Lowville

Church Drama Group
State Street
Lowville, NY 13367

Massapequa

Pequa Players
25 Grover Avenue
Massapequa, NY 11758

Monticello

Periwinkle Productions
19 Clinton Avenue
Monticello, NY 12701
Tel: 914-794-1666; 914-794-4992
Address Inquiries to: Sunna Rasch, Executive
  Producer

Alfred Rasch, Treasurer
Founded in: 1963
Member: AEA; TCG; ACA; ATA; PACT;
Annual Budget: $100,000
Description: One of the oldest on-going Equity Children's Theatres in the United States. It is a not-for-profit, award-winning, professional touring theatre for young audiences. Periwinkle presents shows for every age level. They offer in depth study guides, as well as workshops.

Sullivan Company Drama
4 Lakewood Avenue
Monticello, NY 12701

Sullivan County Dramatic Workshop
4 Lakewood Avenue
Monticello, NY 12701
Tel: 914-794-4114
Address Inquiries to: Kenneth Wells,
  President
  Helen Graham, Vice President
Founded in: 1950
Member: NYSCA;

Naples

Bristol Valley Playhouse
Route 3
Naples, NY 14512

Newark

Newark Players
Post Office Box 306
Newark, NY 14513

New Hartford

Players of Utica
19 Oxford Road
New Hartford, NY 13413

New Paltz

90 Miles Off Broadway
Post Office Box 565
New Paltz, NY 12561

Newtonville

Colonie Players
Post Office Box 35
Newtonville, NY 12128

New York

The Acting Company
420 West 42nd Street, 3rd Floor
New York, NY 10019
Tel: 212-564-3450
Address Inquiries to: John Houseman,
  Artistic Director
  Porter Van Zandt, Executive Director

The Ambassador Theatre
219 West 49th Street
New York, NY 10019
Tel: 212-541-6490; 212-944-4100, Shubert
  Group Sales
Founded in: 1921
Description: A 1,125 seat playhouse originally constructed in 1921, the Ambassador was purchased by the Shubert organization in 1955 and returned to use as a legimate

theatre after serving as a movie theatre, radio, and television studio.

American Center for Stanislavski Theatre
485 Park Avenue
New York, NY 10022
Tel: 212-755-5120
Address Inquiries to: Sonia Moore, Artistic Director
Michael Bertin, General Manager
Founded in: 1965
Member: TCG; ATA; ART/NY;
Annual Budget: $50,000

American Place Theatre
111 West 46th Street
New York, NY 10036
Tel: 212-246-0393
Address Inquiries to: Wynn Handman, Artistic Director
Julia Miles, Director APT Women's Project
Founded in: 1964
Member: AEA; ART/NY; TDF; NYSCA;
Description: Wynn Handman, Michael Tolan, Sidney Lanier and Myrna Loy were the founders of the American Place Theatre. Moving to it's present location in 1971 the APT produces many original plays and sponsors the American Humorist Series and the Women's Project.

American Puppet Arts Council
59 Barrow Street
New York, NY 10014
Tel: 212-989-7060
Address Inquiries to: William B. Baird, Executive Director
William Glass, General Manager
Founded in: 1966

American Stanislavski Theatre
141 West 13th Street
New York, NY 10014
Tel: 212-755-5120
Address Inquiries to: Sonia Moore, Artistic Director
Member: NYSCA; ART/NY; TDF;
Description: Sonia Moore, artistic director, offers training in the method.

Appleby Studio-Theatre
579 Broadway
New York, NY 10012
Tel: 212-431-8489
Member: NYSCA; ART/NY; TDF;

Arts Mix
400 West End Avenue
New York, NY 10024
Member: AEA;

Arts Projects at St. Mark's Church
10th Street and Second Avenue
New York, NY 10003
Tel: 212-533-4650; 212-674-0910
Member: NYSCA; ART/NY; TDF;

The Ethel Barrymore Theatre
243 West 47th Street
New York, NY 10036
Tel: 212-246-0390
Founded in: 1924

Description: Opened originally in 1928 with The Kingdom of God, the Ethel Barrymore has a seating capacity of 1096.

The Martin Beck Theatre
302 West 45th Street
New York, NY 10036
Tel: 212-246-6363
Founded in: 1924
Description: Martin Beck was the chief of the Orpheum Vaudeville circuit. His theatre opened on November 11, 1924 and now houses 1,280.

The Belasco Theatre
111 West 44th Street
New York, NY 10036
Tel: 212-354-4490
Founded in: 1907
Description: Named for the playwright and producer, David Belasco, who used to live above the theatre, it currently houses 1,018 and was built in 1907.

The Bijou Theatre
209 West 45th Street
New York, NY 10036
Tel: 212-221-8500
Founded in: 1917
Description: Built in 1917, the Bijou opened with The Knife and has a seating capicity of 365.

The Biltmore Theatre
261 West 47th Street
New York, NY 10036
Tel: 212-582-5340
Address Inquiries to: David Cogan, Operator
Description: Owned by the Biltmore Nederlander organization the Biltmore was opened on December 7, 1925 and has a seating capacity of 948.

Bond Street Theatre Coalition
2 Bond Street
New York, NY 10012
Tel: 212-244-4270
Member: NYSCA; ART/NY; TDF;

The Booth Theatre
222 West 45th Street
New York, NY 10036
Tel: 212-246-5969
Founded in: 1913
Description: Opened on Octover 16, 1913, the Booth has a seating capacity of 783.

The Broadhurst Theatre
235 West 44th Street
New York, NY 10036
Tel: 212-247-0472
Founded in: 1917
Description: The Broadhurst opened on September 27, 1917 with a seating capacity of 1,155

The Broadway Theatre
Broadway at 53rd Street
New York, NY 10019
Tel: 212-247-3600; 212-398-8383
Address Inquiries to: Shubert Organization
Founded in: 1924
Description: Originally a movie theatre, the

Broadway opened as a legitimate theatre in 1929 and currently houses 1,765.

Broadway-Times Theatre Company
250 West 43rd Street
New York, NY 10036
Tel: 212-391-1880
Member: NYSCA; ART/NY; TDF;

The Brooks Atkinson Theatre
256 West 47th Street
New York, NY 10036
Tel: 212-245-3430
Founded in: 1926
Member: LNYTP;
Description: Known originally as the Mansfield, the theatre opened on February 15, 926, with The Night Duel. The Brooks Atkinson Theatre has a seating capacty of 1,088

Brook Theatre
40 West 17th Street
New York, NY 10011
Tel: 212-929-9554
Member: NYSCA; ART/NY; TDF;

Cathedral of St. John the Divine
1047 Amsterdam Avenue, at 112th Street
New York, NY 10025
Tel: 212-678-6962
Member: NYSCA; ART/NY; TDF;

Center for the Performing Arts
939 Eighth Avenue
New York, NY 10019
Tel: 212-246-4818
Member: NYSCA; ART/NY; TDF;

The Century Theatre
235 West 46th Street
New York, NY 10036
Tel: 212-354-6644
Address Inquiries to: Jeffery Watchtell
Description: This theatre has had several names in the past including the Mayfair and the Staircase. The theatre houses 299, just meeting the seating requirement to qualify as an official 'Broadway' theatre.

The Changing Space
120 West 28th Street
New York, NY 10001
Tel: 212-242-6663
Member: NYSCA; ART/NY; TDF;

Circle in the Square
1633 Broadway
New York, NY 10019
Tel: 212-581-3270; 212-581-0720
Address Inquiries to: Theodore Mann, Artistic Director
Paul Libin, Managing Director
Founded in: 1951
Annual Budget: $200,000
Description: Circle in the Square, well know for Off Broadway revivals of classical material, offers a professional training program two years in length, a staff of prominent actors and directors affiliated with the professional theatre and auditions held in major cities. For the latest schedules and information contact E. Colin O'Leary, Executive Director of the Theatre School.

The Circle in the Square Theatre
1633 Broadway
New York, NY 10019
Tel: 212-581-0720

Circle Repertory Company
99 Seventh Avenue South
New York, NY 10014
Tel: 212-924-7100
Founded in: 1969
Member: NYSCA; ART/NY; TDF;

Cithaeron
55 Mercer Street
New York, NY 10013
Tel: 212-966-6183
Member: NYSCA; ART/NY; TDF;

Classic Theatre
20 Bleecker Street
New York, NY 10012
Tel: 212-242-3900
Member: NYSCA; ART/NY; TDF;

Coachlight Dinner Theatre
10 East 49th Street
New York, NY 10017
Address Inquiries to: Samuel Belkin,
    Producer

Colonnades Theatre Lab
428 Lafayette Street
New York, NY 10003
Tel: 212-673-2222, Theatre; 212-598-4620,
    Lab
Address Inquiries to: Mary T. Nealon,
    General Manager
    Robin Rose, Business Manager
Member: NYSCA; ART/NY; TDF;
Description: An Off-Off Broadway theatre lab
and showcase for professional theatre oper-
ating under the AEA code.

Comedia Puppet Player/Wallace Puppets
Post Office Box 129
Cooper Station
New York, NY 10003
Tel: 212-254-9074
Address Inquiries to: Lea Wallace,
    Director/Manager
Founded in: 1950
Member: ATA; AFTRA; AGVA; PA;

Common Ground
29 Wooster Street
New York, NY 10012
Tel: 212-431-5446
Member: NYSCA; ART/NY; TDF;

Compania de Teatro Repertoria Espanol
138 East 27th Street
New York, NY 10016
Tel: 212-889-2850
Address Inquiries to: Gilbert Zaldivar,
    Producer
    Robert Federico, Associate Producer
Founded in: 1969
Member: ART/NY;
Annual Budget: $100,000

Conway Studio
35 Bond Street
New York, NY 10012

Tel: 212-674-8034
Member: NYSCA; ART/NY; TDF;

The Cort Theatre
138 West 48th Street
New York, NY 10036
Tel: 212-489-6392
Address Inquiries to: Shubert Organiztion
Founded in: 1912
Description: With 1,089 seats the Cort theatre
opened with the play Peg O' My Heart which
ran for two years and gave the theatre a
reputation as a lucky place to book for a
show.

Counterpoint Theatre
152 West 66th Street
New York, NY 10023
Member: NYSCA; ART/NY; TDF;

CSC Repertory
136 East 13th
New York, NY 10003
Tel: 212-677-4210
Address Inquiries to: Christopher Martin,
    Artistic Director
    Dan Martin, Managing Director
Founded in: 1967

Cuban Cultural Center of New York
601 West 51st Street
New York, NY 10019
Tel: 212-586-8564
Member: NYSCA; ART/NY; TDF;

Cubiculo
414 West 51st Street
New York, NY 10019
Tel: 212-265-2138; 212-265-2139
Member: NYSCA; ART/NY; TDF;

Direct Theatre
39 Grove Street
New York, NY 10014
Tel: 212-362-0470
Member: NYSCA; ART/NY; TDF;
Description: Produces new and experimental
theatre.

Dmitri, Swiss Mime
Lehman College
Performing Arts Center
Boulevard West and Paul Avenue
New York, NY 10468
Tel: 212-245-2885
Member: NYSCA; ART/NY; TDF;
Description: Off-Off Broadway theatre special-
izing in Swiss Mime.

Double Image Theatre
444 West 56th Street
New York, NY 10019
Tel: 212-245-2489
Member: NYSCA; ART/NY; TDF;
Description: Looking for new performing and
writing talent.

Drama Committee Repertory Theatre
17 West 20th Street
New York, NY 10011
Tel: 212-929-8377
Member: NYSCA; ART/NY; TDF;
Description: Produces prose classics adapted

for the stage and new plays.

Drama Ensemble Repertory Company
108 Wooster Street
New York, NY 10012
Tel: 212-925-9016
Member: NYSCA; ART/NY; TDF;
Description: New plays and ensemble work.

Dramatis Personae
114 West 14th Street
New York, NY 10011
Tel: 212-675-9922
Member: NYSCA; ART/NY; TDF;
Description: Operates under the AEA show-
case code.

DTW at American Theatre Laboratory
219 West 19th Street
New York, NY 10011
Tel: 212-924-0077; 212-691-6500
Member: NYSCA; ART/NY; TDF;
Description: Space available for perfor-
mances.

DTW's Economy Tires Theatre
219 West 19 Street
New York, NY 10011
Tel: 212-924-0077
Address Inquiries to: Robert Applegarth,
    Associate Director
    David White, Executive Director
Member: NYSCA; ART/NY; TDF;
Description: An Off Off Broadway showcase
theatre.

The Edison Theatre
240 West 47th Street
New York, NY 10036
Tel: 212-757-7164; 212-586-7870
Address Inquiries to: Norma Kean
Doris Buberl
Description: A 500 seat Broadway Musical
Playhouse currently presenting 'Oh! Calcut-
ta!', now in its 15th year.

Encore Theatre Company
424 West 49th Street
New York, NY 10019
Tel: 212-732-6712
Member: NYSCA; ART/NY; TDF;

Ensemble Studio Theatre
549 West 52nd Street
New York, NY 10019
Tel: 212-247-4982
Address Inquiries to: Debra Dahl, Managing
    Director, Production Supervisor
    Kent Lanataff, Business Manager
Founded in: 1971
Member: Billy Rose Foundation; Ford
    Foundation; Hale Matthews Foundation;
    Jerome Foundation; John Golden Fund;
    Lucille Lortel Foundation; Magowan
    Family Foundation; NEA; NYSCA; New
    York City Department of Cultural
    Affairs; ART/NY; Shubert Foundation;
    TCG; TDF;
Annual Budget: $390,000
Description: A not-for-profit Off Off Broadway
theatre with a membership of over 300 ac-
tors, directors and technical people. EST

supports artists and the profession by developing new works for the stage.

Fanfare Theatre Ensemble
100 East 4th Street
New York, NY 10003
Member: AEA;

First All Children's Theatre
37 West 65th Street
New York, NY 10023
Tel: 212-873-6400
Address Inquiries to: Meridee Stein, Artistic
 Director
 Tom Fordham, Business Manager
Member: NYSCA; ART/NY; TDF;

The Floating Rep
146 Chambers Street
New York, NY 10007
Tel: 212-267-5756
Member: NYSCA; ART/NY; TDF;

Flying Eight Ball Productions
145 West 18th Street
New York, NY 10003
Tel: 212-255-3310
Member: NYSCA; ART/NY; TDF;

Fools Company, Inc.
484 West 43rd Street, #19M
New York, NY 10036

Fourth Wall Repertory Company
79 East 4th Street
New York, NY 10003
Tel: 212-254-5060
Member: NYSCA; ART/NY; TDF;

Four Winds Theatre
37 West 10th Street
New York, NY 10011
Tel: 212-260-3939
Address Inquiries to: Dr. Jenny Egan,
 Director
 Aaron Schwatz, Administrator
Founded in: 1959
Annual Budget: $50,000

Frank Silvera Writers' Workshop
317 West 125th Street
New York, NY 10027
Tel: 212-622-8463; 212-864-8307
Address Inquiries to: Frank Silvera, Artistic
 Director
Member: NEA; NYSCA; ART/NY;
Description: A theatre which emphasizes the work of developing new playwrights, with workshops for writers, actors and directors.

Fredrick Douglass Creative Arts Center
83 East 4th Street
New York, NY 10003
Tel: 212-831-6113
Member: NYSCA; ART/NY; TDF;
Description: New plays of Black and Hispanic writers.

Garden Variety Mime Theatre
870 Bowery
New York, NY 10003
Tel: 212-929-7328
Member: NYSCA; ART/NY; TDF;
Description: All woman collective mime theatre.

Gene Frankel Theatre Workshop
342 East 63rd Street
New York, NY 10021
Tel: 212-421-1666
Address Inquiries to: Gene Frankel, Creative
 Director
 Mrs. Theodore Newhouse, Chairperson
Founded in: 1974

The Gershwin Theatre
Broadway at 51st Street
New York, NY 10019
Tel: 212-586-6510; 212-398-8383
Description: No Broadway houses were built from 1928 until the Uris was built in 1972. Designed by Ralph Alswang, the Gershwin seats 1,933 and houses the Theatre Hall of Fame in its rotunda.

Gilbert and Sullivan Players
270 West 89th Street
New York, NY 10024
Tel: 212-724-9159
Member: NYSCA; ART/NY; TDF;

The Golden Theatre
252 West 45th Street
New York, NY 10036
Tel: 212-246-6740; 212-398-8383
Founded in: 1927
Description: The John Golden Theatre, named for the 1930's theatre producer, originally opened in 1927 and now seats 805.

Hampton Playhouse
405 East 54th Street
New York, NY 10022
Address Inquiries to: John Vari, Managing
 Director
 Alfred Christie, Managing Director
Annual Budget: $50,000

Hand Over Mouth Hidden Theatre
16 Thompson Street
New York, NY 10013
Tel: 212-925-0695
Member: NYSCA; ART/NY; TDF;

HB Playwrights Foundation
122 Bank Street
New York, NY 10014
Tel: 212-989-6540
Address Inquiries to: Herbert Berghof,
 Artistic Director
 Marlene Mancini, Administrative
 Director
Founded in: 1964

The Mark Hellinger Theatre
236 West 51st Street
New York, NY 10019
Tel: 212-757-7064; 212-398-8383
Founded in: 1930
Description: Originally named the Hollywood, the Mark Hellinger was a movie house. It seats 1,603.

Henry Street's New Federal Theatre
466 Grand Street
New York, NY 10002
Tel: 212-766-9295

Address Inquiries to: Woodie King, Director
Founded in: 1970

Henry Street Theatre
466 Grand Street
New York, NY 10002
Tel: 212-766-9334
Member: NYSCA; ART/NY; TDF;
Description: Space available for performances.

Hudson Guild Theatre
441 West 26th Street
New York, NY 10001
Tel: 212-760-9810; 212-760-9847
Address Inquiries to: David Kerry Heefner,
 Producing Director
 Judson Barteaux, Managing Director
Member: NYSCA; ART/NY; TDF;

Hunter College Playwrights
Little Theatre
695 Park Avenue
New York, NY 10021
Member: NYSCA; ART/NY; TDF;
Description: Presents full productions of plays developed in the Hunter College playwrighting seminars.

The Imperial Theatre
249 West 45th Street
New York, NY 10036
Tel: 212-265-4311
Founded in: 1923
Description: Known for hit musicals, the theatre opened in 1923 and currently houses 1,453.

Impossible Ragtime Theatre
120 West 28th Street
New York, NY 10001
Tel: 212-243-7494
Member: NYSCA; ART/NY; TDF;
Description: A theatre for directors focusing on audience participation.

Interart Theatre
549 West 52nd Street
New York, NY 10019
Tel: 212-246-1050
Address Inquiries to: Margot Lewitin, Artistic
 Director
 Abigail Franklin, Managing Director
Member: NYSCA; ART/NY; TCG; TDF;
Annual Budget: $500,000
Description: A not-for-profit professional Off Off Broadway showcase theatre.

Jean Cocteau Repertory
330 Bowery
New York, NY 10012
Tel: 212-677-0060
Address Inquiries to: Andy Cohn, Managing
 Director
 Craig Smith, Production Manager
Member: NYSCA; ART/NY; TDF;

Jewish Repertory Theatre
344 East 14th Street
New York, NY 10003
Tel: 212-777-0033
Address Inquiries to: Ran Avni, Artistic
 Director

Edward M. Cohen, Director, Writers
 Laboratory
Member: NYSCA; ART/NY; TDF;

Just a Bunch of Us Kids
10 East 18th Street
New York, NY 10003
Member: AEA;
Description: An AEA theatre for young audiences.

Kopa Kids Productions
8 East 64th Street
New York, NY 10021
Member: AEA;
Description: An AEA theatre for young audiences.

Lakes Region Playhouse
301 West 45th Street
New York, NY 10036
Tel: 603-293-7561
Address Inquiries to: Eloise Armeen, Director
Founded in: 1948

La Mama ETC
74A East 4th Street
New York, NY 10003
Tel: 212-475-7710; 212-475-7908
Address Inquiries to: Ellen Stewart, Executive
 Director
 Jim Moore, Business Manager
Member: Ford Foundation; NEA; NYSCA;
 ART/NY; Rockefeller Foundation; TDF;
Description: The first and most famous of the
New York Off Off Broadway theatres. Ellen
Stewart, Executive Director of La Mama,
oversees programs that include La Mama
ETC, The Third World Institute of Theatre
Arts Studies, The La Mama Annex and other
exciting theatre programs. Founded by playwright Paul Foster and Ellen Stewart in 1964.

Latin American Theatre Ensemble
356 West 36th Street
New York, NY 10018
Tel: 212-362-9447
Member: NYSCA; ART/NY; TDF;
Description: Holds active and literary workshops and presents plays.

Library of the Performing Arts
65th Street and Broadway
New York, NY 10021
Tel: 212-799-2200

Lion Theatre Company
422 West 42nd Street
New York, NY 10036
Tel: 212-947-4224
Member: NYSCA; ART/NY; TDF;
Description: An acting company that to covers
the entire range of dramatic repertory and is
one of the most repected on 42nd Street
Theatre Row.

Lister Complex Theatre
60 West 25th Street
New York, NY 10001
Tel: 212-243-7758
Member: NYSCA; ART/NY; TDF;
Description: Multi-discipline, multi-dimensional approach to theatre.

The Longacre Theatre
230 West 48th Street
New York, NY 10036
Tel: 212-246-5639; 212-944-4100
Founded in: 1913
Description: Open on May 1, 1913 the Longacre now seats 1452.

The Lunt Fontanne Theatre
205 West 46th Street
New York, NY 10036
Tel: 212-586-5555
Description: Owned and operated by the Nederlander theatre group. The theatre holds
1,478.

The Lyceum Theatre
149 West 45th Street
New York, NY 10036
Tel: 212-582-3897; 212-944-3700
Founded in: 1903
Description: The Lyceum, designated a city
landmark, is owned by the Shubert Organization. Originally built as a theatre and
apartment for producer Daniel Frohman,
the theatre is known for its architecture and
now houses 928.

Lyric Theatre
145 West 18th Street
New York, NY 10011
Tel: 212-595-5065; 212-244-4270
Member: NYSCA; ART/NY; TDF;
Description: Develops musical theatre and
theatre artists. Presents original works and
unusual revivals.

The Majestic Theatre
247 West 44th Street
New York, NY 10036
Tel: 212-246-0730
Founded in: 1927
Description: One of the most beautiful houses
on Broadway, the Majestic opened on March
28, 1927 and now seats 1,629 with management by the Shubert theatrical organization.

Manhattan Punch Line
410 West 42nd Street
New York, NY 10036
Tel: 212-288-8288; 212-921-1455, Box
Office
Address Inquiries to: Steve Kaplan, Artistic
 Director
 Mitch McGuire, Executive Director
Founded in: 1979
Member: NEA; NYSCA; ART/NY; TDF;
Description: A theatre devoted completely to
comedy.

Manhattan Theatre Club
321 East 73rd Street
New York, NY 10021
Tel: 212-472-0600; 212-288-2500
Member: NYSCA; ART/NY; TDF;
Description: Presents contemporary work,
cabaret musical events, with performances
by poets of their own works.

Manna House Workshops
338 East 106th Street
New York, NY 10029

Tel: 212-722-8223; 212-722-8224
Founded in: 1967
Member: NYSCA; ART/NY; TDF;
Description: Provides East Harlem with music
education, concerts and musical theatre.

Market Players
134 Reade Street
Morgans Tavern
New York, NY 10013
Tel: 212-254-0474
Member: NYSCA; ART/NY; TDF;
Description: Revivals of original musicals in an
ongoing program.

Masterworks Laboratory Theatre
40 West 22nd Street
New York, NY 10011
Tel: 212-691-4367
Member: NYSCA; ART/NY; TDF;
Description: Fresh approach to world classics
in drama, opera, literature and song.

Maximillion Productions
98 Riverside Drive, #7-H
New York, NY 10024
Member: AEA;
Description: An AEA theatre for young audiences.

Maximus Productions
Cathedral of St. John the Divine
New York, NY 10025
Tel: 212-678-6888
Member: NYSCA; ART/NY; TDF;
Description: Great classic works presented in
the world's largest Gothic cathedral.

The Meat and Potatoes Company
58 West 39th Street
New York, NY 10018
Tel: 212-391-2346
Member: NYSCA; ART/NY; TDF;

Medicine Show Theatre Ensemble
6 West 18th Street
New York, NY 10003
Tel: 212-255-4991
Address Inquiries to: Barbara Vannn, Artistic
 Director
 Chris Brandt, Production Manager
Member: NYSCA; ART/NY; TDF;

Medusa's Revenge
10 Bleecker Street at the Bowery
New York, NY 10012
Tel: 212-532-4151
Member: NYSCA; ART/NY; TDF;
Description: A women's experimental theatre.

The Minskoff Theatre
1515 Broadway at 45th Street
New York, NY 10036
Tel: 212-869-0550
Address Inquiries to: Jerry Minskoff
Founded in: 1973
Description: The Minskoff Theatre was built
on the site of the Astor Hotel and is located
in the 55 story office building that replaced
it. The theatre seats 1,621 and is fully
equipped for handicapped theatregoers.

Morse Mime Repertory Company
224 Waverly Place
New York, NY 10014
Tel: 212-242-0530
Member: NYSCA; ART/NY; TDF;

Music-Theatre Group/Lenox Arts Center
Lenox Arts Center
c/o Lyn Austin
18 East 68th Street
New York, NY 10021
Tel: 212-371-9610; 212-582-1978, Box
Office
Address Inquiries to: Lyn Austin and Margo
Lion, Co Producing Directors
Diane Wondisford, Administrator
Founded in: Lenox Arts Center 1970, Music
Theatre Group 1975
Member: Ford Foundation; Hale Matthews
Foundation; NOI; NYSCA; ART/NY;
Polaroid; Rockwell; TDF;
Annual Budget: $225,000
Description: A winner of five Obie awards, the
center is dedicated to a searching out writ-
ers, composers, directors and performers to
create a new kind of music theatre.

The Nameless Theatre
125 West 22nd Street
New York, NY 10011
Tel: 212-242-9768
Member: NYSCA; ART/NY; TDF;
Description: Aims to present theatrical prod-
uctions with timeless themes.

National Arts on Bond
30 Bond Street
New York, NY 10012
Tel: 212-674-9710
Member: NYSCA; ART/NY; TDF;
Description: Presents classical repertory and
new works.

National Black Theatre
9 East 125th Street
New York, NY 10035
Tel: 212-427-5615
Member: NYSCA; ART/NY; TDF;

National Theatre Company
165 West 6th Street, Suite 1202
New York, NY 10036
Tel: 212-575-1044; 212-575-1046
Address Inquiries to: Barry Weissler,
President
Fran Weissler, Vice President
Founded in: 1964
Member: AEA; ACCUCA; ISPA; NECAA;
Description: A nationwide booking agency
producing shows for children, high schools,
colleges, universities and on Broadway.

Nederlander Theatre
208 West 41st Street
New York, NY 10036
Tel: 212-586-6150
Address Inquiries to: The Nederlanders
Founded in: 1921
Description: Originally the National, the
theatre is now owned by The Nederlanders
and named in honor of David Tobias Neder-
lander housing 1,168. It is the only Broadway

class house open below 42nd street.

The New Apollo Theatre
234 West 43rd Street
New York, NY 10036
Tel: 212-921-8558, Box Office;
212-730-0320
Member: LNYTP;
Annual Budget: $1,500,000
Description: Recently refurbished for a re-
markable low $350,000 the theatre was first
opened in 1910. The original entrance was
on 42nd street and the New Apollo is an
example of one of the several Broadway
houses still used for movies that could be
returned to legimate theatre use.

New Cycle Theatre
657 Fifth Avenue
New York, NY 10022
Tel: 212-788-7098
Member: NYSCA; ART/NY; TDF;
Description: An experimental theatre company whose members are actors and playwrights performing works with feminist and
pacifist themes.

New Federal Theatre
466 Grand Street
New York, NY 10002
Tel: 212-766-9334
Address Inquiries to: Woodie King Jr.,
Producing Director
Steve Tennen, Co-Producer
Member: NYSCA; ART/NY; TDF;

New World Theatre
c/o Wonderhorse Theatre
83 East 4th Street
New York, NY 10003
Tel: 212-838-3704
Address Inquiries to: Jane Stanton, Producer
Andrew Krawetz, Co Manager
Member: NYSCA; ART/NY; TDF;

New York Art Theatre Institute
116 East 14th Street
New York, NY
Tel: 212-228-1470
Member: NYSCA; ART/NY; TDF;

New York Stage Works
15 West 18th Street
New York, NY 10011
Tel: 212-242-3967; 212-242-8108
Member: NYSCA; ART/NY; TDF;
Description: Promotes and develops public
performances of new works for the Ameri-
can stage.

New York Street Theatre Caravan
336 West 20th Street
New York, NY 10011
Tel: 212-242-1869; 212-454-8551
Address Inquiries to: Marketa Kimbrell,
Producer
Founded in: 1968
Member: Campus Activities Association;
NYSCA; National Entertainment
Association; North Star Foundation;
ART/NY;
Annual Budget: $150,000

Description: Winner of a 1978 Obie award,
company travels thousands of miles each
year bringing theatre to Americans outside
the cultural mainstream.

New York Theatre Ensemble
62 East 4th Street
New York, NY 10003
Tel: 212-477-4126
Member: Arts and Business Council;
ART/NY; VLA;
Description: An Off Off Broadway company.

New York Theatre Studio
130 West 80th Street
New York, NY 10024
Tel: 212-595-6656
Address Inquiries to: Cheryl Faraone,
Managing Director
Sally Burnett, Administrative Director
Member: NYSCA; ART/NY; TDF;

No Smoking Playhouse
354 West 45th Street
New York, NY 10036
Tel: 212-245-9808; 212-582-7862
Member: NEA; NYSCA; ART/NY; TDF;
Annual Budget: $75,000
Description: Available for rental.

Nuestro Teatro
112 East 23rd Street
New York, NY 10010
Tel: 212-673-9430
Address Inquiries to: Luz Castanos, Artistic
Director
James Caparelli, Theatre Manager
Founded in: 1972
Member: NEA; NYSCA; ART/NY; TDF;
Annual Budget: $40,000
Description: Performs in Spanish producing
three or four full scale producions each year,
and tours with Alegria, a bilingual story
theatre for children. Accepts unsolicited
manuscripts.

Off Center Theatre
436 West 18th Street
New York, NY 10011
Tel: 212-929-8299
Member: NYSCA; ART/NY; TDF;
Description: Trying to offer low cost and free
entertainment to those who cannot afford
commercial theatre.

The Eugene O'Neill Theatre
230 West 49th Street
New York, NY 10019
Tel: 212-246-0220
Address Inquiries to: David W. Payne,
Manager
Nancy Enterprises, Incorporated
Founded in: 1925
Description: Named for playwright Eugene
O'Neill in 1959, the theatre was originally
named for the first great American actor,
Edwin Forrest. Today it houses 1,101.

Ontological-Histeric Theatre
491 Broadway
New York, NY 10012
Tel: 212-966-7509

Member: NYSCA; ART/NY; TDF;
Description: Presents exclusively the experimental works of Richard Foreman.

The Open Space in Soho
65 Wooster Street
New York, NY 10012
Tel: 212-966-3729
Member: NYSCA; ART/NY; TDF;
Description: New plays by American playwrights and productions of new works by established experimentalists.

The Open Space
133 Second Avenue
New York, NY 10003
Tel: 212-254-8630
Address Inquiries to: Lynn Michels, Artistic Director
    Harry A. Baum, Administrative Director
Founded in: 1971
Member: American Chai Trust; Lever Brothers Foundation; Metropolitan Life Foundation; NEA; NYSCA; ART/NY; Peg Santvoord Foundation; TDF;
Annual Budget: $75,000
Description: Committed to the exploration and development of new plays, production ideas and conceptual forms.

The Palace Theatre
1564 Broadway
New York, NY 10036
Tel: 212-757-2626
Founded in: 1913
Description: Purchased in 1966 by the Nederlanders, the Palace was the place to play and currently houses 1,686.

Pan Asian Repertory Theatre
305 Riverside Drive
New York, NY 10025
Tel: 212-662-7171; 212-475-7710
Address Inquiries to: Tisa Chang, Artistic Director
    Tom Madden, General Manager
Member: NYSCA; ART/NY; TDF;
Description: Uses the La Mama ETC as it's performing home, 74A East 4th Street, New York City.

Performance Group
33 and 35 Wooster Street
New York, NY 10013
Tel: 212-966-3651
Member: NYSCA; ART/NY; TDF;
Description: An experimental theatre company in its 15th season.

Performance Theatre Center
746 Broadway
New York, NY 10003
Tel: 212-982-4499
Description: Explores contemporary theatre in mime.

Performing Garage
33-35 Wooster Street
New York, NY 10013
Tel: 212-966-3651
Member: NYSCA; ART/NY; TDF;

The Playhouse
359 West 48th Street
New York, NY 10036
Tel: 212-489-9237
Address Inquiries to: Actors Group, Incorporated
Description: Costing $700,000 to convert into a legimate theatre, the building was originally a church amd now houses 700.

Playwrights Horizons
416 West 42nd Street
New York, NY 10036
Tel: 212-564-1235
Description: Under the direction of Robert Moss, Playwrights Horizons was the keystone theatre of the 42nd Street Theatre complex. It encourages American playwrights working on new material.

The Plymouth Theatre
236 West 45th Street
New York, NY 10036
Tel: 212-730-1760
Address Inquiries to: Shubert Organization
Founded in: 1917
Description: Built by the famed producer Arthur Hopkins, the theatre opened in 1917 with actor William Gillette appearing in A Successful Calamity and now houses 1077.

Potter's Field Theatre Company
2 Bond Street
New York, NY 10012
Tel: 212-260-1213
Address Inquiries to: Tulis McCall, Producing Director
    Timothy Jude, Producer
Founded in: 1977
Member: ART/NY;
Description: Well known actor, Michael Moriority is the mentor for this company that offers training, inspiration and disipline.

Princess
200 West 48th Street
New York, NY 10019
Tel: 212-586-3903
Founded in: 1935
Description: Remodeled as a theatre in 1979 the Princess seats 499.

Prince Street Players
228 West Houston Street
New York, NY 10014
Member: AEA;
Description: An AEA theatre for young audiences.

Priory
2162 Broadway
New York, NY 10023
Tel: 212-595-2026
Member: NYSCA; ART/NY; TDF;
Description: New works, new musicals, new drama and dance.

The Production Company
249 West 18th Street
New York, NY 10011
Tel: 212-691-7359
Address Inquiries to: Norman Rene, Artistic

Director
    Caren Harder, Managing Director
Member: NYSCA; ART/NY; TDF;
Description: Serving the needs of playwrights, actors, directors, designers and technicians.

Puerto Rican Traveling Theatre
304 West 47th Street
New York, NY 10036
Tel: 212-354-1293; 212-354-1974
Address Inquiries to: Miriam Colon Edgar, Artistic Director
    Jacklyn D. Beck, Administrator
Member: NYSCA; ART/NY; TDF;
Description: Hispanic theatre presented in a bilingual format.

Quaigh Theatre
108 West 43rd Street
New York, NY 10036
Tel: 212-221-9088
Address Inquiries to: William H. Liberson, Artistic Director
    Dey Gosse, Managing Director
Member: NYSCA; ART/NY; TDF;
Description: A theatre dedicated to the playwright.

Repertorio Espanol
138 East 27th Street
New York, NY 10016
Tel: 212-889-2850
Address Inquiries to: Fred Crecca, Managing Director
    Tsipi Zurla, Business Manager
Member: NYSCA; ART/NY; TDF;

Rialto Theatre
1481 Broadway at 43rd Street
New York, NY 10036
Tel: 212-354-5236
Founded in: 1932
Description: One of the grand Times Square Movie palaces it was refurbished in 1980 and now seats 499.

Richard Morse Mime Theatre
224 Waverly Place
New York, NY 10014
Tel: 212-242-0530
Member: NYSCA; ART/NY; TDF;
Description: A repertory company performing original mime works for adults and children.

Ridiculous Theatrical Company
One Sheridan Square
New York, NY 10014
Tel: 212-691-5434
Member: NYSCA; ART/NY; TDF;
Description: An original theatre of professionals with wildly original ideas.

Riverdale Showcase
174th Street at Broadway
Broadway Methodist Temple
New York, NY 10033
Member: NYSCA; ART/NY; TDF;
Description: A showcase for undiscovered playwrights, actors and directors.

Riverside Shakespeare Company
165 West 86th Street
New York, NY 10024

Tel: 212-877-6810
Member: NYSCA; ART/NY; TDF;

Riverside Theatre Workshop
2710 Broadway
New York, NY 10025
Tel: 212-864-9672; 212-663-5420
Address Inquiries to: W. Stuart McDowell,
Artistic Director
Gloria Skurski, Executive Director
Member: NYSCA; ART/NY; TDF;
Description: A poets' theatre also presenting experimental and classical works.

Rodger Hess Productions
509 Madison Avenue
New York, NY 10022
Member: AEA;
Description: An AEA theatre for young audiences.

Royal Court Repertory
301 West 55th Street
New York, NY 10019
Tel: 212-997-9582
Member: NYSCA; ART/NY; TDF;

The Royale Theatre
242 West 45th Street
New York, NY 10036
Tel: 212-245-5760
Founded in: 1927
Description: Opened on January 11, 1927, the Royale opend with a show called Piggy (no relation to today's Miss Piggy) and had some excitment during its early years when Mae West was fined $500 and 10 days in jail for her performance in a show titled Sex. The theatre is under Shubert Organization management and seats 1058.

Royal Playhouse
219 Second Avenue
New York, NY 10003
Tel: 212-475-9647
Member: NYSCA; ART/NY; TDF;
Description: Perform new musicals, classical and contemporary plays and children's musicals.

Saint Bart's Players
109 East 50th Street
New York, NY 10022

The Saint James Theatre
246 West 44th Street
New York, NY 10036
Tel: 212-398-0280
Member: LNYTP;
Description: Opened in 1927 the house holds 1,601 today. It was one the theatres in the Erlanger Theatrical Syndicate.

Saint Stephen's Church
120 West 69th Street
New York, NY 10023
Tel: 212-787-2755
Member: NYSCA; ART/NY; TDF;
Description: Space available for performances.

The Second Stage
200 West 72nd Street, Suite 20

New York, NY 10023
Tel: 212-787-8302
Address Inquiries to: Robin Goodman,
Artistic Director
Carole Rothman, Artistic Director
Member: NYSCA; ART/NY; TDF;
Description: An Off Off Broadway showcase code theatre with performance space at 23 West 73rd Street, New York City.

Seventy-Eighth Street Theatre Lab
236 West 78th Street
New York, NY 10024
Tel: 212-595-5240
Founded in: 1975
Member: ART/NY; TDF;
Description: A not-for-profit Off Off Broadway theatre.

Shandol Theatre
137 West 22nd Street
New York, NY 10011
Tel: 212-691-7950; 212-695-4964
Member: NYSCA; ART/NY; TDF;
Description: Presents old and new plays.

Shelter West Company
217 Second Avenue
New York, NY 10003
Tel: 212-673-6341
Address Inquiries to: Judy Joseph, Artistic
Director
Member: NYSCA; ART/NY; TDF;
Description: Presents new works, old works and translation of foreign plays.

Shirtsleeve Theatre
c/o John Vaccaro
10 Park Avenue
New York, NY 10016
Address Inquiries to: John Adams Vaccaro,
Artistic Director
James J. Wisner, Artistic Director
Founded in: 1976
Member: ART/NY;
Annual Budget: $30,000
Description: Full professional productions of originals, musicals and non-musicals.

The Shubert Theatre
225 West 44th Street
New York, NY 10036
Tel: 212-246-5990
Founded in: 1913
Description: This theatre also houses what was originally Lee Shubert's apartment, now used as Shubert Organization Executive offices. Opening on October 2, 1913 the Shubert houses A Chorus Line, Broadway longest running musical to date and seats 1483.

Sidewalks of New York Productions
44 Beaver Street, 2nd Floor
New York, NY 10004
Tel: 212-668-9074
Address Inquiries to: Gary Beck, Artistic
Director
Nancy Guarino, Company Manager
Member: NYSCA; ART/NY; TDF;
Description: Presenting plays in the commedia dell'arte style as well as classical comedies.

The Neil Simon Theatre
250 West 52nd Street
New York, NY 10019
Tel: 212-757-8646; 212-398-8383, Group Sales
Address Inquiries to: Arthur Rubin, General
Manager, Nederlander Corperation
Gordon Forbes, House Manager, Alvin
Theatre
Founded in: 1927
Description: The Alvin was named for Alex Aarons and Vinton Freeley, a combination of the names of the two producers who built it. On November 22, 1927, the Alvin opened with Fuuny Face by George and Ira Gershwin and today houses 1,334.

Soho Artists Theatre
465 West Broadway
New York, NY 10012
Founded in: 1960
Description: Develops new works, holds public readings and workshops, and runs a summer program.

Soho Repertory Theatre
19 Mercer Street
New York, NY 10013
Tel: 212-925-2588
Address Inquiries to: Jerry Engelbach, Artistic
Director
Marlene Swartz, Artistic Director
Founded in: 1975
Member: Billy Rose Foundation; Canal Street Association; Metropolitan Life Foundation; NYSCA; ART/NY; Rodgers and Hammerstein Foundation; TCG; TDF;
Annual Budget: $70,000
Description: One of the most popular Off Off Broadway theatres presenting unusual plays and neglected classics. Has a thrust stage for major productions, workshops of original works and staged readings. Winners of awards from the *Village Voice, Showbusiness* and *SoHo News.*

South Street Seaport Museum Theatre
16 Fulton Street
New York, NY 10038
Tel: 212-766-9042
Member: NYSCA; ART/NY; TDF;
Description: Space available for performances.

South Street Theatre Company;
424 West 42nd Street
New York, NY 10036
Tel: 212-265-5997

Theatre Matrix
750 Eighth Avenue
New York, NY 10036
Tel: 212-221-9495
Member: NYSCA; ART/NY; TDF;
Description: New plays and experimental productions.

Theatre Off Park
28 East 35 Street
New York, NY 10016
Tel: 212-683-4991

Member: NYSCA; ART/NY; TDF;

Theatre of Riverside Church
490 Riverside Drive
New York, NY 10027
Tel: 212-864-2929
Member: NYSCA; ART/NY; TDF;
Description: Presents the Riverside Dance Festival, Children's Theatre Workshop and the West End Poetry series.

Theatre of the Open Eye
316 East 88th Street
New York, NY 10028
Tel: 212-534-6363
Address Inquiries to: Jean Erdman, Artistic Director
  Ann Schofield, Director, Program Development
Member: NYSCA; ART/NY; TDF;

The Theatre Within
247 West 72nd Street
New York, NY 10023
Tel: 212-799-1847
Member: NYSCA; ART/NY; TDF;

Theatre 22
54 West 22nd Street
New York, NY 10011
Tel: 212-243-2805
Member: NYSCA; ART/NY; TDF;
Description: Presents monologues and scenes.

Thirteenth Street Theatre
50 West 13th Street
New York, NY 10014
Tel: 212-675-6677
Member: NYSCA; ART/NY; TDF;

Time and Space Limited
139-41 West 22nd Street
New York, NY 10011
Tel: 212-741-1032; 212-243-9268
Address Inquiries to: Linda Mussman, Art Director
  Claudia Bruce, Artist
Founded in: 1973
Member: NYSCA; ART/NY; TDF;
Description: An arts organization that provides radical and distinct approaches to theatre, music, and the to performing arts. It is a multi media group.

Touchstone Theatre Company
133 Second Avenue
New York, NY 10003
Tel: 212-254-8630
Member: NYSCA; ART/NY; TDF;

Trinity Theatre
164 West 100th Street
New York, NY 10025
Tel: 212-222-6641
Member: NYSCA; ART/NY; TDF;

Troupe
335 West 39th Street
New York, NY 10018
Tel: 212-244-9699
Member: NYSCA; ART/NY; TDF;
Description: Productions of new plays and classics.

Venture Stage Artists
230-12 Eighth Avenue
New York, NY 10011
Tel: 212-924-4791
Member: NYSCA; ART/NY; TDF;
Description: Presents experimental works, classics, and new plays.

The Virginia Theatre
245 West 52nd Street
New York, NY 10019
Tel: 212-246-6270; 212-840-8181
Address Inquiries to: Howard Rogut, Manager
Founded in: 1925
Member: LNYTP;
Description: A 1,177 seat Broadway house, constructed in 1925 and had been owned and operated from 1943 by ANTA (American National Theatre and Academy).

Vital Arts Center
325 West 16th Street
New York, NY 10011
Tel: 212-675-1136
Member: NYSCA; ART/NY; TDF;
Description: Space available for performances.

West-Park Theatre
165 West 86th Street
New York, NY 10024
Tel: 212-877-1671
Member: NYSCA; ART/NY; TDF;
Description: A community oriented cooperative theatre.

Westside Community Repertory Theatre
252 West 81st Street
New York, NY 10024
Tel: 212-874-9400; 212-666-3521
Address Inquiries to: Andres Castro, Artistic Director
  Timothy Hurley, Managing Director
Member: NYSCA; ART/NY; TDF;
Description: Classics with a contemporary approach.

The Winter Garden Theatre
1634 Broadway
New York, NY 10019
Tel: 212-245-4878; 212-944-4100
Founded in: 1911
Description: This is one theatre built and still owned by the Shuberts to challenge the supremacy of the 42nd street theatres and opened by Al Jolson on March 20, 1911. The theatre holds 1,529 and the hit 42nd Street is currently playing.

Women I Have Known Theatre
81 Perry Street
New York, NY 10014
Tel: 212-929-1071
Address Inquiries to: M. Tulis McCall
Member: AEA;
Description: M. Tulis McCall's one woman show, Women I Have Known, has toured colleges throughout the U.S. and has played in New York to critical acclaim. Characteriza-tions of Sojourner Truth and Susan B. Anthony are just two of the many women woven into Ms. McCall's presentation available for touring.

Women's Interart Center
549 West 52nd Street
New York, NY 10019
Tel: 212-246-1050
Founded in: 1969
Member: Media Alliance; NYSCA; ART/NY; TCG; TDF;
Annual Budget: $500,000
Description: New works primarily by women playwrights, composers, choreographers, visual artists, filmakers and video artists.

WPA Theatre
138 Fifth Avenue at 19th Street
New York, NY 10011
Tel: 212-691-2274
Address Inquiries to: Kyle Resnick, Producing Director
  Michael Kartzmer, Business Manager
Member: NYSCA; ART/NY; TDF;
Description: Presents American plays and revivals of neglected works.

York Players
2 East 90th Street
New York, NY 10028
Tel: 212-289-3402
Member: NYSCA; ART/NY; TDF;
Description: Presents Shakespeare, classics and important modern plays.

13th Street Repertory Company
50 West 13th Street
New York, NY 10014
Tel: 212-675-6677
Founded in: 1972
Member: Accountants for the Public Interest; Materials for the Arts; ART/NY; TDF;
Annual Budget: $50,000
Description: Emphasis on new works by established playwrights and composers, with special attention given to original works.

The 46th Street Theatre
226 West 46th Street
New York, NY 10036
Tel: 212-246-0246
Founded in: 1924
Description: Opened on Christmas Eve, 1925, the 46th Street theatre opened with Greenwich Follies and houses 1342.

Ninetto

Oswego Players Inc.
Post Office Box 486
Ninetto, NY 13115

North Bellmore

Lantern Theatre Incorporated
North Bellmore Public Library
North Bellmore, NY 11710

Norwich

Chenango Community Players
Post Office Box 646
Norwich, NY 13815

Ogdenberg

Community Players
333 Ford Street
Ogdenberg, NY 13669

Old Bethpage

Tobay Players of Plainview
7 Donald Drive
Old Bethpage, NY 11804

Oneida

Oneida Area Little Theatre
Elksclub Main Street
Oneida, NY 13421

Palmyra

America's Witness for Christ Theatre
Bureau of Information
Hill Cumorah
Palmyra, NY 14522

Hill Cumorah Pageant
Post Office Box 117
Palmyra, NY 14522
Tel: 315-597-5851
Address Inquiries to: W. Lynn Fluckiger,
   Producer
   Jack Tederholm, Director
Founded in: 1937
Annual Budget: $65,000
Description: Presented annually is a pageant
portraying the story of the Book of Mormon.
The pageant is staffed entirely by volunteers
who pay their own expenses. Performance
period is two weeks each year.

Pearl River

Hudson Vagabond Puppets
72 Hunt Avenue
Pearl River, NY 10965
Member: AEA;
Description: An AEA theatre for young audi-
ences.

Pleasantville

Music Theatre
Post Office Box 63
Pleasantville, NY 10570

Queens

Gingerbread Players and Jack
35-06 88th Street
Queens, NY 11372
Member: AEA;

Golden Center for the Performing Arts
Queens College
Queens, NY 11367
Tel: 212-390-7558
Member: NYSCA; ART/NY; TDF;

Little Theatre Forest Hills
15 Borage Place
Queens, NY 11375

Queens Community Theatre, Inc.
Post Office Box 1
Queens, NY 11365
Tel: 212-939-9030
Address Inquiries to: Ronald B. Hellman,
   Chairman
Founded in: 1953

Theatre in the Park
Flushing Meadow/Corona Park
Queens, NY
Tel: 212-592-5700
Member: NYSCA; ART/NY; TDF;

Riverdale

Community Theatre
5521 Mosholu Avenue
Riverdale, NY 10471

Rochester

Community Players
820 Clinton Avenue South
Rochester, NY 14620

Nazareth Arts Center
4245 East Avenue
Rochester, NY 14610

Rockville Center

Universal Players
21 Argyle Place
Rockville Center, NY 11570

Rome

Rome Community Theatre
Post Office Box 91
Rome, NY 13440

Sayville

Musical Workshop
Post Office Box 565
Sayville, NY 11782

Scarsdale

Greenville Community Theater
Scarsdale, NY 10583
Tel: 914-472-0679
Address Inquiries to: Valerie Gehn, President
Lois Alterman, Vice President
Founded in: 1965
Member: NYSCA;

Greenville Players
11 High Point Terrace
Scarsdale, NY 10583

Saralta and Friends
42 Montrose Road
Scarsdale, NY 10583
Tel: 914-723-4762
Founded in: 1976
Member: PA;

Schenectady

Civic Players
12 South Church Street
Schenectady, NY 12305

Seaford

Lantern Theatre
2480 Abby Lane
Seaford, NY 11783

Sidney

Tri-Town Theatre
Post Office Box 423
Sidney, NY 13838

Slingerlands

Slingerlands Community Theatre
Post Offfice Box 21
Slingerlands, NY 12159

Smithtown

Masque Theatre
26 Stengel Place
Smithtown, NY 11787

Springville

Springville Players
Post Office Box 62
Springville, NY 14141

Stonybrook

Carriage House Players
Box 1148 Archer Drive
Stonybrook, NY 11790

Syosset

The Contemporary Theater
290 Southwood Circle
Syosset, NY 11791

Tarrytown

Hackley Drama Group
293 Benedict Avenue
Tarrytown, NY 10591

Utica

Mt. Carmel Players
109 Jewett Place
Utica, NY 13501
Address Inquiries to: L. Damel

Valhalla

Hartford Players
75 Grasslands Road
Valhalla, NY 10595

Vestal

Starry Night Puppet Theatre
233 Main Street
Vestal, NY 13850
Address Inquiries to: Jan Hacha

Walton

Little Theatre
17 Franklin Road
Walton, NY 13856

Watertown

Little Theatre
Pearl Street
Watertown, NY 13601

Watertown Lyric Theatre
5989 Sunset Ridge
Watertown, NY 13601

White Plains

Fort Hill Players
Gedney Way
White Plains, NY 10605

Williamsville

Circle Theatre
1595 Hopkins Road
Williamsville, NY 14221

Williamsville Theatre
1595 Hopkins Road
Williamsville, NY 14221

Woodstock

Performing Arts
Post Office Box 517
Woodstock, NY 12498

Yonkers

Seton Players
1061 North Broadway
Yonkers, NY 10701

Yorktown Heights

Yorktown Community Players
3285 Deerhoun Street
Yorktown Heights, NY 10598

Youngstown

Four Nations Players
315 Lockport Street
Youngstown, NY 14174

NORTH CAROLINA

Ahoskie

Gallery Theatre
Post Office Box 544
115 West Main
Ahoskie, NC 27940

Ashboro

Randolf Players
Post Office Box 1009
Ashboro, NC 27203

Asheboro

Park Street Players
210 East Salisbury Street
Asheboro, NC 27203

Asheville

Community Theatre
Post Office Box 7066
Asheville, NC 28807

Livingston Art and Recreational Theatre
Post Office Box 7148
Asheville, NC 28801

Montford Park Players
246 Cumberland Avenue
Asheville, NC 28801

Atlantic Beach

Coastal Playhouse
Post Office Box 239
Atlantic Beach, NC 28512

Bath

Blackbeard
Post Office Box 209
Bath, NC 27808

Boone

Horn in the West
Post Office Box 295
Boone, NC 28607-0295
Tel: 264-212-; 264-908-
Address Inquiries to: William R. Winkler III,
 General Manager
 Ed Pilkington, Art Director
Founded in: 1951
Member: IOD; AASLH; CHC;
Annual Budget: $180,000
Description: The nation's third oldest outdoor
drama theatre plays nightly except Monday
at 8:30 p.m. June 18 through August 14.

Brevard

Little Theatre
Route 4, Box 142
Brevard, NC 28712

Carrboro

Gallery Theatre
150 East Main
Carrboro, NC 27510

Charlotte

Actor's Contemporary Ensemble
1017 East Morehead Street
Charlotte, NC 28204

Central Piedmont Community Theatre
Post Office Box 4009
Charlotte, NC 28204

Ebony Group and Company
1730 Northbrook Drive
Charlotte, NC 28216

Little Theatre of Charlotte
501 Queen Road
Charlotte, NC 28207

Mint Museum Drama
501 Hempstead Place
Charlotte, NC 28207

Cherokee

Unto These Hills
Post Office Box 398
Cherokee, NC 28719

Cherryville

Cherryville Little Theatre
Post Office Box 412
Cherryville, NC 28021

Clinton

Theater Workshop
303 Elizabeth Street
Clinton, NC 28328

Concord

Old Courthouse Theatre
South Union Street
Concord, NC 28025

Dunn

Harnett Regional Theatre
Post Office Box 1325
Dunn, NC 28334

Durham

Durham Savoyards
810 Proctor Street
Durham, NC 27707

Pocket Theatre
1204 North Mangum Street
Durham, NC 27701

Edenton

Edenton Little Theatre
200 West Church Street
Edenton, NC 27932

Elizabeth City

Albemarle Players
1002 West Williams Circle
Elizabeth City, NC 27909

Fayetteville

Circa Productions
1126 Offshore Drive
Fayetteville, NC 28305

Little Theatre
Post Office Box 53723
Fayetteville, NC 28305

Flat Rock

Flat Rock Playhouse
Flat Rock, NC 28731

Franklin

Nantahala Players
Post Office Box 482
Franklin, NC 28734
Address Inquiries to: Al Massengill

Gastonia

Little Theatre
Post Office Box 302
Gastonia, NC 28052

Goldsboro

Berkley Players
509 Greenbriar Drive
Goldsboro, NC 27530

Goldwing Community Theatre
Post Office Box 826
Goldsboro, NC 27530

South Johnson Repertory Theatre
217 South Hillcrest Drive
Goldsboro, NC 27530

Graham

Gallery Players
135 West Elm Street
Graham, NC 27253

Greensboro

Community Theatre of Greensboro
200 North Davie Street
Greensboro, NC 27401
Address Inquiries to: Keith Martin

Greenville

East Carolina Summer Theatre
Post Office Box 2717
Greenville, NC 27835

Halifax

First for Freedom
Post Office Box 1776
Halifax, NC 27839

Hayesville

Licklog Players Community Theatre
Post Office Box 223
Hayesville, NC 28904

Henderson

Henderson Recreation Players
Post Office Box 1556
Henderson, NC 27536

Hendersonville

Pentogram Players
Post Office Box 339
Hendersonville, NC 38739

High Point

Children's Carousel Theatre
1102 Greenway Drive
High Point, NC 27262
Address Inquiries to: Mrs. Robert B. Lett,
    Chairperson
Founded in: 1969

Jacksonville

Onslow Community Theatre
602 Henderson Drive
Jacksonville, NC 28540

Kenansville

The Liberty Cart
Post Office Box 470
Kenansville, NC 28349
Tel: 919-296-1550
Address Inquiries to: Jim Johnson, General
    Manager
    David T. Thomas, Artistic Director
Founded in: 1975
Member: STC; IOD; NCTC;
Annual Budget: $105,000
Description: Produces the outdoor drama
'The Liberty Cart' annually for six weeks
during July and August. An alternate prod-
uction runs one night each week with the
main production.

Lexington

YMCA Community Theatre
119 West 3rd Avenue
Lexington, NC 27292

Louisburg

Louisburg Players
College Box 716
Louisburg, NC 27549

Lumberton

Roberson Little Theatre
Post Office Box 613
Lumberton, NC 28358

Manteo

The Lost Colony
Post Office Box 40
Manteo, NC 27954
Tel: 919-473-2127; 919-473-2128
Founded in: 1937
Member: STC; IOD; ASTW; OBCC;

Monroe

Monroe Little Theatre
1009 Lancaster Avenue
Monroe, NC 28110

Morehead

Carteret Community Theatre
Route 2
Morehead, NC 28557

Mount Airy

Fine Arts Center
Post Office Box 1005
Mount Airy, NC 27030

North Carolina Theatre Conference
523 Board Street, #C
Mount Airy, NC 27030
Address Inquiries to: Jane Tesh

Mt. Airy

Andy Griffith Playhouse
Post Office Box 141
Mt. Airy, NC 27030
Description: Seating capacity 348.

New Bern

Civic Theatre
1316 Spencer Avenue
New Bern, NC 28560

Oxford

Granville Little Theatre
Post Office Box 315
Oxford, NC 27565

Pembroke

Strike at the Wind Theatre
Post Office Box 1059
Pembroke, NC 28372
Tel: 919-521-2489
Address Inquiries to: Carmell Lockleor,
    General Manager
    Gale Herut, Fiscal Affairs Officer
Founded in: 1975
Member: TA;

Annual Budget: $80,000
Description: The story of Henry Lomey and
The Indians of Robean County during a ten
year span, 1864 to 1874.

Raleigh

Raleigh Community Theatre
1008 Canterbury Road
Raleigh, NC 27607

Reidsville

The Studio Group
300 Griffin Road
Reidsville, NC 27320

Roanoke

Roanoke Valley Players
Post Office Box 695
Roanoke, NC 27870

Rockingham

Richmond Community Theatre
111 East Washington Street
Rockingham, NC 28379

Rocky Mount

Tank Theatre
Post Office Box 2031
Rocky Mount, NC 27801

Roxboro

Person Players Theatre
314 North Main Street
Roxboro, NC 27573

Roxboro Little Theatre
211 Barnette Avenue
Roxboro, NC 27573

Salisbury

Piedmont Players Theatre
Post Office Box 762
Salisbury, NC 28144
Address Inquiries to: F. Royster

Sandford

Adult Theatre Park and Recreation
Armory Building 147 McIwer
Sandford, NC 27330

Sanford

Footlight Players
400 North Steele Street
Sanford, NC 27330

Shelby

Greater Shelby Community Theatre
Brown Auditorium
East Dixon Boulevard
Shelby, NC 28150

Smithfield

Neuse Little Theatre
912 South 2nd Street
Smithfield, NC 27577

Snow Camp

The Sword of Peace
Box 535
Snow Camp, NC 27349
Founded in: 1970
Member: STC; IOD;
Description: A historical outdoor drama portraying our new nation at war and the struggles of Patriots, Tories, and the Quakers. Critics throughout the southeast have praised this stirring and dramatic tribute to the Quakers.

Statesville

Little Theatre
517 Holland Drive
Statesville, NC 28677

Stagefront Music Theatre
2517 Heritage Circle
Statesville, NC 28677

Stoneville

Pendleton Little Theatre
Route 1
Stoneville, NC 27048

Tarboro

Edgecombe Community Theatre Group
Post Office Box 550
Tarboro, NC 27886

Taylorsville

Alexander Company Community Theatre
Post Office Box 121
Taylorsville, NC 28681

Thomasville

Chair City Players
406 Unity Street-Finch Avenue
Thomasville, NC 23760

Tryon

Tryon Little Theatre
Fine Arts Center
Tryon, NC 28782

Valdese

From This Day Forward
Post Office Box 112
Valdese, NC 27839
Tel: 704-847-0176
Founded in: 1967
Member: IOD;
Annual Budget: $43,000
Description: A historical outdoor drama telling the story of the Waldenses family, who emigrated from Europe to Western North Carolina to escape poverty and religious persecution.

Old Colony Players
Post Office Box 112
Valdese, NC 28690

Waxhaw

Listen and Remember
Post Office Box 1776
Waxhaw, NC 28173

West Jefferson

Ashe Company Little Theatre
Post Office Box 229, Route 3
West Jefferson, NC 28694

Wilkesboro

The Legend of Tom Dooley
Post Office Box 24
Wilkesboro, NC 28687

Wilmington

SRO Straw-Hat Theatre
UNC-W
Post Office Box 3725
Wilmington, NC 28401
Tel: 419-791-9695
Address Inquiries to: Doug W. Swink,
  Producer/Director
Founded in: 1968

Thespians of Hanover
1802 Market Street
Wilmington, NC 28401

Willis Richardson Players
363 South Kerr Avenue
Wilmington, NC 28403

Wilson

The Playhouse
205 Gray Street
Wilson, NC 27893

Wilson Jester's Theatre
205 Gray Street
Wilson, NC 27893

Winston-Salem

Little Theatre
610 Coliseum Drive
Winston-Salem, NC 27106
Address Inquiries to: C.East Radar

Winston-Salem Experimental Theatre
Miller Park Recreation Center
Winston-Salem, NC 27102

NORTH DAKOTA

Fargo

Fargo-Moorhead Community Theatre
333 South 4th Street, Box 644
Fargo, ND 58021

The Little Country Theatre
North Dakota State University
Fargo, ND 68102
Tel: 701-237-7705; 701-237-7784
Address Inquiries to: Dr. Tal Russell, Director
  of Theatre
Founded in: 1914
Member: ATA; U/RTA; USITT;

Grand Forks

Greater Grand Forks Community Theatre
Post Office Box 895
Grand Forks, ND 58201
Tel: 701-775-4562
Address Inquiries to: Ivan Jensen, President
Lee Barnum, Treasurer
Member: ATA;

Minot

Mouse River Players
Post Office Box 1101
Minot, ND 58701
Tel: 701-839-3486; 701-852-1331
Address Inquiries to: Jo Ann Zoller, Resident
  Director
Founded in: 1972

OHIO

Akron

Weathervane Community Playhouse
1301 Weathervane Lane
Akron, OH 44313
Address Inquiries to: Bob Belfance

Alliance

Carnation City Players
Post Office Box 961
Alliance, OH 44601

Ashtabula

G B Repertory Theatre
2928 West 13th Street
Ashtabula, OH 44004

Athens

Ohio Valley Summer Theatre
Kantner Hall-Ohio UN
Athens, OH 45701
Address Inquiries to: L. Fraze

Bowling Green

The Huron Playhouse
School of Speech Communication
Bowling Green State University
Bowling Green, OH 43403
Tel: 419-372-2350
Address Inquiries to: Robert C. Hansen,
  Manager
Founded in: 1949

Bryan

Williams Company Playhouse
Post Office Box 643
Bryan, OH 43606

Bucyrus

Bucyrus Little Theatre
Post Office Box 741
Bucyrus, OH 44820

Cambridge

Cambridge Area Theatre
Post Office Box 611
Cambridge, OH 43725

Living Word Passion Play
6639 Klass Road
Cambridge, OH 43725
Tel: 614-439-2761; 614-432-3661
Founded in: 1975
Member: IOD;
Annual Budget: $30,000
Description: An outdoor drama based upon the life of Christ. The Living Word Passion Play is first and foremost a ministry dedicated to the spreading of the gospel in dramatic form.

Canton

Players Guild of Canton
1001 Market Avenue
Canton, OH 44702
Tel: 216-453-7619
Address Inquiries to: Jerry M. Lowe, Artistic Director
Founded in: 1933
Member: OCTA; ANTA; OTA;

Players Guild Youth Theatre
1001 North Market Avenue
Canton, OH 44702

Centerville

Town Hall Players
300C Jamestown Circle
Centerville, OH 45459

Chagrin Falls

Chagrin Valley Little Theatre
40 River Street
Chagrin Falls, OH 44022

Chillicothe

Paint Street Playhouse
33 North Paint Street
Chillicothe, OH 45601
Address Inquiries to: Kenneth Breidenbaugh

Tecunseh Theatre
Post Office Box 73
Chillicothe, OH 45601

Cincinnati

Art Reach Touring Theatre
3340 Whitfield Avenue
Cincinnati, OH 45220

Beechmont Players
1601 Turquoise Drive
Cincinnati, OH 45230
Address Inquiries to: R. Brown

The Cincinnati Playhouse in the Park
Post Office Box 6537
Cincinnati, OH 45206
Tel: 513-421-3888, Box Office;
513-421-5440, Administrative
Address Inquiries to: Michael Murray, Producing Director
Baylor Landrum, Managing Director
Founded in: 1960
Member: LORT; AAA; TCG; OTA;
Annual Budget: $1.6 million
Description: The purpose and goal of the Playhouse is to provide top-notch, quality professional theatre for the tri-state region

(Ohio, Northern Kentucky, Eastern Indiana). Playhouse takes theatre into the community with the Speakers' Bureau, Project Interact to the schools (with the Playhouse Intern Company), backstage theatre tours, touring productions, student previews, and senior programs.

Footlighters
3315 Monteith Avenue
Cincinnati, OH 45208
Address Inquiries to: R. Wehrmeyer

Queen City Players
6368 Sharlene Drive
Cincinnati, OH 45211
Address Inquiries to: E. Wanner

Saint James Players
Chevoit Road
Cincinnati, OH 45239

School for Creative and Performing Arts
1310 Sycamore Street
Cincinnati, OH 45210

Stagecrafters
1580 Summit Road
Cincinnati, OH 45237

Tri-County Theatre
6 Village Square-Glendale
Cincinnati, OH 45246

University of Cincinnati Showboat Majestic
Foot of Broadway
Cincinnati, OH 19681
Tel: 513-241-6550
Address Inquiries to: F. Paul Rutledge, Producer
Founded in: 1968
Annual Budget: $190,000
Description: The last original floating theatre in America, the Showboat Majestic is listed in both the state of Ohio and on the National Register of Historic Places. It runs a full seven months of musicals, comedies and mystery plays.

Circleville

Roundtown Players
Post Office Box 431
Circleville, OH 43113

Cleveland

Big Mama Poetry Theatre
1649 Coventry Road
Cleveland, OH 44118
Tel: 216-371-0441
Address Inquiries to: Barbara Angell

Humanist Theatre
8134 Euclid Avenue
Cleveland, OH 44103

Playhouse Square Foundation
1621 Euclid Avenue
Cleveland, OH 44115
Address Inquiries to: Virginia Pfaff

Cleveland Heights

Dobama Theatre
1846 Conventry Road
Cleveland Heights, OH 44118
Tel: 216-932-6838
Address Inquiries to: Ronald J. Newell, Managing and Artistic Director
Donald A. Bianchi, Artistic Director
Founded in: 1960
Member: OTA;
Annual Budget: $25,000

Halle Theatre
3505 Mayfield Road
Cleveland Heights, OH 44118

Columbus

Columbus Junior Theatre
115 West Main Street
Columbus, OH 43215
Member: CTAA;

Gallery Players
c/o Columbus Jewish Center
Columbus, OH 43220
Address Inquiries to: Harold M. Eisenstein

Players Club Theatre
549 Franklin Avenue
Columbus, OH 43215
Address Inquiries to: E. Graczyk

Players Theatre of Columbus
549 Franklin Avenue
Columbus, OH 43215
Tel: 614-224-6971; 614-224-0831
Address Inquiries to: Ed Graczyk, Executive Director
Founded in: 1923
Member: ATA; OTA;
Annual Budget: $277,000

Worthington Company Theatre
Josephinum Seminary
Columbus, OH 43220

Coshocton

Footlighters
962 Green Drive
Coshocton, OH 43812
Address Inquiries to: P. Neal

Dayton

Dayton Community Theatre
1728 East 3rd Street
Dayton, OH 45403

Dover

Trumpet in the Land
Post Office Box 275
Dover, OH 44622
Address Inquiries to: Rachel Redinger, Producer

Dublin

Dublin Abbey Players
Post Office Box 82
Dublin, OH 43017

Euclid

Euclid Little Theatre
22305 Lakeshore Boulevard
Euclid, OH 44123

Fairborn

Fairborn Playhouse
Post Office Box 547
Fairborn, OH 45324

Findlay

Fort Findlay Playhouse
Post Office Box 521
Findlay, OH 45840

Fostoria

Footlighters
South and Poplar Street
Fostoria, OH 44830

Fremont

Fremont Community Theatre
Post Office Box 423
Fremont, OH 43420

Grove City

Little Theatre Off Broadway
Post Office Box 52
Grove City, OH 43121

Lakewood

Lakewood Little Theatre
17801 Detroit Avenue
Lakewood, OH 44107
Tel: 216-521-2540
Address Inquiries to: Karl A. Mackey,
　Managing Director
　Patricia A. Strauss, Operations Manager
Founded in: 1930
Member: AOCAA; OCTA; ATA; ACTA;
　CTAA;
Annual Budget: $600,000

Lima

Amil Dramatics
991 North Shore Drive
Lima, OH 45805

Mansfield

Mansfield Playhouse
95 East 3rd Street
Mansfield, OH 44902

Maple Heights

Maple Heights Little Theatre
18401 Waterbury Avenue
Maple Heights, OH 44137
Address Inquiries to: R. Olenski

Southeast Summer Theatre
17825 Libby Road
Maple Heights, OH 44137

Marietta

Mid-Ohio Players
423 4th Street
Marietta, OH 45750

Marion

Marion Community Theatre
Post Office Box 981
Marion, OH 43302
Tel: 614-383-2101
Founded in: 1963
Member: OCTA; OTA;
Annual Budget: $25,000

Marion Little Theatre
Post Office Box 1002
Marion, OH 43302

Martins Ferry

Heritage Playhouse
High School Auditorium
Martins Ferry, OH 43935

Medina

Masquers Theatre
Post Office Box 3
Medina, OH 44256

Minster

Crescent Players
193 South Main
Minster, OH 45865

Montpelier

Williams Company Playhouse
Lawrence and SE Avenue
Montpelier, OH 43543

Mt. Vernon

Mt. Vernon Players
Post Office Box 182
Mt. Vernon, OH 43050

Napoleon

Maumee Valley Civic Theatre
Napoleon High School
Napoleon, OH 43545

Nelsonville

Berean Theatre
Fort Street
Nelsonville, OH 45764

Newark

Weathervane Playhouse
Post Office Box 607
Newark, OH 43055

Welsh Hills Players
3 Wilwood Avenue
Newark, OH 43055

North Royalton

Royalton Players
Post Office Box 8217
North Royalton, OH 44133

Oxford

Village Playhouse
Center of Performing Arts
Oxford, OH 45056

Parma

Cuyahoga Community College
Western Campus Theatre
11000 Pleasant Valley Road
Parma, OH 44130
Tel: 216-845-4000; 216-842-9770
Address Inquiries to: Ms. Toba Jeffrey
　Lawrence Vincent
Founded in: 1966
Member: ATA; USITT;
Annual Budget: $25,000
Description: An educational theatre serving
the purpose of their institution in the train-
ing of students and members of our com-
munity in the theatre arts.

Piqua

Piqua Players
Post Office Box 345
Piqua, OH 45356

Plainville

Marimont Players
Walton Creek and Much More
Plainville, OH 45227

Port Clinton

Playmakers Civic Theatre
Post Office Box 149
Port Clinton, OH 43452

Portsmouth

Portsmouth Little Theatre
Post Office Box 1251
Portsmouth, OH 45662

Ravenna

Carousel Dinner Theatre
Post Office Box 427
Ravenna, OH 44266
Tel: 216-296-3866
Address Inquiries to: C. David Fulford,
　Producer
　Prescott F. Griffith, Producer
Founded in: 1973
Member: ADTI;
Annual Budget: $1,500,000
Description: Rental of theatrical costumes.

Reading

Reading Community Theatre
1 East Lakeview Drive
Reading, OH 45215
Address Inquiries to: V. Casey

Sagamore Hills

Brandywine Players
Post Office Box 113
Sagamore Hills, OH 44067

Sandusky

The Harlequins
Post Office Box 1582
Sandusky, OH 44870

Shaker Heights

Unitarian Players
1st Unitarian Church
Shaker Heights, OH 44122

Shelby

Blackfork Players
10 West Main Street
Shelby, OH 44875

Toledo

Toledo Repetoire Theatre
16 10th Street
Toledo, OH 43620

Village Players
2740 Upton Avenue
Toledo, OH 43606

Troy

Troy Civic Theatre
1130 Fairway Drive
Troy, OH 45373
Address Inquiries to: B. Scranton

Van Wert

Civic Theatre
118 South Race Street
Van Wert, OH 45891

Warren

Trumbull New Theatre
Post Office Box 374
Warren, OH 44482
Tel: 216-652-1103; 216-856-2282
Address Inquiries to: Mrs. Paul Murray,
    President
    Stan Killingsworth, Vice President
Founded in: 1948
Description: All activities performed by volunteers. The governing body is a six member Board of Trustees elected annually by the membership for a three year term. They produce five shows a year during the season and sometimes an extra summer show along with a Jun ior Workshop for youth in junior high or high school.

Westerville

Curtain Players
Westerville Armory
Westerville, OH 43081

Westlake

Claque Playhouse
1371 Claque Road
Westlake, OH 44145

West Richfield

Bath Players
Town Barn-Everett Road
West Richfield, OH 44286

Willoughby

Fine Arts Association
38660 Mentor Avenue
Willoughby, OH 44094
Address Inquiries to: Gwen Yarnell
Member: CTAA;

Youngstown

Civic Children's Theatre
600 Playhouse Lane
Youngstown, OH 44511
Tel: 216-782-3402
Address Inquiries to: Sherry Weinblatt,
    President
    J. Douglas Wilson, Jr., Executive
    Director
Founded in: 1950
Member: CTAA; ATA; OTA;
Annual Budget: 62,000
Description: Civic Children's Theatre of Youngstown serves as management for CCTY Productions, a touring professional company performing for children. It produces four mainstage shows yearly for children using mixed casts of adult and student volunteers.

Youngstown Playhouse
600 Playhouse Lane
Youngstown, OH 44511
Address Inquiries to: Bentley Lenhoff

Zanesville

Community Theatre
Post Office Box 2375
Zanesville, OH 43701

OKLAHOMA

Ada

Ada Community Theatre
1017 East 17th Place
Ada, OK 74820
Address Inquiries to: E. Hunter

Alva

Alva Community Theatre
913 Apache Drive
Alva, OK 73717

Arapaho

Southwest Playhouse
Post Office Box 304
Arapaho, OK 73620

Ardmore

Ardmore Little Theatre
Post Office Box 245
Ardmore, OK 73401
Tel: 405-223-6387
Address Inquiries to: Beverly Wellnitz
Founded in: 1955
Member: OCTA;
Annual Budget: $16,000

Bartlesville

Little Theatre Guild
Post Office Box 604
Bartlesville, OK 74005
Tel: 918-336-5668; 918-661-4995
Address Inquiries to: J.P. Liggett, President
S. Carleton Guptill, Artistic Director
Founded in: 1927
Member: OCTA;

Annual Budget: $40,000
Description: Produces a four show season plus two other community productions. The season includes musicals as well as straight plays. All actors and production personnel are drawn from the local community, as is major funding. They sell approximately 1000 season tickets per season.

Bristow

Starlite Theatre
Post Office Box 714
Bristow, OK 74010

Broken Arrow

Community Playhouse
316 South Main
Broken Arrow, OK 74021

Chickasha

Chickasha Community Theatre
Post Office Box 236
Chickasha, OK 73081

Clinton

Southwest Playhouse
Post Office Box 204
Clinton, OK 73601

Duncan

Little Theatre
405 East Chestnut
Duncan, OK 73533

Elk City

Red Carpet Theatre
Post Office Box 852
Elk City, OK 73644

El Reno

El Reno Community Theatre
519 South Williams
El Reno, OK 73036

Enid

Enid Gaslight Theatre
216 East Maple
Enid, OK 73701

Fort Sill

Cabaret Supper Theatre
Fort Sill, OK 73503

Grandfield

Harvest Playhouse
Post Office Box 509
Grandfield, OK 73546

Henryetta

Tulledega Playhouse
Post Office Box 1090
Henryetta, OK 74437

Hobart

Shortgrass Playhouse
424 West Ash Street
Hobart, OK 73651

Hugo

Hugo Community Theatre
1212 East Duke
Hugo, OK 74743

Idabel

McCurtain Community Players
108 SE Avenue J
Idabel, OK 74745

Lawton

Lawton Community Theatre
715 North 13th Street
Lawton, OK 73502

Marietta

Frontier Playhouse
1500 Washington Parkway
Marietta, OK 73448

Miami

Miami Little Theatre
2130 Rockdale
Miami, OK 74354

Muskogee

Muskogee Little Theatre
1517 Boston
Muskogee, OK 74401

Norman

Norman Community Players
1013 North Flood
Norman, OK 73069

Renegade Art Theatre
Post Office Box 2731
Norman, OK 73069

Oklahoma City

CAST
2725 Northwest 23rd
Oklahoma City, OK 73107

Lyric Theatre
2501 North Blackwelder
Oklahoma City, OK 73106

Oklahoma Community Theatre
Association
400 West Sheridan
Oklahoma City, OK 73102

Perry

Stagecoach Community Theatre
511 ½ Grove Street
Perry, OK 73077

Ponca City

Ponca Playhouse
Post Office Box 1414
Ponca City, OK 74601

Poteau

Good Times Community Theatre
Post Office Box 821
Poteau, OK 74953

Prague

Prague Community Theatre
The Clothes Closet
Prague, OK 74864

Seminole

Seminole Community Theatre
611 Morningside Drive
Seminole, OK 74868

Shawnee

Little Theatre
Post Office Box 937
Shawnee, OK 74801

Stillwater

Town and Gown Theatre
3514 South Husband
Stillwater, OK 74074

Tahlequah

The Trail of Tears
Post Office Box 515
Tahlequah, OK 74464

20th Century Players
710 Janet Street
Tahlequah, OK 74464

Tulsa

American Indian Theatre
Post Office Box 2140
Tulsa, OK 74101

Tulsa Theatre
1511 South Delaware
Tulsa, OK 74104

Watonga

Watonga Community Theatre
519 North Hampton
Watonga, OK 73772

Weatherford

Weatherford Community Theatre
Chamber of Commerce
Weatherford, OK 73096

Wewoka

Wewoka Little Theatre
Post Office Box 108
Wewoka, OK 74884

Woodward

Woodward Little Theatre
311 22nd Street
Apartment 90
Woodward, OK 73801

OREGON

Ashland

Oregon Shakespeare Festival Association
Post Office Box 158
Ashland, OR 97520
Tel: 503-482-2111
Address Inquiries to: William W. Patton,
Executive Director

Paul E. Nicholson, General Manager
Founded in: 1935
Annual Budget: $3.4 million
Description: Operates three theatres in three distinctive modes: the Elizabethan outdoor playhouse, dedicated mainly to Shakespeare and presenting plays in the Elizabethan manner without interruption; the Angus L. Bowman Theatre, which houses classics and modern plays with relatively wide appeal and the intimate Black Swan, designed for less commercial, more specialized pieces. The festival produces 10 to 12 plays each year drawing on the works of Shakespeare as well as other classic and modern playwrights. In 1984 over 500 new performances will be presented to an expected audience of 270,000 in addition to films, concerts, and lectures, and an actors-in-schools program that reaches 80,000 each year.

Condon

Condon Masquers
Little Theatre Group
Condon, OR 97823

Coos Bay

Little Theatre on the Bay
Post Office Box 722
Coos Bay, OR 97420

Eugene

Very Little Theatre
2350 Hilyard Street
Eugene, OR 97405

Forest Grove

Civic Theatre
Post Office Box 263
Forest Grove, OR 97116

Gardiner

Umpqua Little Theatre
Post Office Box 247
Gardiner, OR 97441

Lake Oswego

Community Theatre
1033 North Shore Road
Lake Oswego, OR 97034

McMinnville

Gallery Players
150 Linfield Avenue
McMinnville, OR 97128

Newport

Porthole Players
5020 North West Agate Way
Newport, OR 97365

Pendleton

Pendleton Little Theatre
119 NW 6th
Pendleton, OR 97801

Portland

Civic Theatre
1530 SW Yamhill
Portland, OR 97205

Firehouse Theatre
1432 SW Montgomery
Portland, OR 97201

Landmark Theatre
906 SW Chestnut
Portland, OR 97201

The New Theater
1839 SW Primrose Street
Portland, OR 97219

Portland Actors Ensemble
1824 SW 11th 22
Portland, OR 97201

Store Front Theatre
1017 SW Morrison, #401
Portland, OR 97205

Roseburg

Children's Theatre
Post Office Box 1391
Roseburg, OR 97470
Address Inquiries to: Kevin J. Henegan
Member: CTAA;

Salem

Pentacle Theatre
Post Office Box 186
Salem, OR 97308

The Dalles

Masquerades
Post Office Box 210
The Dalles, OR 97058

PENNSYLVANIA

Aldan

Colonial Playhouse
Ridley Avenue Below Magnolia
Aldan, PA 19018

Allentown

Civic Little Theatre
519-527 North 19th Street
Allentown, PA 18104

Allison Park

Red Barn Theatre
3101 Mc Cully Road
Allison Park, PA 15101
Address Inquiries to: Martin Streiff

Altoona

Altoona Community Theatre
1208 12th Avenue
Altoona, PA 16601

Bala Cynwyd

Allegro Productions
406 Gary Lane
Bala Cynwyd, PA 19004
Member: AEA;

Bellfonte

Project for Performing Arts
Post Office Box 52
Bellfonte, PA 16823
Address Inquiries to: Mrs. Robert Fisher

Berwyn

Footlighters
58 Main Street
Berwyn, PA 19312

Bethel Park

South Park Conservatory Theatre
Post Office Box 254
Bethel Park, PA 15102
Address Inquiries to: Shirley Custer

Stage 62
5933 Glen Hill Drive
Bethel Park, PA 15102

Bethlehem

Pennsylvania Playhouse
Post Office Box 1461
Bethlehem, PA 18018

Bloomsburg

Bloomsburg Theatre Ensemble
Post Office Box 66
Bloomsburg, PA 17815

Broomall

Marple-Newton Players
Paxton Hollow Road
Broomall, PA 19008

Brownsville

Brownsville Civic Theatre
207 Catherine Street
Brownsville, PA 15417

Bryn Mawr

Main Line Playhouse
Morris and Montgomery
Bryn Mawr, PA 19010

Buckingham

Town and Country Players
Route 263
Buckingham, PA 18912

Butler

Butler Little Theatre
1 Howard Street
Butler, PA 16001

Silver Fox Playhouse
Pitts-Wisr
Butler, PA 16001

Chambersburg

Community Theatre
Post Office Box 2
Chambersburg, PA 17201

Cheltenham

Cheltenham Playhouse
439 Ashbourne Road
Cheltenham, PA 19012

Chester County

Stone Barn Dinner Theatre
Route 842 Near Unionville
Chester County, PA 19375

Clearfield

Saint John Studio Theatre
3rd and Pine Streets
Clearfield, PA 16830
Address Inquiries to: Fred C. Gearhart

Corapolis

R. Morris Colonial Theatre
Narrows Run Road
Corapolis, PA 15108

Drexel Hill

Children's Repertory Company
3707 Garrett Road
Drexel Hill, PA 19206
Member: CTAA;

Ellwood City

Red Barn Players
Post Office Box 628
Ellwood City, PA 16117

Erie

Erie Civic Theatre
Post Office Box 2042
Erie, PA 16512

Forest City

Coal Company Theatre
58 River Street
Forest City, PA 18421
Address Inquiries to: Mrs. Margaret Shemro

Hanover

Hanover Community Players
Road 3
Hanover, PA 17331
Address Inquiries to: Richard King

Hatboro

Village Players
Summit and Jefferson
Hatboro, PA 19040

Havertown

Falcon House Dinner Theatre
525 West Chester Pike
Havertown, PA 19083

Hazelton

Community Players
Jewish Community Center
Hazelton, PA 18201

Irwin

White Barn Theatre
101 Colonial Manor
Irwin, PA 15642

Jeffersonville

Dramateurs Playhouse
Rittenhouse Boulevard
Jeffersonville, PA 19401

Johnstown

Penn Wood Players
Post Office Box 775
Johnstown, PA 15907
Address Inquiries to: Bob Wechtenhiser

Kennett Square

Three Little Bakers
Route 1
Kennett Square, PA 19348

Lancaster

Actors Company of Pennsylvania
318 North Arch, Box 1153
Lancaster, PA 17604
Address Inquiries to: Jeanne Clemson

Fulton Opera House Foundation
12 North Prince Street
Lancaster, PA 17603
Address Inquiries to: Guner Gery

Lebanon

Lebanon Community Theatre
Post Office Box 592
Lebanon, PA 17042

Lewistown

Stone Arch Players
Post Office Box 604
Lewistown, PA 17044

Malvern

Peoples's Light and Theatre
39 Conestoga Road
Malvern, PA 19355

Media

De City Drama Company
Media Line Road
Media, PA 19063

Mercersburg

Tuscarara Area Community Theatre
Post Office Box 26
Mercersburg, PA 17236
Address Inquiries to: Clara L. Green

Merion

Group Theatre East
119 Glenwood Road
Merion, PA 19066
Address Inquiries to: J. Ruckdeschel

Mountainhome

Pocono Playhouse
Mountainhome, PA 19432

Moyland

Hedgerow Theatre
Rose Valley Road
Moyland, PA 19065

Narbeth

Marbeth Community Theatre
Post Office Box 223
Narbeth, PA 19072

New Kensington

Civic Theatre
Stevenson Boulevard
New Kensington, PA 15068

Sherwood Forest Theatre
876 Constitution Boulevard
New Kensington, PA 15068

Oil City

Oil City Community Playhouse
1042 West 1st Street
Oil City, PA k16301

Philadelphia

American Theatre Arts for Youth
1511 Walnut Street
Philadelphia, PA 19102
Member: AEA;

Cafe Theatre
Allen Lane and McCallum
Philadelphia, PA 19119
Address Inquiries to: K. Schaffmester

Freedom Theatre
Broad and Master Streets
Philadelphia, PA 19121

Germantown Theatre Guild
4821 Germantown Avenue
Philadelphia, PA 19144

Irish Theatre of Philadelphia
c/o John Kane
7019 Paschall Ave.
Philadelphia, PA 19142
Tel: 215-729-0936
Address Inquiries to: John Kane, Chairman
Timothy Dugan, Literary Manager
Founded in: 1980
Member: Philadelphia Ceili Group;
Description: A newly formed group presenting plays about the Irish experience in both
the United States and abroad. The group
presents little known plays and has also presented new plays by emerging Irish Playwrights.

Old Academy Players
3544 Indian Queen Lane
Philadelphia, PA 19129

Phil Drama Workshop
105 South 18th Street
Philadelphia, PA 19103

Plays and Players
1714 Delancey Street
Philadelphia, PA 19102

Primary Players
1326 Oak Lane
Philadelphia, PA 19126

Repertory Company
1924 Chestnut Street
Philadelphia, PA 19103

Rittenhouse Players
1906 South Rittenhouse
Philadelphia, PA 19103

Society Hill Playhouse
507 South 8th Street
Philadelphia, PA 17147
Tel: 215-923-0210
Address Inquiries to: Deen Kogan, Managing
Director
Founded in: 1959
Member: GPCA;
Description: Since its inception, the Playhouse
has presented 175 area premiers, developed
and trained countless performers and tech-
nicians, encouraged native playwrights and
maintained on-going community service
programs.

Stagecrafters
8132 Germantown Avenue
Philadelphia, PA

Studio Players Community Theatre
Red Lion Road and Jamison
Philadelphia, PA 19116
Address Inquiries to: Cynthia Kolker

Theater Center Philadelphia
622 South 4th Street
Philadelphia, PA 19147

Phoenixville

Forge Theatre
241-43 1st Avenue
Phoenixville, PA 19460

Pitcairn

Monroeville Civic Theatre
Pitcairn, PA 15140

Pittsburgh

Camelot Production Company
4765 Liberty Avenue
Pittsburgh, PA 15224
Address Inquiries to: Dann Howard

Civic Light Opera
Heinz Hall, 600 Pennsylvania Avenue
Pittsburgh, PA 15222

Penn Hills Players
517 Macbeth Drive
Pittsburgh, PA 15235
Address Inquiries to: Nicholas D. Pranis

The Pittsburgh Laboratory Theatre Center
c/o Karen Foster
420 North Craig
Pittsburgh, PA 15213
Tel: 412-621-2876; 412-621-7261
Founded in: 1971

Member: Mid Atlantic Consortium; APT;
Alcoa Foundation; Vira I. Heinz Fund;
Levinson Steel Corporation Foundation;
A.W. Mellon Educational and Charitable
Trust; PCA; Pittsburgh Foundation;
WEF;
Description: A sponsoring organization subsi-
dizing The Pittsburgh Laboratory Theatre
and The Pittsburgh Comedy Alliance.

Richeyville

Olde Trail Players
119 Oak Street
Richeyville, PA 15358

Ridgeway

Footlighter of Elk Company
Post Office Box 91
Ridgeway, PA 15853

Ridley Park

Barnstormers
Ward and Tome Streets
Ridley Park, PA 19078

Scranton

Scranton Public Theatre Inc.
512-514 Brooks Building
Scranton, PA 18503
Address Inquiries to: Robert Shesimber

Scranton Theatre Libre
512-514 Brooks Building
Scranton, PA 18503
Tel: 717-961-1377
Address Inquiries to: John J. White, Executive
Director
Founded in: 1970
Member: ATA; TCG; Pennsylvania Arts
Council; Northeastern Pennsylvania Arts
Council;

Selinsgrove

Valley Players
Post Office Box 294
Selinsgrove, PA 17870

Shamokin Dam

Brookside Playhouse Inc.
Shamokin Dam, PA 17876
Tel: 717-743-1311
Address Inquiries to: Deborah Z. Prather,
General Manager
Founded in: 1971

Skippack

Playcrafters
Store Road Route 73
Skippack, PA 19474

Spangler

Cresson Lake Playhouse
Post Office Box 767
Spangler, PA 15775

State College

Penn State College Community Theatre
Post Office Box 23
State College, PA 16801
Tel: 814-238-1993
Address Inquiries to: Richard B. Gidez,
President
Founded in: 1957
Member: TAP;
Annual Budget: $50,000

Stroudsburg

Phoenix Players Center of Poconos
Post Office Box 533
Stroudsburg, PA 18360

Swarthmore

Players of Swarthmore
Fairview Road
Swarthmore, PA 19081

Tullytown

Sandbox Dinner Theatre
156 Fallsington Road
Tullytown, PA 19007

Uniontown

Actors and Artists of Fayette Company
62 Rear West Peter Street
Uniontown, PA 15401
Address Inquiries to: Michael J. Slavin

University Park

The Pennsylvania Festival Theatre
137 Arts Building
Penn State University
University Park, PA 16803
Tel: 814-863-0381; 814-865-7586
Address Inquiries to: John R. Bayless, General
Manager
Founded in: 1956
Member: U/RTA; ATA;
Description: Seating capacity 318 in the Pavil-
ion Theatre (Arena). Seating capacity 500 in
the Playhouse Theatre (Proscenium/
Thrust). Full production support facilities.
Season June through August. Internships
available for approximately 75 too 100 ad-
vanced theatre students. Actors' Equity Posi-
tions available. Normal season of four plays;
two musicals and two straight plays. Applica-
tion for internship available in November.
Audition and interviews held in late March at
Penn State and at the national U/RTA Auditions.

Upper Darby

Playmakers
Hampton and Locust Streets
Upper Darby, PA 19082

Wayne

Big Little Theatre Company
489 Old Eagle School Road
Wayne, PA 19087
Address Inquiries to: M. Stone

Footlighters
West Wayne Avenue
Wayne, PA 19087

West Chester

Barley Sheaf Players
Post Office Box 445
West Chester, PA 19380

West Grove

Community Players
Post Office Box 124
West Grove, PA 19390
Address Inquiries to: L. Beaver

Wyncote

Wyncote Players
Bent Road and Greenwood
Wyncote, PA 19095

York

Life Sciences Theatre
Country Club Road
York, PA 17405
Address Inquiries to: Richard Farrell

Princess Players
301 East Philadelphia
York, PA 17403
Address Inquiries to: Ethel Laws

The Theatre Box
120 East Market Street
York, PA 18017

York Little Theatre
26 South Belmont Street
York, PA 17403
Address Inquiries to: Marcia Salvatore

RHODE ISLAND

Barrington

Barrington Players
Post Office Box 107
Barrington, RI 02806
Address Inquiries to: Joan Lussier, President
Founded in: 1930

Coventry

Coventry Players, Inc.
Post Office Box 25
Coventry, RI 02816
Tel: 401-821-9888
Address Inquiries to: Matt Siravo, President
Founded in: 1959

East Greenwich

Academy Players
Post Office Box 282
East Greenwich, RI 02818

Harrisville

Assembly Players
Post Office Box 81
Harrisville, RI 02830

Hopkington

The Mal Angelo Heritage Playhouse
Post Office Box 100
Hopkington, RI 02833
Tel: 401-377-2413
Address Inquiries to: Bernice Bronson,
   Artistic Director
Founded in: 1970

Pawtucet

Pawtucket Community Players
Slater Park
Pawtucet, RI 02861

Providence

Improvise, Incorporated
Post Office Box 2335
Providence, RI 02906
Address Inquiries to: Naida D. Weisberg

Rhode Island Feminist Theatre
Post Office Box 9083
Providence, RI 02940
Tel: 401-331-4578
Founded in: 1973

Scitamard Players
221 Howell Street
Providence, RI 02906

Theatre-Jewish Community Center
170 Sessions Street
Providence, RI 02906

Rumford

Seekonk Stage
172 Hoyt Avenue
Rumford, RI 02916

Westerly

Theatre Workshop
Post Office Box 24
Westerly, RI 02891
Founded in: 1972

West Kingston

South County Players
100 Acre Pond Road
West Kingston, RI 02892

SOUTH CAROLINA

Abbeville

Abbeville Community Theatre
Post Office Box 700
Abbeville, SC 29620

Opera House Players
c/o Abbeville Opera House
Box 1976
Abbeville, SC 29620
Tel: 803-459-2157
Address Inquiries to: George W. Settles,
   Manager
   Missy Cromer, Artistic Director
Founded in: 1958
Description: This historic Opera House was
built in 1908. Fannie Brice, George M. Co-
han and many others once played on its

stage. A regional theatre promoting quality live theatre in an historic setting.

Aiken

Aiken Community Playhouse
Post Office Box 125
Aiken, SC 29801
Tel: 803-648-1438
Founded in: 1952
Description: A community theatre run by
volunteers presenting four plays per season
(September through May). Summer theatre
at city gardens is free to the public. Work-
shops, both acting and technical as well as
one children's play per year.

Anderson

Anderson Community Theatre
Post Office Box 413
Anderson, SC 29621

Beaufort

Beaufort Little Theatre
305 East Street
Beaufort, SC 29902

Bennettsville

Marboro Players
1308 East Main
Bennettsville, SC 29512

Charleston

Footlight Players
Post Office Box 62
Charleston, SC 29401
Address Inquiries to: E. Robinson

Chester

Chester Community Theatre
Chester, SC 29706

College Park

Gaffney Little Theatre
c/o J.E. Moss
214 Crestview Drive
College Park, SC 29340
Founded in: 1970

Columbia

Columbia Lyric Theatre
1527 Senate Street
Columbia, SC 29201

Hadassah Players
3908 Beverly Drive
Columbia, SC 29204

South Carolina Arts Community
1001 Main
Columbia, SC 29201

South Carolina Theatre Conference
1705 Quail Lake Drive
Columbia, SC 29169
Address Inquiries to: Cliff Fagan

Town Theatre
1012 Sumter
Columbia, SC 29201
Address Inquiries to: A. Graves

Workshop Theatre
432 Spring Lake Road
Columbia, SC 29206
Address Inquiries to: C. Gilliam

Workshop Theatre of South Carolina
Post Office Box 11555
Columbia, SC 29211
Tel: 803-799-4876; 803-799-6551, Box
   Office
Address Inquiries to: Leonard H. Metz,
   Business Manager
Founded in: 1967

Conway

Theatre of the Republic
c/o Conway Chamber of Commerce
Box 831
Conway, SC 29526
Tel: 803-248-2275
Founded in: 1969

Florence

Florence Little Theatre
Box 583
Florence, SC 29501
Address Inquiries to: V. Alley

Greenville

Greenville Feminist Theater
304 Chick Springs Road
Greenville, SC 29609
Tel: 803-233-1446
Address Inquiries to: Anne Davis, Artistic
   Director
Founded in: 1973

Greenville Little Theatre
444 College Street
Greenville, SC 29601
Address Inquiries to: B. McLane

Newberry

Newberry Community Players
1403 Nance Street
Newberry, SC 29108

Pendleton

Where Free Men Shall Stand
125 East Queen Street
Pendleton, SC 29670

Rock Hill

Piedmont Players
York County National Museum
Rock Hill, SC 29730

Sumter

Sumter Little Theatre
719 Henderson Street
Sumter, SC 29150
Address Inquiries to: K. Dameron

Winnsboro

Pine Tree Players
Post Office Box 357A
Winnsboro, SC 29180
Address Inquiries to: Chris Blackwelder,
   President
Founded in: 1971

SOUTH DAKOTA

Armour

Armour Star Ham Players
Armour High School
Armour, SD 57313
Address Inquiries to: M. Martin

Custer

Black Hills Playhouse Company
Custer, SD 57730
Tel: 605-255-4242
Address Inquiries to: Warren M. Lee,
    Executive Director
Founded in: 1946

Faulkton

Faulkton Community Theatre
Post Office Box 70
Faulkton, SD 57438
Address Inquiries to: L. Bartholomew

Gettysburg

Gettysburg Summer Theatre
Gettysburg, SD 57442
Address Inquiries to: J. Briscoe

Gregory

Gregory Community Players
115 West 11th
Gregory, SD 57533

Milbank

Pied Piped Theatre
Milbank High School
Milbank, SD 57252
Address Inquiries to: E. Reed

Mitchell

Pioneer Players
119 West 3rd
Mitchell, SD 57301

Oldham

Interlake Players
Oldham, SD 57051
Address Inquiries to: K. Folsland

Pierre

Pierre Players
Post Office Box 933
Pierre, SD 57501
Address Inquiries to: R. Nash

Platte

Plaster of Paris Players
Post Office Box 603
Platte, SD 57062
Address Inquiries to: C. McDonnell

Rapid City

Group Theatre
Dahl Art Center
713 7th Street
Rapid City, SD 57701
Address Inquiries to: G. Thatcher

Sioux Falls

Sioux Falls Community Playhouse
4105 Louise Street
Sioux Falls, SD 57106
Address Inquiries to: Larry Etten

Watertown

Town Players
208 NE 5th Avenue
Watertown, SD 57201
Address Inquiries to: F. Bruhn

Winner

Winner Community Theatre
Post Office Box 5
Winner, SD 57580
Address Inquiries to: J. Miller

TENNESSEE

Brentwood

Pull Tight Players
Murray Lane
Brentwood, TN 37027

Bristol

Dogwood Playhouse
The Malaba
Route 3
Bristol, TN 37620

Chattanooga

Chattanooga Little Theatre
400 River Street
Chattanooga, TN 37405
Tel: 615-267-8534
Address Inquiries to: Albert L. Gresham,
    Director
Founded in: 1923

Little Theatre
400 River Road
Chattanooga, TN 37405

Cookeville

Playmakers
Post Office Box 235
Cookeville, TN 38501

Covington

Covington Little Theatre
521 South Main
Covington, TN 38019

Crossville

Cumberland Company Playhouse
Post Office Box 484
Crossville, TN 38555

Cumberland County Playhouse
Post Office Box 484
Crossville, TN 38555
Tel: 615-484-5000; 615-484-2300
Address Inquiries to: James Crabtree,
    Producing Director
    Mary Crabtree, Producing Director
Founded in: 1965
Member: TCG; SETC;

Description: Serves a rural area the size of
Connecticut as the only performing arts resource in the region. Situated in a low income area in a town of 5000 persons, the
productions must draw from the greater
Knoxville, Nashville, and Chattanooga envi-
rons, each a distance of 100 miles. A community theatre under professional management and staffing, utilizing a mixture of
community avocational players with non-
Equity professionals and Equity guest artists. A major season of eight shows (a total
of 35 playing wee ks).

Dyersburg

Dyersburg Little Theatre
Post Office Box 1
Dyersburg, TN 38024
Tel: 901-285-4604
Address Inquiries to: Jim Godsey, Director
Founded in: 1961
Member: Tennessee Arts Commission;
Annual Budget: $5,000

East Gatlinburg

Hunter Hill Theatre
Highway 73
East Gatlinburg, TN 37738
Tel: 615-436-5062
Address Inquiries to: Tom Cooke, Director
Founded in: 1966
Annual Budget: $50,000

Greeneville

Little Theatre-Greeneville
Post Office Box 3246
Greeneville, TN 37743

Humboldt

Humboldt Little Theatre
Post Office Box 231
Humboldt, TN 38343

Johnson City

Little Theatre Players
Post Office Box 452
Johnson City, TN 37601

Kingsport

Kingsport Theatre Guild
c/o Fine Arts Center
Church Circle
Kingsport, TN 37660
Tel: 615-246-9351
Address Inquiries to: Gerald S. Cassell,
    President
    James W. Johnson, Treasurer
Founded in: 1948
Member: STC;
Description: Provides practical experience in
all phases of theatre. Workshops provide
programs for civic clubs, and assistance for
community events.

Olde West Dinner Theatre
Post Office Box 5001
Kingsport, TN 37743
Tel: 615-323-4151
Address Inquiries to: Patricia L. Gardner,

Manager
Founded in: 1966

Lawrenceburg

The Gentlemen from the Cane
Post Office Box 14
Lawrenceburg, TN 38464
Address Inquiries to: Jerry Henderson,
Director

Lawrenceburg Community Theatre
229 Caperton Avenue
Lawrenceburg, TN 38464

Memphis

Harleton Players
4899 Stage Road
Memphis, TN 38128
Tel: 901-386-1355
Address Inquiries to: Jim Crosthwait,
Manager
Founded in: 1965
Member: Tennessee Arts Commission;

Memphis Children's Theatre
2599 Avery Avenue
Memphis, TN 38112
Tel: 901-275-0835
Founded in: 1953
Member: ACTA;
Annual Budget: $25,000

Theatre Memphis
630 Perkins Extended
Memphis, TN 38119
Tel: 901-682-8323; 901-682-0264
Address Inquiries to: Carol Hensen,
Administrative Director
Sherwood Lohrey, Executive Director
Founded in: 1919
Member: ATA; ACTA; SETC; TTA;
Annual Budget: $350,000
Description: Produces 10 to 12 shows utilizing
a total of 2,000 volunteers (from ushers to
actors and technicians) under the guidance
of a professional staff of 14.

Morristown

Straw Hat Players
1707 Solod Drive
Morristown, TN 37814

Theatre Guild, Inc.
Post Office Box 1502
Morristown, TN 37814
Tel: 615-586-9260
Address Inquiries to: L. Glenn Lester, Artistic
Director
Linda Dietrich, President
Founded in: 1936
Member: STC;
Annual Budget: $16,000
Description: A community theatre organiza-
tion using local amatuer talent with a profes-
sonal director.

Murfreesboro

Murfreesboro Little Theatre
Post Office Box 952
Murfreesboro, TN 37130
Tel: 615-893-9825

Address Inquiries to: John R. StClair,
President
Annual Budget: $10,000

Sing Me No Sad Songs
Post Office Box 1355
Murfreesboro, TN 37130

Nashville

Arts Commission
507 State Office Building
Nashville, TN 37219

Circle Players
4120 Hillsboro Road
Nashville, TN 37215

East Side Players
WLAC Radio
Nashville, TN 37219

Fisk University Little Theatre
17th Avenue North
Nashville, TN 37202
Tel: 615-329-8633; 615-329-8513
Address Inquiries to: Gladys Forde, Manager
Founded in: 1866
Member: ATA; NADAA; ACA; SCA;
Description: A University Theatre which pre-
sents four major shows per year, several play
readings and one act plays directed by stu-
dents. Seating capacity is 104.

Nashville Academy Theatre
724 2nd Avenue
Nashville, TN 37210
Tel: 615-254-9103; 615-254-6020
Address Inquiries to: Mrs. Stephen R.
McDowell, President
Founded in: 1931
Member: ATA; STC; CTAA;
Annual Budget: $225,000
Description: Theatre for children and youn
people.

Norris

Norris Little Theatre
126 Reservoir Road
Norris, TN 37828

Oak Ridge

Oak Ridge Community Playhouse
Post Office Box 3223
Oak Ridge, TN 37830
Tel: 483-122-
Address Inquiries to: Paul Ebert, Director

Sewanee

Sewanee Community Theatre
Brill Keppler
Sewanee, TN 37375

Shelbyville

Bedford Players
Post Office Box 69
Shelbyville, TN 37160

Sneedville

Hancock County Drama Association
Sneedville, TN 37869
Address Inquiries to: Mrs. Howard W. Rhea,
Manager
Founded in: 1968
Annual Budget: $25,000

Townsend

Smoky Mountain Passion Play
Post Office Box 3
Townsend, TN 37882
Tel: 615-984-4111, Year Round;
615-448-2244, Box Office - Summer
Only
Address Inquiries to: Robert E. Temple,
Producer/General Manager
Christian H. Moe, Director
Founded in: 1972
Member: STC; IOD; NTBA;
Annual Budget: $150,000
Description: Outdoor drama of the life of
Jesus is performed nightly, Monday through
Saturday, from mid-June through August.
Passion Play Amphitheatre is in Townsend
25 miles from Knoxville on State Highway
73, near the entrance to the Great Smoky
Mountains National Park. Rehearsal season
is May 27 through June 11 opening night,
and continues one week into the season.

Tullahoma

Community Playhouse Inc.
Post Office Box 7
Tullahoma, TN 37388

TEXAS

Abilene

Dyess Playhouse
Post Office Box 625
Abilene, TX 79607

Teen and Children's Theatre
801 South Mockingbird
Abilene, TX 79065
Tel: 915-673-6271
Address Inquiries to: Robert B. Foard,
Manager
Founded in: 1965
Description: Seating capacity 600.

Albany

Fort Griffin Fandangle Association
Post Office Box 185
Albany, TX 76430
Tel: 817-762-2525
Address Inquiries to: Watt R. Matthews,
Manager
Founded in: 1938
Annual Budget: $10,000

Amarillo

Little Theatre
Post Office Box 2424
Amarillo, TX 79109
Address Inquiries to: P. Fox

Texas Non-Profit Theatre
2410 Teckla
Amarillo, TX 79106
Address Inquiries to: M. Pool

Arlington

Creative Arts Theatre and School
605 East Border Street
Arlington, TX 76010
Address Inquiries to: Linda M. Lee
Member: CTAA;

Athens

Aggie Players
Post Office Box 813
Athens, TX 75751

Athens Little Theatre
Post Office Box 102
Athens, TX 75751

Austin

Austin Civic Theatre
Post Office Box 244
Austin, TX 78767

Austin Theatre Group
119 Laurel Lane
Austin, TX 78705
Tel: 512-477-1421
Address Inquiries to: Betty Weber, Producer

Center Stage
Post Office Box 1501
Austin, TX 78767

Creek Theatre
4007 Avenue B
Austin, TX 78751
Address Inquiries to: L. Carey

Fine Arts Community
Box 13406
Austin, TX 78711

Parks and Recreation Department
Post Office Box 1088
Austin, TX 78767

Union Theatre
105B Bulian Lane
Austin, TX 78746

Zachary Scott Theatre
Post Office Box 244
Austin, TX 78767

Baytown

Baytown Little Theatre
1500 Lakeview Vill
Baytown, TX 77250

Beaumont

Community Players
Post Office Box 3827
Beaumont, TX 77704

Lamar University
Post Office Box 10050
Beaumont, TX 77710

Betton

Beu Fine Arts Theatre
2010 Northeast Street
Betton, TX 76513
Address Inquiries to: J. Barnes

Big Spring

Little Theatre
Post Office Box 643
Big Spring, TX 79720

Brownsville

Camille Players
One Dean Porter Park
Brownsville, TX 78520
Tel: 512-542-8900; 512-542-7334
Address Inquiries to: Laurence Siegle,
    Director
    Richard Moore, Business Manager
Founded in: 1964
Member: ATA;

Brownwood

Brownwood Civic Theatre
1201 Cottage
Brownwood, TX 76801

Bryan

Stage Center
312 Dunn Street
Bryan, TX 77801

Canyon

Branding Iron Theatre
West Texas State University
Canyon, TX 79016
Tel: 806-656-3248
Address Inquiries to: Dr. Ray Ewing,
    Chairman
    Larry Menefer, Artistic Director
Founded in: 1959
Annual Budget: $4,000
Description: Three shows are produced each
year in the BIT and twelve are staged in the
Initmate Theater as part of the West Texas
State University program in theatre.

Texas Musical Drama
Post Office Box 268
Canyon, TX 79015
Tel: 806-655-2181; 806-488-2220
Address Inquiries to: Raymond Raillard,
    Manager
Founded in: 1966
Member: Discover Texas Association;
    NTBA; DMA; Texas Tourist Council;
    Tourism Industry of America;
Annual Budget: $600,000
Description: An outdoor presentation recreat-
ing the settling of the panhandle of Texas
with drama, music and dance. Runs from
June through August and seats 1742. You
can arrive early and down a great barbeque.

Colorado City

Colorado City Playhouse
975 East 17th Street
Colorado City, TX 79512

Corpus Christi

Little Theatre
1801 North Water
Corpus Christi, TX 78401

Corsicana

Corsicana Community Playhouse
202 East Collin
Corsicana, TX 75110
Tel: 214-872-5421
Address Inquiries to: Joe B. Brooks, Manager
Founded in: 1972
Annual Budget: $25,000

Dallas

American Indian Theatre
3061 Cridelle
Dallas, TX 75220

Country Dinner Playhouse
6526 North Central Expressway
Dallas, TX 75206
Address Inquiries to: Bill McHale, Producer

Dallas Repertory Theatre
Post Office Box 12208
Dallas, TX 75019
Tel: 214-369-8966
Address Inquiries to: Ed Delatte, Producer
Founded in: 1969
Annual Budget: $50,000

Dallas Theater Center
3636 Turtle Creek Boulevard
Dallas, TX 75219
Tel: 214-526-8210; 214-526-8857
Address Inquiries to: Paul Baker, Manager
Founded in: 1959
Member: TCG; AAA;
Annual Budget: $2,600,000
Description: Led by its founding/artistic di-
rector Paul Baker, the Dallas Theatre Center
is firmly committed to professional excel-
lence and strong community involvment.
Seeking to appeal to varied audiences, the
Center presents a selection of classics, con-
temporary plays and premieres in the Kalita
Humphreys Theatre, the principal play-
house at the Center.

Granny's Dinner Playhouse
12205 Coit Road
Dallas, TX 75230
Tel: 214-239-0153
Address Inquiries to: Perry Cloud, Producer
Founded in: 1972

Greenhill School
14255 Midway Road
Dallas, TX 75234

Harlequin Players
4626 Abbott Avenue
Dallas, TX 75205
Address Inquiries to: Anthony A. Vincent,
    Producer
Founded in: 1965

Theater Across America
104 North Saint Mary
Dallas, TX 75214

Theatre Three
2800 Routh Street
Dallas, TX 75201
Tel: 214-748-5191
Address Inquiries to: Norma Young, Manager
Founded in: 1961
Member: AEA;
Annual Budget: $100,000

Denton

Denton Community Theatre
Post Office Box 1931
Denton, TX 76201
Tel: 817-382-7014
Address Inquiries to: Darrell W. Woolwine,
    Managing/Artistic Director
Founded in: 1970
Member: ACTA; TNPTI; ATA;
Annual Budget: $46,000

Edinburg

Pan American Fine Arts Auditorium
Pan American University
Edinburg, TX 78539
Tel: 512-381-3471
Founded in: 1967
Description: Seating capacity 1,000.

El Paso

Eastwood High School Little Theatre
2430 McRae
El Paso, TX 79925

Fort Hood

Fort Hood Community Theatre
Building 515
Fort Hood, TX 76544

Fort Worth

Casa Manana Playhouse
Post Office Box 9054
Fort Worth, TX 76107
Tel: 817-332-9319
Address Inquiries to: Sharon Benge,
    Executive Director
Founded in: 1962
Member: ATA;

Greater Fort Worth Community Theatre
3505 West Lancaster
Fort Worth, TX 76107
Tel: 817-738-7491
Address Inquiries to: Bill Garber, Artistic
    Director

Metropolitan Community Theatre
4713 Madella
Fort Worth, TX 76117

Wing and Masquerade Players
4800 Bryant-Irvin Road
Fort Worth, TX 76109

Ft. Worth

Town and Gown Theatre
3505 West Lancaster
Ft. Worth, TX 76107

Galveston

Galveston Civic Theatre
1819 Broadway, Apartment B
Galveston, TX 77550

The Lone Star
Post Office Box 5253
Galveston, TX 77551

Gatesville

Cultural Arts Community
Gatesville Messenger
Gatesville, TX 76528
Address Inquiries to: W. Mack

Georgetown

Georgetown Area Theatre
Post Office Box 567
Georgetown, TX 78626

Harlington

Country Playhouse
Post Office Box 1201
Harlington, TX 78550

Hereford

Hereford Community Theatre
116 Kingwood
Hereford, TX 79045

Houston

Alley Theatre
615 Texas Avenue
Houston, TX 77002
Tel: 713-228-9341
Address Inquiries to: Pat Brown, Artistic
    Director
Founded in: 1947
Member: AEA; AAA; AAT;
Annual Budget: $3,500,000
Description: Founded by Nina Vance, was one
of the first resident professional theatres in
America and still continues to be a leader in
the regional theatre movement.

Channing Players, Inc.
5210 Fannin
Houston, TX 77004
Tel: 713-526-1571
Founded in: 1955

Country Playhouse
720 Town and Country Lane
Houston, TX 77024

Houston Civic Theatre
2212 Loosean Lane
Houston, TX 77019

Houston Upstairs Theatre School
3410 Austin
Houston, TX 77004

Plays for Living
3635 West Dallas
Houston, TX 77109
Tel: 713-524-3881
Address Inquiries to: Mary Beth Splaine,
    Director

Reunion Theatre
709 Franklin
Houston, TX 77002
Tel: 713-228-2267
Address Inquiries to: Camille Waters,
    Producer

Spring Branch Little Theatre
9000 Westview
Houston, TX 77055

Theatre Suburbia
1410 West 43rd Street
Houston, TX 77018
Tel: 713-682-3525
Address Inquiries to: Jim Harvey, Manager
Founded in: 1960
Annual Budget: $25,000

Humble

Humble Little Theatre
Humble, TX 77338

Ingram

Point Theatre
Hill Country Foundation
Ingram, TX 78025

Lake Jackson

Brazosport LIttle Theatre
Post Office Box 375
Lake Jackson, TX 77566

Lancaster

Lancaster Community Theatre
Post Office Box 322
Lancaster, TX 75146

League City

Clear Creek Country Theater
Post Office Box 253
League City, TX 77573
Tel: 713-332-CCCT
Address Inquiries to: Mary Andrews,
    President
    Jinny Young, 1st Vice President
Founded in: 1965
Member: Clear Lake Chamber of
    Commerce;
Annual Budget: $25,000
Description: A community theatre, producing
four major shows and a summer musical.
First Stage, a children's apprentice group,
presents two showcases a year and dance
classes are also held to prepare the dancers
for the summer musical. Novice directors
are given a special production when budgets
and schedules allow.

Liberty

Valley Players
Post Office Box 1063
Liberty, TX 77571

Longview

Longview Community Theatre
Post Office Box 1854
Longview, TX 75601

Midland

Texas Non-Profit Theatres
2000 Wadley
Midland, TX 79701
Address Inquiries to: Enid Holm

Odessa

Globe of the Great Southwest
C. Mc Cally-Shakespeare Road
Odessa, TX 79760

Olton

Olton Community Theatre
Parsons Funeral Home
Olton, TX 79064

Orange

Orange Community Players
Post Office Box 442
Orange, TX 77630
Tel: 713-886-9881
Address Inquiries to: Charlotte Smith,
   Manager
Founded in: 1957
Annual Budget: $10,000

Pasadena

Pasadena Little Theatre
Post Office Box 4193
Pasadena, TX 77502

Port Arthur

Port Arthur Little Theatre
249 Avant Lane
Port Arthur, TX 77640

Raymondville

Raymondville Little Theatre
Raymondville, TX 78580

Rockport

Repertory Theater of America
Post Office Box 1296
Rockport, TX 78382
Tel: 512-729-6274
Address Inquiries to: Drexel H. Riley,
   Director
Founded in: 1967
Member: NECAA;
Annual Budget: $100,000
Description: A professional touring company
available with a complete repertory to col-
leges, arts councils and other bookings.
Over half of RTA's bookings are in dinner
theatres throughout the country.

Rosenberg

Terry's Theatre Arts Troupe
5500 Avenue North
Rosenberg, TX 77471
Address Inquiries to: Suzanne White

San Angelo

San Angelo Civic Theatre
Post Office Box 3525
San Angelo, TX 76901

San Antonio

Fort Sam Houston Playhouse
Fort Sam Houston
San Antonio, TX 78200

Learning About Learning Foundation
411 East Mulberry
San Antonio, TX 78212

Music Theatre
334 Senova
San Antonio, TX 78216

Schulenburg

Backstage, Incorporated
Bermuda Valley Farm
Schulenburg, TX 78956

Sherman

Sherman Community Players
FNLY Playhouse, 500 North Elm
Sherman, TX 75090

Temple

Temple Civic Theatre
Post Office Box 3732
Temple, TX 76501

Texarkana

Texarkana Little Theatre
721 East 12th Street
Texarkana, TX 75501

Vernon

Vernon Civic Theatre
Vernon, TX 76384

Wichita Falls

Backdoor Theatre
Post Office Box 896
Wichita Falls, TX 76307

UTAH

Brigham City

Brigham City Community Theatre
75 North 6th East
Brigham City, UT 84302
Tel: 801-723-8184
Address Inquiries to: Drauca J. Holmes,
   Manager
Founded in: 1970
Annual Budget: $10,000

Kanab

Old Barn Theatre
Kanab, UT 84741

Logan

Old Lyric Repertory Society
382 North 4th East
Logan, UT 84322

Moab

Moab Community Theatre
Apache Motel
Moab, UT 84325

Mount Pleasant

Ephraim Community Theatre
Mount Pleasant, UT 84647

Payson

Payson Community Theatre
Payson, UT 84651

Pleasant Grove

The Alhambra
2755 North 100th Street, East
Pleasant Grove, UT 84062

Provo

Sundance Theatre
Post Office Box 837
Provo, UT 84601

Salt Lake City

Pioneer Memorial Theatre Company
University of Utah
Salt Lake City, UT 84112
Tel: 801-581-6960
Address Inquiries to: Keith Engar, Executive
   Director
Founded in: 1895
Member: ATA; U/RTA;
Annual Budget: $100,000

Promise Valley Playhouse
1350 Brookshire
Salt Lake City, UT 84106

Salt Lake Acting Company
755 Third Avenue
Salt Lake City, UT 84103

Spanish Fork

Castle Summer Theatre
1026 East 20th Street
Spanish Fork, UT 84660

Springville

Springville Playhouse
373 East 400th North
Springville, UT 84663

VERMONT

Barre

Barre Area Theatre Group
Post Office Box 858
Barre, VT 05641

Bennington

Oldcastle Theatre Company
Southern Vermont College
Bennington, VT 05201
Tel: 802-442-9463; 902-447-0564
Address Inquiries to: Eric Peterson,
   Producing Director
   Shelli Duboff, Associate Director
Founded in: 1972
Member: TCG;
Annual Budget: $40,000
Description: A professional regional theatre
company in residence at Southern Vermont
College.

Brandon

Players Club
Brandon, VT 05733

Chelsea

Chelsea Hometowners
Chelsea, VT 05038

East Craftsbury

East Hill Players
Brassknocker Farm
East Craftsbury, VT 05835

Essex Junction

Community Players
12 Church Street
Essex Junction, VT 05452

Marlboro

Marlboro Players
Route 9
Marlboro, VT 05344

Middlebury

Community Players
11 Adirondack View
Middlebury, VT 05753

Plainfield

Two Penny Circus
Post Office Box 128
Plainfield, VT 05667
Tel: 802-476-7873
Address Inquiries to: Don Osman, Artistic
 Director
Founded in: 1973
Annual Budget: $50,000

Richford

Richford Players
Richford, VT 05476

Richmond

Vermont Women's Theater
c/o Roz Payne
Box 164
Richmond, VT 05477
Tel: 206-866-1830
Founded in: 1974
Description: The theatre makes the personal
and political aspects of its members lives
public. An exciting sharing experience
which makes them one with their audience.

Saint Albans

Saint Albans Theatre
17 Barlow Street
Saint Albans, VT 05478

Saint Johnsbury

Saint Johnsbury Players
8 Watiomer Circle
Saint Johnsbury, VT 05819

Shelburne

Champlain Valley Players
Shelburne, VT 05482

Lilliput Children's Program
Post Office Box 266
Shelburne, VT 05482
Tel: 802-985-3522
Address Inquiries to: Kay H. Ryder, Manager
Founded in: 1966
Annual Budget: $5,000

Shoreham

Shoreham Players
Watch Point
Shoreham, VT 05770

South Strafford

South Strafford Players
South Strafford, VT 05070

Springfield

Springfield Community Players
19 Orchard Street
Springfield, VT 05156

White River Junction

Green Mountain Guild
Old Town Farm
White River Junction, VT 05001
Tel: 802-295-7016
Address Inquiries to: Majorie O'Neil-Butler,
 Manager
Founded in: 1971
Member: ATA; NETC;

Woodstock

New Woolhouse Players
Post Office Box 111
Woodstock, VT 05091
Address Inquiries to: J. Soule

Woodstock Community Theatre
Woodstock Community Center
Woodstock, VT 05091

VIRGINIA

Abingdon

Barter Theatre
Main Street
Abingdon, VA 24210
Tel: 703-628-2281
Address Inquiries to: Rex Partington,
 Manager
Founded in: 1932

Alexandria

Fairfax Community Theatre
4601 Spring Green Road
Alexandria, VA 22312

Fairlington Players
804 Circle Terrace
Alexandria, VA 22302

Little Theatre of Alexandria
600 Wolf Street
Alexandria, VA 22314

Arlington

Arlington Players
2352 North Vernon Street
Arlington, VA 22207
Address Inquiries to: B. Cohen

Fairlington Players
3308 South Stafford Street
Arlington, VA 22206

Opera Theatre of North Virginia
125 South Old Glebe Road
Arlington, VA 22204

Bedford

Bedford Little Theatre
Post Office 272
Bedford, VA 24523

Buena Vista

Rockbridge Players
155 Ridge Avenue
Buena Vista, VA 24416

Fairfax

Fairfax Community Theatre
4309 Olley Lane
Fairfax, VA 22030

Falls Church

Falls Church Players
7124 Broad Street
Falls Church, VA 22046
Address Inquiries to: M. Abbey

Franklin

Franklin Little Theatre
113 Woodland Drive
Franklin, VA 23851
Tel: 804-562-2862
Founded in: 1969
Annual Budget: $5,000

Fredericksburg

Children's Musical Theatre
408 Canal Street
Fredericksburg, VA 22401
Address Inquiries to: Anita W. Price

Harrisburg

Charlottetowne Players
Post Office Box 203
Harrisburg, VA 28075

Harrisonburg

Valley Players
Post Office Box 933
Harrisonburg, VA 22801
Address Inquiries to: Anna Mae Crist,
 President
Founded in: 1961

Kilmarnock

North Neck Theatre
Kilmarnock, VA 22482

Leesburg

Blue Ridge Players
Route 2, Post Office Box 95
Leesburg, VA 22075

Lexington

Troubadour Theatre
Main and Henry Streets
Lexington, VA 24450

Lynchburg

Fine Arts Center
Thomson Drive
Lynchburg, VA 24503

Martinsville

Playmakers Community Theatre
Post Office Box 300
Martinsville, VA 24112

McLean

McLean Center Theatre
Post Office Box 652
McLean, VA 22101

Middletown

Wayside Theatre on Tour
Wayside Theatre
Middletown, VA 22645
Tel: Box Office, 703 839 1776;
    Administrative Office, 703-869-1782
Address Inquiries to: C. Edward Steele,
    Managing Director
    Dennis McLynch, General Manager
Founded in: 1962
Member: AEA; SETC; VTC;
Annual Budget: $140,000
Description: Wayside Foundation for the Arts
is a not-for-profit organization. It has three
divisions, Wayside theatre, a summer stock
theatre, Wayside Theatre on Tour, an educa-
tional tour and Wayside Youth Ensemble,
theatre for young people.

Narrows

Giles City Little Theatre
Main Street
Narrows, VA 24124

Norfolk

Little Theatre of Norfolk
801 Claremont Avenue
Norfolk, VA 23507
Tel: 804-855-6033
Address Inquiries to: Wayne Price, Manager
Founded in: 1926

Portsmouth

Little Theatre
3518 High Street
Portsmouth, VA 23507

Radford

The Long Way Home
Post Office Box 711
Radford, VA 24141

Reston

Great Falls Players
11182 Saffold Way
Reston, VA 22070
Address Inquiries to: D. Jameson

Reston Players
11495 Waterview Clus
Reston, VA 22090

Richmond

Barn Dinner Theatre
Patterson Avenue
Richmond, VA 23229

Children's Theatre of Richmond
6317 Mallory Drive
Richmond, VA 23239
Tel: 804-288-6634
Address Inquiries to: Frank Howarth,
    Executive Director
Founded in: 1926
Member: ATA; SETC; Virginia Theatre
    Council;
Annual Budget: $50,000

Dogwood Dell Players
900 East Broad Street
Richmond, VA 23219

Virginia Museum Theatre Company
Boulevard and Grove
Richmond, VA 23221
Tel: 804-786-6333
Address Inquiries to: Loraine Slade, Manager
Founded in: 1955
Annual Budget: $100,000

Roanoke

The Showtimes
Post Office Box 136114
Roanoke, VA 23704

Sandston

Community Actors Playhouse
109 Federal Street
Sandston, VA 23150

Smithfield

The Cotton Gin
938 South Church Street
Smithfield, VA 23430

South Boston

Halifax Company Little Theatre
Post Office Box 23
South Boston, VA 24592

Springfield

Phoenix Theatre
Post Office Box 202
Springfield, VA 22150

Staunton

Oak Grove Theatre
437 East Beverly Street
Staunton, VA 24401

Vienna

Falls Church Community Players
8601 Cottage Street
Vienna, VA 22180
Address Inquiries to: R. Proctor

Lakevale Players
2531 West Meredith Drive
Vienna, VA 22180
Address Inquiries to: G. Ross

Waterford

Waterford Players
Waterford, VA 22190

Williamsburg

Williamsburg Players
Post Office Box 91
Williamsburg, VA 23185

Woodbridge

Woodbridge Players
13618 Kerrydale Road
Woodbridge, VA 22193
Address Inquiries to: H. Davis

WASHINGTON

Anacortes

Anacortes Community Theatre
Post Office Box 35
Anacortes, WA 98221

Auburn

Candlestick Players
4205 Auburn Way, South
Auburn, WA 98002

Bellevue

Snoqualamie Falls Theatre
Post Offfice Box 1705
Bellevue, WA 90889

Bremerton

Community Theatre
599 Lebo Boulevard
Bremerton, WA 98310

Cathlamet

Cathlamet Little Theatre
Cathlamet, WA 98612

Centralia

Evergreen Playhouse
West 226 Center
Centralia, WA 98531

Colville

Colville Balley Players
KCVL Radio Station
Colville, WA 99114

Edmonds

Edmonds Driftwood Players
950 Main Street
Edmonds, WA 98020
Tel: 206-744-9600

Founded in: 1958

Everett

Snohomish Community Theatre
Post Offfice Box 743
Everett, WA 98203

Fort Lewis

Centurion Playhouse
North 1st and Colorado Avenue
Fort Lewis, WA 98433

Friday Harbor

Straits of Juan De Fuca Theatre
Post Office Box 662
Friday Harbor, WA 98250

Gig Harbor

Peninsula Playhouse
15705 Goodrich Drive North West
Gig Harbor, WA 98335

Hoquim

Driftwood Players
Post Office Box 95
Hoquim, WA 98550

Kirkland

Eastside Theatre Wing
620 Market Street
Kirkland, WA 98033

The Children's Theatre
Grasmere Center
5801 112th Place, NE
Kirkland, WA 98033
Address Inquiries to: Aurore Leigh Barrett

Leavenworth

Amberleaf Theatre
Post Office Box 14
Leavenworth, WA 98826
Tel: 509-548-7787
Founded in: 1961

Longview

Cascade Players
Post Office Box 264
Longview, WA 98632

Olympia

Co-Respondents Readers Theatre
c/o Larsen/Ninet
235 West 19th Street
Olympia, WA 98501
Tel: 206-866-1830

Olympia Little Theatre
Post Office Box 1215
Olympia, WA 98507

Omak

Medicine Show Player
Post Office Box 1625
Omak, WA 98841

Port Angeles

Port Angeles Community Players
1203 South Laurel Street
Port Angeles, WA 98362

Port Townsend

Key City Players
Post Office Box 194
Port Townsend, WA 98368
Tel: 206-385-3721
Address Inquiries to: Vern Jones, President
Bruce Lewis, Vice President
Founded in: 1958

Pullman

Pullman Community Theatre
SE 510 Water Street
Pullman, WA 99163

Raymond

Willapa Players
544 Ballantine Street
Raymond, WA 98577

Renton

Carco Theatre
200 Mill Avenue South
Renton, WA 98055

Richland

Richland Players
Post Office Box 603
Richland, WA 99352

Seattle

Bathouse Theatre
7312 West Green Lake Drive, North
Seattle, WA 98103
Tel: 206-524-9141; 206-524-9110
Address Inquiries to: Mary-Claire Burke,
Producer
Arne Zaslove, Artisitic Director
Founded in: 1970
Member: ACTA; SAC; King County Arts
Commission; WSAC; CCFA; Seattle
Department of Arts and Recreation;
Annual Budget: $220,000

Burien Workshop Theatre
17003 4th Avenue, South
Seattle, WA 98148

The Forest Theatre
719 Pike Street
Seattle, WA 98111

The Mountaineers Players
719 Pike Street
Seattle, WA 98101
Tel: 206-633-4398; 206-623-2314
Founded in: 1923
Description: A committee of Mountaineers,
financed by the organization, own their 'Forest Theatre'. They present one play or musical a year, opening on Memorial Day weekend for six performances. In addition they
present a play in the fall at the clubroom or
at branches of the club.

Poncho Theater
100 Dexter Avenue North
Seattle, WA 98109

Rain Country Players
17171 Bothell Way, NE
Seattle, WA 98155

Seattle Puppetry Theatre
13002 10th Avenue, NW
Seattle, WA 98177
Tel: 206-365-0100
Address Inquiries to: Kelly Reed, President
Jean M. Mahson, Director
Founded in: 1973
Member: SAC; WSAC; King County Arts
Commission; POA;
Annual Budget: $25,000
Description: Produces children's and family
shows. Most productions involve handpup-
pets and live actors.

The Skid Road Theatre
85 South Washington, #306
Seattle, WA 98104
Tel: 206-622-0251
Address Inquiries to: Amy Solomon,General
Manager
Roberta Levitow, Artistic Director
Founded in: 1971
Member: SAC; Wyman Family Trust; CCFA;
Poncho Organization; Seattle Trust and
Savings Bank;
Annual Budget: $225,000

Sumner

Valley Theatre
3814 Conrad Johnson
Sumner, WA 98390

Tacoma

Lakewood Players
Villa Plaza
Tacoma, WA 98499

Lakewood Puppeteer Productions
11812 Woodbine Lane SW
Tacoma, WA 98499
Tel: 206-584-4759
Address Inquiries to: Jeanne Murray
Charlton, Director
Founded in: 1966
Annual Budget: $5,000

Tacoma Little Theatre
210 North 'Eye' Street
Tacoma, WA 98403
Tel: 206-272-2492
Founded in: 1919

Vancouver

Old Slocum High School Theatre
605 Esther Street
Vancouver, WA 98660

Wenatchee

Music Theatre
Post Office Box 926
Wenatchee, WA 98801

Yakima

The Capitol Theatre
Post Office Box 102
Yakima, WA 98907

Yakima Little Theatre Group
5000 West Lincoln
Yakima, WA 98908
Tel: 509-966-0930
Address Inquiries to: Mrs. Stuart Semon,
    President
    Randall K. Pugh, Manager
Founded in: 1948
Member: ACTA;
Annual Budget: $25,000

WEST VIRGINIA

Beckley

Theatre Arts of West Virginia
Post Office Box 1205
Beckley, WV 25801
Tel: 304-253-8131
Address Inquiries to: John S. Benjamin,
    Artistic Director
    Stuart B. Gordon, Business Manager
Founded in: 1964
Member: IOD; TCG; NECAA; ACUAA;
    OTA; NTBA; SETC;
Description: Produces the outdoor dramas,
Hatfields and McCoys, Honey in the Rock
and Theatre West Viriginia, a professional
touring company. Theatre Arts also pro-
duces a professional company of mari-
onettes.

Theatre West Virginia
Post Office Box 1205
Beckley, WV 25801
Tel: 304-253-8317
Address Inquiries to: John S. Benjamin,
    Artistic Director
    Stuart B. Gordon, Business Manager
Founded in: 1972.
Member: NECAA; TCG; IOD; OTA; NTBA;
    SETC;
Description: A professional touring repertory
company founded to bring live theatrical
performances to those who may not other-
wise have an opportunity to experience live
theatre.

Buckhannon

Buckhannon Community Theatre
16 Gum Street
Buckhannon, WV 26201
Address Inquiries to: J. Knorr

Buckley

Hatfields and McCoys/Honey in the Rock
Post Office Box 1205
Buckley, WV 25801-1205
Tel: 304-253-8313; 304-253-8314
Address Inquiries to: John S. Benjamin,
    Artistic Director
    Stuart B. Gordon, Business Manager
Founded in: 1955
Member: IOD; TCG; NECCA; OTA; SETC;

ACUCAA; NTBA;
Description: Two of the oldest outdoor
dramas in the U.S. Each year they attract
thousands of tourists to southern West Virginia, giving young performers an opportunity for professional experience. The
dramas are produced by Theatre Arts of
West Virginia.

Cameron

Cameron Community Theatre
Route 3, Box 3
Cameron, WV 26033
Address Inquiries to: S. Kennedy

Charleston

Children's Theatre of Charleston
1105 Quarrier Street
Charleston, WV 25301
Member: CTAA;

Health Awareness Theatre
Post Office Box 3401
Charleston, WV 25334

Charlestown

Old Opera House
Liberty and George Street
Charlestown, WV 25414
Address Inquiries to: B. Angel

Clarksburg

Clarksburg Art Center
Post Office Box 148
Clarksburg, WV 25701
Address Inquiries to: M. Spelsburg

West Virginia Theatre Conference
Post Office Box 148
Clarksburg, WV 25301
Address Inquiries to: Sharon Callis

Fairmont

Creative Garden Theatre
Post Office Box 1541
Fairmont, WV 26554
Address Inquiries to: E. Klein

Masquers/Town and Gown Players
Fine Arts Department
Fairmont State College
Fairmont, WV 26554
Tel: 304-367-4248; 304-367-4240
Address Inquiries to: Leta N. Carlson, Ph.D.;
    Chairman, Fine Arts Division
    Jo Ann Lough, Production Manager
Founded in: Masquers, 1923; Town and
    Gown, 1960
Member: WVAHC;
Annual Budget: Masquers, $12,000; Town
    and Gown, $12,000
Description: Masquers, an arm of the theatre
department of the college, has four major
productions, two reader's theatres, and of-
ten a short touring childrens play and sup-
ports the intercollegiate Oral Interpretation
Team. The Town and Gown Players, an arm
of the college academics, along with volunteers from the community, produces at least
two shows a summer with a paid resident

company.

Huntington

Community Players
610 Terrace
Huntington, WV 25705
Address Inquiries to: N. Calleds

Huntington Theatre Ensemble
1010 13th Street
Huntington, WV 25701
Address Inquiries to: E. Blue

Hurricain

Mountaineer Dinner Theatre
3973 Teays Valley Road
Hurricain, WV 25526
Address Inquiries to: M. Michele

Lewisburg

Greenbrier Repertory Theatre
Post Office Box 494
Lewisburg, WV 24901
Address Inquiries to: A. Benedict

MacArthur

Curtain Callers
Post Office Box 589
MacArthur, WV 25873
Address Inquiries to: J. Sisk

Martinsburg

Berkeley Community Theatre
Post Office Box 1505
Martinsburg, WV 25401
Address Inquiries to: J. Taylor

Moorefield

Hardy City Community Theatre
Post Office Box 625
Moorefield, WV 26836
Address Inquiries to: R. Updegraff

Morgantown

Bridgegate Dinner Theatre
241 ½ Walnut Street
Morgantown, WV 26505
Address Inquiries to: D. Hoffstetter

Wellsburg

Brooke Hills Playhouse
Post Office Box 186
Wellsburg, WV 26070

Wheeling

Oglebay Institute
Oglebay Park
Wheeling, WV 26003
Address Inquiries to: S. Greer

Wheeling Park Players
Oglebay Institute
Wheeling, WV 26003

WISCONSIN

Amery

Amery Community Theatre
Route 2
Amery, WI 54001
Address Inquiries to: C. Obrian

Appleton

Appleton YMCA Theatre
218 East Lawrence Street
Appleton, WI 546911
Address Inquiries to: M. Vanevenhoven

Attic Theatre
Post Office Box 41
Appleton, WI 54911
Tel: 414-733-2945
Address Inquiries to: Carl H. Wenzel,
    President
    K.K. DuVall, Vice President
Founded in: 1950

Ashland

Chequamagon Bay Players
Post Office Box 225
Ashland, WI 54806
Address Inquiries to: L. Glousky

Beaver Dam

Beaver Dam Community Theatre
Post Office Box 216
Beaver Dam, WI 53916
Address Inquiries to: Terry Schmitt

Beloit

Beloit Civic Theatre
Post Office Box 214
Beloit, WI 53511

Black River Falls

Black River Community Theatre
Harrison Street
Black River Falls, WI 54615
Address Inquiries to: G. Strand

Boscobel

Boscobel Community Theatre
832 Wisconsin Avenue
Boscobel, WI 53805
Address Inquiries to: D. Larkosh

Brookfield

Brookfield Players
17535 Oak Park Row
Brookfield, WI 53005
Address Inquiries to: Carol Thiene

Brown Deer

Brown Deer Theatre
8387 North Grandview Drive
Brown Deer, WI 53223
Address Inquiries to: M. Svoboda

Burlington

Burling Haylofters
509 East Jefferson
Burlington, WI 53105
Address Inquiries to: J. Phillips

Durand

Durand Community Theatre
910 Auth Street
Durand, WI 54736
Address Inquiries to: J.A. Peterson

Eau Claire

Eau Claire Community Theatre
1502 Park Avenue
Eau Claire, WI 54701
Address Inquiries to: D. Cox

Elkhorn

Lakeland Players
Post Office Box 234
Elkhorn, WI 53121

Elm Grove

Sunset Playhouse
800 Elm Grove Road
Elm Grove, WI 53122
Tel: 414-782-4430
Founded in: 1953
Member: ATA; WCT;
Annual Budget: $120,000
Description: Entirely supported by box office
receipts and its dedicated volunteers. The
theatre has a regular paid staff of four.

Evansville

Evansville Community Theatre
437 West Church Street
Evansville, WI 53535
Address Inquiries to: G. Knuckles

Fish Creek

Penninsula Players Theatre Foundation
Fish Creek, WI 54212
Tel: 414-868-3287
Address Inquiries to: Tom Connors, General
    Manager
    James B. McKenzie, President
Founded in: 1935

Theatre-in-a-Garden
Fish Creek, WI 54212
Tel: 414-868-3287; 414-868-3288
Address Inquiries to: Tom Birmingham,
    General Manager
    James B. McKenzie, Producer
Founded in: 1935
Member: AEA; WTA; NEA; WAB;
Description: An AEA approved summer
theatre with a house capacity of 300.

Fond Du Lac

Fond Du Lac Community Theatre
2602 Valley Creek Road
Fond Du Lac, WI 54935
Address Inquiries to: S.A. King

Grantsburg

Grantsburg Players
United Methodist Church
Grantsburg, WI 54840

Green Bay

Green Bay Community Theatre
Post Office Box 282
Green Bay, WI 54301

Harlequin Players
Post Office Box 625
Green Bay, WI 54305
Address Inquiries to: J. Frisch

Greendale

Suburban Players
Post Oofice Box 39
Greendale, WI 53129

Hartland

Lake Country Players
North 56, Highway K
Hartland, WI 53029
Address Inquiries to: Dorothy Blish

Hayward

Hayward Community Players
Courthouse
Hayward, WI 54843

Janesville

Clinton Goodtime Players
Route 3
Janesville, WI 53545
Address Inquiries to: Lyn Howard

Lewis

Seven Pines Players
7 Pines Lodge
Lewis, WI 54851
Address Inquiries to: Joan Simpson

Madison

Madison Savoyards
4217 Wanetah Trail
Madison, WI 53711
Address Inquiries to: Frank Parker

Madison Theatre Guild
2410 Monroe Street
Madison, WI 53711
Tel: 608-238-9322
Address Inquiries to: Mary S. Gill, President
Founded in: 1946
Member: ATA; ACTA;

National Theatre Festival
120 East Wilson
Madison, WI 53703

Savoyards LTD
Post Office Box 1612
Madison, WI 53701

Strollers Theatre Limited
354 Kent Lane, #203
Madison, WI 53713

Wisconsin Children's Theatre
621 Pickford Street
Madison, WI 53711
Tel: 608-233-7854
Address Inquiries to: R.J. Sandler, Manager
    J.K. Jallings, Vice President
Founded in: 1971

Manitowoc

Manitowoc Masquers
616 North 8th Street
Manitowoc, WI 54220

Mayville

Marrias Players
10 Tower Drive
Mayville, WI 53050
Address Inquiries to: M. Bachhuber

Menomonie

Menomonie Theatre Guild
Post Office Box 325
Menomonie, WI 54571
Tel: 715-235-0001
Address Inquiries to: Mary Riodan, President
Wallace Smetana, Vice President
Founded in: 1958
Annual Budget: $10,000

Menomonie Falls

Patio Players
Menomonie Falls, WI 53051
Address Inquiries to: Maggie Brooks

Merrill

Lincoln Community Theatre
708 Merrill Avenue
Merrill, WI 54452
Address Inquiries to: M. Rajeck

Middleton

Middleton Civic Theatre
1701 Henry Street
Middleton, WI 53562
Address Inquiries to: B. Cutlip

Milwaukee

Bell Players
722 North Broadway
Milwaukee, WI 53202

Bill-Bart Enterprises
Theatre East, on Oakland
Milwaukee, WI 53211

Cameo Players
314 West Sugar Lane
Milwaukee, WI 53217
Address Inquiries to: L. Bollow

Melody Top Theatre
7201 West Good Hope Road
Milwaukee, WI 53202
Address Inquiries to: Guy Little, Director

Milwaukee Players
Post Office Drawer 10k
Milwaukee, WI 53201

Milwaukee Repertory Theatre
929 North Water Street
Milwaukee, WI 53202
Tel: 414-273-7121 - Business Office;
414-273-7206 - Box Office
Address Inquiries to: Sara O'Connor,
Managing Director
Peggy Haessler Rose, Business Manager
Founded in: 1954
Member: LORT; AAA; MUPAF; WTA;

Annual Budget: $1,740,000
Description: The MRT is counted as a major force in American theatre, an organization that recognizes and develops new talent in acting, playwriting, design, and production. Through the years, the MRT has forged close ties with theatre people throughout Europe and the Orient.

People's Heritage
4240 West Fond Du Lac
Milwaukee, WI 53216
Address Inquiries to: Ben Bradley

Peoples Theatre
2208 North 3rd Street
Milwaukee, WI 53212
Address Inquiries to: G. Wallace

Present Company
2401 West Medford #101
Milwaukee, WI 53206

West Allis Players
535 South 68th Street
Milwaukee, WI 53214
Address Inquiries to: L. Kordus

2563 North Farwell
2679 North Lake Drive
Milwaukee, WI 53211
Address Inquiries to: H. E. Felsenfeld

Mineral Point

Shakerag Players
705 Ridge
Mineral Point, WI 53565
Address Inquiries to: J. Adams

Mount Horeb

Mt. Horeb Community Theatre
512 Green Street
Mount Horeb, WI 53572
Address Inquiries to: J. Sutter

Song of Norway
Post Office Box 132
Mount Horeb, WI 53572
Founded in: 1966
Annual Budget: $12,000
Description: A light romantic musical based on the life of composer Edward Grieg. Performances last Saturday night in June and all Saturdays in July. Performances begin at 8 p.m. on an outdoor stage.

Mukwonago

Village Players
Post Office Box 165
Mukwonago, WI 53149
Address Inquiries to: Pam McGuire

Neenah

Riverside Players
409 Quarry Street
Neenah, WI 54956
Address Inquiries to: B. Tungate

New Glarus

William Tell Players
William Tell Drama Center
New Glarus, WI 535740875
Founded in: 1938
Description: William Tell Drama's sole purpose is to help provide funds for worthwhile community projects.

Oak Creek

Oak Creek Community Theatre
331 East Wynbrook Drive
Oak Creek, WI 53154
Address Inquiries to: K. Wegerbauer

Oconomowoc

Oconomowoc Players
519 West Labelle Avenue
Oconomowoc, WI 53066
Address Inquiries to: N. Rentmeester

Osceola

Saint Croix Valley Community Theatre
Route 1
Osceola, WI 54020

Oshkosh

Drama Lab
113 Baldwin Avenue
Oshkosh, WI 54901
Address Inquiries to: Betty Butcher

Oshkosh Community Players
1045 Eastman
Oshkosh, WI 54901
Address Inquiries to: P.J. Nebel

Portage

Portage Players
2214 Woodcrest
Portage, WI 53901
Address Inquiries to: N. Kinney

Racine

Fellowship Players
2041 Georgia Avenue
Racine, WI 53404
Address Inquiries to: Lawrence Weaver

Rice Lake

Hardscrabble Players
Route 3, Box 67
Rice Lake, WI 54868
Address Inquiries to: N. Klauss

Richland Center

Richmond Community Theatre
648 North Main Street
Richland Center, WI 53581
Address Inquiries to: M. Collins

Salem

Gaslite Players
Route 3, Post Office Box 350
Salem, WI 53168
Address Inquiries to: J.A. Gabriel

Shawano

Mielke Theatre
Post Office Box 87
Shawano, WI 54166
Address Inquiries to: M.M. Winter

Sheboygan

Sheboygan Community Players
830 Virginia Avenue
Sheboygan, WI 53081
Address Inquiries to: Rob Dippel

Spooner

Spooner Community Player
Post Offfice Box 123
Spooner, WI 54801
Address Inquiries to: M. Coquilette

Spring Green

River Valley Community Theatre
Post Office Box 356
Spring Green, WI 53588
Address Inquiries to: Harlan Ferstl

Stevens Point

Area Community Theatre
900 South Marie Avenue
Stevens Point, WI 54481
Address Inquiries to: Diana Bailiff

Stoughton

Stoughton Village Players
916 Roby Road
Stoughton, WI 53589
Address Inquiries to: Dwayne Berg

Sun Prairie

Sun Prairie Civic Theatre
Post Office Box 132
Sun Prairie, WI 53590

Superior

Paul E. Holden Fine Arts Center
University of Wisconsin
Superior, WI 54880
Tel: 715-392-8101
Address Inquiries to: Arthur Kruk, Manager
Founded in: 1973
Description: A total seating capacity of 1,200.

Waukesha

Chancel Players
1114 North Bel-Ayr Drive
Waukesha, WI 53186
Address Inquiries to: Nadine Stromberg

Waukesha Civic Theatre
218 Debbie Drive
Waukesha, WI 53186
Address Inquiries to: D. Parris

Wausau

Agape Community Theatre
810 Grant Street
Wausau, WI 54401
Address Inquiries to: Elsie Waterman

RC Community Theatre
620 North 5th Avenue

Wausau, WI 54401
Address Inquiries to: M. Collins

Wauwatosa

Village Playhouse
4085 North 111th Street
Wauwatosa, WI 53222
Address Inquiries to: Byrll E. Hoelke

West Bend

Stage Door Players
1404 Sandra Lane
West Bend, WI 53095
Address Inquiries to: O.W. Styve

Whitefish Bay

Bay Players
4900 North Hollywood Avenue
Whitefish Bay, WI 53217
Address Inquiries to: L. Verhaagh

Wisconsin Rapids

Wisconsin Rapids
810 Witter Street
Wisconsin Rapids, WI 54494
Address Inquiries to: C. Meils

WYOMING

Casper

The Playhouse
Post Office Box 1018
Casper, WY 82601

Red Dog Saloon Players
2705 East 71st Street
Casper, WY 82601

Cheyenne

Cheyenne Little Theater Players
Post Office Box 1086
Cheyenne, WY 82001
Tel: 307-638-6543
Founded in: 1930

Glenrock

Glenrock Little Theatre
Post Office Box 622
Glenrock, WY 82637

Lander

Landers Littles Theatre
680 Bellue
Lander, WY 82520

Sheridan

Sheridan Civic Theatre Guild
Post Office Box 1
Sheridan, WY 82801
Founded in: 1953

Worland

Worland Community Theatre
701 South 14th Street
Worland, WY 82401

CANADA

Calgary, Alberta

Basement-Fine Arts Centre
2519 Richmond Road SW
Calgary, Alberta, Canada

Les Marionettes Merinat
412 - 3500 Varsity Drive Northwest
Calgary, Alberta, Canada T2L 1Y3
Tel: 403-282-2226
Address Inquiries to: Eric Merinat, Artistic Director
Isabelle Grenier, Publicity Director
Founded in: 1969
Member: Union des Artistes;
Description: A theatre for children that performs in French using marionettes.

Loose Moose Theatre Company
1610 Bowness Road Northwest
Calgary, Alberta, Canada T2N 3J9
Tel: 403-283-9960
Address Inquiries to: Keith Johnstone, Artistic Director
Mel Tonken, General Manager
Founded in: 1976
Description: A theatre that performs on Sunday nights.

Lunchbox Theatre
Post Office Box 9027
Calgary, Alberta, Canada T2P 2W4
Tel: 403-265-4292
Address Inquiries to: Bartley Bard, Artistic Director
Joi Beckett, Administrator/Publicity Director
Founded in: 1975
Description: A professional theatre that presents one-act plays at noon.

Stage Coach Players
830 8th Avenue South West
Calgary, Alberta, Canada T2P 1L7
Tel: 403-262-2146
Address Inquiries to: Rick McNair, Artistic Director
Queenie Day, Extensions Co-ordinator
Founded in: 1977
Description: Stagecoach tours communities and schools in Alberta.

Sun Ergos
2205, 700 - 9th Street, South West
Calgary, Alberta, Canada T2P 2B5
Tel: 403-264-4621
Address Inquiries to: Robert Greenwood, Artistic Director
Dana Luebke, Artistic Director
Founded in: 1978
Description: Provides open space staging for performing arts groups.

Theatre Calgary
830 9th Avenue South West
Calgary, Alberta, Canada T2P 1L7
Tel: 403-262-2146; 403-265-6700
Address Inquiries to: Rick McNair, Artistic Director
Marcia E. Lane, General Manager
Founded in: 1967

Description: Presents a full season of plays.

Canmore, Alberta

The Five Star Theatre of Alberta
Post Office Box 722
Canmore, Alberta, Canada T0L 0M0
Address Inquiries to: Jerome Ackhurst,
    Artistic Director
    Lynn Borrowman, General Manager
Founded in: 1977
Description: A professional theatre that pre-
sents shows for children.

Edmonton, Alberta

Catalyst Theatre Society
9903 80 Avenue
Edmonton, Alberta, Canada T6E 1T2
Tel: 403-452-3557
Address Inquiries to: Jan Selman, Artistic
    Director
    Denise Roy, Administrative Director
Founded in: 1977
Description: Makes use of theatre for public
education.

The Citadel On Wheels/Wings
9828 - 101A Avenue
Edmonton, Alberta, Canada T5J 3C6
Tel: 403-426-4811
Address Inquiries to: Margaret Mooney
Founded in: 1968
Description: A professional theatre that cre-
ates and presents new productions for chil-
dren and adults.

The Citadel Theatre
9828 - 101A Avenue
Edmonton, Alberta, Canada T5J 3C6
Tel: 403-426-4811; 403-425-1820
Address Inquiries to: Peter Coe, Artistic
    Director
    Wayne Fipke, General Manager
Founded in: 1965
Description: Edmonton's largest municipal
theatre that produces a full season of plays.

Edmonton Actors' Workshop
8909 - 112 Street
Hub Building
Edmonton, Alberta, Canada T6G 2C5
Tel: 403-433-2421
Address Inquiries to: Martin Fishman, Artistic
    Director
    Heather Lea MacCallum, Publicity
    Director
Description: An actors' workshop.

Mime-Light Theatre
11018 - 83 Avenue
Edmonton, Alberta, Canada T6G 0T7
Tel: 403-439-4068
Address Inquiries to: Kenneth J. Noster,
    Artistic Director
    Marlane Herklotz, Administrative
    Director
Description: A theatre that presents mime
shows year-round.

Northern Light Theatre
10189 - 99 Street
Edmonton, Alberta, Canada T5J 0N2

Tel: 403-426-4292; 403-429-3110
Address Inquiries to: Scott Swan, Artistic
    Director
    Allan Lysell, General Manager
Founded in: 1975
Description: A theatre that presents shows
during lunch-hour and in the evenings.

Savage God
9527 - 87th Avenue
Edmonton, Alberta, Canada T6C 1K4
Tel: 403-469-9204
Address Inquiries to: John Juliani, Artistic
    Director
    Donna Wong-Juliani, General
    Manager/Publicity Director
Founded in: 1966
Description: A theatre that presents shows at
various places throughout Canada.

Stage West
16615 109 Avenue
Edmonton, Alberta, Canada T5P 4K8
Tel: 403-484-0841; 403-483-4051
Address Inquiries to: William Fisher, Artistic
    Director
    Howard Pechet, General Manager
Founded in: 1972
Description: Stage West produces full-length
plays.

Theatre Network
Post Office Box 4926
Edmonton, Alberta, Canada T6E 5G8
Tel: 403-425-8761
Address Inquiries to: Mark Manson, Artistic
    Director
    Marion Hyde, Administrator
Founded in: 1975
Description: Researches and produces works.

Theatre 3
10426 95 Street
Edmonton, Alberta, Canada T5H 2C1
Tel: 403-426-3394
Address Inquiries to: Keith Digby, Artistic
    Director
    Tim Crighton, Technical Director
Founded in: 1970
Description: Offers productions from the na-
tional and international repertoire.

Workshop West Playwrights' Theatre
#5, 11020 65 Avenue
Edmonton, Alberta, Canada T6H 1V9
Tel: 403-436-7378
Address Inquiries to: Gerry Potter, Artistic
    Director
    Steven Heatley, Associate Director
Founded in: 1978
Description: Develops and produces plays.

Kelowna, British Columbia

Sunshine Theatre
4132 Lakeshore Road
Kelowna, British Columbia, Canada V1W
1V6
Address Inquiries to: Joan Panton, Artistic
    Director
Member: AEA;
Annual Budget: $20,000

Description: An equity theatre that presents a
full summer season.

New Westminster, British Columbia

New Westminster Secondary School
Hyack Theatre
835 8th Street
New Westminster, British Columbia,
Canada V3M 359
Address Inquiries to: Owen A. Erwin

Vancouver, British Columbia

Women's Theatre Co-operative
c/o Nicola Cavendish
1742 Jumbar
Vancouver, British Columbia, Canada

Saint-Boniface, Manitoba

Le Cercle Moliere
C.P.1
Saint-Boniface, Manitoba, Canada R2H
3B4
    Tel: 204-233-8053
Address Inquiries to: Roland Mahe, Artistic
    Director
    Ernest Gautron, General Manager
Founded in: 1925
Description: Canada's oldest continuing
theatre company, and produces plays in
French from a national and international
repertoire.

Winnipeg, Manitoba

Confidential Exchange
133 Albert Street
Winnipeg, Manitoba, Canada R3B 1G6
Tel: 204-452-7195
Address Inquiries to: Rory Kyle, Artistic
    Director/Publicity Director
    Brian Richardson, General Manager
Founded in: 1974
Description: A professional theatre that pro-
duces plays.

Interlake Festival Theatre
201 - 297 Smith Street
Winnipeg, Manitoba, Canada
Address Inquiries to: Frank Adamson, Artistic
    Director
    Beverly Buddick, General Manager
Description: A theatre that performs during
the summer.

Manitoba Puppet Theatre
300 Memorial Boulevard
Winnipeg, Manitoba, Canada R3C 1V1
Tel: 204-943-1302
Address Inquiries to: Chris Hurley
Founded in: 1973
Description: A theatre that performs for chil-
dren year-round.

Manitoba Theatre Centre
174 Market Avenue
Winnipeg, Manitoba, Canada R3B 0P8
Tel: 204-956-1340; 204-942-6537
Address Inquiries to: Richard Ouzounian,
    Artistic Director
    Joe Konrad, General Manager
Founded in: 1958

Description: Canada's first modern regional theatre that produces plays from the national and international repertoire.

Manitoba Theatre Workshop
160 Princess Street
Winnipeg, Manitoba, Canada R3B 1K9
Tel: 204-942-7291
Address Inquiries to: Deborah Baer Quinn,
Artistic Director
Michael Utgaard, Administrative
Director
Founded in: 1973
Description: A theatre that presents new Canadian works.

The Neighborhood Theatre
160 Princess Street
Winnipeg, Manitoba, Canada R3B 1K9
Tel: 204-942-7291
Address Inquiries to: Deborah Baer Quinn,
Artistic Director
Michael Utgaard, Administrative
Director
Founded in: 1977
Description: A theatre that creates plays based on the lives of young people.

Puppet Tree Company
160 Princess Street
Winnipeg, Manitoba, Canada R3B 1K9
Tel: 204-942-7291
Address Inquiries to: Shawn Kimelman,
Artistic Director
Michael Utgaard, Administrative
Director
Founded in: 1977
Description: A puppet theatre for children.

Rainbow Stage
500 - 352 Donald Street
Winnipeg, Manitoba, Canada R3B 2H8
Tel: 204-942-2091; 204-942-3032
Address Inquiries to: Jack Shapira, Managing
Director
Walter Burgess, Resident
Director/Choreographer
Founded in: 1954
Description: Presents musical comedies outdoors.

Sundog Productions
29 Scotia Street
Winnipeg, Manitoba, Canada R2W 3W6
Tel: 204-582-7578
Address Inquiries to: Edward Lee Stebbing,
Artistic Director
Ray Turner, General Manager
Founded in: 1976
Description: Produces musical comedies during the winter.

Caraquet, New Brunswick

Theatre Populaire
C.P. 608
Caraquet, New Brunswick, Canada E0B
1K0
Tel: 506-727-2712
Address Inquiries to: Rejean Poirier
Marcel Albert
Description: Theatre Populaire is a touring

company which performs in French.

Fredericton, New Brunswick

Theatre New Brunswick
Post Office Box 566
Fredericton, New Brunswick, Canada E3B
5A6
Tel: 506-455-3222
Address Inquiries to: Malcolm Black
Donald A. Grant
Founded in: 1968
Member: AEA;

Theatre New Brunswick
Young Company
Post Office Box 566
Fredericton, New Brunswick, Canada E3B
5A6
Tel: 506-455-3080
Address Inquiries to: Malcolm Black
Susan Montague
Founded in: 1974
Description: Theatre New Brunswick Young Company presents new works for children.

Moncton, New Brunswick

Theatre De L'Esaouette
c/o Gracia Couturier
120 rue Victoria
Moncton, New Brunswick, Canada E1C
1P9
Tel: 506-845-7093

Saint John's, Newfoundland

Mummers Troupe of Newfoundland
281 Duckworth Street
Saint John's, Newfoundland, Canada
Tel: 709-754-1692
Address Inquiries to: Rhonda Payne
Founded in: 1972
Description: The Mummers Troupe creates its own works in Newfoundland. Their home is in Saint John's, and they often tour their shows around the province and through Canada.

Rising Tide Theatre
Post Office Box 7371
Saint John's, Newfoundland, Canada A1E
3Y5
Tel: 709-579-4438
Address Inquiries to: Ann Narvaez
Joel Rogers
Founded in: 1978

Theatre Newfoundland and Labrador
c/o Arts and Culture Centre
Prince Philip Drive
Saint John's, Newfoundland, Canada A1C
5P9
Tel: 709-737-3650
Address Inquiries to: Maxim Mazumdar
Founded in: 1979

Chester, Nova Scotia

Canadian Puppetfestivals
Chester, Nova Scotia, Canada B0J 1J0
Tel: 902-275-3171
Address Inquiries to: Dora Velleman
Leo Velleman

Founded in: 1950
Description: Canadian Puppet Festivals is Canada's oldest continuing professional puppet theatre.

Guysborough, Nova Scotia

Mulgrave Road Co-operative Theatre
Compay
Post Office Box 219
Guysborough, Nova Scotia, Canada B0H
1N0
Tel: 902-533-2092
Address Inquiries to: Michael Fahey
Ed McKenna
Description: A touring company.

Halifax, Nova Scotia

Neptune Theatre
1593 Argyle Street
Halifax, Nova Scotia, Canada B3J 2B2
Tel: 902-429-7300
Address Inquiries to: John Neville
Christopher Banks
Founded in: 1963
Member: AEA;
Description: A major regional theatre.

Wolfville, Nova Scotia

Mermaid Theatre
Post Office Box 837
Wolfville, Nova Scotia, Canada B0P 1X0
Tel: 902-542-3641
Address Inquiries to: Evelyn Garbary
Sara Lee Lewis
Founded in: 1972
Member: AEA;
Description: Produces original works for young people usually based on regional folklore and history.

Barrie, Ontario

Gryphon Theatre Company
103 Dunlop Street East
Barrie, Ontario, Canada L4M 4T7
Tel: 705-728-4613
Address Inquiries to: Vernon Chapman,
Administrator
Ev Johnstone, Publicity Director
Founded in: 1970
Description: Presents plays from the international repertoire year round.

Blyth, Ontario

Blyth Summer Festival
Post Office Box 291
Blyth, Ontario, Canada N0M 1H0
Tel: 519-523-9300
Address Inquiries to: Janet Amos, Artistic
Director
Keith Roulston, General Manager
Founded in: 1975
Description: Produces original Canadian works.

Grand Bend, Ontario

Huron Country Playhouse
Grand Bend, Ontario, Canada N0M 1T0
Tel: 519-238-8387; 519-238-8451
Address Inquiries to: Marc L. Quinn, General

Manager
Heather Redick, Publicity Director
Founded in: 1972
Description: Presents musicals and comedies.

Gravenhurst, Ontario

Muskoka Summer Theatre
Box 1055
Gravenhurst, Ontario, Canada P0C 1G0
Tel: 705-687-2762
Address Inquiries to: Michael Ayoub, Artistic
   Director
   Michael Cole, General
   Manager/Publicity Director
Founded in: 1948
Description: Produces plays and musicals.

Guelph, Ontario

The Road Show Theatre Company
122 Harris Street
Guelph, Ontario, Canada N1H 6L8
Tel: 519-823-2381
Address Inquiries to: Norman L. Mackay,
   General Director
   Dennis Johnson, Publicity Director
Founded in: 1974
Description: The Road Show presents plays
from a national and international repertoire
during the fall and winter seasons.

Theatre Max
Post Office Box 1744
Guelph, Ontario, Canada N1H 6Z9
Tel: 519-824-2714
Address Inquiries to: Dy Maass, General
   Manager
   Brenda Campbell, Publicity Director
Description: Theatre Max presents plays for
adults and children.

Hamilton, Ontario

Hamilton Place Theatre
Box 2080, Station A
Hamilton, Ontario, Canada L8N 3Y7
Tel: 416-525-3100; 416-525-7710
Address Inquiries to: Thomas B. Burrows,
   General Manager
   Mary Webb, Publicity Director
Founded in: 1973

Theatre Aquarius
50 Murray Street West
Hamilton, Ontario, Canada L8L 1B3
Tel: 416-529-1195
Address Inquiries to: Gordon Neufeld,
   General Manager
   Deborah Horridge, Publicity
Founded in: 1973
Description: Presents a season of five plays,
two children's plays, a tour of Ontario and a
summer theatre school.

Islington, Ontario

Theatre On The Move
Post Office Box 462
Islington, Ontario, Canada M9A 4X4
Tel: 416-445-1966
Address Inquiries to: James Biros, Artistic
   Director
   Bev Wilson, Business Manager

Founded in: 1970
Description: A professional touring company
that presents plays to schools. It offers special programs for children.

Jackson's Point, Ontario

The Red Barn Theatre
Post Office Box 291
Jackson's Point, Ontario, Canada L0E 1L0
Tel: 416-722-3741
Address Inquiries to: Ernest Schwarz, Artistic
   Director
Description: The Red Barn Theatre presents
plays from the international repertoire dur-
ing the summer season.

Kingston, Ontario

Theatre 5
370 King Street West
Kingston, Ontario, Canada K7L 4Y8
Tel: 613-546-5460
Address Inquiries to: Gordon Robertson,
   General Manager
   David Prosser, Publicity Director
Founded in: 1973
Description: Presents plays from the national
and international repertoire. They also op-
erate a children's touring company.

Lindsay, Ontario

Kawartha Summer Theatre
2 Lindsay Street South, Box 161
Lindsay, Ontario, Canada K9V 4S1
Tel: 705-324-9111
Address Inquiries to: Dennis D. Sweeting,
   Artistic Director
   Margaret Sweeting, General Manager
Founded in: 1968
Description: Presents summer plays.

London, Ontario

Centre Stage Theatre
380 Wellington Street
London, Ontario, Canada N6A 5B5
Tel: 519-433-5241; 519-433-4700
Address Inquiries to: Ken Livingstone,
   Artistic Director
   Janina Barrett, General
   Manager/Publicity Director
Founded in: 1976
Description: Presents plays from the modern
repertoire during the winter.

Theatre London
471 Richmond Street
London, Ontario, Canada N6A 3E4
Tel: 519-672-9030; 519-672-8800
Address Inquiries to: Paul Eck, Administrative
   Director
   Rob Wellan, Publicity Director
Founded in: 1971
Description: One of Canada's oldest continu-
ing community theatres.

Niagara-on-the-Lake, Ontario

Shaw Festival Theatre Foundation
Post Office Box 774
Niagara-on-the-Lake, Ontario, Canada L0S
1J0

Annual Budget: $2.5 million
Description: A theatre that presents a full season from May to October.

Theatre Beyond Words
Post Office Box 759
Niagara on the Lake, Ontario, Canada L0S
1J0
Tel: 416-468-3964
Address Inquiries to: Harro Maskow, Artistic
   Director
   David Satterthwaite, Technical Director
Founded in: 1977
Description: A professional touring company.

Ottawa, Ontario

Great Canadian Theatre Company
Post Office Box 4223, Station E
Ottawa, Ontario, Canada K1S 5B2
Tel: 613-236-5192
Address Inquiries to: Larry McDonald,
   Artistic Director
   Larry Laxdal, Administrator
Founded in: 1975
Description: A theatre that presents Canadian
plays.

Le Theatre des Lutins
C.P. 7065
Ottawa, Ontario, Canada K1L 7065
Tel: 613-523-8621
Address Inquiries to: Gilles Provost, Artistic
   Director
   Monique P. Landry, Administrator
Founded in: 1971
Description: A touring theatre that presents
plays for children in French.

L'Hexagone
C.P. 1534, Succursale B
Ottawa, Ontario, Canada K1P 5W1
Tel: 613-996-5051
Address Inquiries to: Jean Herbiet, Artistic
   Director
   Claude Ranger, Touring Director
Founded in: 1972
Member: Union des Artistes;
Description: L'Hexagone is a school touring
company that performs in French.

National Arts Centre
Box 1534, Station B
Ottawa, Ontario, Canada K1P 5W1
Tel: 613-996-5051; 613-237-4400
Address Inquiries to: Donald MacSween,
   General Director
   Andis Celms, Administrator
Founded in: 1969
Description: Presents plays in French and En-
glish from the national and international
repertoire.

Penguin Theatre Company
Post Office Box 4353, Station E
Ottawa, Ontario, Canada K1S 5B3
Tel: 613-233-9281; 613-233-1841
Address Inquiries to: Maureen LaBonte,
   Acting Artistic Director
   Susan Renouf, General Manager
Founded in: 1976
Description: A touring company producing

four main stage and two school touring shows.

Theatre 2000
62 George Street
Ottawa, Ontario, Canada K1N 5V9
Tel: 416-233-2957
Address Inquiries to: Ron Zwierchowski, Publicity Director
Elizabeth C. Lundy, Business Administrator
Description: Presents Canadian plays.

Versailles Academy of Make-Up Arts and Scientists
35 O'Connor Street, Suite 203
Ottawa, Ontario, Canada K1P 5M4

Peterborough, Ontario

Arbor Theatre Company
Post Office Box 1414
Peterborough, Ontario, Canada K9J 7H6
Tel: 705-748-3022; 705-748-3111
Address Inquiries to: John Plank, Artistic Director
Founded in: 1979
Description: Performs both classics and commercial works.

Petrolia, Ontario

Theatre Go Round
Post Office Box 1180
Petrolia, Ontario, Canada N0N 1R0
Tel: 519-882-1221
Address Inquiries to: Patricia Mahoney, Artistic Director/General Manager
Mark Cole, Technical Director
Founded in: 1977
Description: Presents plays for children and adults.

Victoria Playhouse
Post Office Box 1180
Petrolia, Ontario, Canada N0N 1R0
Tel: 416-822-1221
Address Inquiries to: Patricia Mahoney, Artistic Director/General Manager
Mark Cole, Technical Director
Founded in: 1973
Description: A community theatre.

St. Catharines, Ontario

Brock Centre For The Arts
Brock University
St. Catharines, Ontario, Canada L2S 3A1
Tel: 416-684-3332; 416-684-6377
Address Inquiries to: Donald Acaster, Director
Al Anderson, Production Director
Founded in: 1969
Description: Hosts local companies.

Escarpment Theatre Co-Op
Post Office Box 372
St. Catharines, Ontario, Canada L2R 6T7
Tel: 416-682-8326; 416-684-6377
Address Inquiries to: Duncan McGregor, Artistic Director
Al Anderson, Technical Director
Founded in: 1977
Description: Presents plays for children and adults.

Press Theatre
85 Church Street
St. Catharines, Ontario, Canada L2R 6Y3
Tel: 416-684-1133, Administration;
416-684-6377, Box Office
Address Inquiries to: Elaine Stevenson, Publicity Director
Simon Johnston, Artistic Director
Founded in: 1973
Description: Plays from around the world are offered during the winter season.

St. Catherines, Ontario

Carousel Players
Post Office Box 372
St. Catherines, Ontario, Canada L2R 6T7
Tel: 416-682-8326
Address Inquiries to: Duncan McGregor, Artistic Director
Al Anderson, Technical Director
Founded in: 1971
Description: Presents plays for children.

Sudbury, Ontario

Sudbury Theatre Centre
90 King Street
Sudbury, Ontario, Canada P3E 4P8
Tel: 705-674-8381
Address Inquiries to: Helen Doig, General Manager
Jenny Turner, Publicity Director
Founded in: 1971
Description: Presents plays from around the world.

Theatre du Nouvel-Ontario
79 rue Ignatius
Sudbury, Ontario, Canada P3E 4P8
Tel: 705-675-5606
Address Inquiries to: Alain Poirier, Administrator
Marc O'Sullivan, Publicity Director
Founded in: 1971
Description: Presents plays from the national and international repertoire, in French.

Thunder Bay, Ontario

Kam Theatre Lab
316 Bay Street
Thunder Bay, Ontario, Canada P7B 1S1
Tel: 807-344-1122
Founded in: 1973
Description: A touring company.

Magnus Theatre North-West
639 McLaughlin Street
Thunder Bay, Ontario, Canada P7C 3B6
Tel: 807-623-1337; 807-623-1321
Address Inquiries to: Tibor Feheregyhazi, Artistic Director
Jonathon Shaw, Publicity Director
Founded in: 1971
Description: Magnus Theatre presents plays from the national and international repertoire during the winter months.

Toronto, Ontario

Actors Ensemble Theatre
6 Howard Street, Suite 8
Toronto, Ontario, Canada M4X 1J5
Tel: 416-922-2996
Address Inquiries to: Stephen D. Litchen, Artistic Director
M.E. Samstag, General Manager
Description: Presents works from the international repertoire.

Actor's Lab
95 Danforth Avenue
Toronto, Ontario, Canada M4K 1N2
Tel: 416-461-1644
Address Inquiries to: Richard Nieoczym, Artistic Director
Dawn Obokata, General Manager
Founded in: 1972
Description: Actor's Lab presents classical plays.

Actors' Trunk Company
152 Indian Road
Toronto, Ontario, Canada M6R 2V8
Tel: 416-532-1660
Address Inquiries to: Henry K. Martin, Artistic Director
Norbert Kondracke, General Manager
Founded in: 1975
Description: Presents plays and fables for children.

Black Theatre Canada
109 Vaughan Road, Suite 1
Toronto, Ontario, Canada M6C 2L9
Tel: 416-656-2716
Address Inquiries to: Vera Cudjoe, Artistic Director
Poe Mutuma, Business Administrator
Founded in: 1973
Description: Presents plays by black writers.

Equity Showcase Theatre
417 Queen's West, Suite 500
Toronto, Ontario, Canada
Tel: 416-364-7127, ext. 235; 416-364-5739
Address Inquiries to: Reg Higgens, Artistic Director
Debbie Westphal, Publicity Director
Description: A professional AEA showcase theatre.

Erewhon Theatre
Box 229 Station M
Toronto, Ontario, Canada M6S 4T3
Tel: 416-241-5407
Address Inquiries to: Santo Cervello, Artistic Director
Kathryn Popham, Administrator
Description: Presents plays for children year round.

Errant Productions
651 Yonge Street
Toronto, Ontario, Canada M4Y 1Z9
Tel: 416-961-7675
Address Inquiries to: Heinar Piller, Artistic Director
David Wallett, General Manager
Description: Presents modern plays.

Factory Theatre Lab
207 Adelaide Street East
Toronto, Ontario, Canada M5A 1M8
Tel: 416-864-9971
Address Inquiries to: Bob White, Director of
Programming and Play Development
Dian English, General Manager
Founded in: 1970
Description: Produces new Canadian plays.

Paul Gaulin Mime Theatre
89 Pleasant Boulevard
Toronto, Ontario, Canada M4T 1K2
Tel: 416-924-1373
Address Inquiries to: Paul Gaulin, Artistic
Director
Ron Arnold, General Manager
Founded in: 1973
Description: Tours both nationally and inter-
nationally. Their shows are for family audi-
ences.

Homemade Theatre
4 Maitland Street
Toronto, Ontario, Canada M4Y 1C5
Tel: 416-922-7129; 416-923-0898
Address Inquiries to: Ed Fisher, General
Manager
Barry Flatman, Publicity Director
Founded in: 1970
Description: Performs plays in open spaces.

The Inner Stage
9 - 11 St. Nicholas Street
Toronto, Ontario, Canada M4Y 1W5
Tel: 416-967-3548
Address Inquiries to: Elizabeth Szathmary,
Artistic Director
Marion Dahl, Administrator
Founded in: 1976
Description: A touring company that presents
works for children.

Lampoon Puppet Theatre
332 Brunswick Avenue
Toronto, Ontario, Canada M5R 2Y9
Tel: 416-967-7620
Address Inquiries to: Johan Vandergun,
Director
Founded in: 1972
Description: A touring company that presents
shows for children and families.

Le Theatre du Petit Bonheur
57 Adelaide Street Eastt
Toronto, Ontario, Canada M5C 1K6
Tel: 416-363-4977; 416-363-6401
Address Inquiries to: Claudia Lebeuf-Nasr,
Administrator
Founded in: 1967
Description: Presents plays in French.

The Mime Company Unlimited
Box 361, Station J
Toronto, Ontario, Canada M4J 4Y8
Tel: 416-461-6551
Address Inquiries to: Ron East, Artistic
Director
Larry Tayler, Administrator
Founded in: 1975
Description: Tours schools.

The NDWT Company
736 Bathurst Street
Toronto, Ontario, Canada M5S 2R4
Tel: 416-536-9255; 416-536-6663
Address Inquiries to: Richard Carson,
Business Manager
Florence George, Publicity Director
Founded in: 1975
Description: The NDWT Company presents
tours extensively, and presents a full season
during the fall and winter months.

Necessary Angel Theatre
20 Dupont Street, Unit 3
Toronto, Ontario, Canada M5R 1V2
Tel: 416-932-6119
Address Inquiries to: Richard Rose, Artistic
Director
Scott Dickson, General Manager
Founded in: 1978
Description: Presents classical theatre.

New Theatre
57 Adelaide Street, East
Toronto, Ontario, Canada M5C 1K6
Tel: 416-363-6429; 416-363-6401
Address Inquiries to: Jonathan Stanley,
Artistic Director
Michael Langford, Publicity Director
Description: Presents plays from the national
and international repertoire.

O'Keefe Centre
1 Front Street East
Toronto, Ontario, Canada M5E 1B2
Tel: 416-366-8131; 416-698-2626
Address Inquiries to: Christopher Holman,
Director of Operations
Founded in: 1960
Description: Presents plays from several coun-
tries.

Open Circle Theatre
57 Adelaide Street East
Toronto, Ontario, Canada M5C 1K6
Tel: 416-363-6443, Administrative;
416-363-6401, Box Office
Address Inquiries to: Alain Goldfarb, General
Manager
Michael Langford, Publicity Director
Founded in: 1972
Description: Plays from the national and inter-
national repertoire during the winter
months.

Phoenix Theatre
390 Dupont Street
Toronto, Ontario, Canada M5R 1V9
Tel: 416-922-7835
Address Inquiries to: Graham D. Harley,
Artistic Director
Ann Antkiw, Administrative Director
Founded in: 1974
Description: A professional theatre repertoire
is offered during the fall and winter seasons.

Royal Alexandra Theatre
260 King Street West
Toronto, Ontario, Canada M5V 1H9
Tel: 416-593-4233, Administration;
416-363-4211, Box Office
Address Inquiries to: Yale Simpson, General

Manager
Gino Empry, Publicity Director
Founded in: 1907
Description: One of the oldest touring
theatres in Canada. The Royal Alexander
present shows from Broadway and London's
West End.

Second City
110 Lombard Street
Toronto, Ontario, Canada M5C 1M3
Tel: 416-363-0461, Administrative;
416-363-1674, Box Office
Address Inquiries to: Andrew Alexander,
Producer
Sally Cochrane, General Manager
Founded in: 1973
Description: A dinner theatre which performs
in its own theatre, on radio and television,
and on tours.

Smile Theatre Company
121 Avenue Road
Toronto, Ontario, Canada M5R 2G3
Tel: 416-961-0050
Address Inquiries to: Peter J. McConnell,
Artistic Director
Brian P. Robinson, General
Manager/Publicity Director
Founded in: 1972
Description: Presents plays for senior audi-
ences.

Solar Stage Lunchtime Theatre
149 Yonge Street
Toronto, Ontario, Canada M5C 1W4
Tel: 416-368-5135
Address Inquiries to: Susan Barrable, General
Manager
Tony Hardingham, Publicity Director
Founded in: 1978
Description: Presents short plays, revues and
musicals to lunchtime audiences.

Studio Lab Theatre
235 Macdonell
Toronto, Ontario, Canada M6R 2A9
Tel: 416-531-4832
Address Inquiries to: Ernest J. Schwarz,
Artistic Director
Akiko Lamb, General Manager
Founded in: 1968
Description: A touring company that presents
plays for schools and community groups.

Tarragon Theatre
30 Bridgman Avenue
Toronto, Ontario, Canada M5R 1X3
Tel: 416-531-1827
Address Inquiries to: Mallory Gilbert, General
Manager
David McCaughna, Publicity Director
Founded in: 1971
Description: Presents Canadian translations of
foreign plays.

Teller's Cage Dinner Theatre
Commerce Court South
Wellington Street
Toronto, Ontario, Canada
Tel: 416-862-1565, Administration;
416-862-1434, Box Office

Address Inquiries to: Peter Johns, General
Manager
Founded in: 1974
Description: A professional dinner theatre.

Theatre Compact
730 Yonge Street
Toronto, Ontario, Canada M4Y 2B7
Tel: 416-922-6159
Address Inquiries to: Burton Lancaster,
Artistic Director
Gino Empry, Publicity Director
Founded in: 1975
Description: Presents works from the national
and international repertoire during the
spring and fall seasons.

Theatre Direct Canada
Box 356, Station P
Toronto, Ontario, Canada M5S 2S8
Tel: 416-537-5770; 416-537-8424
Address Inquiries to: David S. Craig, Artistic
Director
Moira J. Canes, Publicity Director
Founded in: 1976
Description: A professional touring company.

Theatre Fountainhead
47 Wembley Road
Toronto, Ontario, Canada M6C 2G1
Tel: 416-738-9300
Address Inquiries to: Jeff Henry, Artistic
Director/General Manager
Ann Wallace, Publicity Director
Founded in: 1974
Description: Presents African and Caribbean
plays, as well as Canadian black plays.

Theatre Hour Company
3 Church Street, Suite 33
Toronto, Ontario, Canada M5E 1M2
Tel: 416-366-1656
Address Inquiries to: Margaret Ann Cain,
Administrator
Sandra Fresco, Publicity Director
Founded in: 1962
Description: Canada's oldest professional
touring company. They present plays for
secondary schools and colleges.

Theatre in the Dell
300 Simcoe Street
Toronto, Ontario, Canada M5T 1T5
Tel: 416-598-4802
Address Inquiries to: William DeLaurentis,
General Manager
Hazel Forbes, Publicity Director
Founded in: 1962
Description: Presents night-club-style musi-
cals.

Theatre Passe Muraille
16 Ryerson Avenue
Toronto, Ontario, Canada M5T 2P3
Tel: 416-363-8988; 416-363-0555
Address Inquiries to: Paul Thompson, Artistic
Director
Susan Serran, General Manager
Founded in: 1971
Description: A professional theatre.

Theatre Plus
35 Front Street East
Toronto, Ontario, Canada M5E 1B3
Tel: 416-869-1255; 416-366-7723
Address Inquiries to: Helen Parr, Business
Manager
Ellen Pomer, Publicity Director
Founded in: 1973
Description: Presents plays by world-re-
nowned authors during the summer.

Tomorrow's Eve Theatre Company
c/o Prologue to the Performing Arts
252 Bloor Street West
Toronto, Ontario, Canada
Tel: 416-920-9100
Address Inquiries to: Mary Giffin,
Co-producer
Marion Gilsenan, Co-producer
Founded in: 1975
Description: Presents plays by and about wom-
en.

Toronto Arts Productions
3 Church Street
Toronto, Ontario, Canada M5E 1M2
Tel: 416-366-1656, Administration;
416-366-7723, Box Office
Address Inquiries to: Martin E. Wiener,
Administrative Director
Sandra Fresco, Publicity Director
Founded in: 1970
Description: Presents both modern and classi-
cal works.

Toronto Free Theatre
26 Berkeley Street
Toronto, Ontario, Canada M5A 2W3
Tel: 416-368-7601, Administration;
416-368-2856, Box Office
Address Inquiries to: Judith Hendry, General
Manager
Catherine Sargalis, Publicity Director
Founded in: 1972
Description: Presents plays by Canadian play-
wrights, as well as foreign works.

Toronto Truck Theatre
94 Belmont Street
Toronto, Ontario, Canada M5R 1P8
Tel: 416-922-0577; 416-922-0084
Address Inquiries to: Peter Peroff, Artistic
Director/General Manager
Don Valiere, Publicity Director
Founded in: 1971
Description: Presents comedies and mystery
plays.

Toronto Workshop Productions
12 Alexander Street
Toronto, Ontario, Canada M4Y 1B4
Tel: 416-925-0526; 416-925-8640
Address Inquiries to: John Stammers, General
Manager
Ruth Batey, Publicity Director
Founded in: 1958
Description: Presents original plays as wel as
plays from the international repertoire.

Upstairs At Old Angelo's
45 Elm Street
Toronto, Ontario, Canada

Tel: 416-597-0155
Address Inquiries to: Shirley Robertson,
Publicity Director
Description: A dinner theatre available for
rental to guest producers.

Video Cabaret
357 College Street
Toronto, Ontario, Canada
Tel: 416-960-4881
Address Inquiries to: Michael Hollingsworth,
Artistic Director
Bobbee Besold, Publicity Director
Description: A touring theatrical company.

Warrack Productions
651 Yonge Street
Toronto, Ontario, Canada M5R 2Z2
Tel: 416-964-6464, Administration
Address Inquiries to: David Warrack, Artistic
Director
Jane Holland, General Manager
Founded in: 1972
Description: Presents cabaret-style plays.

Young People's Theatre
165 Front Street East
Toronto, Ontario, Canada M5A 3Z4
Tel: 416-363-5131, Administration;
416-864-9732, Box Office
Address Inquiries to: T.B.A., Artistic Director
Elizabeth Bradley, Publicity Director
Founded in: 1966
Description: A touring company that presents
plays for schools.

West Hill, Ontario

Frog Print Theatre
449 Lawson Road
West Hill, Ontario, Canada M1C 2K2
Tel: 416-363-1938
Address Inquiries to: Nikki Tilroe, Artistic
Director
Pat Lewis, Administrator
Founded in: 1969
Description: A puppet theatre that tours
schools and holds classes that teach puppe-
try.

Willowdale, Ontario

Leah Posluns Theatre
4588 Bathurst Street
Willowdale, Ontario, Canada M2J 4E4
Tel: 416-636-2720
Address Inquiries to: Reva Tward, Artistic
Director
Andrea Bricks, Publicity Director
Founded in: 1977
Description: Presents shows to the local com-
munity.

Pepi Puppet Theatre
253 McNicoll Avenue
Willowdale, Ontario, Canada M2H 2C6
Tel: 416-497-0916
Address Inquiries to: Andrew F. Taryan,
Artistic Director
Kathy Taryan, General Manager
Founded in: 1973
Description: A touring group presenting chil-
dren's puppet shows.

Charlottetown, Prince Edward Island

Charlottetown Festival
Post Office Box 848
Charlottetown, Prince Edward Island,
Canada C1A 7L9
Tel: 902-892-2464
Address Inquiries to: Alan Lund
Ron Francis
Founded in: 1964
Member: AEA;
Description: A summer theatre specializing in musicals. Their most successful musical, *Ann of Green Gables*, is produced every year.

Ancienne-Lorette, Quebec

Theatre de la Feniere
1500 rue de la Feniere
Ancienne-Lorette, Quebec, Canada
Tel: 418-651-3218
Address Inquiries to: Georges Delisle
Raynald Belanger
Founded in: 1958
Member: Union des Artistes;
Description: Le theatre de la Feniere is a summer theatre presenting comedies and other traditional summer fare in French.

Aylmer, Quebec

Le Theatre des Lutins
C.P. 132
Aylmer, Quebec, Canada
Tel: 819-684-9598
Address Inquiries to: Gilles Provost
Monique P. Landry

Boucherville, Quebec

Theatre-Soleil
C.P. 205
Boucherville, Quebec, Canada J4B 5E6
Tel: 514-524-1332
Address Inquiries to: Micheline Pomrenski
Founded in: 1971
Member: Union des Artistes;
Description: A touring company performing in French and producing original plays.

Drummondville, Quebec

Theatre Lacannerie
Centre culturel
175 rue Ringuet
Drummondville, Quebec, Canada J2C 2P7
Tel: 819-472-6694
Founded in: 1973
Description: French-language touring theatre for children.

Hull, Quebec

Le Theatre de l'Ile
1 rue Wellington
Hull, Quebec, Canada
Tel: 819-777-9164
Address Inquiries to: Gilles Provost
Jean-Claude Pigeon
Founded in: 1976
Member: Union des Artistes;

Le Theatre des Filles du Roi
430 boul. Tache
3eme etage C.P. 2141, succ. B

Hull, Quebec, Canada J9A 1M7
Tel: 819-771-4389
Address Inquiries to: Marie Paule Vachon
Danielle Boyer-Lanthier
Founded in: 771 4389
Member: Union des Artistes;
Description: Les Filles du Roi performs for both adults and children.

Joliette, Quebec

L'Atelier de Theatre La Grosse Valise
638 Base de Roc
Joliette, Quebec, Canada J6E 5P7
Tel: 514-756-6880
Address Inquiries to: Maryse Baillargeon
Founded in: 1975
Description: A touring theatrical company.

Lennoxville, Quebec

Festival Lennoxville
Box 60
Lennoxville, Quebec, Canada J1M 1Z3
Tel: 819-563-9056; 819-363-4966
Address Inquiries to: Peter Stephens, General Manager
Jane Buss, Publicity Director
Description: Presents Canadian plays during the summer.

Longueuil, Quebec

Theatre De La Marmaille
820 rue Lasalle
Longueuil, Quebec, Canada J4K 3G5
Tel: 514-677-6220
Address Inquiries to: Monique Rioux
Jeanne LeRoux
Founded in: 1973
Member: Union des Artistes;

Montreal, Quebec

Centaur Theatre Company
453 Saint Francois-Xavier Street
Montreal, Quebec, Canada H2Y 2T1
Tel: 514-288-1229
Address Inquiries to: Ted Worth, Business Manager
Judy Cutler, Public Relations Director
Founded in: 1969
Description: Presents plays from an international repertoire.

Compagnie de Quat'Sous
100 Avenue des Pins, Est
Montreal, Quebec, Canada H2W 1N7
Tel: 514-845-7278, Administrative;
514-845-7279, Box Office
Address Inquiries to: Paul Buissonneau, Artistic Director
Lorraine Richard, General Manager/Publicity Director
Founded in: 1965
Description: Performs plays in French.

Compagnie Jean Duceppe
1400 rue Saint-Urbain
Montreal, Quebec, Canada H2X 2M5
Tel: 514-842-8194
Address Inquiries to: Lorraine Richard, General Manager/Publicity Director
Serge Turgeon, Publicity Director

Founded in: 1975
Description: Presents plays from a national and international repertoire.

Co-Operative du Grand Cirque Ordinaire
7360 St-Hubert, 3e Etage
Montreal, Quebec, Canada
Tel: 514-271-7822

La Compagnie des Deux Chaises
3823 Melrose
Montreal, Quebec, Canada H4A 2S3
Address Inquiries to: John C. Goodwin, General Manager
Founded in: 1971
Description: A touring company that performs in French.

La Rallonge
5278 rue Waverly
Montreal, Quebec, Canada H27 2X7
Tel: 514-273-3028
Address Inquiries to: Louise Saint-Pierre
Daniel Simard
Founded in: 1974
Member: Union Des Artistes;
Description: La Rallonge presents new works of authors working collectively.

La Troupe De Theatre L'Atrium
1101 Boulevard Saint Joseph Est, #4
Montreal, Quebec, Canada H2J 1L3
Address Inquiries to: Yvon LeLievre
Francois Ostiguy
Founded in: 1974
Member: Union des Artistes;
Description: Theatre L'Atrium performs in French and works with graduates of the National Theatre School.

Les Enfants du Paradis
B.P. 883, Succ. A
Montreal, Quebec, Canada H3C 2V8
Tel: 514-845-5598
Address Inquiries to: Gilles Maheu, Artistic Director
Daniele de Fontenay, Publicity Director
Founded in: 1975
Description: Focuses on non-traditional theatre.

Le Theatre de la Manufacture
3763 St-Andre
Montreal, Quebec, Canada H2C 3V6
Tel: 514-523-1603
Founded in: 1975
Member: Union des Artistes;
Description: A theatrical collective.

Saidye Bronfman Centre
5170 Cote Saint Catherine Road
Montreal, Quebec, Canada H3W 1M7
Tel: 514-739-2301
Address Inquiries to: Muriel Gold
Sheila Roth
Founded in: 1967
Member: AEA;
Description: The Saidye Bronfman is a stock theatre company producing works from the national and international dramatic repertoire.

Theatre D'Aujourd'Hui
1297 Papineau
Montreal, Quebec, Canada H2K 4H3
Tel: 514-521-4149
Address Inquiries to: Jean Claude Germain
Danyelle Morin
Founded in: 1968
Member: UDA;
Description: Theatre d'Aujourd'hui is one of
Quebec's foremost alternative theatres.

Theatre de L'Oeil
4848 Henri Julien
Montreal, Quebec, Canada H2T 2E1
Tel: 514-845-1045
Address Inquiries to: Andre Laliberte
Jeanine William
Founded in: 1973
Description: L'Oeil is a children's school tour-
ing company.

Theatre de Marjolaine
1500 rue Stanley, Suite 320
Montreal, Quebec, Canada H3A 1R3
Tel: 514-845-0917
Address Inquiries to: Louis-Georges Carrier
Daniel Gadouas
Founded in: 1960
Member: Union des Artistes;
Description: Theatre de Marjolaine produces
Canadian musicals during the summer.

Theatre Denise Pelletier
4353 St-Catherine East
Montreal, Quebec, Canada H1V 1Y2
Tel: 514-253-8974
Address Inquiries to: Gilles Pelletier
Francoise Graton
Founded in: 1964
Member: Union des Artistes;
Description: Theatre Denise Pelletier per-
forms in French from the national and inter-
national dramatic repertoire.

Theatre Des Pissenlits
C.P. 458, Station H
Montreal, Quebec, Canada H3G 2L1
Tel: 514-931-0731
Address Inquiries to: Joseph Saint Gelais
Jean-Yves Gaudreault
Founded in: 1968
Member: Union des Artistes;
Description: Theatre des Pissenlits is a
French-language children's company.

Theatre Des Prairies
1400 rue St. Urbain
Montreal, Quebec, Canada H2X 2M5
Address Inquiries to: Louise Duceppe
Member: Union des Artistes;
Description: A summer theatre, with works in
French.

Theatre du Nouveau Monde
84 Ouest rue Ste-Catherine
Montreal, Quebec, Canada H2X 1Z6
Tel: 514-932-3137
Address Inquiries to: Jean-Louis Roux
Lucien Allen
Founded in: 1952
Member: Union des Artistes;
Description: Canada's foremost French-lan-

guage regional theatre.

Theatre Du Rideau Vert
355 rue Gilford
Montreal, Quebec, Canada H2T 1M6
Tel: 514-845-0267
Address Inquiries to: Yvette Brind'Amour
Mercedes Palomino
Founded in: 1948
Member: Union des Artistes;
Description: One of Montreal's major French-
language theatre companies. The theatre
concentrates on the production of original
Canadian plays.

Theatre International de Montreal
1455 rue Peel, Suite G-20
Montreal, Quebec, Canada H3A 1T5
Tel: 514-526-0821
Address Inquiries to: Jeanine C. Beaubien
Gisele Perrault
Founded in: 1958
Member: AEA; Union des Artistes;
Description: Theatre International has per-
formed in English, French, Italian, Spanish
and German.

Theatre National de Mime du Quebec
4459 boul. St-Laurent
Montreal, Quebec, Canada H2W 1Z8
Tel: 514-521-2985
Address Inquiries to: Elie Oren
Guy Mignault
Member: Union des Artistes;
Description: A mime troupe.

Theatre Populaire du Quebec
5015 rue Boyer
Montreal, Quebec, Canada H2J 3E8
Tel: 514-849-2285
Address Inquiries to: Jean-Yves Gaudreault
Nicole Filion
Founded in: 1963
Member: Union des Artistes;

Theatre Sans Fil
2665 Rouen
Montreal, Quebec, Canada H2K 1M9
Tel: 514-522-4637
Address Inquiries to: Andre Viens
Claire Ranger
Founded in: 1971
Member: Union des Artistes;
Description: A puppet theatre company pro-
ducing English as well as French.

Voyagements
5145 Boulevard St-Laurent
Montreal, Quebec, Canada
Tel: 514-274-7985
Address Inquiries to: Michel Cote
Paul Langlois
Founded in: 1975
Member: Union des Artistes;

Youtheatre
408 Saint James Street West, Suite 10
Montreal, Quebec, Canada H2Y 1S2
Tel: 514-844-8781
Address Inquiries to: Doreen Fines
Stephen Nowell
Founded in: 1968

Member: AEA;
Description: Youtheatre presents original
plays which incorporate audience participation.

Quebec City, Quebec

Theatre de la Bordee
109 ½ St-Jean
Quebec City, Quebec, Canada
Tel: 418-529-5237
Address Inquiries to: Claude Binet
Ginnette Guay
Founded in: 1979

Theatre Du Trident
975 Place d'Youville
Quebec City, Quebec, Canada G1R 3P1
Tel: 418-692-2202
Address Inquiries to: Guillermo de Andrea
Denis Mailloux
Founded in: 1970
Member: Union des Artistes;
Description: Quebec City's major repertory
theatre.

Sherbrooke, Quebec

Theatre de l'Atelier
Parc Jaques-Cartier
Sherbrooke, Quebec, Canada J1H 5H2
Tel: 819-562-1982
Address Inquiries to: Pierre Gobeil
Michel Bernier
Founded in: 1960
Member: Union des Artistes;
Description: A touring company.

St-German, Quebec

Theatre Les Ancetres
C.P. 398
St-German, Quebec, Canada J0C 1K0
Tel: 514-677-6217
Address Inquiries to: Georges Dor
Margot Jacob
Founded in: 1976
Member: Union des Artistes;
Description: A summer theatre which features
Quebecois comedies.

Ste. Adele, Quebec

Theatre Sun Valley
C.P. 105
Ste. Adele, Quebec, Canada J0R 1L0
Address Inquiries to: Louis Lalande
Founded in: 1965
Member: Union des Artistes;

Ste-Sophie-de-Lacorne, Quebec

Le Studio Theatre Da Silva
1155 rue Morel
Ste-Sophie-de-Lacorne, Quebec, Canada
J0R 1S0
Tel: 514-436-1304
Address Inquiries to: Jean-Marie da Silva
Lise Leclerc
Founded in: 1368
Member: Union des Artistes;
Description: Le Studio Theatre Da Silva pre-
sents works from the national and interna-
tional repertoire using its own artists and

guests.

Trois-Rivieres Ouest, Quebec

Theatre des Marguerites
Avenue Jean XXIII
Trois-Rivieres Ouest, Quebec, Canada
H2V 2C3
Tel: 819-377-3223
Address Inquiries to: Georges Carrere
Phil Cossette
Founded in: 1967
Member: Union des Artistes;
Description: A summer theatre performing in French.

Victoriaville, Quebec

Theatre Parminou
C.P. 158
312 rue Olivier
Victoriaville, Quebec, Canada G6P 6S8
Tel: 819-758-0577
Address Inquiries to: Jean-Leon Rondeau
Founded in: 1974
Member: Union des Artistes;

Ville Laval, Quebec

Theatre D'Art Du Quebec
459 Place Deauville
Ville Laval, Quebec, Canada H7N 3S6
Tel: 514-387-9344
Address Inquiries to: Luiz Saraiva
Louise Bauchesi
Founded in: 1968
Description: Theatre d'Art du Quebec is a French-language company touring schools and theatres.

Theatre De Polucginellle
459 Place Deauville
Ville Laval, Quebec, Canada H7N 3S6
Tel: 514-387-9344
Address Inquiries to: Luiz Saraiva
Louise Bauchesi
Founded in: 1968
Description: Theatre de Polichinelle is a French-language company producing works for children featuring masks, mime, and puppets.

Regina, Saskatchewan

Globe School Tour Company
1850 Smith Street
Regina, Saskatchewan, Canada S4P 2N3
Tel: 306-525-9553
Address Inquiries to: Kenneth Kramer,
  Artistic Director
Founded in: 1966
Description: A theatre that performs for schools in Saskatchewan.

Globe Theatre
1850 Smith Street
Regina, Saskatchewan, Canada S4P 2N3
Tel: 306-525-9553
Address Inquiries to: Kenneth Kramer,
  Aritistic Director
  John McCullough, Publicity Director
Founded in: 1966
Description: Regina's major professional theatre, and produces a full season of plays.

The Prairie Players
3257 Retallack Street
Regina, Saskatchewan, Canada S4S 1T7
Tel: 306-586-5839; 306-586-1353
Address Inquiries to: Bruce Lawson, Artistic Director
  Pamela Lawson, General Manager
Founded in: 1977
Description: A theatre that presents plays and musicals.

Stage West
Regina Inn
Regina, Saskatchewan, Canada
Tel: 306-565-0611
Address Inquiries to: Geoffrey Saville-Read,
  Artistic Director
  Howard Pechet, Executive Producer
Founded in: 1978
Description: Stage West produces comedies.

Saskatoon, Saskatchewan

Persephone Theatre
Post Office Box 1642
Saskatoon, Saskatchewan, Canada S7K 2R8
Tel: 306-664-2110
Address Inquiries to: Eric Schneider, Artistic Director
  Dan Mooney, Technical Director
Founded in: 1974
Description: Presents plays from a national and international repertoire.

25th Street Theatre
Post Office Box 542
Saskatoon, Saskatchewan, Canada S7K 3L6
Tel: 306-664-2239; 306-343-9966
Address Inquiries to: Andy Tahn, Artistic Director
  Julianne Krause, General Manager
Founded in: 1973
Description: A theatre that produces plays based on life in Western Canada.

Whitehorse, Yukon Territory

Palace Grand Theatre
Post Office Box 4609
Whitehorse, Yukon Territory, Canada Y1A 2R8
Address Inquiries to: Jason W. Murdoch
Annual Budget: $9,000
Description: A theatre that presents a vaudeville production with dancers and singers.

17
Ticket Agencies

Only those companies engaged in the sale of admission tickets to a variety of theatre and other entertainment events are listed in this section of the *Guide*. Companies selling quantities of printed tickets and manufacturers of printed tickets are listed under "Suppliers".

As North American theatre has become more regionalized, so too has the marketing of theatre tickets expanded beyond the box office. Computerized, nationwide agents now include tickets to many theatre events along with sports, music, and other mass media entertainment events.

Users of the *Guide* will find listed in this category a variety of locations other than the box office where they may purchase theatre tickets, primarily to major theatre events. Further changes in ticket buying and selling are likely as smaller theatres lean toward computerized sales and seek outside assistance with marketing to expand their audience and simplify administrative procedures.

NEW JERSEY

Union City

Active Ticket Service
408 32nd Street
Union City, NJ 07087
Tel: 212-869-3700

Colony
Post Office Box 15
Union City, NJ 07087
Tel: 212-245-2345

Mc Bride's
3208 Bergenline Avenue
Union City, NJ 07087
Tel: 212-868-5800
Description: Theatrical ticket agency.

Mutual
4000 Bergenline Avenue
Union City, NJ 07087
Tel: 212-757-2440
Description: Theatrical ticket agency.

NEW YORK

New York

ABC Ticket Agency
255 West 43rd Street
New York, NY 10036
Tel: 212-840-2230

Ace
1560 Broadway
New York, NY 10036
Tel: 212-944-2525

Americana Theatre Service
201 West 52nd Street
New York, NY 10019
Tel: 212-581-6660

Chargit
1501 Broadway
New York, NY 10036
Tel: 212-944-9300

Downtown Theatre Center
71 Broadway
New York, NY 10006
Tel: 212-425-6410

Golden Penn
207 West 45th Street
New York, NY 10036
Tel: 212-757-2300

Group Sales Box Office
234 West 44th Street
New York, NY 212 398 8383
Tel: 800-223-7565
Description: Group Sales arranges tickets for Broadway shows for groups of twenty or more people.

Jacobs Theatre Ticket Service
1501 Broadway
New York, NY 10036
Tel: 212-947-1300

KPI
810 Seventh Avenue
New York, NY 10019
Tel: 212-397-3200

Leblang's
207 West 45th Street
New York, NY 10036
Tel: 212-757-2300

Liberty
210 West 45th Street
New York, NY 10036
Tel: 212-757-6677
Description: Theatrical ticket agency.

Mackey's
210 West 44th Street
New York, NY 10036
Tel: 212-736-6400
Description: Theatrical ticket agency.

Manhattan Theatre Ticket Service
1501 Broadway
New York, NY 10036
Tel: 212-582-3600
Description: Theatrical ticket agency.

Jack Rubin
165 West 46th Street
New York, NY 10036
Tel: 212-354-3000
Description: Theatrical ticket agency.

Supreme
301 West 46th Street
New York, NY 10036
Tel: 212-246-5454
Description: Theatrical ticket agency.

Ticketron Incorporated
1350 Avenue of Americas
New York, NY 10019
Tel: 212-977-9020
Description: Theatrical ticket agency.

Ticketworld
866 Third Avenue
New York, NY 10022
Description: Tickets to a wide variety of events, including theatre.

Times Square Theatre Centre (TKTS)
Broadway and 47th Street
New York, NY 10036
Tel: 212-354-5800
Description: Theatrical ticket agency.

18
Unions

Unions represent all types of performers and technical personnel in the performing arts, negotiating contracts and conducting a wide variety of everyday business dealings with management. The unions act as watchdogs to insure ongoing adherence to rules regarding pay, staffing levels, hours, and other details.

Aside from these functions, the unions establish and maintain professional standards for their crafts. Some require competency examinations of prospective members, while others (such as the Screen Actors Guild) require a prescribed level of professional experience for admission. Questions concerning these and other functions of the unions should be addressed to the closest local chapter.

ALABAMA

Birmingham

Birmingham Musicians' Protective Association, Local 256-733
2115 Pershing Road
Birmingham, AL 35214
Tel: 205-786-1201
Address Inquiries to: Johnny D. Jacobs, President
Robert L. (Bob) Summers, Secretary
Founded in: 1902

Montgomery

Montgomery Federatiton of Musicians
1310 Magnolia Avenue
Montgomery, AL 36106
Tel: 205-262-5154
Address Inquiries to: William R. Norwood, President
V.H. Humphries, Secretary
Founded in: 1908

Tuscaloosa

Tuscaloosa Musicians' Protective Association
53 Arcadia
Tuscaloosa, AL 35401
Tel: 205-553-0645
Address Inquiries to: Bernard Rosenbush, President
Marcia Winter, Secretary
Founded in: 1935

ALASKA

Anchorage

Anchorage Musicians' Association
1851 East 53rd
Anchorage, AK 99507
Tel: 907-344-4665
Address Inquiries to: Richard T. Schopf, President
Howard 'Bud' Quimby, Secretary
Founded in: 1939

Fairbanks

Musicians' Protective Union
Post Office Box 1128
Fairbanks, AK 99701
Tel: 907-456-3199
Address Inquiries to: Bruce Shileika, President
Harlon C. Walrath, Secretary
Founded in: 1947

Juneau

Musicians' Protective Union
534 5th Street
Juneau, AK 99801
Tel: 907-586-1367
Address Inquiries to: James R. Gregg, President
Anita Garnick Kodzoff, Secretary
Founded in: 1940

ARIZONA

Phoenix

Phoenix Federation of Musicians
1202 East Oak Street
Phoenix, AZ 85006
Tel: 602-254-8838
Address Inquiries to: Hal C. Sunday, President
Joanne Drum, Secretary
Founded in: 1912

Scottsdale

Screen Actors Guild, (SAG)
7343 Scottsdale Mall
Scottsdale, AZ 85251

ARKANSAS

Jasper

Musicians' Protective Union, Local 273
Post Office Box 321
Jasper, AR 72641
Tel: 501-442-4100
Address Inquiries to: Kenneth E. Murphy, President
Arlene Murphy, Secretary
Founded in: 1939

Little Rock

Musicians' Protective Union, Local 266
Post Office Box 6142
Little Rock, AR 72116
Tel: 501-835-0337
Address Inquiries to: C. W. Newth, President
Ben F. Thompson, Secretary
Founded in: 1903

CALIFORNIA

Aptos

Musicians' Protective Union
520 Humes Avenue
Aptos, CA 95003
Tel: 408-426-1776
Address Inquiries to: William H. Newman, President
Mrs. Frances Doherty, Secretary
Founded in: 1903

Bakersfield

Musicians' Mutual Protective Association, Local 263
5261 Stine Road, Number 182
Bakersfield, CA 93309
Tel: 805-834-1278
Address Inquiries to: Harry S. Passehl, President
Lucia K. Evans, Secretary
Founded in: 1906

Central Valley

Musicians' Protective Union, Local 113
FPost Office Box 696
Central Valley, CA 96019
Tel: 916-241-2441
Address Inquiries to: Roy J. Warmack, President
Maxine Merrifield, Secretary
Founded in: 1938

El Centro

Imperial Valley Federation of Musicians
1611 Pepper Drive
El Centro, CA 92243
Tel: 714-352-4025
Address Inquiries to: Jimmie Cannon,
President
Creon Thomas, Secretary
Founded in: 1950

Eureka

Musicians' Association
Post Office Box 3379
Eureka, CA 95501
Tel: 707-442-3375
Address Inquiries to: Sal Nygard, President
Robert H. Armstrong, Secretary
Founded in: 1903

Fresno

American Federation of Television and
Radio Artists
Post Office Box 11961
Fresno, CA 93776

Musicians' Protective Association, Local
210
1739 West Celeste
Fresno, CA 93711
Tel: 209-439-3793
Address Inquiries to: Ralph Manfredo,
President
Mrs. Margaret Bettencourt, Secretary
Founded in: 1902

Hollywood

American Federation of Television and
Radio Artists, (AFTRA)
1717 North Highland Avenue
Hollywood, CA 90028

Musicians' Union, Local 47
817 North Vine Street
Hollywood, CA 90038
Tel: 213-462-2161
Address Inquiries to: Max Herman, President
Marl Young, Secretary
Founded in: 1897

Screen Actors Guild (SAG)
7750 Sunset Boulevard
Hollywood, CA 90045
Tel: 213-876-3030
Address Inquiries to: Ken Orsatti, National
Executive Secretary
Ed Asner, President
Founded in: 1933
Member: AFL/CIO; AAA;
Annual Budget: $7,500,000
Description: Screen Actors Guild (SAG)
represents and has jurisdiction over all per-
formers (including dancers) in the film
medium.

Long Beach

Musicians' Association
5215 Arbor Road
Long Beach, CA 90808
Tel: 213-421-4747
Address Inquiries to: John Hollenbeck,

President
Therise R. Wilkinson
Founded in: 1914

Los Angeles

Actors' Equity Association (AEA)
6430 Sunset Boulevard
Los Angeles, CA 90028
Tel: 213-HO2-2334
Address Inquiries to: Edward Western,
Assistant Executive Secretary

American Guild of Variety Artists, (AGVA)
6430 Sunset Boulevard
Los Angeles, CA 98028
Description: See New York AGVA description.

Screen Actors Guild, (SAG)
7750 Sunset Boulevard
Los Angeles, CA 90046

Screen Extras Guild, (SEG)
3629 Cahuenga Boulevard, West
Los Angeles, CA 90068

Marysville

Marysville Musicians' Association, Local
158
Post Office Box 1552
Marysville, CA 95901
Tel: 916-743-9760
Address Inquiries to: William S. Honsinger,
President
Stephen A. Balough, Secretary
Founded in: 1909

Merced

Musicians' Protective Union
1660 Merced Avenue
Merced, CA 95340
Tel: 209-722-9371
Address Inquiries to: Verner H. Taylor,
President
William M. Wivell, Secretary
Founded in: 1920

Modesto

Musicians' Association
1613 Silver Court
Modesto, CA 95351
Tel: 209-522-8015
Address Inquiries to: Mr. Lynn Russell,
President
Mrs. Blanche A. Matthews, Secretary
Founded in: 1913

Monterey

Musicians' Association of Monterey
Country
591 Lighthouse Avenue
Monterey, CA 93940
Tel: 408-375-6166
Address Inquiries to: Millard M. Hawkins,
Presidentt
Founded in: 1925

Napa

Musicians' Protective Union
3545 Oxford Street
Napa, CA 94558
Tel: 707-226-7736
Address Inquiries to: Donald Meehan,
President
Elmer A. Bradley, Secretary
Founded in: 1925

Paradise

Musicians' Protective Union
260 Tranquil Drive
Paradise, CA 95969
Tel: 916-872-0978
Address Inquiries to: Vergie Beatty, President
AL Biegler, Secretary
Founded in: 1912

Pinole

Musicians' Protective Union
2854 Jordan Way
Pinole, CA 94564
Tel: 415-758-2336
Address Inquiries to: As Del Simone,
President
Joe Pallotta, Jr., Secretary
Founded in: 1907

Redlands

Orange Belt Musicians' Association, Local
167
405 Palm Avenue
Redlands, CA 92373
Tel: 714-824-1450
Address Inquiries to: Charles De Mirjyn,
President
James Macintosh, Secretary
Founded in: 1913

Sacramento

American Federation of Television and
Radio Artists, (AFTRA)
8590 Erinbrook Way
Sacramento, CA 95826

Musicians' Protective Union, Local 12
2623 ½ J Street
Sacremento, CA 95816
Tel: 916-444-6660
Address Inquiries to: Thomas P. Kenny,
President
Frank Giordano, Secretary
Founded in: 1896

San Diego

American Federation of Television and
Radio Artists,(AFTRA)
3045 Rosecrans Street #206
San Diego, CA 92110

Musicians' Association of San Diego
County
1717 Morena Blvd
San Diego, CA 92110
Tel: 714-276-4324
Address Inquiries to: John Adamo, President
C. Patric Oakley, Secretary

Founded in: 1903

Screen Actors Guild, (SAG)
3045 Rosecrans Boulevard
San Diego, CA 92110

San Francisco

Actors' Equity Association (AEA)
465 California Street, Suite 210
San Francisco, CA 94104
Tel: 415-781-8660
Address Inquiries to: Jay Moran

Musicians' Union, Local 6
230 Jones Street
San Francisco, CA 94102
Tel: 415-775-8118
Address Inquiries to: J.J. Spain, President
Don Menary, Secretary
Founded in: 1897

Screen Actors Guild, (SAG)
100 Bush Street, 26th Floor
San Francisco, CA 94104

San Fransisco

American Federation of Television and
Radio Artists, (AFTRA)
100 Bush Street
San Fransisco, CA 94104

Screen Extras Guild, (SEG)
100 Bush Street
San Fransisco, CA 94106

San Leandro

Musicians' Protective Union
1303 Breckenridge Avenue
San Leandro, CA 94579
Tel: 415-483-5470
Address Inquiries to: Tony Cervone,
President
Irene Acosta, Secretary
Founded in: 1909

Santa Ana

Musicians' Association, Local 7
2050 South Main Street
Santa Ana, CA 92707
Tel: 714-546-8166
Address Inquiries to: B. Douglas Sawtelle,
President
Robert W. Stava
Founded in: 1923

Santa Barbara

Musicians' Mutual Protective Association
2904 ½ De La Vina Street
Santa Barbara, CA 93105
Tel: 805-687-3519
Address Inquiries to: Harry Chanson,
President
Earl Smith, Secretary
Founded in: 1906

Santa Maria

Musicians' Protective Union
660 Majestic Drive
Santa Maria, CA 93454
Tel: 805-937-2333
Address Inquiries to: Joseph Bardelli,

President
Joseph Bardelli, Act. Secretary
Founded in: 1936

Santa Rosa

Musicians' Mutual Protective Associatiton
1140 Spencer Street
Santa Rosa, CA 95404
Tel: 707-545-1434
Address Inquiries to: Robert Norman,Jr,
President
Nick Bardes, Secretary
Founded in: 1903

Saratoga

San Jose Federation of Musicians, Local
153
14584 Westcott Drive
Saratoga, CA 95070
Tel: 408-867-0456
Address Inquiries to: Orrin Blattner,
President
Don Hoque, Secretary
Founded in: 1901

Stockton

Stockton Musicians' Association, Local
1902
2626 North California Street
Stockton, CA 95204
Tel: 209-464-4016
Address Inquiries to: James Urbani, President
Buddy L. Walter, Secretary
Founded in: 1902

Vallejo

Musicians' Protective Union
2761 Webb Street
Vallejo, CA 94590
Tel: 707-642-5834
Address Inquiries to: Alton G. Robinson,
President
Wilfred Yeaman, Secretary
Founded in: 1907

Ventura

Musicians' Mutual Protective Association
857 Main Street
Ventura, CA 93001
Tel: 805-643-9953
Address Inquiries to: Darrell E. Larson,
President
James C. Hallowell, Secretary
Founded in: 1938

COLORADO

Boulder

University Musicians' Association, Local
275
4654 Harwick
Boulder, CO 80301
Tel: 303-530-1912
Address Inquiries to: Stephen C. Christopher,
President
William K. Matthiesen, Secretary
Founded in: 1947

Colorado Springs

Pike's Peak Musicians' Association, Local
154
1210 North Tejon Street
Colorado Springs, CO 80903
Tel: 303-632-5033
Address Inquiries to: Allen E. Uhles,
President
Charles Gilbert, Secretary
Founded in: 1901

Denver

American Federation of Television and
Radio Artists, (AFTRA)
6825 East Tennessee
Denver, CO 80222

Denver Musicians' Association, Local
20-623
1535 Logan Street
Denver, CO 80203
Tel: 303-861-1112
Address Inquiries to: Tasso Harris, President
James Griggsmiller, Secretary
Founded in: 1897

Screen Actors Guild, (SAG)
6825 East Tennessee Avenue, Suite 639
Denver, CO 80224

Grand Junction

Musicians' Protective Union, Local 164
3162 East Half Road
Grand Junction, CO 81501
Tel: 303-434-6565
Address Inquiries to: Clyde Jorgensen,
President
Roy Weaver, Secretary
Founded in: 1901

Leadville

Musicians' Protective Association, Local 28
425 Elm Street
Leadville, CO 80461
Tel: 303-486-0252
Address Inquiries to: Joe Jakopic, President
Leonard J. Fuchtman, Secretary
Founded in: 1897

Pueblo

Pueblo Musicians' Association, Local 69
Post Office Box 452
Pueblo, CO 81002
Tel: 303-544-4725
Address Inquiries to: Charles Quaranta,
President
Constance M. Bregar, Secretary
Founded in: 1897

CONNECTICUT

Bridgeport

Musicians' Union, Bridgeport Musicians
Association, Local 63-549
448 Willow Street
Bridgeport, CT 06610
Tel: 203-333-2017; 203-334-8972
Address Inquiries to: Raymond M. Svetz,

President and Secretary
Founded in: 1897

Bristol

Musicians' Protective Association
105 Vance Drive
Bristol, CT 06010
Tel: 203-582-5245
Address Inquiries to: Hugo A. Grignoli,
    President
    Walter Osenkowski, Secretary
Founded in: 1908

Danbury

Danbury Musicians' Association, Local 87
8 Grandview Drive
Danbury, CT 06810
Tel: 203-743-9713
Address Inquiries to: Kenneth M. Lee,
    President
    Evelyn Dewan, Secretary
Founded in: 1899

Hamden

New Haven Federation of Musicians, Local
    234-486
26 Glebrook Avenue
Hamden, CT 06514
Tel: 203-387-4765
Address Inquiries to: John F. Beesmer,
    President
    R. George D'Alessio, Secretary
Founded in: 1902

Meriden

Meriden Federation of Musicians, Local 55
30 Briarwood Drive
Meriden, CT 06450
Tel: 203-238-0321
Address Inquiries to: Nicholas Azzolina,
    President
    Robert E. Erdos, Secretary
Founded in: 1900

Middletown

Middletown Musicians' Protective
    Association
Post Office Box 955
Middletown, CT 06457
Tel: 203-347-7805
Address Inquiries to: Michael D. Moroni,
    President
    Clifford E. Hamlin, Secretary
Founded in: 1908

Mystic

Musicians' Protective Association
Post Office Box 1
Mystic, CT 06355
Tel: 203-536-7362
Address Inquiries to: Francis R. Fain,
    President
    Edward Brennan, Secretary
Founded in: 1903

New Britain

New Britain Musicians' Association
20 Carroll Street
New Britain, CT 06053
Tel: 203-229-4037
Address Inquiries to: Joseph DeFazio,
    President
Founded in: 1907

Norwalk

Norwalk Musicians' Association, Local 52
70 Bouton Street
Norwalk, CT 06854
Tel: 203-866-9368
Address Inquiries to: Anthony Santella,
    President
    Mrs. Marie A. Bossert, Secretary
Founded in: 1898

Stamford

American Federation of Television and
    Radio Artists, (AFTRA)
117 Prospect Street
Stamford, CT 06901

Torrington

Torrington Musicians' Association
88 County Road
Torrington, CT 06790
Tel: 203-482-4097
Address Inquiries to: Leo R. Liddle, President
    Joseph Languell, Secretary
Founded in: 1909

Waterbury

Musicians' Association of Waterbury,
    Local 186
442 Farmington Avenue
Waterbury, CT 06710
Tel: 203-753-1354
Address Inquiries to: James F. Saginario,
    President
    Robert Mobilio, Secretary
Founded in: 1902

West Redding

Stamford Musicians' Association
140 Picketts Ridge Road
West Redding, CT 06896
Tel: 203-325-1651
Address Inquiries to: E. Richard Zaffino,
    President
    Anthony J. Matteis, Secretary
Founded in: 1912

DELAWARE

Claymont

Delaware Musical Society
2704 Society Drive
Claymont, DE 19703
Tel: 302-798-6060
Address Inquiries to: Manny Klein, President
    Helen T. Rairgh, Secretary
Founded in: 1907

DISTRICT OF COLUMBIA

Washington

American Federation of Television and
Radio Artists, (AFTRA)
Chevy Chase Center Building, 2nd Floor
Washington, DC 20015

District of Columbia Federation of
Musicians, Local 161-710
5020 Wisconsin Avenue, North West
Washington, DC 20016
Tel: 202-244-8833
Address Inquiries to: Sam Kaufman, President
    Robert D'Arcy, Secretary
Founded in: 1901

FLORIDA

Coral Gables

Screen Actors Guild, (SAG)
3226 Ponce de Leon Boulevard
Coral Gables, FL 33134

Daytona Beach

Daytona Beach Federation of Musicians
115 Seabreeze Boulevard
Daytona Beach, FL 32018
Tel: 904-252-6333
Address Inquiries to: Joe Pace, President
William Benton, Secretary
Founded in: 1938

Jacksonville

Musicians' Association of Jacksonville
2030 Schumacher Avenue
Jacksonville, FL 32207
Tel: 904-398-9735
Address Inquiries to: John Arnold, President
J.P. Pitts, Secretary
Founded in: 1907

Key West

Key West Federation of Musicians, Local
    202
1508 19th Street
Key West, FL 33040
Tel: 305-296-2276
Address Inquiries to: Orlando Caraballo,
    President
    Jim Vagnini, Secretary
Founded in: 1940

Miami

American Federation of Television and
    Radio Artists, (AFTRA)
6660 Biscayne Boulevard
Miami, FL 33138

Miami Federation of Musicians
1779 Northwest 28th Street
Miami, FL 33142
Tel: 305-633-3235
Address Inquiries to: Frank Casiola, President
    Porter Thomas, Secretary
Founded in: 1913

Pensacola

Pensacola Federation of Musicians
4976 Prieto Drive
Pensacola, FL 32507
Tel: 904-456-1643
Address Inquiries to: Frank S. Horne,
    President
    Ron Craig, Secretary
Founded in: 1947

South St. Petersburg

Greater St. Petersburg Musician's
    Association
911 Third Street
South St. Petersburg, FL 33733
Tel: 813-894-5059
Address Inquiries to: Robert E. Burklew,
    President
    Dick Crockett, Secretary
Founded in: 1922

GEORGIA

Atlanta

American Federation of Television and
Radio Artists, (AFTRA)
3252 Peachtree Road, NW
Atlanta, GA 30305

Federation of Musicians, Local 148-462
110 Laurel Forest Circle, North East
Atlanta, GA 30342
Tel: 404-237-1204
Address Inquiries to: Karl A. Bevins,
    President
    James A. Taylor, Secretary
Founded in: 1901

Screen Actors Guild, (SAG)
3252 Peachtree Road,NW, Number 205
Atlanta, GA 30305

Columbus

Columbus Musicians' Protective
    Association
6232 Lyndridge Avenue
Columbus, GA 31904
Tel: 404-323-0515
Address Inquiries to: Robert C. Money,
    President
    Lewis B. Carver, Secretary
Founded in: 1937

Warner Robins

Macon Federation of Musicians
204 Sunnydale
Warner Robins, GA 31093
Tel: 912-923-3242
Address Inquiries to: Roger Dennison,
    President
    Charles E. Steeley Jr., Secretary
Founded in: 1969

Westwood Heights, Rincon

Savannah Federation of Musicians
258 A Mulberry Way
Westwood Heights, Rincon, GA 31326
Tel: 912-826-5905

Address Inquiries to: Russell Sena, President
Henry B. Hill, Secretary
Founded in: 1937

HAWAII

Honolulu

American Federation of Television and
Radio Artists,(AFTRA)
547 Halekauwila Street
Honolulu, HI 96813

Screen Extras Guild, (SEG)
1127 Eleventh Avenue
Honolulu, HI 96826

IDAHO

Caldwell

Musicians' Protective Union
706 East Linden
Caldwell, ID 83605
Tel: 208-459-7503
Address Inquiries to: Loris W. Stewart,
    President
    Carolyn Patterson, Secretary
Founded in: 1935

Hayden Lake

Musicians' Protective Union, Local 225
2038 Avon
Hayden Lake, ID 83835
Tel: 208-773-7971
Address Inquiries to: Richard B. Kuck,
    President
    Jon H. Harwood, Secretary
Founded in: 1946

Pocatello

Musicians' Protective Association
1108 Cherry Lane
Pocatello, ID 83001
Tel: 208-233-3483
Address Inquiries to: Eddie Ashcraft,
    President
    John Miller, Secretary
Founded in: 1903

Saint Anthony

Musicians' Protective Union
Route 2
Saint Anthony, ID 83445
Tel: 208-624-7073
Address Inquiries to: Ross E. Dunn, President
    Garr Gibson, Secretary
Founded in: 1935

Spalding

Musicians' Protective Union
Post Office Box 85
Spalding, ID 83551
Tel: 208-843-2486
Address Inquiries to: James W. Albright,
    President
    Mrs. Bonnie Albright, Secretary
Founded in: 1950

Twin Falls

Sun Valley Musicians' Association
302 Elm Street
Twin Falls, ID 83301
Tel: 208-726-9681
Address Inquiries to: Reed Coulam, President
    Joe Maccarillo Jr., Secretary
Founded in: 1948

ILLINOIS

Alton

Musicians' Protective Association
1905 Washington Avenue
Alton, IL 62002
Tel: 618-466-7385
Address Inquiries to: Henry Lenhardt,
    President
    Phillip H. Youngberg, Secretary
Founded in: 1903

Aurora

Musicians' Protective Union, Local 181
821 Talma Street
Aurora, IL 60505
Tel: 312-851-1386; 312-897-6894
Address Inquiries to: Ralph B. Hesselbaum,
    President
    Richard Bates Sr., Secretary
Founded in: 1902

Belleville

Belleville Musical Union, Local 19
325 North 45th Street
Belleville, IL 62223
Tel: 618-234-2578
Address Inquiries to: Donald L. James,
    President
    Elmer R. Humphries, Secretary
Founded in: 1897

Bloomington

Federation of Musicians, Local 102
508 North East Street
Bloomington, IL 61701
Tel: 309-828-6814
Address Inquiries to: W. J. Donovan,
    President
    Hazel J. Cambron, Secretary
Founded in: 1899

Boise

Musicians' Protective Association
7676 Carriage Lane
Boise, IL 83704
Tel: 208-375-8008
Address Inquiries to: Russell Mamerow,
    President
    James C. Johnson, Secretary
Founded in: 1910

Boubonnais

Kankakee Musicians' Association
740 Armour Road
Boubonnais, IL 60914
Tel: 815-932-6662
Address Inquiries to: Mel Blanchette,

President
Mrs. Josephine Leone, Secretary
Founded in: 1903

Carterville

Herrin Federation of Musicians
390 Mulberry
Carterville, IL 62918
Tel: 618-985-4704
Address Inquiries to: Robert Ledbetter,
President
Bruce Groll, Secretary
Founded in: 1903

Champaign

Champaign Federation of Musicians, Local
196
804 West Vine Street
Champaign, IL 61820
Tel: 217-356-4151
Address Inquiries to: Marion Gulick,
President
Paul E. Karlstrom, Secretary
Founded in: 1902

Chicago

Actors' Equity Association (AEA)
360 North Michigan Avenue
Chicago, IL 60601
Tel: 312-641-0393

American Federation of Television and
Radio Artists, (AFTRA)
307 North Michigan Avenue
Chicago, IL 60601

Chicago Federation of Musicians, Local 10
175 West Washington Street
Chicago, IL 60602
Tel: 312-782-0063
Address Inquiries to: Nicholas G. Bliss,
President
Emil Posada, Secretary
Founded in: 1901

Screen Actors Guild, (SAG)
307 North Michigan Avenue
Chicago, IL 60601

Collinsville

Musicians' Protective Union
414 Ridgemont
Collinsville, IL 63234
Tel: 618-344-3197
Address Inquiries to: Robert W. Sale,
President
Tom Hopper, Secretary
Founded in: 1909

Danville

Musicians' Association, Local 90
301 East 14th Street
Danville, IL 61832
Tel: 217-446-7515
Address Inquiries to: Herbert Johnson,
President
Carolyn Tooker, Secretary
Founded in: 1899

DeKalb

Musicians' Protective Association
246 Miller Avenue
DeKalb, IL 60115
Tel: 815-758-3952
Address Inquiries to: Dee Palmer, President
Edwin W. Harding, Secretary
Founded in: 1911

Dixon

Dixon Musicians' Union
503 South Dixon Avenue
Dixon, IL 61021
Tel: 815-284-3057
Address Inquiries to: Robert J.
McConnaughay, President
Richard Snyder, Secretary
Founded in: 1919

East Peoria

American Federation of Television and
Radio Artists, (AFTRA)
2907 Springfield Boulevard
East Peoria, IL 61614

Effingham

Musicians' Protective Union, Local 224
Post Office Box 94
Effingham, IL 62401
Tel: 217-837-2077
Address Inquiries to: Chuck White, President
Gene Trimble, Secretary
Founded in: 1902

Elgin

Musicians' Union, Local 48
169 East Chicago Street
Elgin, IL 60120
Tel: 312-742-3757
Address Inquiries to: Charles O. Brinckley,
President
Mrs. Lucille (Lucy) Kerber, Secretary
Founded in: 1901

Freeport

Freeport Musical Association
605 East Jefferson Street
Freeport, IL 61032
Tel: 815-233-1040
Address Inquiries to: W. 'Curly' Robbins,
President
Richard Moore, Secretary
Founded in: 1903

Galesburg

Musicians' Protective Union, Local 178
702 North Henderson Street
Galesburg, IL 61401
Tel: 309-342-3007
Address Inquiries to: Gene Fanning,
President
Dick Higbee, Secretary
Founded in: 1902

Gillespie

Tri-County Musicians' Union, Local 88
Post Office Box 85
Gillespie, IL 62033
Tel: 217-835-4539
Address Inquiries to: Richard Sies, President
Ferdinand Girardi, Secretary
Founded in: 1899

Hillsboro

Musicians' Protective Union
1439 Vandalia Road
Hillsboro, IL 62049
Tel: 217-532-3862
Address Inquiries to: Hermon Guile,
President
Founded in: 1909

Jacksonville

Musicians' Protective Union, Local 128
1421 South West Street
Jacksonville, IL 62650
Tel: 217-245-9723
Address Inquiries to: Larry Brennan,
President
Earl Rabjohns, Secretary
Founded in: 1900

Joliet

Joliet Federation of Musicians, Local 37
265 North Ottawa Street
Joliet, IL 60431
Tel: 815-723-1645
Address Inquiries to: Dominick Paone,
President
Roy Carloss, Secretary
Founded in: 1897

Kewanee

Musicians' Protective Association, Local
100
281 Rockwell Street
Kewanee, IL 61443
Tel: 309-853-8668
Address Inquiries to: Dennis Kubiak,
President
Julian Heene, Secretary
Founded in: 1899

LaSalle

Musicians' Protective Union
956 Eighth Street
LaSalle, IL 61301
Tel: 815-CAp-tol 3 4793
Address Inquiries to: Ralph F. Schmoeger,
President
Joseph M. DeZutti, Secretary
Founded in: 1903

Lincoln

Musicians' Protective Union, Local 268
1802 Pekin Street
Lincoln, IL 62656
Tel: 217-732-9482
Address Inquiries to: Dan Hardin, President
Don W. Smith, Secretary
Founded in: 1903

Macon

Decatur Association of Musicians, Local 89
342 West Eckhardt
Macon, IL 62544
Tel: 217-877-8158
Address Inquiries to: Hallie Bafford, President
  Stan Kupish, Secretary
Founded in: 1899

Metropolis

Paducah Federation of Musicians, Local 200
Route 3, Post Office Box 28
Metropolis, IL 62960
Tel: 618-524-3516
Address Inquiries to: Gary D. Moore, President
  James E. Windsor, Secretary
Founded in: 1932

Morris

Musicians' Protective Union
511 West Jefferson Street
Morris, IL 60450
Tel: 815-942-3566
Address Inquiries to: Robert Peterson, President
  Gerald R. Belt, Secretary
Founded in: 1903

Mount Vernon

Musicians' Protective Association
719 South 15th Street
Mount Vernon, IL 62864
Tel: 618-242-7613
Address Inquiries to: Rolland Mays, President
  Wilma Chambers, Secretary
Founded in: 1937

Pekin

Musicians' Protective Union
803 North 14th
Pekin, IL 61554
Tel: 309-347-2350
Address Inquiries to: Lyle Hauser, President
  Kim L. Streenz, Secretary
Founded in: 1908

Peoria Heights

Peoria Federation of Musicians, Local 26
5215 Glen Elm Drive
Peoria Heights, IL 61614
Tel: 309-682-7517
Address Inquiries to: Svata Ciza, President
  Walter B. Coughlin, Secretary
Founded in: 1896

Princeton

Musicians' Protective Union
Rural Route Number 1
Princeton, IL 61356
Tel: 309-895-2544
Address Inquiries to: Glenn C. Russell, President
  Marvin Stone, Secretary
Founded in: 1918

Quincy

Musicians' Protective Union, Local 265
1 Sherwood Drive
Quincy, IL 62301
Tel: 217-222-0941
Address Inquiries to: James Delabar, President
  Carl Landrum, Secretary
Founded in: 1903

Rock Falls

Musicians' Protective Union
1904 1st Avenue, Apartment 5
Rock Falls, IL 61071
Tel: 815-625-3623
Address Inquiries to: Philip Stein, President
  Lorrie Lee, Secretary
Founded in: 1903

Rockford

Musical Union, Local 240
119 North Church Street
Rockford, IL 61101
Tel: 815-965-2132
Address Inquiries to: Vincent F. LaLoggia, President
  Morry Hill, Secretary
Founded in: 1902

Rushville

Musicians' Protective Union
214 North Congress Street
Rushville, IL 62681
Tel: 217-322-6428
Address Inquiries to: Robert L. Boyd, President
  William D. DeJong, Secretary
Founded in: 1937

Springfield

Springfield Musicians' Association, Local 19-675
37 North Koke Mill Lane
Springfield, IL 62707
Tel: 217-546-6260
Address Inquiries to: Howard E. Wikoff, President
  Horace Sweet, Secretary
Founded in: 1897

St. David

Fulton County Musicians' Protective Union
Post Office Box 374
St. David, IL 61563
Tel: 309-688-2468
Address Inquiries to: Greg D. Sims, President
  C. Bruce Donaldson, Secretary
Founded in: 1903

Streator

Musicians' Protective Union, Local 131
227 La Salle Street
Streator, IL 61364
Tel: 815-672-7431
Address Inquiries to: George Nichols, President
  Robert Yedinak, Secretary
Founded in: 1901

Trenton

Musicians' Protective Union, Local 175
422 North Olive Street
Trenton, IL 62293
Tel: 618-224-9460
Address Inquiries to: Wilson Dorries, President
  Darlene Frank, Secretary
Founded in: 1902

Virden

Musicians' Protective Union
238 Olive Street
Virden, IL 62690
Tel: 217-965-4113
Address Inquiries to: William F. Keirs, President
  W. W. Manning, Secretary
Founded in: 1966

Waukegan

Waukegan Federation of Musicians
2500 North Walnut
Waukegan, IL 60087
Tel: 312-662-4738
Address Inquiries to: Leonard Yotko, President
  Jack Maynard, Secretary
Founded in: 1903

Wood River

Musicians' Protective Union, Local 98
437 North 6th Street
Wood River, IL 62095
Tel: 618-254-1488
Address Inquiries to: Ervin Mouish, President
  Robert Wehling, Secretary
Founded in: 1899

INDIANA

Anderson

Musicians' Protective Association, Local 32
2420 Lafayette Street
Anderson, IN 46012
Tel: 317-642-3993
Address Inquiries to: James C. Clark, President
  Chet Carter, Secretary
Founded in: 1896

Decatur

Musicians' Protective Union
Rural Route 5
Decatur, IN 46733
Tel: 219-724-7670
Address Inquiries to: Vernon Hebble, President
  Robert J. Rice, Secretary
Founded in: 1912

Elkhart

Elkhart Musicians' Association, Local 192
320 West Dinehart
Elkhart, IN 46514
Tel: 219-522-5453
Founded in: 1903

Evansville

Musicians' Association, Local 35
2733 Lake Drive
Evansville, IN 47711
Tel: 812-476-4754
Address Inquiries to: David Holzman,
    President
    Rudy Hillenbrand, Secretary
Founded in: 1896

Fort Wayne

Musicians' Protecive Association, Local 58
4022 West State Street
Fort Wayne, IN 46898
Tel: 219-483-7778
Address Inquiries to: Louis Pooler, President
Harold Stout, Secretary
Founded in: 1897

Frankfort

Musicians' Protective Union
Rural Route Number 15
Frankfort, IN 46041
Tel: 317-654-8209
Address Inquiries to: Ray E. Nease, President
    Charles V. Benge
Founded in: 1933

Hammond

Musicians' Guild, Local 203
7414 Indianapolis Blvd.
Hammond, IN 46324
Tel: 219-845-0666
Address Inquiries to: George R. Adams,
    President
    Red Arbuckle, Secretary
Founded in: 1902

Indianapolis

American Federation of Television and
    Radio Artists, (AFTRA)
606 Board of Training Building
Indianapolis, IN 46204

Indianapolis Musicians' Association, Local
3
325 North Delaware Street
Indianapolis, IN 46204
Tel: 317-636-3595
Address Inquiries to: Thomas C. Berry,
    President
    Hal Bailey, Secretary
Founded in: 1897

Kokomo

Kokomo Federation of Musicians, Local
141
3813 Candy Lane
Kokomo, IN 46901
Tel: 317-453-3261
Address Inquiries to: James L. Porter,
    President
    Henry Tilley, Jr., Secretary
Founded in: 1901

Lafayette

Lafayette Federation of Musicians, Local
162
24 Prairie Court
Lafayette, IN 47904
Tel: 317-447-2051
Address Inquiries to: James D. Rardon,
    President
    Mr. Ardith Huff, Secretary
Founded in: 1901

La Porte

La Porte Federations of Musicians
1103 Weller Avenue
La Porte, IN 46350
Tel: 219-324-0332
Address Inquiries to: John Diedrich, President
    Altus Salzwedel, Secretary
Founded in: 1905

Logansport

Musicians' Protective Association, Local 53
101 East Clay Street
Logansport, IN 46947
Tel: 219-753-8416
Address Inquiries to: Robert J. Parente,
    President
    Stewart Gordon, Secretary
Founded in: 1938

Marion

Musicians' Protective Association, Local 45
323 South Adams Street
Marion, IN 46952
Tel: 317-664-0400
Address Inquiries to: Russell L. Fenton,
    President
    Calvin Snapp, Secretary
Founded in: 1897

Michigan City

Michigan City Federation of Musicians
811 Greenwood Avenue
Michigan City, IN 46360
Tel: 219-874-5394
Address Inquiries to: George Ludtke,
    President
    Richard L. Anderson, Secretary
Founded in: 1916

Muncie

Musicians' Protective Union, Local 245
Route 4, Post Office Box 2
Muncie, IN 47302
Tel: 317-282-2134
Address Inquiries to: Roland Eastman,
    President
    Don Tuttle, Secretary
Founded in: 1902

South Bend

American Federation of Television and
    Radio Artists, (AFTRA)
1220 Victory Avenue
South Bend, IN 46615

Musicians' Protective Union
120 West LaSalle Avenue
South Bend, IN 46601

Tel: 219-233-8111
Address Inquiries to: Eddie Jarrett, President
Craig Heitger, Secretary
Founded in: 1903

Terre Haute

Terre Haute Federation of Musicians,
    Local 25
1337 Drieser Square
Terre Haute, IN 47807
Tel: 812-234-6750
Address Inquiries to: Virgil E. Dean,
    President
    Charles L. Seward, Secretary
Founded in: 1897

IOWA

Boone

Musicians' Protective Union
1817 West Third Street
Boone, IA 50036
Tel: 515-432-4092
Address Inquiries to: Leonard Sternquist,
    President
    Herbert Forbell, Secretary
Founded in: 1911

Burlington

Musicians' Protective Union
1106 South 12th
Burlington, IA 52601
Tel: 319-754-4705
Address Inquiries to: Richard Poindexter,
    President
    George D. Briggs, Secretary
Founded in: 1913

Cedar Falls

Waterloo Federation of Musicians
2903 Alameda
Cedar Falls, IA 50613
Tel: 319-266-1521
Address Inquiries to: David Kennedy,
    President
    Jack Dunlevy, Secretary
Founded in: 1903

Cedar Rapids

Musicians' Protective Union, Local 137
718 4th Street, North West
Cedar Rapids, IA 52405
Tel: 319-362-7902
Address Inquiries to: Vern Josifek, President
Miles Adams, Secretary
Founded in: 1901

Clinton

Clinton Musicians' Protective Association,
    Local 79
910 Fifth Avenue, South
Clinton, IA 52732
Tel: 319-242-6257
Address Inquiries to: Thorvald Morsing,
    President
    Warren Wiggins, Secretary
Founded in: 1900

Davenport

Tri-City Musical Society, Local 67
422 East 14th Street
Davenport, IA 52803
Tel: 319-322-7088
Address Inquiries to: Peter H. Schumaker,
    President
    Vincent A. Petersen, Secretary
Founded in: 1897

Des Moines

Musicians' Association, Local 75
640 19th Street
Des Moines, IA 50314
Tel: 515-244-2058
Address Inquiries to: Francis M. Hrubetz,
    President
    Ms. Jo Lene Millang, Secretary
Founded in: 1898

Dubuque

Dubuque Musicians' Association
1030 Boyer
Dubuque, IA 52001
Tel: 319-588-3240
Address Inquiries to: Paul E. Hemmer,
    President
    Roger Svoboda, Secretary
Founded in: 1903

Fort Dodge

Fort Dodge Musicians' Association
1108 North 19th Street
Fort Dodge, IA 50501
Tel: 515-576-3452
Address Inquiries to: Arch Thorson,
    President
    Russell Thorson, Secretary
Founded in: 1908

Hampton

Musicians' Protective Union, Local 230
9 Seventh Avenue, North West
Hampton, IA 50441
Tel: 915-357-4421
Address Inquiries to: Mike Smith, President
G. F. Barney Reynolds, Secretary
Founded in: 1908

Iowa City

Musicians' Protective Union
2116 Friendship Street
Iowa City, IA 52240
Tel: 319-337-4677
Address Inquiries to: Steve Held, President
Julia Munson, Secretary
Founded in: 1937

Marshalltown

Marshalltown Federation of Musicians,
    Local 176
139 Debra Estates
Marshalltown, IA 50158
Tel: 515-753-7650
Address Inquiries to: Frank Brees, President
Leonard Rasmussen, Secretary
Founded in: 1902

Muscatine

Musicians' Protective Union
2318 Houser Street
Muscatine, IA 52761
Tel: 319-263-0649
Address Inquiries to: Donald Olson, President
    Albert Knapp, Secretary
Founded in: 1910

Oelwein

Musicians Protective Union
218 Second Avenue Northeast
Post Office Box 15
Oelwein, IA 50662
Tel: 319-427-3485
Address Inquiries to: Jack Passick, President
Leo L. Fritz, Secretary
Founded in: 1918

Sioux City

Musicians' Protective Union, Local 254
3263 Idlewood
Sioux City, IA 51104
Tel: 712-258-1288
Address Inquiries to: Clyde Wagner,
    President
    Rockley W. Beck, Secretary
Founded in: 1902

KANSAS

Coffeyville

Musicians' Protective Union
Rural Route Number 4
Post Office Box 118-A
Coffeyville, KS 67337
Tel: 316-251-3522
Address Inquiries to: Mike Mason, President
Milford A. Unruh, Secretary
Founded in: 1934

Hutchinson

Musicians' Protective Association, Local
    110
10281 Golden Arrow Drive
Hutchinson, KS 67501
Tel: 316-663-2653
Address Inquiries to: Leo Ashcraft, President
Roland S. Gunn, Secretary
Founded in: 1913

Lawrence

Musicians' Protective Union
2524 Jasu Drive
Lawrence, KS 66044
Tel: 913-843-4966
Address Inquiries to: William L. Kelly,
    President
    J. Roger Stoner, Secretary
Founded in: 1926

Manhattan

Manhattan Musicians Association, Local
    169
828 Allison Road
Manhattan, KS 66502
Tel: 915-537-1928

Address Inquiries to: J. Vaughn Bolton,
    President
    Ferrol K. Oberhelman, Secretary
Founded in: 1935

Parsons

Musicians' Protective Union, Local 250
2430 Appleton
Parsons, KS 67357
Address Inquiries to: Frank Stevenson,
    President
    John H. Hensley, Secretary
Founded in: 1902

Pittsburg

Musicians' Protective Union
Post Office Box 566
Pittsburg, KS 66762
Tel: 316-231-5220
Address Inquiries to: Mike Loy, President
J. Phil Kurtz, Secretary
Founded in: 1912

Salina

Salina Musicians' Association, Local 207
801 Choctow
Salina, KS 67401
Tel: 913-827-7352
Address Inquiries to: Steven Freed, President
Ken Fowler, Secretary
Founded in: 1910

Topeka

Topeka Musical Association, Local 36-665
1737 Randolph
Topeka, KS 66614
Tel: 913-234-4465
Address Inquiries to: Gilbert W. Anderson,
    President
    James H. Parker, Secretary

Wichita

Wichita Musicians' Association
4323 East Kellogg
Wichita, KS 67218
Tel: 316-684-1311
Address Inquiries to: Dennis Danders,
    President
    Vernon K. Nydegger, Secretary
Founded in: 1903

KENTUCKY

Lexington

Lexington Musicians' Association
116 Westgate Drive
Lexington, KY 40504
Tel: 606-255-4721
Address Inquiries to: Fredrick F. Moore,
    President
    William M. McGinnis, Secretary
Founded in: 1910

Louisville

American Federation of Television and
    Radio Artists, (AFTRA)
410 South Third Street
Louisville, KY 40202

Louisville Federation of Musicians, Local
    11-637
1436 Bardstown Road
Louisville, KY 40204
Tel: 502-451-7509
Address Inquiries to: Herbert E. Hale,
    President
    Don R. Shumate, Secretary
Founded in: 1897

LOUISIANA
Baton Rouge

Baton Rouge Musicians' Association
8367 Airline Highway
Baton Rouge, LA 70815
Tel: 504-926-5088
Address Inquiries to: Cleo Yarbrough,
    President
    Matt Omari, Secretary
Founded in: 1938

New Orleans

American Federation of Television and
    Radio Artists, (AFTRA)
1110 Royal Street
New Orleans, LA 70116

Musicians' Mutual Protective Union, Local
    174-496
2401 Esplanade Avenue
New Orleans, LA 70119
Tel: 504-947-1700
Address Inquiries to: David Winstein,
    President
    John Scheuermann, Jr., Secretary
Founded in: 1902

Shreveport

Shreveport Federation of Musicians, Local
    116
517 Creswell
Shreveport, LA 71101
Tel: 318-222-5183; 318-424-3513
Address Inquiries to: Gilbert Phillips,
    President and Secretary
Founded in: 1900

West Monroe

Musicians' Protective Union
1205 North 5th
West Monroe, LA 71291
Tel: 318-387-5030
Address Inquiries to: Les Winslow, President
Les Winslow, Secretary
Founded in: 1937

MAINE
Portland

Portland Musicians' Association
27 Fleetwood Street
Portland, ME 04102
Tel: 207-774-6757
Address Inquiries to: Miss GLoria J.
    McCullough, President
    Jerry Der Boghostan, Secretary
Founded in: 1904

MARYLAND
Baltimore

Musicians' Asociation of Metropolitan
Baltimore, Local 40-543
1055 Taylor Avenue, Suite 203
Baltimore, MD 21204
Tel: 301-337-7277
Address Inquiries to: Albert Sigismondi,
    President
    Jack Hook, Secretary
Founded in: 1903

Salisbury

Salisbury Federation of Musicians, Local
    44
Route 10, Cedarhurst Village
Salisbury, MD 21801
Tel: 301-749-3948
Address Inquiries to: Kendall A. Martin,
    President
    Russell M. Miles, Secretary
Founded in: 1935

MASSACHUSETTS
Adams

Musicians' Protective Association, Local 96
24 Crandall Street
Adams, MA 01220
Tel: 413-743-2943
Address Inquiries to: Gregory S. Mitchell,
    President
    Ronald Lively, Secretary
Founded in: 1899

Boston

American Federation of Television and
    Radio Artists, (AFTRA)
11 Beacon Street
Boston, MA 02108

Boston Musicians' Association, Local
    9-535
56 St. Botolph Street
Boston, MA 02116
Tel: 617-536-2486
Address Inquiries to: Joseph MacDonald,
    President
    Howard Garniss, Secretary
Founded in: 1897

Screen Actors Guild, (SAG)
11 Beacon Street, Room 1103
Boston, MA 02108

Bridgewater

Musicians' Protective Union, Local 231
533 Walnut Street
Bridgewater, MA 02324
Tel: 617-697-4979
Address Inquiries to: Louis E. Perry,
    President
    Richard J. Furtado, Secretary
Founded in: 1902

Brockton

Brockton Federation of Musicians, Local
    138
13 North Ash Street
Brockton, MA 02401
Tel: 617-583-0192
Address Inquiries to: Abraham Dumanis,
    President
    James R. Dowling, Secretary
Founded in: 1901

Chicopee

Holyoke Musicians' Union, Local 144
38 Keddy Blvd.
Chicopee, MA 01020
Tel: 413-533-5235
Address Inquiries to: Charles L. Will,
    President
    Donald J. Baptiste, Secretary
Founded in: 1901

Easthampton

Northampton Federation of Musicians,
    Local 220
31 Davis Street
Easthampton, MA 01027
Tel: 413-527-4094
Address Inquiries to: Edmund J. Schott,
    President
    Raymond B. Black, Secretary
Founded in: 1911

Fall River

Fall River Federation of Musicians, Local
    216
746 Hood Street
Fall River, MA 02720
Tel: 617-679-6235
Address Inquiries to: James M. Considine,
    President
    David Nadien, Secretary
Founded in: 1902

Fitchburg

Musicians' Mutual Association, Local 173
188 South Street
Fitchburg, MA 01420
Tel: 617-345-7191
Address Inquiries to: John R. Pacetti,
    President
    Charles F. Miller, Secretary
Founded in: 1902

Greenfield

Franklin County Musicians' Association
151 Davis Street
Greenfield, MA 01301
Tel: 413-773-9769

Address Inquiries to: James J. Gallagher,
President
Mrs. Mary G. Scoville, Secretary
Founded in: 1917

Haverhill

Haverhill Musicians' Association
92 North Avenue
Haverhill, MA 01830
Tel: 617-373-5200
Address Inquiries to: William Fasulo,
President
Emery Hollerer, Secretary
Founded in: 1903

Hopedale

Musicians' Protective Union
164 Hopedale Street
Hopedale, MA 01747
Tel: 617-473-0473
Address Inquiries to: John Ghiringhelli,
President
Peter A. Paradiso, Secretary
Founded in: 1929

Lowell

Greater Lowell Musicians' Association,
Local 83
200 Parker Street
Lowell, MA 01851
Tel: 617-453-5621
Address Inquiries to: William J. Notini,
President
Angelo L. Bergamini, Secretary
Founded in: 1898

Methuen

Musicians' Protective Union
163 Oakside Avenue
Methuen, MA 01844
Tel: 617-686-2744
Address Inquiries to: Raymond E. DiFiore,
President
Irene Mazzaglia, Secretary
Founded in: 1904

New Bedford

Greater New Bedford Association of
Musicians, Local 214
79 Hunter Street
New Bedford, MA 02740
Tel: 617-994-3049
Address Inquiries to: Frank C. Monteiro,
President
John A. Couto, Secretary
Founded in: 1903

Pittsfield

Pittsfield Federation of Musicians, Local
109
397 Partridge Road
Pittsfield, MA 01201
Tel: 413-442-9755
Address Inquiries to: Morton Wayne,
President
Edgar J. Wood, Secretary
Founded in: 1900

Plymouth

Musicians Protective Union
30 Allerton Street
Plymouth, MA 02360
Tel: 617-746-2247
Address Inquiries to: John Pacheco, President
Donald C. Besegai, Secretary
Founded in: 1903

Randolph

Musicians' Protective Union
11 Adams Drive
Randolph, MA 02368
Tel: 617-963-0151
Address Inquiries to: Robert Seixas, President
Robert G. Schuller, Secretary
Founded in: 1904

Saugus

North Shore Musicians' Association, Local
126
16 Jefferson Avenue
Saugus, MA 01906
Tel: 617-581-3550; 617-233-1366
Address Inquiries to: Louis Amico, President
Arthur Axelrod, Secretary
Founded in: 1900

Springfield

Greater Springfield Musicians'
Association, Local 171
134 Chestnut Street
Springfield, MA 01103
Tel: 413-736-5187
Address Inquiries to: John J. Brogan Jr.,
President
George T. Lull, Secretary
Founded in: 1901

Sutton

Southbridge Musicians' Association
20 Colonial Road
Sutton, MA 01527
Tel: 617-865-2714
Address Inquiries to: Bernard J. Baldyga,
President
Richard J. Bergeron Sr., Secretary
Founded in: 1937

West Dennis

Cape Cod Musicians' Association, Local
155
8 Ridgedale Avenue, Post Office Box 221
West Dennis, MA 02670
Tel: 617-394-4537
Address Inquiries to: Russell Kelsey,
President
Mrs. Jane Ross, Secretary
Founded in: 1932

Worcester

Worcester Musicians' Association, Local
143
38 Patch Reservoir Drive
Worcester, MA 01602
Tel: 617-798-2228
Address Inquiries to: George Cohen,
President

Rudolph J. Forge, Secretary
Founded in: 1901

MICHIGAN
Battle Creek

Battle Creek Federation of Musicians
1349 West Michigan Avenue
Battle Creek, MI 49016
Tel: 616-962-3063
Address Inquiries to: John D. Anglin,
President
George H. Pendill, Secretary
Founded in: 1918

Bay City

Federation of Musicians, Local 127
291 Donahue Beach
Bay City, MI 48706
Tel: 517-684-6834
Address Inquiries to: John Lipinski, President
Clarence Fanger, Secretary
Founded in: 1900

Belmont

Grand Rapids Federation of Musicians,
Local 56
4622 Cannonsburg, NE
Belmont, MI 49505
Tel: 616-874-7421
Address Inquiries to: Robert Gold, President
Clyde Falk, Secretary
Founded in: 1905

Caspian

Iron County Musicians' Association
Post Office Box 482
Caspian, MI 49915
Tel: 906-265-3600
Address Inquiries to: Joseph Shepich,
President
Joseph E. DeAmicis, Secretary
Founded in: 1941

Detroit

Federation Of Musicians, Local 5
19161 Schaefer Highway
Detroit, MI 48235
Tel: 313-345-6200
Address Inquiries to: Merle M. Alvey,
President
Fred Netting, Secretary
Founded in: 1903

Escanaba

Musicians' Protective Union
2122 20th Avenue, South
Escanaba, MI 49829
Tel: 906-786-0271
Address Inquiries to: Robert Shepich,
President
Ray Richards, Secretary
Founded in: 1914

Flint

Flint Federation of Musicians
1502 Woodcroft
Flint, MI 48503
Tel: 313-233-4264
Address Inquiries to: Russell G. Berryman,
    President
    Earl L. Durkee, Secretary
Founded in: 1910

Iron Mountain

Musicians' Protective Union, Local 249
204 5th Street
Iron Mountain, MI 49801
Tel: 906-774-9629
Address Inquiries to: Anthony J. Giovannini,
    President
    Carlo Calo, Secretary
Founded in: 1932

Kalamazoo

Kalamazoo Federation of Musicians, Local
    228
3332 Wedgewood Drive
Kalamazoo, MI 49008
Tel: 616-344-0049
Address Inquiries to: William Morris,
    President
    Don Brocato, Secretary
Founded in: 1902

Lansing

Lansing Federation of Musicians
2703 North Turner Street
Lansing, MI 48906
Tel: 517-484-4461
Address Inquiries to: Darwin D. Hart,
    President
    Otto H. VanSickle, Secretary
Founded in: 1903

Lathrup Village

Screen Actors Guild, (SAG)
28690 Southfield Road
Lathrup Village, MI 48067

Marquette

Musicians' Federation, Local 218
808 West Kaye Avenue
Marquette, MI 49855
Tel: 906-228-8800
Address Inquiries to: John G. Major,
    President
    Mark H. French, Secretary
Founded in: 1931

Menominee

Twin City Musicians' Association of
    Marinette Wisconsin and Menominee
    Michiggan, Local 39
2034 Tenth Avenue
Menominee, MI 49858
Tel: 906-863-2073
Address Inquiries to: William Plemel,
    President
    Elmer Vojcihoski, Secretary
Founded in: 1902

Muskegon Heights

Muskegon Musicians' Association, Local
    252
169 East Broadway
Muskegon Heights, MI 49444
Tel: 616-733-2227
Address Inquiries to: Raymond J. Stralko,
    President
    Jack Lupien, Secretary
Founded in: 1902

Port Huron

Port Huron Federation of Musicians, Local
    33
2601 10th Avenue
Port Huron, MI 48060
Tel: 313-982-8390
Address Inquiries to: Charles Nelson,
    President
    Donald C. Vincent, Secretary
Founded in: 1896

Saginaw

Saginaw Musical Association, Local 57
2456 Barnard Street
Saginaw, MI 48602
Tel: 517-793-1877
Address Inquiries to: Leroy E. Brandimore,
    President
    Paul W. Daines, Secretary
Founded in: 1897

Saint Ann Arbor

Ann Arbor Federation of Musicians
Wolverine Building
202 East Washington, Suite 310
Saint Ann Arbor, MI 48108
Tel: 313-668-8041
Address Inquiries to: Max W. Crosman,
    President
    Reade S. Pierce, Secretary
Founded in: 1912

Saint Joseph

Twin City Federation of Musicians, Local
    232
2182 Hanley Road
Saint Joseph, MI 49085
Tel: 616-429-8777
Address Inquiries to: Al Davino Jr., President
Dorothy Elmer, Secretary
Founded in: 1929

Sault Ste.

Musicians' Mutual Protective Union
Post Office Box 243
Sault Ste., MI 49783
Tel: 906-635-5371
Address Inquiries to: Americo Metro,
    President
    John Quigley, Secretary
Founded in: 1912

Southfield

American Federation of Television and
    Radio Artists, (AFTRA)
24901 Noth Western Highway
Southfield, MI 48703

MINNESOTA

Albert Lea

Musicians' Protective Union
1208 Crestview Road
Albert Lea, MN 56007
Tel: 507-377-1363
Address Inquiries to: Steve Oman, President
Harlan S. Erickson, Secretary
Founded in: 1911

Brainerd

Musicians' Protective Associaton
Route 4, Post Office Box 64
Brainerd, MN 56401
Tel: 218-764-2438
Address Inquiries to: Clinton Wheeler,
    Predident
    Mrs. Carolyn Kassulker, Secretary
Founded in: 1937

Duluth

Duluth Musicians' Association, Local 18
67 Calvary Road
Duluth, MN 55803
Tel: 218-728-1990
Address Inquiries to: Sigurd Erickson,
    President
    Jean Moore, Secretary
Founded in: 1913

Eveleth

Musicians' Protective Association
609 North Court
Eveleth, MN 55734
Tel: 218-744-5402
Address Inquiries to: Harry Angerelli,
    President
Founded in: 1937

Fairbault

Musicians' Protective Association
Rural Route 5, Box 111
Fairbault, MN 55021
Tel: 507-334-6668
Address Inquiries to: James Maas, President
Mrs. Lynda Bougreau, Secretary
Founded in: 1938

Hibbing

Musicians' Protective Union
1320 East 11th Street
Hibbing, MN 55746
Tel: 218-262-2941
Address Inquiries to: Ben A. Martella,
    President
    Ronald P. Gazelka, Secretary
Founded in: 1916

International Falls

Border Musicians' Association, Local 156
Post Office Box 347
International Falls, MN 56649
Tel: 218-283-2251
Address Inquiries to: Art De Benedet,
    President
    Werner Schuschke, Secretary
Founded in: 1936

Lewiston

Winona Musicians' Association
190 West Main Street
Lewiston, MN 55952
Tel: 507-523-3657
Address Inquiries to: Richard Ahrens,
    President
    Catherine Ingvalson, Secretary
Founded in: 1937

Madelia

Musicians' Protective Union
313 First Northwest
Madelia, MN 56062
Tel: 507-625-3339
Address Inquiries to: Andy Lawrence,
    President
    Roy Perry, Secretary
Founded in: 1925

Minneapolis

American Federation of Television and
    Radio Artists, (AFTRA)
105 South Fifth Street
Minneapolis, MN 55402

Musicians' Association, Local 73
127 North Seventh Street
Minneapolis, MN 55403
Tel: 612-333-8205
Address Inquiries to: Robert Biglow,
    President
    Russell J. Moore, Secretary
Founded in: 1901

Screen Actors Guild, (SAG)
924 Soo Line Building
Minneapolis, MN 55402

New Prague

Musicians' Protective Union
Route 4, Post Office Box 377
New Prague, MN 56071
Tel: 612-758-4566
Address Inquiries to: Harold Picha, President
George Maxa, Secretary
Founded in: 1938

New Ulm

Musicians' Protective Association
Route 1, Post Office Box 89-1
New Ulm, MN 56073
Tel: 507-354-6807
Address Inquiries to: Arley Rolloff, President
LeRoy Dewanz, Secretary
Founded in: 1937

Northwest Rochester

Musicians' Protective Union
701 9th Avenue
Northwest Rochester, MN 55901
Tel: 507-288-1519
Address Inquiries to: Duane Johnson,
    President
    Kendall Heins, Secretary
Founded in: 1916

Owatonna

Owatonna Area Musicians' Association
1419 Hemlock
Owatonna, MN 55060
Tel: 507-451-8593
Address Inquiries to: Werner Halvorson,
    President
    Ron Brey, Secretary
Founded in: 1937

Saint Cloud

Musicians' Protective Union
1616 Third Street North
Saint Cloud, MN 56301
Tel: 612-253-6981
Address Inquiries to: William Bach, President
Norman Scherer, Secretary
Founded in: 1920

St. Paul

Musicians' Protective Union, Local 30
1369 Eleanor Avenue
St. Paul, MN 55116
Tel: 612-698-0877; 612-699-9591
Address Inquiries to: Ed Corcoran, President
Patrick J. Rian, Secretary
Founded in: 1897

MISSISSIPPI

Hattiesburg

Hattiesburg Federation of Musicians
326 Venetian Way
Hattiesburg, MS 39401
Tel: 601-544-2834
Address Inquiries to: Gerald Johnston,
    President
    Frank S. Uher, Secretary
Founded in: 1938

Jackson

Jackson Federation of Musicians
Route 2, Post Office Box 270F
Jackson, MS 39209
Tel: 601-924-9313
Address Inquiries to: Jimmy E. Mullen Jr.,
    President
    W.C. Van Devender, Secretary
Founded in: 1917

MISSOURI

Jefferson City

Professional Musicians' Association, Local
217
322 Carl Lane
Jefferson City, MO 65101
Tel: 314-636-7788
Address Inquiries to: Archie Stegmen,
    President
    Frank E. Ovaitt, Secretary
Founded in: 1907

Joplin

Joplin Musicians' Association
1801 South Saint Louis
Joplin, MO 64801
Tel: 417-781-2486
Address Inquiries to: Robert T. Estes,
    President
    Charles B. Konkol, Secretary
Founded in: 1938

Kansas City

American Federation of Television and
    Radio Artists, (AFTRA)
4530 Madison Upper Level
Kansas City, MO 64111

Kansas City Federation of Musicians, Local
34-627
1017 Washington
Kansas City, MO 64105
Tel: 816-221-6934
Address Inquiries to: Ruel L. Joyce, President
    John W. Kost, Secretary
Founded in: 1897

Saint Joseph

Musicians' Association, Local 50
1212 Faraon Street
Saint Joseph, MO 64501
Tel: 816-232-9348
Address Inquiries to: G. Deon Jensen,
    President
    Robert Speer, Secretary
Founded in: 1897

Sedalia

Sedalia Musicians' Association, Local 22
508 West Broadway
Sedalia, MO 65301
Tel: 816-826-3807
Address Inquiries to: Lloyd H. Knox,
    President
    James L. Eschbacher, Secretary
Founded in: 1897

Springfield

Association of Musicians, Local 150
915 East Elm
Springfield, MO 65806
Tel: 417-869-5226
Address Inquiries to: John R. Mongell,
    President
    Willard Shunk, Secretary
Founded in: 1901

St. Louis

American Federation of Television and
    Radio Artists, (AFTRA)
818 Olive Street, Suite 671
St. Louis, MO 63101

Musicians' Association of St. Louis, Local
2-197
2103 59th Street
St. Louis, MO 63110
Tel: 314-781-6612
Address Inquiries to: Louis C. Nauman Jr.,
    President
    Harry A. Gosling, Secretary

Founded in: 1896

MONTANA
Anaconda

Musical Society, Local 81
205 Liden Street
Anaconda, MT 59711
Tel: 406-563-3385
Address Inquiries to: Donald Loranger,
  President
  Louis C. Mertzig Jr., Secretary
Founded in: 1898

Butte

Mutual Protective Union, Local 241
2933 Burke Lane
Butte, MT 59701
Tel: 406-494-4251
Address Inquiries to: Joseph E. Hughes,
  President
  Ms. Louise Zanchi, Secretary
Founded in: 1902

Great Falls

Musicians' Protective Union
1100 First Avenue, SW
Great Falls, MT 59401
Tel: 406-452-3962
Address Inquiries to: Frank C. McKenna,
  President
  Jack D. Harper, Secretary
Founded in: 1904

Helena

Musicians' Protective Union
822 Breckenridge
Helena, MT 59601
Tel: 406-442-5827
Address Inquiries to: Harry Harlen, President
  N.C. Slead, Secretary
Founded in: 1939

Livingston

Musicians' Protective Association
206 South C
Livingston, MT 59047
Tel: 406-222-1274
Address Inquiries to: Edward Tecca,
  President
  Louis J. Armentaro, Secretary
Founded in: 1903

Miles City

Musicians' Association
1602 Palmer
Miles City, MT 59301
Tel: 406-232-4494
Address Inquiries to: Eugene Forsyth,
  President
  Keith W. Keller, Secretary
Founded in: 1909

Missoula

Missoula Professional Musicians'
  Association
315 Westview Drive
Missoula, MT 59802
Tel: 406-728-3473
Address Inquiries to: Charles E. Hurt,
  President
  Mrs. Mardell J. Lockwood
Founded in: 1908

North Billings

Billings Professional Musicians'
  Association
2822 3rd Avenue, #210
North Billings, MT 59101
Tel: 406-245-3360
Address Inquiries to: Roderick R. Wright,
  President
  Frank N. Holzer, Secretary
Founded in: 1935

Somers

Musicians' Protective Union
Post Office Box 142
Somers, MT 59932
Tel: 406-857-3560
Address Inquiries to: Herb White, President
Robert McCandles, Secretary
Founded in: 1910

NEBRASKA
Lincoln

Lincoln Musicians' Association
1730 Crestline Drive
Lincoln, NE 68506
Tel: 402-474-3868
Address Inquiries to: Ruben Haun, President
Keith W. Heckman, Secretary
Founded in: 1907

North Platte

Musicians' Association
315 South Willow
North Platte, NE 69101
Tel: 308-532-5351
Address Inquiries to: Larry Romeiser,
  President
  Hadley Barrett, Secretary
Founded in: 1912

Omaha

American Federation of Television and
  Radio Artists, (AFTRA)
3555 Farnam Street
Omaha, NE 68131

Musicians' Association, Local 70-558
3925 Terrace Drive
Omaha, NE 68134
Tel: 402-571-2722
Address Inquiries to: Ron Ellis, President
Shorty Vest, Secretary
Founded in: 1897

NEVADA
Las Vegas

Musicians' of Las Vegas
Post Office Box 7467
Las Vegas, NV 89101
Tel: 702-739-9369
Address Inquiries to: Mark Tully Massagli,
  President
  Larry O'Brien, Secretary
Founded in: 1931

Screen Actors Guild, (SAG)
440 North 21st Street
Las Vegas, NV 89101

Reno

Reno Musicians' Union
Post Office Box 208
Reno, NV 89504
Tel: 702-323-2116
Address Inquiries to: Stan Rutherford,
  President
  Merle L. Snider, Secretary
Founded in: 1909

NEW HAMPSHIRE
Concord

Concord Federation of Musicians
1 Perkins Street
Concord, NH 03301
Tel: 603-746-3937
Address Inquiries to: Joseph Anicciarico,
  President
  Frank Doyle Jr., Secretary
Founded in: 1904

Manchester

Manchester Federation of Musicians
89 Pennacook Street
Manchester, NH 03104
Tel: 603-622-9084
Address Inquiries to: Albert L'Heureux,
  President
  Raymond T. Pare, Secretary
Founded in: 1903

Marlborough

Associated Musicians of Keene, New
  Hampshire
Fitch Court
Marlborough, NH 03455
Tel: 603-876-3963
Address Inquiries to: Richard Hutchins,
  President
  James F. Fletcher, Secretary
Founded in: 1940

NEW JERSEY
Burlington

Burlington Musical Society
126 Mott Avenue
Burlington, NJ 08016
Tel: 609-386-4793
Address Inquiries to: Robert J. Bell, President

William Parker, Secretary
Founded in: 1903

Dover

Musicians' Protective Union, Local 237
54 Windsor Avenue
Dover, NJ 07801
Tel: 201-366-7640
Address Inquiries to: Thomas J. Casapulla,
President
Arthur Weiner, Secretary
Founded in: 1902

East Orange

Musicians' Guild of Essex County, Local
16
Suburban Office Plaza
141 South Harrison Street
East Orange, NJ 07018
Tel: 201-675-1333
Address Inquiries to: Lew Mallett, President
Philip J. Failla, Secretary
Founded in: 1897

Edison

Association of Professional Musicians,
Local 204
146 Highway No. 1, #25
Edison, NJ 08817
Tel: 201-572-2832
Address Inquiries to: Louis Melia, President
Eddie Shanholtz, Secretary
Founded in: 1902

Garwood

Musicians' Association, Local 151
248 Myrtle Avenue
Garwood, NJ 17127
Tel: 201-SU9-0109
Address Inquiries to: Nick Sabbatelli,
President
James Drake, Secretary
Founded in: 1901

Jersey City

Musicians' Protective Union
130 Central Avenue
Jersey City, NJ 07306
Tel: 201-653-0750
Address Inquiries to: Wilson Bonito,
President
George T. Triano, Secretary
Founded in: 1909

Morristown

Musicians' Protective Union, Local 177
8 Lake Road
Morristown, NJ 07960
Tel: 201-539-2619
Address Inquiries to: Rudolph Spagnola,
President
Edward Dorman, Secretary
Founded in: 1928

Paterson

Musicians' Mutual Protective and
Benevolent Union, Local 248
77 Prospect Street
Paterson, NJ 07505

Tel: 201-278-8418; 201-278-8420
Address Inquiries to: Fred Dittamo, President
Isadore Freeman, Secretary
Founded in: 1902

Pleasantville

Atlantic City Musicians' Association
418 North Main Street
Pleasantville, NJ 08232
Tel: 609-645-7740
Address Inquiries to: Victor J. Marrandino,
President
George A. Fognano, Secretary
Founded in: 1914

Trenton

Trenton Musical Association, Local 62
28 Assumpink Blvd.
Trenton, NJ 08619
Tel: 609-586-0022
Address Inquiries to: Lawrence (Stan)
Kennedy, President
Frank Herrera, Secretary
Founded in: 1901

Vineland

Musicians' Protective Union
40 Southwest Avenue
Vineland, NJ 08360
Tel: 609-692-1039
Address Inquiries to: Frank Testa, President
Enrico Serra, Secretary
Founded in: 1916

Woodbridge

Musicians' Protective Union
414 Elmwood Avenue
Woodbridge, NJ 07095
Tel: 201-634-0750
Address Inquiries to: Frank J. Kreisel,
President
Andy Kuchtyak, Secretary
Founded in: 1904

NEW MEXICO

Alburquerque

Musicians' Protective Union
5301 Central Avenue NE, #807
Alburquerque, NM 87108
Tel: 505-255-2069
Address Inquiries to: Orlie Wagner, President
Raymond Alt, Secretary
Founded in: 1915

Roswell

Roswell Federation of Musicians
1103 South Michigan Avenue
Roswell, NM 88201
Tel: 505-622-7125
Address Inquiries to: Reid Atchley, President
Hank Harral, Secretary
Founded in: 1951

Santa Fe

Screen Actors Guild, (SAG)
410 Taos Highway
Santa Fe, NM 87501

NEW YORK

Albany

American Federation of Television and
Radio Artists, (AFTRA)
341 Northern Boulevard
Albany, NY 12204

Albion

Musicians' Protective Union
123 South Main Street
Albion, NY 14411
Tel: 716-589-7760
Address Inquiries to: Luther Burroughs,
President
Charles L. Piazza, Secretary
Founded in: 1903

Amsterdam

Musicians' Protective Union, Local 133
Road Number 4
Amsterdam, NY 12010
Tel: 518-883-5713
Address Inquiries to: Stanley Czelusniak,
President
David J. Dybas, Secretary
Founded in: 1901

Auburn

Musical Union, Local 239
243 West Genesee Street
Auburn, NY 13021
Tel: 315-253-3345
Address Inquiries to: James Mamuscia,
President
Walter Light, Secretary
Founded in: 1906

Batavia

Musicians Protective Union
9 Woodrow Road
Batavia, NY 14020
Tel: 716-343-4020
Address Inquiries to: Daniel Martino,
President
John J. Stone, Secretary
Founded in: 1938

Binghamton

American Federation of Television and
Radio Artists, (AFTRA)
50 Front Street
Binghamton, NY 13905

Buffalo

American Federation of Television and
Radio Artists, (AFTRA)
615 Brisbane Building
Buffalo, NY 14203

Buffalo Musicians' Association, Local 92
452 Franklin Street

Buffalo, NY 14202
Tel: 716-873-1275
Address Inquiries to: Vincent Impellitter,
    President
    Angelo J. Callea, Secretary
Founded in: 1969

Musicians' Association of East Aurora
452 Franklin Street
Buffalo, NY 14202
Tel: 716-886-5902
Address Inquiries to: Allen Schwartz,
    President
    Clarence H. Hopper, Secretary
Founded in: 1940

Burnt Hills

Saratoga Musical Union
27 High Mills Roads
Burnt Hills, NY 12027
Tel: 518-584-4223
Address Inquiries to: Ronald H. Partch,
    President
    George Kaulfers, Secretary
Founded in: 1918

Cortland

Cortland Musicians' Association
17 Stevenson Street
Cortland, NY 13045
Tel: 607-753-8563
Address Inquiries to: Sam Forcucci, President
    David W. Perfetti, Secretary
Founded in: 1909

Dunkirk

Musicians' Protective Association, Local
    108
5072 West Lake Road
Dunkirk, NY 14048
Tel: 716-366-1773
Address Inquiries to: Richard Kalfas,
    President
    Ron Bialaszewski, Secretary
Founded in: 1900

Elizaville

Musicians' Protective Union
Road Number 1, Box 190
Elizaville, NY 12534
Tel: 518-828-3140
Address Inquiries to: Fred Stark, President
Raymond H. Ringer, Secretary
Founded in: 1940

Fulton

Musicians' Protective Union, Local 267
218 Oneida Street
Fulton, NY 13069
Tel: 315-592-4347
Address Inquiries to: Joseph Cortini,
    President
    Allen Boyce, President
Founded in: 1935

Geneva

Geneva Musicians' Association
187 Genessee Street
Geneva, NY 14456
Tel: 315-789-5441
Address Inquiries to: George J. Telarico,
    President
    George J. Telarico, Secretary
Founded in: 1941

Glen Falls

Adirondack Association of Musicians,
    Local 129
4 Hillcrest Avenue
Glen Falls, NY 12801
Tel: 518-793-4801
Address Inquiries to: John Marine Jr.,
    President
    Theodore C. Firth, Secretary
Founded in: 1901

Gloversville

Musicians' Protective Association, Local
    163
17 South Hollywood Avenue
Gloversville, NY 12078
Tel: 518-725-1256
Address Inquiries to: Milton G. Brookins,
    President
    Ralph J. Gardner, Secretary
Founded in: 1901

Hamburg

Musicians' Protective Union
77 George Street
Hamburg, NY 14075
Tel: 716-649-2251
Address Inquiries to: Eugene Zugger,
    President
    Ronald A. Norris, Secretary
Founded in: 1934

Hornell

Musicians' Protective Union
74 Platt Street
Hornell, NY 14843
Tel: 607-698-4566
Address Inquiries to: John Koskie, President
Clifford Dennis, Secretary
Founded in: 1937

Ithaca

Musicians' Protective Union, Local 132
365 West King Road
Ithaca, NY 14850
Tel: 607-272-8170
Address Inquiries to: Amandus Teeter,
    President
    Edward J. Moore Jr., Secretary
Founded in: 1901

Jamestown

Jamestown Musical Association, Local 134
7 Campbell Avenue
Jamestown, NY 14701
Tel: 716-665-3458
Address Inquiries to: Allan K. Swanson,
    President

Vincent F. Mallare, Secretary
Founded in: 1901

Larchmont

Musicians' Association of Westchester,
    Local 38
132 Larchmont Avenue
Larchmont, NY 10538
Tel: 914-834-0823
Address Inquiries to: Thomas Minichino,
    President
    Peter Pugliese, Secretary
Founded in: 1949

Latham

Troy Musicians, Inc., Local 13
25 Carolina Street
Latham, NY 12110
Tel: 518-274-8275
Address Inquiries to: Romeo Mitri, President
Frank Vadala, Secretary
Founded in: 1897

Lockport

Lockport Federation of Musicians, Local
    97
6279 Hamm Road
Lockport, NY 14094
Tel: 716-434-2229
Address Inquiries to: Frank R. Loiars,
    President
    Robert C. Foster, Secretary
Founded in: 1899

Loudonville

Albany Musicians' Association, Local 14
452 Albany-Shaker Road
Loudonville, NY 12211
Tel: 518-459-4743
Address Inquiries to: Vincent Catalano,
    President
    Joseph A. Lauria, Secretary
Founded in: 1896

Lycoming

Musicians' Protective Union
Post Office Box 91
Lycoming, NY 13093
Tel: 315-343-0557
Address Inquiries to: Kenneth E. Goodness,
    President
    David B. Brown, Secretary
Founded in: 1934

Newburgh

Musicians' Union
3 Wintergreen Avenue
Newburgh, NY 12550
Tel: 914-561-5872
Address Inquiries to: Thomas V. Wison,
    President
    Anthony J. Martini, Secretary
Founded in: 1903

New York

Actors' Equity Association (AEA)
165 West 46th Street
New York, NY 10036
Tel: 212-869-8530

Address Inquiries to: Alan Eisenberg,
  Executive Secretary
  Guy Pace, Executive Assistant
Founded in: 1913
Description: Protects the rights of, and enforces, Equity rules for actors, singers, and dancers in live dramatic and musical theatre in the United States.

American Federation of Musicians (AFM)
1500 Broadway
New York, NY 10038
Tel: 212-869-1330
Founded in: 1896
Description: American Federation of Musicians unites 605 locals in the United States and Canada, representing over 300,000 professional instrumental musicians, promoting good faith and enforcing fair dealing in cases involving members' employment.

American Federation of Television and
Radio Artists (AFTRA)
National Headquuarters
1350 Avenue of the Americas
New York, NY 10019
Tel: 212-719-9570; 212-265-7700
Address Inquiries to: Dick Moore, Press
  Representative
Description: American Federation of Television and Radio Artists (AFTRA) represents and protects performers in phonograph recordings, live and taped television and radio.

American Guild of Musical Artists
(AGMA)
1841 Broadway
New York, NY 10023
Tel: 212-265-3687
Description: American Guild of Musical Artists protects the rights of and adjudicates for dance, operatic and instrumental artists in the concert field.

American Guild of Variety Artists (AGVA)
184 5th Avenue
New York, NY 10010
Tel: 212-675-1003
Address Inquiries to: Rod McKuen, President
Francis Gear, Vice President
Founded in: 1939
Description: American Guild of Variety Artists (AGVA) protects the contractual rights of performers in live variety entertainment.

Association of Theatrical Press Agents and
Managers (ATPAM)
165 West 46th Street
New York, NY 10036
Tel: 212-719-3666
Address Inquiries to: Richard B. Weaver,
  Executive Secretary
Description: Association of Theatrical Press Agents and Managers (ATPAM) represents press agents and company managers in the dance, theatrical and entertainment fields.

International Alliance of Theatrical Stage
Employees (IATSE)
1515 Broadway
New York, NY 10036

Tel: 212-730-1770
Description: International Alliance of Theatrical Stage Employees (IATSE) represents a wide variety of theatrical stage employees through various locals, including stage hands, lighting technicians, wardrobe mistresses and makeup artists.

Screen Actors Guild (SAG)
1700 Broadway
New York, NY 10019
Tel: 212-957-5370
Description: Screen Actors Guild (SAG) represents and has jurisdiction over all performers (including dancers) in the film medium.

Screen Extras Guild, (SEG)
551 Fifth Avenue
New York, NY 10017

Society of Stage Directors and
Choreographers (SSDC)
1501 Broadway
New York, NY 10036
Tel: 212-391-1070
Description: Society of Stage Directors and Choreographers (SSDC) represents and has jurisdiction over directors and choreographers in the Broadway and Off-Broadway theatre, stock resident and dinner theatres.

United Scenic Artists (USA)
1540 Broadway
New York, NY 10036
Tel: 212-575-5120
Description: United Scenic Artists (USA) represents and protects the rights of scenic, costume and lighting designers in all areas of theatre, concert entertainment, motion pictures and television.

Niagra Falls

Musicians' Association of Niagara Falls,
  Local 106
1736 La Salle Avenue
Niagra Falls, NY 14301
Tel: 716-284-6247
Address Inquiries to: Sam Cassano, President
  Salvatore L. Paonessa, Secretary
Founded in: 1900

North Tonawanda

Tonawandas Musicians' Association, Local
  209
1408 Forbes Street
North Tonawanda, NY 14120
Tel: 716-692-7109
Address Inquiries to: Herm J. Janus,
  President
  Gerald Ryan, Secretary
Founded in: 1910

Olean

Olean-Salmanca Musicians' Union, Local
  115-614
122 North 21st Street
Olean, NY 14760
Tel: 716-372-3583
Address Inquiries to: Angelo Melaro,
  President

Walter L. Hedlund, Secretary
Founded in: 1900

Oneonta

Musicians' Protective Association
10 Grove Street
Oneonta, NY 13820
Tel: 607-432-7162
Address Inquiries to: Charles Schneider,
  President
  Linus Houck, Secretary
Founded in: 1907

Pine City

Elmira-Corning Musicians' Association
1001 Pinewood Drive
Pine City, NY 14871
Tel: 607-734-0131
Address Inquiries to: Vincent Stepules,
  President
  William F. Young, Secretary
Founded in: 1906

Poland

Mohawk Valley Musicians' Association,
  Local 51
R.D. 1
Poland, NY 13431
Tel: 315-251-
Address Inquiries to: Stewart J. Wagner,
  President
  Thomas M. Notman, Secretary
Founded in: 1898

Poughkeepsie

Professional Musicians Association, Local
  238
42 Styvestandt Drive
Poughkeepsie, NY 12601
Tel: 914-471-2305
Address Inquiries to: George F. Cacchione,
  President
  Retta Gelormino, Secretary
Founded in: 1902

Rochester

American Federation of Television and
  Radio Artists, (AFTRA)
Suite 900, One Exchange Place
Rochester, NY 14614

Rochester Musicians' Association, Local 66
83 Clinton Avenue, North
Rochester, NY 14604
Tel: 716-546-7633
Address Inquiries to: Joseph DeVitt, President
  Charles LaCava, Secretary
Founded in: 1897

Rome

Musicians' Protective Association
227 East Garden Street
Rome, NY 13440
Tel: 315-336-3534
Address Inquiries to: Joseph J. Trophia,
  President
  Robert J. Kahler
Founded in: 1903

Schenectady

American Federation of Television and
   Radio Artists, (AFTRA)
1400 Balltown Road
Schenectady, NY 12309

Musical Union, Local 85
444 Mc Clellan Street
Schenectady, NY 12304
Tel: 518-346-2086
Address Inquiries to: Abe Rapp, President
Eugene J. Sennes, Secretary
Founded in: 1900

Sparrowbush

Port Jervis Musicians' Protective
   Association
Route 97
Sparrowbush, NY 12780
Tel: 914-856-5612
Address Inquiries to: Douglas R. Bachelder,
   President
   G. Earl Cummings, Secretary
Founded in: 1925

Syracuse

Syracuse Musicians Protective Association,
   Local 78
131 Butler Street
Syracuse, NY 13210
Tel: 315-472-3056
Address Inquiries to: Phillip R. MacArthur,
   President
   Herbert LaHood, Secretary
Founded in: 1898

Woodstock

Musicians' Union, Local 215
49 Plochmann Lane
Woodstock, NY 12498
Tel: 914-679-6227
Address Inquiries to: Harry Castiglione,
   President
   William F. Paulus, Secretary
Founded in: 1902

NORTH CAROLINA

Charlotte

Charlotte Musicians' Association
2122 Eastway Drive
Charlotte, NC 28205
Tel: 704-568-3465
Founded in: 1934

Greensboro

Musicians Protective Union
526 Hilwood Court
Greensboro, NC 27410
Tel: 919-855-1333
Address Inquiries to: Richard L. Wells,
   President
   M Howard Waynick, Secretary
Founded in: 1926

Raleigh

Musicians' Association
123 East Drewry Lane
Raleigh, NC 27609
Tel: 919-782-2040
Address Inquiries to: Richard E. Southwick,
   President
   Russell Olson, Secretary
Founded in: 1908

NORTH DAKOTA

Grand Forks

Musicians' Protective Union
1020 Letnes Drive
Grand Forks, ND 58201
Tel: 701-775-9843
Address Inquiries to: Hartley Brown,
   President
   Bill Henderson, Secretary
Founded in: 1908

Mandan

Musicians' Protective Association, Local
   229
201 Missouri River Road
Mandan, ND 58554
Tel: 701-667-1077; 701-663-5775
Address Inquiries to: Gerry Serhienko,
   President
   Vern Cermak, Secretary
Founded in: 1931

Minot

Minot Musician's Association
1001 38th Street Northeast
Minot, ND 58701
Tel: 701-838-0845
Address Inquiries to: Jeff Lesmeister,
   President
   Marliss Hanson, Secretary
Founded in: 1939

OHIO

Akron

Akron Federation of Musicians, Local 24
Room 315, Metropolitan Building
Akron, OH 44308
Tel: 216-376-8174
Address Inquiries to: Eldon Motz, President
Jack Faller, Secretary
Founded in: 1897

Alliance

Alliance Federation of Musicians, Local 68
130 Shadyside Court
Alliance, OH 44601
Tel: 216-821-2761
Address Inquiries to: Wilbur T. Fites,
   President
   Charles Moushey, Secretary
Founded in: 1902

Ashtabula

Musicians Protective Association, Local
   107
2207 Harbor Avenue
Ashtabula, OH 44004
Tel: 216-992-0970
Address Inquiries to: William F. Giannel,
   President
   Francis J. Montanaro, Secretary
Founded in: 1900

Bolivar

Canton Federation of Musicians, Local 111
Post Office Box 72
Bolivar, OH 44612
Tel: 216-454-7430
Address Inquiries to: Frank L. Corbi,
   President
   John C. Smith, Secretary
Founded in: 1900

Cambridge

Musicians' Protective Union
Road 3
Cambridge, OH 43725
Tel: 614-432-2397
Address Inquiries to: Leonard Patterson,
   President
   Sara Ann Vergari, Secretary
Founded in: 1905

Cardington

Marion Musicians' Association
Route 2
Cardington, OH 43315
Tel: 614-389-4226
Address Inquiries to: Harold L. Ebert,
   President
   Edward A. Miller, Secretary
Founded in: 1920

Cincinnati

American Federation of Television and
   Radio Artists, (AFTRA)
15 West Sixth Street, Suite 607
Cincinnati, OH 45202

Cincinnati Musicians Association, Local 1
19 West Court
Cincinnati, OH 45202
Tel: 513-241-0900
Address Inquiries to: Eugene V. Frey,
   President
   Kenneth S. Mc Laughlin, Secretary
Founded in: 1897

Cleveland

American Federation of Television and
   Radio Artists (AFTRA)
1276 West Third Street
Cleveland, OH 44113

Screen Actors Guild, (SAG)
1276 West 3rd Street
Cleveland, OH 44113

The Cleveland Federation of Musicians,
   Local 4
2200 Carnegie Avenue
Cleveland, OH 44115

Tel: 216-771-1802
Address Inquiries to: Anthony Granata,
  President
  Michael Scigliano, Secretary
Founded in: 1896

Columbus

American Federation of Television and
  Radio Artists (AFTRA)
6600 Busch Boulevard
Columbus, OH 43229

Federation of Musicians, Local 103
2829 Cleveland Avenue
Columbus, OH 43224
Tel: 614-261-9826; 614-261-9827
Address Inquiries to: Lucian Tiberi, President
  Tommy Dale, Secretary
Founded in: 1900

Coshocton

Coshocton Federation of Musicians
44206 South Route 36
Coshocton, OH 43812
Tel: 614-622-8072
Address Inquiries to: Randy Pierce, President
Michael Williams, Secretary
Founded in: 1942

Dayton

Dayton Musicians' Association, Local
  101-473
415 Troy Street
Dayton, OH 45404
Tel: 513-223-6962
Address Inquiries to: Paul W. Rogers,
  President
  Mrs. Mae W. Jean, Secretary
Founded in: 1889

East Liverpool

Musicians' Mutual Protective Association,
  Local 172
1579 Holiday Street
East Liverpool, OH 43920
Tel: 216-385-8949
Address Inquiries to: Robert L. Hall,
  President
  Frank R. Craven, Secretary
Founded in: 1901

Fairfield

Hamilton Musicians' Association, Local 31
4716 Fairfield Avenue
Fairfield, OH 45014
Tel: 513-892-7922
Address Inquiries to: Dominic Roberts,
  President
  Rita Line, Secretary
Founded in: 1897

Fostoria

Fostoria Federation of Musicians, Local
  121
118 West Center Street
Fostoria, OH 44830
Tel: 419-435-5437
Address Inquiries to: Ernest Duffield,

President
  John L. Peck, Secretary
Founded in: 1907

Greenville

Greenville Musicians' Association
Post Office Box 73
Greenville, OH 45331
Tel: 513-548-6714
Address Inquiries to: Richard Locke,
  President
  Ralph T. Plessinger, Secretary
Founded in: 1926

Lima

Lima Federation of Musicians
320 West Market Street
Lima, OH 45801
Tel: 419-228-0045
Address Inquiries to: Donald Lippincott,
  President
  Ed McElderry, Secretary
Founded in: 1910

Lorain

Musicians' Union, Local 146
2601 Eastlawn Avenue
Lorain, OH 44052
Tel: 216-288-0408
Address Inquiries to: Vince Perrier, President
  Pete Galanic, Secretary
Founded in: 1901

Mansfield

Musicians' Protective Association, Local
  159
161 Hilltop Road
Mansfield, OH 44906
Tel: 419-529-2754
Address Inquiries to: Luis A. Mendez Jr.,
  President
  'Eddie' Chiudioni, Secretary
Founded in: 1901

Marietta

Musicians' Protective Union, Local 179
102 Gates Street
Marietta, OH 45750
Tel: 614-374-5473
Address Inquiries to: Donald Shafer,
  President
  Dick Goddard, Secretary
Founded in: 1903

Mentor

Lake and Geauga County Federation of
  Musicians
7621 Chillicothe Road
Mentor, OH 44060
Tel: 216-255-2628
Address Inquiries to: Ken Fleckenstein,
  President
  Roger K. Kraft, Secretary
Founded in: 1939

Middletown

Musicians' Protective Union
Post Office Box 1175
Middletown, OH 45042
Tel: 513-423-6854
Address Inquiries to: Robert C. Farmer,
  President
  Garwood Wells, Secretary
Founded in: 1903

Mount Vernon

Mount Vernon Musicians' Association
111 Miller Avenue
Mount Vernon, OH 43050
Tel: 614-397-4302
Address Inquiries to: F. William Fetters,
  President
  Doris F. Moran, Secretary
Founded in: 1935

Newark

Newark Federation of Musicians, Local
  122
459 Courtney Drive
Newark, OH 43055
Tel: 614-366-1757
Address Inquiries to: Lawrence Griffin,
  President
  Mrs. Nora Mae Huffman, Secretary
Founded in: 1900

Piqua

Piqua Musicians' Association
1201 Park Avenue
Piqua, OH 45356
Tel: 513-773-2665
Address Inquiries to: Kenneth K. McMaken,
  President
  Frand W. Neville Jr., Secretary
Founded in: 1918

Salem

Salem Federation of Musicians, Local 222
Route 4
Salem, OH 44460
Tel: 216-332-1281
Address Inquiries to: Gerald Goddard,
  President
  Michael Kupinski, Secretary
Founded in: 1902

Sandusky

Sandusky Musicians' Association
Post Office Box 2224
Sandusky, OH 44870
Tel: 419-625-1499
Address Inquiries to: Frank Fosco, President
Robert E. Frand, Secretary
Founded in: 1938

Springfield

Springfield Musicians' Association, Local
  160
1500 Malden Avenue
Springfield, OH 45504
Tel: 513-390-0618; 513-390-2351
Address Inquiries to: Robert A. Ware,
  President

John R. Dessinger, Secretary
Founded in: 1901

Steubenville

Steubenville Musicians' Association, Local
223
507 First National Bank Building
Steubenville, OH 43952
Tel: 614-282-5212
Address Inquiries to: Paul Paolisso, President
W. C. Powelson, Secretary
Founded in: 1902

Toledo

Toledo Federation of Musicians, Local
15-286
308 Hillcrest Hotel
Toledo, OH 43624
Tel: 419-243-2017
Address Inquiries to: Steve Chromik,
President
Randall J. Richie, Secretary
Founded in: 1896

Warren

Warren Federation of Musicians, Local
118
3207 Youngstown Road SE
Warren, OH 44484
Tel: 216-369-6745
Address Inquiries to: Roy C. Billion,
President
Rudy Sulek, Secretary
Founded in: 1900

Wheelersburg

Musicians' Protective Union
Route 5
Wheelersburg, OH 45694
Tel: 614-574-6756
Address Inquiries to: Gary Billups, President
Edwards Hughes, Secretary
Founded in: 1929

Youngstown

Youngstown Federation of Musicians,
Local 86-242
2520 South Avenue
Youngstown, OH 44502
Tel: 216-788-8451
Address Inquiries to: Herbert MacPherson,
President
Danny Barber, Secretary
Founded in: 1898

Zanesville

Musicians' Protective Association, Local 54
1030 Richey Road
Zanesville, OH 43701
Tel: 614-452-5691
Address Inquiries to: Clarence E. Shirer,
President
Paul Mitter, Secretary
Founded in: 1897

OKLAHOMA
Bartlesville

Musicians' Union
4421 Woodland Drive
Bartlesville, OK 74003
Tel: 918-333-2054
Address Inquiries to: Don Berger, President
C.H. VanSant, Secretary
Founded in: 1911

Tulsa

Tulsa Musicians' Protective Association,
Local 94
5525 East 32nd Place
Tulsa, OK 74105
Tel: 918-742-5097
Address Inquiries to: Jamie L. McIntosh,
President
Weymouth B. Young, Secretary
Founded in: 1906

OREGON
Klamath Falls

Musicians' Protective Union
303 Acosta Street
Klamath Falls, OR 97601
Tel: 503-882-1795
Address Inquiries to: Steven G. Battis,
President
W.R. 'Baldy' Evans, Secretary
Founded in: 1927

Medford

Medford Federation of Musicians
2722 East McAndrews Street
Medford, OR 97501
Tel: 503-772-2431
Address Inquiries to: Shirley G. Christensen,
President
Founded in: 1942

Pendleton

Musicians' Protective Union
Route 2, Box 258
Pendleton, OR 97801
Tel: 503-276-6220
Address Inquiries to: Bufford Kinnison,
President
Thomas C. Branstetter, Secretary
Founded in: 1952

Portland

American Federation of Television and
Radio Artists, (AFTRA)
111 American Bank Building
Portland, OR 97205

Musicians' Mutual Association, Local 99
325 North East 20th Avenue
Portland, OR 97232
Tel: 503-235-8791
Address Inquiries to: Joe Dardis, President
Robert L. Findley, Secretary
Founded in: 1899

PENNSYLVANIA
Allentown

Allentown Musicians' Association
Suite BBB, 44 South Fulton Street
Allentown, PA 18102
Tel: 215-432-0156
Address Inquiries to: Homer G. Schlenker Jr.,
President
Founded in: 1911

Altoona

Musical Association
212 27th Avenue
Altoona, PA 16602
Tel: 814-943-3220
Address Inquiries to: Richard Potter,
President
Loy W. Applenma, Secretary
Founded in: 1911

Belle Vernon

Charleroi Musical Society
1212 Monongahela Avenue
Belle Vernon, PA 15012
Tel: 412-929-7500
Address Inquiries to: William D. Fries,
President
Joseph G. Yadrick, Secretary
Founded in: 1912

Bethlehem

Musicians' Association
1529 Spring Street
Bethlehem, PA 18018
Tel: 215-866-8131
Address Inquiries to: George J. Kanuck,
President
Stephen P. Reisteter, Secretary
Founded in: 1916

Bradford

Musical Union, Local 84
1144 South Avenue
Bradford, PA 16701
Tel: 814-368-7421
Address Inquiries to: Michael Figula,
President
Raymond A. Arnold, Secretary
Founded in: 1898

Brookhaven

Musicians' Protective Union
Grant Plaza
Brookhaven, PA 19015
Tel: 215-874-7158
Address Inquiries to: Vincent Caruso,
President
Edward Grueninger, Secretary
Founded in: 1908

Butler

Butler Federation of Musicians, Local 188
142 Remil Drive
Butler, PA 16001
Tel: 412-287-1591
Address Inquiries to: John J. Chiprean Jr.,
President
Norman E. Gour, Secretary

Founded in: 1902

Canonsburg

Canonsburg Federation of Musicians
545 Ridge Avenue
Canonsburg, PA 15317
Tel: 412-745-2814
Address Inquiries to: Lee Barrett, President
Val Kerin, Secretary
Founded in: 1914

Carbondale

Musicians' Protective Union, Local 130
87 Belmont
Carbondale, PA 18407
Tel: 717-282-3155
Address Inquiries to: Bernard Cerra,
    President
    Egidio S. Lemoncelli, Secretary
Founded in: 1901

Coaldale

Musicians' Association
151 Fourth Street
Coaldale, PA 18218
Tel: 717-645-9484
Address Inquiries to: Wash King, President
John F. Davis, Secretary
Founded in: 1907

Cochranton

Meadville Musical Society
Road 2
Cochranton, PA 16314
Tel: 814-333-1104
Address Inquiries to: James Ried, President
Samuel Marks, Secretary
Founded in: 1917

Connellsville

Musical Society
512 West Murphy Avenue
Connellsville, PA 15425
Tel: 412-628-1530
Address Inquiries to: Amedeo Molinaro,
    President
    Charles E. Gross, Secretary
Founded in: 1905

Coopersburg

Musicians' Protective Union
Post Office Box 371
Coopersburg, PA 18036
Tel: 215-282-4476
Address Inquiries to: A. Richard Allem,
    President
    Everett Afflerbach, Secretary
Founded in: 1911

Delaware Water Gap

Musicians' Protective Union
Post Office Box 250
Delaware Water Gap, PA 18327
Tel: 717-421-1325
Address Inquiries to: Duane Walck, President
Phillip A. DeMilo Jr., Secretary
Founded in: 1925

Elizabethtown

Musicians' Protective Union
R.D. No. 4, Post Office Box 277
Elizabethtown, PA 17022
Tel: 717-684-7138
Address Inquiries to: James M. Smith Jr.,
    President
    John P. Metzer
Founded in: 1903

Ellwood City

Musicians' Protective Union
224 Spring Avenue
Ellwood City, PA 16117
Tel: 412-758-5991
Address Inquiries to: Charles Navolio,
    President
    E.W. Moncrief, Secretary
Founded in: 1910

Ephrata

Greater Lancaster Federation of Musicians
812 Pointview Avenue
Ephrata, Pa 17522
Tel: 717-733-3410
Address Inquiries to: Gerald S. Wingenroth,
    President
    Mrs. Jo Wingenroth, Secretary
Founded in: 1903

Erie

Musicians' Protective Association, Local 17
3103 Melrose Avenue
Erie, PA 16501
Tel: 814-864-5846
Address Inquiries to: Bernard F. Pacy,
    President
    William M. Fairgraves, Secretary
Founded in: 1896

Franklin

Musical Association, Local 61
604 Buffalo Street
Franklin, PA 16323
Tel: 814-432-5088
Address Inquiries to: William Snyder,
    President
    Fran Fry Jr., Secretary
Founded in: 1898

Freeland

Musicians' Protective Union
Road 1
Freeland, PA 18224
Tel: 717-636-0600
Address Inquiries to: Francis Carr, President
Emil E. Harakal, Secretary
Founded in: 1911

Greenville

Musicians' Protective Union
55 Rosedale Avenue
Greenville, PA 16125
Tel: 412-588-7604
Address Inquiries to: John Baird, President
Ronald C. Rohland, Secretary
Founded in: 1937

Hanover

Hanover Musicians' Association, Local 49
Post Office Box 448
Hanover, PA 17331
Tel: 717-637-7393
Address Inquiries to: Gary L. Urick, President
    William A. Sanders, Secretary
Founded in: 1917

Harrisburg

Musical Association, Local 269
1927 Paxton Street
Harrisburg, PA 17104
Tel: 717-234-8400
Address Inquiries to: Robert A. Cox,
    President
    Charles R. Morrison, Secretary
Founded in: 1903

Hazelton

Musicians' Protective Union, Local 139
408 West Green Street
Hazelton, PA 18201
Tel: 717-455-5160
Address Inquiries to: Joseph Buglio,
    President
    Peter M. Notaro, Secretary
Founded in: 1901

Indiana

Indiana Musicians' Association, Local 251
367 Walnut Street
Indiana, PA 15701
Tel: 412-463-0814
Address Inquiries to: Kenneth F. Maurey,
    President
    Enrico Vincent Colonna, Secretary
Founded in: 1937

Johnstown

Musical Society, Local 41
621 Goucher Street
Johnstown, PA 15905
Tel: 814-536-0751
Address Inquiries to: Sam S. Signorino,
    President
    Harry W. Anderson, Secretary
Founded in: 1913

Kittanning

Musicians' Union
Road Number 1
Kittanning, PA 16201
Tel: 412-543-4359
Address Inquiries to: Joseph A. Alese,
    President
    Ethel Fahlor, Secretary
Founded in: 1912

Leighton

Carbon Musical Society
450 South 7th Street
Leighton, PA 18235
Tel: 215-377-2350
Address Inquiries to: Paul David, President
Donald F. Mantz, Secretary
Founded in: 1939

Minersville

Portsville Musical Society
B & Pottsville Streets
Minersville, PA 17954
Tel: 717-544-4589
Address Inquiries to: John J. Direnzo,
    President
    F. John Tucci, Secretary
Founded in: 1914

New Brighton

Musicians' Protective Union, Local 82
205 Craig Street
New Brighton, PA 15066
Tel: 412-774-2602
Address Inquiries to: Andrew A. Mignanelli,
    President
    Steve E. Blanda
Founded in: 1901

New Castle

Musical Union, Local 27
321 Edison Avenue
New Castle, PA 16101
Tel: 412-654-5182
Address Inquiries to: Mike Isabella, President
Michael Phillips, Secretary
Founded in: 1900

New Kensington

Mew Kensington Musical Society
Sons of Italy Building
1010 Fifth Avenue
New Kensington, PA 15068
Tel: 412-335-6651
Address Inquiries to: Joseph S. DeSimone,
    President
    Edmond P. Manganelli, Secretary
Founded in: 1912

Norristown

Norristown Musicians' Association
Hamilton Hall
Norristown, PA 19401
Tel: 215-272-6210
Address Inquiries to: William S. March,
    President
    Sal L. Nave, Secretary
Founded in: 1903

Philadelphia

American Federation of Television and
    Radio Artists, (AFTRA)
1405 Locust Street, Suite 811
Philadelphia, PA 19102

Philadelphia Musical Society, Local 77
120 North 18th Street
Philadelphia, PA 19103
Tel: 215-567-1071
Address Inquiries to: Lee Herman, President
Tibby Tiberini, Secretary
Founded in: 1903

Screen Actors Guild, (SAG)
1405 Locust Street, Number 811
Philadelphia, PA 19102

Pittsburgh

American Federation of Television and
    Radio Artists, (AFTRA)
1000 Band Tower
Pittsburgh, PA 15222

Pittsburgh Musical Society, Local 60-471
709 Forbes Avenue
Pittsburgh, PA 15219
Tel: 412-281-1822
Address Inquiries to: Herbert I. Osgood,
    President
    Joseph E. Schafer, Secretary
Founded in: 1897

Pottstown

Musicians' Protective Association, Local
    211
170 Mount Vernon Street
Pottstown, PA 19464
Tel: 215-323-3136
Address Inquiries to: Frank Buttaro, President
    Daniel Lutz, Secretary
Founded in: 1902

Punxsutawney

Musicians' Protective Union
Lewis Street
Punxsutawney, PA 15767
Tel: 814-938-5854
Address Inquiries to: John Parise, President
Michael A. Catanzarito, Secretary
Founded in: 1919

Reading

Reading Musical Society, Local 135
214 West 46th Street
Reading, PA 19606
Tel: 215-779-1651
Address Inquiries to: Vernon A. Deysher Jr.,
    President
    Daniel W. Youse, Secretary
Founded in: 1901

Ridgway

Ridgway Musicians' Association
445 Montomorenci Road
Ridgway, PA 15853
Tel: 814-776-1203
Address Inquiries to: Richard G. Butterfuss,
    President
    Frank S. Frederico, Secretary
Founded in: 1946

Sayre

Musicians' Protective Association
613 North Wilbur Avenue
Sayre, PA 18840
Tel: 717-888-0569
Address Inquiries to: Thomas Sandroni,
    President
    Charles A. Hammond, Secretary
Founded in: 1913

Scranton

Musicians' Protective Association, Local
    120
1110 Grandview Street
Scranton, PA 18509

Tel: 717-342-4366; 717-344-5656
Address Inquiries to: Irving T. Miller,
    President
    James Parette, Secretary
Founded in: 1900

Shamokin

Musicians' Protective Association
2106 Stetler Drive
Shamokin, PA 17872
Tel: 717-648-0883
Address Inquiries to: Charles L. Verano,
    President
    William Porto, Secretary
Founded in: 1910

Sharon

Sharon Musicians' Association, Local 187
840 Smith Avenue
Sharon, PA 16147
Tel: 412-981-5760
Address Inquiries to: Joseph Cantelupe,
    President
    Tony Antonino, Secretary
Founded in: 1902

Shenandoah

Musicians' Protective Union, Local 170
102 West Laurel Street
Shenandoah, PA 17976
Tel: 717-462-3075
Address Inquiries to: John F. Dempsey,
    President
    Anthony Liscusky, Secretary
Founded in: 1912

State College

State College Area Musicians' Association
1151 William Street
State College, PA 16801
Tel: 814-237-2689
Address Inquiries to: Elmer C. Wareham Jr.,
    President
    Hubert H. Haugh, Secretary
Founded in: 1913

Sunbury

Sunbury Federation of Musicians
506 Catawissa
Sunbury, PA 17801
Tel: 717-286-9449
Address Inquiries to: August F. Korten,
    President
    Ray M. Fulmer, Secretary
Founded in: 1912

Uniontown

Uniontown Musical Society
121 Mayflower Drive
Uniontown, PA 15401
Tel: 412-438-7587
Address Inquiries to: George Salay, President
    Pete P. Porreca, Secretary
Founded in: 1912

Vandergrift

Vandergrift Musical Society
131 Sherman Avenue
Vandergrift, PA 15690
Tel: 412-845-7273
Address Inquiries to: Carl Spaniel, President
Leo Allera, Secretary
Founded in: 1937

Washington

Wahington Musical Society, Local 277
865 William Street
Washington, PA 15301
Tel: 412-225-9790
Address Inquiries to: James Hill, President
John W. McCreight, Secretary
Founded in: 1903

Wilkes-Barre

Musicians' Protective Union, Local 140
17 Grove Street
Wilkes-Barre, PA 18702
Tel: 717-822-4426
Address Inquiries to: Alfred R. Seidel,
President
Anthony F. Kane Jr., Secretary
Founded in: 1901

York

Musicians' Protective Union
925 North Briar Drive
York, PA 17404
Tel: 717-764-5807
Address Inquiries to: Donald R. Miller,
President
Clair H. Brenner, Secretary
Founded in: 1908

Yukon

Greensburg Musical Society
Post Office Box 67
Yukon, PA 15698
Tel: 412-834-5596
Address Inquiries to: John Faulk, President
Julius Falcon, Secretary
Founded in: 1903

RHODE ISLAND

Newport

Newport Federation of Musicians
235 Eustis Avenue
Newport, RI 02840
Tel: 401-849-3649
Address Inquiries to: Sylvia Stoun, President
Founded in: 1914

Providence

Federation of Musicians, Local 198-457
528 Pleasant Valley Parkway
Providence, RI 02098
Tel: 401-751-2717
Address Inquiries to: Joseph Conte, President
Aime Triangolo, Secretary
Founded in: 1902

Woonsocket

Musicians' Protective Union, Local 262
241 Winter Street
Woonsocket, RI 02895
Tel: 401-762-5146
Address Inquiries to: Chester J. Krajewski,
President
Paul Kazanowski, Secretary
Founded in: 1903

SOUTH CAROLINA

Aiken

Augusta Federation of Musicians
219 Marion Street Southeast
Aiken, SC 29801
Tel: 803-648-7276
Address Inquiries to: Robert E. Maxwell,
President
James A. Kitchings, Secretary
Founded in: 1954

Charleston

Charleston Federation of Musicians
140 Darlington Avenue
Charleston, SC 29403
Tel: 803-722-0936
Address Inquiries to: John D. Droze,
President
Willard Bolchoz, Secretary
Founded in: 1908

SOUTH DAKOTA

Sioux Falls

Musicians' Unions, Local 114
720 South Grange Avenue
Sioux Falls, SD 57104
Tel: 605-338-5818
Address Inquiries to: Robert Niblick,
President
Leonard E. Martinek, Secretary
Founded in: 1906

Yankton

Musicians' Association, Local 255
606 East 17th Street
Yankton, SD 57078
Tel: 605-665-2488
Address Inquiries to: Harry C. Turen,
President
Rex Hays, Secretary
Founded in: 1936

TENNESSEE

Chattanooga

Chattanooga Musicians' Union, Local 80
Memorial Auditorium
Chattanooga, TN 37402
Tel: 615-266-1725; 615-266-5918
Address Inquiries to: Jimmy Tawater,
President
J. R. (Bob) Watkins

Founded in: 1905

Jackson

Jackson Federation of Musicians
140 Highland
Jackson, TN 38301
Tel: 901-427-8348
Address Inquiries to: James Allen, President
James Petty, Secretary
Founded in: 1938

Kingsport

Musicians' Association
201 McTeer Drive
Kingsport, TN 37660
Tel: 615-246-6351
Address Inquiries to: Charles Goodwin,
President
Rudolph Brinkley, Secretary
Founded in: 1938

Knoxville

Musicians' Protective Association
3104 North Broadway, #22C
Knoxville, TN 37917
Tel: 615-687-8350
Address Inquiries to: G.W. Collins, President
AL Smith, Secretary
Founded in: 1910

Memphis

Memphis Federation of Musicians, Local
71
2282 Young Avenue
Memphis, TN 38104
Tel: 901-272-1746
Address Inquiries to: Bob Taylor, President
Russ Spotswood, Secretary
Founded in: 1898

Nashville

American Federation of Television and
Radio Artists, (AFTRA)
1012 17th Avenue South
Nashville, TN 37212

Association of Musicians, Local 257
Post Office Box 120399
Nashville, TN 37212
Tel: 615-244-9514
Address Inquiries to: Johnny DeGeorge,
President
C. L. 'Dutch' Gorton, Secretary
Founded in: 1902

TEXAS

Amarillo

Amarillo Federation of Musicians
2608 Northwest 2nd Avenue
Amarillo, TX 79106
Tel: 806-374-2532
Address Inquiries to: Richard McMillen,
President
John D. Roberts, Secretary
Founded in: 1913

Austin

Austin Federation of Musicians
302 West 15th, Suite 204
Austin, TX 78701
Tel: 512-476-6798
Address Inquiries to: Leon Grizzard,
  President
  Randy McCall, Secretary
Founded in: 1907

Corpus Christi

Corpus Christi Musicians' Association
326 Dolphin Place
Corpus Christi, TX 78411
Tel: 512-852-4128
Address Inquiries to: Edward Galvan,
  President
  Mrs. Billie Ferrell, Secretary
Founded in: 1939

Dallas

American Federation of Television and
  Radio Artists (AFTRA)
3220 Lemmon Avenue, #102
Dallas, TX 75204

Dallas Federation of Musicians, Local 147
2829 West North Highway 235
Dallas, TX 75220
Tel: 214-358-4447
Address Inquiries to: Richard B. Cole,
  President and Secretary
Founded in: 1901

Screen Actors Guild, (SAG)
3220 Lemmon Avenue, #102
Dallas, TX 75204

El Paso

El Paso Federation of Musicians
10288 Saigon Drive
El Paso, TX 79925
Tel: 915-859-7982
Address Inquiries to: John T. Bracey,
  President
  Robert H.W. Booth, Secretary
Founded in: 1907

Fort Worth

Musicians Association, Local 72
3458 Blue Bonnet Circle
Fort Worth, TX 76109
Tel: 817-927-8478
Address Inquiries to: Ken Foeller, President
  and Secretary
Founded in: 1898

Galveston

Musicians' Protective Association, Local 74
1309 Marine
Galveston, TX 77550
Tel: 713-763-3754
Address Inquiries to: R. S. Graunard,
  President
  Carlos Pena, Secretary
Founded in: 1898

Houston

Professional Musicians' Association, Local
  65
609 Chenevert
Houston, TX 77003
Tel: 713-236-8676
Address Inquiries to: E. C. Holland, President
  Don Cannon, Secretary
Founded in: 1897

Knickerbocker

Musicians' Protective Union
Post Office Box 681
Knickerbocker, TX 76939
Tel: 915-653-2690
Address Inquiries to: Calvin Bell, President
  Bill Aylor, Secretary
Founded in: 1947

Port Neches

Professional Musicians' Association
2314 3rd Street
Port Neches, TX 77651
Tel: 713-727-3393
Address Inquiries to: Larry Pulliam, President
  Lowell Benoit, Secretary
Founded in: 1916

San Antonia

Musicians' Society, Local 23
233 Zephyr Drive
San Antonia, TX 78239
Tel: 512-227-3582
Address Inquiries to: Don Kraft, President
  Ishamel Gonzalez, Secretary
Founded in: 1897

Waco

Waco Musicians' Association
8918 Valley Brook Circle
Waco, TX 76710
Tel: 817-772-7929
Address Inquiries to: Shep Barrier, President
  John H. Vanston, Secretary
Founded in: 1903

UTAH

Ogden

Musicians' Protective Union
1473 Lewis Street
Ogden, UT 84404
Tel: 801-393-9558
Address Inquiries to: Ronald K. Nichols,
  President
  Jeff W. Benson, Secretary
Founded in: 1913

Provo

Musicians Protective Union, Local 272
2701 North 700 East
Provo, UT 84601
Tel: 801-377-0857
Address Inquiries to: Don L. Earl, President
  Robert H. Bird, Secretary
Founded in: 1946

Salt Lake City

Federated Musicians, Local 104
3714 East 3800 South
Salt Lake City, UT 84109
Tel: 801-581-8707
Address Inquiries to: Loel T. Hepworth,
  President
  David J. Wilkins, Secretary
Founded in: 1901

VERMONT

Burlington

Burlington Musicians' Association
106 Heinberg Road
Burlington, VT 05401
Tel: 802-862-9858
Address Inquiries to: Edwin Arey, President
  Robert J. Mario, Secretary
Founded in: 1946

VIRGINIA

Covington

Musicians' Protective Union
Post Office Box 689
Covington, VA 24426
Tel: 703-962-3346
Address Inquiries to: Roy U. Arritt, President
  Gary Williams, Secretary
Founded in: 1946

Lynchburg

Musicians' Protective Union, Local 157
3068 Forest Hills Circle
Lynchburg, VA 24501
Tel: 804-845-8794; 804-845-2383
Address Inquiries to: Richard Reed, President
  Ted Simopoulos, Secretary
Founded in: 1937

Norfolk

Norfolk Musicians' Association, Local 125
Post Office Box 201
Norfolk, VA 23501
Tel: 804-622-8095
Address Inquiries to: Bob Sawyer, President
  Herb Sebren, Secretary
Founded in: . 1900

Richmond

Musical Protective Association, Local 123
2006 Dresden Road
Richmond, VA 23229
Tel: 804-270-7963
Address Inquiries to: Robert C. Barker,
  President
  James A. Whitely, Secretary
Founded in: 1900

Roanoke

Musicians' Protective Union, Local 165
3101 Tomaranne Avenue, South West
Roanoke, VA 24018
Tel: 703-342-8933
Address Inquiries to: E. E. Wiggins, President

Adrian Willis, Secretary
Founded in: 1937

Yorktown

Peninsula Musical Society, Local 199
104 Seven Hollis Drive
Yorktown, VA 23692
Tel: 804-380-1022
Address Inquiries to: Edward V. D'Alfonso,
  President
  W. H. Smith, Secretary
Founded in: 1921

WASHINGTON

Aberdeen

Musicians' Protective Union, Local 236
724 Terrace
Aberdeen, WA 98520
Tel: 206-532-0583
Address Inquiries to: Charles Fradenberg,
  President
  R. J. Brawley, Secretary
Founded in: 1902

Everett

Musicians' Association, Local 184
4801 Seahurst
Everett, WA 98203
Tel: 206-259-3802
Address Inquiries to: R. E. Draper, President
Mrs. Janis C. Fifield, Secretary
Founded in: 1902

Ferndale

Musicians' Protective Union
5519 Poplar Drive
Ferndale, WA 98248
Tel: 206-733-2670
Address Inquiries to: Lew Nordby, President
Robert J. Wood, Secretary
Founded in: 1935

Kent

Musicians' Protective Union
10820 South East 231st
Kent, WA 98031
Tel: 206-852-6695
Address Inquiries to: Donald L. McLean,
  President
  Mrs. Evelyn Allyn, Secretary
Founded in: 1914

Longview

Musicians' Mutual Protective Union
Post Office Box 1852
Longview, WA 98632
Tel: 206-423-5010
Address Inquiries to: Jarrett Dailey, President
Gerald E. Philbrook, Secretary
Founded in: 1923

Oak Harbor

Musicians' Association of Skagit
Post Office Box 46
Oak Harbor, WA 98277
Tel: 206-424-4995

Address Inquiries to: Dean Davis, President
Lawrence M. Seitz, Secretary
Founded in: 1907

Olympia

Musicians' Association, Local 124
119 Capitol Way
Olympia, WA 98501
Tel: 206-357-5220
Address Inquiries to: Lyall Smith, President
Deena Tveden, Secretary
Founded in: 1936

Pasco

Tri-City Musicians Association
521 West Sylvester Street
Pasco, WA 99301
Tel: 509-547-6698
Address Inquiries to: Wayne E. McGuffin,
  President
  Ted O. Myrick, Secretary
Founded in: 1950

Seattle

American Federation of Television and
  Radio Artists, (AFTRA)
158 Thomas Street
Seattle, WA

Musicians' Association, Local 76
2620 Third Avenue
Seattle, WA 98121
Tel: 206-623-0025
Address Inquiries to: Chet Ramage, President
  Carl H. Challstedt, Secretary
Founded in: 1898

Spokane

Musicians' Association, Local 105
4025 South Lee Street
Spokane, WA 99203
Tel: 509-448-0627
Address Inquiries to: Joseph T. Baker,
  President
  Richard Q. Totusek, Secretary
Founded in: 1900

Sumner

Musicians' Association, Local 117
Route 5, Post Office Box 759
Sumner, WA 98390
Tel: 206-863-2144
Address Inquiries to: George A. Doll,
  President
  Robert L. Colombini Jr., Secretary
Founded in: 1900

Walla Walla

Musicians' Protective Union
847 Bowman
Walla Walla, WA 99362
Tel: 509-525-7576
Address Inquiries to: Darrell P. Ovens,
  President
  Carl B. Brittain, Secretary
Founded in: 1937

Yakima

Musicians' Protective Union
206 South 16th Avenue
Yakima, WA 98902
Tel: 509-453-9813
Address Inquiries to: John R. Schactler,
  President
  Bill Davison, Secretary
Founded in: 1907

WEST VIRGINIA

Bluefield

Bluefield Federation of Musicians
304 Jones Street
Bluefield, WV 24701
Tel: 304-327-8743
Address Inquiries to: E.G. Watkins, President
John R. Palmer, Secretary
Founded in: 1940

Bridgeport

Clarksburg Federation of Musicians
320 Front Street
Bridgeport, WV 26330
Tel: 304-842-3088
Address Inquiries to: Sam B. Folio, President
William T. Kirkpatrick, Secretary
Founded in: 1911

Charleston

Charleston Musicians' Union, Local 136
1562 Kanawha Boulevard, East
Charleston, WV 25311
Tel: 304-346-9693; 304-343-7778
Address Inquiries to: Ned H. Guthrie,
  President
  Frank C. Thompson, Secretary
Founded in: 1907

Fairmont

Fairmont Federation of Musicians
1627 Otlahurst Drive
Fairmont, WV 26554
Tel: 304-366-1635
Address Inquiries to: Walter Kloc, President
Mrs. Edna D. Kopp, Secretary
Founded in: 1911

Huntington

Musicians' Protective Union
2711 Emmons Avenue
Huntington, WV 25702
Tel: 304-697-2617
Address Inquiries to: Stanley Husk, President
Max Whitley, Secretary
Founded in: 1906

Morgantown

Musicians' Protective Union
1502 Eastern Avenue
Morgantown, WV 26505
Tel: 304-599-0793
Address Inquiries to: Richard E. Powell,
  President
  Kennith Vance, Secretary
Founded in: 1918

Moundsville

Musicians Protective Union
3 Maple Avenue
Moundsville, WV 26041
Tel: 304-845-3796
Address Inquiries to: J. Ryland Cox, President
Harold Kirby, Secretary
Founded in: 1935

Parkersburg

Musicians' Mutual Protective Union, Local
259
104 Bliarwood Drive, Liberty Hills
Parkersburg, WV 26101
Tel: 304-422-1331
Address Inquiries to: Richard Leonhart,
President
Miss Margaret A. Alexander, Secretary
Founded in: 1902

Wheeling

Wheeling Musical Society, Local 142
17th and Jacobs Streets
Wheeling, WV 26003
Tel: 304-233-0620
Address Inquiries to: Logan C. Daugherty,
President
L. F. Meyers, Secretary
Founded in: 1901

WISCONSIN

Algoma

Kewaunee Federation of Musicians
320 Church Street
Algoma, WI 54201
Tel: 414-845-5021
Address Inquiries to: Gene LeBotte, President
Melvin A. Gaedtke, Secretary
Founded in: 1938

Appleton

Musicians' Protective Association
1231 East Hanson Drive
Appleton, WI 54911
Tel: 414-734-0021
Address Inquiries to: Raymond P. Brock,
President
Gary Laabs, Secretary
Founded in: 1903

Beloit

Beloit Musicians' Association, Local 183
1715 Strong Avenue
Beloit, WI 53511
Tel: 608-362-8356
Address Inquiries to: Pete Galiano, President
Vernard Saborn, Secretary
Founded in: 1902

Bonduel

Shawnano Federation of Musicians, Local
227
301 State Street
Bonduel, WI 54107
Tel: 715-758-8944
Address Inquiries to: Willard Kumm,

President
Frank Cheyka, Secretary
Founded in: 1939

Eau Claire

Chippewa Valley Musicians' Association
2915 North Ninth Street
Eau Claire, WI 54701
Tel: 715-832-1937
Address Inquiries to: Roy Rankin, President
Mrs. Marion Peplau, Secretary
Founded in: 1903

Fond Du Lac

Fond du Lac Musicians' Association
261 East Bank Street
Fond Du Lac, WI 54935
Tel: 414-921-9248
Address Inquiries to: AL Buerger, President
James Sabel, Secretary
Founded in: 1903

Green Bay

Green Bay Federation of Musicians, Local
205
2330 Libal Street
Green Bay, WI 54301
Tel: 414-432-2467
Address Inquiries to: Fred J. Orland,
President
Richard J. Conley, Secretary
Founded in: 1902

Janesville

Janesville Musicians' Association
27 South Randall Avenue
Janesville, WI 53545
Tel: 608-754-7474
Address Inquiries to: John Kerr, President
Ilene Kerr, Secretary
Founded in: 1903

Kenosha

Kenosha Federation of Musicians, Local 59
711 Washington Road
Kenosha, WI 53140
Tel: 414-652-1465
Address Inquiries to: Joe Perry, President
Ben Strobl, Secretary
Founded in: 1897

La Crosse

Musicians' Association, Local 201
2315 Losey Blvd., South
La Crosse, WI 54601
Tel: 608-788-6592
Address Inquiries to: Kenneth G. Bye,
President
Edgar Wuensch, Secretary
Founded in: 1902

Lena

Musicians' Protective Association
Route 2
Lena, WI 54139
Tel: 414-834-5153
Address Inquiries to: Mr. Fay Hessil,
President
Joe Melton, Secretary

Founded in: 1939

Madison

Madison Musicians' Association
222 South Hamilton
Madison, WI 53703
Tel: 608-238-3421
Address Inquiries to: Robert Ramsdell,
President
Robert Johnson, Secretary
Founded in: 1901

Manitowoc

Manitowoc Musicians' Association, Local
195
1511 Cherry Road
Manitowoc, WI 54220
Tel: 414-793-1235
Address Inquiries to: Arthur Nickels,
President
Clarence F. Doleysh, Secretary
Founded in: 1902

Marshfield

Musicians' Protective Union, Local 270
807 South Peach Street
Marshfield, WI 54449
Tel: 715-387-4928
Address Inquiries to: Ray Kraemer, President
Lynn Winch Jr., Secretary
Founded in: 1942

Menasha

Musicians' Protective Union, Local 182
342 Elm Street
Menasha, WI 54952
Tel: 414-722-5226
Address Inquiries to: Richard Remmel,
President
Mildred Yost, Secretary
Founded in: 1902

Milwaukee

Musicians' Association, Local 8
2200 North 45th Street
Milwaukee, WI 53208
Tel: 414-444-5234
Address Inquiries to: James Higgins,
President
Robert Couey, Secretary
Founded in: 1896

Monroe

Musicians' Protective Union, Local 243
1723 21st Street
Monroe, WI 53566
Tel: 608-325-5764
Address Inquiries to: Leo C. Peterson,
President
Stanley Neuberger, Secretary
Founded in: 1932

North Wisconsin Rapids

Central Wisconsin Musicians' Association
2830 37th Street
North Wisconsin Rapids, WI 54494
Tel: 715-421-0066
Address Inquiries to: George Middlecamp,
President

Wally Ives, Secretary
Founded in: 1919

Oshkosh

Oshkosh Musicians' Association, Local 46
3159 Omro Road
Oshkosh, WI 54901
Tel: 414-235-3461
Address Inquiries to: Frank Novotny,
  President
  Milton H. Galow, Secretary
Founded in: 1897

Racine

American Federation of Television and
  Radio Artists, (AFTRA)
WRJN, Sentry Broadcasting Co.
Racine, WI 53405

Musicians' Union, Local 42
1535 Melvin Avenue
Racine, WI 53405
Tel: 414-633-7922
Address Inquiries to: Norman Sill, President
John Shelby, Secretary
Founded in: 1897

Rhinelander

Musicians' Protective Associatton
Route 5, Box 1970
Rhinelander, WI 54501
Tel: 715-362-2787
Address Inquiries to: Howard Olsen,
  President
  Elmer R. Luebcke, Secretary
Founded in: 1937

Rock Springs

Association Musicians
Route No 1
Rock Springs, WI 53961
Tel: 608-522-4486
Address Inquiries to: Charles Pfaff, President
Ira E. Perry, Secretary
Founded in: 1937

Rothschild

Musicians' Protective Association
21 Brown Boulevard
Rothschild, WI 54474
Tel: 715-359-2505
Address Inquiries to: Garen Reich, President
Brian Seehafer, Secretary
Founded in: 1908

Sheboygan

Musicians' Association, Local 95
2505 North Avenue
Sheboygan, WI 53081
Tel: 414-452-4435
Address Inquiries to: Michael Brendze,
  President
  Mrs. Gloria Witte, Secretary
Founded in: 1899

Stevens Point

Musicians' Protective Union, Local 213
3004 North Campsite Drive
Stevens Point, WI 54481
Tel: 715-344-7550
Address Inquiries to: Herman Bella, President
  Anton C. Kunst, Secretary
Founded in: 1936

Sturgeon Bay

Sturgeon Bay Federation of Musicians
936 North Seventh Place
Sturgeon Bay, WI 54235
Tel: 414-743-6319
Address Inquiries to: Gerald Mickelson,
  President
  John W. Schack, Secretary
Founded in: 1943

Superior

Musicians' Protective Union, Local 260
1712 Logan Avenue
Superior, WI 54880
Tel: 715-394-5749
Address Inquiries to: Robert Skudstad,
  President
  Henry A. Koski, Secretary
Founded in: 1933

Watertown

Watertown Musicians' Association
Route 2
Watertown, WI 53094
Tel: 414-261-5839
Address Inquiries to: Will Eske, President
Eugene Kelm, Secretary
Founded in: 1937

Waukesha

Musicians' Association, Local 193
1228 Hickory Drive
Waukesha, WI 53186
Tel: 414-542-2425
Address Inquiries to: Mr. Laurel I. Houlihan,
  President
  Dale Nickel, Secretary
Founded in: 1901

Waupun

Musicians' Protective Union
306 Roundville Street
Waupun, WI 53963
Tel: 414-885-5548
Address Inquiries to: Carl Neuman, President
  George Freeman, Secretary
Founded in: 1935

WYOMING

Cheyenne

Musicians' Protective Union
5900 Townsend Place
Cheyenne, WY 82001
Tel: 307-632-2186
Address Inquiries to: Johnnie W. Grant,
  President
  Florence Miller, Secretary

Founded in: 1912

CANADA

Calgary, Alberta

Calgary Musicians' Association
630 Eighth Avenue SW, #703
Calgary, Alberta, Canada T2P 1G6
Tel: 403-264-4727
Address Inquiries to: John Mackie, President
Ray Petch, Secretary
Founded in: 1938

Vancouver, British Columbia

Musicians' Association, Local 145
The Dominion Bank Building
510-207 West Hastings Street
Vancouver, British Columbia, Canada V6B
  1J6
Tel: 604-684-1564
Address Inquiries to: Robert Reid, President
Founded in: 1901

Victoria, British Columbia

Victoria Musicians' Association, Local 247
1241 Topaz Avenue
Victoria, British Columbia, Canada V8T
  2N1
Tel: 604-382-7351
Address Inquiries to: Thomas Tucker,
  President
  Benjamin C. Manning, Secretary
Founded in: 1902

Brandon, Manitoba

Brandon Musicians' Association
1057 5th Street
Brandon, Manitoba, Canada
Tel: 204-727-8506
Address Inquiries to: W.F. Dinsdale, President
  R.A. Patterson, Secretary
Founded in: 1939

Winnipeg, Manitoba

Winnipeg Musicians' Association, Local
  190
409 Royal Tower, 504 Main Street
Winnipeg, Manitoba, Canada R3B 1B8
Tel: 204-WH3-4803
Address Inquiries to: David J. Jandrisch,
  President
  Joseph H. Karr, Secretary
Founded in: 1902

Halifax, Nova Scotia

Atlantic Federation of Musicians
6307 Chebucto Road
Halifax, Nova Scotia, Canada B3L 1K9
Tel: 902-422-6492
Address Inquiries to: Peter J. Power,
  President
  Ervin F. Street, Secretary
Founded in: 1938

Sidney, Nova Scotia

Cape Benton Musicians' Association
Post Office Box 1282
Sidney, Nova Scotia, Canada
Address Inquiries to: Ivan Melanson,
  President
  Eddie Parris, Secretary
Founded in: 1966

Brantford, Ontario

Brantford Musicians' Association
15 Mayflower Avenue
Brantford, Ontario, Canada N3R 1N9
Tel: 519-752-7973
Address Inquiries to: Albert Chowhan,
  President
  Howard G. Johnson, Secretary
Founded in: 1907

Chatham, Ontario

Chatham Federation of Musicians
14 Forest Street
Chatham, Ontario, Canada N71 1Z7
Tel: 519-352-3902
Address Inquiries to: Bill Neff, President
Bill Mankiss, Secretary
Founded in: 1951

Hamilton, Ontario

Hamilton Musicians' Guild
101 Iverness Court
Hamilton, Ontario, Canada L9C 1A6
Tel: 416-388-0140
Address Inquiries to: Samuel Taylor,
  President
  James H. Begg, Secretary
Founded in: 1903

Kingston, Ontario

Kingston Musicians' Union
18 ½ Division Street
Kingston, Ontario, Canada K7K 3Y9
Tel: 613-542-3732
Address Inquiries to: Brian Thrasher,
  President
  Richard Baldwin, Secretary
Founded in: 1937

London, Ontario

London Musician's Association
149 Wortley Road
London, Ontario, Canada N6C 3P4
Tel: 519-438-3870
Address Inquiries to: George Ross, President
Ron Shadbolt, Secretary
Founded in: 1903

Niagara Falls, Ontario

Niagara Falls Musicians' Association
5848 Main Street
Niagara Falls, Ontario, Canada L2G 5Z5
Tel: 416-357-4642
Address Inquiries to: Robert D. Keppy,
  President
  Robert F. Carpenter, Secretary
Founded in: 1933

North Bay, Ontario

North Bay Musicians' Association
2405 Queensway Road
North Bay, Ontario, Canada
Tel: 705-472-6966
Address Inquiries to: L.D. Barham, President
Norm Mauro, Secretary
Founded in: 1974

Ottawa, Ontario

District Federation of Musicians, Local 180
49 Bank Street
Ottawa, Ontario, Canada K2P 1Z2
Tel: 613-233-5301
Address Inquiries to: Edward Hall, President
Robert Langley, Secretary
Founded in: 1902

Peterbourough, Ontario

Federation of Musicians, Local 191
Route No. 1
Peterbourough, Ontario, Canada K9J 6X2
Tel: 705-292-7082
Address Inquiries to: Clifford Endicott,
  President
  Gary W. Warriner, Secretary
Founded in: 1902

Plainfield, Ontario

Belleville Federation of Musicians
Rural Route Number 1
Plainfield, Ontario, Canada K0K 2V0
Tel: 613-477-2003
Address Inquiries to: Charles Tilbrook,
  President
  J.R. Burchill, Secretary
Founded in: 1966

Sarnia, Ontario

Sarnia Musicians' Association
150 North Brock Street
Sarnia, Ontario, Canada N7T 5ZI
Tel: 519-337-5838
Address Inquiries to: John Chevalier,
  President
  Karl Starkman, Secretary
Founded in: 1912

St. Catharines, Ontario

Saint Catharines Musicians' Association
32 Canal Street
St. Catharines, Ontario, Canada L2N 4S9
Tel: 416-935-6673
Address Inquiries to: Ron Simpson, President
  Stephen Boyuk, Secretary
Founded in: 1903

Strafford, Ontario

Strafford Musicians' Association
52 Jones Street
Strafford, Ontario, Canada
Tel: 519-271-1362
Address Inquiries to: Norman M. Carnegie,
  President
  Ronald Coulthard, Secretary
Founded in: 1920

Thunder Bay, Ontario

Musicians' Protective Association
1206 Victoria Avenue
Thunder Bay, Ontario, Canada P7C 4X8
Tel: 807-623-0122
Address Inquiries to: Roy Coran, President
James Watts, Secretary
Founded in: 1938

Toronto, Ontario

Actors Equity Association, (AEA)
54 Shutter Street
Toronto, Ontario, Canada M5B 2G7

ACTRA
105 Carlton Street
Toronto, Ontario, Canada M5B 1M2
Tel: 416-977-6335
Address Inquiries to: Jack Gray

Associated Designers of Canada
600 Lonsdale Road
Apartment 8
Toronto, Ontario, Canada M5P 1R7
Tel: 416-652-3293
Address Inquiries to: Tom Doherty

Guild of Canadian Playwrights
The Writers Centre
24 Ryerson Avenue
Toronto, Ontario, Canada M5T 2P3
Tel: 416-868-6917
Address Inquiries to: Sheldon Rosen
Jane Adams

International Alliance of Theatrical Stage
  Employees
696 Yonge Street, #404
Toronto, Ontario, Canada M4Y 2A7
Tel: 416-923-4161
Address Inquiries to: Pat Travers

Toronto Musicians' Association, Local 149
101 Thorncliffe Park Drive
Toronto, Ontario, Canada M4H 1M1
Tel: 416-421-1020
Address Inquiries to: Sam Levine, President
Victor Bridgewater, Secretary
Founded in: 1901

Union, Ontario

Federation of Musicians
Rural Route Number 1
Union, Ontario, Canada N5R 3A8
Tel: 519-633-3730
Address Inquiries to: Eber J. Rice, President
Richard Butterwick, Secretary
Founded in: 1913

Waterloo, Ontario

Central Ontario Musicians' Association,
  Local 226
125 Union Street East
Waterloo, Ontario, Canada N2J 4E5
Tel; 519-744-4891
Address Inquiries to: John T. Conrad,
  President
  Douglas Janke, Secretary
Founded in: 1905

West Sudbury, Ontario

Sudbury Federation of Musicians
194 Elm Street
West Sudbury, Ontario, Canada P3C 1V3
Tel: 705-674-4241
Address Inquiries to: Con DiSalle, President
Carole Ann Lefebvre, Secretary
Founded in: 1969

Windsor, Ontario

Windsor Federation of Musicians
Suite 202, 744 Ouellette Avenue
Windsor, Ontario, Canada N9A 1C3
Tel: 519-258-2288
Address Inquiries to: Carm Adams, President
Stanley Grose, Secretary
Founded in: 1911

Montreal, Quebec

Association Des Directeurs de Theatre
1501 rue Jeanne Mance, Suite 951
Montreal, Quebec, Canada H2X 1Z9
Tel: 514-842-0923
Address Inquiries to: Mercedes Palomino

Union des Artistes
1290 rue St-Denis
Montreal, Quebec, Canada H2X 3J7
Tel: 514-862-7087
Address Inquiries to: Louise Deschatelets

Quebec City, Quebec

Quebec Musicians' Association, Local 119
1406 West Street
Quebec City, Quebec, Canada G1S 1X2
Tel: 418-688-1722
Address Inquiries to: Robert Vocelle,
   President
   Jean Pierre Gagnon, Secretary
Founded in: 1917

Regina, Saskatchewan

Regina Musicians' Association
1365 Princess Street
Regina, Saskatchewan, Canada S4T 3Y9
Tel: 306-527-3871
Address Inquiries to: William A. Winters,
   President
   N. Mosienko, Secretary
Founded in: 1912

Names & Addresses Index

A

Aaberg, Helen, Liberty County Arts Council Post Office Box 555 Chester, MT 59522 406-759-5476 (5)

Aaron, Stephen, Washington Theatre Club 1101 23rd Street Washington, DC 20037 202-296-2386 (16)

Abad, Marilyn, Gavilan College Department of Theatre 5055 Santa Teresa Boulevard Gilroy, CA 95020 408-847-1400 (4)

Abad, Marylyn C., Gavilan Joint Community College Department of Theatre Gilroy, CA 95020 408-842-8221 (4)

Abbey, Harold, Harold Abbey 165 West 57th Street New York, NY 10019 212-841-9678 (12)

Abbey, M., Falls Church Players 7124 Broad Street Falls Church, VA 22046 (16)

Aberg, Bob, Standard Photo Supply 43 East Chicago Avenue Chicago, IL 60611 312-440-4920 (15)

Aberson, Dan, Major Corporation 455 Academy Drive Northbrook, IL 60062 312-564-4550 (15)

Abraham, N., Gaslite Players 1807 Bayou Circle Bossier City, LA 71010 (16)

Acaster, Donald, Brock Centre For The Arts Brock University St. Catharines, Ontario, Canada L2S 3A1 416-684-3332; 416-684-6377 (16)

Ackhurst, Jerome, The Five Star Theatre of Alberta Post Office Box 722 Canmore, Alberta, Canada T0L 0M0 (16)

Ackley, Marilyn, Phoenix Council Hebron Academy Hebron, ME 04238 207-966-2100 (5)

Ackly, Robert, Loyola Marymount University Department of Theatre Los Angeles, CA 90045 213-642-2837 (4)

Acosta, Irene, Musicians' Protective Union 1303 Breckenridge Avenue San Leandro, CA 94579 415-483-5470 (18)

Adamo, John, Musicians' Association of San Diego County 1717 Morena Blvd San Diego, CA 92110 714-276-4324 (18)

Adams, Carm, Windsor Federation of Musicians Suite 202, 744 Ouellette Avenue Windsor, Ontario, Canada N9A 1C3 519-258-2288 (18)

Adams, Don, Duro-Test Light Center 347a Serramonte Plaza Daly City, CA 94015 415-994-3393 (15)

Adams, Fred C., Southern Utah State College Department of Theatre Arts 351 West Center Cedar City, UT 84750 801-856-3636 (4)

Adams, Fred C., Utah Shakespearean Festival Southern Utah State College 351 West Center Cedar City, UT 84720 801-586-7880, Administration Office;

801-586-7878, Box Office (9)

Adams, George R., Musicians' Guild, Local 203 7414 Indianapolis Blvd. Hammond, IN 46324 219-845-0666 (18)

Adams, J., Shakerag Players 705 Ridge Mineral Point, WI 53565 (16)

Adams, Jane, Guild of Canadian Playwrights The Writers Centre Toronto, Ontario, Canada M5T 2P3 416-868-6917 (18)

Adams, Miles, Musicians' Protective Union, Local 137 718 4th Street, North West Cedar Rapids, IA 52405 319-362-7902 (18)

Adams, Rachel, Lincoln Arts Council Pollard Road Lincoln, NH 03251 603-745-2289 (5)

Adamson, Frank, Interlake Festival Theatre 201 - 297 Smith Street Winnipeg, Manitoba, Canada (16)

Adler, C., Library Theatre 6805 Florida Street Chevy Chase, MD 20015 (16)

Adler, Richard, Richard Adler, Producer 870 United Nations Plaza New York, NY 10017 212-838-5907 (13)

Admanson, Eve, Bouwerie Lane Theatre 330 Bowery New York, NY 10012 212-677-0060 (8)

Adrian, William, William Adrian Agency 520 South Lake Drive Pasadena, CA 91101 213-681-5750 (2)

Afflerbach, Everett, Musicians' Protective Union Post Office Box 371 Coopersburg, PA 18036 215-282-4476 (18)

Ahart, John, Great American People Show Summer: Box 401; Off Season: Box 2178 Summer: Petersburg; Off Season: Champaign, IL Summer: 61675; Off Season: 61820 217-632-7755; 217-632-7754 (16)

Ahrens, Richard, Winona Musicians' Association 190 West Main Street Lewiston, MN 55952 507-523-3657 (18)

Aiken, Carl, Sturgis Art Council 201 North Nottawa Road Sturgis, MI 49091 616-651-8541 (5)

Albers, Everett, Chataqua Post Office Box 948 Bismarck, ND 701-663-1948 (9)

Albert, Allan, Berkshire Theatre Festival East Main Street Stockbridge, MA 01262 413-298-3618 (9)

Albert, Allan, Proposition Workshop 245 Hampshire Street Cambridge, MA 02139 617-661-1776 (16)

Albert, Marcel, Theatre Populaire C.P. 608 Caraquet, New Brunswick, Canada E0B 1K0 506-727-2712 (16)

Albright, Mrs. Bonnie, Musicians' Protective Union Post Office Box 85 Spalding, ID 83551 208-843-2486 (18)

Albright, James W., Musicians' Protective Union Post Office Box 85 Spalding, ID 83551 208-843-2486 (18)

Alegria, Alonso, Waynesburg College Department of Theatre Waynesburg, PA 15370 412-627-8191 (4)

Alese, Joseph A., Musicians' Union Road Number 1 Kittanning, PA 16201 412-543-4359 (18)

Alexalder, Mrs. Q.H., Pismo Beach Arts Council 1545 Hillcrest Street Arroyo Grande, CA 93420 (5)

Alexander, Andrew, Second City 110 Lombard Street Toronto, Ontario, Canada M5C 1M3 416-363-0461, Administrative; 416-363-1674, Box Office (16)

Alexander, Lawrence D., A and W Publishers Incorporated 95 Madison Avenue New York, NY 10016 212-725-4970 (14)

Alexander, Miss Margaret A., Musicians' Mutual Protective Union, Local 259 104 Bliarwood Drive, Liberty Hills Parkersburg, WV 26101 304-422-1331 (18)

Alexander, Ruth, Lon Morris College Department of Theatre Lon Morris College Station Jacksonville, TX 75766 214-586-2471 (4)

Alfred, Penny, Oklahoma Theatre Center 400 West Sheridan Oklahoma City, OK 73102 405-239-6884 (8)

Alkofer, David W., Frazier Auditorium Idaho State University Pocatello, ID 83201 208-236-3695 (8)

Allan, David, Minnetonka Theatre 14300 Excelsior Boulevard Minnetonka, MN 55343 (16)

Alleluka, Renata, Old Town Players 1718 North Northpark Chicago, IL 60614 312-645-0145 (16)

Allem, A. Richard, Musicians' Protective Union Post Office Box 371 Coopersburg, PA 18036 215-282-4476 (18)

Allen, Derek, Hammond Industries Post Office Box 2229 Toluca Lake Station, CA 91602 213-846-0500 (15)

Allen, Georgia K., Arts Council of Spartanburg County 385 South Spring Street Spartanburg, SC 29301 803-583-2776 (5)

Allen, Jacquie, Niagara Council of the Arts Box 937, Falls Station Niagara Falls, NY 14303 716-278-8881; 716-278-8147 (5)

Allen, James, Jackson Federation of Musicians 140 Highland Jackson, TN 38301 901-427-8348 (18)

Allen, Kermit, Rustic Barn Dinner Theatre Route 20, Lake Street Bloomingdale, IL 62220 (16)

Allen, Lucien, Theatre du Nouveau Monde 84 Ouest rue Ste-Catherine Montreal, Quebec, Canada H2X 1Z6 514-932-3137 (16)

Allen, Michael, Keystone Junior College Department of Theatre LaPlume, PA 18440 717-945-5141 (4)

Allen, Ralph G., University of Tennessee, Knoxville Department of Theatre Cumberland Avenue Knoxville, TN 37916 615-974-2591 (4)

Allen, Richard, Village Green Summer Playhouse 25A and Park Avenue Huntington, NY 11743 516-549-4065 (16)

Allera, Leo, Vandergrift Musical Society 131 Sherman Avenue Vandergrift, PA 15690 412-845-7273 (18)

Alley, V., Florence Little Theatre Box 583 Florence, SC 29501 (16)

Allison, John C., The Legend of Daniel Boone Post Office Box 365 Harrodsburg, KY 40330 (16)

Allsopp, Clarence, Clarence Allsopp 55 West 42 Street, Room 1547 New York, NY 10036 (12)

Allvin, Dr. Raynold, Oakland University Department of Theatre Rochester, MI 48063 313-377-2030 (4)

Allyn, Mrs. Evelyn, Musicians' Protective Union 10820 South East 231st Kent, WA 98031 206-852-6695 (18)

Alonzo, Cecil, The Alonzo Players 395 Clinton Avenue Brooklyn, NY 11238 718-622-9058 (16)

Alpaugh, John, Jamestown Area Arts Council Municipal Building Jamestown, NY 14701 (5)

Alpaugh, Robert, The Whole Theater Company 544 Bloomfield Avenue Montclair, NJ 07042 201-744-2996; 201-744-2989 (8)

Alpaugh, Robert, The Whole Theatre Company 544 Bloomfield Avenue Montclair, NJ 07042 201-744-2989; 201-744-2996 (16)

Alpert, Michael, Alpert/Levine Public Relations 1501 Broadway, Suite 1502 New York, NY 10036 212-354-5940 (12)

Alt, Raymond, Musicians' Protective Union 5301 Central Avenue NE, #807 Alburquerque, NM 87108 505-255-2069 (18)

Altbaum, Barry, Life-Like Products, Ltd. 24 Ronson Drive Rexdale, Ontario, Canada M9W 1B4 (15)

Alterman, Lois, Greenville Community Theater Scarsdale, NY 10583 914-472-0679 (16)

Althaver, Holly, Cass City Arts Council 4618 Kennebec Drive Cass City, MI 48726 517-872-3465 (5)

Altoni, Buddy, Buddy Altoni Esquire Incorporated 1680 North Vine Street New York, NY 90028 213-467-4939 (2)

Alvarado, Carlos, Carlos Alvarado Agency 8820 Sunset Boulevard Los Angeles, CA 90069 213-652-0272 (2)

Alvarer, Zenobia, Tampa Players Post Office Box 124 Tampa, FL 33601 813-877-2684 (16)

Alvarez, Luis, Luis Alvarez 11264 Sunshine Terrace Studio City, CA 91604 213-877-8779; 213-339-5907 (12)

Alvey, Merle M., Federation Of Musicians, Local 5 19161 Schaefer Highway Detroit, MI 48235 313-345-6200 (18)

Ambrose, Bonnie, Performing Arts Supply Company 10161 Harwin Drive, Suite 115 Houston, TX 77036 713-776-8900 (15)

Ames, Harold Jr., Three Continents Press 1346 Connecticut Avenue NW, Suite 1131 Washington, DC 20036 202-457-0288 (14)

Amico, Louis, North Shore Musicians' Association, Local 126 16 Jefferson Avenue Saugus, MA 01906 617-581-3550; 617-233-1366 (18)

Amos, Janet, Blyth Summer Festival Post Office Box 291 Blyth, Ontario, Canada N0M 1H0 519-523-9300 (16)

Anastasia, Tricia, Atlantic City Stage Lighting Company 28 Old Turnpike Pleasantville, NJ 08232 609-641-8447 (15)

Ancha, Robert F., Ancha Electronics 713 Edgebrook Champaign, IL 61820 217-398-6600; 217-398-6601 (15)

Andersen, R., Strobelite Company, Incorporated 10 East 23rd Street New York, NY 10010 212-677-9220 (15)

Anderson, Al, Brock Centre For The Arts Brock University St. Catharines, Ontario, Canada L2S 3A1 416-684-3332; 416-684-6377 (16)

Anderson, Al, Escarpment Theatre Co-Op Post Office Box 372 St. Catharines, Ontario, Canada L2R 6T7 416-682-8326; 416-684-6377 (16)

Anderson, Al, Carousel Players Post Office Box 372 St. Catherines, Ontario, Canada L2R 6T7 416-682-8326 (16)

Anderson, Dayna A., East Mississippi Junior College Department of Theatre Scooba, MS 39358 601-476-3421 (4)

Anderson, Donald, Lafayette Arts Council Post Office Box E Franconia, NH 03580 603-823-8056 (5)

Anderson, Donna, The Players Theatre 2811 West Magnolia Boulevard Burbank, CA 213-842-4755; 213-845-1193 (4)

Anderson, Donna, Players Theatre Company 2811 West Magnolia Boulevard Burbank, CA 91505 213-842-4755; 213-845-1193 (16)

Anderson, Edward, Miami-Dade Community College-North Campus Department of Theatre 11011 Southwest 104th Street Miami, FL 33176 305-596-1203 (4)

Anderson, Gary, Mitchell Fine Arts Center Transylvania University Lexington, KY 40508 606-233-8179 (8)

Anderson, Gilbert W., Topeka Musical Association, Local 36-665 1737 Randolph Topeka, KS 66614 913-234-4465 (18)

Anderson, Harry W., Musical Society, Local 41 621 Goucher Street Johnstown, PA 15905 814-536-0751 (18)

Anderson, Jay, Mille Lacs Community Theatre Isle, MN 56342 (16)

Anderson, Mary, Maysville Players Opera House 116 2nd Street Maysville, KY 41056 606-564-3666 (8)

Anderson, Nancy, Edina Theatre Company 555 West 70th Street Edina, MN 55435 (16)

Anderson, Paul J., Decor Electronics Corporation 4711 East Fifth Street Austin, TX 78702 512-385-0277 (15)

Anderson, Richard L., Michigan City Federation of Musicians 811 Greenwood Avenue Michigan City, IN 46360 219-874-5394 (18)

Anderson, Roger, Roger Anderson 635 Navarre Drive Stone Mountain, GA 30087 404-469-2864 (15)

Anderson, Terry, Civic Summer Theatre Post Office Box 169 Fairmont, MN 56031 (16)

Anderson, Thomas, Blackburn College Department of Theatre Carlinville, IL 62626 217-854-3231 (4)

Anderson, Walter C.J., Collegium Misericordia Theatre Arts College Dallas, PA 18612 717-675-2181 (4)

Anderson, Wendy L., Off-Broadway Musical Theatre 8955 47-½ Avenue North New Hope, MN 55428 (16)

Andre, James L., Blue Mountain College Department of Theatre Box 333 Blue Mountain, MS 38610 601-685-4711 (4)

Andrea, Guillermo de, Theatre Du Trident 975 Place d'Youville Quebec City, Quebec, Canada G1R 3P1 418-692-2202 (16)

Andrews, Jessica L., Foundation for the Extension and Development of the American Professional Theatre (FEDAPT) 165 West 46th Street, Suite 310 New York, NY 10036 212-869-9690 (5)

Andrews, John, Prichard Arts and Humanities Congress 4559 Old Citronelle Highway Prichard, AL 36613 (5)

Andrews, Mary, Clear Creek Country Theater Post Office Box 253 League City, TX 77573 713-332-CCCT (16)

Andrucki, Martin, Bates College Department of Theatre Lewiston, ME 04240 207-738-8772 (4)

Andrus-Hughes, Mr. Bruce, Tennessee Performing Arts Center 505 Deaderick Street Nashville, TN 37219 615-741-7975; 615-741-5633 (8)

Angel, B., Old Opera House Liberty and George Street Charlestown, WV 25414 (16)

Angel, Dr. Grover L., Madison County Arts Council Route 3, California Creek Road Mar Hills, NC 28754 704-689-4168 (5)

Angell, Barbara, Big Mama Poetry Theatre
1649 Coventry Road Cleveland, OH
44118 216-371-0441 (16)

Angelo, J., Plummer Mummers 1200
North Vista Los Angeles, CA 90046 (16)

Angelo, John, Pixie Players-Plummer Park
1300 North Vista Los Angeles, CA
90046 213-876-1725 (16)

Angerelli, Harry, Musicians' Protective
Association 609 North Court Eveleth,
MN 55734 218-744-5402 (18)

Angermeier, Thomas E., Repertory People
of Evansville Old Courthouse Evansville,
IN 47708 812-423-2060 (16)

Anglin, John D., Battle Creek Federation
of Musicians 1349 West Michigan
Avenue Battle Creek, MI 49016
616-962-3063 (18)

Anlauf, Celeste, Children's Theatre
Festival 6253 Hollywood Boulevard,
#222 Los Angeles, CA 90028 (16)

Annicciarico, Joseph, Concord Federation
of Musicians 1 Perkins Street Concord,
NH 03301 603-746-3937 (18)

Antisdel, Richard, The Theatre Service
Group 1792 Union Avenue Chipper Mill
Park Baltimore, MD 21211 301-467-1225
(15)

Antkiw, Ann, Phoenix Theatre 390 Dupont
Street Toronto, Ontario, Canada M5R
1V9 416-922-7835 (16)

Antonino, Tony, Sharon Musicians'
Association, Local 187 840 Smith
Avenue Sharon, PA 16147 412-981-5760
(18)

Antrum, R.H., Lane College Department
of Theatre 545 Lane Avenue Jackson,
TN 38301 901-424-4600 (4)

Appel, Libby, California Institute of the
Arts 24700 McBean Parkway Valencia,
CA 91355 805-255-1050 (4)

Applegarth, Robert, Dance Theater
Workshop 219 West 19th Street New
York, NY 10011 212-691-6500 (5)

Applegarth, Robert, DTW's Economy
Tires Theatre 219 West 19 Street New
York, NY 10011 212-924-0077 (16)

Applegett, J., Community Theatre 202
Cabrillo San Clemente, CA 92627 (16)

Applenma, Loy W., Musical Association
212 27th Avenue Altoona, PA 16602
814-943-3220 (18)

Appleton, David R., High Point College
Department of Theatre 933 Montlieu
Avenue High Point, NC 27262
919-885-5105 (4)

Arbuckle, Red, Musicians' Guild, Local 203
7414 Indianapolis Blvd. Hammond, IN
46324 219-845-0666 (18)

Arden, Marty, Florida Studio Theatre 4619
Bay Shore Drive Sarasota, FL 33580
813-355-4096 (16)

Ardenne, Michael, Nova Scotia Cultural
Affairs Division Post Office Box 864
Halifax, Nova Scotia, Canada B3J 2V2
902-424-4378 (5)

Arey, Edwin, Burlington Musicians'
Association 106 Heinberg Road
Burlington, VT 05401 802-862-9858 (18)

Argo, Elizabethe B., Orleans Arena
Theatre Old Town Hall, Main Street
Orleans, MA 02653 617-255-0695 (16)

Arlon, Ary, Peter Wolf Associates, Inc.
8181 Hoyle Dallas, TX 75227
214-388-3461 (15)

Armeen, Eloise, Lakes Region Playhouse
301 West 45th Street New York, NY
10036 603-293-7561 (16)

Armentaro, Louis J., Musicians' Protective
Association 206 South C Livingston, MT
59047 406-222-1274 (18)

Armstrong, Robert H., Musicians'
Association Post Office Box 3379
Eureka, CA 95501 707-442-3375 (18)

Arnold, John, Musicians' Association of
Jacksonville 2030 Schumacher Avenue
Jacksonville, FL 32207 904-398-9735
(18)

Arnold, Maxine, Maxine Arnold Agency
8350 Santa Monica Los Angeles, CA
90069 213-650-4999 (2)

Arnold, Raymond A., Musical Union, Local
84 1144 South Avenue Bradford, PA
16701 814-368-7421 (18)

Arnold, Richard, Richard Arnold and
Associates 331 West Arden Avenue
Glendale, CA 91203 213-240-3677 (15)

Arnold, Ron, Paul Gaulin Mime Theatre
89 Pleasant Boulevard Toronto, Ontario,
Canada M4T 1K2 416-924-1373 (16)

Arnold, Dr. William, Arizona State
University Tempe, AZ 85281
602-965-6536 (4)

Arnott, Peter D., Prologue Tufts
University Arena Theatre Medford, MA
02155 617-623-3880 (box office);
617-628-5000 ext237 (office) (14)

Aronheim, Ralph E., Civic Theatre of
Waterbury Post Office Box 85
Waterbury, CT 06702 203-756-6666 (16)

Arritt, Roy U., Musicians' Protective
Union Post Office Box 689 Covington,
VA 24426 703-962-3346 (18)

Arthur, Indus, Theater East Company
12655 Ventura Boulevard Studio City,
CA 91604 213-766-6111 (16)

Aschkenes, Anna M., Middlesex County
Cultural Commission 841 George Road
North Brunswick, NJ 08902
201-745-4489 (5)

Ashcraft, Eddie, Musicians' Protective
Association 1108 Cherry Lane Pocatello,
ID 83001 208-233-3483 (18)

Ashcraft, Leo, Musicians' Protective
Association, Local 110 10281 Golden
Arrow Drive Hutchinson, KS 67501
316-663-2653 (18)

Ashwill, Gary, Direct Safety Company 511
Osage Kansas City, KS 66110
913-281-0504 (15)

Asner, Ed, Screen Actors Guild (SAG)
7750 Sunset Boulevard Hollywood, CA
90045 213-876-3030 (18)

Atchley, Nelda, North Arts Council 425
Albert Drive Gardendale, AL 35071
205-631-7438 (5)

Atchley, Reid, Roswell Federation of
Musicians 1103 South Michigan Avenue
Roswell, NM 88201 505-622-7125 (18)

Aten, Gary, Crawford Cultural Center 337
Second Street Crawford, NB 69339
308-665-2389 (5)

Atkins, Ruissell, Free Lance 6005 Grand
Avenue Cleveland, OH 44104
216-431-7118 (14)

Atkins, Thomas, Hollins College
Department of Theatre Post Office Box
9602 Hollins College, VA 24020
703-362-6518 (4)

Atkins, Tom, Little Theater Hollins
College Hollins College, VA 24020 (8)

Atkinson, Richard, Hollywood Playhouse
Little Theatre of Hollywood 2640
Washington Street Hollywood, FL 33020
305-922-0404; 305-927-4239 (16)

Atlee, Howard, Howard Atlee 1560
Broadway, Suite 507 New York, NY
10036 212-575-9415 (12)

Auer, Miles Bohm, Miles Bohm Auer
Agency 8344 Melrose Avenue Los
Angeles, CA 90069 213-462-6416 (2)

Auger, Carol, Fort Lauderdale Children's
Theatre, Incorporated Post Office Box
4779 Fort Lauderdale, FL 33338
305-763-6882 (16)

Augustine, Larry D., Susquehanna
University Department of
Communications Selinsgrove, PA 17870
717-374-9700 (4)

Aukeman, Juanita, Washington County
Arts Council 202 Oak Circle
Williamsport, MD 21740 301-733-5600
(5)

Ausink, Adele, Nevada Community
Theatre 223 West Cherry Street Nevada,
MO 64772 (16)

Austermann, Mary, Fine Arts Community
Theatre 104 Hannah Street Mankato,
MN 56001 (16)

Austin, Deborah, Arts Councils of Western
North Carolina Post Office Box 507
Ashville, NC 28802 704-258-0710 (5)

Austin, Gary, The Groundlings 1089
North Oxford Avenue Los Angeles, CA
90029 213-462-4415 (16)

Ausubel, Bobbi, Caravan Theatre 1555
Masachusetts Avenue Cambridge, MA
02138 617-868-8520 (16)

Averill, Richard, Seem-To-Be-Players 630
Elm Lawrence, KS 66044 (16)

Avni, Ran, Jewish Repertory Theatre 344
East 14th Street New York, NY 10003
212-777-0033 (16)

Axelrod, Arthur, North Shore Musicians'
Association, Local 126 16 Jefferson
Avenue Saugus, MA 01906
617-581-3550; 617-233-1366 (18)

Ayers, Josephine E., Alabama Shakespeare
Festival Post Office Box 141 Anniston,
AL 36201 205-236-7503; 205-237-2332
(Summer Box Office) (9)

Ayers, Richard G., Bob Hope Theatre Southern Methodist University Dallas, TX 75275 214-692-2558 (8)

Ayers, Richard G., Margo Jones Experimental Theatre Southern Methodist University Dallas, TX 75275 214-692-2558 (8)

Aylem, Linda, Plastic Reel Corporation of America 1234 Roundtable Drive Dallas, TX 75247 214-634-7774 (15)

Aylor, Bill, Musicians' Protective Union Post Office Box 681 Knickerbocker, TX 76939 915-653-2690 (18)

Ayoub, Michael, Muskoka Summer Theatre Box 1055 Gravenhurst, Ontario, Canada P0C 1G0 705-687-2762 (16)

Ayres, James B., Shakespeare at Winedale Box 11 Round Top, TX 78954 713-278-3530 (9)

Azzolina, Nicholas, Meriden Federation of Musicians, Local 55 30 Briarwood Drive Meriden, CT 06450 203-238-0321 (18)

B

Babajko, Judy A., YMCA Nassau Youth Theatre Company 1 Plainfield Avenue Elmont, NY 11033 516-328-8358 (16)

Babb, Susan Thomas, Golden West College Department of Theatre Huntington Beach, CA 92647 714-892-7711, ext. 450 (4)

Babcock, Dr. Alberta, Allied Arts Council 1500 Compromise Line Road Glendora, CA 91740 213-335-1782 (5)

Bach, William, Musicians' Protective Union 1616 Third Street North Saint Cloud, MN 56301 612-253-6981 (18)

Bachelder, Douglas R., Port Jervis Musicians' Protective Association Route 97 Sparrowbush, NY 12780 914-856-5612 (18)

Bachhuber, M., Marrias Players 10 Tower Drive Mayville, WI 53050 (16)

Bachmann, D., Topeka Civic Theatre Post Oofice Box 893 Topeka, KS 66601 (16)

Bacon, Mike, Third Century Community Theatre Lexington, NE 68850 (16)

Baer, Clinton, The Arts Exchange 16 Whipple Building Lebanon, NH 03766 603-448-4353 (5)

Bafford, Hallie, Decatur Association of Musicians, Local 89 342 West Eckhardt Macon, IL 62544 217-877-8158 (18)

Bagg, Richard, National College of Education Department of Theatre 2840 Sheridan Road Evanston, IL 60201 312-256-5150 (4)

Bagley, Edythe S., Cheyney State College Department of Theatre Cheyney, PA 19319 215-399-2000 (4)

Bahs, C. W., University of Wyoming Box 3951, University Station Laramie, WY 82071 307-766-2197 (4)

Bailey, Hal, Indianapolis Musicians' Association, Local 3 325 North Delaware Street Indianapolis, IN 46204 317-636-3595 (18)

Bailey, Opal, Trueblood Theatre State Street at Washington Ann Arbor, MI 48104 313-764-5687 (8)

Bailiff, Diana, Area Community Theatre 900 South Marie Avenue Stevens Point, WI 54481 (16)

Baillargeon, Maryse, L'Atelier de Theatre La Grosse Valise 638 Base de Roc Joliette, Quebec, Canada J6E 5P7 514-756-6880 (16)

Baird, Beth, Grand Island Area Arts Council 111 West Second Street Grand Island, NB 68801 308-384-2130 (5)

Baird, John, Musicians' Protective Union 55 Rosedale Avenue Greenville, PA 16125 412-588-7604 (18)

Baird, William B., American Puppet Arts Council 59 Barrow Street New York, NY 10014 212-989-7060 (16)

Baisley, Robert W., Schwab Auditorium 103 University Auditorium, Penn. State University University Park, PA 16802 814-863-0388 (8)

Baker, Ellis B., Williston Summer Theatre Williston-Northampton School Easthampton, MA 01027 413-527-1520 (16)

Baker, James, Pacific College Department of Theatre Fresno, CA 93702 (4)

Baker, Joseph T., Musicians' Association, Local 105 4025 South Lee Street Spokane, WA 99203 509-448-0627 (18)

Baker, Paul, Dallas Theatre Center Down Center Stage 3636 Turtle Creek Boulevard Dallas, TX 75219 214-526-0107 (8)

Baker, Paul, Dallas Theatre Center Kalita Humphreys Theatre 3636 Turtle Creek Boulevard Dallas, TX 75219 214-526-8210; 214-526-8857 (8)

Baker, Paul, Trinity University Fine Arts Center Trinity University San Antonio, TX 78284 512-225-6351 (8)

Baker, Paul, Dallas Theater Center 3636 Turtle Creek Boulevard Dallas, TX 75219 214-526-8210; 214-526-8857 (16)

Baker, Ramona, The Arts Council Von Braun Civic Center Huntsville, AL 35801 205-533-6565 (5)

Baldwin, Ken, Earl and Brown Company 7719 Southwest Capitol Highway Portland, OR 97219 503-245-2283 (15)

Baldwin, Lois K., County Commission on the Arts and Sciences 124 Olde Courthouse Baltimore, MD 21204 301-494-2757 (5)

Baldwin, Richard, Kingston Musicians' Union 18 ½ Division Street Kingston, Ontario, Canada K7K 3Y9 613-542-3732 (18)

Baldyga, Bernard J., Southbridge Musicians' Association 20 Colonial Road Sutton, MA 01527 617-865-2714 (18)

Ball, Linda L., Paramount Arts Center Winchester and 12th Ashland, KY 41101 606-324-3175 (8)

Ballantyne, Bruce, Listec Television Equipment Corporation 39 Cain Drive Plainview, NY 11803 516-694-8963 (15)

Ballantyne, William J., Ballantyne Flamproofing Company 2722 North Lincoln Avenue Chicago, IL 60614 312-348-7770 (15)

Ballet, Houston, Rowland Bachman Jones Hall Houston, TX 77002 (6)

Ballew, Leighton M., University of Georgia Department of Theatre Athens, GA 30601 404-542-2836 (4)

Ballok, Irene, Polka Dot Playhouse Post Office Box 50 Bridgeport, CT 06601 203-374-1777 (16)

Balof, Dr. Eugene, University of North Alabama Florence, AL 35630 205-766-4100, Ext.247; 205-766-4100, Ext.358 (4)

Balough, Stephen A., Marysville Musicians' Association, Local 158 Post Office Box 1552 Marysville, CA 95901 916-743-9760 (18)

Balson, Carl G., Beloit College Department of Theatre Beloit, WI 53511 608-365-3391 (4)

Banard, John P., Frank Phillips College Department of Theatre Borger, TX 79007 806-274-5311 (4)

Bandringa, Gary, Westroads Dinner Theatre 46 Town Hall Road Omaha, NB 68114 402-397-0300 (16)

Bangham, Jerry, Alcorn State University Department of Theatre Lorman, MS 39096 601-877-3711 (4)

Bankes, Gary, Omega Center for the Performing Arts Building 5226 Fort Lewis, WA 98433 206-968-4097 (8)

Banks, Christopher, Neptune Theatre 1593 Argyle Street Halifax, Nova Scotia, Canada B3J 2B2 902-429-7300 (16)

Baptiste, Donald J., Holyoke Musicians' Union, Local 144 38 Keddy Blvd. Chicopee, MA 01020 413-533-5235 (18)

Barash, Roberta, Roberta Barash Agency 404 North La Cienega Los Angeles, CA 90048 213-820-3383 (2)

Barber, Danny, Youngstown Federation of Musicians, Local 86-242 2520 South Avenue Youngstown, OH 44502 216-788-8451 (18)

Barber, Michael, Madison Area Technical College Department of Theatre 211 North Carroll Street Madison, WI 53703 608-266-5054 (4)

Barber, Rupert T., Davidson College Department of Theatre Davidson, NC 28036 704-892-2000 (4)

Barbush, Lillian, Islip Town Council on the Arts Post Office Box 85 Islip, NY 11751 516-581-2448 (5)

Bard, Bartley, Lunchbox Theatre Post Office Box 9027 Calgary, Alberta, Canada T2P 2W4 403-265-4292 (16)

Bardelli, Joseph, Musicians' Protective Union 660 Majestic Drive Santa Maria, CA 93454 805-937-2333 (18)

Bardelli, Joseph, Musicians' Protective Union 660 Majestic Drive Santa Maria, CA 93454 805-937-2333 (18)

Bardes, Nick, Musicians' Mutual Protective Associatiton 1140 Spencer Street Santa Rosa, CA 95404 707-545-1434 (18)

Barham, L.D., North Bay Musicians' Association 2405 Queensway Road North Bay, Ontario, Canada 705-472-6966 (18)

Barker, Robert C., Musical Protective Association, Local 123 2006 Dresden Road Richmond, VA 23229 804-270-7963 (18)

Barlow, Curtis, International Theatre Institute c/o Professional Association of Canadian Theatres Toronto, Ontario, Canada 416-366-0159 (5)

Barlow, Curtis, Professional Association of Canadian Theatres 3 Church Street, Suite 301 Toronto, Ontario, Canada M5E 1M2 416-366-0159 (5)

Barne, B., Tree County Players 321 North Franklin Greensburg, IN 47240 (16)

Barnes, J., Beu Fine Arts Theatre 2010 Northeast Street Betton, TX 76513 (16)

Barnes, Karen, Burke Arts Council 115 East Meeting Street Morganton, NC 28655 704-433-7282 (5)

Barnes, M., Way Off-Broadway Players Post Office Box 1284 Dodge City, KS 67801 (16)

Barnum, Lee, Greater Grand Forks Community Theatre Post Office Box 895 Grand Forks, ND 58201 701-775-4562 (16)

Barr, Barbara, Film Actors Workshop 5004 Vineland North Hollywood, CA 91601 213-766-5108 (16)

Barr, Eric, University of California, Riverside Department of Theatre Post Office Box 112 Riverside, CA 92521 714-787-3343 (4)

Barr, P., Throop Players 300 South Los Robles Pasadena, CA 91106 (16)

Barr, Richard, League of New York Theatres and Producers 266 West 47th Street New York, NY 10036 212-764-1122 (5)

Barr, Tony, Film Actors Workshop 5004 Vineland North Hollywood, CA 91601 213-766-5108 (16)

Barrable, Susan, Solar Stage Lunchtime Theatre 149 Yonge Street Toronto, Ontario, Canada M5C 1W4 416-368-5135 (16)

Barranger, M.S., Tulane University Department of Theatre New Orleans, LA 70118 504-865-6205 (4)

Barrett, Aurore Leigh, The Children's Theatre Grasmere Center 5801 112th Place, NE Kirkland, WA 98033 (16)

Barrett, Edwin B., Playhouse on the Hill c/o Ijams Route 28 Barneveld, NY 13304 315-896-4441 (16)

Barrett, Hadley, Musicians' Association 315 South Willow North Platte, NE 69101 308-532-5351 (18)

Barrett, Janina, Centre Stage Theatre 380 Wellington Street London, Ontario, Canada N6A 5B5 519-433-5241; 519-433-4700 (16)

Barrett, Laura J., Kansas City Community College Department of Theatre Kansas City, KS 66112 (4)

Barrett, Lee, Canonsburg Federation of Musicians 545 Ridge Avenue Canonsburg, PA 15317 412-745-2814 (18)

Barrier, Shep, Waco Musicians' Association 8918 Valley Brook Circle Waco, TX 76710 817-772-7929 (18)

Barry, Ellen, The New Jersey Shakespeare Festival Drew University Madison, NJ 07940 201-377-4487; 201-377-5330, Administrative (16)

Barry, John, John Barry 815 North East 172nd Terrace North Miami Beach, FL 33162 (15)

Barry, Paul, The New Jersey Shakespeare Festival Drew University Madison, NJ 07940 201-377-4487; 201-377-5330, Administrative (16)

Bart, June, Foster Sound Incorporated 505 Harvester Court Wheeling, IL 60090 312-541-7510 (15)

Barteaux, Judson, Hudson Guild Theatre 441 West 26th Street New York, NY 10001 212-760-9810; 212-760-9847 (16)

Bartek, Gloria, Metropolitan Arts Council Post Office Box 1077 Omaha, NB 68101 402-341-7910 (5)

Bartholomew, L., Faulkton Community Theatre Post Office Box 70 Faulkton, SD 57438 (16)

Bartholomew, Linda, Faulkton Area Arts Council Post Office Box 70 Faulkton, SD 57538 605-598-4187 (5)

Bartke, Bill, Bartke's Dinner Theatre 2500 Rocky Point Drive Tampa, FL 33607 813-884-0478 (16)

Bartlett, James D., Southern West Virginia Community College Department of Theatre Willimson, WV 25601 304-235-2800 (4)

Barton, John, Northwestern Oklahoma State University Department of Theatre Alva, OK 73717 405-327-1700 (4)

Bartruff, Jim, Carroll College Little Theatre Helena, MT 59625 406-442-3450 Ext. 276; 406-442-3455 (4)

Barulich, Richard M., California Theatrical Supply 745 Polk Street San Francisco, CA 94109 415-928-5824; 415-957-1686 (15)

Barulich, Richard M., Kryolan Corporation 747 Polk Street San Francisco, CA 94109 415-928-5824; 415-957-1686 (15)

Baschnagel, Carol, Baschnagel Brothers, Incorporated 150-25 14th Avenue Whitestone, NY 11357 212-767-1919 (15)

Baschnagel, Robert Jr., Baschnagel Brothers, Incorporated 150-25 14th Avenue Whitestone, NY 11357 212-767-1919 (15)

Basney, Lionel, Houghton College Department of Theatre Houghton, NY 14744 716-567-2211 (4)

Basset, Clyde, State University College Department of Theatre Brockport, NY 14420 716-395-2478 (4)

Bassett, Suzanne P., Wapole Arts Council Post Office Box 182 Wapole, MA 02081 617-668-6882 (5)

Bates, Joseph E., Iddings Paint Company 3486 Union Pacific Avenue Los Angeles, CA 90023 213-268-4744 (15)

Bates, Richard Sr., Musicians' Protective Union, Local 181 821 Talma Street Aurora, IL 60505 312-851-1386; 312-897-6894 (18)

Batey, Ruth, Toronto Workshop Productions 12 Alexander Street Toronto, Ontario, Canada M4Y 1B4 416-925-0526; 416-925-8640 (16)

Battis, Steven G., Musicians' Protective Union 303 Acosta Street Klamath Falls, OR 97601 503-882-1795 (18)

Bauchesi, Louise, Theatre D'Art Du Quebec 459 Place Deauville Ville Laval, Quebec, Canada H7N 3S6 514-387-9344 (16)

Bauchesi, Louise, Theatre De Polucginellle 459 Place Deauville Ville Laval, Quebec, Canada H7N 3S6 514-387-9344 (16)

Bauer, Bob, Theatrix, Incorporated 5138 East 39th Avenue Denver, CO 80207 303-388-9345 (15)

Baum, Harry A., The Open Space 133 Second Avenue New York, NY 10003 212-254-8630 (16)

Bay, Rich, Video TechniLites, Incorporated Post Office Box 226 Union, MO 63084 314-583-9914; 314-583-3754 (15)

Bayer, Robert F., Theatrical Services and Supplies, Incorporated 205C Brook Avenue Deer Park, NY 11729 516-242-5454 (15)

Bayless, John R., Playhouse Theatre Arts Building, Penn. State University University Park, PA 16803 814-863-0381 (8)

Bayless, John R., The Pennsylvania Festival Theatre 137 Arts Building University Park, PA 16803 814-863-0381; 814-865-7586 (16)

Beagan, Carol, Lincoln Council on the Arts Post Office Box 213 Lincoln, RI 02865 401-725-4990 (5)

Beagle, T., Community Theatre Post Office Box 638 Antioch, CA 94509 (16)

Bearce, Dr. W.H., Missouri Valley College Department of Theatre 500 East College Street Marshall, MO 65340 816-866-6924 Extension 147 (4)

Bearden, June, Lubbock Christian College Department of Theatre Lubbock, TX 79407 806-792-3221 (4)

Beasley, Mrs. Robin J., Fort Ruger Theatre Makapu and Aloha Avenues Honolulu, HI 96816 808-734-0274 (8)

Beasley, Ms. Robin R., Honolulu Community Theatre Makapuu and Aloha Avenue Honolulu, HI 96816 808-734-0274; 808-737-8108 (16)

Beatty, Vergie, Musicians' Protective Union 260 Tranquil Drive Paradise, CA 95969 916-872-0978 (18)

Beaubien, Jeanine C., Theatre International de Montreal 1455 rue Peel, Suite G-20 Montreal, Quebec, Canada H3A 1T5 514-526-0821 (16)

Beaudry, Fred, Fred T. Beaudry and Associates, Incorporated 1520 Northway Mall Pittsburgh, PA 15237 412-364-0788 (15)

Beaulieu, Victor-Levy, VLB Editeur 5840 Boulevard Gouin Est Montreal-Nord, Quebec, Canada 514-326-5029 (14)

Beautyman, William, Limelight Productions, Incorporated Post Office Box 816, Yale Hill Stockbridge, MA 01262 413-298-3771 (15)

Beaver, L., Community Players Post Office Box 124 West Grove, PA 19390 (16)

Beck, Gary, Sidewalks of New York Productions 44 Beaver Street, 2nd Floor New York, NY 10004 212-668-9074 (16)

Beck, Jacklyn D., Puerto Rican Traveling Theatre 304 West 47th Street New York, NY 10036 212-354-1293; 212-354-1974 (16)

Beck, Rockley W., Musicians' Protective Union, Local 254 3263 Idlewood Sioux City, IA 51104 712-258-1288 (18)

Becker, Brian, Becker Studios 2824 West Taylor Street Chicago, IL 60612 312-722-4040 (15)

Becker, D., Argo Center of Cultural Art 4276 Crenshaw Boulevard Los Angeles, CA 90008 (16)

Beckerman, Bernard, Columbia University Department of Theatre 116th Street New York, NY 10027 212-280-3408 (4)

Beckett, Joi, Lunchbox Theatre Post Office Box 9027 Calgary, Alberta, Canada T2P 2W4 403-265-4292 (16)

Beckman, Jack, Rushmore Plaza Civic Center 444 Mount Rushmore Road North Rapid City, SD 57701 605-394-4115 (8)

Beddoe, John, Orrie De Nooyer Auditorium 200 Hackensack Avenue Hackensack, NJ 07061 201-343-6000 (8)

Bednerik, Marya, Colorado Women's College Department of Theatre Denver, CO 80220 303-394-6012 (4)

Beebe, Ralph P., Power Center for the Performing Arts 121 Fletcher Street Ann Arbor, MI 48109 313-763-3333 (8)

Beebe, Sheriden, Long Beach Regional Arts Council 130 Pine Avenue Long Beach, CA 90802 213-436-6822 (5)

Beeck, Cheryl L., Slagle Auditorium University of South Dakota Vermillion, SD 57069 605-677-5481 (8)

Beesmer, John F., New Haven Federation of Musicians, Local 234-486 26 Glebrook Avenue Hamden, CT 06514 203-387-4765 (18)

Begg, James H., Hamilton Musicians' Guild 101 Iverness Court Hamilton, Ontario, Canada L9C 1A6 416-388-0140 (18)

Behan, David F., Tusculum College Department of Theatre Tusculum Station Greenville, TN 37743 615-639-2701 (4)

Behan, George, Seattle University Auditorium 12th and East Columbia Seattle, WA 98122 (8)

Behl, Jack R., Village Theatre Incorporated Post Office Box 32 Arlington Heights, IL 60006 312-259-3200 (16)

Behm, Tom, University of North Carolina Department of Theatre 1000 Spring Garden Street Greensboro, NC 27412 919-379-5562 (4)

Behr, Robert E., Foellinger Outdoor Theater in Franke Park 1 East Main Street Fort Wayne, IN 46802 219-482-2785 (8)

Behr, Robert E., Arena Theatre 816 Ewing Street Fort Wayne, IN 46802 219-742-0135 (16)

Behr, Robert E., Theatre Workshop Park Board 1 East Main Street Fort Wayne, IN 46802 219-423-7015 (16)

Behrend, Jack, Behrend's Incorporated 541 North Franklin Chicago, IL 60610 312-527-3060 (15)

Behringer, Fred, University of Tennessee, Chattanooga Department of Theatre 323 Fine Arts Building Chattanooga, TN 37402 615-755-4374; 615-755-4297 (4)

Beige, Joel, Rubie's Costume Company Incorporated 1 Rubie Plaza Richmond Hill, NY 11418 202-846-1008 (15)

Belanger, Raynald, Theatre de la Feniere 1500 rue de la Feniere Ancienne-Lorette, Quebec, Canada 418-651-3218 (16)

Belcher, LeAnn, Gardendale Cultural Arts Council Post Office Box 38 Gardendale, AL 35071 205-631-5679 (5)

Belfance, Bob, Weathervane Community Playhouse 1301 Weathervane Lane Akron, OH 44313 (16)

Belkin, Samuel, Coachlight Dinner Theatre 10 East 49th Street New York, NY 10017 (16)

Bell, Calvin, Musicians' Protective Union Post Office Box 681 Knickerbocker, TX 76939 915-653-2690 (18)

Bell, C.E., Norfolk Scope Cultural/Convention Center Scope Plaza Norfolk, VA 23510 804-441-2764 (8)

Bell, Howard R., Mole-Richardson Company 937 North Sycamore Avenue Hollywood, CA 90038 213-851-0111 (15)

Bell, Robert J., Burlington Musical Society 126 Mott Avenue Burlington, NJ 08016 609-386-4793 (18)

Bell, Vicky E., Arts Council of Wilson 205 Gray Street Wilson, NC 27893 919-291-4329 (5)

Bella, Herman, Musicians' Protective Union, Local 213 3004 North Campsite Drive Stevens Point, WI 54481 715-344-7550 (18)

Bellah, Donald W., Texas Wesleyan Fine Arts Auditorium Texas Wesleyan College Box 3277 Fort Worth, TX 76105 817-534-0251 (8)

Bellamy, Dr. G., Southwestern State College Department of Theatre Weatherford, OR 73096 405-772-5511 (4)

Bellini-Sharp, Carol, Hamilton College Department of Theatre and Dance Clinton, NY 13323 315-859-4257 (4)

Bellows, Louise O., Maysville Players 116 North 2nd Street Maysville, KY 41056 606-564-3666 (16)

Belt, Gerald R., Musicians' Protective Union 511 West Jefferson Street Morris, IL 60450 815-942-3566 (18)

Benberg, Vernon, Hibbing Community College Department of Theatre Hibbing, MN 55746 (4)

Benbow, Loren, Loren Benbow and Assocciates Post Office Box 244 Groveland, IL 61535 309-387-6556 (15)

Bender, Jack, University of Michigan Professional Theatre Program 227 South Ingalls Ann Arbor, MI 48109 313-764-5350 (4)

Benedet, Art De, Border Musicians' Association, Local 156 Post Office Box 347 International Falls, MN 56649 218-283-2251 (18)

Benedict, A., Greenbrier Repertory Theatre Post Office Box 494 Lewisburg, WV 24901 (16)

Benett, Stuart, San Jose City College San Jose, CA 95128 (4)

Benge, Charles V., Musicians' Protective Union Rural Route Number 15 Frankfort, IN 46041 317-654-8209 (18)

Benge, Sharon, Casa Manana Playhouse Post Office Box 9054 Fort Worth, TX 76107 817-332-9319 (16)

Benjamin, John S., Theatre Arts of West Virginia Post Office Box 1205 Beckley, WV 25801 304-253-8131 (16)

Benjamin, John S., Theatre West Virginia Post Office Box 1205 Beckley, WV 25801 304-253-8317 (16)

Benjamin, John S., Hatfields and McCoys/Honey in the Rock Post Office Box 1205 Buckley, WV 25801-1205 304-253-8313; 304-253-8314 (16)

Benndett, David, David Benndett, Incorporated 2431 Briarcrest Road Beverly Hills, CA 90210 213-278-5657 (2)

Bennet, Ted, Sphere Associates 11250-14 Roger Bacon Drive Reston, VA 22090 703-471-1230 (15)

Bennett, Gordon C., Eastern College Department of Communication Arts Fairview Drive Saint Davids, PA 19087 215-688-3300 (4)

Bennett, Maria, Potpourri Players, Ltd. 17 University Circle Longmont, CO 80501 303-772-1430 (16)

Bennett, William J., National Endowment for the Humanities 806 15th Street Washington, DC 20506 202-786-0438 (5)

Benoit, Lowell, Professional Musicians' Association 2314 3rd Street Port Neches, TX 77651 713-727-3393 (18)

Benson, Eugene, Canadian Drama/L'Art Dramatique Canadien Department of English University of Guelph Guelph, Ontario, Canada 519-821-4120 (14)

Benson, Jeff W., Musicians' Protective Union 1473 Lewis Street Ogden, UT 84404 801-393-9558 (18)

Benson, June, Pioneer Players 622 Cantor Street New Ulm, MN 56073 (16)

Benson, Lois J., Lois J. Benson Agency 2221 West Olive Burbank, CA 91502 213-849-5647 (2)

Benson, Mickey, North Park College Department of Theatre 5125 North Spaulding Chicago, IL 60115 312-583-2700 (4)

Benson, Dr. Richard, Eastern Kentucky University Department of Speech and Theater Richmond, KY 40475 606-622-0111; 606-622-5851 (4)

Benson, Robert L., Skirpan Lighting Control Corporation 61-03 32nd Avenue Woodside, NY 11377 212-274-7222 (15)

Bent, J., Indiana Arts Council 915 School Street Indiana, PA 15701 412-687-2397 (5)

Benton, William, Daytona Beach Federation of Musicians 115 Seabreeze Boulevard Daytona Beach, FL 32018 904-252-6333 (18)

Benzil, Naomi, Carroll County Arts Council 129 East Main Street Westminster, MD 21157 301-848-7272 (5)

Berg, Dwayne, Stoughton Village Players 916 Roby Road Stoughton, WI 53589 (16)

Bergamini, Angelo L., Greater Lowell Musicians' Association, Local 83 200 Parker Street Lowell, MA 01851 617-453-5621 (18)

Berger, Don, Musicians' Union 4421 Woodland Drive Bartlesville, OK 74003 918-333-2054 (18)

Berger, Jeniva, Toronto Drama Bench c/o Theatre Ontario, 8 York Street, 7th Floor Toronto, Ontario, Canada M5J 1R2 416-366-2938 (5)

Berger, Jeniva, Scene Changes Theatre Ontario, 8 York Street, 7th Floor Toronto, Ontario, Canada M5J 1R2 416-366-2938 (14)

Berger, Sidney, University of Houston, Central Campus Department of Theatre 4800 Calhoun Houston, TX 77004 713-749-1011 (4)

Berger, Sidney L., Houston Shakespeare Festival University of Houston Houston, TX 77004 713-749-1427 (9)

Bergeron, Richard J. Sr., Southbridge Musicians' Association 20 Colonial Road Sutton, MA 01527 617-865-2714 (18)

Berghof, Herbert, HB Playwrights Foundation 122 Bank Street New York, NY 10014 212-989-6540 (16)

Berkeley, Norma, Montgomery College Department of Theatre Rockville, MD 20854 301-762-7400 (4)

Berkowsky, Paul, League of OffBroadway Theatres and Producers 1540 Broadway, Suite 711 New York, NY 10036 212-869-8282 (5)

Berkson, Dennis, Oakton Community College Department of Theatre Morton Grove, IL 60053 312-967-5120 (4)

Berlin, Richard M., Carlow College Department of Theatre Pittsburgh, PA 15213 412-683-4800; 412-578-6036 (4)

Berlin, Zeke, Rutgers University Department of Theatre 311 North Fifth Street Camden, NJ 08102 609-757-6246 (4)

Berman, Jack, Jack Berman Company, Incorporated 8925 South LaCienga Boulevard Inglewwood, CA 90301 213-649-6101; 910-328-6184 (15)

Berman, Lois, Lois Berman Agency 240 West 44th Street New York, NY 10036 212-581-0670 (2)

Bernier, Michel, Theatre de l'Atelier Parc Jaques-Cartier Sherbrooke, Quebec, Canada J1H 5H2 819-562-1982 (16)

Berns, Charlene, Seward Arts Council 1160 Eastridge Seward, NB 68434 (5)

Bernstein, Jeffrey, Pocket Mime Theatre Post Office Box 269 Boston, MA 02117 617-266-2770 (16)

Berrick, Lawrence, Adelphian Players 8515 Ridge Boulevard Brooklyn, NY 11209 718-273-3781 (16)

Berry, Carlton F., Norwich University Department of English/Theatre Northfield, VT 05663 802-485-5011 (4)

Berry, Thomas C., Indianapolis Musicians' Association, Local 3 325 North Delaware Street Indianapolis, IN 46204 317-636-3595 (18)

Berryman, Russell G., Flint Federation of Musicians 1502 Woodcroft Flint, MI 48503 313-233-4264 (18)

Bert, Dr. Norman, Messiah College Department of Theatre Grantham, PA 17027 717-766-2511 (4)

Bertin, Michael, American Center for Stanislavski Theatre 485 Park Avenue New York, NY 10022 212-755-5120 (16)

Bertolino, Angelo, Italian American Drama Group 1051 North Broadway Los Angeles, CA 90012 213-664-7435 (16)

Besegai, Donald C., Musicians Protective Union 30 Allerton Street Plymouth, MA 02360 617-746-2247 (18)

Besold, Bobbee, Video Cabaret 357 College Street Toronto, Ontario, Canada 416-960-4881 (16)

Bestwina, Joesph G., The Feed Store 5408 South Harlem Summit, IL 60501 312-458-1327 (15)

Beswick, Melville, Progress Feather Company 657 West Lake Street Chicago, IL 60606 312-726-7443 (15)

Bethel, Audrey, Arts and Crafts Center of Pittsburgh Fifth and Shady Avenue Pittsburgh, PA 15232 412-361-0873 (5)

Bettenbender, John, Rutgers State University of New Jersey, Department of Theatre Mason Gross School of the Arts New Brunswick, NJ 08903 201-932-9891; 201-932-9816 (4)

Bettenbender, John, Rutgers University Mason Gross School of the Arts New Brunswick, NJ 08903 201-932-9816 (4)

Bettenbender, John, Rutgers University, Douglass College Department of Theatre New Brunswick, NJ 08903 201-932-9721 (4)

Bettencourt, Mrs. Margaret, Musicians' Protective Association, Local 210 1739 West Celeste Fresno, CA 93711 209-439-3793 (18)

Bettendorf, Pat, Duck Soup Players 948 Carmel Court Saint Paul, MN 55112 (16)

Betterly, J.E., Globe Ticket Company 680 Blair Mill Road Horsham, PA 19044 215-657-4230 (15)

Bettin, Val, Theatre of Western Springs Hampton at Hillgrove, Box 29 Western Springs, IL 60558 312-246-4043 (16)

Bevins, Karl A., Federation of Musicians, Local 148-462 110 Laurel Forest Circle, North East Atlanta, GA 30342 404-237-1204 (18)

Bialaszewski, Ron, Musicians' Protective Association, Local 108 5072 West Lake Road Dunkirk, NY 14048 716-366-1773 (18)

Bialosky, Marshall, California State College Playbox 1000 East Victoria Street Dominguez Hills, CA 90247 213-532-4300 (8)

Bianchi, Donald A., Dobama Theatre 1846 Conventry Road Cleveland Heights, OH 44118 216-932-6838 (16)

Bianco, Patty, University of Pittsburgh Department of Theatre Bradford, PA 16791 814-362-3801 (4)

Biegler, AL, Musicians' Protective Union 260 Tranquil Drive Paradise, CA 95969 916-872-0978 (18)

Biel, Rosemary, Big Stone Community Theatre 229 South East 2nd Street Ortonville, MN 56278 (16)

Bielecki, Donald, Page Hall Washington Avenue Albany, NY 12207 513-457-7600 (8)

Biggers, John, University of Houston, Downtown College Department of Theatre 1 Main Street Houston, TX 77002 713-749-1011 (4)

Biglow, Robert, Musicians' Association, Local 73 127 North Seventh Street Minneapolis, MN 55403 612-333-8205 (18)

Bill, Mary, Great Lakes Shakespeare Festival Ohio Theatre Playhouse Square Cleveland, OH 44115 216-228-1225 (9)

Billion, Roy C., Warren Federation of Musicians, Local 118 3207 Youngstown Road SE Warren, OH 44484 216-369-6745 (18)

Billups, Gary, Musicians' Protective Union Route 5 Wheelersburg, OH 45694 614-574-6756 (18)

Binet, Claude, Theatre de la Bordee 109 ½ St-Jean Quebec City, Quebec, Canada 418-529-5237 (16)

Birch, Robert A., Rochester Civic Theatre Mayo Park Rochester, MN 55901 507-282-8401; 507-282-7633 (16)

Bird, Robert H., Musicians Protective Union, Local 272 2701 North 700 East Provo, UT 84601 801-377-0857 (18)

Birkett, Margaret Jean, University of Wisconsin, Richland Center Department of Theater Richland Center, WI 53581 608-647-6186 (4)

Birkey, Mary, Montevideo Arts Council 513 North Ninth Street Montevideo, MN 56265 (5)

Birmingham, Tom, University Theatre University of Wisconsin Green Bay Green Bay, WI 54302 414-465-2256; 414-465-2217 (8)

Birmingham, Tom, Theatre-in-a-Garden Fish Creek, WI 54212 414-868-3287; 414-868-3288 (16)

Biros, James, Theatre On The Move Post Office Box 462 Islington, Ontario, Canada M9A 4X4 416-445-1966 (16)

Birtwistle, Michael, Pomona College Department of Theatre Claremont, CA 91711 714-621-8186 (4)

Bishop, Kathleen, Willingboro Theatre of the Performing Arts Post Office Box 398 Willingboro, NJ 08046 609-387-3226 (16)

Bissada, Mofid, The Great American Market Box 178, 21133 Costanso Street Woodland Hills, CA 91364 213-883-8182 (15)

Bitch, Carroll P., Springfield College Department of Theatre 263 Alden Street Springfield, MA 01109 413-788-3000 (4)

Bittel, Ann, Jackson County Arts Council Benham Avenue Scottsboro, AL 35768 205-259-1874 (5)

Bittle, Dr. William, Kent State University Professional Arts Center 6000 Frank Avenue Canton, OH 44720-7599 216-499-9600 (4)

Bittner, Jim, Lumatrol Corporation 409 Citizens Bank Building Anderson, IN 46016 317-649-0606 (15)

Black, E. R., Northwestern State University Department of Theatre Natchitoches, LA 71457 (4)

Black, E. Robert, Northwestern State University Little Theatre Fine Arts Building Natchitoches, LA 71457 318-357-6196 (8)

Black, F., Essex Community College Department of Theatre 7201 Rossville Road Baltimore, MD 21237 301-522-1420 (4)

Black, George, University of Virginia Department of Theatre Charlottesville, VA 22903 804-924-3326 (4)

Black, Jean, Concordia College Department of Theatre Saint Paul, MN 5504 612-641-8266 (4)

Black, Malcolm, Theatre New Brunswick Post Office Box 566 Fredericton, New Brunswick, Canada E3B 5A6 506-455-3222 (16)

Black, Malcolm, Theatre New Brunswick Young Company Post Office Box 566 Fredericton, New Brunswick, Canada E3B 5A6 506-455-3080 (16)

Black, Raymond B., Northampton Federation of Musicians, Local 220 31 Davis Street Easthampton, MA 01027 413-527-4094 (18)

Blackwelder, Chris, Pine Tree Players Post Office Box 357A Winnsboro, SC 29180 (16)

Blaine, Dr. I., University of Southern Mississippi Department of Theatre Box 31, Southern Station Hattiesburg, MS 39406 601-266-7225 (4)

Blaine, John, Seattle Arts Commission 305 Harrison Street Seattle, WA 98109 206-625-4223 (5)

Blair, Leonard Buzz, Westwood Players 10886 Le Conte Avenue Los Angeles, CA 90024 213-477-4907 (16)

Blair, Wink, Phoenix Art Council 1202 North Third Street Phoenix, AZ 85004 602-271-9052 (5)

Blake, William, William Blake Agency/West 1888 Century Park East Century City, CA 90067 213-274-0321 (2)

Blakely, Chuck, Charles A. Blakely Company 646 First Street San Francisco, CA 94107 415-431-5563 (15)

Blanchard, G.L., Jackson Community College Department of Theatre 2111 Emmons Road Jackson, MI 49201 517-787-0800 (4)

Blanchard, Nina, Nina Blanchard Agency 1717 North Highland Avenue Los Angeles, CA 90028 213-462-6248 (2)

Blanchette, Mel, Kankakee Musicians' Association 740 Armour Road Boubonnais, IL 60914 815-932-6662 (18)

Blanda, Steve E., Musicians' Protective Union, Local 82 205 Craig Street New Brighton, PA 15066 412-774-2602 (18)

Blanning, Richard, Michigan Technological University Department of Drama Houghton, MI 49931 906-487-2067 (4)

Blattner, Orrin, San Jose Federation of Musicians, Local 153 14584 Westcott Drive Saratoga, CA 95070 408-867-0456 (18)

Blatz, Martin J., Peninsula Players of Nahant 65A Basspoint Road Nahant, MA 01908 617-581-1078 (16)

Blaustone, H. Robert, Santa Ana College Department of Theatre Santa Ana, CA 92706 714-667-3216; 714-667-3215 (4)

Bledsoe, Mary, Omaha Stage Equipment, Incorporated 3873 Leavenworth Street Omaha, NE 68105 402-345-4427 (15)

Blevins, Floyd, Amherst Lumber Company 700 Mill Avenue Amherst, OH 44001 216-988-4431 (15)

Blish, Dorothy, Lake Country Players North 56, Highway K Hartland, WI 53029 (16)

Bliss, Nicholas G., Chicago Federation of Musicians, Local 10 175 West Washington Street Chicago, IL 60602 312-782-0063 (18)

Blomquist, Dr. Allen P., Idaho State University Department of Theatre Pocatello, ID 83209 208-236-2431 (4)

Blondeau, Betty, Atlanta Children's Theatre Post Office Box 77324 Atlanta, GA 30357 404-892-7607 (16)

Bloodworth, Robert, Coker College Department of Theatre Hartsville, SC 29550 803-332-1381 (4)

Bloom, J. Michael, J. Michael Bloom 9220 Sunset Boulevard Los Angeles, CA 90069 213-275-6800 (2)

Bloom, Phillip, Phillip Bloom 1995 Broadway New York, NY 10023 212-243-5363 (12)

Blossom, Katie, Adirondack Children's Troupe Star Route, Pilot Knob Road Glen Falls, NY 12801 (16)

Blouke, Jessie, Washington County Arts and Crafts Association Post Office Box 278 Chatom, AL 36518 205-847-2714 (5)

Blue, E., Huntington Theatre Ensemble 1010 13th Street Huntington, WV 25701 (16)

Blutstein, H., Seasoned Players 7017 16th Avenue Takoma Park, MD 20012 (16)

Boarman, Randal K., Repertory People of Evansville Old Courthouse Evansville, IN 47708 812-423-2060 (16)

Boarts, Delbert, EMS Products 242 South Gill Street State College, PA 16801 814-237-6702 (15)

Boarts, Vonny, EMS Products 242 South Gill Street State College, PA 16801 814-237-6702 (15)

Boatner, James K., Manchester Institute of Arts and Sciences 148 Concord Street Manchester, NH 03101 603-623-0313 (5)

Boddie, B.F., WILLCO Foundation One Williams Center Tulsa, OK 74103 918-588-2111 (10)

Boe, H., Barn Players 121 North 12th Street Miles City, MT 59301 (16)

Boehm, Lorenz, Central YMCA Community College Department of Theatre Chicago, IL 60601 312-222-8150 (4)

Boesing, Martha, At the Foot of the Mountain 3144 Tenth Avenue, South Minneapolis, MN 55407 612-375-9487; 612-825-2820 (16)

Boevers, Eileen, Performing Arts Workshop 881 Apple Tree Lane Highland Park, IL 60035 (16)

Bogan, S., Regis College Department of Theatre 235 Wellesley Street Wheaton, MA 02193 617-893-1820 (4)

Boghostan, Jerry Der, Portland Musicians' Association 27 Fleetwood Street Portland, ME 04102 207-774-6757 (18)

Bogos, Jacques, La Salle Audio 2500 Bates Road Montreal, Quebec, Canada H3S 1A6 514-342-4503 (15)

Bogos, Jacques, Radio Service Incorporated 2500 Bates Road Montreal, Quebec, Canada H3S 1A6 514-342-4503 (15)

Bohlen, Jeanne, Foundation Center Field Office 739 National City Bank Building Cleveland, OH 44114 216-861-1933; 800-424-9836, Publications (5)

Bohlken, Dr. Robert, Northwest Missouri State University Department of Theatre Maryville, MO 64468 816-582-7141 (4)

Boivin, James A., Community Arts Development Group 125 South Topanga Canyon Boulevard Topanga, CA 90290 213-455-1351 (5)

Boksa, Bill, Superscope Texas, Incorporated 3214 Beltling Road Dallas, TX 75234 214-241-9712 (15)

Bolchoz, Willard, Charleston Federation of Musicians 140 Darlington Avenue Charleston, SC 29403 803-722-0936 (18)

Bolen, Dr. Jane, Greenwood Council of the Arts 210 West Cambridge Avenue Greenwood, SC 29646 803-223-2546 (5)

Bolen, Robert, Arkansas Tech University Russeville, AR 72801 501-968-0274 (4)

Bollow, L., Cameo Players 314 West Sugar Lane Milwaukee, WI 53217 (16)

Bolton, J. Vaughn, Manhattan Musicians Association, Local 169 828 Allison Road Manhattan, KS 66502 915-537-1928 (18)

Boma, Weldon, Theatre 707 1707 Brunswick Street Halifax, Nova Scotia, Canada 902-429-7777 (8)

Bonanno, Russell, Adelphian Players 8515 Ridge Boulevard Brooklyn, NY 11209 718-273-3781 (16)

Bond, Wayne, Montclair State College Department of Theatre Upper Montclair, NJ 07043 201-893-4217 (4)

Bonito, Wilson, Musicians' Protective Union 130 Central Avenue Jersey City, NJ 07306 201-653-0750 (18)

Booth, Robert H.W., El Paso Federation of Musicians 10288 Saigon Drive El Paso, TX 79925 915-859-7982 (18)

Booth, Dr. Roscoe, University of Nevada, Reno Department of Theatre Reno, NV 89557 702-784-6155 (4)

Booth, Willard, Delta State University Department of Theatre Cleveland, MS 38733 601-843-2434 (4)

Booth, Willard C., George Peabody College Department of Drama 21st Avenue South Nashville, TN 37203 615-327-8121 (4)

Boozer, Tom, Arts and Humanities Council Tuscaloosa County Post Office Box 1117 Tuscaloosa, AL 35401 205-758-8083 (5)

Boozer, Tom, Acadiana Arts Council Post Office Box 53762 Lafayette, LA 70505 318-233-7060 (5)

Borak, Julia, Roscommon Chamber Music Society Post Office Box 88 Roscommon, MI 48653 517-275-5826 (5)

Bordeau, J. William, Marymount Manhattan College Department of Theatre 221 East 71st Street New York, NY 10021 212-472-3800 (4)

Borden, Jack, Washington's Crossing Association Post Office Box 1776 Titusville, NJ 08560 (16)

Borden, L., Salina Community Theatre 228 ½ East Republic Salina, KS 66604 (16)

Bordner, Kenneth E., Fort Lewis College Department of Theatre College Heights Durango, CO 81301 303-247-7410 (4)

Bordy, Bill, Hollywood Drama-Logue Post Office Box 38771 Los Angeles, CA 90028 213-464-5079 (14)

Borgert, David J., Saint Cloud Community Arts Council Post Office Box 323 Saint Cloud, MN 56302 612-252-2105 (5)

Born, Walter L., Creative Productions 2 Beaver Place Matawan, NJ 07747 201-566-6985 (16)

Borrowman, Lynn, The Five Star Theatre of Alberta Post Office Box 722 Canmore, Alberta, Canada T0L 0M0 (16)

Boske, JoAnna, Arts Council of Montgomery 1010 Forest Avenue Montgomery, Al 36106 205-265-8593 (5)

Bossert, Mrs. Marie A., Norwalk Musicians' Association, Local 52 70 Bouton Street Norwalk, CT 06854 203-866-9368 (18)

Bostic, L.S., Panoak Lighting Systems 6809 East 40th Street Tulsa, OK 74145 918-664-1111 (15)

Bottom, Michael, Cuba Arts Council Route 1, Box 242 Cuba, MO 65453 (5)

Bouchard, Elizabeth, Malcolm X College Theatre Program Chicago, IL 60612 312-942-3000 (4)

Bouchaud, Sally, Sketch Club Players Glover and Logan Box 674 Woodbury, NJ 08096 609-848-8089 (16)

Bougreau, Mrs. Lynda, Musicians' Protective Association Rural Route 5, Box 111 Fairbault, MN 55021 507-334-6668 (18)

Bouland, Michael, Three Rivers Community College Department of Theatre 507 Vine Street Poplar Bluff, MO 63901 314-785-7794 (4)

Bourne, Becky, Eastern College Department of Communication Arts Fairview Drive Saint Davids, PA 19087 215-688-3300 (4)

Bower, Tom, Santa Rosa Junior College Department of Theatre Arts 1501 Mendocino Avenue Santa Rosa, CA 95401 707-527-4418; 707-527-4328 (4)

Bowlett, T.E., Lee College Department of Fine Arts Post Office Box 818 Baytown, TX 77520 713-427-5611 (4)

Bowman, Dr. Georgia, William Jewell College Department of Theatre Liberty, MO 64068 816-781-3806 (4)

Bowman, Gordon, United Technologies Corporation One Financial Plaza Hartford, CT 06101 203-728-7000 (10)

Boxer, Paula, Belden Communications 25 West 45th Street, Room 1206 Chicago, IL 60612 212-730-0172 (15)

Boyars, Marion, Marion Boyars Publishers 99 Main Street Salem, NH 03079 617-686-6407 (14)

Boyce, Allen, Musicians' Protective Union, Local 267 218 Oneida Street Fulton, NY 13069 315-592-4347 (18)

Boyce, Bruce C., ARA Services Incorporated Independence Square West Philadelphia, PA 19106 215-574-5379 (10)

Boyce, Mary, Warner Pacific College Department of Theatre 2219 Southeast 68th Street Portland, OR 97215 503-775-4368 (4)

Boyd, Robert L., Musicians' Protective Union 214 North Congress Street Rushville, IL 62681 217-322-6428 (18)

Boyer-Lanthier, Danielle, Le Theatre des Filles du Roi 430 boul. Tache 3eme etage C.P. 2141, succ. B Hull, Quebec, Canada J9A 1M7 819-771-4389 (16)

Boyle, Tom, Research Technology International 4700 Chase Avenue Lincolnwood, IL 60646 312-677-3000; 800-323-7520 (15)

Boyuk, Stephen, Saint Catharines Musicians' Association 32 Canal Street St. Catharines, Ontario, Canada L2N 4S9 416-935-6673 (18)

Bozenhard, Cushing C., Worcester Foothills Theatre Company Post Office Box 236 Worcester, MA 01602 617-754-3314 (16)

Bracey, John T., El Paso Federation of Musicians 10288 Saigon Drive El Paso, TX 79925 915-859-7982 (18)

Braddy, Robert E., Colorado State University Division of Theatre Arts Johnson Hall Fort Collins, CO 80523 303-491-5116; 303-491-5561 (4)

Bradford, Jim, Dallas Stage 2813 Florence Dallas, TX 75204 214-630-0297 (15)

Bradford, Mrs. Lillian, Madhatters Community Theatre 609 2nd Street Wadena, MN 56482 (16)

Bradley, Ben, People's Heritage 4240 West Fond Du Lac Milwaukee, WI 53216 (16)

Bradley, Denny, Capitol Communication Incorporated Post Office Box 481 Olympia, WA 98507 206-943-5378 (15)

Bradley, Elizabeth, Young People's Theatre 165 Front Street East Toronto, Ontario, Canada M5A 3Z4 416-363-5131, Administration; 416-864-9732, Box Office (16)

Bradley, Elmer A., Musicians' Protective Union 3545 Oxford Street Napa, CA 94558 707-226-7736 (18)

Bradley, George, Sul Ross State University Alpine, TX 79830 915-837-8221 (4)

Bradley, Dr. Robert, Springfield Little Theatre 311 East Walnut Street Springfield, MO 65806 417-869-1334 (16)

Bradley, Dr. Robert H., Southwest Missouri State University Department of Theatre 901 South National Springfield, MO 65802 417-836-5000 (4)

Brady, Kevin, Northwestern Theatre Association 146 Eisenhower Lane, North Lombard, IL 60148 312-629-4165 (15)

Brady, Martie, Loup Valley Arts Council 607 North 22nd Ord, NB 68862 308-728-3874 (5)

Braithwaite, Dr. Roland, Talladega Arts Festival Talladega College Talladega, AL 35160 (9)

Branch, Darr, Jupiter Theatre 516 North Harbor Boulevard Fullerton, CA 92632 714-525-4725 (8)

Brandenburg, Maxine N., Arts Development Services 237 Main Street Buffalo, NY 14203 716-856-7520 (5)

Brandimore, Leroy E., Saginaw Musical Association, Local 57 2456 Barnard Street Saginaw, MI 48602 517-793-1877 (18)

Brandow, Roland, D'Youville College Department of Theatre 320 Porter Avenue Buffalo, NY 14201 716-886-8100 (4)

Brandt, Chris, Medicine Show Theatre Ensemble 6 West 18th Street New York, NY 10003 212-255-4991 (16)

Branstetter, Thomas C., Musicians' Protective Union Route 2, Box 258 Pendleton, OR 97801 503-276-6220 (18)

Brant, Mary B., Community Center for the Performing Arts 303 East Main Street Fort Wayne, IN 46802 219-422-4226 (8)

Bratman, Garry S., Carroll Sound, Incorporated 895 Broadway New York, NY 10036 212-868-4120 (15)

Braun, Charles F., Wheeling College Department of Theatre Post Office Box 18 Wheeling, WV 26003 (4)

Braun, Daryl, Daryl Braun Associates 15691 Container Lane Huntington Beach, CA 92647 213-594-8764 (15)

Bravar, A. James, School of Fine Arts Auditorium California State University Long Beach, CA 90840 213-498-4364 (8)

Brawley, R. J., Musicians' Protective Union, Local 236 724 Terrace Aberdeen, WA 98520 206-532-0583 (18)

Breen, Gertrude, Zeta Phi Eta 518 Greenwood Boulevard Evanston, IL 60201 (16)

Breen, Dr. Kermit, Cookeville Arts Council Breen Lane Cookeville, TN 38501 (5)

Brees, Frank, Marshalltown Federation of Musicians, Local 176 139 Debra Estates Marshalltown, IA 50158 515-753-7650 (18)

Bregar, Constance M., Pueblo Musicians' Association, Local 69 Post Office Box 452 Pueblo, CO 81002 303-544-4725 (18)

Bregstein, Barbara, Cambridge Ensemble 1151 Massachusetts Avenue Cambridge, MA 02138 617-876-2544 (16)

Breidenbaugh, Kenneth, Paint Street Playhouse 33 North Paint Street Chillicothe, OH 45601 (16)

Brendze, Michael, Musicians' Association, Local 95 2505 North Avenue Sheboygan, WI 53081 414-452-4435 (18)

Brenmark, Erik, Mark Taper Forum Laboratory 2580 Cahuenga Boulevard Hollywood, CA 90068 213-972-7357 (16)

Brennan, Edward, Musicians' Protective Association Post Office Box 1 Mystic, CT 06355 203-536-7362 (18)

Brennan, Jimmy, Cinema Services 3050 Sheridan Street Las Vegas, NV 89102 702-876-4667 (15)

Brennan, J.J., East Stroudsburg State College Department of Theatre East Stroudsburg, PA 18301 717-424-3233 (4)

Brennan, Larry, Musicians' Protective Union, Local 128 1421 South West Street Jacksonville, IL 62650 217-245-9723 (18)

Brennan, Ruth, Rapid City Fine Arts Council 713 Seventh Street Rapid City, SD 57701 605-394-4101; 605-394-4102 (5)

Brenner, Clair H., Musicians' Protective Union 925 North Briar Drive York, PA 17404 717-764-5807 (18)

Brenner, Marylou, Alliance College Department of Theatre Cambridge Springs, PA 16403 814-398-4611 (4)

Breslauer, Mr. Tom, Monroe County Arts Council County Courthouse Stroudsburg, PA 18360 717-992-5157 (5)

Breslin, Herbert, Herbert Breslin 119 West 57th Street New York, NY 10019 212-246-5480 (12)

Breton, Ulric, Grand Theatre du Quebec 269 boulevard Saint Cyrille East Quebec City, Quebec, Canada G1R 2B3 418-643-8111, Administrative; 418-643-8131, Box Office (8)

Brett, Roger, Brett Theatrical, Ltd. 91 Beach Road Bristol, RI 02809 401-253-5624 (15)

Brey, Ron, Owatonna Area Musicians' Association 1419 Hemlock Owatonna, MN 55060 507-451-8593 (18)

Bricks, Andrea, Leah Posluns Theatre 4588 Bathurst Street Willowdale, Ontario, Canada M2J 4E4 416-636-2720 (16)

Bridges, E., Galilean Players 580 West 6th Street San Pedro, CA 90731 (16)

Bridgewater, Victor, Toronto Musicians' Association, Local 149 101 Thorncliffe Park Drive Toronto, Ontario, Canada M4H 1M1 416-421-1020 (18)

Briezke, Milton W., Missouri Southern State College Department of Theatre Newman and Duquesne Roads Joplin, MO 64801 417-624-8100 (4)

Briggs, Douglas M., Northwestern College Department of Theatre Roseville, MN 55113 612-636-4840 (4)

Briggs, George D., Musicians' Protective Union 1106 South 12th Burlington, IA 52601 319-754-4705 (18)

Briggs, Patricia, Palo Alto Children's Theatre 1305 Middlefield Road Palo Alto, CA 94301 (16)

Briggs, Wallace N., University of Kentucky Department of Theatre Lexington, KY 40506 606-257-2797 (4)

Brignac, Jack, Rapco Associates, Incorporated Post Office Box 7885 Metairie, LA 70010 504-887-9500 (15)

Brill, Frank A., Elmo Manufacturing Corporation 70 New Hyde Park Road New Hyde Park, NY 11040 516-775-3200 (15)

Brimhall, Mary, Copper Village Museum and Arts Center Post Office Box 29 Anaconda, MT 59711 406-563-3604 (5)

Brinckley, Charles O., Musicians' Union, Local 48 169 East Chicago Street Elgin, IL 60120 312-742-3757 (18)

Brind'Amour, Yvette, Theatre Du Rideau Vert 355 rue Gilford Montreal, Quebec, Canada H2T 1M6 514-845-0267 (16)

Brindley, Robert L., Washington and Jefferson College Department of Theatre Lincoln Street Washington, DC 15301 412-222-4400 (4)

Brink, Lois, Association for the Visual Arts 1001 North Saint Joseph Hastings, NB 68901 (5)

Brinkley, Rudolph, Musicians' Association 201 McTeer Drive Kingsport, TN 37660 615-246-6351 (18)

Brinson, Louise, Meridian Municipal Junior College Department of Theatre Meridian, MS 39301 (4)

Brinson, Steve, Image Devices Incorporated 1615 Phoenix Boulevard Atlanta, GA 30349 404-996-0000 (15)

Briscoe, J., Gettysburg Summer Theatre Gettysburg, SD 57442 (16)

Britch, Carroll P., Springfield Profile Ensemble Theatre 586 Main Street Wilbraham, MA 01095 413-596-8449 (16)

Britch, Florea M., Springfield Profile Ensemble Theatre 586 Main Street Wilbraham, MA 01095 413-596-8449 (16)

Brittain, Carl B., Musicians' Protective Union 847 Bowman Walla Walla, WA 99362 509-525-7576 (18)

Brocato, Don, Kalamazoo Federation of Musicians, Local 228 3332 Wedgewood Drive Kalamazoo, MI 49008 616-344-0049 (18)

Brocato, Thomas, Tom Brocato and Associates, Incorporated 6380 Wilshire Boulevard, Suite 1411 Los Angeles, CA 90048 213-653-9570 (12)

Brock, Raymond P., Musicians' Protective Association 1231 East Hanson Drive Appleton, WI 54911 414-734-0021 (18)

Brockington, John, University of British Columbia Department of Theatre Vancouver, British Columbia, Canada V6T 1W5 604-228-3880; 604-228-2678 (4)

Brockway, Bob, Concession Supply Company 1016 North Summit Street, Box 1007 Toledo, OH 43697 419-241-7711 (15)

Brockway, Brad, Concession Supply Company 1016 North Summit Street, Box 1007 Toledo, OH 43697 419-241-7711 (15)

Brodley, Michael, State Community College of East Saint Louis Department of Theatre East Saint Louis, IL 62201 (4)

Brody, Alan, Skidmore College Department of Theatre Saratoga Springs, NY 12866 518-584-5000 (4)

Brody, Stanley, Stanley Brody 649 East 14th Street New York, NY 10009 212-228-7863 (12)

Brogan, John J. Jr., Greater Springfield Musicians' Association, Local 171 134 Chestnut Street Springfield, MA 01103 413-736-5187 (18)

Bronson, Bernice, The Mal Angelo Heritage Playhouse Post Office Box 100 Hopkington, RI 02833 401-377-2413 (16)

Brooking, Jack T., Agnes Scott College Department of Theatre Decatur, GA 30030 404-373-2571 (4)

Brookins, Milton G., Musicians' Protective Association, Local 163 17 South Hollywood Avenue Gloversville, NY 12078 518-725-1256 (18)

Brooks, Alfred G., State University of New York, Stony Brook Department of Theatre Arts Stony Brook, NY 11794 516-246-5670 (4)

Brooks, Darryl E., Flynns Fabric Design Supplies 1154 Howard Street San Francisco, CA 94103 415-621-5968, Flynns; 415-431-8214, Fibrec (15)

Brooks, Gwen, Poor Alex Theatre 296 Brunswick Avenue Toronto, Ontario, Canada M5S 2M7 416-920-8370 (8)

Brooks, Joe B., Corsicana Community Playhouse 202 East Collin Corsicana, TX 75110 214-872-5421 (16)

Brooks, Maggie, Patio Players Menomonie Falls, WI 53051 (16)

Brooten, Opal, Citizens Council for the Arts Art on the Green Post Office Box 901 Coeur d'Alene, ID 83814 208-664-9052; 208-664-2259 (9)

Brothers, David H., David H. Brothers, Company 19 Old Court Road Baltimore, MD 21208 301-764-7189 (15)

Brown, Arvin, Long Wharf Theatre 222 Sargent Drive New Haven, CT 06511 203-787-4284; 203-787-4282 (Box Office) (16)

Brown, Bob, Brown Lighting Sales 3214 Sunridge Drive Manlius, NY 13104 315-682-8916 (15)

Brown, C., Hidden Hills Players 5791 Jed Smith Road Hidden Hills, CA 91302 (16)

Brown, Carl, AUM Publications Post Office Box 32433 Queens, NY 11431 212-523-3471 (14)

Brown, Curtis, Curtis Brown, Ltd. 575 Madison Avenue New York, NY 10022 212-840-8272 (2)

Brown, David, Town Players, Incorporated Post Office Box 211 Newton, CT 06470 (16)

Brown, David B., Musicians' Protective Union Post Office Box 91 Lycoming, NY 13093 315-343-0557 (18)

Brown, Elva, Oconee County Arts Commission Post Office Box 217 Walhalla, SC 29691 803-638-5049 (5)

Brown, Firman, Dillingham Center for the Performing Arts Ithaca College Ithaca, NY 14850 607-274-3345 (8)

Brown, Firman H., Dillingham Center Ithaca College Ithaca, NY 14850 607-274-3345 (8)

Brown, Dr. Firman H., Ohio State University Department of Theatre 1849 Cannon Drive Columbus, OH 43210 614-422-5821 (4)

Brown, Gladys T., Area Council on the Arts and Humanities Post Office Box 21 Sylacauga, AL 35150 205-249-2700; 205-245-5383 (5)

Brown, Hartley, Musicians' Protective Union 1020 Letnes Drive Grand Forks, ND 58201 701-775-9843 (18)

Brown, Jack, Jack Brown Electronic Sales 207 Rosedale Road Yonkers, NY 10910 914-779-7330 (15)

Brown, James, James Brown Associates 25 West 43rd Street New York, NY 10036 212-276-1131 (2)

Brown, Johnny, Johnny Brown 2019 Mansfield Street Montreal, Quebec, Canada (15)

Brown, Kaleta, Cypress College Department of Theatre 9200 Valley View Cypress, CA 90630 714-826-2220; 714-821-6320 (4)

Brown, Larry, Strand Century, Incorporated 303 West Greenfield Lombard, IL 60148 312-629-1664 (15)

Brown, Pat, Alley Theatre 615 Texas Avenue Houston, TX 77002 713-228-9341 (16)

Brown, R., Beechmont Players 1601 Turquoise Drive Cincinnati, OH 45230 (16)

Brown, Sally Stearns, Peterborough Players Box 1 Peterborough, NH 03458 603-924-3601 (16)

Brown, Timothy E., Saint Mary of the Woods College Department of Theatre Saint Mary of the Woods, IN 47876 812-535-4141 (4)

Brubaker, David, Dickinson College Department of Theatre Carlisle, PA 17013 717-243-5121 (4)

Bruce, Claudia, Time and Space Limited 139-41 West 22nd Street New York, NY 10011 212-741-1032; 212-243-9268 (16)

Bruce, Irene, Sumter County Fine Arts Council Post Office Drawer 1038 Livingston, AL 35470 205-652-2298 (5)

Bruhn, F., Town Players 208 NE 5th Avenue Watertown, SD 57201 (16)

Bruhn, Florence, Watertown Area Arts Council 912 North Broadway Watertown, SD 57201 605-886-5542 (5)

Brumm, Beverly, Pace University Department of Theatre 78 North Broadway White Plains, NY 10603 914-682-7000 (4)

Bruner, Mrs. Marty, Pixie Playhouse Post Office Box 845 Mobile, AL 36608 205-344-1537 (8)

Brunner, Marty, Pixie Players Post Office Box 81 Mobile, AL 36608 205-344-1537 (16)

Brunson, Nancy Cowart, Coffee County Arts Alliance Post Office Box 848 Enterprise, AL 36330 205-347-2623 (5)

Brunyate, Roger, Peabody Conservatory Theatre Department 1 East Mount Vernon Place Baltimore, MD 21202 301-659-8100 (4)

Brustein, Robert, Yale Repertory Theatre 222 York Street New Haven, CT 06511 203-436-1587 (16)

Bryant, Hazel J., Afro-American Total Theatre Grant Arts Foundation, Inc. New York, NY 10023 (3)

Bryant, Mary, Mary Bryant 165 West 46th Street New York, NY 10036 212-575-1166 (12)

Bryant, R.L., Brazosport Fine Arts Council Post Office Box 684 Lake Jackson, TX 77566 713-265-6427 (5)

Buberl, Doris, The Edison Theatre 240 West 47th Street New York, NY 10036 212-757-7164; 212-586-7870 (16)

Buckland, C.S., Holophane-Manville Canada Incorporated 1620 Steeles Avenue Brampton, Ontario, Canada L6T 1A5 416-793-3111 (15)

Buckwald, Charles, The Theater Post Office Box 330 Moorestown, NJ 08057 609-234-9737 (8)

Bucky, J.B., Williams College Department of Theatre Williamstown, MA 02766 413-597-3131 (4)

Buddick, Beverly, Interlake Festival Theatre 201 - 297 Smith Street Winnipeg, Manitoba, Canada (16)

Calvin, M. J., Whittier Community Theatre Post Office Box 601 Whittier, CA 90605 (16)

Cambron, Hazel J., Federation of Musicians, Local 102 508 North East Street Bloomington, IL 61701 309-828-6814 (18)

Campbell, Brenda, Theatre Max Post Office Box 1744 Guelph, Ontario, Canada N1H 6Z9 519-824-2714 (16)

Campbell, Kenneth, Virginia Commonwealth University 901 West Franklin Street Richmond, VA 23284 (4)

Campbell, Lisa, Gatson College Department of Theatre Dallas, NC 28034 704-922-3136; 704-554-6080 (4)

Campbell, Tricia, Edison Recreational Center Municipal Boulevard, Plainfield Avenue Edison, NJ 08817 201-287-0900 (5)

Campbell, William, State University Agricultural and Technical College Department of Theatre New Delhi, NY 13753 607-746-4216; 607-746-4222 (4)

Campbell, William, The Little Theatre State University Agricultural and Technical College Delhi, NY 13753 607-746-4216 (8)

Canes, Moira J., Theatre Direct Canada Box 356, Station P Toronto, Ontario, Canada M5S 2S8 416-537-5770; 416-537-8424 (16)

Canine, William, Newberry Arts Council 1508 College Street Newberry, SC 29108 803-276-5012 (5)

Cannon, Don, Professional Musicians' Association, Local 65 609 Chenevert Houston, TX 77003 713-236-8676 (18)

Cannon, James, Bash Theatrial Lighting 1515 A Pacific Avenue Atlantic City, NJ 08404 (15)

Cannon, Jimmie, Imperial Valley Federation of Musicians 1611 Pepper Drive El Centro, CA 92243 714-352-4025 (18)

Cannon, Robert, Bash Theatrical Lighting 2012 86th Street North Bergen, NJ 07047 201-869-1400; 212-279-9265 (15)

Canon, Robert, Arts Council of San Antonio 235 East Commerce San Antonio, TX 78205 512-224-5532 (5)

Cantelupe, Joseph, Sharon Musicians' Association, Local 187 840 Smith Avenue Sharon, PA 16147 412-981-5760 (18)

Canter, Louis, Mount San Jacinto Community College Department of Theatre 21400 Highway 79 San Jacinto, CA 92383 (4)

Cantin, Pierre, Quebec Ministry of Cultural Affairs 955 chemin St-Louis Quebec, Quebec, Canada G1A 1A3 418-643-2110 (5)

Caparelli, James, Nuestro Teatro 112 East 23rd Street New York, NY 10010 212-673-9430 (16)

Capo, Larry, Rider College Department of Theatre 2083 Lawrenceville Road Lawrenceville, NJ 08648 609-896-5168; 609-896-0800 (4)

Caporaso, Barbara, Ticket Craft Incorporated 1925 Bellmore Avenue Bellmore, NY 11710 516-826-1500; 800-645-4944 (15)

Cappel, John, Cappel Display Company, Incorporated 920 Elm Street Cincinnati, OH 45202 513-621-0952 (15)

Cappel, Ray, Cappel Display Company, Incorporated 920 Elm Street Cincinnati, OH 45202 513-621-0952 (15)

Capron, George, Merrimack Valley Council on the Arts 4 Summer Street Haverhill, MA 08130 617-373-0421 (5)

Caraballo, Orlando, Key West Federation of Musicians, Local 202 1508 19th Street Key West, FL 33040 305-296-2276 (18)

Card, Russ, Arjay Lighting Sales 3832 North Hubbard Milwaukee, WI 53212 414-961-1690 (15)

Carey, L., Creek Theatre 4007 Avenue B Austin, TX 78751 (16)

Carey, Orlin, Anchorage Press Post Office Box 8067 New Orleans, LA 70182 504-283-8868 (14)

Carlberg, Carl T., C.T. Carlburg and Associates Incorporated 2530 Washington North East Albuquerque, NM 87110 505-888-3883 (15)

Carlbon, Lawrence, Hunterdon Art Center Old Stone Mill Clinton, NJ 08809 (5)

Carlock, J. Bruce, Erskine College Department of English Due West, SC 29639 803-379-2131 (4)

Carloss, Roy, Joliet Federation of Musicians, Local 37 265 North Ottawa Street Joliet, IL 60431 815-723-1645 (18)

Carlson, Carolyn, Arts Council of Fayetteville Post Office Box 318 Fayetteville, NC 28302 919-323-1776 (5)

Carlson, Fredrick B., Citrus College Azusa, CA 91024 213-355-0521 (4)

Carlson, Mrs. James, Verdigre Arts Council Post Office Box C Verdigre, NB 68783 (5)

Carlson, Leta N., Masquers/Town and Gown Players Fine Arts Department Fairmont, WV 26554 304-367-4248; 304-367-4240 (16)

Carlson, P., Theatre Upstairs 10622 Fable Row Columbia, MD 21044 (16)

Carlson, Pat, Stromsburg Area Arts Council 416 Main Street Stromburg, NB 68666 (5)

Carmen, Beverly, Cape Cod Melody Tent Hyannis, MA 02601 617-775-5630; 617-775-9100 (16)

Carmen, William, Cape Cod Melody Tent Hyannis, MA 02601 617-775-5630; 617-775-9100 (16)

Carmichael, Mrs. Georgia, Craven Community Arts Council Post Office Box 596 New Bern, NC 28560 919-638-2577; 919-637-4064 (5)

Carnaby, Michael, Tracy Costumes 63 Melcher Street Boston, MA 02210 617-542-9100 (15)

Carnaby, Michael, Mikan Theatricals 54 Tide Mill Road Hampton, NH 03842 603-926-2744; 617-542-9101 (15)

Carnegie, Norman M., Strafford Musicians' Association 52 Jones Street Strafford, Ontario, Canada 519-271-1362 (18)

Carner, Ann L., Arts and Sciences Center 14 Court Street Nashua, NH 03060 603-883-1506 (5)

Carone, Gary, Visuals Ltd. 1485-C Landmeier Road Elk Grove Village, IL 60007 312-640-1185 (15)

Carozza, G.N., Johns-Manville Sales Corporation 600 Sylvan Avenue Englewood Cliffs, NJ 07632 215-543-0701 (15)

Carpenter, Robert F., Niagara Falls Musicians' Association 5848 Main Street Niagara Falls, Ontario, Canada L2G 5Z5 416-357-4642 (18)

Carr, Francis, Musicians' Protective Union Road 1 Freeland, PA 18224 717-636-0600 (18)

Carre, Jerry L., Mobile Theatre Guild Post Office Box 1265 Mobile, AL 36601 205-433-7513 (16)

Carrere, Georges, Theatre des Marguerites Avenue Jean XXIII Trois-Rivieres Ouest, Quebec, Canada H2V 2C3 819-377-3223 (16)

Carrier, Louis-Georges, Theatre de Marjolaine 1500 rue Stanley, Suite 320 Montreal, Quebec, Canada H3A 1R3 514-845-0917 (16)

Carroad, Andrea, Cherry Lane Theatre 38 Commerce Street New York, NY 10014 212-989-2020 (8)

Carrol, Bill, Falls City Theatre Equipment Company 427-429 South Third Street Louisville, KY 40202 502-584-7375 (15)

Carrol, John R., Thomas More Theatre Company 5430 Torrance Boulevard Torrance, CA 90503 213-540-2021 (16)

Carroll, Barbara, Barbara Carroll 1501 Broadway New York, NY 10036 212-391-6994 (12)

Carroll, John W., John W. Carroll 1133 Marlowe Avenue Orlando, FL 32809 305-855-1993 (15)

Carroll, Kay, Comco Plastics of Illinois 4920 South Monitor Avenue Chicago, IL 60638 312-496-1800; 312-581-3000 (15)

Carrother, Richard, Waldorf Astoria Playhouse Tiffany's Attic Dinner Playhouse 5028 Main Street Kansas City, MO 64112 816-523-1706; 816-361-2661 (16)

Carshen, Charles, Sarah Lawrence College Department of Theatre 1 Meadway Bronxville, NY 10708 914-337-0700 (4)

Carson, Chuck, Fresno Community Theatre Post Office Box 1308 Fresno, CA 93715 209-233-6213; 209-233-6214 (16)

Carson, John, Garden State Arts Center Post Office Box 116 Holmdel, NJ 07733 (8)

Carson, Richard, The NDWT Company 736 Bathurst Street Toronto, Ontario, Canada M5S 2R4 416-536-9255; 416-536-6663 (16)

Carstairs, Hobart C., FaceMakers, Incorporated 140 Fifth Street Savanna, IL 61074 815-273-3944 (15)

Carstens, Dr. Jerald, University of Wisconsin, River Falls Department of Theatre River Falls, WI 54022 715-425-3911 (4)

Carter, Chet, Musicians' Protective Association, Local 32 2420 Lafayette Street Anderson, IN 46012 317-642-3993 (18)

Carter, Lois, Kaleidoscope Theatre Post Office Box 4272 Panama City, FL 32401 904-763-6878 (16)

Carter, Ralph, Johnson State College Department of Performing Arts Johnson, VT 05656 802-635-2356 (4)

Carter-Cox, Ann, Robbins-Zust Marionettes and Theatre East Road Richmond, MA 01254 413-698-2591 (16)

Caruso, Vincent, Musicians' Protective Union Grant Plaza Brookhaven, PA 19015 215-874-7158 (18)

Carver, Lewis B., Columbus Musicians' Protective Association 6232 Lyndridge Avenue Columbus, GA 31904 404-323-0515 (18)

Carver, Raymond E., Angelo State University Department of Drama San Angelo, TX 76902 915-942-2031; 915-942-2032 (4)

Casapulla, Thomas J., Musicians' Protective Union, Local 237 54 Windsor Avenue Dover, NJ 07801 201-366-7640 (18)

Casey, Richard, Fort Wayne Civic Theatre 303 East Main Street Fort Wayne, IN 46802 (16)

Casey, V., Reading Community Theatre 1 East Lakeview Drive Reading, OH 45215 (16)

Cashman, Daniel E., Southern Connecticut State College Department of Theatre 501 Crescent Street New Haven, CT 06515 203-397-4432; 203-397-4431 (4)

Casiola, Frank, Miami Federation of Musicians 1779 Northwest 28th Street Miami, FL 33142 305-633-3235 (18)

Cassano, Sam, Musicians' Association of Niagara Falls, Local 106 1736 La Salle Avenue Niagra Falls, NY 14301 716-284-6247 (18)

Cassell, Gerald S., Kingsport Theatre Guild c/o Fine Arts Center Church Circle Kingsport, TN 37660 615-246-9351 (16)

Casstevens, William, Yadkin Arts Council Route 3, Box 142 Yadkinville, NC 27055 919-679-2941 (5)

Cast, Dick, The Crosby Group Post Office Box 3128 Tulsa, OK 74101 918-834-4611 (15)

Castanos, Luz, Nuestro Teatro 112 East 23rd Street New York, NY 10010 212-673-9430 (16)

Castellanos, Jose F., Bacardi Imports 2100 Biscayne Boulevard Miami, FL 33137 305-573-8511 (10)

Castiglione, Harry, Musicians' Union, Local 215 49 Plochmann Lane Woodstock, NY 12498 914-679-6227 (18)

Castro, Andres, Westside Community Repertory Theatre 252 West 81st Street New York, NY 10024 212-874-9400; 212-666-3521 (16)

Castro, Mark, Industrial Safety Products, Incorporated 5775 Canal Road Cleveland, OH 44125 216-524-0360 (15)

Catalano, Vincent, Albany Musicians' Association, Local 14 452 Albany-Shaker Road Loudonville, NY 12211 518-459-4743 (18)

Catanzarito, Michael A., Musicians' Protective Union Lewis Street Punxsutawney, PA 15767 814-938-5854 (18)

Cecil, Dr. Herbert, Weber State College Fine Arts Center Main Auditorium 3750 Harrison Boulevard Ogden, UT 84408 801-399-5941 (8)

Celms, Andis, National Arts Centre Box 1534, Station B Ottawa, Ontario, Canada K1P 5W1 613-996-5051; 613-237-4400 (16)

Cercone, Samuel P., Cercone Vincent Associates, Incorporated 5020 Richmond Road Bedford Heights, OH 44146 216-292-2550 (15)

Cercone, Samuel P., Cercone Vincent Associates, Incorporated 2741 Noblestown Road Pittsburgh, PA 15205 412-922-0901 (15)

Cermak, Vern, Musicians' Protective Association, Local 229 201 Missouri River Road Mandan, ND 58554 701-667-1077; 701-663-5775 (18)

Cerniglia, Anthony P.J., Lincoln Land Community College Department of Theatre Springfield, IL 62708 217-786-2314 (4)

Cerra, Bernard, Musicians' Protective Union, Local 130 87 Belmont Carbondale, PA 18407 717-282-3155 (18)

Cervello, Santo, Erewhon Theatre Box 229 Station M Toronto, Ontario, Canada M6S 4T3 416-241-5407 (16)

Cervone, Tony, Musicians' Protective Union 1303 Breckenridge Avenue San Leandro, CA 94579 415-483-5470 (18)

Chadwick, W.R., University of Waterloo Department of Theatre Humanities, Room 148 Waterloo, Ontario, Canada N2L 3G1 519-885-1211 (4)

Chafee, Mike, Michael Chafee Enterprises 2215 Alpine Avenue Sarasota, FL 33579 813-621-7725 (15)

Challstedt, Carl H., Musicians' Association, Local 76 2620 Third Avenue Seattle, WA 98121 206-623-0025 (18)

Chambers, Lois, Valley Art Association 2120 Main Street Forest Grove, OR 97110 503-357-3703 (5)

Chambers, Wilma, Musicians' Protective Association 719 South 15th Street Mount Vernon, IL 62864 618-242-7613 (18)

Chambless, John, Bathouse Theatre 7312 West Green Lake Drive Seattle, WA 98103 206-524-9110 (8)

Chang, Tisa, Pan Asian Repertory Theatre 305 Riverside Drive New York, NY 10025 212-662-7171; 212-475-7710 (16)

Chang, T.T., Chinese Cultural and Community Center 125 North Tenth Street Philadelphia, PA 19107 215-NA3-6767 (5)

Changstrom, Bob, R.W. Changstrom and Associates Route #8 Lincoln, NE 68506 402-723-3367 (15)

Changstrom, Tom, R.W. Changstrom and Associates Route #8 Lincoln, NE 68506 402-723-3367 (15)

Chanson, Harry, Musicians' Mutual Protective Association 2904 ½ De La Vina Street Santa Barbara, CA 93105 805-687-3519 (18)

Chapman, James, Seattle Pacific University Department of Theatre 3307 3rd Avenue West Seattle, WA 98119 206-281-2036 (4)

Chapman, James W., Alfred University Division of Performing Arts Alfred, NY 14802 607-871-2251; 607-871-2252 (4)

Chapman, Lonny, The Group Theatre 1276 Van Ness Hollywood, CA 90028 213-466-2273 (16)

Chapman, Robert, Bakersfield College 1801 Panorama Drive Bakerfield, CA 93305 805-395-4011 (4)

Chapman, Vernon, Gryphon Theatre Company 103 Dunlop Street East Barrie, Ontario, Canada L4M 4T7 705-728-4613 (16)

Chappell, Fred, Alliance Theatre Company/Atlanta Children's Theatre 12801 Peachtree Street NE Atlanta, GA 30309 404-898-1132 (16)

Chappell, Wallace, The Repertory Theatre of Saint Louis 130 Edgar Road Post Office Box 28030 Saint Louis, MO 63119 314-968-7340; 314-968-4925, Box Office (16)

Charles, Melisande, Minneapolis Arts Commission 302 City Hall Minneapolis, MN 55415 612-348-5486 (5)

Charlton, Jeanne Murray, Lakewood Puppeteer Productions 11812 Woodbine Lane SW Tacoma, WA 98499 206-584-4759 (16)

Chavez, Edmund M., University of Idaho Department of Theatre Moscow, ID 83843 208-885-6465 (4)

Chernack, Peter A., Company Theatre 1653 South La Cienega Boulevard Los Angeles, CA 90035 213-274-5153 (16)

Chernuck, Dorothy, Corning Summer Theatre Post Office Box 51 Corning, NY 14830 607-936-4634 (16)

Cherry, Wal, Temple University Department of Theatre Philadelphia, PA 19122 212-787-8413 (4)

Chevalier, John, Sarnia Musicians' Association 150 North Brock Street Sarnia, Ontario, Canada N7T 5ZI 519-337-5838 (18)

Cheyka, Frank, Shawnano Federation of Musicians, Local 227 301 State Street Bonduel, WI 54107 715-758-8944 (18)

Chichester, Professor W. T., Palmer Auditorium University of Montevallo Montevallo, AL 35115 205-665-2521 (8)

Childs, Don, Concordia University Department of Theatre Loyola Campus, 7141 Sherbrooke Street West Montreal, Quebec, Canada H4B 1R6 514-482-0320; 514-879-5855 (4)

Chiles, Suzanne, New Stage Theatre Post Office Box 4792 Jackson, MS 39216 (16)

Chilocote, J., Clayton Players Clayton, NM 88415 (16)

Ching, James C., Hamline University Department of Theatre 1536 Hewitt Avenue Saint Paul, MN 55104 612-641-2229 (4)

Chiprean, John J. Jr., Butler Federation of Musicians, Local 188 142 Remil Drive Butler, PA 16001 412-287-1591 (18)

Chiudioni, "Eddie", Musicians' Protective Association, Local 159 161 Hilltop Road Mansfield, OH 44906 419-529-2754 (18)

Chmel, Patrick, Rider College Department of Theatre 2083 Lawrenceville Road Lawrenceville, NJ 08648 609-896-5168; 609-896-0800 (4)

Chow, Alan, Chinese-American Arts Council 45 Canal Street New York, NY 10002 212-431-9740; 212-284-6083 (5)

Chowhan, Albert, Brantford Musicians' Association 15 Mayflower Avenue Brantford, Ontario, Canada N3R 1N9 519-752-7973 (18)

Christensen, Shirley G., Medford Federation of Musicians 2722 East McAndrews Street Medford, OR 97501 503-772-2431 (18)

Christenson, Gary, Clear Light Systems Company 608 19th Avenue East Seattle, WA 98112 206-322-8811 (15)

Christern, Ann, Arena Civic Theatre Inc. Post Office Box 744 Greenfield, MA 01301 413-773-8111 (16)

Christie, Alfred, Hampton Playhouse 405 East 54th Street New York, NY 10022 (16)

Christopher, Stephen C., University Musicians' Association, Local 275 4654 Harwick Boulder, CO 80301 303-530-1912 (18)

Chromik, Steve, Toledo Federation of Musicians, Local 15-286 308 Hillcrest Hotel Toledo, OH 43624 419-243-2017 (18)

Chuck, John, Theatre Vision 5426 Fair Avenue North Hollywood, CA 91601 213-769-0928 (15)

Church, Charles F., Sikeston Activity Center 201 South Kings Highway Sikeston, MO 63801 314-471-4113 (8)

Church, K., Brown Grand Community Theatre 333 East 16th Street Concordia, KS 66901 (16)

Churko, John G., Lighting Services, Incorporated 150 East 58th Street New York, NY 10022 212-838-8633 (15)

Chvany, Lawrence, Metropolitan Cultural Alliance 250 Boylston Street Boston, MA 02116 617-247-1460 (5)

Ciesil, Dennis, Columbus College Department of Theatre Algonquin Drive Columbus, GA 31907 404-568-2030 (4)

Cinelli, Lou, Gaslight Players Turlock, CA 95380 (16)

Civitillo, Don F., Cine 60 Incorporated 630 Ninth Avenue New York, NY 10036 212-586-8782 (15)

Ciza, Svata, Peoria Federation of Musicians, Local 26 5215 Glen Elm Drive Peoria Heights, IL 61614 309-682-7517 (18)

Claire, James M. St., Shippensburg State College Department of Theatre Shippensburg, PA 17257 717-532-1732 (4)

Clancy, James F., Century 11 Convention Hall 225 West Douglas Wichita, KS 67202 316-264-9121 (8)

Clancy, James F., Century 11 Theatre 225 West Douglas Wichita, KS 67202 316-264-9121 (8)

Clancy, J.R., J.R. Clancy Incorporated 7041 Interstate Island Road Syracuse, NY 13209 315-451-3440 (15)

Clapp, Harvey, Chilton County Arts and Humanities Council 100 First Avenue Clanton, AL 35045 205-366-2921 (5)

Clapp, Harvey, Chilton County Fine Arts Guild 100 First Avenue Clanton, AL 35045 205-366-2921 (5)

Clapsaddle, Joseph, Performing Arts Council Music Center of Los Angeles County 135 North Grand Avenue Los Angeles, CA 90012 213-972-7265 (5)

Clare, Jeanette, Our Lady of Angels College Humanities Department Aston, PA 19014 215-GL9-0905 (4)

Clark, C.N., General Electric Lamp Products Division Nela Park Cleveland, OH 44112 216-266-2121 (15)

Clark, Mrs. Faye, Dekalb Community College Department of Theatre 555 North Indian Creek Clarkston, GA 31907 404-292-1520 (4)

Clark, Ginna, Wayne Art Center 413 Maplewood Avenue Wayne, PA 19087 215-688-3553 (5)

Clark, Dr. Graham, Jones Auditorium School of the Ozarks Point Lookout, MO 65726 417-334-6411 (8)

Clark, James, Morgan Hall Auditorium c/o Clark Box 2906 University, AL 35486 205-348-7007 (8)

Clark, James C., Musicians' Protective Association, Local 32 2420 Lafayette Street Anderson, IN 46012 317-642-3993 (18)

Clark, Dr. Jay D., Pittsfield Area Arts Council 32 Manchester Street Pittsfield, NH 03263 (5)

Clark, Leroy, Berry College Department of Theatre Mount Berry, GA 30149 404-232-5374 (4)

Clark, Mort, Westchester Community College Department of Theatre Valhalla, NY 10595 914-592-3038 (4)

Clark, Richard M., Loretto Heights College Department of Theatre Denver, CO 80236 303-936-4265 (4)

Clark, Dr. Richard M., Ithaca College Department of Theatre Arts Ithaca, NY 14850 607-274-3345 (4)

Clark, Thomas P., Parma Area Fine Arts Council 7441 West Ridgewood Drive Parma, OH 44129 216-888-4514 (5)

Clarke, Glenn, Avon Product Foundation 9 West 57th Street New York, NY 10019 212-593-5605 (10)

Clarke, V., Lyceum Players Post Office Box 3659 Wilmington, DE 19807 (16)

Clayman, A. East, Liberty Community Theatre 7909 Brookford Circle Baltimore, MD 21208 (16)

Clegg, Oliver, Magnolia Arts Council 128 South Jackson, Drawer A Magnolia, AR 71753 501-234-3550 (5)

Clemens, Donald R., Peabody ABC Corporation Post Office Box 77 Warsaw, IN 46580 219-267-5166 (15)

Clemson, Jeanne, Actors Company of Pennsylvania 318 North Arch, Box 1153 Lancaster, PA 17604 (16)

Cleveland, John, Greater Gary Arts Council 504 Broadway, Suite 1037 Gary, IN 46402 219-885-8444 (5)

Cleveland, William, De Anza College 21250 Stevens Creek Boulevard Cupertino, CA 95014 408-996-4567 (4)

Clevenger, Theodore, Association for Communication Administration 5105 Backlick Road, Suite E Annandale, VA 22003 703-053- (5)

Clewis, Buddy, Mobile Municipal Theatre 401 Auditorium Drive Mobile, AL 36601 205-438-7261 (8)

Clifton, Randy J., The Cast Theatre Incorporated 804 North El Centro Avenue Hollywood, CA 90038 213-462-9872, Production Office; 213-462-0265, Box Office (16)

Clinton, John, Sterling Heights Cultural Commission 40555 Utica Road Sterling Heights, MI 48078 313-268-8500 (5)

Cloud, Perry, Granny's Dinner Playhouse 12205 Coit Road Dallas, TX 75230 214-239-0153 (16)

Clover, Alice M., Clarion State College Department of Theatre 165 Warwick Boyd Fine Arts Center Clarion, PA 16214 814-226-2282 (4)

Cloyd, Royal, Boston Center for the Arts 539 Tremont Street Boston, MA 02116 617-426-5000 (5)

Clum, John M., Duke University Drama Program 6936 College Station Durham, NC 27708 919-684-6285 (4)

Coatney, James E., Theatrical Equipment Rental, Incorporated 600 Atlantic Avenue Knoxville, TN 37917 615-546-2082 (15)

Coatney, Jim, TERI Productions 600 Atlantic Avenue Knoxville, TN 37917 615-546-2082 (15)

Cochrane, Sally, Second City 110 Lombard Street Toronto, Ontario, Canada M5C 1M3 416-363-0461, Administrative; 416-363-1674, Box Office (16)

Cocks, Harvey, Youtheatre 303 East Main Street Fort Wayne, IN 46802 (16)

Coe, Peter, American Shakespeare Theatre/Connecticut Center for the Performing Arts (Stratford) 1850 Elm Street Stratford, CT 06497 203-378-7321; 212-966-3900 (16)

Coe, Peter, The Citadel Theatre 9828 - 101A Avenue Edmonton, Alberta, Canada T5J 3C6 403-426-4811; 403-425-1820 (16)

Coe, Shirley, Suffolk County Community College Department of Theatre Selden, NY 11784 516-233-5252 (4)

Coffey, Jim, Jim Coffey 14352 Ehlen Way Tustin, CA 92680 714-832-6152 (15)

Cogan, David, The Biltmore Theatre 261 West 47th Street New York, NY 10036 212-582-5340 (16)

Cohen, B., Arlington Players 2352 North Vernon Street Arlington, VA 22207 (16)

Cohen, Bruce, Bruce Cohen 2054 Broadway New York, NY 10023 212-580-9548 (12)

Cohen, Edward M., Jewish Repertory Theatre 344 East 14th Street New York, NY 10003 212-777-0033 (16)

Cohen, George, Worcester Musicians' Association, Local 143 38 Patch Reservoir Drive Worcester, MA 01602 617-798-2228 (18)

Cohen, Robert, University of California, Irvine Department of Theatre Irvine, CA 96717 714-883-6614 (4)

Cohen, Sam, Southern Importers 4825 San Jacinto Street Houston, TX 77004-5620 713-524-8236 (15)

Cohen, William, Paco Electronics, Ltd. 45 Stinson Street Montreal, Quebec, Canada H4N 2E1 514-748-6787 (15)

Cohn, Andy, Jean Cocteau Repertory 330 Bowery New York, NY 10012 212-677-0060 (16)

Cohnstaedy, Joy, Saskatchewan Arts Board 200 Lakeshore Drive Regina, Saskatchewan, Canada S4S 0B3 306-565-4056 (5)

Coker, Charmaine, Medieval Festival, Fullerton University Activities Center Fullerton, CA 92634 (9)

Colbath, Anorld, University of Maine, Orono Department of Theatre 123 Lord Hall Orono, ME 04473 207-581-7534 (4)

Colberg, Clyde, Peninsula Arts Appreciation Council Post Office Box 273 Ishpeming, MI 49849 906-486-4401 (5)

Cole, Mark, Theatre Go Round Post Office Box 1180 Petrolia, Ontario, Canada N0N 1R0 519-882-1221 (16)

Cole, Mark, Victoria Playhouse Post Office Box 1180 Petrolia, Ontario, Canada N0N 1R0 416-822-1221 (16)

Cole, Michael, Muskoka Summer Theatre Box 1055 Gravenhurst, Ontario, Canada P0C 1G0 705-687-2762 (16)

Cole, Nancy, University of South Florida Department of Theatre Tampa, FL 33620 813-974-2701; 813-974-2603 (4)

Cole, Richard B., Dallas Federation of Musicians, Local 147 2829 West North Highway 235 Dallas, TX 75220 214-358-4447 (18)

Cole, Robin, Central Wyoming College Department of Theatre Riverton, WY 82501 307-856-9291 (4)

Cole, Susan S., Appalachian State University Department of Communication Boone, NC 28608 704-262-3028; 704-262-3029 (4)

Colebank, Mrs. Forrest R., Natchez Little Theatre Post Office Box 1232 Natchez, MS 39120 601-442-2233 (8)

Coleman, F.R., Coleman Puppet Theatre 1516 Second Avenue South Maywood, IL 61455 312-344-2920 (16)

Coleman, James, Resident Theatre/Jewish Community Center 8201 Holmes Road Kansas City, MO 64131 816-361-5200 (16)

Coleman, Dr. V.J., University of Arkansas, Pine Bluff Cedar Street Pine Bluff, AR 71601 501-535-6700 (4)

Coll, Ron, Bozak, Incorporated 587 Connecticut Avenue South Norwalk, CT 06854 203-838-6521 (15)

Collins, G.W., Musicians' Protective Association 3104 North Broadway, #22C Knoxville, TN 37917 615-687-8350 (18)

Collins, Joseph Stephen, Modesto Junior College Department of Theatre College Avenue Modesto, CA 95350 209-526-2000 (4)

Collins, K. Lee, Oblong Valley Players Post Office Box 1582 Lakeville, CT 06039 (16)

Collins, M., Richmond Community Theatre 648 North Main Street Richland Center, WI 53581 (16)

Collins, M., RC Community Theatre 620 North 5th Avenue Wausau, WI 54401 (16)

Colombini, Robert L. Jr., Musicians' Association, Local 117 Route 5, Post Office Box 759 Sumner, WA 98390 206-863-2144 (18)

Colonna, Enrico Vincent, Indiana Musicians' Association, Local 251 367 Walnut Street Indiana, PA 15701 412-463-0814 (18)

Colvin, Ron, Ithaca Theatre Lighting, Incorporated 1001 West Seneca Street Ithaca, NY 14850 607-272-2131 (15)

Comer, Carol, Women's Jazz Festival Post Office Box 22321 Kansas, MO 64113 816-361-1901 (9)

Como, William, Dance Magazine 1180 Avenue of the Americas New York, NY 10036 212-921-9300 (14)

Compton, David, Logan County Council for the Arts Post Office Box 218 Logan, WV 25601 304-752-1324 (5)

Comtios, M. E., Rutgers State University of New Jersey, Department of Theatre Mason Gross School of the Arts New Brunswick, NJ 08903 201-932-9891; 201-932-9816 (4)

Comtrois, Dr. Mary E., Rutgers University Mason Gross School of the Arts New Brunswick, NJ 08903 201-932-9816 (4)

Cone, S., Community Council for the Arts Post Office Box 3554 Kinston, NC 28501 919-527-2517 (5)

Conley, Richard J., Green Bay Federation of Musicians, Local 205 2330 Libal Street Green Bay, WI 54301 414-432-2467 (18)

Conlon, George R., David Clark Company Incorporated 360 Franklin Street Worcester, MA 01604 617-756-6216 (15)

Connaire, Chris, The People's Theatre 1253 Cambridge Street Cambridge, MA 02138 617-547-4930 (16)

Conneen, George M., George M. Conneen Company, Inc. 24 South Newtown Street Road Newtown Square, PA 19073 215-353-2241; 215-353-2242 (15)

Connell, Michael, Kliegl Brothers 32-32 48th Avenue Long Island City, NY 11101 212-786-7474 (15)

Connor, Helen M., Theater Workshop-Boston 551 Tremont Street Boston, MA 02116 617-482-4778 (4)

Connors, Tom, Penninsula Players Theatre Foundation Fish Creek, WI 54212 414-868-3287 (16)

Conolly, Leonard, University of Guelph Department of Drama Guelph, Ontario, Canada N1G 2W1 519-824-4120 (4)

Conrad, John T., Central Ontario Musicians' Association, Local 226 125 Union Street East Waterloo, Ontario, Canada N2J 4E5 519-744-4891 (18)

Considine, James M., Fall River Federation of Musicians, Local 216 746 Hood Street Fall River, MA 02720 617-679-6235 (18)

Craver, Joe L., Schofield Drama Center Recreation Services, Schofield Barracks Wahiawa, HI 96786 808-655-0891 (8)

Crawford, James, Lakeland College Department of Theatre Sheboygan, WI 53081 414-565-2111 (4)

Crawford, Toni, Pleasant Hill Arts Council 3300 North Main Street Pleasant Hill, CA 94523 415-934-6050 (5)

Crecca, Fred, Repertorio Espanol 138 East 27th Street New York, NY 10016 212-889-2850 (16)

Credgington, Nicholas, Centurion Playhouse Building 5300 Fort Lewis, WA 98433 206-968-3402 (8)

Creech, J.G., Cleveland County Arts Council First National Bank, Box 168 Shelby, NC 28150 704-482-3831 (5)

Creedon, Eugene W., Parker School Children's Theatre 148 Billings Road North Quincy, MA 02171 (16)

Crenshaw, George, Imagination Theater, Incorporated 7535 North Washtenaw Avenue Chicago, IL 60645 312-262-4195 (16)

Crenshaw, Mrs. Henry F., Community Arts and Activities Commission Post Office Box 280 Fort Deposit, AL 36032 205-227-4940 (5)

Crew, Marie, Kent Civic Arts Commission Post Office Box 223 Kent, WA 98031 (5)

Crighton, Tim, Theatre 3 10426 95 Street Edmonton, Alberta, Canada T5H 2C1 403-426-3394 (16)

Cripton, John, Canada Council Touring Office Post Office Box 1047 Ottawa, Ontario, Canada K1P 5V8 613-238-7413 (5)

Crist, Anna Mae, Valley Players Post Office Box 933 Harrisonburg, VA 22801 (16)

Crist, Mrs. D.A., Prairie Theatre Rural Route 1 Quinter, KS 67752 (16)

Crocken, William E., Pennsylvania State University Auditorium Pennsylvania State University University Park, PA 16802 814-863-0388 (8)

Crockett, Dick, Greater St. Petersburg Musician's Association 911 Third Street South St. Petersburg, FL 33733 813-894-5059 (18)

Crom, Richard, West Nebraska Art Center Post Office Box 62 Scottsbluff, NB 69361 308-632-2226 (5)

Cromer, Missy, Opera House Players c/o Abbeville Opera House Abbeville, SC 29620 803-459-2157 (16)

Crone, W. B., Verdigris Valley Players Madison, KS 66860 (16)

Croom, Marion, Duro-Test Light Center 1950 Century Boulevard NE, Suite 4 Atlanta, GA 30345 404-633-0132 (15)

Crosland, Marvin, Rowe Theatre UNCC Department of Creative Arts Charlotte, NC 28223 707-597-2477 (8)

Crosman, Max W., Ann Arbor Federation of Musicians Wolverine Building 202 East Washington, Suite 310 Saint Ann Arbor, MI 48108 313-668-8041 (18)

Crosthwait, Jim, Harleton Players 4899 Stage Road Memphis, TN 38128 901-386-1355 (16)

Crowder, Charles, American University Academy for the Performing Arts Massachusetts Avenue at Nebraska, NW Washington, DC 20016 202-686-2315 (4)

Crowder, Sara C., Birmingham Festival of Arts 1927 First Avenue North Birmingham, AL 35203 205-323-5461, Ext. 52 (9)

Crowell, Josephine, Katherine Cornell Memorial Theatre Vineyard Haven, MA 02568 (8)

Crowley, Dorothy, Dale County Council on the Arts Post Office Box 971 Ozark, AL 36360 205-774-6232 (5)

Crum, Jane Ann, Odessa College Department of Theatre Post Office Box 3752 Odessa, TX 79760 915-337-5381 (4)

Crum, Mrs. Mike, Grand Prairie Art Council Post Office Box 65 Stuttgart, AR 72160 501-673-8586; 501-673-7278 (5)

Crump, Janice, Soul City Cultural Arts and Historical Society Post Office Box 38 Soul City, NC 27553 919-456-3111 (5)

Cubbage, Jerry, Coast Recording Equipment Supply Incorporated 6114 Santa Monica Boulevard Hollywood, CA 90038 213-462-6058 (15)

Cudjoe, Vera, Black Theatre Canada 109 Vaughan Road, Suite 1 Toronto, Ontario, Canada M6C 2L9 416-656-2716 (16)

Culbertson, Ruth, Monmouth-Independence Community Art Association Post Office Box 114 Monmouth, OR 97361 503-838-2834 (5)

Cullison, Larry, Lincoln College Department of Theatre 300 Keokuk Street Lincoln, IL 62656 217-732-3155 (4)

Culver, Dr. C.D., Jackson State Community College Department of Theatre Post Office Box 2467 Jackson, TN 38301 901-424-3520 (4)

Culver, Edwin R., Municipal Theatre Association Forest Park Saint Louis, MO 63112 314-361-1900, General Office; 314-367-8686, Box Office (16)

Cumerford, Peter, Eager Plastics 3701 South Halsted Street Chicago, IL 60609 312-927-3484; 312-927-3515 (15)

Cummings, E., Marlboro Masquers 9122 Old Burton Circle Upper Marlboro, MD 20870 (16)

Cummings, G. Earl, Port Jervis Musicians' Protective Association Route 97 Sparrowbush, NY 12780 914-856-5612 (18)

Cummings, Louise, A Contemporary Theatre 100 West Roy Street Seattle, WA 98119 206-285-3220; 206-285-3220 (8)

Cunetto, Dominic J., Mississippi State University Department of Theatre State College, MS 39762 (4)

Cunetto, Dr. Dominic J., Mississippi State University Department of Theatre Mississippi State, MS 39762 601-325-3320; 601-323-4746 (4)

Curcio, Christopher, Parks and Recreation Department Cultural Arts Division Room 102, 2425 Fresno Street Fresno, CA 93721 209-488-1012 (5)

Currie, Fergus G., Emory University Department of Theatre Atlanta, GA 30322 404-329-6187 (4)

Curtis, Bob, Bob Curtis 708 Lincoln Green Drive Arlington, TX 76011 817-261-6859 (15)

Curtis, Geoffrey, Malabar Ltd. 14 McCaul Street Toronto 2B, Ontario, Canada M5T 1V6 416-598-2581 (15)

Custer, Shirley, South Park Conservatory Theatre Post Office Box 254 Bethel Park, PA 15102 (16)

Cutler, Judy, Centaur Theatre Company 453 Saint Francois-Xavier Street Montreal, Quebec, Canada H2Y 2T1 514-288-1229 (16)

Cutlip, B., Middleton Civic Theatre 1701 Henry Street Middleton, WI 53562 (16)

Cuttingham, George, American Academy of Dramatic Arts 120 Madison Avenue New York, NY 10016 212-686-9244 (4)

Czajka, Mary, Dimatronics Incorporated 171 South Main Street Crystal Lake, IL 60014 815-455-4400 (15)

Czelusniak, Stanley, Musicians' Protective Union, Local 133 Road Number 4 Amsterdam, NY 12010 518-883-5713 (18)

D

Dadson, Ann, Secretary of State, Arts and Culture 66 Slater Street Ottawa, Ontario, Canada K1A 0M5 613-996-3711 (5)

Dahl, Debra, Ensemble Studio Theatre 549 West 52nd Street New York, NY 10019 212-247-4982 (16)

Dahl, Marion, The Inner Stage 9 - 11 St. Nicholas Street Toronto, Ontario, Canada M4Y 1W5 416-967-3548 (16)

Dahlin, Marshall B., Little Theatre Building 18-24 East Second Street Jamestown, NY 14701 716-483-1095 (8)

Dailey, Jarrett, Musicians' Mutual Protective Union Post Office Box 1852 Longview, WA 98632 206-423-5010 (18)

Daines, Paul W., Saginaw Musical Association, Local 57 2456 Barnard Street Saginaw, MI 48602 517-793-1877 (18)

Dale, Patt, Patt Dale 159 West 53rd Street New York, NY 10019 212-245-5855 (12)

Dale, Tommy, Federation of Musicians, Local 103 2829 Cleveland Avenue Columbus, OH 43224 614-261-9826; 614-261-9827 (18)

D'Alessio, R. George, New Haven Federation of Musicians, Local 234-486 26 Glebrook Avenue Hamden, CT 06514 203-387-4765 (18)

Daley, Dr. Mary P., Ursuline College Department of Theatre 2550 Lander Road Cleveland, OH 44124 216-449-4200 (4)

D'Alfonso, Edward V., Peninsula Musical Society, Local 199 104 Seven Hollis Drive Yorktown, VA 23692 804-380-1022 (18)

Dalrymple, Jean, Jean Dalrymple Associates 150 West 55th Street New York, NY 10019 212-246-7820 (12)

Dalton, Pat, Shure Brothers, Incorporated 222 Hartrey Avenue Evanston, IL 60204 312-866-2547 (15)

Dalzell, Joy S., Manoa Valley Theatre 2833 East Manoa Road Honolulu, HI 96822 808-988-6131 (8)

Damel, L., Mt. Carmel Players 109 Jewett Place Utica, NY 13501 (16)

Dameron, K., Sumter Little Theatre 719 Henderson Street Sumter, SC 29150 (16)

Dampman, Allan, Sullivan County Council for the Arts Review Committee Loch Sheldrake, NY 12759 914-434-5750 (5)

Danch, Elmer J., Da-Lite Screen Company, Incorporated 3100 State Road 15 North Warsaw, IN 46580 219-267-8101; 219-Tel-x 23 2649 (15)

Danders, Dennis, Wichita Musicians' Association 4323 East Kellogg Wichita, KS 67218 316-684-1311 (18)

Daniel, E. Mc, Gallup Community Theatre Post Office Box 1032 Gallup, NM 87301 (16)

Danko, Ronald C., Hartnell Community College Department of Theatre Salinas, CA 93901 (4)

D'Antoni, Nicholas J., Phillips Hall/Santa Ana College 17th at Bristol Santa Ana, CA 92706 714-667-3395; 714-667-3216 (16)

Darby, Louise, Chowan Arts Council 108 South Granville Street Edenton, NC 27932 919-482-4112 (5)

D'Arcy, Robert, District of Columbia Federation of Musicians, Local 161-710 5020 Wisconsin Avenue, North West Washington, DC 20016 202-244-8833 (18)

Dardis, Joe, Musicians' Mutual Association, Local 99 325 North East 20th Avenue Portland, OR 97232 503-235-8791 (18)

Darling, Beverly, Masters Costumes 303 Federal Plaza West Youngstown, OH 44503 216-744-2571 (15)

Dasher, Harriet, Fullerton Civic Light Opera Company, Incorporated 218 West Commonwealth Avenue Fullerton, CA 92632 714-526-3832 (15)

Daugherty, Logan C., Wheeling Musical Society, Local 142 17th and Jacobs Streets Wheeling, WV 26003 304-233-0620 (18)

David, Barbara, Bell Road Barn Playhouse 6008 Bell Road Parkville, MO 64152 816-587-0218 (16)

David, Jenkin K., Bell Road Barn Playhouse 6008 Bell Road Parkville, MO 64152 816-587-0218 (16)

David, Jenkin R., Bell Road Barn Playhouse 6008 Bell Road Parkville, MO 64152 816-587-0218 (8)

David, Paul, Carbon Musical Society 450 South 7th Street Leighton, PA 18235 215-377-2350 (18)

Davidson, Bob, Bob Davidson Post Office Box 962 Bennington, VT 05201 802-447-0311 (15)

Davidson, Charles, Colortran, Incorporated 24 Lake Avenue Trumbull, CT 06611 203-261-7835 (15)

Davidson, Lowell, Lumatrol Corporation 409 Citizens Bank Building Anderson, IN 46016 317-649-0606 (15)

Davies, Harry, Harry Davies 350 West 57th Street New York, NY 10019 212-247-8522 (12)

Davies, J., Dramedians 8024 Cole Downey, CA 90242 (16)

Davino, Al Jr., Twin City Federation of Musicians, Local 232 2182 Hanley Road Saint Joseph, MI 49085 616-429-8777 (18)

Davis, Anne, Greenville Feminist Theater 304 Chick Springs Road Greenville, SC 29609 803-233-1446 (16)

Davis, Britt D., The Houston Festival 1950 West Gray #6 Houston, TX 77019 713-521-9329; 713-521-9559 (9)

Davis, David, Fordham University Department of Theatre Lincoln Center New York, NY 10023 212-841-5269 (4)

Davis, Dean, Musicians' Association of Skagit Post Office Box 46 Oak Harbor, WA 98277 206-424-4995 (18)

Davis, Frank E., Frank E. Davis Associates 524 Virginia Avenue Rochester, PA 15704 412-774-2133 (15)

Davis, H., Woodbridge Players 13618 Kerrydale Road Woodbridge, VA 22193 (16)

Davis, H. Barrett, Lincoln University Department of Theatre Lincoln, PA 18015 215-691-7000 (4)

Davis, Jared T., Phenix City Arts Council Post Office Box 1132 Phenix City, AL 36867 404-561-0364 (5)

Davis, Jerry L., West Memphis Fine Arts Center Post Office Box 1434 West Memphis, AR 72301 501-735-6923 (5)

Davis, John F., Musicians' Association 151 Fourth Street Coaldale, PA 18218 717-645-9484 (18)

Davis, Lawrence, Indiana University Auditorium Indiana University Bloomington, IN 47401 812-337-1103 (8)

Davis, Marie A., The Free Library of Philadelphia Logan Square Philadelphia, PA 19103 215-686-5322 (11)

Davis, Shethar, Wabash Instrument Company 1801 Grand Street Wabash, IN 46992 219-563-8406 (15)

Davis, William, Alternative Light 2972 Gale Road Ann Arbor, MI 48105 313-994-5700 (15)

Davison, Bill, Musicians' Protective Union 206 South 16th Avenue Yakima, WA 98902 509-453-9813 (18)

Dawson, Taylor, Jasmine Hill Arts Council Post Office Box 6001 Montgomery, AL 36106 205-265-2837; 205-263-1440 (5)

Day, Queenie, Stage Coach Players 830 8th Avenue South West Calgary, Alberta, Canada T2P 1L7 403-262-2146 (16)

DeAmicis, Joseph E., Iron County Musicians' Association Post Office Box 482 Caspian, MI 49915 906-265-3600 (18)

Dean, Virgil E., Terre Haute Federation of Musicians, Local 25 1337 Drieser Square Terre Haute, IN 47807 812-234-6750 (18)

DeCell, Betty, Yazoo Arts Council Post Office Box 985 Yazoo City, MS 39194 601-746-6062 (5)

Dechario, Barbara, Genesee Valley Council on the Arts 4241 Lakeville Road Genesee, NY 14454 716-245-5401 (5)

DeDee, Edward A., Michael C. Rockefeller Arts Center State University College Fredonia, NY 14063 716-673-3217 (8)

Deems, Jadene, Costumes Unlimited Pittsburgh, Incorporated 1031 Forbes Avenue Pittsburgh, PA 15219 412-281-3277 (15)

DeFazio, Joseph, New Britain Musicians' Association 20 Carroll Street New Britain, CT 06053 203-229-4037 (18)

DeGeorge, Johnny, Association of Musicians, Local 257 Post Office Box 120399 Nashville, TN 37212 615-244-9514 (18)

DeGraffenreid, Dean, DeGraffenreid Associates Box 3518 Reno, NV 89505 702-826-2313 (18)

DeHart, Dr. Stan, Tallahassee Community College Department of Theatre Tallahassee, FL 32304 904-576-5181, Extension 257 (4)

deJaager, Alfred R, Hall of Fine Arts Theater West Liberty State College West Liberty, WV 26074 304-336-8006; 304-336-8003 (8)

DeJaager, Alfred R., West Liberty College Hall West Liberty State College West Liberty, WV 26074 304-336-8006 (8)

DeJong, William D., Musicians' Protective Union 214 North Congress Street Rushville, IL 62681 217-322-6428 (18)

Delabar, James, Musicians' Protective Union, Local 265 1 Sherwood Drive Quincy, IL 62301 217-222-0941 (18)

Delatte, Ed, Dallas Repertory Theatre Post Office Box 12208 Dallas, TX 75019 214-369-8966 (16)

DeLaurentis, William, Theatre in the Dell 300 Simcoe Street Toronto, Ontario, Canada M5T 1T5 416-598-4802 (16)

Delaurier, S., PR George Little Theatre 5906 Bedford Lane Clinton, MD 20735 (16)

Delgado, Alex, Penrod-Plastino Movement Theatre 4645 Greentree Irving, CA 97215 714-552-7472 (16)

Delisle, Georges, Theatre de la Feniere 1500 rue de la Feniere Ancienne-Lorette, Quebec, Canada 418-651-3218 (16)

DellaGrotte, Anthony, Knights of Columbus Hall Relay Road Nahant, MA 01908 (8)

Dellinger, D., Valley Center Players 809 North Colby Valley Center, KS 67147 (16)

DelPlunkett, Rubye, LBW Community Arts Council Post Office Box 1418 Andalusia, AL 36420 205-222-6591 (5)

Delponte, Joanne, Connecticut Commission on the Arts 340 Capitol Avenue Hartford, CT 06106 (3)

DelTufo, Liz, Essex County Division of Cultural Affairs 115 Clifton Avenue Newark, NJ 07039 201-482-6400; 201-482-0967 (5)

Demayo, Frank, Lake Systems 55 Chapel Street Newton, MA 02160 617-244-6881 (15)

DeMent, Robert, San Diego Stage and Lighting Supply 2002 State Street San Diego, CA 92101 714-235-8379 (15)

DeMilo, Phillip A. Jr., Musicians' Protective Union Post Office Box 250 Delaware Water Gap, PA 18327 717-421-1325 (18)

Dempsey, John F., Musicians' Protective Union, Local 170 102 West Laurel Street Shenandoah, PA 17976 717-462-3075 (18)

Denninger, Lucinda, Lighting Specialties Division of D.A. Olson Company 5001 25th Avenue, NE Seattle, WA 98105 206-522-6594 (15)

Dennis, Clifford, Musicians' Protective Union 74 Platt Street Hornell, NY 14843 607-698-4566 (18)

Dennis, Margaret, Pixie Players Post Office Box 81 Mobile, AL 36608 205-344-1537 (16)

Dennison, Roger, Macon Federation of Musicians 204 Sunnydale Warner Robins, GA 31093 912-923-3242 (18)

Dente, Bob, Strand Century, Incorporated 20 Bushes Lane Elmwood Park, NJ 37347 201-791-7000 (15)

Deo, Joe, Superscope New York, Incorporated 37-04 57th Street Woodside, NY 11377 212-446-7227 (15)

Derfner, Carol A., Anchorage Arts Council 419 West 7th Avenue Anchorage, AK 99501 907-274-7324 (5)

Derrickson, Lew, Old Dominion Center Theatre Old Dominion University Norfolk, VA 23508 804-489-6210 (8)

Deschatelets, Louise, Union des Artistes 1290 rue St-Denis Montreal, Quebec, Canada H2X 3J7 514-862-7087 (18)

DeSimone, Joseph S., Mew Kensington Musical Society Sons of Italy Building New Kensington, PA 15068 412-335-6651 (18)

Dessinger, John R., Springfield Musicians' Association, Local 160 1500 Malden Avenue Springfield, OH 45504 513-390-0618; 513-390-2351 (18)

Deuser, Lew J., Commercial Actors Agency 8500 Wilshire Boulevard Beverly Hills, CA 90212 213-553-8611 (2)

Devender, W.C. Van, Jackson Federation of Musicians Route 2, Post Office Box 270F Jackson, MS 39209 601-924-9313 (18)

Devin, Lee, Swarthmore College Department of Theatre Swarthmore, PA 19081 215-447-7149 (4)

DeVitt, Joseph, Rochester Musicians' Association, Local 66 83 Clinton Avenue, North Rochester, NY 14604 716-546-7633 (18)

Devlin, Sandra, Devlin Productions, Incorporated 150 West 55th Street New York, NY 10019 212-582-5572 (15)

Dewan, Evelyn, Danbury Musicians' Association, Local 87 8 Grandview Drive Danbury, CT 06810 203-743-9713 (18)

Dewanz, LeRoy, Musicians' Protective Association Route 1, Post Office Box 89-1 New Ulm, MN 56073 507-354-6807 (18)

Dewey, Peter, Festival Theatre 56 Centre Street Dover, MA 02030 617-785-1260 (8)

Dewey, Priscilla B., North End-Waterfront Arts Council 20 Paramenter Street Boston, MA 02113 617-227-2927 (5)

Dewey, Priscilla B., Charles River Creative Arts Program 56 Center Street Dover, MA 02030 617-785-0068 (5)

Dewey, Priscilla B., Festival Theatre 56 Centre Street Dover, MA 02030 617-785-1260 (8)

DeWille, Tom, Luna Tech 822 Demasters Street Huntsville, AL 35801 205-533-1487; 205-533-1489 (15)

Deyo, George H., Anniston Little Theatre Post Office Box 1454 Anniston, AL 36202 205-236-8342 (16)

Deysher, Vernon A. Jr., Reading Musical Society, Local 135 214 West 46th Street Reading, PA 19606 215-779-1651 (18)

DeZutti, Joseph M., Musicians' Protective Union 956 Eighth Street LaSalle, IL 61301 815-CAp-tol 3 4793 (18)

Dichersm, Lisa, Springfield Arts Council Post Office Box 745 Springfield, OH 45501 513-324-2712 (5)

Dickens, Richard, Richard Dickens Agency 5550 Wilshire Boulevard Los Angeles, CA 90036 213-937-3080 (2)

Dickson, Kathleen, Mabel Tainter Memorial Theater 205 Main Street Menomonie, WI 54751 715-235-9725 (8)

Dickson, Scott, Necessary Angel Theatre 20 Dupont Street, Unit 3 Toronto, Ontario, Canada M5R 1V2 416-932-6119 (16)

Diedrich, John, La Porte Federations of Musicians 1103 Weller Avenue La Porte, IN 46350 219-324-0332 (18)

Diercks, Dr. John, Bradley Hall Hollins College Hollins College, VA 24020 703-362-6512 (8)

Diers, Herman, University of Miami Department of Theatre Coral Gables, FL 33124 305-284-4474; 305-284-3178 (4)

Dietrich, Linda, Theatre Guild, Inc. Post Office Box 1502 Morristown, TN 37814 615-586-9260 (16)

Dietz, Dr. Charles, Zanesville Art Center 1145 Maple Avenue Zanesville, OH 43701 614-452-0741 (8)

DiFiore, Raymond E., Musicians' Protective Union 163 Oakside Avenue Methuen, MA 01844 617-686-2744 (18)

Digby, Keith, Theatre 3 10426 95 Street Edmonton, Alberta, Canada T5H 2C1 403-426-3394 (16)

Dill, Janet, Stillman College Tuscaloosa, AL 35402 205-752-2548 (4)

DiMeo, Claire Jr., Discovery Workshop 486 Main Street Melrose, MA 02176 617-665-8870 (16)

DiMeo, Claire E., Discovery Workshop 486 Main Street Melrose, MA 02176 617-665-8870 (16)

DiMeo, Claire E., North Shore Discovery Workshop 486 Main Street Melrose, MA 02176 617-665-8870 (16)

Dingman, Anthony, Raleigh Amphitheatre 301 Pogue Street Raleigh, NC 27607 919-832-3519 (8)

Dini, Richard, Combined Arts Corporate Campaign c/o R.F. Dini Associates 600 Jefferson Suite 502 Houston, TX 77002 713-654-9217 (5)

Dinsdale, W.F., Brandon Musicians' Association 1057 5th Street Brandon, Manitoba, Canada 204-727-8506 (18)

Dion, Gerald J., Dion Products 78 Amber Street Buffalo, NY 14220 716-823-4381 (15)

Dionne, Normand, D.I.M. Lighting Company Cedar Hill Road Salem, MA 01970 617-744-8859 (15)

Dippel, Rob, Sheboygan Community Players 830 Virginia Avenue Sheboygan, WI 53081 (16)

Director, Assistant Travel, International Festival of the Arts, Dunseith North Dakota State Highway Department Bismarck, ND 58505 800-437-2077; 701-224-2525 (9)

Director, Lawrence Lane; Managing, The Glines 28 Willow Street Brooklyn, NY 11201 718-522-5567 (16)

Directors, ALT Board of, Anniston Little Theatre 1620 Leighton Avenue Anniston, AL 36201 205-236-8342 (8)

Direnzo, John J., Portsville Musical Society B & Pottsville Streets Minersville, PA 17954 717-544-4589 (18)

Diringer, Lila, The Arts Council at Freeport Post Office Box 97 Freeport, NY 11520 516-223-2522; 516-223-4769 (5)

DiSalle, Con, Sudbury Federation of Musicians 194 Elm Street West Sudbury, Ontario, Canada P3C 1V3 705-674-4241 (18)

Disbrow, James W., Costumes Unlimited, Incorporated 1685 Elmwood Avenue Buffalo, NY 14207 716-873-0709; 412-281-3277 (15)

Dittamo, Fred, Musicians' Mutual Protective and Benevolent Union, Local 248 77 Prospect Street Paterson, NJ 07505 201-278-8418; 201-278-8420 (18)

Dixon, Robert, Saint Louis Community College at Meramec Department of Theatre 11333 Big Bend Boulevard Saint Louis, MO 63122 314-966-7500 (4)

Dnrerr, M.H., Maryland Childrens' Theatre 4930 Cordell Avenue Bethesda, MD 20814 301-652-7999; 301-654-9820 (16)

Dodds, Cranston, Warehouse Living Arts Center 202 East Collin Corsicana, TX 75110 214-872-5421 (8)

Dodds, Cranston H., Firehouse Theatre 221 North Elm Denton, TX 76201 817-382-7014 (8)

Dodge, Grace, Camden County Cultural Commission 250 South Park Drive Haddon Township, NJ 08108 609-858-0063 (5)

Doepel, Robert F., Chicago Scenic Studios 2217 West Belmont Avenue Chicago, IL 60618 312-942-1483, Shop; 312-477-8366, Office (15)

Doheen, Margaret, Independence Community Junior College Department of Theatre Box 708 Independence, KS 67301 316-331-4100 (4)

Doherty, Carmel, Hammond Industrial Imports 7270 -1 Torbram Road Malton, Ontario, Canada L4T 3Y7 (15)

Doherty, Mrs. Frances, Musicians' Protective Union 520 Humes Avenue Aptos, CA 95003 408-426-1776 (18)

Doherty, Tom, Associated Designers of Canada 600 Lonsdale Road Apartment 8 Toronto, Ontario, Canada M5P 1R7 416-652-3293 (18)

Doig, Helen, Sudbury Theatre Centre 90 King Street Sudbury, Ontario, Canada P3E 4P8 705-674-8381 (16)

Dolan, Muriel, Piccadilly Square Theatre Company 93 Union Street Newton Centre, MA 02159 617-237-2679 (16)

Dolde, Lillian, Albuquerque National Bank 303 Roma North West Albuquerque, NM 87103 505-765-2104 (10)

Doleysh, Clarence F., Manitowoc Musicians' Association, Local 195 1511 Cherry Road Manitowoc, WI 54220 414-793-1235 (18)

Doll, George A., Musicians' Association, Local 117 Route 5, Post Office Box 759 Sumner, WA 98390 206-863-2144 (18)

Dolphin, John R., Mid-West Scenic and Stage Equipment Company, Ltd. 224 East Bruce Street Milwaukee, WI 53204 414-276-2707 (15)

Doms, Keith, The Free Library of Philadelphia Logan Square Philadelphia, PA 19103 215-686-5322 (11)

Donahue, John Clark, The Children's Theatre Company 2400 Third Avenue Minneapolis, MN 55404 612-874-0500 (16)

Donahue, Judy, Alexandria Community Theatre Route 1 Post Office Box 341 Alexandria, IN 46001 317-724-2927 (16)

Donaldson, C. Bruce, Fulton County Musicians' Protective Union Post Office Box 374 St. David, IL 61563 309-688-2468 (18)

Donchey, Sheryl, Phillips Hall/Santa Ana College 17th at Bristol Santa Ana, CA 92706 714-667-3395; 714-667-3216 (16)

Donnell, Beulah, Hot Springs Arts Council 505 North River Hot Springs, SD 57747 605-745-6696; 605-745-4225 (5)

Donohue, James, Olivet College Department of Theatre Rochester, MI 48063 616-749-7620 (4)

Donohue, James R., Western New Mexico University Department of Theatre College Avenue Silver City, NM 88061 605-538-6011 (4)

Donovan, W. J., Federation of Musicians, Local 102 508 North East Street Bloomington, IL 61701 309-828-6814 (18)

Dor, Georges, Theatre Les Ancetres C.P. 398 St-German, Quebec, Canada J0C 1K0 514-677-6217 (16)

Doran, Carter, Mount San Antonio College Department of Theatre 1100 North Grand Avenue Walnut, CA 91789 714-598-2811 (4)

Dorman, Edward, Musicians' Protective Union, Local 177 8 Lake Road Morristown, NJ 07960 201-539-2619 (18)

Dorries, Wilson, Musicians' Protective Union, Local 175 422 North Olive Street Trenton, IL 62293 618-224-9460 (18)

Dorsey, Dave, Willmar Community Theatre Rural Route 4 Willmar, MN 56201 (16)

Dorsey, Linda, Hardin County Arts Council Post Office Box 903 Elizabeth, KY 42701 (5)

Dorwaldt, Carl, Rauland-Borg 3535 West Addison Street Chicago, IL 60618 312-267-1300 (15)

Dotten, Robert, Dearborn Community Arts Council Post Office Box 572 Dearborn, MI 48126 (5)

Dougherty, Charles, Sketch Club Players Glover and Logan Box 674 Woodbury, NJ 08096 609-848-8089 (16)

Doughty, Charles L., Atlanta Children's Theatre Post Office Box 77324 Atlanta, GA 30357 404-892-7607 (16)

Doveton, M., Lawrence Community Theatre Post Office Box 3205 Lawrence, KS 66044 (16)

Dowd, Dr. John A., Seeger Memorial Chapel Milligan College Milligan College, KY 37682 615-929-0116 (8)

Dowling, James R., Brockton Federation of Musicians, Local 138 13 North Ash Street Brockton, MA 02401 617-583-0192 (18)

Dowling, Vincent, Great Lakes Shakespeare Festival Ohio Theatre Playhouse Square Cleveland, OH 44115 216-228-1225 (9)

Downer, M., Don Juan Playhouse 80 Cascabel Los Alamos, NM 87544 (16)

Doyle, Frank Jr., Concord Federation of Musicians 1 Perkins Street Concord, NH 03301 603-746-3937 (18)

Doyle, Tim, Society to Save the Stage Post Office Box 69A07 Los Angeles, CA 90069 282-948- (16)

Dozier, Cornelia, Coconut Grove Childrens Theatre Department of Theatre 3043 Grand Avenue Post Office Box 331002 Miami, FL 33133 305-442-0489 (16)

Dozier, Phyllis, Arts Council of Brazos Valley Post Office Drawer CL College Station, TX 77840 713-244-8883 (5)

Drake, Edwin B., Middlesex County College Department of Theatre Edison, NJ 08817 201-548-6000, Ext. 367 (4)

Drake, James, Nashville War Memorial Auditorium 7th and Union Streets Nashville, TN 37219 615-741-3132 (8)

Drake, James, Musicians' Association, Local 151 248 Myrtle Avenue Garwood, NJ 17127 201-SU9-0109 (18)

Drapeau, Donald A., Virginia Polytechnic Institute Department of Theatre Blacksburg, VA 24061 703-951-5200 (4)

Draper, D., Aprenda Players 2007 Avenue Aprenda San Pedro, CA 90700 (16)

Draper, R. E., Musicians' Association, Local 184 4801 Seahurst Everett, WA 98203 206-259-3802 (18)

Drayna, Roger, Wausau Insurance Companies 2000 Westwood Drive Wausau, WI 54401 715-842-6092 (10)

Driml, Richard L., McCook Area Arts Council 1205 East Third Street McCook, NB 69001 308-345-6303, Ext. 65 (5)

Driscoll, Christine, Cheboygan Area Arts Council Post Office Box 95 Cheboygan, MI 49721 616-627-2739 (5)

Driver, William, Bard College Department of Drama and Dance Annandale-on-Hudson, NY 12504 914-758-6822, Ext. 245; 914-758-8622 (4)

Droze, John D., Charleston Federation of Musicians 140 Darlington Avenue Charleston, SC 29403 803-722-0936 (18)

Drum, Joanne, Phoenix Federation of Musicians 1202 East Oak Street Phoenix, AZ 85006 602-254-8838 (18)

Dryden, Bob, Brainerd Community College Department of Theatre College Drive Brainerd, MN 56401 612-829-1791 (4)

Dubblerly, Ronald A., Seattle Public Library-Main Branch 1000 Fourth Avenue Seattle, WA 98104 206-625-2665 (8)

Duboff, Shelli, Oldcastle Theatre Company Southern Vermont College Bennington, VT 05201 802-442-9463; 902-447-0564 (16)

Dubois, J., Atchison Community Theatre Post Office Box 175 Atchison, KS 66002 (16)

Duceppe, Louise, Theatre Des Prairies 1400 rue St. Urbain Montreal, Quebec, Canada H2X 2M5 (16)

Duckwall, Ralph W., California State University Department of Theatre Arts 1250 Bellflower Boulevard Long Beach, CA 90840 213-498-5356 (4)

Duckworth, Aidron, New Hampshire West Council for the Arts Review Committee Meriden, NH 03770 603-469-3232 (5)

Duffield, Ernest, Fostoria Federation of Musicians, Local 121 118 West Center Street Fostoria, OH 44830 419-435-5437 (18)

Dugan, Barbara, Lewisburg Council on the Arts Post Office Box 418 Lewisburg, PA 17837 (5)

Dugan, Timothy, Irish Theatre of Philadelphia c/o John Kane Philadelphia, PA 19142 215-729-0936 (16)

Dumanis, Abraham, Brockton Federation of Musicians, Local 138 13 North Ash Street Brockton, MA 02401 617-583-0192 (18)

Duncan, Jan, Fullerton Civic Light Opera Company, Incorporated 218 West Commonwealth Avenue Fullerton, CA 92632 714-526-3832 (15)

Duncan, Lee A., Victor Duncan, Inc. 2659 Fondren Dallas, TX 75206 214-369-1165 (15)

Dunlevy, Jack, Waterloo Federation of Musicians 2903 Alameda Cedar Falls, IA 50613 319-266-1521 (18)

Dunn, Ross E., Musicians' Protective Union Route 2 Saint Anthony, ID 83445 208-624-7073 (18)

Dunnerman, Bob Sr, F.G. Lighting Sales Post Office Box 20186 Phoenix, AZ 85036 602-277-7901 (15)

Dunngan, Michael, Baker Street Productions 139 Esperanza Sierra Madre, CA 91204 (16)

Dunnigan, M., Heinks Memorial Theatre Players 526 West Highland Sierra Madre, CA 91024 (16)

Dunnington, George B., The Williston Theatre Williston-Northampton School Easthampton, MA 01027 413-527-1520 (8)

duPont, Marian "Mitch", Vagabond Players Gadsden State Jr. College Gadsden, AL 35999 205-546-5960; 205-546-0484 ext. 255 (4)

Durkee, Earl L., Flint Federation of Musicians 1502 Woodcroft Flint, MI 48503 313-233-4264 (18)

Dussault, Larry, Greater Marion Arts Council Post Office Box 448 Marion, OH 43302 614-387-2732 (5)

DuVall, K.K., Attic Theatre Post Office Box 41 Appleton, WI 54911 414-733-2945 (16)

Dybas, David J., Musicians' Protective Union, Local 133 Road Number 4 Amsterdam, NY 12010 518-883-5713 (18)

Dyer, Bob, Richland College Department of Theatre 12800 Abrams Road Dallas, TX 75081 214-746-4550 (4)

Dym, Barry, Theater Workshop-Boston 551 Tremont Street Boston, MA 02116 617-482-4778 (4)

Dyreng, R. Morgan, Manti Temple Grounds Manti, UT 84642 801-835-2333 (8)

Dyreng, R. Morgan, The Morman Miracle Pageant 420 A Street Salt Lake City, UT 84103 801-835-2333; 801-835-1094 (9)

Dzubay, Greg, Telex Communications, Incorporated 9600 Aldrich Avenue South Minneapolis, MN 55420 612-884-4051 (15)

E

Eakins, Mike, Beams Company 11503 West 75th Street Shawnee Mission, KS 66214 913-631-0301 (15)

Eakins, Tim, Beams Company 2318 Harding Road Station 14B Des Moines, IA 50314 515-255-1148 (15)

Eales, H.S., H.S. Eales Company Post Office Box 45465 Los Angeles, CA 90045 213-776-4410 (15)

Earl, Don L., Musicians Protective Union, Local 272 2701 North 700 East Provo, UT 84601 801-377-0857 (18)

Earl, Mike, Earl and Brown Company, Incorporated 320 Second West Seattle, WA 98119 206-284-1121 (15)

Earley, William, Cabriolet Dinner Theatre Routes 21 and 63 Libertyville, IL 60048 312-367-1313 (16)

East, Ron, The Mime Company Unlimited Box 361, Station J Toronto, Ontario, Canada M4J 4Y8 416-461-6551 (16)

Eastman, Robert, Musician Supply Company 1001 Vernon Way El Cajon, CA 92020 714-448-7137 (15)

Eastman, Roland, Musicians' Protective Union, Local 245 Route 4, Post Office Box 2 Muncie, IN 47302 317-282-2134 (18)

Eastwood, David, Lake George Dinner Theatre Route 9 Lake George, NY 12845 518-668-5787 (16)

Eatman, Rodney H., University of Pittsburgh Department of Theatre Johnstown, PA 15904 814-266-9661 (4)

Eaves, Winslow, Creative Arts Association of Andover Post Office Box 71 Andover, NH 03216 603-735-5371 (5)

Eaves, Winslow, Creative Arts Association of Andover Arts and Crafts Festival Post Office Box 71 Andover, NH 03216 603-735-5371 (9)

Eberly, Dr. J.W., Redland Auditorium Texas Women's University Denton, TX 76204 817-387-1412 (8)

Ebert, Harold L., Marion Musicians' Association Route 2 Cardington, OH 43315 614-389-4226 (18)

Ebert, Paul, Oak Ridge Community Playhouse Post Office Box 3223 Oak Ridge, TN 37830 483-122- (16)

Eck, Paul, Theatre London 471 Richmond Street London, Ontario, Canada N6A 3E4 519-672-9030; 519-672-8800 (16)

Eckart, Rick, Monmouth Arts Center 99 Monmouth Street Red Bank, NJ 07701 201-842-9000 (5)

Eckersley, Art, Tupelo Community Theatre 611 North Thomas Street Tupelo, MS 38801 601-842-4518 (16)

Eckles, Mrs. Marvin, Fine Arts Associates 17822 Summer Avenue Artesia, CA 90701 (5)

Edelson, Stan, Caravan Theatre 1555 Masachusetts Avenue Cambridge, MA 02138 617-868-8520 (16)

Edgar, Miriam Colon, Puerto Rican Traveling Theatre 304 West 47th Street New York, NY 10036 212-354-1293; 212-354-1974 (16)

Edinborough, Arnold, Council for Business and the Arts in Canada Box 7, Suite 1507, 401 Bay Street Toronto, Ontario, Canada M5H 2Y4 416-869-3016 (5)

Edison, Dr. Don, Central Methodist College Department of Theatre Fayette, MO 65248 816-248-3391 (4)

Edmonson, Dr. W.T., Itawamba County Arts Council 310 Cedar Street Fulton, MS 38843 601-862-4926 (5)

Edward, Lee, Baton Rouge Little Theatre Post Office Box 1943 Baton Rouge, LA 70821 504-924-6496 (16)

Edwards, F., Mechanicsville Repertory Theatre 7349 Springfield Avenue Sykesville, MD 21784 (16)

Efston, Evan, Efston Line 3500 Bathhurst Street Tonronto, Ontario, Canada M6A 2C6 416-787-5140 (15)

Egan, Dr. Jenny, Four Winds Theatre 37 West 10th Street New York, NY 10011 212-260-3939 (16)

Egan, John G., Container Corporation of America One First National Plaza Chicago, IL 60603 312-786-5340 (10)

Eggebrecht, David, Concordia College Department of Humanities Milwaukee, WI 53140 414-344-3400 (4)

Eggleston, A., Masque Players 1316 West Pine Alhambra, CA 91801 (16)

Eichler, Alan L., Alan L. Eichler 333 West 14th Street New York, NY 10014 212-929-1130 (12)

Eis, Joel, Lassen Community College Department of Theatre Susanville, CA 96130 (4)

Eisen, Max, Max Eisen 234 West 44th Street New York, NY 10036 212-391-1072 (12)

Eisenberg, Alan, Actors' Equity Association (AEA) 165 West 46th Street New York, NY 10036 212-869-8530 (18)

Eisenstein, Harold M., Gallery Players c/o Columbus Jewish Center Columbus, OH 43220 (16)

Eisner, Ted, Road Company of Audubon 302 8th Avenue Haddon Heights, NJ 08035 (16)

Eje, John, Le Sueur Community Theatre 115 Sunset Circle Le Sueur, MN 56058 (16)

Elbaum, S., Rollerwall Incorporated Post Office Box 757 Silver Spring, MD 20901 301-649-4422 (15)

Elder, Judith, Beaver College Department of Theatre Glenside, PA 19038 215-884-3500 (4)

Eley, Ed, Atmos Corporation Box 173 Carrollton, TX 75006 214-242-6581 (15)

Eley, Robert, East Los Angeles College Department of Theatre Monterey Park, CA 91754 213-265-8941 (4)

Elgood, Ann, Flint Youth Theatre 924 East Sixth Street Flint, MI 48503 (16)

Elkin, Saul, State University of New York at Buffalo Department of Theatre Buffalo, NY 14214 716-831-3742 (4)

Elkin, Saul, Green Mountain College Department of Theatre Poultney, VT 05764 802-287-9313 (4)

Elkins, Mrs. James, Oxford Little Theatre 520 North Lamar Oxford, MS 38655 (16)

Elleman, Robert P., On Stage Repertory Company c/o Advent Lutheran Church Brooklyn, NY 11229 718-743-6819 (16)

Ellin, Kathy, Ellen Jacobs 252 West 73rd Street New York, NY 10023 212-496-8353 (12)

Ellingsen, Mike, Blur Earth Town and Country Players 312 North Holland Street Blue Earth, MN 56013 (16)

Elliott, Rita, Corrales Adobe Theatre Post Office Box 546 Corrales, NM 87048 505-898-3323 (16)

Ellis, John W., West Virginia University Arts Center West Virginia University Morgantown, WV 26506 304-293-4642 (8)

Ellis, Joshua, Joshua Ellis 45 West 34th Street New York, NY 10001 212-947-0515 (12)

Ellis, Lydia, Thunderbird Products Company 1042 West Van Buren Chicago, IL 60607 312-733-2340 (15)

Ellis, Mary, New Berlin Art Forum Post Office Box 329 New Berlin, NY 13411 607-847-9810; 607-847-8890 (5)

Ellis, Ron, Musicians' Association, Local 70-558 3925 Terrace Drive Omaha, NE 68134 402-571-2722 (18)

Ellison, Joan, San Francisco Arts Commission c/o City Hall San Francisco, CA 94102 415-558-3465; 415-558-3463 (5)

Elmer, Dorothy, Twin City Federation of Musicians, Local 232 2182 Hanley Road Saint Joseph, MI 49085 616-429-8777 (18)

Emmes, David, Long Beach City College Department of Theatre Long Beach, CA 90808 (4)

Emmett, Nathalie D., McMaster University Department of Theatre Hamilton, Ontario, Canada 416-525-9140, extension 4660, 4661 (4)

Empey, Tom, Casper College Department of Theatre 125 College Drive Casper, WY 82601 307-268-2216 (4)

Empry, Gino, Royal Alexandra Theatre 260 King Street West Toronto, Ontario, Canada M5V 1H9 416-593-4233, Administration; 416-363-4211, Box Office (16)

Empry, Gino, Theatre Compact 730 Yonge Street Toronto, Ontario, Canada M4Y 2B7 416-922-6159 (16)

Emrick, William E., Major Holmes Auditorium Harder Hall, Alfred University Alfred, NY 14802 607-871-2411 (8)

Endicott, Clifford, Federation of Musicians, Local 191 Route No. 1 Peterbourough, Ontario, Canada K9J 6X2 705-292-7082 (18)

Engar, Keith, University of Utah Department of Theatre College of Fine Arts Salt Lake City, UT 84112 801-581-6356 (4)

Engar, Keith, Pioneer Memorial Theatre Company University of Utah Salt Lake City, UT 84112 801-581-6960 (16)

Engbers, Dick, Evansville Civic Theatre 717 North Fulton Avenue Evansville, IN 47708 812-423-2060 (8)

Engbers, Dick, Evansville Civic Theatre 717 North Fulton Evansville, IN 47710 812-423-2616 (16)

Engel, Mike, Studio Theatre 141 South Welwood Avenue Lindenhurst, NY 11757 516-884-1877 (8)

Engel, Mike, List Theatricals "Studio Theatre" 141 South Welwood Avenue Lindenhurst, NY 11757 516-884-1877 (16)

Engelbach, Jerry, Soho Repertory Theatre 19 Mercer Street New York, NY 10013 212-925-2588 (16)

Engers, Kathleen M., College of Notre Dame of Maryland Department of Theatre 4701 North Charles Street Baltimore, MD 21210 301-435-0100 (4)

England, Mrs. Edsel, Arts Guild of Sparta Post Office Box 305 Sparta, TN 38583 615-761-2367 (5)

English, Dian, Factory Theatre Lab 207 Adelaide Street East Toronto, Ontario, Canada M5A 1M8 416-864-9971 (16)

Ensign, Walter G., University of Alaska College of Arts and Letters Fairbanks, AK 99701 907-479-7211 (4)

Enterprises, Nancy, The Eugene O'Neill Theatre 230 West 49th Street New York, NY 10019 212-246-0220 (16)

Epp, Richard, University of Lethbridge Department of Dramatic Arts 4401 University Drive Lethbridge, Alberta, Canada T1K 3M4 403-329-2675 (4)

Epstein, Barbara, Zephyr Theatre 7458 Melrose Avenue Hollywood, CA 90046 213-852-9399 (8)

Epstein, Lawrence S., Lawrence S. Epstein Associates 1634 59th Street Brooklyn, NY 11204 212-232-8468; 212-837-2881, Data Line (1)

Epstein, Lawrence S., Lawrence S. Epstein Playwriting Award 1634 59th Street Brooklyn, NY 11204 212-232-8468 (3)

Erath, John F., Shakespeare '70 Incorporated 121 Grand Street Trenton, NJ 08611 609-392-1704 (16)

Erdman, Jean, Theatre of the Open Eye 316 East 88th Street New York, NY 10028 212-534-6363 (16)

Erdoffy, Alan, Sharon Arts Center Route 2, Post Office Box 361 Peterborough, NH 03458 603-924-7256 (5)

Erdos, Robert E., Meriden Federation of Musicians, Local 55 30 Briarwood Drive Meriden, CT 06450 203-238-0321 (18)

Erickson, Harlan S., Musicians' Protective Union 1208 Crestview Road Albert Lea, MN 56007 507-377-1363 (18)

Erickson, Jack, North Central Nebraska Area Arts Council 527 North Hall Valentine, NB 62901 402-376-3234 (5)

Erickson, Sigurd, Duluth Musicians' Association, Local 18 67 Calvary Road Duluth, MN 55803 218-728-1990 (18)

Erickson, Dr. Vernon, Grand Rapids Players Post Office Box 26 Grand Rapids, MN 55744 (16)

Ericson, Joan, Textile Resources 3763 Durango Avenue Los Angeles, CA 90034 213-838-9179 (15)

Ernst, Jane K., Andy's Summer Playhouse Box 601 Wilton, NH 03086 603-654-2613 (16)

Erwin, Donna, Hobbs Community Players 1700 North Grimes Hobbs, NM 88240 505-393-9524 (16)

Erwin, Linda, University Theatre University of Wisconsin Green Bay Green Bay, WI 54302 414-465-2256; 414-465-2217 (8)

Erwin, Owen A., New Westminster Secondary School Hyack Theatre 835 8th Street New Westminster, British Columbia, Canada V3M 359 (16)

Faulkner, June, Shaw Festival Post Office Box 774 Niagara on the Lake, Ontario, Canada L0S 1J0 416-468-2153; 416-468-3201 (9)

Faulkner, Seldon, University of Mississippi Department of Theatre University, MS 38677 601-232-7170 (4)

Faulkner, Seldon, University of Wisconsin, Stevens Point Department of Theatre 2100 Main Street Stevens Point, WI 54481 715-346-0123 (4)

Favorini, Attilio, University of Pittsburgh Department of Theatre Cathedral of Learning Pittsburgh, PA 15260 412-633- (4)

Fearey, Jack, Seattle Center 305 Harrison Street Seattle, WA 98109 206-625-4227; 206-625-4254 (8)

Feary, Jack, Seattle Center Arena 305 Harrison Seattle, WA 98109 206-625-4254 (8)

Febyszn, Stan, Norfolk Theatre Center 345 West Freemason Street Norfolk, VA 23510 804-627-1234 (8)

Federico, Robert, Compania de Teatro Repertoria Espanol 138 East 27th Street New York, NY 10016 212-889-2850 (16)

Fedigan, Jim, Fedigan Lighting Associates 12 Fanshaw Avenue Yonkers, NY 10705 914-968-6636 (15)

Feheregyhazi, Tibor, Magnus Theatre North-West 639 McLaughlin Street Thunder Bay, Ontario, Canada P7C 3B6 807-623-1337; 807-623-1321 (16)

Feidner, Edward J., University of Vermont Department of Theatre Burlington, VT 05405 802-656-2095 (4)

Feidner, Edward J., Royall Tyler Theatre University of Vermont Burlington, VT 05401 802-656-2095 (8)

Felsenfeld, H. E., 2563 North Farwell 2679 North Lake Drive Milwaukee, WI 53211 (16)

Fendrich, Shubert, Pioneer Drama Service 2172 South Colorado Boulevard Denver, CO 80222 (14)

Fenton, Russell L., Musicians' Protective Association, Local 45 323 South Adams Street Marion, IN 46952 317-664-0400 (18)

Ferguson, Paul, Lake City Community College Department of Theatre Lake City, FL 32055 904-752-1822 (4)

Feris, Manny, Manny Feris 76 Ninth Avenue, Room 1531 New York, NY 10011 212-924-7783; 212-625-4357 (15)

Ferlita, Ernest, Loyola University Department of Theatre 6363 Saint Charles Avenue New Orleans, LA 70118 504-865-2011 (4)

Ferrell, Mrs. Billie, Corpus Christi Musicians' Association 326 Dolphin Place Corpus Christi, TX 78411 512-852-4128 (18)

Ferrell, Dr. David M., Hartwick College Department of Theatre Oneonta, NY 13820 607-432-4200 (4)

Ferstead, J., Ascension Players 10154 Mountain Tujunga, CA 91042 (16)

Ferstl, Harlan, River Valley Community Theatre Post Office Box 356 Spring Green, WI 53588 (16)

Fetters, F. William, Mount Vernon Musicians' Association 111 Miller Avenue Mount Vernon, OH 43050 614-397-4302 (18)

Feuer, Michael, Fabri-Centers of America 23550 Commerce Park Road Beachwood, OH 44122 216-464-2500 (15)

Fieckenstein, Joan, Northwest Connecticut Community College Theatre Department of Theatre Winsted, CT 06518 (4)

Fielding, Lisabeth, American National Theatre and Academy Post Office Box 3221 Los Angeles, CA 90028 (16)

Fielding, Thomas G., British Columbia Cultural Fund Ministry of Provincial Secretary and Government Services Victoria, British Columbia, Canada V8W2Y2 604-387-5848 (5)

Fifield, Mrs. Janis C., Musicians' Association, Local 184 4801 Seahurst Everett, WA 98203 206-259-3802 (18)

Figler, Janet, Mid-Susquehanna Arts in Education Council 54 Parker Street Carlisle, PA 17013 717-783-2554 (5)

Figula, Michael, Musical Union, Local 84 1144 South Avenue Bradford, PA 16701 814-368-7421 (18)

File, David C., Iowa Wesleyan College Department of Theatre Mount Pleasant, IA 52641 319-385-8021 (4)

Filion, Nicole, Theatre Populaire du Quebec 5015 rue Boyer Montreal, Quebec, Canada H2J 3E8 514-849-2285 (16)

Filippo, I., Austin Peay State University Department of Theatre Clarksville, TN 37040 615-648-7378 (4)

Fincke, Ray, Plastic Reel Corporation of America 43 West 61st Street New York, NY 10023 212-541-1950 (15)

Findley, Robert L., Musicians' Mutual Association, Local 99 325 North East 20th Avenue Portland, OR 97232 503-235-8791 (18)

Fine, Naomi, Allied Arts Council 821 Las Vegas Boulevard, North Las Vegas, NV 89101 702-384-1208 (5)

Finell, Judith, Danceservices New York, NY 10023 212-580-4500 (12)

Fines, Doreen, Youtheatre 408 Saint James Street West, Suite 10 Montreal, Quebec, Canada H2Y 1S2 514-844-8781 (16)

Finklestein, Nini, Nini Finklestein 850 Third Avenue, 14th Floor New York, NY 10022 212-752-1408 (12)

Finn, Kay, Coach House Players 12 Augusta Street Kingston, NY 12401 (16)

Finnegan, Vincent G. Jr., Litelab 5200 Venice Boulevard Los Angeles, CA 90019 213-936-6206 (15)

Finnegan, Vincent G. Jr., Litelab 251 Elm Street Buffalo, NY 716-856-4300 (15)

Finnegan, Vincent G. Jr., Litelab Corporation 76 Ninth Avenue New York, NY 10011 212-675-4357 (15)

Finney, Collin, Collin Finney 807 Bradford Avenue Nashville, TN 37024 615-383-1358 (15)

Fipke, Wayne, The Citadel Theatre 9828 - 101A Avenue Edmonton, Alberta, Canada T5J 3C6 403-426-4811; 403-425-1820 (16)

Firor, Thomas, Pendleton County Committee for the Arts Post Office Box 572 Franklin, WV 268017 304-358-2506 (5)

Firth, Theodore C., Adirondack Association of Musicians, Local 129 4 Hillcrest Avenue Glen Falls, NY 12801 518-793-4801 (18)

Fischer, P., Musicomedy Productions 2211 Hindle Bowie, MD 20715 (16)

Fishbein, Ms. Janice, Frieda Fishbein Ltd. 353 West 57th Street New York, NY 10019 212-247-4398; 212-265-6100 (2)

Fishel, Richard, Gilbert and Sullivan Very Light Opera Company 1715 West Franklin Minneapolis, MN 55405 (16)

Fisher, Ed, Homemade Theatre 4 Maitland Street Toronto, Ontario, Canada M4Y 1C5 416-922-7129; 416-923-0898 (16)

Fisher, Edward, Jackson State College Department of Theatre Jackson, MS 39217 601-948-8533 (4)

Fisher, Jean-Marie, Vanilla Press 2400 Colfax Avenue South Minneapolis, MN 55405 612-374-4726 (14)

Fisher, Mrs. Robert, Project for Performing Arts Post Office Box 52 Bellfonte, PA 16823 (16)

Fisher, William, Stage West 16615 109 Avenue Edmonton, Alberta, Canada T5P 4K8 403-484-0841; 403-483-4051 (16)

Fisherman, Leslie D., On Stage Repertory Company c/o Advent Lutheran Church Brooklyn, NY 11229 718-743-6819 (16)

Fishman, Martin, Edmonton Actors' Workshop 8909 - 112 Street Hub Building Edmonton, Alberta, Canada T6G 2C5 403-433-2421 (16)

Fitch, Polly, Victor Valley College Department of Theatre Victor Ville, CA 92392 714-245-4271 (4)

Fites, Wilbur T., Alliance Federation of Musicians, Local 68 130 Shadyside Court Alliance, OH 44601 216-821-2761 (18)

Fitzgerald, Ed, Clear-Com Intercom Systems (CCI) 1111 17th Street San Francisco, CA 94107 415-861-6666 (15)

Fitzgerald, Hugh, Quincy College Department of Theatre 1831 College Avenue Quincy, IL 62301 217-222-8020 (4)

Fitzgerald, Jewell, Regina Theatre Edlewood College Madison, WI 53711 608-257-4861 (8)

Fitzgerald, Jewell P., Edgewood College Department of Performing Arts 855 Woodrow Street Madison, WI 53711 608-257-4861 (4)

Flach, Robert D., Hudson County Public Theatre 244 New York Avenue Jersey City, NJ 07307 201-653-7143 (16)

Flaherty, John, Putnam Color and Dye Post Office Box 1267 Galesburg, IL 61401 309-343-6181 (15)

Flam, Theodore, Viking Press 625 Madison Avenue New York, NY 10022 212-755-4330 (14)

Flammia, Sue, Citizens Council for the Arts Art on the Green Post Office Box 901 Coeur d'Alene, ID 83814 208-664-9052; 208-664-2259 (9)

Flannery, Dennis, Pittsburg Arts and Cultural Commission Post Office Box 1518 Pittsburg, CA 94565 415-439-4978 (5)

Flannery, James W., University of Rhode Island Department of Theatre Kingston, RI 02881 401-792-1000 (4)

Flatman, Barry, Homemade Theatre 4 Maitland Street Toronto, Ontario, Canada M4Y 1C5 416-922-7129; 416-923-0898 (16)

Flavell, Joe, Joe Flavell 1539 Brookside Drive Findlay, OH 45848 419-422-4235 (15)

Flaxman, Harvey, Fairleigh Dickenson University Department of Theatre Madison, NJ 07940 201-377-4700 (4)

Fleckenstein, Ken, Lake and Geauga County Federation of Musicians 7621 Chillicothe Road Mentor, OH 44060 216-255-2628 (18)

Fleisher, Mary, Marymount Manhattan College Department of Theatre 221 East 71st Street New York, NY 10021 212-472-3800 (4)

Fleishhacker, Mrs. Walter, Tupelo Community Theatre 611 North Thomas Street Tupelo, MS 38801 601-842-4518 (16)

Fleitell, Neil, National Stage Lighting 1232 9th Street, NW Washington, DC 20001 202-483-7090 (15)

Fletcher, James, Westmar College Department of Theatre 1002 Third Avenue Southeast Le Mars, IA 51031 712-546-7081 (4)

Fletcher, James F., Associated Musicians of Keene, New Hampshire Fitch Court Marlborough, NH 03455 603-876-3963 (18)

Flippo, Dr. Joe, Margaret Fort Theatre Austin Peay State University Clarksville, TN 37040 615-648-7378 (8)

Floore, Russell, Artesia Arts Council Post Office Box 782 Artesia, NM 88210 505-746-3226 (5)

Flora, Becky, Becky Flora 247 West 21st Street New York, NY 10011 212-242-7379 (12)

Fluckiger, W. Lynn, Hill Cumorah Pageant Post Office Box 117 Palmyra, NY 14522 315-597-5851 (16)

Flynn, Mary, Saint Mary College Department of Theatre Leavenworth, KS 66048 913-682-5151 (4)

Flynn, Michael W., Flynns Fabric Design Supplies 1154 Howard Street San Francisco, CA 94103 415-621-5968, Flynns; 415-431-8214, Fibrec (15)

Flynn, Rosemarie, Mercer County Community College Department of Theatre 1200 Old Trenton Road Trenton, NJ 08690 609-586-4800 (4)

Foard, Robert B., Teen and Children's Theatre 801 South Mockingbird Abilene, TX 79065 915-673-6271 (16)

Focht, Constance, Upper Merion Cultural Center 700 Moore Road King of Prussia, PA 19406 215-337-1393 (5)

Foeller, Ken, Musicians Association, Local 72 3458 Blue Bonnet Circle Fort Worth, TX 76109 817-927-8478 (18)

Fogg, Robert H., Millersville State College Department of Theatre Millersville, PA 17751 717-872-5411 (4)

Fognano, George A., Atlantic City Musicians' Association 418 North Main Street Pleasantville, NJ 08232 609-645-7740 (18)

Folio, Sam B., Clarksburg Federation of Musicians 320 Front Street Bridgeport, WV 26330 304-842-3088 (18)

Folsland, K., Interlake Players Oldham, SD 57051 (16)

Fonseca, Bryan, The Company Players 3729 Broadway Gary, IN 46409 (16)

Fontenay, Daniele de, Les Enfants du Paradis B.P. 883, Succ. A Montreal, Quebec, Canada H3C 2V8 514-845-5598 (16)

Forbell, Herbert, Musicians' Protective Union 1817 West Third Street Boone, IA 50036 515-432-4092 (18)

Forbes, Gordon, The Neil Simon Theatre 250 West 52nd Street New York, NY 10019 212-757-8646; 212-398-8383, Group Sales (16)

Forbes, Hazel, Theatre in the Dell 300 Simcoe Street Toronto, Ontario, Canada M5T 1T5 416-598-4802 (16)

Forcucci, Sam, Cortland Musicians' Association 17 Stevenson Street Cortland, NY 13045 607-753-8563 (18)

Ford, Judith, Southwest Gas Corporation Post Office Box 15015 Las Vegas, NV 89114 702-876-7241; 702-876-7222 (10)

Forde, Gladys, Fisk University Little Theatre 17th Avenue North Nashville, TN 37202 615-329-8633; 615-329-8513 (16)

Forde, Gladys I., Fisk University Department of Theatre 17th Avenue N Nashville, TN 37203 615-329-8765 (4)

Fordham, Tom, First All Children's Theatre 37 West 65th Street New York, NY 10023 212-873-6400 (16)

Foreman, Mrs. Foster, Berkeley Civic Art Commission Berkeley Art Center Berkeley, CA 94709 415-849-4120 (5)

Forge, Rudolph J., Worcester Musicians' Association, Local 143 38 Patch Reservoir Drive Worcester, MA 01602 617-798-2228 (18)

Fornes, Maria Irene, INTAR Playwrights-in-Residence Lab 420 West 42nd Street New York, NY 10036 212-695-6134 (3)

Forney, Dolores, Thief River Falls Arts Council 1524 Cartway Drive Thief River Falls, MN 56701 218-681-5916 (5)

Forsyth, Eugene, Musicians' Association 1602 Palmer Miles City, MT 59301 406-232-4494 (18)

Forsythe, Eric, Tufts Arena Theater Tufts University Medford, MA 02155 617-623-3880 (8)

Fortner, Michael, Coastal Carolina College Department of Theatre Conway, SC 29526 803-347-3161 (4)

Fortner, Michael, Upstage Company Coastal Carolina College Conway, SC 29526 803-347-3161 (8)

Fosco, Frank, Sandusky Musicians' Association Post Office Box 2224 Sandusky, OH 44870 419-625-1499 (18)

Foster, Mrs. Doris, Annual Outdoor Arts Festival School of Fine Arts Willoughby, OH 44094 216-951-7500 (9)

Foster, Gene, Mel Foster Technical Sales, Inc. 7611 Washington Avenue, South Edina, MN 55435 612-941-9800 (15)

Foster, Jack, Stage Lighting Discount Corporation 70 Haight Street Deerpark, NY 11729 516-242-7865 (15)

Foster, Robert C., Lockport Federation of Musicians, Local 97 6279 Hamm Road Lockport, NY 14094 716-434-2229 (18)

Fouch, Doris A., Tubac Center for the Arts Post Office Box 282 Tubac, AZ 85640 602-398-2371 (5)

Fowler, Ken, Salina Musicians' Association, Local 207 801 Choctow Salina, KS 67401 913-827-7352 (18)

Fox, Chester, Chester Fox 3 West 57th Street New York, NY 10019 212-371-1799 (12)

Fox, P., Little Theatre Post Office Box 2424 Amarillo, TX 79109 (16)

Fradenberg, Charles, Musicians' Protective Union, Local 236 724 Terrace Aberdeen, WA 98520 206-532-0583 (18)

France, Charles, Charles France 57 West 75th Street New York, NY 10023 212-362-9243 (12)

France, Richard, Lawrence University Department of Theatre Post Office Box 599 Appleton, WI 54911 414-739-3681 (4)

Francis, Ron, Charlottetown Festival Post Office Box 848 Charlottetown, Prince Edward Island, Canada C1A 7L9 902-892-2464 (16)

Francis, Vicky, Broadway Melody
Entertainment Tours Post Office Box
1634 Studio City, CA 91604
213-766-5875; 213-227-8370 (1)

Frand, Robert E., Sandusky Musicians'
Association Post Office Box 2224
Sanddusky, OH 44870 419-625-1499
(18)

Frank, Darlene, Musicians' Protective
Union, Local 175 422 North Olive
Street Trenton, IL 62293 618-224-9460
(18)

Frank, Jerry L., Reno Little Theater Post
Office Box 2088 Reno, NV 89505
702-329-0661; 702-322-3244 (16)

Frankel, Gene, Gene Frankel Theatre
Workshop 342 East 63rd Street New
York, NY 10021 212-421-1666 (16)

Franklin, Abigail, Interart Theatre 549
West 52nd Street New York, NY 10019
212-246-1050 (16)

Franklin, Maureen, Assembly of
Community Arts Councils Tennessee
Arts Commission Nashville, TN 37219
615-741-1701 (5)

Franklin, Wendy, Third Sector Press 2000
Euclid Avenue Cleveland, OH 44118
216-932-6066 (14)

Franks, Bud, Casa Manana 3101 West
Lancaster Fort Worth, TX 76112
817-332-9319 (8)

Fraze, L., Ohio Valley Summer Theatre
Kantner Hall-Ohio UN Athens, OH
45701 (16)

Frederico, Frank S., Ridgway Musicians'
Association 445 Montomorenci Road
Ridgway, PA 15853 814-776-1203 (18)

Fredman, Donald M., University of
California, Berkeley Department of
Dramatic Arts Berkeley, CA 94720
415-642-1677 (4)

Fredman, Doris, Public Arts Council 25
Central Park West New York, NY 10009
212-586-7527 (5)

Freebody, Barbara, Rising Sun Cultural
Arts Program Post Office Box 182
Ambler, PA 19002 215-646-2015 (5)

Freed, Steven, Salina Musicians'
Association, Local 207 801 Choctow
Salina, KS 67401 913-827-7352 (18)

Freeman, B., Antrim Players Spookrock
Road Suffern, NJ 10901 (16)

Freeman, B. Pope, Santa Barbara
Repertory Theatre James R. Garvin
Memorial Theatre Santa Barbara, CA
93109 805-965-0581, Ext. 375 (16)

Freeman, Dexter, The Actors Workshop
6111 West Olympic Boulevard Los
Angeles, CA 90048 213-931-4662 (4)

Freeman, Ed, Life-Like Products 1600
Union Avenue Baltimore, MD 21211
301-889-1023 (15)

Freeman, George, Musicians' Protective
Union 306 Roundville Street Waupun,
WI 53963 414-885-5548 (18)

Freeman, Isadore, Musicians' Mutual
Protective and Benevolent Union, Local
248 77 Prospect Street Paterson, NJ
07505 201-278-8418; 201-278-8420 (18)

French, Mark H., Musicians' Federation,
Local 218 808 West Kaye Avenue
Marquette, MI 49855 906-228-8800 (18)

Fresco, Sandra, Theatre Hour Company 3
Church Street, Suite 33 Toronto,
Ontario, Canada M5E 1M2
416-366-1656 (16)

Fresco, Sandra, Toronto Arts Productions
3 Church Street Toronto, Ontario,
Canada M5E 1M2 416-366-1656,
Administration; 416-366-7723, Box
Office (16)

Frey, Eugene V., Cincinnati Musicians
Association, Local 1 19 West Court
Cincinnati, OH 45202 513-241-0900 (18)

Fricker, Helen, Riverside Theatre Post
Office Box 3788 Vero Beach, FL 32960
305-567-8860 (8)

Fricker, Helen M., Vero Beach Theatre
Guild Post Office Box 4019 Vero Beach,
FL 32960 305-562-1621 (16)

Friedlander, Norman, Dazian's
Incorporated 40 East 29th Street New
York, NY 10016 212-686-5300 (15)

Friedman, Jane, Jane Friedman 250 West
57th Street New York, NY 10107
212-245-5587 (12)

Friedman, Sidney J., Washington
University Department of Theatre Saint
Louis, MO 63130 314-863-0100 (4)

Fries, William D., Charleroi Musical
Society 1212 Monongahela Avenue Belle
Vernon, PA 15012 412-929-7500 (18)

Friese, Arthur, Salem Press 550 Sylvan
Avenue Engelwood Cliffs, NJ 07632
201-871-3700 (14)

Frisch, J., Harlequin Players Post Office
Box 625 Green Bay, WI 54305 (16)

Fritsch, Robert, Port City Playhouse 1336
Sanford Street Muskegan, MI 49441 (16)

Fritz, Leo L., Musicians Protective Union
218 Second Avenue Northeast Post
Office Box 15 Oelwein, IA 50662
319-427-3485 (18)

Frost, M.A. III, Southern Importers 4825
San Jacinto Street Houston, TX
77004-5620 713-524-8236 (15)

Fry, Fran Jr., Musical Association, Local 61
604 Buffalo Street Franklin, PA 16323
814-432-5088 (18)

Fry, J., Bridge Street Players 3115 P
Street, NW Washington, DC 20007 (16)

Frye, Steven, Ohio Valley College
Department of Theatre Parkersburg, WV
25304 304-485-7384 (4)

Fuchtman, Leonard J., Musicians'
Protective Association, Local 28 425 Elm
Street Leadville, CO 80461
303-486-0252 (18)

Fujii, Mort, Cetec Gauss 13035 Saticoy
Street North Hollywood, CA 91605
213-875-1900 (15)

Fulford, C. David, Carousel Dinner
Theatre Post Office Box 427 Ravenna,
OH 44266 216-296-3866 (16)

Fulkerson, Gerald, Freed-Hardeman
College Department of
Communication/Theatre 158 East Main
Street Henderson, TN 38340

901-989-4611 (4)

Fuller, P., New Dimension Theatre Studio
c/o YMHA of Bergen County
Hackensack, NJ 07601 201-489-5900
(16)

Fulmer, Ray M., Sunbury Federation of
Musicians 506 Catawissa Sunbury, PA
17801 717-286-9449 (18)

Funking, Robert J., An Evening Dinner
Theatre 11 Clearbrook Road Elmsford,
NY 10523 914-592-2268 (16)

Furlong, Gregory W., The Joyce-Cridland
Company Post Office Box 1630 Dayton,
OH 45401 513-294-6261 (15)

Furman, Lou, Wayside Theatre
Middletown, VA 22645 703-869-1782 (8)

Furman, Paul, Festival Repertory Company
1401 Flatbush Avenue Brooklyn, NY
11210 718-859-9459 (16)

Furnaux, Don, The Group Theatre 1276
Van Ness Hollywood, CA 90028
213-466-2273 (16)

Furtado, Richard J., Musicians' Protective
Union, Local 231 533 Walnut Street
Bridgewater, MA 02324 617-697-4979
(18)

G

Gaalipeau, Teri, Halfpenny
Playhouse/Upsala Theatre Edgerton
Terrace East Orange, NJ 07019 (8)

Gaber, Lee, Lee Gaber Company Post
Office Box 8237 Honolulu, HI 96815
808-839-9059 (15)

Gabriel, J.A., Gaslite Players Route 3, Post
Office Box 350 Salem, WI 53168 (16)

Gadberry, Glenn, University of Minnesota
Department of Theatre Minneapolis,
MN 55455 612-373-3118; 612-373-4882
(4)

Gadouas, Daniel, Theatre de Marjolaine
1500 rue Stanley, Suite 320 Montreal,
Quebec, Canada H3A 1R3 514-845-0917
(16)

Gaedtke, Melvin A., Kewaunee Federation
of Musicians 320 Church Street Algoma,
WI 54201 414-845-5021 (18)

Gaffney, John P., Bay Path Junior College
Department of Theatre 588
Longmeadow Longmeadow, MA 01106
413-567-0621 (4)

Gafrein, Jack, Actors and Directors
Laboratory 254 South Robertson
Boulevard Beverly Hills, CA 90211
213-652-6483 (16)

Gagnon, Jean Pierre, Quebec Musicians'
Association, Local 119 1406 West Street
Quebec City, Quebec, Canada G1S 1X2
418-688-1722 (18)

Gaither, Pearino, Harwell Auditorium 414
Oak Street Talladega, AL 35160
205-362-2203 (8)

Galanic, Pete, Musicians' Union, Local 146
2601 Eastlawn Avenue Lorain, OH
44052 216-288-0408 (18)

Galia, Frank, F.G. Lighting Sales Post Office Box 20186 Phoenix, AZ 85036 602-277-7901 (15)

Galiano, Pete, Beloit Musicians' Association, Local 183 1715 Strong Avenue Beloit, WI 53511 608-362-8356 (18)

Gallagher, Ed, Santa Monica College Department of Theatre 1900 West Pico Boulevard Santa Monica, CA 90405 213-450-5150 (4)

Gallagher, James J., Franklin County Musicians' Association 151 Davis Street Greenfield, MA 01301 413-773-9769 (18)

Gallagher, Kent G., Northern Illinois University Department of Theatre Arts DeKalb, IL 60115 815-753-1334; 815-753-1335 (4)

Gallagher, Mary B., Radford College Studio Theatre Norwood Street Radford, VA 24141 703-731-5152 (8)

Gallagher, Wayne, Fair Park Bandshell Dallas, TX 75226 (8)

Galo, Al, Sound Creations 1309 Bingham Northwest Warren, OH 44485 216-399-8752 (15)

Galow, Milton H., Oshkosh Musicians' Association, Local 46 3159 Omro Road Oshkosh, WI 54901 414-235-3461 (18)

Galvan, Edward, Corpus Christi Musicians' Association 326 Dolphin Place Corpus Christi, TX 78411 512-852-4128 (18)

Gambini, Lindsay, Producer's Collaborative 240 West 44th Street New York, NY 10036 212-390-1030 (13)

Gandy, Irene, Irene Gandy 234 West 44th Street New York, NY 10036 212-391-1072 (12)

Gandy, Mary, Hattiesburg Little Theatre Post Office Box 1291 Hattiesburg, MS 39401 (16)

Gannon, Harold, The Arcus Ticket Company 348 North Ashland Avenue Chicago, IL 60607 312-733-7440 (15)

Gannon, Thomas, Buckeye Woodland Community Service 10613 Lamontier Cleveland, OH, 44104 216-368-1070 (5)

Ganshaw, Robert, Robert Ganshaw 157 West 57th Street New York, NY 10019 212-489-6745 (12)

Garbary, Evelyn, Mermaid Theatre Post Office Box 837 Wolfville, Nova Scotia, Canada B0P 1X0 902-542-3641 (16)

Garber, Bill, William Edrington Scott Theatre 3505 West Lancaster Fort Worth, TX 76107 817-738-1938 (8)

Garber, Bill, Greater Fort Worth Community Theatre 3505 West Lancaster Fort Worth, TX 76107 817-738-7491 (16)

Garbutt, Robert, Sharp Electronics Corporation 10 Keystone Place Paramus, NJ 07652 201-265-5600 (15)

Garcia, Federico, Westinghouse Electric Supply Company Box 144, La Ceramica Annex Carolina, PR 00630 (15)

Gardella, Elizabeth, Alliance of Resident Theatres, New York 325 Spring Street New York, NY 10013 212-989-5257 (5)

Gardiner, Robert, Cosumnes River College Department of Theatre Sacramento, CA 95823 916-421-1000, Ext. 292 (4)

Gardner, Joseph T., Davidson College Department of Theatre Davidson, NC 28036 704-892-2000 (4)

Gardner, Patricia L., Olde West Dinner Theatre Post Office Box 5001 Kingsport, TN 37743 615-323-4151 (16)

Gardner, Ralph J., Musicians' Protective Association, Local 163 17 South Hollywood Avenue Gloversville, NY 12078 518-725-1256 (18)

Gardner, Robert, Gustavus Adolphus College Department of Theatre Saint Peter, MN 56082 507-931-4300 (4)

Gardner, William, Academy Festival Theatre Barat College Lake Forest, IL 60045 312-234-6750 (16)

Garfein, Jack, Harold Clurman Theatre 412 West 42nd Street New York, NY 10036 212-575-9654 (8)

Garfield, John David, City Theatre Project 2653 Hollyridge Drive Los Angeles, CA 90028 213-464-5031 (16)

Garguilo, Alfred V., Delray Beach Playhouse Post Office Box 1056 Delray Beach, FL 33444 305-272-1281 (8)

Garner, Nathan, George Washington University Department of Theatre Washington, DC 20052 202-676-7072 (4)

Garniss, Howard, Boston Musicians' Association, Local 9-535 56 St. Botolph Street Boston, MA 02116 617-536-2486 (18)

Garren, Lois Z., Auburn University Department of Theatre Auburn, AL 36849 205-826-4748 (4)

Garrett, Mason, Easley Arts Council Post Office Box 841 Easley, SC 29640 802-859-5351 (5)

Garrick, Harris, Garrick Associates 3925 Loch Drive Highland, MI 48031 313-887-2140 (15)

Garrison, Robert, Theatre Arts Corporation 905 Saint Frances Drive Santa Fe, NM 87501 505-983-9815 (10)

Garrison, Robert, Theatre Arts Corporation 724 Canyon Road Santa Fe, NM 87501 505-983-9815 (16)

Gasche, John, Houston Cinema and Sound Equipment 3732 North Shepard Houston, TX 77018 713-691-4379 (15)

Gasper, Raymond D., Queens College Department of Theatre 67-30 Kissena Boulevard Flushing, NY 11367 212-520-7572; 212-520-7573 (4)

Gates, John C., Capron Lighting and Sound 278 West Street Needham Heights, MA 02194 617-444-8850 (15)

Gatewood, E.C., E.C. Gatewood 3120 Arundel Drive Charlotte, NC 28209 704-523-3499 (15)

Gathings, Joseph G., University of the District of Columbia Department of Theatre Washington, DC 20001 202-727-2351 (4)

Gatwood, Dr. Robin, Hickory Arts Council Post Office Box 1004 Hickory, NC 28601 704-328-1741 (5)

Gaudette, Richard L., Natick Drama Workshop 5 Summer Street Natick, MA 01760 (16)

Gaudreault, Jean-Yves, Theatre Des Pissenlits C.P. 458, Station H Montreal, Quebec, Canada H3G 2L1 514-931-0731 (16)

Gaudreault, Jean-Yves, Theatre Populaire du Quebec 5015 rue Boyer Montreal, Quebec, Canada H2J 3E8 514-849-2285 (16)

Gaulin, Paul, Paul Gaulin Mime Theatre 89 Pleasant Boulevard Toronto, Ontario, Canada M4T 1K2 416-924-1373 (16)

Gautron, Ernest, Le Cercle Moliere C.P.1 Saint-Boniface, Manitoba, Canada R2H 3B4 204-233-8053 (16)

Gavahan, John, Las Vegas Arts Council Post Office Box 1506 Las Vegas, NV 87701 505-425-7400 (5)

Gavura, John J., White Product Company 200 East Main Street Washingtonville, OH 44490 216-747-8116; 216-427-6542 (15)

Gaydos, Thomas V., Robert Morris College Department of Theatre Pittsburgh, PA 15219 412-264-9300 (4)

Gazelka, Ronald P., Musicians' Protective Union 1320 East 11th Street Hibbing, MN 55746 218-262-2941 (18)

Gear, Francis, American Guild of Variety Artists (AGVA) 184 5th Avenue New York, NY 10010 212-675-1003 (18)

Gearhart, Fred C., Saint John Studio Theatre 3rd and Pine Streets Clearfield, PA 16830 (16)

Gedney, J.A., Bozak, Incorporated c/o Gedney Company 476 East 58th Avenue Denver, CO 80216 303-572-1900 (15)

Geer, Faith, Faith Geer 485 West 22nd Street New York, NY 10011 212-243-3353 (12)

Gehn, Valerie, Greenville Community Theater Scarsdale, NY 10583 914-472-0679 (16)

Geike, Siegfried H., Kryolan Corporation 14316 Victory Boulevard Van Nuys, CA 91401 213-789-1465; 213-787-5054 (15)

Gelais, Joseph Saint, Theatre Des Pissenlits C.P. 458, Station H Montreal, Quebec, Canada H3G 2L1 514-931-0731 (16)

Gelormino, Retta, Professional Musicians Association, Local 238 42 Styvestandt Drive Poughkeepsie, NY 12601 914-471-2305 (18)

Genauer, Mark, Stagelight Cosmetics 630 Ninth Avenue New York, NY 10036 212-757-4851 (15)

Gladstone, Herbert, Condec Corporation 1700 East Putnam Avenue Old Greenwich, CT 06870 203-637-4511 (10)

Glass, Dr. Robert, Missouri Valley College Department of Theatre 500 East College Street Marshall, MO 65340 816-866-6924 Extension 147 (4)

Glass, William, American Puppet Arts Council 59 Barrow Street New York, NY 10014 212-989-7060 (16)

Glendinning, Alex B., Dodd Company, The 13123 Shaker Square Cleveland, OH 44120 216-561-1500 (15)

Glenn, Barbara, Barbara Glenn 234 West 44th Street New York, NY 10036 212-391-1072 (12)

Glenn, Margaret, Downey Civic Light Opera Association Post Office Box 429 Downey, CA 90241 213-923-1714; 213-861-3994 (16)

Glenn, Todd V., Fullerton College Department of Theatre Fullerton, CA 92634 714-871-8000 (4)

Glines, John, The Glines 28 Willow Street Brooklyn, NY 11201 718-522-5567 (16)

Glousky, L., Chequamagon Bay Players Post Office Box 225 Ashland, WI 54806 (16)

Gluck, Jeff, Saturday Review Post Office Box 6024 Columbia, MO 65205 314-875-3003 (14)

Gnat, Ray, Bailey's Incorporated 25 West Van Buren Street Chicago, IL 60605 312-939-2172 (15)

Gobeil, Pierre, Theatre de l'Atelier Parc Jaques-Cartier Sherbrooke, Quebec, Canada J1H 5H2 819-562-1982 (16)

Goddard, Dick, Musicians' Protective Union, Local 179 102 Gates Street Marietta, OH 45750 614-374-5473 (18)

Goddard, Gerald, Salem Federation of Musicians, Local 222 Route 4 Salem, OH 44460 216-332-1281 (18)

Godsey, Jim, Dyersburg Little Theatre Post Office Box 1 Dyersburg, TN 38024 901-285-4604 (16)

Godwin, Randy, Jefferson Civic Center 1 Civic Center Plaza Birmingham, AL 35202 205-328-8160 (8)

Goehring, Doris P, Juniata College Department of Theatre Huntington, PA 16652 814-643-4310 (4)

Goff, Warren, Diversified Lighting 120 Pennsylvania Avenue Oreland, PA 19075 215-887-7480 (15)

Gogdan, Frank, Trenton War Memorial Auditorium West Lafayette Street Trenton, NJ 08608 609-393-4866 (8)

Gohn, Lamar E., Gohn Brothers Post Office Box 111 Middlebury, IN 46540 219-825-2400 (15)

Gold, Muriel, Saidye Bronfman Centre 5170 Cote Saint Catherine Road Montreal, Quebec, Canada H3W 1M7 514-739-2301 (16)

Gold, Robert, Grand Rapids Federation of Musicians, Local 56 4622 Cannonsburg, NE Belmont, MI 49505 616-874-7421 (18)

Golden, David A., Alexandria Bay Convention Hall James Street Alexandria Bay, NY 13601 315-482-3320 (8)

Goldfarb, Alain, Open Circle Theatre 57 Adelaide Street East Toronto, Ontario, Canada M5C 1K6 416-363-6443, Administrative; 416-363-6401, Box Office (16)

Goldman, Harris, Theatre Marketplace Post Office Box 181 New York, NY 10024 212-724-0248 (15)

Goldman, Mia, Massachusetts Assembly of Community Arts Councils Council on the Arts and Humanities 1 Ashburton Place Boston, MA 02108 617-727-3668 (5)

Goldman, Stephen M., Ekedahl Tool and Supply Company Post Office Box 13198 Pittsburgh, PA 15243 412-531-2850 (15)

Goldrich, Henry, Manny's Music 156 West 48th Street New York, NY 10036 212-747-0576 (15)

Goldsmith, O.E., Barstow Community Players Barstow, CA 92311 (16)

Goldsmith, Ted, Ted Goldsmith 125 West 12th Street New York, NY 10011 212-929-7226 (12)

Goldstaub, Mark, Mark Goldstaub 312 West 48th Street New York, NY 10036 212-582-2879 (12)

Goldstayn, Lily, Jackson County Arts Council 200 Grandview Jackson, OH 45640 (5)

Goldstein, David, D.O. Industries, Incorporated 317 East Chestnut East Rochester, NY 14445 716-385-4920 (15)

Goldstein, Nathan L., Chicago Hair Goods 428 South Wabash Avenue Chicago, IL 60605 312-427-8600 (15)

Goloub, Janet, Valley Arts Council Post Office Box 4504 Allentown, PA 18105 215-776-0204 (5)

Gom, Leona, Event Kwantlen College, Box 9030 Surrey, British Columbia, Canada V3T 5H8 (14)

Gombar, Mary Lou, Mira Costa Community College Department of Theatre 1 Bernard Drive Oceanside, CA 92054 714-757-2121 (4)

Gompertz, Erich, Erich Gompertz and Associates 941 South West 70th Avenue Plantation, FL 33314 305-583-5819 (15)

Gonzales, C., Ana Modjeska Players Post Office Box 3354 Anaheim, CA 92802 (16)

Gonzalez, Ishamel, Musicians' Society, Local 23 233 Zephyr Drive San Antonia, TX 78239 512-227-3582 (18)

Gonzalez, Rene J., Spanish Little Theatre 1704 Seventh Avenue Tampa, FL 33605 813-248-3594 (16)

Gooder, David M., Festival of American Community Theaters in Spokane c/o David M. Gooder Downers Grove, IL 60515 (9)

Goodman, Arlene, Frank Goodman Publicity 1776 Broadway New York, NY 10019 212-246-4180 (12)

Goodman, Frank, Frank Goodman Publicity 1776 Broadway New York, NY 10019 212-246-4180 (12)

Goodman, Irving, Viking Press 625 Madison Avenue New York, NY 10022 212-755-4330 (14)

Goodman, Robin, The Second Stage 200 West 72nd Street, Suite 20 New York, NY 10023 212-787-8302 (16)

Goodman, William W., American Shakespeare Theatre/Connecticut Center for the Performing Arts (Stratford) 1850 Elm Street Stratford, CT 06497 203-378-7321; 212-966-3900 (16)

Goodness, Kenneth E., Musicians' Protective Union Post Office Box 91 Lycoming, NY 13093 315-343-0557 (18)

Goodridge, Edythe, New Foundland and Labrador Arts Council Prince Philip Drive, Box 1854 Saint John's, Newfoundland, Canada A1C 5P9 709-722-0711 (5)

Goodwin, Charles, Musicians' Association 201 McTeer Drive Kingsport, TN 37660 615-246-6351 (18)

Goodwin, John C., La Compagnie des Deux Chaises 3823 Melrose Montreal, Quebec, Canada H4A 2S3 (16)

Gordean, Meg, Meg Gordean c/o Gurfman and Murtha Associates New York, NY 10019 212-245-4771 (12)

Gordey, Gordon, Alberta Culture Council CN Tower, 10004-104 Avenue Edmonton, Alberta, Canada T5J 0K5 403-427-2553 (5)

Gordon, Joann, Canton Community Players 229 East North Street Canton, MS 39046 (16)

Gordon, Mary, Central Oregon Arts Association Post Office Box 175 La Pine, OR 97739 503-536-2770 (5)

Gordon, Sidney, Falmouth Playhouse Falmouth, MA 02540 617-563-6622 (16)

Gordon, Stewart, Musicians' Protective Association, Local 53 101 East Clay Street Logansport, IN 46947 219-753-8416 (18)

Gordon, Stuart B., Theatre Arts of West Virginia Post Office Box 1205 Beckley, WV 25801 304-253-8131 (16)

Gordon, Stuart B., Theatre West Virginia Post Office Box 1205 Beckley, WV 25801 304-253-8317 (16)

Gordon, Stuart B., Hatfields and McCoys/Honey in the Rock Post Office Box 1205 Buckley, WV 25801-1205 304-253-8313; 304-253-8314 (16)

Gorlin, B., Conrad-Hanovia, Incorporated 100 Chestnut Street Newark, NJ 07105 201-589-4300 (15)

Gorsky, Edwin, Pratt Community College Department of Theatre Highway 61 Pratt, KS 67124 316-672-5641 (4)

Gorton, C. L. "Dutch", Association of Musicians, Local 257 Post Office Box 120399 Nashville, TN 37212 615-244-9514 (18)

Gosling, Harry A., Musicians' Association of St. Louis, Local 2-197 2103 59th Street St. Louis, MO 63110 314-781-6612 (18)

Gosse, Dey, Quaigh Theatre 108 West 43rd Street New York, NY 10036 212-221-9088 (16)

Gossett, Jon K., High Point Arts Council 220 East Commerce Street High Point, NC 27260 919-882-0710; 919-882-9721 (5)

Gould, Ann, Corry Area Fine Arts Council 209 North Center Street Corry, PA 16406 (5)

Gour, Norman E., Butler Federation of Musicians, Local 188 142 Remil Drive Butler, PA 16001 412-287-1591 (18)

Gouran, Patrick D., Iowa State University Department of Theatre Ames, IA 50011 515-294-4111 (4)

Gowdy, Anne R., Anchorage Press Post Office Box 8067 New Orleans, LA 70182 504-283-8868 (14)

Goyette, John, White Mountains Center for the Arts Post Office Box 145 Jefferson, NH 03585 603-586-7754 (5)

Graczyk, E., Players Club Theatre 549 Franklin Avenue Columbus, OH 43215 (16)

Graczyk, Ed, Players Theatre of Columbus 549 Franklin Avenue Columbus, OH 43215 614-224-6971; 614-224-0831 (16)

Gradert, Catherine Heber, Kennedy-Webster Electric Company 133 North Jefferson Street Chicago, IL 60606 312-876-1612 (15)

Grady, Mary, Mary Grady Artists Manager 10850 Riverside North Hollywood, CA 91602 213-985-9800 (2)

Graham, Helen, Sullivan County Dramatic Workshop 4 Lakewood Avenue Monticello, NY 12701 914-794-4114 (16)

Graham, Marian, Marian Graham 135 East 50th Street New York, NY 10022 212-753-7110 (12)

Graham, William H., Catholic University of America Department of Theatre Washington, DC 20064 202-635-5353 (4)

Granata, Anthony, The Cleveland Federation of Musicians, Local 4 2200 Carnegie Avenue Cleveland, OH 44115 216-771-1802 (18)

Grandgeorge, William, Roger Williams College Department of Theatre Bristol, RI 02809 401-253-1000 (4)

Granich, Ron, Cerulean Blue, Ltd. Post Office Box 5126 Seattle, WA 98105 206-625-9647 (15)

Grant, Donald A., Theatre New Brunswick Post Office Box 566 Fredericton, New Brunswick, Canada E3B 5A6 506-455-3222 (16)

Grant, Johnnie W., Musicians' Protective Union 5900 Townsend Place Cheyenne, WY 82001 307-632-2186 (18)

Grant, Sis, Jasper Arts Council Post Office Box 622 Jasper, AL 35501 205-384-3461 (5)

Grantham, Ken, Franconia College Department of Theatre Franconia, NH 03580 603-823-5545 (4)

Grass, R., Arena Stages 19 Lindsey Place Wilmington, DE 19809 (16)

Graton, Francoise, Theatre Denise Pelletier 4353 St-Catherine East Montreal, Quebec, Canada H1V 1Y2 514-253-8974 (16)

Graunard, R. S., Musicians' Protective Association, Local 74 1309 Marine Galveston, TX 77550 713-763-3754 (18)

Graunke, Dean F., University of Wisconsin Fine Arts Theater University of Wisconsin Sheboygan Sheboygan, WI 53081 414-459-3750 (8)

Graves, A., Town Theatre 1012 Sumter Columbia, SC 29201 (16)

Gray, D., Christina Cultural Arts 88 East 7th Street Wilmington, DE 19801 (16)

Gray, Donovan, Spectrum Theatre of Allied Arts 118 East Johnson Lake Chelan, WA 98816 509-682-5041 (8)

Gray, Jack, ACTRA 105 Carlton Street Toronto, Ontario, Canada M5B 1M2 416-977-6335 (18)

Green, Barry, Ciro Equipment, Corporated 6820 Romaine Street Hollywood, CA 90038 213-467-1296 (15)

Green, Clara L., Tuscarara Area Community Theatre Post Office Box 26 Mercersburg, PA 17236 (16)

Green, Mrs. Donna, Arts Institute of Western Maine Corner of Main and Anson Streets Farmington, ME 04938 207-778-3475 (5)

Green, Evan, Cine 60 Incorporated 6430 Sunset Boulevard Hollywood, CA 90028 213-461-3046 (15)

Green, Robert, Rual Industries, Incorporated 1700 South 740 West Salt Lake City, UT 84104 801-972-1317; 801-972-1318 (15)

Green, Thomas K., Gatson College Department of Theatre Dallas, NC 28034 704-922-3136; 704-554-6080 (4)

Greenberg, Gail, Camden County Cultural Commission 250 South Park Drive Haddon Township, NJ 08108 609-858-0063 (5)

Greenberg, Jan, Jan Greenberg 420 Riverside Drive New York, NY 10025 212-864-3306 (12)

Greenberg, Mara, Pentacle 200 W 72nd St., Suite 20 New York, NY 10023 212-580-8107 (12)

Greene, Dr. Grady, New Mexico Highlands University Department of Theatre Las Vegas, NM 87701 505-425-7511 (4)

Greene, Randy, Illinois State University Auditorium Illinois State University Normal, IL 61761 309-438-2222 (8)

Greenfield, Dan, Robart-Green Commpany 17-21 Newark Way Maplewood, NJ 07040 201-761-7400 (15)

Greenhoe, Mary, Sweetwater Valley Citizens for the Arts Post Office Box 188 Sweetwater, TN 37874 615-337-6014 (5)

Greenwell, Andrew D., Hampton Coliseum Post Office Box 7309 Hampton, VA 23666 804-838-5650 (8)

Greenwood, Robert, Sun Ergos 2205, 700 - 9th Street, South West Calgary, Alberta, Canada T2P 2B5 403-264-4621 (16)

Greer, S., Oglebay Institute Oglebay Park Wheeling, WV 26003 (16)

Gregg, Dianne, Women's Jazz Festival Post Office Box 22321 Kansas, MO 64113 816-361-1901 (9)

Gregg, Gail, Lynn Canal Community Players Post Office Box 75 Haines, AK 99827 907-766-2540; 907-766-2763 (9)

Gregg, James R., Musicians' Protective Union 534 5th Street Juneau, AK 99801 907-586-1367 (18)

Gregory, William A., United States Steel Foundation 600 Grant Street Pittsburgh, PA 15230 412-433-5238 (10)

Greiner, Arthur S., Friendship Garden Pavilion Post Office Box 911 Brownsville, TX 78520 512-542-3367 (8)

Greiner, Arthur S., Jacob Brown Auditorium Post Office Box 911 Brownsville, TX 78520 512-542-3367 (8)

Grenier, Isabelle, Les Marionettes Merinat 412 - 3500 Varsity Drive Northwest Calgary, Alberta, Canada T2L 1Y3 403-282-2226 (16)

Gresham, Albert L., Chattanooga Little Theatre 400 River Street Chattanooga, TN 37405 615-267-8534 (16)

Grey, Mrs. John, Nine O'Clock Players 1367 North Andrews Place Los Angeles, CA 90028 213-469-1973, Assistance League Switchboard; 213-499-1970 (16)

Gries, Ursula, Jiffy Mixer Company, Incorporated 17981-G Sky Park Circle Irvine, CA 92714 714-557-1272 (15)

Griffin, Bill, L.D.A. Sales 2221 Freemont Memphis, TN 38114 901-743-3111 (15)

Griffin, J., Foundry Players 1500 16th Street NW Washington, DC 20036 (16)

Griffin, Lawrence, Newark Federation of Musicians, Local 122 459 Courtney Drive Newark, OH 43055 614-366-1757 (18)

Griffith, Danny, Imperial Players Imperial Hotel Cripple Creek, CO 80813 303-689-2292 (16)

Griffith, J. Sharon, Mountain View College Arena Theatre 4849 West Illinois Avenue Dallas, TX 75211 214-746-4132 (8)

Griffith, Patsy, Choctaw County Arts Council 1106 Cliff Road Butler, AL 36904 205-459-3666 (5)

Griffith, Prescott F., Carousel Dinner Theatre Post Office Box 427 Ravenna, OH 44266 216-296-3866 (16)

Griffiths, Mrs. Clark, Friends of Lebanon Opera House 74 Prospect Street Lebanon, NH 03766 603-448-2966 (5)

Griffth, E.E., Hobart and William Smith Colleges Department of Theatre Geneva, NY 14456 315-789-5500 (4)

Grigg, Beth, Klamath Arts Association Post Office Box 995 Klamath, OR 97601 503-884-6157 (5)

Griggsmiller, James, Denver Musicians' Association, Local 20-623 1535 Logan Street Denver, CO 80203 303-861-1112 (18)

Grignoli, Hugo A., Musicians' Protective Association 105 Vance Drive Bristol, CT 06010 203-582-5245 (18)

Grimes, D., Chris-Mar Players 6914 Freeport Street Hyattsville, MD 20784 (16)

Grimm, Ben, 5 Corners Library Auditorium Network and Summit Avenues Jersey City, NJ 07306 (8)

Grimsley, Lynn, Allied Arts Fund of Greater Chattanooga 16 Pattern Parkway Chattanooga, TN 37402 615-266-7318 (5)

Grindinger, G., Audiotronics 7428 Bellaire North Hollywood, CA 91605 213-765-2645 (15)

Grinnell, Robert, Herkimer County Arts Council Post Office Box 25 Herkimer, NY 133350 315-866-0300 (5)

Grissom, Sandy, Kaleidoscope Theatre Post Office Box 4272 Panama City, FL 32401 904-763-6878 (16)

Grizzard, Leon, Austin Federation of Musicians 302 West 15th, Suite 204 Austin, TX 78701 512-476-6798 (18)

Groll, Bruce, Herrin Federation of Musicians 390 Mulberry Carterville, IL 62918 618-985-4704 (18)

Grose, Stanley, Windsor Federation of Musicians Suite 202, 744 Ouellette Avenue Windsor, Ontario, Canada N9A 1C3 519-258-2288 (18)

Grose, Virginia M., South Carolina National Bank 101 Greystone Boulevard Columbia, SC 29226 803-765-3756 (10)

Gross, Charles E., Musical Society 512 West Murphy Avenue Connellsville, PA 15425 412-628-1530 (18)

Gross, Ken, Birmingham-Bloomfield Art Association 1516 South Cranbrook Road Birmingham, MI 48009 313-644-0866 (5)

Gross, Roger, University and College Theatre Association 1010 Wisconsin Avenue, NW Washington, DC 20007 (5)

Grossberg, Richard, Brooklyn Center for the Performing Arts Brooklyn College Campus Road at Hillel Place Brooklyn, NY 11210 212-780-5296, Operations and Rentals; 212-780-5291, Programming (8)

Grossman, Howard, NE Pennsylvania Arts Alliance Post Office Box 777 Avoca, PA 18641 717-655-5581 (5)

Grosz, Mike, Stage Equipment and Lighting, Incorporated Post Office Box 61000F Miami, FL 33161 305-891-2010 (15)

Group, Actors, The Playhouse 359 West 48th Street New York, NY 10036 212-489-9237 (16)

Grueninger, Edward, Musicians' Protective Union Grant Plaza Brookhaven, PA 19015 215-874-7158 (18)

Guarino, Nancy, Sidewalks of New York Productions 44 Beaver Street, 2nd Floor New York, NY 10004 212-668-9074 (16)

Guarnieri, Gerald Edward, Shakespeare '70 Incorporated 121 Grand Street Trenton, NJ 08611 609-392-1704 (16)

Guay, Ginnette, Theatre de la Bordee 109 ½ St-Jean Quebec City, Quebec, Canada 418-529-5237 (16)

Guenther, Carl, SGL Waber Electric 300 Harvard Avenue Westville, NJ 609-456-5400 (15)

Guffey, Sara, Rangeley Friends of the Performing Arts Review Committee Oquossoc, ME 04964 207-864-3617 (5)

Guile, Hermon, Musicians' Protective Union 1439 Vandalia Road Hillsboro, IL 62049 217-532-3862 (18)

Guinan, Ed, Kansas Wesleyan University Department of Theatre South Santa Fe Salina, KS 67401 913-827-5541, Extension 257 (4)

Gulas, Joseph D., Carroll Sound, Incorporated 895 Broadway New York, NY 10036 212-868-4120 (15)

Gulbranson, Dr. Bruce, William Paterson College Department of Theatre 300 Pompton Road Wayne, NJ 07470 201-595-2335; 201-595-2314 (4)

Gulick, Marion, Champaign Federation of Musicians, Local 196 804 West Vine Street Champaign, IL 61820 217-356-4151 (18)

Gunderson, Hal, Saint Francis College Department of Theatre Fort Wayne, IN 46808 219-432-3551 (4)

Gunderson, Joanna, Red Dust Incorporated Box 630, Gracie Station New York, NY 10028 212-348-4388 (14)

Gunderson, Warren, Red Dust Incorporated Box 630, Gracie Station New York, NY 10028 212-348-4388 (14)

Gunn, Roland S., Musicians' Protective Association, Local 110 10281 Golden Arrow Drive Hutchinson, KS 67501 316-663-2653 (18)

Guptill, S. Carleton, Little Theatre Guild Post Office Box 604 Bartlesville, OK 74005 918-336-5668; 918-661-4995 (16)

Gurtman, Bernard, Gurtman and Murtha Associates, Incorporated 162 West 56th Street New York, NY 10019 212-245-4771; 212-245-4772 (12)

Gustavson, Robert E., Corporate Council for the Arts 421 Skinner Building Seattle, WA 98101 206-682-3663 (5)

Guthrie, Ned H., Charleston Musicians' Union, Local 136 1562 Kanawha Boulevard, East Charleston, WV 25311 304-346-9693; 304-343-7778 (18)

Gutman, Madeleine, Town of Greenburgh Arts and Cultural Committee Post Office Box 205 Elmsford, NY 10523 914-478-3559; 914-682-5200 (5)

H

Haarbauer, Dr D. Ward, Bell Auditorium University of Alabama 13th Street and Seventh Avenue Birmingham, AL 35294 205-934-3236 (8)

Haarbauer, Dr. Ward, University of Alabama Department of Theatre University Station Birmingham, AL 35294 205-934-3236 (4)

Haas, Thomas B., Weathervane Theatre Whitfield, NH 03598 603-837-9010 (16)

Hacha, Jan, Starry Night Puppet Theatre 233 Main Street Vestal, NY 13850 (16)

Haddaway, Kenneth, Southeastern Bible College Department of Theatre Lakeland, FL 33801 (4)

Hadley, Dr. Charles O., Queens College Department of Theatre 1900 Selwyn Avenue Charlotte, NC 28274 704-332-7121 (4)

Hager, Nancy, Academy Theatre 3317 Piedmont Road Northeast Atlanta, GA 30305 404-261-8550 (16)

Hager, R.M., Barn Dinner Theatre Post Office Box 257 Cedar Crest, NM 87008 (16)

Hagerman, Christine, Sundance Lighting Corporation 9801 Variel Avenue Chatsworth, CA 91311 213-882-4321 (15)

Hahn, Jean, Great American People Show Summer: Box 401; Off Season: Box 2178 Summer: Petersburg; Off Season: Champaign, IL Summer: 61675; Off Season: 61820 217-632-7755; 217-632-7754 (16)

Hailey, Robert C., Lynchburg College Department of Dramatic Arts Lynchburg, VA 24501 804-845-9071 (4)

Hale, Herbert E., Louisville Federation of Musicians, Local 11-637 1436 Bardstown Road Louisville, KY 40204 502-451-7509 (18)

Haley, Douglas R., Pocket Mime Theatre Post Office Box 269 Boston, MA 02117 617-266-2770 (16)

Haley, Kathryn, Allied Arts of Tacoma 600 Commerce Street Tacoma, WA 98402 (5)

Hall, Carol J., Hays Art Center 112 East 11th Hays, KS 67601 913-625-7522 (8)

Hall, Dr. Charles, Central Arizona College Signal Peak Coolidge, AZ 85228 602-723-4141 (4)

Hall, Edward, District Federation of Musicians, Local 180 49 Bank Street Ottawa, Ontario, Canada K2P 1Z2 613-233-5301 (18)

Hall, Jaqueline A., Lincoln Community Arts Council Room 508, Center Building Lincoln, NB 68508 402-477-5930 (5)

Hall, Leonard, Lancaster Arts Council White Moutain Regional High School Lancaster, NH 03584 603-788-2076 (5)

Hall, Pugsley, South Dakota State University Department of Theatre Brookings, SD 57006 605-688-6131 (4)

Hall, Robert L., Musicians' Mutual Protective Association, Local 172 1579 Holiday Street East Liverpool, OH 43920 216-385-8949 (18)

Hall, Robert N., Association for Communication Administration 5105 Backlick Road, Suite E Annandale, VA 22003 703-053- (5)

Halliburton, Jeanne, Jeanne Halliburton Agency 5205 Hollywood Boulevard Los Angeles, CA 90027 213-466-6183 (2)

Hallowell, James C., Musicians' Mutual Protective Association 857 Main Street Ventura, CA 93001 805-643-9953 (18)

Halverson, Dr. Bruce, Denison University Department of Theatre Granville, OH 43023 614-587-0810 (4)

Halvorson, Werner, Owatonna Area Musicians' Association 1419 Hemlock Owatonna, MN 55060 507-451-8593 (18)

Hamaty, Emile, Theatre 40 241 Moreno Drive Beverly Hills, CA 90210 213-277-4221 (16)

Hambleton, T. Edward, Phoenix Theatre 1540 Broadway New York, NY 10036 212-730-0787 (13)

Hamilburg, Mitchell, Mitchell Hamilburg Agency 292 South La Cienega Boulevard Beverly Hills, CA 90069 213-652-2409 (2)

Hamilton, Betty, Fine Arts Association of SE Kentucky 1210 Pine Street Corbin, KY 40701 606-528-4824 (5)

Hamilton, Stephen, Virginia Fine Arts Center Little Theatre Virginia Intermont College Bristol, VA 24201 703-669-6101 (8)

Hamlin, Clifford E., Middletown Musicians' Protective Association Post Office Box 955 Middletown, CT 06457 203-347-7805 (18)

Hamlin, George, Harvard Summer Repertory Theatre Loeb Drama Center 64 Brattle Street Cambridge, MA 02138 617-495-2668 (16)

Hammack, Dr. Henry, Texas Christian University Theatre Landreth Hall School of Fine Arts Fort Worth, TX 76129 817-926-2461 (8)

Hammet, Rick, Embassy Theatre 121 West Jefferson Fort Wayne, IN 46802 219-424-5665 (8)

Hammond, Charles A., Musicians' Protective Association 613 North Wilbur Avenue Sayre, PA 18840 717-888-0569 (18)

Hammond, Doug, Corinth Theatre Arts, Inc. Post Office Box 127 Corinth, MS 38834 (16)

Han, William I., Barrington College Department of Theatre Middle Highway Barrington, RI 02806 401-246-1200 Extension 146 (4)

Hancock, Jim, Wyborny Sales Company, Incorporated 9450 Skillman Suite 113 Dallas, TX 75243 214-348-9657 (15)

Hand, Dave, Stage Engineering and Supply 325 Karen Lane Colorado Springs, CO 80901 303-635-2935 (15)

Handley, John, Prince Georges Community College Department of Theatre 301 Largo Road Largo, MD 20870 301-336-6000 (4)

Handman, Wynn, American Place Theatre 111 West 46th Street New York, NY 10036 212-246-3730 (13)

Handman, Wynn, American Place Theatre 111 West 46th Street New York, NY 10036 212-246-0393 (16)

Hankins, Robert J., Wausau Area Performing Arts Foundation Post Office Box 783 Wausau, WI 54401 715-842-0988 (10)

Hanna, Gene, Strand Century, Incorporated 4618 Conwell Drive Annandale, VA 22003 703-941-9025 (15)

Hannan, Robert, Willapa Harbor Arts Commission 544 BAllentine Raymond, WA 98577 206-942-2944 (5)

Hannum, Charles R., Limestone College Department of Theatre College Drive Gaffney, SC 29340 803-489-7151 (4)

Hannum, Charles R., Bluefield College Department of Theatre Bluefield, WV 24605 703-327-7137 (4)

Hanoud, Paul, Hanoud Associates 711 County Street Fall River, MA 02723 617-675-2489 (15)

Hansen, Mrs. Edward A., Delia Austrian Medal Drama League of New York New York, NY 1002 212-838-5859; 212-MU8-3233 (3)

Hansen, Harold C., Sioux City Municipal Auditorium 401 Gordon Drive Sioux City, IA 51101 712-279-6157 (8)

Hansen, Richard, B and B Electrical Products Incorporated 2605 East and 3300 South Salt Lake City, UT 84109 801-486-3943 (15)

Hansen, Robert C., The Huron Playhouse School of Speech Communication Bowling Green, OH 43403 419-372-2350 (16)

Hansen, Ruth, Greenville Creative Arts Council 409 South Lauray Greenville, MI 48838 616-754-4264 (5)

Hanson, Arthur, Ernest L. Silver Hall Plymouth State College Plymouth, NH 03264 603-536-1550 (8)

Hanson, Marliss, Minot Musician's Association 1001 38th Street Northeast Minot, ND 58701 701-838-0845 (18)

Hanson, Mr. Richard, Moorhead State University Department of Theatre Moorhead, NM 56560 218-236-2762; 218-236-2126 (4)

Hanson, Tillie, Center Youth Theatre 3003 West Touhy Chicago, IL 60645 312-761-9100 (16)

Hanson, Wendy, Wendy Hanson 1001 Park Avenue New York, NY 10028 212-734-3406 (12)

Happe, Pete, Theatrix, Incorporated 5138 East 39th Avenue Denver, CO 80207 303-388-9345 (15)

Harakal, Emil E., Musicians' Protective Union Road 1 Freeland, PA 18224 717-636-0600 (18)

Haraway, David A., Gene Russell Theatre Gonzaga University Spokane, WA 99202 509-328-4200 (8)

Harbin, Shirley, Southeast Michigan Arts Forum 2735 West Warren Detroit, MI 48208 313-898-6340 (5)

Harbour, Charles C., University of Montevallo Department of Theatre Montevallo, AL 35115 205-665-2521, ext 413 (4)

Harder, Caren, The Production Company 249 West 18th Street New York, NY 10011 212-691-7359 (16)

Hardin, Dan, Musicians' Protective Union, Local 268 1802 Pekin Street Lincoln, IL 62656 217-732-9482 (18)

Hardin, Mary, Gadsden Civic Theater 310 North 27th Street Gadsden, AL 35904 205-547-7960 (16)

Hardin, W.E., Greenville City Arts Commission Post Office Box 507 Greenville, AL 36037 205-382-3111 (5)

Harding, Edwin W., Musicians' Protective Association 246 Miller Avenue DeKalb, IL 60115 815-758-3952 (18)

Hardingham, Tony, Solar Stage Lunchtime Theatre 149 Yonge Street Toronto, Ontario, Canada M5C 1W4 416-368-5135 (16)

Hardy, James, Simon's Rock Early College Department of Theatre Alford Road Great Barrington, MA 02130 413-528-0771 (4)

Hargus, Warran, Community Council on the Arts 1212 North Olive Street Nevada, MO 64772 417-667-3994 (5)

Harlen, Harry, Musicians' Protective Union 822 Breckenridge Helena, MT 59601 406-442-5827 (18)

Harley, Graham D., Phoenix Theatre 390 Dupont Street Toronto, Ontario, Canada M5R 1V9 416-922-7835 (16)

Harman, William, Lawrence Academy Theatre Powderhouse Road Groton, MA 01450 617-448-3344 (8)

Harmon, Lewis, Lewis Harmon 205 West 57th Street New York, NY 10019 212-247-0354 (12)

Harnick, Sarah-Ann, Rider College Cultural Programs Post Office Box 6400 Lawrenceville, NJ 08648 608-896-0800 (8)

Harper, Dorothy, Burien Arts Association 421 Southwest 146th Seattle, WA 98166 206-244-7808 (5)

Harper, Jack D., Musicians' Protective Union 1100 First Avenue, SW Great Falls, MT 59401 406-452-3962 (18)

Harral, Hank, Roswell Federation of Musicians 1103 South Michigan Avenue Roswell, NM 88201 505-622-7125 (18)

Harris, Albert J., University of Louisville Department of Theatre Louisville, KY 40208 502-588-6814 (4)

Harris, Tasso, Denver Musicians' Association, Local 20-623 1535 Logan Street Denver, CO 80203 303-861-1112 (18)

Harris, Terri, Southeast Community College-Fairbury Campus Department of Theatre 924 K Street Fairbury, NB 68352 402-729-6148 (4)

Harrison, Dolly, Federated Arts of Manchester 148 Concord Street Manchester, NH 03104 603-668-6186 (5)

Harrison, Dolly, Merrimack Valley Arts Council 148 Concord Street Manchester, NH 03104 603-668-6186 (5)

Hart, Darwin D., Lansing Federation of Musicians 2703 North Turner Street Lansing, MI 48906 517-484-4461 (18)

Hart, Leonard, Greensboro College Department of Theatre 815 West Market Street Greensboro, NC 27420 919-272-7102 (4)

Hartburg, Warren, Niagara Falls Little Theatre, Inc. 419 Tryon Drive Lewiston, NY 14092 716-282-9119 (16)

Hartigan, W.C., Alhambra Dinner Theatre 12000 Beach Boulevard Jacksonville, Fl 32216 904-641-1212 (16)

Hartley, Patricia B., Stanley County Arts Council Post Office Box 909 Albermarie, NC 28001 704-982-8116 (5)

Hartman, Albert A., Lawrence S. Epstein Associates 1634 59th Street Brooklyn, NY 11204 212-232-8468; 212-837-2881, Data Line (1)

Hartman, June, Theatre House Incorporated 400 West Third Street Covington, KY 41012 606-431-2414 (15)

Hartman, Roger, Theatre House Incorporated 400 West Third Street Covington, KY 41012 606-431-2414 (15)

Harvard, Bernard, Alliance Theatre Company/Atlanta Children's Theatre 12801 Peachtree Street NE Atlanta, GA 30309 404-898-1132 (16)

Harvey, Jim, Theatre Suburbia 1410 West 43rd Street Houston, TX 77018 713-682-3525 (16)

Harvey, John, Theatrebooks Limited 659 Yonge Street, 2nd Floor Toronto, Ontario, Canada M4Y 1Z9 416-922-7175 (14)

Harwood, Jon H., Musicians' Protective Union, Local 225 2038 Avon Hayden Lake, ID 83835 208-773-7971 (18)

Hasen, Robert, College of Saint Scholastica Department of Theatre Duluth, MN 55811 218-728-3631 (4)

Hasenberg, Estelle, Middlesex County Arts Council 37 Oakwood Avenue Edison, NJ 08817 201-549-4684 (5)

Haslam, Herb, Texas Assembly of Arts Councils c/o Charles Lansden, President Houston, TX 77002 713-651-1313 (5)

Haslam, Richard P., Snow College Department of Theatre 140 East College Avenue Ephraim, UT 84627 (4)

Haslun, Robert A., Highfield Theatre Drawer F Falmouth, MA 02541 617-548-0668 (8)

Hatfield, Carl, Barbour County Arts and Humanities Council 100 Keyes Avenue Philippi, WV 26416 304-457-1700 (5)

Hatfield, D., MacAlester College Department of Theatre Saint Paul, MN 55101 612-647-6221 (4)

Hatfield, M.P., Macon Little Theatre Post Office Box 7121 Macon, GA 31204 (16)

Hatz, Mrs. Russell C., Lebanon Valley Council on the Arts Post Office Box 786 Lebanon, PA 17042 (5)

Haugh, Hubert H., State College Area Musicians' Association 1151 William Street State College, PA 16801 814-237-2689 (18)

Haun, Ruben, Lincoln Musicians' Association 1730 Crestline Drive Lincoln, NE 68506 402-474-3868 (18)

Hauser, Lyle, Musicians' Protective Union 803 North 14th Pekin, IL 61554 309-347-2350 (18)

Hawes, Carol Ann, San Jose State University Department of Theatre Arts San Jose, CA 95192 408-277-2763; 408-277-2764 (4)

Hawkins, Clyde, Tivoli Theatre Broad Street Chattanooga, TN 37402 615-267-1676 (8)

Hawkins, Clyde M., Chattanooga Memorial Auditorium 399 McCallie Avenue Chattanooga, TN 37402 615-266-2642 (8)

Hawkins, Jo Ann, On Stage Players 419 Amvets Drive De Soto, MO 63020 (16)

Hawkins, Kenneth J., Cumberland College Auditorium South Greenwood Street Lebanon, TN 37087 615-444-2562 (8)

Hawkins, Millard M., Musicians' Association of Monterey Country 591 Lighthouse Avenue Monterey, CA 93940 408-375-6166 (18)

Hawkins, Mr. Robert, Broadway Theatre League of Pueblo, Incorporated Post Office Box 3145 Pueblo, CO 81005 303-545-4721; 303-542-1211 (16)

Hawley, C. Robert, University of Central Arkansas Conway, AR 72032 501-329-2931; 501-450-3165 (4)

Hawley, L. Alison, National Association of Dramatics White Horse Beach Plymouth, MA 02381 617-224-3967 (16)

Hawthorn, Pamela, Vancouver Professional Theatre Alliance c/o New Play Centre Vancouver, British Columbia, Canada V6H 3R6 (5)

Hay, Peter, Talonbooks 201-1019 East Cordova Vancouver, British Columbia, Canada M5J 1R2 604-255-5915 (14)

Hayde, Barbara A., Montgomery County Memorial Hall 125 East First Street Dayton, OH 45422 513-223-7581 (8)

Hayes, D., Cochran Players 2773 East Larned-101 Detroit, MI 48207 (16)

Hayes, Don, City-County Arts Council Post Office Box 301 Paducah, KY 42001 502-444-7713 (5)

Hayes, Stephen E., Stage/West 1511 Memorial Avenue West Springfield, MA 01089 413-781-4470 (16)

Haynie, Phil, Parkersburg Community College Department of Theatre Parkersburg, WV 26101 304-424-8266 (4)

Hays, David, National Theatre of the Deaf Little Theatre 305 Great Neck Road Waterford, CT 06385 203-442-0066; 203-443-7406 (16)

Hays, Rex, Musicians' Association, Local 255 606 East 17th Street Yankton, SD 57078 605-665-2488 (18)

Hays, Stephen E., Horace A. Moses Building-Stage/West Eastern State Grounds West Springfield, MA 01089 413-736-7092 (8)

Healy, Jerry, Springfield Civic Center 1277 Main Street Springfield, MA 01103 413-781-7080 (8)

Heard, Ann, Arts Bulletin 141 Laurier Avenue West, Suite 707 Ottawa, Ontario, Canada K1P 5J3 613-238-3561 (14)

Heard, Doreen, Lexington Children's Theatre Division of the Living Arts and Science Center Lexington, KY 40512 606-252-1381 (16)

Heaselden, Patricia, New American Theatre 117 South Wyman Street Rockford, IL 61108 815-963-9454 (16)

Heath, Richard G., Queensborough Community College Department of Theatre 56th Avenue and Springfield Boulevard Bayside, NY 11364 212-631-6284 (4)

Heatley, Steven, Workshop West Playwrights' Theatre #5, 11020 65 Avenue Edmonton, Alberta, Canada T6H 1V9 403-436-7378 (16)

Hebble, Vernon, Musicians' Protective Union Rural Route 5 Decatur, IN 46733 219-724-7670 (18)

Hebert, Lorraine, Jeu, Cahiers de Theatre Post Office Box 1600, Station E Montreal, Quebec, Canada H2T 3B1 514-523-1757 (14)

Heckman, Keith W., Lincoln Musicians' Association 1730 Crestline Drive Lincoln, NE 68506 402-474-3868 (18)

Hedlund, Walter L., Olean-Salmanca Musicians' Union, Local 115-614 122 North 21st Street Olean, NY 14760 716-372-3583 (18)

Hedrick, Elizabeth, Brenau College Washington Street Gainesville, GA 30501 404-532-4341 (4)

Heefner, David Kerry, Hudson Guild Theatre 441 West 26th Street New York, NY 10001 212-760-9810; 212-760-9847 (16)

Heene, Julian, Musicians' Protective Association, Local 100 281 Rockwell Street Kewanee, IL 61443 309-853-8668 (18)

Heflin, Ann, Daytona Playhouse 100 Jessamine Boulevard Daytona Beach, FL 32018 904-255-2431; 904-255-2432 (16)

Heflin, Julia, Mount Vernon College Department of Theatre 2100 Foxhill Road Washington, DC 20007 202-331-34444 (4)

Hegland, P., Appleton Theatre Board Route 3, Post Office Box 63 Appleton, MN 56208 (16)

Hegle, Dick, Wenger Corporation 555 Park Drive Owatonna, MN 55060 800-533-0393 (15)

Heide, Christopher, Dramatists' Co-Op of Nova Scotia Box 3608, South Post Office Halifax, Nova Scotia, Canada B3J 3K6 902-423-8116 (5)

Heino, Thomas K., Stephen F. Austin State University Department of Theatre 6204 SFA Nacogdoches, TX 75961 713-569-4004 (4)

Heins, Kendall, Musicians' Protective Union 701 9th Avenue Northwest Rochester, MN 55901 507-288-1519 (18)

Heise, Vern, Braham Community Theatre RR 2, Box 46 Stanchfield, MN 55080 (16)

Heitger, Craig, Musicians' Protective Union 120 West LaSalle Avenue South Bend, IN 46601 219-233-8111 (18)

Held, Steve, Musicians' Protective Union 2116 Friendship Street Iowa City, IA 52240 319-337-4677 (18)

Heller, Donald R., Automatic Devices Company 212 South 12th Street Allentown, PA 18103 215-797-6000 (15)

Hellman, Ronald B., Queens Community Theatre, Inc. Post Office Box 1 Queens, NY 11365 212-939-9030 (16)

Hellmuth, Lynn A., City Cultural Affairs Committee 202 Monona Avenue Madison, WI 53703 608-266-4611; 608-255-8177 (5)

Hemmer, Paul E., Dubuque Musicians' Association 1030 Boyer Dubuque, IA 52001 319-588-3240 (18)

Henderson, Bill, Musicians' Protective Union 1020 Letnes Drive Grand Forks, ND 58201 701-775-9843 (18)

Henderson, James, McLennan Community College Department of Theatre 1400 College Drive Waco, TX 76708 817-756-6551 (4)

Henderson, Jerry, The Gentlemen from the Cane Post Office Box 14 Lawrenceburg, TN 38464 (16)

Henderson, Rena, Jones County Arts Council Post Office Box 69 Trenton, NC 28585 919-448-3131 (5)

Hendler, Peter, Fine Arts Auditorium 2000 West Fifth Street Marchfield, WI 54449 715-387-1147 (8)

Hendry, Judith, Toronto Free Theatre 26 Berkeley Street Toronto, Ontario, Canada M5A 2W3 416-368-7601, Administration; 416-368-2856, Box Office (16)

Henegan, Kevin J., Children's Theatre Post Office Box 1391 Roseburg, OR 97470 (16)

Henehan, Eileen, Huntington Park Civic Theatre 3401 East Florence Avenue Huntington Park, CA 90255 213-582-6162 (16)

Henes, John B., Menominee Arts Council 1502 First Street Menominee, MI 49858 906-863-2524 (5)

Henkin, Frank, G. Fishman's Sons, Incorporated 1101 South Desplaines Street Chicago, IL 60607 312-922-7250; 312-922-725½ /3 (15)

Hennessy, Dennis, Waldorf Astoria Playhouse Tiffany's Attic Dinner Playhouse 5028 Main Street Kansas City, MO 64112 816-523-1706; 816-361-2661 (16)

Henning, Cassandra, Cassandra Henning Division of L and M Stagecraft 1446 Mayson Street Atlanta, GA 30324 404-875-2683; 404-872-6686 (15)

Henning, Roy, Rauland-Borg Corporation 244 Murdock Waterloo, Ontario, Canada N2J 2M7 519-885-1043 (15)

Henry, Jeff, Theatre Fountainhead 47 Wembley Road Toronto, Ontario, Canada M6C 2G1 416-738-9300 (16)

Henry, Joyce, Ursinus College Department of Theatre Collegeville, PA 19426 215-489-4111 (4)

Henry, Patrick, Free Street Theater 59 West Hubbard Chicago, IL 60610 312-822-0460 (16)

Hensen, Carol, Theatre Memphis 630 Perkins Extended Memphis, TN 38119 901-682-8323; 901-682-0264 (16)

Hensley, John H., Musicians' Protective Union, Local 250 2430 Appleton Parsons, KS 67357 (18)

Henson, Eben, Pioneer Playhouse of Kentucky Danville, KY 40422 606-236-2747 (8)

Henzler, Paul, Luther College Field House Speech and Theater Department Decorah, IA 52101 319-387-1245 (8)

Hepworth, Loel T., Federated Musicians, Local 104 3714 East 3800 South Salt Lake City, UT 84109 801-581-8707 (18)

Herbert, D., Publick Playhouse 5445 Landover Road Hyattsville, MD 20784 (16)

Herbert, D., Prince George Playhouse 6600 Kenilworth Avenue Riverdale, MD 20840 (16)

Herbertson, Don, Theatre Ontario 8 York Street, 7th Floor Toronto, Ontario, Canada N5J 1R2 416-366-2938 (5)

Herbiet, Jean, L'Hexagone C.P. 1534, Succursale B Ottawa, Ontario, Canada K1P 5W1 613-996-5051 (16)

Herd, Kermit, Northwest Community College Department of Theatre Powell, WY 82435 (4)

Herdeck, Donald E., Three Continents Press 1346 Connecticut Avenue NW, Suite 1131 Washington, DC 20036 202-457-0288 (14)

Herder, Gary, Indiana Electrical Sales 5160 East 65th Streeet Indianapolis, IN 46220 317-849-3880 (15)

Herklotz, Marlane, Mime-Light Theatre 11018 - 83 Avenue Edmonton, Alberta, Canada T6G 0T7 403-439-4068 (16)

Herman, Lee, Philadelphia Musical Society, Local 77 120 North 18th Street Philadelphia, PA 19103 215-567-1071 (18)

Herman, Max, Musicians' Union, Local 47 817 North Vine Street Hollywood, CA 90038 213-462-2161 (18)

Heron, William J., Hale County Council for the Arts Post Office Box 490 Greensboro, AL 36774 205-624-8793 (5)

Herrera, Frank, Trenton Musical Association, Local 62 28 Assumpink Blvd. Trenton, NJ 08619 609-586-0022 (18)

Herrington, Jeanette, Thumb Council for the Arts Post Office Box 63 Bad Axe, MI 48913 517-269-7604 (5)

Herron, Clifford D., Chipola Junior College Department of Theatre Marianna, FL 32446 904-526-2761 (4)

Hershberger, Rick, D. Rick Hershberger 3403 Overton Drive Greensboro, NC 27408 919-288-2742 (15)

Herson, Edward, Worcester Children's Theatre 1782 Wachasett Street Jefferson, MA 01522 617-829-3411 (16)

Hertzberg, Steven, Superscope Canada, Ltd. 3710 Nashua Drive Mississauga, Ontario, Canada L4V 1M5 416-676-1720 (15)

Herut, Gale, Strike at the Wind Theatre Post Office Box 1059 Pembroke, NC 28372 919-521-2489 (16)

Herz, Shirley, Shirley Herz 165 West 48th Street New York, NY 10036 212-221-8466 (12)

Hess, Emil, Parisian Stores, Alabama 1101 North 26th Street Birmington, AL 35234 205-251-1300 (10)

Hess, Robert L., Brooklyn College Arts Management Circle Brooklyn College Department of Theatre Brooklyn, NY 11210 (14)

Hesselbaum, Ralph B., Musicians' Protective Union, Local 181 821 Talma Street Aurora, IL 60505 312-851-1386; 312-897-6894 (18)

Hessil, Mr. Fay, Musicians' Protective Association Route 2 Lena, WI 54139 414-834-5153 (18)

Hester, Jesse, Dorchester Arts Center 120 High Street Cambridge, MD 21613 301-228-8870 (5)

Hetzel, R.J., R.J. Hetzel 2893 Aldgate Drive Bloomfield Hills, MI 48013 313-333-7672 (15)

Heuer, J. Vincent, Heuer Publishing Company Postal Drawer 248 Cedar Rapids, IA 52406 (14)

Hevey, Will, Show Lighting Corporation 26 South George Street Meriden, CT 06450 203-238-2000 (15)

Hewitt, Frakie, Ford's Theatre Society 511 10th Street Washington, DC 20004 202-638-2941 (16)

Hickey, T. Earl, Prince Edward Island, Cultural Affairs Post Office Box 2000 Charlottetown, P.E.I., Canada C1A 7N8 902-894-4738 (5)

Hickin, Janette, Shaw Festival Post Office Box 774 Niagara on the Lake, Ontario, Canada L0S 1J0 416-468-2153; 416-468-3201 (9)

Hickman, L., Bel Pre Players 2605 Baywood Court Silver Spring, MD 20906 (16)

Hider, Ruth, Ruth Hider 310 West 56th Street New York, NY 10019 212-757-6734 (12)

Higbee, Dick, Musicians' Protective Union, Local 178 702 North Henderson Street Galesburg, IL 61401 309-342-3007 (18)

Higgens, Reg, Equity Showcase Theatre 417 Queen's West, Suite 500 Toronto, Ontario, Canada 416-364-7127, ext. 235; 416-364-5739 (16)

Higginbotham, Rodney, Bethel College Department of Theatre Cherry Street McKenzie, TN 38201 901-352-5896 (4)

Higgins, James, Musicians' Association, Local 8 2200 North 45th Street Milwaukee, WI 53208 414-444-5234 (18)

Higgins, J.C., Memorex Corporation Post Office Box 1000 Santa Clara, CA 95052 408-987-1072 (15)

Higgins, John J., Mayor's Committee on the Arts Redevelopment Authority Sharon, PA 16146 (5)

Higgins, Roy, Harbourfront Studio Theatre 235 Queen's Quay West Toronto, Ontario, Canada M5J 2G8 416-364-7127; 416-869-8412 (8)

Highlander, James L., Central Missouri State University Department of Theatre Warrensburg, MO 64093 816-429-4020; 816-429-4330 (4)

Hightower, Frank, Tullahoma Fine Arts Center 401 South Jackson Street Tullahoma, TN 37388 615-455-1234; 615-455-0097 (5)

Higuera, Jean, BankAmerica Foundation Post Office Box 37000 San Francisco, CA 94137 415-622-8674 (10)

Hill, Henry B., Savannah Federation of Musicians 258 A Mulberry Way Westwood Heights, Rincon, GA 31326 912-826-5905 (18)

Hill, James, Wahington Musical Society, Local 277 865 William Street Washington, PA 15301 412-225-9790 (18)

Hill, Mars, Black Experience Ensemble 5 Homestead Avenue Albany, NY 12203 518-452-3306 (16)

Hill, McCoy, James G. Hanes Community Center Theatre 610 Coliseum Drive Winston-Salem, NC 27106 919-722-2585 (8)

Hill, Morry, Musical Union, Local 240 119 North Church Street Rockford, IL 61101 815-965-2132 (18)

Hill, Philip G., Furman University Department of Drama Greenville, SC 29613 803-294-2051; 803-294-2125 (4)

Hill, Richard, Rainy River Community College Department of Theatre International Falls, MN 55649 (4)

Hill, Ronald W., Stagecraft Industries, Incorporated 13022 North West Kearney Street Portland, OR 97209 503-226-7351 (15)

Hill, R.S., Southwestern at Memphis Department of Theatre 2000 North Parkway Memphis, TN 38112 (4)

Hillenbrand, Rudy, Musicians' Association, Local 35 2733 Lake Drive Evansville, IN 47711 812-476-4754 (18)

Hilzen, Hy, Packaged Lighting Systems, Incorporated Post Office Box 285 Walden, NY 12586 914-778-3515 (15)

Hinds, Jackson C., The Houston Festival 1950 West Gray #6 Houston, TX 77019 713-521-9329; 713-521-9559 (9)

Hines, Steve, Illinois Bell Telephone Company 225 West Randolph Street Chicago, IL 60606 312-427-4691 (10)

Hjelmeland, Tim, Bertha Community Theatre Bertha, MN 56437 (16)

Hobday, John, Canadian Conference of the Arts 141 Laurier Avenue West, Suite 707 Ottawa, Ontario, Canada K1P 5J3 613-356- (5)

Hock, Dennis, The Wilson Paint Company 1616 Harrison Avenue Cincinnati, OH 45214 513-251-5300 (15)

Hodges, Earl, Olean Community Arts Council Post Office Box 141 Olean, NY 14760 716-373-2522 (5)

Hodges, Owen, Northwest College Learning Center Northwest College Kirkland, WA 98033 206-822-8266 (8)

Hodgin, Jo, Library Theatre, Incorporated 418 Seventh Street, NW Washington, DC 20004 (16)

Hoelke, Byrll E., Village Playhouse 4085 North 111th Street Wauwatosa, WI 53222 (16)

Hoff, Alvin, Buffalo Creek Players Rural Route 2 Glencoe, MN 55336 (16)

Hoffman, G., Huron Area Arts Council 1742 McClellan Drive, SW Huron, SD 57350 605-352-8651 (5)

Hoffman, Mary K., Arts Council of Franklin County Post Office Box 364 Greenfield, MA 01301 413-774-3131 (5)

Hoffman, Richard H., Reedley College Department of Theatre Reedley, CA 93654 (4)

Hoffstetter, D., Bridgegate Dinner Theatre 241 ½ Walnut Street Morgantown, WV 26505 (16)

Hofland, Neal, Chokio Community Theatre Chokio, MN 55101 (16)

Hogan, Thomas R., Lemoyne College Department of Theatre LeMoyne Heights Syracuse, NY 13214 315-446-2882 (4)

Hogstrom, Harold A., Trenton State College Department of Theatre Pennington Road Trenton, NJ 08625 609-771-1855 (4)

Holbert, N. Terry, Greater Newburgh Arts Council 427 Grand Street Newburgh, NY 12550 914-562-9028 (5)

Holden, Virginia, Virginia Holden 4 East 88th Street New York, NY 10028 212-534-5382 (12)

Holder, Robert, University of North Alabama Florence, AL 35630 205-766-4100, Ext.247; 205-766-4100, Ext.358 (4)

Holl, Edward, Dover Little Theatre Box 82 Elliot Street Dover, NJ 07801 201-366-9890 (16)

Holland, Charlene, Chemung Valley Arts Council 171 Cedar Street Corning, NY 14830 607-967-5871 (5)

Holland, Charles A., Western Texas College Department of Theatre Snyder, TX 79549 915-573-8511 (4)

Holland, E. C., Professional Musicians' Association, Local 65 609 Chenevert Houston, TX 77003 713-236-8676 (18)

Holland, Jane, Warrack Productions 651 Yonge Street Toronto, Ontario, Canada M5R 2Z2 416-964-6464, Administration (16)

Holland, Sally, Coosa County Arts Council Route 2 Rockford, AL 35136 205-377-4540 (5)

Holland, T. Shandy, Carthage College Department of Theatre Kenosha, WI 53140 414-551-8500 (4)

Hollenbeck, John, Musicians' Association 5215 Arbor Road Long Beach, CA 90808 213-421-4747 (18)

Hollerer, Emery, Haverhill Musicians' Association 92 North Avenue Haverhill, MA 01830 617-373-5200 (18)

Hollers, Mrs. Bennie, Montgomery County Arts Council Post Office Box 206 Candor, NC 27229 919-974-4774 (5)

Hollingsworth, Dawn, Chicago Spotlight 4036 West Waveland Chicago, IL 60641 312-777-8824 (15)

Hollingsworth, Dawn, Grand Stage
Lighting Company 630 West Lake Street
Chicago, IL 60606 312-332-5611;
800-621-2181 (15)

Hollingsworth, June J., Burke Arts Council
115 East Meeting Street Morganton, NC
28655 704-433-7282 (5)

Hollingsworth, Michael, Video Cabaret
357 College Street Toronto, Ontario,
Canada 416-960-4881 (16)

Hollis, Lucie F., Tullahoma Fine Arts
Center 401 South Jackson Street
Tullahoma, TN 37388 615-455-1234;
615-455-0097 (5)

Holm, Enid, Texas Non-Profit Theatres
2000 Wadley Midland, TX 79701 (16)

Holman, Christopher, O'Keefe Centre 1
Front Street East Toronto, Ontario,
Canada M5E 1B2 416-366-8131;
416-698-2626 (16)

Holmes, Drauca J., Brigham City
Community Theatre 75 North 6th East
Brigham City, UT 84302 801-723-8184
(16)

Holmes, S., Detroit Crusade 3015 East
Outer Drive Detroit, MI 48234 (16)

Holroyd, Frank J., The Players Post Office
Box 2277 Sarasota, FL 33578
813-958-1577 (16)

Holst, Frank A., River Cities Sound 1025
West Fourth Street Davenport, IA 52802
319-323-7398 (15)

Holt, Bob, University of Wisconsin Center
Department of Theatre Rock County
Janesville, WI 53545 608-755-2811 (4)

Holzborn, Hermione, Brewton Arts
Council Post Office Box 432 Brewton,
AL 36426 205-867-4832 (5)

Holzemer, Mercene, Prairie Arts Group
721 Parkview Lane Madison, MN 56256
(16)

Holzer, Frank N., Billings Professional
Musicians' Association 2822 3rd
Avenue, #210 North Billings, MT
59101 406-245-3360 (18)

Holzman, David, Musicians' Association,
Local 35 2733 Lake Drive Evansville, IN
47711 812-476-4754 (18)

Homertz, Fred R., Okoboji Summer
Theatre Post Ofice Box 341 Spirit Lake,
IA 53160 712-332-2773 (8)

Homrighous, Mary, Salem College
Department of Theatre Winston-Salem,
NC 27108 919-723-7961 (4)

Hong, Mae, Mae Hong 525 East 14th
Street New York, NY 10009
212-475-7393 (12)

Honsinger, William S., Marysville
Musicians' Association, Local 158 Post
Office Box 1552 Marysville, CA 95901
916-743-9760 (18)

Hood, Ann, SE North Carolina Arts
Council Route 2 Elizabethtown, NC
28337 919-588-4898 (5)

Hood, Mary, Owensboro Arts Commission
122 East 18th Street Owensboro, KY
42301 502-685-3141 (5)

Hook, Jack, Musicians' Asociation of
Metropolitan Baltimore, Local 40-543
1055 Taylor Avenue, Suite 203
Baltimore, MD 21204 301-337-7277 (18)

Hooper, Robert, Festival-in-the-Park
Incorporated (Roanoke) Post Office Box
12745 Roanoke, VA 24028 703-342-2640
(9)

Hoot, Fred, Fred Hoot 230 West 55th
Street New York, NY 10019
212-246-3346 (12)

Hopewell, Alton, Martin County Arts
Council Post Office Box 1134
Williamston, NC 27892 919-792-1575;
919-792-4361 (5)

Hopkins, John B., Erpf Catskill Cultural
Center Route 28 Arkville, NY 12406
904-586-3326 (5)

Hopkins, K., Chelm Players 6125
Montrose Road Rockville, MD 20852
(16)

Hopkins, Mary, Dalles Art Association
Post Office Box 882 The Dalles, OR
97058 503-296-4759 (5)

Hopkinson, Deborah, Hawaii Performing
Arts Company 2833 East Manda Road
Honolulu, HI 96822-1893 808-988-6131;
808-988-7388 (16)

Hopper, Dr. Arthur, Millikin University
Department of Theatre 1184 West Main
Street Decatur, IL 62522 217-424-6211;
217-424-6282 (4)

Hopper, Clarence H., Musicians'
Association of East Aurora 452 Franklin
Street Buffalo, NY 14202 716-886-5902
(18)

Hopper, Tom, Musicians' Protective
Union 414 Ridgemont Collinsville, IL
63234 618-344-3197 (18)

Hoque, Don, San Jose Federation of
Musicians, Local 153 14584 Westcott
Drive Saratoga, CA 95070 408-867-0456
(18)

Horlacher, Jack, Greater Birmingham Arts
Alliance Post Office Box 2152
Birmingham, AL 35201 205-251-1228
(5)

Hormaechea, Cory, Alpine Playhouse Post
Office Box 753 McCall, ID 83638
208-634-9945 (8)

Horne, Frank S., Pensacola Federation of
Musicians 4976 Prieto Drive Pensacola,
FL 32507 904-456-1643 (18)

Horne, Henry, Biloxi Little Theatre Post
Office Box 955 Biloxi, MS 39533 (16)

Horne, Nat, Nat Horne Musical Theatre
440 West 42nd Street New York, NY
10036 212-736-7128 (4)

Horridge, Deborah, Theatre Aquarius 50
Murray Street West Hamilton, Ontario,
Canada L8L 1B3 416-529-1195 (16)

Horst, Donald P., Pierce College
Department of Theatre Woodland Hills,
CA 91371 213-347-0551 (4)

Hosey, James T., United States Steel
Foundation 600 Grant Street Pittsburgh,
PA 15230 412-433-5238 (10)

Hotsoll, Frank, National Endowment for
the Arts 2401 E Street Washington, DC
20506 202-682-5400 (5)

Hott, Jordan, Pratt Institute Department of
Theatre 215 Ryerson Street Brooklyn,
NY 11205 212-636-3600; 212-636-3583
(4)

Hotta, Tay, Teac Corporation of America
7733 Telegraph Road Montebello, CA
90640 213-726-0303 (15)

Houchin, Thomas D., Saint John's
University Department of Theatre Grand
Central and Utopia Parkway Jamaica, NY
11432 212-969-8000 (4)

Houck, Linus, Musicians' Protective
Association 10 Grove Street Oneonta,
NY 13820 607-432-7162 (18)

Houghton, Ruth, Ithaca Repertory Theater
313 North Tioga Street Ithaca, NY
14850 607-273-8588 (16)

Houlihan, Mr. Laurel I., Musicians'
Association, Local 193 1228 Hickory
Drive Waukesha, WI 53186
414-542-2425 (18)

Houseman, Joe, Barbizon Electric
Company, Incorporated 426 West 55th
Street New York, NY 10019
212-586-1620 (15)

Houseman, John, The Acting Company
420 West 42nd Street, 3rd Floor New
York, NY 10019 212-564-3450 (16)

Housman, Arthur L., University of North
Carolina Department of Theatre Chapel
Hill, NC 27514 919-933-1132 (4)

Houston, Cora, Central Oregon Arts
Society Route 1, Box 1207 Prineville,
OR 97754 (5)

Houtz, Warren, Tulsa Performing Arts
Center Third and Cincinnati Tulsa, OK
74103 918-581-5641 (8)

Hovick, Marcia G., Children's
Experimental Theatre Post Office Box
3381 Carmel, CA 9321 (16)

Howard, Bruce, Anniston Little Theatre
Post Office Box 1454 Anniston, AL
36202 205-236-8342 (16)

Howard, Dana, Tech Theatre Incorporated
Post Office Box 401 Naperville, IL
60540 312-971-0855 (15)

Howard, Dann, Camelot Production
Company 4765 Liberty Avenue
Pittsburgh, PA 15224 (16)

Howard, Elizabeth H., Alliance of New
York State Arts Councils 198 New York
Avenue Huntington, NY 11743
516-423-1818 (5)

Howard, Lyn, Clinton Goodtime Players
Route 3 Janesville, WI 53545 (16)

Howard, Natalie N., Center Stage 229
Klondyke Road Long Beach, MS 39560
(16)

Howarth, Frank, Children's Theatre of
Richmond 6317 Mallory Drive
Richmond, VA 23239 804-288-6634 (16)

Howlett, John, John Howlett 48 West 89th
Street New York, NY 10024
212-799-3003 (12)

Hoyer, Christopher, Concordia College Department of Theatre 171 White Plains Road Bronxville, NY 10708 914-337-9300 (4)

Hoyt, Peggy, Allied Arts Council of Walla Walla Valley 109 South Palouse Street Walla Walla, WA 99362 509-529-5978 (5)

Hrubetz, Francis M., Musicians' Association, Local 75 640 19th Street Des Moines, IA 50314 515-244-2058 (18)

Hubner, Donald A., Central/Shippee, Incorporated 46 Star Lake Road Bloomingdale, NJ 07403 201-838-1100; 800-631-8968 (15)

Hueur, Kathy, Northern Lights Players Route 2 Nevis, MN 56467 (16)

Huff, Mr. Ardith, Lafayette Federation of Musicians, Local 162 24 Prairie Court Lafayette, IN 47904 317-447-2051 (18)

Huffington, Dale, Chimera Theatre Company 30 East 10th Street Saint Paul, MN 56221 (16)

Huffman, Mrs. Nora Mae, Newark Federation of Musicians, Local 122 459 Courtney Drive Newark, OH 43055 614-366-1757 (18)

Huggins, Beverly, Theatre Magic 1282 Nantucket Columbus, OH 43220 614-459-3222 (15)

Huggins, Richard, Theatre Magic 1282 Nantucket Columbus, OH 43220 614-459-3222 (15)

Hughes, Edwards, Musicians' Protective Union Route 5 Wheelersburg, OH 45694 614-574-6756 (18)

Hughes, Joseph E., Mutual Protective Union, Local 241 2933 Burke Lane Butte, MT 59701 406-494-4251 (18)

Hull, Kathryn B., Glendale Regional Arts Council Post Office Box 8292 LaCrescenta, CA 91214 213-249-6510 (5)

Hulse, Larry, Creative Artists Public Service Program Fellowships 250 West 57th Street New York, NY 10019 (3)

Hume, Charles V., California State University, Sacramento 6000 J. Street Sacramento, CA 95819 916-454-6011 (4)

Hume, George, Melrose Memorial Hall Main Street Melrose, MA 02176 (8)

Humphrey, David R., Florida School of the Arts Department of Theatre Tallahassee, FL 32077 (4)

Humphrey, Richard, D/H Productions 250 West 57th Street, #1921 New York, NY 10019 212-582-5656 (13)

Humphries, Elmer R., Belleville Musical Union, Local 19 325 North 45th Street Belleville, IL 62223 618-234-2578 (18)

Humphries, V.H., Montgomery Federatiton of Musicians 1310 Magnolia Avenue Montgomery, AL 36106 205-262-5154 (18)

Hunt, Betty Lee, Betty Lee Hunt 1501 Broadway New York, NY 10036 212-354-0880 (12)

Hunt, Gaddis, Lee Hall Auditorium Mississippi State University State College, MS 39762 601-325-5646 (8)

Hunt, George B., George B. Hunt Agency 8350 Santa Monica Los Angeles, CA 90046 213-654-6600 (2)

Hunter, E., Ada Community Theatre 1017 East 17th Place Ada, OK 74820 (16)

Huntoon, Wallace, Golden West College Community Theatre 15744 Golden West Street Huntington Beach, CA 92647 714-892-7711 (16)

Hurley, Chris, Manitoba Puppet Theatre 300 Memorial Boulevard Winnipeg, Manitoba, Canada R3C 1V1 204-943-1302 (16)

Hurley, Timothy, Westside Community Repertory Theatre 252 West 81st Street New York, NY 10024 212-874-9400; 212-666-3521 (16)

Hurt, Charles E., Missoula Professional Musicians' Association 315 Westview Drive Missoula, MT 59802 406-728-3473 (18)

Husk, Stanley, Musicians' Protective Union 2711 Emmons Avenue Huntington, WV 25702 304-697-2617 (18)

Hussong, Barbara, Chinese Cultural and Community Center 125 North Tenth Street Philadelphia, PA 19107 215-NA3-6767 (5)

Hustoles, Paul J., Tarkio College Department of Theatre Tarkio, MO 64491 816-736-4131 (4)

Huston, Hollis W., Tougaloo College Department of Theatre Tougaloo, MS 39174 601-982-4242 (4)

Hutchins, Alex, Alamance County Arts Council 135 West Elm Street Graham, NC 27253 919-226-4495; 919-226-4496 (5)

Hutchins, Richard, Associated Musicians of Keene, New Hampshire Fitch Court Marlborough, NH 03455 603-876-3963 (18)

Hutmacher, Ray R., Ray R. Hutmacher Associates, Inc. 7205 West Pratt Chicago, IL 60631 312-631-3248 (15)

Hyatt, Karen Kinnett, National Arts Jobbank 141 East Palace Avenue Santa Fe, NM 87501 505-988-1166 (14)

Hyde, Marion, Theatre Network Post Office Box 4926 Edmonton, Alberta, Canada T6E 5G8 403-425-8761 (16)

Hymes, Virginia, Virginia Hymes 465 West End Avenue New York, NY 10024 212-873-8616 (12)

I

Iacobucci, Dr. Richard, Roctronics Entertainment Lighting 22-TC Wendell Street Cambridge, MA 02138 617-826-8888 (15)

Iannucci, Michael P., Storrowton Theatre Exposition Park West Springfield, MA 01089 413-732-1105 (16)

Iddings, Paul, Behrend College Department of Theatre Erie, PA 16563 814-898-1511 (4)

Ijams, Maitland T., Playhouse on the Hill c/o Ijams Route 28 Barneveld, NY 13304 315-896-4441 (16)

Impellitter, Vincent, Buffalo Musicians' Association, Local 92 452 Franklin Street Buffalo, NY 14202 716-873-1275 (18)

Ingvalson, Catherine, Winona Musicians' Association 190 West Main Street Lewiston, MN 55952 507-523-3657 (18)

Irwin, P., Texas College Department of Theatre Tyler, TX 75701 214-594-3200 (4)

Isabella, Mike, Musical Union, Local 27 321 Edison Avenue New Castle, PA 16101 412-654-5182 (18)

Isola, Dick, Superscope Detroit, Incorporated 591 Executive Drive Troy, MI 48084 313-588-7200 (15)

Isserman, Ronald, South African Feather Company, Incorporated 401 N. Broad Street, Suite 242 Philadelphia, PA 19108 215-925-5219; 215-925-5220 (15)

Ives, Wally, Central Wisconsin Musicians' Association 2830 37th Street North Wisconsin Rapids, WI 54494 715-421-0066 (18)

Iwanicki, John, D.I.M. Lighting Company Cedar Hill Road Salem, MA 01970 617-744-8859 (15)

J

Jache, David, Titusville Playhouse Post Office Box 1234 Titusville, FL 32780 305-267-9684 (8)

Jackman, Phillip H., El Centro College Department of Theatre Main and Lamar Street Dallas, TX 75202 (4)

Jacksina, Judy, Jacksina and Freedman 1501 Broadway New York, NY 10036 212-921-7979 (12)

Jackson, Charles, Huntsville Little Theatre 700 Monroe Street Huntsville, AL 35801 205-533-6565 (16)

Jackson, Frank E., Lander College Department of Speech and Theatre Stanley Avenue Greenwood, SC 29646 803-229-8211; 803-229-8213 (4)

Jackson, G. Craig, Ohlone College Department of Theatre Post Office Box 909 Fremont, CA 94538 415-657-2100 (4)

Jackson, Mazella, George B. Carpenter and Company 401 North Ogden Chicago, IL 60647 312-666-8700 (15)

Jackson, Tommy, Paspoint Little Theatre Post Office Box 231 Pascagoula, MS 39567 (16)

Jackson, Wally, Odessa College Fine Arts Center Odessa College Odessa, TX 79760 915-337-5381 (8)

Jacob, Margot, Theatre Les Ancetres C.P. 398 St-German, Quebec, Canada J0C 1K0 514-677-6217 (16)

Johnson, Lawrence H., Duro-Test Corporation 2321 Kennedy Boulevard North Bergen, NJ 07047 201-867-7000 (15)

Johnson, Mason, Texas Wesleyan College Department of Theatre Post Office 3277 Fort Worth, TX 76105 817-534-0251 (4)

Johnson, Nancy, Foothills Civic Theatre Post Office Box 319 LaPorte, CO 80535 303-484-8182 (16)

Johnson, Ms. Pat, Mora Area Community Theatre 1235 South Union Mora, MN 55051 (16)

Johnson, Robert, Madison Musicians' Association 222 South Hamilton Madison, WI 53703 608-238-3421 (18)

Johnson, Roland D., California State University Cedar and Shaw Fresno, CA 93740 209-487-9011 (4)

Johnson, Ronald E., J.R. Russell Electric 714 South Niel Champaign, IL 61820 217-356-8700 (15)

Johnson, S., British Embassy Players 3100 Massachusetts NW Washington, DC 20008 (16)

Johnson, Tom, Telex Communications, Incorporated 9600 Aldrich Avenue South Minneapolis, MN 55420 612-884-4051 (15)

Johnson, Yankee, King County Arts Commission Room W-140, County Courthouse Seattle, WA 98104 206-344-4040 (5)

Johnston, Gerald, Hattiesburg Federation of Musicians 326 Venetian Way Hattiesburg, MS 39401 601-544-2834 (18)

Johnston, Simon, Press Theatre 85 Church Street St. Catharines, Ontario, Canada L2R 6Y3 416-684-1133, Administration; 416-684-6377, Box Office (16)

Johnstone, Ev, Gryphon Theatre Company 103 Dunlop Street East Barrie, Ontario, Canada L4M 4T7 705-728-4613 (16)

Johnstone, Keith, Loose Moose Theatre Company 1610 Bowness Road Northwest Calgary, Alberta, Canada T2N 3J9 403-283-9960 (16)

Jones, Cecil D. Jr., Vanderbuilt University Department of Drama and Speech Nashville, TN 37235 615-033- 2404 (4)

Jones, Dewitt, Bob Jones University Department of Theatre Wade Hampton Boulevard Greenville, SC 29614 803-242-5100 Extension 238 (4)

Jones, Edwin, Edwin Jones Company 6445 Prestonshire Dallas, TX 75225 214-789-9447 (15)

Jones, Harley, Duro-Test Sales and Service 1200 Kirk Street Elk Grove Village, IL 60007 312-766-0042 (15)

Jones, Dr. Janie, West Hills College Department of Theatre 300 Cherry Lane Coalinga, CA 93210 209-935-0801 (4)

Jones, Jinny, Macon County Cultural Arts Council Post Office Box 726 Franklin, NC 28734 704-524-7683 (5)

Jones, Keith, Metropolitan Community College Department of Theatre 50 Willow Street Minneapolis, MN 55403 612-339-9441 (4)

Jones, Lloyd H., Lehigh Electric Products Company R.D. 1, Box J1, Route 222 Wescosville, PA 18106 215-395-3386 (15)

Jones, Dr. Lloyd S., California State University, Chico Chico, CA 95929 916-985-5351 (4)

Jones, Mick, University of LaVerne Department of Theatre La Verne, CA 91750 714-593-3511, Ext. 248, 364, 365; 213-629-1066 (4)

Jones, Mike, Mike Jones 314 Cane Ridge Drive Antioch, TN 37013 615-331-2164 (15)

Jones, R. A., Canby Southwest Association Arts and Humanities Council 606 Oscar North Canby, MN 56220 507-223-5962 (5)

Jones, Richard L., Russell Sage College Department of Theatre Troy, NY 12180 518-270-2263 (4)

Jones, Robert E., Saint Petersburg College Department of Theatre Saint Petersburg, FL 33710 813-381-6681 (4)

Jones, Robert W., Metropolitan Lansing Fine Arts Council 507 South Grand Avenue Lansing, MI 48933 517-487-2424 (5)

Jones, Vern, Key City Playhouse Post Office Box 194 Port Townsend, WA 98368 206-385-3721 (8)

Jones, Vern, Key City Players Post Office Box 194 Port Townsend, WA 98368 206-385-3721 (16)

Jordan, Casper L., Free Lance 6005 Grand Avenue Cleveland, OH 44104 216-431-7118 (14)

Jorgensen, Clyde, Musicians' Protective Union, Local 164 3162 East Half Road Grand Junction, CO 81501 303-434-6565 (18)

Josal, Wendell, University of Minnesota Department of Theatre Minneapolis, MN 55455 612-373-3118; 612-373-4882 (4)

Joseph, Bernard L., Foamcraft Incorporated 947 West Van Buren Street Chicago, IL 60607 312-243-6262 (15)

Joseph, Fred, Design Concepts 5365 Polaris Avenue Las Vegas, NV 89118 702-736-8333 (15)

Joseph, Judy, Shelter West Company 217 Second Avenue New York, NY 10003 212-673-6341 (16)

Joseph, Michael, S.A.E. (Scientific Audio Electronics) 701 E. Macy Street Los Angeles, CA 90012 213-489-7600 (15)

Joseph, Robert, Duro-Test International Corporation Post Office Box 1893 Carolina, PR 00628 809-768-2711; 809-762-1485 (15)

Josifek, Vern, Musicians' Protective Union, Local 137 718 4th Street, North West Cedar Rapids, IA 52405 319-362-7902 (18)

Joyce, Ruel L., Kansas City Federation of Musicians, Local 34-627 1017 Washington Kansas City, MO 64105 816-221-6934 (18)

Joynt, Martha L., Community Arts Council 812 Oakland Drive Mount Pleasant, MI 48858 517-722-2543 (5)

Judd, Garda M., Colgate University Dana Arts Center Hamilton, NY 13346 315-824-1000, Ext. 639, 631 (4)

Judd, Jerome D., Arts in Middleton Post Office Box 441 Middleton, OH 45042 (5)

Jude, Timothy, Potter's Field Theatre Company 2 Bond Street New York, NY 10012 212-260-1213 (16)

Judge, Diane, Diane Judge 38 East 38th Street New York, NY 10016 212-685-2690 (12)

Juergens, Robert O., Rollins College Department of Theatre Winter Park, FL 32789 305-646-2000; 305-646-2501 (4)

Julian, Donald H., Union College Department of Theatre 1033 Springfield Avenue Cranford, NJ 07016 201-276-2600 (4)

Juliani, John, Savage God 9527 - 87th Avenue Edmonton, Alberta, Canada T6C 1K4 403-469-9204 (16)

K

Kabatchnik, Amnon, Elmira College Department of Theatre Elmira, NY 14901 607-734-3911 (4)

Kadlerek, Patricia, Renville County Arts Centre Post Office Box 25 Olivia, MN 56277 (16)

Kahler, Robert J., Musicians' Protective Association 227 East Garden Street Rome, NY 13440 315-336-3534 (18)

Kahn, Sy M., Ventura College Department of Theatre Stockton, CA 93003 (4)

Kainer, R., Bleeker Street Players 3622 Ordway Street, NW Washington, DC 20016 (16)

Kalfas, Richard, Musicians' Protective Association, Local 108 5072 West Lake Road Dunkirk, NY 14048 716-366-1773 (18)

Kamarck, Edward, University of Wisconsin Department of Theatre Madison, WI 53706 608-263-6320 (4)

Kamins, Patrick, F.P.C. Corporation 615 West Colfax Palatine, IL 60067 312-359-3838 (15)

Kamlot, Robert, New York Shakespeare Festival 425 Lafayette Street New York, NY 10003 212-598-7100 (9)

Kane, Anthony F. Jr., Musicians' Protective Union, Local 140 17 Grove Street Wilkes-Barre, PA 18702 717-822-4426 (18)

Keppy, Robert D., Niagara Falls Musicians' Association 5848 Main Street Niagara Falls, Ontario, Canada L2G 5Z5 416-357-4642 (18)

Kerber, Mrs. Lucille (Lucy), Musicians' Union, Local 48 169 East Chicago Street Elgin, IL 60120 312-742-3757 (18)

Kerin, Val, Canonsburg Federation of Musicians 545 Ridge Avenue Canonsburg, PA 15317 412-745-2814 (18)

Kerr, Ilene, Janesville Musicians' Association 27 South Randall Avenue Janesville, WI 53545 608-754-7474 (18)

Kerr, John, Janesville Musicians' Association 27 South Randall Avenue Janesville, WI 53545 608-754-7474 (18)

Kesper, Jeffrey A., Middlesex County Cultural Commission 841 George Road North Brunswick, NJ 08902 201-745-4489 (5)

Kestel, M., Buena Vista Community Theatre 110 West 2nd Street Storm Lake, IA 50588 (16)

Keyser, M., Otitiani Study Club Post Office Box 145 Council Grove, KS 66846 (16)

Kiebitz, Ashley, Huntington Arts Council 12 New Street Huntington, NY 11743 516-271-8423 (5)

Kiensler, Kenny, Hill Parents Association Post Office Box 7005 New Haven, CT 06511 203-777-6371 (16)

Kiley, Daniel, Mikan Theatricals 55 Walker Street Concord, NH 03301 (15)

Kilgore, David and Nancy, Barksdale Theatre Hanover Tavern Hanover, VA 23069 804-838-5650 (8)

Killam, Mike, Stokes County Arts Council Post Office Box 56 Danbury, NC 27106 919-593-8159 (5)

Killingsworth, Stan, Trumbull New Theatre Post Office Box 374 Warren, OH 44482 216-652-1103; 216-856-2282 (16)

Kimberlin, Barbara, Florence City Arts Commission Kennedy-Douglas Arts Center Florence, Al 35630 205-764-7271 (5)

Kimbrell, Marketa, New York Street Theatre Caravan 336 West 20th Street New York, NY 10011 212-242-1869; 212-454-8551 (16)

Kimbrough, Mildred, Ivy Green Theatre 300 W Worth Common Tuscumbia, AL 35674 205-383-4066 (16)

Kimelman, Shawn, Puppet Tree Company 160 Princess Street Winnipeg, Manitoba, Canada R3B 1K9 204-942-7291 (16)

Kincaid, Dennis, Grand Piano Company Post Office Box 1238 Morganton, NC 28665 (15)

King, Dennis W., Denalee Productions 3070 Montair Avenue Long Beach, CA 90808 213-425-1759 (16)

King, H.C., H.C. King and Associates, Incorporated 800 Compton Road Cincinnati, OH 45231 513-521-5511 (15)

King, Richard, Hanover Community Players Road 3 Hanover, PA 17331 (16)

King, S.A., Fond Du Lac Community Theatre 2602 Valley Creek Road Fond Du Lac, WI 54935 (16)

King, Wash, Musicians' Association 151 Fourth Street Coaldale, PA 18218 717-645-9484 (18)

King, Woodie, Henry Street's New Federal Theatre 466 Grand Street New York, NY 10002 212-766-9295 (16)

King, Woodie Jr., New Federal Theatre 466 Grand Street New York, NY 10002 212-766-9334 (16)

Kinney, N., Portage Players 2214 Woodcrest Portage, WI 53901 (16)

Kinney, Tom, Brazosport College Department of Theatre Post Office Drawer 955 Brazosport, TX 7754 713-265-6131 (4)

Kinnison, Bufford, Musicians' Protective Union Route 2, Box 258 Pendleton, OR 97801 503-276-6220 (18)

Kirby, Harold, Musicians Protective Union 3 Maple Avenue Moundsville, WV 26041 304-845-3796 (18)

Kirby, Michael, Drama Review,The New York University New York, NY 10012 212-598-2597 (14)

Kirkby, Jack W., Costumes Unlimited 814 North Franklin Chicago, IL 60610 312-642-0200 (15)

Kirkpatrick, Barbara, Gainesville Spring Arts Festival Santa Fe Community College Gainesville, FL 32601 (9)

Kirkpatrick, Mr. John E., Kirkpatrick Foundation 1300 North Broadway Oklahoma City, OK 73103 405-235-5621 (10)

Kirkpatrick, William T., Clarksburg Federation of Musicians 320 Front Street Bridgeport, WV 26330 304-842-3088 (18)

Kirschman, Marvin, Hillsborough Community College, YBOR Campus Department of Theatre Post Office Box 22127 Tampa, FL 33622 813-879-7222 (4)

Kirshenblatt-Gimblett, Barbara, New York University Tisch School of the Arts 300 South Building, 51 West 4th Street New York, NY 10003 212-598-4651; 212-598-2596 (4)

Kirtley, Robert C., Arts in Action Council 501 Southridge Drive Riverton, WY 82501 347-856-9565 (5)

Kissinger, Beverly, Columbus Community Theatre Post Office Box 83 Columbus, MS 39701 (16)

Kitchings, James A., Augusta Federation of Musicians 219 Marion Street Southeast Aiken, SC 29801 803-648-7276 (18)

Klaiman, Ralph, Bilt-Rite Fabrics, Incorporated 16121 Euclid Avenue Cleveland, OH 44112 216-451-2900 (15)

Klass, Richard, Norfolk Arts Council 501 Norfolk Avenue Norfolk, NB 68701 (5)

Klassen, Robert, Marquette University Department of Theatre Arts 615 North 11th Street Milwaukee, WI 53233 414-224-7504 (4)

Klassen, Rose, Cardinal Stritch College Department of Theatre 6801 North Yates Road Milwaukee, WI 53217 414-352-5400, Ext. 291 (4)

Klausner, Bertha, Bertha Klausner Literary Agency 71 Park Avenue New York, NY 10016 212-685-2642; 212-532-8638 (2)

Klauss, N., Hardscrabble Players Route 3, Box 67 Rice Lake, WI 54868 (16)

Kleeman, Kay E., Meadville Council on Arts Post Office Box 337 Meadville, PA 16335 814-336-5051 (5)

Klein, E., Creative Garden Theatre Post Office Box 1541 Fairmont, WV 26554 (16)

Klein, Manny, Delaware Musical Society 2704 Society Drive Claymont, DE 19703 302-798-6060 (18)

Klein, Stanley F., Foothill Playhouse Beechwood Avenue Middlesex, NJ 08846 201-356-0462 (8)

Kleir, Mary E., Seattle Public Library-Main Branch 1000 Fourth Avenue Seattle, WA 98104 206-625-2665 (8)

Kline, Charles, State University of New York, Plattsburgh Department of Theatre Broad Street Plattsburgh, NY 12901 518-564-2000; 518-564-2181 (4)

Kline, Norman, Emelin Theatre Library Lane Mamaroneck, NY 10543 914-698-3045 (8)

Kloc, Walter, Fairmont Federation of Musicians 1627 Otlahurst Drive Fairmont, WV 26554 304-366-1635 (18)

Knapp, Albert, Musicians' Protective Union 2318 Houser Street Muscatine, IA 52761 319-263-0649 (18)

Knaub, Donald E., Civic Arts Division/City of Davis 212 D Street Davis, CA 95616 916-756-3740 (5)

Knell, Dick, Dick Knell 2533 Cottle Avenue San Jose, CA 95125 408-267-0720 (15)

Knentsch, Piet, Burnett Center for Performing Arts Bethany College Lindsberg, KS 67456 913-227-3312 (8)

Knoll, Evelyn E., Albany Civic Auditorium 19 Clinton Avenue Albany, NY 12207 518-465-3333 (8)

Knorr, J., Buckhannon Community Theatre 16 Gum Street Buckhannon, WV 26201 (16)

Knotts, Allan, North County Arts Council White Mountain Center for the Arts Jefferson, NH 03583 603-586-7754 (5)

Knower, Barry, Goucher College Department of Theatre 1021 Dulaney Valley Road Baltimore, MD 21204 301-825-3300 (4)

Knowles, Judith, Shasta College Department of Theatre Redding, CA 96001 916-241-3523 (4)

Kriley, James D., Masquer Theater Department of Drama Missoula, MT 59801 406-243-4481 (8)

Krislov, E., Studio Players Incorporated 1008 Gainesway Drive Lexington, KY 40501 (16)

Kristensen, Kent, The Cutawl Company Bethel, CT 06801 203-792-8622 (15)

Kronen, H.B., Dance Scope 1133 Broadway New York, NY 10010 212-691-4564 (14)

Krowe, Elliot B., See Factor, Incorporated 84 Thomas Street New York, NY 10013 212-732-1464; 710-581-4327 (15)

Kruggel, Bob, Four Star Stage Lighting, Incorporated 3935 North Mission Road Los Angeles, CA 90031 213-221-5114 (15)

Kruggel, G., Bluff Players 8321 Palmetto Lane Indianapolis, IN 46217 (16)

Kruk, Arthur, Paul E. Holden Fine Arts Center University of Wisconsin Superior, WI 54880 715-392-8101 (16)

Kubiak, Dennis, Musicians' Protective Association, Local 100 281 Rockwell Street Kewanee, IL 61443 309-853-8668 (18)

Kuchtyak, Andy, Musicians' Protective Union 414 Elmwood Avenue Woodbridge, NJ 07095 201-634-0750 (18)

Kuck, Richard B., Musicians' Protective Union, Local 225 2038 Avon Hayden Lake, ID 83835 208-773-7971 (18)

Kuhl, Darwin, Bellevue Community Arts Council 201 West Street Bellevue, MI 49021 616-763-9413 (5)

Kuhn, Sarah Sappington, Los Angeles Feminist Theatre 8700 Skyline Drive Los Angeles, CA 90046 213-656-9044 (16)

Kukuk, Jack, Kennedy Center for the Performing Arts Alliance for Arts Education Washington, DC 20566 (16)

Kullen, A., Montgomery Players 7723 Groton Road Bethesda, MD 20014 (16)

Kulp, Ted, Contra Costa College Department of Theatre San Pablo, CA 94806 415-235-7800 (4)

Kumm, Willard, Shawnano Federation of Musicians, Local 227 301 State Street Bonduel, WI 54107 715-758-8944 (18)

Kunst, Anton C., Musicians' Protective Union, Local 213 3004 North Campsite Drive Stevens Point, WI 54481 715-344-7550 (18)

Kunz, James T., Theatrical Rigging Systems, Incorporated 4060 West Broadway Minneapolis, MN 55422 612-533-3311 (15)

Kupinski, Michael, Salem Federation of Musicians, Local 222 Route 4 Salem, OH 44460 216-332-1281 (18)

Kupish, Stan, Decatur Association of Musicians, Local 89 342 West Eckhardt Macon, IL 62544 217-877-8158 (18)

Kurtz, J. Phil, Musicians' Protective Union Post Office Box 566 Pittsburg, KS 66762 316-231-5220 (18)

Kushnar, William Lawrence, Glassboro State College Department of Theatre Glassboro, NJ 08028 609-445-5288; 609-445-5787 (4)

Kyle, Rory, Confidential Exchange 133 Albert Street Winnipeg, Manitoba, Canada R3B 1G6 204-452-7195 (16)

L

Laabs, Gary, Musicians' Protective Association 1231 East Hanson Drive Appleton, WI 54911 414-734-0021 (18)

Labeille, Daniel C., Cayuga County Community College Department of Theatre Franklin Street Auburn, NY 13021 315-253-7345 (4)

LaBerge, Molly, Compas 700 Saint Paul Building Saint Paul, MN 55102 612-227-8241 (5)

LaBonte, Maureen, Penguin Theatre Company Post Office Box 4353, Station E Ottawa, Ontario, Canada K1S 5B3 613-233-9281; 613-233-1841 (16)

LaCava, Charles, Rochester Musicians' Association, Local 66 83 Clinton Avenue, North Rochester, NY 14604 716-546-7633 (18)

Lafferty, Kerry, College of Saint Benedict Department of Theatre Saint Joseph, MN 56374 612-363-5713 (4)

Laffoon, Don R., Stop-Gap 630 Anita Street Laguna Beach, CA 92651 (16)

LaHood, Herbert, Syracuse Musicians Protective Association, Local 78 131 Butler Street Syracuse, NY 13210 315-472-3056 (18)

Lalande, Louis, Theatre Sun Valley C.P. 105 Ste. Adele, Quebec, Canada J0R 1L0 (16)

Laliberte, Andre, Theatre de L'Oeil 4848 Henri Julien Montreal, Quebec, Canada H2T 2E1 514-845-1045 (16)

LaLoggia, Vincent F., Musical Union, Local 240 119 North Church Street Rockford, IL 61101 815-965-2132 (18)

Lamb, Akiko, Studio Lab Theatre 235 Macdonell Toronto, Ontario, Canada M6R 2A9 416-531-4832 (16)

Lammers, Raymond J., University of Minnesota, Morris Department of Theatre Morris, MN 56267 612-589-2211 (4)

Lampe, Michael, Springfield Little Theatre 311 East Walnut Street Springfield, MO 65806 417-869-1334 (16)

Lanataff, Kent, Ensemble Studio Theatre 549 West 52nd Street New York, NY 10019 212-247-4982 (16)

Lancaster, Burton, Theatre Compact 730 Yonge Street Toronto, Ontario, Canada M4Y 2B7 416-922-6159 (16)

Landes, Gloria, Mamaroneck Council on the Arts 169 Mount Pleasant Avenue Mamaroneck, NY 10543 914-698-7400 (5)

Landress, John R., Copiah-Lincoln Community Junior College Department of Theatre Wesson, MS 39191 (4)

Landrum, Baylor, The Cincinnati Playhouse in the Park Post Office Box 6537 Cincinnati, OH 45206 513-421-3888, Box Office; 513-421-5440, Administrative (16)

Landrum, Carl, Musicians' Protective Union, Local 265 1 Sherwood Drive Quincy, IL 62301 217-222-0941 (18)

Landry, Monique P., Le Theatre des Lutins C.P. 7065 Ottawa, Ontario, Canada K1L 7065 613-523-8621 (16)

Landry, Monique P., Le Theatre des Lutins C.P. 132 Aylmer, Quebec, Canada 819-684-9598 (16)

Landy, James E., Landy Associates Incorporated 1890 East Marlton Pike Cherry Hill, NJ 08003 609-424-4660 (15)

Lane, Barton, Puppet Theatre of War 2753 West 15th Street Brooklyn, NY 11224 718-373-2810 (16)

Lane, John F., Marymount Palos Verdes College Department of Theatre Rancho Palos Verdes, CA 90274 (4)

Lane, Marcia E., Theatre Calgary 830 9th Avenue South West Calgary, Alberta, Canada T2P 1L7 403-262-2146; 403-265-6700 (16)

Lane, Ted, Alan Gordon Enterprises, Inc. 1430 North Cahuenga Boulevard Hollywood, CA 90028 213-466-3561 (15)

Langdon, Harry, Saint Mary of the Plains College Department of Theatre Dodge City, KS 67801 316-225-4171 (4)

Langernbruch, Linda, Mercer University, Atlanta Department of Drama 3000 Flowers Road Atlanta, GA 30341 404-451-0331 (4)

Langford, Michael, New Theatre 57 Adelaide Street, East Toronto, Ontario, Canada M5C 1K6 416-363-6429; 416-363-6401 (16)

Langford, Michael, Open Circle Theatre 57 Adelaide Street East Toronto, Ontario, Canada M5C 1K6 416-363-6443, Administrative; 416-363-6401, Box Office (16)

Langham, Michael, Julliard School, Theatre Center Lincoln Center New York, NY 10023 212-799-5000 (4)

Langhans, Edward A., University of Hawaii Department of Drama 1770 East West Road Honolulu, HI 96822 808-948-7677; 808-948-7622 (4)

Langley, Robert, District Federation of Musicians, Local 180 49 Bank Street Ottawa, Ontario, Canada K2P 1Z2 613-233-5301 (18)

Langley, Stephen, Brooklyn College School of Performing Arts Department of Theatre Brooklyn, NY 11210 212-780-5800 (4)

Langley, Stephen, Performance-Management Brooklyn College, Department of Theatre Brooklyn, NY 11210 (14)

Lemoncelli, Egidio S., Musicians' Protective Union, Local 130 87 Belmont Carbondale, PA 18407 717-282-3155 (18)

Lengyel, Cornel, Living Playwrights Award Dragon Teeth Press Georgetown, CA 95634 916-333-4224 (3)

Lenhardt, Henry, Musicians' Protective Association 1905 Washington Avenue Alton, IL 62002 618-466-7385 (18)

Lenhoff, Bentley, Youngstown Playhouse 600 Playhouse Lane Youngstown, OH 44511 (16)

Leonard, George, Department of Parks and Recreation Hempstead Executive Plaza Hempstead, NY 11550 516-489-5000 (5)

Leone, Mrs. Josephine, Kankakee Musicians' Association 740 Armour Road Boubonnais, IL 60914 815-932-6662 (18)

Leone, Leonard, Wayne State University Department of Theatre 1400 Chrysler Freeway Detroit, MI 48202 313-961-7302 (4)

Leonhart, Richard, Musicians' Mutual Protective Union, Local 259 104 Bliarwood Drive, Liberty Hills Parkersburg, WV 26101 304-422-1331 (18)

LeRoux, Jeanne, Theatre De La Marmaille 820 rue Lasalle Longueuil, Quebec, Canada J4K 3G5 514-677-6220 (16)

Leslie, Chuck, Leslie Sales 25 Three Fountains Mesa, AZ 85203 602-969-5729 (15)

Lesmeister, Jeff, Minot Musician's Association 1001 38th Street Northeast Minot, ND 58701 701-838-0845 (18)

Lester, Jean, Fullerton College Community Services 321 East Chapman Avenue Fullerton, CA 92634 714-871-8000, ext. 252 (4)

Lester, L. Glenn, Theatre Guild, Inc. Post Office Box 1502 Morristown, TN 37814 615-586-9260 (16)

Lett, Mrs. Robert B., Children's Carousel Theatre 1102 Greenway Drive High Point, NC 27262 (16)

Leuning, Glenn, Chabot College Department of Theatre Hayward, CA 91245 (4)

Levendorf, Marvin, Weirton Area Arts Council Post Office Box 482 Weirton, WV 26062 304-748-7110 (5)

Levenson, Jill, University of Toronto, Massey College Toronto, Ontario, Canada M5S 2E1 416-978-2092 (14)

Lever, Elayne, Al Lever and Associates 12607 Waverly Place Bowie, MD 20715 301-262-7678 (15)

Levey, Alan, Sundown Theatre Route 3, Box 640 Livingston, TX 77351 713-563-4391 (8)

LeVine, David E., Dramatists Guild 234 West 44th Street New York, NY 10036 212-398-9366 (5)

LeVine, Marilyn, Alpert/Levine Public Relations 1501 Broadway, Suite 1502 New York, NY 10036 212-354-5940 (12)

Levine, Mark, Mark Levin Association 328 South Beverly Drive Beverly Hills, CA 90212 213-277-8881 (2)

Levine, Robert L., Miami-Dade Community College Department of Theatre 300 North East 2nd Avenue Miami, FL 33132 305-577-6740 (4)

Levine, Sam, Toronto Musicians' Association, Local 149 101 Thorncliffe Park Drive Toronto, Ontario, Canada M4H 1M1 416-421-1020 (18)

Levitow, Roberta, The Skid Road Theatre 85 South Washington, #306 Seattle, WA 98104 206-622-0251 (16)

Levitt, Bruce, University of Iowa Department of Drama Iowa City, IA 52242 319-353-5791; 319-353-6589 (4)

Levy, Albert, Mattew Players East McChurch Street Randallstown, MD 21133 (16)

Levy, Sidney, Gilly/Levy Agency 8721 Sunset Boulevard Los Angeles, CA 90069 213-657-5660 (2)

Lewis, Bruce, Key City Players Post Office Box 194 Port Townsend, WA 98368 206-385-3721 (16)

Lewis, Kathryn, Mississippi Gulf Coast Junior College Department of Theatre Perkinston, MS 39573 601-928-5211 (4)

Lewis, Linda, City Cultural Affairs Committee 202 Monona Avenue Madison, WI 53703 608-266-4611; 608-255-8177 (5)

Lewis, Mark, Point Park College 201 Wood Street Pittsburgh, PA 15222 412-391-4100 (4)

Lewis, Mary Kay, Susan Howell Hall Alfred University Alfred, NY 14802 607-871-2193 (8)

Lewis, Pat, Frog Print Theatre 449 Lawson Road West Hill, Ontario, Canada M1C 2K2 416-363-1938 (16)

Lewis, Richard, Richard Lewis Sales 222 South Easton Road Glenside, PA 19038 215-886-1555; 215-886-1556 (15)

Lewis, Rose, Beaufort County Arts Council Post Office Box 634 Washington, NC 27889 919-946-2504 (5)

Lewis, Sara Lee, Mermaid Theatre Post Office Box 837 Wolfville, Nova Scotia, Canada B0P 1X0 902-542-3641 (16)

Lewis, Terral S., Amarillo College Department of Theatre Amarillo, TX 79178 806-376-5111 (4)

Lewitin, Margot, Interart Theatre 549 West 52nd Street New York, NY 10019 212-246-1050 (16)

L'Heureux, Albert, Manchester Federation of Musicians 89 Pennacook Street Manchester, NH 03104 603-622-9084 (18)

Liberman, Frank, Frank Liberman and Associates, Incorporated 9021 Melrose Avenue, Suite 308 Los Angeles, CA 90069 213-278-1993; 213-276-5716 (12)

Liberson, William H., Quaigh Theatre 108 West 43rd Street New York, NY 10036 212-221-9088 (16)

Libert, David, David Libert Agency 1108 North Sherbourne Los Angeles, CA 90069 213-659-6776 (2)

Libin, Paul, League of OffBroadway Theatres and Producers 1540 Broadway, Suite 711 New York, NY 10036 212-869-8282 (5)

Libin, Paul, Circle in the Square 1633 Broadway New York, NY 10019 212-581-3270; 212-581-0720 (16)

Librach, Mathew B., The Repertory Theatre of Saint Louis 130 Edgar Road Post Office Box 28030 Saint Louis, MO 63119 314-968-7340; 314-968-4925, Box Office (16)

Lichtman, Terry, Terry Lichtman Agency 9301 Wilshire Boulevard Beverly Hills, CA 90210 213-550-4550 (2)

Liddle, Leo R., Torrington Musicians' Association 88 County Road Torrington, CT 06790 203-482-4097 (18)

Lieberman, Douglas L., Center Youth Theatre 3003 West Touhy Chicago, IL 60645 312-761-9100 (16)

Lien, Dee Ann, Proscenium Players, Inc. Post Office Box 1165 Carson City, NV 89701 702-882-4503 (16)

Liggett, J.P., Little Theatre Guild Post Office Box 604 Bartlesville, OK 74005 918-336-5668; 918-661-4995 (16)

Light, Walter, Musical Union, Local 239 243 West Genesee Street Auburn, NY 13021 315-253-3345 (18)

Linborg, H.J., Marian College Department of Theatre 45 South National Avenue Fond Du Lac, WI 54935 414-921-3900 (4)

Lind, Gloria, University of Wisconsin, Oshkosh Department of Theatre Oshkosh, WI 54901 414-424-4422 (4)

Lindberg, Mark, Walnut Hill School of Performing Arts 912 Highland Street Natick, MA 01760 617-653-4312 (4)

Lindsay, Beverly, Bryan Fine Arts Council Post Office Box 525 Bryan, OH 43506 419-636-1144 (5)

Line, Rita, Hamilton Musicians' Association, Local 31 4716 Fairfield Avenue Fairfield, OH 45014 513-892-7922 (18)

Link, Jean, Old Mission Gallery Arts Council Kettle Falls Realty, East 250 Third Kettle Falls, WA 99141 509-738-6225 (5)

Linke, Curtis G., Consolidated Foods Corporation 135 South LaSalle Chicago, IL 60603 312-726-6414 (10)

Linz, William M., William M. Linz Associates, Inc. 821 Skokie Boulevard Northbrook, IL 60062 312-498-9600 (15)

Lion, Lyn Austin and Margo, Music-Theatre Group/Lenox Arts Center Lenox Arts Center c/o Lyn Austin New York, NY 10021 212-371-9610; 212-582-1978, Box Office

(16)

Lipinski, John, Federation of Musicians, Local 127 291 Donahue Beach Bay City, MI 48706 517-684-6834 (18)

Lippincott, Donald, Lima Federation of Musicians 320 West Market Street Lima, OH 45801 419-228-0045 (18)

Lipscomb, Nancy, Charles County Arts Council Post Office Box 368 La Plata, MD 20646 301-934-9305 (5)

Liscusky, Anthony, Musicians' Protective Union, Local 170 102 West Laurel Street Shenandoah, PA 17976 717-462-3075 (18)

Lister, Stephen, McMannus Enterprises 111 Union Avenue Bala Cynwyd, PA 19004 215-664-8600; 800-523-0348 (15)

Litchen, Stephen D., Actors Ensemble Theatre 6 Howard Street, Suite 8 Toronto, Ontario, Canada M4X 1J5 416-922-2996 (16)

Little, Guy, Melody Top Theatre 7201 West Good Hope Road Milwaukee, WI 53202 (16)

Little, Margaret, Little Stage Lighting Company 10507 Harry Hines Boulevard Dallas, TX 75220 214-358-3511 (15)

Little, Paul J., University of Redlands Department of Theatre 1200 East Colton Avenue Redlands, CA 92373 714-793-7104 (4)

Littleton, W. Thomas, Southbury Playhouse Post Office Box 361 Southbury, CT 06488 203-264-8215; 203-264-8216 (16)

Lively, Ronald, Musicians' Protective Association, Local 96 24 Crandall Street Adams, MA 01220 413-743-2943 (18)

Livingstone, Ken, Centre Stage Theatre 380 Wellington Street London, Ontario, Canada N6A 5B5 519-433-5241; 519-433-4700 (16)

Lloyd, Robert, Arts Council of Tamworth Post Office Box 71 Chocorua, NH 03817 (5)

Lobisco, Michael J., Auburn Players Community Theatre Post Office Box 543 Auburn, NY 13021 (16)

Lochead, Glen H., Putnam County Arts Council 1817 Putnam Unionville, MO 63565 816-947-2284 (5)

Locke, Richard, Greenville Musicians' Association Post Office Box 73 Greenville, OH 45331 513-548-6714 (18)

Locklear, Carolyn, Decatur Arts Council Post Office Box 173 Decatur, AL 35601 205-355-3422 (5)

Lockleor, Carmell, Strike at the Wind Theatre Post Office Box 1059 Pembroke, NC 28372 919-521-2489 (16)

Lockrow, A., Indiana University Department of Theatre Theatre by the Grove Indiana, PA 15705 412-357-2965 (4)

Lockwood, Mrs. Mardell J., Missoula Professional Musicians' Association 315 Westview Drive Missoula, MT 59802 406-728-3473 (18)

Lockwood, Dr. Patton, Longwood College Department of Theatre Farmville, VA 23901 804-392-9371 (4)

Loeffler, Donald L., University and College Theatre Association 1010 Wisconsin Avenue, NW Washington, DC 20007 (5)

Loessin, Edgar R., East Carolina University Department of Theatre Greenville, NC 27834 919-757-6390 (4)

Loftesness, Roy, Sioux Empire Arts Council 1817 South Sherman Sioux Falls, SD 57105 605-336-2850 (5)

Logan, Billie, Peeko Puppet Productions Post Office Box 363 Park Ridge, IL 60068 312-823-8778 (16)

Logan, Chuck, Elmo Manufacturing Corporation Post Office Box 828 Woodland Hills, CA 91367 213-346-4500 (15)

Logan, Drewry, Friends of the Hopkins Center Dartmouth College Hanover, NH 03755 603-646-2006 (5)

Logan, Leroy, Bennington College Department of Theatre Bennington, VT 05201 802-442-5401 (4)

Logan, Nedda Harrigan, Actors' Fund Medal, Award of Merit Actor's Fund of America New York, NY 10036 212-221-7300 (3)

Logothetis, Richard F., Lycian Stage Lighting 385 Central Avenue Bohemia, NY 11716 516-589-3939 (15)

Lohrey, Sherwood, Theatre Memphis 630 Perkins Extended Memphis, TN 38117 901-682-8323 (8)

Lohrey, Sherwood, Theatre Memphis 630 Perkins Extended Memphis, TN 38119 901-682-8323; 901-682-0264 (16)

Loiars, Frank R., Lockport Federation of Musicians, Local 97 6279 Hamm Road Lockport, NY 14094 716-434-2229 (18)

loisMarshall, Dean, Bergen County Cultural Commission Bergen Community College, 400 Paramus Road Paramus, NJ 07652 201-477-1500 (5)

Lomax, Mrs. Dan, Waynesboro Little Theatre Post Office Box 281 Waynesboro, MS 39367 (16)

Lombard, John, Scottish Rite Auditorium 431 West Berry Street Fort Wayne, IN 46802 219-423-2593 (8)

Lombard, Joseph P., Needham Drama Workshop 5 Manning Street Needham, MA 02194 617-444-1178 (16)

Long, Dayton, Atmore Council of Fine Arts 102 South Pensacola Atmore, AL 36502 205-368-3640 (5)

Long, Greg, Back Stage Lighting 878 Pearl Street Eugene, OR 97400 (15)

Long, J., Morgan City Players Post Office Box 157 Fort Morgan, CO 80701 (16)

Long, Kenneth, Fairmount Center for Performing Arts Department of Theatre 1925 Coventry Road Cleveland Heights, OH 44118 216-932-2000 (4)

Longacre, Allan, City Arts Department 250 Hamilton Avenue Palo Alto, CA 94306 405-329-2122 (5)

Loo, Bessie, Bessie Loo Agency 8730 Sunset Boulevard Los Angeles, CA 90069 213-657-5888 (2)

Loosemore, Marianna, Cedar Crest College Department of Theatre Allentown, PA 18104 215-437-4471 (4)

Lopez, Miguel A., Miguel A. Lopez 825 West 31st Street Hialeah, FL 33012 305-822-6853 (15)

Loranger, Donald, Musical Society, Local 81 205 Liden Street Anaconda, MT 59711 406-563-3385 (18)

Lord, Kathleen, Unity College Department of Theatre Unity, ME 04988 207-948-3131 (4)

Lord, William, Ontario Arts Council 151 Bloor Street West Toronto, Ontario, Canada M5S 1T6 416-961-1660 (5)

Lorden, T.C., Souhegan Valley Theatre Mount Vernon Street Milford, NH 03055 (8)

Lorendeau, Yvon, ASSITEJ-Canadian Centre 4808 Saint Denis Street Montreal, Quebec, Canada H2J 2L6 514-288-9343 (5)

Lott, Robert C., Asphalt Players Post Office Box 7377 Birmingham, AL 35223 205-879-0411 (16)

Lottrall, David L., W.B. Geary Auditorium University of Charleston Charleston, WV 25304 304-346-9471 (8)

Loubier, Mrs. C. B., Waterville Players Augusta Road Waterville, ME 04901 (16)

Loucks, Grant, Alan Gordon Enterprises, Inc. 1430 North Cahuenga Boulevard Hollywood, CA 90028 213-466-3561 (15)

Lough, JoAnn, Fairmont State College Department of Theatre Fairmont, WV 26554 304-367-4219 (4)

Lough, Jo Ann, Masquers/Town and Gown Players Fine Arts Department Fairmont State College Fairmont, WV 26554 304-367-4248; 304-367-4240 (15)

Lough, Jo Ann, Masquers/Town and Gown Players Fine Arts Department Fairmont, WV 26554 304-367-4248; 304-367-4240 (16)

Louis, William J., Avila College Department of Performing and Visual Arts 11901 Wornall Road Kansas City, MO 64145 816-942-8400; 816-942-8408 (box office) (4)

Louis, Dr. William J., Goppert Theatre 11901 Wornall Road Kansas City, MO 64145 816-942-8400 (8)

Louis, Dr. William J., Goppert Theatre 11901 Wornall Road Kansas City, MD 64145 816-942-8400 (16)

Lounzer, William, University of South Florida Department of Theatre Tampa, FL 33620 813-974-2701; 813-974-2603 (4)

Loup, Alfred J., University of Michigan, Flint Department of Theatre 1321 East Court Flint, MI 48503 313-762-3230 (4)

Love, Dr. Herschel D., Southern Appalachia Consortium Arts Council Southern Union State Junior College Wadley, AL 36276 205-395-2211

Extension 39 (5)

Love, Marion H., Lenior-Rhyne College Department of Theatre Hickory, NC 28603 704-328-1741, Ext. 253 (4)

Love, Matt, Apple Core Playhouse Post Office Box P Lake Chelan, WA 98816 509-682-2814 (8)

Lovegren, Joseph, Greater Portland Arts Council 334 Fore Street Portland, ME 04111 207-774-5743 (5)

Low, Roy, Lowel-Light Mfg., Incorporated 3407 West Olive Avenue Burbank, CA 91505 213-846-7740 (15)

Lowe, Jerry M., Players Guild of Canton 1001 Market Avenue Canton, OH 44702 216-453-7619 (16)

Lowenstein, Henry E., Denver Center for the Performing Arts-Bonfils Theatre East Colfax at Elizabeth Denver, CO 80206 303-322-7725, Box Office; 303-399-5418, Other Departments (16)

Lowman, Zel, Nevada Alliance for the Arts 821 Las Vegas Boulevard Las Vegas, NV 89101 702-384-1208 (5)

Lowrey, Glynn, Free Street Theater 59 West Hubbard Chicago, IL 60610 312-822-0460 (16)

Loy, Harold W., Pittsburg State University Department of Theatre Pittsburg, KS 66762 316-231-7000, Ext. 340 (4)

Loy, Mike, Musicians' Protective Union Post Office Box 566 Pittsburg, KS 66762 316-231-5220 (18)

Loyd, Al, Ed Landreth Auditorium School of Fine Arts Fort Worth, TX 76129 817-926-2461 (8)

Lubeley, George, Arts and Science Center 14 Court Street Nashua, NH 03060 603-883-1506 (8)

Lucas, Charles, Charles Lucas Sales Company Post Office Box 24632 Dallas, TX 75224 214-330-8181 (15)

Lucas, John R., Charles Beseller Company 8 Fernwood Road Florham Park, NJ 07932 201-822-1000 (15)

Lucke, Ron, San Antonio College Department of Theatre 1300 San Pedro Avenue San Antonio, TX 78284 512-734-5381 (4)

Ludlow, Merrel B., Beck Studios, Incorporated 5614 Wooster Pike Cincinnati, OH 45227 513-271-0080 (15)

Ludtke, George, Michigan City Federation of Musicians 811 Greenwood Avenue Michigan City, IN 46360 219-874-5394 (18)

Luebcke, Elmer R., Musicians' Protective Association Route 5, Box 1970 Rhinelander, WI 54501 715-362-2787 (18)

Luebke, Dana, Sun Ergos 2205, 700 - 9th Street, South West Calgary, Alberta, Canada T2P 2B5 403-264-4621 (16)

Lueke, Betsy, Burbank Fine Arts Federation 110 West Clark Burbank, CA 91510 (5)

Lull, George T., Greater Springfield Musicians' Association, Local 171 134 Chestnut Street Springfield, MA 01103 413-736-5187 (18)

Lumsden, Doland, Kean College of New Jersey Department of Theatre Morris Avenue Union, NJ 07083 201-527-2107 (4)

Lunceford, Mrs. Bolton, Georgia Theatre Conference Pembroke Hall Crawfordville, GA 30631 (5)

Lund, Alan, Charlottetown Festival Post Office Box 848 Charlottetown, Prince Edward Island, Canada C1A 7L9 902-892-2464 (16)

Lund, Marlene, Southeast Alaska Regional Arts Council c/o Sitka Community College, Box 2133 Sitka, AK 99835 907-747-6653 (5)

Lundahl, Lester, Richard Daley College Department of Theatre Chicago, IL 60652 (4)

Lundberg, Clifford, Elk River Community Theatre 310 King Street Elk River, MN 55330 (16)

Lundrigan, Paul J., High Point College Department of Theatre 933 Montlieu Avenue High Point, NC 27262 919-885-5105 (4)

Lundy, Elizabeth C., Theatre 2000 62 George Street Ottawa, Ontario, Canada K1N 5V9 416-233-2957 (16)

Lupien, Jack, Muskegon Musicians' Association, Local 252 169 East Broadway Muskegon Heights, MI 49444 616-733-2227 (18)

Lussier, Joan, Barrington Players Post Office Box 107 Barrington, RI 02806 (16)

Luter, Gary, University of Tampa Department of Drama 401 West Kennedy Tampa, FL 33606 813-253-8861 (4)

Lutz, Daniel, Musicians' Protective Association, Local 211 170 Mount Vernon Street Pottstown, PA 19464 215-323-3136 (18)

Luzine, Elaine, Guilderland League of Arts Post Office Box 305 Guilderland Center, NY 12085 716-456-2913 (5)

Lydecker, Mrs. John, Stagecrafters 153 Elder Avenue Bergenfield, NJ 07621 201-385-1298 (16)

Lynch, Robert, Arts Extension Service University of Massachusetts Amherst, MA 01003 413-545-2360 (5)

Lynde, Gail, Brattleboro Museum and Art Center Post Office Box 800 Brattleboro, VT 05301 802-257-0124 (8)

Lynn, A., Potomac Playhouse 4949 Battery Lane Bethesda, MD 20014 (16)

Lynn, Margaret, American Theatre Association 1010 Wisconsin Avenue, NW Washington, DC 20005 202-342-7530 (5)

Lyon, Yoland, Roosevelt University Department of Theatre 430 South Michigan Avenue Chicago, IL 60605 312-341-3720 (4)

Lyons, Charles, Stanford University Department of Theatre Stanford, CA 94305 415-497-2300 (4)

Lyons, Helen E., National Arts Jobbank 141 East Palace Avenue Santa Fe, NM 87501 505-988-1166 (14)

Lyons, Ian R., Pontiac Arts Council 47 Williams Street Pontiac, MI 48053 313-333-7849 (5)

Lyons, James E., University Press of America 4720 Boston Way Lanham, MD 20706 301-459-3366 (14)

Lysell, Allan, Northern Light Theatre 10189 - 99 Street Edmonton, Alberta, Canada T5J 0N2 403-426-4292; 403-429-3110 (16)

M

Maas, Mrs. Al, Watertown Arts Council Post Office Box 204 Watertown, WI 53180 414-261-6913 (5)

Maas, James, Musicians' Protective Association Rural Route 5, Box 111 Fairbault, MN 55021 507-334-6668 (18)

Maass, Dy, Theatre Max Post Office Box 1744 Guelph, Ontario, Canada N1H 6Z9 519-824-2714 (16)

MacArthur, Phillip R., Syracuse Musicians Protective Association, Local 78 131 Butler Street Syracuse, NY 13210 315-472-3056 (18)

Macbeth, Bruce, Fine Arts Committee Hardy County Library Association Post Office Box 653 Moorefield, WV 26836 304-538-6560 (5)

MacCallum, Heather Lea, Edmonton Actors' Workshop 8909 - 112 Street Hub Building Edmonton, Alberta, Canada T6G 2C5 403-433-2421 (16)

Maccarillo, Joe Jr., Sun Valley Musicians' Association 302 Elm Street Twin Falls, ID 83301 208-726-9681 (18)

MacDonald, Joseph, Boston Musicians' Association, Local 9-535 56 St. Botolph Street Boston, MA 02116 617-536-2486 (18)

Macdonald, Samuel K., Samuel K. Macdonald, Inc. 1531 Spruce Street Philadelphia, PA 19102 215-545-1205 (15)

Maceda, Joseph, Broadway Productions, Incorporated 51-02 27th Street Long Island City, NY 11101 212-392-0020 (15)

Macintosh, James, Orange Belt Musicians' Association, Local 167 405 Palm Avenue Redlands, CA 92373 714-824-1450 (18)

Mack, W., Cultural Arts Community Gatesville Messenger Gatesville, TX 76528 (16)

Mackay, Norman L., The Road Show Theatre Company 122 Harris Street Guelph, Ontario, Canada N1H 6L8 519-823-2381 (16)

MacKay, Patricia, Theatre Crafts 250 West 57th Street, Suite 312 New York, NY 10019 212-582-4110 (14)

Mackey, Karl A., Lakewood Little Theatre 17801 Detroit Avenue Lakewood, OH 44107 216-521-2540 (16)

Mackie, John, Calgary Musicians' Association 630 Eighth Avenue SW, #703 Calgary, Alberta, Canada T2P 1G6 403-264-4727 (18)

Mackinnon, Mrs. Cyrus L., Actors Theatre of Louisville, Incorporated 316-320 West Main Street Louisville, KY 40202 502-584-1265 (16)

MacKinnon, Theresa, Canadian Child and Youth Drama Association 318 Towerview Place Sydney, Nova Scotia, Canada B1S 3B8 902-539-1995 (5)

MacMahon, Paul, Elmo Canada Manufacturing Corporation 44 West Drive Brampton, Ontario, Canada L6T 3T6 416-453-7880 (15)

MacNeil, Lynn, South Florida Junior College Department of Theatre Avon Park, FL 33825 813-453-6661, Ext. 192 (4)

MacPherson, Herbert, Youngstown Federation of Musicians, Local 86-242 2520 South Avenue Youngstown, OH 44502 216-788-8451 (18)

MacSween, Donald, National Arts Centre Box 1534, Station B Ottawa, Ontario, Canada K1P 5W1 613-996-5051; 613-237-4400 (16)

Madden, Edward L., Florida Atlantic University Department of Theatre Boca Raton, FL 33431 305-395-5100; 305-395-2502 (4)

Madden, Tom, Pan Asian Repertory Theatre 305 Riverside Drive New York, NY 10025 212-662-7171; 212-475-7710 (16)

Maddox, Craig, Electronic Services, Incorporated 690-G Kakoi Street Honolulu, HI 96816 808-847-4891 (15)

Maddox, Ester, Spring Arbor College Department of Theatre Spring Arbor, MI 49283 517-750-1200, Ext. 265 (4)

Madel, R. P., Waseca Players 304 North East 6th Waseca, MN 56093 (16)

Maffongelli, Ralph, Pit and Six Balcony Theatre 805 North Hamilton Saginaw, MI 48602 (16)

Magill, Frank N., Salem Press 550 Sylvan Avenue Engelwood Cliffs, NJ 07632 201-871-3700 (14)

Maginnis, Mrs. E.J., Baton Rouge Little Theater Post Office Box 1943 Baton Rouge, LA 70821 504-924-6496 (8)

Magnus, Ilene, Wellesley Children's Theatre 4 Mansfield Road Wellesley, MA 02181 617-235-5–29 (16)

Mahe, Roland, Le Cercle Moliere C.P.1 Saint-Boniface, Manitoba, Canada R2H 3B4 204-233-8053 (16)

Maher, Robert C., Worcester Cultural Commission 253 Belmont Street Worcester, MA 01605 617-799-1325; 617-799-1326 (5)

Maheu, Gilles, Les Enfants du Paradis B.P. 883, Succ. A Montreal, Quebec, Canada H3C 2V8 514-845-5598 (16)

Mahoney, John, Four Star Stage Lighting 585 Gerard Avenue Bronx, NY 10451 212-993-0471 (15)

Mahoney, Patricia, Theatre Go Round Post Office Box 1180 Petrolia, Ontario, Canada N0N 1R0 519-882-1221 (16)

Mahoney, Patricia, Victoria Playhouse Post Office Box 1180 Petrolia, Ontario, Canada N0N 1R0 416-822-1221 (16)

Mahson, Jean M., Seattle Puppetry Theatre 13002 10th Avenue, NW Seattle, WA 98177 206-365-0100 (16)

Mailloux, Denis, Theatre Du Trident 975 Place d'Youville Quebec City, Quebec, Canada G1R 3P1 418-692-2202 (16)

Main, Peter, Co-ordinated 137 Yonge Street Toronto, Ontario, Canada M5C 1W6 416-368-1024 (5)

Main, William E., Frederick Town Players 501 Prospect Boulevard Frederick, MD 21701 (16)

Maingast, Jack, Decorators Supply Corporation 3610-12 South Morgan Street Chicago, IL 60609 312-847-6300 (15)

Mainwarling, Donald, Principia College Department of Theatre Elsah, IL 62028 618-966-2131 (4)

Major, Claire, Gingnol Puppet Theater Gooding High School Route 1 Gooding, ID 83330 208-934-4831 (16)

Major, James R., Panola Playhouse Post Office Box 13 Sardis, MS 38666 (16)

Major, John G., Musicians' Federation, Local 218 808 West Kaye Avenue Marquette, MI 49855 906-228-8800 (18)

Majur, Dr. Charles E., Depot-In-The-Park Orr Municipal Park Montevallo, AL 35115 205-665-1591 (8)

Majure, Charles E., Shelly County Community Theatre Post Office Box 33 Montevallo, AL 35115 205-344-1537 (16)

Malek, John, James Fackert Cae Incorporated Post Office Box 430 Hamburg, MI 48139 313-231-9373 (15)

Mallardi, Vincent, Mutual Hardware Corporation 5-45 49th Avenue Long Island City, NY 11101 212-361-2480 (15)

Mallare, Vincent F., Jamestown Musical Association, Local 134 7 Campbell Avenue Jamestown, NY 14701 716-665-3458 (18)

Mallett, Lew, Musicians' Guild of Essex County, Local 16 Suburban Office Plaza 141 South Harrison Street East Orange, NJ 07018 201-675-1333 (18)

Malmgren, D.E., Colorado Children's Theatre 1750 Willow Street Denver, CO 80220 (16)

Malmgren, Donald E., Temple Buell College Department of Theatre Denver, CO 80220 (4)

Malstream, David, Geneva County Arts and Crafts Association Post Office Box 62 Samson, AL 36477 (5)

Mamerow, Russell, Musicians' Protective Association 7676 Carriage Lane Boise, IL 83704 208-375-8008 (18)

Mamuscia, James, Musical Union, Local 239 243 West Genesee Street Auburn, NY 13021 315-253-3345 (18)

Manchester, Charles, Allied Arts Council of Metropolitan Mobile 401 Auditorium Drive Mobile, AL 36602 205-432-9796 (5)

Mancini, Marlene, HB Playwrights Foundation 122 Bank Street New York, NY 10014 212-989-6540 (16)

Mancuso, Charles, Omaha Civic Auditorium 1804 Capitol Avenue Omaha, NB 68102 402-346-1323 (8)

Mancuso, Charles J., Orpheum Theater 409 South 16th Street Omaha, NB 68102 402-346-1323 (8)

Manfredo, Ralph, Musicians' Protective Association, Local 210 1739 West Celeste Fresno, CA 93711 209-439-3793 (18)

Manganelli, Edmond P., Mew Kensington Musical Society Sons of Italy Building New Kensington, PA 15068 412-335-6651 (18)

Mange, Diana, Unicorn Theatre Workshop 3514 Jefferson Kansas City, MO 64111 (16)

Manifold, Gay, University of LaVerne Department of Theatre La Verne, CA 91750 714-593-3511, Ext. 248, 364, 365; 213-629-1066 (4)

Mankiss, Bill, Chatham Federation of Musicians 14 Forest Street Chatham, Ontario, Canada N71 1Z7 519-352-3902 (18)

Mann, Ted, Circle in the Square 1633 Broadway New York, NY 10019 212-581-3270 (13)

Mann, Theodore, Circle in the Square 1633 Broadway New York, NY 10019 212-581-3270; 212-581-0720 (16)

Manning, Benjamin C., Victoria Musicians' Association, Local 247 1241 Topaz Avenue Victoria, British Columbia, Canada V8T 2N1 604-382-7351 (18)

Manning, Lois, Cultural and Performing Arts Division Department of Community Services Town Hall-Audrey Avenue Oyster Bay, NY 11771 (5)

Manning, Thomas J., Teachers College of Columbia University Department of Theatre New York, NY 10027 212-678-3278 (4)

Manning, W. W., Musicians' Protective Union 238 Olive Street Virden, IL 62690 217-965-4113 (18)

Mansole, Phil, A World of Plastic 1517 South Elmhurst Road Elk Grove Village, IL 60007 312-956-6161 (15)

Manson, Mark, Theatre Network Post Office Box 4926 Edmonton, Alberta, Canada T6E 5G8 403-425-8761 (16)

Maxwell, Robert E., Augusta Federation of Musicians 219 Marion Street Southeast Aiken, SC 29801 803-648-7276 (18)

Mayer, Bob C., Tulsa Performing Arts Center Third and Cincinnati Tulsa, OK 74103 918-581-5641 (8)

Mayer, Harry, Mayer and Fisher, Incorporated 15 West 38th Street New York, NY 10018 212-840-8438 (15)

Mayer, John, Seaport Marketing 2054 127th South East Bellevue, WA 90085 206-641-5721 (15)

Mayer, Lyle, Ferris State College, Department of Theatre Department of Theatre Big Rapids, MI 49307 616-296-9971 (4)

Mayer, Ms. Sandi, Alabama League Community Theatre Division 1067 Cloverdale Drive Mobile, AL 36606 (16)

Maylett, William, Maylett Associates 4747 Kandel Court Annandale, VA 22003 703-354-6055; 703-354-5368 (15)

Maynard, Jack, Waukegan Federation of Musicians 2500 North Walnut Waukegan, IL 60087 312-662-4738 (18)

Maynard, Mrs. Neil, Grand Prairie Art Council Post Office Box 65 Stuttgart, AR 72160 501-673-8586; 501-673-7278 (5)

Mays, Rolland, Musicians' Protective Association 719 South 15th Street Mount Vernon, IL 62864 618-242-7613 (18)

Mazumdar, Maxim, Theatre Newfoundland and Labrador c/o Arts and Culture Centre Saint John's, Newfoundland, Canada A1C 5P9 709-737-3650 (16)

Mazzaferri, Dr. Annette, Kutztown State College Department of Theatre College Hill Kutztown, PA 19530 215-683-4400 (4)

Mazzaglia, Irene, Musicians' Protective Union 163 Oakside Avenue Methuen, MA 01844 617-686-2744 (18)

Mazzucchi, Tony, See Factor Pacific, Incorporated 1420 Beachwood Drive Hollywood, CA 90028 213-469-7214 (15)

McAdams, Dr. Charles, Grayson County College Department of Theatre 6101 Highway 691 Denison, TX 75020 214-893-6834 (4)

McAnaulty, Sara, Lurleen B. Wallace State Junior College Post Office Box 1418 Andalusia, AL 36420 205-222-6591 (4)

McAuley, Muriel, Barksdale Theatre Hanover Tavern Hanover, VA 23069 804-838-5650 (8)

McAuliffe, Mike, Westinghouse Electric Corporation Post Office Box 519 Granby, Quebec, Canada 514-378-0470 (15)

McBride, Bill, Luna Tech 822 Demasters Street Huntsville, AL 35801 205-533-1487; 205-533-1489 (15)

McBride, Jo, Grant Arts and Humanities Council Post Office Box 70 Grant, AL 205-728-4205 (5)

McCachren, Hoyt M., Catawa College Department of Theatre West Innes Street Salisbury, NC 28144 704-637-4417 (4)

McCall, Fiona, Harbourfront Studio Theatre 235 Queen's Quay West Toronto, Ontario, Canada M5J 2G8 416-364-7127; 416-869-8412 (8)

McCall, M. Tulis, Women I Have Known Theatre 81 Perry Street New York, NY 10014 212-929-1071 (16)

McCall, Randy, Austin Federation of Musicians 302 West 15th, Suite 204 Austin, TX 78701 512-476-6798 (18)

McCall, Tulis, Potter's Field Theatre Company 2 Bond Street New York, NY 10012 212-260-1213 (16)

McCandles, Robert, Musicians' Protective Union Post Office Box 142 Somers, MT 59932 406-857-3560 (18)

McCarter, Brooke, Klopf Audio/Video Company 3381 Successful Way Dayton, OH 45414 513-236-5500 (15)

McCarthy, Fran, Kenyon Martin Mime Troupe-National Mime Theatre 419 Boylston, Suite 510 Boston, MA 02116 617-353-1440 (16)

McCarthy, Tom, George Mitchell 6 Adams Road Framingham, MA 01701 617-872-7610; 612-941-1700 (15)

McCaughna, David, Tarragon Theatre 30 Bridgman Avenue Toronto, Ontario, Canada M5R 1X3 416-531-1827 (16)

McClain, Dr. Barbara, Trevecca Nazarene College Department of Theatre 333 Murfreesboro Road Nashville, TN 37210 615-244-6000 Extension 374 (4)

McClain, Don, Don McClain 1345 Northeast 109th Portland, OR 97220 503-253-5527 (15)

McCloskey, James R., Los Angeles City College Department of Theatre Los Angeles, CA 90029 (4)

McClung, Marcia, Marcia McClung c/o National Ballet of Canada Toronto, Ontario, Canada M5C 1G9 416-362-1041 (12)

McConnaughay, Robert J., Dixon Musicians' Union 503 South Dixon Avenue Dixon, IL 61021 815-284-3057 (18)

McConnell, Peter J., Smile Theatre Company 121 Avenue Road Toronto, Ontario, Canada M5R 2G3 416-961-0050 (16)

McCord, Dr. Clarence, Georgia Southern College Department of Theatre Milledgville, GA 30458 912-681-5600 (4)

McCoy, Dr. William, Wayside Foundation for the Arts Wayside Theatre Middletown, VA 22645 703-869-1782 (10)

McCreight, John W., Wahington Musical Society, Local 277 865 William Street Washington, PA 15301 412-225-9790 (18)

McCrory, Jerry, Thomasville Arts and Humanities Council Post Office Box 107 Thomasville, AL 36784 205-636-5731 (5)

McCullough, Douglas, University of Calgary Department of Drama 2500 University Drive, NW Calgary, Alberta, Canada T2N 1N4 403-284-5421 (4)

McCullough, Miss GLoria J., Portland Musicians' Association 27 Fleetwood Street Portland, ME 04102 207-774-6757 (18)

McCullough, John, Globe Theatre 1850 Smith Street Regina, Saskatchewan, Canada S4P 2N3 306-525-9553 (16)

McCullough, Mary, Peter Wolf Associates, Inc. 8181 Hoyle Dallas, TX 75227 214-388-3461 (15)

McCullough, R.B., Smith-Victor Corporation 301 North Colfax Griffith, IN 46319 219-924-6136; 800-348-9862 (15)

McCully, Carol, Queens Council on the Arts 161-04 Jamaica Avenue Jamaica, NY 11432 212-291-1100 (5)

McDaniel, Craig, John Michael Kohler Arts Center 608 New York Avenue Sheboygan, WI 53081 414-458-6144 (8)

McDaniel, Henry A. Jr., Freed-Hardeman College Department of Communication/Theatre 158 East Main Street Henderson, TN 38340 901-989-4611 (4)

McDonald, Arthur, Saint Andrews Presbyterian College Department of Theatre McCall Highway Laurinburg, NC 28352 919-276-3652 (4)

McDonald, Larry, Great Canadian Theatre Company Post Office Box 4223, Station E Ottawa, Ontario, Canada K1S 5B2 613-236-5192 (16)

McDonald, Mike, Mid-West Scenic and Stage Equipment Company, Ltd. 224 East Bruce Street Milwaukee, WI 53204 414-276-2707 (15)

McDonnell, C., Plaster of Paris Players Post Office Box 603 Platte, SD 57062 (16)

McDougall, Charles A., L and M Stagecraft, Incorporated 2110 Superior Avenue Cleveland, OH 44114 216-621-4752 (15)

McDowell, Mrs. Stephen R., Nashville Academy Theatre 724 2nd Avenue Nashville, TN 37210 615-254-9103; 615-254-6020 (16)

McDowell, W. Stuart, Riverside Theatre Workshop 2710 Broadway New York, NY 10025 212-864-9672; 212-663-5420 (16)

McElderry, Ed, Lima Federation of Musicians 320 West Market Street Lima, OH 45801 419-228-0045 (18)

McEnnerney, Matthew, Performing Arts Guild Post Office Box 44 Forest City, NC 28043 704-245-8676 (5)

McFadden, John L., Laurie Auditorium Trinity University San Antonio, TX 78284 512-736-8119 (8)

McGauley, Walter, Actor's Theater for Children 3625 Yale Drive Santa Rosa, CA 95405 707-545-4307 (16)

McGee, George J., Palm Beach Atlantic College Department of Theatre West Palm Beach, FL 33401 305-883-8592 (4)

McGiffin, Mike, Potomac Lighting 105 North Virginia Avenue Falls Church, VA 22046 703-534-4550 (15)

McGill, Raymond D., James T. White and Company 1700 State Highway 3 Clifton, NJ 07013 201-773-9300 (14)

McGinnis, Bob, M.E.R. and Associates 7317 Cahill Road Edina, MN 55435 (15)

McGinnis, William M., Lexington Musicians' Association 116 Westgate Drive Lexington, KY 40504 606-255-4721 (18)

McGovern, Catherine, Mount Mary College Department of Oral Communication 1100 West 8th Yankton, SD 57078 605-668-1533 (4)

McGovern, Terrence, Peace College Department of Theatre 15 East Peace Street Raleigh, NC 27604 919-832-2881 (4)

McGraw, Rex, University of Nebraska, Lincoln Department of Theatre Lincoln, NB 68588 402-472-2072; 402-472-1619 (4)

McGraw, Rex, University of Nebraska Department of Theatre 103 Temple Building Lincoln, NB 68508 402-472-1606; 402-472-2072 (8)

McGraw, Rex, Nebraska Repertory Theatre 103 Temple Building Lincoln, NB 68508 402-472-1606,2072 (16)

McGregor, Duncan, Escarpment Theatre Co-Op Post Office Box 372 St. Catharines, Ontario, Canada L2R 6T7 416-682-8326; 416-684-6377 (16)

McGregor, Duncan, Carousel Players Post Office Box 372 St. Catherines, Ontario, Canada L2R 6T7 416-682-8326 (16)

McGuffin, Wayne E., Tri-City Musicians Association 521 West Sylvester Street Pasco, WA 99301 509-547-6698 (18)

McGuire, Mitch, Manhattan Punch Line 410 West 42nd Street New York, NY 10036 212-288-8288; 212-921-1455, Box Office (16)

McGuire, Pam, Village Players Post Office Box 165 Mukwonago, WI 53149 (16)

McHale, Bill, Country Dinner Playhouse 6526 North Central Dallas, TX 75206 (16)

Mchale, Michael, Bloomsburg State College Bloomsburg, PA 17815 717-389-3817 (4)

McHardy, Leonard, Stratford Festival Post Office Box 520 Stratford, Ontario, Canada N5A 6V2 519-271-4040; 416-273-1600 (9)

McIllrath, Dr. Patricia, University of Missouri, Kansas City Department of Theatre 51st and Rockhill Road Kansas City, MO 64110 816-276-2701 (4)

McIlrath, Patricia, Missouri Repertory Theatre 5100 Rockhill Road Kansas City, MO 64110 816-276-2701 (16)

McIntire, Lucy, Marlboro Area Arts Council 927 East Main Street Bennettsville, SC 29512 803-479-2192 (5)

McIntosh, Jamie L., Tulsa Musicians' Protective Association, Local 94 5525 East 32nd Place Tulsa, OK 74105 918-742-5097 (18)

McIntrye, Barbara M., University of Victoria Department of Theatre Post Office Box 1700 Victoria, British Columbia, Canada V8W 2Y2 604-477-6911; 604-721-7992 (4)

McIntyre, Bob, Seven Arts Society Reformed Church of Bronxville Bronxville, NY 10708 914-337-6776 (16)

McIntyre, James, Durham Arts Council 810 West Proctor Street Durham, NC 27707 919-682-5519 (5)

McIrvin, Calvin C., Stagecraft Industries, Incorporated Post Office Box 660 Bellevue, WA 98009 206-454-3089; 503-226-7351 (15)

McIrvin, Dan, Stagecraft Industries, Incorporated 913 Tanklage Road San Carlos, CA 94070 415-592-8885 (15)

McKay, M.L., Tennessee Technological University Department of Theatre Cookeville, TN 38501 615-528-3478 (4)

McKenna, Ed, Mulgrave Road Co-operative Theatre Compay Post Office Box 219 Guysborough, Nova Scotia, Canada B0H 1N0 902-533-2092 (16)

McKenna, Frank C., Musicians' Protective Union 1100 First Avenue, SW Great Falls, MT 59401 406-452-3962 (18)

McKenzie, James B., Penninsula Players Theatre Foundation Fish Creek, WI 54212 414-868-3287 (16)

McKenzie, James B., Theatre-in-a-Garden Fish Creek, WI 54212 414-868-3287; 414-868-3288 (16)

McKenzie, Ken, Cetec Gauss 13035 Saticoy Street North Hollywood, CA 91605 213-875-1900 (15)

McKinney, Bud, Belden Communications Preferred Distributing Los Angeles, CA 90028 213-461-4201 (15)

McKinney, Jack F., Jack F. McKinney Sales Co. 1303 Chemical Street Dallas, TX 76207 214-631-9450 (15)

McKuen, Rod, American Guild of Variety Artists (AGVA) 184 5th Avenue New York, NY 10010 212-675-1003 (18)

McLane, B., Greenville Little Theatre 444 College Street Greenville, SC 29601 (16)

McLauglin, Robert, Drew University Department of Theatre 36 Madison Avenue Madison, NJ 07940 201-377-3000 (4)

McLean, Donald L., Musicians' Protective Union 10820 South East 231st Kent, WA 98031 206-852-6695 (18)

McLeran, P.D., Community College of Denver Department of Theatre 3645 West 112th Avenue Westminster, CO 80030 (4)

McLynch, Dennis, Wayside Theatre on Tour Wayside Theatre Middletown, VA 22645 Box-Off-ce 703 839 1776; Adm-nis-rative Office, 703 869 1782 (16)

McMahon, J., The Superior Electric Company 383 Middle Street Bristol, CT 06020 203-582-9561 (15)

McMaken, Kenneth K., Piqua Musicians' Association 1201 Park Avenue Piqua, OH 45356 513-773-2665 (18)

McMillan, Mrs. George L., Bullock County Arts Council Route 1 Union Springs, AL 36089 205-474-3385 (5)

McMillan, Hazel, Hazel McMillan Agency 7805 Sunset Boulevard Los Angeles, CA 90046 213-276-9823 (2)

McMillen, Richard, Amarillo Federation of Musicians 2608 Northwest 2nd Avenue Amarillo, TX 79106 806-374-2532 (18)

McMillen, William E., Colorado College Department of Theatre Colorado Springs, CO 80903 303-473-2233 (4)

McMullan, Marion, Rohnert Park Cultural Arts Corporation 435 Southwest Boulevard Rohnert Park, CA 94928 707-795-5416 (5)

McNair, Rick, Stage Coach Players 830 8th Avenue South West Calgary, Alberta, Canada T2P 1L7 403-262-2146 (16)

McNair, Rick, Theatre 830 9th Avenue South West Calgary, Alberta, Canada T2P 1L7 403-262-2146; 403-265-6700 (16)

McPhee, Norman C., Racine Memorial Hall 72 Seventh Street Racine, WI 53404 414-636-9169 (8)

McPhee, Norman C., Racine Theatre Guild 2519 Northwestern Avenue Racine, WI 53404 414-633-1250 (8)

McPherson, Frank C., Frank C. McPherson Associates Post Office Box 800 Pinellas Park, FL 33565 813-577-3300 (15)

McReynolds, Shirley, Maryland National Capital Park/Planning Commission Arts Division 6600 Kenilworth Avenue Riverdale, MD 20737 301-699-2450; 301-699-2452 (5)

McTeague, James, University of Alberta Department of Theatre Edmonton, Alberta, Canada T6G 2C9 403-432-2771 (4)

McVey, Carol, Lincoln Community Playhouse 2500 South 56th Street Lincoln, NE 68506 402-489-9608 (16)

McWilliam, W., Playcrafters Coaltown Road and 49th Moline, IL 61265 (16)

Mead, Hyrum, Electro Controls, Incorporated 2975 South 300 West Salt Lake City, UT 84115 801-487-9861 (15)

Meagher, Joel, Ansell-Simplex Ticket Company 2970 Maria Avenue Northbrook, IL 60062 312-291-0696 (15)

Medoff, Mark, New Mexico State University Department of Theatre Arts Las Cruces, NM 88003 505-646-4517 (4)

Meduitz, Richard, Theatre Vision 5426 Fair Avenue North Hollywood, CA 91601 213-769-0928 (15)

Meehan, Donald, Musicians' Protective Union 3545 Oxford Street Napa, CA 94558 707-226-7736 (18)

Meekins, G. Page, Waterside Theatre Post Office Box 40 Manteo, NC 27954 919-473-2127 (8)

Mego, Dr. Joseph, Hatford County Cultural Advisory Commission Essex Community College Baltimore County, MD 21237 301-682-6000 (5)

Mehl, Dr. James, Missouri Western State College Department of Theatre 4525 Downs Drive Saint Joesph, MO 64507 816-271-4397 (4)

Meier, Nancy N., Arts Alliance of Washington State c/o Edmonds Community College Lynwood, WA 98036 206-775-8551 (5)

Meier, Paul, Market House Theatre Paducah, KY 42001 (16)

Meikle, James L., Beacon Hill Theatre School of the Ozarks Point Lookout, MO 65726 417-334-6411, ext. 339, summer; 417-334-6411, ext. 437, all year (16)

Meils, C., Wisconsin Rapids 810 Witter Street Wisconsin Rapids, WI 54494 (16)

Melanson, Barbara S., Auburn Players Community Theatre Post Office Box 543 Auburn, NY 13021 (16)

Melanson, Ivan, Cape Benton Musicians' Association Post Office Box 1282 Sidney, Nova Scotia, Canada (18)

Melaro, Angelo, Olean-Salmanca Musicians' Union, Local 115-614 122 North 21st Street Olean, NY 14760 716-372-3583 (18)

Melhuish, Paul S., University of Portland Department of Theatre 5000 North Willamette Boulevard Portland, OR 97203 503-283-7228 (4)

Melia, Louis, Association of Professional Musicians, Local 204 146 Highway No. 1, #25 Edison, NJ 08817 201-572-2832 (18)

Melonian, Gary, Fraerman Yard Goods and Draperies Company 314 West Adams Street Chicago, IL 60606 312-236-6886; 312-236-6887 (15)

Melton, Joe, Musicians' Protective Association Route 2 Lena, WI 54139 414-834-5153 (18)

Melville, Lee, Hollywood Drama-Logue Post Office Box 38771 Los Angeles, CA 90028 213-464-5079 (14)

Memmel, R.O., Cameo House, Ltd. 3828 W. North Avenue Milwaukee, WI 53208 414-449-1281 (15)

Menary, Don, Musicians' Union, Local 6 230 Jones Street San Francisco, CA 94102 415-775-8118 (18)

Mendelson, Steven, New London Barn Players Post Office Box 285 New London, NH 03257 603-526-4631 (16)

Mendez, Luis A. Jr., Musicians' Protective Association, Local 159 161 Hilltop Road Mansfield, OH 44906 419-529-2754 (18)

Menefer, Larry, Branding Iron Theatre West Texas State University Canyon, TX 79016 806-656-3248 (16)

Meng, John, Old Dominion Technology Theatre Old Dominion University 46th and Hampton Boulevard Norfolk, VA 23508 804-440-4373; 804-440-4423 (8)

Menke, James E., Jim Menke Marionette Theatre 99 Northwood Drive Kenmore, NY 14233 716-876-7869 (16)

Meredith, D.G., Johns-Manville Sales Corporation Ken-Caryl Ranch Denver, CO 80217 303-979-1000 (15)

Merinat, Eric, Les Marionettes Merinat 412 - 3500 Varsity Drive Northwest Calgary, Alberta, Canada T2L 1Y3 403-282-2226 (16)

Merkel, Robert P., Monroe City-County Fine Arts Council 1555 South Raisinville Road Monroe, MI 48161 313-242-7300 (5)

Mermes, Harriet, Needham Youth Summer Theatre 651 Central Avenue Needham, MA 02194 617-444-7351 (16)

Merrifield, Maxine, Musicians' Protective Union, Local 113 FPost Office Box 696 Central Valley, CA 96019 916-241-2441 (18)

Merrill, Frank E., Merrill Stage Equipment 6520 Westfield Boulevard Indianapolis, IN 46220 317-255-4666 (15)

Merrill, Henry, Earlham College Department of Theatre Richmond, IN 47374 317-962-6561 (4)

Merrill, James, University of Delaware Press 326 Hullihen Hall Newark, DE 19711 302-738-1149 (14)

Merrill, Mrs. Katherine, Arts Institute of Western Maine Corner of Main and Anson Streets Farmington, ME 04938 207-778-3475 (5)

Merson, Georges, Duro-Test Electric Ltd. 419 Attwell Drive Rexdale, Ontario, Canada M9W 5W5 416-675-1623; 416-675-1624 (15)

Mertzig, Louis C. Jr., Musical Society, Local 81 205 Liden Street Anaconda, MT 59711 406-563-3385 (18)

Mesner, Paul, Puppet Theater Museum 511 South 11th Omaha, NB 68102 402-342-1313 (16)

Mesnick, Jack, Jack Mesnick Sales 13 Juneberry Lane Liverpool, NY 13088 315-622-3211 (15)

Messer, Miriam, Iowa Wesleyan Chapel Auditorium Iowa Wesleyan College Mount Pleasant, IA 52641 319-385-8021 (8)

Metcalfe, Dr. William, Ira Allen Chapel University of Vermont Burlington, VT 05401 802-656-3040 (8)

Metro, Americo, Musicians' Mutual Protective Union Post Office Box 243 Sault Ste., MI 49783 906-635-5371 (18)

Metz, Leonard H., Workshop Theatre of South Carolina Post Office Box 11555 Columbia, SC 29211 803-799-4876; 803-799-6551, Box Office (16)

Metzer, John P., Musicians' Protective Union R.D. No. 4, Post Office Box 277 Elizabethtown, PA 17022 717-684-7138 (18)

Meyer, Daniel P., Consolidated Papers, Inc. c/o Consolidated Civic Foundation, Inc. Wisconsin Rapids, WI 54494 715-442- 3368 (10)

Meyers, D., Memorex Corporation 1621 Walnut Hill Irving, TX 75062 (15)

Meyers, L. F., Wheeling Musical Society, Local 142 17th and Jacobs Streets Wheeling, WV 26003 304-233-0620 (18)

Michaud, George, George Michaud Agency 4950 Densmore Encino, CA 91436 213-981-6680 (2)

Michele, M., Mountaineer Dinner Theatre 3973 Teays Valley Road Hurricain, WV 25526 (16)

Michels, Lynn, The Open Space 133 Second Avenue New York, NY 10003 212-254-8630 (16)

Michelson, Catherine, Goddard College Department of Theatre Plainfield, VT 05667 802-454-8311 (4)

Mickelson, Gerald, Sturgeon Bay Federation of Musicians 936 North Seventh Place Sturgeon Bay, WI 54235 414-743-6319 (18)

Middlecamp, George, Central Wisconsin Musicians' Association 2830 37th Street North Wisconsin Rapids, WI 54494 715-421-0066 (18)

Middleton, Linda, Vero Beach Theatre Guild Post Office Box 4019 Vero Beach, FL 32960 305-562-1621 (16)

Mignanelli, Andrew A., Musicians' Protective Union, Local 82 205 Craig Street New Brighton, PA 15066 412-774-2602 (18)

Mignault, Guy, Theatre National de Mime du Quebec 4459 boul. St-Laurent Montreal, Quebec, Canada H2W 1Z8 514-521-2985 (16)

Milam, Marvin, Mintzer Auditorium Municipal Building Main Street Harrisonburg, VA 22801 (8)

Mildred, Sister M., Caldwell College Student Union Building Caldwell College Caldwell, NJ 07006 201-228-4424 (8)

Miles, Julia, American Place Theatre 111 West 46th Street New York, NY 10036 212-246-0393 (16)

Miles, Russell M., Salisbury Federation of Musicians, Local 44 Route 10, Cedarhurst Village Salisbury, MD 21801 301-749-3948 (18)

Milet, Jeffrey, Lehigh University Department of Theatre Bethlehem, PA 18015 215-861-3640 (4)

Miley, Frank, Northbrook Civic Theatre Post Office Box 534 Northbrook, IL 60062 312-498-2178 (16)

Millang, Ms. Jo Lene, Musicians' Association, Local 75 640 19th Street Des Moines, IA 50314 515-244-2058 (18)

Miller, Anna, Texas Southmost College Department of Theatre Brownsville, TX 78520 512-541-1241 (4)

Miller, Bob, Flexitrol Lighting 237 Morrison Drive Pittsburgh, PA 15216 412-531-4733 (15)

Miller, Charles F., Musicians' Mutual Association, Local 173 188 South Street Fitchburg, MA 01420 617-345-7191 (18)

Miller, D., Memorex Corporation 741 Fifth Avenue King of Prussia, PA 19406 (15)

Miller, Dale E., Purdue University Department of Theatre West Lafayette, IN 47907 317-749-2695 (4)

Miller, Dale E., Purdue University Loeb Playhouse/Stewart Theatre West Lafayette, IN 47907 317-749-2649 (8)

Miller, David A., Burlington County Cultural and Heritage Commission 49 Rancocas Road Mount Holly, NJ 08060 609-261-5068 (5)

Miller, Donald R., Musicians' Protective Union 925 North Briar Drive York, PA 17404 717-764-5807 (18)

Miller, Edward A., Marion Musicians' Association Route 2 Cardington, OH 43315 614-389-4226 (18)

Miller, Mrs. E.J., Charleston Council on Arts 423 East Main Charleston, MS 38921 601-647-3382 (5)

Miller, Eleanor C., Joseph P. Hays Surflight Summer Theatre Box 155 Beach Haven, NJ 08008 609-492-9477; 609-492-4112 (16)

Miller, Eleanor C., Surflight Summer Theatre 29 West Indiana Avenue Beach Haven Terrace, NJ 08008 609-492-4112; 609-492-9477 (16)

Miller, Florence, Musicians' Protective Union 5900 Townsend Place Cheyenne, WY 82001 307-632-2186 (18)

Miller, Frank M., University of the South Department of Theatre Sewanee, TN 37375 615-598-5931 (4)

Miller, Irving T., Musicians' Protective Association, Local 120 1110 Grandview Street Scranton, PA 18509 717-342-4366; 717-344-5656 (18)

Miller, J., Winner Community Theatre Post Office Box 5 Winner, SD 57580 (16)

Miller, John, Musicians' Protective Association 1108 Cherry Lane Pocatello, ID 83001 208-233-3483 (18)

Miller, John M., The Joyce-Cridland Company Post Office Box 1630 Dayton, OH 45401 513-294-6261 (15)

Miller, K., Canton Festival Theatre Route 2 Kenton, MO 63435 (16)

Miller, M.J., Brock University Department of Theatre Saint Catherines, Ontario, Canada L25 416-684-7201 (4)

Miller, Ronnie, Meridian Junior College Theatre 5500 Highway 19, North Meridian, MS 39301 601-483-8241 (8)

Miller, Stan, Rosco Labs, Incorporated 36 Bush Avenue Port Chester, NY 10573 914-937-1300 (15)

Mills, Dennis, Council of Drama in Education 336 Markham Street Toronto, Ontario, Canada M6G 2K9 (5)

Mills, Francis, Cordiner Hall Whitman College Walla Walla, WA 99362 509-529-5100 (8)

Mills, Julie, Theatre of Western Springs Hampton at Hillgrove, Box 29 Western Springs, IL 60558 312-246-4043 (16)

Mills, Ray, Lenior-Rhyne College Department of Theatre Hickory, NC 28603 704-328-1741, Ext. 253 (4)

Milne, William P., Ann Arbor Arts Association 117 West Liberty Ann Arbor, MI 48104 313-994-8004 (5)

Milner, Alan, Sonoma County Arts Council 1049 Fourth Street Santa Rosa, CA 95404 707-528-8220 (5)

Milsk, R., R. Milsk Company 22420 Telegraph Road Southfield, MI 48034 313-354-3310 (15)

Mindlin, Freda, Opportunity Resources for the Arts, (OR) 1501 Broadway New York, NY 10036 212-575-1688 (5)

Minichino, Thomas, Musicians' Association of Westchester, Local 38 132 Larchmont Avenue Larchmont, NY 10538 914-834-0823 (18)

Minnaugh, Patricia, Barry College Department of Theatre 11300 North East 2nd Street Miami, Florida 33161 305-751-0044; 305-758-3392 Ext. 223 (4)

Minnich, A., Carroll Community Theatre 1748 Quinit Avenue Carroll, IA 51401 (16)

Minskoff, Jerry, The Minskoff Theatre 1515 Broadway at 45th Street New York, NY 10036 212-869-0550 (16)

Mintz, Herbert, Sheffield Bronze Paint Corporation 17814 South Waterloo Road Cleveland, OH 44119 216-481-8330 (15)

Mires, Clark G., Grossmont Community College Department of Theatre El Cajon, CA 92020 714-465-1700 (4)

Mirjyn, Charles De, Orange Belt Musicians' Association, Local 167 405 Palm Avenue Redlands, CA 92373 714-824-1450 (18)

Misegadis, Mary, Barton County Community Department of Theatre Route 1 Great Bend, KS 67530 316-792-2701 (4)

Missimi, Dominic, University of Detroit, Marygrove College Department of Theatre 8425 West McNichols Detroit, MI 43221 313-341-1838 (4)

Mitchell, George, George Mitchell 6 Adams Road Framingham, MA 01701 617-872-7610; 612-941-1700 (15)

Mitchell, Gregory S., Musicians' Protective Association, Local 96 24 Crandall Street Adams, MA 01220 413-743-2943 (18)

Mitri, Romeo, Troy Musicians, Inc., Local 13 25 Carolina Street Latham, NY 12110 518-274-8275 (18)

Mittelman, Arnold, The Whole Theatre Company 544 Bloomfield Avenue Montclair, NJ 07042 201-744-2989; 201-744-2996 (16)

Mitter, Paul, Musicians' Protective Association, Local 54 1030 Richey Road Zanesville, OH 43701 614-452-5691 (18)

Mobilio, Robert, Musicians' Association of Waterbury, Local 186 442 Farmington Avenue Waterbury, CT 06710 203-753-1354 (18)

Moe, Christian H., Smoky Mountain Passion Play Post Office Box 3 Townsend, TN 37882 615-984-4111, Year Round; 615-448-2244, Box Office - Summer Only (16)

Moe, Robert E., Coeur D'Alene Community Theatre Post Office Box 622 Coeur D'Alene, ID 83814 208-667-1323 (16)

Moeser, James, Hoch Auditorium University of Kansas Lawrence, KS 66045 913-864-3421 (8)

Moffett, Phyllis, Greater Harrisburg Arts Council 114 Walnut Street Harrisburg, PA 17101 717-234-5454 (5)

Molen, Jan, Napa College Department of Theatre 2277 Napa Valley Highway Napa, CA 94558 707-255-2100 (4)

Molete, Carlton W., Texas Southern University Department of Theatre 3201 Wheeler Avenue Houston, TX 77004 713-527-7360 (4)

Molinaro, Amedeo, Musical Society 512 West Murphy Avenue Connellsville, PA 15425 412-628-1530 (18)

Molthen, David, Carroll College Department of Theatre Arts Waukesha, WI 53186 414-547-1211 (4)

Moltz, Sidney, Saul S. Siegal Company 847 West Jackson Boulevard Chicago, IL 60607 312-738-3400 (15)

Moncrief, E.W., Musicians' Protective Union 224 Spring Avenue Ellwood City, PA 16117 412-758-5991 (18)

Money, Robert C., Columbus Musicians' Protective Association 6232 Lyndridge Avenue Columbus, GA 31904 404-323-0515 (18)

Mongell, John R., Association of Musicians, Local 150 915 East Elm Springfield, MO 65806 417-869-5226 (18)

Monta, Marian, Pan American University Department of Communication Edinburg, TX 78935 512-381-3581 (4)

Montague, Susan, Theatre New Brunswick Young Company Post Office Box 566 Fredericton, New Brunswick, Canada E3B 5A6 506-455-3080 (16)

Montanaro, Francis J., Musicians Protective Association, Local 107 2207 Harbor Avenue Ashtabula, OH 44004 216-992-0970 (18)

Monteiro, Frank C., Greater New Bedford Association of Musicians, Local 214 79 Hunter Street New Bedford, MA 02740 617-994-3049 (18)

Montgomery, A.E., Lighting by Monty 11528 89th Street Edmonton, Alberta, Canada 403-477-5077 (15)

Montgomery, J. Patrick, Bath Civic Theatre Bath, ME 14530 (16)

Montgomery, Robert W., ACF Foundation, Incorporated 750 Third Avenue New York, NY 10017 212-986-8600 (10)

Montpetit, Jacques, Department of External Affairs 125 Sussex Drive Ottawa, Ontario, Canada K1A 0G2 613-992-9948 (5)

Mooberry, Marion, Omaha Community Playhouse 6915 Cass Street Omaha, NB 68132 402-553-4890 (16)

Moock, R., Parkland Community Theatre 4610 West Frankfort Drive Rockville, MD 20853 (16)

Moody, James L., Sundance Lighting Corporation 9801 Variel Avenue Chatsworth, CA 91311 213-882-4321 (15)

Moonan, William, Bedford Players 4 Rodney Road Bedford, MA 01730 617-275-8147 (16)

Mooney, Dan, Persephone Theatre Post Office Box 1642 Saskatoon, Saskatchewan, Canada S7K 2R8 306-664-2110 (16)

Mooney, Margaret, The Citadel On Wheels/Wings 9828 - 101A Avenue Edmonton, Alberta, Canada T5J 3C6 403-426-4811 (16)

Moonschein, Henry, Corning Community College Department of Theatre Corning, NY 14830 607-962-9011; 607-962-9271 (4)

Moore, Barbara, Lakewood Cultural Arts Council Post Office Box 158 Lakewood, CA 90714 213-866-9771 (5)

Moore, Dick, American Federation of Television and Radio Artists (AFTRA) National Headquarters 1350 Avenue of the Americas New York, NY 10019 212-719-9570; 212-265-7700 (18)

Moore, Donald E., Coast Junior College Department of Theatre Gulfport, MS 39501 601-896-3355 (4)

Moore, Edward J. Jr., Musicians' Protective Union, Local 132 365 West King Road Ithaca, NY 14850 607-272-8170 (18)

Moore, Fredrick F., Lexington Musicians' Association 116 Westgate Drive Lexington, KY 40504 606-255-4721 (18)

Moore, Gary D., Paducah Federation of Musicians, Local 200 Route 3, Post Office Box 28 Metropolis, IL 62960 618-524-3516 (18)

Moore, James R., Alexandria Community Theatre Route 1 Post Office Box 341 Alexandria, IN 46001 317-724-2927 (16)

Moore, Jane, Clay County Historical and Arts Council Post Office Box 5 Hayesville, NC 28904 404-896-2244 (5)

Moore, J. Chris, Springfield Arts Council Post Office Box 745 Springfield, OH 45501 513-324-2712 (5)

Moore, Jean, Duluth Musicians' Association, Local 18 67 Calvary Road Duluth, MN 55803 218-728-1990 (18)

Moore, Jim, La Mama ETC 74A East 4th Street New York, NY 10003 212-475-7710; 212-475-7908 (16)

Moore, Lester L., Rutgers University, Newark Department of Theatre 392 High Street Newark, NJ 07102 201-648-5205 (4)

Moore, Mary, Albion Community Arts Program Post Office Box 588 Albion, MI 49224 517-629-8072 (5)

Moore, Richard, Camille Players One Dean Porter Park Brownsville, TX 78520 512-542-8900; 512-542-7334 (16)

Moore, Richard, Freeport Musical Association 605 East Jefferson Street Freeport, IL 61032 815-233-1040 (18)

Moore, Russell J., Musicians' Association, Local 73 127 North Seventh Street Minneapolis, MN 55403 612-333-8205 (18)

Moore, Sonia, Sonia Moore Studio 485 Park Avenue New York, NY 10022 212-755-5120 (4)

Moore, Sonia, American Center for Stanislavski Theatre 485 Park Avenue New York, NY 10022 212-755-5120 (16)

Moore, Sonia, American Stanislavski Theatre 141 West 13th Street New York, NY 10014 212-755-5120 (16)

Moore, Woody S., Commission on the Arts and Humanities 213 Polk Street Marion, AL 36756 205-683-2871 (5)

Moorhouse, William, Milligan College Department of Theatre Milligan College, TN 37682 (4)

Moosenick, Marilyn, Lexington Council of the Arts 755 Brookhill Drive Lexington, KY 40502 (5)

Moot, Weles V., Studio Arena Theatre 681 Main Street Buffalo, NY 14203 716-856-5650 (16)

Morales, Jose, Duro-Test International Corporation Post Office Box 1893 Carolina, PR 00628 809-768-2711; 809-762-1485 (15)

Moran, Doris F., Mount Vernon Musicians' Association 111 Miller Avenue Mount Vernon, OH 43050 614-397-4302 (18)

Moran, Jay, Actors' Equity Association (AEA) 465 California Street, Suite 210 San Francisco, CA 94104 415-781-8660 (18)

Moran, Terry, W.B. Geary Auditorium University of Charleston Charleston, WV 25304 304-346-9471 (8)

Morehouse, William, West Chester State College Department of Theatre West Chester, PA 19380 215-436-2500 (4)

Morely, Jim, University of New Mexico Department of Theatre Albuquerque, NM 87131 505-277-4332; 505-277-2111 (4)

Morgan, Carl, Council on the Arts and Humanities 820 King Street Selma, AL 36701 205-874-4061 (5)

Morgan, James, Northern Oklahoma College Department of Theatre 1220 East Grand Tonkawa, OK 74563 405-628-2581 (4)

Morgan, Rachel R., Bryan College Department of Theatre Dayton, TN 37321 775-204-, ext. 286 (4)

Morin, Danyelle, Theatre D'Aujourd'Hui 1297 Papineau Montreal, Quebec, Canada H2K 4H3 514-521-4149 (16)

Moritz, George, Sedona Arts Center Post Office Box 569 Sedona, AZ 86336 602-282-3809 (5)

Morley, Jim, University of Albuquerque Department of Theatre Albuquerque, NM 87120 505-842-8500 (4)

Moroni, Michael D., Middletown Musicians' Protective Association Post Office Box 955 Middletown, CT 06457 203-347-7805 (18)

Morreale, Thelma R., Baker University Department of Theatre 606 Eighth Street Baldwin City, KS 66006 913-594-6451 (4)

Morris, E., Pembroke State University Department of Theatre Pembroke, NC 28372 919-521-4214, Extension 287; 919-521-0778, Box Office (4)

Morris, Larry, Newton Country Players Post Office Box 9 Newton Centre, MA 02161 617-244-2160 (16)

Morris, T., The Crown Players 1407 North Armour Wichita, KS 67026 (16)

Morris, William, Kalamazoo Federation of Musicians, Local 228 3332 Wedgewood Drive Kalamazoo, MI 49008 616-344-0049 (18)

Morrison, Charles R., Musical Association, Local 269 1927 Paxton Street Harrisburg, PA 17104 717-234-8400 (18)

Morrison, Cliff, Greater Pell City Arts Council Post Office Box 169 Pell City, Al 35125 205-522-5873 (5)

Morrison, Dorothy, Seminole Community College Department of Theatre Sanford, FL 32771 305-323-1450 (4)

Morrison, Jeannie, Winona Community Theatre Post Office Box 735 Winona, MN 55987 (16)

Morrison, Lynn, Neligh Arts Council Post Office Box 194 Neligh, NB 69756 402-887-5090 (5)

Morrison, Malcolm, North Carolina School of the Arts Department of Theatre Post Office Box 12189 Winston-Salem, NC 27107 919-784-7170 (4)

Morrison, Norma, Iredell Arts Council Post Office Box 134 Statesville, NC 28677 704-873-6100; 704-873-6400 (5)

Morrison, R., Roseville Community Theatre 15250 Martin Roseville, MI 48066 (16)

Morrow, Lynn, Albright College Department of English Reading, PA 19604 (4)

Morsing, Thorvald, Clinton Musicians' Protective Association, Local 79 910 Fifth Avenue, South Clinton, IA 52732 319-242-6257 (18)

Morterson, L., Paola Civic Theatre 609 East Wea Paola, KS 66071 (16)

Morton, Susana, Salem College Department of Theatre Salem, WV 26426 304-782-5217 (4)

Moseley, Mary L., Centreville/Brent Arts Council Post Office Box 398 Centreville, AL 35094 205-926-4631 (5)

Moser, J., Rockville Little Theatre 208 Upton Street Rockville, MD 20850 (16)

Moses, Hal, Mutual Display 1748 East 27th Street Cleveland, OH 44114 216-621-3685 (15)

Mosher, Allyn, Backstage Theatre Post Office Box 97 Breckenridge, CO 80424 303-453-0199; 303-453-2297 (16)

Mosienko, N., Regina Musicians' Association 1365 Princess Street Regina, Saskatchewan, Canada S4T 3Y9 306-527-3871 (18)

Moskowitz, Eric, BML Stage Lighting Company, Incorporated 27 Steele Avenue Somerville, NJ 08876 201-725-0810 (15)

Moss, Janes S., Alliance of Resident Theatres, New York 325 Spring Street New York, NY 10013 212-989-5257 (5)

Moss, Michael, Plantation Playhouse Saint Louis, MO 63138 (8)

Motz, Eldon, Akron Federation of Musicians, Local 24 Room 315, Metropolitan Building Akron, OH 44308 216-376-8174 (18)

Mouish, Ervin, Musicians' Protective Union, Local 98 437 North 6th Street Wood River, IL 62095 618-254-1488 (18)

Mount, Harry, Gloucester County College Department of Theatre Sewell, NJ 08080 609-468-5000 (4)

Mount, Phyllis, Lake Forest Country Day School Theatre 270 South Western Lake Forest, IL 60045 (16)

Moushey, Charles, Alliance Federation of Musicians, Local 68 130 Shadyside Court Alliance, OH 44601 216-821-2761 (18)

Mowcomber, Howard, Amherst Fabric and Trim 205 North Leavitt Road Amherst, OH 44001 216-988-2116 (15)

Moxley, Bob, McFarlin Memorial Auditorium 6400 Hillcrest Avenue Dallas, TX 75205 214-699- 3129 (8)

Moyer, Ronald L., University of South Dakota, Vermillion Department of Theatre Vermillion, SD 57069 605-677-5418 (4)

Mraz, Doyne, Foothill College Department of Theatre Los Altos, CA 94022 415-948-8590 (4)

Mrochinski, Mel, Interlochen Arts Academy Department of Theatre Interlochen, MI 49643 616-392-5111 (4)

Mueller, Richard L., Firehouse Dinner Theatre 11th and Jackson Omaha, NE 68102 402-346-8833 (16)

Mueller, Robert E., Peacock Puppet Theater Britton House Roosevelt, NJ 08555 609-448-2605 (16)

Mulkey, Dr. Gwendel, Tarrant County Junior College, South Campus Department of Theatre 5301 Campus Drive Fort Worth, TX 76119 817-534-4861 (4)

Mullen, B., Center Playhouse 5870 West Olympic Los Angeles, CA 90036 (16)

Mullen, Charles J., Foothills Civic Theatre Post Office Box 319 LaPorte, CO 80535 303-484-8182 (16)

Mullen, Jimmy E. Jr., Jackson Federation of Musicians Route 2, Post Office Box 270F Jackson, MS 39209 601-924-9313 (18)

Mullikin, Mildred B., Broward Community College Department of Theatre Fort Lauderdale, Florida 33314 305-475-6840; 305-475-6840 (4)

Mundell, W.L., Scioto Society Post Office Box 73 Chillicothe, OH 45601 614-775-4100 (5)

Mundy, Frank M., South Carolina State College Department of Theatre College Avenue Orangeburg, SC 29117 803-536-7123 (4)

Munn, James, Colortran, Incorporated 958 Paulsboro Drive Rockville, MD 20850 301-340-7405 (15)

Munson, Mrs. Joan M., Dover Little Theatre Post Office Box 82 Dover, NJ 07801 201-366-9890 (8)

Munson, Miss John M., Dover Little Theatre Box 82 Elliot Street Dover, NJ 07801 201-366-9890 (16)

Munson, Julia, Musicians' Protective Union 2116 Friendship Street Iowa City, IA 52240 319-337-4677 (18)

Murdoch, Jason W., Palace Grand Theatre Post Office Box 4609 Whitehorse, Yukon Territory, Canada Y1A 2R8 (16)

Murphy, Arlene, Musicians' Protective Union, Local 273 Post Office Box 321 Jasper, AR 72641 501-442-4100 (18)

Murphy, Don B., Georgetown University Department of Theatre State One, 3620 P Street NW Washington, DC 20057 202-625-4085 (4)

Murphy, Gene, Strand Century Incorporated 5432 West 102nd Street Los Angeles, CA 90045 213-776-4600 (15)

Murphy, Gretchen, Itasca Community College Department of Theatre Grand Rapids, MN 55744 218-326-9451 (4)

Murphy, Kenneth E., Musicians' Protective Union, Local 273 Post Office Box 321 Jasper, AR 72641 501-442-4100 (18)

Murphy, N.R., Playhouse Post Office Box 251 Huntington Beach, CA 92646 (16)

Murphy, William J., United Performing Arts Fund 929 North Water Street Milwaukee, WI 53202 414-237-7121 (5)

Murray, Michael, The Cincinnati Playhouse in the Park Post Office Box 6537 Cincinnati, OH 45206 513-421-3888, Box Office; 513-421-5440, Administrative (16)

Murray, Michael M., Technical Audio/Visual Services, Incorporated 5569 West Washington Boulevard Los Angeles, CA 90016 213-938-2858 (15)

Murray, Mrs. Paul, Trumbull New Theatre Post Office Box 374 Warren, OH 44482 216-652-1103; 216-856-2282 (16)

Murray, Robert, Salem Cultural Arts Center 32 Derby Square Salem, MA 01970 617-744-4580 (8)

Murtha, James, Gurtman and Murtha Associates, Incorporated 162 West 56th Street New York, NY 10019 212-245-4771; 212-245-4772 (12)

Musgrave, Gary, Kelly-Deyong Sound 2145 West Broadway Vancouver, British Columbia, Canada V6K 2C7 (15)

Mussman, Linda, Time and Space Limited 139-41 West 22nd Street New York, NY 10011 212-741-1032; 212-243-9268 (16)

Muth, Tom, Topeka Public Library Gallery of Fine Arts 1515 West Tenth Street Topeka, KS 66604 913-233-3040 (11)

Mutuma, Poe, Black Theatre Canada 109 Vaughan Road, Suite 1 Toronto, Ontario, Canada M6C 2L9 416-656-2716 (16)

Myers, Charles, Humboldt State University Department of Theatre Arcata, CA 95521 707-826-3011 (4)

Myers, Ken, Kenneth Sawyer Goodman Memorial Theatre 200 South Columbus Drive Chicago, IL 60603 312-236-3238 (16)

Myers, Roland W., Wayland Baptist University Department of Theatre 1900 W 7th Street Plainview, TX 79072 806-296-5521 (4)

Myerson, Bess, Department of Cultural Affairs 830 Fifth Avenue New York, NY 10021 212-360-8211 (5)

Myrick, Ted O., Tri-City Musicians Association 521 West Sylvester Street Pasco, WA 99301 509-547-6698 (18)

N

Nadien, David, Fall River Federation of Musicians, Local 216 746 Hood Street Fall River, MA 02720 617-679-6235 (18)

Nail, William A., Zenith Radio Corporation 1000 Milwaukee Avenue Glenview, IL 60025 312-391-8181 (10)

Nakano, Jack, Santa Barbara Gazebo Theatre One 631 Alameda Padre Serra Santa Barbara, CA 93103 805-962-6587; 213-657-3270 (16)

Nalbach, D.F., University of Saskatchewan Department of Theatre Saskatoon, Saskatchewan, Canada 306-343-2656 (4)

Nalbach, Kay C., Hart, Schaffner and Marx Foundation 101 North Wacker Drive Chicago, IL 60606 312-372-6300 (10)

Nalibow, H., Center Players 2601 Grand Avenue Long Beach, CA 90815 (16)

Nance, Don, Surry Arts Council Post Office Box 141 Mount Airy, NC 27030 919-786-7998 (5)

Nanney, David, Lynn Canal Community Players Post Office Box 75 Haines, AK 99827 907-766-2540; 907-766-2763 (9)

Nardi, Lou, San Joaquin Delta College Department of Theatre 5151 Pacific Avenue Stockton, CA 95207 209-478-2011 (4)

Narramore, W.D., Austin College Department of Theatre Sherman, TX 75090 214-892-9101 (4)

Narvaez, Ann, Rising Tide Theatre Post Office Box 7371 Saint John's, Newfoundland, Canada A1E 3Y5 709-579-4438 (16)

Nash, R., Pierre Players Post Office Box 933 Pierre, SD 57501 (16)

Nauman, Louis C. Jr., Musicians' Association of St. Louis, Local 2-197 2103 59th Street St. Louis, MO 63110 314-781-6612 (18)

Navas, Judy, Sonoma State University Department of Theatre Rohnert Park, CA 94928 707-664-2474 (4)

Nave, Sal L., Norristown Musicians' Association Hamilton Hall Norristown, PA 19401 215-272-6210 (18)

Navolio, Charles, Musicians' Protective Union 224 Spring Avenue Ellwood City, PA 16117 412-758-5991 (18)

Naylor, James N., Long Beach Community Players 5021 East Anaheim Street Long Beach, CA 90804 213-438-0356 (16)

Neal, Miss Julia, Shaker Festival, South Union Shakertown South Union, KY 42283 (9)

Neal, P., Footlighters 962 Green Drive Coshocton, OH 43812 (16)

Neal, Tom, Hollywood Lights, Incorporated 0625 SW Florida Portland, OR 97219 503-244-5808; 503-245-2236 (15)

Nealon, Mary T., Colonnades Theatre Lab 428 Lafayette Street New York, NY 10003 212-673-2222, Theatre; 212-598-4620, Lab (16)

Nease, Ray E., Musicians' Protective Union Rural Route Number 15 Frankfort, IN 46041 317-654-8209 (18)

Nebel, P.J., Oshkosh Community Players 1045 Eastman Oshkosh, WI 54901 (16)

Neben, Mike, Art Drapery Studios 6252 North Pulaski Chicago, IL 60646 312-736-9700 (15)

Nederlanders, The, Nederlander Theatre 208 West 41st Street New York, NY 10036 212-586-6150 (16)

Neeson, Jack H., Chatham College Department of Theatre Woodland Road Pittsburgh, PA 15232 412-441-8200 (4)

Neff, Bill, Chatham Federation of Musicians 14 Forest Street Chatham, Ontario, Canada N71 1Z7 519-352-3902 (18)

Neilson, George L., University of Windsor Department of Dramatic Arts Windsor, Ontario, Canada N9B 3P4 519-253-4232 (4)

Neilson, Steven S., Annie Russell Theatre Box 37 Rollins College Winter Park, FL 32789 305-646-2501 (16)

Nellist, Glenn F., Stage-Brite 695 Lowry Avenue North East Minneapolis, MN 55418 612-788-9476 (15)

Nelsen, Paul, Windham College Theatre Windham College Parkway Putney, VT 05346 802-387-5511 (8)

Nelson, Bob, B and B Electronic Products 500 South Quebec Denver, CO 80237 303-773-6700 (15)

Nelson, Charles, Port Huron Federation of Musicians, Local 33 2601 10th Avenue Port Huron, MI 48060 313-982-8390 (18)

Nelson, David E., Montana Assembly of Community Arts Council Montana Arts Council Missoula, MT 59801 406-543-8286 (5)

Nelson, Jeffrey, Mount Washington Valley Theatre Company Eastern Slope Playhouse North Conway, NH 03860 603-356-5776 (16)

Nelson, Mark E., Ohlone College Department of Theatre Post Office Box 909 Fremont, CA 94538 415-657-2100 (4)

Nelson, Polly, Short Grass Arts Council Post Office Box 757 Pierre, SD 57501 605-224-7402 (5)

Nemeth, Terence, Theatre Communications Group (TCG) 355 Lexington Avenue New York, NY 10017 212-697-5230 (5)

Nemoyten, William, San Mateo County Arts Council Twin Pines Cultural Center Belmont, CA 94002 415-593-1816 (5)

Nester, Beverly, Lawrence Arts Council Municipal Square Lawrence, NJ 08648 609-883-0873 (5)

Netting, Fred, Federation Of Musicians, Local 5 19161 Schaefer Highway Detroit, MI 48235 313-345-6200 (18)

Netzky, Lester, Tom Thumb Players Company 4737 East Towner Tucson, AZ 85712 (16)

Neuberger, Stanley, Musicians' Protective Union, Local 243 1723 21st Street Monroe, WI 53566 608-325-5764 (18)

Neufeld, Gordon, Theatre Aquarius 50 Murray Street West Hamilton, Ontario, Canada L8L 1B3 416-529-1195 (16)

Neuman, Carl, Musicians' Protective Union 306 Roundville Street Waupun, WI 53963 414-885-5548 (18)

Neville, Frand W. Jr., Piqua Musicians' Association 1201 Park Avenue Piqua, OH 45356 513-773-2665 (18)

Neville, John, Neptune Theatre 1593 Argyle Street Halifax, Nova Scotia, Canada B3J 2B2 902-429-7300 (16)

Newell, John, Country Playhouse Playwright Competition 12802 Queensbury Houston, TX 77024 713-467-4497 (3)

Newell, Ronald J., Dobama Theatre 1846 Conventry Road Cleveland Heights, OH 44118 216-932-6838 (16)

Newhouse, Mr. John, Southwestern Community College Department of Theatre 900 Otay Lakes Road Chula Vista, CA 92010 714-421-6700, Ext. 346 (4)

Newhouse, Mrs. Theodore, Gene Frankel Theatre Workshop 342 East 63rd Street New York, NY 10021 212-421-1666 (16)

Newman, Christine, Chicago Magazine 500 North Michigan Chicago, IL 60611 312-751-7150 (14)

Newman, Geoffrey W., Howard University Department of Theatre 2400 Sixth Street NW Washington, D.C. 20059 202-636-7050; 202-636-7051 (4)

Newman, Iris, Reed Whipple Cultural Arts Center 821 Las Vegas Boulevard Las Vegas, NV 89101 702-386-6211 (5)

Newman, William H., Musicians' Protective Union 520 Humes Avenue Aptos, CA 95003 408-426-1776 (18)

Newson, Mike, Kings Theater Guild 304 East 3rd Street Brooklyn, NY 12223 718-844-4241 (16)

Newth, C. W., Musicians' Protective Union, Local 266 Post Office Box 6142 Little Rock, AR 72116 501-835-0337 (18)

Niblick, Robert, Musicians' Unions, Local 114 720 South Grange Avenue Sioux Falls, SD 57104 605-338-5818 (18)

Nichols, A. Richard, University of Nebraska, Lincoln Department of Theatre Lincoln, NB 68588 402-472-2072; 402-472-1619 (4)

Nichols, George, Musicians' Protective Union, Local 131 227 La Salle Street Streator, IL 61364 815-672-7431 (18)

Nichols, Ronald K., Musicians' Protective Union 1473 Lewis Street Ogden, UT 84404 801-393-9558 (18)

Nicholson, Paul E., Oregon Shakespeare Festival Association Post Office Box 158 Ashland, OR 97520 503-482-2111 (16)

Nicholson, R.E., R.E. Nicholson 75 West Main Street East Bloomfield, NY 14443 716-657-6145 (15)

Nickel, Dale, Musicians' Association, Local 193 1228 Hickory Drive Waukesha, WI 53186 414-542-2425 (18)

Nickels, Arthur, Manitowoc Musicians' Association, Local 195 1511 Cherry Road Manitowoc, WI 54220 414-793-1235 (18)

Niedeerkorn, Thomas, Ithaca Repertory Theater 313 North Tioga Street Ithaca, NY 14850 607-273-8588 (16)

Niederkorn, Thomas, Center for the Arts at Ithaca 313 North Tioga Street Ithaca, NY 14580 607-273-8588 (5)

Niel, Pieter J. Van, Compton Community College 1111 East Artesia Boulevard Compton, CA 90221 213-635-8081 (4)

Nieman, Maureen, Capitol City Theatre 617 South Smith Avenue St. Paul, MN 55107 (16)

Nieoczym, Richard, Actor's Lab 95 Danforth Avenue Toronto, Ontario, Canada M4K 1N2 416-461-1644 (16)

Nigh, J., Gingerbread Players 422 Montgomery Street Laurel, MD 20810 (16)

Nimmons, J., Rappa House Theatre 96 East Fisher Freeway Detroit, MI 48201 (16)

Nipson, Herbert, Ebony 820 South Michigan Avenue Chicago, IL 60605 312-322-9320 (14)

Nixon, William R., Sport Seating Company, Incorporated 1540 Chestnut Street Emmaus, PA 18049 215-967-5450 (15)

Noble, Pauline, Shorter College Department of Theatre Shorter Hill Rome, GA 31404 404-232-2463 (4)

Noel, Craig, Old Globe Theatre Simon Edison Center Post Office Box 2171 San Diego, CA 92112 714-231-1941; 714-231-1942 (16)

Nolen, Bill, Tipton County Art Association Post Office Box 575 Covington, TN 38019 (5)

Nordby, Lew, Musicians' Protective Union 5519 Poplar Drive Ferndale, WA 98248 206-733-2670 (18)

Nordheimer, Clyde L., Jean Rosenthal Associates, Inc. 765 Vose Avenue Orange, NJ 07050 201-674-1530 (1)

Norflett, Linda K., North Carolina Central University Department of Drama Durham, NC 27707 919-682-2172 (4)

Norman, Robert, Musicians' Mutual Protective Associatiton 1140 Spencer Street Santa Rosa, CA 95404 707-545-1434 (18)

Norquist, Richard, Northern State College Department of Drama Jay and 12th Street Aberdeen, SD 57401 605-622-2503 (4)

Norris, Ronald A., Musicians' Protective Union 77 George Street Hamburg, NY 14075 716-649-2251 (18)

North, Halsey M., Arts and Science Council 110 East Seventh Street Charlotte, NC 28202 704-372-9664 (5)

North, Keath, Park Players, Ltd. Post Office Box 1259 Hot Springs National Park, AR 71901 501-767-2351 (16)

Norton, Clinton E., International Society of Performing Arts Administrators c/o Clinton E. Norton, President Thomas Performing Arts Hall University of Akron Akron, OH 44325 216-375-7595 (5)

Norwood, William R., Montgomery Federatiton of Musicians 1310 Magnolia Avenue Montgomery, AL 36106 205-262-5154 (18)

Noster, Kenneth J., Mime-Light Theatre 11018 - 83 Avenue Edmonton, Alberta, Canada T6G 0T7 403-439-4068 (16)

Notaro, Peter M., Musicians' Protective Union, Local 139 408 West Green Street Hazelton, PA 18201 717-455-5160 (18)

Notini, William J., Greater Lowell Musicians' Association, Local 83 200 Parker Street Lowell, MA 01851 617-453-5621 (18)

Notman, Thomas M., Mohawk Valley Musicians' Association, Local 51 R.D. 1 Poland, NY 13431 315-251- (18)

Novak, Elaine A., Marshall University Department of Theatre Huntington, WV 25701 304-696-6786 (4)

Novellino, Mary, Costume Armour, Incorporated and Christo-Vac Post Office Box 325 Shore Road Cornwall-on-Hudson, NY 12520 914-534-9120 (15)

Novotny, Frank, Oshkosh Musicians' Association, Local 46 3159 Omro Road Oshkosh, WI 54901 414-235-3461 (18)

Nowell, Stephen, Youtheatre 408 Saint James Street West, Suite 10 Montreal, Quebec, Canada H2Y 1S2 514-844-8781 (16)

Nydegger, Vernon K., Wichita Musicians' Association 4323 East Kellogg Wichita, KS 67218 316-684-1311 (18)

Nygard, Sal, Musicians' Association Post Office Box 3379 Eureka, CA 95501 707-442-3375 (18)

Nyren, R., R. Nyren Company 2222 West Diversey Chicago, IL 60647 312-276-5515 (15)

O

Oakley, C. Patric, Musicians' Association of San Diego County 1717 Morena Blvd San Diego, CA 92110 714-276-4324 (18)

Oathour, Edward N., Crowder College Department of Theatre Neosho, MO 64850 417-451-3223 (4)

Oberhelman, Ferrol K., Manhattan Musicians Association, Local 169 828 Allison Road Manhattan, KS 66502 915-537-1928 (18)

Obokata, Dawn, Actor's Lab 95 Danforth Avenue Toronto, Ontario, Canada M4K 1N2 416-461-1644 (16)

Obrian, C., Amery Community Theatre Route 2 Amery, WI 54001 (16)

O'Brien, Jack, Old Globe Theatre Simon Edison Center Post Office Box 2171 San Diego, CA 92112 714-231-1941; 714-231-1942 (16)

O'Brien, Larry, Musicians' of Las Vegas Post Office Box 7467 Las Vegas, NV 89101 702-739-9369 (18)

O'Connell, F.K., Johns-Manville Sales Corporation 2222 Kensington Court Oak Brook, IL 60521 312-887-7400 (15)

O'Connell, Jerry, Widl Video 5425 West Diversey Chicago, IL 60639 312-622-9606 (15)

O'Conner, J. Regis, Western Kentucky University Department of Theatre Bowling Green, KY 42101 502-745-3296 (4)

O'Connor, Sara, Milwaukee Repertory Theatre 929 North Water Street Milwaukee, WI 53202 414-273-7121 - Business Office; 414-273-7206 - Box Office (16)

O'Connor, Sheila, Silver Lake College Fine Arts Theatre Silver Lake College, 2406 South Alverno Road Manitowoc, WI 54220 414-684-6691 (8)

O'Dea, Nancy, Genesee Valley Council on the Arts 4241 Lakeville Road Genesee, NY 14454 716-245-5401 (5)

Ogawa, Junso, Pearson Auditorium 1900 North Main Street Roswell, NM 88201 505-622-6250; 505-623-9338 (8)

O'Hehir, Diana, Mills College Department of Theatre Oakland, CA 94613 415-632-2700 (4)

Okarski, Ruth H., Council for Arts in Rock County 110 Virginia Street Luverne, MN 56165 507-283-2598 (5)

Oldfather, Germaine, Kearney Area Arts Council Post Office Box 2001 Kearney, NB 68847 308-234-4949 (5)

Olendory, Ken, Theatre Art Nouveau Post Office Box 613 Olympia, WA 98501 206-491-6504 (8)

Olenski, R., Maple Heights Little Theatre 18401 Waterbury Avenue Maple Heights, OH 44137 (16)

Olich, Michael E., Saint Joseph's College Department of Theatre Moutain View, CA 94040 (4)

Oliver, George, Henderson County Junior College Abilene, TX 79601 915-677-7281 (4)

Oliver, Lee, Arizona Cine Equipment Company 1660 E. Winsett Street #220 Tucson, AZ 85719 602-623-8268 (15)

Oliver, Maurine, Maurine Oliver and Associates 8730 Sunset Boulevard Los Angeles, CA 90069 213-657-1250 (2)

Olley, Francis R., Saint Joseph's College Department of Fine Arts and English Philadelphia, PA 19131 (4)

Olsen, Howard, Musicians' Protective Associatton Route 5, Box 1970 Rhinelander, WI 54501 715-362-2787 (18)

Paul, Theodore, Mankato State University
Department of Theatre Mankato, MN
56001 507-389-2119 (4)

Paulus, William F., Musicians' Union,
Local 215 49 Plochmann Lane
Woodstock, NY 12498 914-679-6227
(18)

Paxon, Omar M., Occidental College
Department of Theatre Los Angeles, CA
90041 213-259-2771 (4)

Payne, Darwin R., Southern Illinois
University Department of Theatre
Carbondale, IL 62901 618-692-2773 (4)

Payne, David W., The Eugene O'Neill
Theatre 230 West 49th Street New York,
NY 10019 212-246-0220 (16)

Payne, Gerald, Payne Motion Picture
Service 20 High Street Westerly, RI
02891 401-596-4739 (15)

Payne, Rhonda, Mummers Troupe of
Newfoundland 281 Duckworth Street
Saint John's, Newfoundland, Canada
709-754-1692 (16)

Payne, Rod, Seattle Center 305 Harrison
Street Seattle, WA 98109 206-625-4227;
206-625-4254 (8)

Payne, Rod, Seattle Center Opera House
305 Harrison Seattle, WA 98109
206-625-4254 (8)

Pazereskis, John, Carl Sandburg College
Department of Theatre Galesburg, IL
61401 309-344-2518 (4)

Peace, Douglas, Duro-Test Electric Ltd.
419 Attwell Drive Rexdale, Ontario,
Canada M9W 5W5 416-675-1623;
416-675-1624 (15)

Pearson, A.J., Presser Hall Auditorium
Bethany College Lindsborg, KS 67456
913-227-3312 extension 42 (8)

Pearson, Gordon, State Wide Lighting
Incorporated 21516 West Greenfield
Avenue New Berlin, WI 53151 (15)

Pearson, Phyllis, Maplewood Barn Theatre
701 Manor Drive Columbia, MO 65201
(16)

Peart, Liz, Kings Theater Guild 304 East
3rd Street Brooklyn, NY 12223
718-844-4241 (16)

Pechet, Howard, Stage West 16615 109
Avenue Edmonton, Alberta, Canada T5P
4K8 403-484-0841; 403-483-4051 (16)

Pechet, Howard, Stage West Regina Inn
Regina, Saskatchewan, Canada
306-565-0611 (16)

Peck, John L., Fostoria Federation of
Musicians, Local 121 118 West Center
Street Fostoria, OH 44830 419-435-5437
(18)

Pecor, Dr. Charles, Macon Junior College
Department of Theatre US 80 and I-475
Macon, GA 31206 912-474-2700 (4)

Pedersen, Mr. Dave, Racine Arts
Council,Inc. Post Office Box 263 Racine,
WI 53401 414-553-2367 (5)

Peel, Joel, Producers
Foundation/Association 2095 Broadway,
Suite 405 New York, NY 10023
212-496-9121; 212-496-9122/¾ (13)

Pegg, Thomas B., Pine Manor College
Department of Theatre 400 Heath Street
Chestnut Hill, MA 02167 617-731-7000
(4)

Pegler, B., Television Equipment
Associates Post Office Box 260 South
Salem, NY 10599 914-763-8893 (15)

Pelech, Michael, Reynolds Auditorium
Hawthorne Road Winston-Salem, NC
27104 919-727-2180 (8)

Pelletier, Gilles, Theatre Denise Pelletier
4353 St-Catherine East Montreal,
Quebec, Canada H1V 1Y2 514-253-8974
(16)

Pellowe, Susan, Aurora College
Department of Theatre Aurora, IL
60506 312-892-6431 (4)

Pena, Carlos, Musicians' Protective
Association, Local 74 1309 Marine
Galveston, TX 77550 713-763-3754 (18)

Pendill, George H., Battle Creek
Federation of Musicians 1349 West
Michigan Avenue Battle Creek, MI
49016 616-962-3063 (18)

Pendleton, Gary, Gary Pendleton 10329
Ash Overland Park, KS 66207
913-381-5035 (15)

Pentecost, Max, Martin Arts Commission
Post Office Box 197 Martin, TN 38237
901-587-9502 (5)

Peplau, Mrs. Marion, Chippewa Valley
Musicians' Association 2915 North
Ninth Street Eau Claire, WI 54701
715-832-1937 (18)

Perfetti, David W., Cortland Musicians'
Association 17 Stevenson Street
Cortland, NY 13045 607-753-8563 (18)

Perina, Peter, Dalhousie University
Department of Theatre Halifax, Nova
Scotia, Canada B3H 3J5 902-424-2233;
902-424-2234 (4)

Perius, Rose, Rose Perius c/o Continental
Promotions, 2749 Erie San Diego, CA
92117 714-298-8858; 714-276-6521 (12)

Perkins, Mac, P.N.T.A. 316 Westlake
Avenue, North Seattle, WA 98109
206-622-7850 (15)

Perlin, John, Newfoundland Cultural
Affairs Prince Philip Drive, Box 1854
Saint John's, Newfoundland, Canada
A1C 5P9 709-737-3650 (5)

Perlin, John C., The Arts and Culture
Centre Post Office Box 1854, Prince
Philip Drive Saint John's, Newfoundland,
Canada A1C 5P9 709-737-3650 (8)

Peroff, Peter, Canadian Independent
Theatrical Producers c/o 94 Belmont
Street Toronto, Ontario, Canada M5R
1P3 416-922-0084 (5)

Peroff, Peter, Bayview Playhouse 1605
Bayview Avenue Toronto, Ontario,
Canada M4G 3B5 416-481-6191 (8)

Peroff, Peter, Toronto Truck Theatre 94
Belmont Street Toronto, Ontario,
Canada M5R 1P8 416-922-0577;
416-922-0084 (16)

Perrault, Gisele, Theatre International de
Montreal 1455 rue Peel, Suite G-20
Montreal, Quebec, Canada H3A 1T5
514-526-0821 (16)

Perrier, Ronald G., Saint Cloud State
University Department of Theatre Saint
Cloud, MN 56301 612-255-3229 (4)

Perrier, Vince, Musicians' Union, Local
146 2601 Eastlawn Avenue Lorain, OH
44052 216-288-0408 (18)

Perry, George F., Marywood College
Department of Theatre Scranton, PA
18509 717-343-6521 (4)

Perry, Gregg, Alexander and Baldwin,
Incorporated Post Office Box 3440
Honolulu, HI 96801 808-525-6640 (10)

Perry, Ira E., Association Musicians Route
No 1 Rock Springs, WI 53961
608-522-4486 (18)

Perry, Jack, Crooked Tree Arts Council
461 East Mitchell Petoskey, MI 49770
616-347-4337; 616-347-7870 (5)

Perry, Joe, Kenosha Federation of
Musicians, Local 59 711 Washington
Road Kenosha, WI 53140 414-652-1465
(18)

Perry, Louis E., Musicians' Protective
Union, Local 231 533 Walnut Street
Bridgewater, MA 02324 617-697-4979
(18)

Perry, Robert, Magic Circle Theatre 615
West Wellington Avenue Chicago, IL
60657 312-929-0542 (16)

Perry, Roy, Musicians' Protective Union
313 First Northwest Madelia, MN 56062
507-625-3339 (18)

Perry, William Wade, Alexander
Auditorium Friends University Witchita,
KS 67213 316-263-9131 (8)

Petch, Ray, Calgary Musicians' Association
630 Eighth Avenue SW, #703 Calgary,
Alberta, Canada T2P 1G6 403-264-4727
(18)

Petek, Gary, Petek Sales 1541 Westlake
Avenue North Seattle, WA 98109
206-285-9006 (15)

Peters, Steven J., East Texas Baptist
College Department of Theatre 1209
North Grove Marshall, TX 75670
214-938-3911 (4)

Petersen, Vincent A., Tri-City Musical
Society, Local 67 422 East 14th Street
Davenport, IA 52803 319-322-7088 (18)

Peterson, Carl R., Cranford Dramatic Club
78 Winans Avenue Cranford, NJ 07016
201-276-7611 (16)

Peterson, Eric, Oldcastle Theatre
Company Southern Vermont College
Bennington, VT 05201 802-442-9463;
902-447-0564 (16)

Peterson, Harold, Kansas City Municipal
Auditorium 1310 Wyandotte Street
Kansas City, MO 64105 816-421-8000
(8)

Peterson, Harold R., Kansas City
Convention Center 301 West 13th Street
Kansas City, MO 64145 816-421-8000
(8)

Peterson, J.A., Durand Community Theatre 910 Auth Street Durand, WI 54736 (16)

Peterson, Larry, L.P. Marketing 2036 Livingston Street, #5 Oakland, CA 94606 415-532-5600 (15)

Peterson, Leo C., Musicians' Protective Union, Local 243 1723 21st Street Monroe, WI 53566 608-325-5764 (18)

Peterson, Pat, Marshall Arts Association 606 South First Street Marshall, MN 56258 (5)

Peterson, R., Fort Scott Community Theatre 2108 South Horton Fort Scott, KS 66701 (16)

Peterson, Richard F., Prairie State College Department of Theatre Chicago Heights, IL 60411 312-756-3110 (4)

Peterson, Robert, Musicians' Protective Union 511 West Jefferson Street Morris, IL 60450 815-942-3566 (18)

Peterson, William A., Lansing Community College Department of Theatre 419 North Capitol Lansing, MI 48914 517-373-7400 (4)

Petrafesa, John, Connecticut Theatre Supply/Theatre Concepts 282 Woodmont Road Milford, CT 06460 203-877-4507 (15)

Petrafesa, John, Connecticut Theatre Supply/ Theatre Concepts 40 Richmond Street Providence, RI 02903 401-331-7288 (15)

Petrik, D., Carson-Newman College Department of Theatre Russel Street Jefferson City, TX (4)

Petrik, Virgil, University of South Dakota, Springfield Department of Theatre Springfield, SD 57062 605-369-5414 (4)

Petro, Joseph J., Diversified Lighting 120 Pennsylvania Avenue Oreland, PA 19075 215-887-7480 (15)

Pettengill, Emma C., Orleans Arena Theatre Old Town Hall, Main Street Orleans, MA 02653 617-255-0695 (16)

Petterson, George F., Art Drapery Studios 6252 North Pulaski Chicago, IL 60646 312-736-9700 (15)

Pettit, Bonnie, Cochise Fine Arts Council Post Office Box 1783 Bisbee, AZ 85603 602-432-9951 (5)

Petty, James, Jackson Federation of Musicians 140 Highland Jackson, TN 38301 901-427-8348 (18)

Peuchen, W., Brandywiners 8725 Kennett Pike Centerville, DE 19807 (16)

Peyrose, Jack, Methodist College Department of Theatre Raleigh Road Fayetteville, NC 28301 919-488-7110; 919-488-4598 (4)

Peyrouse, Jack, East Tennessee State University Department of Theatre ETSU Station Johnson City, TN 37601 (4)

Pfaff, Charles, Association Musicians Route No 1 Rock Springs, WI 53961 608-522-4486 (18)

Pfaff, Virginia, Playhouse Square Foundation 1621 Euclid Avenue Cleveland, OH 44115 (16)

Pfanstiehl, Eliot, Montgomery County Arts Council 6400 Democracy Boulevard Bethesda, MD 20034 301-468-4172 (5)

Pfeiffer, F., Trojan Playhouse Willowbrook Road Cumberland, MD 21502 (16)

Pfisterer, Audrey, Kemmerer Council on the Arts 613 Emerald Kemmerer, WY 83101 307-877-6652 (5)

Ph.D, Douglas Duncan, McMaster University Department of Theatre Hamilton, Ontario, Canada 416-525-9140, extension 4660, 4661 (4)

Phelps, Jane, United Arts Rhode Island 45 Arcade Building Providence, RI 02903 401-351-2451 (5)

Phifer, Larry, Rend Lake College Department of Theatre Rural Route 1 Ina, IL 62846 618-437-5321 (4)

Philbrook, Gerald E., Musicians' Mutual Protective Union Post Office Box 1852 Longview, WA 98632 206-423-5010 (18)

Philibert, Robert A., Rapco Associates, Incorporated Post Office Box 7885 Metairie, LA 70010 504-887-9500 (15)

Phillip, J., Short Grass Players 204 West 7th Street Hays, KS 67601 (16)

Phillips, Gilbert, Shreveport Federation of Musicians, Local 116 517 Creswell Shreveport, LA 71101 318-222-5183; 318-424-3513 (18)

Phillips, Henry W., Henry W. Phillips Company 110 Mansel Circle Roswell, GA 30075 404-992-3070 (15)

Phillips, J., Burling Haylofters 509 East Jefferson Burlington, WI 53105 (16)

Phillips, J. Ward, Edmonds Art Festival Post Office Box 9344 Seattle, WA 98109 (9)

Phillips, Michael, Musical Union, Local 27 321 Edison Avenue New Castle, PA 16101 412-654-5182 (18)

Piacentive, Carmella V., Olin Corporation Charitable Trust 120 Long Ridge Road Stamford, CT 06904 203-356-3301; 203-356-3021 (10)

Piazza, Charles L., Musicians' Protective Union 123 South Main Street Albion, NY 14411 716-589-7760 (18)

Picha, Harold, Musicians' Protective Union Route 4, Post Office Box 377 New Prague, MN 56071 612-758-4566 (18)

Pickrell, H. Alan, Emory and Henry College Department of English Emory, VA 24327 (4)

Pierce, Jan, Warren Cultural Commission 29500 Van Dyke City Hall Warren, MI 48093 313-573-9500 (5)

Pierce, Paul, Anoka Theatre Ensemble 1500 South Ferry Street Anoka, MN 55303 (16)

Pierce, Randy, Coshocton Federation of Musicians 44206 South Route 36 Coshocton, OH 43812 614-622-8072 (18)

Pierce, Reade S., Ann Arbor Federation of Musicians Wolverine Building 202 East Washington, Suite 310 Saint Ann Arbor, MI 48108 313-668-8041 (18)

Piety, Gene, Gene Piety Factors 861 Mapunapuna Street Honolulu, HI 96802 808-839-9059 (15)

Pigeon, Jean-Claude, Le Theatre de l'Ile 1 rue Wellington Hull, Quebec, Canada 819-777-9164 (16)

Pigfird, Jimmy, Meridian Little Theatre Post Office Box 3055 Meridian, MS 39301 (16)

Pigford, Jimmy, Meridian Little Theatre Post Office Box 3055, North Station Meridian, MS 38301 601-482-6371 (8)

Pilkington, Ed, Horn in the West Post Office Box 295 Boone, NC 28607-0295 264-212-; 264-908- (16)

Pillar, Heinar, Canadian Independent Theatrical Producers c/o 94 Belmont Street Toronto, Ontario, Canada M5R 1P3 416-922-0084 (5)

Piller, Heinar, Errant Productions 651 Yonge Street Toronto, Ontario, Canada M4Y 1Z9 416-961-7675 (16)

Pincu, Thomas L., Colortran, Incorporated 1015 Chestnut Street Burbank, CA 91502 213-843-1200 (15)

Pine, Ralph, Drama Book Specialists Publishers 821 Broadway New York, NY 10003 212-582-1475 (14)

Pinker, Carole, Plastic Reel Corp. of America 7165 Willoughby Avenue Hollywood, CA 90046 213-851-7532 (15)

Piquette, Julia C., State University College Department of Theatre Buffalo, NY 14222 716-862-5900 (4)

Pisanesch, John, Luzern College Department of Drama Nanticoke, PA 18634 (4)

Pittmon, John, Tupelo Community Theatre 1014 Main Street Tupelo, MS 38801 601-842-4518 (8)

Pitts, J.P., Musicians' Association of Jacksonville 2030 Schumacher Avenue Jacksonville, FL 32207 904-398-9735 (18)

Plank, John, Arbor Theatre Company Post Office Box 1414 Peterborough, Ontario, Canada K9J 7H6 705-748-3022; 705-748-3111 (16)

Plant, Richard, Theatre History in Canada Massey College, University of Toronto Toronto, Ontario, Canada M5S 2E1 (14)

Platt, Martin L., Alabama Shakespeare Festival Post Office Box 141 Anniston, AL 36201 205-236-7503; 205-237-2332 (Summer Box Office) (9)

Plemel, William, Twin City Musicians' Association of Marinette Wisconsin and Menominee Michigan, Local 39 2034 Tenth Avenue Menominee, MI 49858 906-863-2073 (18)

Plessinger, Ralph T., Greenville Musicians' Association Post Office Box 73 Greenville, OH 45331 513-548-6714 (18)

Plonkey, Dr. Ken, USC Summer Theatre 2200 North Bonforts Boulevard Pueblo, CO 81001 303-549-2169; 303-584-3227 (16)

Plumb, Flora, Theatre 40 241 Moreno Drive Beverly Hills, CA 90210 213-277-4221 (16)

Pocase, Tom, Mobile Theatre Guild 14 North Lafayette Street Mobile, AL 36604 205-433-7513 (8)

Pochase, Tom, Mobile Theatre Guild Post Office Box 1265 Mobile, AL 36601 205-433-7513 (16)

Podolny, James H., James H. Podolny Co. 124 W. Washington Street Medina, OH 44256 216-725-8814 (15)

Poe, Fred, Murray State College Department of Theatre Tishomingo, OK 73460 405-371-2371 (4)

Poindexter, Richard, Musicians' Protective Union 1106 South 12th Burlington, IA 52601 319-754-4705 (18)

Poirier, Alain, Theatre du Nouvel-Ontario 79 rue Ignatius Sudbury, Ontario, Canada P3E 4P8 705-675-5606 (16)

Poirier, Rejean, Theatre Populaire C.P. 608 Caraquet, New Brunswick, Canada E0B 1K0 506-727-2712 (16)

Poland, Albert, Astor Place Theatre 434 Layfayette Street New York, NY 10003 212-254-4370 (8)

Polinsky, Joe, Theatre Two and Theatre Two Workshops 376 Boyleston Boston, MA 02116 617-864-1700 (16)

Pomer, Ellen, Theatre Plus 35 Front Street East Toronto, Ontario, Canada M5E 1B3 416-869-1255; 416-366-7723 (16)

Pomrenski, Micheline, Theatre-Soleil C.P. 205 Boucherville, Quebec, Canada J4B 5E6 514-524-1332 (16)

Pool, M., Texas Non-Profit Theatre 2410 Teckla Amarillo, TX 79106 (16)

Pooler, Louis, Musicians' Protective Association, Local 58 4022 West State Street Fort Wayne, IN 46898 219-483-7778 (18)

Popham, Kathryn, Erewhon Theatre Box 229 Station M Toronto, Ontario, Canada M6S 4T3 416-241-5407 (16)

Porcher, Nananne, Jean Rosenthal Associates, Inc. 765 Vose Avenue Orange, NJ 07050 201-674-1530 (1)

Porreca, Pete P., Uniontown Musical Society 121 Mayflower Drive Uniontown, PA 15401 412-438-7587 (18)

Porter, Mrs. H.W., Jackson Arts and Crafts Association 331 High Acres Drive Jackson, AL 36545 205-246-3545 (5)

Porter, James L., Kokomo Federation of Musicians, Local 141 3813 Candy Lane Kokomo, IN 46901 317-453-3261 (18)

Portlock, Cindy, Frap Company Post Office Box 40097 San Francisco, CA 94114 415-431-9350 (15)

Portlock, Miles, Orkney Springs Pavilion Orkney Springs Hotel Orkney Springs, VA 22845 703-856-2610 (8)

Porto, William, Musicians' Protective Association 2106 Stetler Drive Shamokin, PA 17872 717-648-0883 (18)

Posada, Emil, Chicago Federation of Musicians, Local 10 175 West Washington Street Chicago, IL 60602 312-782-0063 (18)

Potter, Gerry, Workshop West Playwrights' Theatre #5, 11020 65 Avenue Edmonton, Alberta, Canada T6H 1V9 403-436-7378 (16)

Potter, Richard, Musical Association 212 27th Avenue Altoona, PA 16602 814-943-3220 (18)

Poupart, Homer, Jean Dalrymple Associates 150 West 55th Street New York, NY 10019 212-246-7820 (12)

Powell, Gwendolyn C., Southwest Cultural Heritage Festival Oklahoma State University Stillwater, OK 74078 405-624-6217; 405-624-6142 (9)

Powell, J. P., Wilmington Black Theatre 313 North Broom Street Wilmington, DE 19805 (16)

Powell, Richard E., Musicians' Protective Union 1502 Eastern Avenue Morgantown, WV 26505 304-599-0793 (18)

Powell, William R., The Wilson Paint Company 1616 Harrison Avenue Cincinnati, OH 45214 513-251-5300 (15)

Powelson, W. C., Steubenville Musicians' Association, Local 223 507 First National Bank Building Steubenville, OH 43952 614-282-5212 (18)

Power, Dick, Needham Drama Workshop 5 Manning Street Needham, MA 02194 617-444-1178 (16)

Power, Peter J., Atlantic Federation of Musicians 6307 Chebucto Road Halifax, Nova Scotia, Canada B3L 1K9 902-422-6492 (18)

Powers, Harvey M., Bucknell University Department of Theatre Lewisburg, PA 17837 717-523-1271 (4)

Powers, Richard, McLane Center Alfred University Alfred, NY 14802 607-871-2193 (8)

Powers, William, Cranford Dramatic Club 78 Winans Avenue Cranford, NJ 07016 201-276-7611 (16)

Pranis, Nicholas D., Penn Hills Players 517 Macbeth Drive Pittsburgh, PA 15235 (16)

Prater, George, Cultural Activities Center Post Office Box 3292 Temple, TX 76501 817-773-9926 (5)

Prather, Deborah Z., Brookside Playhouse Inc. Shamokin Dam, PA 17876 717-743-1311 (16)

Pratt, Sydney W., Cowley County Community College Department of Theatre 125 East Second Street Arkansas, KS 67005 316-442-0430 (4)

Prendergast, Gabriel, University of Regina Department of Theatre Regina, Saskatchewan, Canada S4S 0A2 306-584-4866 (4)

Prentiss, Brett, Stephens College Department of Theatre East Broadway Columbia, MO 65201 314-442-2211 (4)

Presar, Charles J., West Virginia Wesleyan College Department of Drama Buckhannon, WV 26201 304-473-8044 (4)

President, Bennett Katz; , Brunswick Music Theatre/Coastal Theatre Workshop Post Office Box 656 Brunswick, ME 04011 207-725-8769; 207-882-7607 (16)

Press, Stephen, Dutchess Community College Department of Theatre Pindell Road Poughkeepsie, NY 12601 914-471-4500 (4)

Pressgrove, D., Wellington Community Theatre Post Office Box 573 Wellington, KS 67152 (16)

Pressnall, Lonn, Richland Community College Department of Theatre Decatur, IL 62526 217-875-7200 Extension 266; 217-875-7200 Extension 262 (4)

Preston, Mrs. William H., Northeast Mississippi Junior College Department of Theatre Booneville, MS 38829 602-728-6208 (4)

Price, Anita W., Children's Musical Theatre 408 Canal Street Fredericksburg, VA 22401 (16)

Price, Sylvia, Lighting Associates 2626 Lakeview, Suite 2008 Chicago, IL 60614 312-348-6767 (15)

Price, Wayne, Little Theatre of Norfolk 801 Claremont Avenue Norfolk, VA 23507 804-855-6033 (16)

Priest, Roberta P., Jonesboro Fine Arts Council Post Office Box 224 Jonesboro, AR 72401 501-932-1151 (5)

Priest, Stefani, San Francisco Actors Ensemble 2940 16th Street, Studio B-1 San Francisco, CA 94103 415-861-9015 (16)

Printer, Calvin Lee, Illinois State University Department of Theatre Normal, IL 61761 309-436-6683 (8)

Pritner, Calvin Lee, Illinois State University Department of Theatre Normal, IL 61761 309-436-8321 (4)

Prober, David, Ansell-Simplex Ticket Company 2970 Maria Avenue Northbrook, IL 60062 312-291-0696 (15)

Proctor, R., Falls Church Community Players 8601 Cottage Street Vienna, VA 22180 (16)

Prosser, David, Theatre 5 370 King Street West Kingston, Ontario, Canada K7L 4Y8 613-546-5460 (16)

Prouse, Peter, University of New Mexico Department of Theatre Albuquerque, NM 87131 505-277-4332; 505-277-2111 (4)

Provost, Gilles, Le Theatre des Lutins C.P. 7065 Ottawa, Ontario, Canada K1L 7065 613-523-8621 (16)

Provost, Gilles, Le Theatre des Lutins C.P. 132 Aylmer, Quebec, Canada 819-684-9598 (16)

Provost, Gilles, Le Theatre de l'Ile 1 rue Wellington Hull, Quebec, Canada 819-777-9164 (16)

Provosty, Mrs. Ledoux, Rapides Art Council Post Office Box 1064 Alexandria, LA 71301 318-443-3219 (5)

Pudzuvelis, Kathleen, Mount Mercy College Department of Theatre Cedar Rapids, IA 52402 (4)

Puff, Jean, Governor Wentworth Arts Council Post Office Box 743 Wolfeboro, NH 03894 603-569-2744 (5)

Pugh, Randall K., Yakima Little Theatre Group 5000 West Lincoln Yakima, WA 98908 509-966-0930 (16)

Pugliese, Peter, Musicians' Association of Westchester, Local 38 132 Larchmont Avenue Larchmont, NY 10538 914-834-0823 (18)

Pugliese, Dr. Rudolph E., University of Maryland Department of Theatre College Park, MD 20742 301-454-2740 (4)

Puia, Chub, Teco, Incorporated 1033 North East 44th Street Ft. Lauderdale, FL 33334 305-772-0242; 305-947-8751 (15)

Pulliam, Larry, Professional Musicians' Association 2314 3rd Street Port Neches, TX 77651 713-727-3393 (18)

Pullins, William, Candelight Dinner Playhouse 5620 South Harlem Avenue Summit, IL 60501 312-735-7400 (16)

Pulzynski, Donald, Mount Holly Recreation Center Brainerd Street Mount Holly, NJ 08060 609-267-0178 (8)

Purcell, Gerald W., Gerald W. Purcell Associates 133 Fifth Avenue New York, NY 10003 (2)

Purkiss, William, Orange Coast College Department of Theatre 2701 Fairview Road Costa Mesa, CA 92626 714-556-5725 (4)

Putnam, Linda, Normandale Community College Department of Theatre Bloomington, MN 55431 612-831-1 5001 (4)

Pyeatt, Woody, Albany Little Theatre Post Office Box 552 Albany, GA 31702 912-439-7141 (16)

Q

Quade, Patrick, Saint Olaf College Department of Theatre Northfield, MN 55057 507-663-3370 (4)

Qualls, Larry, Visual Resources, Incorporated 152 West 42nd Street, Suite 1219 New York, NY 10036 (15)

Quam, Sylvester, Northwestern College Department of Theatre Watertown, WI 53094 414-261-4352 (4)

Quaranta, Charles, Pueblo Musicians' Association, Local 69 Post Office Box 452 Pueblo, CO 81002 303-544-4725 (18)

Quave, Obra, William Carey College Department of Theatre Hattiesburg, MS 39401 601-582-5051 Extension 228 (4)

Quigley, John, Musicians' Mutual Protective Union Post Office Box 243 Sault Ste., MI 49783 906-635-5371 (18)

Quimby, Howard "Bud", Anchorage Musicians' Association 1851 East 53rd Anchorage, AK 99507 907-344-4665 (18)

Quinn, Deborah Baer, Manitoba Theatre Workshop 160 Princess Street Winnipeg, Manitoba, Canada R3B 1K9 204-942-7291 (16)

Quinn, Deborah Baer, The Neighborhood Theatre 160 Princess Street Winnipeg, Manitoba, Canada R3B 1K9 204-942-7291 (16)

Quinn, Marc L., Huron Country Playhouse Grand Bend, Ontario, Canada N0M 1T0 519-238-8387; 519-238-8451 (16)

Quirmbach, Wilford P., Robert Cooley Auditorium Milwaukee Technical College Milwaukee, WI 53203 414-278-6300; 414-278-6310 (8)

R

Rabbitt, Michael L., Drexel University Department of Theatre 32nd and Chestnut Street Philadelphia, PA 19104 215-895-2528 (4)

Rabjohns, Earl, Musicians' Protective Union, Local 128 1421 South West Street Jacksonville, IL 62650 217-245-9723 (18)

Rachow, Louis A., The Players, New York 16 Gramercy Park South New York, NY 10003 212-475-6116 (11)

Racine, Phyllis, Superwinch, Incorporated Connecticut Route 52 at Exit 95 Putnam, CT 06260 203-928-7787 (15)

Radar, C.East, Little Theatre 610 Coliseum Drive Winston-Salem, NC 27106 (16)

Radick, Al, Al Radick Post Office Box 26667 San Diego, CA 92126 815-886-3135 (15)

Raillard, Raymond, Texas Panhandle Heritage Foundation, Incorporated Post Office Box 268 Canyon, TX 79015 806-655-2181 (10)

Raillard, Raymond, Texas Musical Drama Post Office Box 268 Canyon, TX 79015 806-655-2181; 806-488-2220 (16)

Rainbow, Donald C., Bethel College Department of Theatre Saint Paul, MN 55112 (4)

Rains, Dale O., Presbyterian College Department of Fine Arts South Broad Street Clinton, SC 29325 803-833-2820 (4)

Rains, G.R., Heritage High School Theatre 7109 South Gallup Littleton, CO 80120 (16)

Rairgh, Helen T., Delaware Musical Society 2704 Society Drive Claymont, DE 19703 302-798-6060 (18)

Raitnover, Mrs. Lynn P., Nine O'Clock Players 1367 North Andrews Place Los Angeles, CA 90028 213-469-1973, Assistance League Switchboard; 213-499-1970 (16)

Rajeck, M., Lincoln Community Theatre 708 Merrill Avenue Merrill, WI 54452 (16)

Ramage, Chet, Musicians' Association, Local 76 2620 Third Avenue Seattle, WA 98121 206-623-0025 (18)

Ramage, Robert, Taconic Art Center Post Office Box 383 Hopewell Junction, NY 12533 914-226-9266 (5)

Ramp, Jim, Weatherford College Department of Theatre 308 East Park Weatherford, TX 76086 817-594-5471, Ext. 36 (4)

Ramsay, Mrs. Louis L., Pine Arts Council 2001 Country Club Lane Pine Bluff, AR 71601 501-535-1655 (5)

Ramsdell, Robert, Madison Musicians' Association 222 South Hamilton Madison, WI 53703 608-238-3421 (18)

Ramsden, Rob, National Electric Supply 5311 North Kedzie Avenue Chicago, IL 60625 312-463-1470 (15)

Ramsey, Carolyn, Berks County Arts Council Post Office Box 854 Reading, PA 19603 215-755-2104 (5)

Ramsey, Jack R., Moravian College Department of Theatre Bethlehem, PA 18018 215-865-0741; 214-861-1489 (4)

Ramsey, Margaret, Free Association 8707 Cranbrook Court Bethesda, MD 20817 301-365-0037 (16)

Ramsey, Val, Council of Arts, Greater San Jose 123 South Third Street San Jose, CA 95113 408-279-1131 (5)

Rane, Jeanie R., Abbeville Arts Council Post Office Box 172 Abbeville, AL 36310 205-585-2598 (5)

Ranger, Claire, Theatre Sans Fil 2665 Rouen Montreal, Quebec, Canada H2K 1M9 514-522-4637 (16)

Ranger, Claude, L'Hexagone C.P. 1534, Succursale B Ottawa, Ontario, Canada K1P 5W1 613-996-5051 (16)

Rankin, Dorothy, Puppet Studio and Little Theatre Marionettes 67 Lake Shore Road Peabody, MA 01960 617-595-4455 (16)

Rankin, Lindon, Worcester Foothills Theatre 6 Chatham Street Worcester, MA 01608 617-754-3314 (8)

Rankin, Rebecca, Florida Theatre Conference 100 Narvaez Drive Pensacola Beach, FL 32561 (5)

Rankin, Roy, Chippewa Valley Musicians' Association 2915 North Ninth Street Eau Claire, WI 54701 715-832-1937 (18)

Ransford, George, Indiana Electrical Sales 5160 East 65th Streeet Indianapolis, IN 46220 317-849-3880 (15)

Rapp, Abe, Musical Union, Local 85 444 Mc Clellan Street Schenectady, NY 12304 518-346-2086 (18)

Resnick, Sam, Barbizon Electric Company, Incorporated 426 West 55th Street New York, NY 10019 212-586-1620 (15)

Revitte, F., Dodge City Community College Department of Theatre Dodge City, KS 67801 (4)

Reynolds, Chris, Winthrop College Department of Theatre 319 Kinard Boulevard Rock Hill, SC 29733 803-323-2171 (4)

Reynolds, G. F. Barney, Musicians' Protective Union, Local 230 9 Seventh Avenue, North West Hampton, IA 50441 915-357-4421 (18)

Reynolds, Joan, Bemidji State College Department of Theatre Bemidji, MN 56601 281-755-3935 (4)

Rhea, Mrs. Howard W., Hancock County Drama Association Sneedville, TN 37869 (16)

Rhodes, Bob, Playhouse 196 3160 145 Street West Rosemount, MN 55024 (16)

Rhodes, Lucille, C.W. Post Center of Long Island University Department of Theatre Greenvale, NY 11548 516-299-2395 (4)

Rhodes, Milton, American Council on the Arts 570 5th Avenue New York, NY 10018 212-354-6655 (5)

Rian, Patrick J., Musicians' Protective Union, Local 30 1369 Eleanor Avenue St. Paul, MN 55116 612-698-0877; 612-699-9591 (18)

Rice, Eber J., Federation of Musicians Rural Route Number 1 Union, Ontario, Canada N5R 3A8 519-633-3730 (18)

Rice, Eugene, Saint Anselm's Commission on the Arts Saint Anselm's Drive Manchester, NH 03102 603-669-1030; 603-237-1030 (5)

Rice, Richard, Eckerd College Department of Theatre Saint Petersburg, FL 33733 813-867-1166 (4)

Rice, Richard A., Memphis State University Department of Drama Memphis, TX 38152 901-454-2565 (4)

Rice, Richard A., Memphis State University Department of Drama Memphis, TN 38152 901-454-2565 (8)

Rice, Robert J., Musicians' Protective Union Rural Route 5 Decatur, IN 46733 219-724-7670 (18)

Rice, Walter G., Dundalk Community College Department of Theatre Baltimore, MD 21222 (4)

Rich, Joseph A., Butte College Department of Theatre Route 1, Box 183A Oroville, CA 95965 916-895-2581 (4)

Richard, Lorraine, Compagnie de Quat'Sous 100 Avenue des Pins, Est Montreal, Quebec, Canada H2W 1N7 514-845-7278, Administrative; 514-845-7279, Box Office (16)

Richard, Lorraine, Compagnie Jean Duceppe 1400 rue Saint-Urbain Montreal, Quebec, Canada H2X 2M5 514-842-8194 (16)

Richards, J.W., Mendota Community Theatre Post Office Box 304 Mendota, IL 61342 (16)

Richards, Ray, Musicians' Protective Union 2122 20th Avenue, South Escanaba, MI 49829 906-786-0271 (18)

Richardson, Brian, Confidential Exchange 133 Albert Street Winnipeg, Manitoba, Canada R3B 1G6 204-452-7195 (16)

Richardson, Clair, Skylight Theatre 813 North Jefferson Street Milwaukee, WI 53202 414-271-8815 (8)

Richardson, Susan C., The Skid Road Theatre Pioneer Square Performing Arts Association Seattle, WA 98104 206-622-0251 (8)

Richie, Randall J., Toledo Federation of Musicians, Local 15-286 308 Hillcrest Hotel Toledo, OH 43624 419-243-2017 (18)

Richman, Mrs. Walter, University of California at Los Angeles Arts Council 405 Hilgard Avenue Los Angeles, CA 90024 213-825-3264 (5)

Richmond, Charles, Richmond Sound Design Ltd. 1234 West 6th Avenue Vancouver, British Columbia, Canada V6H 1A5 604-734-1217; 604-734-0705 (15)

Richter, Charles, Muhlenberg College Center for the Arts and Theatre Allentown, PA 18104 215-433-3191 (4)

Riddick, John, Sea and Sound Arts Council Post Office Box 1029 Manteo, NC 27954 (5)

Ridenour, Don, Pompano Players, Incorporated Post Office Box 2045 Pompano Beach, FL 33061 305-946-4646 (16)

Ridge, Sam, Puppet Theater Museum 511 South 11th Omaha, NB 68102 402-342-1313 (16)

Ridley, Robert, Southwest State University Department of Speech and Theatre Marshall, MN 56258 507-537-7103 (4)

Ried, James, Meadville Musical Society Road 2 Cochranton, PA 16314 814-333-1104 (18)

Rieffel, Karen, Fine Arts Committee 304 North Center Street Flora, IN 46929 219-967-3671 (5)

Rifkin, Lawrence J., Georgia State University Speech and Drama Department University Plaza Atlanta, GA 30303 404-658-2921 (4)

Riford, Susan C., Auburn Civic Theatre Post Office Box 506 Auburn, NY 13021 315-252-5876 (16)

Riley, Drexel H., Repertory Theater of America Post Office Box 1296 Rockport, TX 78382 512-729-6274 (16)

Riley, Ervin, Davie County Arts Council Post Office Box 744 Mocksville, NC 27028 704-634-2188 (5)

Riley, Perry, San Jacinto College Department of Theatre 5800 Uvalde Houston, TX 77049 713-458-4050 (4)

Rimmer, Mel, Colortran, Incorporated 3805 Cheyenne Drive Rowlett, TX 75088 214-375-4211 (15)

Rindfleisch, Greg, University of Wisconsin, Marshfield Department of Theatre Marshfield, WI 54449 715-387-1147 (4)

Ringel, Harriet M., Central Illinois Light Company 300 Liberty Street Peoria, IL 61602 309-672-5260 (10)

Ringer, Raymond H., Musicians' Protective Union Road Number 1, Box 190 Elizaville, NY 12534 518-828-3140 (18)

Riodan, Mary, Menomonie Theatre Guild Post Office Box 325 Menomonie, WI 54571 715-235-0001 (16)

Rioux, Monique, Theatre De La Marmaille 820 rue Lasalle Longueuil, Quebec, Canada J4K 3G5 514-677-6220 (16)

Rippy, Frances Mayhew, Ball State University Forum Ball State University Muncie, IN 47306 (14)

Riska, Robert D., Winward Theatre Guild Post Office Box 624 Kailua, HI 96734 808-254-2356 (16)

Ritch, Andrew J., Schreiner College Department of Fine Arts Post Office Box 4498 Kerrville, TX 78028 512-896-5411 (4)

Ritchie, Carl, Colegio Cesar Chevez Department of Theatre Mount Angel, OR 97362 503-843-2234 (4)

Ritchie, Harry M., University of Denver Department of Theatre University Park Denver, CO 80208 303-753-2518 (4)

Ritter, Don, Aim Community College Department of Theatre Greeley, CO 80631 (4)

Ritz, R., Stage Lighting Discount Corporation 5 Ferndale Road New City, NY 10956 914-634-9494 (15)

Rivers, Benny Anthony, Jaceo Community Theatre - Black Fire Company 1823 Avenue E Ensley Birmingham, AL 35218 205-780-7510, Ext. 24 (16)

Roach, Clara, Cleburne Arts and Crafts League Route 4, 101 Evans Bridge Road Heflin, AL 36264 205-463-7917; 205-463-2223 (5)

Roach, Jim, Panhandle State University Department of Theatre Goodwell, OK 73939 405-349-2611 Extension 255 (4)

Roach, Ray, Ballantyne Flamproofing Company 2722 North Lincoln Avenue Chicago, IL 60614 312-348-7770 (15)

Robb, Mr. Phillip, Kent State University Professional Arts Center 6000 Frank Avenue Canton, OH 44720-7599 216-499-9600 (4)

Robbins, Herm, Herm Robbins Associates 34B Pilgrims Harbor Wallingford, CT 06492 203-265-5045 (15)

Robbins, Kenneth R., Newberry College Department of Theatre Newberry, SC 29108 803-276-8104 (4)

Robbins, Linda B., Worcester Children's Theatre 1782 Wachasett Street Jefferson, MA 01522 617-829-3411 (16)

Robbins, Richard L., Robbins-Zust Marionettes and Theatre East Road Richmond, MA 01254 413-698-2591 (16)

Robbins, Sanford, University of Wisconsin, Milwaukee School of Fine Arts Milwaukee, WI 53201 414-963-4762 (4)

Robbins, W. "Curly", Freeport Musical Association 605 East Jefferson Street Freeport, IL 61032 815-233-1040 (18)

Robel, R., Dharma Trading Company Post Office Box 916 San Rafael, CA 94902 415-456-1211; 415-841-7722 (15)

Roberts, Dominic, Hamilton Musicians' Association, Local 31 4716 Fairfield Avenue Fairfield, OH 45014 513-892-7922 (18)

Roberts, Gerald, Chateau De Ville Dinner Theatre 2 Dinsmore Avenue Framingham, MA 01701 (16)

Roberts, John D., Amarillo Federation of Musicians 2608 Northwest 2nd Avenue Amarillo, TX 79106 806-374-2532 (18)

Roberts, Norman, Northampton Community College Department of Theatre Bethlehem, PA 18017 (4)

Roberts, Vera, Hunter College Department of Theatre 695 Park Avenue New York, NY 10021 213-570-5747 (4)

Robertson, Clifton, Worcester Memorial Auditorium Worcester, MA 01608 617-752-6703 (8)

Robertson, Gordon, Theatre 5 370 King Street West Kingston, Ontario, Canada K7L 4Y8 613-546-5460 (16)

Robertson, J., The Adelphians 9539 Riggs Road Adelphi, MD 20783 (16)

Robertson, Martha, Mountain Valley Council on the Arts Post Office Box 592 Albertville, AL 35950 205-593-7505 (5)

Robertson, Shirley, Upstairs At Old Angelo's 45 Elm Street Toronto, Ontario, Canada 416-597-0155 (16)

Robinson, Alton G., Musicians' Protective Union 2761 Webb Street Vallejo, CA 94590 707-642-5834 (18)

Robinson, Arnie, Robart-Green Commpany 17-21 Newark Way Maplewood, NJ 07040 201-761-7400 (15)

Robinson, Brian P., Smile Theatre Company 121 Avenue Road Toronto, Ontario, Canada M5R 2G3 416-961-0050 (16)

Robinson, Charles K., Hudson County Office of Cultural Affairs 595 Newark Avenue Jersey City, NJ 07306 201-659-5062 (5)

Robinson, Don, Don Robinson 1921 Moser #220 Dallas, TX 75206 214-233-0731 (16)

Robinson, E., Footlight Players Post Office Box 62 Charleston, SC 29401 (16)

Robinson, James, Hollywood Lights, Incorporated 0625 SW Florida Portland, OR 97219 503-244-5808; 503-245-2236 (15)

Robinson, William A., Thiel College Department of Theatre Greenville, PA 16125 (4)

Robotti, Eva C., Duquesne University Department of Theatre Pittsburgh, PA 15219 412-434-6460 (4)

Roddey, David, Bozak Incorporated 3819 Oakcliff Industrial Court Atlanta, GA 30340 404-448-3790 (15)

Rodgers, James W., William Paterson College Department of Theatre 300 Pompton Road Wayne, NJ 07470 201-595-2335; 201-595-2314 (4)

Rodriguez, Jeanne, Mayor's Council on the Arts Borough Building, Exchange Street Susquehanna, PA 18847 717-853-4625 (5)

Rodwell, Robert, Florala Area Arts Council 602 East Fifth Avenue Florala, AL 36442 205-858-3227 (5)

Rogers, Bruce, Vassar Playhouse Post Office Box 5 Vassar, KS 66543 913-828-3249 (8)

Rogers, Clark, New Mexico State University Little Theatre New Mexico State University Las Cruces, NM 88003 505-646-2421 (8)

Rogers, Frank B., Sherman Players Jericho Road Sherman, CT 06784 203-354-3622 (16)

Rogers, I., Horseshoe Stage 7458 Melrose Los Angeles, CA 90046 (16)

Rogers, Joel, Rising Tide Theatre Post Office Box 7371 Saint John's, Newfoundland, Canada A1E 3Y5 709-579-4438 (16)

Rogers, Paul W., Dayton Musicians' Association, Local 101-473 415 Troy Street Dayton, OH 45404 513-223-6962 (18)

Rogers, Veda, Vassar Playhouse Post Office Box 5 Vassar, KS 66543 913-828-3249 (8)

Rogers, Mrs. William, Lexington Children's Theatre Division of the Living Arts and Science Center Lexington, KY 40512 606-252-1381 (16)

Roggeveen, Robert H., Aetna Life and Casualty 151 Farmington Avenue Hartford, CT 06156 203-273-2465; 203-273-7589 (10)

Rogut, Howard, The Virginia Theatre 245 West 52nd Street New York, NY 10019 212-246-6270; 212-840-8181 (16)

Rohde, Linda, Chester Fritz Auditorium Box 8282, University Station Grand Forks, ND 58202 701-777-3076; 701-777-4211 (8)

Rohland, Ronald C., Musicians' Protective Union 55 Rosedale Avenue Greenville, PA 16125 412-588-7604 (18)

Rolf, D., Geneva Players 3300 Wilshire Los Angeles, CA 90005 (16)

Roller, Max F., Channon Corporation 1343 West Argyle Chicago, IL 60640 312-475-4700 (15)

Rolloff, Arley, Musicians' Protective Association Route 1, Post Office Box 89-1 New Ulm, MN 56073 507-354-6807 (18)

Rolls, Dan, Holly Fine Arts Council 111 College Street Holly, MI 48442 313-634-7341 (5)

Roloff, Michael, Urizen Books 66 West Broadway New York, NY 10007 212-962-3413 (14)

Rom, Bob, Santa Rosa Junior College Department of Theatre Arts 1501 Mendocino Avenue Santa Rosa, CA 95401 707-527-4418; 707-527-4328 (4)

Romans, Guy, Sangamon State University Department of Theatre Shephard Road Springfield, IL 62708 217-786-6600 (4)

Romeiser, Larry, Musicians' Association 315 South Willow North Platte, NE 69101 308-532-5351 (18)

Rondeau, Jean-Leon, Theatre Parminou C.P. 158 312 rue Olivier Victoriaville, Quebec, Canada G6P 6S8 819-758-0577 (16)

Roney, Edmund, Ripon College Department of Drama Ripon, WI 54971 414-748-8136; 414-748-7525 (4)

Roney, Edmund, Benstead Theatre Rodman Center for the Arts Ripon College Ripon, WI 54971 414-748-8136 (8)

Ronnow, H. Kris, Harris Bank Foundation 111 West Monroe Street Chicago, IL 60690 312-461-6660 (10)

Roof, Susan, University of South Carolina Department of Theatre and Speech The Horseshoe Columbia, SC 29208 803-777-4288; 803-777-5208 (4)

Rooney, Alice, Allied Arts of Seattle 107 South Main Street Seatlle, WA 98104 206-624-0432 (5)

Root, John, Guitar Center 928 Van Ness Avenue San Francisco, CA 94109 415-441-4020 (15)

Rose, Frank, The Playhouse 1700 North Grimes Hobbs, NM 88240 505-393-9524 (8)

Rose, Jack, Jack Rose/Dorothy Day Otis Agency 6430 Sunset Boulevard Los Angeles, CA 90028 213-461-4911 (2)

Rose, Mrs. Jane, Seven Lively Arts Festival, Hollywood Lively Arts Festival Hollywood, FL 33200 (9)

Rose, M.J., Stockton State College Department of Theatre Pamona, NJ 08239 609-652-1776 (4)

Rose, Peggy Haessler, Milwaukee Repertory Theatre 929 North Water Street Milwaukee, WI 53202 414-273-7121 - Business Office; 414-273-7206 - Box Office (16)

Rose, Phyllis Jane, At the Foot of the Mountain 3144 Tenth Avenue, South Minneapolis, MN 55407 612-375-9487; 612-825-2820 (16)

Rose, Richard, Necessary Angel Theatre 20 Dupont Street, Unit 3 Toronto, Ontario, Canada M5R 1V2 416-932-6119 (16)

Rose, Robin, Colonnades Theatre Lab 428 Lafayette Street New York, NY 10003 212-673-2222, Theatre; 212-598-4620, Lab (16)

Roseborough, Timothy E., Hampton Institute Department of Drama Hampton, VA 23668 804-727-5401 (4)

Rosen, Richard, Richards Rosen Press Incorporated 29 East 21st Street New York, NY 10010 212-777-3017 (14)

Rosen, Ruth C., Richards Rosen Press Incorporated 29 East 21st Street New York, NY 10010 212-777-3017 (14)

Rosen, Sheldon, Guild of Canadian Playwrights The Writers Centre Toronto, Ontario, Canada M5T 2P3 416-868-6917 (18)

Rosenberg, L., New Dimension Theatre Studio c/o YMHA of Bergen County Hackensack, NJ 07601 201-489-5900 (16)

Rosenblatt, Bernard S., American Theatre Association 1010 Wisconsin Avenue, NW Washington, DC 20005 202-342-7530 (5)

Rosenblum, Jonathan, Ryan Repertory Company 2445 Bath Avenue Brooklyn, NY 11214 718-373-5208 (16)

Rosenblum, M. Edgar, Long Wharf Theatre 222 Sargent Drive New Haven, CT 06511 203-787-4284; 203-787-4282 (Box Office) (16)

Rosenblum, Murry, Murry Rosenblum Sound Associates, Inc. 21-36 33rd Road Long Island City, NY 11106 212-728-2654 (15)

Rosenblum, Ray H., Marietta Arts Council c/o WMOA Radio, Box 708 Marietta, OH 45750 614-373-1490 (5)

Rosenbush, Bernard, Tuscaloosa Musicians' Protective Association 53 Arcadia Tuscaloosa, AL 35401 205-553-0645 (18)

Rosenthal, Mark, Galena Art Theatre c/o Sue Corbett Galena, IL 61036 815-777-1367 (16)

Ross, Fran, Worcester Jewish Community Center 633 Salisbury Street Worcester, MA 01608 617-756-7109 (8)

Ross, G., Lakevale Players 2531 West Meredith Drive Vienna, VA 22180 (16)

Ross, George, London Musician's Association 149 Wortley Road London, Ontario, Canada N6C 3P4 519-438-3870 (18)

Ross, Dr. James A., Baldwin-Wallace College Department of Theatre 275 Eastland Road Berea, OH 44017 216-826-2900 (4)

Ross, Mrs. Jane, Cape Cod Musicians' Association, Local 155 8 Ridgedale Avenue, Post Office Box 221 West Dennis, MA 02670 617-394-4537 (18)

Ross, Laura, Theatre Communications 355 Lexington Avenue New York, NY 10017 100-7; 212-697-5230 (14)

Ross, Linda, Cleveland Community Theatre Post Office Box 44 Cleveland, MS 38732 (16)

Ross, Norman, Urban Services Cultural Arts Project 1400 Orleans Street Baltimore, MD 21231 (16)

Ross, Dr. Paul, Monroe County Community College Department of Theatre 1555 South Raisinville Road Monroe, MI 48161 313-242-7300 (4)

Ross, R. Kenneth, Municipal Arts Department City Hall, Room 1500 Los Angeles, CA 90012 213-485-2433 (5)

Ross, Ted, Denver Center for the Performing Arts-Bonfils Theatre East Colfax at Elizabeth Denver, CO 80206 303-322-7725, Box Office; 303-399-5418, Other Departments (16)

Ross, W.D., University of Southern California Department of Theatre Los Angeles, CA 90007 415-743-2703 (4)

Rossi, Angelo Del, Cape Playhouse Route 6A Dennis, MA 02638 617-385-3838 (8)

Rossini, Rocky, Amherst Lumber Company 700 Mill Avenue Amherst, OH 44001 216-988-4431 (15)

Roter, T., Group Theatre 1211 4th Street Santa Monica, CA 90401 (16)

Roth, Diane H., Sound Chamber 12041 Burbank Boulevard North Hollywood, CA 91607 213-985-1376; 213-761-1454 (15)

Roth, Sheila, Saidye Bronfman Centre 5170 Cote Saint Catherine Road Montreal, Quebec, Canada H3W 1M7 514-739-2301 (16)

Rothman, Carole, The Second Stage 200 West 72nd Street, Suite 20 New York, NY 10023 212-787-8302 (16)

Rothman, Norman, N.R. Associates 74 Westlyn Drive Bardonia, NY 10954 914-623-6299; 914-623-2063 (15)

Rotta, Julia, Putnam Arts Council Post Office Box 156 Mahopac, NY 10541 914-628-3664 (5)

Rough, William H., Southern Seminary Junior College Department of Theatre Buena Vista, VA 24416 703-261-6181 (4)

Roulston, Keith, Blyth Summer Festival Post Office Box 291 Blyth, Ontario, Canada N0M 1H0 519-523-9300 (16)

Roux, Jean-Louis, Theatre du Nouveau Monde 84 Ouest rue Ste-Catherine Montreal, Quebec, Canada H2X 1Z6 514-932-3137 (16)

Rovine, Milton, Once Upon a Stage 3376 Edgewater Orlando, FL 32804 305-425-8400 (16)

Rowe, Bill, Roberts Arts Center 3626 River Road Salem, OR 97303 503-378-9060 (5)

Rowe, Douglas, Festival of the Arts 1455 Terrace Way Laguna Beach, CA 92651 714-494-8021 (16)

Rowe, Douglas, Laguna Moulton Community Playhouse 606 Laguna Canyon Road Laguna Beach, CA 92651 714-494-8021 (16)

Rowell, Gene A., Gene A. Rowell 1222 Country Club Drive Orlando, FL 32804 305-425-6228 (15)

Rowland, Charles D., Mesabi Community College Department of Theatre 905 West Chestnut Street Virginia, MN 55792 218-741-9200 (4)

Rowley, T. Leonard, Weber State College Department of Theatre 3750 Harrison Boulevard Ogden, UT 84415 801-626-6431 (4)

Roy, Denise, Catalyst Theatre Society 9903 80 Avenue Edmonton, Alberta, Canada T6E 1T2 403-452-3557 (16)

Roys, B., Beta Sigma Fellowship 23369 Longview Dearborn Heights, MI 48127 (16)

Royster, F., Piedmont Players Theatre Post Office Box 762 Salisbury, NC 28144 (16)

Rozak, Irving, R-Columbia Product Company, Incorporated 2008 St. Johns Avenue Highland Park, IL 60035 312-432-7915 (15)

Rozzi, Art, Newco Products, Incorporated 11605 Lebanon Road Loveland, OH 45040 513-683-1825 (15)

Rozzi, Nancy, Newco Products, Incorporated 11605 Lebanon Road Loveland, OH 45040 513-683-1825 (15)

Rubenstein, Lee G., Arena Stage 6th and Maine Avenue SW Washington, DC 20024 202-554-9066 (16)

Rubes, Susan, ASSITEJ-Canadian Centre 4808 Saint Denis Street Montreal, Quebec, Canada H2J 2L6 514-288-9343 (5)

Rubin, Arthur, The Neil Simon Theatre 250 West 52nd Street New York, NY 10019 212-757-8646; 212-398-8383, Group Sales (16)

Rubin, Don, York University Department of Theatre 4700 Keele Street, Room 206A Downsview, Ontario, Canada M3J 1P3 416-667-2247; 416-667-3237 (4)

Rubin, Don, Canadian Theatre Review Publications York University, 4700 Keele Street Downsview, Ontario, Canada M3J 1P3 416-667-3768 (14)

Rubinstein, Lori, San Diego Stage and Lighting Supply 2002 State Street San Diego, CA 92101 714-235-8379 (15)

Ruble, Dr. Ronald, Bowling Green State University, Firelands Department of Theatre 901 Rye Beach Road Huron, OH 44839 419-433-5560 (4)

Ruckdeschel, J., Group Theatre East 119 Glenwood Road Merion, PA 19066 (16)

Rucker, Pat, Eastern New Mexico University Department of Theatre Portales, NM 88130 505-562-2711; 505-562-2712 (4)

Rucker, Ron, Booth Tarkington Civic Theatre 1200 West 38th Street Indianapolis, IN 46322 (16)

Rudall, D. Nicholas, Court Theatre University of Chicago Chicago, IL 60637 312-753-3581 (8)

Schoettler, Robert A., Fresno Convention Center Theatre 700 M Street Fresno, CA 93721 209-488-1515 (8)

Schofield, Ann, Theatre of the Open Eye 316 East 88th Street New York, NY 10028 212-534-6363 (16)

Schons, Alain, Dell'Arte School of Mime and Comedy Department of Theatre Blue Lake, CA 95525 707-668-5411; 707-668-5782 (4)

Schoonmaker, J.Y., J.Y. Schoonmaker Company 10710 Sand Hill Road Dallas, TX 75238 214-349-1650 (15)

Schopf, Richard T., Anchorage Musicians' Association 1851 East 53rd Anchorage, AK 99507 907-344-4665 (18)

Schott, Edmund J., Northampton Federation of Musicians, Local 220 31 Davis Street Easthampton, MA 01027 413-527-4094 (18)

Schrader, Lynn, Klamath Arts Council Post Office Box 1703 Klamath, OR 97601 503-882-1503 (5)

Schrag, Phyllis, Freeman Area Arts Council Route 2 Marion, SD 57043 605-648-3474 (5)

Schramm, R.C., Broadway Costumes 932 West Washington Chicago, IL 60607 312-829-6400 (15)

Schramm, R.C., Odd's 'N Ends Unlimited 932 West Washington Boulevard Chicago, IL 60607 312-666-2660 (15)

Schroeder, Robert, Huntingburg Arts Committee Route 2 Huntingburg, IN 88351 812-683-2324 (5)

Schubert, Gerard, Allentown College of Saint Francis De Sales Department of Theatre Station Avenue Center Valley, PA 18034 215-282-1100 (4)

Schucker, Irv, Swivelier, Incorporated 33 Route 304 Nanuet, NY 10954 914-623-3471 (15)

Schueneman, Warren W., Anoka-Ramsey Community College Department of Theatre Coon Rapids, MN 55443 (4)

Schuller, Robert G., Musicians' Protective Union 11 Adams Drive Randolph, MA 02368 617-963-0151 (18)

Schulman, Rose, Hedgerow Theatre School Rose Valley Road Moylan, PA 19065 215-566-9892 (4)

Schultz, Gary D., Riverside City College Department of Theatre 4800 Magnolia Avenue Riverside, CA 92506 714-684-3240 (4)

Schultz, Ray, Mid-Atlantic Center for the Arts Post Office Box 164 Cape May, NJ 08204 (5)

Schumacher, Thomas, Christian Brothers College Department of Theatre 650 East Parkway South Memphis, TN 38104 901-278-0100 (4)

Schumaker, Peter H., Tri-City Musical Society, Local 67 422 East 14th Street Davenport, IA 52803 319-322-7088 (18)

Schupp, Jim, University Foundation Center Austin Auditorium Oregon State University Corvallis, OR 97331 3102 503-754-2402 (8)

Schuschke, Werner, Border Musicians' Association, Local 156 Post Office Box 347 International Falls, MN 56649 218-283-2251 (18)

Schwab, James E., The Baldwin Foundation 1801 Gilbert Avenue Cincinnati, OH 45202 513-852-7965 (10)

Schwartz, Allen, Musicians' Association of East Aurora 452 Franklin Street Buffalo, NY 14202 716-886-5902 (18)

Schwartz, Inge, Tallahassee Little Theatre Post Office Box 3262 Tallahassee, FL 32303 904-224-8474 (16)

Schwartz, J., Centinela Playhouse 400 West Beach Inglewood, CA 90302 (16)

Schwartz, Moe, Gothic Color Company, Incorporated 727-729 Washington Street New York, NY 10014 212-929-7493; 212-929-7494 (15)

Schwarz, Ernest, The Red Barn Theatre Post Office Box 291 Jackson's Point, Ontario, Canada L0E 1L0 416-722-3741 (16)

Schwarz, Ernest J., Studio Lab Theatre 235 Macdonell Toronto, Ontario, Canada M6R 2A9 416-531-4832 (16)

Schwatz, Aaron, Four Winds Theatre 37 West 10th Street New York, NY 10011 212-260-3939 (16)

Scigliano, Michael, The Cleveland Federation of Musicians, Local 4 2200 Carnegie Avenue Cleveland, OH 44115 216-771-1802 (18)

Scism, Delos Mark, National Theatre of the Deaf Little Theatre 305 Great Neck Road Waterford, CT 06385 203-442-0066; 203-443-7406 (16)

Scott, Michael, Michael Scott Company, Incorporated 20 Walnut Street Wellesley Hills, MA 02181 617-235-0102 (15)

Scott, Virginia, University of Massachusetts at Amherst Department of Theatre 112 Fine Arts Center Amherst, MA 01003 413-545-2214; 413-545-3490 (4)

Scott, Winfield, Richland Community College Department of Theatre Decatur, IL 62526 217-875-7200 Extension 266; 217-875-7200 Extension 262 (4)

Scoville, Mrs. Mary G., Franklin County Musicians' Association 151 Davis Street Greenfield, MA 01301 413-773-9769 (18)

Scranton, B., Troy Civic Theatre 1130 Fairway Drive Troy, OH 45373 (16)

Seaman, B.J., B.J. Seaman and Company 1801 South Lumber Chicago, IL 60634 312-666-6580; 312-733-7911 (15)

Seaman, Grace, Village Theatre Incorporated Post Office Box 32 Arlington Heights, IL 60006 312-259-3200 (16)

Seaman, Jacki, Willingboro Theatre of the Performing Arts Post Office Box 398 Willingboro, NJ 08046 609-387-3226 (16)

Seaman, Janet, Shelby County Arts Council 410 Meadow Road Montevallo, AL 35115 205-665-4132 (5)

Seaver, Avi, Huron College Department of Theatre Huron, SD 57350 605-352-8721 (4)

Sebald, Louis, Canton Memorial Civic Center 1101 North Market Avenue Canton, OH 44702 216-489-3090; 216-489-3000 (8)

Sebren, Herb, Norfolk Musicians' Association, Local 125 Post Office Box 201 Norfolk, VA 23501 804-622-8095 (18)

Sebring, Jerry, Jerry Sebring 505 14th Street, SE Owatonna, MN 55060 507-451-5220 (15)

Second, R.E., Wintario Ministry of Culture and Recreation Toronto, Ontario, Canada M7A 2R9 416-965-0617 (5)

Sederholm, Jack P., Elizabethtown College Department of Drama Elizabethtown, PA 17022 717-367-1151 (4)

Seehafer, Brian, Musicians' Protective Association 21 Brown Boulevard Rothschild, WI 54474 715-359-2505 (18)

Sefton, M., Saints And Sinners 1324 Monoco Parkway Denver, CO 80222 (16)

Seidel, Alfred R., Musicians' Protective Union, Local 140 17 Grove Street Wilkes-Barre, PA 18702 717-822-4426 (18)

Seifter, Sandra, Albany City Arts Office Department of Human Resources Albany, NY 12208 518-472-6147 (5)

Seigerman, Bette, Southern Berkshire Community Arts Council Post Office Box 232 Monterey, MA 02145 413-528-3747 (5)

Seitz, Lawrence M., Musicians' Association of Skagit Post Office Box 46 Oak Harbor, WA 98277 206-424-4995 (18)

Seixas, Robert, Musicians' Protective Union 11 Adams Drive Randolph, MA 02368 617-963-0151 (18)

Selby, Anne, Stratford Festival Post Office Box 520 Stratford, Ontario, Canada N5A 6V2 519-271-4040; 416-273-1600 (9)

Seligman, Marvin, Lowel-Light Mfg., Incorporated 475 Tenth Avenue New York, NY 10019 212-947-0950 (15)

Sellers, Barbara, PCPA Theatrefest Post Office Box 1700 Santa Maria, CA 93456 213-925-4009; 213-925-3288 (9)

Selman, Jan, Catalyst Theatre Society 9903 80 Avenue Edmonton, Alberta, Canada T6E 1T2 403-452-3557 (16)

Semmes, David H., University of Wisconsin, Manitowoc Department of Theatre 705 Viebahn Street Manitowoc, WI 54220 414-682-8251 (4)

Semon, Mrs. Stuart, Warehouse Theatre 5000 West Lincoln Yakima, WA 98908 509-966-0930 (8)

Semon, Mrs. Stuart, Yakima Little Theatre Group 5000 West Lincoln Yakima, WA 98908 509-966-0930 (16)

Semple, Robert B., BASF Wyandotte Corporation 100 Cherry Hill Road Parsippany, NJ 07054 201-282-3300 (10)

Sena, Russell, Savannah Federation of Musicians 258 A Mulberry Way Westwood Heights, Rincon, GA 31326 912-826-5905 (18)

Senecal, Donald G., Cooperative Arts Council of Clark County Post Office Box 1995 Vancouer, WA 98663 206-696-8171 (5)

Seniff, Richard, Richard Seniff R.R. #8, Post Office Box 87 Normal, IL 61761 309-452-2089 (15)

Sennes, Eugene J., Musical Union, Local 85 444 Mc Clellan Street Schenectady, NY 12304 518-346-2086 (18)

Senteney, Jack, West Valley College Department of Theatre 14000 Fruitvale Saratoga, CA 95070 408-867-2200 (4)

Sepler, Eric, Kinetic Artistry 7216 Carroll Avenue Tacoma Park, MD 20012 301-270-6666 (15)

Seralio, Evelyn, DC Community Theatre 2826 Newton Street, SE Washington, DC 20018 (16)

Sergel, Christopher, Dramatic Publishing Company 4150 North Milwaukee Avenue Chicago, IL 60641 312-545-2062 (14)

Serhienko, Gerry, Musicians' Protective Association, Local 229 201 Missouri River Road Mandan, ND 58554 701-667-1077; 701-663-5775 (18)

Serra, Enrico, Musicians' Protective Union 40 Southwest Avenue Vineland, NJ 08360 609-692-1039 (18)

Serran, Susan, Theatre Passe Muraille 16 Ryerson Avenue Toronto, Ontario, Canada M5T 2P3 416-363-8988; 416-363-0555 (16)

Settles, George W., Opera House Players c/o Abbeville Opera House Abbeville, SC 29620 803-459-2157 (16)

Severa, Joan, State Historical Society of Wisconsin 816 State Street Madison, WI 53706 608-262-0459 (15)

Severns, Pat, Traveller's Community Theatre 411 South Halliburton Kirksville, MO 63501 (16)

Seward, Charles L., Terre Haute Federation of Musicians, Local 25 1337 Drieser Square Terre Haute, IN 47807 812-234-6750 (18)

Seward, Harry P., Bankers Life Nebraska Cotner at O Street Lincoln, NE 68501 402-467-1120 (10)

Seward, Roger, Arena Civic Theatre Inc. Post Office Box 744 Greenfield, MA 01301 413-773-8111 (16)

Seyglinski, Leon A., Shakespeare Festival of Woodbridge 428 South Park Drive Woodbridge, NJ 07095 201-634-2496 (9)

Shadbolt, Ron, London Musician's Association 149 Wortley Road London, Ontario, Canada N6C 3P4 519-438-3870 (18)

Shadduck, Barbara, Central Oregon Arts Association 456 Fifth Madras, OR 97741 (5)

Shafer, Donald, Musicians' Protective Union, Local 179 102 Gates Street Marietta, OH 45750 614-374-5473 (18)

Shaff, Dick, Long Beach Convention Center Arena 300 East Ocean Boulevard Long Beach, CA 213 436 3636 213-436-3636 (8)

Shalansky, Ruby, Warwick Arts Foundation Post Office Box 726 Warwick, RI 02888 401-942-2399 (10)

Shambley, Billie, Pittsboro Arts Advisory Committee Post Office Box 753 Pittsboro, NC 27312 919-542-4642 (5)

Shanholtz, Eddie, Association of Professional Musicians, Local 204 146 Highway No. 1, #25 Edison, NJ 08817 201-572-2832 (18)

Shank, Richard, Cornell University Department of Theatre Arts 104 Lincoln Hall Ithaca, NY 14853 607-256-4060 (4)

Shanks, Marian L., Las Medanos College Department of Theatre Pittsburg, CA 94565 (4)

Shannon, Dr. James P., General Mills Foundation Post Office Box 1113 Minneapolis, MN 55440 612-540-3337 (10)

Shapira, Jack, Rainbow Stage 500 - 352 Donald Street Winnipeg, Manitoba, Canada R3B 2H8 204-942-2091; 204-942-3032 (16)

Sharp, Harry, California Polytechnic State University Speech Communications Department San Luis Obispo, CA 93407 805-546-2553 (4)

Shatts, O., Strobelite Company, Incorporated 10 East 23rd Street New York, NY 10010 212-677-9220 (15)

Shaw, John, Bozak, Incorporated c/o Centurian Marketing, Box 1011 Ballwin, MO 63011 314-227-7229 (15)

Shaw, Jonathon, Magnus Theatre North-West 639 McLaughlin Street Thunder Bay, Ontario, Canada P7C 3B6 807-623-1337; 807-623-1321 (16)

Shawgo, Michael C., Centennial Hall Augustana College Rock Island, IL 61201 309-794-7306 (8)

Shea, Andrew J., Sico, Incorporated 7525 Cahill Road Minneapolis, MN 55435 613-941-1700 (15)

Shearwood, James, Manhattanville College Department of Theatre Purchase Street Purchase, NY 10577 914-946-9600 (4)

Sheehan, Deborah, The Learning Theatre Post Office Box 2144 Paterson, NJ 07509 201-345-3220 (16)

Sheehan, Michael T., State University of New York Performing Arts Center 1400 Washington Avenue Albany, NY 12222 518-457-8608 (8)

Sheehan, Michael T., Michael T. Sheehan 914 Richmond Terrace Staten Island, NY 10301 212-448-2500 (12)

Sheid, Walter E., Westminster College Department of Theatre New Wilmington, PA 16142 412-946-8761 (4)

Shelby, John, Musicians' Union, Local 42 1535 Melvin Avenue Racine, WI 53405 414-633-7922 (18)

Shemro, Mrs. Margaret, Coal Company Theatre 58 River Street Forest City, PA 18421 (16)

Shepard, Irving M., Fraerman Yard Goods and Draperies Company 314 West Adams Street Chicago, IL 60606 312-236-6886; 312-236-6887 (15)

Shepard, Richmond, Shepard Theatre Workshop 6468 Santa Monica Boulevard Hollywood, CA 90038 213-462-9033 (16)

Shepard, Sue, Northfield Arts Guild Post Office Box 21 Northfield, MN 55057 507-645-8877; 507-645-8878 (5)

Shepich, Joseph, Iron County Musicians' Association Post Office Box 482 Caspian, MI 49915 906-265-3600 (18)

Shepich, Robert, Musicians' Protective Union 2122 20th Avenue, South Escanaba, MI 49829 906-786-0271 (18)

Sheppard, C.A., Chaffey College Department of Theatre Alta Loma, CA 91701 714-987-1737 (4)

Sherman, Carol C., Cushing Junior College Department of Theatre Bryn Mawr, PA 19010 (4)

Shesimber, Robert, Scranton Public Theatre Inc. 512-514 Brooks Building Scranton, PA 18503 (16)

Shestack, Charles, Charles Shestack Associates 8400 Bustleton Avenue, Suite 200 Philadelphia, PA 19152 215-745-4044 (15)

Shestak, David, Nodaway Arts Council Post Office Box 55 Maryville, MO 64468 816-582-5687 (5)

Shields, Joan E., Arapahoe Community College Department of Theatre 5900 South Santa Fe Drive Littleton, CO 80122 303-794-1550 (4)

Shileika, Bruce, Musicians' Protective Union Post Office Box 1128 Fairbanks, AK 99701 907-456-3199 (18)

Shine, Ted, Prairie View A and M College Department of Theatre Prairie View, TX 77445 713-857-2356 (4)

Shipp, Charles, Dekalb County Arts Council Post Office Box 520 Fort Payne, AL 35967 205-845-0714 (5)

Shirer, Clarence E., Musicians' Protective Association, Local 54 1030 Richey Road Zanesville, OH 43701 614-452-5691 (18)

Shirk, Margaret, Burlington County Cultural and Heritage Commission 49 Rancocas Road Mount Holly, NJ 08060 609-261-5068 (5)

Shirle, Joan, Dell'Arte School of Mime and Comedy Department of Theatre Blue Lake, CA 95525 707-668-5411; 707-668-5782 (4)

Shoehalter, Nathan , Newark College of Arts and Sciences Department of Theatre Arts 392 High Street Newark, NJ 07102 201-648-5248; 201-648-5119 (4)

Shores, Barbara, Associated Arts of Ocean Shores Post Office Box 241 Ocean Shores, WA 98043 (5)

Short, Linda, Lake Agassiz Arts Council Post Office Box 742 Fargo, ND 58107 701-237-6133 (5)

Short, Ray L. Jr., Research Technology International 4700 Chase Avenue Lincolnwood, IL 60646 312-677-3000; 800-323-7520 (15)

Shulz-Keil, Wieland, Urizen Books 66 West Broadway New York, NY 10007 212-962-3413 (14)

Shumate, Don R., Louisville Federation of Musicians, Local 11-637 1436 Bardstown Road Louisville, KY 40204 502-451-7509 (18)

Shunk, Willard, Association of Musicians, Local 150 915 East Elm Springfield, MO 65806 417-869-5226 (18)

Sickle, Mrs. Kathleen Van, Moorhead State University Department of Theatre Moorhead, NM 56560 218-236-2762; 218-236-2126 (4)

Sidwell, Sandy, Sonoma State University Department of Theatre Rohnert Park, CA 94928 707-664-2474 (4)

Siefred, Bud, Florida Theatre Festival 681 North Halifax Ormand Beach, FL 32074 (9)

Siegel, Leon, Saul S. Siegal Company 847 West Jackson Boulevard Chicago, IL 60607 312-738-3400 (15)

Siegfried, Jay D., Wilkes College Department of Theatre Wilke-Barre, PA 18072 717-824-4651 (4)

Siegle, Frank, Taproot Theatre 1523 Portland Avenue South Minneapolis, MN 55404 (16)

Siegle, Laurence, Camille Players One Dean Porter Park Brownsville, TX 78520 512-542-8900; 512-542-7334 (16)

Siemers, Paul W., Golden Valley Lutheran College Department of Theatre 6125 Olson Highway Minneapolis, MN 55422 612-542-1245 (4)

Sies, Richard, Tri-County Musicians' Union, Local 88 Post Office Box 85 Gillespie, IL 62033 217-835-4539 (18)

Sigismondi, Albert, Musicians' Asociation of Metropolitan Baltimore, Local 40-543 1055 Taylor Avenue, Suite 203 Baltimore, MD 21204 301-337-7277 (18)

Signorino, Sam S., Musical Society, Local 41 621 Goucher Street Johnstown, PA 15905 814-536-0751 (18)

Sikes, Dr. Davis, Jacksonville University Department of Theatre College of Fine Arts Jacksonville, FL 32211 904-744-3950 (4)

Silberman, Janice, University of Pennsylvania Department of Theatre Philadelphia, PA 19104 215-243-5000 (4)

Sill, Norman, Musicians' Union, Local 42 1535 Melvin Avenue Racine, WI 53405 414-633-7922 (18)

Silva, Jean-Marie da, Le Studio Theatre Da Silva 1155 rue Morel Ste-Sophie-de-Lacorne, Quebec, Canada J0R 1S0 514-436-1304 (16)

Silvera, Frank, Frank Silvera Writers' Workshop 317 West 125th Street New York, NY 10027 212-622-8463; 212-864-8307 (16)

Simard, Daniel, La Rallonge 5278 rue Waverly Montreal, Quebec, Canada H27 2X7 514-273-3028 (16)

Simkins, Paula, Danciger Auditorium 8201 Holmes Road Kansas City, MO 64131 816-361-5200 (8)

Simkins, Paula, Resident Theatre/Jewish Community Center 8201 Holmes Road Kansas City, MO 64131 816-361-5200 (16)

Simmonds, A.C., Simmonds and Sons, Ltd. 975 Dillingham Road Pickering, Ontario, Canada L1W 3B2 416-839-8041 (15)

Simmons, Harold, Briarcliff College Department of Theatre Elm Road Briarcliff Manor, NY 10510 914-941-6400 (4)

Simon, Mark B., Producer's Collaborative 240 West 44th Street New York, NY 10036 212-390-1030 (13)

Simone, As Del, Musicians' Protective Union 2854 Jordan Way Pinole, CA 94564 415-758-2336 (18)

Simopoulos, Ted, Musicians' Protective Union, Local 157 3068 Forest Hills Circle Lynchburg, VA 24501 804-845-8794; 804-845-2383 (18)

Simpson, Aili, Pompano Players, Incorporated Post Office Box 2045 Pompano Beach, FL 33061 305-946-4646 (16)

Simpson, James, South Shore Cultural Alliance 36 Miller Stile Road Quincy, MA 02169 479-111- (5)

Simpson, Joan, Seven Pines Players 7 Pines Lodge Lewis, WI 54851 (16)

Simpson, Robert, Park Players, Ltd. Post Office Box 1259 Hot Springs National Park, AR 71901 501-767-2351 (16)

Simpson, Ron, Saint Catharines Musicians' Association 32 Canal Street St. Catharines, Ontario, Canada L2N 4S9 416-935-6673 (18)

Simpson, Yale, Royal Alexandra Theatre 260 King Street West Toronto, Ontario, Canada M5V 1H9 416-593-4233, Administration; 416-363-4211, Box Office (16)

Sims, Greg D., Fulton County Musicians' Protective Union Post Office Box 374 St. David, IL 61563 309-688-2468 (18)

Sims, John W., Arts Council of Fort Worth and Tarrant County 2505 West Lancaster Fort Worth, TX 76107 817-738-7191 (5)

Sincerbox, Earl, Chenango County Council on the Arts 47 South Broad Street Norwich, NY 13815 607-334-3286 (5)

Siravo, Matt, Coventry Players, Inc. Post Office Box 25 Coventry, RI 02816 401-821-9888 (16)

Sisk, J., Curtain Callers Post Office Box 589 MacArthur, WV 25873 (16)

Sitton, Fred, Valparaiso University Department of Theatre University Place Valparaiso, IN 46838 219-464-5073 (4)

Skaalen, Jon, Village Players Post Office Box 106 Montevideo, MN 56265 (16)

Skeen, B., Footlighters 767 Price Canyon Pismo Beach, CA 93449 (16)

Skrudland, David, Classic Communications 47 East Fullerton Addison, IL 60101 312-279-8082 (15)

Skudstad, Robert, Musicians' Protective Union, Local 260 1712 Logan Avenue Superior, WI 54880 715-394-5749 (18)

Skurski, Gloria, Riverside Theatre Workshop 2710 Broadway New York, NY 10025 212-864-9672; 212-663-5420 (16)

Slade, Loraine, Virginia Museum Theatre Company Boulevard and Grove Richmond, VA 23221 804-786-6333 (16)

Slattery, Kenneth, Morris Harvey College Department of Theatre Charleston, WV 25304 (4)

Slaughter, Jean, Delaware County Council for the Arts Post Office Box 4883 Farmland, IN 47340 (5)

Slavin, Michael J., Actors and Artists of Fayette Company 62 Rear West Peter Street Uniontown, PA 15401 (16)

Slead, N.C., Musicians' Protective Union 822 Breckenridge Helena, MT 59601 406-442-5827 (18)

Slinker, Eva, Eastern Oregon Arts Council Route 1, Post Office Box 219 Enterprise, OR 97828 503-426-3393 (5)

Sloane, James M., Newton Country Players Post Office Box 9 Newton Centre, MA 02161 617-244-2160 (16)

Slocum, Richard, Our Lady of the Lake College Department of Theatre 411 South West 24th Street San Antonio, TX 78285 512-434-6711 (4)

Sloshberg, Leah P., New Jersey State Museum Auditorium 205 West State Street Trenton, NJ 08626 609-292-6300 (8)

Slusher, Preston, Pine Mountain Park Amphitheatre Pineville, KY 40977 606-337-3800 (8)

Slusher, Preston, The Book of Job Pineville, KY 40977 606-337-3800 (16)

Slutske, Robert A., Skirpan Lighting Control Corporation 1155 North LaCienega Boulevard Los Angeles, CA 90069 213-657-6383 (15)

Smalley, Cathy, Toronto Theatre Alliance 25 Lennox Avenue Toronto, Ontario, Canada M6G 3W6 416-536-1101 (5)

Smetana, Wallace, Menomonie Theatre Guild Post Office Box 325 Menomonie, WI 54571 715-235-0001 (16)

Smith, AL, Musicians' Protective
Association 3104 North Broadway,
#22C Knoxville, TN 37917
615-687-8350 (18)

Smith, Archie, Archie Smith 4482 Lindell
Boulevard St. Louis, MO 63108
314-533-8458 (15)

Smith, Barry K., Union College
Department of Theatre Schenectady, NY
12308 (4)

Smith, Charles B., PMC College
Department of Theatre Chester, PA
19013 (4)

Smith, Charles E., Truman College
Department of Theatre Chicago, IL
60640 312-878-1700 (4)

Smith, Charlotte, Orange Community
Players Post Office Box 442 Orange, TX
77630 713-886-9881 (16)

Smith, Craig, Jean Cocteau Repertory 330
Bowery New York, NY 10012
212-677-0060 (16)

Smith, David W., Gardner-Webb College
Department of Theatre Boiling Springs,
NC 28017 704-434-2361 (4)

Smith, Delbert, Iowa Western Community
College Department of Theatre
Clarinda, IA 51632 712-542-5117 (4)

Smith, Don W., Musicians' Protective
Union, Local 268 1802 Pekin Street
Lincoln, IL 62656 217-732-9482 (18)

Smith, Dora, Clay County Arts and Crafts
League Post Office Box 566 Ashland, AL
36251 205-354-2183 (5)

Smith, Doyle D., Tarrant County Junior
College Northeast Department of
Theatre 828 Harwood Road Hurst, TX
76053 (4)

Smith, Earl, Musicians' Mutual Protective
Association 2904 ½ De La Vina Street
Santa Barbara, CA 93105 805-687-3519
(18)

Smith, Estelle, Cherokee County Arts
Council Post Office Box 366 Centre, AL
35906 205-927-3337 (5)

Smith, Francine, Dance Plant,
Incorporated Post Office Box 66 West
Medford, MA 02156 617-395-2199 (12)

Smith, Harry W., Florida Technological
University Department of Theatre Post
Office Box 25000 Orlando, FL 32816
305-275-9101 (4)

Smith, James M. Jr., Musicians' Protective
Union R.D. No. 4, Post Office Box 277
Elizabethtown, PA 17022 717-684-7138
(18)

Smith, John, Producers
Foundation/Association 2095 Broadway,
Suite 405 New York, NY 10023
212-496-9121; 212-496-9122/¾ (13)

Smith, John C., Canton Federation of
Musicians, Local 111 Post Office Box 72
Bolivar, OH 44612 216-454-7430 (18)

Smith, Joyce, Lower Adirondack Regional
Arts Council Post Office Box 659 Glen's
Falls, NY 12801 518-789-1144 (5)

Smith, L., Concept East 5826 Hazlett
Street Detroit, MI 48210 313-875-3150
(16)

Smith, Lamont E., Cape Playhouse Route
6A Dennis, MA 02638 617-385-3838 (8)

Smith, Lyall, Musicians' Association, Local
124 119 Capitol Way Olympia, WA
98501 206-357-5220 (18)

Smith, M., Newton Community Theatre
616 Park Road Newton, KS 67114 (16)

Smith, Marc P., Worcester Foothills
Theatre 6 Chatham Street Worcester,
MA 01608 617-754-3314 (8)

Smith, Marc P., Worcester Foothills
Theatre Company Post Office Box 236
Worcester, MA 01602 617-754-3314 (16)

Smith, Marvin, Loomis Camera Company
413 Broad Street Elyria, OH 44035
216-322-3325 (15)

Smith, Mike, Musicians' Protective Union,
Local 230 9 Seventh Avenue, North
West Hampton, IA 50441 915-357-4421
(18)

Smith, P., Chula Vista Playhouse 4180
Acacia Bonita, CA 92002 (16)

Smith, Richard, Fine Arts Council of Hot
Springs 815 Whittington Avenue Hot
Springs, AR 71901 501-623-0836 (5)

Smith, Robert W., Central Telephone and
Utilites Corporation 5725 East River
Road Chicago, IL 60631 312-399-2767
(10)

Smith, Viki, Coquille Valley Art
Association 587 North Elliot Coquille,
OR 97423 503-396-3968 (5)

Smith, W. H., Peninsula Musical Society,
Local 199 104 Seven Hollis Drive
Yorktown, VA 23692 804-380-1022 (18)

Snapp, Calvin, Musicians' Protective
Association, Local 45 323 South Adams
Street Marion, IN 46952 317-664-0400
(18)

Snead, Mrs. Sam, Eufaula Arts Council
403 North Randolph Eufala, AL 36027
205-687-3121 (5)

Snider, Merle L., Reno Musicians' Union
Post Office Box 208 Reno, NV 89504
702-323-2116 (18)

Snowden, Barbara, Currituck County Arts
Council Post Office Box 111 Currituck,
NC 27929 919-232-2311 (5)

Snowden, Robert L., Dover
Corporation/Elevator Division Post
Office Box 2177 Memphis, TN 38101
601-393-2110 (15)

Snyder, Richard, Dixon Musicians' Union
503 South Dixon Avenue Dixon, IL
61021 815-284-3057 (18)

Snyder, Richard D., C.Y. Stephens
Auditorium Iowa State University Ames,
IA 50011 515-294-3347 (8)

Snyder, Dr. Richard D., T.H. Benton
Auditorium Iowa State Center Ames, IA
50011 515-294-3347 (8)

Snyder, Sherwood, Chicago State
University Department of Theatre 95th
and King Drive Chicago, IL 60628
312-995-2190 (4)

Snyder, Steve, Tracey Arts Council Tracey
Community Foundation Tracey, MN
56175 507-629-3437 (5)

Snyder, William, University of Tennessee,
Martin Department of Theatre Martin,
TN 38237 901-587-7133 (4)

Snyder, William, Musical Association,
Local 61 604 Buffalo Street Franklin, PA
16323 814-432-5088 (18)

Soares, George, George Soares and
Associates 12735 Ventura Boulevard
Studio City, CA 91604 213-980-0400 (2)

Soden, Carol, Great Bend City Auditorium
1214 Stone Great Bend, KS 67530
316-793-3755 (8)

Soller, Robert A., Croswell Opera House
and Fine Arts Association Post Office
Box 724 Adrian, MI 49221
517-263-5674; 517-263-6415 (5)

Solloway, J., Ottuma Heights College
Grandview and Elm Street Ottuma, IA
52501 (8)

Solomon, Amy, The Skid Road Theatre 85
South Washington, #306 Seattle, WA
98104 206-622-0251 (16)

Soltker, Gertrude, Old Town Players 1718
North Northpark Chicago, IL 60614
312-645-0145 (16)

Sommers, Stan, Pro Audio Marketing Post
Office Box 153 Jackson Heights, NY
11372 212-898-0200 (15)

Sossi, Ron, Odyssey Theatre Ensemble
c/o Odyssey Theatre Foundation Los
Angeles, CA 90025 213-826-1626;
213-879-5221 (16)

Sostek, Edward L., Carleton College
Department of Theatre Northfield, MN
55057 507-645-4431 (4)

Soule, J., New Woolhouse Players Post
Office Box 111 Woodstock, VT 05091
(16)

South, L., Allegheny Arts Council 8 Green
Street Cumberland, MD 21502
301-777-9137 (5)

Southard, Charles, Roswell Area Arts
Council 1708 West Third Street Roswell,
NM 88201 505-662-7648 (5)

Southern, Hugh, National Endowment for
the Arts 2401 E Street Washington, DC
20506 202-682-5400 (5)

Southern, Hugh, Theatre Development
Fund 1501 Broadway New York, NY
10036 212-221-0013, General Office;
212-221-0885, Administrative Office (5)

Southwick, Richard E., Musicians'
Association 123 East Drewry Lane
Raleigh, NC 27609 919-782-2040 (18)

Sowle, John, Dominican College
Department of Theatre San Rafael, CA
94901 (4)

Soyk, Arthur, Feller Precision,
Incorporated 378 Canal Place Bronx,
NY 10451 212-292-1004 (15)

Spady, D., Liberal Community Theatre 510
North Jordan Liberal, KS 67901 (16)

Spagnola, Rudolph, Musicians' Protective
Union, Local 177 8 Lake Road
Morristown, NJ 07960 201-539-2619
(18)

Spain, J.J., Musicians' Union, Local 6 230 Jones Street San Francisco, CA 94102 415-775-8118 (18)

Spalding, George, Guthrie Management Systems c/o The Guthrie Theater Minneapolis, MN 55403 612-347-1100 (1)

Spalteholz, Hans, Concordia College Department of Theatre 2811 Northeast Holman Portland, OR 97211 503-284-1148 (4)

Spanabel, Robert, University of Hawaii at Hilo Department of Theatre Post Office Box 1357 Hilo, HI 96720 808-961-9311 (4)

Spaniel, Carl, Vandergrift Musical Society 131 Sherman Avenue Vandergrift, PA 15690 412-845-7273 (18)

Sparks, Donna J., Cosumnes River College Department of Theatre Sacramento, CA 95823 916-421-1000, Ext. 292 (4)

Sparling, Judd, Prattville Council on the Arts Post Office Box 178 Prattville, AL 36067 205-365-6727 (5)

Spataro, Carlo V., Greater Muskegon Council for the Arts 1336 Sanford Street Muskegon, MI 49443 616-773-1115 (5)

Spaugh, Dan, Augustana College Department of Theatre 639 38th Street Rock Island, IL 61201 309-794-7000 (4)

Speegle, Nill, Wyrborny Sales Company, Incorporated 9630 Clairewood Suite B2A Houston, TX 77036 713-772-0961 (15)

Speer, Alexander, Actors Theatre of Louisville 316-320 West Main Street Louisville, KY 40202 502-584-1265 (8)

Speer, Robert, Musicians' Association, Local 50 1212 Faraon Street Saint Joseph, MO 64501 816-232-9348 (18)

Spelman, Jon W., Florida Studio Theatre 4619 Bay Shore Drive Sarasota, FL 33580 813-355-4096 (16)

Spelsburg, M., Clarksburg Art Center Post Office Box 148 Clarksburg, WV 25701 (16)

Spence, David, Ontario Ministry of Culture and Recreation 77 Bloor Street West Toronto, Ontario, Canada M7A 2R9 416-965-7690 (5)

Spence, J., University of North Carolina Department of Theatre Charlotte, NC 28223 704-597-2387 (4)

Spencer, Walter J., Rauland-Borg Corporation 40 High Ridge Road Monroe, NY 10950 914-783-4151 (15)

Spendlooe, W., Lanark Drama Workshop 21816 Lanark Canoga Park, CA 91304 (16)

Sperling, A., Burtonsville Players 3413 Kilkenny Street Silver Spring, MD 20904 (16)

Sperling, A., Calverton Players 3413 Kilkenny Street Silver Spring, MD 20904 (16)

Spiegel, Stan, Duro-Test Light Center One Times Square New York, NY 10036 212-391-8190 (15)

Spieler, H.E., Consumers Power Company 212 West Michigan Avenue Jackson, MI 49201 517-788-0430 (10)

Spiess, Tom, Fayette Community Fine Arts Council Post Office Box 355 Fayette, OH 43521 419-237-2683 (5)

Spisto, Louis, Committee for Arts and Lectures University of California 101 Zellerbach Hall Berkeley, CA 94720 415-642-0212 (16)

Spitzer, Philip G., Philip G. Spitzer Literary Agency 111-25 76th Avenue Forest Hills, NY 11375 212-263-7592; 212-793-4149 (2)

Splaine, Mary Beth, Plays for Living 3635 West Dallas Houston, TX 77109 713-524-3881 (16)

Spotswood, Russ, Memphis Federation of Musicians, Local 71 2282 Young Avenue Memphis, TN 38104 901-272-1746 (18)

Spraeberry, Sam, L.D.A. Sales 2221 Freemont Memphis, TN 38114 901-743-3111 (15)

Spriggs, Ted, Fullerton College Community Services 321 East Chapman Avenue Fullerton, CA 92634 714-871-8000, ext. 252 (4)

Springer, C.M., Westinghouse Electric Fund Westinghouse Building, Gateway Center Pittsburgh, PA 15222 412-255-3017 (10)

Springford, Norma, Concordia University Department of Theatre Loyola Campus, 7141 Sherbrooke Street West Montreal, Quebec, Canada H4B 1R6 514-482-0320; 514-879-5855 (4)

Springmeyer, Thomas R., Wenger Corporation 555 Park Drive Owatonna, MN 55060 800-533-0393 (15)

Sproul, Atlee, Colgate University Dana Arts Center Hamilton, NY 13346 315-824-1000, Ext. 639, 631 (4)

Spurrier, James, Vincennes University Department of Theatre 1002 North First Avenue Vincennes, IN 47591 812-885-4256; 812-885-4580 (4)

Stabley, Stewart H., Air Products and Chemicals, Incorporated Post Office Box 538 Allentown, PA 18105 215-398-6587 (10)

Stacey, Betty, Tift College Department of Theatre Forsyth, GA 31209 912-994-6689 (4)

Stafford, Ed, Otero Junior College Department of Theatre 18th and Colorado La Junta, CO 81050 303-384-4446 (4)

Stafford, Suzanne, Lafayette Art Center 101 South Ninth Street Lafayette, IN 47901 317-742-4470 (5)

Stagg, Doris, Players Theatre Incorporated Post Office Box 909 Eunice, LA 70535 (16)

Stahl, Steve, Riverside Theatre Post Office Box 3788 Vero Beach, FL 32960 305-567-8860 (8)

Stahura, Raymond, Demmer Concert Hall Rodman Center for the Arts Ripon College Ripon, WI 54971 414-748-8120 (8)

Stalsky, Igor, Mercyhurst College Department of Theatre Erie, PA 16546 814-864-0681 (4)

Stammers, John, Toronto Workshop Productions 12 Alexander Street Toronto, Ontario, Canada M4Y 1B4 416-925-0526; 416-925-8640 (16)

Stanko, Thomas, Edinboro State College Department of Drama Edinboro, PA 16444 814-732-2736; 814-732-2537 (4)

Stanley, Audrey, Canada College 4200 Farm Hill Boulevard Redwood City, CA 95064 408-429-2292 (4)

Stanley, Jonathan, New Theatre 57 Adelaide Street, East Toronto, Ontario, Canada M5C 1K6 416-363-6429; 416-363-6401 (16)

Stansbury, Raymond, Diablo Valley College Department of Theatre Pleasant Hill, CA 94523 415-685-1230 (4)

Stanton, Jane, New World Theatre c/o Wonderhorse Theatre New York, NY 10003 212-838-3704 (16)

Stapsy, Ira, Buhl Optical 1009 Beech Avenue Pittsburgh, PA 15233 412-321-0076 (15)

Stark, Fred, Musicians' Protective Union Road Number 1, Box 190 Elizaville, NY 12534 518-828-3140 (18)

Starkman, Karl, Sarnia Musicians' Association 150 North Brock Street Sarnia, Ontario, Canada N7T 5ZI 519-337-5838 (18)

Starnes, Leland, Salisbury State College Department of Theatre Salisbury, MD 21801 301-546-3261 (4)

Starr, D., New Bordentown Community Player 272 Ward Avenue 7L Bordentown, NJ 08505 (16)

Starr, Morgan, The Starr Agency Post Office Box 546 Jacksonville, FL 32201 904-743-5807 (2)

Statler, George W., Central Florida Community College Department of Theatre Post Office Box 1388 Ocala, FL 32670 904-237-2111 (4)

Staub, August W., Georgia Resident Theatre Company University of Georgia Athens, GA 30602 404-542-2836 (16)

Stava, Robert W., Musicians' Association, Local 7 2050 South Main Street Santa Ana, CA 92707 714-546-8166 (18)

StClair, John R., Murfreesboro Little Theatre Post Office Box 952 Murfreesboro, TN 37130 615-893-9825 (16)

Stebbing, Edward Lee, Sundog Productions 29 Scotia Street Winnipeg, Manitoba, Canada R2W 3W6 204-582-7578 (16)

Steck, Janet B., Council on the Arts for Cortland 19 Main Street Cortland, NY 13045 607-753-0722 (5)

Steckler, William, Gannon University Department of Drama Perry Square Erie, PA 16541 814-871-7327 (4)

Steckman, Eleanor, Blair County Arts Foundation 1208 12th Avenue Altonna, PA 16601 814-944-9434 (5)

Steele, Byron, Artists Showcase Theatre 1150 Indiana Avenue Trenton, NJ 08611 609-392-2433 (8)

Steele, C. Edward, Wayside Theatre on Tour Wayside Theatre Middletown, VA 22645 Box-Off-ce 703 839 1776; Adm-nis-rative Office, 703 869 1782 (16)

Steele, William P., University of Maine Department of Theatre College Avenue Gorham, ME 04038 207-839-6771 (4)

Steeley, Charles E. Jr., Macon Federation of Musicians 204 Sunnydale Warner Robins, GA 31093 912-923-3242 (18)

Steerman, James B., Vassar College Department of Theatre Poughkeepsie, NY 12603 914-452-7000 (4)

Stegmen, Archie, Professional Musicians' Association, Local 217 322 Carl Lane Jefferson City, MO 65101 314-636-7788 (18)

Stein, Howard, State University of New York Department of Theatre Purchase, NY 10577 914-253-5016 (4)

Stein, Jack, Jack Stein Make-Up Awards 50 Exchange Street Waltham, MA 02154 (3)

Stein, Judith, Art and the Law 36 West 44th Street New York, NY 10036 212-575-1150 (14)

Stein, Meridee, First All Children's Theatre 37 West 65th Street New York, NY 10023 212-873-6400 (16)

Stein, Philip, Musicians' Protective Union 1904 1st Avenue, Apartment 5 Rock Falls, IL 61071 815-625-3623 (18)

Stein, Sophie, Jack Stein Make-Up Center 80 Boylston Street Boston, MA 02116 617-542-7865; 617-542-8334 (15)

Steinberg, Ron, Rent Com Incorporated 9550 Berwyn Rosemont, IL 60018 312-678-0071 (15)

Steinharter, Fred P., Southbury Playhouse Post Office Box 361 Southbury, CT 06488 203-264-8215; 203-264-8216 (16)

Stell, W. Joseph, Georgia Resident Theatre Company University of Georgia Athens, GA 30602 404-542-2836 (16)

Stephens, C., Hunting Community Players 1700 Huntington Drive San Marino, CA 91108 (16)

Stephens, Gene, Las Vagas Convention Center 3150 South Paradise Road Las Vegas, NV 89109 702-735-2323 (8)

Stephens, Peter, Festival Lennoxville Box 60 Lennoxville, Quebec, Canada J1M 1Z3 819-563-9056; 819-363-4966 (16)

Stephenson, R. Rex, Ferrum College Department of Theatre Post Office Box 85 Ferrum, VA 24088 703-365-2121 (4)

Stepules, Vincent, Elmira-Corning Musicians' Association 1001 Pinewood Drive Pine City, NY 14871 607-734-0131 (18)

Sterling, Irene, The Learning Theatre Post Office Box 2144 Paterson, NJ 07509 201-345-3220 (16)

Stern, Alfred, Alfred Stern 408 West 57th Street New York, NY 10019 212-246-9866 (15)

Stern, Charles H., Charles H. Stern Agency 9220 Sunset Boulevard Los Angeles, CA 90069 213-273-6890 (2)

Stern, Don, Bash Theatrical Lighting 2012 86th Street North Bergen, NJ 07047 201-869-1400; 212-279-9265 (15)

Stern, Irving, Jewish Community Center Players 3960 Montclair Road Birmingham, AL 35223 205-879-0411 (16)

Sterngold, Dini, Circle of Friends Children's Theatre 428 North West 70th Avenue, #136 Plantation, FL 33317 (16)

Sternlicht, Sanford, State University of New York, Oswego Tyler Hall Oswego, NY 13126 315-341-2140; 315-341-2147 (4)

Sternquist, Leonard, Musicians' Protective Union 1817 West Third Street Boone, IA 50036 515-432-4092 (18)

Stevens, George, Oregon Memorial Union Lounge Oregon State University Corvallis, OR 97330 754-241-; 754-210- (8)

Stevenson, Elaine, Press Theatre 85 Church Street St. Catharines, Ontario, Canada L2R 6Y3 416-684-1133, Administration; 416-684-6377, Box Office (16)

Stevenson, Frank, Musicians' Protective Union, Local 250 2430 Appleton Parsons, KS 67357 (18)

Stevenson, Isabelle, Antoinette Perry Award 250 West 57th Street New York, NY 10022 212-765-0609 (3)

Stevenson, N., Union University Department of Theatre Arts North 45 Bypass Jackson, TN 38301 901-668-1818 (4)

Stevenson, Ruth, Chaska Civic Theatre 110914 Van Hersen Circle Chaska, MN 55318 (16)

Steward, John, Masque Players 629 Darfield Avenue Covina, CA 91724 213-966-9360 (16)

Stewart, Carole, Carole Stewart Agency 8230 Beverly Boulevard Los Angeles, CA 90048 213-655-4330 (2)

Stewart, Earl, Charles H. Stewart and Company 8 Clarendon Avenue Somerville, MA 02144 617-625-2407 (15)

Stewart, Ellen, La Mama ETC 74A East 4th Street New York, NY 10003 212-475-7710; 212-475-7908 (16)

Stewart, Frank, A.T.C. 307 West 80th Street Kansas City, MO 64114 816-523-1655 (15)

Stewart, Loris W., Musicians' Protective Union 706 East Linden Caldwell, ID 83605 208-459-7503 (18)

Stewart, Patricia W., Monroe County Arts Council Post Office Box 924 Monroeville, AL 36460 205-575-3282 (5)

Stewart, Richard, Grand Rapids Baptist College Department of Drama 1001 East Beltline, Northeast Grand Rapids, MI 49505 616-949-5300 (4)

Stewart, S., Glenmont Players 3608 Isabil Street Silver Spring, MD 20906 (16)

Stewart, Tom, Associated Theatrical Contractors 307 West 80th Street Kansas City, MO 64114 816-523-1655 (15)

Stewart, Virginia, Littleton Arts Council Fowler Hill Road Littleton, NH 03561 603-444-5014 (5)

Stieg, Rose Marie, Hala Kahiki 2832 River Road River Grove, IL 60171 312-456-3222 (15)

Stigant, Ernest, Manitoba Arts Council 555 Main Street Winnipeg, Manitoba, Canada R3B 1C3 204-944-2237 (5)

Stilwill, Charles, Waterloo Community Playhouse Post Office Box 433 Waterloo, IA 50704 319-235-0367 (16)

Stobie, Richard, Rapport Entertainment Corporation 1023 North Labrea Avenue Hollywood, CA 90028 213-876-9033 (13)

Stock, Morgan, Monterey Peninsula College Department of Theatre Monterey, CA 93940 408-649-1150 (4)

Stockhausen, Patti, Seaway Arts Council Saint Clair County Community College 323 Erie St. Port Huron, MI 48060 313-982-3881 (5)

Stohn, Carl Jr., Pheasant Run Playhouse Post Office Box 64 Saint Charles, IL 60174 312-584-1454 (8)

Stokely, Dr. Frederick, Waltham Arts Council 205 Bacon Street Waltham, MA 02154 617-893-8050 (5)

Stoker, Richard, The Arts and Culture Centre Post Office Box 1854, Prince Philip Drive Saint John's, Newfoundland, Canada A1C 5P9 709-737-3650 (8)

Stollman, Irving, Oak Park Arts and Cultural Commission 14200 Oak Park Boulevard Oak Park, MI 48237 313-548-7230 (5)

Stolper, Carolyn L., National Corporate Fund for the Dance, Inc. 130 West 56th Street New York, NY 10019 212-582-0130 (10)

Stone, Edwin C., Business in the Arts Awards 1501 Broadway New York, NY 10036 (3)

Stone, Frank T., Studio Arena Theatre 681 Main Street Buffalo, NY 14203 716-856-5650 (16)

Stone, John J., Musicians Protective Union 9 Woodrow Road Batavia, NY 14020 716-343-4020 (18)

Stone, Len, Stage Lighting Ottawa 2097 Street Lawrence Boulevard Ottawa, Ontario, Canada (15)

Stone, M., Big Little Theatre Company 489 Old Eagle School Road Wayne, PA 19087 (16)

Stone, Marvin, Musicians' Protective Union Rural Route Number 1 Princeton, IL 61356 309-895-2544 (18)

Stone, Norman, The Music Box Theatre 239 West 45th Street New York, NY 10036 212-246-4636 (8)

Stone, Peter, Dramatists Guild 234 West 44th Street New York, NY 10036 212-398-9366 (5)

Stoner, J. Roger, Musicians' Protective Union 2524 Jasu Drive Lawrence, KS 66044 913-843-4966 (18)

Storch, Arthur, Syracuse University Department of Theatre Syracuse, NY 13210 315-423-2708 (4)

Storey, M., Singing Players-Dover 333 Pennsylvania Avenue Dover, DE 19901 (16)

Stork, John R., Genesee Community College Department of Theatre College Road, Post Office Box 718 Batavia, NY 14020 716-343-0055 (4)

Storm, Susan, Crooked Tree Arts Council 461 East Mitchell Petoskey, MI 49770 616-347-4337; 616-347-7870 (5)

Stoun, Sylvia, Newport Federation of Musicians 235 Eustis Avenue Newport, RI 02840 401-849-3649 (18)

Stout, Harold, Musicians' Protecive Association, Local 58 4022 West State Street Fort Wayne, IN 46898 219-483-7778 (18)

Stowe, Sydney, Happiness Bag Players 1519 South 7th Street Terre Haute, IN 47802 (16)

Strafford, Dr. Merrille, Los Angeles Southwest Community College Department of Theatre 1600 West Imperial Highway Los Angeles, CA 90047 213-757-9521 (4)

Stralko, Raymond J., Muskegon Musicians' Association, Local 252 169 East Broadway Muskegon Heights, MI 49444 616-733-2227 (18)

Strand, G., Black River Community Theatre Harrison Street Black River Falls, WI 54615 (16)

Strauss, Patricia A., Lakewood Little Theatre 17801 Detroit Avenue Lakewood, OH 44107 216-521-2540 (16)

Streenz, Kim L., Musicians' Protective Union 803 North 14th Pekin, IL 61554 309-347-2350 (18)

Street, Ervin F., Atlantic Federation of Musicians 6307 Chebucto Road Halifax, Nova Scotia, Canada B3L 1K9 902-422-6492 (18)

Street, Irene N., Warren County Cultural Commission County Court House Belvedere, NJ 07823 (5)

Streett, J. Bruce, New Mexico State University Department of Theatre Arts Las Cruces, NM 88003 505-646-4517 (4)

Streiff, Martin, Red Barn Theatre 3101 Mc Cully Road Allison Park, PA 15101 (16)

Streightoff, Lynn, Greater Huntingdon Fine Arts Council Post Office Box 216 Huntingdon, PA 16652 717-253-3080 (5)

Strel, Donald, Saint Francis Auditorium Museum of New Mexico Santa Fe, NM 87501 505-827-2351 (8)

Stribling, Donald W., Loras College Department of Theatre 1450 Alta Visa Dubuque, IA 52001 319-588-7127 (4)

Stringe, Suzanne, Ashland-Bayfield Arts Council Post Office Box 577 Mellen, WI 54546 (5)

Strobl, Ben, Kenosha Federation of Musicians, Local 59 711 Washington Road Kenosha, WI 53140 414-652-1465 (18)

Stromberg, Nadine, Chancel Players 1114 North Bel-Ayr Drive Waukesha, WI 53186 (16)

Stromme, Chris, Albuquerque Civic Light Opera Association 4201 Ellison Northeast Albuquerque, NM 87109 505-345-6577 (15)

Strong, Mrs. G.B., City of Demopolis Arts Committee 400 South Main Demopolis, AL 36732 205-289-0396 (5)

Strother, E.S., Ball State University Department of Theatre 2000 University Avenue Muncie, IN 47306 317-285-4028 (4)

Struckman, R., City College of San Francisco Department of Theatre 50 Phelan Ave San Francisco, CA 94112 415-239-3100; 415-239-3132 (4)

Stuart, Alfred, Mendelssohn Theatre 227 South Ingalls Ann Arbor, MI 48104 313-763-1085 (8)

Stuart, Ross, Association for Canadian Theatre History Department of Theatre Downsview, Ontario, Canada M3J 1P3 416-667-3975 (5)

Stucker, Howard, Marvin Jacobs Optical Engineering 4527 San Fernando Road Glendale, CA 91204 213-244-0838 (15)

Studnicky, George, Creative Stage Lighting Company Post Office Box 51 Johnsburg, NY 12843 518-251-3302 (15)

Studnicky, Lily M., Creative Stage Lighting Company Post Office Box 51 Johnsburg, NY 12843 518-251-3302 (15)

Stump, Walter R., University of Southern Maine Department of Theatre Gorham, ME 04038 207-780-5481 (4)

Sturdivant, Bill, Bill Sturdivant and Associates 3050 West 7th Street Los Angeles, CA 90025 213-382-8483 (2)

Stutler, William B., An Evening Dinner Theatre 11 Clearbrook Road Elmsford, NY 10523 914-592-2268 (16)

Styers, Mrs. W. W., Gatson Fine Arts Council Post Office Box 565 Belmont, NC 28012 704-825-5146 (5)

Styve, O.W., Stage Door Players 1404 Sandra Lane West Bend, WI 53095 (16)

Subers, Anita, Bucks County Council on the Arts Room 315, Building G Doylestown, PA 18901 215-343-2800 (5)

Sublette, Tim, Greater Columbus Arts Council 33 North Third Street Columbus, OH 43215 614-234-2606 (5)

Suchower, John, Armstrong State College Drama-Speech Section 11935 Abercorn Street Savannah, GA 31406 912-927-5354 (4)

Suergiu, Kathy, Coconut Grove Childrens Theatre Department of Theatre 3043 Grand Avenue Post Office Box 331002 Miami, FL 33133 305-442-0489 (16)

Sulek, Rudy, Warren Federation of Musicians, Local 118 3207 Youngstown Road SE Warren, OH 44484 216-369-6745 (18)

Sullivan, J.R., The New American Theatre 118 South Main Street Rockford, IL 61108 815-963-9454 (8)

Sullivan, J.R., New American Theatre 117 South Wyman Street Rockford, IL 61108 815-963-9454 (16)

Sullivan, Kaylynn, KLS Management, Ltd. 76 Pearl Street New York, NY 10004 212-741-0368 (12)

Sullivan, Margaret, The Summertree Players Post Office Box 480 Estes Park, CO 80517 913-584-6512; 303-586-6100 (16)

Sullivan, Paul, Huntington Beach Playhouse, Incorporated Post Office Box 451 Huntington Beach, CA 92648 714-847-4465; 714-536-9072 (16)

Summers, Dr. L.J., Arkansas College Post Office Box 2317 Batesville, AR 75201 501-793-9813 (4)

Summers, Robert L. (Bob), Birmingham Musicians' Protective Association, Local 256-733 2115 Pershing Road Birmingham, AL 35214 205-786-1201 (18)

Sumners, Mr. Warren K., Tennessee Performing Arts Center 505 Deaderick Street Nashville, TN 37219 615-741-7975; 615-741-5633 (8)

Sumrall, Mary Ann, Laurel Little Theatre Post Office Box 2131 Laurel, MS 39440 (16)

Sunday, Hal C., Phoenix Federation of Musicians 1202 East Oak Street Phoenix, AZ 85006 602-254-8838 (18)

Suntherland, Jerry, Sacramento City College Department of Theatre Sacramento, CA 95882 916-449-7480 (4)

Susser, Harvey, College of Marin Department of Theatre Kentfield, CA 94904 415-457-8811 (4)

Sutherland, James, Lyric Theatre 11th and Central Kansas City, MO 64105 816-471-4933 (8)

Sutter, J., Mt. Horeb Community Theatre 512 Green Street Mount Horeb, WI 53572 (16)

Sutton, Ralph, M and J Trimming Company 1008 Sixth Avenue New York, NY 10018 212-391-9072 (15)

Svela, Myrl, Gold Crown Dinner Theatre 7676 Fireston Boulevard Downey, CA 90241 213-861-7117 (16)

Svetz, Raymond M., Musicians' Union, Bridgeport Musicians Association, Local 63-549 448 Willow Street Bridgeport, CT 06610 203-333-2017; 203-334-8972 (18)

Svoboda, M., Brown Deer Theatre 8387 North Grandview Drive Brown Deer, WI 53223 (16)

Svoboda, Roger, Dubuque Musicians' Association 1030 Boyer Dubuque, IA 52001 319-588-3240 (18)

Swan, Richard C., Leland Powers School Department of Theatre 70 Brookline Avenue Boston, MA 02115 617-247-1300 (4)

Swan, Scott, Northern Light Theatre 10189 - 99 Street Edmonton, Alberta, Canada T5J 0N2 403-426-4292; 403-429-3110 (16)

Swanson, Allan K., Jamestown Musical Association, Local 134 7 Campbell Avenue Jamestown, NY 14701 716-665-3458 (18)

Swartz, Dan, Brooklyn Center for the Performing Arts Brooklyn College Campus Road at Hillel Place Brooklyn, NY 11210 212-780-5296, Operations and Rentals; 212-780-5291, Programming (8)

Swartz, F. Randolph, F. Randolph Associates 1300 Arch Street Philadelphia, PA 19107 215-567-6662 (12)

Swartz, Marlene, Soho Repertory Theatre 19 Mercer Street New York, NY 10013 212-925-2588 (16)

Swearingen, Ginger, Sedalia Community Theatre 717 West 6th Street Sedalia, MO 65301 (16)

Sweeney, Paul J., University of North Carolina Department of Theatre University Heights Ashville, NC 28814 704-258-6610; 704-253-5778 (4)

Sweet, Benjamin, Community College of Denver Red Rocks Campus 12600 West 6th Avenue Golden, CO 80401 (4)

Sweet, Horace, Springfield Musicians' Association, Local 19-675 37 North Koke Mill Lane Springfield, IL 62707 217-546-6260 (18)

Sweet, Linda, Opportunity Resources for the Arts, (OR) 1501 Broadway New York, NY 10036 212-575-1688 (5)

Sweeting, Courtney, The Venice Little Theatre Tampa Avenue Venice, FL 33595 813-488-2419; 813-488-1115 (16)

Sweeting, Dennis D., Kawartha Summer Theatre 2 Lindsay Street South, Box 161 Lindsay, Ontario, Canada K9V 4S1 705-324-9111 (16)

Sweeting, Margaret, Kawartha Summer Theatre 2 Lindsay Street South, Box 161 Lindsay, Ontario, Canada K9V 4S1 705-324-9111 (16)

Swink, Doug W., Sarah Graham Kenan Auditorium UNC-W, Post Office Box 3725 Wilmington, NC 28401 919-791-9695 (8)

Swink, Doug W., SRO Straw-Hat Theatre UNC-W Post Office Box 3725 Wilmington, NC 28401 419-791-9695 (16)

Sydney, Albert, Albert Sydney and Associates 143 Hoffman Avenue Cranston, RI 02920 401-943-3530 (15)

Sygoda, Ivan, Pentacle 200 W 72nd St., Suite 20 New York, NY 10023 212-580-8107 (12)

Sylvester, Audrey, Library Arts Center 58 North Main Street Newport, NH 03773 03 -63 -040 (5)

Symons, James M., College of Saint Thomas Department of Theatre Saint Paul, MN 55105 612-647-5265 (4)

Symons, James M., State University of New York Department of Theatre Albany, NY 12222 518-457-8360 (4)

Symons, James M., Trinity University Department of Drama 715 Stadium Drive San Antonio, TX 78284 512-736-8511 (4)

Szathmary, Elizabeth, The Inner Stage 9 - 11 St. Nicholas Street Toronto, Ontario, Canada M4Y 1W5 416-967-3548 (16)

T

Tabakin, Ralph, Maryland Academy of Dramatic Arts and Theatre 4930 Cordell Avenue Bethesda, MD 20814 301-652-7999; 301-654-9820 (4)

Tabakin, Ralph, Maryland Childrens' Theatre 4930 Cordell Avenue Bethesda, MD 20814 301-652-7999; 301-654-9820 (16)

Tahn, Andy, 25th Street Theatre Post Office Box 542 Saskatoon, Saskatchewan, Canada S7K 3L6 306-664-2239; 306-343-9966 (16)

Tait, Vicki, Eastern Montana College 1500 North 30th Billings, MT 59101 406-657-2011 (4)

Talbot, P., Unitarian Players 2900 Connecticut NW Washington, DC 20008 (16)

Tambellini, P., Civic Playhouse Post Office Box 1200 Costa Mesa, CA 92626 (16)

Tancke, Henry, Thermoplastic Processes Valley Road Stirling, NJ 07980 201-647-1000 (15)

Tangren, Marion, Watertown Area Arts Council 912 North Broadway Watertown, SD 57201 605-886-5542 (5)

Taryan, Andrew F., Pepi Puppet Theatre 253 McNicoll Avenue Willowdale, Ontario, Canada M2H 2C6 416-497-0916 (16)

Taryan, Kathy, Pepi Puppet Theatre 253 McNicoll Avenue Willowdale, Ontario, Canada M2H 2C6 416-497-0916 (16)

Tasca, Jules, Gwynedd Mercy College Department of Theatre Gwynedd Valley, PA 19437 215-646-7300 (4)

Tasco, Rai, Hollywood Theater Company 12838 Kling Street Studio City, CA 91604 213-984-1867 (16)

Tastle, William, Delaware County Council on the Arts c/o Delhi College, 149 Bush Hall Delhi, NY 13753 607-746-4161 (5)

Taufer, Carol, Security Pacific Foundation 333 South Hope Street Los Angeles, CA 90051 213-613-6688 (10)

Tawater, Jimmy, Chattanooga Musicians' Union, Local 80 Memorial Auditorium Chattanooga, TN 37402 615-266-1725; 615-266-5918 (18)

Tawny, Lee, Oneonta Community Arts Center Post Office Box 20 Oneonta, NY 13820 607-433-2555 (5)

Tayler, Larry, The Mime Company Unlimited Box 361, Station J Toronto, Ontario, Canada M4J 4Y8 416-461-6551 (16)

Taylor, Bob, Memphis Federation of Musicians, Local 71 2282 Young Avenue Memphis, TN 38104 901-272-1746 (18)

Taylor, Colin, North Platte Area Art Council c/o Chamber of Commerce North Platte, NB 69101 308-532-6888 (5)

Taylor, Frederick S., Lower Manhattan Cultural Council 32 Broadway New York, NY 10004 212-269-0320 (5)

Taylor, J., Berkeley Community Theatre Post Office Box 1505 Martinsburg, WV 25401 (16)

Taylor, Jack, The Venice Little Theatre Tampa Avenue Venice, FL 33595 813-488-2419; 813-488-1115 (16)

Taylor, James A., Federation of Musicians, Local 148-462 110 Laurel Forest Circle, North East Atlanta, GA 30342 404-237-1204 (18)

Taylor, Ron, Hillside Cultural Center Post Office Box 88351 Indianapolis, IN 46208 317-925-9861 (5)

Taylor, Samuel, Dramatists Play Service 440 Park Avenue South New York, NY 10016 212-683-8960 (14)

Taylor, Samuel, Hamilton Musicians' Guild 101 Iverness Court Hamilton, Ontario, Canada L9C 1A6 416-388-0140 (18)

Taylor, Verner H., Musicians' Protective Union 1660 Merced Avenue Merced, CA 95340 209-722-9371 (18)

Taylor, W.R., Stage Decoration and Supplies, Incorporated 1204 Oakland Avenue Greensboro, NC 27403 919-275-6488 (15)

Teall, M. J., Wichita Community Theatre 110 South Battin Wichita, KS 67218 (16)

Tearle, David, Consolidated Photographic Sales 4548 Ewing Avenue North Minneapolis, MN 55422 612-535-2254 (15)

Tecca, Edward, Musicians' Protective Association 206 South C Livingston, MT 59047 406-222-1274 (18)

Tederholm, Jack, Hill Cumorah Pageant Post Office Box 117 Palmyra, NY 14522 315-597-5851 (16)

Tedesco, John, Phoebus Company, Incorporated 145 Bluxome Street San Francisco, CA 94107 415-543-7626 (15)

Tedford, Harold C., Wake Forest University Department of Theatre Box 7264 Reynolda Station Winston-Salem, NC 27109 919-761-5294; 919-761-5295 (4)

Teeter, Amandus, Musicians' Protective Union, Local 132 365 West King Road Ithaca, NY 14850 607-272-8170 (18)

Teeter, Tom, Tom Teeter 901 Forest Hill Drive Greensboro, NC 27401 919-855-6238 (15)

Teitzman, Dr. Peter A., Jersey City State College Department of Theatre 2039 Kennedy Memorial Boulevard Jersey City, NJ 07305 201-547-3348 (4)

Telarico, George J., Geneva Musicians' Association 187 Genessee Street Geneva, NY 14456 315-789-5441 (18)

Telarico, George J., Geneva Musicians' Association 187 Genessee Street Geneva, NY 14456 315-789-5441 (18)

Temple, Robert E., Smoky Mountain Passion Play Post Office Box 3 Townsend, TN 37882 615-984-4111, Year Round; 615-448-2244, Box Office - Summer Only (16)

Tennen, Steve, New Federal Theatre 466 Grand Street New York, NY 10002 212-766-9334 (16)

Terrell, H., Sikeston Little Theatre 835 William Street Sikeston, MO 63801 (16)

Teschan, Walter, Music and Arts Institute of San Francisco Department of Theatre 2622 Jackson Street San Francisco, CA 94115 415-567-1445 (4)

Tesh, Jane, North Carolina Theatre Conference 523 Board Street, #C Mount Airy, NC 27030 (16)

Tessa, Johanne, Play of Light Company 2702 North Maryland Avenue Baltimore, MD 21218 301-366-3758 (1)

Testa, Frank, Musicians' Protective Union 40 Southwest Avenue Vineland, NJ 08360 609-692-1039 (18)

Thatcher, G., Group Theatre Dahl Art Center 713 7th Street Rapid City, SD 57701 (16)

Thayer, David, University of Iowa Department of Drama Iowa City, IA 52242 319-353-5791; 319-353-6589 (4)

Thayer, Robert, Crane School of Music State University College Potsdam, NY 13676 315-267-2413; 315-267-2415 (9)

Thayer, Robert W., State University of New York, Potsdam Department of Theatre Pierrepont Avenue Potsdam, NY 13676 315-267-2413; 315-267-2414 (4)

Thieling, Jane, Charleston Performing Arts Council Post Office Box 2749 Charleston, WV 25330 304-348-8173 (5)

Thiene, Carol, Brookfield Players 17535 Oak Park Row Brookfield, WI 53005 (16)

Thomas, Creon, Imperial Valley Federation of Musicians 1611 Pepper Drive El Centro, CA 92243 714-352-4025 (18)

Thomas, David T., The Liberty Cart Post Office Box 470 Kenansville, NC 28349 919-296-1550 (16)

Thomas, George A., George Thomas Associates 4040 East McDowell Road Phoenix, AZ 85008 602-244-8143 (1)

Thomas, Jack, Thomas-Redwine, Incorporated 427 Breesport San Antonio, TX 78216 512-349-2131 (15)

Thomas, James W., Mars Hill College Department of Theatre Mars Hill, NC 28754 704-689-1203 (4)

Thomas, Jean, Grand Marais Playhouse Grand Marais, MN 55604 (16)

Thomas, Porter, Miami Federation of Musicians 1779 Northwest 28th Street Miami, FL 33142 305-633-3235 (18)

Thomas, Roger, Amarillo Theatre Centre and Academy Box 2424 Amarillo, TX 79109 806-355-9991 (4)

Thomason, Sally, Memphis Arts Council Post Office Box 40682-9990 Memphis, TN 38104 901-278-2950 (5)

Thomason-Bergner, James, Lone Mountain College Department of Theatre 2800 Turk Boulevard San Francisco, CA 94118 415-752-7000 (4)

Thompson, Ben F., Musicians' Protective Union, Local 266 Post Office Box 6142 Little Rock, AR 72116 501-835-0337 (18)

Thompson, Claire S., Bellflower Cultural Arts Council 9729 East Flower Bellflower, CA 90706 213-867-1744 (5)

Thompson, Frank C., Charleston Musicians' Union, Local 136 1562 Kanawha Boulevard, East Charleston, WV 25311 304-346-9693; 304-343-7778 (18)

Thompson, I.D., Lemoyne-Owen College Department of Theatre 807 Walker Avenue Memphis, TN 38126 901-948-6626 (4)

Thompson, J., Drama Workshop Bell Avenue and Casady Drive Des Moines, IA 56315 (16)

Thompson, John F., John F. Thompson Company 5003 Brittany Drive South St. Petersburg, FL 33715 813-866-0045 (15)

Thompson, Larry, Capitol Stage Equipment Company 3121 North Pennsylvania Oklahoma City, OK 73112 405-524-9552 (15)

Thompson, Paul, Theatre Passe Muraille 16 Ryerson Avenue Toronto, Ontario, Canada M5T 2P3 416-363-8988; 416-363-0555 (16)

Thompson, Paula, Landers Theatre 311 East Walnut Street Springfield, MO 65806 417-869-1334 (8)

Thompson, Robert L., Springs Mills, Incorporated Fort Mill, SC 29715 803-547-2901 (10)

Thon, Carol, Delaware County Community College Department of Theatre Media, PA 19063 215-353-5400 (4)

Thornton, E., Brandon Stage 280 Linda K Lane Ortonville, MI 48462 (16)

Thorp, Cora, Bisbee Council on the Arts Post Office Box 451 Bisbee, AZ 85603 602-432-7071 (5)

Thorson, Arch, Fort Dodge Musicians' Association 1108 North 19th Street Fort Dodge, IA 50501 515-576-3452 (18)

Thorson, Russell, Fort Dodge Musicians' Association 1108 North 19th Street Fort Dodge, IA 50501 515-576-3452 (18)

Thrasher, Brian, Kingston Musicians' Union 18 ½ Division Street Kingston, Ontario, Canada K7K 3Y9 613-542-3732 (18)

Thronson, Ron, Chapman College Department of Communication 333 North Glassell Orange, CA 92666 714-997-6856; 714-997-6625 (4)

Thurston, Ellen, Center for Arts Information 1625 Broadway New York, NY 10012 212-677-7548 (1)

Tiberi, Lucian, Federation of Musicians, Local 103 2829 Cleveland Avenue Columbus, OH 43224 614-261-9826; 614-261-9827 (18)

Tiberini, Tibby, Philadelphia Musical Society, Local 77 120 North 18th Street Philadelphia, PA 19103 215-567-1071 (18)

Tilbrook, Charles, Belleville Federation of Musicians Rural Route Number 1 Plainfield, Ontario, Canada K0K 2V0 613-477-2003 (18)

Tilghman, Romalyn, Association of Community Arts Councils 509A Kansas Avenue Topeka, KS 6603 913-296-4092 (5)

Tilley, Henry, Kokomo Federation of Musicians, Local 141 3813 Candy Lane Kokomo, IN 46901 317-453-3261 (18)

Tilroe, Nikki, Frog Print Theatre 449 Lawson Road West Hill, Ontario, Canada M1C 2K2 416-363-1938 (16)

Timm, H.C., Alverno College, Department of Theatre 3401 South 39th Street Milwaukee, WI 53215 414-671-5400 (4)

Tinapp, Richard, University of Wisconsin Department of Theatre 1725 State Street La Crosse, WI 54601 608-785-8523 (4)

Tingle, Brian E., Council For the Arts of Greater Lima Post Office Box 1124, Memorial Hall Lima, OH 45802-1124 419-225-9165 (5)

Tipton, David L., Tipton Sound and Lighting 36 South Pennsylvania Indianapolis, IN 46204 317-631-2703 (15)

Titlow, Robert, College of Notre Dame Department of Theatre Belmont, CA 94002 415-593-1601 (4)

Tobias, Herb, Herb Tobias and Associates 1901 Avenue of the Stars Century City, CA 90067 213-277-6211 (2)

Todd, Donna Edwards, Jaceo Community Theatre - Black Fire Company 1823 Avenue E Ensley Birmingham, AL 35218 205-780-7510, Ext. 24 (16)

Todd, Hal J., San Jose State University Department of Theatre Arts San Jose, CA 95192 408-277-2763; 408-277-2764 (4)

Todd, Hal J., San Jose State University Company Comique Theatre Arts Department San Jose, CA 95192 408-277-2763; 408-277-2764 (16)

Tomlinson, Tom, Allied Arts Council of the Yakima Valley 5000 West Lincoln Avenue Yakima, WA 98902 509-966-0930 (5)

Tong, Olga, Chinese-American Arts Council 45 Canal Street New York, NY 10002 212-431-9740; 212-284-6083 (5)

Tonken, Mel, Loose Moose Theatre Company 1610 Bowness Road Northwest Calgary, Alberta, Canada T2N 3J9 403-283-9960 (16)

Tooker, Carolyn, Musicians' Association, Local 90 301 East 14th Street Danville, IL 61832 217-446-7515 (18)

Toomer, Lamar C., Arts Council of Oak Ridge Post Office Box 324 Oak Ridge, TN 37830 (5)

Topp, Robert F., Flagstaff Art Association Post Office Box 1901 Flagstaff, AZ 86001 602-774-0822 (5)

Topper, Evelyn, Mill Valley Arts Commission Post Office Box 132 Mill Valley, CA 94941 415-383-6664 (5)

Totusek, Richard Q., Musicians' Association, Local 105 4025 South Lee Street Spokane, WA 99203 509-448-0627 (18)

Tower, Gael, Mount Hood Community College Department of Theatre 26000 Southeast Stark Street Gresham, OR 97030 503-667-1561 (4)

Towey, Augustine, Niagara University Department of Theatre Niagara Falls, NY 14109 716-285-1212, Extension 526,525 (4)

Tracie, Jo, Gallaudet College Department of Theatre 7th and Florida Avenue, NE Washington, D.C. 20002 202-651-5606; 202-651-5710 (4)

Trapp, Richard, Tacoma-Pierce County Civic Arts Commission 705 South Ninth, Suite 105 Tacoma, WA 98492 206-593-4754 (5)

Trask, Dr. A. Franklin, National Association of Dramatics White Horse Beach Plymouth, MA 02381 617-224-3967 (16)

Trask, Franklin, Plymouth Drama Festival National Association of Dramatics Manomet, MA 02345 617-224-3697 (9)

Trauth, Suzanne, Fort Hays State University Department of Theatre Hays, KS 67601 913-628-4226 (4)

Travers, Pat, International Alliance of Theatrical Stage Employees 696 Yonge Street, #404 Toronto, Ontario, Canada M4Y 2A7 416-923-4161 (18)

Traxier, Ralph III, North Carolina Wesleyan College Department of Theatre Highway 301 North Rocky Mount, NC 27801 919-422-7121 (4)

Triangolo, Aime, Federation of Musicians, Local 198-457 528 Pleasant Valley Parkway Providence, RI 02098 401-751-2717 (18)

Triano, George T., Musicians' Protective Union 130 Central Avenue Jersey City, NJ 07306 201-653-0750 (18)

Trimble, Gene, Musicians' Protective Union, Local 224 Post Office Box 94 Effingham, IL 62401 217-837-2077 (18)

Trophia, Joseph J., Musicians' Protective Association 227 East Garden Street Rome, NY 13440 315-336-3534 (18)

Trotter, Jim, Jim Trotter Post Office Box 44316 Tacoma, WA 98444 206-531-1201 (15)

Troutman, Denise E., Bennett College Department of Theatre Greensboro, NC 27420 914-273-4431 (4)

Truesdale, Nancy, Meredith College Department of Theatre Hillborough Street Raleigh, NC 27611 919-883-6461 (4)

Truex, Duane, Roberson Center for the Arts and Sciences 30 Front Street Binghamton, NY 13905 607-772-0660 (5)

Truitt, Wesley M., Villanova University Department of Theatre Villanova, PA 19085 215-645-4760 (4)

Tucci, F. John, Portsville Musical Society B & Pottsville Streets Minersville, PA 17954 717-544-4589 (18)

Tucker, Brian, Pro Audio Sales 111 South Drive Tower Lakes Barrington, IL 60010 312-381-4559 (15)

Tucker, Irma, City Players 3207 Washington Avenue Saint Louis, MO 63108 (16)

Tucker, Thomas, Victoria Musicians' Association, Local 247 1241 Topaz Avenue Victoria, British Columbia, Canada V8T 2N1 604-382-7351 (18)

Tudor, Bronwen, Forum-A University of Maine, Augusta Augusta, ME 04330 207-662-7131, Ext. 212 (5)

Tungate, B., Riverside Players 409 Quarry Street Neenah, WI 54956 (16)

Turchen, Michael, Dakota Wesleyan University Department of Theatre Mitchell, SD 57301 605-996-6511 (4)

Turen, Harry C., Musicians' Association, Local 255 606 East 17th Street Yankton, SD 57078 605-665-2488 (18)

Turgeon, Serge, Compagnie Jean Duceppe 1400 rue Saint-Urbain Montreal, Quebec, Canada H2X 2M5 514-842-8194 (16)

Turk, Thomas, Michigan Association of Community Arts Agencies 608 Whitehills Drive East Lansing, MI 48823 517-355-2300 (5)

Turk, Thomas L., Cultural Activities Center Post Office Box 3292 Temple, TX 76501 817-773-9926 (5)

Turnbull, Keith, Toronto Theatre Alliance 25 Lennox Avenue Toronto, Ontario, Canada M6G 3W6 416-536-1101 (5)

Turner, Jenny, Sudbury Theatre Centre 90 King Street Sudbury, Ontario, Canada P3E 4P8 705-674-8381 (16)

Turner, Jerry, Oregon Shakespearean Festival Association 15 South Pioneer Street Ashland, OR 97520 503-482-2111 (8)

Turner, Jerry, Oregon Shakespearean Festival Post Office Drawer 158 Ashland, OR 97520 503-482-2111 (9)

Turner, Marguerite, Anniston Council on the Arts Post Office Box 1252 Anniston, AL 36201 205-237-6767 (5)

Turner, Ray, Sundog Productions 29 Scotia Street Winnipeg, Manitoba, Canada R2W 3W6 204-582-7578 (16)

Turoff, Robert, Golden Apple Dinner Theatre 25 North Pineapple Avenue Sarasota, FL 33577 813-266-2646 (16)

Tushinsky, Joseph S., Marantz Company, Incorporated 20525 Nordoff Street Chatsworth, CA 91311 213-998-9333 (15)

Tuttle, Barry, Barry Tuttle Summer Theatre East Rochester, NY 14603 (16)

Tuttle, Don, Musicians' Protective Union, Local 245 Route 4, Post Office Box 2 Muncie, IN 47302 317-282-2134 (18)

Tveden, Deena, Musicians' Association, Local 124 119 Capitol Way Olympia, WA 98501 206-357-5220 (18)

Tward, Reva, Leah Posluns Theatre 4588 Bathurst Street Willowdale, Ontario, Canada M2J 4E4 416-636-2720 (16)

Tweedie, David, Gallaudet College Department of Theatre 7th and Florida Avenue, NE Washington, D.C. 20002 202-651-5606; 202-651-5710 (4)

Twist, Paul L.P., Hammond Industries 8000 Madison Pike Madison, AL 35758 205-772-9626; 205-772-3870 (15)

Tyler, Richard, Carmel Cultural Commission Post Office Box 5066 Carmel, CA 93921 408-624-3996 (5)

Tyler, Rick, Mc Pherson College Department of Theatre 1600 East Euclid Mc Pherson, KS 67460 316-241-0731 (4)

U

Ubans, Maris U., California State University Department of Theatre 5151 State University Drive Los Angeles, CA 90032 213-224-3345; 213-224-3344 (4)

Uber, Mrs. Jay J., Island Players Anna Maria, FL 33501 813-778-5755 (16)

Udouj, Joe, Joe Udouj Post Office Box 1851 Fort Smith, AR 72901 501-783-1468 (15)

Uher, Frank S., Hattiesburg Federation of Musicians 326 Venetian Way Hattiesburg, MS 39401 601-544-2834 (18)

Vincent, Anthony A., Harlequin Players 4626 Abbott Avenue Dallas, TX 75205 (16)

Vincent, Donald C., Port Huron Federation of Musicians, Local 33 2601 10th Avenue Port Huron, MI 48060 313-982-8390 (18)

Vincent, Lawrence, Cuyahoga Community College Western Campus Theatre 11000 Pleasant Valley Road Parma, OH 44130 216-845-4000; 216-842-9770 (16)

Vincent, Paul, Cercone-Vincent Associates, Inc. 5020 Richmond Road Bedford Heights, CT 44146 216-292-2550 (15)

Vincent, Paul E., Cercone Vincent Associates, Incorporated 5020 Richmond Road Bedford Heights, OH 44146 216-292-2550 (15)

Vincent, Paul E., Cercone Vincent Associates, Incorporated 2741 Noblestown Road Pittsburgh, PA 15205 412-922-0901 (15)

Vocelle, Robert, Quebec Musicians' Association, Local 119 1406 West Street Quebec City, Quebec, Canada G1S 1X2 418-688-1722 (18)

Vogel, Fred, Foundation for the Extension and Development of the American Professional Theatre (FEDAPT) 165 West 46th Street, Suite 310 New York, NY 10036 212-869-9690 (5)

Vogel, J., Chapel Theatre 2222 Lomita Boulevard Lomita, CA 90717 (16)

Vojcihoski, Elmer, Twin City Musicians' Association of Marinette Wisconsin and Menominee Michigan, Local 39 2034 Tenth Avenue Menominee, MI 49858 906-863-2073 (18)

Volland, R. Michael, Volland Studios, Incorporated 1425 Hanley Industrial Court Street Louis, MO 63105 314-962-5555 (15)

Vollman, Hellen, Leech Lake Community Theatre Route 2, Post Office Box 50 Akeley, MN 56433 (16)

Vrieze, Jack W., Frostburg State College Department of Theatre East College Avenue Frostburg, MD 21532 (4)

Vukasin, Helen, Ulster County Council for the Arts 95 Maiden Lane Kingston, NY 12401 914-339-4330 (5)

Vunovich, Dr. Nancy, University of Tulsa Department of Theatre 600 South College Tulsa, OK 74104 918-939-6351 (4)

Vunovich, Dr. Nancy, Leta Chapman Theatre University of Tulsa 600 South College Tulsa, OK 74104 918-592-6000 (8)

Vunovich, Dr. Nancy, Theatre Two University of Tulsa 600 South College Tulsa, OK 74104 918-592-6000 (8)

Vyzralek, Frank, Chataqua Post Office Box 948 Bismarck, ND 701-663-1948 (9)

W

Waal, Carla, University of Missouri-Columbia Department of Theatre 129 Fine Arts Building Columbia, MO 65211 314-882-2021 (4)

Wachtel, George S., Connecticut Mutual Life Insurance Company 140 Garden Street Hartford, CT 06115 203-549-4111 (10)

Wade, George F., Lakewood Community College Department of Theatre White Bear Lake, MN 55110 612-770-1331 (4)

Wade, Jere D., California State College Department of Theatre 801 Monte Vista Turlock, CA 95380 209-667-3451 (4)

Wadleigh, Director, University of Washington Department of Theatre Pullman, WA 99164 509-335-4581 (4)

Wagenschein, Dr. Miriam, Corpus Christi State University Department of Theatre Post Office Box 6010 Corpus Christi, TX 78411 512-991-6810 (4)

Wages, Wayne, R.W. Wages Agency Box 5356 Missoula, MT 59806 406-549-3283 (15)

Waggoner, Marion, Scioto Society Post Office Box 73 Chillicothe, OH 45601 614-775-4100 (5)

Wagner, Authur, University of California, La Jolla Department of Theatre La Jolla, CA 92037 (4)

Wagner, Carl E., King's College Department of Theatre Wilkes-Barre, PA 18711 717-826-5900, extension 762, 763 (4)

Wagner, Clyde, Musicians' Protective Union, Local 254 3263 Idlewood Sioux City, IA 51104 712-258-1288 (18)

Wagner, Orlie, Musicians' Protective Union 5301 Central Avenue NE, #807 Alburquerque, NM 87108 505-255-2069 (18)

Wagner, Stewart J., Mohawk Valley Musicians' Association, Local 51 R.D. 1 Poland, NY 13431 315-251- (18)

Wagner, W.E., Actors Incorporated 318 ½ Main Street Ames, IA 50010 (16)

Wahl, Thomas, Austin Wahl Agency Ltd. 332 South Michigan Avenue Chicago, Il 60604 312-922-3329; 312-922-3331 (2)

Wain, Erika, Webster Artists Management 13615 Victory Boulevard Van Nuys, CA 91404 213-780-2558 (2)

Wakin, Eleanor, New Rochelle Council on the Arts 45 Wellington Avenue New Rochelle, NY 10804 914-632-9227 (5)

Walck, Duane, Musicians' Protective Union Post Office Box 250 Delaware Water Gap, PA 18327 717-421-1325 (18)

Waldman, Authr, Ocean County College Department of Theatre College Drive Toms River, NJ 08753 201-255-4000 (4)

Walker, Charles, Herschel-Harrington Scenic and Lighting Studio 132-A Tenth North East Atlanta, GA 30309 404-892-0065 (15)

Walkiewicz, Edward P., Southwest Cultural Heritage Festival Oklahoma State University Stillwater, OK 74078 405-624-6217; 405-624-6142 (9)

Wall, Mary, Perle Roland Perfume Shop 946 West Rush Street Chicago, IL 60611 312-944-1432 (15)

Wallace, Ann, Theatre Fountainhead 47 Wembley Road Toronto, Ontario, Canada M6C 2G1 416-738-9300 (16)

Wallace, Cliff, Von Braun Civic Center 700 Monroe Street, SW Huntsville, AL 35801 205-533-1953 (8)

Wallace, G., Peoples Theatre 2208 North 3rd Street Milwaukee, WI 53212 (16)

Wallace, Lea, Comedia Puppet Player/Wallace Puppets Post Office Box 129 Cooper Station New York, NY 10003 212-254-9074 (16)

Wallace, Vickie, Four Star Stage Lighting 585 Gerard Avenue Bronx, NY 10451 212-993-0471 (15)

Wallach, Susan, Theatre Crafts 250 West 57th Street, Suite 312 New York, NY 10019 212-582-4110 (14)

Wallett, David, Errant Productions 651 Yonge Street Toronto, Ontario, Canada M4Y 1Z9 416-961-7675 (16)

Walling, Mel, Omaha Stage Equipment, Incorporated 3873 Leavenworth Street Omaha, NE 68105 402-345-4427 (15)

Walrath, Harlon C., Musicians' Protective Union Post Office Box 1128 Fairbanks, AK 99701 907-456-3199 (18)

Walsh, Frederick G., North Dakota State University Department of Theatre Fargo, ND 58203 701-237-8011 (4)

Walsh, Luis, Electronics Diversified, Incorporated 1675 Northwest 216th Street Hillsboro, OR 97123 503-645-5533 (15)

Walter, Buddy L., Stockton Musicians' Association, Local 1902 2626 North California Street Stockton, CA 95204 209-464-4016 (18)

Walter, William S., Stagecraft Industries, Incorporated Post Office Box 660 Bellevue, WA 98009 206-454-3089; 503-226-7351 (15)

Walton, William F., Allegheny College Department of Drama Meadville, PA 16335 (4)

Waltz, Mary, Snohomish Arts Commission 1009 First Street Snohomish, WA 98290 206-568-3115 (5)

Wamble, V., R B Harrison Players 4730 Penrose Street St. Louis, MO 63115 (16)

Wamsley, Howard, New York Institute of Technology Department of Theatre Old Westbury, NY 11568 516-686-7616 (4)

Wanner, E., Queen City Players 6368 Sharlene Drive Cincinnati, OH 45211 (16)

Warburton, John Michael, Southern College Theatre 800 Eighth Avenue West Birmingham, AL 35204 205-328-5250, Ext. 324 (8)

Ware, Robert A., Springfield Musicians' Association, Local 160 1500 Malden Avenue Springfield, OH 45504 513-390-0618; 513-390-2351 (18)

Wareham, Elmer C. Jr., State College Area Musicians' Association 1151 William Street State College, PA 16801 814-237-2689 (18)

Warmack, Roy J., Musicians' Protective Union, Local 113 FPost Office Box 696 Central Valley, CA 96019 916-241-2441 (18)

Warrack, David, Warrack Productions 651 Yonge Street Toronto, Ontario, Canada M5R 2Z2 416-964-6464, Administration (16)

Warren, James H., Scarritt College for Christian Workers Department of Theatre 19th and Grand Avenue Nashville, TN 37203 615-327-2700 (4)

Warren, Dr. J., Florida League of the Arts 76 West Church Street Orlando, FL 32801 305-843-2787 (5)

Warren, Dr. Jerry L., Belmont College Department of Theatre 1900 Belmont Boulevard Nashville, TN 37203 615-383-7001 (4)

Warren, Skelly, Christopher Newport College Campus Center Theatre Shoe Lane Newport News, VA 23606 804-599-7005; 804-599-7088 (8)

Warriner, Gary W., Federation of Musicians, Local 191 Route No. 1 Peterbourough, Ontario, Canada K9J 6X2 705-292-7082 (18)

Wasserman, Hillel, Hillel Wasserman Agency 328 South Beverly Drive Beverly Hills, CA 90212 213-553-5337 (2)

Watchtell, Jeffery, The Century Theatre 235 West 46th Street New York, NY 10036 212-354-6644 (16)

Waterman, Adele, Festival Repertory Company 1401 Flatbush Avenue Brooklyn, NY 11210 718-859-9459 (16)

Waterman, Elsie, Agape Community Theatre 810 Grant Street Wausau, WI 54401 (16)

Waters, Camille, Reunion Theatre 709 Franklin Houston, TX 77002 713-228-2267 (16)

Waters, T., The Conejo Players Post Office Box 1695 Thousand Oaks, CA 91320 (16)

Watford, Roy W., Arts and Humanities Council Post Office Box 1369 Dothan, AL 36301 205-792-2914 (5)

Watkins, Edwin, McCraney Arts Council 622 Hudson Place Tallassee, AL 36078 205-283-4606 (5)

Watkins, E.G., Bluefield Federation of Musicians 304 Jones Street Bluefield, WV 24701 304-327-8743 (18)

Watkins, J. R. (Bob), Chattanooga Musicians' Union, Local 80 Memorial Auditorium Chattanooga, TN 37402 615-266-1725; 615-266-5918 (18)

Watkinson, Dr. Sharon O., Niagara University Department of Theatre Niagara Falls, NY 14109 716-285-1212, Extension 526,525 (4)

Watsol, Evelyn, City of Troy Council on the Arts and Humanities Post Office Box 606 Troy, AL 36081 205-566-3685 (5)

Watson, Albert, Delta Center Stage Post Office Box 14 Greenville, MS 38701 (16)

Watson, Chrystal, Pasadena City College Department of Theatre 1570 East Colorado Boulevard Pasadena, CA 91106 213-578-7216 (4)

Watson, Harmon S., Morgan State College Department of Theatre Baltimore, MD 21239 301-323-2270 (4)

Watts, James, Musicians' Protective Association 1206 Victoria Avenue Thunder Bay, Ontario, Canada P7C 4X8 807-623-0122 (18)

Waugh, Ann, Ann Waugh Talent Agency 4731 Laurel Canyon Boulevard North Hollywood, CA 91607 213-980-0141 (2)

Wawak, William F., William Wawak Company 2235 Hammond Drive Schaumburg, IL 60195 312-397-4850 (15)

Waymire, John, Anthenaeum Turners Building 401 East Michigan Street Indianapolis, IN 46204 317-635-6336 (8)

Wayne, Morton, Pittsfield Federation of Musicians, Local 109 397 Partridge Road Pittsfield, MA 01201 413-442-9755 (18)

Waynick, M Howard, Musicians Protective Union 526 Hilwood Court Greensboro, NC 27410 919-855-1333 (18)

Weart, Nancy Ruth, Albuquerque Civic Light Opera Association 4201 Ellison Northeast Albuquerque, NM 87109 505-345-6577 (15)

Weaver, D., Black Swan Players 11316 South Crestline Romeo, MT 48065 (16)

Weaver, David Jr., Globe of the Great Southwest Shakespeare Festival 2808 Shakespeare Road Odessa, TX 79761 915-332-1586; 915-332-1587 (9)

Weaver, Lawrence, Fellowship Players 2041 Georgia Avenue Racine, WI 53404 (16)

Weaver, Richard A., Texas Tech University Department of Theatre Arts Post Office Box 4298 Lubbock, TX 79409 806-742-3601 (4)

Weaver, Richard B., Association of Theatrical Press Agents and Managers (ATPAM) 165 West 46th Street New York, NY 10036 212-719-3666 (18)

Weaver, Roy, Musicians' Protective Union, Local 164 3162 East Half Road Grand Junction, CO 81501 303-434-6565 (18)

Webb, Mary, Hamilton Place Theatre Box 2080, Station A Hamilton, Ontario, Canada L8N 3Y7 416-525-3100; 416-525-7710 (16)

Webb, Ruth, Ruth Webb Agency 7500 Devista Drive Los Angeles, CA 90046 213-874-1700 (2)

Weber, Betty, Austin Theatre Group 119 Laurel Lane Austin, TX 78705 512-477-1421 (16)

Weber, Dale G., Dale G. Weber Co. 1226 S.E. 7th Avenue Portland, OR 97214 503-234-7671 (15)

Webster, Don, Little Stage Lighting Company 10507 Harry Hines Boulevard Dallas, TX 75220 214-358-3511 (15)

Webster, H. Wayne, Wood Junior College Department of Theatre Mathiston, MS 39752 601-263-9321 (4)

Webster, James E., Festival-in-the-Park Incorporated (Roanoke) Post Office Box 12745 Roanoke, VA 24028 703-342-2640 (9)

Wechesser, John C., College of Santa Fe Department of Theatre Saint Michaels Drive Santa Fe, NM 87501 505-473-6131; 505-473-6439 (4)

Wechtenhiser, Bob, Penn Wood Players Post Office Box 775 Johnstown, PA 15907 (16)

Weedman, Sidney H., Clowes Memorial Hall 4600 Sunset Avenue Indianapolis, IN 46208 317-924-6321 (8)

Wegerbauer, K., Oak Creek Community Theatre 331 East Wynbrook Drive Oak Creek, WI 53154 (16)

Wegley, Joyce, Kings Players, Incorporated 514 East Visalia Street Hanford, CA 93230 209-584-7241 (16)

Wehling, Robert, Musicians' Protective Union, Local 98 437 North 6th Street Wood River, IL 62095 618-254-1488 (18)

Wehrmeyer, R., Footlighters 3315 Monteith Avenue Cincinnati, OH 45208 (16)

Weider, Les, Moorpark Community College Department of Theatre Moorpark, CA 93021 805-529-2321 (4)

Wein, Lawrence, American Place Theatre 111 West 46th Street New York, NY 10036 212-246-0393 (8)

Weinberger, Martin, Claremont Intercultural Council Claremont Courier Claremont, CA 91711 714-621-4761; 714-621-4762 (5)

Weinblatt, Sherry, Civic Children's Theatre 600 Playhouse Lane Youngstown, OH 44511 216-782-3402 (16)

Weiner, Arthur, Musicians' Protective Union, Local 237 54 Windsor Avenue Dover, NJ 07801 201-366-7640 (18)

Weiner, Shirley G., Adirondack Community College Department of Theatre Glen Falls, NY 12801 518-793-4491 (4)

Weisberg, Naida D., Improvise, Incorporated Post Office Box 2335 Providence, RI 02906 (16)

Weiss, Jean, Queens Council on the Arts 161-04 Jamaica Avenue Jamaica, NY 11432 212-291-1100 (5)

Weiss, Robert O., DePauw Speech Hall DePauw University Greencastle, IN 46135 317-653-9721 (8)

Weiss, Robert O., De Pauw University Performing Arts Center De Pauw University Greencastle, IN 46135 317-653-9721 (8)

Weissler, Barry, National Theatre Company 165 West 6th Street, Suite 1202 New York, NY 10036 212-575-1044; 212-575-1046 (16)

Weissler, Fran, National Theatre Company 165 West 6th Street, Suite 1202 New York, NY 10036 212-575-1044; 212-575-1046 (16)

Welch, Karen West, Bush Theatre 690 Cleveland Avenue South Saint Paul, MN 55101 (16)

Welch, Robert, Fort Worth College of the Holy Names Department of Theatre West 4000 Randolph Road Spokane, WA 99204 509-328-2970 (4)

Welk, Robert W., University of Nebraska, Omaha Department of Theatre 60th and Dodge Streets (Box 688) Omaha, NB 68101 402-554-2200 (4)

Wellan, Rob, Theatre London 471 Richmond Street London, Ontario, Canada N6A 3E4 519-672-9030; 519-672-8800 (16)

Wellborn, Charles, Tallahassee Little Theatre Post Office Box 3262 Tallahassee, FL 32303 904-224-8474 (16)

Wellborne, C.L., Southeastern Community College Department of Theatre Whiteville, NC 28472 (4)

Wellnitz, Beverly, Ardmore Little Theatre Post Office Box 245 Ardmore, OK 73401 405-223-6387 (16)

Wells, Garwood, Musicians' Protective Union Post Office Box 1175 Middletown, OH 45042 513-423-6854 (18)

Wells, Kenneth, Sullivan County Dramatic Workshop 4 Lakewood Avenue Monticello, NY 12701 914-794-4114 (16)

Wells, Richard L., Musicians Protective Union 526 Hilwood Court Greensboro, NC 27410 919-855-1333 (18)

Welsbacher, Richard, Wichita State University Department of Theatre 1845 Fairmount Witchita, KS 67208 316-689-3368; 316-689-3360 (4)

Welsh, Grace R., McKendree College Department of Theatre Lebanon, IL 62254 618-537-4481 (4)

Welton, John, Carson-Newman College Communication Arts Department Russel Street Jefferson Street, TN 37760 615-745-9061 (4)

Wengrow, Arnold, University of North Carolina Department of Theatre University Heights Ashville, NC 28814 704-258-6610; 704-253-5778 (4)

Wente, Jean R., Alameda County Art Commission c/o Office of Administration Oakland, CA 94612 415-874-6751 (5)

Wentworth, Jeff, Lake Tahoe Community College Department of Theatre South Lake Tahoe, CA 95702 916-541-4660 (4)

Wenzel, Carl H., Attic Theatre Post Office Box 41 Appleton, WI 54911 414-733-2945 (16)

Werch, Henry, Superscope Chicago, Incorporated 1300 Norwood Avenue Itasca, IL 60143 312-569-2147 (15)

Werts, D., Little Theatre Post Office Box 305 Junction City, KS 66441 (16)

West, Carolyn, Studio West, Incorporated 421 South Rockford Tulsa, OK 74120 918-582-3512 (15)

West, C.E., Studio West, Incorporated 421 South Rockford Tulsa, OK 74120 918-582-3512 (15)

West, R., Community Theatre North West Missouri State Maryville, MO 64468 (16)

West, William C., Benedict College Department of Theatre Columbia, SC 29204 803-779-4930 (4)

Western, Edward, Actors' Equity Association (AEA) 6430 Sunset Boulevard Los Angeles, CA 90028 213-HO2-2334 (18)

Westfall, Jeanette, Greater Gulf Coast Arts Council Post Office Box 4091 Biloxi, MS 39531 601-388-1976 (5)

Westin, Jack, College of the Mainland Department of Theatre 8001 Palmer Highway Texas City, TX 77590 713-938-1211 (4)

Westphal, Debbie, Equity Showcase Theatre 417 Queen's West, Suite 500 Toronto, Ontario, Canada 416-364-7127, ext. 235; 416-364-5739 (16)

Weyand, Ronald, Marymount College Department of Drama Tarrytown, NY 10592 914-631-3200; 212-898-1073 (4)

Whalen, Mike, Sing-Sing Lighting Post Office Box 664 Notre Dame, IN 46556 219-232-5707 (15)

Whaley, Frank L., Fayetteville State University Department of Theatre Murchinson Road Fayetteville, NC 28301 919-486-1275; 919-486-1443 (4)

Whaley, Regina, Duplin County Arts Council Post Office Box 36 Kenansville, NC 28349 919-296-1341 (5)

Wheeler, Clinton, Musicians' Protective Associaton Route 4, Post Office Box 64 Brainerd, MN 56401 218-764-2438 (18)

Wheeler, David, Yuba Community College Marysville, CA 95901 216-742-7351 (4)

Wheless, Bobbi, Metropolitan Arts Council 301 College Street Greenville, SC 29601 803-232-2402 (5)

Whitaker, Claudine, Harnett County Arts Council 1011 North Orange Avenue Dunn, NC 28334 919-892-8344 (5)

White, Bob, Factory Theatre Lab 207 Adelaide Street East Toronto, Ontario, Canada M5A 1M8 416-864-9971 (16)

White, Bonnie, Peoria Players Theatre House 4300 North University Avenue Peoria, IL 61614 309-688-4473 (8)

White, Chuck, Musicians' Protective Union, Local 224 Post Office Box 94 Effingham, IL 62401 217-837-2077 (18)

White, David, DTW's Economy Tires Theatre 219 West 19 Street New York, NY 10011 212-924-0077 (16)

White, Herb, Musicians' Protective Union Post Office Box 142 Somers, MT 59932 406-857-3560 (18)

White, John J., Scranton Theatre Libre 512-514 Brooks Building Scranton, PA 18503 717-961-1377 (16)

White, John W. Jr., Paper Mill Playhouse Brookside Drive Millburn, NJ 07041 201-379-3636 (16)

White, Julie, College of Saint Catherine Department of Theatre 2004 Randolph Avenue Saint Paul, MN 55105 612-698-5571 (4)

White, Lee, The Pringle Group 30 Scarsdale Road Don Mills, Ontario, Canada M3B 2R7 (15)

White, Dr. Roi, Plymouth State College Department of Theatre Plymouth, NH 93264 603-536-1550 (4)

White, Shirl, Northeastern Oklahoma Agricultural and Mechnical College Department of Theatre 2nd and 1, North East Miami, OK 74354 918-542-8441 (4)

White, Suzanne, Terry's Theatre Arts Troupe 5500 Avenue North Rosenberg, TX 77471 (16)

White, Terry, East Grand Forks Community Theatre Community Education East Grand Forks, MN 56721 (16)

White, William H., James T. White and Company 1700 State Highway 3 Clifton, NJ 07013 201-773-9300 (14)

Whitehead, Bruce, Lumitrol Limited 5 Walker Avenue Toronto, Ontario, Canada M4V IG3 416-921-6060; 416-921-6688 (15)

Whitehead, Paul C., Stage Light-Tronics 2536 South 700 East Salt Lake City, UT 84106 801-485-9886 (15)

Whitely, James A., Musical Protective Association, Local 123 2006 Dresden Road Richmond, VA 23229 804-270-7963 (18)

Whiter, J., Clinton Repertory Theatre Democrat Clinton, MO 64735 (16)

Whiting, L. E., Tennessee Wesleyan College Department of Theatre Post Office Box 112 Athens, TN 37303 615-745-5093 (4)

Whitlatch, R. C., Eleanor Abbott Ford Center Knox College Galesburg, IL 61401 309-343-0112 (8)

Whitley, Max, Musicians' Protective Union 2711 Emmons Avenue Huntington, WV 25702 304-697-2617 (18)

Whitmore, Jon, West Virginia University Department of Theatre Morgantown, WV 26506 304-293-4022 (4)